C Purcell
303-756-2739

D1120228

Psychological Evaluations for the Courts
Second Edition

Psychological Evaluations for the Courts

A HANDBOOK FOR MENTAL HEALTH PROFESSIONALS
AND LAWYERS

Second Edition

GARY B. MELTON
JOHN PETRILA
NORMAN G. POYTHRESS
CHRISTOPHER SLOBOGIN

The Guilford Press

New York   *London*

Printed in the United States of America

This book is printed on acid-free paper.

Last digit is print number: 9 8 7 6 5 4 3 2 1

Library of Congress Cataloging-in-Publication Data

Psychological evaluations for the courts : a handbook for
    mental health professionals and lawyers / Gary B. Melton
. . . [et al.].—2nd ed.
        p. cm. —
    Includes bibliographical references and index.
    ISBN 1-57230-236-4 (hardcover)
    1. Psychology, Forensic. 2. Forensic psychiatry.
3. Evidence, Expert—United States. 4. Insanity—
Jurisprudence—United States.
I. Melton, Gary B. II. Series.
KF8922.P767 1997
347.73'67—DC21   97-10163
                                                        CIP

About the Authors

Gary B. Melton, PhD, received his doctorate from Boston University. He is Director of the Institute for Families in Society at the University of South Carolina, where he is also Professor of Neuropsychiatry and Behavioral Science and Adjunct Professor of Law, Pediatrics, and Psychology. He is Director of the Consortium on Children, Families, and the Law, a national network of interdisciplinary centers for policy research, and President of Childwatch International, a global network. He is a past President of the American Psychology–Law Society and the American Psychological Association Division of Child, Youth, and Family Services. Melton has received awards for distinguished contributions to the public interest from the American Psychological Association, two of its divisions, Psi Chi (the national honor society in psychology), and the National Committee to Prevent Child Abuse. The author of more than 225 publications, Melton leads a regular briefing series for congressional staff, and his work has been cited by U.S. courts at all levels, including the U.S. Supreme Court.

John Petrila, JD, LLM, received his law degrees from the University of Virginia. He is Professor and Chair of the Department of Mental Health Law and Policy at the Louis de la Parte Florida Mental Health Institute, University of South Florida. He also holds appointments at the University of South Florida College of Public Health and at Stetson University College of Law. Petrila was previously Counsel to the New York State Office of Mental Health, and Director of Forensic Services in the Missouri Department of Mental Hygiene. He has written and lectured widely on mental health law and policy issues. He is coeditor of *Mental Health Services: A Public Health Perspective* (with Bruce Levin; Oxford University Press, 1996), and *Law and Mental Health Professionals: Florida* (with Randy Otto; American Psychological Association, 1996).

Norman G. Poythress, AB, PhD, received his undergraduate degree at Indiana University and his doctorate at the University of Texas at Austin. He is a Professor in the Department of Mental Health Law and Policy at the Louis de la Parte Florida Mental Health Institute, University of South Florida. He is a former President of the American Psychology–Law Society and was the 1990 recipient of the American Academy of Forensic Psychology's Award for Distinguished Contribution to Forensic Psychology. From 1989–1996 he was a member of the Criminal Competence Subgroup of the MacArthur Foundation Research Network on Mental Health and the Law. He presently serves on an expert panel for the development of a benchbook for state court judges on psychiatric and psychological evidence, a project of the American Bar Association's Commission on Mental and Physical Disability Law.

Christopher Slobogin, JD, LLM, received his law degrees from the University of Virginia. He is currently Professor of Law, Alumni Research Scholar, and Associate Dean at the University of Florida College of Law. He is also an Affiliate Professor of Psychiatry at the University of Florida's Department of Psychiatry (where he teaches forensic psychiatry interns) and an Adjunct Professor at the University of South Florida's Mental Health Institute (for which he conducts frequent training programs for mental health professionals). He is coauthor of the leading law school casebook on mental health law. He has served as Chair of the Law and Mental Disability section of the American Association of Law Schools, reporter for the American Bar Association's Standards on the Insanity Defense, and editor/reviewer for *Law and Human Behavior,* the *American Journal of Psychiatry,* and the *Journal of Psychology, Public Policy and Law.* In the early 1980s he helped establish Virginia's outpatient forensic evaluation system as Director of the University of Virginia's Forensic Evaluation Center and also directed a legal aid program at a state mental hospital.

Preface

General Remarks

The second edition of this book, like the first edition published ten years ago, is aimed at two groups: mental health professionals who are involved in performing psychological evaluations for the courts, and lawyers and judges who request such evaluations. Its purpose is to provide these groups with a comprehensive guide to the issues the legal system has most commonly asked clinicians to address. This second edition not only updates and significantly revises the first edition, but adds four new chapters on subjects not covered in the first edition.

The contexts examined in this book are thus quite diverse. They include insanity and competence determinations; sentencing and civil commitment proceedings; probate and guardianship hearings; personal injury, workers' compensation, and Social Security claims; juvenile delinquency and status offense adjudications; custody and neglect disputes; and, new with this edition, federal discrimination claims and educational "mainstreaming" issues. In each of these areas, we first summarize the relevant legal rules and their jurisprudential underpinnings. We then try to analyze the law's approach critically—both to increase the mental health professional's understanding of the issues, and to enhance the lawyer's ability to argue for change. Additionally, unlike many works on "forensics," we incorporate or refer to research on each topic—from studies concerning the reliability of clinical opinions and specific evaluation techniques, to actuarial data on the persons subject to evaluation, to empirical assessments of the manner in which the legal process actually works. Finally, we offer suggestions about evaluation procedures and ways of communicating information to the courts. These recommendations are not offered solely for the benefit of the clinician; they should also help demystify the clinical process for the lawyer.

The collective experience culminating in this book is wide-ranging. Two of the authors (J. P. and C. S.) are lawyers with specialized educational backgrounds in mental health law, one of whom (C. S.) is a law school professor who at one time represented individuals with mental disabilities, and the other of whom (J. P.) now directs an interdisciplinary program of research and policy on law and mental health, after serving for many years as chief counsel to the New York State Office of Mental Health. The other two (G. B. M. and N. G. P.) are doctorate-level psychologists, one (G. B. M.) a university professor with a special research interest in children, the other (N. G. P.) a practicing clinician and university professor who devotes increasingly more of his time to studies of the forensic process. Each author has trained both mental health professionals and legal practitioners in mental health law, and we have all observed or performed scores of psychological evaluations for the courts. The idea for this book grew out of a training program in Virginia, which involved two of us (G. B. M. and C. S.) in establishing a statewide community outpatient evaluation system.*

While the diversity in our backgrounds has led to differing areas of specialization, we have reached some common conclusions about psychological evaluations for the courts. These themes permeate the book and are worth stating here at the outset.

First, we obviously believe that there is a place for mental health professionals in the legal system. To put this somewhat differently, we feel that in most contexts the potential contributions of mental health professionals outweigh the prejudice and systemic inefficiency that may result from their use. Contrary to the assertions of some writers, clinicians do have specialized knowledge that can assist judges and juries in arriving at better-informed decisions.

On the other hand, it is apparent that mental health professionals are frequently misused, overused, and, on occasion, underused by the legal system, depending upon the specific issue. At times the law appears interested only in obtaining a conclusory "expert imprimatur," which hides the moral (and uncomfortable) nature of the decision being made [see § 9.09(c) on dangerousness assessments]. At other times, the legal system demands data and inferences from a clinician, but in situations in which lay testimony and common sense are all that are required [see § 16.01(a) on custody determinations]. And at still other times, the courts completely disregard valid scientific findings, apparently out of fear that the factfinder will pay too much attention to them [see § 18.05(a) on judicial acceptance of actuarial evidence].

One of the primary reasons we wrote this book was to try to sort through this often contradictory approach to clinical expertise and to provide some rough guidelines for its use in the legal areas we cover. Put in general terms, we urge

throughout this volume, first of all, that lawyers and judges look carefully at the foundations of clinical opinions and that mental health professionals not overstep the bounds of their existing knowledge. More specifically, we admit a strong preference for research-based testimony, although we would not bar evidence founded on theoretical constructs or "educated intuition" in most contexts. Second, we believe that mental health professionals have an obligation to make clear the uncertainty of their offerings, whether research based or theory based, and that lawyers should not attempt to deny or gloss over the probabilistic nature of clinical decisionmaking. Perhaps most controversially from the practitioner's point of view, we also feel that mental health professionals should neither be permitted nor cajoled to give so-called "ultimate" legal opinions lacking in clinical content, even when they make clear that the opinions are nonscientific. All of these stipulations stem from our belief that if mental health professionals are to assist the legal system, they and the lawyers who seek their aid must tread a delicate balance between co-opting the legal decisionmaker and condoning legal results uninformed by credible information concerning human behavior.

Assuming that mental health professionals can contribute constructively in the legal process, the task becomes one of maximizing their usefulness. First and foremost, this requires making clinicians (and lawyers) aware of the legal framework in which they will participate, and making lawyers (and clinicians) at least cognizant of basic forensic evaluation procedures. Most of the chapters in this book are devoted to this enterprise. It also requires, in our opinion, that forensic evaluations be tailored to the specific legal problems at hand. At several points in this volume, we stress that lawyers should not request, and that clinicians should not perform, global evaluations aimed at discovering "what's wrong" with clients. Nor should either distort legal issues to fit clinical constructs. Competency evaluations, for instance, primarily require an assessment of the clients' current functioning, not categorization by diagnosis, regurgitation of family and social histories, or intricate psychodynamic formulations.

Adopting these precautions will go far toward achieving full use of clinical expertise. But we be-

*See GARY MELTON, LOIS WEITHORN, & CHRISTOPHER SLOBOGIN, COMMUNITY MENTAL HEALTH CENTERS AND THE COURTS: AN EVALUATION OF COMMUNITY-BASED FORENSIC SERVICES (1985).

lieve that if mental health professionals are to be as useful to the courts as they possibly can be, conceptual as well as practical steps need to be taken. First, it is important for members of both professions to develop a better understanding of the paradigmatic differences between them. Second, it is crucial that both groups become sensitive to the ethical and legal dilemmas raised when a court asks a member of the "helping" profession to assess the mental condition of a person whose interests may be harmed by the results of the evaluation. Although these issues are most directly addressed in Chapters 1 and 4, respectively, they too are interwoven throughout the entire book.

A final pervasive theme of this volume has to do with the forensic clinician's "job description." It has become commonplace to characterize the mental health professional involved in the legal system as a "hired gun." Assuming, as we feel confident in assuming, that most professionals honestly believe in their testimony, it is still true that the adversary process tends to define differences sharply. This should not mean, however, that the clinician must be pigeonholed as the mere puppet of the attorney who happens to have retained him or her. At several points in this book, we recommend that the best way to conceptualize the clinician's role is an exercise in consultation and dissemination of information. That is, the mental health professional is often utilized most efficiently in advising various members of the legal system—judges, lawyers, jail personnel, or parole officers—about the behavioral idiosyncrasies of the individual in question. Certainly, this may involve testimony in an adversarial setting. But this testimony should above all be informative; moreover, there are other less dramatic ways in which the clinician as evaluator can aid the legal system prior to adjudication. In this book, we try to identify some of these nontraditional uses of clinical expertise.

The Content of the Book

With these themes in mind, the specific subjects covered in the book can be described. The book is divided into five parts: " "General Considera-

tions," "The Criminal Process," "Noncriminal Adjudications," "Children and Families," and "Communicating with the Courts."

Part I, "General Considerations," contains five chapters examining topics of overarching consequence to the book, two of them new with this edition. Chapter 1, "Law and the Mental Health Professions: An Uneasy Alliance," sets the conceptual stage for the rest of the book by addressing two central questions, both briefly alluded to above. The first of these focuses on the implications of the philosophical differences between the legal and mental health professions: What, if any, are the implications of these differences for clinical participation in the legal system? Perhaps members of the two professions are so far apart in their basic worldviews that understanding one another on any more than a superficial level is a hopeless task. Perhaps their assumptions about what motivates behavior, the concept of "knowledge," or the process of discovering "truth" (to name a few points of contention) are so divergent that the law, if it is to maintain its integrity, must either change its basic tenets or refrain from relying on mental health professionals at all.

The second question addressed in Chapter 1 assumes that paradigmatic differences can be resolved short of taking either of these two drastic steps, but is nonetheless also fundamental: Is the type of information a mental health professional is able to provide of any use to the legal system, or are clinical offerings so flimsy that the courts are better off seeking evidence from more traditional sources? That is, are mental health professionals really "experts" who can assist factfinders on the issues raised by the law? As noted above, under the most modern definition of the term, we think the answer to this question is a qualified yes, despite the courts' increasing insistence on a "scientific" basis for opinion testimony.

Chapter 2, "An Overview of the Legal System: Sources of Law, the Court System, and the Adjudicative Process," is on a decidedly different level than Chapter 1, but, like that chapter, its objective is to provide a backdrop for subsequent parts to this book. It is essentially a primer on the "infrastructure" of the law—where the law comes from, the procedures governing its application, and the points at which it seeks clinical testimony. It has been our experience that concepts considered part of the lawyer's daily armamentarium sometimes befuddle mental health professionals, thereby reducing their effectiveness as forensic clinicians. Chapter 2 provides answers to a number of basic questions: For example, what does it mean to say that a law is "constitutional"? Is there a difference between a state and federal court? What are the stages of the criminal process, and how do they differ from the stages of a "civil" proceeding? These questions should illuminate the legal arena for the clinician and thus should facilitate interdisciplinary cooperation. The chapter should also help the mental health professional put the legal discussions in the following chapters in context.

Chapter 3, "The Nature and Method of Forensic Assessment," is new with this edition. It describes in more concrete terms than Chapter 1 the "attitude adjustment" that is necessary when clinical therapists become forensic evaluators. The chapter begins with a general exploration of the multiple practical differences between a therapeutic and a forensic interview, emphasizing the investigative nature of the latter. It then discusses the limited usefulness, for forensic purposes, of traditional clinical tools such as psychological tests and diagnostic procedures, describes various ways of gathering all-important third-party information, and analyzes a number of forensic evaluation methods, including selected specialized evaluation protocols, "truth-seeking" devices such as hypnosis and narcoanalysis, and other procedures for detecting malingering. It ends by describing the evidentiary rules that govern the admissibility of testimony based on use of these techniques.

Chapter 4, "Constitutional, Common-Law, and Ethical Contours of the Evaluation Process: The Mental Health Professional as Double Agent," examines the complex, interwoven legal and ethical principles that control the process of evaluation, ranging from the Fifth Amendment's privilege against self-incrimination to the "Tarasoff duty" and the confidentiality rule. From the clinician's point of view, each of these principles aims at answering a single question, "Who is the client?" Unfortunately, the answers they suggest often conflict. Although this chapter attempts to reconcile the various legal and ethical pressures on the clinician, it is probably impossible to do so entirely satisfactorily, at least in the abstract. The

primary goal of the chapter, therefore, is to identify concisely these pressures so that judges, lawyers, and mental health professionals will be sensitive to them in individual cases. In pursuing this goal, the chapter explicitly analyzes the professional guidelines that have been developed since the last edition.

Like the other chapters in Part I, Chapter 5, "Establishing a Forensic System and Practice," deals with issues that affect all of the substantive evaluation contexts discussed in Chapters 6 through 17. New with this edition, it looks at three separate topics. The first part of the chapter examines different types of systems for delivering forensic evaluations and offers suggestions as to how to implement them. The second part is aimed at the individual practitioner, providing hints on how to establish and maintain a forensic "business." The third part discusses ways of diffusing behavioral science research to legal policymakers. The overarching theme of the chapter is that, in order to protect the integrity of traditional mental health practice, ensure a viable forensic system, and systematize the transfer of behavioral knowledge to the legal system, specialization in forensic work is necessary.

With the general backdrop provided by Part I, the reader is better equipped to tackle specific areas of forensic assessment. The next three parts of the book deal with over 20 "substantive" evaluation areas. Any such treatment of forensic issues that attempts to be comprehensive must describe basic legal rules and procedures and must recognize fundamental clinical realities. But we have also tried to add fresh material from the legal, empirical, and clinical archives and to mix in our own insights when we think we have something to offer. In the brief descriptions of Parts II, III, and IV that follow, these latter aspects of the book are emphasized. The table of contents should be consulted to obtain a more complete overview of each chapter's scope.

Part II, "The Criminal Process," is devoted to psychological evaluations performed for the criminal justice system. The classic example of the mental health profession's involvement in this system has been expert testimony about "insanity." But responsibility assessments are only one small aspect of current clinical participation in the criminal process.

Chapter 6, "Competency to Stand Trial," discusses an issue that demands the services of more mental health professionals each year than all other types of criminal evaluations combined. As a way of combating the abuses associated with the huge and easily manipulated system that fitness determinations have spawned, the chapter emphasizes the narrow focus of the competency evaluation and points out the opportunities clinicians have for consulting with the legal profession about alternative pretrial dispositions. It also examines critically the various psychometric instruments designed to aid in assessing competency, including the instruments developed by the MacArthur Foundation Research Network on Mental Health and the Law since the last edition.

Chapter 7, "Other Competencies in the Criminal Process," deals with even less frequently acknowledged areas of clinical input in the criminal justice system. Specifically, it covers competency to consent to a search (new with this edition), competency to confess, competency to plead guilty, competency to waive one's right to an attorney, competency to refuse an insanity defense, and competency to be sentenced and executed—subjects not normally addressed in forensic volumes. It also discusses competency to testify and, new with this edition, the related issue of expert testimony on the credibility of a witness, both of which arise in the civil as well as the criminal context. Of particular note is the chapter's attempt to provide some framework for assessing "voluntariness"—a problematic concept for both lawyers and clinicians, but one that is nevertheless extremely relevant in any situation involving the waiver of rights like the right to remain silent or right to counsel.

Chapter 8, "Mental State at the Time of the Offense," confronts perhaps the core issue of the criminal law: the scope of one's responsibility for one's actions. Because the insanity defense still triggers the mental health profession's most visible forensic endeavor, the legal portion of this chapter is largely a discussion of that doctrine's historical development, its component parts, and the popular myths that surround it. But this part of the chapter also investigates other doctrines relevant to the responsibility inquiry, such as the defenses of automatism, diminished capacity, and intoxication and the verdict of guilty but mentally ill. For the first time in this edition, it also addresses the use of psychiatric testimony in connection with more traditional defenses such as self-defense and duress, and tackles the difficult issue of when "character evidence," independently of other defenses, should be admissible. As in the legal section, the research and clinical sections of this chapter are particularly careful to address whether mental health professionals have anything to offer in these areas. To that end, we investigate studies concerning various novel "syndromes" popularly accorded exculpatory significance (including, as of this edition, dissociative states and posttraumatic stress disorders); examine research on recently developed techniques for evaluating past mental impairment; look at the usefulness of "psychodynamic," as opposed to "behavioral," formulations; and offer our own recommendations for conducting a "reconstructive" evaluation of mental state at the time of the offense.

The final chapter in Part II, "Sentencing," considers the area of the criminal law that has long been thought to be a special preserve of the mental health professions. Chapter 9 describes the rise of the "rehabilitative ideal," which led to this notion; the advent of "determinate" sentencing; and the research suggesting that clinical opinion generally has minimal impact under either system. Among other additions, discussion of "sexual predator" statutes and of recent developments in capital sentencing law is new with this edition. The chapter then examines the extent to which clinicians can offer useful sentencing information, focusing on the three "clinical" issues that most often arise in this context—amenability to treatment, culpability, and dangerousness. We pay particular attention to the last of these areas, since much has been said about the "inability" of clinicians to predict violence proneness. We closely examine the research on the topic (updated through the mid-1990s) and address its evidentiary and ethical implications, concluding that a combination of clinical, actuarial, and anamnestic assessment is necessary in this area.

The four chapters in Part III, "Noncriminal Adjudication," leave the criminal arena and deal with contexts that have traditionally been described as "civil" in character. As Chapter 10, "Civil Commitment," makes clear, however, the term is a misnomer when applied to commitment. The deprivation of liberty associated with involuntary hospitalization—combined with the extensive empirical findings indicating the failure of efforts to "legalize" the commitment process and other data suggesting the relative ineffectiveness of hospital care—lead us to the conclusion that clinical participation in this area should be steeped in caution. Recognizing that professionals must work within the commitment system despite its defects, we criticize the Supreme Court's decisions relaxing strictures on the process, recommend an adversarial role for the attorney, and supply clinicians with current data on the predictability of short-term dangerousness to self and others. New with this edition is a discussion of outpatient commitment, a relatively recent phenomenon. The chapter also deals with the commitment of "special" populations—minors, people with mental retardation, prisoners, insanity acquittees and, new in this edition, people who abuse substances.

Chapters 11 and 12 look at areas that are more accurately deemed "civil" in nature. Chapter 11, "Civil Competencies," discusses a number of contexts involving assessments of current functioning: competency to handle one's financial and personal affairs (i.e., guardianship), competency to consent to treatment (experimental or otherwise), and competency to make a will. As in Chapters 6 and 7 on criminal competencies, this chapter stresses the focused nature of the capacity assessment and the consultative role available to the clinician; significant new research is also reported in this edition.

Chapter 12, "Compensation for Mental Injuries," describes the two primary systems for reimbursing the individual injured through the "fault" of another: workers' compensation and tort law. Both systems compensate "mental injury," but both have great difficulty designating the circumstances under which such compensation should occur. This chapter exposes the conceptual gap between the legal and clinical professions on the key compensation issue of "causation," and offers some hints as to how mental health professionals should approach it. Developments since the last edition that have tended to restrict recovery for mental injury are highlighted.

The final chapter in Part III, "Discrimination

and Entitlement Law," is largely new with this edition. It focuses on three federal laws—the Americans with Disabilities Act, the Fair Housing Act, and the Social Security Act—which have a significant impact on those suffering from mental disability. The first two laws, both relatively recent, prohibit unnecessary discrimination against people with mental and physical disabilities in the employment and housing contexts. The third law, which is of much older vintage (and was covered in the first edition), provides those who are more severely disabled with a modicum of financial security (although recent amendments governing eligibility of children, discussed in this edition, significantly diminish that security for that group). After canvassing the complicated legal rules created by these statutes, the chapter details the relatively rigid evaluation procedures the government has imposed in these areas.

Part IV, "Children and Families," is the final "substantive" section of the book, devoted entirely to the subject of children's involvement in the legal process—a topic that has received considerable legal and empirical attention in recent years. Its first three chapters, entitled "Juvenile Delinquency," "Child Abuse and Neglect," and "Child Custody in Divorce," are all organized around a triad of themes. First, clinicians know very little about the treatability of children and the dynamics of family systems. Second, because of this ignorance, they should view their evaluative role primarily as one of providing information about these issues, not judging what the information means legally (even when sound research of the type recapitulated in these chapters strongly suggests a particular disposition). Third, these investigative data should come not only from the child and the family, but from a wide range of other sources as well; that is, the evaluation should be ecological in nature. All three chapters are updated to take into account the significant legal, empirical, and therapeutic developments over the past decade in connection with children, including the movement to "shrink" the juvenile court by increasing transfer jurisdiction to adult court; new information about juvenile treatment programs, abuse reporting statutes, and joint custody; and the extremely vituperous "repressed memory" debate.

The fourth chapter in Part IV, "Education and

Habilitation," is new with this edition. Although it also sounds the above themes, it focuses on a single federal law, the Individuals with Disabilities Education Act, which requires the evaluator to address additional issues connected with "mainstreaming" handicapped children into the public school system. This chapter was included because the Act has given rise to a vast disability education "industry" which might benefit from a structured inquiry into the purposes of the law and how best to implement them.

Following the parts dealing with specific evaluation issues, Part V, "Communicating with the Courts," concludes the book by delving into the important task of communicating the results of an evaluation to the legal system. Chapter 18, which provides suggestions to mental health professionals and lawyers about "Consultation, Report Writing, and Expert Testimony" (including new material on social psychology research relevant to being an effective expert) is the principal chapter in this part. But because reports are often the primary way in which many mental health professionals and lawyers communicate, we also include Chapter 19, containing sample evaluation reports on several of the issues covered in this book (for a total of 16 sample reports). This chapter serves two different purposes. First, it provides examples of the type of reports we think should be presented to the courts (although no doubt they can be improved upon substantially). Second, the reports, and the commentary that accompanies each of them, provide concrete illustration of the abstract legal and clinical points made in earlier chapters.

The final chapter in the book, Chapter 20, contains two glossaries, one of legal terms, the other of clinical and research terms. These glossaries, both significantly larger than in the first edition, define many of the "jargon terms" used in this book, as well as other words that might pose obstacles to communication between the lawyer and the clinician.

Some Comments on the Book's Structure

As noted at the beginning of this preface, all of the chapters on the substantive evaluation issues follow a simple format designed to benefit both types of professionals: They begin with analysis of the law; then examine the research, if any, on the subject; and end with a discussion of the proper method for performing an evaluation in the area. While the legal sections are written with the layperson in mind, lawyers should find them useful because they try to canvass the relevant legal positions, often include state-by-state reviews of the law, and provide citations to leading cases, statutory material, and secondary resources. At the same time, our hope is that this depth of coverage will help clinicians better appreciate the policies that find expression in "the law."

The research and clinical sections stress precepts unique to forensic practice. While it is obvious that, without basic knowledge about human behavior and psychopathology, one cannot hope to be a skilled forensic clinician, we felt that the most efficient approach to take in this volume would be to assume such knowledge rather than rehearse it. This approach should not frighten the legally trained reader away, however. As already noted, the research and clinical sections can provide lawyers with insights into the clinical process, as well as with means of measuring the quality of any evaluations or reports they request. Thus, we recommend that lawyers as well as clinicians read both the legal and clinical sections.

A new feature in the second edition is the inclusion of one or more case studies or problems in most of the chapters (for obvious reasons, we did not construct problems for the report writing and glossary chapters). Each of the case studies describes a fact situation, occasionally with variations, and then asks questions that raise legal and/or clinical issues covered in the relevant chapter; the problems, in contrast, are not fact based, but policy oriented. The primary reason we include these exercises in the book is to assist those who use it as a pedagogical text in understanding and explicating the subject matter. However, the relative veteran in the forensic field might also find them helpful as "self-test" mechanisms. Not all the exercises have definitive answers, but we tried to provide, in close proximity to each, enough material to provoke incisive thought on the issues raised.

Each chapter is divided into numbered sections and lettered and numbered subsections—an organizational device which is perhaps somewhat "bureaucratic," but which we think makes the contents of the chapters more accessible, provides ease of cross-referencing, and facilitates updating (through future biennial supplements). If the practitioner is interested in discovering the relevant law or research on a particular topic, a quick look at the table of contents should generally suffice, although referring to the extensive index may be helpful as well.

The reader interested in exploring further the topics covered in the book should find it useful to consult the bibliography at the end of each chapter. These bibliographies are not meant to be comprehensive. Rather, they represent a compilation of some of the books and articles in each subject area that are noteworthy for their conceptual contributions and their thoroughness. We have also included leading cases. The reader who seeks still further information can find many other sources in the Notes section at the end of the book.

A word about the terminology used in this book is in order. As should already be clear, we use the word "clinician" interchangeably with "mental health professional" to designate any professional in the mental health system, including social workers and psychiatric nurses as well as psychiatrists and psychologists. As we indicate in Chapter 1, many of the distinctions among these groups that are imposed by the law and guild concerns are meaningless in forensic practice. We also try to use "consumer-oriented" language when referring to people who have a mental disability. Any lapses in this regard are a matter of oversight.

We hope this book will improve the contributions mental health professionals make to the legal system. We also encourage criticisms and comments about its content so that this improvement can continue.

GARY B. MELTON
JOHN PETRILA
NORMAN G. POYTHRESS
CHRISTOPHER SLOBOGIN

Contents

Part III.   Noncriminal Adjudication

Chapter 10.   Civil Commitment   297

Part IV.   *Children and Families*

Chapter 14.   *Juvenile Delinquency*   *417*

Online Updates

A special website maintained by the authors provides ongoing updates to the information contained in this edition. Go to: **http//www.guilford.com/courts**

Psychological Evaluations for the Courts
Second Edition

PART I

General Considerations

CHAPTER ONE

Law and the Mental Health Professions: An Uneasy Alliance

1.01. The Context for Law and Behavioral Science

There can be no doubt that the legal system's use of expert opinions from mental health professionals and other behavioral scientists is a matter of considerable controversy. Members of the general public, the legal profession, and even the mental health profession have all been highly critical of such testimony and the way it is proffered.

The public's antipathy toward clinical opinion appears to stem from the belief that much "expert" testimony is based on "junk science" from professionals who, for a fee, will find evidence of almost anything.[1] Although seldom successful,[2] highly publicized psychological defenses—often associated with such flamboyant names as the "abuse excuse" or the "urban survival syndrome"[3]—have led many in the general public to question the objectivity and expertise of the mental health professions.[4] More generally, since the earliest explicit use of social and behavioral sciences in judicial opinions, popular commentators have worried that psychologists and other experts use the legal process to undermine the political judgments of less liberal legislators elected by the people.[5]

Lawyers have echoed these concerns. Even the late Judge David Bazelon, perhaps the paradigmatic liberal advocate of extensive use of behav-ioral science in legal decisionmaking, ultimately described himself as a "disappointed lover" chagrined by clinicians' overreaching into moral and political domains.[6] Indeed, the issues associated with use of the behavioral sciences in the courtroom have become sufficiently common and important that traditional mental health law has been joined in law schools by entire courses on use of expert social science evidence.[7]

As intense as the concerns of the public and the legal world are, they are at least matched, if not overshadowed, by the ferocity of the debate among behavioral science researchers and mental health professionals themselves, as even casual readers of journals in mental health disciplines and psycholegal studies can attest.[8] The fundamental nature of this conflict was illustrated when Jay Ziskin and David Faust argued in *Science* and other prestigious journals that clinical opinions are insufficiently reliable and valid to warrant their use in the legal arena.[9] Although more scholarly arguments to the same effect have been made by others,[10] the prestige of the forum in which Ziskin and Faust's views appeared led to a remarkable professional brouhaha. Their articles not only stimulated special symposia at professional meetings but also provoked replies from both the chief executive officer and the president of the American Psychological Association.[11]

To some degree, the debate reflects the fact

that courtrooms are foreign territory for psychologists, psychiatrists, and social workers. As this chapter makes clear, the legal rules for admission and consideration of evidence do not necessarily conform to the norms of mental health practice and scientific inquiry. The resulting culture clashes create ambiguity and conflict about the standards to be applied, leading naturally to the following question: Does forensic work inevitably result in some compromise of mental health professionals' principles or at least in their mode of operation?[12]

The intensity of the debate is also heightened by the stakes involved, not just in terms of the public and private interests at issue in litigation but also in terms of image. Much of the emotion in the controversy over mental health professional expertise is traceable to the fact that public perceptions—and, to some degree, self-perceptions—of the science and the profession are closely tied to clinicians' and researchers' status in courtrooms and judges' chambers. On the one hand, lack of recognition by legal authorities is perceived as a challenge to the usefulness of the mental health professions. On the other hand, acceptance of professional opinions that are not consensually accepted in the field is perceived as a threat to the explicit and implicit canons of science and practice, thus undermining the behavioral sciences and the mental health professions themselves.

We believe that the various controversies about the use of mental health professionals' opinions in the legal process have been blown out of proportion and that they reflect a misunderstanding of the purpose of expert evidence and the standard for its admission. In scientific terms, the law expects *incremental*—not absolute—validity. The question is whether mental health professionals' opinions will *assist* legal decisionmakers, not whether the opinions meet a particular standard of scientific rigor. At the same time, we believe that professional credentials by themselves are not enough to guarantee that opinions will be sufficiently helpful to warrant their admission into evidence.

The "moderate" view that we express in this chapter and throughout the book may take some of the sting from both the arguments posed by advocates of outright exclusion and the contentions of those who defend professional prerogatives. Nonetheless, it is important to understand the underlying conflicts because they involve fundamental differences of epistemology and worldview; they will not disappear with a good-natured exchange of views. Thus, the purposes of this chapter are to analyze the sources of the current ambivalence about the interaction between law and mental health and to address generally the limits of expertise possessed by mental health professionals. In the discussion of these questions, we make some initial inquiry into the problems of defining who is an expert and for what purpose—questions that recur throughout this volume.

1.02. Some Preliminary Problems in Law and Mental Health

CASE STUDY 1.1

Below are excerpts of expert testimony from two different proceedings involving Mike Simpson, who is charged with embezzlement. The issue addressed in the first proceeding, a criminal trial on the embezzlement charges, is whether Simpson was "insane" at the time of the offense. Insanity in this jurisdiction is defined as a "mental disease or defect that causes a substantial inability to appreciate the wrongfulness of the act or to conform behavior to the requirements of the law."

Q: Now, doctor, your testimony is that the respondent is suffering from a pathological gambling disorder?

A: Yes.

Q: And this is a mental disease?

A: Yes, it is in the fourth edition of the American Psychiatric Association's *Diagnostic and Statistical Manual,* and I suppose there are twenty or thirty psychologists like myself who specialize in this area and are convinced it's a serious problem.

Q: What led you to give him this diagnosis?

A: This individual admits he is preoccupied with gambling, and can't stop himself from doing it. He feels anxious unless he is gambling or planning a gambling trip. He's now at the point where, even though he's never been in trouble with the law before, he's embezzling from his company.

Q: Does this make him incapable of distinguishing right from wrong?

A: Well, here's a man who normally knows the law well, who knows about right and wrong, but a man who is in a desperate strait. He is under a tremendous amount of stress, does not consider right and wrong. Based on my experience with these people, I don't think that becomes part of his thinking process. His process is to survive. He's losing his job, his family, his children, his reputation, everything is going down. So he functions this way, in an irrational way which leaves his judgment impaired.

Q: And what about his ability to conform his acts to the requirements of the law?

A: He has virtually none. While he probably intends to return the money, he can't help himself from embezzling because of the urge to gamble. Again, based on my experience, people like this are prone to commit crimes to get money. There's also a study of 70 people with this disorder which shows that one out of five have committed crimes like forgery, theft, or embezzlement. Whereas, as a conservative estimate, only one of 200 people in the general population commit such crimes, meaning pathological gamblers are 40 times more likely to commit these crimes than the average person. This man needs treatment, not punishment.

Q: So would you say he's insane?

A: I would, yes.

Mike is acquitted by reason of insanity and is committed to an institution for observation. At the end of a month a commitment hearing is held to determine whether he should remain in the hospital, which is permitted only if Mike is shown to be "dangerous to self or others," defined as "a likelihood that, as a result of mental disorder, the individual will cause substantial harm to himself or another." The lone expert witness at the 15-minute hearing, a member of the hospital staff, testifies as follows:

Q: What is Mr. Simpson's condition at this time?

A: He's unresponsive to treatment.

Q: Does that make him dangerous to others or self?

A: He is still dangerous [here the doctor describes the same study described at trial]. There is no guarantee he won't steal again to feed his habit. Also, according to DSM-IV, of individuals in treatment for pathological gambling, 20% are reported to have attempted suicide.

QUESTIONS: Applying the test of *Frye v. United States* [see § 1.04(c) for a discussion of this case], at least one court has held that clinical testimony attempting to link the pathological gambling diagnosis to insanity is inadmissible.[13] On the facts of this case, do you agree? Assuming that such testimony is admissible as a general matter, is any of the specific language of the witness legally or ethically prohibited? Assuming the studies described by the witnesses are accurately depicted, should their results be admissible? What else would you like to know about them? Does it matter whether the clinical or research testimony is presented in a criminal trial by the defendant as opposed to the state at a commitment proceeding? Would your answer to any of these questions change in a jurisdiction that followed *Daubert v. Dow Pharmaceutial* [see § 1.04(c) for a description of this case]?

As suggested in the introduction, some of the perceived "clashes" between law and the mental health professions reflect fundamental conceptual differences. These are discussed in the next section. Here we tackle some of the more practical reasons for tension between lawyers and mental health professionals.

(a)   Bridging Gaps in Training

Discussions of what is "wrong" in the relationship between law and the mental health professions have tended to focus on relatively superficial problems of communication. Typically, there is a suggestion that the core problem is that lawyers and mental health professionals do not "speak the same language." Hence, lawyers may be awed when a mental health professional appears to be able to sweep away the complexities of the human mind with profundities about "diffuse ego boundaries," and mental health professionals may complain that the sorts of questions that lawyers ask force them to compartmentalize their observations in foreign and untenable ways. If the tension between law and mental health is the result of semantic difficulties, it should be erasable by facilitating communication between the two professional groups. Thus, problems should be remediable through some combination of cross-disciplinary training and transformation of legal tests into language and concepts commonly used by mental health professionals.

Such a view strikes us as naive. We do not mean to minimize the need for training, of course. Indeed, this book is oriented toward facilitation of an understanding of the kinds of questions that the law poses for mental health professionals. We, like others, have been troubled by "expert" mental health professionals who testify on a particular legal issue without any understanding of the nature of the issue they are purporting to address. We are also troubled when legal authorities claim ignorance of "medical" problems in the law and effectively avoid hard decisions by demanding conclusory opinions from mental health professionals. Both examples are indicative of inappropriate avoidance of "confusion by the facts." Professionals whose practice takes them into interdisciplinary matters, whether legally or behaviorally trained, have an ethical obligation to learn enough to be able to function competently in such a context.

Such training will not eliminate interdisciplinary problems, however. Simply inculcating a common understanding of key terms will not eradicate the philosophical problems inherent in interdisciplinary endeavors. A well-known example of this fact was the failure of the District of Columbia Circuit's experiment in the 1950s with the *Durham* rule (or product test) of insanity. Concerned with the unhelpfulness of much psychiatric testimony in insanity cases, that court, in an opinion by Judge Bazelon, concluded that the problem would be alleviated if the test language were reformed to make it congruent with the jargon of the mental health professions. Accordingly, rather than force mental health professionals to compartmentalize the mind into specific faculties (as the historic *M'Naghten* test appears to demand), the *Durham* test asked mental health professionals to determine whether the criminal act was the "product of mental disease or defect" [see § 8.02(b) for further discussion of these tests]. Essentially, the question was simply one of whether the legally relevant behavior was caused by the defendant's mental illness, a concept assumed to be well within the repertoire of mental health professionals.

It should have come as no surprise that *Durham* ultimately failed, however.[14] As discussed later in this chapter [§ 1.03(a)], there is no coherent conceptual basis for determining which behaviors are produced by "free choice" and which behaviors are the product of mental illness. The question makes little sense in a deterministic paradigm. Simply medicalizing the terms of the insanity test does not eliminate the much more fundamental philosophical differences between the law and the behavioral sciences. (In Case Study 1.1, for example, the "medical" conclusion that Mr. Simpson's embezzlement was the product of a pathological gambling syndrome would still not answer the ultimate legal question of whether he should be held responsible for it.) Similarly, these conceptual differences between law and the behavioral sciences will not be eliminated, although they may be unmasked, by acquisition of a working knowledge of key concepts in the law (for mental health professionals) or the behavioral sciences (for lawyers).

(b)   Bridging Attitudinal Differences

Just as it is naive to believe that problems in the interaction between law and mental health will be eliminated through training programs, so too is it simplistic to view these conflicts as mere reflections of attitudinal differences. Those who emphasize the significance of these differences tend to perceive lawyers as concerned primarily with the sanctity of legal principles in the abstract and, accordingly, with the vigorous advocacy of civil liberties for people with mental illness without regard to their needs. Conversely, mental health professionals are perceived as paternalistic and prone "to try to help" regardless of the cost of liberty, with the result that they advocate hospitalization and treatment whether the context is civil commitment, criminal trial, or sentencing. Such perceptions lead to the conclusion that conflicts between the law and the mental health professions would be largely eliminated if some middle ground of attitudes toward people with mental disabilities were reached; the issues then are simply ones of consciousness-raising.

Undoubtedly, there are substantial differences in the socialization of the professions. However, we believe that differences between libertarian and paternalist attitudes are overemphasized as a source of disciplinary conflict. First, the attitudinal differences among the mental health professions themselves may be as great as, or perhaps even greater than, those between lawyers and mental health professionals generally.[15] Thus, the American Psychiatric Association has commonly advocated less deference to patients' wishes and less legalistic procedures in decisionmaking about treatment than have the American Psychological Association and the American Orthopsychiatric Association.[16] Second, research suggests that lawyers tend to be paternalists themselves when they are actually confronted with people who have been labeled as having a mental illness. Poythress, for example, was unable to train lawyers to adopt a more adversary stance when representing respondents in civil commitment actions.[17] Although the lawyers were taught the inadequacies of testimony by mental health professionals (e.g., problems of reliability and validity of diagnosis), they persisted in avoiding careful cross-examination of expert witnesses in commitment proceedings because of a belief that it was in the best interests of their clients to be hospitalized and deprived of liberty. In short, particular attitudes are not the province of any one profession. Rather they are, again, the product of fundamental philosophical positions that may not be reconcilable.

(c)   The State of the Art

A more significant source of trouble between law and the mental health professions, although still one that is practical rather than philosophical, is the paucity of scientific knowledge concerning human behavior in many contexts. Even if both language and assumptions can be matched sufficiently to allow relatively easy translation of knowledge from the behavioral sciences into legal concepts, there is often little legally relevant knowledge to apply. Moreover, if there is a relevant body of psychological knowledge, the conclusions that can be drawn from it may not be sufficiently reliable to warrant their use in legal decisionmaking.

The state-of-the-art problems may be divided into three types. First, there are general problems of uncertainty in the behavioral sciences. That is, often there is a question of whether there is sufficient rigor in the behavioral sciences to warrant the admissibility of opinions based on these disciplines or, if admitted, to warrant placing much weight on them. It is important in this regard to distinguish between *scientific* opinions about processes of human behavior (e.g., evidence from experiments about precipitants of aggression) and *clinical* opinions about psychological functioning of particular individuals (e.g., formulation of the causes of aggression committed by a particular individual at a particular time). In the former instance, the weight placed on opinions will be limited by the level of explanation achieved,[18] the degree of control for extraneous sources of variance in the relevant studies,[19] and the degree of generalizability in the findings of the relevant studies to situations outside the laboratory.[20] Clinical opinions also should be derived from general, scientifically verifiable principles of behavior, and their rigor can often be determined through studies (many of which are described in this book) of their reliability[21] and validity,[22] yet ultimately they are often more art and intuition than science.[23]

Irrespective of general uncertainties in the behavioral sciences, a second type of state-of-the-art problem stems from gaps in the current state of knowledge with respect to questions asked by the law. For example, there is a substantial literature on the effects of divorce on children. However, as discussed in Chapter 16, little of that research is directly applicable to questions pertaining to dispositions of child custody disputes, either in individual cases or as a matter of policy. Similarly, although there are numerous studies concerning the efficacy of training people with mental retardation in self-help and social skills, there is virtually no research on training women with moderate or severe mental retardation in use of contraceptives, avoidance of sexual abuse, and maintenance of menstrual hygiene—all skills relevant to determinations of whether a person should be involuntarily sterilized.[24] Thus, although the *general* state of knowledge with respect both to effects of divorce and to training of people with mental retardation may be rather advanced, the literature may be virtually barren with respect to *specific* legally relevant questions.

A third state-of-the-art problem arises when questions asked by the law are inherently unanswerable. Sometimes the differences between possible dispositions are sufficiently subtle that it is extremely unlikely that behavioral science would ever advance to a point where their effects would be distinguishable. To give an extreme example, one of us was once asked to evaluate a child in a divorce dispute in order to assess the relative impact of spending one week a year versus two weeks a year with his mother.

1.03.   Paradigm Conflicts

While it may be difficult to reconcile variations in attitutde, flaws in training, or tensions created by state-of-the-art problems, it is differences in paradigm that are mostly likely to cause rifts between the law and the behavioral sciences. This section addresses the following questions: How is interaction between lawyers and mental health professionals likely to be affected by differing ways of conceptualizing problems? Do the differences in the philosophies of law and science imply inherent conflict?

(a)   Free Will versus Determinism

Perhaps the most obvious philosophical difference between the law and the behavioral sciences is that the former is predicated on an assumption of free will whereas the sciences are generally solidly deterministic. Indeed, the behavioral sciences are generally directed toward an explanation or prediction of the factors determining behavior. On the other hand, the law holds individuals responsible for their conduct, unless the behavior appears to be the product of a will overborne by external pressure or internal compulsion, or of a mind so irrational as to raise questions about the individual's capacity to function in the community of independent moral actors.[25]

In the present context, the significance of these differing underlying assumptions about motivation and freedom is that there is no basis in any of the prevailing models of abnormal behavior to differentiate "caused" or "overborne" behavior from behavior that is the product of free and rational choice. In a provocative analysis of the use of voluntariness in determining the validity of confessions, Grano recognized this point:

> [E]ven assuming a person's will can be overborne without rendering the person unconscious, the tools do not exist to tell us whether the breaking point has been reached. If we reject, as we must, a literal notion of overborne wills, our only alternative is to shift from the empirical inquiry regarding what happened to a professedly normative inquiry regarding the degree of mental freedom necessary to produce a "voluntary" [act].[26]

A cursory review of major models of abnormal behavior underscores the incompatibility of their basic assumptions with legal decisionmaking. The most marked example of such incompatibility is the behaviorist model, which conceptualizes behavior as the product of the individual's history of rewards and punishments in combination with the specific contingencies of reward and punishment present in a given situation.[27] Because *all* behavior is thought to be so determined, there is no basis in behaviorist thinking for identifying "voluntary" behavior.

Even models of abnormal behavior that superficially are more compatible with legal assumptions about the origins of conduct on closer examination fail to fit. Psychoanalytic theories of behavior provide individual, intrapsychic explanations of conduct. Because they may "explain" the underlying motivations of people, they may appear to provide a measure of which behavior was in fact compelled. The problem with such application is that psychoanalytic psychology is *generally* deterministic. As reflected in Freud's paper "Psychopathology of Everyday Life,"[28] psychoanalysis posits that much behavior that may be partially the result of rational decisions or conscious choices (e.g., embezzling money in order to pay one's bills) may also be "overdetermined" by unconscious motives (e.g., a desire to be punished). In the example given, most people would view the thief as criminally responsible and in control of his or her behavior; there is no basis in psychoanalytic theory for making such a determination, however. Even if one makes a distinction, as do later psychoanalytic theorists,[29] between behavior that is motivated initially by conflict-laden experiences (and therefore "driven") and behavior that is "conflict free," such a distinction does not provide a tenable basis for identifying compelled versus free behavior.[30] As May, an eminent existential theorist, pointed out, a concept of "autonomy of the ego" (i.e., the rational, "executive" part of the psyche) "becomes something akin to Descartes' theory that the pineal gland, the organ at the base of the brain between body and head, was the place where the soul was located."[31] If the personality as a whole is not free, it is hard to conceptualize a *part* of the personality as autonomous outside its totality.

Unlike members of the two schools of thought discussed thus far, humanistic/existential theorists (e.g., Viktor Frankl, Abraham Maslow, Rollo May, and Carl Rogers) have generally started from a fundamental premise that human behavior is the result of free choice. In this instance, however, the problem is that the psychological model is *too* undeterministic to match legal assumptions. Existentialists generally hold that, even in the most dire circumstances, people ultimately have choices.

A final model of abnormal behavior, which more closely matches legal assumptions about the causation of behavior, is a true (organic) medical model.[32] To use a common textbook example, suppose a man standing near the edge of a cliff has an epileptic seizure. As he falls to the ground, he bumps a bystander and knocks that person off the cliff. The seizure behavior was clearly not the product of voluntary, conscious choice. Punishment for a symptom of disease would offend most people's sense of justice.[33] Analogously, if legally relevant behavior could be shown to result directly from a disease process, that behavior would also be excused. This principle is embedded in the language of insanity standards, which generally require that a threshold of "mental disease or defect" be crossed.

Rarely, however, is there such a direct relationship between organic condition and behavior. For example, with respect to severe mental disorders for which there appears to be a genetic basis, the relationship is generally one in which genetic factors account for only a portion of the variance. Commonly, genetic background is thought merely to *predispose* the individual to psychopathology, such that psychopathology is activated only when

the individual has experienced a pathogenic, stressful environment.[34] Moreover, neither the specific anatomical or biochemical abnormality that is inherited nor the specific mechanism of genetic transmission is likely to be definitively known, although such knowledge is rapidly growing.[35]

Even with wholly organic explanations for behavior, moreover, we inevitably uncover a tension between determinism and free will. Lest an untenable dualism remain, we are left with an assumption that *all* behavior is controlled by the nervous system. There is no apparent philosophical basis for distinguishing between behavior resulting from a central nervous system lesion and behavior resulting from a "normal" system, as it is shaped by genetic composition in interaction with life experiences.

In short, if the clinician is theoretically consistent, the paradigm within which mental health professionals (of whatever theoretical orientation) work would appear to be in inherent conflict with legal worldviews. Notwithstanding attempts at reconciliation by some commentators,[36] the philosophical assumptions that govern these disciplines seem to a large extent mutually exclusive. These conflicts are of substantial significance as a matter of policy in attempting to apply the behavioral sciences or clinical opinions to legal problems.

However, the individual expert need not be paralyzed by this dilemma. Indeed, there is at least a partial solution: Mental health professionals should be neither permitted nor cajoled to give opinions on the ultimate legal issue (i.e., the conclusion that the factfinder must ultimately draw—e.g., was the act voluntary?). Although practical problems result from this position [see § 18.05], we feel that clinicians should, whenever possible, resist drawing causal conclusions with respect to voluntariness or responsibility when the concept does not make sense within a scientific paradigm. Rather, the relevant factual findings should be presented so that the factfinder (i.e., the judge or the jury) may fit them into the legal framework and may make whatever moral–legal judgments follow. Thus, for example, in assessing the "voluntariness" of Mr. Simpson's embezzlement [see Case Study 1.1] the clinician might assist the factfinder by describing the types of choices Simpson confronted, given his particular characteristics and his specific situation. However, whether his behavior was "involuntary"—whether the choice was so hard as to represent an "overbearing" context—should be left to the factfinder. This "ultimate issue issue" is discussed at greater length below [§ 1.04].

(b)   The Process of Factfinding

Still another source of potential stress in the relationship between the law and the mental health professions lies in the nature of the process of inquiry on which the disciplines rely. It is commonplace for mental health professionals to express discomfort with the adversary process employed in Anglo-American law. Part of this discomfort probably stems from the differing social purposes of the law and the behavioral sciences. The behavioral sciences (even more so, the mental health professions specifically) are dedicated to the development and application of knowledge designed to promote positive interpersonal relations—in a sense, to *prevent* or at least to dampen social conflict. Although the ultimate social function of law in resolving disputes is compatible with the ends served by the behavioral sciences, the law accomplishes this function by *sharpening* conflict, so as to ensure that issues in dispute are carefully posed and that they are resolved fairly in accordance with societal values. In view of these differing functions, it would be unsurprising to find disciplinary differences in the comfort experienced when dealing with conflict generally and adversariness in particular.

Although procedural differences may stimulate interdisciplinary problems, this problem may be exaggerated in significance. It can be largely resolved by remembering that the purpose of forensic evaluation differs qualitatively from the purpose of other forms of observation and study in the behavioral sciences or the mental health professions. Although mental health professionals may correctly complain that the adversary system distorts their conclusions by stimulating the presentation of only the evidence that is favorable to one side, they should understand that the legal process is designed not just to uncover *truth* but also to render *justice*. Due process demands that

each side have the opportunity to put forward whatever evidence best makes its case. This is not to say that the law should or does ignore reality, only to indicate that the goal of truthfinding in law is subordinate to the pursuit of justice—a synthesis of two antithetical views.[37] Hence, as long as they maintain intellectual integrity and recognize the limits of their observations and expertise, mental health professionals should be undisturbed if they are "used" by one side in the dispute.[38]

A similar source of tension comes when experts find that their observations are "pigeonholed" into concepts that seem to strip the data of their richness. Thus, one often observes a lawyer straining to have an expert curtail an intricate explanation about the subject's relations with the victim and urging the expert to "stick to the point"—the point being, perhaps, whether the defendant "planned" the attack on the victim. Similarly, clinicians may feel constrained by certain legal rulings, such as the inability to talk about prior criminal offenses. Concern about these practices again arises from a misunderstanding of purpose. The law is fundamentally conservative. As legal scholar Paul Freund noted, "no Nobel Prize is awarded for the most revolutionary judicial decision of the year."[39] The reliance on precedents and rules of law ensures the maintenance of the social fabric and the even-handed and predictable administration of justice. For instance, a single-minded focus on planning may be dictated by the jurisdiction's homicide law which, for reasons developed over scores of years, has pinpointed premeditation as the primary criterion for establishing murder. Similarly, the evidentiary rule barring evidence of past crimes rests on the conclusion, stemming from centuries of trial experiences, that otherwise the factfinder may convict a person for what he or she did in the past rather than deliberate on the current charge. Thus, although at times examination of the evidence within a narrow historical framework may seem to pull attention away from the best interests of the parties, such narrowness of concern ensures that specific points of dispute will be resolved justly.

There is a problem, however, when jurists become so focused on normative analysis and historic legal values that they carry precedent beyond its logical bounds. Sometimes, in their zeal to protect legal values, judges seem to derive an "is" from an "ought"—that is, to assume that the world in fact operates in the way that they think it should. Such blinders to the real world promote unfair decisionmaking. For example, limits placed by the United States Supreme Court on minors' autonomy and privacy have frequently been ostensibly based on empirically unsupportable assumptions about adolescents' competency and family life (e.g., that youth under 18 are not competent to make treatment decisions).[40] It is unjust and intellectually dishonest to base the deprivation of liberty on invalid assumptions. If a decision is in fact based on particular values, those values should be clearly expressed. Thus, in terms of the example given, if the Supreme Court wishes to support a particular view of family autonomy, it should make clear its preference for that policy. On the other hand, if there really are empirical assumptions underlying the analysis, whether of case facts or of legislative facts, the parties should be able to expect that a persuasive display of evidence on point will turn the case.[41]

(c)　The Nature of a Fact

Assuming for argument's sake that the clash in assumptions about causal relations and the difference in means of discovering such relationships need not be major obstacles in the interaction between law and the behavioral sciences, there still remain fundamental but more subtle and probably even more problematic epistemological issues. Specifically, major disciplinary differences exist in the conceptualization of a "fact." This definition issue is closely linked to the process issue just discussed, in that whether the law and the behavioral sciences recognize particular information as a relevant "fact" depends on whether the respective truthfinding process has been followed. However, for clarity of analysis, we separate the process of finding facts from the question of whether a fact exists and turn now to the latter issue.

(1)　From Probability to Certainty

Perhaps the most basic problem rests in differing conceptions about the role of probability assess-

ments. Although the sciences are inherently probabilistic in their understanding of truth, the law demands at least the appearance of certainty, perhaps because of the magnitude and irrevocability of decisions that must be reached in law. As Haney has noted, "there is a peculiar transformation that probabilistic statements undergo in the law. The legal concept of 'burden of proof,' for example, is explicitly probabilistic in nature. But once the burden has been met, the decision becomes absolute—a defendant is either completely guilty or not."[42]

To give an example of this difference in conceptualization of facts, suppose that a construction company is charged with negligence after a bridge that it built collapses. Specifically, the company is alleged to have used steel rods that were too small for the construction needs. A civil engineer is asked, as an expert, to measure the rods and to determine the length that the rods should have been in order to provide a safe structure. The engineer might take several measurements of the rods and conclude that the probability is greater than 0.95 that the true length of the rods was between 1.35 meters and 1.37 meters, when measured at 75°F. The engineer then might note the probability of contraction to a given length at the lowest temperature observed in the particular locality. Still another probability judgment might be made as to the likelihood of an even lower temperature's occurring in the future. On the other hand, from a legal perspective, either the rod was too small or it was not. Although the tolerable risk of error is acknowledged in the standard of proof applied (e.g., preponderance of the evidence), the conclusion of fact is made in all-or-none fashion.

Although this difference may seem rather trivial at first glance, its import is actually quite substantial. There is a danger that, because of the law's preference for certainty, experts will over-reify their observations and reach beyond legitimate interpretations of the data both to appear "expert" and to provide usable opinions. Similarly, legal decisionmakers may discard testimony properly given in terms of probabilities as "speculative" and may defer instead to experts whose judgments are expressed in categorical opinions of what did or will happen. The result is a less properly informed court. The risk of distorting the factfinding process is particularly great in the behavioral sciences given that single variables rarely account for more than 25% of the variance in a particular phenomenon and that the reliability and validity of observations by mental health professionals are far from perfect.

Part of the problem is simply intellectual dishonesty, however well intended. In the desire to be helpful, experts may permit themselves to be seduced into giving opinions that are more certain than the state of knowledge warrants. In our view, experts are ethically obligated to describe the uncertainty in their conclusions, even though such honesty may result in the courts' reducing the weight accorded the testimony, even unduly so.[43]

The problem is not simply one of professional ethics, however, or even of overzealousness by attorneys in their attempt to elicit strongly favorable opinions from experts. The style of clinical decisionmaking itself (as opposed to that of scientific research) often may not be conducive to the truthfinding process. Although researchers customarily report their findings in terms of probability statements, practitioners often must make judgments that are of an all-or-none character. Because of the need to develop and implement treatment plans, clinicians must make decisions as to what the problem is and as to how best to treat it. Moreover, because of placebo effects, the efficacy of treatment may be enhanced as a function of the display of confidence by clinicians in the treatment they are administering. In short, even if mental health professionals are fully cognizant of the weaknesses in the scientific basis of their work, they are probably advised to behave as if there were near-certainty in their formulations and the efficacy of their treatment. The problem in the present context is that if this style of presentation is carried into the reporting of forensic evaluations, the legal factfinder may be misled as to the certainty of the conclusions.

Unfortunately, this style of presentation—especially when it is *idiographic* in nature (i.e., case-centered rather than based on group data)—is preferred by the courts, as well as lawyers. For instance, the testimony in the Simpson proceedings [see Case Study 1.1] that Simpson was irrational or anxious may well be given more credence by the legal system than the testimony describing the

research on the percentage of those with the pathological gambling diagnosis who commit forgery and other crimes. Although we do not wish to denigrate careful clinical testimony, we also find it unfortunate if, as they sometimes do, the courts reject the testimony of researchers whose work sheds light on the behavioral phenomenon in question. This rejection is especially serious if the topic is one on which academic psychologists are more likely to be expert, such as the reliability of eyewitness testimony.[44] In any case, the general point is that clinicians involved in the legal process should be careful to think like scientists to give an accurate picture of the probabilistic nature of their facts, even if this stance heightens the discomfort of both the clinician and the court.

This general admonition is appropriate even in jurisdictions that attempt to transform probabilistic judgments into certain facts by application of a standard of "reasonable medical (psychological, scientific) certainty" when deciding the admissibility of expert testimony. As Martin has pointed out, professionals are likely to have idiosyncratic subjective judgments of "reasonable certainty";[45] moreover, even "uncertain" opinions may still be relevant and of assistance to the trier of fact provided that the conclusions have some probative value and are not unduly prejudicial. Most important, the standard of reasonable certainty may in fact *result* in prejudicial opinions, because the fact that the opinions *are* probabilistic is masked by the certainty standard. Experts should leave to the judge the question of whether the opinions are so uncertain as to be unhelpful.[46]

(2)   From Group to Individual

Assuming that the probabilistic nature of the opinions is acknowledged, another problem arises. As already noted, the scientific data base for the behavioral sciences on which all researchers and many clinicians rely is generally *nomothetic:* That is, principles of behavior are derived from comparisons of *groups* differing on a particular dimension. Given that, in psychology, a particular variable will almost never perfectly account for the variance in another variable, the problem is one of how to apply psychological findings based on group data to individual cases. Although this problem is not one for the experts themselves, it is a major conceptual obstacle for legal factfinders and may result in rejection of the expert's opinions.

Some case examples may indicate the significance of the philosophical dilemmas that are presented when applying nomothetic data to the resolution of individual cases.

Case 1.[47] The defendant's 14-year-old daughter accused him of raping her. Two months later (and on two subsequent occasions), she wrote statements recanting her accusation; she said that she had lied so she could get "out on her own." However, at trial, she returned to her original story. Experts testified that such inconsistency is common among victims of incest.

Case 2.[48] The defendant was charged with third-degree murder of his three-month-old son. An expert on child abuse testified that the pattern of injuries was consistent with "battered child syndrome." He testified further that abusing parents tend to have been abused as children themselves and that they also are prone to a number of negative personality characteristics (e.g., short temper and social isolation). The state then called two witnesses from the defendant's past (his caseworker as a youth; an employee of a therapeutic school he had attended). The caseworker testified that the defendant had been abused; both testified that the defendant had many of the personality traits identified by the first expert. Other witnesses provided additional testimony suggesting that the defendant possessed characteristics identified by the expert as consistent with those common to battering parents.

Case 3.[49] The defendant was stopped by Drug Enforcement Administration (DEA) agents after she disembarked from an airplane at the Detroit Metropolitan Airport. The DEA agent's suspicions were aroused because the defendant's behavior fit a "drug courier profile": (1) the plane on which she arrived had originated in a "source city" (Los Angeles, thought to be the origin of much of the heroin brought to Detroit), (2) she was the last person to leave the plane, (3) she appeared to be nervous and watchful, (4) she did not claim any luggage, and (5) she changed airlines for her flight from Detroit. On questioning, the defendant appeared nervous, and it became known that her ticket had been purchased under an assumed name. A search revealed heroin hidden in her undergarments. The defendant contested the search on the ground that the agents had no reasonable basis for suspecting that she was involved in criminal activity and for stopping her for an investigation. Testimony at trial indicated that during the first 18 months of the surveillance based on behavioral profiles, agents had searched 141 persons in 96 encounters and had found illicit substances in 77 instances.

Case 4. An offender in Michigan is denied parole because he is a "very high" assaultive risk. Of parolees whose behavior fits this category, 40% are rearrested and returned to prison for a violent crime while on parole. The offender protests that he has been placed in the very-high-risk group because of a juvenile arrest for an offense of which he was never convicted. Moreover, he asserts that he has "reformed" and that he should be considered to be among the 60% of very-high-risk offenders who will not be recidivists.

These four cases starkly pose the question of whether attention to probability data in the legal system is legitimate.[50] The cases represent four different problems (respectively, whether a crime occurred, the identity of a past legal actor, the identity of a present legal actor, the identity of a future legal actor). Is the issue of whether to consider this type of probability evidence merely a function of its reliability and explanatory power, or is there something inherently unfair about determinations of past, present, or future guilt on the partial basis of group data?

A thorough consideration of these issues has been presented in an influential article by Tribe,[51] who concluded that, for the most part,[52] the law should bar evidence expressed in mathematical probabilities. Tribe raised a number of objections to "precision" in the consideration of evidence:

1. Probability estimates are themselves inherently probabilistic, in that the validity of the probability itself must be considered. For example, in a case in which eyewitnesses saw a brown-eyed, brown-haired male rob a bank in a small Finnish town, jurors' assessment of the probability that a defendant who meets the physical description and was found in the town is the robber must take into account the probability of the intitial eyewitness's account and the probability of the validity of the statistics indicating how often people with these characteristics are found in small Finnish towns. Consequently, the presentation of a single statistic or even a string of statistics may be deceptive. Moreover, jurors' consideration of the

data may be complicated by statistical interdependence. For example, brown eyes and brown hair are correlated, so one cannot do a simple Bayesian computation[53] to learn the probability of their joint occurrence.

2. The presumption of innocence may be effectively negated by permitting consideration of the probability that a person with X characteristic is guilty.[54] For instance, direct consideration at trial of such probabilities will necessarily force the factfinder to include in the calculus the probability of guilt that is associated merely with having been brought to trial. Presumably, this initial probability is likely to be greater than zero, despite legal assumptions to the contrary.

3. Soft variables will be dwarfed by more easily quantifiable ones.[55] To return to our example of the Finnish bank robber, the attention to the defendant's physical characteristics might divert attention from the probability that he has been framed.

4. The "quantification of sacrifice" (i.e., the recognition of the risk of a wrongful conviction) is intrinsically immoral.[56] There is something intuitively unjust in telling a defendant that the jury is willing to tolerate X risk of error in convicting him.

5. Reliance on statistical evidence dehumanizes the trial process by diminishing jurors' ritualized intuitive expression of community values.[57] Rather than clarify the jury's role in expressing the will of the community, statistical evidence will obscure this role and make the legal process seem alien to the public.

Although Tribe has articulated important issues, we are more persuaded by Saks and Kidd's critique of his article.[58] First, Tribe's analysis relied in part on unverified psychological assumptions (e.g., jurors will be overinfluenced by quantified evidence and jurors in the present system feel subjectively certain in their judgments when they reach a verdict based on a standard of "beyond a reasonable doubt"). Second, research on intuitive information processing of the type preferred by Tribe suggests that jurors will make errors of analysis in their consideration of implicit probabilities unless the actual probabilities are brought to their attention. Third, as Tribe himself acknowledged, all evidence is ultimately probabilistic, regardless of whether it is quantified. Simply pretending that it is not and ignoring the clearest, most specific evidence does not lead to morally superior decisionmaking.

At the same time, accuracy of evidence is not the only concern. Other legal considerations may counsel limiting or excluding even relatively reliable probability evidence in some types of cases. Two such concerns are particularly important. The first is that certain types of information used in probabilistic testimony, although scientifically relevant, may not be legally cognizable. For instance, reliance on race as a statistical predictor may be impermissible for constitutional reasons, even if it is correlated to a legally relevant variable.[59] Indeed, some have argued that, in some settings, *every* factor over which one has no control should be banned as a basis for an actuarial determination.[60]

A second concern is the effect probabilistic information may have on the factfinder. Tribe exaggerated the layperson's inability to understand such information. But there is a danger that, if and when it is understood, statistical information will assume too much prominence in the factfinder's decisionmaking process, at least when it is used by the state to bolster the preconceived and often incorrect notions of the factfinder. This danger of "prejudice," to use the legal term,[61] is probably greatest in the criminal context in cases such as the four described above, where the stakes are high both in terms of threats to individual freedom and to public welfare.

Probably the least prejudicial use of probabilistic information is in connection with police investigation. Using behavioral science techniques to construct a "profile" of offender characteristics that might be associated with a particular kind of crime, law enforcement agents have tried to narrow the range of suspects in a given case (as in Case 3). Although this approach is not without problems,[62] at least it is relegated to the investigative phase of trial, where probability assessments are inherent and thus more easily countenanced.[63]

Use of such evidence in criminal adjudication (Cases 1 and 2), where the legal objective is to determine definitively whether *this* defendant committed a crime, is much more problematic. For instance, when applied to a criminal defendant on trial (as in Case 2), such evidence is character evidence, which is not ordinarily admissible unless the defendant puts character at issue by claiming that he or she is not the type of person who would commit the crime.[64] Even though there may be a substantial correlation, revealed by well-designed research, between particular traits and involvement in particular kinds of offenses, such information is considered too prejudicial to permit except in response to defense assertions. Given a presumption of innocence, defendants must be convicted on the basis of what they did, not who they are.

The character evidence rule is not applicable when profile evidence is used to suggest a crime occurred (Case 1). Thus, initial prosecution use of such evidence has often been permitted, most often as expert testimony to suggest that the purported victim shows behavioral characteristics exhibited by victims of a particular kind of offense [see §§ 8.03(c), 15.04(c)(4)]. Here too, however, syndrome evidence can create problems. Even if it is strong scientifically, it may be inherently misleading because of the difficulty most people have in processing base rates.[65] For example, Table 1.1 presents a hypothetical case in which an extraordinarily valid profile of a sexually abused child—far more valid than anything currently available—still would result in only a 32% probability that a randomly selected child showing the profile (an assumption consonant with the presumption of innocence) would have recently been abused. Yet a judge or jury, once hearing that the victim met the profile, would probably not believe the probability to be so low. Nor would telling them how low it is be likely to diminish the profile's impact, as the mere fact that a prosecution has been brought already has created the strong impression that a crime must have been committed. Thus, a "defendant-first" rule, analogous to the character evidence rule, might be appropriate here as well unless the profile evidence is very strong.

In forward-looking decisions (e.g., sentencing, as in Case 4), the inquiry is, as with investigation and unlike at trial, inherently probabilistic; actuarial data are thus directly relevant [see § 9.09(c)]. Here, too, however, the possibility is great that such data will overly impress the factfinder, at least when used by the state to con-

Table 1.1

Probability That a Child Fitting a Hypothetical Profile of a Sexually Abused Child Actually Has Been Recently Abused

1. There are about 65 million children and youth in the United States.
2. Assume that 5% have been sexually abused recently.[a]
3. Therefore, 3.25 million children and youth have been recently sexually abused; 61.75 million have not.
4. Assume that 90% of the children found to fit the profile of a sexually abused child on the Melton Magnificent Measure (MMM) have recently been sexually abused, while 10% of those who fit the profile have not been abused.[b]
5. Sally Doe fits the MMM profile.

What is the probability that Sally has been recently sexually abused?

3.25 million $\times$ 0.90 = 2.925 million true positives (*TPs*)

61.75 million $\times$ 0.10 = 6.175 million false positives (*FPs*)

2.925 million *TPs* + 6.175 million *FPs* = 9.1 million positives (*Ps*)

2.925 million *TPs* divided by 9.1 million *Ps* = 0.32

Therefore, the hypothetical probability (under a scenario of far more pronounced base-rate differences than is true in reality) is only about 1 in 3!

[a]This hypothetical percentage probably substantially exceeds the actual base rate of recent sexual abuse in the general population of children. Community surveys (most of them retrospective) to determine prevalence *at any point* during childhood have yielded median prevalence rates of 15% for females and 6.5% for males. Stefanie Doyle Peters et al., *Prevalence*, in A SOURCEBOOK ON CHILD SEXUAL ABUSE 15, 20–21 (David Finkelhor ed. 1986).

[b]The development of a profile with such high validity is extremely unlikely given the great diversity of responses among victims of child sexual abuse. See Jon R. Conte & Lucy Berliner, *The Impact of Sexual Abuse of Children: Empirical Findings*, in HANDBOOK OF SEXUAL ABUSE OF CHILDREN 72 (Lenore Walker ed. 1987).

firm the likely assumption of the factfinder that a person who has just committed a crime will offend again. Rebutting these data by pointing to the false positive rate or by trying to distinguish the offender from those in the actuarial profile may well be futile in this situation.[66] At the least, when the false positive rate is high (as is the case, for instance, with actuarial prediction of dangerousness), courts might again do well to consider prohibiting the use of such information unless the defendant uses it first.

1.04. Should Mental Health Professionals Be Considered Experts?

As the preceding discussion illustrates and as we reiterate below, we believe that some controls on mental health testimony are necessary in circumstances in which it is inherently misleading or prejudicial. Nonetheless, we retain our general preference for liberal use of behavioral science expertise. To explain this view, we come now to what may be the core problem in contemporary forensic mental health: Should mental health professionals be recognized as experts by the law and, if so, for what purposes? Before discussing the courts' answer to this question, we will give our own. In doing so, we refer liberally to the Federal Rules of Evidence, the relevant parts of which are listed in Table 1.2. Because most states have adopted all or part of these rules, they will form the baseline for our analysis.

(a)   The Definition of Specialized Knowledge

The first point to note is that, whereas laypersons are generally limited in their testimony to descriptions of direct observations (see Rule 701), experts may testify as to opinions, provided that the "specialized knowledge" of the witness will "assist" the trier of fact in determining a relevant issue (Rule 702). Rule 702's insistence that the expert assist the factfinder is derived in part from the democratic premise that professional education in itself does not confer special status in the legal system. In principle, everyone is equal before the bar of justice. It follows that occupational status should not infringe the societally designated authority of the judge or jury to decide the case at hand.[67] Experts should be able to go further than lay witnesses in offering opinions only if doing so would provide *specialized* information

Table 1.2
Federal Rules of Evidence, Article 7: Opinions and Expert Testimony

Rule 701.
OPINION TESTIMONY BY LAY WITNESSES

If the witness is not testifying as an expert, the witness' testimony in the form of opinions or inferences is limited to those opinions or inferences which are (a) rationally based on the perception of the witness and (b) helpful to a clear understanding of the witness' testimony or the determination of a fact in issue.

Rule 702.
TESTIMONY BY EXPERTS

If scientific, technical, or other specialized knowledge will assist the trier of fact to understand the evidence or determine a fact in issue, a witness qualified as an expert by knowledge, skill, experience, training, or education, may testify thereto in the form of an opinion or otherwise.

Rule 703.
BASES OF OPINION TESTIMONY BY EXPERTS

The facts or data in the particular case upon which an expert bases an opinion or inference may be those perceived by or made known to the expert at or before the hearing. If of a type reasonably relied upon by experts in the particular field in forming opinions or inferences upon the subject, the facts or data need not be admissible in evidence.

Rule 704.
OPINION ON ULTIMATE ISSUE

(a) Except as provided in subdivision (b), testimony in the form of an opinion or inference otherwise admissible is not objectionable because it embraces an ultimate issue to be decided by the trier of fact.
(b) No expert witness testifying with respect to the mental state or condition of a defendant in a criminal case may state an opinion or inference as to whether the defendant did or did not have the mental state or condition constituting an element of the crime charged or of a defense thereto. Such ultimate issues are matters for the trier of fact alone.

that will help the trier of fact in understanding the evidence as it is presented.

In analyzing the import of Rule 702's requirement that opinion evidence be based on specialized knowledge that can assist the factfinder, it should also be recognized that there are several levels of opinion that might be rendered. For example, in considering whether a defendant meets the *M'Naghten* test of insanity [see § 8.02(b)], the following levels of inference might occur, all of which represent increments in opinion formation:

1. Application of meaning (perception) to a behavioral image (e.g., "He was wringing his hands").
2. Perception of general mental state (e.g., "He appeared anxious").
3. "Formulation" of the perception of general mental state to fit into theoretical constructs or the research literature and/or to synthesize observations (e.g., "His anxiety during the interview was consistent with a general obsession with pleasing others").
4. Diagnosis (e.g., "His behavior during the interview and his reported history are consistent with a generalized anxiety disorder").
5. Relationship of formulation or diagnosis to legally relevant behavior (e.g., "At the time of the offense, his anxiety was so overwhelming that he failed to consider the consequences of his behavior").
6. Elements of the ultimate legal issue (e.g., "Although he was too anxious at the time of the offense to *reflect* upon the consequences of his behavior, he *knew* the nature and consequences of his acts and *knew* that what he did was wrong").
7. Ultimate legal issue (e.g., "He was sane at the time of the offense").

In considering the question of which, if any, levels of inference mental health professionals should be permitted to reach in their testimony, on one point there is near-unanimity among scholarly commentators.[68] Despite the fact that such opinions are commonly sought and, unfortunately, are commonly given, *mental health professionals ordinarily should refrain from giving opinions as to ultimate legal issues.* As we have already seen, the constructs about which an opinion might be sought (e.g., voluntariness) are often inconsistent with the model of behavior on which the expert's observations are based. Even when the constructs appear familiar, however, experts should avoid giving ultimate-issue opinions; questions as to

criminal responsibility, committability, and so forth are not based on "specialized" knowledge but are legal and moral judgments outside the expertise of mental health professionals *qua* mental health professionals. For example, the types of behavior that constitute a "mental disorder" as a matter of law may be substantially different from the range of behaviors subsumed under that concept in the expert's mind. Similarly, opinions as to dangerousness require the drawing of legal lines as to how high the probability of particular kinds of behavior must be to warrant state intervention; indeed, the definition of "dangerous" behavior itself involves legal judgments. When experts give such opinions, they usurp the role of the factfinder and may mislead the factfinder by suggesting that the opinions are based on specialized knowledge specific to the profession.

Note in this regard that although Rule 704(a) allows experts to give opinions on ultimate issues, Rule 702 prohibits admission of *any* opinion not based on specialized knowledge, a prohibition which presumably can include ultimate-issue opinions. Indeed, Rule 704(b) (an amendment to the original Rule 704 which was inspired by John Hinckley's acquittal on insanity grounds) makes this point concretely with respect to mental state testimony in criminal cases. The position we take is that the same evidentiary prohibition should apply to *all* types of cases.

In any event, even if a court permits such an opinion to be admitted as a matter of law, it should not be offered as a matter of professional ethics because of the explicit or implicit misrepresentation of the limits of expertise involved when a clinician *acting as an expert witness* gives a legal opinion in the guise of mental health knowledge.[69] The mental health professional should ask himself or herself, "Would the requested opinion be the product of expertise as a clinician, or rather stem from the moral sensibility or common sense of a citizen?" If the latter, the opinion should not be offered; if it is demanded, it should be described as a legal, moral, or commonsense judgment, not a psychological or medical one.

Under this reasoning, there are virtually no circumstances where a clinician should offer an opinion at level 7 in the hierarchy set out earlier. Testifying that a person is "sane," "dangerous," "competent," "parentally fit," or "disabled" (for workers' compensation or social security purposes) trenches on both legal and ethical domains. Testimony at level 6 should also generally be avoided because the clinician will be using legally defined language. It is true that a rigid prohibition on testimony at this level may sometimes be an artificial constraint. Talk about whether criminal defendants "knew" their act was "wrong" (both aspects of the *M'Naghten* test), even if banned, can easily be replaced with testimony about whether defendants were "aware" they were breaking the law (consider, in this regard, the testimony in Case Study 1.1). Similarly, it is often difficult to discuss competency to stand trial without directly discussing the defendant's ability to assist counsel—one of the elements of the competency standard [see Chapter 6]. However, the question of *how much* "knowledge" or "awareness" a defendant must have to be sane, or the *extent to which* defendants must be able to "assist" their attorney to be competent, is a purely legal issue. Consequently, the clinician should at the least avoid parroting the language of the legal test and should be sensitive to using unexplained synonyms as well.

The question is harder with respect to opinions based on intermediate levels of inference (2 though 5 in the list above, as well as statements at level 6 that avoid legal language). The most articulate proponent of exclusion is Morse, who has argued that only two types of testimony by mental health professionals (when testifying in that capacity) should be permitted.[70] First, Morse would permit presentation of "hard actuarial data," when relevant and available. Second, because mental health professionals usually have much more experience with "crazy" persons than do laypersons, and thus are likely to be better observers of the kinds of behavior that may be legally relevant, he would allow them to present their observations of behavior. For example, Morse believes that mental health professionals are likely to be more skilled than laypersons in asking the right questions to elicit information about hallucinations, suicidal plans, and so forth, and should thus be able to describe the answers to those questions.

On the other hand, Morse would not allow opinions as to the meaning of the behavior; he would bar formulations and diagnoses as well as conclusions on ultimate issues. Therefore, the role of mental health professionals would be that of specially trained fact witnesses. Morse has summarized his objections to most expert testimony by mental health professionals on the following grounds:

> [F]irst, professionals have considerably less to contribute than is commonly supposed; second, for legal purposes, lay persons are quite competent to make judgments concerning mental disorder; third, all mental health law cases involve *primarily* moral and social issues and decisions, not scientific ones; fourth, overreliance on experts promotes the mistaken and responsibility-abdicating view that these hard moral questions (i.e., whether and in what way to treat mentally ill persons differently) are scientific ones; and fifth, professionals should recognize this difference and refrain from drawing social and moral conclusions about which they are not expert.[71]

We have already indicated our agreement with Morse as to his third, fourth, and fifth points. We are also in agreement, for the most part, with his second point: Whether a person appears sufficiently disabled to warrant special legal treatment is an intuitive social and moral judgment. Diagnosis, for example, is largely irrelevant to mental health law questions.[72]

However, we part company with Morse with respect to his first point. We recognize the well-known,[73] although at times exaggerated,[74] vagaries of mental health assessment and prediction. The literature with respect to specific forensic questions is reviewed in more detail throughout this volume. But although we share Morse's uneasiness about the state of art in mental health assessment and his preference for testimony based on valid, quantified research, we would still permit mental health professionals to offer other opinions short of the ultimate issue.

In our view, Morse underestimates the degree to which mental health professionals can assist the factfinder in making legal judgments, *provided* that professionals both know and acknowledge the limits of their expertise. As Bonnie and Slobogin have pointed out,[75] the law's approach to the admissibility of expert opinions is *incremental*: The main consideration, as formulated in Rule 702 of the Federal Rules of Evidence, is whether the opinion will assist the factfinder (not whether it is or should be dispositive). Stated somewhat more precisely, the question is whether the probative value of the evidence outweighs its tendency to be inefficient, misleading, or prejudicial.[76] Rather than completely exclude opinions that offer marginal assistance, the modern trend in evidence law, as Morse acknowledges,[77] is to admit the testimony and let the factfinder assign the weight to be given it.

Although Morse argues that the mental health professions' scientific basis is so limited as to warrant a special exception to this general rule,[78] we believe there are two reasons for refusing to single out mental health professionals in this way. First, by way of precedent, expert opinion is commonly admitted in situations in which the opinions are no less speculative and probably more prejudicial than those commonly offered by mental health professionals. For example, the opinions of experts employed by forensic science laboratories, which are rarely challenged, are based on mistaken identifications as much as 70% of the time.[79] Moreover, psychiatric diagnosis is as reliable as numerous other areas of health science diagnosis.[80]

Second, even if speculative opinions from other disciplines have been admitted erroneously, we still would contend that justice is often served by the liberal admission of mental health professionals' opinions. Whatever might be the case with other disciplines, mental health professionals *do* have access to a body of specialized knowledge (i.e., knowledge commonly unshared by the lay public) that may assist legal factfinders in making informed judgments. Melton, Weithorn, and Slobogin administered a test of knowledge about clinical syndromes commonly observed in criminal and juvenile forensic practice and the research relevant to those syndromes to samples of mental health professionals and trial judges.[81] Mental health professionals' performance was generally superior to that of judges; when the latter were compared to mental health professionals specialized in forensic practice, the differences were especially marked.

Even when the research basis of opinions is weak, there may be instances in which the underlying knowledge is sufficiently great to warrant the admission of the opinions. For example, in contrast to Morse, we favor admission of psychological formulations (levels 3 and 4 in the typology of inference set out earlier) in many legal contexts, although we acknowledge, as Morse persuasively shows, that the scientific basis of psychodynamic formulations in particular is often inadequate for their verification. Such opinions are clearly not based on precise "science." However, neither are they folklore nor homespun wisdom. The argument here is analogous to Morse's approval of mental health professionals as trained observers of "crazy" behavior. Mental health professionals are trained and experienced in generating explanations of abnormal behavior. Even if these formulations are at times mere "stories,"[82] their narration may provide plausible explanations of a defendant's behavior that would otherwise be unavailable to the trier of fact. If these possible explanations are delivered with appropriate caution, they may well assist the factfinder in reaching a judgment, despite the fact they have not or cannot be "tested."[83]

(b)　Limitations on the Use of Specialized Knowledge

Admittedly, the conclusions of mental health professionals may provide more assistance in some contexts than in others. They seem particularly germane when the clinical testimony is offered by an individual to rebut allegations made by the state designed to deprive the individual of liberty (as in civil commitment proceedings and criminal trials and sentencing hearings). In such situations, it may often be unjust to deprive a defendant of the option of bringing appropriately framed evidence before the factfinder. More generally, we think behavioral science information is most likely to "assist" factfinders when it challenges their preconceptions (e.g., the assumption that a defendant rationally intends the consequences of his actions), a point we develop in other parts of this volume [see, e.g., § 8.03(b)].

However, similar to our comments in connection with probabilistic data, we are less sanguine about how helpful professional testimony is when the defense has decided *not* to use such testimony. Under such circumstances, the possibility that the factfinder will be unduly influenced by the state's clinician is great, given that the natural assumption is already that any individual who is being tried must be in court for a reason. The probative value of the evidence, which is low, may easily be outweighed by the possibility of prejudice.

We are also leery of reports or testimony using the upper levels of inference if they will not be subjected to the adversarial process. Although the typical insanity trial, capital sentencing proceeding, or parental fitness hearing usually involves rebuttal experts, cross-examination, and other trappings of the truth-testing process, some types of proceedings—civil commitment and competency to proceed hearings to name but two—often resemble star-chambers, where a lone expert's word is dispositive. In such situations, clinicians must be particularly careful, at the least, to explain their inferences and may even want to abide by Morse's injunction to avoid straying beyond level-1 type testimony.[84]

In summary, although the range of opinions with which mental health professionals provide the courts should be narrowed to exclude opinions of a purely moral or legal nature, the door should be left open to professional opinions that might assist the trier of fact, especially when they are likely to challenge factfinders' intuitive assumptions about human behavior and motivation. At the same time, such subultimate opinion testimony should be used cautiously. Lawyers and judges should be sensitive to the prejudicial impact this testimony can have when its use is initiated by the state or will be untested by the adversarial process, while mental health professionals, as a matter of ethics, should always assess their ability and willingness to indicate the validity or certainty of their opinions and to explain them.[85]

(c)   Expertise under **Frye** and **Daubert**[86]

With the foregoing in mind, the law's current approach to admission of testimony from mental health professionals can be more easily understood and critiqued. The courts follow virtually none of our suggested prescriptions, much less those proposed by Morse. Indeed, traditionally, testimony from clinicians has been left alone; whether framed in ultimate terms or not, it has been routinely admitted, without any consideration of its prejudicial impact, the party introduc-

ing it, or the type of proceeding involved. Although courts in recent times have been somewhat more active in monitoring such testimony, they have not done so in the nuanced way we recommend. Rather, while continuing to allow ultimate issue pronouncements about traditional mental disorders, psychodynamic causes and dangerousness, they have often barred all evidence that speaks in terms of syndromes (e.g., battered spouse syndrome) and novel-sounding diagnoses (e.g., pathological gambling), even when presented by the defense.

Until 1993, the dominant analytical vehicle for evaluating clinical testimony in federal court and many state courts was the *Frye* rule, so-called because it originated in the 1923 case of *Frye v. United States*.[87] That decision, involving an attempt to introduce the results of a polygraph test, held that the admissibility of scientific evidence should be conditioned on its being "sufficiently established to have gained general acceptance in the particular field to which it belongs."[88] As noted, traditional clinical testimony has generally been immune from a *Frye* challenge, with some courts simply claiming that the behavioral sciences should not be governed by rules relating to the "physical sciences,"[89] and others apparently assuming that most mental health professionals would agree it is based on "generally accepted" theory.[90] At the same time, more novel clinical testimony has frequently been prohibited under *Frye*, either because at the time of the decision the diagnosis at issue had not yet appeared in the *Diagnostic and Statistical Manual of Mental Disorders* (DSM),[91] or because, even if it had, the relevant field was too small or the relevant theory was too untested.[92]

Critics of the *Frye* rule regard it as unduly conservative. By requiring general acceptance, the rule results in exclusion of evidence that is novel but still reliable (valid, in scientific terms). At the same time, the *Frye* test seems to permit admission of unreliable evidence whenever it achieves general acceptance, even in a field with little or no scientific credibility (e.g., clinical predictions of dangerousness). Nonetheless, many courts retained it because of the time and expertise required in case-by-case determination of the scientific merit of experts' opinions. Under *Frye*, the court need merely hear evidence as to whether a particular technique is "generally accepted," rather than carefully balance its relevance against is prejudicial impact.[93]

In 1993, however, the analytical landscape seemed to change with the United States Supreme Court's decision in *Daubert v. Merrell Dow Pharmaceuticals.*[94] The Court's unanimous holding rested on a straightforward legal analysis: Congress adopted the Federal Rules of Evidence more than half a century after the D.C. Circuit's decision in *Frye*, and it did not intend to incorporate the "austere" *Frye* standard into the new Rules promoting "liberal" admission of evidence.[95] The Court's opinion added extensive dicta,[96] joined by seven of the nine justices, about factors to be considered in weighing scientific evidence. By implication, that discussion, written by Justice Blackmun, provides guidance to experts and attorneys preparing the presentation of opinions.

Probably the most important point made in the dicta is that bright-line indicia of reliability (e.g., whether general acceptance has been obtained or even whether peer review has occurred) are inconsistent with the balancing test implicit in the requirement for specialized knowledge that will assist the trier of fact. Thus, *Frye*'s establishment of a "threshold" standard of scientific reliability or expert credibility is misguided. The Rules of Evidence, Justice Blackmun wrote, are "designed not for cosmic understanding but for the particularized resolution of legal disputes."[97]

As to how the admissibility of scientific evidence should now be gauged, the *Daubert* dicta made clear that the opinion must be based on "an inference or assertion . . . derived by the scientific method"; that is, the court should decide "whether the reasoning or methodology underlying the testimony is scientifically valid and . . . whether that reasoning or methodology properly can be applied to the facts in issue."[98] Although expressly noting that its list of factors was not exhaustive or dispositive, the Court offered some criteria to use in forming such an impression: These included the "testability" of the theoretical basis for the opinion and the error rate associated with the methods used, as well as *Frye*-like factors such as approval by peer reviewers and the level of acceptance of those methods by experts in the field. Blackmun emphasized that Rule 702 is intended to guide a "flexible" inquiry, with the

"overarching" focus to be on "the scientific validity—and thus the evidentiary relevance and reliability—of the principles that underlie a proposed submission." He further clarified that "the focus, of course, must be solely on principles and methodology, not on the conclusions that they generate."[99] Thus, new ideas not yet generally accepted in the scientific community are not barred from admission into legal decisionmaking.

Although these latter comments sound more "liberal" than *Frye*, it remains to be seen whether *Daubert* significantly changes the admissibility inquiry, especially given its retention of peer review as one factor to consider. Indeed, the decision's emphasis on scientific validity may well have a "conservative" effect. With respect to the specific issues considered in this book, *Daubert* raises two major questions. First, will state courts follow it? Second, is the admissibility of clinical opinion governed by it?

Although most states have adopted the Federal Rules of Evidence, sometimes even to the point of using the same numbering in their code, they often vary in adoption or interpretation of particular rules. In any event, they are not bound to adopt the prevailing interpretation in the federal courts, although that understanding is often influential. In approximately the first two years after the *Daubert* ruling by the Supreme Court, appellate courts in 32 states cited it in their decisions. Eleven adopted it,[100] and five rejected it,[101] although one of the five explicitly left the door open to adopting *Daubert* at a later point.[102] The remainder cited the case without ruling on its applicability because the issue was not presented by the parties or its resolution was unnecessary to the case at bar. Some of the states adopting the *Daubert* approach had already rejected *Frye*, whereas the California and Nebraska supreme courts explicitly stated a preference for the *Frye* test.[103] Therefore, readers should be careful to determine *Daubert*'s application in their own state. Nonetheless, it appears that the trend is to reject the general acceptance test in state as well as federal law and to require, at least in theory, a more searching judicial inquiry to determine the scientific validity of expert opinions before they are admitted.

With respect to the second question, *Daubert*'s dicta do not make clear whether the guidance that they provide about determination of "scientific" knowledge also apply to "technical or other specialized knowledge" referred to in Rule 702.[104] If it does not, and clinical opinion is considered technical or specialized knowledge rather than "scientific," any admissibility inquiry that takes place may well be relatively cursory; examination of the empirical underpinnings of such opinion may occur only if such underpinnings exist.[105] If, on the other hand, opinion testimony from mental health professionals *is* seen as "scientific" in nature or, to the same effect, *Daubert's* regulation of scientific evidence is applied to *all* types of expertise, the question becomes whether its basis is scientifically "valid."[106]

Certainly in some cases it is. The type of probabilistic data discussed earlier, as well as information about some types of clinical diagnoses, has often resulted from hypothesis testing in the traditional scientific manner. But much clinical testimony would not meet this threshold. Indeed, as Bonnie and Slobogin have pointed out,

> the central etiological theories and conceptual categories of the clinical behavioral disciplines have not been scientifically validated. . . . At best, opinions about psychological processes—beyond merely descriptive observations—are clinical probability judgments rooted in theoretical constructs that are more or less widely shared among mental health professionals.[107]

In our view, transformation of *Daubert* into a new bright-line rule barring such clinical testimony as "unscientific" would be unwise. Such a stance would eliminate ways of thinking about human behavior that may be helpful to the trier of fact and that are not merely common sense. Consider, for instance, these statements taken from the sample reports set out in Chapter 19 of this book:

> One characteristic stress response is for individuals to "relive" through their own thoughts and fantasies the original stressful episodes in an apparent effort to bring about more successful (i.e., psychologically acceptable) solutions. (p. 561)

> It is probable that the death of his father contributes to his . . . loss of self-esteem. (p. 584)

> Tom's impulse control may often be tenuous, at least partially because of his poor verbal skills and resulting inability to label feelings. (p. 592)

Under a strict *Daubert* approach none of these statements could be made unless the expert could point to research articles supporting their underlying propositions, for example, that people "relive" their original stress episodes, that this reliving can be an attempt to heal, that loss of a father can contribute to loss of self-esteem, and that poor verbal skills can lead to poor impulse control. The second and third propositions cannot easily be subjected to scientific testing; the other two can be (and, to some extent, have been), but not necessarily with any definitive results. If *Daubert* were to lead to exclusion of any or all of these statements, it would be at least as arbitrary as *Frye* or its corollary requirement (as applied by the lower courts in *Daubert*) that scientific opinions must be peer reviewed. Such a result is contrary to the spirit of Rule 702 and its focus on incremental validity of decision making by the trier of fact, as many have pointed out.[108]

Unfortunately, some courts have not followed this admonition. Rather, they have relied on or referred to *Daubert* in deciding that clinical testimony should not be permitted. For instance, in *State v. Cressey*,[109] the New Hampshire Supreme Court cited *Daubert*, apparently with approval, in conducting a searching analysis of whether psychological evaluations of sexually abused children were properly admitted in a triad of cases decided on the same day. In determining that they were not, the court's decision noted that although it did not "seek to disparage the work being done in psychology and the behavioral sciences . . . the psychological evaluation of a child suspected of being sexually abused is, at best, an inexact science" that "does not present the verifiable results and logical conclusions that work to ensure the reliability required in the solemn matter of a criminal trial." It is likely that, using reasoning like that in *Cressey*, courts will increasingly demand proof that testimony from mental health professionals have some scientific basis.[110]

Of course, as stated previously, we are not adverse to this scrutiny to the extent it requires clinicians to produce the available evidence supporting their position (an approach we advocate throughout this book); for instance, basing assertions on one's "experience," without more (see Case Study 1.1), may be insufficient. But whatever the validity of the specific result in *Cressey*,[111] we think its requirement that clinical testimony be "verifiable" is too demanding. A rigid rule of exclusion for theories about human behavior that have not been subjected to the "scientific method"—including those which for ethical or practical reasons may never be so tested[112]—is overbroad.

It is also too narrow. Merely because something is "verifiable" does not mean that testimony based on it will be helpful to the jury. We agree with *Cressey*, and with O'Connor, Sales, and Shuman,[113] that juror skepticism and cross-examination cannot always be relied on to ferret out unreliable clinical testimony. But we are even less sure that jurors will be skeptical of research-based testimony or that cross-examination can detect when it is unreliable.[114] The point is that there is good and bad clinical testimony, good and bad research, and good and bad cross-examination. Rather than relying solely on verifiability as the gauge of admissibility, the better answer, we believe, is to take the nuanced approach to admissibility we developed earlier and, at the same time, try to improve the performance of both mental health professionals and lawyers, a task to which this book is devoted.

1.05. Which Professionals Should Be Considered Experts?

Assuming that mental health professionals' opinions should be admissible in at least some instances, the question arises as to *which* mental health professionals should be considered experts by the courts. Traditionally, this question has been answered by examining educational credentials, particularly with respect to discipline. In general, physicians have been considered experts in mental health matters, often without regard to psychiatric training. In recent years, courts have also admitted testimony by clinical psychologists, although some jurisdictions require psychologists to meet special experiential or training requirements before they can be acknowledged as experts, and many do not permit civil commitment orders to be filed by psychologists. Psychiatric social workers are often considered experts in juvenile and domestic relations matters and some-

times at sentencing in criminal cases but are generally not permitted to offer opinions about a defendant's competency to stand trial or mental state at the time of the offense.[115]

These general guidelines have evolved more from the internecine conflicts among the mental health guilds and the law's comfort with a medical model than from any systematic attempt to identify which mental health professionals possess sufficient specialized knowledge to assist the trier of fact on particular forensic issues. A survey of psychiatrists and psychologists indicated the depth of interdisciplinary antipathy.[116] Members of both professions were asked to evaluate their relative competence in 11 tasks performed by mental health professionals, including assessment, treatment, program administration, and expert testimony. Psychiatrists viewed themselves as more competent on eight of the tasks (including testimony), equally competent on two of the tasks, and less competent only with respect to administration of psychological tests. In contrast, psychologists perceived themselves as superior to psychiatrists on nine of the tasks, equal with respect to testimony, and inferior only with respect to the management of medication. In the face of such marked differences in perception of expertise, any comparison of disciplinary differences in knowledge and skills is likely to be fraught with controversy. Although reliance on objective indicators of expertise (e.g., form of training) clearly is the easiest method of determining qualifications as an expert, it is not the best.

Our own preference is for establishment of qualifications that are both broader and narrower than those commonly used; these should focus not only on educational attainments but also on experience in the relevant area and on the evaluation procedures used. This preference is based on an assumption that the law should use a functional approach to evaluation of qualifications, as in fact is suggested in Rule 702 (which uses a criterion of probable assistance to the trier of fact). The prevailing standard as to qualifications should be broader in that the available research gives no basis in most contexts for the historic preference for medically trained experts. The level of knowledge about forensic practice is not predictable by discipline, either among general clinicians or among clinicians with special forensic training.[117] As we point out in Chapter 6, for example, there is no basis for excluding social workers from competency evaluations; indeed, trained laypersons reach conclusions similar to those of mental health professionals.

On the other hand, the standard as to qualifications should be narrower, in that training as a mental health professional by itself is insufficient to guarantee a specialized knowledge of forensic mental health. For example, to the extent that there are observed disciplinary differences, they suggest some bias against medically trained experts in many types of forensic assessments. Petrella and Poythress[118] found that psychologists and social workers tended to do more thorough forensic evaluations and more comprehensive and more relevant forensic reports than their psychiatric colleagues.[119] There may be some specific topics on which medically trained clinicians are more likely to be expert, but even on these topics there is not likely to be exclusive expertise. For example, psychiatrists by training are more likely than other mental health professionals to have specialized knowledge about the effects of psychotropic medication; however, some psychologists specialized in psychopharmacology may be more expert on such matters than the average psychiatrist. Conversely, although psychologists are more likely to be knowledgeable about research methods, some psychiatrists active in research are likely to be more expert on research design than the average psychologist.[120]

In short, the various mental health professions should be perceived as equally qualified as experts with respect to *general* training in legally relevant assessment, but attention should be given to the specific spheres of specialized knowledge that the expert may offer. For example, clinicians without detailed knowledge of the available research on predictions of violent behavior should not be rendering opinions as to dangerousness. Mental health professionals should not perform evaluations of competency to stand trial without knowledge of the standard. Even more generally, clinicians without sensitivity to the special ethical and legal problems raised by forensic evaluation itself [see Chapter 4] should avoid participating in forensic work. The knowledge level and evalua-

tion procedures appropriate for a given type of testimony should become apparent as one examines the relevant portions of this book.

1.06.   Conclusion

In titling this chapter "an uneasy alliance" between the law and the mental health professions, we have called attention both to the conflicts in perspective—some of them inherent—between lawyers and clinicians and to the points of alliance. Readers will recognize this ambivalent theme throughout this volume. On the one hand, there are paradigmatic disciplinary differences in conceptualizing and finding facts, and the state of the art in the mental health professions renders a level of certainty far lower than the law would like in many instances. On the other hand, there is a corpus of knowledge in the behavioral sciences that, if available to legal decisionmakers, would result in more informed judgments on many issues. Our primary admonition to mental health professionals and to lawyers who would consult them is that both aspects of this theme should be kept in mind. Mental health professionals who exaggerate the state of knowledge (either their own as individuals or that of the field as a whole), or who ignore problems in translating the behavioral sciences into legal findings, do the law no service. At the same time, lawyers who ignore the behavioral sciences or, conversely, who swallow whole the conclusions of mental health professionals fail to exercise proper diligence in generating the facts necessary for the pursuit of justice. We hope that readers from both perspectives will find this volume useful in developing an interdisciplinary alliance wherever doing so would improve the quality of legal decisionmaking. Less globally, this volume is intended to demystify the arcane aspects both of the courts and of the mental health system.

Bibliography

Hal R. Arkes, *Principles in Judgment / Decision Making Research Pertinent to Legal Proceedings,* 7 BEHAVIORAL SCIENCES & THE LAW 429 (1989).

DAVID BARNES, STATISTICS AS PROOF: FUNDAMENTALS OF QUANTITATIVE EVIDENCE (1983). (An overview of statistics for lawyers.)

Richard J. Bonnie & Christopher Slobogin, *The Role of Mental Health Professionals in the Criminal Process: The Case for Informed Speculation,* 66 VIRGINIA LAW REVIEW 427 (1980).

Craig Haney, *Psychology and Legal Change: On the Limits of a Factual Jurisprudence,* 4 LAW & HUMAN BEHAVIOR 147 (1980).

Craig Haney, *Psychology and Legal Change: The Impact of a Decade,* 17 LAW & HUMAN BEHAVIOR 371 (1993).

LAW AND PSYCHOLOGY: THE BROADENING OF THE DISCIPLINE (James R. P. Ogloff ed. 1992).

Gary B. Melton, *Expert Opinions: "Not for Cosmic Understanding,"* in PSYCHOLOGY IN LITIGATION AND LEGISLATION 55 (Bruce D. Sales & Gary Van den Bos eds. 1994).

JOHN MONAHAN & LAURENS WALKER, SOCIAL SCIENCE IN LAW: CASES, MATERIALS AND PROBLEMS (3d ed. 1994).

John Monahan & Laurens Walker, *Social Science Research in Law: A New Paradigm,* 43 AMERICAN PSYCHOLOGIST 465 (1988).

MICHAEL MOORE, LAW AND PSYCHIATRY: RETHINKING THE RELATIONSHIP (1984).

Stephen J. Morse, *Crazy Behavior, Morals, and Science: An Analysis of Mental Health Law,* 51 SOUTHERN CALIFORNIA LAW REVIEW 527 (1978).

Stephen J. Morse, *Failed Explanations and Criminal Responsibility: Experts and the Unconscious,* 68 VIRGINIA LAW REVIEW 971 (1982).

Michael J. Saks & Robert Kidd, *Human Information Processing and Adjudication: Trial by Heuristics,* 15 LAW & SOCIETY REVIEW 123 (1980–81).

Alan J. Tomkins & Joe S. Cecil, *Treating Social Science Like Law: An Assessment of Monahan and Walker's Social Authority Proposal,* 2 SHEPARD'S EXPERT & SCIENTIFIC EVIDENCE QUARTERLY 343 (1994).

Laurence H. Tribe, *Trial by Mathematics: Precision and Ritual in the Legal Process,* 84 HARVARD LAW REVIEW 1329 (1971).

CHAPTER TWO

An Overview of the Legal System: Sources of Law, the Court System, and the Adjudicative Process

2.01. Introduction

The forensic specialist works in a world defined largely, if not exclusively, by "the law." The law regulates forensic practice through administrative licensing agencies, legal rules governing malpractice and confidentiality [see § 4.04], and constitutional principles limiting evaluation procedures [see §§ 4.02, 4.03]. Legal officials—judges, attorneys, probation officers, and clerks—initiate forensic referrals, and sheriffs and other law enforcement officers transport the client to and from hospital and jail. And, of course, legal factfinders—judges and juries—are the ultimate arbiters of those cases evaluated by the forensic specialist.

Most important, at least from the perspective of this book, the law establishes the guidelines that define the scope of forensic evaluation. Chapters 6 through 17 describe this law in detail. But before undertaking an investigation of these legal rules, it is important to understand whence they come, and when and by whom they are applied. The "law" is not derived from a single, readily accessible or static source. Nor is it always implemented by a judge or jury. To function competently, the forensic specialist must have a basic knowledge of the sources of law, the institutions that shape it, the various points in the legal process at which it can be applied (especially those points at which "mental health law" is applied), and the types of individuals who apply it. This chapter is devoted to an acquisition of that basic knowledge. Much of its content will probably be familiar to the lawyer; it is aimed primarily at the clinician with no legal training.

2.02. Sources of Law

PROBLEM 2.1

Through the sources discussed in this chapter, find the law that applies in your state on the following topics: (1) the insanity defense; (2) the extent to which mental retardation is a mitigating factor in capital sentencing proceedings; (3) the extent to which mental injury is compensable under worker's compensation law; (4) the scope of the psychotherapist–patient privilege; (5) eligibility for social security; (6) the standard for competency to stand trial; (7) when an arrested person must be taken before a judge; and (8) when the defendant in a civil case can require a mental examination of the plaintiff. In which areas is the law federal and in which is it state? In which areas is there *both* federal and state law and when does each apply? In which areas is the source of law constitutional? Statutory? Regulatory? In which areas is the source of law judicial, either in origin or as a matter of interpreting constitutional, statutory or regulatory law?

Tradition has it that the legislature "makes" the law, the executive branch enforces the law, and the judicial branch interprets the law. In actuality, each of these governmental institutions produces legal rules. Moreover, they are not the only sources of law; in particular, constitutional provisions can often affect legal analysis. In addition, federal and state systems each have their own constitutions, and their own legislative, executive, and judicial arms, each of which develops legal principles. Before discussing the various ways in which law is manufactured, a word must be said about this latter aspect of our form of government.

(a)   Federal–State Relations

The United States is a "federation" of states. This means that although each state has retained its own government and its own system of laws, the states have collectively ceded certain powers to the central government. The United States Constitution is the document that sets out the various powers held by the federal government on the one hand and the state governments on the other. For instance, it states that the power to regulate interstate commerce and provide for the national defense rests exclusively in the hands of the federal government. On the other hand, the Tenth Amendment to the Constitution reserves to the states those "powers not delegated to the United States by the Constitution, nor prohibited by it to the States."

Although the federal government's authority under these constitutional provisions was originally narrowly construed, it is now clear that Congress may pass laws affecting any activity that can conceivably be said to involve either the "public welfare" (assuming that federal funds are part of the statutory package) or "interstate commerce." Thus, under its public welfare authority, the federal government has been able to affect dramatically the provision of health care in this county; it has set institutional and staffing standards under which Medicare and Medicaid monies will be made available to state facilities,[1] attempted to stimulate the growth of community mental health services through the Community Mental Health Centers Act,[2] and has significantly advanced the habilitation opportunities of people with developmental disabilities through the Individuals with Disabilities Education Act.[3] Similarly, relying on its authority to regulate interstate commerce, Congress has passed a number of laws affecting people with mental disability, many of which are only tangentially related to business activity. The most prominent such bill is the Americans with Disabilities Act, which limits employment discrimination against those with physical and mental problems.[4]

The federal laws most likely to raise evaluation issues fall into four categories: (1) federal criminal law, which includes offenses in which the victim was a federal official, violations of federal civil rights, offenses involving federal property, and interstate crimes (such as mail fraud, robbery of federally insured banks, and narcotics violations involving interstate and international transactions); (2) the social security laws, which call for certain types of disability determinations [see § 13.04]; (3) the aforementioned Individuals with Disabilities Education Act, which requires treatment and habilitation plans for children with disability [see Chapter 17]; and (4) the aforementioned Americans with Disabilities Act, which can require evaluation of a person's competency to work under certain conditions [see § 13.02].

Virtually all other substantive areas that might call for forensic evaluations are governed primarily by state law. When crimes other than those federal offenses noted above are committed, for example, state law is the basis for criminal prosecution; not only does state law define the relevant violations in such cases, it also determines the scope of defenses (such as the insanity defense) and the appropriate punishment (e.g., the death penalty vs. life imprisonment). State law controls most civil disputes as well. For instance, state law usually governs the following areas related to this book: civil commitment; guardianship; wills; "torts" (or wrongs) such as personal injury, malpractice, and breach-of-confidentiality claims; worker's compensation; juvenile delinquency; and domestic matters such as divorce and custody. It also governs licensing of mental health professionals. Thus, in these areas, the evaluator and lawyer must determine the approach of the particular state in which a case is located; with the exception of those relatively few situations in which the federal constitution imposes limits on state law (discussed below), there is no "national" or uniform law on these subjects.

There are some instances in which federal and state laws overlap. In the criminal area, they usually coexist. For instance, an armed robbery of a federally insured bank in Missouri could be punishable under Missouri's armed robbery statute and federal law as well. Because the state and federal governments are seen as separate "sovereigns," both may prosecute for the same robbery without fear of violating the double jeopardy clause of the Constitution. In the noncriminal area, state and federal law may also coexist. Occasionally, however, certain federal enactments are said to "preempt" the substantive area with which they deal, to the exclusion of state law. The preemption doctrine is designed to promote a unified approach to "federal" problems. As a result, a federal law that deals with a preempted issue will supersede all state laws on the subject. For example, the Department of Health and Human Services regulations governing confidentiality in substance abuse treatment programs have been found to preempt the area; state statutes in conflict with these regulations are thus inapplicable.[5]

With these points about federal–state relations in mind, we can now turn to an investigation of how the various sources of law at the federal and state levels operate.

(b) Constitutions

The United States has a "constitutional" form of government, meaning that the United States Constitution is the ultimate authority in the country. The rules found in all other forms of law must be consistent with it; in other words, they must be "constitutional." Thus, as noted above, the Constitution places limits on what state (as well as federal) law can provide.

Provisions of the United States Constitution that affect forensic practice most significantly are the Fifth, Sixth, and Fourteenth Amendments to the Constitution. The Fifth Amendment establishes the so-called privilege against self-incrimination, and the Sixth Amendment provides each person accused of crime with the "right to counsel"; the implications of these concepts for foren-

sic evaluation are discussed in Chapter 4. The Fourteenth Amendment guarantees that no state shall deprive any citizen of the United States of life, liberty, or property without "due process of law" and that no state shall deny an individual "equal protection" of the laws. Relying on these provisions, principally the due process clause, the courts have issued rulings that have significantly affected the standards for competency to stand trial [see § 6.02(b)] and other competencies in the criminal process [see §§ 7.03–7.05, 7.08], the admissibility of clinical testimony in criminal trials on issues other than insanity [see § 8.03(b)], the procedures to be followed in capital sentencing proceedings [see § 9.05(b)], the criteria and procedures for civil and criminal commitments [see §§ 10.03, 10.04], and the scope of the right to refuse treatment [see § 11.03(b)].

Within the parameters set by the United States Constitution, the federal and state branches of government may devise legal rules. The state branches are further limited in their actions by the constitutions of the particular states, although in practice the provisions of most state constitutions are similar to those in the federal constitution.

(c) Statutes and Regulations

As noted earlier, the federal government and the various state governments parallel one another. Each has a legislative branch (Congress at the federal level; "general assemblies," "houses of delegates," etc., at the state level), an executive branch (the President and the federal departments in the federal system; the governor and state agencies in the state system), and a judicial branch. This section looks at the type of law produced by the first two branches.

The laws that legislatures pass are called statutes and are codified, or collected, into codes, which are organized by subject. In the federal system, for instance, Title 18 is the section of the United States Code that deals with federal crimes. State codes may also be organized according to titles or by chapters, sections, or some other nomenclature, but each represents the product of the state legislature's deliberations.

As might well be imagined, legislatures often

find themselves unable to treat by statute all situations or circumstances they want to address. Accordingly, they have increasingly delegated rule-making authority to government agencies, which are units of the executive branch. In the federal system, for instance, in establishing "conditions of participation" that facilities must meet under Medicare and Medicaid statutes, Congress merely drafted general standards and left it up to the Department of Health and Human Services to decide, within the ambit of those standards, the precise conditions that must be met. Similarly, a state legislature might direct its Department of Mental Health to devise guidelines for the provision of forensic evaluation services. This administrative law, usually promulgated in the form of "regulations" and also found in "codes," has become so complex in some areas that legislatures have required several of the executive's agencies to set up their own "judicial" bodies to adjudicate disputes arising under the regulations. Alleged violations of regulations must first be considered by these administrative hearing boards before they are considered by a court. More will be said about administrative proceedings below [see § 2.04(c)].

(d)   The Judiciary

Despite the advent of administrative hearing boards, the primary interpretive institution within both the federal and state systems remains the judicial system (indeed, most administrative findings are appealable to a court). The interpretation performed by courts takes place through deliberation on individual cases that raise an issue concerning a particular legal principle. The holding and reasoning of the courts in these cases are recorded in *Reports* or *Reporters*, which are organized according to the type and level of court. Thus, for instance, for the federal court system, *United States Reports* and the *Supreme Court Reporters* contain opinions of the United States Supreme Court; the *Federal Reporters* contain the decisions of the federal circuit courts of appeals; and the *Federal Supplement* contains opinions of the federal district courts (the next section describes the various levels of courts in detail).

The United States Supreme Court has con-

ferred upon itself and the lower federal courts the authority to review all federal enactments to determine their constitutionality, their meaning, and, in the case of regulations, whether they exceed the delegation made by Congress.[6] The federal courts also have the authority to consider the validity, under the United States Constitution, of any *state* constitutional, statutory, or regulatory provision[7] (although the state courts are the ultimate arbiter of the *meaning* of state law).

Of particular significance here is the fact that the review and explication functions of the courts imbue them with frequent opportunities to "make" law. Thus, as noted earlier, federal and state courts construing the constitutionality of state civil commitment statutes have not only found state provisions unconstitutional but have also indicated what they felt were permissible criteria and procedures for commitment [see Chapter 10]. Some commentators have argued that such instances are examples of inappropriate "legislating" by the courts, but in fact they occur with frequency.

A second situation in which the courts make law occurs when the textual sources of law (e.g., constitutions and statutes) are silent on a particular issue. In performing their interpretive function, courts will first look at the plain words of any relevant constitutional provision, statute, or regulation and then review the legislative history of a given law, including statements made by the law's sponsors or during committee or public hearing sessions. But if neither of these sources is helpful, or if no relevant law exists, the courts themselves must devise principles to govern the case before them. The principles articulated by courts when they create law are collectively known as common law, or judge-made law.

Thus, in many areas of civil law, such as tort and family law, many of the guiding legal principles are found in reported judicial decisions rather than statutes or regulations. In these areas, the law has developed through an accretion of judicial holdings which legislatures have often been reluctant to change or even "codify." In the criminal area, on the other hand, common-law pronouncements are rare, because virtually all crimes are now defined by statute. However, some defenses to crimes are not statutorily defined. For instance, until recently Congress had not passed a statute setting forth a test of insanity for federal criminal cases; the federal courts thus adopted their own common-law standards for insanity [see § 8.02(b)]. Moreover, in both the civil and criminal areas, even when statutes do apply, they may use terms that have been developed in common law (such as "malice aforethought") and that are left undefined in the statute. In such cases, the courts rely on the common-law tradition for interpretive aid.

As should be apparent from this last statement, the common law—unlike statutory and regulatory law, which often create rules out of whole cloth—usually develops according to the principle of *stare decisis*, which holds that present controversies should be decided according to past cases, or "precedents." This doctrine tends to make judge-made law conservative in nature, but it has the advantage of avoiding abrupt and perhaps ill-reasoned changes; it also serves to provide notice to those who come before the courts of the general principles that will govern resolution of their cases.

In sum, there are several sources of law: the United States Constitution; state constitutions; statutes passed by legislatures; regulations promulgated by agencies; and interpretive and common law handed down by the courts. There are other sources of law as well: "executive orders" issued by the President's office are one example. In addition, international law (e.g., the International Convention on Civil and Political Rights, the Convention on the Rights of the Child) or Native American law (which "preempts" national law in many situations involving the particular Native American tribe) may occasionally be relevant to evaluators. However, generally clinicians are concerned only with the types of federal and state law described above.

2.03. The Court System

Just as the federal and state governments have parallel branches of government, they have roughly parallel judicial structures. Both the federal and state judiciaries have two types of courts: "trial courts" and "appellate courts." The primary functions of the trial court are to ascertain the

facts of the case before it and then to apply "the law" to those facts. The facts are gleaned through an "adversarial" process, which, as described in § 1.03(c), envisions an impartial "trier of fact" (either a judge or a jury) considering evidence chosen by the parties to the dispute. (An "adversarial" process can be distinguished from an "inquisitorial" process, found in some European countries, which combines the investigative and decision-making roles). In most instances, the trial court's decision may be appealed to an appellate court, which determines whether the correct legal principles were applied by the trial court. Usually, no "trial" takes place at the appellate level[8]; rather, the court bases its decision on the record developed by the trial court, the briefs (written memoranda of law) submitted by opposing counsel, and, occasionally, oral argument by counsel.

Beyond this basic structure, the federal and state judicial systems tend to diverge.

(a)   The Federal Court System

In the federal system, the "district court" serves as the trial court. Each state is divided into one or more districts over which a district court judge presides. The district courts have jurisdiction over many types of cases, but most relevant to this book is their authority over cases arising under federal law. Thus, any claim that a federal or state statute or practice is unconstitutional under the United States Constitution may be brought in federal court. So, too, may any claim for an entitlement under federal statutes and regulations (e.g., welfare benefits and discrimination claims under the American with Disabilities Act, although both require administrative proceedings first). All defendants charged with federal offenses are also tried in federal court.

There are two levels of appellate courts in the federal system: the circuit courts of appeals and the United States Supreme Court. The country is divided into 12 circuits, each including several states (except the District of Columbia Circuit); the judges on the circuit courts of appeal hear appeals from the district courts within their circuit. A decision by a particular court of appeals determines the law only for that particular circuit.

The United States Supreme Court, consisting

of nine justices, is the highest court in the country. Its decisions regarding the United States Constitution and federal and state enactments apply nationwide and are final—that is, unappealable. Its jurisdiction is primarily appellate, although it has original trial jurisdiction over some types of cases, such as controversies between a state and the United States and between a state and citizens of another state.[9] The Court is required to take certain types of cases on appeal, including cases in which a district court declares a federal statute unconstitutional and in which a circuit court declares a state statute unconstitutional.[10] For the most part, however, the Court may exercise its discretion in deciding which cases to consider; otherwise, it would be overwhelmed. The primary mechanism for petitioning the Court to hear a case is called a writ of certiorari. The Court denies or grants certiorari on a particular case depending on its legal and systemic significance. For instance, the Court often "grants cert" in cases that provide an opportunity to resolve a conflict between courts of appeal or those in which a state supreme court has interpreted a federal constitutional or statutory provision in a questionable manner. Many significant "mental health law cases" were certiorari cases (e.g., *Addington v. Texas*,[11] establishing the standard of proof in civil commitment cases, and *Washington v. Harper*,[12] setting forth the Supreme Court's views on the right to refuse psychoactive medication).

(b)   State Judicial Systems

Most states have at least two levels of "general-jurisdiction trial courts"—one that tries civil matters involving small sums of money and minor crimes and another that handles major civil and criminal trials. With a few exceptions (most important, federal criminal cases), a state court with general jurisdiction may hear cases involving federal as well as state law.

Moreover, most states have "special-jurisdiction courts" for designated subject areas, such as civil commitment, domestic relations, juvenile matters, and probate. Many of the special-jurisdiction courts and the lower-level general-jurisdiction courts are relatively informal. The proceedings are not transcribed as a matter of routine, the rules of evidence may not apply, and witnesses may not be required to testify under oath. Litigation over the level of formality that should adhere in these types of courts has achieved mixed results [see, e.g., §§ 10.02(c), 10.04(a), 14.02(d)].

Like the federal system, most states also have two appellate levels—an intermediate appeals court and a supreme court—although some states have only the latter. The state supreme court is the ultimate authority on the interpretation of state law; even the United States Supreme Court must respect the state court's decision with respect to its own law, unless it is in conflict with the United States Constitution or a federal enactment that has preempted the area.

Figure 2.1 illustrates in simplified form the relationship between the federal court system and the typical state court system.

2.04.   The Adjudicative Process

There are four major types of judicial proceedings: criminal, civil, administrative, and what this chapter calls quasi-criminal. Each process aims at different objectives, has different rules of evidence and procedure, and involves different types

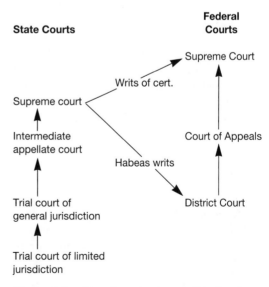

Figure 2.1. *The relationship between federal and state courts.*

of personnel. The forensic clinician should be aware of the principal differences among these proceedings in order to understand the context in which clinical input is sought.

(a)   The Criminal Process

A criminal prosecution occurs when the government (federal or state) charges an individual with the commission of an act that is forbidden by statute and punishable either by imprisonment or by a fine. Conviction of and punishment for a criminal offense have traditionally been viewed as the most severe actions society can take against one of its members. Accordingly, the criminal process is the most highly formalized of any adjudicatory proceeding. The prosecution must prove each element of the crime charged "beyond a reasonable doubt" (a level of certainty that can reasonably be quantified at above 90%).[13] The defendant is afforded the right to counsel, not only at trial but at any "critical" stage before trial, including post-indictment lineup identifications and custodial interrogations.[14] To prevent "star-chamber proceedings," the defendant is entitled to a public jury trial, the right to compel witnesses to testify in his or her behalf, and the right to cross-examine the prosecution's witnesses.[15]

There are two generic types of offenses: misdemeanors and felonies. A misdemeanor is usually defined as an offense punishable by imprisonment up to one year, a fine, or both. The place of imprisonment, if it occurs, is usually the local jail rather than a state prison. Felons, on the other hand, are incarcerated in the state prison system, for terms ranging from a few months up to life—depending, of course, upon the crime. Roughly 36 states also authorize the death penalty [see § 9.05].

(1)   The Stages of a Criminal Prosecution

A criminal prosecution is a highly structured event, established by statute, court rule, or long tradition. Although the details vary from jurisdiction to jurisdiction, the following topology is representative.

1.   *Detention.* The state has authority to detain an individual on a criminal charge if there is "prob-

able cause" (a degree of certainty perhaps roughly equivalent to 40–50%) to believe that the individual has committed the crime charged. Information constituting probable cause can come from direct police observation, reports from informants, or complaints by ordinary citizens. Once sufficient grounds exist for believing there is probable cause to arrest an individual, the police may seek an arrest warrant from a judge or magistrate (a judicial officer who presides over pretrial hearings). However, if there is no time to seek a warrant, the arrest is in public, or some other extenuating circumstance exists, the police may make a warrantless arrest. In rare cases (e.g., those involving political corruption), an arrest may be made pursuant to a grand jury indictment or based on an "information" from the prosecutor, both indicating that, after a formal investigation, grounds exist for detaining the named individual. As will be noted later, however, the indictment or information usually follows, rather than precedes, arrest.

2.   *Booking.* Immediately after arrest the defendant is taken to the station house, where appropriate paperwork is completed, and if necessary, fingerprinting and photographing take place.

3.   *The initial hearing.* The United States Supreme Court has held that, as soon as possible after arrest (i.e., within 48 hours), the government must afford the accused a hearing to determine whether there is probable cause to detain him or her, unless the arrest is based on a warrant or an indictment (because in the latter instances a judicial determination of probable cause has already been made).[16] Those charged with misdemeanors may be tried at this time. Those charged with felonies will usually have counsel appointed if they cannot afford one and will either have their bail set or be released on their own recognizance. In many states, as well as in federal prosecutions, the government has the authority to "preventively detain" an arrested individual who is proven likely to commit a crime if released prior to trial.[17]

4.   *Defensive motions and discovery.* Once the defendant has obtained counsel, several events may occur, depending on the nature of the case and the competence of counsel. First, defense counsel may try to "discover" the prosecution's case, which he or she can do by making a motion to the court asking for "exculpatory information" in the prosecution's files,[18] as well as other information that the

prosecution plans to use at trial (e.g., confessions by the defendant, statements of prosecution witnesses). In an increasing number of states, the prosecution may do the same whether or not the defense makes a discovery motion (although it may not obtain incriminating statements from the defendant, for Fifth Amendment reasons). Most other states follow a "reciprocity" principle with respect to discovery, meaning that prosecution discovery is contingent upon a discovery request from the defense; in practice, given the limited resources of the defense and the vast resources of the state, such a request usually occurs. Thus, in virtually all states, the discovery rules permit prosecution access to the results of the defendant's clinical evaluations, either "independently" or once the defendant makes a discovery motion. As § 4.02(b) indicates, however, in some circumstances operation of these rules may be unconstitutional.

The defense attorney may also make a "motion to suppress" (or render inadmissible) certain evidence. For instance, the attorney may argue that evidence was illegally seized from the defendant's house, or that a confession the defendant made to the police was invalidly obtained [see §§ 7.02; 7.03]; these issues are addressed at a "suppression hearing."

5. *The* prima facie *showing.* At some point following the initial hearing, it is incumbent upon the prosecution to formally "make its case" in front of a judicial body—either a judge, a magistrate, or a grand jury. This stage is designed to ensure that the prosecutor has a "*prima facie* case" (i.e., a case good on its "face," with sufficient evidence to justify going forward with the criminal prosecution). To meet this burden, the prosecutor will often present the results of lineup identifications, police interrogations, searches of the defendant's home or the crime scene, and any discovery that he or she is able to make of information that the defense counsel has in his or her possession. In many states, this presentation is made to a magistrate or judge at a preliminary hearing, at which the defendant and counsel are present. In addition, most states east of the Mississippi River,[19] as well as the federal courts, require an indictment by a grand jury; here the public and the defendant are barred from the proceedings.

6. *The arraignment.* Although the term "arraignment" is sometimes used to refer to the ini-

tial hearing (step 3), technically it is the stage at which the accused pleads, which may not occur until well after that hearing (and with felonies often occurs just before trial). In most states, there are four possible pleas: "guilty," "not guilty," "*nolo contendere*" (by which the defendant indicates he or she will not contest the state's charges), and "not guilty by reason of insanity." In about 12 states, it is also possible to plead "guilty but mentally ill" [see § 8.03(f)]. Most jurisdictions permit a defendant to plead not guilty and not guilty by reason of insanity simultaneously (on the theory that the defendant should not be barred from asserting other defenses—e.g., self-defense—just because he or she claims insanity). If one or both of the latter pleas are entered, the case is usually set for trial. If the plea is guilty, the judge must ascertain whether it was voluntarily, intelligently, and knowingly made[20]; if so, the defendant is sentenced, either at arraignment (in misdemeanor cases) or at a later proceeding (step 8).

Most guilty pleas are the result of "plea bargaining," which involves an agreement between the defendant (through his or her attorney) and the prosecutor providing that if the defendant pleads guilty to a specified charge, the prosecutor will recommend to the judge that the plea be accepted. To encourage such pleas, the prosecutor will often reduce the charges, drop one or more charges, or pledge to recommend a lenient sentence to the judge. Because more than 90% of all criminal cases are disposed of through a bargained plea,[21] this relatively hidden procedure is an extremely significant aspect of the criminal process.

7. *Trial.* If the defendant chooses to go to trial and does not waive his or her right to a jury, a jury is selected through "*voir dire.*" This process permits each side to exclude individuals from the jury using a limited number of "peremptory challenges" (which require no stated reason) and an unlimited number of "for-cause challenges" (which must be justified). Most states require 12-member juries in felony cases, although six-member juries are becoming more common. Once a jury is properly impaneled, the trial begins. After opening arguments, the state presents its evidence, through submission of exhibits and direct examination of witnesses. The defendant may challenge this evidence through cross-examination and, in the court's discretion, rebuttal wit-

nesses. The defendant then puts on his or her evidence, if any, which the state may contest. If insanity is an issue, some states permit a "bifurcated trial," with the insanity evidence introduced at the second stage [see § 8.02(b)]. After closing arguments, the judge provides the jury, if there is one, with instructions on the law it is to apply to the facts of the case. In a case in which insanity is raised as a defense, for instance, the jury will be told the jurisdiction's test for insanity. After instructions are given, the jury retires until it can produce a verdict, which usually must be unanimous (although the Supreme Court has held that 11–1, 10–2, and 9–3 decisions are not unconstitutional).[22] If the jury is "hung" (i.e., cannot reach a proper verdict), a new trial may be held.

8. *Disposition: sentencing and commitment.* A few states permit the jury to sentence the defendant once it finds the defendant guilty. However, most states leave the sentencing decision up to the judge, who will often request a "presentence report" from the probation officer and will occasionally hold a sentencing hearing before announcing the penalty. Except in death penalty cases, the latter hearing is usually much more informal than a trial [see § 9.03(b)], although again both sides are given the opportunity to present evidence. The sentencing authority may impose any sentence within the statutory range and may also impose probation, with conditions. An individual acquitted by reason of insanity, on the other hand, is usually required to undergo a short commitment for evaluation purposes and is then subjected to a hearing that results in prolonged commitment if he or she is found to be mentally disordered and dangerous [§ 10.10(c)].

9. *Appeal.* After conviction and sentencing, a defendant has the option of appealing the trial court's decision. An appeal must be taken within a certain period of time and must be based on factual issues (e.g., insufficient evidence to convict) or legal ones (e.g., the defendant's confession was obtained in violation of the Fifth Amendment) that have been objected to before or during trial. The prosecution may not appeal an acquittal (under the double jeopardy clause of the United States Constitution), although in a few states it may appeal a sentence.

10. *Collateral attack.* Once appeal routes are exhausted, it is still possible for both the offender and the insanity acquittee to attack their confinement "collaterally" through a writ of "*habeas corpus*" (or, in some states, a writ of "*coram nobis*"). The gist of these writs is an allegation that the state is illegally detaining the person. Once the state *habeas* process is exhausted, the state criminal defendant might also be able to raise claims on a federal writ of *habeas corpus*. Although the scope of federal *habeas* for state prisoners has been narrowed in recent years, it does enable the prisoner or acquittee to make certain claims regarding the fairness and adequacy of the trial or plea bargain that resulted in incarceration. Several mental health law cases, in particular those challenging the death penalty, have reached the U.S. Supreme Court through this procedural mechanism, including *Barefoot v. Estelle*,[23] affirming the use of psychiatric prediction testimony in capital sentencing proceedings, and *Ford v. Wainwright*,[24] prohibiting execution of the incompetent.

11. *Dispositional review.* Most offenders and insanity acquittees are not released via appeal or collateral attack. Instead, most are released through state-initiated review of their status. Although some states have abolished parole in favor of "fixed" sentences [see § 9.03(a)(4)], in most states convicted offenders who have served a minimum period of time are entitled to have a parole board determine their eligibility for early release, based on the individual's criminal record, behavior in prison, and perceived tendency to recidivate. Similarly, in most states insanity acquittees are entitled to periodic reviews of their mental state and dangerousness either by a probate court or by a board of mental health professionals.

12. *Postsentence treatment hearings.* Many states transfer prisoners needing psychiatric care to secure mental hospitals until they no longer need inpatient treatment; others seek such treatment for prisoners under the new "guilty but mentally ill" statutes. The United States Supreme Court decision has required that, before an involuntary transfer from prison to a hospital takes place, some type of hearing be held.[25]

(2) Clinical Input: Issues, Points of Entry, and Contacts

During the process described above, myriad issues arise that may call for clinical expertise. Due process requires that before an accused pleads guilty or undergoes trial, he or she must be competent to do so. Thus, the clinician may be asked to evaluate the accused's "competency to plead guilty" [see § 7.04] at virtually any point prior to arraignment; an assessment of the defendant's "competency to stand trial" [see Chapter 6] could be called for at any time up *through* the conclusion of trial. Occasionally, the evaluator may even be asked to address these issues retrospectively if, for instance, the competency issues are raised via a writ of *habeas corpus.*

If the defendant confesses, the clinician may be requested to determine whether, at the time of the incriminating statement, the defendant was "competent to confess" [see § 7.03] and may be asked to explain his or her findings at a suppression hearing. If the defendant wants to proceed *pro se* at either arraignment or trial, or both, the clinician may be asked to evaluate the defendant's "competency to waive an attorney" [see § 7.05]. A final competency issue that the clinician may address is whether the defendant (or, more likely, one of the trial witnesses) is "competent to testify" [see § 7.07]. All these evaluations are likely to be ordered at some time between the initial hearing and the trial.

Both the defense and the prosecution may also want an evaluation of the defendant's "mental state at the time of the offense" [see Chapter 8]. Most states require the defendant to give the state formal notice of an intent to raise an insanity defense at least ten days before trial, so the defense will usually ask the clinician to evaluate the defendant's sanity well before this time. The prosecution, on the other hand, arguably does not need its own evaluation or any information on this issue until after the defendant raises it [see § 4.02(b)]. Nonetheless, in practice, the prosecution often requests an evaluation before notice occurs. Occasionally, the defense may actually encourage such action; the available data indicate that a large percentage of insanity acquittals are the result of quasi-plea bargaining [see Chapter 8, note 24], which may occur well before notice by the defendant is required.

If the defendant is convicted, either the state or the defendant may want a presentence evaluation of the defendant focusing on his or her "dangerousness," "treatability," mental state at the time

of the offense (or "culpability"), or other issues [see Chapter 9]. Frequently, such evaluations take place before the determination of guilt or innocence, either because, as is the case with capital sentencing procedures in most states, the sentencing hearing immediately follows trial or because both sides want to reach a bargain and the defendant's treatability is an issue that will influence the ultimate plea and recommended sentence. Another issue that may require clinical expertise at or after sentencing is competency to be sentenced or executed [see § 7.08(b)].

Finally, in the context of parole board decisionmaking and release hearings for insanity acquittees, the clinician may be asked to evaluate the defendant's mental state and dangerousness. In the context of prison transfers, treatability may also be an issue [see § 10.10(b)(1)].

The mental health professional should also be aware of the different actors involved in the criminal process. The prosecutor is perhaps the most powerful, at least during the pretrial stages, as he or she is the official responsible for deciding what charges to bring against the defendant: Indeed, the prosecutor has the authority to dismiss the charges entirely even if the victim wants them pressed. Moreover, the prosecutor's discretion during the plea bargaining process to reduce charges and fashion a disposition is enormous.

Obviously, the defense attorney is also of extreme importance. Without this individual the process would probably not be adversarial in any real sense. Because most defendants are indigent, few defense attorneys are retained. Most are either court-appointed attorneys or public defenders. Both types of defense attorneys are paid by the state, the former on a per-case basis, the latter by salary. Increasingly, states are moving toward public defender offices as the method for providing legal services to indigent defendants; whereas public defenders may represent only criminal defendants, court-appointed attorneys are often marginally involved in criminal practice and may resent having to take time out from the rest of their caseload. At the same time, attorneys working for public defender offices tend to be young and inexperienced, overworked, and prone to plea bargain to keep their caseload manageable.[26]

Other actors in the system have already been briefly described. Judges make rulings of law and instruct the jury at trial as to the proper law to apply. Magistrates issue warrants and preside over preliminary hearings. Probation officers prepare presentence reports and supervise offenders put on probation. Court clerks issue the judge's orders and organize the court docket. The sheriff and jail personnel provide security and transportation. All these individuals are important to the evaluator because of their control over various aspects of the criminal process. Moreover, each can provide useful information about the person being evaluated. Serious forensic practitioners need to establish a credible relationship with each of them if evaluations are to reflect a comprehensive assessment of the client and if reports and testimony are to receive the full attention they deserve.

The evaluator should also be aware of the types of information that may be available from various stages of the criminal process. The police report, filed soon after detention, can be an invaluable source of data about the mental state of an accused. The initial hearing is usually not transcribed, and in any event will usually not produce anything probative of mental state. But the documents supporting evaluation, discovery or suppression motions, made at that stage or soon thereafter, can be very useful to the evaluator, as can the transcripts of suppression hearings and any information obtained through the discovery process. Preliminary hearings are also virtually always transcribed and can be made available to evaluators (grand jury testimony, on the other hand, is usually kept sealed until shortly before or during trial). Of course, if a presentence report exists, it can be very helpful in addressing dispositional and perhaps other issues.

(b)   Civil Proceedings

Unlike a criminal adjudication, a truly civil proceeding involves a dispute between private parties. The government merely provides the forum for resolving the dispute. A simple civil suit might involve a claim by one party (the "plaintiff") that the other party (the "defendant") negligently operated his or her automobile and caused injury to the plaintiff. More relevant to this book are suits that attempt to obtain damages for breach of con-

fidentiality or malpractice by a mental health professional. A different type of civil suit involves custody over children during a divorce proceeding[27]; here the goal is not money damages but possession of the children. The common thread among these cases is that all involve disputes between citizens rather than between a citizen and the state.

Because a civil proceeding of this type does not result in a loss of liberty and is viewed as a conflict between parties with roughly equivalent resources, the degree of certainty required to reach a decision is much lower than in the criminal process. Although the plaintiff has the burden of proof, he or she can meet it merely by a "preponderance of the evidence," meaning a showing that the plaintiff's version of the facts is more likely than the defendant's.

Nor are the stages of civil adjudication as highly ritualized as those in the criminal context. Under the federal rules of civil procedure, which many states have also adopted in whole or in part, a civil suit is commenced by filing a "complaint," to which the defendant responds with an "answer." No further steps are required until trial.

Typically, of course, both sides make numerous "pretrial motions." The most frequent are those designed to "discover" the other side's case. The scope of discovery has expanded in the past several decades in order to avoid surprise at trial. A number of mechanisms are available to facilitate this process, including "depositions" (during which witnesses are questioned and their testimony transcribed), "interrogatories" (sets of written questions that are answered in writing), requests to produce documents and other tangible evidence, mental and physical examinations, and requests to admit facts relevant to the case.

Of particular importance here are motions to obtain a mental examination and motions to discover the content and basis of opinions held by a party's experts. Under the rules applicable in federal court, a party can obtain a mental examination only of another party to the case or a person in that party's "custody or control"; for privacy reasons, examinations of nonparties cannot usually be obtained. Moreover, before a mental examination of a party can be obtained, the court must be convinced that his or her mental condition is "in controversy" and that there is "good cause" for the evaluation.[28] In contrast, discovery of expert opinion is facilitated by the rules. A party that will use an expert as a witness must automatically give the other side a report containing the opinions, data and reasoning of the expert; in addition, that expert may be deposed at any time.[29] The identities of experts who are consulted but will not testify must also be disclosed[30]; however, these experts may not be deposed or sent interrogatories unless exceptional circumstances exist making the information they possess difficult to obtain through other means.[31]

As indicated above, experts are often deposed during the discovery process. A deposition involves questioning of the witness by the deposing party's attorney, with the witness's attorney present. The transcript of this deposition may be used at trial to impeach the expert's testimony at trial or as a substitute for it if the expert is unavailable. Although objections to questions asked during deposition may be made, they are usually merely noted for the record; experts must generally answer all questions put to them, even if the answers will not later be admissible at trial. The most relevant exception to this rule is when the questions ask for privileged information or information that the expert's attorney can convince the court is entitled to protection for confidentiality reasons.[32] As § 4.04 makes clear, in most jurisdictions neither objection affords much protection.

Frequently, once discovery is complete the parties settle rather than go to trial. Although "settlement" is analogous to plea bargaining, the terms of the settlement agreement need not be approved by, or even divulged to, the judge. The settlement rate is almost as high as the guilty plea rate in criminal trials.

If settlement is not reached, *voir dire* of the jury venire is conducted and the trial begins. The civil adjudication, like the criminal trial, is adversarial in nature. The plaintiff's evidence is presented first and his or her witnesses subjected to cross-examination; the defendant's case follows. Again illustrating the differing stakes involved, however, in many states the civil jury need only produce a majority verdict for one party to prevail (in the federal courts, a unanimous verdict is required unless the parties stipulate otherwise before trial[33]).

The psychological issues that arise in civil cases will depend, of course, on the substantive nature of the case. In the typical personal injury, or tort, case, the plaintiff may claim that the defendant's negligence caused not only physical harm but mental pain and suffering as well and may request an evaluation gauging the nature and extent of this pain and suffering [see Chapter 12]. In custody disputes, the issues are whether one or either of the parents is fit to care for the child and, in a larger sense, what is in the best interests of the child [see Chapters 15 and 16]. As in the criminal context, several competency issues may arise in a civil adjudication, all discussed in Chapter 11. In probate cases, clinicians may be asked to evaluate whether the deceased was competent to make a will at the time it was executed; in guardianship cases, they may have to assess whether the proposed ward was competent to make personal or business decisions; and, in contract cases, a question may arise as to whether a party to the agreement was competent to enter into a contractual relationship. As in criminal cases, there may also be a need to determine whether a particular witness is competent to testify [see § 7.07].

(c)   Administrative Hearings

Virtually all administrative hearings in front of executive adjudicative bodies are also deemed "civil" in nature. However, in these cases the government is a party and is often acting to confer property on or take it away from a citizen (e.g., licensing and Social Security determinations). Therefore, the standard of proof used in these proceedings is often the "clear and convincing" standard, which falls between the "beyond a reasonable doubt" rule used in criminal cases and the "preponderance of the evidence" standard used in the typical civil case. In contrast, rules of evidence are often relaxed at administrative proceedings because of the absence of a jury [see, e.g., §§ 12.02(a), 13.02(d)].

Probably the most common psychological issue in administrative adjudication is the level of mental disability suffered by an applicant for government benefits in the form of Social Security [see § 13.04] or worker's compensation [see § 12.02]. As legislatures begin conferring authority on administrative bodies to hear issues traditionally heard in the courts, such as the right to refuse treatment [see § 11.03(b)],[34] greater clinical participation in administrative hearings can be expected.

(d) Quasi-Criminal Proceedings: Civil Commitment and Juvenile Delinquency

There exist entirely discrete types of cases that have traditionally been labeled "civil" in nature but, because they potentially involve a significant deprivation of liberty, are best characterized as "quasi-criminal." The two types of quasi-criminal cases discussed in this book are "civil commitment" and "juvenile delinquency" cases. Civil commitment is the process by which the state institutionalizes those found to be mentally disordered and either dangerous or in need of care. Juvenile court provides a mechanism separate from the adult criminal justice system for trying allegedly antisocial juveniles. Traditionally, both civil commitment and the juvenile courts were seen as means of providing state resources to relatively helpless groups within society; their objective was not punishment but rehabilitation. But since the 1960s, the courts have recognized that the primary result under both systems is a "deprivation of liberty" that often does little to help and may actually harm those involved.

As a result of this shift in perspective, significant changes have occurred in both areas, described in detail in Chapters 10 (on civil commitment) and 14 (on juvenile delinquency). For present purposes, only a few recent developments need be noted. In the civil commitment context, the United States Supreme Court has held unconstitutional state statutes that permit commitment by the civil "preponderance of the evidence" standard; instead, it has required the higher "clear and convincing evidence" test to be met.[35] Lower federal courts and some state courts have also held that formal evidentiary rules and the rights to subpoena and cross-examine witnesses apply in commitment hearings.[36] In the juvenile context, the United States Supreme Court has, in effect, equated juvenile delinquency proceedings with adult criminal trials. With a few exceptions (e.g., the right to jury trial),[37] every right afforded

adult criminal defendants must also be afforded juveniles charged with committing a crime, including the right to require proof beyond a reasonable doubt that the crime was committed.[38] It would be naive to conclude that the "therapeutic ideal" no longer exerts a strong influence on the civil commitment and delinquency adjudicatory systems; in practice, the new procedural requirements have often been disregarded. Nonetheless, with a few exceptions, those subjected to these types of proceedings are theoretically entitled to the same type of adversarial proceeding that adult criminal defendants are.

As described in detail in Chapter 10, the issues that will confront the clinician performing civil commitment evaluations focus on the need to hospitalize the individual in question. State statutes vary but usually require a finding that the individual is mentally ill plus either dangerous to others, dangerous to himself or herself, or in need of care or treatment before involuntary commitment may occur. The clinician may also be asked to evaluate the individual's competency to make treatment decisions [see § 11.03].

Juvenile delinquency proceedings, as Chapter 14 makes clear, may require a number of different decisions that can be informed through clinical expertise. Just as in the criminal process, issues of competency to stand trial and waive certain rights may arise, as well as the question of whether the juvenile was insane at the time of the offense. On the other hand, unique to the juvenile system is the determination of whether certain children (usually between 14 and 18 years of age) are "amenable to treatment" within the juvenile system; if not, there may be a transfer of the juvenile to adult court jurisdiction, a procedure also known as "waiver" of juvenile court jurisdiction. Finally, the child who remains in the juvenile court system and is convicted will as a matter of course be evaluated, often by a mental health professional, to determine the best disposition. This presentence evaluation is much more wide-ranging than the analogous adult assessment; most states provide several types of rehabilitative services for children, all of which must be considered by the evaluator.

It should be remembered that both civil commitment and juvenile courts are often special-jurisdiction courts, with separate personnel and facilities. Many states do not appropriate funds for a prosecutor in either civil commitment or juvenile cases. In the former context, often the committing judge or the examining clinician fills that role; in the latter area, many states confer prosecutorial discretion on the juvenile probation officer.

2.05. Conclusion: The Interplay of Systems

Lest the impression be created that the criminal, civil, and quasi-criminal systems described above operate entirely independently of one another, it may be helpful to conclude this chapter with a hypothetical situation that illustrates the extent to which they can overlap. The reader may also wish to refer to Figure 2.2, which depicts in a schematic fashion many of these connections.

Assume that a quarrel erupts between a husband and wife, which climaxes in the husband's beating the wife as well as the couple's child. Of course, the woman may decide not to report the event to anyone in authority. Or she may contact the local police, triggering the criminal process. Finally, if she thinks her husband may have mental problems, she may attempt to seek professional intervention, possibly triggering the civil commitment process. If the police are called in, they may decide to book the husband for assault and battery, take him to a hospital for mental evaluation, or do nothing. Whatever their decision, the prosecutor, assuming that he or she hears of the case, may decide to handle the case quite differently. Moreover, in many states, an offense against a child is tried in juvenile court; if charges are pressed, the whole matter may end up there and the husband's fitness as a parent may become an issue. Simultaneously, the wife may decide to sue the husband for divorce, custody of the child, and damages on the assault and battery; all three claims are heard in civil court, but the first two may be tried in juvenile court (or "family" or "domestic relations" court) and the latter in a court of general jurisdiction.

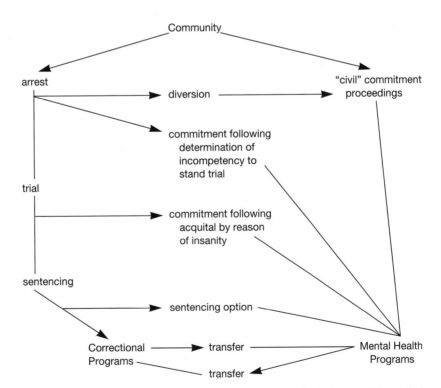

Figure 2.2.   *The mental health process. [From THE MENTAL HEALTH PROCESS (F. Miller, R. Dawson, G. Dix, & R. Parnas eds. 2d ed. 1976). Reprinted by permission of Foundation Press, Mineola, NY.]*

This hypothetical illustrates two different points. First, whether a case enters the criminal, civil, or quasi-criminal system depends, in many instances, on the preferences of the victim, the predilections of the police and the prosecutor, and the relevant state law. Especially when mental disorder is an issue, the room for discretion and flexibility is quite large. "Criminal" cases may be "diverted" to civil commitment or juvenile court jurisdiction or to private psychiatric care. Or, they may result in hospitalization following a finding of incompetency to stand trial or an insanity finding. If conviction occurs, psychiatric care may take place in prison or after a transfer from prison to a mental hospital.

A second point to be garnered from this brief hypothetical situation is the importance of finding out the context of an evaluation. A mental health professional who is asked to evaluate an individual needs to know who is asking for the evaluation, what court will use the evaluation results, and, most crucially, precisely what is to be evaluated. For example, the husband of the hypothetical victim could be evaluated on the following issues, depending on which "process" has been triggered and the stage to which it has progressed: (1) his competency to plead guilty, stand trial, or waive an attorney; (2) his sanity at the time of the offense; (3) his "intent" to hit his wife (relevant to the civil assault and battery claim as well as the criminal charge); (4) the extent to which he is presently mentally ill and dangerous either to himself or to others; (5) his fitness as a parent; and (6) his "treatability" for sentencing purposes. And this list does not exhaust the possibilities.

Ideally, a court order or the party making the referral clarifies these contextual issues. If no clarification is forthcoming, the professional must find out personally. Otherwise, the evaluation may yield results that are useless to the legal system. This theme is one sounded throughout this volume.

Bibliography

Jack H. Friedenthal, Mary Kay Kane & Arthur R. Miller, Civil Procedure chs. 1 & 7 (1993).

Richard Ross, American National Government: An Introduction To Political Institutions (1972).

Charles H. Whitebread & Christopher Slobogin, Criminal Procedure: An Analysis Of Cases And Concepts ch. 1 (3d ed. 1993).

The Nature and Method of Forensic Assessment

3.01. Introduction

This chapter examines the nature of the forensic evaluation process. It does so primarily by exploring the differences between "forensic" assessments, conducted at the behest of the legal system, and traditional therapy, which occurs at the request of the patient. Although the previous two chapters have alluded to several such differences, this chapter explicitly compares these two types of clinical work, particularly in terms of the types of information sought and the strategies for gathering it. In the course of doing so, it discusses typical and newly developed techniques of forensic evaluation.

More specifically, after describing in general terms the differing demands of therapeutic and forensic assessment, this chapter examines the forensic enterprise from the following perspectives: (1) the utility of conventional diagnostic tests and procedures; (2) the use of specialized forensic assessment instruments; (3) the use of archival and third-party information; (4) information recovery procedures from allegedly amnesic clients; and (5) the assessment of malingering. Despite its primarily clinical content, this chapter is as important to lawyers as it is to mental health professionals. Its explanation of the forensic craft clarifies the nature and basis of forensic "expertise." Furthermore, the final sub-

stantive section of the chapter reviews the extent to which evidence law may limit use of particular forensic techniques, information that should be useful to the attorney as well as to the clinician planning an evaluation.

3.02. Distinctions between Therapeutic and Forensic Assessment

PROBLEM 3.1

You run a forensic training program in your state, and have just begun a session with 30 psychiatrists and psychologists who on average have provided therapy for five years but have never conducted a forensic evaluation. They will have several training sessions on various aspects of civil and criminal law. But your present task is to tell them how the skills they presently possess may or may not be useful in forensic practice. What will you tell them? What is the role of diagnosis, clinical interviewing, and psychological testing in forensic work? Will they have to learn new techniques and, if so, what types of techniques? Will they need to approach forensic clients differently than therapy clients?

In the therapeutic context a variety of tools are available for the purposes of diagnosing mental disorder and planning treatment. Probably the most important such method is the clinical interview, a dialogue with the patient exploring present mental state, past experiences, and desires for the future. Additional or corroborating diagnostic information may be gleaned from psychological tests (e.g., personality inventories and projective tests) and specialized laboratory procedures (e.g., neuropsychological tests and imaging techniques). Treating clinicians also occasionally rely on archival information (e.g., records of prior treatment) and third-party information (e.g., independent psychosocial history from family members) to flesh out the client's clinical picture and inform treatment decisions. In short, mental health professionals in traditional clinical settings are accustomed to gathering, sifting, and synthesizing complex data from diverse sources.

These same methods—interviewing, testing, and retrieval of archival or third-party information—are also useful in forensic evaluations. However, the nature of forensic work may affect both the extent to which they are relied on and the manner in which they are used. Because it is a creature of the legal system, forensic assessment differs from a therapeutic assessment on a number of dimensions. Summarized in Table 3.1, they include such fundamental aspects of assessment as the focus of the examiner, the cooperativeness of the client, and the dynamics and pace of the evaluation. Unless aware of these differences, otherwise competent clinicians may prove to be naive forensic examiners, selecting familiar but less than optimal procedures for conducting their assessments.

Table 3.1
Dimensions Distinguishing Therapeutic from Forensic Assessment

1. **Scope.** In clinical settings, broad issues, such as diagnosis, personality functioning and treatment to effect behavior change are primary. Forensic evaluations more commonly address narrowly defined events or interactions of a nonclinical nature; clinical issues (e.g., diagnosis or treatment needs) are often background rather than foreground issues.

2. **Importance of client's perspective.** Although accuracy of information is important in both settings, the treating clinician's focus is on understanding the client's unique view of the situation or problem; a more "objective" appraisal is secondary. The forensic examiner is concerned primarily with accuracy; the client's view, while important, is secondary.

3. **Voluntariness.** Persons seeking mental health therapy commonly do so voluntarily. Persons undergoing forensic assessment commonly do so at the behest of a judge or an attorney.

4. **Autonomy.** As voluntary consumers of therapeutic services, people have greater autonomy and input regarding assessment objectives and procedures. The objectives in forensic evaluations are determined by the relevant statutes or common law "tests" that define the legal dispute.

5. **Threats to validity.** Therapist and client seek to develop a common agenda, based on the client's treatment needs, that will guide their interactions. Although unconscious distortion of information is a threat to validity in both contexts, the threat of conscious and intentional distortion is substantially greater in the forensic context.

6. **Relationship and dynamics.** Treatment oriented interactions emphasize caring, trust, and empathic understanding as building blocks for a developing therapeutic alliance. Forensic examiners may not ethically nurture the client's perception that they are there in a "helping" role; divided loyalties, limits on confidentiality, and concerns about manipulation in the adversary context dictate more emotional distance between forensic clinician and client.

7. **Pace and setting.** In the therapeutic setting, evaluations may proceed at a more leisurely pace. Diagnoses may be reconsidered over the course of treatment and revised well beyond the initial interviews. In the forensic setting, a variety of factors, including court schedules and limited resources, may limit the opportunities for contact with a client and place time constraints on getting closure on the evaluation or reconsidering formulations. At the same time, the importance of accuracy is enhanced by the finality of legal dispositions.

(a) Scope

The most obvious difference between the forensic evaluation and the typical therapeutic encounter is that the focus of the former is determined by a legal system that is only occasionally interested in treatment information. Although therapeutic concerns may dominate some forensic evaluations (e.g., dispositional assessments in juvenile delinquency cases), a person's psychological well-being is only of tangential relevance in most such encounters. Assessments of a criminal defendant's insanity, a parent's fitness, or a person's competence to manage his or her affairs require answering legal questions focusing on whether there is impairment, not on what to do about it.

Our experience has been that some clinicians, schooled in conventional professional values which put the clients' treatment needs above all else, have difficulty adapting to this changed emphasis. Yet part of developing forensic expertise is the capacity to conceptualize and focus on the legally relevant aspects of the case. More tersely: *Not all clients should be perceived as "patients."*

At the same time, it is important to note that virtually any forensic evaluation permits at least some attention to clients' treatment needs, if only in an informal manner. Even when immediate treatment considerations are not the focal point of a forensic assessment, clinicians usually can suggest a consultation or note therapeutic issues connected with the case. Therefore, it is neither proper nor *necessary* to subvert the forensic assessment process with a misplaced emphasis on diagnostic and treatment concerns.

(b) Importance of the Client's Perspective

Related to the scope issue is the extent to which the client's views are important to the clinician. In the therapeutic enterprise, the primary interest of the clinician is the client's perspective, revealed gradually and more candidly over the course of repeated contacts. The better the therapist understands the client's worldview the more effective the therapist becomes, at least in theory, at developing interventions or offering interpretations that facilitate change. A more "objective"

understanding, although desirable, is of secondary importance because useful clinical interpretations (e.g., suggestions to the client of an alternative perspective) do not necessarily depend on an accurate account of the client's situation.[1]

In contrast, because the legal system is interested in the just adjudication of disputes, accuracy is the primary goal in the forensic context. Thus, information should be sought not only from the client but from *all* relevant sources, including sources that the client does not know about or would rather not have consulted. In short, because of the greater need to consider alternative views and to corroborate client reports about legally relevant events, the client's unique perspective is only of secondary importance in forensic evaluations.

(c) Voluntariness and Autonomy

A third dimension in which the forensic and therapeutic endeavors differ is the attitude of the client. The typical therapy patient enters into the clinician–patient relationship voluntarily. In contrast, forensic clients are often forced or cajoled into confronting the evaluator, by either the court or an attorney.

Forensic clients may resist the evaluation for at least two reasons. First, they may fear its outcome. For instance, a criminal defendant asserting an insanity defense may be leery of a mental health professional performing an evaluation for the state; alternatively, some defendants may prefer going to prison to being labeled "crazy" and sent to a mental hospital and thus will resent any clinician who has the power to affix such a label. Second, even if they are willing to live with the outcome of the evaluation, forensic clients may resent its intrusiveness and insult to autonomy. For instance, parents in divorce and custody proceedings may view psychological evaluations as unnecessarily invasive, despite their attorney's or the court's insistence that the evaluation take place. And in virtually all forensic settings, the evaluator may be given personal information by an attorney or the court, disclosure of which the client did not explicitly authorize.

In short, to a much greater extent than the therapist, the forensic evaluator will be confronted with sullen, recalcitrant, guarded, or otherwise uncooperative individuals, a situation that may be exacerbated by ethical rules requiring that the client be fully informed of the evaluator's role [see § 4.05(d)]. Later portions of this chapter make some suggestions as to how to adapt to such client resistance. For now, the important point is that the client in forensic evaluations will often not be a willing participant in the process, which leads to the next difference between forensic and therapeutic work.

(d)   Threats to Validity

Generally, voluntary clients seeking relief from psychological suffering will have few motives for conscious or intentional distortion,[2] and most of the third parties to whom professionals might turn for archival or collateral information, such as other service providers or friends and family members, will have little reason to be biased in their reporting of information. To the extent inaccuracy is a concern, its principal source is likely to be the client's shyness or lack of self-awareness.

In the forensic context, on the other hand, there are numerous other threats to validity. Because of the relatively coerced nature of the evaluation process and the importance of its outcome, noted above, clients already have added incentive to distort the truth. Beyond that, lawyers may pressure the client to provide misinformation or, at the least, be uncooperative. For example, some defense attorneys may view state requested or court-ordered evaluations of pretrial competency as "fishing expeditions" designed to circumvent the defendant's Fifth Amendment right to silence by obtaining client's statements about the crime that are communicated to the examiner [see § 6.03(c)]. Accordingly, they may instruct their clients to participate only minimally in the evaluation and to refrain from discussing certain issues (such as the facts of the crime) that the clinician may be obligated to explore in order to respond to the court order.

Other sources of information besides the client may also have an interest in the examiner's findings and thus may also be tainted. Consciously or unconsciously, these parties—most likely the attorneys, but also relatives and friends of the client, police, health service workers who might end up caring for the client, and potential beneficiaries of any money involved—may further distort the fact-gathering process by sharing only certain information with the examiner or presenting it in a biased light.

(e)   Relationship Dynamics

Because of the need for accurate information, the relationship between the forensic clinician and the client may differ dramatically from conventional therapeutic practice. The typical therapist usually tries to be empathetic with the patient. Confrontation, when used, will be carefully timed and will be attempted only after the bond with the client is judged strong enough to withstand it. Maintenance of the relationship takes priority over resolving conflicting reports or convincing the client to recant information or endorse a different view.

A forensic evaluator, on the other hand, is usually much more detached. Although evaluators may approach clients with compassion for their difficult legal circumstances, their primary goal is answering the law's questions. Having abandoned the formal caregiver's role, forensic examiners do not rely on the development of a trusting relationship over time to break down either conscious or unconscious barriers to disclosure, nor are they likely to rely extensively on the interpretation of transference in the assessment process. Indeed, one commentator has argued that using empathy to obtain information from a forensic client is unethical.[3] Although we do not adopt that view, we do believe that clients must be alerted to the potentially adversarial role the evaluator will play [see § 4.05(c)].

Forensic examiners may be not only more distant than therapists but also more confrontational. Because forensic clients are more likely to malinger, and because the clinician's conclusions are more likely to be scrutinized by others, the evaluator's inquiries tend to be more focused and probing than are assessments in the therapeutic context. Forensic examiners are more likely to challenge and confront clients whose reports are dubious and inconsistent or do not comport with credible information from other sources. More will be said about these different techniques later in this chapter [see § 3.07].

(f)   Pace and Setting

Ideally, both the therapeutic and forensic processes would permit the opportunity for repeated contact and observation with the client, under optimum assessment conditions and unfettered by external constraints.[4] As Table 3.1 notes, however, these conditions may be met less often in the forensic context. In the criminal justice system in particular, access to clients for multiple observations may be limited by conditions of incarceration, the costs involved in commuting to and from jails or prisons, or the unwillingness of police or corrections officials to transport clients to examiners' offices. Further, in many jails and prisons clinicians will find the physical settings to be far below the optimum. Generally, time constraints associated with scheduled depositions or court proceedings may affect forensic evaluations adversely.

Finally, as noted in Table 3.1, the forensic evaluation process is relatively finite, resulting from the fact of adjudication. In contrast to the therapeutic enterprise, opportunities to reconsider and revise clinical forensic information over a long period are rare. Once submitted to the court, the forensic product is likely to become part of the "record" and not subject to change.

With this general discussion of some of the important dimensions that distinguish therapeutic from forensic assessment as a backdrop, we now consider the utility, and limitations, of some particular assessment techniques and strategies.

3.03.   Conventional Psychological Tests and Diagnostic Procedures

Mental health professionals have a vast array of structured assessment tools and laboratory procedures to aid in the diagnostic enterprise. A major resource for information about psychological tests is the *Mental Measurements Yearbook*,[5] which periodically publishes updated lists of available

tests and comprehensive reviews of research on selected instruments. Of more relevance to the subject matter of this book, Heilbrun has identified 11 different categories of tests that may play a role in forensic assessment.[6]

Rather than considering individual tests in detail, we provide a brief description of the some of the more commonly utilized types of instruments and review the role of conventional tests in forensic evaluations in light of contemporary analyses and criticisms. These analyses identify several issues that forensic evaluators should consider in deciding whether and how to use conventional psychological tests in forensic assessments.

(a)   Categories of Tests

Table 3.2 identifies some of the more common types of tests that have been developed and lists some of the more popular instruments currently in use for each type. Some, like the SCID (see Table 3.2 for full names of this and other tests), are highly structured interviews that formalize inquiries about symptoms and yield outcomes that closely track diagnostic categories of the *Diagnostic and Statistical Manual of Mental Disorders* (DSM).[7] Others are self-report personality inventories, such as the MMPI and MCMI, that consist of objectively scored items (e.g., true/false) and produce protocols and indices that have been related, through empirical research on persons with known clinical diagnoses, to global symptom patterns, likely diagnoses, and characteristics of general personality functioning and behavior. They may inform judgments about specific diagnoses, and may also, in conjunction with interpretive manuals, provide hypotheses about general behavioral patterns to look for with a particular individual.

A third type of personality test is the projective test, like the Rorschach or TAT. However, these tests do not rely on self-reports of symptoms or experiences; rather, they require the client to view, interpret, and describe complex and ambiguous stimuli. The Rorschach stimuli are monochrome and multicolor "inkblots," whereas the TAT stimuli are pictures, most of which portray individuals or interpersonal interactions, about which the client must develop sto-

Table 3.2
Conventional Diagnostic Tests

Structured clinical diagnostic interviews
    Psychiatric Diagnostic Interview—Revised
      (PDI-R)
    Schedule for Affective Disorders and Schizophrenia
      (SADS)
    Structured Clinical Interview for DSM-IV (SCID)

Checklists
    Child Behavior Checklist (CBCL)
    Symptom Checklist 90—Revised (SCL-90-R)

Personality inventories
    California Psychological Inventory (CPI)
    Millon Clinical Multiaxial Inventory
      (MCMI/MCMI-II)
    Minnesota Multiphasic Personality Inventory
      (MMPI/MMPI-2)

Projective personality tests
    Draw-a-Person (DAP)
    Rorschach Inkblot Technique
    Thematic Apperception Test (TAT)

Tests of general intellectual functioning
    Stanford–Binet
    Wechsler Adult Intelligence Scale—Revised
      (WAIS-R)
    Wechsler Intelligence Scale for Children
      (WISC-III)

Tests of memory functioning
    Wechsler Memory Scale—Revised
      (WMS/WMS-R)

Tests for neuropsychological impairment
    Halstead–Reitan Neuropsychological Battery
    Luria–Nebraska Neuropsychological Battery

Tests for specific disorders
    Beck Depression Inventory (BDI)
    Michigan Alcohol Screening Test (MAST)
    Psychopathy Checklist—Revised (PCL-R)

ries. By "projecting" their own perceptions and interpretations onto these ambiguous stimuli, clients reveal something about the ways in which they view and comprehend their environment. Clinicians then interpret the client's responses (often aided by reference to published norms) to develop hypotheses and draw inferences about diagnosis and personality functioning.

Still different in structure are neuropsychological, achievement, and intelligence tests. These instruments often contain multiple subtests consisting of problems to be solved or other kinds of items that have objectively or normatively "correct" answers. Individuals' scores on these tests can often be interpreted in light of the performance norms of relevant populations to delineate specific strengths and weaknesses in cognitive functioning, general abilities, or aspects of intelligence.

In addition to radical structural differences, tests vary in the range of psychopathology to which they are sensitive. The personality inventories and projective tests may be sensitive to a variety of symptoms but are best used to assess mental disorders that are not usually accompanied by impaired consciousness or significant deficits in cognitive functioning. In contrast, neuropsychological tests such as the Halstead–Reitan or Luria–Nebraska, and even some standard intelligence tests, are preferred where neurological injury (e.g., brain lesion) is the suspected etiological factor; these tests may provide evidence for impaired cognitive functioning (memory, capacity for abstraction, etc.) and permit inferences regarding the site of possible brain injury that may explain impaired abilities. Other tests such as BDI (depression), the MAST (alcohol abuse), and the WMS-R (memory impairment) are used when a particular diagnosis or facet of cognitive impairment is suspected. The BDI, for example, addresses only depressive symptomatology and contains subscales to help clinicians determine the particular manifestations of the illness in an individual (e.g., cognitive [despondency] vs. behavioral [lethargy] symptoms).

By reference to professional guidelines for the development of psychological tests and the test manuals and published research on a particular test, clinicians can determine which tests are most appropriate for different kinds of clinical applications. Test manuals and published research reports also provide information about the reliability and validity of tests, both for a given population and for the different purposes for which the tests have been developed. As noted, the *Yearbook*, published by the Buros Institute of the University of Nebraska, also periodically provides critical reviews that can help both clinicians and attorneys determine the relative strengths and limitations of the tests.[8]

(b) Forensic Applications

For a number of reasons, testing has become a significant aspect of forensic evaluation. Historically, conventional psychological testing played an important role in justifying the participation of psychologists (as opposed to psychiatrists) in the legal process.[9] Further, some clinicians believe that any forensic assessment is incomplete unless a battery of tests that permits insights into all aspects of functioning (cognitive, intellective, personality) is administered.[10] Finally, the legal system may demand comprehensive testing; a graduate adviser counseled one of us to administer psychological tests in every forensic assessment whether or not they would inform the legal issue being addressed, simply because the lawyers and judges have come to expect it.

Recently, however, more critical analyses have identified several limitations of conventional tests and laboratory procedures.[11] To some extent, these limitations may result from the nature of the population tested. For instance, the Rorschach requires an ample number of responses for scoring and interpretation. But in forensic cases the number of responses to such a projective test will often be low, either because subjects intentionally reduce responses to avoid evaluation or because (as is often true with clients charged with crime for instance) they have below-average IQ scores, which correlate with response production. This problem aside, the reviews suggest, and we concur, that conventional diagnostic testing procedures—as opposed to the specialized forensic assessment instruments (FAIs) examined in the next section—are of minimal usefulness in many forensic contexts. Deciding whether, when, and how to use these tests as part of a forensic evaluation requires consideration of several factors, identified below.

(1) Relevance to Specific Legal Inquiry

The test should be relevant to the legal issue, or to a psychological construct underlying the legal issue. Whenever possible, this relevance should be supported by the availability of validation research published in referreed journals.[12]

The primary determinant of whether to administer diagnostic tests in any assessment, clinical or forensic, should be the degree to which test results will inform the judgment that has to be made. Accordingly, forensic examiners should be concerned with the scientific research base that links specific test results to relevant legal outcomes. If good research studies show a positive correlation between the results of a particular test and legally relevant behaviors or legal outcomes, administration of the tests may be well advised. On the other hand, if tests inform the clinician only about diagnosis or general level of functioning and will permit only speculative inferences about legally relevant behavior, the clinician should consider whether there are other, more direct ways to address the problem (e.g., FAIs or archival or third-party information).[13]

Unfortunately, most traditional tests have neither been developed nor validated specifically to inform judgments about legally relevant behavior. This fact should caution against their indiscriminate use. Instead, a first consideration in deciding whether to use conventional testing should be whether the information it provides is of "primary" importance or of only a "secondary" (background) concern for the particular evaluation being performed.

Examples of evaluations in which testing information might be particularly useful include dispositional decisions (e.g., sentencing), personal injury cases involving neuropsychological assessments or alleged emotional pain and suffering (e.g., tort suits), and some entitlement cases (e.g., social security disability applications), all of which hinge to a significant degree on information about the nature and extent of an individual's current psychopathology. In many forensic contexts, however, this type of information is of secondary concern even when present mental state is the primary focus. For example, competence to stand trial depends on present ability to assist counsel and to adequately understand the legal proceedings.[14] These abilities are defined in functional, not clinical, terms, and if such capacities are present, lingering doubts about clinical issues such as differential diagnoses may not need to be resolved. Unless and until legitimate concerns about the person's functional abilities arise, the clinical issues should remain in the background. Similarly, diagnosis and treatment information is generally only of secondary importance in addressing the many other criminal and civil competency issues that arise in the legal system [see Chapters 6, 7, and 11].

A Michigan case in which three mental health professionals testified regarding a juvenile's competence to stand trial is illustrative. After reciting the Supreme Court's competency standard[15] and its emphasis on the specific functional criteria of consulting with counsel and understanding the proceedings, the trial judge expressed concern that

> [a]ll three of the experts seemed to be preoccupied with what kinds of pictures he drew, the difference between his verbal and non-verbal skills, how much he remembered about his early childhood . . . and his ability to separate fantasy from *their* reality. Dr. C____ admitted that he believed that anyone with below average intelligence was incapable of being able to reasonably consult with his lawyer. One must wonder about Dr. C____'s reality.[16]

Because the forensic examiners employed general personality and diagnostic procedures and attempted to draw inferences about legal functioning from diagnostic categories (below-average IQ) or broad personality indicators (projective drawings), their test results could not be tied in a reasonably direct way to the legal criteria applicable in the case, resulting in an icy reception by the court and a scathing opinion about the clinicians' capacity to inform the court on the issue.

(2)   Hypothetical Nature of Test Results

Some clinicians fall quickly into the trap of concluding that "testing shows that this individual has characteristics or tendencies *x, y,* and *z*." Yet norm-referenced interpretive guides for most tests merely represent compilations of features found in groups of individuals who produced a particular testing profile. When a clinical or forensic client produces a particular profile, the chances increase that the client shares at least some of the behavioral characteristics that are associated with other members of that profile

group. But the degree of fit between this individual and the reference group's general characteristics can be determined only by gathering other information about the client.

Accordingly, as we suggested in Chapter 1 [see § 1.03(c)], the interpretive results of psychological tests are best considered as hypotheses about the nature of the client's psychological disorder or personality or behavioral functioning. In the therapeutic context, confirmation of the hypothesis often comes in the form of observations made over the course of therapy. But in the forensic context, where client contact may be limited to one or a very small number of contacts, archival or third-party information may be necessary before these test-generated hypotheses can be accepted or rejected.

Such corroboration can be crucial. Consider a hypothetical evaluation of a female plaintiff in a sexual harassment suit originating in an employment setting. It would be one thing to assert that testing results suggest the presence of a personality disorder commonly associated with a manipulative and seductive interpersonal style; it is quite another to assert, on the basis of testing alone, that this individual was seductive in her relationship with her employer and thus may have contributed to or caused the situation that gave rise to the complaint. In the absence of corroborating information, forensic evaluators should be cautious in the conclusions they draw regarding specific behavioral tendencies or characteristics implicated by test(s) profiles.

(3)   Limitations in Reconstructive Contexts

There are a number of forensic assessments in which the examiner is asked to develop information about a person's mental condition at a prior point in time. Perhaps most common and familiar are evaluations of criminal defendants for purposes of an insanity defense; retrospective inquiries also occasionally arise regarding competence to stand trial or to waive rights[17] or in connection with testamentary capacity [see § 11.05(b)].

Conventional psychological testing will clearly have less utility in reconstructive evaluations than in assessments that focus on current mental state. Although some aspects of personality such as general intellectual functioning may be expected to remain relatively stable over time (assuming no acute trauma), personality test profiles and clinical diagnostic test indices are likely to be sensitive to a wide range of intervening factors. The more remote in time the focus of the evaluation, the greater the likelihood that natural processes (e.g., normal forgetting or the natural course of some illnesses) or situational factors (e.g., treatment received or the stress of incarceration or adverse life events) will influence the test results. At most they may suggest whether or not a particular disorder was present and active in the past. For these reasons, we encourage the use of archival methods (e.g., prior records and investigative interviewing) as superior data sources in reconstructive evaluations [see § 3.05].

(4) Face Validity Considerations

The ultimate practical utility of a forensic report, or testimony based on that report, is as a persuasive message. In persuasive communications the audience is a key factor in determining the effectiveness of the message.[18] Therefore, in selecting among available procedures, clinicians should also be concerned with how their methods are likely to be received by the legal system.

Receptivity may vary somewhat from attorney to attorney or court to court, and anticipating the reception that certain methods or data will receive may be difficult. It is fair to say, however, that courts are generally conservative and perhaps inclined to view many of the methods of psychiatry and psychology as arcane.[19] They are likely to prefer explanatory formulations based on idiographic rather than nomothetic data [see §1.03(c)(2)] and to distrust evidence that relies excessively on statistics to dispose individual matters.[20]

Judges and attorneys understand interviewing; they are less sanguine toward inkblots. They can comprehend behavioral trends gleaned from record reviews, but intricate inference chains that begin with projective drawings and end with opinions on legal issues will be less well received, as illustrated by hostile judicial reaction to such testimony in the competency case described earlier. This is not to say that traditional diagnostic testing and laboratory procedures should not be utilized simply because lay jurors and legal professionals may be unfamiliar with them; mental health professionals should select methods that will enable them to address satisfactorily the referral questions. Other things being equal, however, consideration should be given to the differential face validity of available methods so as to facilitate legal consumers' understanding of the bases for clinical inferences and opinions.

3.04. Specialized Forensic Assessment Instruments

In recognition of the limitations of traditional diagnostic tests and procedures in addressing forensic issues, mental health professionals have developed a variety of interview schedules, surveys, and tests that attempt to focus more directly on discrete legal issues. Increasingly, these specialized instruments are used in forensic evaluations to supplement, if not replace, some of the more traditional procedures.

A comprehensive review and discussion of FAIs available through 1986 was published by Grisso.[21] Table 3.3 identifies some of the instruments currently available and the legal issues they were developed to address.

FAIs have the potential to alleviate some of the problems noted in the previous section. Most are not broad-band forensic instruments but are narrowly focused to a specific legal application. Thus, the chain of inferences from test behavior to legal criterion is typically reduced; further, when normative data have been gathered, FAI developers have often tested relevant legal populations. However, as is the case with conventional tests, all FAIs are not created equal—or equally well. Most FAIs appear to be facially valid instruments. Authors and developers have typically incorporated content that makes clear the focus on the legally relevant behavior that the test purports to measure. But an investigation of the conceptual development, psychometric sophistication, and validating research for the various instruments reveals radical differences among them.

Some FAIs are simply interview guides that provide a list of topics to help clinicians structure their interviews around appropriate legal issues; they offer no pretense of rigorous administration,

Table 3.3
Forensic Assessment Instruments

Competence to waive *Miranda*
   Comprehension of *Miranda* Rights
   Comprehension of *Miranda* Vocabulary
   Function of Rights in Interrogation

Competence to stand trial
   Competency Screening Test (CST)
   Competence to Stand Trial Assessment Instrument
      (CAI)
   Interdisciplinary Fitness Interview (IFI)
   Georgia Court Competency Tests (GCCT)

Legal insanity
   Rogers's Criminal Responsibility Assessment Scales
      (RCRAS)

Child custody/parental fitness
   Ackerman–Schoendorf Scales for Parent Evaluation
      of Custody (ASPECT)
   Bricklin Perceptual Scales

Guardianship and conservatorship
   Multidimensional Functional Assessment
      Questionnaire
   Community Competence Scale

**Competence for medical treatment
decisionmaking**
   Hopkins Competency Assessment Test

objective scoring criteria, quantification of the level or degree of performance, or research on known groups' performance to facilitate norm-referenced interpretation.[22] Even more problematic are instruments that provide some of the trappings of sophisticated instruments, with multiple scales and apparently quantified measures, but are conceptually flawed[23] or have little empirical research to validate the authors' claims about the instruments' capabilities.[24] On the other side of the ledger, there are some very good instruments that appear to have been solidly constructed from conceptualization to validation.[25]

It is beyond the scope of this handbook to undertake a microscopic analysis of each FAI that is currently available. We will mention some of the more prominent instruments in appropriate chap-

ters throughout the book [see, e.g., §§ 6.06, 8.05(c); 11.02(b)(2), 16.04(d)]. Attorneys and clinicians seeking more information may avail themselves of Grisso's excellent (but now somewhat dated) review[26] and the subsequent research literature.[27] When testing is judged appropriate, we encourage the use of the FAIs over conventional personality and diagnostic tests. We caution practitioners, however, that there are a number of legal issues (e.g., insanity) for which valid, structured assessment instruments do not exist. Other methods, such as investigative interviewing, may be more appropriate in these instances.

3.05. Archival and Third-Party Information

In addition to the client and testing sources, a wide variety of documentary and third party sources of information will often inform the forensic evaluation. After explaining why archival and third-party information play such a significant role in the forensic context, this section describes, in a general way, the process of obtaining such information. Specific suggestions on the type of third-party information to seek for particular examinations is left to the relevant chapter.

(a)   Reasons for Seeking Third-Party Data

As suggested earlier in this chapter, forensic evaluators are more likely than therapists to rely on third-party data for two reasons: a greater need for accuracy and the fact that the evaluator's conclusions will be scrutinized by the legal system. The first goal is probably the more important. By stating that evaluators should be concerned about accuracy, we do not mean to suggest that they must resolve conclusively all conflicting accounts about the case; that is the job of the legal system. However, some understanding of what has happened or is happening to the client will obviously facilitate the evaluation; furthermore, reconciliation of different points of view may occasionally be possible, and clients sometimes recant an earlier account when confronted with the truth. Thus, the evaluator should endeavor to understand which accounts of relevant events and family, medical, and social history are feasible.

Given this goal, archival and third-party information is a mandatory component of most forensic evaluations.[28] Traditional clinical methods (i.e., interviewing and testing the client) have inherent limitations as means of obtaining accurate information. Obviously, they rely on the client; even if the client does not malinger, normal forgetting, impaired memory, the effects of treatment received since the legally relevant event, and other factors may limit the extent of his or her recall. Concern about these considerations aside, traditional techniques may still fail the forensic examiner because they tend to produce only a general diagnosis based on present functioning, whereas making judgments about the contribution of psychopathology to legally relevant behavior often requires developing information about specific symptoms, experienced at a circumscribed point in time. For example, testing and interviewing may confirm that a person has schizophrenia, but those techniques may not provide enough information to assess the person's parental behavior in the past two years, or his or her motivation for a particular crime (e.g., was a theft for "crazy" reasons or to obtain money?). As these examples illustrate, archival and third-party information is particularly important in reconstructive evaluations (e.g., insanity, testamentary capacity, and psychological conditions preexisting an accident), where the focus is the client's mental state at a remote point in the past. [See § 8.06(b)(1) and Table 8.5 for a case-specific illustration of how useful third-party information can be.]

Such information is also important in terms of enhancing the examiner's credibility with the judge, jury, and attorneys. To the degree that these parties view the forensic examiner as the mouthpiece for the client's self-serving story, they will discount and potentially disregard the examiner's testimony or report. Efforts to corroborate statements provided by clients and to weigh it against information from other sources can significantly improve the weight assigned to the examiner's conclusions.

(b)   The Process of Obtaining the Data

The first goal of the evaluator seeking archival and third-party information should be to identify the types of information needed. For instance, records of former treatment providers and family history are usually essential in dispositional evaluations but usually unnecessary in competency evaluations. As noted earlier, each chapter of this book describes in more detail the most useful third-party information in the forensic context it covers. But the types of information so identified are not exclusive. Initial data may yield a variety of unanticipated leads, and in many kinds of forensic assessments the sources of potentially valuable third-party information are numerous and unpredictable. In many cases, the examiner may find that a multistage evaluation is optimal, on the theory that the earlier stage or stages will clarify the third-party information needed for subsequent evaluations.[29]

Ideally, once all the information needed is identified, it will be provided by the referral source (usually an attorney, occasionally the court, and at times a government agency). In reality, this source cannot be depended on. Some attorneys appear to think of examiners as "black boxes" into which one inputs the client and out of which spurts a report. Other attorneys who are willing to do the legwork to gather collateral information may still not be helpful because they are not familiar with the process for obtaining information (e.g., the fact that client consent must be obtained before medical and other types of records are released), or are familiar with it but have been stymied [see, e.g., § 2.04(b) on discovery].

There are various ways of responding to these obstacles. When the referring party balks at providing assistance, it is not inappropriate to issue a reminder that the examiner has something the party wants (i.e., the report), and that it will not be forthcoming until the examiner has obtained all the necessary data; in the alternative, the examiner can submit an incomplete report, with a notation about why it is incomplete. Those attorneys who are willing to help but ignorant of the process can be educated. And an explanation of the specific information needed and the reason it is desired should provide sufficient ammunition to those attorneys whose efforts have been blocked by the opposing side to draft a motion for judicial sanctions. Even if such sanctions are not pursued, proof of a specific request can be invaluable at trial, especially if, during cross-examination, the party who refused to provide the information tries to suggest the evaluator was negligent in not obtaining it.

A final alternative for the frustrated forensic examiner is to contact third parties or possessors of relevant documents directly, by phone or letter. Generally, however, this approach should be a last resort, or used only when custom and commonsense have established its permissibility (e.g., contact with jail personnel during a competency evaluation, or the police during an insanity evaluation). If the clinician is an agent of an attorney, it is unethical, under legal ethics rules, to make such contact with a person represented by counsel.[30] Although it is not unethical to contact witnesses (as opposed to parties), the witness may be misled about the adversarial nature of the process by the fact that a mental health professional rather than a lawyer is calling.[31] Furthermore, the clinician may end up working at cross-purposes with attorneys who are simultaneously collecting information from the witness. At the least, the clinician should notify the attorney of the contact, and, when contact is made, make clear immediately for whom he or she is working.

3.06. Amnesia: Hypnosis and Narcoanalysis

Forensic examiners often encounter individuals who report memory problems for some period that is pertinent to the forensic assessment.[32] In such situations, the forensic clinician might consider an interview under the influence of hypnosis or a general anesthetic (i.e., narcoanalysis), both techniques that may recover lost memories [see, e.g., the Wertz report, § 19.04(a)]. Before carrying out such procedures, however, the clinician should go through several steps.

First, of course, it is important to determine whether the amnesia claim is legitimate. Amnesia is easily feigned; some studies indicate that a large proportion of amnesia claims are fabricated.[33]

When amnesia is claimed, the examiner should attempt to corroborate it or confront the client with contrary information; in criminal cases, the client may also be told that amnesia is not a defense (which might encourage a suddenly "restored" memory). Other methods of detecting malingered amnesia are discussed in the next section (on malingering).

If the amnesia is considered legitimate, the second step is to ascertain whether the amnesia present is potentially recoverable. Generally, amnesia can be divided into two types: "registration amnesia" and "recall amnesia." With registration amnesia, the memories sought to be recovered were never permanently stored because some incident (e.g., a blow to the head) or some agent (e.g., certain drugs, such as hypnotic sedative compounds[34] or some types of psychedelics[35]) interfered with the encoding process. The individual with this type of amnesia has no record of prior events waiting to be retrieved; recovery using special interviewing techniques is thus (theoretically) impossible. When the problem is one of recall amnesia, on the other hand, hypnosis or narcoanalysis may be able to facilitate retrieval of the forgotten material. In these cases, the original memories were registered but access to them has been disrupted, in theory (according to Freud) because the memories are too psychologically painful to be admitted into consciousness and therefore have been repressed.[36] Hypnosis and narcoanalysis may be useful in this situation because they apparently bypass the individual's psychological defenses and allow repressed material to surface, allowing access to thoughts, feelings, and memories that are not accessible during normal consciousness.

Assuming hypnosis or narcoanalysis is indicated, the clinician should next advise the attorney(s) in advance of the procedure and the nature of any memories that might be recovered. All parties should be warned that hypnosis and narcoanalysis have no demonstrated value as "truth serums" and that no particular claims about the "honesty" or objective validity of the subject's report can be made. Contrary to common wisdom, memories are not photographic recordings. What a person remembers may be influenced by a great number of factors, both situational and personal, and there is no assurance that a person's recovered memories will be either complete or accurate by some objective standard.[37] Individuals' own needs, beliefs, prejudices, attitudes, and other personal factors may influence the events attended to or their interpretation of them. Furthermore, defendants may report as personal "memories" what are in fact variations of accounts of their behavior previously provided by others or they may develop "memories" by patching together clues from the examiner's questions (leading or otherwise).[38] Finally, the clinician should warn all parties that these procedures may not recover any information, tainted or otherwise; some clients may prove unsusceptible to the hypnotic or chemical induction, and in many other cases memory will not be enhanced even when an altered state is induced.

If, after these admonitions, the parties still want to pursue the memory recovery procedure and the client gives informed consent [see §4.04(d)(1)], the fourth step is administering the technique. Because of the potential that memory recall will be affected by situational variables when these special procedures are used, a number of authorities have recommended special guidelines for forensic applications.[39] These include the use of clinicians who are both specially trained in hypnosis or narcoanalysis and highly skilled in nonleading interrogation, maintaining careful records of preprocedure knowledge on the part of both the subject and the interrogator, a preprocedure briefing in which no specific expectations about the session are communicated to the subject (to minimize demand characteristics), and a videotape recording of the session.[40] Even with all these precautions, the possibility of malingering exists, however.[41] Experimental studies have shown that subjects under hypnosis or the influence of drugs may persist in presenting a previously rehearsed and untruthful story[42] or may prevaricate for the first time while in the altered state.[43]

Given the problems associated with these techniques, memories "recovered" employing these special procedures will usually be useful only to the degree that they confirm or corroborate other information. When the behavior or memories recalled are entirely subjective and not subject to verification (e.g., "Just as I was strangling her, her face looked like my mother's face!"), no assertion of the truth or validity of the information should be offered, and clinicians should be cautious in endorsing formulations that hinge on such "memories." When corroborable information is provided, however, the implications for the case may prove to be fairly dramatic. A colleague reported the use of hypnosis with a woman charged with attempted murder of her estranged husband.[44] Unable to recall her behavior at the time of the alleged crime, under hypnosis she recounted events that placed her several miles from the scene of the crime at the time of the shooting. Credible witnesses were located who could confirm her story, leading to a dismissal of the charges.

In contrast to the last illustration, forensic clinicians will usually use hypnosis or narcoanalysis in the process of forming an expert opinion about the mental state of someone who did commit the crime. Accordingly, a final important consideration [discussed in detail in § 3.08(c)] is the extent to which opinions based on hypnotically or drug-induced interviews are admissible. Even if the foregoing precautions are taken, some courts do not permit such opinions or allow the opinion but do not allow the expert to recount the subject's statements. In the latter two types of jurisdictions, the evaluator may be well advised to seek other alternatives. In jurisdictions in which the matter is undecided, or the attorney decides to proceed despite adverse precedent, the clinician should be particularly careful to make clear that although hypnosis and narcoanalysis have the capacity to produce an account of otherwise unrecallable behavior, they can also produce statements that are unreliable or unverifiable.

3.07.   Malingering

CASE STUDY 3.1

Stanley is bringing a personal injury claim against a grocery store for injuries he allegedly sustained after slipping on a banana peel in the store. He claims that, as a result of the fall, he injured his back. He has since withdrawn from his job as a plumber, claiming an inability to work bending over. His attorney has arranged for him to see you because he also claims that, since leaving his job, he has been severely depressed. The attorney is interested primarily in the extent of Stanley's present depression. Within minutes of entering your office, Stanley starts crying and professes to be unable to talk because of his depression. After letting him cry for a few moments, you ask him if he is ready to talk, at which point he dries his eyes and says yes. He then, matter-of-factly, describes the accident.

QUESTIONS: At this point, what further steps might you take to investigate Stanley's claim of depression? What questions might you ask, what tests, if any, might you administer, and what third-party information would you want?

Clients in therapeutic settings may unconsciously distort the information they provide to clinicians, but they rarely have any incentive to practice conscious deception and manipulation. In contrast, as noted in § 3.02, the typical forensic client has much to gain from a particular finding or formulation about the case. Thus, many forensic clients manipulate their presentation to appear more or less "crazy," depending on the context. Fabrication or exaggeration of symptoms may often occur in cases in which aberrant mental condition is an excuse for unacceptable behavior (e.g., insanity cases), can help avoid sanctions (e.g., capital sentencing), or will be useful in obtaining entitlements (e.g., disability evaluations or personal injury claims). Minimizing evidence of psychological dysfunction, a response style termed *defensiveness*,[45] may occur when the client wants to preserve certain entitlements or have them restored (e.g., when the issue is competency to manage one's affairs, eligibility for parole or release from the hospital, or custody in a divorce proceeding).

These machinations by the client can obviously affect the validity of a forensic assessment. Furthermore, opposing attorneys routinely raise inquiries about possible self-serving claims. Thus, implicitly or explicitly, the forensic examiner must make judgments about the client's response style.

Given the significant potential for deception and the implications for the validity of their findings, mental health professionals should develop a low threshold for suspecting deceptive responding. At the same time, because the label of "malingerer" may carry considerable weight with legal decisionmakers and potentially tarnish all aspects of the person's legal position, conclusions that a person is feigning should not be reached hastily.

Thus, the forensic examiner's low threshold for suspecting dissimulation should be accompanied by a conservative stance with respect to reaching conclusions on that issue.

A number of strategies are available for systematically investigating response style. We first provide an overview of interview approaches, followed by a consideration of psychological testing and the use of third-party information. Given the problems that afflict each of the methods, information from more than one source should be sought before coming to any conclusions.

(a) Interviewing Approaches to Assessing Malingering

The most common and venerable method used to assess malingering is the clinical interview, usually consisting of a mental status examination or other relatively unstructured interview procedure. The cues and indicators of "faking bad" that skilled interviewers look for have developed over decades of clinical experience and comprise part of clinical lore passed on during professional education.[46] They are based on the etiology, onset, course of treatment, prognosis, and other aspects of various mental disorders.

Rogers's review of the literature identified several indicators of malingering that might be detected during an interview.[47] These include:

- *An overplayed and dramatic presentation,* including such features as theatrical style, eagerness to discuss symptoms, reports of extreme symptom severity, and indiscriminant endorsement of symptoms.
- *Deliberateness and carefulness,* including such features as slower rate of speech, extensive use of qualifiers, more hesitations, and repeating of interviewer questions.
- *Inconsistency with psychiatric diagnosis,* including report of rapid onset and resolution of symptoms, and the report of rare symptoms or unusual symptom combinations.
- *Inconsistency of self-report,* including report of contradictory symptoms and disparity between reported and observed symptomatology.

- *Endorsement of obvious symptoms,* including endorsement of positive (vs. negative) and blatant (vs. subtle) symptoms, and more impaired content than mental process.

Experienced forensic clinicians develop their own interview questions to explore for these kinds of cues. For example, persons who appear all too ready to endorse a wide range of positive or dramatic symptoms may be enticed by inquiries about exotic symptoms or ludicrous symptom combinations, such as, "When you hear voices, do you also experience slight dizziness and the sudden smell of hamburger?" As another example, Schacter suggests that defendants claiming amnesia for a particular event be asked whether they feel they could remember the incident with sufficient prodding; his research suggests that simulators are more likely to deny a "feeling-of-knowing" than those who truly cannot remember.[48] When subjects fall into one or more of these interviewing traps laid by the clinician, a diagnosis of malingering may follow.

However, this approach to detecting malingering, although popular, is limited. Because the specific questions employed to investigate malingering will vary from one clinician to another, there will often be no systematically gathered data (e.g., explicit norms) to facilitate an objective interpretation of a subject's responses. Rather, the clinician's basis for concluding that the subject is malingering will be his or her "clinical experience," which may be subject to a number of biases in judgment and memory. The accuracy of clinical judgments of malingering in research studies has not been impressive.[49] Increasingly, mental health professionals have been criticized for exclusive reliance on the interview-based approach, and some have questioned whether expert testimony about malingering should be admissible in court if not corroborated by information gathered by other methods [see generally § 7.07(d)].[50]

One approach to overcoming the problems noted is to employ highly structured clinical diagnostic interviews. As Rogers and colleagues have demonstrated[51] (using the Schedule of Affective Disorders and Schizophrenia),[52] repeated administrations of such instruments to the same individual permit an analysis of consistency of self-report. In addition, with respect to norming, reli-

able administration procedures associated with such interviews ensure a high degree of replicability across clinicians, and consistent structure permits quantification of variables of interest (number of rare symptoms endorsed, number of symptom areas/categories reported, contradictory symptoms endorsed, etc.). Unfortunately, to date, the extent to which this approach has been employed in forensic practice is unknown and thus collated data are unavailable.

An even more promising interview approach to the detection of malingering is the Structured Interview of Reported Symptoms (SIRS).[53] This 172-item instrument comprises multiple scales, each of which represents a different strategy to detect malingering of psychopathological symptoms.[54] The eight primary scales contain items that permit more *systematic* exploration of the various malingering strategies found in Rogers's survey of the literature that is summarized above. For example, one scale (RS) records a person's endorsement of rare symptoms that do not often occur even in true psychotic individuals; another scale (IA) captures the reporting of improbable or absurd symptoms; yet another scale (SU) is sensitive to the overreporting of everyday problems that are not indicative of a major psychiatric disorder.

Rogers and his colleagues have investigated the capacity of the SIRS to detect malingering in a series of studies that have included both simulation and known groups designs.[55] The scores on the SIRS have consistently discriminated known[56] or simulated[57] malingerers from normal and clinical control groups instructed to respond honestly, even when the feigning subjects have been provided with information regarding the detection strategies employed in the test[58] or were psychologically knowledgeable about specific disorders to be feigned.[59] Research on the SIRS has also consistently reported respectable indices of *sensitivity*[60] and *specificity*.[61] Consistent with our earlier recommendation that forensic clinicians be conservative in judgments that label someone a malingerer, the interpretation of the SIRS scales is geared to minimize the risk that a respondent will be inappropriately identified as malingering.

The highly structured SIRS interview, which resembles a mental status examination in format, takes about 45 minutes to administer. Because it incorporates most of the interview strategies that clinicians might employ anyway, but in a structured and objectively scored protocol, the SIRS overcomes many of the specific limitations and concerns expressed about unstructured interviewing approaches. Thus, the SIRS is worthy of serious consideration by forensic clinicians investigating the malingering of symptoms of psychopathology.

(b) Psychological Testing

The second primary approach to detection of malingering involves the use of psychological tests, such as intelligence tests, personality inventories, or projective tests. As noted in § 3.03, most of these tests have been developed and validated for other purposes (i.e., the assessment of intelligence, personality characteristics, abilities, clinical symptoms, and diagnosis). Some of these tests do contain validity scales designed to assess the client's posture and attitude toward testing. With some of the remaining tests, researchers have attempted to develop indices of malingering through empirical studies. Nonetheless, few of these malingering-detection techniques are deserving of unqualified endorsements.[62] The research supporting use of these tests for this purpose is suspect because of limitations in the research design and failure to cross-validate promising findings with new samples, among other problems. Further, many studies indicate that although test scores have reliably distinguished *groups* of individuals who were either feigning or not, they have not demonstrated satisfactory levels of accuracy in classifying individual cases.

The most useful categorization of psychological tests comes from Rogers and his colleagues,[63] who note an important distinction between strategies for detecting psychopathology and those necessary to diagnose neuropsychological impairment: "In the former case the would-be malingerer must generate and amplify on a believable set of bogus symptoms. . . . In the case of feigned organic deficits, the would-be malingerer must simply deny his/her abilities and make deliberate mistakes. . . ."[64] The following discussion addresses the use of psychological tests to detect these two types of malingering before summarizing the findings.

(1) Feigning Psychopathology

A number of psychological tests might be useful in detecting malingered emotional disorders. Beginning with the projective tests, various studies of the Rorschach have suggested that malingering is correlated with slow reaction times, dramatic contents, frequent card rejections, and inconsistencies (e.g., failure to give easy, popular responses while providing more difficult ones).[65] But Schretlen has criticized this research as lacking methodological rigor,[66] a conclusion echoed by other scholars in the area.[67] Regarding the Bender–Gestalt, Schretlen similarly concluded that "additional well-controlled studies are needed before the Bender can be assumed to provide a valid and reliable index of malingering."[68]

Among personality tests, the instrument most extensively researched and widely used in the assessment of dissimulation is the MMPI/MMPI-2. The determination of profile validity is a significant topic in any handbook or text describing the clinical use of the MMPI/MMPI-2,[69] and the assessment of dissimulation using the MMPI and other personality inventories has been thoroughly discussed by Greene.[70] Potential indices of dissimulation on the MMPI/MMPI-2 include elevations and configurations of the traditional validity scales (L, F, and K; F-K index), profile configuration, subtle versus obvious symptom endorsement, special scales (the Ds scale), and new measures of response consistency developed for the MMPI-2 (FB, VRIN, and TRIN)[see Glossary entry MMPI, § 20.02].

Although a number of studies have supported the use of one or more of these indices as useful in the detection of malingering, the literature reveals several potential problems as well. First, various of these indices have performed inconsistently across studies. In a number of recent studies and reviews, support has been voiced most often for those indices associated with F scale elevation (F, F-K),[71] whereas the subtle-obvious item differential has performed less well, yielding unacceptably high false positives in malingering studies.[72] In some other studies, however, the opposite pattern of results has been obtained.[73] Second, although the research literature appears to establish an empirical relationship between high scores on the F scale or F-K index and malingering, some investigators have concerns about the cutoff scores traditionally recommended for these indices.[74] Schretlen, for instance, noted that the F-K index may be subject to misinterpretation because severity of psychopathology correlates positively with F scores, whereas socioeconomic status (SES) correlates negatively. Thus, he suggests that conservative values (e.g., F-K > 17) should be used in assessing possible malingering by African Americans, other persons of lower SES, and in persons suspected of severe psychopathology.[75] Finally, Greene cautions against the overinterpretation of MMPI dissimulation indicators, warning that "[i]t is not necessary to use several of these scales/indexes simultaneously since they are correlated highly and consequently are very redundant."[76] Despite these cautions, the MMPI/MMPI-2 appears to have the most empirical support, among conventional psychological tests, for use in the assessment of malingered psychopathology.

In the past decade investigators have also attempted to develop structured psychological tests specifically for the assessment of malingered psychopathology. One such instrument is the M test,[77] which has been the subject of a number of empirical studies but has not yet emerged as a viable clinical instrument. A self-report test containing only 33 items, its developers envisioned a clinically useful tool that could be used in such places as jails and emergency rooms, where time and restrictive conditions make administration of lengthy instruments like the MMPI burdensome. Although an initial simulation design study yielded impressive results (accurate identification of 93.7% of the controls and detection of 78.2% of the malingering subjects), this level of performance has not been approached in subsequent studies.[78]

(2) Feigning Cognitive Impairment

One might assume that detection of malingered brain damage or feeble-mindedness would rely primarily on intelligence tests. But a review by Schretlen revealed that much of the research on the usefulness of such tests for this purpose is dated and focused on instruments not currently in wide use.[79] Further, Schretlen found, even the more popular contemporary intelligence tests [see Table 3.2] are not well adapted to the kind of "scatter analysis" that has been the best indicator of malingering.[80] Thus, Schretlen's review offers little support even for the use of intelligence tests in assessing malingered cognitive impairment.

Rogers and colleagues reviewed several studies in which skilled clinicians have attempted to detect malingering of cognitive deficits using intelligence tests, or a combination of those tests with neuropsychological tests and other clinical protocols. In most of these studies as well clinicians performed poorly, even below chance in some cases.[81] The review also discerned six different detection strategies that are potentially available to detect the feigning of neuropsychological impairment.[82] Although several of these strategies have shown promise in isolated studies, few have been systematically utilized in commonly employed measures for the detection of malingered cognitive deficits.

(3) Summary

In conclusion, clinicians should be cautious about their use of psychological tests to investigate malingering. Although judicious use of the MMPI/MMPI-2 appears warranted, the track record of most other strategies has not been impressive. Many experienced clinicians advocate the use of a battery of tests of different types as an approach to overcoming the limitations associated with any one test. This approach is theoretically sound, and its potential has been demonstrated in some recent studies by Schretlen and colleagues.[83] However, these studies used a combination of experimental and conventional testing indices, and they utilized strictly statistical, as opposed to clinical, interpretations to attain their results. Our review did not reveal studies in which clinicians, using clinical interpretations of combinations of tests, had demonstrated any extraordinary ability to detect malingering.

(c) Use of Third-Party Information

Of course, as indicated in § 3.02, one of the most useful means of detecting malingering is third-party information. Indeed, obtaining information contradicting the client's version of events is probably the most accurate means of detecting fabrication and may be the only viable one with clients who sabotage interview and testing efforts. Although this point probably does not require further elaboration, we offer a description of a case in which one of us was involved as an illustration of the critical role that collateral information can play:

The defendant was a 24-year-old, married, white male charged with rape. On a Wednesday morning in 1982 he was admitted to a forensic psychiatric hospital for an inpatient evaluation of competency to stand trial. Early the next day he was interviewed in his room by the examiner. He appeared unfamiliar with the surroundings and stated that he believed the year to be 1978 and that he was currently in an army field hospital in Korea. He reported that his last memory prior to waking up was being with his military unit.

This defendant presented as puzzled and perplexed, and he was reluctant to participate in a formal evaluation without first receiving confirmation/explanation from "somebody I trust" regarding his current legal circumstances and hospitalization. He advised that this could probably be accomplished if he could talk on the phone to his wife. When an offer was made to call his wife from the examiner's office, he stated "she works at McDonald's and doesn't get home from work until 4:00 P.M.," and it was agreed that the call would be placed later in the day.

The defendant had indicated that he and his wife lived with his mother. The examiner immediately called the defendant's mother, who confirmed that the wife did live with her, was at work at McDonald's, and was expected home at about 4:00 in the afternoon. She also reported, however, that the wife had obtained this job only six months earlier (1981) and that this was her first employment in the five years (1977–1982) of their marriage. Thus, the defendant could not have known about his wife's employment and work schedule in 1981 if he truly believed that he was still in the army in Korea in 1978.

In assessing malingering, forensic clinicians who possess contradictory information like that in the above example might consider a tactic sometimes employed by polygraph examiners. Although not usually admissible in court [see § 3.08(b)], the results of polygraph tests may be used "clinically" to confront subjects with the evidence of deviant responding. Such confrontation

occasionally results in a confession of deception, if not guilt, by the subject. Similarly, forensic clinicians may use evidence from interviewing, testing, or other sources (e.g., third-party information that is incongruent with the person's self-report or presentation) to confront clients with suspicions of feigning. Little is lost if the client does not admit to feigning, but much is gained if the client admits to the deception. Whatever the weaknesses in the interview or testing data that gave rise to the suspicions, the client's admission is a compelling piece of clinical information that brings closure to the issue. If handled tactfully and empathically, the clinician may now have a relieved, cooperative and candid respondent for any remaining issues to be explored as part of the forensic referral.[84]

3.08. Challenges to the Basis of Expert Testimony

CASE STUDY 3.2

Gloria, charged with murder of her husband, claims she can remember nothing about the commission of the homicide. She recalls preparing dinner, but next remembers sitting in the living room with a bloody knife in her hand and the body of her husband on the kitchen floor (at which point she called the police). You have been hired by her attorney to evaluate her mental state at the time of the offense. From her history, there is no past evidence of dissociation. She repeatedly, and from what you can tell, sincerely, states that she has no memory of killing her husband; she also claims to be deeply sorry about his death. You decide to conduct an interview of her while under the influence of sodium pentothal. After advising her attorney of your objectives and obtaining Gloria's consent for the procedure, you administer the drug and ask her what she can remember about the night of the offense. Speaking in slurred tones, she at first says she remembers nothing. Then, after you prod her by suggesting she must remember something, she spends the next ten minutes describing, in an uninterrupted, disorganized monologue, how she killed her husband. She says that while she was fixing dinner, her husband came up behind her and started to take off her clothes. When she resisted, he forced her to the floor. He started choking her, at which point she found a knife on the floor and stabbed him several times. When you ask her whether her husband had ever done anything like this before, she started crying and stated that he "forced" her all the time. When the drug wore off she claimed to remember nothing of the interview, and expressed surprise at the story she had told while under the influence of the drug. She continued to insist she had no memory of killing her husband, or of any "rapes" by her husband in years past.

You also talk to one of Gloria's neighbors, who says that over the years he has heard loud yells and "slapping sounds" coming from Gloria's house at night. The police report contains a statement from a police detective, who says he saw indentations in Gloria's neck as he talked to her on the night of the killing. Finally, Gloria's attorney has obtained the criminal records of her husband, which indicate that he had served time for aggravated battery against another woman some ten years ago, and include a prison psychologist's report stating, among other things, that the defendant had "psychopathic tendencies" and had stated that he "got off hurting women."

QUESTIONS: Assume Gloria's attorney wants to put you on the stand to bolster an argument that Gloria should at most be guilty of manslaughter. Is there any legal or clinical reason why you might not be able to testify about what you have discovered through the various sources described above? If a court decided you could not testify as to the contents of the sodium pentothal interview, but that you could, based on that interview and other information, offer an opinion as to Gloria's mental state at the time of the offense, would you do so? In addition to the material in this chapter, you might want to consult § 4.04(d).

As this chapter has made clear, expert forensic testimony can and should be based on multiple sources of information. Suppose an expert bases an opinion about insanity on a clinical interview of the accused, a diary of his that police seized from his home, psychological testing, interviews with the criminal defendant's family, police and medical records, and the results of a polygraph test. It may be that, given common practice in the jurisdiction, the other side will not object to these various bases for the testimony. However, if in doubt on this score, the wise attorney should seek, prior to trial, either a stipulation from the other side or a judicial determination that the opinion and its foundations are admissible. In practice, perhaps only the polygraph results will

give rise to serious challenge, but the admissibility of any one of these sources of information might be attacked.

The legal basis for such challenges are diverse. The results of a clinical interview might be tainted if the defendant's Fifth Amendment rights were not honored [see § 4.02]. The diary might be "suppressed" if it was illegally seized [see § 2.04(a)(1), § 7.02]. The results of the psychological tests might be considered inadmissible because their orientation to the present and their nomothetic nature render them irrelevant [see § 3.03(b)]. The interviews with the family, as well as the police and medical records, might be challenged as inadmissible "hearsay" [see below]. And the polygraph results could be challenged either under the *Frye* test (which bars testimony unless "the thing [on which it is based] is sufficiently established to have gained general acceptance in the particular field in which it belongs"), or *Daubert* and federal Rule 702 (which prohibit testimony based on evidence which is "unhelpful," in light of its low probative value, error rate, lack of general acceptance and other factors) [see § 1.04(c)].

If any of these challenges is successful, is the expert's testimony also rendered inadmissible? In the federal courts, this question is answered by Federal Rule of Evidence 703, which provides that facts or data underlying an expert opinion "need not be admissible in evidence" if "of a type reasonably relied upon by experts in the particular field in forming opinions or inferences upon the subject." Although this language is similar to *Frye*'s, note that the rule focuses on whether it is "reasonable" to rely on certain information, not whether it is "generally acceptable" to do so, and is meant to deal with situations involving *any* type of information, not just scientific information. Many states have adopted a version of Rule 703 as well. Some, however, do not permit expert testimony unless its basis is *independently* admissible.[85]

In the previous insanity case hypothetical, assume a court finds all the information underlying the expert's opinion admissible except the polygraph results (on the ground that they are not based on a "generally accepted" technique and thus run afoul of *Frye*). The last group of courts described in the previous paragraph would, as a result of this ruling, also prohibit the expert testimony that relies on it. On the other hand, in federal court, and in those state courts that follow the federal approach, the question would be whether forensic clinicians in the type of case at issue reasonably rely on polygraph results. Given the similarity between this inquiry and the *Frye* test (under which the court has already ruled the results inadmissible on their own), the court might answer this question negatively. However, when the results constituted only a "corroborative" rather than a crucial component of the expert's case, a court might well agree with the argument that relying on polygraph testing is reasonable despite its lack of "general acceptance."

One further complication must also be noted. Most courts that permit an opinion under Rule 703 analysis would probably allow the expert not only to voice the opinion but also to explain its entire basis (including, in this case, the results of the polygraph test).[86] But other courts, although allowing the opinion, prohibit informing the jury about any data that are not independently admissible.[87] For ethical (if not legal) reasons, this second position is problematic. A clinician should not offer an opinion that cannot be explained [see § 1.04(a)]. Nor should the law allow unexplained opinions to be given because this maneuver "usurps" the jury's credibility assessment role. Thus, if the challenged information is important to the clinician's opinion and the court insists that it not be mentioned, the clinician should generally not testify [see § 4.05(b)(1)].

These general points should be kept in mind in reading the following discussion, which addresses special issues connected with four differing types of information that might underlie expert testimony: hearsay, polygraph tests, narcoanalysis and hypnosis, and other types of novel "clinical" evidence.

(a) Hearsay

"Hearsay" is simply an out-of-court statement sought to be used in a trial or similar proceeding to prove the truth of the matter asserted in the statement. Thus, statements obtained from the subject's family, the police, or the clinician's own colleagues who have assisted in the evaluation are hearsay (in Case Study 3.2, the reports from the neighbors, the detective, and the various records

are hearsay). A hearsay statement is generally not admissible because its reliability cannot be assessed through cross-examination of the declarant at the time the statement is made. However, there are several exceptions to the hearsay rule, normally applying in situations in which the hearsay is considered reliable despite its out-of-court nature, or when it is the only available evidence. The most significant such exception is the "party admission" exception, which admits statements made by a criminal defendant or a party to a civil lawsuit[88]; analogously, declarations against interest, made by individuals who are not parties and are not available at trial, are admissible.[89] Testimony given at a preliminary hearing will also generally be admissible,[90] whereas testimony given at a grand jury proceeding usually will not be (because in the latter case there has been no opportunity for cross-examinaton).[91] Hearsay statements found in official and medical records are admissible *if* they are of the type routinely recorded in such records (e.g., statements in psychiatric records from mental health professionals and patients about mental condition, but not statements by a patient about how her husband constantly beat her up).[92] One important caveat to the so-called business records rule is that the prosecution may not use hearsay statements found in law enforcement "business" records against a criminal defendant given the latter's constitutional right to confront accusers.[93]

As this brief and incomplete survey of the hearsay rules makes clear, much of the standard hearsay information on which a mental health professional relies in court will be independently admissible, but at least some types of information (e.g., statements from family members, statements in police reports used against a defendant) may not be. In the latter situation, most trial courts allow the expert to testify in any event, either under Rule 703 or simply because the judge and the parties have not given the situation any thought. It has been argued, however, that Rule 703's reasonable reliance language should be narrowly construed to permit the clinician to report only those hearsay statements the validity of which can be demonstrated (e.g., through a hearsay exception, or through in-court cross-examination of the declarant about the out-of-court statement).[94] According to this view, the jury should not be forced to judge the credibility of an unavailable source based solely on what the clinician says.

At the least, one can make a strong argument that everyone who is a *significant* source of information should be required to testify in court, including, for instance, all members of an evaluation team who have conducted independent components of the evaluation. But in those situations in which the hearsay data are trivial or unlikely to be contested, or when they are significant but the source is practically unavailable,[95] a strict rule seems counterproductive. In any event, clinicians, aided by their lawyers, should be prepared to explain why sources they have relied on are not available and why they nonetheless feel comfortable in relying upon them.

(b) Polygraph Results

The modern polygraph machine measures various autonomic physiological functions (such as pulse and respirations rates, blood pressure, and perspiration) as the subject is questioned by an interrogator. If these physical measures differ or are more persistent when the subject responds to "relevant" questions as opposed to "control" questions, the usual conclusion is that the subject is lying when answering the "relevant" questions.[96] However, the validity (accuracy) of the polygraph process is much in dispute. Although some proponents of the device claim accuracy rates of between 90% and 100%, some of the studies on which these claims are based are really *reliability* studies, measuring interrater agreement, and others use as the criterion variable the subsequent conviction of the subject, in jurisdictions in which the conviction rate is between 90% and 100%.[97] Other, better done studies estimate false-positive rates of more than 30%.[98] Research on the accuracy of voice stress analyzers (which detect subaudible, involuntary tremors that supposedly result from stress, and therefore fabrication) is even less encouraging.[99]

A second type of lie detection technique that has generated better results does not attempt to evaluate the truthfulness of any given response, but rather measures the reaction to questions or stimuli to which (it is hypothesized) only guilty

people would react. Typically, the subject is given a multiple-choice question about facts that only a guilty subject would know (e.g., the subject is shown a series of photographs, including one of a teller in the bank that was robbed). Consistently high physiological responses to the incriminating part of the question are supposed to indicate involvement in the offense. The false-positive rate using this technique is said to approach 10%.[100]

Even so, if polygraph results are the *only* or principal basis of an expert opinion, their admissibility is questionable. The reported false-positive rates of 10% to 35%, the possibility that juries will nonetheless attribute undue significance to testimony that has such a "scientific" aura, and the fact that juries are assumed to be adequate evaluators of credibility on their own (and thus will not be "helped" by polygraph results), in combination, lead to this conclusion under *Daubert* (which requires focusing on the helpfulness of the information). Whether *Frye*'s general-acceptance-in-the-field test dictates the same result depends on how one defines the relevant "field" of reference—professional polygraph operators are likely to disagree with researchers on the topic. In any event, most courts reject polygraph results[101] or admit them only if their admissibility is stipulated by the parties before the test takes place[102]; only a few leave their admissibility up to the judge or permit them to be used to impeach.[103] As indicated previously, however, if the results are only a secondary basis for the expert opinion, even the former group of courts might lean toward finding both the opinion and the results admissible.

(c) Narcoanalysis and Hypnosis

These two techniques are treated together because both raise similar problems from an evidentiary perspective. As discussed in an earlier part of this chapter [§ 3.06], whether under the influence of "truth serums," such as sodium amytal or pentothal, or hypnotized, the subject is thought to be more likely to recall "repressed" memories. At the same time, however, the subject is apparently very susceptible to suggestions, unconscious or not, from the interviewer. Indeed, as discussed earlier, some commentators indicate that the subject may confabulate "memories" in an effort to cooperate with an interviewer, even one who merely presses the subject to remember anything he or she possibly can.[104] Furthermore, at least as far as hypnosis is concerned, the person hypnotized may no longer be able to separate actual memories from "suggested" ones.[105]

With this in mind, many legislatures and courts generally bar admission of drug or hypnosis-induced statements. However, since 1987 this stance has been modified to some extent. In that year, in *Rock v. Arkansas,*[106] the United States Supreme Court held that, given a defendant's right to testify under the Fifth and Sixth Amendments and the due process clause, a rigid prohibition on hypnotically induced statements is unconstitutional in criminal cases when the statements are the defendant's. The court reasoned that a per se prohibition does not take into account the reasons for undergoing hypnosis, the circumstances under which it took place, or any independent verification of the information it produced; nor does it recognize that cross-examination, expert testimony, and cautionary instructions might counteract the inadequacies of posthypnotic testimony. A case-by-case approach is mandated, the Court held, unless the state can show "that hypnotically enhanced testimony is always so untrustworthy and so immune to the traditional means of evaluating credibility that it should disable a defendant from presenting her version of the events for which she is on trial."

Although *Rock* was limited to cases involving defendants' statements, its reasoning could apply to drug or hypnosis-induced statements of others as well. The decision suggests that courts should conduct a sensitive appraisal of such evidence. Most courts limit *Rock* to its facts, however; using *Frye* or a *Daubert*-type probative value/prejudicial impact balancing test, they continue to adhere to a per se exclusionary rule except in cases in which the hypnotically-induced statements are sought to be introduced in a criminal case and are essential to the defendant's claim.[107] A few courts are willing to permit testimony under other circumstances, but only if rigorous safeguards are observed. For instance, in *State v. Hurd,*[108] the court outlined an analysis that essentially makes admissibility contingent on the elaborate guidelines that were described in § 3.06.[109]

Hurd and the other cases mentioned previously dealt with attempts to introduce the results of narcoanalysis or hypnosis on their own. A question more relevant to the subject matter of this book is: What if, instead, these results are described by mental health professionals as a basis for their testimony? *McCormick on Evidence,* perhaps the leading evidence treatise, asserts that "[w]hen an expert uses narcoanalysis or hypnosis in his or her examination of a person to determine whether the individual is insane, incompetent or mentally incapacitated, the case for admissibility is much stronger."[110] Consistent with earlier statements in this section, if the induced statements are only corroborative, we believe this position makes sense. However, if they are a principal component of the testimony, this position is less defensible; the vagaries of the techniques at issue here do not disappear just because an expert opinion is based on their results.

(d)   Other Clinical Techniques

Virtually any other "novel" or "scientific" clinical technique—ranging from projective tests to syndrome or profile analysis—could give rise to admissibility challenges under *Frye* or *Daubert*; to the extent such techniques are discussed in this book, the relevant admissibility issues are discussed there [see, e.g., §§ 8.03(c), 803(d)]. The main point to be made here is that, as with the other techniques discussed previously, clinicians and lawyers should be alert to the fact that even if information from these sources is not independently admissible, an expert opinion partially based upon it may be.

3.09.   Conclusion

Moving from therapeutic to forensic work requires several adjustments in attitude and technique. Treatment considerations are more likely to be secondary, subjects are less likely to be cooperative and candid, investigation of other sources is more likely to be necessary, and "conventional" interview and testing techniques are less likely to be useful. Furthermore, even sources that a clinician may feel are forensically helpful (e.g., third-party statements, hypnotic interviews, and profile information) may be anathema to a legal system worried about unreliable information and thus may legally taint the resulting clinical opinion. The clinician who fails to recognize the need for these adjustments or neglects to make them will be of limited aid to a legal system which, as the next chapter makes even clearer, is the forensic clinician's ultimate client.

Bibliography

CLINICAL ASSESSMENT OF MALINGERING AND DECEPTION (Richard Rogers ed. 2d ed. 1997).

THOMAS GRISSO, EVALUATING COMPETENCIES: FORENSIC ASSESSMENTS AND INSTRUMENTS (1986).

Kirk Heilbrun, *The Role of Psychological Testing in Forensic Assessment*, 16 LAW & HUMAN BEHAVIOR 257 (1992).

Kirk Heilbrun, Barry Rosenfeld, Janet Warren, & Steven Collins, *The Use of Third Party Information in Forensic Assessments: A Two State Comparison*, 22 BULLETIN OF AMERICAN ACADEMY OF PSYCHIATRY & LAW 399 (1994).

MCCORMICK ON EVIDENCE § 206 (4th ed. 1992) (admissibility of scientific evidence).

Martin Orne, *The Use and Misuse of Hypnosis in Court*, 27 INTERNATIONAL JOURNAL OF CLINICAL & EXPERIMENTAL HYPNOSIS 311 (1979).

Martin Reiser, *Investigative Hypnosis*, in PSYCHOLOGICAL METHODS IN CRIMINAL INVESTIGATION AND EVIDENCE 151 (David C. Raskin ed. 1989).

Richard Rogers, Ernest H. Harrell, & Christine D. Liff, *Feigning Neuropsychological Impairment: A Critical Review of Methodological and Clinical Considerations*, 13 CLINICAL PSYCHOLOGY REVIEW 255 (1993).

David J. Schretlen, *The Use of Psychological Tests to Identify Malingered Symptoms of Mental Disorder*, 8 CLINICAL PSYCHOLOGY REVIEW 451 (1988).

Constitutional, Common-Law, and Ethical Contours of the Evalution Process: The Mental Health Professional as Double Agent

4.01. Introduction

The mental health professional who performs evaluations for the courts and the lawyer who represents those evaluated must be aware of several constitutional, common-law, and ethical principles that have a direct bearing on the conduct of forensic evaluations. The first two sections of this chapter discuss when an "accused" who is being evaluated has a Fifth Amendment right to remain silent during the evaluation or to prevent state use of its results, and how the Sixth Amendment's right to counsel applies to forensic assessment. The third section addresses the evaluator's common-law and statutory duties toward the person being evaluated and toward the court and society at large: Here the focus is on privilege and confidentiality rules, the somewhat opposed "*Tarasoff* duty" to take preventive measures when a defendant being evaluated appears dangerous, and the doctrines of informed consent and negligent misdiagnosis. The final section of the chapter examines several ethical issues that are closely related to many of these legal doctrines but that stem from the mental health professions' own attempts to regulate their evaluation practices.

In discussing the often controversial issues covered in this chapter, we take the view that, whenever possible, legal and ethical principles should be formulated to facilitate the interchange between the evaluator and the person being evaluated. Unfortunately, the conflicting and complex demands made on the evaluator by these principles make it impossible to develop an entirely consistent approach to many problems that arise in the evaluation process. The aim of this chapter, therefore, is to provide answers when they seem clear and to present the available alternatives when, as is frequently the case, the answers seem less than obvious.

CASE STUDY 4.1

Suppose you are a psychologist ordered by the court, upon motion of the prosecutor, to evaluate the trial competency of a criminal defendant. When you arrive at the jail to interview the man, he seems very disturbed and agitated. After you identify yourself and tell him the purpose of the interview, he blurts out that he is charged with murder, that his brother was also involved in the crime, and that he would have killed the victim's sister as well if he'd had the chance. He also says he threw the murder weapon in a pond, because he did so the last time he killed someone and was never caught. When you are finally successful in stopping his tirade, you ask if he has seen a defense attorney, to which the answer is no.

QUESTIONS: Should you refuse to evaluate the defendant further, despite the court order, until an attorney has been appointed for him? Should you have told him as soon as he began to talk that he has a "right to remain silent" and that anything he says could be used against him? You have heard the man incriminate himself in two crimes, incriminate his brother in the most recent crime, and reveal an intention to kill a third person. You have also heard him describe the location of the murder weapon for the most recent crime. Do you have a duty to disclose all or any part of this information to someone (and, if so, to whom, and when—now or only at some later point in time)? Could you be liable financially if you do not disclose and the man either is not convicted of murder or harms the victim's sister or someone else? Could you be held liable if you *do* reveal the information, on the ground that you have breached confidentiality?

Suppose instead you are the lawyer appointed (somewhat tardily) to represent the defendant and that, based on an opinion from another mental health professional, you formally assert to the court that your client is incompetent to stand trial and that he was insane at the time of the offense. Can you prevent the clinician described earlier from disclosing what he or she knows to the prosecution, or at least keep the prosecution from using this information on either the competency or the insanity issue? If you have hired other private clinicians to evaluate your client but found their opinions unfavorable, can you "muzzle" them as well? Finally, can you prevent the state from obtaining an evaluation on insanity? (At this point the state has sought only a competency evaluation.) If not, can you at least sit in on, and ask questions during, the prosecution's evaluation of the man's mental state at the time of the offense?

4.02. The Fifth Amendment and the Right to Remain Silent

The principle behind the Fifth Amendment's privilege against "self-incrimination" is that persons accused of a crime should not be forced to provide evidence against themselves; the state should be required to prove its case on its own, without bringing its formidable power to bear on the accused. Thus, as presently construed by the United States Supreme Court, the Amendment prohibits the state from using at a criminal trial any (1) "testimonial" statement (2) of an "incriminating" nature (3) that it "compelled" from the defendant being tried.[1]

The requirement of testimonial evidence comes from a long line of cases distinguishing between "testimonial" or "communicative" evidence on the one hand and "noncommunicative" or "physical" evidence on the other. The latter type of evidence does not fall within the scope of Fifth Amendment protection. To hold otherwise, pointed out Justice Holmes in *Holt v. United States*, "would forbid a jury to look at a prisoner and compare his features with a photograph in proof."[2] Using similar reasoning, the Supreme Court has held that the state may require a defendant to submit to a blood test, give a writing example, stand in a lineup, and try on articles of clothing, even if these actions assist the state in securing a conviction.[3]

A few lower courts have held that clinical evaluations do not implicate the Fifth Amendment because the defendant's disclosures during such evaluations are not relied on for their content but rather serve merely to identify mental traits of the accused, much as a fingerprint measures certain physical characteristics. But by far the majority of courts agree with the D.C. Court of Appeals that "the words of the accused are critically important in determining his mental condition."[4] The Supreme Court itself appears to agree with this conclusion. In *Estelle v. Smith*[5]—the primary case in which the Court has considered the application of the Fifth and Sixth Amendments to psychological evaluations, and therefore one that is referred to frequently throughout this and the following section—the Court cited approvingly a statement from the American Psychiatric Association's amicus brief that "absent a defendant's willingness to cooperate as to the verbal content of his communications a psychiatric examination . . . would be meaningless."[6]

It appears settled, then, that the disclosures typically made during a clinical evaluation are testimonial rather than noncommunicative. When particular disclosures by the defendant are "incriminating" and when they may be compelled from the defendant and used at trial have been more controversial topics. To a great extent, the answers to these questions depend on the type of evaluation at issue and the purpose for which the results of the evaluation will be used. The following discussion looks at these issues in connection with evaluations of competency, mental state, sentencing, quasi-criminal, and civil law issues.

(a)   Competency Evaluations

As Chapter 2 indicated, there are several different types of legal competencies that can arise in the criminal process: competency to stand trial, competency to plead guilty, competency to waive certain rights, and so forth. With a few exceptions, a competency evaluation involves an assessment of the defendant's present mental state rather than his or her mental state at the time of the offense. Thus, at first glance, it may seem unlikely that anything "incriminating" will be revealed during such assessments.

As Chapters 6 and 7 make clear, however, any comprehensive competency evaluation of a defendant, regardless of the specific competency in question, can involve delving into incriminating matters. In an evaluation of competency to stand trial, for example, the clinician may inquire into the defendant's memory of his or her behavior at the time of the offense to ascertain whether the individual can adequately assist an attorney in preparing a defense. Similarly, an examination of competency to plead guilty will probably involve asking questions about the offense to determine the extent to which the defendant understands the implications of the plea.

As Case Study 4.1 illustrates, even without such direct questions, the defendant could easily divulge information during a competency evaluation that could prove "incriminating." This is especially so given the broad scope of that term: The Supreme Court has held that any disclosure by the defendant is potentially self-incriminating if it might "furnish a link in the chain of evidence needed to prosecute."[7] Thus, not only outright "confessions" but statements that provide investigative leads (e.g., "I threw the gun in the bushes" or "My wife saw me do it") implicate the Fifth Amendment.

There is a good possibility, then, that incriminating evidence will be produced during a competency evaluation. Yet virtually every state permits the prosecution to compel the defendant to undergo a competency evaluation upon showing that the defendant's competency is in question. The central justification for permitting this state coercion is that the state's interest in protecting the integrity of the criminal process by ensuring that the defendant understands what he or she is

doing overrides the defendant's Fifth Amendment interest in remaining silent. In many jurisdictions, a second justification, at least in the context of competency to stand trial, is that statutory provisions prohibit the use of the evaluation results at trial.[8] In these states, disclosures made during an evaluation of competency to stand trial may be used by the prosecution only to determine the defendant's competency, not to determine guilt; incrimination of defendants through their own words is thereby avoided. When there are no such statutory limitations (e.g., in the context of competency to plead guilty or to confess), defense attorneys can accomplish the same result by inserting language in the court order to the effect that use of the results of the evaluation at trial is prohibited.

In *Estelle v. Smith*, the Court spoke approvingly of limiting use of competency results to the competency issue, at least when that is the only psychiatric issue raised by the defense (as was the case in *Estelle*). In that case, the prosecution's psychiatrist, Dr. Grigson, used the results of his court-ordered competency evaluation not only to address Smith's competency but also to give opinions about Smith's sanity at trial and his dangerousness at sentencing. The Supreme Court held that "if the application of [Grigson's] findings had been confined to serving that function [of determining the defendant's competency], no Fifth Amendment issue would have arisen."[9]

Even with statutory or court-ordered protection barring use of evaluation statements at trial, however, there remains the possibility that the competency evaluation report will contain disclosures by the defendant that could lead to incriminating evidence (e.g., the murder weapon). In such cases, the mental health professional who is ordered to submit a competency report to the prosecution has two options: (1) to retain the incriminating information in the report and leave it to the court to decide whether the prosecution's trial evidence is in fact the fruit of the defendant's evaluation statements or (2) to refrain from including in the prosecution's report any possibly incriminating disclosures by the defendant. Admittedly, the latter approach may require deletion of some probative information. But the alternative—the inclusion of potentially incriminating information—may lead to difficult-to-detect prosecutorial abuse of the evaluation process (with prosecutors relying on tidbits from clinical reports to help make their cases).[10]

Based on this latter concern, Virginia provides by statute that "no statement of the defendant relating to the time period of the alleged offense shall be included in the [competency] report."[11] This approach does not prevent a general statement in the report to the effect that the defendant could (or could not) recount events during the time period of the alleged offense. Nor does it prevent including statements by others, such as eyewitnesses and police, because these are not *self*-incriminating and thus do not receive Fifth Amendment protection. It merely protects against adjudicative use of statements made by the defendant during a competency examination; it has the added benefit of encouraging the defendant to be communicative during the competency evaluation.

What if, rather than being forced to undergo the competency evaluation by the prosecution, the defendant "voluntarily" seeks such an evaluation? Here one could argue that the defendant's statements are not "compelled," but one could also argue that allowing prosecution use of these statements would affect the defendant's candor during his or her own competency examination and thus chill the right to an effective consultation. Those states that bar the use of competency evaluation results on the issue of guilt do not distinguish between prosecution- and defense-requested evaluations, thereby implicitly recognizing the latter point.

However, according to the Supreme Court, when the prosecution wants to use the results of a defense-requested competency examination on a *mental state* issue (as opposed to whether the defendant committed a criminal act), it may do so without violating the Fifth Amendment, even if the mental state issue is not competency. In *Buchanan v. Kentucky*,[12] the prosecution rebutted the defendant's psychiatric defense at trial with the results of a competency and treatment evaluation that had been jointly requested by the prosecution and the defense. The Supreme Court found that the Constitution was not violated by this use of competency evaluation results because, unlike in *Estelle*, the defendant had raised a psychiatric defense and the defendant had joined

in the evaluation motion. The Court held, in effect, that by requesting a competency evaluation the defendant forfeits Fifth Amendment protection against use of its results on any psychiatric issues he or she subsequently raises. *Buchanan* obviously could have a chilling effect on defense evaluation requests and thus does not facilitate exploration of competency issues. Note, however, that the decision merely concludes that the Fifth Amendment does not bar the practice described above; local statutory rules may still do so.[13]

(b) Evaluations of Mental State at the Time of the Offense

It should be obvious that the various legal doctrines addressing an accused's mental state at the time of the offense require the forensic evaluator to ask questions of the accused that could easily lead to incriminating disclosures [see Chapter 8]. A comprehensive evaluation on issues of insanity, automatism, or diminished capacity necessitates detailed inquiry into the defendant's thoughts and actions during the time period of the crime. For this reason, most courts that have addressed the issue do not permit the state to *compel* an evaluation of defendants before they have formally indicated a desire to assert one of these defenses.[14] On the other hand, by far the majority of courts impose sanctions on defendants who refuse to cooperate with a state-requested evaluator once the defense gives notice of intent to raise a defense (as the lawyer did in Case Study 4.1).[15] In *Estelle v. Smith*, the Supreme Court implicitly condoned this practice on the ground that to permit a defendant to assert the right to remain silent after giving notice "may deprive the state of the only effective means it has of controverting his proof on an issue that he interjected into the case."[16]

In the event the defendant does refuse to cooperate with the state in the postnotice context, most courts prohibit the defendant from presenting expert evidence. A second, less frequently utilized sanction is permitting the defendant's expert to take the stand but allowing the prosecutor to inform the jury that the defendant will not talk to the state's expert.[17] A difficult issue, which has yet to be resolved, is when the defendant deserves such sanctions. Outright refusal to talk might normally be considered noncooperation. But some truly disordered defendants will be hostile to the evaluator for irrational reasons having nothing to do with the constitutional right to remain silent. Indeed, as one court put it: "The fact, amply demonstrated over the years, is that a failure of a defendant . . . to cooperate most often reflects an even greater degree of insanity rather than less."[18] The court attempting to decide whether sanctions should be imposed on the recalcitrant defendant needs to consult the evaluating clinician as well as the defense attorney to determine both the extent of the defendant's resistance and whether his or her attorney condones it.

As in the competency context, not only does the Fifth Amendment dictate when the prosecution can compel a mental state at the time of the offense evaluation, it also places restrictions on when the state can use its results. The modern trend, similar to that in the competency context, is to limit trial use of disclosures made during such an evaluation to the issue being evaluated. To this effect, the Model Penal Code formulation, which has been adopted in several states, reads: "A statement made by a person subjected to a psychiatric examination or treatment . . . shall not be admissible in evidence against him in any criminal proceeding on any issue other than that of his mental condition."[19]

The Federal Rule of Criminal Procedure concerning this issue provides even more comprehensive protection:

> No statement made by the defendant in the course of any [psychiatric] examination . . . whether the examination be with or without the consent of the defendant, no testimony by the expert based upon such statement, and no other fruits of the statement shall be admitted in evidence against the defendant in any criminal proceeding except on an issue respecting mental condition on which the defendant has introduced testimony.[20]

Thus, the Federal Rules not only prohibit direct use of the defendant's evaluation statements on issues other than those he or she has raised but also forbid use of the defendant's disclosures for investigative purposes. In several other jurisdictions, similar Fifth Amendment protection has been extended to the defendant through judicial decision.[21] Where statutory or judicial provisions do not exist, the defense attorney can request the court to provide such protection via court order.

Even this protection may not be enough. To prohibit "fruits" of the defendant's statements from being admitted at trial, one must be able to discover when the state's evidence is in fact such a fruit—a task that, as pointed out earlier, may often be impossible. Therefore, the best method of reducing the potential for prosecutorial and police abuse of the evaluation process is to restrict state access to the results as much as possible. When the clinician is retained by the defendant, this objective is easily achieved: Virtually every court that has considered the matter has held that the retained professional is an "agent" of the attorney, and that the results of such an evaluation are therefore protected by the "attorney–client privilege" until the defense "waives" the privilege by putting the defendant's mental state at the time of the offense at issue.[22] Unfortunately, the dictates of the attorney–client privilege and the Constitution have not generally been recognized in those cases in which a state-employed clinician performs an assessment requested by an indigent defendant. Typically, the report of the clinician employed by the state is sent to all parties, whether or not notice of a defense has been given. Yet, if the indigent defendant has requested the evaluation, he or she should be able to rely on the same protection (whether based on Fifth Amendment or privilege principles) as one who can afford a private clinician.

Thus, we recommend that whenever a mental state at the time of the offense evaluation is defense-requested, and the law or court order does not otherwise specify, the full evaluation report not be sent to the prosecution or the court (barring defense consent or a court order) unless and until the defendant affirmatively indicates that a defense will be asserted. Only at that point does the prosecution need to know the content of the defendant's statements. Up to that point, delivering the report to the prosecution is unnecessary, provides the state with too great a temptation to use the information therein for investigative purposes even if it is barred from using it directly at trial, and tends to discourage full disclosure by the defendant who knows the clinician is a conduit to the prosecutor.

Thus, for example, in Virginia it is provided by statute that, prior to notice of a mental state defense, the prosecution is to receive only a summary of the clinical report, from which all statements by the defendant about the time period of the alleged offense have been deleted.[23] After notice is given, the prosecution can obtain the full report, as well as its own evaluation, if it wants one.[24] An innovative proposal having much the same effect has been put forward by the American Bar Association (ABA) in its Criminal Justice Mental Health Standards. Under standard 7-3.4, the prosecutor may compel the defendant to undergo an evaluation within 48 hours of the defendant's own evaluation, but the results of the prosecution's evaluation are sealed until formal notice of an intent to raise a defense based on mental abnormality is given by the defendant. (The results of the defendant's own evaluation are, of course, protected by the attorney–client privilege.) This device honors the defendant's Fifth Amendment interest but also gives the prosecution access to evaluation results "as fresh" as those obtained by the defendant's expert.

The whole issue of pretrial disclosure of evaluation results is complicated by "reciprocal discovery" provisions in many states (usually incorporated in the state's rules of criminal procedure), allowing the prosecution to "discover" the reports and statements of the defense's experts once the defense asks for information from the prosecution, even if the defense request precedes the defendant's decision to raise a defense.[25] To the extent that such discovery rules require prenotice disclosure of defense evaluation results, they would seem to be in violation both of the Fifth Amendment and of the attorney–client privilege.

A final point with respect to the application of the Fifth Amendment in this context has to do with the courts' treatment of testimony derived from an evaluation of mental state at the time of the offense. If and when the state's expert takes the stand and testifies, he or she will probably reveal incriminating information disclosed by the defendant, even if the testimony is limited to a discussion of the defendant's mental condition. Clinical testimony about the defendant's sanity, for instance, will usually reveal admissions by the defendant with respect to the act associated with the crime in question. But preventing disclosure

of this information would probably seriously undermine the credibility of the testimony.

This problem has been dealt with in two ways. At one time, several states provided for mandatory "bifurcation" of the trial process, with the first stage focusing on the "guilt" of the defendant and the second stage, if necessary, reserved for trying the sanity of the defendant found to have committed the offense charged. In this way, the potentially incriminating testimony of the clinician is reserved until after the defendant is found "guilty." Unfortunately for this approach, most state courts that have addressed the issue have declared that prohibiting admission of clinical testimony at the initial stage of the process is unconstitutional because it denies defendants the opportunity to introduce all relevant testimony in their defense.[26] Thus, under constitutionally correct procedures, the bifurcated trial does not always avoid the incrimination problem and will often produce duplicative proceedings.[27] For these reasons, most of the states that adopted a mandatory bifurcation procedure have since abandoned it.[28] However, several states still permit bifurcation at the defendant's request if the court agrees.[29]

A second approach to the problem of trial incrimination, followed by most states, is to hold a unitary trial but to caution the jury to consider the clinician's testimony only on the issue of mental condition, and not on other issues that the jury must decide.[30] Such an instruction will not prevent misapplication of the clinician's testimony by the jury. Nonetheless, provided that the other protections discussed in this chapter are available, a unitary trial is not likely to create much actual prejudice to the defendant's Fifth Amendment interest. Moreover, the defendant will often have an expert of his own describing the offense in detail, and the prosecution will usually have evidence independent of the clinical evidence sufficient to prove that the defendant committed the act associated with the crime. Perhaps the best approach, endorsed by the ABA in Criminal Justice Standard 7-6.7, is to hold a unitary trial with a precautionary instruction under most circumstances but to allow bifurcation if the court considers it appropriate (as when the defendant is presenting clinical testimony on the insanity issue and also has a colorable nonclinical defense, such as self-defense, which might be prejudiced by the clinical testimony if heard at the same proceeding).

(c)   Sentencing Evaluations

The few courts that have addressed the issue have all declared that the Fifth Amendment does not apply to the typical sentencing evaluation.[31] Initially, this result seems logical because if the defendant is being considered for sentencing, he or she presumably has been convicted and thus can no longer be "incriminated." Yet in reality, presentence evaluations often take place before trial and thus can provide still another source of investigative leads. In addition, the postconviction sentencing process itself can result in a type of incrimination. In the typical first-degree murder case, for instance, the judge may have authority to impose a sentence ranging from a few years to life. Arguably, the defendant should not be forced by the state to reveal information that may tend to increase the sentence in such a case.

The Supreme Court has obliquely accepted this line of argument in the unique context of capital sentencing. In *Estelle v. Smith* the Court found that when the defendant's statements to a clinician who later testifies for the state expose the defendant to the "ultimate penalty of death," there is "no basis to distinguish between the guilt and penalty phases of a capital murder trial so far as the protection of the Fifth Amendment privilege is concerned."[32] After *Estelle*, it appears that, procedurally, the capital sentencing evaluation should be treated like an evaluation of mental state at the time of the offense. That is, until the defendant indicates a desire to use a clinician at the capital sentencing hearing, the state should not be able to obtain its own clinical evaluation on capital sentencing issues. After such notice is given, on the other hand, the prosecution should be entitled to obtain its own assessment as well as the results of the defendant's evaluation.

It is important to note, however, that *Estelle* is limited to capital sentencing. The Court was careful to point out that its decision in *Estelle* did "not hold that the same Fifth Amendment concerns are necessarily presented by all types of interviews and examinations that might be ordered or relied upon to inform a sentencing determina-

tion."[33] Thus, although the lawyer or mental health professional may want to seek court-ordered restrictions on the state's access to and use of noncapital presentence evaluation results, there is no clear constitutional foundation for such restrictions.

(d)   Juvenile Delinquency and Commitment Proceedings

Technically, the Fifth Amendment only prohibits use of incriminating statements at criminal trials. But as § 2.04(d) points out, modern courts have consistently characterized juvenile delinquency proceedings and civil commitment as "quasi-criminal" in nature, given the "massive deprivation" of liberty that may result from a finding that a person should be punished as a delinquent or institutionalized in a mental hospital. It is not surprising, therefore, that the Supreme Court held, in *In re Gault*,[34] that the Fifth Amendment applies in juvenile delinquency proceedings. Presumably, the same constitutional rules that govern adult evaluations should also apply to these proceedings.

The judiciary's approach to civil commitment has been more cautious, however. Some courts have applied the Fifth Amendment to civil commitment proceedings and evaluations,[35] on the ground that a defendant's disclosures during a commitment hearing or a prehearing assessment are "incriminating" (even though they may not constitute admission of a crime) if they could lead to involuntary hospitalization, and that they are "compelled" if the individual is not told of the right to remain silent. Most courts, however, have concluded that although a civil commitment hearing is analogous to the criminal process in many ways, it is not a criminal trial and should not be encumbered with all the procedures afforded the criminal defendant.[36]

The Supreme Court appears to have endorsed the latter position. In *Allen v. Illinois*,[37] the Court held, 5–4, that commitment under a "sexually dangerous offender" statute is not a "criminal" proceeding for purposes of the Fifth Amendment, at least when the statute permits the prosecution to seek commitment in lieu of criminal conviction for a sexual offense. (Some states provide for special commitment of the "sexually dangerous" *after* conviction [see § 9.04(b)].) Thus, the state may, without violating the federal constitution, compel an individual charged under such a statute to undergo a psychiatric evaluation of his or her dangerousness, as long as the results are used only as a basis for seeking commitment under the statute; similarly, the individual may not exclude compelled statements from such commitment proceedings. The Court's justification for this holding was that the primary purpose of the Illinois statute in question was treatment, not punishment. Thus, there is no danger of "incrimination" at this type of commitment proceeding, unless the consequences of such a proceeding turn out to be identical to those faced by a felon. Allen had been confined for five years in the psychiatric unit of the state's maximum security prison under authority of the Illinois Sexual Offender Act. (Had he been convicted of the offense which led to his commitment, he would have received at most a year's imprisonment and a $500 fine.) Yet because he made no showing that the state had failed to afford him treatment different in kind from that afforded felons, he was not entitled to Fifth Amendment protection.

Allen is important because it firmly repudiates the suggestion in *Gault* that the Fifth Amendment should apply whenever the proceeding in question may lead to loss of liberty. Rather, after *Allen*, the sole question for Fifth Amendment purposes is whether the primary purpose of the proceeding in question is treatment or punishment. One could certainly argue that the type of commitment at issue in *Allen* more resembled punishment than treatment, particularly because under these types of statutes confinement is indeterminate and release is conditioned on a finding that the individual is no longer dangerous; the primary purpose of such statutes would seem to be incapacitation bordering on retribution, not treatment. Moreover, as Justice Stevens pointed out in his dissenting opinion in *Allen*, the Illinois statutory framework is decidedly criminal in flavor: Commitment is triggered by a criminal offense, is initiated by the state prosecutor, requires the criminal standard of proof, and results in confinement in prison. But after the Court's holding in *Allen*, it seems clear that not only sexually dangerous offender proceedings of the type at issue in

Allen but also civil commitment proceedings and post-insanity-acquittal hearings will be considered "civil" for Fifth Amendment purposes.[38]

(e) Other Civil Proceedings

It is possible that incriminating information will be revealed during evaluations that are more properly labeled "civil" in nature. Because several states render child neglect a criminal offense, for instance, incriminating statements may be made during a child custody evaluation. Generally, such incriminating information is admissible at a subsequent criminal trial if it is not protected by the attorney–client privilege (i.e., if the evaluation is conducted at the behest of the other side or the state). During such evaluations, it is up to the individual's attorney to ensure that the client "takes the Fifth" when asked questions that might reveal incriminating information. If the privilege is not asserted, it is very likely that the disclosures will be admissible in any criminal proceeding initiated against the individual. If, on the other hand, the privilege is asserted, the client may not be held in contempt; otherwise, the Fifth Amendment would be meaningless.

(f) The "Miranda Warnings"

In *Estelle v. Smith*, the Supreme Court held that when the defendant "neither initiates [a] psychiatric evaluation nor attempts to introduce any psychiatric evidence" at a subsequent capital sentencing proceeding,[39] statements made by the defendant during the evaluation are inadmissible at the capital sentencing proceeding unless the defendant has first been given warnings to this effect: "You have the right to remain silent, and anything you say may be used against you in later proceedings." *Estelle* has caused considerable confusion among mental health professionals; on a first reading, the decision seems to require that every forensic evaluation be preceded by "*Miranda* warnings" (so-called because the above-described litany is taken from the Supreme Court's famous decision in *Miranda v. Arizona*[40]).

In the typical criminal case, however, such warnings are not required; indeed, they would be inaccurate. As noted earlier, the defendant generally has no right to remain silent during a court-ordered competency evaluation (such as that involved in Case Study 4.1), a postnotice state-requested evaluation of mental state at the time of the offense or capital sentencing issues, or a noncapital sentencing evaluation. And if his or her evaluation disclosures are protected by the attorney–client privilege [see § 4.02(b)], the defendant has no reason to remain silent. Only when, as in *Estelle* itself, the defense has not yet indicated an intent to use psychiatric evidence and the evaluation is designed to obtain sanity or sentencing information for the state does the clinician need to tell the defendant, "You may refuse to talk, and anything you say may be used against you."

Whether persons subjected to civil commitment evaluations must be warned of the right to remain silent depends, of course, on whether such a right has been found to exist by the relevant tribunal. If individuals are entitled to such a right, they should be told they possess it; otherwise their Fifth Amendment guarantee is likely to be meaningless. The fact that such warnings might inhibit disclosure is legally irrelevant, although perhaps clinically unfortunate.[41] Courts consistently refuse to abate the Fifth Amendment right in the criminal context merely on the ground that its implementation might complicate the state's efforts to secure a conviction.

Although the law may not require that "warnings" be given prior to most forensic evaluations, the mental health professions' own ethical guidelines may necessitate a short preevaluation discussion with the subject, describing the content of the evaluation and its possible uses. This topic is dealt with at greater length in § 4.05(d).

4.03. The Right to Counsel

The Sixth Amendment promises the criminal defendant the "assistance of counsel for his defense." The Supreme Court has held that the Amendment actually guarantees two different rights: (1) the right to presence of counsel and (2) the right to effective assistance of counsel. Both rights have implications for the conduct of forensic evaluations in criminal cases. With respect to counsel in civil cases, on the other hand, the relevant law on these issues is likely to be statutory rather than constitutional and varies from jurisdiction to jurisdiction.

(a) Counsel's Presence during the Evaluation

Over the past two decades, the Supreme Court has decided a number of cases granting the criminal defendant a constitutional right to counsel not only at the trial itself but also at several so-called critical stages of the criminal process that precede trial. Thus, for instance, the defendant has the right to have counsel present at a postindictment lineup, at a preliminary hearing to determine whether there is probable cause to prosecute, and at arraignment.[42] A minority of courts have equated the pretrial clinical evaluation with these stages of the criminal process and have held that the Sixth Amendment guarantee applies to forensic assessments.[43] Most courts, however, have held that the defendant does not have a right to counsel's presence during the actual evaluation.[44] In *Estelle v. Smith*, the Supreme Court intimated that it agreed with this latter approach. While the Court established that the state must inform the defendant's attorney about any evaluation that it plans to conduct (which suggests that the clinician in Case Study 4.1 may have an obligation to ensure the defense attorney knows about the evaluation), it also cited with approval a lower court's opinion that the attorney's actual presence during the psychiatric interview "could contribute little and might seriously disrupt the examination."[45]

A cogent argument can be made that the Supreme Court's caution on this issue is unfounded. The leading Court case on the right to counsel is *United States v. Wade*,[46] which held that a criminal defendant has the right to counsel during postindictment identification lineups. The Court appeared to rely primarily on two justifications for its ruling. First, an attorney should be present because the identification made at the lineup might substantially prejudice the defendant's interests. Second, reconstructing at trial what actually occurred during the lineup identification might be difficult if counsel did not observe it.

The Court noted, for instance, that "neither witnesses nor line-up participants are apt to be alert for conditions prejudicial to the suspect," and that "[i]mproper influences may go undetected by a suspect, guilty or not, who experiences the emotional tension which we might expect in one being confronted with potential accusers." The Court also pointed out that "any protestations by the suspect of the fairness of the line-up at trial are likely to be in vain; the jury's choice is between the accused's unsupported version and that of the police officers present."

The analogy to the clinical evaluation process should be apparent. The results of state-requested competency, insanity, and sentencing evaluations can have a substantially adverse impact on the defendant's case.[47] And a defendant with mental problems is unlikely to be able to reconstruct accurately for the attorney what occurred during such an evaluation, nor is such a person's testimony alone likely to fare well against the testimony of a mental health professional.

Even accepting these points, however, one might argue that the attorney's presence during the evaluation is not necessary. It has been suggested, for instance, that a videotape or audiotape of the evaluation would afford the attorney with a sufficient record of the relevant events.[48] Further, when the attendance of the defendant's attorney would be inimical to the efficiency of the evaluation (as can the case when the evaluation takes place far from the trial court or over a long period), taping or written records may prove to be the only possible solution. Finally, and most important to most clinicians, the presence of the defendant's attorney can affect the defendant's responses (whether the attorney has that intention or not).

Nonetheless, in those cases in which attorney access is practicable, we suggest that criminal defense counsel be permitted to observe the evaluation process. Even a videotape will not accurately transmit all the possible contextual variables at work during an evaluation. And it is not a foregone conclusion that the attorney will have a negative impact on the evaluation process. As noted in § 4.02, in the typical state-requested evaluation the defendant does not have the right to remain silent, and the attorney risks sanctions against the client if he or she advises noncooperation or pre-

vents the client from cooperating. Indeed, because the relationship between the state's clinician and the defendant may be somewhat strained to begin with, the attorney's presence is unlikely to harm, and may even contribute to, development of an evaluation dialogue. It should also be kept in mind that, regardless of constitutional demands, practical considerations connected with certain types of evaluations may warrant the presence of an attorney. In particular, when one of the issues to be assessed is the relationship between the attorney and a client, as in evaluations of competency to stand trial like that involved in Case Study 4.1, it may make good sense to allow the attorney to be present at, if not participate in, the assessment.[49]

Given the possibility of disruption by the attorney, however, most courts confronted with this issue will, at most, permit the defense attorney to tape the clinician's evaluation—an option that is consistent with *Estelle*'s reasoning. An alternative is to have the defendant's own expert observe the evaluation in place of the attorney. Even if the actual presence of an attorney is not constitutionally required in criminal cases, one of these "substitute" procedures may be constitutionally mandated in those cases where the defendant requests it.

The reluctance of most courts to permit defense attorneys to attend evaluations in criminal cases stands in contrast to the willingness of many courts to allow opposing counsel at evaluations in civil cases, a contrast that is particularly striking given the fact that the Constitution does not mandate counsel in such cases. The courts that are most likely to permit attorney presence in civil litigation are those that perceive the expert as an advocate engaged in discovery, as compared to those that perceive the expert to be an impartial authority.[50] If the presence of counsel is viewed as too disruptive, tape-recording the evaluation is also an option; it has the advantage of being "self-regulating" in that, unlike criminal cases involving indigent clients, the recording party will normally have to bear the expense. Some clinicians may object even to the presence of a recording device, on the ground that it is impractical (imagine, e.g., a child custody evaluation involving prolonged interviews of hyperactive children and home visits) or on the ground that evaluees will be defensive or inhibited by knowledge that their statements may be reported verbatim. These concerns, although valid, must be balanced against the parties' legitimate interest in access to an accurate account of the expert's data.

(b) Presenting an Effective Defense

Two issues involving the criminal defendant's right to effective assistance of counsel are briefly mentioned here. The first is the indigent defendant's right to an independent state-funded evaluation. The second is the nonindigent defendant's right to prevent the prosecution from using experts the defendant has decided not to call. Although the focus here will be on criminal cases, reference to practice in other types of cases is also made.

(1) The Right to an Independent Evaluation

Although virtually every state provides indigent criminal defendants with free evaluation services at state institutions, less than half provide funds on a systematic basis for the indigent who wishes to consult a private forensic specialist. At least three arguments have been advanced for providing indigents with funds for an "exploratory" evaluation (also called "ex parte" or "confidential" evaluations). First, the results of such evaluations are more likely to be kept confidential than the results of evaluations by state hospital employees, thus better protecting the Fifth Amendment rights discussed earlier. Second, failing to provide funds for exploratory evaluation forces clients to rely on potentially biased state-employed clinicians, thus undermining the defense attorney's ability to represent his or her client adequately.[51] Finally, it has been argued that making indigents rely on state clinicians violates notions of equal protection, as wealthier defendants can choose from as many clinicians as their resources permit.[52] These arguments can be coupled with empirical proof that the costs associated with an independent evaluation program that pays community clinicians on a per-evaluation basis is likely to be much less expensive than transporting defendants to hospitals for prolonged stays.[53]

Yet these arguments usually fail, because courts make the dubious assumption that state evaluations are "impartial." Thus, for instance, in *Ake v. Oklahoma*,[54] the Supreme Court held that indigent defendants are guaranteed psychiatric assistance under the Sixth Amendment when raising an insanity defense or mitigating circumstances at capital sentencing, but it also decided that indigent individuals do not have the right to a clinician of their own choosing. Rather, the states may determine how the right to such assistance is to be implemented. For instance, the states are not compelled by *Ake* to provide funds for private, as opposed to state employee, clinical assistance.[55] Moreover, *Ake* specifically held that an indigent is entitled to only one state-funded evaluation.

A few states do permit defendants to seek an independent evaluation if they are dissatisfied with the evaluator selected by the court or the results of the evaluation.[56] Many states have also decentralized their evaluation system; in these states community mental health professionals, as well as state hospital personnel, are usually available to provide evaluations, thereby offering indigent defendants a greater variety of clinicians from which to choose (if the state allows such a choice).[57] Furthermore, even under *Ake*, the clinician who reaches an opinion contrary to that sought by the defense must still "consult" with the attorney; the majority opinion in *Ake* requires the professional to "conduct an appropriate examination and assist in evaluation, preparation and presentation of the defense." Thus, if the defense is able to construct an insanity defense using lay witnesses, the expert who disagrees with the defense must still assist counsel in preparing for direct examination, as well as assist in preparing for cross-examination of any witnesses the prosecution proffers.

A separate question concerns the circumstances under which the indigent is entitled to the state-paid clinician. The majority in *Ake* stated that "[w]hen the defendant is able to make an *ex parte* threshold showing to the trial court that his sanity is likely to be a *significant* factor in his defense, the need for the assistance of a psychiatrist is readily apparent" [Emphasis added]. And the defendant is entitled to an expert on dangerousness "when the State presents psychiatric evidence of defendant's future dangerousness." Although the latter standard is relatively clear, many lower courts have held that to obtain an *Ake* evaluation on insanity the defendant must make a "clear showing" that mental state is a "genuine" or "real" issue, a showing that may be difficult without psychiatric assistance.[58]

It should also be emphasized that *Ake* only dealt with insanity and capital sentencing evaluations. Although states usually finance competency evaluations as well, only a few courts have found that funds for independent evaluations are constitutionally mandated in civil commitment and like contexts.[59] In some settings, such as Social Security assessment, statutes require the government to pay for evaluations that cannot be afforded by the claimant [see § 13.04(b)]. In most civil contexts, however, the evaluation cost must be borne by the requesting party.

(2) Use of Experts Retained by the Opposing Party

A quite different problem arises when, as hypothesized in Case Study 4.1, the *non*indigent defendant consults more than one expert, decides to raise a psychiatric defense using only some of the experts, and the opposing side then subpoenas the remaining expert or experts. In *United States ex rel. Edney v. Smith*,[60] the court held that, in criminal cases, the state should have access to the experts the defendant has decided not to use once the issue of mental state at the time of the offense is properly raised. Otherwise, the circuit court stated, the defendant would "be permitted to suppress any unfavorable psychiatric witness whom he had retained in the first instance, under the guise of the attorney–client privilege, while he endeavors to shop around for a friendly expert, and take unfriendly experts off the market." Several courts have followed *Edney*'s lead.[61]

A slightly smaller number of courts follow *United States v. Alvarez*,[62] which held that the defendant's right to effective assistance of counsel is curtailed when the state is permitted to use experts the defendant has discarded. According to the *Alvarez* court, the "attorney must be free to make an informed judgment with respect to the best course for the defense without the inhibition of creating a potential government witness."

It is clear that the *Edney* rule has more of an inhibiting effect on open disclosure during the evaluation. Furthermore, because the state is entitled to its own evaluation once the defendant gives notice of an intent to raise a psychiatric defense, the prosecution will rarely be severely hampered by the *Alvarez* rule. Yet if the defense attorney is able to gag experts merely by consulting them, however briefly, the prosecution could be denied access to valuable, and arguably much fresher, data if the former approach is not followed. Deciding which rule is best in a particular case may depend largely on the number of experts available in the particular community and on whether the defense attorney has acted in good faith when consulting with the various experts.[63] This approach would also comport with typical practice in civil cases, where, as detailed in § 2.04(b), one side may depose another side's unused experts only upon a showing of substantial need.

4.04. Common-Law and Statutory Duties of the Evaluator

This section discusses various nonconstitutional legal principles governing the conduct of forensic evaluations. In particular, it focuses on the types of acts or omissions for which the evaluator may be legally liable or which may violate a "privilege." As will be seen, the evaluator (as opposed to the therapist) has little to be concerned about in either regard.

(a) Liability for Breach of Confidentiality

In the typical therapeutic relationship, in which the mental health professional and another individual enter into an arrangement designed to provide therapy for the latter, the law encourages confidentiality. A clinician who divulges information about a patient to unauthorized parties without the patient's consent is liable for any resulting damage to that patient's reputation and privacy interests.[64] In the purely evaluative relationship, however, clinicians are *required* to give third parties information about the person evaluated regardless of that person's wishes. This is so even when the court record in which the report will be filed is public record, as is often the case in both civil and criminal cases.[65] Such openness may seem anathema to the mental health professional trained to honor the patient's privacy and may run afoul of central ethical precepts [see § 4.05(d)]. But it stems from the conviction, rooted in the First Amendment, that the public has the right to monitor the judicial process—a concept that has been reemphasized by the United States Supreme Court in several decisions.[66]

Thus, as long as the evaluator's disclosures do not stray beyond the terms of the court order, it is extremely unlikely that he or she could be found liable for breach of privacy or damage to reputation. In fact, several courts have held that an evaluator is absolutely immune from a claim that an evaluation report defames or violates the privacy of the subject of the report if the report was requested by the government for purposes of litigation pending against the subject.[67] Of course, this type of protection against personal liability should not lead evaluators to neglect their ethical duty toward people whom they see professionally. As discussed more fully in § 4.05(e), because of the public nature of their product, evaluators should not include material of only marginal relevance in their reports unless, as discussed below, they are required to do so.

(b) The Duty to Protect the Public (Tarasoff)

Under limited circumstances having to do with protection of the public the law may require information beyond that requested by the court order. Virtually every state, for instance, provides that clinicians who observe or suspect child abuse must notify the appropriate agency, even if the information is obtained through a confidential relationship.[68] Similarly, some states require clinicians to contact the authorities if patients tell them of plans to commit a crime.[69] Whether these requirements apply to clinicians acting as *evaluators* depends on the context. When the clinician is an agent of a criminal defense attorney or a civil attorney (rather than the prosecutor or court), disclosure probably should be governed by the attorney–client privilege. This privilege and associated ethical rules prohibit disclosure of

information about past crime (so as to encourage revelation of material necessary to facilitate effective representation). Thus, the evaluator retained by an attorney should keep confidential past crimes related by the client (including information about past child abuse), at least until the client and the attorney indicate otherwise. On the other hand, the rules dealing with the attorney–client relationship allow disclosure of information necessary to *prevent* serious crime.[70] If the attorney resists disclosure even in the latter situation, the evaluator will have to be guided by his or her own ethical rules, which may or may not mandate disclosure [see § 4.05(d)(3)]. When the evaluator is not an agent of the attorney, as is the case in Case Study 4.1, the attorney–client privilege does not apply and the ethical rules govern disclosure of both past and future crime.

A separate legal development, which began in the courts rather than the legislatures, has created the possibility of significant monetary liability in the latter situation; that is when the clinician concludes, or should have concluded, that the person evaluated is dangerous, yet fails to protect against the danger. In the famous case of *Tarasoff v. Regents of the University of California*,[71] the Supreme Court of California imposed a duty on therapists to take preventive measures whenever it would appear to a reasonable and competent therapist that a patient is likely to harm another person in the near future. Applying this rule to the facts in *Tarasoff*, the court found that the two therapists involved could be sued by the family of a woman who was killed by one of their patients, on the ground that they had failed to inform the victim that the patient had threatened to harm her or to take other measures to protect her.

Although most jurisdictions now recognize a *Tarasoff*-type duty, the vast majority that do limit it to situations in which, to use the words of the California statute enacted after *Tarasoff*, "the patient has communicated to the psychotherapist a serious threat of physical violence against a reasonably identifiable victim or victims."[72] Moreover, application of the duty to therapists does not necessarily mean it also applies to evaluators, even in those situations where the attorney–client privilege would permit disclosure.[73] A person does not normally have a legal obligation to help another unless he or she stands in a "special relationship" to that person. *Tarasoff* found that the therapist does have such a relationship with potential victims of patients, in part because the therapist's involvement with and control over the party's potential assailant is "significant," and in part because, according to the court, the therapist possesses expertise in predicting who may be violent. But the *evaluator* may not have as much contact with the subject of an evaluation as a therapist does with a patient; moreover, malpractice law has traditionally made a distinction between "treating" and "examining" doctors and placed less of a duty on the latter.[74]

On the other hand, the evaluator, as a clinician, can initiate commitment and take other steps to "control" a dangerous individual. And although there is some question whether any mental health professional is adept at predicting dangerousness [see § 9.09(b)], to the extent such expertise exists, distinguishing between a therapist and an evaluator may make little sense. Moreover, it is arguable that, given the minimal degree of confidentiality associated with evaluations, even less reason exists to refrain from disclosure than in the therapeutic context.

If *Tarasoff* is applied to evaluations, what type of obligation does it impose on the evaluator? First, as indicated above, most jurisdictions, including the one in which *Tarasoff* was decided, provide that no duty exists unless the potential victim is specifically identified or reasonably foreseeable; threats directed at groups or "types" of individuals are usually considered too amorphous to trigger any legal obligation on the part of the clinician.[75] Second, contrary to popular perception, *Tarasoff* did not create an automatic "duty to warn" the potential victim if and when the victim is identified. Courts and statutes recognize several alternatives to a warning, including notification of the police and commitment of the individual—in short, any steps reasonably necessary under the circumstances.[76] If, as is often the case in criminal cases, the person being evaluated is already in custody, the clinician's *Tarasoff* duty may be met merely by notifying the court or the custodial agency of this suspicion. If the individual is not in custody, on the other hand, other measures, including commitment, should be considered in lieu of or in addition to notification of the court. In criminal cases, standard 7-3.2(b) of the ABA's

Criminal Justice Mental Health Standards suggests that, when the evaluation is initiated by the defense attorney, the attorney should be notified of any imminent risk to self or others posed by the defendant, and when the evaluation is initiated by the court or prosecution, both the court and the defense attorney should be notified.

There is evidence to suggest that *Tarasoff* has inhibited the therapeutic process and that applying its rule to either the therapeutic or evaluative context does more harm than good.[77] On the other hand, the American Psychiatric Association has indicated it may be proper to hold a psychiatrist liable for "flagrantly negligent" failures to protect others from harm, and ethical rules mandate a duty to protect the public.[78] Given the controversy surrounding *Tarasoff*, it is impossible to predict what those states that have not considered the issue will decide with respect to either therapy or evaluations. In states in which the law is indefinite, professional evaluators are probably best advised to act as if they were in a *Tarasoff* jurisdiction, remembering that disclosure should occur only when there are sufficient indications of dangerousness to lead a competent clinician reasonably to conclude the individual will act out violently toward a specific person, and that only the information that is necessary to prevent the foreseen dangerous act should be divulged.

(c)   Clinician–Patient Privileges

Although many states recognize only a physician–patient or psychiatrist–patient privilege, an increasing number have also established psychotherapist–patient, psychologist–patient, and social worker–patient privileges.[79] Under limited circumstances, these evidentiary privileges allow the patient, and in some jurisdictions the therapist as well,[80] to prevent testimony or disclosure of records from the therapist. As with the attorney–client privilege discussed in § 4.02, these privileges are designed to encourage discussion between the professional and the person seeking the professional's services by protecting against unwarranted disclosures to third parties.

As should be clear from the foregoing discussion, however, in the purely *evaluative* relationship, these privileges are irrelevant. The clinician–patient privileges do not apply when the clinician–"patient" relationship is the creature of the court, as is the case with court-ordered evaluations. And, as noted in § 4.02, even the attorney–client privilege applies only when the clinician is an agent of the defendant's attorney. In short, the law takes the position that, for purposes of evidence law, the evaluator's client is the party that requests the evaluation, not the person being evaluated. Consistent with previous discussion, therefore, the evaluator must report any information about the person that is relevant to the questions specified by the requesting party, regardless of assertions of a clinical privilege.

A separate privilege issue arises when the evaluator is (or was) also the therapist of the person being evaluated. Although, as an ethical matter, the therapist should avoid this situation [see § 4.05(c)(2)], it may occasionally arise. When it does occur, the evaluator may feel particularly concerned about the competing duties of confidentiality and obedience to the court.

As might be expected, the law gives precedence to the latter duty. In civil cases, for instance, most jurisdictions hold that patients waive the privilege whenever they have initiated litigation or raised a defense that might involve the issue of their mental status; other states abrogate the privilege when the benefit to be gained by the disclosure outweighs its negative effects, but the result is usually the same as under the first approach. In criminal cases, the privilege is even less useful. A small number of states follow the balancing approach just described; most, however, simply state that the privilege is not available when mental state is at issue.[81] Thus, in the typical case, the privilege provides little protection; the therapist or the therapist *cum* evaluator can usually be required to reveal what has been learned about the individual through therapy. The only recourse in the face of a subpoena for records or testimony is to argue that the adverse effects of disclosure outweigh the benefits or that the material sought is irrelevant to the pending litigation because the issue of mental state has not been squarely raised.

Jaffee v. Redmond[82]—a 1996 decision in which the United States Supreme Court finally affirmed that there is a psychotherapist (including social worker)–patient privilege in federal court—

might eventually swing the pendulum in the other direction, although its ultimate import is not clear. *Jaffee* specifically rejected the balancing approach described above, stating that "[m]aking the promise of confidentiality contingent upon a trial judge's later evaluation of the relative importance of the patient's interest in privacy and the evidentiary need for disclosure would eviscerate the effectiveness of the privilege." It also made other strong statements endorsing the need for the privilege. But it did not address whether the traditional patient–litigant exception to the privilege would be recognized. It merely held that on the facts of the case—which involved the therapy records of a police officer being sued for negligently killing someone—the privilege prevented disclosure. Because the officer had not raised her mental state as an issue, and the therapy took place after, rather than before, the legally relevant event (the shooting), the Court's holding says nothing explicit about the typical situation raised in the forensic evaluation context. Moreover, as noted, it speaks only to the scope of the privilege in federal court.

As should be obvious from the previous discussion, common-law and statutory principles—in particular rules establishing the duty to protect third parties and the patient–litigant exception to therapeutic privileges—may tend to discourage communication between the clinician and the subject. The problem is exacerbated if the clinician feels ethically compelled to "warn" the person being evaluated of the potential for disclosure to third parties, an issue taken up in § 4.05(d)(3).

(d)   Other Tort Doctrines Relevant to Evaluations

Although it is extremely unlikely, the evaluator may be sued for damages on a number of other claims arising out of civil tort law. The two most probable such claims, and the only two to be discussed here, are informed consent and negligent misdiagnosis.

(1)   The Informed Consent Doctrine

If a doctor treats a competent individual in a non-emergency situation without obtaining that person's consent, the doctor is liable for battery and any damages resulting from the treatment. Both to define the criteria for a valid consent and to encourage consensual treatment, courts developed the doctrine of "informed consent." Recently, the doctrine has become relatively sophisticated. As discussed in detail in § 11.03(a), it requires, in the treatment context, that the clinician provide the patient with information that would be material to the decision whether to accept the proposed treatment, that the consent not be "coerced," and that the individual from whom consent is sought be competent or have a guardian protecting his or her interests.[83]

The relevance of the doctrine to the evaluation process is minimal in the typical case because the evaluation is court-ordered and will proceed whether the subject wants it or not; in fact, as noted earlier, in criminal cases the defendant may risk sanctions upon a refusal to cooperate. However, if the evaluator decides to use evaluation techniques other than the usual verbal or written question-and-answer modes, the doctrine may come into play. For example, before administering sodium amytal to an individual [see § 3.06], the subject should be told of the possible dangers of the drug, and the clinician should make sure that any consent obtained is given intelligently and voluntarily. Otherwise, the clinician might be held liable for any harm caused by the procedure, even if it is performed in a competent manner.[84] Of course, potential liability should not be the only concern of the forensic evaluator. As developed in §4.05(d), the clinician should feel ethically compelled to inform any person subject to evaluation of its nature.

(2)   Negligent Misdiagnosis

Generally, a mental health professional is not liable for negligent misdiagnosis unless the failure to diagnose correctly results in the administration of the wrong treatment and subsequent harm. The standard for deciding what is negligent focuses on prevailing professional norms.[85] Usually, a mistake in diagnosis will not be viewed as negligent if the clinician can show (1) the existence of reasonable doubt as to the nature of the condition involved, or (2) a split of medical authority as to the diagnostic procedure to be followed when

one of the conflicting procedures was, in fact, used; or (3) the diagnosis was made after a conscientious effort by the physician to inform himor herself about the patient's condition.[86]

Recall also that forensic examiners have tradiionally been given much more leeway than therapists, in part to encourage full disclosure to the court or agency ordering the examination. Therefore, it is unlikely that a person who was found "incompetent," "insane," or "unfit as a parent" (or "competent," "sane," or "fit") on the basis of a professional's testimony could successfully sue the professional on the ground that the clinician's opinion was arrived at negligently and that it caused harm. Indeed, it is probable that, as discussed in § 4.04(a), absent a showing of bad faith, clinicians would be given immunity from such a suit if their information or opinions were the result of a court order. In the commitment context, several states go further and grant clinicians who testify at commitment hearings absolute immunity from claims based on their hearing testimony.[87]

4.05.   Ethical Considerations in the Evaluation Process

CASE STUDY 4.2

You are a mental health professional working at a state forensic facility but maintain a part-time private practice. In your private practice you have been providing individual therapy for several months to John Doe, who is going through a divorce. An attorney representing Mr. Doe calls and requests to retain your services as an expert witness in an upcoming custody hearing; she asks that you evaluate Mr. Doe regarding parental fitness and be prepared to offer an opinion, hopefully one that will support his request for custody of a minor child. The attorney advises that Mr. Doe has agreed to this arrangement.

QUESTIONS: What are the relevant considerations in your decision whether to accept this referral? Assume you take the referral and that, during the divorce process, Mr. Doe and his estranged wife have a physical altercation resulting in Mr. Doe's arrest and placement in jail, whence he is referred to your forensic facility for a court-ordered evaluation regarding competency to stand trial. What factors would you consider in deciding whether to conduct this evaluation as part of your duties at the forensic facility? Assume you are able to arrange to have a colleague perform the evaluation. What factors should you or your colleague consider in becoming involved in the treatment of Mr. Doe in the forensic facility if he is ultimately adjudicated incompetent? If Mr. Doe is convicted, what factors should govern your colleague's actions if the state later requests that she testify at the sentencing hearing?

CASE STUDY 4.3

You are a psychologist who has been ordered by the court, upon motion of the prosecution and the defense, to evaluate the competency and mental state at the time of the offense of a Mr. Smith. Your report is to go to all parties. Smith's current charge is attempted murder of a police officer; he also has a three-page rap sheet listing prior offenses ranging from property crimes to violent offenses. According to the police report, Smith was shot in the head during his altercation with the officer; since his brain surgery, he claims total amnesia for the period of the offense, as well as transient confusion and disorientation. His wife, whom he married three months prior to his arrest, reported that he appeared very regressed during recuperation, having to relearn self-care habits (use of toilet, dressing, feeding). Based on this information, a previous evaluator concluded that Smith was incompetent.

When you arrive to interview Smith, you identify yourself and your purpose. Smith responds with a grunt and the statement, "One of you has already been here." He then says that he doesn't feel like talking today because he feels "down." You express sympathy for his situation, noting that, if you were in his situation, you would be feeling depressed and disoriented as well. He responds, "Yeah, plus my wife is leaving me." When you press him on why, he refuses to answer. You threaten to tell the court he is not cooperating, but he persists in his refusal, ultimately telling you to leave. Suspicious now that Smith may be malingering, you contact the wife for confirmation of her earlier observations about her husband's behavior during convalescence. The wife is vague about confirming or denying her previous reports; she speaks cautiously and inquires whether her husband might ever learn of her answers to your questions. You confirm that you may have to make reference to your conversation with her in disclosing the basis of your findings. The wife blurts out, "I did what I thought was the right thing to do at the time," but she refuses to

provide substantive responses to inquiries about her husband's behavior. When pressed, she confesses that the defendant has made threats toward her and her children if she does not "play along with his story." When you ask if she is scared, she says, "He's killed before," but refuses to say anything further.

QUESTIONS: What is the propriety of your actions to this point? Was there anything "unethical" about empathizing with Smith's situation? Should you have threatened him? Must you reveal the wife's allusion to another crime? Can you mention the wife's information in support of an opinion that Smith is malingering? If so, must you tell the wife you are doing so?

The preceding sections of this chapter discuss a variety of legal principles that may influence forensic evaluation practice. Forensic clinicians must also be aware, however, of potentially conflicting concerns that derive from professional practice standards and codes of ethics. In this section we examine the most significant such concerns and discuss them in light of the parallel (and sometimes competing) legal principles.

Although there is no uniform set of standards that apply to all mental health professionals, the professional organizations representing various health care disciplines—medicine, nursing, psychology, and social work—have independently established general ethical guidelines for their respective members. Until recently these general guidelines were the primary resource documents for practitioners. However, in recent years, two national professional organizations have developed explicit guidelines for forensic practice. These are the *Ethical Guidelines for the Practice of Forensic Psychiatry* promulgated by the American Academy of Psychiatry and the Law (AAPL)[88] and the *Specialty Guidelines for Forensic Psychologists* adopted by the American Psychology–Law Society (APLS).[89]

Although these documents vary somewhat in breadth, detail, and organization, both cover many of the essential ethical concerns that arise in providing forensic mental health services, particularly forensic evaluations, reports, and expert testimony that result from such evaluations. The remainder of this chapter is organized around these essential concerns, and excerpts from the APLS and AAPL guidelines are presented to guide the discussion. Readers are urged to obtain and employ the full guidelines as appropriate to their respective disciplines and practices.

(a)   Competence and Qualifications in Forensic Practice

> Expertise in the practice of forensic psychiatry is claimed only in areas of actual knowledge and skills, training and experience. . . . [T]here are areas of special expertise that may require special training and expertise.[90]

> Forensic psychologists are responsible for a fundamental and reasonable level of knowledge and understanding of the legal and professional standards that govern their participation as experts in legal proceedings. . . .[F]orensic psychologists have an obligation to maintain current knowledge of scientific, professional and legal developments within their area of claimed competence.[91]

With relatively few exceptions, mental health professionals who perform evaluations for the courts need more than basic clinical training. In addition to a good generalist training, forensic work in the criminal and civil justice system requires, at a minimum, familiarity with (1) the legal system [as discussed in Chapter 2]; (2) forensic assessment instruments and other special forensic techniques [as discussed in Chapter 3]; (3) the legal doctrines that give relevance to the mental health evaluation [described in Parts II, III, and IV of this book]; (4) research about syndromes, propensities, and similar phenomena that one may have been exposed to only minimally, if at all, as part of basic clinical training [Parts II, III, and IV]; and (5) the demands of being an expert witness [Chapter 18].

The need for specialty training for forensic mental health practice has been noted in the professional literature,[92] and it is reflected in the growth in recent years of interdisciplinary programs in forensic psychiatry[93] and psychology and law.[94] But it remains the case that most mental health professionals will obtain the significant part of their forensic training through self-study, on-the-job opportunities with experienced colleagues, and continuing education programs.[95] Obviously, if the state in which a clinician hopes to practice offers training and continuing education

programs, the clinician should take advantage of the opportunity, especially if certification as a forensic examiner is offered [see § 5.04(b)]. There are also nationally affiliated training programs, such as the one sponsored by the American Academy of Forensic Psychology. "Board" (as opposed to state) certification is also offered by the American Board of Forensic Psychiatry[96] and the American Board of Forensic Psychology.[97] Analogous certification is provided for social workers.[98] Finally, the American Academy of Psychiatry and Law[99] and the American Psychology-Law Society[100] sponsor annual or biannual conferences that focus significantly on forensic issues, and the annual conferences of the American Psychiatric Association and the American Psychological Association both include several sessions on forensic topics. These organizations also offer free-standing training programs on forensic evaluation and treatment, approved for continuing education credits, as do many experienced forensic clinicians.

A wealth of reading material on forensic issues also exists. In additional to this book and books like it,[101] there are numerous specialized professional publications that contain articles of interest to the forensic clinicians, including the *Bulletin of the American Academy of Psychiatry and Law*, the *Journal of Psychiatry and Law*, the *International Journal of Law and Psychiatry*, the *American Journal of Forensic Psychology, Forensic Reports, Law & Human Behavior, Behavioral Sciences and the Law,* and the *Mental Health and Physical Disability Law Reporter* (which reports on all new legal developments in disability law four times a year). Of course, general journals in mental health and general law reviews also often contain articles germane to forensic mental health, as do specialized journals in related areas (e.g., criminology and child protection).

Whether through formal or informal training, clinicians should come to understand the special demands of the various types of cases in which they hope to become involved. Three brief and, we hope, somewhat obvious comments regarding special forensic training are worth noting. First, competence in one area of forensic evaluation practice does not necessarily establish one's competence in another area. Some areas of forensic practice are significantly dissimilar from one another (e.g., insanity evaluations vs. parental fitness for custody evaluations) and little if any forensic expertise would be expected to generalize from one area to the other. Clinicians should obtain training in each of the areas in which they offer services.[102]

Second, an important but sometimes underemphasized aspect of forensic competence is an appreciation of the limits of what the behavioral/medical sciences have to offer the legal system. Grisso has noted that the development of new forensic research and technology is "a double-edged sword. Acquiring the benefits of a more rigorous empirical approach often requires that [forensic clinicians] also acknowledge more clearly the limits to the reach of their testimony."[103] This aspect of competence, stressed throughout this book [see in particular § 1.04], may have particular import in situations in which attorneys seek to use expert testimony in novel ways (e.g., assertion of a posttraumatic stress "defense" or a seizure "defense").[104]

Finally, as infrequent but sobering anecdotal reports attest, the accumulation of workshop diplomas and diplomate certificates is no guarantee against error or marginal clinical practice. In one instance, a board-certified forensic psychologist developed a report opining that the defendant was incompetent to stand trial as a result of a suspected brain lesion. The testing that "revealed" the precise location of the brain lesion was one subtest from the verbal portion and one subtest from the performance portion of the Wechsler Adult Intelligence Scale—Revised. In another instance a board-certified forensic psychologist promulgated the "*M'Naghten* competence test" in an effort to standardize interviews for competency to stand trial.[105] The title of the proposed "test" invited confusion by using a name (*M'Naghten*) historically associated with insanity rather than competency, and its content cited out-of-date rules of criminal procedure as authority.

(b) Clarifying Referrals with Legal Agents

> During initial consultation with the legal representative of the party seeking services, forensic psychologists have an obligation to inform the party of factors that might reasonably affect the decision to contract with the forensic psychologist.[106]

Depending on the attorney's experience in working with mental health professionals and the particular type of litigation, the range of issues needing clarification may be quite broad.[107] In the discussion that follows, these issues are classified as legal issues, issues concerning fees, and issues concerning prior relationships.

(1) Legal Issues

Clarification of the precise legal topic to be addressed in the evaluation is crucial for three reasons. First, as just discussed, clinicians should not take on an evaluation they are not competent to conduct. To advise the attorney of the extent to which their expertise will be useful, as required by the passage above,[108] clinicians need to discover the motivation for the referral. In doing so, even a clinician with solid credentials on a particular forensic issue may find that the angle or theory the attorney seeks to advance would draw the clinician beyond the boundaries of personal expertise. For example, some clinicians who are quite competent and confident testifying in insanity cases based on traditional medical model formulations may nonetheless feel uncomfortable with a case in which the attorney intends to pursue a novel theory (e.g., a "premenstrual syndrome" or "battered spouse" defense) with which they are not familiar. Advising the attorney of such concerns at the beginning of the consultation may persuade the attorney that another evaluator should be sought.

Second, clarifying issues will tend to ensure that later conflict does not develop about the conduct of the evaluation or testimony. For example, the mental health professional should explore any particular expectations that the attorney has about the methods and rigor of procedures that will be used in the evaluation.[109] Some attorneys may insist on the use of particular tests or procedures because of a belief that juries can be more readily persuaded or influenced if a tangible product (e.g., an X-ray or a test protocol) can be displayed at trial, whether or not the clinician plans to use the procedure, believes that it can contribute to the evaluation, or is skilled in its use. Clinicians should also discuss their posture with respect to providing ultimate-issue testimony so that the attorney can judge whether the anticipated testimony will enhance the case presentation [for more discussion on the latter issue, see § 18.05]. Finally, mental health professionals who can anticipate the use of procedures whose validity will likely be challenged (e.g., hypnosis) should so advise the attorney so that the attorney can deal with admissibility concerns early in the litigation [see, e.g., § 3.08]. Clarifications such as these at the early stages of consultation will result in a smoother relationship as the case proceeds.

A third reason for clarifying issues at the outset is that, as discussed in detail at other points in this chapter, the scope of the evaluation affects both the type of notification the clinician must give the client and the extent to which information learned by the clinician must be kept confidential. In this regard, clinicians should be particularly alert to referrals that are overly vague ("I need a psychiatric work-up on my client"). When such referrals are received, consultation with the referring source (i.e., one or both attorneys, the judge, or all three) is advised. Even when an evaluation request seems clear, such consultation is useful. For example, the attorney who moves for an evaluation or the judge who authorizes it may have a particular issue or range of issues in mind, yet the court clerk may have used standard (and perhaps dated) form orders that fail to reflect the specific referral issues of concern.

A final legal topic implicated by the ethical duty to clarify relationships is the individual's right to counsel. If the individual has not had an opportunity to confer with an attorney about the evaluation, that should be arranged. If no counsel has been retained or appointed, the mental health professional should go through the proper channels to notify the court and defer the evaluation until the opportunity for legal consultation can be arranged. In criminal cases, these steps would seem to be compelled by *Estelle v. Smith* [see § 4.03(a)]. In civil cases, they are mandated by common sense; unless the individual has the advantage of legal advice, the nature of the clinician–party relationship may be clouded or even misunderstood.

(2)   Professional Fees

Another factor that almost always requires clarification is the fee structure for professional services. The clinician must make clear to the client and his or her attorney what the fee structure will be (e.g., hourly or by the type of service rendered), the cost of specialized tests, how unanticipated services will be compensated, and when payment should be made (e.g., up front, in installments, or at the completion of services).[110] Practical concerns related to these aspects of billing are discussed in more detail in § 5.05(a), on operating a forensic practice.

Occasionally, the client's straitened financial situation may affect the clinician's willingness to take a case. If so, this consideration should also be communicated to the potential client. Relevant in this regard, both the AAPL Guidelines[111] and the APLS Guidelines[112] prohibit forensic examiners from contracting to provide services on a contingency-fee basis. As an ethical matter, forensic evaluators should not agree to financial arrangements in which their fees are paid only if the party retaining them prevails. Furthermore, some courts have held that such arrangements, when made by medical doctors, are void on public policy grounds.[113] Contingency arrangements are most likely to be proposed in personal injury cases in which an indigent (or at least, nonwealthy) plaintiff will have sufficient funds to pay for litigation expenses only if an award or settlement is paid by the defendants. Such arrangements trigger a conflict of interest, or at least the appearance of one, because they create a significant temptation to give an opinion that favors compensation for the plaintiff (and therefore compensation for the expert); in other words, contingent arrangements make it look as if the clinician is selling his or her opinion. This problem can only be avoided by making clear in the agreement that the lawyer/law firm is responsible for the expert's fees, not the lawyer's client; the expert's fees then become part of the upfront costs committed by the law firm that must be paid regardless of the outcome of either the forensic evaluation or the case itself.

A possible consequence of this "hard line" stance on contingency arrangements is an inhibition of indigent access to forensic evaluations. It might also curtail "class action" litigation on important public policy issues involving groups represented by small or not-for-profit legal organizations. Rather than yielding on the prohibition against contingency arrangements, however, we recommend that forensic clinicians be responsive to ethical guidelines that encourage pro bono service and devote a portion of their practices to such cases.[114] Under such arrangements, reimbursement would consist of, at most, travel expenses and possibly a nominal fee; there would be no expectation of reimbursement at one's hourly rate for time committed to the case. The clinicians' benefit will come from contributing to the public good and in the subsequent "paying" cases that such goodwill should attract.

(3)   Prior Relationships

Also implicating the ethical requirement that relationships be clarified are current or prior activities, obligations, or relationships of the clinician that might produce a conflict of interest in the case.[115] For example, an attorney might call a clinician who has been providing therapy to the attorney's client and request that the clinician become involved in a case as a forensic examiner. Alternatively, an attorney may contact a clinician to serve as an expert witness in a malpractice case against an agency that formerly employed the clinician. In the first example the preexisting therapeutic relationship with the client should discourage the clinician from accepting the referral in order to avoid problems of dual relationships [see § 4.05(c) (2)].[116] In the second example the attorney should be alerted to the possible appearance of conflict of interest stemming from the clinician's prior employment.

(c)   Confused Roles and Dual Roles

> [B]efore beginning a forensic evaluation, the psychiatrist should inform the evaluee that although he is a psychiatrist, he is not the evaluee's "doctor."[117]

Due both to training and the socializing forces within mental health practice, clinicians are disposed to be helpers. The focus of therapeutic evaluation is to develop strategies that advance the psychological growth and well-being of the client. Alleviation of anxiety, depression, or other subjective symptoms of psychological stress and the extrication from or the development of improved skills for coping with stressful situations are among the primary concerns of the caregiving professional. These goals and objectives are typically discussed and developed collaboratively by the clinician and client. The therapeutic relationship and the trust that it engenders are viewed as positive developments.

As Chapter 3 developed in detail, participation in forensic evaluations poses a dilemma for clinicians strongly committed to this helping posture. First, the focus of the evaluation will have been dictated by third parties (courts, attorneys) usually not present for the evaluation. How and whether the evaluation results will be used to advance personal goals or objectives of the client will often be secondary, perhaps even incidental, to considerations of legal strategy and the mandates of the rules of evidence.

Second, given the complexities of issues raised in forensic evaluations and the conflicting interests of the social institutions and individuals involved, clinicians may have difficulty adhering to the "helping ethic." In child custody proceedings, for example, a clinician may feel conflicted about providing data and recommendations that potentially enhance the well-being of one or more family members at the cost of increased psychological discomfort for others. In guardianship proceedings the clinician's assessment may indicate that a conservator be appointed to protect an elderly person's accumulated material resources, possibly at the expense of that individual's sense of autonomy, competence, or self-worth. In capital sentencing proceedings a clinician's findings regarding the offender's potential for future violent behavior may be pivotal in the jury's decision to invoke the death penalty.

Further, the style and tone of clinician–client interactions in forensic evaluations may be much different from those in common therapeutic interactions. A more skeptical, if not confrontational style is likely to prove useful in some forensic evaluations, where evaluators will have a lower threshhold for suspecting malingering and a higher degree of concern for the accuracy of information provided by the person being evaluated [see § 3.02].

In our view, the resolution to the caregiver's dilemma stems from the realization that there are numerous situations in which the mental health professional may be asked to serve more than one client.[118] The problem then becomes one of recognizing the various legitimate claims on the professional's findings and establishing priorities through a process of explicit role clarification. At the most general level, there are two recurring situations: when the evaluation is the only contact with a client and when the evaluation precedes or is subsequent to a therapeutic relationship with the client.

(1)　Forensic Contacts Alone

In most evaluations for the courts, the clinician's involvement begins through contact with a court or an attorney; the clinician has no prior or ongoing relationship with the person to be evaluated. The primary goal of the assessment is not to ensure the individual's optimal psychological adjustment or well-being but to assist the court in making a fully informed disposition. In these situations there is (or should be) no conflict with the helping ethic because there is no explicit or assumed understanding that the examiner–individual encounter will be for therapeutic purposes.

To prevent examinees from being misled or deceived, forensic evaluators are charged to dispel explicitly any beliefs or preconceptions, stereotypical or otherwise, that clients may have regarding the "helpful" intent of the clinician in the forensic evaluation. Although this disclosure is important in any forensic evaluation, it may be particularly so in dealing with criminal defendants ordered to undergo a court-ordered, pretrial evaluation. Such individuals often will have been detained in the unfriendly and, for some, unfamiliar confines of a jail. Contact with friends and family, and even with their own attorney (if one has been appointed), may have been extremely limited. These clients may be the most vulnerable to misperceptions of the forensic evaluator's role and to premature disclosure of personal or sensitive material.

If the examiner makes a serious effort to correct any erroneous preconceptions about the clinician's role and purpose of the evaluation, he or she should not feel precluded from approaching forensic clients with understanding and compassion. We disagree with Shuman's argument that use of "empathy" during a forensic evaluation is unethical.[119] Occasionally, empathy may be necessary to ensure successful emergency treatment.[120] More commonly, it may be the only way information desired by the referring party can be obtained (consider Case Study 4.3). It is precisely this fact that leads Shuman to conclude that the use of empathy is "unfair," at least when the evaluation is "involuntary." But, in our opinion, empathetic questioning is not coercive and need not be deceptive; appropriately used, therefore, it is no more unfair than any other forensic technique that provides useful information. As discussed in §4.02(b), a defendant can be sanctioned for not cooperating with state-requested "involuntary" evaluations. Surely empathetic questioning does not add to the coercion associated with this situation; it may even help a client avoid unwanted sanctions (e.g., prohibition of the defense's expert testimony on insanity) by facilitating cooperation. Nor need the use of empathy be deceptive, as long as the professional makes clear who will get the report and does not fabricate expressions of empathy. Indeed, from an ethical standpoint, empathy could be considered superior to the type of brusque confrontation that might otherwise be necessary to elicit information from a client [see § 3.02(e)].

Nonetheless, Shuman's concern that forensic clients may be misled by a therapeutic approach should be kept in mind. Clinicians should not intentionally try to deceive clients into believing that they are there to treat rather than evaluate; indeed, as the American Psychiatric Association has suggested, "the psychiatrist should consider terminating the examination whenever it appears that the subject is confused about the purpose of the encounter."[121] To this extent, Shuman's admonitions are very appropriate.

(2) Dual Forensic / Therapeutic Relationships

Some clinicians may be asked to be forensic experts in cases involving persons with whom the clinician has a preexisting therapeutic relationship, as in Case Study 4.2. An adult therapy client having difficulty in the work setting may file a civil suit for damages attributed to perceived discrimination or hostile working conditions; the client's attorney may request that the therapist conduct additional assessments and give expert testimony regarding the "causes" of the client's psychological discomfort. Similarly, an attorney may ask a therapist to provide an assessment and provide an expert opinion regarding the parental fitness of one or both parents seen in therapy prior to divorce proceedings.

Mental health professionals should be alert to situations that threaten to involve them in such dual relationships and, *when possible*, should decline the forensic evaluator role. To take on this role would violate ground rules mutually agreed to at the beginning of therapy regarding the objectives of the clinician–client interactions and the clinician's avowed intention to protect confidentiality of client disclosures. Similarly, to function effectively as a forensic evaluator the clinician may adopt a more challenging or skeptical posture that might threaten if not destroy the therapeutic relationship. The client may lose a valuable ally needed to see him or her through the additional stress associated with the legal proceedings because of the clinician's willingness to adopt a role fundamentally inconsistent with that of therapist.

As noted in § 4.04(c), the client's privilege protecting against disclosure of therapeutic communications is often waived by involvement in a legal matter. As a result, the clinician may be required (e.g., by force of subpoena) to testify in the case anyway. However, by declining to become involved as forensic evaluator the clinician can preserve the therapeutic role; to the extent he or she testifies, it will be only as a "fact" witness (i.e., a witness who testifies to facts and opinions based on information revealed in therapy). Although this approach may not completely eliminate the client's sense of betrayal, at least it will be clear that the testimony is coerced by the court rather than based on a "voluntary" evaluation requested and paid for by the court or one of the parties.

Other obvious dual-role situations occur when the evaluative encounter *initiates* contact with the legal system (a scenario also illustrated by Case Study 4.2). For example, a psychologist who conducts a presentence evaluation of a sex offender may later be asked to accept the offender into therapy as a condition of probation; a psychiatrist who evaluates an individual in a worker's compensation claim may be asked to provide therapy or other treatment to diminish the worker's emotional problems; a plaintiff in a successful torts action later may seek therapy from a mental health expert who testified for the plaintiff in the prior civil action. In contrast to the examples in the preceding paragraph, in none of these examples is there an obvious conflict between the evaluative and therapeutic roles; theoretically, at least, the therapy can proceed without being infected by the earlier evaluative stance. However, a more subtle conflict may arise if there are formal or informal "arrangements" by which the evaluator is assigned (and is paid for) treatment of those he or she evaluates. Only if the subsequent therapeutic request is wholly unanticipated should it be accepted.

The above caveat that dual-role arrangements should be avoided *when possible* is an important one, however. In rural areas, where all mental health services may be provided by a small number of clinicians, some dual-role situations may have to be tolerated if services are going to be provided at all. Generally, there is one other forensic context in which it may be extremely difficult, if not impossible, to completely avoid dual-role relationships. In hospitals that provide treatment services to forensic clients (e.g., to restore competence to stand trial or care for persons adjudicated not guilty by reason of insanity), members of a client's treatment team may be required to participate in, if not conduct, evaluations that are used to determine discharge readiness. In this context the clinician serves both as a therapist and as a gatekeeper; information (e.g., about dangerous propensities or sexual fantasies) that a client would willingly disclose in confidence to a therapist might well be withheld from a forensic examiner who will report to the court. Similar role conflicts may arise in corrections settings, where clinicians who evaluate and/or treat inmates for therapeutic purposes may also be involved in evaluations that inform parole board decisions.[122]

In these settings it may be difficult for mental health professionals to avoid dual-role status.[123] Individual clinician's roles may be dictated by state law, administrative policy, and organizational structure. Of course, mental health professionals should alert facility administrators to ethical problems related to dual-role assignments and work with them to design services in a way that minimizes the risk.[124] Yet even when administrative policy is sufficiently enlightened and flexible to develop a structure that maximally separates treatment from discharge evaluation duties, concerns that discharge decisions be based on the most complete and relevant information dictate that some input from the therapist be made available to the ultimate decisionmaker.[125] In smaller forensic hospitals with limited staff resources, a handful of clinicians may handle all therapeutic and evaluation duties, and the treatment–evaluator roles with individual patients may be inextricably related.

In these situations the clinician should take great care to inform the client/patient of the clinician's dual responsibilities and the limits on confidentiality in therapy imposed by the duty to perform, or inform, collateral forensic evaluations. Because contact with such persons may occur over extended periods of time in these settings, the clinician should periodically remind the person of this dual-role obligation and clarify which role the clinician is playing in any particular session.[126]

(d) Confidentiality and Informed Consent

> Respect for the individual's right of privacy and the maintenance of confidentiality are major concerns of the psychiatrist performing forensic evaluations. The psychiatrist maintains confidentiality to the extent possible given the legal context. . . . An evaluation for forensic purposes begins with notice to the evaluee of any limitations on confidentiality.[127]

> Forensic psychologists inform their clients of the limitations to the confidentiality of their services and their products by providing them with an understandable statement of their rights, privileges, and the limitations of confidentiality.[128]

As the preceeding discussion on dual roles amply demonstrated, a major issue for mental health professionals involved in forensic evaluations is the question of confidentiality.[129] In treatment settings clinicians consider confidentiality of paramount importance—so much so that they are reluctant to disclose information obtained from a client even when there are explicit legal or countervailing ethical mandates to do so (such as when a patient might harm another). For reasons that should be obvious by now, such an attitude is unrealistic in the forensic context. Forensic evaluations inevitably and routinely involve disclosure of information to third parties. The clinician will have to report to the attorney and/or appointing court, and often there is the further possibility of disclosure in testimony (either in deposition or in open court).

Some clinicians may have concerns that announcing explicit limitations on confidentiality will discourage some clients from freely disclosing all the information that the examiner seeks. However, as an ethical matter, the tension between the need to obtain information and the need to respect the client's privacy and autonomy has clearly been resolved in favor of clients' rights.[130] Both general ethical guidelines and the specialty forensic guidelines excerpted above make clear that forensic examiners must advise clients of reasonably foreseeable disclosures and uses of information that in the nonforensic context would be confidential.[131]

After such a warning is given, the individual's decision whether or not to disclose personal material that might later become public is one best made after being advised by the attorney of the legal implications for both disclosing and witholding information. As discussed in § 4.02, the risks for disclosure vary depending on (1) which side has requested the evaluation, (2) the type of evaluation requested, and, in certain criminal contexts (3) whether the evaluation takes place before or after notice of an intent to use clinical testimony is given. The mental health professional can best facilitate the client's understanding of these risks by ensuring that the individual is informed of these alternatives and has an opportunity to confer with counsel.

Consider, for example, an actual case involving a defendant referred for an evaluation of mental state at the time of the offense after he shot and killed his wife and then shot himself. When informed that the evaluation results might be presented in court if the insanity defense were raised, the defendant elected not to discuss the case to avoid public humiliation for himself, his children, and the memory of his wife. A preliminary report was submitted, indicating that no substantive findings could be offered and advising that the defendant have further consultation with his attorney to reconsider the desirability of a defense based on mental state. While the individual eventually decided to cooperate, failure to disclose the possible uses of the evaluation could have had seriously detrimental consequences.

A more difficult case for the clinician is the individual who appears to be cooperating only partially, leaving the forensic examiner with the suspicion that the picture obtained is an incomplete one [see § 4.02(b)]. In many cases external time constraints imposed by the court may limit the examiner's ability to develop a relationship with the individual that permits greater openness and candor in the evaluation. The examiner may decide that no report, or only a very qualified report, can be submitted. Either of these options is preferable to eliciting more complete information through false promises of confidentiality.

(1) Basic Elements of Notification

The full scope of the notification that forensic clients should be given varies with legal context and jurisdiction. Notifications may range in form and in force from a Miranda-like notification in situations such as those involved in *Estelle v. Smith* to communications that state that the individual has no legal basis for declining to participate [see § 4.02(f)]. Obviously, good-faith professional judgments will be required on some occasions. Forensic examiners would do well to consider the basic considerations that underlie informed consent in the treatment context [see § 11.03(a)]. Clinicians are obligated to provide that information a person would reasonably want to know in order to make an informed decision about whether to participate, and to provide that information in a fashion that facilitates the person's comprehension. Clinicians are not required to provide information based on remote or unrealistic possibilities that do not have clearly negative implications for the client; the object is to encourage the client's involvement through an informed dialogue, not to scare the client or discourage involvement by intimidating or overwhelming the client with excessive detail and speculation.

We suggest that minimum standards for notice

about the limits of confidentiality in a forensic context require that the mental health professional provide the following information:

(1) The name or role of the person(s) or agencies for whom the clinician is conducting the evaluation and to whom the clinician will submit a report.

(2) The legal issues that will be addressed in the evaluation (e.g., pretrial competency, parental fitness, capacity to work).

(3) The kinds of information most likely to be material to the evaluation and the proposed techniques (interview, testing, etc.) to be used to gather that information.

(4) The legal proceeding(s) (e.g., hearing; trial; posttrial sentencing hearing) at which testimony is anticipated.

(5) The kinds of information that may require special disclosure to third parties (e.g., an admission that one has abused a child) and the potential consequences for the individual.

(6) Whether there is a legal right to decline/limit participation in the evaluation and any known sanctions for declining.

Table 4.1 provides a sample notification form that contains much of this information. As in the treatment context, providing notification and obtaining consent is *not* simply obtaining a client signature on a form; rather, it is a process that requires an interactive dialogue between forensic examiner and client to enable the client to understand relevant information and to make an informed decision about participation. We recommend that the forensic evaluator keep a signed copy of the notification in the file and provide a second copy to be retained by the person being evaluated.

(2) Additional Considerations Regarding Confidentiality in Criminal Cases

It is also appropriate to advise clients of other considerations that may be peculiar to particular circumstances or evaluations. In the criminal context, whether, and to what degree, any assurances of confidentiality can be offered to protect self-incrimination interests will depend on the applicability of the attorney–client privilege, if any, and

Table 4.1
Sample Notification

AGENCY NAME
NOTIFICATION: Competence to Stand Trial

Purpose

You have been referred by the <u>Court/Your Attorney/(or Name)</u> for an evaluation of your competence to stand trial. I will be assessing your understanding of your legal situation, as well as your ability to assist your lawyer.

Procedures

You will be asked about the circumstances surrounding the alleged crime(s), your understanding of the case against you, how legal proceedings work, and your past and current psychological functioning. You may be given psychological tests or asked to complete forms that will assist us in learning more about you. It may be necessary for us to talk with other professionals or family members and to review prior records to obtain additional background information that may be important to the case.

Reporting

The information that is collected during the evaluation will be prepared for <u>(the referrer; if court referred, indicate if reports will also go to State/Defense attorney)</u> in the form of a report. I may be subpoenaed to Court and required to testify at a pretrial competency hearing.

Other Limits on Confidentiality

Other than our report to <u>(the person(s) who referred you)</u>, and the possible testimony just noted, all information given by you is treated as confidential, except under the following circumstances. The State requires that information related to known or suspected child abuse, or abuse of a person over 65 be reported to the state health department. Also, information may be released if you present a risk to yourself or someone else.

Possible Outcomes

The findings may result in a recommendation for you to receive treatment prior to proceeding with your case, or the evaluation may indicate that your case should proceed at this time.

My signature below indicates that I have read this statement (or have had it read to me). I have had an opportunity to ask questions about the evaluation and to have issues explained in terms that I understand. By my signature below, I agree to the evaluation under the conditions stated herein.

Signature of Participant   Date

Note. Language may need to be simplified, depending upon client.

the rules of evidence governing testimony by defense retained witnesses. For instance, as suggested by the discussion in § 4.03(b)(2), in jurisdictions that follow *Alvarez*, clinicians retained by the defense to evaluate the sanity of the defendant may be able to offer strong assurances that the attorney will be able to exercise considerable control over whether, and how, the results of the evaluation will be used, thus allaying the client's fears about possible self-incrimination. In jurisdictions that follow *Edney*, such assurances should not be made.

As noted in § 4.02, there may also be statutory protections that limit prosecution use of defendants' statements regarding mental state at the time of the offense (or clinicians' full documentation of defendants' statements) until such time as the defense places the individual's mental condition at issue in the proceedings. Although such statutes do restrict the use of a person's disclosures, they do not restrict access to those disclosures. Thus, in these states examiners appointed by the state or the court should inform individuals that nothing is entirely confidential. Only in those jurisdictions, such as Virginia, that direct clinicians to avoid including self-incriminating material in a prenotice report can complete confidentiality be guaranteed contingent upon the defense's decision to assert a defense.

(3)   The "Duty to Protect"

As discussed in § 4.04(b), although a number of jurisdictions have adopted the *Tarasoff* rule requiring therapists to protect the public from their dangerous patients, most have not made clear the precise scope of the rule. Most important for purposes of this book, few have established whether the rule extends to evaluators as well as to therapists. Although ethical provisions reflect the concern for public safety underlying the *Tarasoff* ruling by permitting disclosure "to protect the patient or client or others from harm,"[132] they leave the decision whether to disclose up to the clinician. Given these uncertainties, formulating a simple rule for forensic examiners is difficult. We recommend that forensic evaluators advise evaluees about the circumstances (e.g., threats to harm self or others) that might give rise to disclosures to third parties. If the forensic examiner does determine that the client poses a serious threat to harm a third party, advising the referral source (e.g., the attorney or court) is probably the most appropriate step to take, absent clear legal direction to the contrary. These officers of the court may then consider the next step to take (e.g., issuing warnings or denying/revoking bail).

(e)   Autonomy and Privacy Concerns

Psychologists accord appropriate respect to the fundamental rights, dignity, and worth of all people. They respect the rights of individuals to privacy, confidentiality, self-determination, and autonomy, mindful that legal and other obligations may lead to inconsistency and conflict with the exercise of these rights.[133]

(1)   Freedom of Choice to Participate

In therapeutic settings mental health professionals acknowledge that competent individuals have freedom of choice with regard to participation in assessment procedures. In the forensic setting, this assumed freedom of choice may be restricted in two ways. First, the law may provide for specific sanctions for nonparticipation; for example, as discussed in § 4.02(b), most states have provisions barring the use of the insanity defense by defendants who fail to cooperate with state-appointed examiners. In other contexts, there may be *de facto* informal sanctions. For instance, individuals who refuse to participate in court-ordered hospital treatment may be left in the hospital by the courts (or, worse, by the clinicians) to "think about it," in effect punishing the person for his or her refusal.

Second, freedom of choice to participate may be a moot issue in some situations. For example, an individual who is detained in a hospital pending a civil commitment hearing [see § 10.04(a)(1)] may not consent to, yet be unable to avoid, observation by nurses and psychiatric aides which provides evidence supporting commitment (e.g., voicing delusional beliefs or resisting the staff). Similarly, during the brief period of explaining to a criminal defendant the purpose of a pretrial competency evaluation, the defendant may appear guarded, voice persecutory delusions involving his or her attorney as a central figure, or provide other evidence of mental disturbance sufficient to indicate a compromised ability to assist counsel.

The ethically proper course of action when the individual refuses to cooperate is not clear. If, as in the examples above, an evaluation of some sort can be completed and a report generated from the informal data, the question remains: Should the clinician offer a report of the findings? Clinicians who take a strong stance favoring the individual's right to nonparticipation may view the submission of a report based on informal observation and third-party data as unethical. At an emotional level, such a position is easier to maintain with clients who appear relatively undisturbed than it is when individuals are babbling incoherently or engaging in self-injurious behavior. Others may feel that there is no ethical dilemma in submitting a report or testifying when informal observation and third-party data provide adequate and potentially useful information to the attorney or to the court.

When the individual has been informed of the

purpose and nature of the evaluation and has declined to participate, we recommend the following course of action, which overlaps substantially with recommendations made earlier in connection with clarifying relationships and ensuring informed consent. First, advise the person of any known sanctions that may be imposed as a result of a refusal (e.g., a prohibition of the insanity defense). Second, arrange for the individual to talk with the attorney for further explanations or guidance. Third, advise the person whether or not a report may be sent anyway and of the implications of the refusal for the completeness or validity of the report. Fourth, take precautions against the use of undue pressure or "scare tactics" to coerce the individual's participation (e.g., threats by any staff members that "You're going to stay in seclusion until you talk to the doctor!"). If a report is ultimately sent, the fact of the individual's noncooperation should be clearly stated and any inferences drawn by the clinician from the refusal or reasons for the refusal should be indicated. Appropriate qualifications regarding the completeness or validity of the findings should also be included.

(2) Invasion of Privacy

Whether a referral is for a voluntary or involuntary evaluation, orders for forensic evaluation do not constitute a *carte blanche* license for examiners to do with individuals what they will. Clinicians should tailor their evaluation procedures to avoid undue invasion of privacy. In respecting the individuals' right to privacy, forensic clinicians must be careful to avoid two types of intrusions: (1) seeking or obtaining clinical information not relevant to the referral question and (2) addressing forensic issues not raised in the referral order. When forensic evaluations are conducted on an inpatient basis at a psychiatric hospital, mental health professionals must also be alert to the possibility that overzealous staff will provide information to the examiner that the person being evaluated would not voluntarily disclose.

Recognition of the first problem should drive the clinician's choice of evaluation procedures and techniques. As noted in § 4.02, there are many situations in which a forensic clinician may have to delve into personal, secret, and sensitive mate-

rial with an individual. However, some forensic referral questions are appropriately addressed in a more straightforward manner. The assessment of competency to stand trial [see Chapter 6] is a good example. As noted earlier, the focus in a competency assessment is the defendant's ability to understand the nature and object of pending legal proceedings (that he or she is on trial, that his or her liberty is in jeopardy, that the proceeding is adversarial and that certain parties have explicit roles and responsibilities, etc.) and the defendant's ability to assist counsel in a reasonable manner (to answer questions with relevant, coherent responses, to choose among alternative courses of action, etc.). In the majority of referrals, the competency assessment can be completed in a relatively short time (one to two hours), using a structured interview or assessment procedure designed expressly for competency evaluations. One may question whether a "deep" psychological evaluation is appropriate in such cases. Clinicians who find themselves performing extensive batteries of tests or conducting in-depth, psychodynamically oriented interviews routinely in such situations might well explore their motivations for doing so.

Occasionally, some censorship of information may be advisable even when the information is relevant. This scenario occurs most often in evaluations of criminal defendants who reveal information protected by the Fifth Amendment [see § 4.02]. One situation not discussed earlier involves defendants who, in the course of the clinical interview, admit their involvement in other, as yet unsolved, crimes (as in Case Study 4.1; consider also, the wife's information in Case Study 4.3). Although such information may be relevant to establishing a clinical diagnosis (e.g., antisocial personality) or in making an appraisal of certain tendencies (e.g., violence-proneness), we recommend—in view of both privacy and Fifth Amendment considerations—that clinicians exercise caution in their manner of documentation and disclosure to avoid becoming unwitting agents of the prosecution in establishing new charges against the individual. Rather than detailed descriptions of previous assaults, global statements, such as "The defendant reported being involved in three prior fights in which weapons were used," may suffice for the needs of the present evaluation and will avoid unnecessary betrayal of the client by the examiner.

The second aspect of invasion of privacy involves applying the evaluation findings or inferences to legal issues other than those about which the individual was informed. This is what occurred in *Estelle v. Smith*, in which clinical information was obtained ostensibly for a competency determination prior to a capital murder trial but was later introduced at the sentencing phase [see § 4.02(a)]. Clinicians may violate the individual's right to privacy by soliciting cooperation in addressing one question and then applying the findings to a different one.

Mental health professionals employed in state facilities are particularly subject to administrative pressure to violate this ethical consideration. In one case, an individual was committed by the court for an evaluation of competency to stand trial. A comprehensive evaluation was completed including, in accordance with hospital policy, a psychiatric mental status examination, ratings by a psychologist using the Competency Assessment Instrument, and a social history study. Extensive information about the defendant's behavior at the time of the offense was also available in the form of the police investigation report, which included statements of several eyewitnesses. After the competency evaluation was completed, the defendant was discharged from the hospital and transported back to the county jail, which was located quite some distance from the hospital. At a later date, the prosecutor requested an amended report to include the clinical staff's opinion regarding mental state at the time of the offense. Considering the imminent court date, the significant expense of recommitting the patient, and the fact that most of the required information was already available, the hospital administrator directed the evaluation team to prepare an amended report as requested by the prosecutor. This directive led to a major confrontation with the clinical staff members, who refused to submit a report because the defendant had not been advised of this possible use of the clinical data at the time of the evaluation.[134]

As indicated earlier, clinicians may avoid problems of this type by seeking confirmation, early in the referral procedure, of all forensic issues to be addressed. The court or the attorneys may intend that the evaluation address other questions or provide general clinical information beyond what would be obtained by adhering literally to the order. In such cases, amended orders can be obtained, or the examiner may provide a much broader "notification of rights" to the individual to ensure that all intended uses of the data are explained. Where the individual has not been informed of a particular use for the evaluation findings, however, it would appear to be a breach of ethics to submit amended reports, as in the example above.

Finally, in inpatient evaluation settings, mental health professionals must be alert to invasions of privacy by overzealous staff members who inappropriately seize personal items of an individual—letters or diaries, for example—and secure them for the clinicians conducting the evaluation. Consistent with privacy considerations and respect for the individual's right to volunteer or withhold information of a personal nature, personal items should be returned to the patient and should not be examined or used by the forensic examiner without first obtaining the patient's permission to do so. Note that if such information is somehow included in a clinical report, it may not be admissible anyway, depending on local law and how it was obtained [see § 3.08].

4.06. Summary: Competence in Forensic Practice

As this overview reveals, forensic evaluations may be influenced by legal and ethical considerations that seem foreign to, if not incongruent with, traditional clinical practice. As such, this discussion underscores the point in Chapter 1 and 3 that mental health professionals can benefit from special training to become competent forensic examiners. They need to be sensitive to a variety of legal principles as well as to the specialty guidelines for ethical forensic practice that have been promulgated by professional organizations. Through such training they may gain an enhanced appreciation of the potential conflicts that can occur in forensic practice and develop skills for resolving tensions among the various forces that influence or constrain the evaluation effort. This chapter's subtitle—"The Mental Health Professional as Double Agent"—alludes to the abandonment of the traditional therapist's role and the assumption of divided loyalties. Forensic examiners who conduct evaluations without careful consideration of the legal and ethical implications of their actions may truly become "double agents" in the worst sense of the term: They may offer, and then betray, the confidence of their clients.

Table 4.2 outlines a series of steps that clini-

cians may follow to ensure that proper attention is paid to important legal and ethical issues discussed in this chapter and in other portions of the text. This outline is offered as a guide to help clinicians avoid some of the conflict situations that have been discussed. However, familiarity with the caveats and countervailing considerations that apply at each step is important as well; to this end citations to relevant portions of the text are also provided. Although this summary provides the

Table 4.2
Steps to Ensure Ethical Evaluation Procedures

Stage of evaluation	Relevant text by section
I. Preevaluation	
A. Clarify ambiguous or overly general referral orders.	4.05(b)
B. Ensure that client has counsel, who has talked to client about evaluation.	4.03(a), 4.05(b)(1)
C. Assess your competence to perform the evaluation.	4.05(a)
D. Assess conflicts of interest.	4.05(b)
E. Establish payment arrangement.	4.05(b)(2)
F. Decline to review information *known* to have been illegally obtained that may jeopardize admissibility of report.	4.05(e)(2), 18.05
II. During clinical evaluation	
A. Notify the person of all legal issues to be addressed in the evaluation.	4.02, 4.05(d)(1)
B. In those few situations in which a right to remain silent pertains, inform person using *Miranda* language.	4.02(f)
C. Advise the person of the limited confidentiality afforded.	4.02(d), 4.03(b)(2),
1. Identify persons or agencies to whom reports may be sent.	4.04(a), 4.05(d)
2. Identify legal proceedings in which testimony is anticipated.	
3. Advise the person of other uses of the clinical report.	
4. (Optional) Administer *Tarasoff* warnings.	4.04(b), 4.05(d)(3)
D. Make clear evaluative role; dispel notions that you are a therapist	4.05(c)
E. Request the person's participation in the evaluation and advise of any sanctions if participation is declined.	4.02, 4.04(a), 4.05(e)(1)
F. Respect privacy interests and Fifth Amendment concerns.	4.05(e)(2)
1. Keep clinical inquiry within the boundaries of referral question.	
2. Do not gratuitously address issues not in the referral order.	
3. Assist the person in limiting disclosure of information not relevant to the present evaluation.	
III. Postevaluation	
A. *Relevance* should guide the content of reports and testimony.	4.05(e), 18.03(b)(2)
1. Avoid detail that might unnecessarily embarrass the person or jeopardize other rights.	
2. Refrain from conclusions that are the factfinder's responsibility.	1.04, 18.05
B. In *Tarasoff* situations, notify the referral source of the existing threat.	4.04(b)

basic legal and ethical principles, it cannot anticipate all or even most of the myriad dilemmas that
might confront the evaluator or lawyer. There are
other resources that can be called on for assistance. In particular, attorneys general can provide
advisory opinions regarding the priority of conflicting legal principles, the ethics committees of
the appropriate state and national organizations
can help resolve ethical quandaries, and the trial
court (upon motion by an evaluator's lawyer) can
help delineate application of constitutional and
privilege doctrine in individual cases.

Bibliography

American Academy of Psychiatry and the Law, *Ethical
Guidelines for the Practice of Forensic Psychiatry AAPL
Guidelines,* in AMERICAN ACADEMY OF PSYCHIATRY
AND THE LAW MEMBERSHIP DIRECTORY xi–xiv
(1993).

American Psychological Association, *Ethical Principles
of Psychologists and Code of Conduct*, 47 AMERICAN
PSYCHOLOGIST 1597 (1992).

Committee on Ethical Guidelines for Forensic Psychologists, *Specialty Guidelines for Forensic Psychologists*, 15 LAW & HUMAN BEHAVIOR 655 (1991).

Estelle v. Smith, 451 U.S. 454 (1981).

*Final Report of the National Institute of Mental Health
(NIMH) Ad Hoc Forensic Advisory Panel*, 12 MENTAL &
PHYSICAL DISABILITY LAW REPORTER 77 (1988).

R. J. Freeman & Ronald Roesch, *Psycholegal Education:
Training for Forum and Function*, in HANDBOOK OF
PSYCHOLOGY AND LAW 568 (Dorothy K. Kagehiro
& William S. Laufer eds. 1992).

Thomas Grisso, *The Economic and Scientific Future of
Forensic Psychological Assessment*, 42 AMERICAN PSY-
CHOLOGIST 831 (1987).

Kenneth E. Meister, *Miranda on the Couch: An Approach
to Problems of Self-Incrimination, Right to Counsel and
Miranda Warnings in Pre-Trial Psychiatric Examinations
of Criminal Defendants,* 11 COLUMBIA JOURNAL OF
LEGAL SOCIAL PROBLEMS 403 (1975).

Vanessa Merton, *Confidentiality and the "Dangerous Patient": Implications of Tarasoff for Psychiatrists and
Lawyers*, 31 EMORY LAW JOURNAL 263 (1982).

Christopher Slobogin, *Estelle v. Smith: The Constitutional
Contours of the Forensic Evaluation*, 31 EMORY LAW
JOURNAL 71 (1982).

United States v. Byers, 740 F.2d 1104 (D.C. Cir.
1984).

WHO IS THE CLIENT? (John Monahan ed. 1981).

CHAPTER FIVE

Managing Public and Private Forensic Services

5.01. Introduction

In the previous two chapters we discussed the methodological and ethical differences between forensic and therapeutic mental health services. This chapter deals with a third way that forensic and therapeutic services differ: the various practical issues involved in setting up and sustaining a forensic practice. Because of the need to interact with the legal system, forensic mental health programs often face formidable implementation problems (e.g., communicating with nonclinicians, integrating the legal system's rules, uncertain scheduling, security problems, and involvement with litigious people). As a result, leaders in law and mental health have begun to focus on the need to develop a *system* of forensic services.[1]

This chapter begins by discussing the optimal staffing of such a system; we take the position that forensic mental health should be regarded as a *specialty within the community mental health system*. Applying this perspective, the next two sections of the chapter address systemic issues. Focusing on evaluations in criminal cases,[2] we describe the alternatives for forensic systems and discuss the process of establishing a statewide evaluation system once a particular approach is selected. Next we examine how individual clinicians, whether part of such a system or on their own, might establish or expand a forensic practice. Finally, we

discuss ways of alerting lawyers and judges to scientific findings.

PROBLEM 5.1

You are the director of forensic services in your state. Your governor has appointed you to head and select a commission that is to recommend an ideal forensic evaluation system for your state. What considerations are most likely to be important in accomplishing the commission's objective? Who will you want on your commission?

5.02. The Case for Specialization[3]

Whether the focus is on criminal or civil questions, our preference is for use of forensic specialists whenever possible. By "forensic specialists" we mean mental health professionals whose work consists *primarily or solely* of conducting evaluations and consultation for the legal system. Our preference for specialists rests primarily on (1) the possible adverse effects of forensic work on other aspects of mental health practice and (2) the need for a special system to maximize legal professionals' access to forensic expertise. Although we also discuss how such a policy might result in a better match between the legal system's needs and experts' knowledge, that positive effect is in the end only a secondary reason for our advocacy of specialization in forensic mental health.

(a) Avoiding Adverse Effects on General Mental Health Practice

Perhaps the strongest reason for reliance on specialists to deliver forensic services is that neither conventional nor optimal clinical practice is fully compatible with the forensic clinicians' proper emphasis on uncertainty. Maximum assistance to the factfinder requires adoption of a scientist's mind-set, with a skeptical view of the validity of inferences and careful scrutiny of the probabilities involved [see § 1.04]. Although there is no question that both the design and the delivery of clinical services should be informed by empirical research, continuous self-scrutiny—in effect, self-doubt—about the validity of one's impressions and plans is likely to undermine therapeutic efficacy.[4]

The techniques involved in forensic assessment also may be antitherapeutic [see § 3.02]. Forensic evaluations typically must be conducted in a relatively short time, are not for the subject's own benefit, often focus on highly emotionally charged events, and commonly involve matters about which there is motivation to lie. As a result, forensic interviews often are confrontational and address traumatic memories faster than would be common in therapeutic assessment and intervention.

Role confusion is another likely outcome for the mental health professional who undertakes both forensic and therapeutic work. Such a clinician may easily forget the fact that the ultimate client in the forensic evaluation context is not the person being evaluated. Role conflict is especially likely if the clinician becomes involved as a therapist for someone he or she has evaluated [see § 4.05(c)]. Accordingly, professional associations generally discourage such dual involvement.[5]

Similarly, because of the exercise of authority that may be involved (e.g., directly in evaluations for emergency civil commitment and indirectly in evaluations for sentencing and competency to be executed), forensic practice may alter clinicians' perspective or reputation in ways that interfere with therapeutic evaluations and interventions

with clients without legal-system involvement. Indeed, this effect may occur even when the clinician's opinions do not directly translate into loss of a defendant's liberty or life. Mere association with the justice system may be enough to compromise the clinician's current and potential therapeutic relationships. To use the most blatant example, the presence in a clinician's waiting room of defendants bound in leg chains and guarded by armed deputies is not likely to enhance the delivery of mental health services or the trust that clients have in their therapist's benevolence.[6]

(b) Building a Forensic Service System

Reliance on forensic specialists makes sense not only because of the potential adverse effects of forensic work on general mental health practice but also because of the effort needed to build a forensic service system. Overcoming the obstacles to sustained relations between the mental health and justice systems requires a level of commitment that may be unrealistic for clinicians for whom forensic work is a secondary task.

For example, in summarizing the efforts involved in establishing a community-based forensic services system in Virginia, we concluded:

> Successful implementation of community-based forensic services requires much more than simply training community mental health clinicians in the techniques of forensic assessment. Notably, the system can fall apart without active involvement—or without cooptation—of all the relevant parties (e.g., state mental health and court administrators, judges, prosecutors, defense attorneys, sheriffs, directors of community mental health centers, guild organizations of the various mental health professions).[7]

As described in detail later in this chapter [§ 5.04], implementation of the Virginia program required not only correcting economic disincentives for community-based services[8] but also developing and disseminating model court orders, interagency agreements, and routine referral procedures and arranging transportation and security for defendants in custody. Most important, various legal constituencies had to be educated to overcome their intuition that brief community-based evaluations are inherently low-quality and defense-oriented. Consensus, much of it eventually incorporated into statutes,[9] also had to be reached about complex legal issues (e.g., whether clinicians could address problems of diminished capacity and whether prosecutors could obtain potentially incriminating evaluation information at will).

Our experience confirmed the conclusions of other observers of interaction between the mental health and justice systems.[10] If such interaction is to go smoothly, there must be *boundary spanners*—staff whose job is to provide the necessary coordination.[11] Such positions are necessary at both state and local levels. Accordingly, clinicians who plan to undertake a limited forensic practice are unlikely to have incentives to invest the time needed to create and sustain working relationships with authorities in the justice system, master the practical issues raised by forensic mental health services, and negotiate solutions to such problems.[12]

(c)   The Need for Specialized Knowledge

The nature and complexity of a successful forensic mental health system suggests that clinicians who wish to operate adequately in this area need a forensic focus. One might reasonably believe that a third reason for such a focus is the need to acquire the relevant expertise; the level of familiarity with the literature that is necessary for optimal education of the trier of fact may be difficult to achieve amid the demands of full-time general clinical practice. Yet, ultimately, this reason for specialization is not as persuasive.

As discussed in § 4.05(a), forensic practice requires knowledge and skills more specialized than those developed in general training as a mental health professional, regardless of one's disciplinary pedigree. Appropriately trained forensic clinicians have specialized knowledge about relevant legal standards and issues, the technology of various forms of forensic assessment, and the effects of various dispositions. They probably also are more aware than general clinicians of potential threats to the rights of subjects of evaluations (e.g., use of the fruits of evaluations of competency to stand trial for the purpose of discovering incriminating information [see § 4.02(a)]). Indeed,

our research has shown that the knowledge base of forensic clinicians about legal issues, empirical research, and clinical theory commonly encountered in forensic practice is substantially greater than that of community mental health professionals engaged in general practice.[13] Such a finding should be unsurprising. Simply put, mental health professionals are unlikely to encounter rapists and murderers in either their training or their practice. Similarly, the information about legal issues, research, and clinical practice presented in this volume still is not a staple of training in any of the mental health professions.

The fact that this body of knowledge is specialized does not mean, however, that specialization is necessary to acquire it. In fact, we found that it can be learned at an acceptable level relatively quickly. Our experience in Virginia showed that a knowledge level about criminal law commensurate with that of forensic diplomates can be attained by general mental health clinicians (regardless of specific discipline) in an eight-day training program [see § 5.04(b)(1)].

Thus, although, we favor development of a specialty in forensic mental health, that position is not based on a belief that the skills involved are so difficult or the relevant knowledge so vast. Rather, our preference for specialty clinics in forensic mental health is derived from the conviction that the organizational and role demands of forensic assessment are incompatible with general clinical practice. Acquisition of specialized knowledge, including an appreciation of the philosophical, methodological, and ethical issues in forensic practice, can be seen as a positive by-product of the specialization that is needed to establish and manage the intersystem relations that a forensic practice requires.

5.03.   Types of Evaluation Systems[14]

Historically, most states have administered forensic services that were not only specialized but isolated. States provided pretrial psychological evaluations on criminal issues such as competency and sanity through court-ordered commitments to forensic inpatient institutions operated by the states' departments of mental health. In recent years, however, a number of alternatives to the institution-based, inpatient model have emerged. We first describe contemporary models of service delivery and the extent to which they have been adopted. We then evaluate these models and discuss the related issues of quality assurance and professional training that must be considered in the effective implementation of any model.

(a) Descriptions of Models

At least five models for delivering forensic evaluations on a system-wide basis can be imagined: the traditional institution-based inpatient model, the institution-based outpatient model, the community-based outpatient model, the community-based private practitioner model, and a mixture of these models.

(1) Model I: Institution-Based, Inpatient Model

The traditional model is characterized by service delivery at a centralized location, either a maximum security forensic hospital or a secure forensic unit within a state hospital. Transportation of the defendant to and from the hospital is usually provided by law enforcement officers from the jurisdiction of the referring court. The defendant is admitted for an inpatient evaluation that typically involves a multidisciplinary assessment over a period of several days or weeks. In some settings, the final report to the court is developed by a committee or team that is usually chaired by the attending psychiatrist and composed of other clinical and administrative staff. Because the defendant will have been in the institution for several days or weeks, during which time collateral information (prior records, arrest reports, etc.) can be obtained and reviewed, the report to the court is often available at the time of discharge when the defendant is returned to the custody of the appropriate authorities. Perhaps 15 states still depend primarily on the institution-based, inpatient model, typically relying on one or two institutions to conduct forensic evaluations.

However, several developments have led other states to move away from this model. The inpatient approach evolved and thrived in an era in which incompetence to stand trial and insanity

were thought by clinicians to be tantamount to the presence of psychosis.[15] Now that determination of clinical–legal issues has shifted from emphasizing clinical symptomatology to a more direct assessment of functional behavior [see, e.g., §§ 6.07(b), 8.07], evaluations can often be completed in a much shorter time. Furthermore, because of litigation requiring states to provide services in less restrictive settings[16] and related policy changes, today much greater emphasis is placed on providing services, whether for treatment or evaluation, in outpatient settings. Pushed by these broader trends, many states have found alternatives to inpatient forensic evaluations to be less expensive and more efficient. These developments have led to new systems of forensic services.

(2) Model II: Institution-Based, Outpatient Model

In the institution-based, outpatient model—the dominant evaluation method in perhaps five states—the locus of evaluations remains the forensic unit or state hospital site, but the evaluations are performed on an outpatient basis. Because defendants are not admitted to the hospital's inpatient service, many of the procedures required for inpatient admissions that are not directly germane to forensic issues (e.g., a medical examination by a physician; routine laboratory work) may be eliminated. In contrast to the multidisciplinary evaluation usually relied on in Model I, the evaluation under Model II is often conducted by one clinician, who uses structured interview procedures or assessment devices that focus specifically on the areas of legal functioning raised by the court order.[17] In those cases requiring multiple sources of data (e.g., sanity evaluations), the clinician arranges to gather the desired records and information by working with the court (e.g., through requests that police reports be sent to the hospital) and the defendant (e.g., by asking for authorization to release prior records).

The defendant typically is returned to the jail (if bail has not been posted) following a two- to four-hour evaluation, and the clinician examines and integrates the clinical interview data with the archival information as it is obtained. Depending on the type of evaluation performed, the examiner's report may not be available until several days after the evaluation is completed, but the entire process is still briefer than that associated with a full inpatient evaluation (Model I).

(3)   Model III: Community-Based, Outpatient Model

Another model, followed in more than ten states, combines the outpatient evaluation approach with decentralization of services. Rather than providing services through a forensic hospital or forensic unit at a state hospital, evaluations are provided through local agencies that serve either a legal jurisdiction or a mental health catchment area. Some states, such as Virginia, have relied primarily on community mental health centers (CMHCs). Other states, such as Ohio, have used private service providers as well as CMHCs. In still other jurisdictions, court clinics operated by counties or municipalities provide most pretrial examinations. When state mental health departments are involved in providing services under this model, their role is primarily to negotiate contracts with service providers and to provide training and quality assurance.

Under a community-based, outpatient model, evaluations of defendants in custody may be conducted either at the agency, with transportation provided by local law enforcement authorities, or at the county jail. Defendants on bond usually present themselves for evaluation at the agency. Evaluation procedures are similar to those used in the hospital-based, outpatient model described previously. The community-based model, however, facilitates follow-up interviews with the defendant, because of the proximity of the service provider to the defendant.

(4)   Model IV: Community-Based, Private Practitioner Model

A fourth model, describing the dominant evaluation system in perhaps ten states, also utilizes the outpatient evaluation approach but relies on neither state hospitals nor community agencies to provide services. Rather, pretrial forensic evaluations are provided by individual practitioners, located in the community, who are appointed by the court. Usually, these practitioners become known to the courts through contacts with the clerk of the court, who places their names on a list from which judges may select the evaluator. As with Model III, the evaluations may take place either at the clinician's office or at the county jail.

State mental health administrators' involvement in this model may be quite limited, unless the legislature requires the state agency either to provide financing for forensic evaluations or to assure their quality. In Florida, for example, involvement by the Department of Health and Rehabilitative Services in the pretrial evaluation process is limited to training community practitioners and maintaining a list for the courts of clinicians with such forensic training. Funding for pretrial evaluations resides with the courts.

(5)   Model V: Mixed

The models described above offer alternative approaches to providing pretrial evaluation services. Several states, probably as many as ten, have found it beneficial to mix models, for a variety of reasons. The peculiar geography of Michigan, with its rural upper peninsula located far from its Center for Forensic Psychiatry in Ann Arbor, led to its adoption of such an approach. To relieve the cost and burden on small-town police departments of transporting defendants to and from Ann Arbor for evaluations, the Forensic Center made provisions for a clinician to "ride the circuit" among the upper peninsula counties on a periodic basis. Similarly, in an effort to capitalize on existing resources in various communities as well as the forensic hospital, Alabama recently implemented a model of service that utilizes outpatient evaluations conducted by a state forensic hospital, selected CMHCs, and various private practitioners.

(b)   Evaluation of Models

Each of the models has specific strengths and weaknesses. Mental health administrators might consider a number of factors when comparing the various models of forensic evaluation.

(1)   Cost

Cost is a major concern of administrators comparing the utility of the different models. One would suspect that outpatient evaluations are generally less expensive than inpatient evaluations, given the costs inherent in an inpatient stay. This supposition is confirmed by a number of studies.

After conducting a nationwide survey, Grisso and his colleagues estimated that the cost per defendant of inpatient evaluations ranged between $1,300 and $6,000, whereas a local outpatient evaluation system cost between $350 and $650 per defendant, and a statewide hospital-based outpatient evaluation system cost between $175 and $350 per defendant.[18] Grisso et al. also found that the site of the evaluation had some effect on the time from the issuance of the court order to the completion of the evaluation: inpatient, 21–36 days; local outpatient, 15–23 days; hospital-based outpatient, 15–35 days.[19]

Two other studies comparing inpatient and outpatient evaluation reached similar results. In their study of an outpatient evaluation system implemented in Virginia,[20] Melton et al. made three principal findings about the efficiency of community-based evaluations. First, as expected, the outpatient evaluation program decreased forensic hospital admissions. Specifically, during the pilot year of the community-based evaluation program, admissions to state hospitals for forensic evaluations dropped 46% for those catchment areas using the outpatient model, but admissions remained constant for defendants from comparison areas continuing to use the inpatient model. Second, implementation of the community-based evaluation system did not result in a substantial increase in the total number of forensic evaluations requested, although some increase was noted in two areas adopting the outpatient approach. Third, the state saved 40% when the community-based system of evaluation was used instead of the institution-based system.

In his evaluation of the Alabama outpatient program, Poythress reported similar findings.[21] The estimated cost of outpatient forensic evaluations (approximately $300) was only a small fraction of the average cost of an inpatient evaluation ($6,000 to $7,000) when the latter was calculated by multiplying the median number of inpatient days required for an inpatient evaluation by the per diem cost of hospitalization. Unlike Melton et al., Poythress also found that adoption of the outpatient approach resulted in a decrease in the number of evaluation requests and therefore presumably a further decrease in the state's total expenditure on forensic evaluations. Poythress attributed this decrease in referrals to two factors: (1) the adoption of a fee-for-service contract with local professionals, which reduced the number of "strategic" referrals (e.g., referrals to create a delay in proceedings or to reduce jail overcrowding), and (2) the participation of community mental health professionals in forensic evaluation training, which made them more sophisticated about competencies in the criminal process and thus better able to avert inappropriate referrals. Poythress identified other financial benefits stemming from adoption of the outpatient model, including more timely evaluations (resulting in fewer legal delays) and decreased transportation and personnel costs borne by local law enforcement authorities.

The studies reviewed all compared inpatient evaluation to outpatient evaluation. Grisso et al.'s data suggest, however, that the various outpatient models may have different fiscal consequences as well.[22] Specifically, Model II (outpatient evaluations at a hospital) may be the least expensive approach on a per-evaluation basis. Further, although there are no data to support the conclusion, it would be unsurprising to find a difference between the two community outpatient options (Models III and IV), with evaluations by CMHCs being less expensive than evaluations by private practitioners. Because of their mission of public service and their coverage of at least some of their overhead expenses through basic program funding, CMHCs may be more likely to contract with the courts to conduct publicly funded forensic evaluations at a price that is below the market rate. Moreover, when evaluators do recover income above their costs in conducting forensic evaluations, profits of CMHCs are probably more likely than those of private practitioners to be "recycled" to support other community mental health services.

(2) Geography

Of course, our discussion of the relation between costs and model of service delivery is in terms of averages. Other factors may affect the practicality—and therefore the cost—of a particular model in a given state or community.

Geography is one such factor. States with largely rural populations might find the outpatient approach impractical because of the difficulty in finding qualified professionals in some rural areas. Particularly when courts expect particular professional credentials (e.g., doctoral training), the cost of attracting qualified professionals may significantly increase the overall cost of community-based evaluations in some rural communities. Even if mental health professionals are present in sufficient number, the cost per evaluation of training and continuing education in forensic services may be prohibitive.

In such a situation, referral to a central evaluation center may be the most practical approach. Alternatively, adoption of a mixed model might be considered. As already noted, Alabama has adopted a model in which evaluations are performed in both central and community-based locations, depending on the professional resources available locally.

However, the fact that low population density increases the cost per evaluation of attracting and training professionals should not lead to the assumption that a centralized or mixed approach is optimal. In large states (e.g., California, Florida, and Texas) and states with mental hospitals far from large population centers, decentralized systems will substantially reduce the costs associated with travel and will increase the ease of communication among the evaluators, potential informants (in regard to the defendant's history), and relevant legal professionals. Moreover, associated benefits of community-based evaluation systems (e.g., consultation to jail administrators) apply at least as much to rural communities as they do to metropolitan areas.[23]

(3) Quality Assurance

Of course, in evaluating the worth of a forensic model, one must consider the quality of the evaluations likely to be provided. The cost of quality assurance efforts may differ depending on the model.

One way of ensuring quality is by providing training for the evaluators; research has confirmed the intuitively obvious relationship between evaluation quality, on the one hand, and knowledge of the relevant legal standards and re-search literature on the other.[24] The cost of providing this training may vary depending on the evaluation model being implemented. By definition, the community-based approach requires that clinicians throughout the state be trained to perform forensic evaluations. By contrast, the number of clinicians to be trained is decreased and the logistics of providing updates are simplified when forensic services are centralized.

Another approach to quality assurance is promotion of standard procedures for evaluation, report writing, and peer review. Although the efficacy of this approach obviously depends on the quality of the standard procedures, centralization may facilitate the standardization. However, this advantage should not be overemphasized. Standardization can also be achieved by uniformity of consumers' demands[25]—a process that can be promoted through model court orders and training of the bar, the judiciary, and clerks of court. Moreover, modern communication technology enables relatively easy continuing education and peer review, and state CMHCs typically already have in place elaborate systems of quality assurance (relating in large part to the recordkeeping necessary to meet the demands of third-party payors).

(4) Other Factors

In addition to relative costs and ease of administration, other, less tangible factors should be considered. These factors generally point to the superiority of community-based systems over those that are hospital-based:

- *Mental health ideology.* A community-based approach is consistent with prevailing trends in mental health services, which are based on the premise that psychological interventions should be available in, and directed toward, the social systems in which people actually experience stress. In that regard, development of a program focused on forensic evaluations in a particular (e.g., criminal) context can foster the development of forensic services in other (e.g., family) contexts[26] as well as treatment services for individuals involved in the legal system (e.g., jail inmates).[27]

- *Legal ideology and constitutional concerns.* Insofar as evaluations can be provided in the community, a hospital-based system violates the least-drastic-means principle[28] and intrudes on defendants' rights to bail, a speedy trial, and the communication necessary for effective assistance of counsel.

• *Facilitation of consultation.* As the previous two points illustrate, forensic evaluation should be seen as part of a consultation system in which both access to and use of information are facilitated by a community base. For example, competency evaluation demands consultation with the defense attorney concerning techniques of communication with a difficult client [see § 6.07(a)]. Many other people in distress—those seeking child custody, worker's compensation, or Social Security, for example—seek help through the legal system. Community mental health centers typically are better situated than hospitals to assist in resolving a client's problems through consultation with legal authorities.

• *Public support.* Integration of forensic services into the regular mental health system minimizes the possibility of their becoming or remaining *de facto* correctional services or "dumping grounds,"[29] the unwanted stepchild of the mental health system, chronically underfunded and understaffed.

• *Recruitment of staff.* In many states, state hospitals are stigmatized among mental health professionals as well as the community at large. Integration of forensic services into the community mental health system may increase the pool of qualified clinicians willing to consider specialization in forensic mental health.

5.04. Establishing a Forensic Evaluation System

The only conclusion that can be reached with certainty from this analysis is that a forensic evaluation system based solely on Model I (inpatient evaluation) is not cost-efficient; preferably, the forensic system should consist of one or more of the other models, or perhaps a combination of Model I and the other models. As discussed previously, most states are moving toward an outpatient evaluation system or a multitier system with outpatient evaluations as the front line resource. On the assumption that some form of outpatient evaluation system is the system chosen, this section presents recommendations about its organization, personnel, management, and financing.[30]

(a)   Organization

Whenever possible, each tier of the forensic evaluation system should be prepared to offer the full range of forensic services. Without such capability, abuse of the system is more likely. Clinicians in the less restrictive settings may seek an "out" to have undesirable (e.g., unprofitable) services provided outside the community, and attorneys, too, may attempt to use the ruse of unavailability of a particular service as a means of hospitalizing the defendant for illegitimate reasons (e.g., delay or detention without bail). Also, if particular forensic services are unavailable, attorneys and judges may couch referral questions in terms of the services that are provided (e.g., a competency evaluation) instead of what is really desired (e.g., emergency treatment or development of information useful in plea bargaining).[31] The result is often unnecessary and costly provision of a particular service that does not adequately fulfill the actual perceived need.

An additional concern in the design of the forensic service system should be finding the most effective way to implement rules generally and the protection of defendants' rights specifically. Many of the constitutional rules governing forensic evaluations are subtle and complex; they are also frequently neglected. For example, as described in § 4.02, the Fifth Amendment has significant implications for the conduct of forensic evaluations and the contents and timing of reports, yet many states have failed to construct their evaluation process accordingly. As another example, as described in § 4.03(b)(1), the Sixth Amendment imposes a duty on the state to provide at least one professional "consultant" to the indigent defendant wishing to raise an insanity defense, again an obligation that is not well implemented by some state systems. Generally, the notion that forensic services should be provided in the least restrictive setting has often been dismissed or ignored by both lawyers and clinicians.

One implication of these observations is that procedures designed to protect defendants' rights in the forensic services system should be spelled out in statutes or regulations to provide clear guidelines for judges, lawyers, forensic clinicians, and administrators.[32] Incorporating statutory provisions into model court orders provides further assurance that these rules will be implemented. Table 5.1 presents an example of a court order used in Virginia. Note how the form informs the judge and the clinician about the relevant substantive and procedural law. Such orders make it harder for participants in the system to avoid the law's dictates.

A second implication of these observations about the necessity of protecting defendants' rights is that lawyers knowledgeable about both mental health law and forensic assessment should be included in the design and implementation of forensic services. Although clinicians and administrators are presumably familiar with the ethical injunction to protect civil rights of clients and others [see § 4.05], they are understandably more likely to be concerned with, and knowledgeable about, the psychological rather than the legal aspects of forensic assessment. Involvement of lawyers can reduce this gap in knowledge.

More generally, it is important to include representatives from all affected groups in policy formulation. Devising a forensic system requires balancing competing interests—between prosecutors and defense attorneys, between the courts and the mental health system, between defendants wanting to avoid hospitalization and the public's desire for safety, and so on. Accordingly, representatives of the diverse interest groups involved (e.g., judges, attorneys, patients' rights groups, hospital, clinic and jail administrators, and forensic clinicians) should be asked whether given policies meet their needs. Although consensus may not be possible, the stakeholders will have an opportunity to be heard, and the system planners and administrators will obtain useful feedback. In Virginia, for example, an advisory panel of lawyers and forensic clinicians provided invaluable assistance: advice about the design and politics of the system, proposals for model orders

and policies, and suggestions about the content of the state's training program.[33]

(b) Personnel

A number of issues arise in connection with the personnel who staff and use the forensic system. Most important among them are training and providing incentives to specialize.

(1) Training

As suggested in earlier, a primary focus in the development of forensic services should be on intensive legally and psychologically sophisticated training in forensic issues. This goal is mandated not only by the desire for quality services but also by ethical mandates [see § 4.05(a)]. Although there has been an increase in programs designed to train new clinicians in a forensic specialty, such programs are still uncommon.[34] Therefore, it remains necessary to train mental health professionals who already have general clinical competence in the additional knowledge and skills to function as a forensic clinician.

The nature of forensic training obviously varies, depending on the area of practice covered. Even subjects that appear to have general applicability (such as ethical concerns or tips on testifying as an expert) should be fine-tuned to fit the substantive area covered. Table 5.2 provides a short outline of a comprehensive training program for clinicians who want to provide evaluations for the criminal justice system. Many training programs might justifiably delete some of the subjects described.

There must also be training of lawyers, so that they become discerning consumers.[35] In Virginia, we found that most lawyers do not have routine dealings with the mental health system. As a result, their misconceptions about forensic practice can be profound. Many lawyers believed, for example, that psychological evaluations require at least a month in the hospital, that psychologists are not qualified to perform forensic evaluations, and that neurological tests are necessary in every case. More surprisingly, many lawyers, even very competent ones, are ignorant about the special-

Table 5.1
Order for Psychological Evaluation

COURT NAME AND ADDRESS

Commonwealth of Virginia V. _____

Type of Evaluation and Report

☐ COMPETENCY TO STAND TRIAL: It appearing to the Court, on motion of
  ☐ Commonwealth's Attorney   ☐ defendant's attorney   ☐ the Court
and upon hearing evidence or representations of counsel, that there is probable cause to believe that the defendant lacks substantial capacity to understand the proceedings against him or to assist in his own defense, the Court therefore appoints the evaluator(s) listed below to evaluate the defendant and to submit a report, on or before the date shown below, to this Court, the Commonwealth's Attorney, and the defendant's attorney, concerning: (1) the defendant's capacity to understand the proceedings against him; (2) his ability to assist his attorney; and (3) his need for treatment in the event that he is found to be incompetent. No statements of the defendant relating to the time period of the alleged offense shall be included in the report.

☐ MENTAL STATE AT THE TIME OF THE OFFENSE: It appearing to the Court, on motion of
  ☐ Commonwealth's Attorney   ☐ defendant's attorney   ☐ the Court
and upon hearing evidence or representations of counsel, that there is probable cause to believe that the defendant's actions during the time of the alleged offense may have been affected by mental disease or defect, the Court therefore appoints the evaluator(s) listed below to evaluate the defendant and submit a report, on or before the date shown below, to the defendant's attorney, and a summary of the report (which shall not include any statements by the defendant about the alleged offense) to the Court and the Commonwealth's Attorney, concerning the defendant's mental state at the time of the offense, including whether he may have had a significant mental disease or defect which rendered him insane at the time of the offense. If further evaluation on this issue is necessary, the evaluator(s) shall so state.

Designation of Evaluator(s)

It appearing to the Court that the evaluation
☐ can be conducted on an outpatient basis in jail or a mental health facility
☐ must be conducted on an inpatient basis because:
  ☐ no outpatient services are available
  ☐ the results of outpatient evaluation (copy attached) indicate that hospitalization for further evaluation is necessary
  ☐ a court of competent jurisdiction has found, pursuant to Va. Code §§ 19.2-169.6 or 37.1-67.3, that the defendant requires emergency treatment on an inpatient basis at this time.
The Court therefore appoints the following evaluator(s) to conduct the evaluation:

☐ _____
OUTPATIENT EVALUATOR(S) NAME(S) AND TITLE(S) OR NAME OF FACILITY

☐ qualified staff at a hospital to be designated by the Commissioner of Mental Health and Mental Retardation or his designeee. Hospitalization for evaluation shall not extend beyond 30 days from the date of admission.

DUE DATE AND TIME: _____

The Court further orders that the Commonwealth's Attorney and the defendant's attorney forward appropriate background information to the evaluator(s) as required by law.

TO EVALUATORS AND ATTORNEYS: See reverse for additional instructions.

_____   _____
DATE   JUDGE

File No. _____

Table 5.1. Continued

ADDITIONAL INSTRUCTIONS TO EVALUATOR(S) AND ATTORNEYS

Providing Background Information

1. *Competency to Stand Trial:* Prior to an evaluation of competency to stand trial, the Commonwealth's Attorney must forward to the evaluator(s):

    (a) a copy of the warrant

    (b) the names and addresses of the Commonwealth's Attorney, the defendant's attorney, and the judge ordering the evaluation

    (c) information about the alleged crime

    (d) a summary of the reasons for the evaluation request

    The defendant's attorney must provide any available psychiatric records and other information that is deemed relevant. Va. Code § 19.2-169.1 (C).

2. *Mental State at the Time of the Offense:* Prior to an evaluation of mental state at the time of the offense, the party making the motion for the evaluation must forward to the evaluator(s):

    (a) a copy of the warrant

    (b) the names and addresses of the Commonwealth's Attorney, the defendant's attorney, and the judge ordering the evaluation

    (c) information about the alleged crime, including statements by the defendant made to the police and transcripts of preliminary hearings, if any

    (d) a summary of the reasons for the evaluation request

    (e) any available psychiatric, psychological, medical or social records that are deemed relevant.

    Va. Code § 19.2-169.5 (C)

Use of Information Obtained during Evaluation

No statement or disclosure by the defendant concerning the alleged offense made during the evaluation may be used against the defendant at trial as evidence, or as a basis for such evidence, except on the issue of his/her mental condition at the time of the offense after the defendant raises the issue pusuant to § 19.2-168 of the Code of Virginia. Va. Code § 19.2-169.7.

---

ized provisions of mental health law.[36] In short, training of lawyers and judges must include attention not only to the prevailing state of the art in forensic mental health services but also to the relevant law.

For both clinical and legal groups, the training should be ongoing and cover developments in both the law and the behavioral sciences.[37] It is obvious that an evaluation based on a legal standard that is no longer in force cannot be valid, and assessments by a clinician unaware of new forensic protocols or tests may be less valid than they could be. Focused training is needed to keep the clinician up-to-date in both areas. Research suggests that changes in mental health law are unlikely to be transmitted quickly to mental health professionals unless there is an active effort to disseminate the new law.[38] Similarly, although new clinical forensic information is usually found in nationally distributed journals or books, the average clinician probably does not have the time to peruse the literature systematically.[39]

Lawyers and judges also need to be kept informed about new laws, changes in the forensic evaluation system, and new research findings that help them make use of—or challenge—the opinions of mental health professionals. As is the case with forensic clinicians, dissemination of new information, even legal information, is not automatic for legal professionals,[40] especially those whose practice seldom includes cases involving criminal mental health law (or whatever area of law is involved).

The form of education may vary. In our experience, initial training programs are enhanced by use of problems, videotapes of actual or simulated

Table 5.2

A Comprehensive Training Program on Criminal Forensic Issues

1. Introduction
   A. Overview of topics for forensic evaluation
   B. The definition of an expert [§§ 1.04 and 1.05]
   C. Stages of the criminal process [§ 2.04(a)]
2. The Nature of Forensic Evaluation [Chapter 3]
3. Constitutional and Ethical Contours of the Evaluation Process [Chapter 4]
4. Competency to Stand Trial [Chapter 6]
5. Other Competencies in the Criminal Process [Chapter 7]
6. Mental State at the Time of the Offense [Chapter 8]
7. Sentencing [Chapter 9]
8. Other Uses of Clinical Evidence in the Criminal Process [§ 7.07]
9. Report Writing and Expert Testimony [Chapters 18 and 19]
10. Developing a Forensic Practice [§ 5.05]

Note. Section references refer to applicable parts of this book.

cases, and participation in evaluations and mock trials. These can supplement outlines and excerpts from relevant legal and clinical materials (of the type that led to the first edition of this book).

Continuing education can also take many forms. The Virginia experience provides a useful illustration. *Developments in Mental Health Law* is a widely distributed newsletter published by the Institute of Law, Psychiatry and Public Policy at the University of Virginia, with funds provided by the state Department of Mental Health and Mental Retardation. The Institute also sponsors an annual two-day symposium on mental health law, which attracts about 200 mental health professionals and lawyers each year. In addition, the Institute conducts periodic continuing education workshops for particular groups (e.g., annual sessions for special justices who hear civil commitment cases and semiannual workshops for clinicians trained and certified by the Institute in forensic evaluation). Institute faculty make periodic visits to community mental health centers to talk with the forensic teams about problems they have encountered and inform them of new developments.

They also give lectures at continuing-education workshops of particular groups (e.g., trial judges) and at the annual meetings of judges, prosecutors, and defense attorneys.[41]

Other states also have adopted innovative approaches, often facilitated by forensic mental health institutes in the respective state universities. For example, the mental health law program of the University of Massachusetts Medical School supports "mentoring," in which an experienced evaluator takes responsibility for monitoring the evaluations and reports of newer evaluators.[42] In Florida, the Florida Mental Health Institute, with state support, sponsors three-day and one-day review programs using lectures, small-group breakout sessions, videotapes, and mock hearings.

There is, of course, an empirical question about the relative effectiveness of various formats for training and continuing education. Without such data, we offer no particular recommendation on formats that should be used. Probably a combination of formats (as in the Virginia program) is optimal because the level of prior knowledge can vary with the particular audience.

For reasons that should be obvious, any training program, whether basic or supplementary, should usually include both lawyers and mental health professionals as faculty. The law usually is best taught by lawyers who understand its nuances, and the state of the forensic art usually is best taught by mental health professionals. An additional benefit of this interdisciplinary interaction is that both groups are more likely to develop a basic understanding of the other discipline.

(2)   Incentives to Specialize

We already have explained our general preference for development of a forensic specialty. Unfortunately, it is likely that forensic practice is not a popular career track among mental health professionals.[43] Thus, special incentives should be given for successful specialization in forensic mental health. An increment in salary or fees is justified in view of the special skills and knowledge necessary for forensic practice and the costs involved in pursuing such training. Job titles and "perks" are other ways of recognizing the expertise that competent forensic clinicians have attained.

The state should also provide certification of expert forensic clinicians. Certification can vary in rigor. In Virginia, a clinician can be certified after completing a course such as that described in Table 5.2 and passing an examination of forensic knowledge. In Massachusetts, the clinician must not only take the course and pass the examination but also make site visits to various forensic mental health services, perform several court-ordered evaluations under the supervision of a state-approved supervisor, and submit work samples for review by a committee of examiners.[44]

Certification has several advantages. First, it assists the court system in deciding who should be allowed to give testimony and file reports. Recall our argument in § 1.05 that the test for admissibility of experts' opinions—whether the specialized knowledge of the expert will assist the factfinder in decisionmaking—demands that judges take a functional approach to the question of whether the opinions of a particular expert or class of experts should be admitted into evidence. The obvious practical difficulty with this approach is that it increases the complexity of the decision the judge must make about the admissibility of a particular expert's opinion. Educational or professional credentials are easy to identify, but evaluating the level of specialized knowledge that an expert possesses (and its probative or prejudicial value in the case) requires more extensive questioning of the expert and a more subjective and probably less reliable decision. The inefficiency and possible unfairness thereby created can be diminished by providing that mental health professionals who successfully complete the state's forensic training and pass an examination on the relevant body of specialized knowledge are presumed to qualify as experts on those types of cases covered in the training program. At the same time, this presumption should apply *only* in those types of cases covered by the training program (e.g., competency and sanity cases) and be subject to rebuttal (if, for instance, the certified clinician has not carried out an adequate evaluation of the specific case at hand).

A side benefit of a certification program is that the title "certified forensic clinician" may come to carry a certain amount of prestige and serve as a recognition of the specialty. Thus, a certification process may be a low-cost way to recruit competent clinicians to forensic practice and provide an incentive for adequate investment of time and energy in the training program. Another benefit is that the existence of veteran certified clinicians can facilitate training via mentoring.[45]

To maximize the incentive to become certified, the state might want to stipulate that all referrals for initial, publicly funded evaluations be made only to certified forensic clinicians (at least when any are available). However, barring noncertified clinicians from other types of expert consultation or testimony in court is probably not justifiable. Some clinicians may have solid background in forensic mental health even though they have not completed a particular training program. Examples might be mental health professionals who are certified as diplomates by the American Board of Forensic Psychiatry or the American Board of Forensic Psychology, who have been trained in one of the few existing specialty programs, or who have attained some other indicator of expertise (e.g., Fellow in the American Psychology–Law Society). Provision could be made for such clinicians to qualify for state certification by examination only (without taking the prescribed training) to ensure that they are familiar with standards and procedures prevailing in the particular jurisdiction.[46]

(c) Management

Previous discussion has suggested, and others have confirmed,[47] that to the extent a forensic system diverges from Models I and II (which rely on hospitals as evaluation sites), administration is more complex. Simply put, there is more to administer when there is a range of programs and levels of services. Coordination of services, standardization of training, and quality control are all more difficult. Although these difficulties are probably outweighed by the benefits of community-based services, it is important that they are recognized and that administrative structures are developed to deal with them. It is also important to provide interagency coordination. By definition, forensic services involve the mental health system in interaction with other agencies (e.g., the sheriff's department, the corrections department, and the court system).

In view of the need for statewide coordination of forensic services, both internally and externally, the state should vest someone with coordination authority at the state level. Moreover, because of the nature of the specific tasks to be accomplished (e.g., establishment of interagency agreements and enforcement of standards for quality of services), it is desirable that the position be at the assistant commissioner level, so that the individual who possesses authority clearly has sufficient standing in the bureaucracy to be able to communicate easily with high-level administrators in other agencies. Also, because forensic services will cut across levels or types of mental health services (e.g., community services and hospitals), the director of forensic services needs to be at a level commensurate with, rather than subordinate to,

the directors of these broad types of services, who will themselves typically be assistant commissioners. Finally, a high-level, independent position for forensic services in the mental health bureaucracy minimizes the possibility that funding for forensic services will be an afterthought in a division with other primary responsibilities.

Each forensic center should also have a coordinator. Analogous to the job of the assistant commissioner, the local director of forensic services must ensure smooth working relationships with the various parties involved (e.g., the prosecutor, clerk of court, judges, defense attorneys, and probation staff). Representatives of the legal system need to know the procedures for referral and whom to call in case of a problem. Table 5.3 presents the information sheet circulated to such in-

Table 5.3
Sample Services Description

Forensic Evaluation Services

Mental Health Services Center of Midtown Area

To arrange evaluation: Please call the Administrative Offices at 999-9999. We prefer several days' notice in order to adjust staff schedules to accommodate the evaluation.

Location: The evaluation will preferably be conducted at the Midtown Office, which is located at 100 First Street (map attached). The evaluation will be conducted in an interior office with no windows and only one exit to facilitate security arrangements. Persons in custody may wear leg chains. If necessary in certain cases a defendant may be evaluated while in the Central County Jail. It may also be possible for persons in custody in the other local jails to be evaluated in the jail facility.

Time of evaluation: The competency evaluation should be expected to take two or two and one-half hours to conduct. The presentence evaluation and evaluation of mental status at the time of the offense will vary in time required depending on the individual case and whether or not we have examined the defendant previously. We will attempt to give the court an estimate of length of time for each case.

Reports: Reports will be returned to the appropriate persons in the judicial system within two weeks of the evaluation.

To board persons in custody overnight, Central County Sheriff John Smith has graciously offered the facilities of the Central County Jail. If you desire to have the prisoner boarded overnight, the Central County Jail should be notified in advance by calling (888) 888-8888. The jail is located at 100 Main Street. They will give you directions over the phone.

In case of questions or concerns, please call the Administrative Offices (999-9999) and ask for Dr. George Williams, Forensic Team Leader, or Dr. Jane Jones, Center Director.

Clinical staff: The Center staff who will be conducting these evaluations have received intensive training through the [name of forensic institute], in addition to their clinical training. Project Staff includes [here list all staff members, their degrees, internship training, position in the CMHC, etc.]

dividuals by one community mental health center whose forensic program served several court jurisdictions. It provides a summary of the details with which local administrators must be concerned.

Ongoing attention should also be given to management information services. As Steadman et al. discovered,[48] many states are not even aware of the number of defendants who enter their forensic service programs or the auspices under which they enter. Without such information, it is impossible to undertake systematic program planning or evaluation involving such matters as where additional evaluation centers should be based, the number of beds needed to ensure adequate treatment of defendants requiring inpatient care, or the effect of a change in law or policy. Well-developed data systems may also assist in identification of unanticipated problems (e.g., changes in referral patterns in a particular local jurisdiction).[49] Such a need is present in human services generally, but it is especially acute in forensic services. The multiplicity of competing interests identified previously makes especially common the "sabotage" of forensic service programs (whether intentional or not). For instance, prosecutors may prefer hospital evaluations to outpatient evaluations, under the impression that the hospital staff is more government-oriented. Similarly, a jail director may consistently refuse to allow defendants restored to competency to be forcibly medicated in jail, thus rendering them incompetent before they can be tried. Although anecdotal reports might uncover these practices, systematic analysis of data obtained from information retrieval systems can identify statistical aberrations that will lead to further investigation.

(d) Financing

Care should be taken to ensure the absence of economic disincentives for implementation of community-based services. As Kiesler has convincingly shown,[50] the national policy of providing mental health services in the least restrictive setting has yet to be translated into practice, largely because public funding mechanisms (e.g., Medicaid) still disproportionately reward use of inpatient services. Analogous disincentives can arise in forensic services. For example, a major factor in the success of the Virginia program was an interagency directive that established that the payment mechanism for outpatient forensic evaluations would be the state judicial administrative office. Prior to the directive, the financial incentive for the courts was to refer evaluations to the forensic hospitals rather than to local mental health professionals because the latter charged the county in which the referring court sat, whereas the former absorbed the cost in their budgets. Although inpatient evaluations were costly to the state, they were free to the referring agency, which led to an inefficient and legally inappropriate use of resources.[51]

Of course, circumvention of the system can also occur if fees are set too low. Apparently some community mental health clinics in Virginia perceived, for example, that screening evaluations were more profitable than comprehensive evaluations and consequently tended to refer cases requiring comprehensive evaluations to the forensic hospital.[52] Similarly, clinics might be inclined to assign their least competent staff to forensic services if the income from the services is perceived as insufficient to justify use of highly trained staff.

Presumably, hospital-based evaluators will receive salaries from the state. However, it is difficult to be specific about how community-based evaluators should be paid because the fiscal structures available will vary across jurisdictions. For example, administrative relationships between state and local mental health agencies vary widely between states. We are reasonably confident, however, in suggesting a mix of fees for services and lump-sum contracts. Assuming that the fees are set at a level commensurate with the actual costs of performing the services, clinics will find it advantageous to perform services efficiently and quickly if they are reimbursed case by case. However, they are likely to find it disadvantageous economically to go beyond the provision of the report. Consequently, a lump-sum contract may be necessary to ensure that clinics carry out consultation and education, as well as direct delivery of services in individual cases. An initial lump-sum incentive may also be useful in covering the upfront costs of training, therefore enabling small clinics to put aside the necessary staff time prior to the receipt of significant fees for forensic services.

The manner of compensating evaluators can also play a role in quality assurance. Compare, for instance, the financing system in Florida to that in Alabama and Massachusetts.[53] In Florida, individual circuit courts are responsible for retaining and reimbursing professionals who conduct forensic evaluations. Accordingly, there is little uniformity across jurisdictions in terms of pay or quality of evaluations. In contrast, the Alabama and Massachusetts departments of mental health are responsible for funding forensic evaluations throughout the state. Because the departments are free to choose among service providers, they contract only with those professionals who meet certain standards and agree to follow specific procedures. Thus, greater statewide uniformity can be ensured by the departments of mental health through the contract and funding process.

5.05.   Operating a Forensic Practice

PROBLEM 5.2

You have been a practicing psychologist for the past ten years. You have just completed an intensive training program in criminal forensic work and another training program in child custody evaluations. You are now interested in obtaining forensic clients. A friend of yours who is a forensic "veteran" suggests that you write every attorney in the area telling them you are willing to work at "discount" prices in both criminal and domestic relations cases, and that you "guarantee acceptable results." He also advises that retainers are not necessary but that you should tell lawyers that you require payment before sending them a report or testifying. Finally, he advises you to keep two "files" for every evaluation: an "official" file, which contains your report and supporting data, to be handed over when files are subpoenaed, and an "office" file which contains other information related to the case and raw test scores from psychological tests. How should you react to this advice?

Consider also whether you will (1) bill services on the basis of time, the nature of the specific services, or the nature of the question asked; (2) bill services at a rate comparable to the same or analogous general clinical services; (3) deliver pro bono services and, if so, under what conditions; and (4) bill the client or the lawyer.

We now shift from the systemic to the individual office level and discuss various management issues that should concern a forensic practitioner. The premise of this section is that forensic practice is a business. It is wise to have in place routine methods for billing, initial consultation, record-keeping, and marketing.

(a)   Billing

Whether for one's own livelihood or for the fiscal health of one's agency, it is obviously important to establish a procedure for setting and obtaining a reasonable fee for evaluation, consultation, report writing, and, if necessary, testimony. For many types of evaluations, the government establishes a fee. For instance, the state may provide that an evaluation and report on competency to stand trial is compensated at $200, regardless of the time spent. Even in these situations, however, statutory provisions exist for further compensation under extraordinary circumstances. In other types of cases (e.g., custody determinations or defense-referred evaluations on insanity), the fees can vary considerably.[54]

Our experience has been that forensic practitioners are far from uniform in their billing practices. Many charge rates for forensic practice that are different (usually higher) from their rates for general clinical services. Some charge more for time in deposition or in court than for the evaluation services that take place out of court. The bottom-line amount a client is willing to pay may also influence a clinician's willingness to accept a case. None of these approaches is necessarily inappropriate. However, the clinician should avoid the temptation to accept payment on a contingent basis—that is, take payment only if the client wins the legal case. As discussed in § 4.05(b)(2), such contingency arrangements are unethical.

Whenever the fee is not set by statute, it is not only wise but ethically required [see § 4.05(b)(2)] to clarify compensation matters from the beginning, preferably in a memorandum of agreement on the attorney's letterhead that makes clear the agreed upon financial arrangement. To facilitate this type of agreement, the clinician may want to draft a standard letter or contract setting forth the following information:

- The hourly rate for the clinician's time (perhaps differentiating among the rates for services provided inside the office, for those provided outside the office, and for expert testimony).
- The hourly rate for other staff time (e.g., secretarial staff and other clinicians).
- The types of services for which these fees will be charged (e.g., interviewing, testing, interpretation of test scores, telephone contacts, and document review).
- Other types of charges (e.g., photocopying and travel expenses).
- The charge when appointments are cancelled by the client (which may be different depending on the length of the cancelled appointment and when the cancellation occurs).
- The date or time that payment is due (e.g., when services are completed), and any fee that will be charged for late payment (which is often limited in amount or percentage by state law).
- The extent to which, if timely payment is not made, the client will be responsible for collection fees (and when such fees shall begin accruing) and legal fees (in the event of a lawsuit).[55]

The clinician may also want to ask for a retainer fee prior to the commencement of services. Law firms have been known not to pay their experts, especially when the expert opinions are not particularly "useful."[56] Thus, the letter regarding fees might include the amount of a retainer fee and when it is due (e.g., 48 hours before the first consultation). It might also note that the amount of time necessary for a psychological consultation can vary and that, depending on the case, additional retainers may be demanded.

The clinician should also make clear that the referring party (e.g., the lawyer or law firm) is financially responsible for the fee, not a third party (such as an insurance company).[57] Lawyers should not be able to avoid payment by blaming nonpayment on an uncooperative insurer. The agreement might also note that if the subject of the evaluation ceases to be represented by an attorney, the clinician may terminate the relationship.

(b)   Establishing a Relationship with the Client[58]

In addition to fees, a number of subjects should be addressed in writing and discussed with the client and the client's lawyer or other referring agent before the evaluation begins. The following list of such subjects is compiled primarily from the detailed discussion of the forensic clinician's ethical obligations in the previous chapter [see §4.05][59]:

- The precise subject matter of the evaluation.
- The need for the client and the referring agent to be as open with the evaluator as possible (with the provision that a significant failure to provide information may result in an inability to provide an opinion).
- The need for the client to provide (revocable) releases for all information and records considered relevant by the evaluator.
- The fact that the clinician may talk to various friends, relatives, acquaintances, employers and so on in order to acquire information.
- The need for the client to permit revelation of confidential information to consulting clinicians and third-party insurers when necessary.
- The fact that damaging or embarrassing information may be revealed as a result of the evaluation.
- The fact that the clinician is an *evaluator*, not a therapist, and will not provide therapy except under special circumstances arranged after the evaluation is completed.
- The types of tests, interviews, and so on to be used, and the usual length of the process.
- The fact that the clinician does not give legal advice.
- The fact that the report goes to the referring agent, not the client (although the client may have a feedback session with the clinician).

The various topics outlined may be spelled out in the form of an agreement to be signed by the client after consultation with the attorney. If that is the approach taken by the clinician, a few other sentences could also be added to relieve the clinician of legal liability for damage caused by disclosure of confidential information. However, this kind of "release" seldom prevents a finding of liability when the clinician's negligence is the cause of such disclosure.[60]

(c) Recordkeeping and Disclosure of Records

Busy clinicians must keep good records. Often they will be required to testify on cases initiated several months or even years earlier. Without records detailing not only conclusions but also the data supporting those conclusions, preparation for testimony will be difficult and the testimony itself will probably be lacking in credibility.

Good records usually contain the following:

- The referral source and reason for the forensic contact.
- Relevant legal documents provided by the referral source (e.g., court order, indictment, and transcripts).
- Information about financial arrangements.
- The date and content of each visit, phone call, and conference, with descriptions about events in the client's or third party's own words whenever possible.
- Results of psychological and other tests.
- Clear separation of opinion from factual matters.
- Initialing of items in the record that are not in the clinician's handwriting.
- A copy of correspondence.[61]

Perhaps the only individual case information that should routinely be discarded from files are trivial notations and draft reports that have been superseded by final products. Copies of articles relied on in forming opinions also need not be kept in the files. Although records of the clinician's facts and opinions should be maintained for the reasons given above, there is no point in providing a possible *outside* source of questions for cross-examination.

As the previous paragraph suggests, the evaluator's files may provide useful "impeachment" information for the cross-examiner. Under some circumstances [as discussed in §§ 4.02 and 4.04], the contents of an evaluator's files are initially protected by the attorney–client privilege or the Fifth Amendment. Once the mental state of the person evaluated becomes a significant issue, however, the contents lose that protection. Indeed, virtually every relevant piece of information in the file (including the scribblings) is generally discoverable. Such discovery is usually accomplished through a subpoena *duces tecum* (literally, bring with you).

Fearful of such subpoenae, some clinicians may keep only minimal information in the file or create separate "court" and "personal" files. Neither approach is a good one. As we discussed earlier, comprehensive file information is important. And merely labeling a file "personal" does not exclude it from the reach of a valid subpoena. If the court learns about the ruse, the clinician might even be held in contempt.[62] The best approach is to keep complete files. Any information that is truly irrelevant can and should be excluded by the judge. Information that is relevant should not embarrass the evaluator who has done an honest job.

Occasionally, even relevant information for which privilege has been waived may be protected from a subpoena. Two such situations are noteworthy. First, the *work-product doctrine* protects information that comes directly from the attorney and that could be construed to pertain to the attorney's "mental impressions" about, or strategy for, the case.[63] Second, raw test data may not be directly discoverable. The American Psychological Association's Ethical Code prohibits "releasing raw test results or raw data to persons, other than to patients or clients as appropriate, who are not qualified to use such information."[64] It also states that "reasonable steps" should be taken to "ensure that appropriate explanation of results are given"[65] and that the "integrity and security of tests and other assessment techniques" are maintained, "consistent with law."[66] Although courts need not abide by psychologists' ethical norms about test security and use (especially in the face of a valid motion for discovery), many have been willing to accept the position that test data should be released only to qualified mental health professionals trained in psychological assessment.[67]

When valid grounds for avoiding a subpoena exist, the clinician can usually depend on the referring attorney to make arguments directed toward "quashing" the subpoena. If there is no such attorney or a third party's interests are at stake (e.g., the files contain private information about a third party otherwise uninvolved in the case), the clinician may need to retain a lawyer (although arguments can also be made *pro se*). Note further that, in the *absence* of a subpoena, signed by a judge, turning over documents may be a violation of confidentiality. It is important to make sure the subpoena is valid.

Occasionally, a forensic clinician may receive a telephone request from the opposing attorney "wondering" whether the clinician would discuss the case or provide access to records. In such situations, the best course of action is to contact the referring party to ascertain its views about such contact. Often the opposing attorney will not be able to engage in such informal discovery. Instead, the adverse party will be required to depose the clinician. The deposition notice may then be accompanied by a subpoena *duces tecum* or formal discovery request for documents [see generally § 2.04(b)].

(d)   Building and Marketing a Practice

Clinicians who wish to expand their forensic practice have several options. For many types of cases (e.g., criminal and juvenile), the courts maintain lists of mental health experts. If a clinician has not already been placed there by virtue of a certification process or a similar procedure related to training, it is a good idea for the clinician to put his or her name on such a list. Clinicians also can introduce themselves via letters to the relevant judges and attorneys, with business cards and resumés enclosed.

Referrals can also be encouraged via word of mouth (i.e., simply "passing the word" about an interest in receiving requests for forensic evaluations). This process can be facilitated by publication of articles on forensic issues (especially in state bar journals and other local fora for practitioners), lectures to lawyers, and membership on local committees established by mental health organizations, bar associations, or government agencies.

Other ways of enhancing one's exposure can be more problematic. For example, Sadoff has recommended that clinicians stay away from expert witness groups that charge fees for advertising experts' names, if only because "one can easily be exposed as belonging to such a factory or mill,

as they are called."[68] Offering pro bono or reduced-fee work in an effort to attract attention can also backfire, at least if such an offer is made in connection with a particular case, because it smacks of result-oriented solicitation.[69]

For similar reasons, advertising in local bar journals and other periodicals likely to be read by lawyers, although a useful marketing device, should be approached cautiously.[70] At one time, the American Psychological Association prohibited advertising that compared skills or services, appealed to the "fears, anxieties, or emotions" of consumers, contained testimonials, or made statements of direct solicitation. However, after Federal Trade Commission intervention under the antitrust laws in 1992, the American Psychological Association agreed to delete the prohibitions from its code.[71] The National Association of Social Workers entered into a similar consent agreement in the same year.[72] Nonetheless, the ethical rules still bar statements intended to create a false or misleading impression (e.g., that favorable results will be obtained), require that paid advertisements be identified as such, and prohibit personal solicitation of potential clients.[73]

Other prohibitions on advertising may apply. For example, the Ethical Code of the California Association of Criminalists (i.e., scientists working in criminal justice system laboratories) proscribes "seeking publicity . . . on specific cases" and "the association of [the professional's] name with development, publications, or organizations in which he [or she] has played no significant part, merely as a means of gaining personal publicity or prestige."[74] Added to these ethical prohibitions are statutory restrictions on advertising, violation of which can lead to loss of license or suspension. The most typical regulatory prohibition is a bar on false or misleading advertising. Florida, in addition, prohibits "obtaining a fee or other thing of value on the representation that beneficial results from any treatment will be guaranteed."[75]

In composing letters or advertising addressed to attorneys, the following items (most of them obvious) might be considered: (1) degrees and education; (2) board certification; (3) specialized forensic training; (3) publications on forensic issues; (4) membership in relevant organizations, universities, research institutes, and so on; (5) areas of practice, types of cases handled and approximate number; (6) jurisdictions in which already qualified as an expert; (7) approximate fees; (8) testimonials; and (9) availability.[76]

5.06. Effective Diffusion of Behavioral Science Research

The foregoing discussion primarily examined how a forensic system should be organized to provide the legal system with useful information on *individual* cases. Another component of a well-functioning forensic system is the continuing *general* education of legal actors about the findings of behavioral research (e.g., the dangerousness of people with mental illness, or the competence of children). Our repeatedly stated preference for the development of a specialty practice in forensic mental health is based in large part on the desirability—and the difficulty—of systematizing legal authorities' access to psychological knowledge that would be useful in their decisionmaking.

A second reason for addressing this topic here is the assumption that such general behavioral research can have a positive impact not just on substantive law but on the forensic system itself. As Grisso has thoughtfully discussed,[77] the nature of the forensic enterprise is such that bad practices can be easily institutionalized or maintained. In the legal system, with its heavy emphasis on precedent and formalization of procedure, "that's the way we've always done it" can be a powerful rationale. Clinicians willing to conform to conventional practice—even if it is not optimal practice—are likely to be favored in the forensic marketplace. Grisso has argued persuasively that two potential antidotes to this problem are (1) to promote professional standards (thus potentially changing conventional practice)[78] and (2) to build structures (e.g., direct support by professional associations) to foster behavioral science research relevant to forensic issues and to facilitate its diffusion to legal policymakers. The rest of this book is devoted to discussing appropriate professional standards. But Grisso's second antidote against forensic system inertia—dissemination of research—needs separate attention.[79]

With the ultimate task of guiding researchers

in diffusing knowledge among potential users in the legal system, a study group of the Society for Research in Child Development examined ways that various actors in the legal system learn about behavioral science research and then use, misuse, or ignore it.[80] Besides applying their experience as law professors, expert witnesses, and authors of amicus briefs, the study group synthesized existing research about knowledge diffusion and use (especially in the legal system), and group members conducted several studies of reading habits of judges and probation officers[81] and citation practices of judges and law professors.[82] The project resulted in several broad recommendations[83]:

1. *Report research where it is accessible to users.* Research on the reading habits and citation practices of those in the legal system showed that for research to be discovered by judges and lawyers who are actively seeking it, it must be available in journals covered by the *Index to Legal Periodicals* (e.g., law reviews and a smattering of interdisciplinary journals). By contrast, the popular media and practitioner journals, such as state bar journals, are at best useful for incidental exposure to legal professionals. Furthermore, the low hit rate for attempts to penetrate the national news media, combined with the virtual certainty of nonpenetration if active efforts are not made,[84] means that use of this source requires a substantial investment of time if researchers want their policy-relevant findings to be used.[85]

2. *Use informal networks to diffuse information.* In light of the foregoing, researchers should consider other methods of disseminating information besides journals and the media. News about the law, like other disciplines, travels primarily by word of mouth.[86] Whether in the legislative or the judicial process, relatively small networks of opinion leaders not only shape policy and practice but also serve as the primary sources of information for their professional peers.

In a project undertaken by the University of Nebraska Center on Children, Families, and the Law and the American Bar Association Center on Children and the Law,[87] the project staff attempted to harness the informal process of knowledge diffusion among judges. A small group of judges, judicial educators, and staff of the National Center for State Courts identified judges in Iowa and

Nebraska whom they believed were likely to be leaders of judicial views about child sexual abuse. The resulting 16 judges were contacted. All agreed to participate in conference-call seminars, read selected background materials, communicate the information to peers, and log such activities.

In brief, the low-cost process proved to have significant impact. The selected judges appreciated the convenience of continuing education at their desks and having the opportunity for direct discussions with respected peers and experts. Most important, virtually all the judges did spread the word, usually through multiple face-to-face interactions with other judges. About three-fourths of these informal brief educational events occurred at the networkers' initiation. The remainder involved "teachable moments" when peers sought information or opinions.[88]

3. *Look for opportunities to apply the research.* Whether in amicus briefs or briefings of advocates or legislators and their staff, the most direct impact comes when researchers bring their information to the decisionmaking fora in which particular behavioral science findings are relevant. In this regard, integration into an issue networks like the one just described can do double duty. Not only can researchers use the networks as avenues for diffusion of knowledge but they also can learn about forthcoming opportunities for its application.

4. *Use professional organizations.* Professional associations play two important roles in the application of scientific information in the legal process. First, they are *de facto* arbiters of good science and practice.[89] Courts are especially prone to use policy statements, practice guidelines, and testimony or briefs by professional associations or government commissions (on which professional associations are often represented) as authoritative statements of the state of knowledge or practical art.

Second, the professional associations commonly have active programs to bring knowledge into the policy arena through lobbying of legislative and administrative officials, contacts with representatives of other professional and advocacy groups, legislative testimony, and amicus briefs. Because of staff integration into issue networks, professional associations can be efficient avenues for diffusion of policy-relevant knowledge.

Given the fact that most legal policy issues are primarily matters of state law, the minimal involvement of most state associations of mental health professionals in issues other than those having direct guild implications[90] is unfortunate. The opportunities for ensuring socially responsive policy—including policies on forensic mental health services that are protective of defendants' rights and facilitative of high quality—are greatest in the state capitols and courtrooms.

5. *Meet legal professionals on their own terms.* If scholarly articles are the method of dissemination, it is important to remember that behavioral science knowledge is most likely to be used when it is presented within the context of a legally sound policy analysis that identifies the important empirical issues and their policy significance. In such presentations, the quality of the legal scholarship is likely to be as important as the rigor of the science in determining whether research is used (and not misused). Although many psycholegal scholars themselves are capable of this integration, there is a need at the very least for effective collaboration between behavioral scientists and law professors. Such a collaboration requires behavioral scientists to master the sociology of law schools, which is quite different from that of psychology and psychiatry departments,[91] and the publication practices of law reviews, which bear little resemblance to those of social science and health journals.

As with the use of clinical opinions in the legal system, the questions that have dominated both legal and psychological discourse about the proper use of research evidence may pale in the face of the practical problems of ensuring decisionmakers' access to information in an easily usable form. The need for systemic development is clear.

Bibliography

Theodore H. Blau, The Psychologist as Expert Witness (1984), ch. 12.

Thomas Grisso, *The Economic and Scientific Future of Forensic Psychological Assessment*, 42 American Psychologist 831 (1987).

Thomas Grisso et al., *The Organization of Pretrial Evaluation Services: A National Profile*, 18 LAW & HUMAN BEHAVIOR 377 (1994).

GARY B. MELTON ET AL., COMMUNITY MENTAL HEALTH CENTERS AND THE COURTS: AN EVALUATION OF COMMUNITY-BASED FORENSIC SERVICES (1985).

James R. P. Ogloff & Ronald Roesch, *Using Community Mental Health Centers to Provide Comprehensive Mental Health Services to Local Jails*, in LAW AND PSYCHIATRY: THE BROADENING OF THE DISCIPLINE 241 (James R. P. Ogloff ed. 1992).

Norman Poythress et al., *Pretrial Evaluations for Criminal Courts: Contemporary Models of Service Delivery*, 18 JOURNAL OF MENTAL HEALTH ADMINISTRATION 198 (1991).

REFORMING THE LAW: IMPACT OF CHILD DEVELOPMENT RESEARCH (Gary B. Melton ed. 1987).

HENRY J. STEADMAN ET AL., THE MENTALLY ILL IN JAIL: PLANNING FOR ESSENTIAL SERVICES (1989).

Symposium, *Justice and Mental Health Systems Interactions*, 16 LAW & HUMAN BEHAVIOR 1 (1992).

PART II

The Criminal Process

CHAPTER SIX

Competency to Stand Trial

6.01. Introduction

The "competency" paradigm permeates the law. An individual must be "competent" to enter a contract; otherwise, that contract may be void. A will written by an individual lacking the "competency" to write it may not be admitted to probate. An individual must be "competent" to consent to medical treatment. And, as discussed in this chapter, the state may not subject an "incompetent" individual to trial on criminal charges. In each of these situations, the law seeks to implement a basic premise: that only the acts of an autonomous individual are to be recognized by society. In doing so, the law attempts to reaffirm the integrity of the individual as well as the interests of society at large.

We devote an entire chapter to competency to stand trial because it is by far the most frequently adjudicated competency issue. Other contexts in which competency is an issue in the criminal process are the subject of Chapter 7, and Chapter 11 discusses competency issues arising in civil litigation. In this chapter, we discuss the genesis of the legal rule that a criminal accused must be mentally fit to stand trial; the current definition of trial competency; the myriad reasons, often unrelated to the defendant's competency, the competency issue is raised; and the consequences of an adjudication of incompetency. We also dis-

cuss a number of empirical studies examining the reliability and validity of competency evaluations, including those using competency-gauging instruments such as the Competency Screening Test mentioned in Case Study 6.1. The chapter concludes with a discussion of the clinical evaluation of competency to stand trial.

CASE STUDY 6.1

Donald is charged with six counts of arson. Each count charges him with intentionally setting fire to a church. He has an IQ of 58. You are asked to evaluate whether he is competent to stand trial. During the evaluation, the following dialogue takes place:

Q: Do you know what you are charged with?
A: I dunno. What's charged mean?
Q: Do you know why you're here in this jail?
A: Yeah. Burnin' down stuff.
Q: What stuff?
A: Goddamn churches.
Q: Have you talked to your attorney about this?
A: Those churches was wrong. They get in the way. I got them out of the way.
Q: Is that what you told your attorney?
A: Yeah.
Q: Do you like your attorney?
A: He doan like me.
Q: Why do you say that?
A: He doan talk to me or nothin'. He doan try to get me off.

Q: Do you want to get off?

A: Yeah.

Q: Is that because you think you are innocent?

A: I got good reasons for doin' what I done. Those churches are bad. I didn't want to hurt no one. The fire, the fire, it cleans everything up. Right up.

Q: Do you hear people talking to you who aren't there?

A: The Lord, he talk to me. And so do the devils, and the angels. They all in there trying to mess me up. But I done right.

Q: Have you ever seen these devils or angels?

A: Nope. They just always shouting at me. Tryin' to mess me up. The fire, it'll clean everything right up.

Q: If your lawyer wanted you to testify, would you do it?

A: I'm goin' to tell everyone what's wrong with the churches.

Q: Would you be willing to tell them you have mental problems, if that would get you off?

A: I ain't crazy. Jus' mad.

Q: Do you think you need any kind of treatment?

A: I jus' tol' you, I ain't crazy, and I don't want to go to no loony bin.

Q: What do you think might happen at a trial?

A: They'll try to put me in prison, but I'll burn it down. They can't stop me from doin' right.

Q: Who will try to put you in prison?

A: The pros'cutor, the jury, the judge, all those people.

Q: Are the judge and jury against you?

A: Depends 'pon whether they know what's right. Maybe they is, maybe they isn't. But the fire will clean everything up.

Q: Let's say the prosecutor comes to your attorney and says he'll recommend only five years in prison if you plead guilty to burning down six churches. What would you do?

A: Five years in prison?

Q: Five years.

A: I shouldn't oughta go to prison.

Q: But what might happen if you go to trial?

A: I tol' you they could put me in prison.

Q: For how long?

A: For as long as they want.

Q: So might it not be a good idea to take the prosecutor's offer of five years?

A: It don't matter, since they ain't goin' to be able to keep me. Look, I don't like this. I ain't talkin' to you no more.

Before the interview, Donald was asked to complete the Competency Screening Test, which he did orally (not being able to write). He scored 17. Some of his completions which did not receive the full two points were: "When I go to court the lawyer will <u>probably not say much</u>." "When they say a man is innocent until proven guilty, I <u>know what they mean</u>." "What concerns Fred about his lawyer <u>is that he don't seem to care much</u>."

QUESTIONS: What other information might you want to assess Donald's competence to stand trial? Assuming you want to interview Donald further, but he still refuses, may the court impose sanctions on Donald [see § 4.02(a)]? If Donald's defense attorney wants Donald to stand trial now, and he agreed, should trial proceed? Alternatively, if Donald's attorney believes Donald needs treatment to restore him to competency, may he seek such treatment over Donald's objection? If Donald were found incompetent due to delusions, and he refused medication because he does not like the side effects, can and should he be forcibly medicated?

6.02.　The Legal Standard

This section examines the historical basis and rationale for the competency test and its most common modern formulations. It also addresses two issues that routinely complicate the competency determination: the extent to which either amnesia or antipsychotic medication might affect a defendant's competency.

(a)　Historic Antecedents

The rule that an individual must be competent to undergo the criminal process originated in the common law and has been traced at least to the 17th century.[1] In those days, as is true today, the defendant was required to plead to the charge prior to trial. Some commentators believe that the concept of competency first arose as a reaction by the English courts to defendants who, rather than making the required plea, stood mute. In such a case, the court would then seek to ascertain whether the defendant was "mute of malice" or "mute by visitation of God." If the individual fell into the first category, the court sought to force a plea by ordering increasingly heavier weights to be placed upon the individual's chest. If the individual fell into the latter category, he or she was spared this ordeal. The category "mute by visitation from God" initially included the literally deaf and mute but over time was expanded to include the "lunatic."[2]

Although the requirement that the defendant be competent may have developed as a practical response to a practical problem, it also seems to have its roots in a more general concern that subjecting certain types of individuals to trial was simply unfair. Thus, in the 18th century Blackstone observed that a defendant who "becomes mad . . . ought not to be arraigned . . . because he is not able to plead to it with that advice and caution that he ought. And if, after he has pleaded, the prisoner becomes mad, he shall not be tried: for how can he make his defense?"[3] This idea was also reflected in early English court decisions. For example, in *Frith's Case*, decided in 1790, the court found that trial must be postponed until the defendant "by collecting together his intellects, and having them entire, he shall be able so to model his defense and to ward off the punishment of the law."[4]

Early American courts, which relied heavily on English common law,[5] also recognized the incompetency plea. In 1835, for instance, the man who attempted to assassinate President Andrew Jackson was declared unfit to stand trial.[6] In 1899, a federal court of appeals went so far as to give the competency doctrine constitutional status; the court held it to be "fundamental that an insane person can neither plead to an arraignment, be subjected to a trial, or, after trial, receive judgment, or, after judgment, undergo punishment; to the same effect are all the common-law authorities. . . . It is not 'due process of law' to subject an insane person to trial upon an indictment involving liberty or life."[7] Since that time, the United States Supreme Court has on several occasions stated that the right of an incompetent defendant to avoid trial is "fundamental to an adversary system of justice."[8]

These holdings have been based on the due process clause but are probably best thought of as attempts to implement the Sixth Amendment, which guarantees criminal defendants the rights to effective counsel, confront one's accusers, and present evidence. Exercise of these rights re-

quires more than physical presence; defendants who are not present mentally cannot help their attorneys rebut the state's case or discover helpful evidence. Put another way, in an ideal world the criminal process should provide a trial between evenly matched adversaries. This process posits defendants able to participate in their own defense. Without the competency doctrine, the rights afforded by the Sixth Amendment would be empty for many individuals.

A second rationale for the competency requirement focuses not on the individual's rights but on society's interests. The defendant must be competent not only to ensure fair results but also to guarantee a dignified criminal process. As one commentator has observed, "The adversary form of the criminal proceeding necessarily rests on the assumption that the defendant will be a conscious and intelligent participant; the trial of a defendant who cannot fulfill this expectation appears inappropriate and irrational."[9] Even a proceeding that produces an accurate guilty verdict would be repugnant to our moral sense if the convicted individual were unaware of what was happening or why.[10] As later discussion develops, this latter rationale for the competency requirement is important, as it seems to underlie many of the substantive and procedural aspects of competency doctrine.

(b)   The Competency Test

In *Dusky v. United States*[11] the United States Supreme Court set forth a definition of competency to stand trial that has since come to be the standard in federal court and most state jurisdictions. The Court stated that "the test must be whether he [the defendant] has sufficient present ability to consult with his attorney with a reasonable degree of rational understanding and a rational as well as factual understanding of proceedings against him."[12] Although actually only a repetition of a test put forth by the Solicitor General in the case, this formulation is now viewed as having constitutional status, with the result that many state statutes and courts follow it verbatim and most others track its basic components.[13]

These components are several in number. First, the Court's test delineates *two prongs* to the competency test: the defendant's capacity to understand the criminal process, including the role of the participants in that process, and the defendant's ability to function in that process, primarily through consulting with counsel in the preparation of a defense. Efforts to define competency further have consistently focused on these two prongs.

Second, *Dusky* makes clear that competency focuses on the defendant's *present* ability to consult with counsel and to understand the proceedings. It therefore differs fundamentally from the test for criminal responsibility, which is a retrospective inquiry focusing on the defendant's state of mind at the time of the offense. It also differs from the predictive inquiry required for civil commitment although, as will be noted below, a degree of prediction may be necessary to determine competency in some instances.

Third, the test emphasizes the defendant's *capacity,* as opposed to willingness, to relate to counsel and understand the proceedings. The defendant who refuses to talk to the attorney even though capable of doing so is making a rational choice knowing the consequences. Unless the lack of motivation is based on irrational factors, thereby calling into question one's capacity to assist in one's defense, it is not ground for an incompetency finding. Similarly, when a suspect's inability to state the precise charge or describe the role of the judge results from failure to be apprised of the relevant information rather than a cognitive deficiency, a finding of incompetency is unwarranted.

Fourth, the requirement that the defendant possess a *reasonable* degree of understanding suggests that the test as applied to a particular case is a flexible one. "Perfect" or complete understanding on the part of the defendant will not be required—in fact, most observers agree that the threshold for a finding of competency is not particularly high.[14] At the same time, that threshold may vary according to context. With respect to the first prong of the competency test, for instance, a level of capacity sufficient to understand simple charges (e.g., driving without a license) may be grossly insufficient when a more complicated offense is involved [*cf.* the Premington report, § 19.02(c)]. Similarly, the defendant's capacity to communicate with counsel may depend

as much on the attorney's personality and the facts of the case as on any aspect of the defendant's mental condition. Relevant in the latter regard, however, is the Supreme Court's decision in *Morris v. Slappy*,[15] which held that the Constitution does not guarantee a "meaningful relationship" between a defendant and his or her attorney (primarily because, according to the Court, such a guarantee is impossible). Although this decision was in the context of claims that counsel's assistance was ineffective, it suggests that the Court will not require a particularly high-quality attorney–client relationship in the competency context either.

A fifth and final component of the *Dusky* standard is its emphasis on the presence or absence of "rational" and "factual" understanding, which suggests an emphasis on cognitive *functioning.* As many courts have held,[16] the mere fact that a defendant has psychotic symptoms or has a particular IQ does not mean that the defendant is incompetent to stand trial. Neither mental illness nor the defendant's need for treatment is sufficient for an incompetency finding. The presence of mental illness is relevant only insofar as that illness affects one's "rational and factual understanding" as one consults with counsel and undergoes trial. At the same time, note that understanding must be factual *and* rational; factual understanding alone is not enough. A defendant who understands that a particular prison term is associated with his charges but believes for irrational reasons that he will never serve any time in prison may be incompetent [consider Case Study 6.1 and the Rhodes report in § 19.02(e)].

There have been a number of efforts by legislators, courts, and clinicians to add content to the rather sparsely worded standard enunciated by the Supreme Court. For example, the Florida Rules of Criminal Procedure provide that "the following factors and any others deemed relevant" should be assessed during a competency evaluation:

the defendant's capacity to:

1. Appreciate the charges or allegations against him;
2. Appreciate the range and nature of possible penalties, if applicable, which may be imposed in the proceedings against him;

3. Understand the adversary nature of the legal process;
4. Disclose to his attorney facts pertinent to the proceedings at issue;
5. Manifest appropriate courtroom behavior;
6. Testify relevantly.[17]

These criteria operationalize both prongs of *Dusky*. The first three criteria relate to the defendant's ability to understand the legal process. Defendants who cannot grasp the charges or possible penalties, or who cannot understand that trial involves an attempt by the prosecutor to obtain a conviction from a jury or judge, are unlikely to be able to confront their accusers or have the motivation to defend themselves. The last three criteria concern defendants' ability to function in the process. The fourth criterion focuses on the ability to communicate facts about the alleged crime to the attorney, obviously an important aspect of confronting accusers and assuring a fair trial (although amnesia for the offense does not necessarily bar a finding of incompetency [see § 6.02(c)]). The fifth and sixth criteria relate to the defendant's ability to function in the courtroom.

Note further that the latter two criteria call for predictions as to how the defendant will fare in the courtroom. Competency to stand trial assessments focus primarily on present mental status. These factors are nonetheless important because a defendant who will disrupt and distract the factfinding process may prejudice the factfinder and make defense counsel's job difficult, and a defendant who is incapable of testifying, even though able to talk to the attorney in private, may be deprived of a fair trial.

The Florida rules provide that examiners should also consider "any other factors deemed relevant." One such factor might be the capacity to relate to one's attorney, one of the two *Dusky* prongs, although that factor is probably subsumed in the fourth criterion, having to do with capacity to disclose pertinent facts. Another nonlisted criterion is the defendant's capacity to weigh the advantages and disadvantages of a guilty plea and make a reasonable decision about whether to make such a plea. This criterion will almost always be relevant in a competency evaluation because, as noted in § 2.04(a)(1), more than 90% of all criminal cases are resolved through a guilty plea rather than trial.[18] Yet most statutory and ju-

dicial formulations of the competency test, like Florida's, fail to take explicit notice of this fact. Perhaps this oversight can be justified on the ground that a person who understands the charges and their consequences can make an adequate decision as to whether to plead guilty; indeed, as discussed in § 7.04 (discussing competence to plead guilty in detail), many courts have so held. Yet, as Bonnie has pointed out,[19] an intelligent guilty plea requires not only understanding of the legal process and the ability to communicate information (the core of competency to stand trial) but also the capacity to make a decision in light of that understanding. This distinction between "decisional" competency and "competency to proceed" is discussed in more detail later in this chapter.

As noted previously, most state statutes are not as detailed as Florida's, instead adopting or providing variations on the test announced in *Dusky*. However, judicial decisions construing these laws often flesh out the *Dusky* test in a fashion similar to Florida's rules.[20] Similarly, the standard proposed by the American Bar Association (ABA) uses the *Dusky* language to define competency, but the commentary to the standard stresses that evaluation should focus on the defendant's skills relative to trial rather than the defendant's general mental condition.[21]

In addition to the efforts of legislators and judges, clinicians have developed a number of checklists and tests designed to assist in the evaluation of competency. For instance, the Group for the Advancement of Psychiatry (GAP), composed primarily of psychiatrists, has derived a 21-item list from existing test instruments [see Table 6.1].[22] Other instruments developed for use by clinicians are discussed in § 6.06. Central to all these tests, again, is an emphasis on specific dysfunction related to the defendant's understanding of the legal process and the capacity to assist in the preparation of his defense.

It is also worth repeating that although criteria such as those found in the Florida rules and the GAP items help operationalize *Dusky*, their meaning in a given case depends heavily on context and in any event will be open to multiple interpretations. Donald, the individual in Case Study 6.1, can recount some of the facts surrounding the offense, but can he give the attorney all the "perti-

Table 6.1

List of Items Relevant to Competency to Stand Trial (Group for the Advancement of Psychiatry)

Competency to Stand Trial may involve the ability of a defendant:

1. To understand his current legal situation.
2. To understand the charges against him.
3. To understand the facts relevant to his case.
4. To understand the legal issues and procedures in his case.
5. To understand legal defenses available in his behalf.
6. To understand the dispositions, pleas, and penalties possible.
7. To appraise the likely outcomes.
8. To appraise the roles of defense counsel, the prosecuting attorney, the judge, the jury, the witnesses, and the defendant.
9. To identify and locate witnesses.
10. To relate to defense counsel.
11. To trust and to communicate relevantly with his counsel.
12. To comprehend instructions and advice.
13. To make decisions after receiving advice.
14. To maintain a collaborative relationship with his attorney and to help plan legal strategy.
15. To follow testimony for contradictions or errors.
16. To testify relevantly and be cross-examined if necessary.
17. To challenge prosecution witnesses.
18. To tolerate stress at the trial and while awaiting trial.
19. To refrain from irrational and unmanageable behavior during the trial.
20. To disclose pertinent facts surrounding the alleged offense.
21. To protect himself and to utilize the legal safeguards available to him.

nent" facts and will he be able to testify relevantly (see criteria 4 and 6 in the Florida rules, and items 20 and 16 on the GAP list)? The answer to these questions is more likely to be yes if an insanity defense will be raised, but Donald seems to resist that tactic. What implications does continued rejection of an insanity defense have for Donald's ability "to understand legal defenses available in his behalf" (item 5 on the GAP list)? What can be said about his ability to collaborate with his attorney (item 14 on the GAP list)? The difficulty

the evaluating clinician might have in answering these types of questions counsels for avoidance of not only the ultimate issue (i.e., competent vs. incompetent) but also the penultimate issues (i.e., able vs. not able to recount pertinent facts and to understand legal defenses).

(c)   The Amnesic Defendant

At first glance, a defendant who cannot remember the criminal act would appear to be incompetent, as recounting to counsel the facts pertinent to the offense would be impossible. As noted earlier, however, amnesia for the period of the crime, by itself, does not bar a finding of competency.[23] This principle appears to be predicated primarily on judicial distrust of the authenticity of such claims. As one court stated, to recognize amnesia as a bar to trial would "turn over the determination of crime and criminal liability to psychiatrists, whose opinions are usually based in large part upon defendant's self-serving statements, instead of to Courts and juries."[24] Another court, after expressing similar concern over the ease with which amnesia could be feigned, observed that a defendant is only entitled to a fair trial, not a perfect trial.[25]

Although the courts have been unanimous in refusing to equate amnesia with incompetency, many have remained sensitive to the threat that amnesia poses to accurate adjudication. Perhaps the most comprehensive attempt to reconcile the competency requirement with the rule regarding amnesia is found in *Wilson v. United States.*[26] In that case, the defendant, charged with assault and robbery, had fractured his skull while being apprehended for the offense; as a result, he claimed (and clinicians verified) that he had no memory of the incidents underlying his charges and was deemed unlikely ever to regain his memory. While finding that his amnesia did not bar prosecution, the federal court of appeals issued the following guidelines to assist the trial court in determining whether the defendant was competent:

1. The extent to which the amnesia affected the defendant's ability to consult with and assist his lawyer.

2. The extent to which the amnesia affected the defendant's ability to testify in his own behalf.

3. The extent to which the evidence could be extrinsically reconstructed in view of the defendant's amnesia. Such evidence would include evidence relating to the crime itself as well as any reasonably possible alibi.

4. The extent to which the government assisted the defendant and his counsel in that reconstruction.

5. The strength of the prosecution's case. The court observed that "most important here will be whether the Government's case is such as to negate all reasonable hypotheses of innocence. If there is any substantial possibility that the accused could, but for his amnesia, establish an alibi or other defense, it should be presumed that he would have been able to do so."

6. Any other facts and circumstances that would indicate whether or not the defendant had a fair trial.[27]

Wilson also required the prosecution to assist the defense in preparing its case, including cooperation in pretrial discovery broader than that ordinarily permitted in criminal cases. A similar approach was taken in *United States v. Stubblefield,*[28] in which the court emphasized the obligation of the prosecution to assist the defense not only in reconstructing the events surrounding the offense but in constructing any reasonably possible alibi or other defense.

(d)   Drug-Induced Competency

Because many of those who are found incompetent are suffering from psychosis [see § 6.05(b)], the most common method of restoring competency is the administration of psychotropic medication. Yet some courts have refused to recognize "drug-induced" competency in the belief that the drugs distort defendants' thought processes.[29] Although such drugs do have side effects, they often can permit an individual to attain the low threshold of understanding required for competency to stand trial. Further, barring such individuals from trial may mean they will never be tried. In recognition of these facts, the vast majority of states do

not prohibit trial of a medicated defendant as long as the functional criteria for competency are met.[30]

At the same time, courts, lawyers and clinicians must be alert to the possibility that inappropriate medication may diminish a defendant's ability to confront accusers. This issue came to the fore in *Riggins v. Nevada,*[31] a United States Supreme Court decision. After being found incompetent to stand trial on capital charges, Riggins was treated with medication, apparently successfully. But by the time he was tried he was receiving 800 milligrams of Mellaril a day, an extremely high dosage. Although the Court avoided a firm conclusion as to whether this dosage compromised Riggins's right to a fair trial, it remanded the case to the trial court, requiring a determination as to whether "the substance of [Riggins's] testimony, his interaction with counsel, or his comprehension at trial were compromised by forced administration of Mellaril." *Riggins* appears to require the trial judge (and thus evaluating clinicians) to calibrate carefully the effect of medication on a defendant's ability to understand and participate in the proceedings and to consult with counsel (i.e., the *Dusky* criteria).

In sum, it is important to remember that competency to stand trial is concerned primarily with present levels of functioning; that a finding of mental illness or need for treatment is not analogous to, or necessarily even relevant to, a finding of incompetency to stand trial; and that the legal test, although sketchy, is concerned with the level of the defendant's cognitive functioning and its impact on his or her ability, as opposed to willingness, to understand and participate meaningfully in the criminal process.

6.03.   Procedural Issues

A request for a competency-to-stand-trial evaluation may occur at any point in the criminal process, although it usually occurs prior to trial. To comprehend the roles of the attorney and the clinician in the competency context, it is important to understand who makes such requests and why, the standard under which such motions are granted, the typical location of the competency examination, and the procedures associated with the formal adjudication of competency.

(a)   Who May Raise the Issue?

The defense attorney most frequently initiates the competency inquiry.[32] However, in most jurisdictions a motion for an evaluation or hearing on competency may also be made by the prosecution or by the court *sua sponte*.[33] Because these motions may be granted even over the defendant's objection, they apparently are justified on the second ground given earlier for the competency requirement: society's (as opposed to the individual's) interest in ensuring a dignified adjudication process.

Two related concerns have arisen in connection with prosecution or court-initiated competency examinations. The first is the possibility that such examinations will occur without the knowledge of defense counsel, or even prior to appointment of counsel for the defendant, thereby prejudicing the constitutional right of the defendant to counsel [see § 4.03(a)]. The American Psychiatric Association has instructed its members that they have an ethical obligation to avoid performing competency examinations prior to the appointment of defense counsel and to ascertain that defense counsel is aware the examination is being conducted.[34] The ABA standards provide similar protection.[35] These positions suggest, as discussed in § 4.05(b)(1), that the clinician asked to evaluate competency has an ethical obligation to ascertain immediately whether the defendant has counsel; if not, the examiner should indicate to the referral source that the examination must be deferred until counsel is obtained.

The second concern about prosecution and court-initiated competency motions attacks head on the notion that society's interest in ensuring competent defendants overrides a defendant's desire to be tried. Put succinctly, the question is whether—once counsel has been provided the defendant and the defendant, on counsel's advice, decides not to raise the competency issue—the prosecution or court may obtain a competency examination over defense objection. In *Pate v. Robinson,*[36] the Supreme Court suggested an affirmative response to this question, when it asserted

that "it is contradictory to argue that a defendant may be incompetent and yet knowingly or intelligently 'waive' his right to have the court determine his capacity to stand trial." But Winick has argued that when, as hypothesized, defense counsel *affirms* the defendant's decision, the court should not be able to override the decision, at least when the client can "clearly articulate" a decision to waive the right. Although such a client may not be fully "competent" to make such a waiver, Winick contends that "[w]hen the competing values at stake are respect for autonomy and a desire to act in the individual's best interests or to protect him from harm, the competency question should turn on an assessment of the degree of autonomy present and the risk/benefit ratio of the activity in question." A presumption in favor of the client's choice to go to trial is merited when counsel concurs, he argues, because the concurrence "will presumably eliminate instances in which the defendant's choice is based on irrelevant reasons . . . or irrational beliefs . . . or outright delusions," and will be "strong evidence that the risk/benefit ratio of his choices is acceptable compared to an adjudication of incompetency."[37]

A separate issue, raised in connection with Case Study 6.1, is whether the client may limit the *defense attorney's* ability to raise the competency issue. The ABA has concluded that defense counsel has an ethical obligation to move for a competency evaluation whenever there is good-faith doubt as to competency, even over the client's objection.[38] This position assumes that the attorney will act in the client's best interests, an assumption that may not be warranted [see § 6.03(c)]. Further, as the commentary to the ABA rule recognizes, in some cases the length of commitment for treatment of an incompetent defendant may exceed the potential sentence if trial proceeds. Nonetheless, the commentary concludes, defense counsel's "obligation to the court" requires the issue to be raised. Uphoff has argued, on the other hand, that this approach will lead to many unnecessary competency evaluations, create distrust between the defendant and counsel, and complicate counsel's role at subsequent competency hearings given the possibility that counsel will need to reveal confidential communications from the client to support an incompetency claim.[39] He also notes that the judge or prosecutor can raise the competency issue if it appears the defendant is being demeaned by the process.

The relevant ethical rules only require the defense attorney to prevent "fraud" by the client[40] and thus provide no definitive resolution of this issue. Defense counsel faced with an objecting client who appears to have mental problems might best be advised to seek an outpatient "exploratory" evaluation on the competency issue first [see § 4.03(b)(1)]. Only if this relatively minimal intrusion into the client's autonomy results in a firm conclusion of incompetency should the attorney contemplate raising the competency issue over the client's objection, keeping in mind that the competency requirement serves two, perhaps competing, goals: fairness to the individual and the integrity of the system.

(b)   The Standard for Raising the Issue

A second issue crucial to the competency evaluation process is when, regardless of who makes it, a motion for an evaluation should be granted. The Supreme Court has ruled that the trial court must order an inquiry into competency if a "bona fide doubt" exists as to the defendant's competency.[41] Further, the Court has made clear that, in deciding whether such doubt exists, the trial court must take into account and weigh any factor suggestive of mental illness. For example, in *Drope v. Missouri*,[42] where the defendant's wife had testified about his "strange behavior" and where the defendant on the second day of trial shot himself in an attempted suicide, the Court ruled that a competency exam should have been ordered and suggested that the threshold for obtaining evaluation on the issue of competency is not very high:

> [E]vidence of defendant's irrational behavior, his demeanor at trial, and any prior medical opinion on competence to stand trial are all relevant in determining whether further inquiry is required, but even one of these factors standing alone may, in some circumstances, be sufficient. There are, of course, no fixed or immutable signs which invariably indicate the need for further inquiry to determine fitness to proceed; the question is often a difficult one in which a wide range of manifestations and subtle nuances are implicated. That they are difficult to evaluate is suggested by the varying opinions trained psy-

chiatrists can entertain on the same facts.[43] [Emphasis added]

In practice, a court will rarely refuse a request for a competency examination if only for fear that an ensuing conviction will be reversed on the ground that the defendant's constitutional right to due process has been violated.[44] This fact emphasizes a point made in the previous section: Preventing trial of an incompetent defendant is sufficiently important to society, irrespective of the individual's desires, that the system tends to resolve marginal cases by calling for a competency inquiry.

(c)   Reasons Evaluation Is Sought

Unfortunately, the low threshold for seeking competency evaluations, although perhaps justifiable from a constitutional perspective, has encouraged misuse of the system. Data on attorneys' rationales for referral suggest that the evaluation is often precipitated by concerns that are in some sense illegitimate. For instance, one prominent reason for evaluation is simply attorney ignorance. Rosenberg and McGarry found that only 10 of 28 trial attorneys they interviewed had any knowledge at all of the legal standards for incompetency.[45] Similarly, attorneys (and clinicians) may confuse incompetency with mental disorder per se or with insanity and may request evaluation of the former when in fact they want an evaluation on the latter issues.[46]

Even when there is no such conceptual confusion, competency evaluation referrals are sometimes inappropriately used to obtain information relevant to an insanity defense or to a dispositional plan. For example, in a questionnaire study of defense attorneys who had referred their clients to Dorothea Dix Hospital in North Carolina for an evaluation of competency to stand trial,[47] almost half indicated that they were actually seeking an opinion as to the defendant's criminal responsibility. They also indicated that they hoped to obtain information relating to sentencing. In fairness, some states have no procedures for obtaining evaluation of an indigent defendant's treatment needs and disposition. Although every state does have procedures for evaluating insanity, these procedures appear to be neglected because they are more cumbersome than those associated with obtaining an evaluation of competency to stand trial.

Of more concern than these abuses is evidence suggesting that incompetency referrals are used as a ruse to force treatment of persons who do not meet dangerousness requirements for civil commitment and who may be acting bizarrely.[48] Because a competency referral can be initiated by any party simply on a showing of bona fide doubt as to competency, a defendant who acts strangely or presents management problems in jail is much more readily placed in the mental health system through such a referral than through a commitment petition requiring a full hearing with counsel [see § 10.04]. Such a shortcut through system boundaries is spurious not only because of the insult to defendants' rights.[49] It may also fail on pragmatic grounds. Forensic units may lack clear authority to provide involuntary treatment to defendants admitted for evaluation.[50] Moreover, hospitals may—and should—limit their intervention to the scope of orders for admission. Consequently, defendants should be returned to the jail immediately after competency is evaluated.

Finally, and perhaps most objectionably, competency referrals may be made for purely strategic reasons unrelated to any concern with defendants' mental status. Perhaps foremost among these purposes is simply delay. In a case in which the alleged offense has created public uproar, defense counsel may succeed in bringing about the defendant's removal from the community until public emotions have calmed by having him or her hospitalized for a competency evaluation. Similarly, if the evidence is weak but the public sentiment for prosecution is strong, prosecutors may have the defendant "put away" for a period through a competency evaluation. The result may be pretrial detention without the opportunity for bail. A similar type of strategic abuse involves prosecution use of competency evaluations as a means of discovery. Even if the defendant's statements during a competency evaluation are inadmissible at trial on the issue of guilt, they may provide the prosecution with leads in its investigation if information from the evaluation is available to all parties [see § 4.02(a)]. In such situations, regardless of the parties' primary inten-

tion, competency evaluations serve as means to interrogate and investigate defendants in derogation of Fifth and Sixth Amendment protections.

As this brief discussion makes clear, the competency issue may be raised for a variety of reasons unrelated to concern over defendants' competency. Exacerbating the problem is the apparent attitude of many judges. In a survey of members of the North Carolina bench, Roesch and Golding found that judges suspect misuse of the competency referral process, especially among defense attorneys who misunderstand the concept or who merely seek delay.[51] Nonetheless, the majority of them reported that they routinely grant motions for competency evaluation even when no evidence of incompetency exists.

Our observations lead us to believe that the practices described above are not as pervasive as they once were. Nonetheless, they have not disappeared, thus creating doubt as to whether prosecutors, judges, or defense attorneys should be able to initiate competency evaluations over defendants' objections [cf. § 6.03(a)]. Further, they suggest that clinicians must be sensitive to the dynamics of the criminal process and the varying impulses that result in referrals. Otherwise, they may become unwitting participants in strategic ploys by one side or the other having nothing to do with competency—the ostensible reason for the referral, and the only issue with which clinicians should be concerned. At the same time, lawyers must ensure that their uses of the competency referral conform with its purposes; failure to do so, although perhaps attaining a short-term strategic goal such as delay, may result in harm to clients (e.g., unnecessary confinement in a mental health facility and exacerbation of evidence staleness if and when trial does take place).

(d)   Competency Examination: Situs and Length

After the court grants the motion for an examination into the defendant's competency, one or more clinicians will examine the defendant. Traditionally, competency examinations were performed by psychiatrists in "remotely located state institutions far from . . . family and community ties," where the defendants were hospitalized for lengthy periods of time often lasting from one to three months.[52] However, beginning in the 1970s, states have moved toward decentralizing their forensic services systems. Some have even mandated that competency examinations be performed locally and on an outpatient basis [see § 5.03].[53] In addition, states have increasingly authorized psychologists and social workers to perform competency examinations,[54] a trend that has facilitated the decentralization of forensic systems by expanding locally available forensic resources.

These developments have occurred for a number of reasons. Most important, research has made evident that a competency evaluation can be performed adequately in a much shorter time and in an outpatient rather than an inpatient setting [see § 6.05(c)].[55] Second, courts have become more attuned to defendants' constitutional rights to a speedy trial and to nonexcessive bail,[56] which may increase the desire to expedite cases and avoid unnecessary incarceration. In addition, fiscal constraints have pressured courts to seek efficient ways of processing cases, which may lead them to favor outpatient examinations performed locally; defendants evaluated in such a system return to court for trial much more quickly than those evaluated on an inpatient basis in remote facilities [see § 5.03(b)(1)]. Despite all these developments, however, unnecessary hospitalization persists [see § 6.04(a)(b)].

(e)   Adjudication of Competency

Wherever performed, the clinical evaluation produces results that are very important to the legal system. Determining whether a person should be tried or instead hospitalized or released may depend heavily on clinical opinion. It must be emphasized, however, that the determination of competency is a legal, not a clinical, decision. The clinician simply offers an opinion; the court decides. As one commentary has observed:

> [M]edical opinion about the defendant's condition should be only one of the factors relevant to the determination [of competency]. A defendant's abilities must be measured against the specific demands trial will make upon him and psychiatrists have little familiarity with either

trial procedure or the complexities of a particular indictment.[57]

Some appellate courts have emphasized this point as well. One federal court of appeals noted, for instance, that

> [t]he chief value of an expert's testimony in this field, as in all other fields, rests upon the material from which his opinion is fashioned and the reasoning by which he progresses from his material to his conclusion. . . . The conclusions, the inferences, from the facts, are for the trier of the facts.[58]

Unfortunately, many trial courts appear to abdicate their role as decisionmaker too readily. State statutes usually call for a court hearing on the issue of competency, but these proceedings rarely occur. For instance, 59% of North Carolina judges reported that they typically did not hold a formal hearing to assess the defendant's competency; rather, they relied on the clinicians' reported conclusions.[59] To some extent, the dearth of hearings reflects the parties' willingness to stipulate to the results of the clinical examination, but that fact does not excuse the lack of court review: In the analogous context of plea bargains, for example, the court must still approve the plea agreement despite its acceptance by the prosecution and the defense.[60] Furthermore, even if a hearing is held, it is likely to be perfunctory. Studies in a number of jurisdictions show judge–clinician agreement to be greater than 90%.[61] In fact, the clearest conclusion that can be reached about the class of incompetent defendants is that its composition depends almost entirely on clinical opinions. That is, whomever examining mental health professionals characterize as incompetent is likely ultimately to be found incompetent.

Presumably, conclusory reliance on diagnosis or unsubstantiated opinion will exacerbate the tendency on the part of courts and lawyers to avoid investigating the competency issue; this abdication, in turn, will ill serve defendants, who deserve a legal, not a clinical, determination of competency. Thus, clinicians should attempt to avoid offering legal conclusions about competency, or, if the court orders otherwise, should couch their conclusions in cautious terms [see § 18.05]. Moreover, they should include in their reports and testimony descriptive details about defendants' functioning that will enable the court to reach its own opinions on the issue [see, e.g., sample reports in § 19.02].

If these admonitions are followed, the evidence presented on the competency issue will occasionally fail to point to a clear conclusion. In such situations, the jurisdiction's rule with respect to which side bears the burden of proof may play an important role because when evidence is in "equipoise," the party bearing the burden of proof loses. In *Medina v. California*,[62] the Supreme Court upheld the constitutionality of a California statute that created a presumption of competency and placed the burden of proving incompetency on the party raising the question (which in *Medina* was the defendant, who was charged with capital murder). The Court conceded that "an impaired defendant might be limited in his ability to assist counsel in demonstrating incompetence" but noted in support of its holding that this instability "can, in and of itself, constitute probative evidence of incompetence." It also asserted that "defense counsel will often have the best-informed view of the defendant's ability to participate in his defense," thus justifying placement of the burden on the defense. As Justice Blackmun's dissent pointed out, however, at least when the defendant has been hospitalized for treatment, the state and its experts have better access to evidence of mental state than the defense counsel, who in any event is not likely to have as great an impact on the judge or the jury as the experts. A better reason for placing the burden on the party raising incompetency is society's and the individual's interests in avoiding delay due to unnecessary competency evaluations and hospitalization; this placement of the burden might also deter malingering and encourage a more positive attitude on the part of the defendant toward treatment.[63]

Medina does not *require* the approach taken in California. Although it would probably be unconstitutional to make the defendant bear the burden of proving competence (given *Drope* and *Pate*), the state could be required to prove its case regardless of whether it is arguing that the defendant is competent or incompetent. However, for the reasons suggested above, the California statute probably arrives at the best solution.

6.04.   Disposition of the Incompetent Defendant

If the court finds the defendant competent, the criminal process resumes. If the defendant is adjudicated incompetent, however, criminal proceedings are suspended. In some of these cases, particularly if the defendant is charged with a nonserious offense, the charges may be dropped (or, in the alternative, *nolle prossed*), in exchange for the defendant seeking treatment as a civil patient. If the criminal proceeding is not short-circuited through an arrangement of this type, the defendant is often committed to the public mental health system for treatment. This section examines the latter disposition, including possible ways of improving current practice.

(a)   *The Rule of* Jackson v. Indiana

The stated purpose of treating the person found incompetent to stand trial is to restore competency so that trial may resume. Until the early 1970s, however, commitment of incompetent individuals often simply meant long-term or even lifetime confinement in a state maximum security unit, with treatment being only a secondary objective.[64] These individuals were literally forgotten by the court system, despite the fact that they were neither tried for nor convicted of a crime.

In 1972, however, the United States Supreme Court decided *Jackson v. Indiana.*[65] In *Jackson,* the Court confronted the case of a deaf-mute defendant charged with two counts of petty theft who had been found incompetent to stand trial and hospitalized "for treatment." Because of his underlying mental condition, he was unlikely ever to be restored to competency and thus faced indefinite and perhaps lifelong hospitalization. The Court found this disposition violated both the equal protection and due process guarantees of the Fourteenth Amendment. Equal protection was violated because Indiana accorded other nonconvicted persons who were involuntarily hospitalized (i.e., those subjected to civil commitment) significantly more procedural protections than people such as Jackson. More important, Jackson's disposition violated the due process clause because it did not rationally relate to the state's avowed interest—

restoration of competency. Accordingly, the Court held:

> A person charged by a State with a criminal offense who is committed solely on account of his incapacity to proceed to trial cannot be held more than a reasonable period of time necessary to determine whether there is a substantial probability that he will attain the capacity in the foreseeable future. If it is determined that this is not the case, then the State must either institute the customary civil commitment proceedings that would be required to commit indefinitely another citizen or release the defendant.[66]

This language means that the state may not commit a person on incompetency grounds unless there is a "substantial probability" that competency will be restored and even then may do so only for a "reasonable period of time" during which restoration is attempted. If, after this period of time, restoration of competency has not occurred, the state may detain the individual in a hospital only upon a finding of mental disability and danger to self or others, using the standards and procedures provided for in its civil commitment laws.

Like most of the Court's decisions in this area, however, *Jackson* offers only a general guideline. The Court did not define what it meant by "substantial probability" or "reasonable period of time." Stone has suggested that in the vast majority of cases six months is sufficient to determine whether the defendant can be restored to competency.[67] Others have agreed, on the ground that "positive responses to medication will occur relatively quickly, if they are to occur at all."[68] For defendants who have developmental disabilities, habilitation may take longer, but for many of these individuals restoration may not be possible, in which case *Jackson* dictates civil commitment or release.

As a result of the *Jackson* decision, many states have revamped their statutes, to limit the length of time that an individual may be confined as incompetent to stand trial. Yet by 1994—more than 20 years after the decision—32 states still had not required periodic judicial review of those found incompetent. Even more significantly, 28 states and the District of Columbia allowed confinement of these people for a period well exceeding what is "reasonable," at least if Stone and other commentators are to be believed. About half these states place no time limit whatever on the confinement of those found incompetent, whereas the rest tie it either to the maximum sentence that could have been received had conviction occurred or to some arbitrary period (e.g., five years in Florida) bearing no relationship to the time needed to restore someone to competency or to determine that they are not restorable.[69]

Another issue left unresolved after *Jackson* is the appropriate disposition of criminal charges pending against a person found unrestorably incompetent. The *Jackson* Court refused to hold that such charges should be dismissed. Thus, in some states the charges of defendants who have not been restored at the end of a "reasonable time" are dismissed "without prejudice" (meaning they can be reinstituted) or not dismissed at all.[70] The practical import of these practices may be that even if the unrestorable person is converted to "civil" status via civil commitment, he or she may continue to be confined in a secure "forensic" facility and provided with fewer privileges. The criminal label may also make staff and courts more willing than would otherwise be the case to extend civil commitment on dangerousness grounds.[71]

(b)　Inappropriate Hospitalization

States have not only failed to impose limits on the length of time an incompetent defendant may be subjected to involuntary treatment but have also ignored concerns about where that treatment takes place. Just as those subject to competency evaluation are often unnecessarily hospitalized, those found incompetent as a result of those evaluations may be needlessly confined. Indeed, many jurisdictions continue to authorize *automatic* commitment of an individual found incompetent; a finding that inpatient hospitalization is necessary is not required.[72] In addition, as Steadman found:

> Overall, for most incompetent defendants, particularly for those who are not indicted, mental hospitals are simply an alternative place to do time. This is particularly true for the unindicted defendants because so few are subsequently convicted. Just over half of the indicted defendants are eventually convicted. Many do get and

serve additional prison time, but many others are given "time-served" sentences in recognition of the length of time they were hospitalized. The detention times of these incompetent defendants make a much stronger case for the use of this diversion as an easy way for the state to detain defendants in very secure facilities without the ordeal of prosecution. [C]ertainly . . . it appears that the length of time most of these defendants are off the street is quite similar to what would have resulted had they remained in jail.[73]

One proposal to eliminate the problem of inappropriate hospitalization comes from the ABA, which proposes that inpatient treatment of an incompetent defendant be permitted only if the court determines by clear and convincing evidence that no less restrictive facility exists.[74] The ABA also recommends that periodic redetermination of the defendant's competency occur at intervals not to exceed 90 days.[75] These proposals have much merit, particularly in keeping the attention of the courts, counsel, and those charged with treatment focused on the issues of competency and the necessity of hospitalization.

(c) Trying the Incompetent Defendant

The various problems that persist after *Jackson* arise from a trilemma described by Roesch and Golding:

> [I]f [the state] tries and punishes the defendant despite his lack of competency to stand trial, he has been denied due process; if it commits him until he is competent to stand trial, which if he is permanently incompetent, he will never be, he has in effect been punished without trial; and if it finds him incompetent to stand trial yet is not allowed to commit him, he may as a practical matter have been given carte blanche to commit other crimes.[76]

Of particular concern to civil libertarians is the second prong of the trilemma—the fact that protecting the defendant's constitutional right to due process by precluding a trial when he or she is found incompetent may paradoxically result in depriving the defendant of other, perhaps equally valuable rights. As one commentator has observed:

Unlike the mentally competent defendant, the accused found incompetent to stand trial may never have his day in court, particularly if he is permanently incompetent. Effectively lost are his rights to jury trial, to confront witnesses, to call witnesses in his own behalf, to take the stand on his own behalf, and to have his guilt determined beyond a reasonable doubt. Arguably, loss of such rights doesn't follow logically from a mere finding of incompetency to stand trial.[77]

Although many jurisdictions permit incompetent defendants to contest issues that do not require the participation of the defendant (e.g., the sufficiency of the indictment), these provisions apply to very few defendants.

One way of breaking this logjam is to try the incompetent individual. For example, Burt and Morris would allow a six-month commitment of an incompetent individual.[78] At the expiration of that period, the state either would have to dismiss the charges, with continuing hospitalization available only through civil commitment, or would have to proceed to trial on guilt or innocence. In the latter instance, analogous to the *Wilson* requirements for trial of defendants with amnesia [see § 6.02(c)], the state would be required to assist the defendant in compensating for the difficulties resulting from disability. For example, (1) the prosecution would have to provide the defense with full pretrial discovery; (2) the prosecution would have to meet the "beyond a reasonable doubt" standard in all phases of the proceeding (including, e.g., when contesting a defendant's motion for a directed verdict of acquittal, which is normally dismissed once the prosecution meets a much lesser burden of proof); (3) a corroborating eyewitness would have to establish some or all elements of the alleged offense; (4) special instructions would be given the jury; and (5) procedural rules governing postconviction relief would be less stringent when new evidence is discovered that was unavailable at trial because of the defendant's incompetence.[79]

The ABA, in contrast, has put forth three alternative solutions to the problem of the permanently incompetent individual, all of which stop short of the Burt and Morris proposal permitting conviction of such a person.[80] The first approach simply establishes a time limit within which the court must hold a hearing to determine whether the defendant is permanently incompetent. The hearing must be held either when the treating professional reports permanent incompetency, or at the expiration of the maximum time of sentence for the crime charged, or five years from the date of adjudication of incompetence, whichever comes first. If found to be permanently incompetent, the defendant could be confined only through involuntary civil commitment. This proposal, similar to the law in many states today, has the advantage of establishing a specific limit to the state's authority to confine an individual as incompetent to stand trial (albeit, for reasons noted above, a limit that is unreasonably long).

The second alternative distinguishes between felonies involving the causation or threat of serious bodily harm and minor offenses. If the defendant is charged with a minor crime and is judged permanently incompetent, the charges are dismissed at the expiration of the maximum time of sentence for the crime charged, or 12 to 18 months from the date of adjudication of incompetence, whichever occurs first. The defendant charged with a serious felony, on the other hand, would be subjected to a hearing on guilt or innocence, either upon adjudication of permanent incompetence or after the expiration of 18 months from the initial adjudication of incompetence.[81] The hearing would be conducted like a criminal trial: It would be adversarial in nature, rules of evidence and constitutional trial rights would apply, and a jury would hear the case. If the defendant were found not guilty, a judgment of acquittal would be entered disposing of the criminal charges. Further confinement would be possible only through civil commitment. The individual found "guilty" would remain in incompetent status, and the criminal charges would remain pending. As the commentary to the proposal points out, prosecutors are generally opposed to this "innocent only" trial because a finding of guilt would not constitute conviction and, assuming a later return to competence, a trial on guilt or innocence would be necessary.[82] This alternative does, however, have the merit of at least allowing for disposition of serious charges if the defendant is found not guilty, as well as permitting the dismissal of nonserious charges.

The third alternative, the one officially adopted by the ABA, is much the same as the second

but differs in one critical respect. If, at the "factual guilt" hearing, the prosecutor has proved beyond a reasonable doubt that the defendant has committed the offense charged, the defendant may be subject to special-commitment proceedings. This alternative would not allow punishment of the defendant through incarceration in prison but would recognize the societal "right to greater scrutiny of the defendant from perspectives of treatment, incapacitation and security, and release, while also permitting the defendant to obtain a judgment of acquittal in those instances where the prosecution cannot prove guilt."[83] Although the standards on special commitment are not specific in terms of the locus of such confinement,[84] the drafters would apparently, at a minimum, allow for use of secure facilities and lengthier periods of confinement than would be allowed for the civilly committed; in other words, the commitment would be analogous to the type of detention typically reserved for insanity acquittees [see §10.10(c)].

Given the interest of the ABA and a growing recognition that the *Jackson* decision provided only incomplete relief to dispositional problems faced by incompetent defendants, legislatures should begin considering one of the aforementioned approaches. In the interim, lawyers and clinicians need to acquaint themselves with the consequences of adjudications of incompetency in their own jurisdictions. As this discussion has suggested, these consequences extend far beyond temporary suspension of trial and may include lengthy hospitalization and an indefinite period in which defendants are charged with but are not tried for a criminal offense.

(d)   Incompetent Defendants' Right to Refuse Medication

If left to their own devices, some defendants might *choose* to remain unrestored, for a number of reasons. Least justifiably, they may simply refuse treatment in the hopes of avoiding trial. Or, as with Donald in Case Study 6.1, they may honestly abhor the side effects of the treatment proposed by the state. A more tactical reason is the negative effect the calmer, more organized demeanor of a treated defendant can have on the potential success of an insanity defense, which is commonly raised in cases involving defendants with mental disability. Indeed, some commentators have suggested that one reason the insanity defense is seldom successful before a jury is that the defendant seems "normal" at trial.[85]

Nonetheless, most courts that have addressed the issue have held that defendants found incompetent to stand trial have no right to refuse appropriate treatment.[86] Whether the Supreme Court would agree has been thrown into some doubt by *Riggins v. Nevada*,[87] in which the Court stated that, given its side effects, involuntary medication of a defendant during trial is not permitted "absent a finding of overriding justification and a determination of medical appropriateness." The Court went on to suggest that this test would be met if "treatment with antipsychotic medication was medically appropriate and, considering less intrusive alternatives, essential for the sake of [the defendant's] own safety or the safety of others." At the same time, as discussed in § 6.02(d), it held that *over*medication which adversely affected a defendant's ability to assist at trial did not meet this test.

Ultimately, however, the *Riggins* decision left open whether the state may forcibly administer treatment that is a "medically appropriate" way of ensuring competence. The Court's eventual answer to this question is likely to be no. Indeed, given its earlier decision in *Washington v. Harper*,[88] the Court appears to believe that even *competent* patients have virtually no constitutional right to refuse medication [see § 11.03(b)]. A criminal defendant who has been found incompetent, albeit incompetent to stand trial rather than incompetent to make a treatment decision, is even less likely to have such a right. Perhaps the Court would view the state's interest in restoring a defendant to competency to be weaker than its interest in ensuring the safety of others (the interest relied on in *Harper* and noted in *Riggins*). But, even if it does, the individual interests to be weighed against the state's desire to restore (e.g., side effects or the need to present an "insane" demeanor at trial) may themselves be relatively weak. If the medication is "medically appropriate" and the "least intrusive alternative," as required by *Riggins*, side effects will be minimized. And the argument that a desire to appear "crazy" at trial

should permit refusal of medication is very unlikely to persuade the Court. The state, it will be remembered, has an independent interest in maintaining the competency requirement [see § 6.02(a)]. Furthermore, other, arguably better ways of reconciling the competency requirement and the defendant's desire to show the factfinder an "insane" demeanor exist. These include providing a videotape of the defendant in an unmedicated state, allowing expert testimony describing that state, or giving instructions cautioning against drawing conclusions from the defendant's medicated demeanor.[89]

In any event, allowing defendant "waiver" of the competency requirement is extremely problematic, as demonstrated by the New Hampshire Supreme Court's attempt to implement this idea. In *State v. Hayes*,[90] that court permitted incompetent defendants to appear at trial without medication, provided that when they decide to do so they are medicated and competent to make such a decision. In those cases in which such a procedure is appropriate, the period between the time that defendants are taken off medication and trial is to equal the period between their last medication before the offense and the offense itself. Putting aside problems with a waiver made when the events at trial cannot be anticipated, this approach is questionable ethically (because it requires taking a person suffering from psychosis off needed medication) and practically (because reactions to being taken off medication are idiosyncratic and not related solely to the duration of the unmedicated state).

In short, the United States Supreme Court is likely to agree with the courts that withhold a right to refuse from defendants found incompetent to stand trial. However, the Court's decisions do accord criminal defendants some important protections. In particular, *Riggins* clearly establishes that medication used for restoration purposes must be "medically appropriate." Perhaps even more significantly, it suggests that the chosen treatment must be the "least intrusive" means of achieving the state's ends. These requirements should reduce unnecessary medication. At the same time, they may beneficially force the state to *use* medication when it is the least intrusive medically appropriate option. For instance, in many jurisdictions a defendant who is restored to competency at a hospital and sent back to the community for trial is then allowed to decompensate, either because the jail has no clinician who can prescribe medication or because jail clinicians believe they have no authority to administer the drugs.[91] This situation results in harm to the defendant and frustration for the courts, which must recommit the defendant to the more intrusive inpatient hospital setting for further treatment. The reading of *Riggins* advocated here might require the state, as a constitutional matter, to continue providing medication in the community once the restored defendant is sent there.

6.05.   Research Relating to Competency Evaluations

Since 1970, a substantial literature has developed about the nature of the competency evaluation.[92] This literature has examined several specific topics, which are discussed here in turn: the frequency with which the question of incompetency is raised; the characteristics of defendants found incompetent; and the reliability and validity of competency evaluations generally. The reliability and validity of structured interview formats for competency are considered in the following section.

(a) Frequency of Competency Evaluations and Findings

Surveys of public defenders indicate that defense lawyers have concerns about their clients' competency in about 10–15% of their cases.[93] However, motions for evaluation are made in fewer than half these cases of doubted competence.[94] Apparently, attorneys are often able to utilize other methods of resolving their concerns about their clients' competence, including consultation with other attorneys or other third parties (e.g., the client's probation officer), or involvement of third parties (e.g., family members) in important case decisions.[95] Nonetheless, certain types of cases typically result in referral. One study comparing referred and nonreferred cases found that the most important predictor of attorneys' deci-

sions to refer was disorganized speech by the defendant.[96] Pressures from defendants' families and strategic considerations were other factors influencing decisions to raise the competency issue.

Despite the fact that many cases of doubted competence do not result in a motion for evaluation, competency still appears to be, in numerical terms, the most significant criminal issue in forensic mental health. Data compiled in the late 1970s indicated that restoration of competency was the most frequent reason for commitment to state forensic hospitals, with 6,420 such commitments nationally.[97] When admissions for *evaluation* of competency are added, the figures become much larger. Roesch and Golding reviewed ten studies reporting the frequency of competency evaluations and findings of incompetency.[98] Averaging the findings across studies, they suggested that only about 30% of defendants referred for competency evaluations are actually found incompetent. Extrapolating from this percentage, competency evaluations in 1978 might well have numbered greater than 20,000. Although these numbers are based on old research, the available evidence indicates that, if anything, competency evaluations have increased significantly in the 1990s.[99]

It is important to note, however, that the percentage found incompetent in the studies reviewed by Roesch and Golding varies widely across jurisdictions (1.2–77.0%) and within jurisdictions across time. The variance appears to result from the fact that in many jurisdictions only one or two hospitals perform forensic evaluations. Consequently, when staff changes in these facilities, a striking change can occur in the proportion of defendants found incompetent. The higher figures for incompetency findings seem to result when clinicians equate incompetency to stand trial with psychosis, or when incompetency is used essentially as a dispositional device for defendants believed to be in need of treatment. When more rigorous (i.e., more valid) evaluation standards and procedures are applied, the percentage found incompetent is typically less than 10%.

Whether the proportion of those found incompetent is 10% or 30% of evaluated defendants, it is clear that the question of incompetency is raised much more frequently than it is answered in the affirmative. In short, as suggested earlier in this chapter [see § 6.03(c)], many defendants are referred for evaluation needlessly. This fact has provided incentive not only to develop outpatient evaluation systems [see §§ 5.02, 5.03] but also to encourage the development of the screening instruments described later in this chapter [§ 6.06].

(b) Characteristics of Incompetent Defendants

The most extensive case study of defendants found to be incompetent was undertaken by Steadman,[100] who conducted a three-year follow-up of 539 males charged with felonies and found incompetent between September 1971 and August 1972. Steadman summarized the demographic characteristics of these defendants as representative of "marginal individuals with much less than average education and few useful job skills. Most have few community ties, either through employment or family. An unusually high proportion have never married."[101] These defendants also usually had a long history of shuttling between the criminal justice and mental health systems.[102] No less than 81% of the sample had been previously hospitalized in psychiatric facilities and more than two-thirds of the study group had been previously arrested.

Unfortunately, Steadman did not compare the study group with a control defendant population. Thus, although the incompetent defendants were "marginal" relative to the general population, whether they differed appreciably from the competent defendant population is unknown. A more recent study supported by the MacArthur Foundation Research Network on Mental Health and the Law has rectified this deficiency.[103] This research looked not only at persons admitted to hospitals in Virginia and Florida for competence restoration but also at two comparison groups—randomly selected (unscreened) pretrial jail detainees and pretrial jail detainees receiving psychiatric treatment for issues other than competence restoration. Table 6.2 displays demographic and social history findings for these three groups; Table 6.3 displays mental status and clinical features.

Table 6.2
Demographic and Social History Characteristics of Three Groups of Pretrial Defendants

Measure	Group HI ($n = 159$)	JT ($n = 113$)	JU ($n = 94$)	Test and significance
Age (years)				
M	34.2	32.4	29.9	$F(2,362) = 7.28$ $p < .001$
Education (years)				
M	11.25	11.79	11.45	n.s.
Ethnicity				
Nonwhite (%)	37%	32%	28%	n.s.
Prior mental health treatment				
Inpatient (%)	79%	64%	10%	$\chi^2(2,365) = 119.45$ $p < .001$
Outpatient (%)	77%	64%	15%	$\chi^2(2,365) = 97.03$ $p < .001$
Prior arrests				
M	1.7	1.7	1.8	n.s.

Note. HI, hospitalized incompetent; JT, pretrial jail detainees receiving psychiatric treatment for reasons other than competence restoration; JU, unscreened pretrial jail detainees.

Table 6.3
Mental Status and Clinical Features of Three Groups of Pretrial Defendants

Measure	Group			Test and significance
	HI ($n = 159$)	JT ($n = 113$)	JU ($n = 94$)	
Prorated Verbal IQ[a]				
M	87.97	92.37	90.39	$F(2,363) = 4.32$ $p < .001$
BPRS total[b]				
M	37.02	38.95	28.72	$F(2,357) = 50.98$ $p < .001$
BPRS subscales				
Psychoticism (M)	6.60	5.71	3.74	$F(2,358) = 36.87$ $p < .001$
Depression (M)	7.58	10.84	7.57	$F(2,358) = 39.96$ $p < .001$
Hostility (M)	6.58	5.79	4.41	$F(2,358) = 23.38$ $p < .001$
Withdrawal (M)	5.89	6.8	5.11	$F(2,357) = 9.96$ $p < .001$
Chart diagnosis				
Schizophrenia (%)	65%	24%	2%	$\chi^2(6,366) = 337.7$ $p < .001$
Affective disorder (%)	28%	59%	0%	
Other diagnosis (%)	7%	17%	7%	

Note. Abbreviations as in Table 6.2.
[a]Based on three subscales of Wechsler Adult Intelligence Scale—Revised.
[b]Brief Psychiatric Rating Scale (18-item, anchored version).

Table 6.2 reveals that although no difference between groups was found in terms of mean years of education or mean number of arrests, the hospitalized incompetent (HI) group members had a more significant history of prior psychiatric treatment, both inpatient and outpatient, than the jail-treated (JT) and jail-unscreened (JU) groups. Turning to Table 6.3 on the clinical data, one notes further differences. First, the HI group had a lower prorated mean verbal IQ score than the other two groups (although the measurement of IQ for the HI group may have been less valid because the prevalence of schizophrenia and active psychotic symptoms may have depressed IQ test performance). Second, although the JT and HI groups did not differ in their total scores on the Brief Psychiatric Rating Scale (BPRS), the pattern of symptoms on BPRS subscales was different for these two groups. Consistent with the greater prevalence of schizophrenia in the HI group, higher scores were found on the BPRS psychoticism subscale. The mean BPRS depression score, on the other hand, was higher among JT inmates, for whom affective disorder more often appeared as a chart diagnosis. These findings regarding diagnosis and symptom patterns are consistent with Roesch and Golding's study of defendants referred for evaluation of competency; 87% of their incompetent defendants were diagnosed as psychotic or, less frequently, mentally retarded, but only 15% of those found competent had such a diagnosis.[104]

In short, the data reveal that persons adjudicated incompetent to stand trial differ from other groups of pretrial defendants on a number of important variables, including history of hospitalization and outpatient mental health treatment, IQ, psychoticism, and depression.

(c)   Quality of Competency Evaluations

Research on the process of forensic evaluation itself is of more direct utility to forensic clinicians and lawyers. How much confidence can be placed in the opinions derived from evaluations of competency to stand trial? That is, how reliable and valid are such opinions? What level of expertise in the mental health professions is required before adequate reliability and validity can be achieved? How intensive or broad does the evaluation need to be to achieve adequate reliability and validity?

A sensible hypothesis would be that these evaluations are more reliable and valid than many other types of forensic evaluations. As noted in § 6.02(b), the competency assessment is *functional* and *present-oriented*; the most pertinent questions are the defendant's ability to assist counsel and to understand the nature of the legal proceedings. There is usually no need to speculate about the defendant's state of mind at some point in the past or future, and issues such as diagnosis and treatment remain in the background unless and until it is determined that a significant impairment in competence-related abilities exists.[105] Thus, high reliability and validity of evaluation results can be expected as long as the evaluators understand their task.

The available research substantiates these hypotheses. A considerable number of studies indicate that competence evaluations are typically highly reliable. Exemplary of this research is Poythress and Stock's examination of interclinician agreement on a series of 44 cases at the Center for Forensic Psychiatry in Michigan.[106] Pairs of clinical psychologists interviewed defendants and then reached opinions without consultation within pairs; 100% agreement was reached as to the ultimate opinion on competence. Similarly high reliability has been reported by several other investigators.[107]

Other research indicates that high reliability occurs even when the evaluators are not mental health professionals, as long as they are given a structure for the interviews and an explanation of the concept of competence to stand trial. Roesch and Golding reported 90% agreement between trained laypersons (members of the local Association for Mental Health) and hospital-based forensic clinicians.[108] Golding, Roesch, and Schreiber

observed 97% agreement between lawyers and clinicians on global assessments of competence to stand trial, although there were varying emphases in their opinion formation (lawyers attended more to "crazy" thinking; clinicians placed greater weight on communication skills and recall ability).[109] In short, reliability tends to be high, without regard to the disciplinary background of the examiners.

However, it should be noted that all these studies used samples of examiners who had been trained together, and all the studies except that of Poythress and Stock involved use of a structured interview format. Consequently, it is possible that "real-world" reliability may be lower than in the reported studies, especially if reliability is compared across evaluation centers. At the same time, it is clear that examiners with a common framework for assessment can easily attain high reliability in competence evaluations, and that this level of reliability does not depend on a particular disciplinary background.

The data with respect to the validity of competency evaluations are less clear. In view of the fact that judges seldom challenge clinicians' opinions as to a defendant's competency [see § 6.03(e)], there is no independent criterion available in the legal system against which to compare clinicians' opinions. Therefore, researchers have had to examine the validity of competency opinions through study of the kinds of variables that predict ultimate opinion,[110] comparison with "blue-ribbon" experts' judgments,[111] and experts' analyses of report quality.[112] Early evidence from these types of studies suggest that clinicians frequently, and erroneously, directly translated diagnoses of psychosis and mental retardation into a finding of incompetency.[113] However, more recent studies, most of them examining the correlates of clinicians opinions regarding defendants' trial competence, have been more encouraging. For instance, a study involving 261 defendants admitted to an Oklahoma State Hospital for pretrial evaluation reported that clinical symptoms and scores on a standard competency screening measure accounted for most of the independent variance in clinicians' judgments regarding competence.[114] A meta-analysis of 30 studies comparing competent and incompetent defendants revealed that the factors most strongly related to clinical findings of incompetency were (1) poor performance on psychological tests or interviews that specifically evaluate competence-related skills, (2) psychotic diagnosis, and (3) severe symptoms of psychopathology.[115] Taken in sum, these studies suggest that examiners trained in the nature of the competency construct typically achieve high validity.

Not only are evaluations of competency to stand trial usually highly reliable and potentially highly valid, but these levels of psychometric rigor can be achieved in a relatively brief interview.[116] It is clear that quality of evaluation is not sacrificed when trained community-based clinicians are used; indeed, quality may even improve.[117] Community clinics are more likely than state hospitals to have easy access to important sources of information (e.g., the defense attorney), and they are less likely to be staffed by foreign-born, foreign-trained physicians who may have difficulty communicating with the client.[118]

6.06.   Structured Evaluation Formats

Over the years, a number of interview formats have been developed to assist in the competency evaluation. Some are screening instruments, designed to facilitate retention in the community of those who are clearly not incompetent. Others are more elaborate devices meant to guide the entire competency evaluation.

Robey was one of the first to take a less "diagnostic" and more "functional" approach to the evaluation of trial competence.[119] His competency checklist, published in 1965, was soon followed by other unstructured, menu-type instruments meant to guide clinicians' inquiries in competence evaluations.[120] The field quickly moved beyond the unstructured interview guide, however. A major research project funded by the National Institute of Mental Health (NIMH) yielded the first two formal "tests" for use by mental health professionals, the Competency Screening Test (CST)[121] and the Competency to Stand Trial Assessment Instrument (CAI).[122] Subsequent instruments offered to the field have included the Interdisciplinary Fitness Interview (IFI),[123] the Georgia Court Competency Test (GCCT),[124] the

Competence Assessment for Standing Trial for Defendants with Mental Retardation (CAST-MR)[125] and the Computer-Assisted Competency Instrument (CADCOMP).[126] We offer a brief description and critique of each of these instruments[127] and then discuss a new instrument developed by the MacArthur Foundation Research Network on Mental Health and the Law, the MacArthur Competence Assessment Tool— Criminal Adjudication (MacCAT-CA).

(a)   Competency Screening Test

The CST (the instrument used in Case Study 6.1) is a 22-item sentence-completion test, to be used in screening defendants for competency. Administration and scoring are both standardized. Each item is scored on a scale of 0–2, with 2 meant to represent a sentence completion showing a high level of legal comprehension and 0 representing a low level.[128] Administration time is about 25 minutes.[129] Representative items include: "When I go to court the lawyer will . . .," "When they say a man is innocent until proven guilty, I . . . ," and "What concerns Fred most about his lawyer. . . ." The test developers empirically established a cutoff score of 20; that is, defendants who score below 20 are to be "screened in" for a more comprehensive evaluation.[130] The developers also intended that the comprehensive evaluation, if necessary, would utilize the CAI, the second instrument developed by NIMH (discussed below).

The CST has been the subject of a number of empirical studies, with mixed results. As shown in Table 6.4, which summarizes the psychometric properties of a number of competence assessment measures, the CST has the lowest mean predictive validity index of any of the instruments shown. However, a more detailed look at the validity studies reveals that most of the "mistakes" are false positives (i.e., competent persons labeled incompetent).[131] If any error occurs, this is probably the type one would want for a competency screening instrument, such as the CST purports to be. At least in serious cases, more harm results from prematurely labeling defendants competent and subjecting them to a trial they may not understand than from subjecting defen-

Table 6.4
Summary of Psychometric Properties: Selected Instruments for Competence to Stand Trial

Instrument	Interscorer reliability		Test–retest reliability	Internal consistency[a]	Predictive validity[b]	Concurrent validity[c]
	Intraclass R	Pearson r				
CST	.89–.94 (2)[d]	.68–.95 (4)	Not reported	.74–.85 (3)	Mean r = .37 (11)	r = .56–.76 (2, GCCT) r = .69 (1, CAI) r = .03 (1, IFI)
CAI	90% agree (1) .87		Not reported	Not reported	Mean r = .52 (2)	r = .69 (1, CST) r = .26 (1, IFI)
GCCT	.96 (2)	.96 (1)	.79–.84 (2)	.80–.88 (3)	Mean r = .42 (4)	r = .56–.76 (2, CST)
CADCOMP	88% agree (1) Kappa = .71 (1)		Not reported	.47–.90 (1)	r = .55 (1)	Across 8 scales, range r = −.56 to .11 (1, CST)[e] r = −.57 to .11 (1, GCCT)[e]
IFI	97% agree (1) Kappa = .93 (1)		Not reported	Not reported	r = .42 (1)	r = .26 (1, CAI) r = .03 (1, CST)

Note. Data from Robert A. Nicholson, Current Methods for Assessing Criminal Competencies (Tables 3–7) (paper presented at the Annual Convention of the American Psychiatric Association, San Francisco, 1993). Reproduced with permission.

[a]Coefficient alpha.

[b]Correlation with clinical opinion regarding competency.

[c]Correlation with alternative measure of competence.

[d]( ) indicates the number of studies in which statistic has been measured.

[e]CADCOMP scales are reverse scored; therefore, high negative correlations indicate good agreement with alternative measures of competence.

dants who are competent to a more thorough evaluation.

At the same time, the false-positive rate should be sufficiently low that the instrument prevents unnecessary full evaluations, especially if they are to take place in the hospital. Unfortunately, the CST's false-positive rate may be undesirably high (ranging from 14.3% to 28.6%). Probably the best explanation for this finding is the CST's apparent bias against defendants with a negative view of the legal system.[132] For example, in response to the stem "Jack felt that the judge . . ." "was fair" is a 2-point (competent) answer, but "was unjust" is a 0-point (incompetent) answer. Similarly, a 0-point response to "What concerns Fred most about his lawyer . . ." is "is tardiness." Presumably, the authors were attempting to differentiate defendants based on their understanding of the way the system *is supposed* to work. However, it has been our experience that defendants who score in the false positive ranges on the CST tend to be either cynical about the system (perhaps correctly in some instances) or simply depressed and expecting (again often accurately) an unfavorable disposition of their cases.

A second problem with the CST, which may create false negatives as well as false positives, is that investigators have not been able to establish a factor structure that is stable across different defendant samples.[133] In other words, it is not clear that the CST adequately samples relevant competence-related abilities; it yields simply a number rather than a descriptive appraisal of different psycholegal abilities. This aspect of the CST may also raise concerns about the instrument's face validity with legal professionals.

Turning again to Table 6.4, one notes that the reliability of the CST is appreciably better than its validity. Yet data informally collected by Melton suggest that the reliability of the CST is also problematic, at least without further clarification of scoring rules. Twenty-seven community mental health clinicians were asked to score three CST protocols as part of their training in forensic assessment. Item-by-item agreement ranged from 36% to 100%, with mean agreement of only 73.3%. Admittedly, the participants in this study were inexperienced in the use of the CST, and the scoring was presented as a training exercise. As a result, items about which the participants were unsure were sometimes left blank, deflating the level of agreement. Nonetheless, the data raise a question about the reliability of the CST when used as a general screening device by persons without substantial training in its use, and when supplementary scoring rules (beyond those in the CST manual) have not been agreed upon.

On the positive side, the research shows that the CST does accurately screen out a relatively high number of individuals (usually over 50% of a sample that has identifiable mental problems). This relatively high true negative rate and the test's ease of administration suggest that it bears promise as a screening instrument. Until there is further development and evaluation of the scoring system, however, it should be used only with great caution in clinical decisionmaking. It is unwise at this point to use a CST score as the primary basis of a decision as to whether a defendant's competency should be further explored.

(b)   Competency Assessment Instrument

For comprehensive evaluations of competency to stand trial, the McGarry group developed the CAI. The CAI is a semistructured interview that is scored with 5-point Likert ratings (1 = "total incapacity" to 5 = "no incapacity") on 13 functions (e.g., "appraisal of available legal defenses"; "planning of legal strategy, including guilty pleas to lesser charges where pertinent"; and "capacity to testify relevantly"). Although the CAI manual emphasizes that the weight to be given particular functions is a matter for the court to decide, it suggests that "a majority or a substantial accumulation" of scores of 3 or less may be cause for inpatient observation.[134]

Unlike the CST, the administration and scoring of the CAI is not standardized and there are no norms for interpreting scores that clinicians might assign to the various functions inquired about. As Grisso has noted, although clinical case examples are given for certain scores on each of the 13 functions/items, "[n]o specific scoring criteria are provided," and "the 13 scores are neither summed nor weighted."[135] Further, as the right-hand columns of Table 6.4 reveal, there have been few empirical studies of the CAI. Thus, whether the CAI scoring system is helpful is essentially unknown.

In light of these facts, use of the CAI scales to reach conclusions about competency is inadvisable. However, the CAI can play an important role in competency evaluations. Grisso has suggested that the CAI is probably most useful as an interview-structuring device,[136] and it has been substantially utilized in that manner.[137] Further, the CAI manual includes a large number of sample interview questions and case examples that may be helpful to clinicians learning to perform competency evaluations.[138] Finally, the 13 functions or content areas have high face validity, which may facilitate the CAI's acceptance among judges and attorneys.

(c)   Interdisciplinary Fitness Interview

One of the more tightly conceptualized competency assessment guides is the IFI, developed by Golding and Roesch[139] and evaluated by Golding, Roesch, and Schreiber.[140] The IFI is a semistructured interview format intended to be administered jointly by a mental health professional and an attorney. It requires ratings from 0 ("no or minimal incapacity") to 2 ("substantial incapacity") on 5 aspects of specific legal functioning (having to do with the *Dusky* prongs), 11 items representing psychopathology (e.g., hallucinations, amnesia, and mental retardation), and 4 items having to do with overall impressions of competency (e.g., overall fitness, rating of confidence in judgment, factors taken into account in reaching the conclusion). The raters also record, again on a scale of 0–2, the weight each particular dimension is given in the formation of the opinion. Golding and Roesch incorporated this second scale (Influence on Decision) on the assumption that the significance of a given dimension will vary with the particular facts of a defendant's case. For example, ability to maintain appropriate courtroom demeanor will be assigned a higher "influence" rating in cases in which a defendant's testimony is considered necessary for a proper defense than in cases when it will not play a crucial role. Similarly, rigid rejection of plea bargaining for irrational reasons would be insignificant if plea bargaining is not a real option.

As Table 6.4 indicates, there has been only one study published on the IFI.[141] Interviewer pairs of one clinician and one attorney used the IFI to evaluate 77 defendants in Massachusetts, on average taking 45 minutes to complete the assessment. On final judgments of competency, the interviewers agreed in 75 of the cases (97%). In those cases, 58 defendants were found to be competent and 17 to be incompetent. Item-by-item, interrater reliability between attorneys and clinicians was greatest for legal items most directly related to competency, was relatively low for legal items not related to competency, and was respectable on psychopathology items, especially with respect to delusional processes. Indeed, overall, reliability was higher for the psychopathology items than for the legal items.

These preliminary data suggest that the IFI is a time-efficient interview format that produces rich observations with high reliability. It is disappointing that no new empirical studies have appeared in the literature since the instrument was introduced in the early 1980s. However, a few observations about the IFI are possible even without such data.

The first point has to do with the Influence on Decisions scale. Although there is appeal to the notion that competency is related to the complexity of the case [see § 6.02(b)], it may be presumptuous for clinicians (or even clinicians in concert with lawyers, as contemplated by the IFI) to decide which factors are important in determining competency to stand trial. Because competency ultimately focuses on the fairness of trial, the law may require defendants to be capable of performing any (or all) psycholegal functions at some minimal level even if in a particular case the defense strategy may not require their use. The uncertainty as to the correct approach in this area illustrates the foibles of providing conclusory, ultimate-issue opinions, even on a "simple" question such as competency to stand trial. However, the second scale on the IFI at least makes the evaluators' judgments explicit, so that the hearing judge can evaluate the calculus used in the opinion.

The second observation concerns the stipulation that the IFI be administered by a mental health professional and a lawyer. As a matter of theory, this practice is commendable. As should be clear by now, the functional nature of the competency test requires the evaluator to have a firm grasp not just of the legal system but of the particular demands of the case in question. Also supporting the utility of adding lawyers' input on a routine basis is the above-reported empirical finding of a relative lack of cross-disciplinary agreement on legal issues not directly related to competency. But this structural strength of the IFI may also be its practical weakness. In our experience most attorneys have neither the time nor the inclination to observe, much less participate in, competency-to-stand-trial evaluations. Thus, these potential benefits of the IFI approach are likely to remain unfulfilled in most applications.

Even used appropriately, the IFI is probably still best characterized as an experimental instrument, given the lack of research.[142] Like the CAI, however, it may serve as a useful interview-structuring device. Further, its clear focus on relevant legal content may result in acceptance in the legal community.

(d)   Georgia Court Competency Test

The GCCT has two versions. The original GCCT consisted of 17 questions administered in a fixed sequence and grouped in six categories:[143] *(1) Picture of Court* (consisting of seven questions about a drawing of a vacant courtroom—e.g., "Where does the Judge sit?"); *(2) Functions* (consisting of five questions concerning roles and functions of key participants—e.g., "What do the witnesses do?"); *(3) Charges* (consisting of two questions— e.g., "What are you charged with?"); *(4) Helping the Lawyer* (one question: "How can you help your lawyer defend you?"); *(5) Alleged Crime* (one question: "What actually happened about the charge you are here on?"); and *(6) Consequences* (one question: "If the jury finds you guilty on this charge, what might they do to you?"). Examiners use explicit scoring criteria to assign weights to various items (from 0 to 10 points, depending on the item) to arrive at a score from 0 to 50. Points are multiplied by 2 to yield a range of 0–100. Like the CST, the GCCT was developed as a screening device to identify defendants who were obviously competent. The authors recommend further clinical examination of defendants who score 69 or below on the instrument.[144] According to Grisso, administration time is about 10 minutes.[145]

A revised, 21-item version of the GCCT was

developed at the Mississippi State Hospital (GCCT-MSH).[146] The additional items focus on the defendant's familiarity with his or her attorney ("What is your attorney's name? How can you contact him/her?") and with expectations about courtroom behavior (e.g., "What will you do during the trial?"). In revising the instrument, item weights were adjusted in order to preserve the 0–100 point range and cutoff score of 69.

Table 6.4, which includes psychometric data from studies of both versions, suggests that the GCCT is comparable with other competence measures on conventional indicia of reliability and validity. Further, the GCCT has been shown to have a stable three-factor structure that has been replicated across samples: I. General Legal Knowledge, II. Courtroom Layout, and III. Specific Legal Knowledge.[147]

These positive indicators notwithstanding, concerns have been raised about the GCCT. The most obvious is its content validity. A full one-third of the items (Picture of Court) deal with relatively cosmetic and superficial issues about "who sits where," which do not appear to tap any meaningful dimension regarding understanding of, or participation in, the legal process. As Nicholson has noted, "A major limitation of the test is that the underlying factors do not correspond clearly to the competency construct as adumbrated by statute and case law. . . . The factors do not reflect an adequate sampling of the domain of relevant abilities."[148]

(e) Computer-Assisted Competence Assessment Tool

Developed by Barnard and his colleagues at the University of Florida School of Medicine,[149] the CADCOMP consists of 272 questions that tap various content areas, including social history, psychological functioning, and legal knowledge. The items are primarily objective in format (yes/no, true/false, multiple choice) and average administration time for the CADCOMP is one to one and a half hours. Output from the program is a computer-generated, narrative report that summarizes the data provided by the defendant's self-report. The data then form the basis for further clinical interview. Developers of the CADCOMP

identified three objectives for the instrument: to "collect relevant data directly from a defendant and organize it into a concise narrative report," to have a report that would "be available to the clinician before seeing the defendant so that he/she could probe the defendant in areas that require further professional consideration," and to provide treatment teams with a measure of competence that might prove sensitive to changes over the course of treatment and thus alert them to restoration status.[150]

Additional research is needed on the CADCOMP to establish its utility for the field. The data in Table 6.4 suggest that it may hold promise. However, problems with the experimental design for the original evaluation study give rise to several concerns. The most significant flaw is the way validity was gauged. The CADCOMP's measure of predictive validity ($r = .55$) is the highest reported among competence assessment instruments.[151] However, the reported figure is almost certainly inflated because competence judgments based on the CADCOMP reports were made by the same clinician (Barnard) who provided the clinical judgments of competence to which the CADCOMP results were compared.[152] Further research is needed in which uncontaminated criteria are used to evaluate the instrument's predictive validity.

A related concern with the CADCOMP is the validity of the defendants' self-reports. Clinicians relying solely on such reports may miss areas in which defendants have problems or fail to detect denial or suppression of problems and impairments. If so, even good predictive validity (based on uncontaminated criterion judgments) would not ensure that specific problem areas would be identified by the CADCOMP procedure.

Other limitations stem from efficiency concerns. The one to one and a half hours of administration time occur *after* an assistant has administered the Wide Range Achievement Test (to yield an estimated reading level) and has oriented the defendant to the computer terminal and responding procedures. Further, as noted previously, once the CADCOMP is completed by the defendant, the clinician conducts an interview, which is of variable length depending on the extent of follow-up required. Thus, the overall length of competence evaluations using the prescribed CAD-

COMP procedure would likely exceed that currently required with the use of other instruments (e.g., the CAI and IFI).[153] It seems doubtful that most mental health professionals conducting competence evaluations in outpatient settings (e.g., jails) will be able or willing to supervise defendants in front of laptop computer screens for one to one and a half hours or to employ assistants to do so. In state hospital settings, where defendants are admitted for lengthy inpatient evaluations, the CADCOMP procedure may be more feasible. As we have noted, however, the current trend in forensic services development is away from such lengthy inpatient evaluations.

(f)   Competence Assessment for Standing Trial for Defendants with Mental Retardation

The CAST-MR was developed specifically for evaluation of persons who are mentally retarded. According to its developers, this population is not served by existing instruments for several reasons. First, open-ended questions such as those contained in conventional interview approaches (CAI, IFI) may not yield accurate results with individuals whose expressive skills may be impaired; an objective format, such as multiple-choice items, is preferable because it "reduces the demand on the respondent to answer independently."[154] Second, existing tests do not necessarily use vocabulary and syntax at an appropriate level for persons of reduced linguistic ability.[155] Third, instruments that focus on symptoms rather than concrete legal functioning are inappropriate with persons who are mentally retarded.[156]

The CAST-MR consists of 50 items in three sections, the first two of which require approximately a grade-4 reading level and the last of which is administered orally. Section I includes 25 multiple-choice items that examine defendants' understanding of basic legal terms (e.g., "What does the judge do?" [(a) defends you, (b) decides the case, (c) works for your lawyer], and "What is a felony?" [(a) a way to get off, (b) a very serious crime, (c) a person who talks in court]). Section II (15 items) utilizes the same format to explore defendants' skills to assist in their defense (e.g.,

"What if the police ask you to sign something and you don't understand it? What would you do?" [(a) refuse to talk to them, (b) sign it anyway, (c) ask to see your lawyer]). The final ten items in section III solicit narrative response from the defendant and relate to the understanding of case events (e.g., "What were you doing that caused you to be arrested?" and "Tell me what happened when the police came?"). The test manual provides scoring guidelines for each item (0, 1/2, or 1).[157]

As indicated in Table 6.4, pilot studies conducted in the development of the CAST-MR indicate that it has satisfactory psychometric properties. In particular, interscorer reliability for section III of the CAST-MR (the nonobjective, narrative section) was at acceptable levels (average agreement = 83% for ten pairs of examiners).[158] Further, face validity for CAST-MR items was established by two groups of experts, which rated the appropriateness of proposed items.[159] A subsequent validation study contrasted CAST-MR scores for four groups of defendants: group No MR (criminal defendants who were not mentally retarded, $n = 46$), group MR (criminal defendants who were mentally retarded but not referred for competency evaluation, $n = 24$), group MR-C (defendants who were mentally retarded and evaluated and recommended as competent to stand trial, $n = 12$) and group MR-I (defendants who were mentally retarded and evaluated and recommended as incompetent to stand trial, $n = 11$). Although the three groups of defendants with mental retardation did not differ significantly in terms of average IQ,[160] their mean scores were significantly different, in the appropriate directions, on all sections of the CAST-MR. A subsequent study comparing CAST-MR scores of MR-C ($n = 15$) and MR-I ($n = 20$) subjects also yielded significant differences for mean scores on sections I and III.[161]

These studies provide support for the use of CAST-MR with defendants who are mentally retarded.[162] However, given the samples they used, some caveats are in order. First, in the pilot studies in which initial psychometric properties were investigated, the subjects with mental retardation were community residents, not defendants with existing criminal charges.[163] Thus, compared to individuals for whom the test was developed, the subjects may have lacked familiarity with the legal system; further, it is not clear how they answered the questions in section III of the CAST-MR, as it requires subjects to describe the events associated with their current case. Second, in the first validation study described earlier the authors note that the MR-I group had a significant number of persons with dual diagnoses. The presence of mental illness in this group could have depressed its IQ scores as well as contributed to some of the differences in outcomes observed between it and the other groups.

A more important observation is that, according to other research conducted by the developers, persons who suffer from mental retardation, even those whose competence is not questioned or whose clinical evaluation suggests they are "competent," score significantly below nonretarded defendants on the CAST-MR.[164] Thus, a relatively high score on the CAST-MR by a person with mental retardation does not necessarily suggest that he or she has competence-related abilities comparable to those of nonretarded defendants. In short, even if the CAST-MR is a viable instrument, judgments about the demands of the case and the abilities they require (i.e., to comprehend and reason) will have to be made by examiners formulating clinical recommendations, and by judges or juries reaching the ultimate decision about competence.

(g) MacArthur Competence Assessment Tool–Criminal Adjudication

In 1990 the MacArthur Foundation Research Network on Mental Health and the Law began an extensive instrument development project which has produced a competency assessment instrument quite different from those described earlier. First, building on the theoretical work of Bonnie,[165] the objective of the competence project was to measure psychological abilities relevant to *competence to proceed to adjudication* rather than competence to stand trial. This change in terminology was meant to reflect the broader scope of the MacArthur measures, which include specific inquiry into defendants' abilities to plead guilty [see § 7.03] as well as their abilities to stand trial. A second novel aspect of the MacArthur

group measures is their dedication of various psycholegal perspectives on competence—having to do with constructs like appreciation and rational thinking as well as understanding and recognition of relevant information—that have been identified in case law dealing with treatment decision-making.[166] Third, the instruments explicitly measure both abstract knowledge and case-specific knowledge about the legal system. In short, the MacArthur measures seek to provide what Nicholson called for: "a new generation of competency assessment instruments[—]multiple scales comprised of homogeneous items that assess specific components of the multifaceted construct."[167]

(1) Structure of the MacArthur Research Protocol

The research prototype from which the MacCAT-CA was developed consists of seven scales, all composed of items that represent various combinations of two legal abilities (assisting counsel and decisionmaking) and four psychological abilities (i.e., understanding, recognizing relevant information, thinking rationally, and appreciation) required for competency.[168] The first three scales address the defendant's *understanding* of various issues: One measures understanding as related to general trial issues and competence to assist counsel (CAC-U), and two others gauge understanding as related to important decisions— whether to plead guilty (DC:U-PG) and to waive jury and request a bench trial (DC:U-WJ). The fourth scale, the CAC:R, examines the capacity to *recognize relevant information* and explain its relevance to counsel. The fifth scale, the DC:R, explores *rational thinking capacity,* including reasoning and logical problem-solving abilities, by having defendants compare and contrast available options (e.g., trial vs. plea), anticipate the consequences of alternative courses of action, and solve concrete logical problems. The final two measures examine defendants' perceptions, beliefs, and reasoning abilities about the same kinds of issues but as applied in their own unique cases (i.e., their *appreciation* of the relevance of these matters). The CAC:A examines defendants' appreciation of matters related to the general assistance of counsel, whereas the DC:A examines the appreciation of issues related to specific case decisions (again, pleading guilty and waiving jury). [For an interesting case regarding the appreciation issue, see the Rhodes report, § 19.02(e).]

(2) Description of Component Measures

Items and measures dealing with understanding, recognizing relevant information, and rational thinking about legal processes are constructed around a hypothetical crime that serves as a stimulus for inquiries into general capacities:

> "Two men, Fred and Reggie, are playing pool at a bar and get into a fight. Fred hits Reggie with a pool stick. Reggie falls and hits his head on the floor so hard that he nearly dies."

Defendants are then asked a series of structured questions, the answers to which reveal their understanding of the legal process and potential decisions that the defendant ("Fred") faces.

The specific measures are as follows. Inquiries into a defendant's *understanding* are presented in three formats. The predisclosure format tests for the knowledge that defendants bring with them to the evaluation. For example, an item from the DC:U-PG examines defendants' understanding about the legal rights and protections surrendered in pleading guilty:

> "Fred may plead not guilty and go to trial, or Fred may plead guilty. Now, if Fred pleads guilty to attempted murder, he would give up some legal rights and protections. What are they?"

The defendant's narrative response is then scored against explicit criteria to determine whether rights waived (right to jury trial, right to confrontation, protection against self-incrimination, certain appeals, etc.) are reported. When defendants' knowledge satisfies scoring criteria, it can be presumed that their ability with respect to the item content has been demonstrated. The second response format, postdisclosure, examines the defendant's ability to hear, assimilate, and understand new information. Thus, for this same item, a defendant is told:

> "If Fred pleads guilty to attempted murder, he will be giving up some of his legal rights and protections. There won't be any jury trial. And,

the prosecutor won't have to prove the charge of attempted murder. In your own words, tell me what Fred just found out about his legal rights and protections."

Again, the defendants' narrative response is based on explicit scoring criteria (loss of jury trial, state will not have to prove its case) for the content of the disclosure. The third format for these understanding measures is a series of four true/false items that test a defendant's ability to recognize the disclosed information.

"Recognizing relevant information" items on the CAC:R challenge defendants to distinguish more relevant from less relevant information and to explain the basis for their choice. An example item based on the previous vignette asks the defendant to respond to the following two bits of information:

> G. At the bar, there was a country and western band playing in the room next to the pool room.
> H. Fred himself called the ambulance because he could see that Reggie was hurt very badly.

Credit is given for selecting the most relevant bit of information for Fred to relate to his attorney (H), and for an explanation that indicates awareness that taking action to help Reggie may be used to challenge assertions that Fred intended to kill Reggie.

The measure of *rational thinking* (DC:R) presents defendants with descriptions of the two routes of case disposition available to Fred, pleading not guilty and proceeding to trial versus pleading guilty. Defendants are asked to discuss these two options, to identify additional information that might inform Fred's choice about how to proceed, and to indicate advantages and disadvantages of each in a way that reveals their capacity to conduct a cost–benefit analysis. Additional DC:R items examine the capacity for logical thinking more abstractly, including formal logical operations problems.

Leaving the case vignette, *appreciation* is measured through inquiries about defendants' views of the legal process as applied to their own cases, in particular how they view their situation as compared to that of other defendants facing similar charges. For example, one item from the DC:A notes that "some people who get into trouble with the law are found guilty of a crime" and asks defendants to indicate their chances of being found guilty relative to similarly situated defendants using a five-point scale ("definitely lower chance," "probably lower chance," "about the same chance," "probably higher chance," "definitely higher chance"). They are then asked to give a reason that explains their choice, and the quality of the reason(s) given are scored for impairment (2 = none, 1 = some, 0 = significant) in appreciation. Reasons scored as indicating no impairment include viable or feasible reasons for a perceived higher risk (e.g., "They've got four eyewitnesses" and "I signed a confession") or lower risk (e.g., "I've got an alibi"). In addition, in contrast to the CST, reasons that reflect political attitudes (e.g., "The D.A. is going after me because it's an election year") or cynical attitudes (e.g., "I don't have much of a chance because the public defenders don't try very hard") are scored as showing no impairment. On the other hand, responses suggestive of psychopathology (e.g., "My attorney is trying to send me up so he can get my inheritance" and "I'm going to be found guilty because I'm the worst sinner in the world") are consid-

ered indicative of impaired appreciation of one's legal situation.

(3) Findings from the MacArthur Field Study

The prototype measures described above were the subject of a major field study in Florida and Virginia,[169] involving three groups of male subjects: 159 defendants hospitalized as incompetent to proceed (group HI), 113 defendants receiving mental health treatment in jail for purposes other than competence restoration (group JT), and 94 unscreened defendants selected from jail inmate populations (group JU). (Sample characteristics of these three groups were presented earlier in Tables 6.2 and 6.3.) For a subgroup of the hospitalized sample, the protocol was readministered after the hospital treatment team judged that competence had been restored (group HR, $n = 97$).

As can be seen by comparing Table 6.4 with Table 6.5, in terms of psychometric properties the MacArthur prototype measures are at least as adequate as other competence assessment instruments. It should also be noted that the predictive validity finding, which used hospital treatment staff's rating on a six-point scale as a criterion,

Table 6.5

MacArthur Structured Assessment of the Competencies of Criminal Defendants (MacSAC-CD): Psychometric Properties

	Understanding			Reasoning		Appreciation	
	CAC:U	DC:U-PG	DC:U-WJ	CAC:R	DC:R	CAC:A	DC:A
Interrater agreement							
Kappa	.60	.74	.75	.60	.60	.48	.36
Percent agreement	75	83	83	82	76	88	75
Internal consistency							
Cronbach's alpha	.87	.88	.88	.68	.71	.74	.40[a]
M item–scale correlation	.53	.54	.50	.41	.32	.48	
r with estimated VIQ	.60	.59	.56	.40	.56	<u>.90</u>	.31
r with psychopathology							
BPRS-A (total)	−.28	−.33	−.31	<u>−.14</u>	−.31	−.22	20
BPRS-A Psychoticism	−.44	−.46	−.47	−.39	−.43	−.41	−.40
r with clinical rating of incompetence (HI)	.39	.46	.40	.41	.39	.34	.29

Note. All correlations in the table are significant at $p < .05$ or less, except those underlined.

[a]Because DC:A consists of only two items, this is simply a Pearson correlation coefficient.

may understate the measure's validity relative to other instruments; the median of 0.39 (with a range over the seven measures of 0.29 to 0.46) was obtained from a study of the 97-member HR group, composed of people who were in the hospital to be restored to competency and were thus presumably harder to differentiate on competency grounds than a sample taken from the community (which is the type of sample used in studying most of the other instruments).

Table 6.5 also provides data concerning construct validity, which indicate that each measure had a modest positive competency correlation with estimated verbal IQ (range = 0.09 to 0.60, median = 0.56), and a negative competency correlation with total score on the Brief Psychiatric Rating Scale (range = –0.14 to –0.33, median = –0.28) and the BPRS's psychoticism subscale (range = –0.39 to –0.47, median = –0.43). Between-group comparisons also provide evidence of the validity and potential clinical utility of the MacArthur measures. As predicted, the HI group performed significantly more poorly on each of the seven measures, whereas the JT and JU groups performed at levels that were not statistically different from each other.

(4)   Development of the MacCAT-CA

Although the MacArthur research protocol performed well in both pilot and extensive field testing, the complete instrument took between one and two hours to administer. Moreover, further analyses revealed redundancy among response formats within some scales and between some of the scales. Finally, some of the measures (DC:U-WJ) address issues that arise only infrequently in attorney–client negotiations about how to proceed, and some items were judged weak in terms of face validity. Based on these considerations, as well as on traditional psychometric considerations (e.g., internal consistency of scales with items deleted), the MacCAT-CA was created by eliminating items and measures from the prototype. The result is a 22-item, clinically portable measure that requires approximately 35–45 minutes to administer and which yields quantitative indices of three competence-related abilities: *understanding, reasoning,* and *appreciation.*

Data extracted from the field study suggest

that the MacCAT-CA subscales have satisfactory internal consistency (range = 0.75 to 0.77). In addition, group differences between the field study groups remain significant when total scores on the extracted Mac-CAT-CA subscales were compared. A study has been funded by the National Institute of Mental Health to developed interpretive norms for the MacCAT-CA based on data from eight states. The new instrument should become available to the field in 1998.

(h)   Summary

This brief review of instruments and interview formats for evaluating competence to stand trial reveals a variety of approaches, differing in design, purpose, scope, and the degree to which they have been examined empirically. The trade-offs involved in instrument development to date are illustrated in Table 6.6, which presents a comparative appraisal of these measures and highlights some of their strengths and weaknesses.

The instruments designed for competency "screening" (e.g., CST and GCCT) offer efficient (i.e., brief) administration as well as the merits of standardized administration and scoring. However, concerns exist regarding their validity as screening measures and their utility beyond screening out defendants who are "obviously competent."[170] Furthermore, of course, cases not "screened out" require further clinical inquiry, which then offsets the efficiency of the screening methods.

The more comprehensive approaches (e.g., CAI and IFI) do a better job of sampling the domain of relevant legal issues and competence-related abilities. However, even these measures provide relatively little focus on the capacity to decide whether to plead guilty, the legal issue that will be paramount in most defendants' cases.[171] A second shortcoming in existing "comprehensive" instruments is the failure to provide the standardized administration and objective, criterion-based scoring that is needed to limit variance in the questions asked and the weights to assign to defendants' responses. The lack of standardized administration also leaves unclear whether examiners using these instruments are evaluating defendants' *ability,* which is the focus of the *Dusky* stan-

Table 6.6
Comparison of Competence Assessment Instruments

Instrument	Purpose[a]	Admin. time (approx.)	Admin./scoring standardized	Norm-referenced interpretation	Comments
CST	S	30 min.	Yes/Yes	Cutoff only	Vague, questionable scoring criteria. Poor face validity and content validity.
CAI	C	30–45 min.	No/No	No	No calculus for "quantified" ratings. Good face validity (legal content). High interexaminer variance in administration.
IFI	C	45 min.	No/No	No	Administration ideally requires attorney presence and involvement in assessment. Facilitates linkage of impairment in competence-related abilities to psychopathology.
GCCT	S	10–15 min.	Yes/Yes	Cutoff only	Inadequate sampling of domain of competence related abilities; superficial item content and overemphasis on trial vs. plea issues.
CADCOMP	S	60–90 min.	Yes/Yes	No	Lengthy setup and administration; requires follow-up interview evaluation. Validity unknown.
CAST-MR	C	30–45 min.	Yes/Yes	Yes	Does not assess competence-related skills beyond "understanding." "Recognition" format may preclude evaluation of depth of understanding legal issues.
MacCAT-CA	C	35–45 min.	Yes/Yes	Available in 1998	Multiple subscales systematically assess multiple competence-related abilities. Criterion-based scoring assesses ability as well as knowledge. Explicit focus on "guilty plea" as potential outcome.

[a]Screening ("S") versus Comprehensive ("C") evaluation.

dard, or simply their *existing knowledge,* which is the level of comprehension that defendants bring with them to the evaluation. To test ability, defendants who exhibit some deficit in knowledge or understanding should be given the relevant information and later asked to restate it in their own words and perhaps draw inferences from it as well. Although the semistructured interviews (CAI, IFI) do not prevent examiners from pro-

ceeding this way, such an approach may not be adopted in practice.

The "new generation" MacCAT-CA tries to rectify many of these problems. It taps legal domains related to both the general capacity to assist counsel and competence for discrete legal decisions, simultaneously examining multiple competence-related abilities such as understanding, reasoning, and appreciation, both before and after competency instruction. It retains the relative efficiency of existing measures, yet it offers standardized administration and, for most of its submeasures, objective, criterion-based scoring that should minimize the subjectivity that plagues existing comprehensive measures.

6.07. Guidelines for Evaluation

(a) Social Context

Although the legal paradigm for competency demands a case-by-case determination, as if competency rested within the individual,[172] it might more properly be viewed as a transactional construct lying somewhere between the attorney and the client. After all, one prong of the competency standard is directly concerned with the *relationship* between the attorney and the client, and the other prong partially depends on the success of the attorney's efforts to educate the defendant about the nature of the proceedings. The cliché that "there are no incompetent defendants, only incompetent attorneys" overstates the case. Nonetheless, it is true that the typical lawyer receives little, if any, formal clinical training in counseling disturbed clients. Moreover, as Golding and Roesch have noted,[173] it is probable that certain kinds of attorneys have more success in counseling clients with particular characteristics, just as therapist and client characteristics interact. Consequently, some attorneys may refer a defendant who clearly passes the threshold for competency due simply to the frustration or discomfort of working with a client perceived to be "strange" or "difficult."

In light of these considerations, clinicians should approach the competency evaluation as a problem in *consultation;* that is, as a means of rendering assistance to the defense attorney in preparing the client for the defense. Careful reporting of the evaluation data should give a sense of the specific points about which the defendant needs further education or counseling [see, e.g., Mills report, § 19.02(a)]. When there seems to be a mismatch between attorney and client, the clinician may be able to offer suggestions as to ways of getting the relationship "unstuck." Careful consultation may also decrease future unnecessary referrals. Indeed, ideally attorneys themselves might profitably initiate such consultation when deciding whether to seek an evaluation. Still more basic, when attorneys do not understand the standard for competency, the forensic clinician may help to clarify the nature of the construct, again with the probable result of decreasing unnecessary referrals.

The consultation process should not be conceptualized as unidirectional, however. The clinician also needs to *obtain* information from the attorney. For instance, to be able to evaluate the defendant's understanding of the charges and potential penalties, the clinician obviously needs to know what they are. Although this information can come from other sources, the attorney can provide details the court documents will not. More important, only the attorney can provide the clinician with information about the length, substance, and nature of previous attorney–client contacts. This information is important to both prongs of the *Dusky* standard. Points of misunderstanding about charges and the legal process will be interpreted differently depending on whether they occur after hours of counseling from the attorney or, as may often be the case given the press of dockets and lawyers' caseloads, after a five-minute meeting at a preliminary hearing. And, as noted previously, information about the quality of the relationship is crucial in addressing the second *Dusky* prong and in fulfilling the consultation role. We strongly recommend that clinicians routinely obtain this type of information from attorneys representing defendants referred for competency evaluations (and, conversely, that referring attorneys routinely provide it). The form shown in Figure 6.1 may be helpful in that regard.

(b) Competency Evaluation Content

Before describing the content and structure of the competency evaluation, an additional word should be said about the traditional legal position on this issue. Despite the relatively focused nature of the competency construct, and the demonstrated fact that it can be evaluated relatively briefly on an outpatient basis, many legal professionals continue to expect the clinician to con-

Defendant: _____ **DOB:** _____

Attorney: _____

Describe the charges for which defendant is standing trial and the underlying facts:

Describe the potential penalties:

Describe the specific behavior of the defendant which leads you to believe that he/she may be incompetent to stand trial or was suffering from significant mental abnormality at the time of the offense (e.g., detached and indifferent; depressed; hostile; chaotic behavior; peculiar speech content; hallucinations; history).

Have you observed this behavior yourself? If not, who are the sources of these observations?

Figure 6.1. *Referral form.*

duct a "full" psychiatric evaluation on the issue, including thorough history taking, psychological testing, and inpatient observation. Illustrative are the results of a study conducted in Virginia.[174] Trial judges ($n = 52$), forensic clinicians ($n = 27$) and general clinicians ($n = 134$) were asked which of the following four items were least likely to be needed for a competency evaluation: projective test results, a copy of the indictment, a mental status examination, or what the defense attorney has told the client about the legal process. Although 96% of the forensic clinicians picked projective tests as the right answer, only 13% of the judges (and only 25% of the general clinicians) picked that answer. The answers for the remaining judges were almost evenly split between the indictment and the mental status examination (40% and 42%, respectively). Similarly, although 100% of the forensic clinicians were willing to say that, compared to sentencing and sanity evaluations, a competency evaluation was the type of evaluation least likely to require a

family history, only 17.3% of the judges chose that answer, with 63.5% stating that family history "is essential" to all three types of evaluations. Especially in jurisdictions in which competency evaluations have customarily been conducted via inpatient admission, there may be some initial resistance from some judges and others in the legal system to evaluation reports that focus primarily on functional criteria. Nonetheless, our position is that clinicians performing these evaluations should adopt such a focus.[175]

(1) Interview Format

As with all forensic evaluations, notification of the purpose, nature, and confidentiality limits of the competency evaluation should precede the interview [see § 4.05(d)]. The precise chronology of the interview after notification may depend in large part on whether one of the interview formats discussed in § 6.06 is used. The Mac-CAT-CA is a highly structured instrument that dictates the general flow of the evaluation, but even the "semistructured" formats, such as the CAI and the IFI, have manuals which contain guidelines for interview content, including specific questions that may reveal pertinent information. Other instruments, such as the CST, GCCT, CAST-MR, and CADCOMP are meant to be used in conjunction with a relatively unstructured clinical interview.

If the latter type of interview is conducted, it should generally consist of three components. One component, having to do with the *offense*, will be an inquiry into the defendant's awareness of the charges and ability to describe the specific allegations. Questions here should be open-ended and phrased in a way that does not assume the defendant's involvement in the alleged offense. Thus, questions such as "What do the police say you did to get your current charges?" or "What can you tell me about your case?" are preferable to "Tell me about the armed robbery" or "Tell me about the fight that led to you being arrested." Ideally, examiners will already be armed with information about the allegations based on communications with the attorney and/or the court. This information may assist in guiding inquiries about the defendant's knowledge or memory of specific elements of the allegations and charges, or provide the basis for confrontation if malingering or deceptive responding is suspected.

A second component of the interview will inquire into the defendant's competence-related abilities in connection with the *legal process*, including the ability to relate to the attorney. Information about the client's understanding of the legal situation can usually be obtained in a nonconfrontive conversational interview. The interview should address such issues as the defendant's understanding of the purpose of a trial, the roles of the various participants at trial, and the trial process itself (e.g., the nature of examination and cross-examination of witnesses), as well as advantages and disadvantages of pleading guilty. The clinician should also inquire about the defendant's perceptions and expectations of the attorney. In that regard, it is useful to have the defendant describe previous interactions, including both their quantity and quality (which responses may be compared with the attorney's referral information).

With respect to both of these components,

and regardless of whether a packaged format or more informal interview process is used, clinicians should generally avoid following a rigid, test-like series of questions. Poorly educated defendants sometimes perceive the list of factual questions about the legal system as a "schoolmarmish" test (as in some sense it is), and they are accordingly reluctant to answer fully lest their ignorance be uncovered. Also, such defendants may be unable to give dictionary definitions of terms, even though they have a basic understanding of the underlying concepts. Various alternative approaches are feasible. For example, defendants who are unable to say in the abstract what the prosecutor does may nonetheless reveal a good understanding of the adversary system if the courtroom situation is discussed in terms of their own case. Similarly, conversations about past experiences in the courtroom (e.g., "Tell me who was there and what they did/were supposed to do") may reveal a more sophisticated understanding of the legal process than does direct questioning (as Table 6.2 suggests, defendants referred for competency evaluations will typically have such experience from previous arrests, or from a pretrial hearing on the current charges). Finally, for defendants who are reluctant to discuss or disclose information about their specific situation, hypothetical inquiries of the type used in the Mac-CAT-CA (e.g., if John were tried for murder, what would happen?) may prove useful, as they put emotional distance between the defendant's case and the specific questions at hand.

The third component of an evaluation is assessment of current *mental status,* which can routinely be accomplished via a brief social history and mental status examination (although bolstering these steps with information from jail personnel and other observers of the defendant may be necessary). As indicated earlier, competence to proceed evaluations do not ordinarily require a detailed social history. But obtaining a brief history has merit on several counts. First, if taken early in the interview (perhaps immediately following the notification/consent), it can serve as a means of facilitating rapport building between the defendant and examiner. Second, it can provide verbal samples of general mental status, including classic indicators of psychopathology (word salad, tangentiality, delusional content, clang associations, etc.), from which inferences may be drawn regarding the defendant's capacity for ordering and expressing thoughts. Third, the history can explore general incapacity to establish or sustain relationships as a means of learning how the defendant might relate to the attorney. Finally, the content of the history, particularly with respect to prior mental health treatment, may become important if significant impairment in competence-related abilities is detected in other parts of the evaluation. In such cases, as discussed in more detail below, clinicians will want to form at least a preliminary diagnostic impression about restorability.

However, at the risk of belaboring a point made throughout this chapter, the presence of mental illness or mental retardation alone should not ordinarily result in a judgment that the defendant is incompetent. The goal of the examination is to determine whether and how specific symptoms impair particular competence-related abilities; in other words, the question to be answered is, "What tasks will be demanded of the defendant's performance of which may be impaired by the symptoms observed?" For example, as noted in § 6.02(b), delusions per se are insufficient to render a defendant incompetent; their discovery during the mental status component of the exam should merely trigger further inquiry, not a conclusion of incompetency. On the other hand, delusions of a certain type may be highly relevant. A belief that one's attorney is part of a conspiracy to poison one's mind would likely interfere substantially with the attorney–client relationship, and a delusion that one is immune from punishment due to supernatural powers is likely to impair one's ability to appreciate the consequences of a guilty verdict and thus one's motivation to work with the attorney in constructing a defense.

(2)   Psychological Testing

Routine administration of conventional psychological tests is unlikely to be a cost-efficient means of gathering information in most competency cases. Because the nature of the cognitive defect in such cases is relatively specific, generalized measures of intelligence or personality are unlikely to pertain.

In a narrow range of cases testing may be use-

ful, however. For instance, if malingering is suspected, the clinician may want to administer one or more of the psychological tests discussed in § 3.07(b) to explore that specific issue. In addition, when the client appears incompetent or marginally competent on the basis of interview data, cognitive testing may be useful for one of the following purposes: (1) corroboration of the degree of mental retardation or other generalized impairment of ego functioning or (2) assessment of the ability to consider alternatives and process information in a structured situation. However, even these goals may often be more efficiently (and perhaps more validly) met by examination of agency records and discussions about the defendant's typical behavior with relatives, employers, and other who know the defendant well.

(3)   Amnesia and Statements about the Offense

One of the most troublesome problems in evaluating competency is the weight to be give reported amnesia. As noted in § 6.02(c), amnesia per se is not a bar to competency. The competency standard emphasizes present ability to communicate with the attorney and to understand the proceedings. Indeed, general memory problems are more likely to be probative on the competency issue than is amnesia for the specific time of the offense because the former may interfere with the defendant's ability to follow a trial and communicate with his or her attorney about it whereas the latter can often be rectified through provision of extrinsic information.

Nonetheless, because amnesia for the time of the offense is sometimes relevant to a competency determination, the clinician should first try to determine whether the amnesia claim is genuine, using the types of techniques discussed in § 3.06. If the amnesia seems fabricated but the defendant persists in remaining mute about the offense, comments about the defendant's *capacity* to relate the events surrounding the crime can still be made. Similarly, even if the amnesia is real, the "usual" competency evaluation should proceed because, as noted previously, the quality of the communication between counsel and client, as well as the defendant's understanding of the criminal process, may well be unimpeded. In addition, the defendant may be able to participate in the defense by evaluating the prosecution's evidence depicting his or her conduct at the time of the offense.

Whatever findings are made about the amnesia issue should be reported to the court. However, as is true anytime potentially self-incriminating statements are involved, the clinician should be alert to Fifth Amendment issues in doing so [see § §4.02(a)]. We recommend that if the report is to go to all parties, it should state simply, "The defendant claims to be unable to remember (or to have difficulty describing) the time period of the alleged offense as a result of a memory deficit." Also, statements by the defendant as to what others (e.g., the police) say he or she did may be included because they are not *self*-incriminating and are germane to the defendant's understanding of the charges. It will also be useful to report information about the probable source of the amnesia and whether it is remediable, as these determinations will be relevant to the defendant's restorability if the defendant is found to be incompetent.

(c)   Treatment and Restorability

As discussed in § 6.04, *Jackson v. Indiana* places limits on the state's ability to confine those found incompetent. Thus, although determining treatment needs is not the primary purpose of a competency evaluation, restorability becomes a foreground issue when the defendant appears to be incompetent or marginally competent.[176] When such is the case, the evaluator should attempt to address, based on diagnostic impressions and the available history of mental health treatment: (1) the probability of the defendant's achieving a higher level of competency under various treatment regimens, (2) whether such treatment can be administered on an outpatient basis, and (3) the length of time that would constitute a reasonable treatment trial under the proposed regimen(s). In addition, in some states the evaluator must address whether the defendant meets the criteria for inpatient commitment (i.e., imminent dangerousness to self or others).[177]

There is relatively little research on the accuracy of clinicians' specific prognostication about which defendants will be restored and in what time frame. The studies that have been reported suggest that precise judgments on these issues are

not particularly accurate.[178] However, forensic evaluators should not be unduly discouraged by this literature. They need only give *estimates* of potential restorability and time frames, because more fine-tuned assessments of these issues will be made by treatment staff if the defendant is judged incompetent.

To ensure this estimate is as accurate as possible, however, knowledge of more general literature on competence restoration might be useful. First, the evaluator may wish to examine reports of clinical interventions that have been found efficacious in competence restortion.[179] Second, the evaluator should be aware of studies reporting length-of-stay (LOS) data regarding competence restoration, summarized in Table 6.7. The studies are relatively consistent in finding that the large majority of defendants referred for treatment are recommended as "restored" within six months, and often earlier.[180] Such findings can provide some empirical bases for clinicians' ballpark estimates of time to competence restoration.

Table 6.7
Competence Restoration: Length-of-Stay Data

State	LOS findings
California[a]	Median LOS = 4.5 months
Colorado[b]	Mean LOS = 3.8 months
Florida[c]	LOS < 1 month: 32% of admissions
	LOS < 3 months: 44%
	LOS < 6 months: 78%
Michigan[d]	Mean LOS = 9.6 months
Oklahoma[e]	Mean LOS = 2.3 months
	LOS > 3 months: 21.9%
	LOS > 6 months: 5.5%
	LOS > 9 months: 3.2%
	LOS > 1 year: 1.6%

[a]*Appropriateness and Outcome,* 44 ARCHIVES GEN. PSYCHIATRY 754 (1987).

[b]Nicola S. Schutte et al., *Incompetency and Insanity: Feasibility of Community Evaluation and Treatment,* 24 COMMUNITY MENTAL HEALTH J. 143 (1988).

[c]Sally Cunningham, personal communication (Forensic Services Division, Central Office of Florida Department of Health and Rehabilitative Services).

[d]Carol T. Mobray, *A Study of Patients Treated as Incompetent to Stand Trial,* 14 SOC. PSYCHIATRY 31 (1979).

[e]Robert Nicholson & John L. McNulty, *Outcome of Hospitalization for Defendants Found Incompetent to Stand Trial,* 10 BEHAVIORAL SCI. & L. 371 (1992).

Another fact that may be helpful to the clinician trying to evaluate restorability is that, barring an irreversible condition (e.g., a severe organic deficit) or a functional disorder that has repeatedly proven treatment resistant, most defendants are restorable. As Table 6.3 indicated, functional psychoses and affective disturbance (e.g., depression) are more often the disorders observed in persons determined incompetent,[181] and these tend to be treatable with medication. Even defendants with significant mental retardation can be "restored" in many cases.[182]

Nonetheless, it bears emphasizing that, under *Jackson*, attempts at restoration in the absence of a substantial probability that a higher level of competency will be achieved constitute an unconstitutional deprivation of liberty. In these cases the examiner's report should advise that competence restoration is not feasible, which should signal the attorneys and court to consider alternative dispositions of the case.

6.08.   Conclusion: The Need for Policy Consultation

A final point is that attorneys and forensic clinicians can be helpful in educating the community, including legislators, about the system of competency evaluations and problems associated with it. Although public outcry is common in connection with the insanity defense [see § 8.02(a)], abuses of competency evaluations and of commitments for restoration of competency are far more common and far more costly in the aggregate [see § 6.03(c)]. Similarly, if attorneys and clinicians often confuse incompetency and insanity, the error is much more common in the general public. Whether directly through public lectures or interviews or indirectly through education of community leaders and the news media, attorneys and forensic clinicians might perform a useful service in teaching the distinctions between these concepts and the legal and moral underpinnings of the competency question. Such education and consultation might ulti-mately prevent some of the abuses of the system (e.g., *de facto* incarceration of "incompetent" defendants who have been arrested on the basis of weak evidence). It might also persuade policymakers to reduce some of the wasteful practices (e.g., routine hospitalization) commonly associated with the forensic mental health system.

Bibliography

American Bar Association, Criminal Justice Mental Health Standards pt. IV (1984).

Robert A. Burt & Norval Morris, *A Proposal for the Abolition of Incompetency Plea,* 40 University of Chicago Law Review 66 (1972).

Drope v. Missouri, 420 U.S. 162 (1975).

Dusky v. United States, 362 U.S. 402 (1960).

Thomas Grisso, Competency to Stand Trial Evaluations: A Manual for Practice (1988).

Thomas Grisso, Evaluating Competencies: Forensic Assessments and Instruments 62–112 (1986).

Thomas Grisso, *Five-Year Research Update (1986–1990):* Evaluations for Competence to Stand trial, 10 Behavioral Science & Law 353 (1992).

Jackson v. Indiana, 406 U.S. 715 (1972).

Laboratory of Community Psychiatry, Competency to Stand Trial and Mental Illness (1974).

Gary Melton, Lois Weithorn, & Christopher Slobogin, Community Mental Health Centers and the Courts: An Evaluation of Community-Based Forensic Services (1985).

Riggins v. Nevada, 112 S. Ct. 1810 (1992).

Robert A. Nicholson & Karen E. Kugler, *Competent and Incompetent Criminal Defendants: A Quantitative Review of Comparative Research,* 109 Psychological Bulletin 355 (1991).

Ronald Roesch & Stephen L. Golding, Competency to Stand Trial (1980).

Henry Steadman & Elliot Hartstone, *Defendants Incompetent to Stand Trial,* in Mentally Disordered Offenders: Perspectives from Law and Social Science (J. Monahan & Henry Steadman eds. 1983).

Alan Stone, Mental Health and Law: A System in Transition ch. 12 (1975).

Bruce Winick, *Incompetency to Stand Trial: Developments in the Law,* in Mentally Disordered Offenders: Perspectives from Law and Social Sciences (John Monahan & Henry Steadman eds. 1983).

CHAPTER SEVEN

Other Competencies in the Criminal Process

7.01. Introduction

The state has traditionally been accorded wide-ranging power to make decisions for those unable to care for themselves under what is known as its *parens patriae* (literally, "state as parent") authority.[1] At the same time, at least since the time of John Stuart Mill,[2] much of Western society has subscribed to the principle that human dignity demands respect for individual autonomy unless compelling reasons to infringe upon that autonomy exist. On this assumption, it is generally held that the state may not invoke its *parens patriae* power as justification for intervening in a person's life unless, at a minimum, the individual is incompetent to make the *specific* decision or to perform the *specific* act at issue.[3] Accordingly, competency to stand trial, the topic of the last chapter, is just one of many criminal competencies that the mental health professional may be asked to evaluate.

This chapter examines the following issues, in roughly the order they might arise during criminal litigation: competency to consent to a search and seizure, competency to confess, competence to plead guilty, competency to waive an attorney, competency to refuse an insanity defense, competency to testify and the associated issue of assessing witness credibility, and competency to be sentenced and executed. Other competency issues that might arise in the *civil* context are discussed primarily in Chapter 11.

CASE STUDY 7.1

Following are the facts of *Godinez v. Moran*,[4] a United States Supreme Court opinion discussed in §§ 7.04 & 7.05.

On August 2, in the early hours of the morning, Tom Moran entered the Red Pearl Saloon in Carson City, Nevada, and shot the bartender and a patron four times each with an automatic pistol. He then walked behind the bar and removed the drawer to the cash register. Nine days later, Moran arrived at the apartment of his former wife and opened fire on her; five of his seven shots hit their target. Moran then shot himself in the abdomen and attempted, without success, to slit his wrists. Of the four victims of Moran's gunshots, only Moran himself survived. On August 13, Moran summoned police to his hospital bed and confessed to the killings.

After Moran was appointed counsel and pleaded not guilty to three counts of first-degree murder, the trial court ordered that he be examined by a pair of psychiatrists, both of whom concluded that he was competent to stand trial. One of the psychiatrists stated that there was "not the slightest doubt" that Moran was "in full control of his faculties" insofar as he had the "ability to aid counsel, assist in his own defense, recall evidence and . . . give testimony if called upon to do so." The other psychiatrist believed that Moran was "knowledgeable of the charges being made against him"; that he had the ability to "assist his attorney, in his own defense, if he so desire[d]"; and that he was "fully cognizant of the penalties if convicted." Both also said, however, that Moran was very depressed, with one noting that his "considerable remorse and guilt" might incline him "to exert less effort towards his own defense."

The prosecution announced its intention to seek the death penalty. Two and a half months after the psychiatric evaluations, Moran again appeared before the trial court. At this time he informed the court that he wished to discharge his attorneys and change his pleas to guilty. When asked to explain the change, Moran responded that he wished to represent himself because he opposed all efforts to mount a defense. His purpose, specifically, was to prevent the presentation of any mitigating evidence on his behalf at the sentencing phase of the proceeding. The trial judge inquired whether Moran was "presently under the influence of any drug or alcohol," and Moran replied: "Just what they give me in, you know, medications." The trial judge did not question him further regarding the type, dosage, or effect of the "medications" to which he referred; in fact Moran was being administered simultaneously four different prescription drugs—phenobarbital, dilantin, inderal, and vistaril—which can cause light-headedness, drowsiness, depression, disorientation, and short-term memory loss.

The court then advised Moran that he had a right both to counsel and to self-representation, warmed him of the "dangers and disadvantages" of self-representation, inquired into his understanding and his awareness of his rights, and asked why he had chosen to represent himself. In a string of affirmative responses, Moran stated that he knew the import of waiving his constitutional rights, that he understood the charges against him, and that he was guilty of those charges. However, when the trial judge asked him whether he killed his ex-wife "deliberately, with premeditation and malice aforethought," Moran unexpectedly responded: "No. I didn't do it—I mean, I wasn't looking to kill her, but she ended up dead." Rather than probing further, the trial judge repeated the question, inquiring again whether Moran acted deliberately. Once again, Moran replied: "I don't know. I mean, I don't know what you mean by deliberately. I mean, I pulled the trigger on purpose, but I didn't plan on doing it; you know what I mean?" The trial judge stated: "Well, I've previously explained to you what is meant by deliberation and premeditation. Deliberate means that you arrived at or determined as a

result of careful thought and weighing the consideration for and against the proposed action. Did you do that?" This time, Moran responded: "Yes."

QUESTIONS: Recall the point made at the end of the introduction—that being competent to stand trial does not necessarily mean one is competent to participate in other aspects of the criminal process. Note that both of the experts found Moran competent to stand trial. Assume the court agrees. Of what relevance is this finding in evaluating his competence to plead guilty or his competence to waive counsel? What else would you want to know?

Assume that the court finds that Moran is *not* competent to waive counsel, and that once counsel is appointed, the attorney makes plans to assert an insanity defense, over Moran's objection. How would you evaluate Moran's competency to waive an insanity plea? If he is competent to stand trial, is he automatically competent to waive an insanity defense?

In the actual case, Moran was found competent to waive his attorney, and represented himself. He pleaded guilty and presented no evidence at his sentencing hearing, which took place shortly after the hearing described above. He was sentenced to death for the saloon murders and received a life sentence for the murder of his wife. As a lawyer, what arguments could you make for or against the proposition that, at the time of the sentencing hearing, he was incompetent to be sentenced? To be executed?

Finally, note that while in the hospital, Moran gave a confession to the police in the absence of counsel (but apparently after *Miranda* warnings). What can you say about his competency to confess at that time? What else would you like to know?

7.02. Competency to Consent to a Search or Seizure

The government obtains much of the evidence used in criminal cases through searches of people's houses, effects, and papers and through seizures and searches of persons. The Fourth Amendment to the United States Constitution prohibits "unreasonable" searches and seizures and requires that warrants authorizing a search or seizure be based on "probable cause."[5] If a court determines, at a pretrial "suppression hearing" [see § 2.04(a) (1)], that a police action violates these strictures, its fruits are generally excluded from the prosecution's case.[6]

Although this legal context can give rise to several matters of interest to behavioral scientists,[7] the Fourth Amendment issue most likely to require clinical evaluation is whether a person who consented to a search or seizure was competent to do so. According to the United States Supreme Court, a valid (competent) consent to a search or seizure is one way the police action can be rendered reasonable. Specifically, a search is reasonable, even if the police do not have cause to conduct it, when a person "voluntarily" consents to the search.[8] Similarly, a police detention of a person, even if lacking in basis, is not considered a Fourth Amendment seizure when the person is found to have "voluntarily" consented to the detention.[9]

The Supreme Court has also held that, for Fourth Amendment purposes, a consent can be "voluntary" even if the person who consents does not know of the right to refuse consent.[10] Thus, in contrast to an assessment of competency to confess, which at least ostensibly involves a determination as to whether the confession is knowingly, as well as voluntarily, made [see § 7.03], evaluation of a person's competency to consent to a search is focused almost entirely on the extent to which police coerced the consenter. A person's knowledge or understanding of the right to refuse is at best a secondary issue.

Some data exist on the circumstances in which such a consent is most likely to be voluntary in the sense of being uncoerced.[11] But the most relevant case law and research about this subject comes from the confession context, where the difficult issues concerning the interaction of police behavior and the subject's vulnerabilities are virtually identical. It is to this subject that we now turn.

7.03. Competency to Confess

Like competency to consent to a search, the question whether a defendant was competent to confess is likely to be raised prior to trial, at a suppression hearing. Typically, the defense will claim that, at the time the defendant made a self-incriminating statement, the individual was incompetent to waive his or her rights under the Fifth

or Sixth Amendments and the statement should therefore be excluded. In such a situation, the evaluator's role is to form an opinion about the defendant's state of mind at the time the statement was made. To perform such an evaluation adequately, some understanding of the law of confessions is necessary.

(a) The Law of Confessions

The law of confessions is fraught with competing values. On the one hand, there is a desire to encourage confessions from guilty defendants. On the other hand, even reliable confessions are seen as unfairly obtained if they were elicited through means calculated to break the suspect's "will"; moreover, some police tactics (e.g., egregious lying, preventing access to one's attorney) might be considered "unfair" regardless of their impact on individuals. In short, the courts have exhibited an ambivalence about the desirability of effective interrogation ploys. Although a thorough discussion of the psychological issues implicated by the law of confessions is beyond the scope of this book, a brief review of the evolution of standards for assessing the admissibility of confessions should illuminate the complexity of clinical evaluation of a defendant's competency to confess.[12].

The Supreme Court's concern with the constitutional limits of police interrogations began in 1936 with *Brown v. Mississippi*.[13] In *Brown*, the Court vacated the convictions of three black defendants whose signatures on confessions to murder had been extorted through physical torture, hanging, and severe beating. The constitutional basis of this decision was the Fourteenth Amendment's admonition that government not deprive its citizens of liberty without "due process of law." In *Brown* and nearly 40 Court cases thereafter,[14] the validity of the confession depended on whether the totality of circumstances combined in such a way as to deprive the defendants of their will to resist the police.[15] For example, the Court ruled inadmissible confessions obtained from a suspect who was questioned continuously for 36 hours without rest or sleep,[16] a man who was told he could not phone his wife or anyone else unless he gave a statement,[17] a woman informed that welfare for her children would be cut off and her children taken away from her if she failed to "cooperate,"[18] and a man hospitalized for a gunshot wound, suffering from extreme pain and under the influence of morphine.[19]

Dissatisfied with the fact-specific nature of this analysis, which usually depended on findings of state courts prone to rely on police version of events, the Court cast about for an alternative approach. In 1964, the Court shifted its focus to whether the Sixth Amendment right to counsel was violated by failure to provide counsel during the interrogation of persons who have been formally charged.[20] Two years later, this approach was superseded by the Court's ruling in *Miranda v. Arizona*,[21] which relied on the Fifth Amendment's "privilege against self-incrimination" as the ground for excluding confessions. Although the due process and Sixth Amendment approaches still apply in certain circumstances,[22] the Fifth Amendment is now the principal constitutional basis for regulating police interrogation.

Besides the doctrinal shift, *Miranda* is important for the adoption of per se rules governing confessions. Unless defendants who are subjected to custodial interrogation are given the famous warnings mandated by *Miranda*, any statements they make are usually inadmissible.[23] If they are read their rights (i.e., that they have a right to remain silent and a right to an attorney during the interrogation), subsequent statements are still not admissible unless the defendant knowingly, intelligently and voluntarily waives them.[24] Moreover, interrogation must cease if a defendant says that he or she does not want to talk or invokes the right to counsel "in any manner and at any stage in the process."[25] These per se rules were designed to provide defendants with a measure of protection against sophisticated psychological ploys of police interrogators,[26] without the necessity of discerning the facts of an essentially "secret inquisition"[27] and engaging in the case-by-case analysis required under the law of voluntariness.[28]

Yet the law of voluntariness remains a key element in confessions cases, and *Miranda* itself is partly responsible. As noted, that decision held that once the warnings are given, the admissibility of any subsequent statements still depends on whether they were "knowingly, intelligently and voluntarily" made. Because police today routinely give the warnings, admissibility analysis in most

cases is therefore conceptually similar to, if not indistinct from, the pre-*Miranda* totality of the circumstances inquiry.[28] Furthermore, although the Supreme Court has shown little inclination to overrule *Miranda* altogether,[30] it has made clear that voluntary statements that are not preceded by warnings are still admissible under certain circumstances. For example, unwarned statements are admissible to impeach a defendant who takes the stand if they were voluntarily made in the totality of the circumstances.[31] Similarly, voluntariness is the only issue when there is no "custodial interrogation," a threshold the Court has interpreted narrowly: For instance, *Miranda* does not apply to interviews in the home,[32] questioning after stops for a traffic arrest,[33] or even some types of questioning at the police station when they do not represent the functional equivalent of arrest.[34]

In interpreting the scope of this rejuvenated voluntariness test, the Court has focused on the volitional rather than the cognitive aspects of "voluntariness." Although *Miranda* prohibited police "trickery,"[35] later Court decisions have indicated that as long as the person subjected to interrogation appears to understand the right to remain silent and the right to counsel subsequent waiver of those rights will usually be "knowing and intelligent"; other types of misunderstandings or misimpressions are not relevant to the admissibility issue. Thus, the Court has admitted confessions given by suspects (1) who thought they were making their admissions to prison inmates rather than police undercover agents,[36] (2) who believed only written statements were admissible and thus willingly gave oral statements,[37] (3) who were led to believe they would be questioned about one crime but were in fact questioned about another,[38] and (4) who were not told that their attorney was trying to reach them at the time of the interrogation.[39] In each case, the Court justified its holding on the ground that, although the police action may have been fraudulent, it did not result in the "compulsion" banned by the Fifth Amendment or the "coercion" prohibited by the due process clause.

As a result, confessions analysis has centered on the "voluntariness" component of the waiver requirement and has brought to the fore the complicated issue of coercion. Although the offensiveness of physical abuse as an interrogation tactic may be widely acknowledged,[40] police conduct that merely exerts "a tug on the suspect to confess" is not as likely to attract the same moral consensus.[41] The courts' decisions themselves make the latter point. *Miranda* castigated police attempts to "persuade" and "cajole" suspects into talking. But in the subsequent decision of *Rhode Island v. Innis*,[42] the Court found admissible the confession of a defendant who was persuaded to talk and reveal the location of the murder weapon by a police conversation to the effect that if the weapon were not found innocent children might find it and be harmed. Similarly, lower courts have found nothing unconstitutional about police "pressure" tactics suggesting that the evidence against the suspect is stronger than it actually is, or that a confession will better the suspect's chances at trial.[43]

When the suspect is demonstrably impaired, the courts have been somewhat more cautious about finding confessions either "intelligent" or "voluntary." For instance, several of the Supreme Court's pre-*Miranda*, due process cases declared that the suspect's mental retardation and mental illness are important factors to consider in gauging voluntariness.[44] At the same time, the courts have made clear that mental dysfunction, even if significant, will not automatically render a confession incompetent.[45] If the person understands the rights, evidence of impairment is unlikely to convince the court to suppress the evidence, unless there is also significant evidence of suggestibility or some other indicia of abnormal vulnerability to police importunings.[46]

Further, the Supreme Court has held that unless the police take advantage of the mental disability, due process and *Miranda* are not implicated because there is no *governmental* coercion. In *Colorado v. Connelly*,[47] the defendant flew from Boston to Denver to confess to police about a murder committed several months earlier in Colorado. Despite *Miranda* warnings and repeated reminders that he did not need to talk, Connelly insisted on giving police self-incriminating details of the murder. The police claimed to observe no signs of mental illness at that time. However, in trying to exclude Connelly's admissions at a subsequent hearing, the defense presented significant evidence of impairment, including the facts that

he had been a mental patient on several occasions and had not taken medication for the past six months. A psychiatrist further testified that although Connelly had understood his right to remain silent at the time he confessed, he had been "compelled" to talk by so-called "command delusions" from God. The Supreme Court held, however, that even assuming such delusions existed, neither voluntariness analysis nor *Miranda* required the exclusion of the admissions in this case because there was no police conduct "causally related to the confession." Although Connelly's illness may have rendered his statements unreliable, this was a matter to be decided under state evidentiary law.[48] After *Connelly*, then, statements not "caused" by the police will be admissible regardless of the defendant's mental state as long as they are considered admissible under state law and as long as the defendant was not so cognitively impaired that the right to remain silent was not understood.

All the Supreme Court's decisions, and most of the lower court cases as well, have been accompanied by vigorous dissents. Part of the difficulty in assessing the voluntariness of a confession emanates from a mix of philosophical paradigms regarding the nature of choice [see § 1.03(a)]: Courts seem to vacillate between a focus on free will (how "hard" did the police make the defendant's choice?) and determinism (was the defendant psychologically incapable of resisting?). On the one hand, no amount of police pressure, even the whipping and hanging involved in *Brown*, entirely breaks a suspect's will in the sense that the ultimate decision to talk is still the product of one's choice. On the other hand, one could also say that, at least for some people (perhaps some like Connelly), *any* degree of police confrontation may "compel" some type of response.

One answer to the difficulties inherent in the "causation–compulsion" issue may be to go beyond *Miranda* and establish new per se rules that explicitly indicate which interrogation tactics are believed to elicit confessions unfairly. White suggests, for instance, a ban on admitting incriminating statements obtained when police underplay the seriousness of the charges, announce that the suspect is known to be guilty, or assume a nonadversary stance (e.g., indicate that their purpose is to help the defendant)[49]—all tactics he claims minimize the import of the warnings.[50]

A second, quite different approach, is to avoid per se rules altogether and instead try to clarify the voluntariness inquiry. One such effort to alleviate the conceptual confusion came from Grano, who suggested that voluntariness doctrine be separated into three subcomponents: a prohibition of undue impairment of mental freedom, a prohibition of police taking undue advantage of the accused, and a prohibition of police creating an unnecessary risk of a false confession.[51] Of most interest to the mental health professional is Grano's definition of "mental freedom." Grano eschewed a "deterministic" definition of this term:

> The vast majority of defendants, weak or strong, initially are disinclined to provide the police self-incriminating statements. The objective of the interrogation session is to overcome this initial unwillingness without creating a risk that an innocent person will falsely confess. To take into account the peculiar weaknesses of each defendant would frustrate this objective, for the permissible level of police pressure would then decrease in direct proportion to the weakness of the suspect, thus leaving room for little more than volunteered statements. . . .
>
> Because the question of undue impairment of mental freedom [thus] requires normative rather than empirical judgements, we have the liberty to select those factors we consider morally relevant. Characteristics that are feigned easily and difficult to verify properly may be excluded, much as they are in everyday discourse and in the substantive criminal law [see §8.03(b)]. We generally do not excuse conduct because of social adversity, peculiar personality traits, abnormal temperament, or low intelligence; rather, we expect an individual to overcome these conditions or characteristics. We do, however, morally empathize with the physically or mentally ill, the feeble, the very young, and the very old. These, moreover, are stark characteristics that an interrogation officer can be expected to recognize.[52]

On these assumptions, Grano concluded: "The mental freedom component of the due process voluntariness test should ask whether a person of ordinary firmness, innocent or guilty, having the defendant's age, physical condition, and relevant mental abnormalities (but not otherwise having the defendant's personality traits, temperament, intelligence, or social background), and strongly preferring not to confess, would find the interrogation pressures overbearing."[53] Although Grano's precise test has not been adopted by any court, it probably captures the typical judicial approach to assessing the voluntariness of confessions by those with some type of mental impairment claim.

(b)   Evaluation Issues

The questions the mental health professional must consider when performing an evaluation of competency to confess are clear, at least in the abstract: Was the defendant's behavior "knowing" (i.e., did the defendant understand that he or she was waiving rights)? Was it "intelligent" (i.e., was the waiver of rights the product of a rational reasoning process)? Most problematic, was it "voluntary" (i.e., was the situation in its totality—and in its interaction with the defendant's state of mind—so coercive that the defendant's will was overborne)?

As is probably apparent from the preceding discussion, however, clinical opinion will rarely be considered very probative on any of these issues. The inquiry is likely to focus instead on two relatively superficial points: (1) whether police "followed the book" (e.g., whether they properly read *Miranda* warnings and subsequently obtained the suspect's acquiescence to talk and whether they refrained from unduly threatening behavior) and (2) whether the defendant "seemed okay" at the time of the interrogation. On both issues, courts will rely primarily on the police and on audiotapes, videotapes, or transcripts when they are available. As the foregoing discussion suggests, expert testimony might sway the judge in cases involving significant mental impairment. But even in these situations the condition that is alleged to have created incompetence (e.g., severe intoxication or misunderstanding of one's rights due to mental illness) may well have disappeared by the time of the evaluation, making credible corroboration difficult to obtain [cf. Mills and Bates reports in §§ 19.02(a), 19.03(a)].

Accordingly, evaluators should be particularly careful in their assessment. With respect to the knowing and intelligent prongs of the waiver issue, they should first question the defendants about their current understanding of the *Miranda* warnings (asking for both definitions and applications). They should then learn step by step what is recalled about the interrogation. What did the defendant think was the consequence of signing the waivers? What choices did the defendant think he or she had? Transcripts of the confession may be helpful corroboration here, although it should be noted that some "transcripts" are in fact police summaries of the defendant's statements which may leave out valuable information about the defendant's "true" mental state.[54] Further, they seldom include any description of the all-important events before the warnings are given.

In addition to reporting defendants' present and claimed past level of understanding of their rights, clinicians can help the courts evaluate this information by reporting norms of comprehension of rights for persons of similar age, socioeconomic status, and court experience. Here Grisso's work might be useful. Grisso found juveniles' understanding of *Miranda* warnings to be particularly likely to be deficient; however, results of interviews with the adult comparison groups showed that many adults from lower socioeconomic strata also lacked adequate comprehension of *Miranda* rights.[55] Furthermore, contrary to the probable assumption of the court, previous court experience was not a predictor of understanding of the *Miranda* warnings,[56] a finding replicated by other studies.[57]

Evaluation of "voluntariness" is more speculative and far-ranging. A step-by-step retrospective interview about the interrogation will still be necessary, but other information may also be needed. If, for example, there is a question about a defendant's being especially suggestible (an issue that is particularly likely to arise in connection with youth and those with mental retardation),[58] the clinician will want to find out more about the defendant's response to authority figures in other situations. Several research-based protocols can assist in this endeavor.[59] Similarly, if a defendant claims to have been intoxicated at the time of interrogation, information will be needed about the individual's previous drug and alcohol history in order to evaluate the report. Police reports and other eyewitness accounts of the defendant's behavior are also sometimes helpful, as of course are transcripts or tapes of the confession itself.

The evaluator may also want to keep in mind that people do confess to crimes they did not commit, even when the techniques used do not involve physical coercion.[60] Kassin and Wrightsman have suggested three different situations in which this might occur[61]: (1) "voluntary" false confessions, in which the individual confesses with little or no police pressure, out of a desire for notoriety, a need to expiate guilt for other wrongdoing, or simply due to an inability to distinguish fact from fantasy[62]; (2) "coerced compliant" false confessions, which occur because the suspect believes confessing is the only way to escape from an intolerably stressful interrogation situation (and which are usually retracted as soon as the confessor does escape); and (3) "coerced-internalized" false confessions, which occur because an innocent person temporarily internalizes the police message of guilt. Based on a small case study, Ofshe suggests that the third type of confession is most likely to occur when the interrogator, during a lengthy, emotionally intense interrogation, repeatedly displays certainty about the suspect's guilt, is able to produce seemingly incontrovertible proof of the suspect's guilt, and is able to suggest reasons why the suspect cannot remember committing the crime.[63]

In view of the fuzziness of the concept in the law and the illogic of the concept in a deterministic paradigm, clinicians should not couch their report in terms of "voluntariness" [see generally § 1.03(a)]. Rather, the clinician should report on those aspects of the defendant's functioning that might make him or her especially vulnerable to influence by the police. Where systematic data are available as to the effectiveness of a given interrogation technique with people of similar characteristics, such research should also be noted.[64] After *Connelly*, the mere presence of a severe mental dysfunction will not support a constitutional claim that a confession was involuntarily made—some proof that police took advantage of the defendant's condition is required. Thus, whenever the defense theory is that a confession was unduly coerced, clinicians should be careful to report from available sources the extent of police interaction with the defendant so that the "causal connection" issue can be addressed intelligently.

7.04.　Competency to Plead Guilty

More than 90% of all criminal cases are resolved through a guilty plea rather than through a verdict reached after a trial.[65] As is true with confessions, such a plea must be "knowing and intelligent," as well as "voluntary."[66] Thus, the defendant must understand at least three aspects of the guilty plea to enter a valid plea: (1) the nature of the charge pled to,[67] (2) the penalties associated with the charge,[68] and (3) the rights waived by the plea of guilt, including the right to remain silent, the right to confront one's accusers, the right to a jury trial, and the right to trial counsel.[69] This determination must be made by a judge, on the record, at a plea hearing (often called the "arraignment" [see § 2.04 (a) (1)]). At the same time, the typical plea-taking process is short; it consists of a series of questions directed at the defendant, who usually answers in monosyllables, as directed by the defense attorney. The assumption is that the attorney has determined that the plea is in the defendant's best interest and has explained to the defendant the consequences of pleading guilty.[70]

Until the early 1990s, a crucial constitutional question in connection with guilty pleas was whether a person who pleaded guilty had to be "more" competent than a person who decided to go to trial. The rationale for so holding, endorsed by the Ninth Circuit in *Seiling v. Eyman*,[71] was that a person who pleads guilty not only has to understand the charge and its consequences (as is true with a person undergoing trial) but also must be able, as indicated above, to understand and waive intelligently various constitutional rights. According to *Seiling*, because "the degree of competency required to waive a *constitutional* right is that degree which enables him to make decisions of very serious import" [Emphasis added], the degree of competency necessary to make a guilty plea valid must be higher than that required for competency to stand trial.[72] Thus, *Seiling* held, "[a] defendant is not competent to plead guilty if a mental illness has substantially impaired his ability to make a reasoned choice among the alternatives presented to him and to understand the nature of the consequences of his plea."[73]

However, in *Godinez v. Moran*,[74] the facts of which are described in Case Study 7.1, the United States Supreme Court rejected this standard, holding with the majority of federal courts that a person who is competent to stand trial is also competent to plead guilty. The principal reason it gave for this conclusion was that, contrary to the insinuation in *Seiling*, a person who stands trial, like a person who pleads guilty, must also be able to decide whether to remain silent (when deciding whether to take the stand), confront accusers (when it comes time for their cross-examination), and waive a jury trial. As Justice Thomas wrote for seven members of the Court:

> [All c]riminal defendants—not merely those who plead guilty—may be required to make important decisions once criminal proceedings have been initiated. And while the decision to plead guilty is undeniably a profound one, it is no more complicated than the sum total of decisions that a defendant may be called upon to make during the course of a trial.

As a practical matter, most defendants who go to trial do not waive their rights to remain silent, confront accusers, or be heard by a jury, and therefore do not have to make the momentous decisions that a person pleading guilty must make; thus, *Moran*'s justification for its conclusion is somewhat disingenuous. But there are other reasons to support its conclusion equating competency to stand trial with competency to plead guilty. As one commentator pointed out, the *Seiling* standard could "create a class of semi-competent defendants who are not protected from prosecution because they have been found competent to stand trial, but who are denied the leniency of the plea bargain process because they are not competent to plead guilty."[75] Moreover, as others have argued,[76] the danger of inappropriate pleas by such "semi-competent" individuals is mitigated by the fact that counsel can be assumed to have already made "a reasoned choice among the alternatives," even if the defendant is incapable of doing so.

In short, in those jurisdictions that follow *Moran* (i.e., all federal jurisdictions and most states), the clinician performing a pretrial evaluation of competency need not "adjust" the competency standard according to whether the defendant is likely to plead guilty or go to trial. On the other hand, to ensure that defendants are competent in the appropriate areas, it is important to quiz *every* defendant about his or her understanding of the rights that are waived through a plea. An instrument that was developed with precisely this objective in mind is the MacArthur Competence Assessment Tool—Criminal Adjudication, described in § 6.06(g).

If the latter "rights" assessment is undertaken in connection with the usual competency-to-stand trial evaluation, the evaluator will have obtained sufficient information for the "knowing" and "intelligence" prongs of the competency to plead guilty inquiry [see Bates report, § 19.03]. That leaves the "voluntariness" component of the inquiry. Most guilty pleas are reached through the plea-bargaining process, in which the prosecutor offers either a reduced charge or the promise of a favorable sentencing recommendation in exchange for a plea of guilty.[77] In short, guilty pleas typically result in less aversive consequences than are risked by going to trial. Are such avoidance responses "voluntary"?

The Supreme Court has answered this question in the affirmative. In *Bordenkircher v. Hayes*,[78] the prosecutor threatened to charge the defendant as an habitual offender, conviction of which would carry a mandatory life sentence, if he did not agree to plead guilty and accept a five-year sentence. The Court found nothing unconstitutional about the prosecutor's action because the habitual offender charge was legitimate under state law and the defendant was free to accept or reject the prosecution's offer. According to the Court, "the imposition of these difficult choices [is] an inevitable—and permissible—attribute of any legitimate system which tolerates and encourages the negotiation of pleas." Similarly, in *Brady v. United States*,[79] the Supreme Court refused to invalidate a guilty plea given in exchange for a life sentence, despite the defendant's claim that he had pleaded guilty out of fear that he might receive the death penalty had he gone to trial. The Court explained that although fear of the death penalty may have "caused" the plea, it did not coerce it; the latter would have been true only if the defendant had proven he "was so gripped by fear of the death penalty or hope of leniency that he did not or could not, with the help of counsel, rationally weigh the advantages of going to trial against the advantages of pleading guilty."

Yet this extreme construction of voluntariness may not be the last word. As in the confession context, there is some precedent indicating that government conduct need not produce or take advantage of "irrationality" to be considered impermissible. The *Brady* Court itself seemed to suggest that some types of government "threats" and "unfulfillable promises" might exert enough pressure on a defendant to invalidate any subsequent guilty plea, regardless of the person's rationality at the time it was made.[80] Further, in contrast to the confession context [see discussion of *Connelly* in § 7.03(a)], the government may not even have to be involved for a plea to be invalid. Suppose, for instance, a defendant with mental retardation places such trust in the attorney that he or she immediately accepts the attorney's suggestion to plea-bargain, without considering any of the options. Should not such a plea be considered "involuntary"? As noted in the preceding section, there is no scientific basis for differentiating these cases on the basis of voluntariness. The mental health professional should report a defendant's reasoning about the decision and any internal or external pressures to accept a bargain and should leave to the judge determination of whether the choice was so hard as to render the plea involuntary.

7.05. Competency to Waive the Right to Counsel

The decision that is probably most likely to have an adverse effect on a defendant's ability to achieve a fair trial is the waiver of the right to trial counsel. Because this decision deprives the defendant of a legally trained advocate, it will seldom, if ever, be in a defendant's best interests. Nonetheless, in *Faretta v. California*,[81] the United States Supreme Court held that the Sixth Amendment guarantees criminal defendants a right to self-representation. Writing for the majority, Justice Stewart emphasized that procedural rights of due process belong to the accused, not his or her counsel:

It [the Sixth Amendment] speaks of the "assistance" of counsel, and an assistant, however expert, is still an assistant. The language and spirit of the Sixth Amendment contemplate that counsel, like the other defense tools guaranteed by the Amendment, shall be an aid to a willing defendant, not an organ of the State interposed between an unwilling defendant and his right to defend himself personally. To thrust counsel upon the accused, against his considered wish, thus violates the logic of the Amendment. In such a case, counsel is not an assistant but a master; and the right to make a defense is stripped of the personal character upon which the Amendment insists.[82]

The Court noted further that although the defendant may ultimately be acting to his or her detriment in deciding to proceed *pro se*, the value of free choice is worthy of constitutional protection even when the choice could increase the likelihood of criminal punishment.

Faretta did not attempt to define competency in this context. But it did emphasize that a person is not incompetent to waive an attorney merely because he or she may be unable to understand technical legal matters such as the hearsay rules or the rules governing selection of the jury. At the same time, earlier Court decisions had suggested, without deciding, that the level of competency required for the decision to waive counsel was "higher" than that required to stand trial or plead guilty with the aid of counsel.[83] This conclusion would seem to follow from the idea, noted earlier, that counsel is crucial to a fair trial in our adversarial system; recall also [from § 7.04] that the primary rationale for equating competency to stand trial and competency to plead guilty is that counsel can ensure that the latter decision is a wise one, which is much less likely if a defendant who is merely competent to stand trial is allowed to discharge the attorney before making a plea.

In *Godinez v. Moran*,[84] however, the Court not only found competency to stand trial and plead guilty to be equivalent (as discussed in the previous section) but also held that a person who is competent to stand trial is competent to waive an attorney. According to the majority, "the competence that is required of a defendant seeking to waive his right to counsel is the competence to waive the right, not the competence to represent himself." Noting, as had *Faretta*, that the right to

self-representation inevitably will mean some defendants will "conduct [their] own defense ultimately to [their] own detriment," it stated that "a criminal defendant's ability to represent himself has no bearing upon his competence to *choose* self-representation."[85] Thus, a person who is competent to stand trial is competent to waive the right to counsel and proceed *pro se*. The fact that such a person may perform inadequately during the adjudication process is irrelevant.

Two limitations on the effect of *Moran* should be noted. First, the Court emphasized that competence to waive an attorney, by itself, does not make a waiver of counsel valid. The trial judge must also determine, as with other waivers of constitutional rights, that the waiver is "voluntary" and "intelligent." To be voluntary a waiver must be uncoerced, in the same way a guilty plea must be uncoerced. To be intelligent, the *Moran* Court stated, the defendant "must be made aware of the dangers and disadvantages of self-representation, so that the record will establish that he knows what he is doing and his choice is made with eyes open." In other words, the defendant must not only be competent to understand, but actually understand, the consequences of the waiver decision.[86]

The second way in which the potentially harsh impact of *Moran* may be cushioned comes from an earlier Court decision, *McKaskle v. Wiggins*.[87] There, the Court held that the person who successfully waives counsel can nonetheless be forced to proceed with "standby counsel" as long as the *pro se* defendant retains actual control over the case presented to the jury and the jury retains the perception that the defendant represents him or herself. Under these conditions, the standby counsel can provide the *pro se* defendant advice about tactics and information about legal rules.

Under *Moran*, then, the clinician performing an evaluation of competency to waive an attorney should conduct a competency-to-stand-trial evaluation and additionally inquire into the reasons for wanting to proceed *pro se* and whether the individual is aware of the disadvantages of doing so. Further inquiry is unnecessary, at least as to whether the decision is knowing and intelligent. *Faretta* established that technical legal knowledge is not required to represent oneself, and *Moran* confirmed this holding. Apparently the monitoring of the judge and the provision of standby counsel are considered sufficient to protect against unfair adjudications in cases involving unrepresented individuals who are merely competent to stand trial. It should be noted, however, that in some states a higher level of competency may be required; *Moran* only established the constitutional minimum. Furthermore, it may be that *Moran* will increase the level of competency associated with competency to stand trial now that judges and evaluators know that the latter finding will also normally permit waiver of counsel.

Regardless of the standard applied, clinicians should be particularly alert to defeatist attitudes (e.g., "A lawyer won't be any help because I'm guilty"), paranoid ideation (e.g., "All lawyers are against me"), clearly fantastic objectives (e.g., a desire to defend oneself on the ground that the President of the United States actually committed the offense), or irrational beliefs (e.g., supernatural powers will prevent the jury from returning a guilty verdict). In the past, courts have been more willing to declare a defendant incompetent in such situations.[88] On the other hand, defendants who want to proceed *pro se* because they think they can do a better job than a lawyer, believe a lawyer will not effectively communicate their message, or disagree with the lawyer's objective are not likely to be found incompetent unless their reasoning is clearly irrational.[89] Because the importance of these variables may differ from case to case and court to court, our usual injunction to avoid the ultimate issue stands here as well.

7.06.   Competency to Refuse an Insanity Defense

A relatively uncommon variant of competency arises when the defense attorney, the prosecution, or the court believes that a defendant may have been insane at the time of the offense, but the defendant does not want to assert such a defense. Does the court have the authority, or perhaps even the duty, to raise the defense over the defendant's objection?

The appellate courts that have considered this question have been divided in their approach.[90]

One line of cases is illustrated by *Whalem v. United States*,[91] in which Judge Bazelon, writing for the federal Court of Appeals for the District of Columbia Circuit, appeared to require trial judges to impose an insanity defense when the defense would be likely to succeed:

> One of the major foundations for the structure of the criminal law is the concept of responsibility, and the law is clear that one whose acts would otherwise be criminal has committed no crime at all if because of incapacity due to age or mental condition he is not responsible for those acts. . . .
>
> In the courtroom confrontations between the individual and society the trial judge must uphold this structural foundation by refusing to allow the conviction of an obviously mentally irresponsible defendant, and when there is sufficient question as to a defendant's mental responsibility at the time of the crime, that issue must become part of the case. Just as the judge must insist that the *corpus delicti* be proved before a defendant who has confessed may be convicted, so too must the judge forestall the conviction of one who in the eyes of the law is not mentally responsible for his actions.[92]

The *Whalem* formulation thus emphasizes society's interests in avoiding the conviction of a morally blameless person. Although it permits judges, in their discretion, to take the defendant's interests into account as well,[93] these interests would not be dispositive.

In contrast, a second line of cases, led by *Frendak v. United States*,[94] requires that the defendant's decision regarding assertion of the defense be followed when the defendant is competent to make it. Pointing to the United States Supreme Court's post-*Whalem* decisions in *North Carolina v. Alford*[95] (which held that a competent defendant is permitted to plead guilty even when denying guilt) and *Faretta v. California*,[96] (establishing, as noted previously, the right to represent oneself), the *Frendak* court concluded that "respect for a defendant's freedom as a person mandates that he or she be permitted to make fundamental decisions about the course of the proceedings."[97] The court then noted several reasons why a defendant might choose to refuse an insanity defense: (1) an insanity acquittal may result in a longer period of confinement than would conviction, (2) the defendant may believe that better treatment will be received in prison than in a mental hospital, (3) the defendant may wish to avoid the stigma associated with mental disorder, (4) commitment to the mental health system may result in collateral loss of legal rights (e.g., the ability to obtain a driver's license), or (5) the defendant may view the crime as a political or religious act, which an insanity defense would negate.[98] The court was persuaded—properly, in our view—that, because the defendant must bear the consequences of any decision, these types of reasons are more compelling than *Whalem's* objective of upholding society's concept of justice. Accordingly, *Frendak* limits the inquiry about whether a defendant may refuse an insanity defense to an investigation of the defendant's competency to waive the defense.[99]

Frendak is clearly the majority view. Indeed, *Whalem* itself was overturned in *United States v. Marble*.[100] But a few jurisdictions still adhere to the *Whalem* approach.[101] In the latter jurisdictions, the scope of the evaluation will be akin to a typical evaluation of mental state at the time of the offense; the primary issue is whether the weight of the evidence points toward a viable insanity defense, although the defendant's reasoning process in rejecting the defense may be considered relevant. On the other hand, in a *Frendak*-style jurisdiction, the nature of the evaluation will be similar to that of competency to stand trial. Indeed, in light of *Godinez v. Moran* (discussed in the preceding sections), it is probable the Supreme Court would hold that a person who is competent to stand trial is competent to waive the insanity defense.[102]

Yet the clinician performing a *Frendak*-type evaluation should be aware that there are differences between the typical decisions made by a person found competent to stand trial and the person who is making the specific decision as to whether to assert an insanity defense. In particular, as *Frendak* recognized,[103] an assessment of the latter decision might need to focus on whether a refusal to pursue an insanity defense is related to a denial of one's mental disorder (e.g., when the defendant's claim that an insanity defense should be rejected rests on the assertion that "there is nothing wrong with me").[104] If so, the scope of the evaluation may go well beyond the typical competency to stand trial evaluation and, as in *Whalem* jurisdictions, require an assessment of

mental state at the time of the offense, at least at a screening level [see § 8.06(a)].

Moreover, even if competency to waive an insanity defense is equated with competency to stand trial, the waiver must be voluntary and intelligent, as is true with competency to plead guilty and to waive an attorney. Thus, the clinician will also need to explore the defendant's understanding of alternative defenses and their consequences, and the perceived probability of their success. In so doing, the inquiry once again may focus on the viability of an insanity defense and whether the defendant's reasons for rejecting it are based on denial. Whether the level of denial is sufficiently severe to warrant a finding of incompetency to refuse an insanity defense is, of course, a matter for the judge to decide.

7.07. Competency to Testify

Based on the principle that only evidence that has some probative value is admissible, courts have long held that people who are incapable of remembering or reporting what they have observed, or have no ability to grasp the importance of accurately doing so, may not testify as witnesses. Thus, testimonial competency is still another competency issue that a forensic clinician might be asked to address. Two differences between this type of competency and the others in this chapter should be apparent, however. First, whereas the other competencies addressed herein concern only the defendant, the issue of testimonial competency may arise in connection with *any* person who may be a witness. Second, testimonial capacity arises in civil as well as criminal trials. It is discussed here because it most often arises in criminal trials, particularly in abuse cases involving children.

Also discussed here is the closely related issue of expert evaluation of and testimony about a witness's *credibility*. Increasingly, mental health professionals have been involved in assessing and commenting upon the truth of testimony offered by witnesses who are competent to testify but whose mental condition raises questions about their veracity. The fourth subsection examines this complex area.

(a) Legal Requirements for Testimonial Competency

Until the 1970s, the law of most states presumed that children under a certain age (e.g., 10 or 14) were incompetent to testify, meaning that the party tendering the witness had to prove competency.[105] Although there was typically no similar presumption with respect to those with mental disability, courts routinely barred persons with significant impairments from testifying.[106] Today, in contrast, the law in most states presumes that everyone is competent to testify.[107] In 1975, the Federal Rules of Evidence added Rule 601, which simply states that "[e]very person is competent to be a witness" unless their testimony is irrelevant or likely to mislead the factfinder, or they are unable or unwilling to declare they will testify truthfully.[108] Describing current law at the federal level, Louisell and Mueller go so far as to state:

> Only in extreme cases—imaginable, but unlikely to be encountered often—should a trial judge exclude a witness [on the grounds of incompetence]. Neither immaturity nor mental or psychological disability, nor even the use of drugs or alcohol, will ordinarily signify that a witness cannot provide relevant evidence, or will inject into the case in undue degree the concerns underlying Rule 403 [which allows exclusion of evidence which will create "unfair prejudice, confusion of the issues or mislead[ ] the jury," or cause "undue delay, waste of time or needless presentation of cumulative evidence"].[109]

Although a few states still set a presumptive age for incompetency, most states have since followed the federal lead or at most set out guidelines for determining whether a witness is competent.

In many jurisdictions, moreover, a witness who claims to be a victim of abuse and is testifying against the alleged abuser is *irrebuttably* presumed to be competent,[110] a rule that has withstood constitutional challenge.[111] These "automatic competency" statutes are principally the result of the same campaign that gave rise to child abuse reporting laws [see § 15.01(c)]. But they are also justifiable on grounds elucidated by the noted evidence authority Dean Wigmore many years ago:

> A rational view of the peculiarities of child-nature, and of the daily course of justice in our courts, must lead to the conclusion that the effort to measure *a priori* the degrees of trustworthiness in children's statements, and to distinguish the point at which they cease to be totally incredible and acquire some degree of credibility, is futile and unprofitable. . . . Recognizing on the one hand the childish disposition to weave romances and to treat imagination for verity, and on the other the rooted ingeniousness of children and their tendency to speak straightforwardly what is in their minds, it must be concluded that the sensible way is to put the child upon the stand and let the story come out for what it may be worth.[112]

It is important to note, however, that except in those jurisdictions requiring the admission of testimony from alleged child abuse victims, modern law merely makes testimony by children and those with mental disability more likely than under the common law; it does not prevent a judge from barring testimony on competency grounds. Just as the common-law presumption of incompetency for children was rebuttable, the modern presumption that everyone is competent may be overcome with sufficient evidence showing that a person's mental incapacity will render his or her testimony irrelevant, misleading, or incredible.[113] Indeed, as Weissenberger has noted, a preliminary hearing on the competency issue "is advisable in any case in which the trial judge has reason to believe that the witness's testimony might be impaired by infancy, counter-probative mental or psychological conditions or chemical influence."[114]

The precise criteria the judge applies at such a hearing vary from state to state but, as summarized by Myers,[115] focus on five capacities: (1) the ability to observe the event, (2) the ability to remember it, (3) the ability to communicate that memory, (4) the ability to tell the difference between truth and falsity, and (5) the ability to understand the obligation to tell the truth in court.[116] Given the language of Rule 601 and its state counterparts, presumably only minimal capacity in each of these areas is necessary. Nonetheless, courts and parties have occasionally sought assistance from the behavioral sciences in making competency determinations. To aid in this endeavor, the following discussion describes empirical research relevant to the five areas described (the last two of which are discussed together). It also attempts to explicate the legal implications of the research.

(b)　Psychological Research

As the previous discussion suggests, the four categories of individuals most likely to trigger testimonial capacity concerns are children, people with mental retardation, people with mental illness and those who have abused substances. Because the literature is most robust in connection with children, this review focuses on what is known about their testimonial capacities. However, a few references to research on the capacities of those with retardation are noted as well; in addition, the developmental literature regarding children should be useful in understanding the likely effects of cognitive immaturity for those with retardation. When the prospective witness is a person with mental illness or substance abuse problems, an individual assessment will need to be made of the severity of impairment in cognitive functioning, though much of the discussion that follows may prove helpful in such cases as well.

(1)　Observation

Unless the child or mentally disabled person has some visual or aural defect, his or her capacity to sense events will usually be sufficient to meet the first prong of testimonial capacity. It is possible, however, that some very young children or people with mental retardation may not have the ability to process all types of events. For instance, although children seem to have the capacity to recognize familiar faces and absorb simple scenarios, Johnson and Foley found that "recognition of more complex events, such as unfamiliar, disguised faces . . . or complex scenes . . . evidently require processes that are more likely to develop with age."[117] Children may also have difficulty grasping the meaning of sophisticated conversations. At the same time, children still seem to be able to register an event even if they do not understand it.[118] Moreover, children who are called on to testify will typically be asked to describe

relatively concrete actions by people they know; if so, little question about their capacity to observe events should exist. A separate issue is their ability to conceptualize and describe what has been observed, a topic discussed in connection with ability to communicate.

(2)　Memory and Suggestibility

Because legal proceedings often occur months or even years after the legally relevant event, the capacity to remember what was observed is as important as the capacity to observe. Furthermore, the capacity to remember events accurately is virtually inseparable from one's capacity to resist suggestion from other sources. Thus, research on both memory and suggestibility is important in evaluating this competency criterion.

Most of the research in this area has been conducted in connection with children. The bottom line appears to be that children are somewhat less likely than adults to retain memory of what they hear or observe, but that all but the youngest children probably have good enough memories to pass the minimal requirements for testimonial capacity. On the closely related issue of the extent to which memory may be affected by outside influences, most studies indicate that young children are more suggestible than adults. Again, however, this finding alone probably should not render the child incompetent to testify; the better approach will normally be to make known the opportunities for suggestion to the factfinder, which can then assess the credibility of the witness.

In assessing memory retention capacity, two different types of memory should be noted: recognition memory, where a person is asked if he or she recognizes a person or a place, and recall memory, where a person is asked to describe an event, person, or place. Even children as young as three and four appear to perform as well as adults on some recognition-memory tasks. For instance, a child who is asked to identify previously seen pictures or faces should be able to do as well as an adult, assuming no intervening suggestions have taken hold.[119] Research also indicates that even when a previously *unfamiliar* perpetrator is present in a lineup, five- and six-year olds' identifications are as accurate as adults'.[120]

However, when the child has had only brief exposure to the perpetrator or is very young, accuracy decreases.[121] Furthermore, when the suspect is *not* present in the lineup, children as old as nine tend to make more errors than adults,[122] and there is some evidence that young children may sometimes place familiar people at an event who were not actually there.[123]

Recall memory requires more sophisticated cognitive processes than recognition memory. Accordingly, a child who is asked to describe a past event, such as an assault, will find the task relatively more difficult than an adult. The difference between the recall memory of children and adults depends primarily on two variables: time and the extent to which other versions of the event have been suggested by third parties (the "suggestibility" issue).

When the time interval between the event and the attempt at memory recall is short, children apparently do not do appreciably worse than adults. For instance, in a study by Marin, Holmes, Guth, and Kovac,[124] students ages 5 to 22 observed a confederate of the experimenter interrupt a session to complain angrily about the experimenter's using a room supposedly already scheduled. Subjects were questioned about the incident after a brief interval (10–30 minutes) and after two weeks. Memory was assessed using free recall, objective questions (including one leading question), and photo identification. Older subjects produced much more material on free recall (mean number of descriptive statements: kindergarten and first grade, 1.42; third and fourth grades, 3.75; seventh and eighth grades, 6.50; college students, 8.25). However, the younger subjects were no worse than the older subjects in answering objective questions and making photo identification (the latter result supporting the findings about recognition memory noted earlier). Furthermore, the youngest subjects were significantly *more* likely than adults to recall the event correctly on those occasions they did produce information (only 3% incorrect).[125]

As the time interval between event and recall lengthens, however, children do not do as well as adults in recalling events. For instance, one study found that the proportion of inaccurate information from six- and nine-year old children doubled from 9% one day after the event to 18% five

months after the event, whereas the error rate for adults for the two time periods remained constant (10% vs. 8%).[126] A similar pattern was found in a study of children ages four to eight years: Although the error rate one week after the event was similar among children and adults (7% on average), two years later the children's error rate was 20% whereas the adults' remained the same.[127] This study also found that two years later, 21% of the children attributed actions to one person that had actually been performed by another, an error not made by any of the adults, and one that has obvious legal implications. Finally, infantile amnesia can obscure memories of very early childhood if enough time elapses.[128] More research needs to be done, however, on whether children's memory fades more quickly than adults' when a particularly negative event is involved.[129]

Presumably, one way of alleviating the effects of memory decay would be to obtain an early account of the legally relevant event. Indeed, several studies have found that "events that are personally significant, emotion-laden, *and* rehearsed are less likely to be lost from memory" [Emphasis added].[130] As Poole and White suggest, a post-event interview may act as a "memory consolidator" for children. However, they also conclude that it will have this effect only if it occurs less than a week after the event, and only if it avoids specific (i.e., yes–no) questions.[131] Unfortunately, neither of these conditions is easily met in legal contexts such as abuse cases. Allegations of abuse may not arise until some time after the alleged event. More important, use of open-ended questions, which is generally a good idea in *any* forensic interview, may not be as productive where children are involved. As suggested by the Marin et al. study described earlier, and as Poole and White themselves note, "it is exceptionally difficult to get children to volunteer information with general questions."[132] In short, young children require direct cues, such as specific, direct questions, to stimulate recall.[133]

These various observations bring to the fore the suggestibility issue, which many courts have recognized as an important component of competency analysis.[134] Although specific questions may be the best method for obtaining information from children, they are also most likely to contain cues as to how to answer. Hence, the "memory" recounted by a child may be suggested inadvertently (or advertently) as an adult helps the child to make sense of the experience.

Here again the research is relatively clear. Although adults as well as children are prone to fill in perceptual and memory gaps with stereotypical information and postevent suggestion,[135] most studies find that young children are more likely to accede to such suggestions, especially when they are from authority figures who act in an intimidating fashion. According to Ceci, children over 10 or 11 years of age tend to show adult levels of resistance to leading questions.[136] But children under 6 may acquiesce fairly frequently, especially when questions are "highly leading, detailed, incriminating, and repeated over multiple interviews," with children in between showing varying levels of vulnerability.[137] Vulnerability to suggestions may be particularly high when, as is often the case with child witnesses in criminal and civil cases, the adult proffering the suggestions is someone who saw the event. For instance, Warren and Lane found that the nine-year-olds in their study were significantly more likely than adults to adhere to the suggestions of adult interviewers who had seen the event in question.[138] Indeed, when the "suggester" has seen the event, his or her age may not be a major determinant of suggestive power. Haugaard et al. showed children ages four to six a videotape of a girl who was approached but not touched by a neighbor and then made up a story about being assaulted by him. Apparently responding to the girl's lie, 29% of the children incorrectly recalled that the assault occurred, whereas none of the undergraduates who saw the tape did.[139]

This correlation between age and suggestibility can be explained in a number of ways, none of them mutually exclusive. It is likely due in part to children's weaker memory over time, discussed previously. It is also likely due to young children's greater respect for authority—an hypothesis bolstered by simple learning theory, which would suggest that children's behavior will be shaped by their perceptions of adults' expectations.[140] Finally, it may have something to do with children's moral development. As Fodor discovered,[141] children who yield to the suggestions of an adult interviewer tend to score lower on assessments of level of moral judgment (according to Kohlberg's criteria) than children who resist such suggestions.

Although the research is not as extensive, studies examining the capacities of those with mental retardation yield results similar to those obtained with children. As with children, the method that is most likely to garner information from those with mental retardation is also the method most likely to taint it. Because of their cognitive deficiencies, mentally retarded individuals are more likely to reveal what they know in response to a yes–no question format; free recall is likely to produce less, if not inaccurate, information.[142] Yet, because of their desire to please, these people are also more likely than others to acquiesce in suggestions by authority figures.[143]

In light of the fact that, by the time of the typical trial, a witness has been interviewed several times by government officials and lawyers, and perhaps been confronted by the alleged perpetrator as well, what are the legal implications of these findings about suggestibility? Myers states that people "are not rendered incompetent to serve as witnesses simply because they are sometimes misled by suggestion" and implies that generally heightened suggestibility should not be a bar to testimony.[144] Christiansen is less sanguine, stating that "when pretrial procedures have falsified a child's memory, the child is not competent to testify to the contents of that memory." He goes on to suggest how the law should respond when suggestive procedures have been used:

> When a child has been the subject of potentially suggestive pretrial procedures the child's competence as a witness cannot be determined unless these procedures have been taken into account and any effects they may have had on the child's memory have been weighed. Competency hearing *voir dire* of the child alone does not satisfy this requirement. The child may not be able to separate out the various interviews she has been through or to respond meaningfully to questions about them. The child may not have been at all aware of more subtle forms of suggestion, such as the phrasing and repetition of questions. . . . Accordingly, competency determinations in such cases must rely upon extrinsic evidence of the pretrial procedures as well, including, but not limited to, the testimony and records of those who conducted the pretrial in-

terviews and other procedures. . . . In some cases, it might also be appropriate to present expert testimony independent of the testimony of the interviewers, to show why the procedures might or might not have affected the child's memory.[145]

At the least, the research recounted earlier suggests that interviewing and evaluation of young children and those with mental retardation must proceed cautiously. Specific guidelines along these lines are taken up in § 7.07(c). As to the special issues that arise when the memory is allegedly "repressed," that topic is discussed in Chapter 15, which deals with abuse and neglect issues [see in particular § 15.07(b)].[146]

(3)   Ability to Communicate

If an event cannot be communicated in a coherent, meaningful way, a witness's observation and memory of it are useless to the factfinder. Consequently, a person's ability to conceptualize complex events and to order them in space and time are of major legal importance. Further, particular kinds of testimony may require further specific competencies. Most notably, testimony about sexual abuse may require verification of the child's comprehension of the meaning of sexual terms and behavior.[147]

Shaffer has stated that "by age 5, children not only understand most of the grammatical rules of their native tongue but are also constructing remarkably complex, adultlike sentences."[148] But children below that age, and indeed some children above it, may not be able to communicate their observations effectively. For example, to Piaget, the well-known theorist of child development,[149] it was a truism that "preoperational" children, often up to age seven, are unable to "decenter" from the most obvious attribute of a stimulus and make use of all relevant information. To cite a classic example, young children who observe a clay string rolled into a ball and then rolled back into a string believe that there is more clay present when it is in a ball, which looks more massive. Children may also have difficulty in understanding time independent of distance and speed (e.g., many believe that the object that travels the furthest has traveled the longest), and thus may have difficulty in describing the chronology

of events. Further, Piaget asserted, the basic egocentrism of young children may make it difficult for them to interpret the actions of others outside a limited frame of reference.[150] All this may affect a child's ability to recite facts accurately.

Some critics of Piagetian theory have suggested that, on many tasks, preschoolers are less illogical and egocentric in their thinking than Piaget believed.[151] Siegel has argued that the classical finding of young children's inability to pass "conservation" tasks (e.g., the ball-of-clay) is often a manifestation of linguistic deficits.[152] That is, young children may not understand the words "more," "bigger," and the like, but they may be able to demonstrate understanding of the concepts nonverbally. Furthermore, Brainerd, Trabasso and others have demonstrated that preschoolers can be trained in conservation skills,[153] contrary to the Piagetian hypothesis that the necessary cognitive structures would not be expected to have developed adequately. With respect to the egocentrism claim, Borke has found that children three to four years old have the capacity to take the perspective of another,[154] provided the specific task is a simple one and involves little use of language.[155]

These studies do not moot the point, however, that young children are likely to have difficulty in conceptualizing complex events. Borke, for example, has admitted that some of Piaget's tasks are "cognitively too difficult" for children below the age of five.[156] And although the work of Brainerd and others indicates that children's capacities can be enhanced with training,[157] such training is not always available or feasible. Given the realities of the courtroom situation, cognitive-developmental factors are an important consideration in evaluating the testimony of children who are younger than seven.[158] They should also be taken into account when interviewing such children.[159]

Nonetheless, young children's immaturity of conceptualization may ultimately have little impact on their competency to testify, for at least two reasons. First, modern courts do not seem overly concerned with these problems. According to most courts, the fact that children use language differently, are occasionally inconsistent, make factual mistakes, have difficulty conceptualizing time, or resort to nonverbal methods are not per se bars to a competency finding.[160] The ultimate question is whether children's testimony is so un-reliable that jurors would be "unduly" influenced by it. Thus, as long as the court thinks a jury (or in a bench trial, the judge) can accurately per-ceive the objective reality of a child, the child's cognitive immaturity is of little significance.

Second, steps can be taken to increase the like-lihood the child's testimony will be understand-able. In the typical abuse case, children *will* appear incompetent if the examiner uses technical vo-cabulary rather than slang or dolls or drawings. Monge et al.[161] found that even ninth-graders are often unfamiliar with "proper" terms for sexual anatomy and physiology.[162] On the other hand, there is evidence that by age four most children are quite aware of sex differences and willing to speak freely about them, provided that questions are direct and in language familiar to a child.[163] Furthermore, at least one court has permitted a child witness to have an "interpreter" (e.g., a par-ent or child psychologist) when it appears that a child cannot express him- or herself in a nonidio-syncratic manner.[164]

(4)   Moral Development: Distinguishing Truth and Falsity

If a witness can relate his or her experiences ade-quately, the principal concern is whether he or she will do so truthfully. Indeed, under the com-mon law, a witness's ability to abide by the "oath" was the focal point of the competency assess-ment; courts would routinely ask child witnesses, for instance, if they believed in God and knew the consequences of telling a lie in court, and would base their competency decision on the an-swers.[165] Even today, the courts tend to gloss over observation, memory, and communication capacities and place primary emphasis on the wit-ness's ability to differentiate truth from false-hood, to comprehend the duty to tell the truth, and to understand the consequences of not fulfill-ing this duty.[166] However, in contrast to the com-mon-law test, the modern witness need not con-firm a belief in God. Most jurisdictions now give the witness the choice of the oath (e.g., swearing to tell the truth "so help me God") or an affirma-tion that the witness will tell the truth.[167] Several states even allow a child to testify without taking an oath if, in the court's discretion, the child does

not understand it but is still likely to give proba-tive testimony.[168]

When it comes to children, the courts' obses-sion with truthtelling seems misplaced. There is in fact little correlation between age and truthtelling.[169] From 1969 to 1974, Michigan po-lice referred to a polygraph examiner 147 chil-dren whose veracity about allegations of sexual abuse was questioned. Only one child was judged to be lying.[170] More recent studies support the view that most young children understand the concept of telling the truth. For instance, Bussey found that "even preschoolers could differentiate between lies and truthful statements about mis-deeds [and] appreciated the naughtiness of ly-ing."[171] Another study of children ages four to six also found that most understand the difference between the truth and a lie.[172] However, consis-tent with the research on suggestibility, these re-searchers did caution that "there may be a small percentage of children whose definition of the truth may be influenced by parental direction or its helpfulness to a friend."[173] Similar general findings have been made with respect to those with mental retardation.[174]

A more likely developmental differentiation is in the reasons people give to justify behavior. For instance, as children grow older, they become more sociocentric and oriented toward respect for persons[175]; in contrast, younger children are likely to say the oath is important on more "prim-itive" grounds involving reification of rules[176] and avoidance of punishment.[177] This difference is un-likely to be relevant in this context, however.[178] Justice will be served if witnesses tell the truth, regardless of their reasons for doing so, and most courts today recognize that fact.[179] If there *is* some reason to ascertain a child's conceptualiza-tion of the duty to tell the truth, however, the yes–no and definition questions traditionally used in the common-law *voir dire* of witnesses are inad-equate measures. One of the philosophical under-pinnings of current cognitive-developmental the-ories of moral development is that a given behav-ior may be motivated by vastly different levels of moral reasoning.[180] Thus, asking a child to ex-plain the meaning of "truth," "oath," or "God" probably tells more about the child's intellectual development than about his or her propensity to tell the truth.[181]

(5)   Conclusions

Although there are some gaps in the relevant literature, the available research suggests that preteen children as young as five have the capacity to observe events, remember them accurately for moderately long periods as long as authority figures do not suggest alternative facts to them, and communicate about them with the understanding that a truthful report is important. Children under the age of five are likely to have more difficulty with long-term memory, resisting suggestions and effectively communicating their observations, but with assistance even some three-year-olds may have the capacity to report their observations accurately and understand the difference between a lie and the truth. The analogues with people who have mental retardation are not precise, but the correlation between testimonial capacity and IQ is probably similar to that between testimonial capacity and age.

A possible caveat to these conclusions is that very little of the research on children's testimonial accuracy has replicated the stress likely to be associated with the courtroom setting. Research on this issue is mixed, although the evidence points to the conclusion that conventional legal procedures are somewhat more likely to be stress inducing than informal environments and that testimony is somewhat more likely to be incomplete in traditional courtrooms.[182] Concern over these effects has led some states to construct elaborate procedures for taking juvenile testimony in abuse cases, including use of screens and television monitors to distance the witness from the defendant and the trappings of the courtroom.[183] Yet these procedures are seldom used,[184] apparently because prosecutors perceive live testimony to be more influential, fear creating appealable issues, and lack the necessary financial resources.[185] In those (predominately foreign) settings in which the procedures are more commonly used, their efficacy is unclear, although it does appear that having the *option* of such a procedure, whether or not it is chosen, alleviates stress.[186]

In any event, stress impairment at trial will normally not reach a level requiring a declaration of incompetency. In view of the small percentage of cases that reach the courtroom,[187] much more important from the standpoint of obtaining the "facts" is avoiding stress, suggestiveness, and other accuracy-reducing aspects of the investigation process, a subject covered in more detail below.

(c)   Guidelines for Evaluation

It is important to recognize that evaluations of witnesses stand on a different footing than evaluations of litigants (which are the usual focus of this book). Although litigants can be said to have placed their mental state at issue by raising or defending a particular claim, witnesses are often "innocent bystanders" in the quarrel. Thus, courts have exhibited some reluctance about ordering psychological evaluations of witnesses, primarily on privacy grounds [see § 7.07(d)(2) for elaboration of this point].[188]

Another preliminary issue clinicians must address is whether they have anything to add to what a trial judge will be able to discern with respect to observational, memory, communication, and moral capacities. At least one commentator has stated that "the trial judge is nearly always capable of reaching a reasoned decision on competence without [a psychiatric] evaluation."[189] Furthermore, as indicated earlier, the clinician should remember that multiple interviews with witnesses like children may tend to distort the ultimate testimony. On the other hand, mental health professionals may well have something useful to say about testimonial competency in selected cases, particularly involving very young children and individuals with mental retardation or severe mental illness.

If an evaluation is undertaken, it should focus on the four factors described above. The witness's observational skills can be directly assessed, although if the event in question took place some time previously when the witness was very young, information about such skills at the time of the event may have to be obtained from parents or other significant others. Memory for events other than the one in question can be tested by asking simple questions about both recent and long-ago events. Communication skills can also be ascertained by having the witness recount an event known to have happened and ascertaining his or her capacity to describe correctly spatial, temporal, and other aspects of the event. Finally, the witness's understanding and commitment to truth telling can be assessed by asking in the abstract what it means to tell the truth and then asking for examples. If more concrete information is needed, the witness can be asked if a statement such as "I am wearing glasses" is true or false and then asked why it is one or the other.

Although such an assessment would cover the basic criteria of testimonial competency, to be useful an evaluation probably should not stop at this point. A court would generally also benefit from insight into whether the witness's memory of *the legally relevant event* is "genuine" and is being accurately recounted or, instead, is the product of suggestion or fantasy. As already indicated, the difficulty is that by the time the question of competency is raised, the potential witness is likely to have been asked about the alleged offense numerous times. If it was perceived as a traumatic event or if a family member is the defendant, the witness may also have been bombarded with diverging interpretations of the event. Moreover, especially with children, when the event in question was one previously outside the witness's experience or one that he or she had not previously identified as deviant, the witness may be dependent upon others to provide meaning to the experience.[190]

Determining with certainty the origins of a witness's memories in such situations may not be possible. But it will obviously be useful in this regard to determine as precisely as one can when and with whom the child has talked and the content and process of these discussions. If depositions have already been taken, they should be reviewed and compared with the interview notes. As Christiansen stated in the excerpt above, a "child's competence as a witness cannot be determined unless these procedures have been taken into account and any effects they may have had on the child's memory have been weighed."[191]

The clinician must also try to avoid "creating" memories. One could avoid asking about the event entirely, instead simply carrying out the third-party investigation described above. The problem with this approach is that there may be no current version of the story with which to compare earlier versions; furthermore, useful information about communication skills may be ob-

tainable only by having the witness recount the event once again. If such an account is viewed as necessary, Yuille has described the following several-stage process as a way of maximizing information while minimizing suggestion: building rapport, asking for a free narrative account and, only if the latter appears ineffective, proceeding to open-ended questions, specific yet nonleading questions, and finally leading questions.[192] Whether the use of anatomically correct dolls or props is helpful at any of these stages is currently in much debate [see § 15.06(d)]. According to one reviewer, "the most important research finding about the use of dolls with very young children is that there is no good evidence that the dolls help,"[193] but others seem to disagree, at least if the doll is used solely to "investigate" abuse claims rather than to "diagnose" abuse.[194]

Although the fact-gathering and evaluation process just described can probably be accomplished by a competent nonprofessional (and indeed is often carried out by judges and lawyers without clinical assistance), there are other ways in which a clinician might be particularly helpful to the legal system in this context. First, when necessary to correct any misconceptions about typical behavior of children at a given age, the clinician might present research of the type described in the previous discussion. In this guise, the clinician—or research psychologist—is providing assistance similar to that of a psychologist giving expert testimony on eyewitness testimony generally.[195]

Second, the clinician can consult with the attorneys seeking—or challenging—the prospective witness's testimony. In the former instance, the clinician may be helpful in preparing the witness for testimony both by desensitizing him or her to the court process and by providing the attorney with advice on ways of interviewing the witness (or, as may be allowed in some courts, conducting the questioning him- or herself). As a consultant to the challenging attorney, the clinician may point out factors likely to affect the reliability of the witness's testimony and ways of highlighting these factors on *voir dire*.

Third, and most controversial, the clinician might, at the behest of the lawyers or the court, attempt to solidify a vulnerable witness's memory. Saywitz tentatively suggests three methods designed to improve "memory performance:" (1) "narrative elaboration," in which the witnesses "learn to organize the elements of an event into five forensically relevant, theoretically driven categories (participants, setting, actions, conversations/affect, and consequences)"; (2) "strategy training to resist misleading questions, including practice, feedback, [and] self-monitoring"; and (3) the "cognitive interview" which, as described by other researchers,[196] relies on mnemonics and other cognitive interventions to enhance the accuracy of recall and testimony.[197] These methods would presumably be used prior to trial, and in preparation for it.

(d) Assessment of Witness Credibility

As just discussed, an evaluation of a witness's competency to testify addresses the person's *capacity* to observe, recall, and report events purportedly witnessed and to understand the oath. Expert testimony on credibility, on the other hand, addresses the likelihood that statements made by a person who has been found competent to testify are *truthful*. As a conceptual matter, the distinction between a competency evaluation and a credibility assessment seems reasonably clear. As a practical matter, however, the line between the two evaluations is likely to be blurred, as should become apparent from the following discussion, which examines the evidentiary rules governing testimony on witness credibility and the extent to which a party may obtain an evaluation for the purpose of preparing such testimony.

CASE STUDY 7.2

John is charged with buying cocaine from an undercover agent named George. The only evidence against John is George's testimony and the fact that cocaine was found in John's car. John admits that George, whom he vaguely knows, asked him if he wanted to buy cocaine when they met by chance at a shopping mall but swears he turned George down flat. Noting that George had access to his car (which he left unlocked) and that undercover informants get paid by the "sting," John asserts that George framed him. You have been hired by John's lawyer to evaluate George's credibility. From records John's attorney has obtained from the prosecution during discovery, you know that George

has been involved in several cases involving similar facts. The records also reveal that he has an extensive criminal history, involving minor drug crimes and assaults against others. Although you haven't had access to George, John's attorney locates an ex-girlfriend of his, who tells you that George beat her, that he has had several girlfriends over the years whom he also had beaten, that he has never held a steady job or stayed in one location for long, that he constantly stole from his friends, and that he always laughed at her when she cried or told him to stop beating her. At trial you observe George testify and notice his eyes constantly shifting.

QUESTIONS: Would you be willing to testify to the effect that George may well be lying about John's actions on the day of the offense? If so, would you offer the factfinder any diagnostic information (e.g., that George has an antisocial personality)? Why or why not?

CASE STUDY 7.3

Susan claims that Jack raped her. Jack admits that he and Susan had intercourse, but claims it was consensual. He asserts that Susan has fabricated the rape claim because he broke up with her the night the rape allegedly occurred. His attorney moves for an evaluation of Susan's mental state, averring that, according to his client Jack, Susan has been seeing a therapist for the past three years and has been on lithium for two of those years. The attorney also subpoenas Susan's psychiatric records and requests a deposition of the therapist.

QUESTIONS: Should the court grant the evaluation, subpoena, and deposition requests? How should Susan's therapist respond? If the court grants the evaluation request, how should the evaluator go about the evaluation? [This problem requires consideration of issues discussed in Chapters 3 and 4 as well.]

---

(1) The Law on Expert Testimony about Witness Credibility

It is a basic premise of the Anglo-American legal system that the jury (or judge, in bench trials) is responsible for assessing the credibility of witnesses.[198] In an effort to avoid "usurping" this function of the jury, ethical rules forbid both the judge and the lawyers from expressing an opinion in front of the jury about the truthfulness of a witness.[199] For some time, the law also significantly restricted the ability of a party to present *testimony* about a witness's credibility. Only statements about the witness's "reputation" for truth-fulness in the community were permitted; the person describing the witness's reputation was prohibited from expressing his or her *own* opinion as to credibility and furthermore was not permitted to describe specific acts of untruthfulness or truthfulness unless queried about them during cross-examination.[200] As Lilly noted, these limitations were designed "to minimize the burdens of delay and distraction caused by the introduction of secondary issues."[201] Furthermore, information about reputation was seen as more reliable than a personal opinion about truthfulness and more relevant and less prejudicial than descriptions of specific acts of fabrication.

Given the "reputation evidence" restriction on credibility testimony in this traditional regime, mental health professionals should have had no role to play in assessing witness credibility (as distinct from witness competency). Nonetheless, some courts did allow expert testimony about the credibility of a witness. One of the first such cases involved the prosecution of Alger Hiss on espionage charges in the early 1950s,[202] a case worth investigating in some detail because it illustrates many of the pitfalls of expert credibility testimony.

The primary prosecution witness against Hiss was Whittaker Chambers. To impeach his testimony, the defense put on Dr. Carl Binger, who testified that Chambers was a "psychopath with a tendency toward making false accusations." He based this testimony on a number of factors: personal observation of Chambers during his trial testimony; the plays, poems, articles, and book reviews Chambers had written; and some information provided by counsel during a hypothetical question that ostensibly described various characteristics of Chambers. Although the prosecution objected to this testimony, the trial judge allowed it in on the theory that "insanity" is relevant to credibility.

Despite Binger's opinion, Hiss was convicted. Two factors undermined whatever impact the expert testimony, standing alone, might have had on the jury. The first factor was a skillful cross-examination of Binger by the prosecutor who, perhaps somewhat unfairly, concentrated on some of the specific psychopathic "symptoms" mentioned by the psychiatrist. For instance, noting that Binger

had called attention to Chambers's "untidiness," the prosecutor elicited a concession that such persons as Albert Einstein, Bing Crosby, and Thomas A. Edison had manifested that trait. Binger had also made much of the fact that, while testifying, Chambers had continuously gazed at the ceiling; the prosecutor pointed out that Binger himself had looked at the ceiling 19 times during the first 10 minutes of his direct testimony, 20 times during the next 15 minutes, and 20 times in the remainder of his testimony. When Binger insisted that stealing was a psychopathic symptom, the prosecutor asked, "Did you ever take a hotel towel or a Pullman towel?," to which Binger replied, "I can't swear whether I did or not. I don't think so." The prosecutor then asked "And if any member of this jury had stolen a towel, would that be evidence of psychopathic personality?," to which Binger replied, "That would have no bearing on it."

The second factor that undercut the impact of the testimony was the instruction the judge gave the jury. Referring to both Binger's testimony and the testimony of a psychologist, who had also given an opinion attacking Chambers's credibility based on "hypothesized" characteristics, he stated the following:

> As is the case with all expert testimony, these opinions are purely advisory. You may reject their opinions entirely if you find the hypothetical situation presented to them in the question to be incomplete or incorrect or if you believe their reasons to be unsound or not convincing. An expert does not pass on the truth of the testimony included in a hypothetical question. Similarly, he does not, and as a matter of law, he cannot pass on the truth of any part or parts of the testimony of the witness about whose mental condition he expresses his opinion. Assuming the facts in the hypothetical question to be true, the expert testifies that in his opinion the witness is suffering from a mental disorder which would tend to reduce his credibility in general. You yourselves have seen and heard Mr. Chambers for several days while he was on the witness stand and you have heard all the evidence. It is for you to say how much weight, if any, you will give to the testimony of the experts—and of Mr. Chambers. . . . Even though you may accept the experts' opinion as to Mr. Chambers' mental condition, you may still find that Mr. Chambers was telling the truth when he testified regarding those particular matters.

Should testimony such as that given in the *Hiss* case by permitted? Under the law at the time, admitting Binger's testimony was clearly erroneous (albeit "harmless," as Hiss was convicted despite the testimony); as noted earlier, the general rule was that a witness's character for truthtelling could only be impeached with testimony about the witness's reputation as an untruthful person. In 1975, however, almost 25 years after the *Hiss* trial, the federal courts adopted Rule 608, which liberalized the approach to credibility testimony. The rule, adopted by most states as well, provides:

> The credibility of a witness may be attacked or supported by evidence in the form of *opinion* or reputation, but subject to these limitations: (1) the evidence may refer only to character for truthfulness or untruthfulness, and (2) evidence of truthful character is admissible only after the character of the witness for truthfulness has been attacked by opinion or reputation evidence or otherwise. [Emphasis added]

As the highlighted language indicates, Rule 608 allows opinion testimony as well as reputation testimony. Thus, under a literal interpretation of subparagraph (1) of the rule, Binger's testimony in *Hiss* would be permitted. And had the prosecution desired to do so, it could have presented an expert to rebut Binger's testimony under a literal interpretation of subparagraph (2).

Interestingly, the legislative history of the rule indicates that it was aimed solely at broadening the basis of *lay* credibility testimony; as the commentary to the rule explained, "[w]hile the modern practice has purported to exclude opinion, witnesses who testify to reputation seem in fact often to be given their opinions, disguised somewhat misleadingly as reputation."[203] Nonetheless, the wording of the rule obviously does not limit opinion testimony about witness credibility to that provided by lay witnesses.

Whatever the correct reading of Rule 608, psychiatric testimony on credibility has been admitted with increasing frequency since its promulgation. A relatively common position was expressed in *United States v. Lindstrom*,[204] where the Court of Appeals for the Eleventh Circuit noted that the kind of conditions that might be relevant to impeaching a witness included "psychoses,

most or all neuroses, defects in the structure of the nervous system, mental deficiency, alcoholism, drug addiction, and psychopathic personality." Several courts similarly leave the admissibility of expert credibility testimony to the discretion of the trial judge, who is to determine whether it is helpful to the jury.[205]

At the same time, such testimony is not routinely admitted. Indeed, many courts still insist that experts should normally *not* be allowed to testify about credibility. There appear to be two reasons for this stance. First, of course, a court might feel that such testimony is not based on specialized knowledge, which is required of all expert testimony [see § 1.04(a)]; perhaps, for instance, Binger's testimony in the *Hiss* case, based on a relatively cursory "evaluation," should have been excluded for this reason. Second, even if the mental health professional's credibility testimony is thought to pass this initial test, the court may believe that its potential for confusing the jury or usurping the jury's traditional role as an assessor of credibility outweighs its probative value. In many cases, this possibility might be curable with an instruction of the type given by the trial judge in *Hiss*, combined with effective cross-examination (along the lines of the cross-examination in *Hiss*). In other cases, however, the courts have concluded these procedural devices do not sufficiently protect against misleading the jury.

Thus, for instance, state courts in California adhere to a strict judicial policy disfavoring the use of psychiatric testimony to impeach. In *People v. Alcala*,[206] the California Supreme Court explained that such testimony may be irrelevant or its basis not generally accepted, that the psychiatrist may not be in any better position to evaluate credibility than the juror, and that such testimony may be distracting, time-consuming, and costly. Several courts in other states have arrived at similar holdings.[207]

Nonetheless, expert testimony on witness credibility has been permitted in enough cases to discern at least four areas in which courts in some jurisdictions may permit it. The first is when the witness is allegedly suffering from significant mental disorder, such as hallucinations.[208] In these cases, expert testimony assessing the credibility of the witness comes closest to the traditional role of assessing witness competency. It is easily distinguished from the kind of testimony involved in *Hiss* (and the contemplated testimony in Case Study 7.2 as well?), in terms of both accuracy and comprehensibility.

Second, courts have traditionally been willing to allow credibility testimony focused on the complainant in rape cases, the situation raised in Case Study 7.3.[209] This stance follows the view of many commentators, who have argued that accusations of rape are particularly likely to be fabricated. As one put it, "the accusation is 'easily to be made and harder to be defended,' the penalties are high, and often the charge incites sympathy for the prosecutrix and prejudice for the defendant."[210] Because this reasoning appears to be based on outdated attitudes amounting to sexism, testimony about the credibility of alleged rape victims is becoming less common.[211] At the same time, the advent of the "rape trauma syndrome," which purportedly helps gauge whether intercourse was consensual [see § 8.03(c)], gives prosecutors and defense attorneys an additional tool for evaluating credibility.[212]

Similar comments can be made about a third common area for expert credibility testimony, having to do with the truthfulness of child witnesses in child abuse cases. Some courts have allowed the prosecution to rebut attacks on a child witness's credibility with expert testimony to the effect that children never or seldom lie about abuse.[213] Like testimony attacking the credibility of rape complaints, testimony unequivocally supporting the credibility of child abuse complainants is based on outmoded assumptions, in this case the assumption that today's children are not able to fabricate stories about sexual abuse. Courts are likely to be more reticent about permitting such testimony as they come to recognize that children *do* lie or, at least, as suggested in § 7.07(b)(2), can be prompted to "remember" events that did not occur. This topic is discussed further in § 15.04(c)(4).

A final common type of credibility testimony has to do with the reliability of eyewitnesses. Whereas the foregoing types of credibility testimony usually address whether a witness is consciously deceiving the factfinder, this testimony typically describes the extent to which unconscious factors may affect the reliability of a witness's account. It seeks to build on the immense

amount of research exploring the difficulties of accurately perceiving and remembering an observed event. Beyond what has already been said in connection with testimonial competency [see in particular § 7.07(b)(2)], a description of these studies will not be attempted here, as quite competent book-length treatments exist elsewhere.[214] It is sufficient for present purposes to note that the research suggests a number of conclusions about eyewitness testimony that, if not counterintuitive, at least may be helpful to a jury considering the credibility of an eyewitness. These include the findings that (1) people tend to be less accurate observers in stressful situations, (2) people have difficulty making cross-racial identifications, (3) people focus on weapons rather than faces, (4) the memory of a perception begins decaying immediately, (5) gaps in memory are easily and often unconsciously replaced by preconceptions about what must have happened or by suggestions implanted by subsequent accounts, the police, or other external forces, and as a result of all this, (6) there is no necessary correlation between the level of certainty evinced by the eyewitness and accuracy.

Despite the helpfulness of such observations, several courts have clung to the view that juries are competent to evaluate eyewitness testimony without expert assistance or, somewhat contradictorily, that the jury will be overly influenced by expert testimony on the topic.[215] Many other courts have permitted such testimony,[216] although some have reasonably prohibited the expert from stating his or her own opinion on the "ultimate issue" of the eyewitness's accuracy.[217]

(2)　Legal Strictures on Evaluations of Credibility

Whether mental health professionals have any ability to evaluate credibility per se is a matter of some controversy.[218] Chapter 3 (in particular § 3.07) provides an assessment of available techniques for detecting conscious malingering. But the usefulness of these techniques is generally limited to inquiries into whether a claim of mental illness (or mental health) is valid; they are unlikely to be helpful in evaluating whether a statement about what *other* people have done or said is false. As just discussed, in some areas (e.g., eyewitness testimony) behavioral science may be able to assist the courts in detecting "unconscious" false testimony. Again, however, detection of intentional deception is not the aim of the experts who testify on this issue. We believe that when the *only* reason an expert is on the stand is to attack a witness's motivations or honesty, there will typically be very little "science" involved. In short, as a general matter, this type of credibility testimony about a witness is highly suspect.

If, however, such testimony *is* undertaken, mental health professionals should conduct an evaluation of that witness. One reason Dr. Binger's testimony in the *Hiss* case was so easily debunked was that it purported to rely primarily on the doctor's in-court observation of the witness and some of his writings; Binger never talked to Chambers.

The issue addressed here is whether there are, or should be, any restrictions on when a witness can be compelled to undergo an evaluation for the purpose of assessing credibility.[219] The relevant procedural rules place significant limitations on when a party can force an evaluation of someone who is not a litigant. As explained in § 2.04(b), out of concern for witness privacy, the Federal Rules of Civil Procedure only allow mental examinations of *parties* and only when there is *good cause* for such an evaluation.[220] The rules do not even mention examination of nonparties (i.e., witnesses other than the plaintiff or defendant or someone in their legal custody). Similarly, the Federal Rules of Criminal Procedure explicitly contemplate only mental examinations of criminal defendants, and only on issues connected with competency and mental state at the time of the offense.[221]

Nonetheless, courts often hold that they have inherent authority to order evaluations when necessary to reach a just result. The question then becomes how a court should balance the competing interests. On the one hand is the witness's interest in maintaining privacy. On the other is the opposing party's interest in discovering relevant information. When, as in Case Study 7.3, the opposing party is a criminal defendant, the latter interest rises to constitutional status, given the Sixth Amendment's guarantees of the right to compulsory process and the right to confront accusers. The fulcrum on which these interests balance is relevance: Only if the examination will

yield relevant results should it be permitted. But how "relevant" must the results be?

In civil cases, one might argue that if "good cause" is required to evaluate a *party* to a dispute, a least that level of cause ought to be required before a third party can be subjected to such an intrusion. Although "good cause" is an amorphous term, it is normally interpreted to mean something more than a possibility of finding relevant evidence.[222] Thus, a good-cause showing in this context might require proof that the witness is known to have mental problems that have led to fabrication in the past; an even more stringent test might require showing there has been fabrication *on similar issues*. According to the Supreme Court, the good-cause standard might also require a showing that no other means exist for assessing the witness's credibility.[223]

In criminal cases, on the other hand, a lesser showing might be permitted, at least when the *defendant* requests such an evaluation (given the constitutional interests involved). However, some commentators have argued that a lesser standard is not appropriate even for defendants, at least in rape and child abuse cases.[224] Noting that parties rarely make, and courts rarely grant, motions for evaluations of witnesses in other types of criminal cases (e.g., a garden-variety assault), and that such evaluations can be particularly damaging to vulnerable subjects such as women or children who have been abused, they claim that permitting routine evaluations of such alleged victims is discriminatory. In short, to the alleged victim's privacy interest, they add an equality interest, which would require the same showing required in any other case. Specifically, these commentators appear willing to grant an evaluation motion only upon a showing that the rape or abuse victim has mental problems that have led (as opposed to might lead) to fabrication about the precise type of event at issue.

In sum, courts should consider motions to compel an evaluation for purposes of assessing credibility with caution. Indeed, the weak scientific basis for most such assessments, combined with the insult to privacy interests, might lead to the conclusion that such evaluations should never be permitted, even when the witness to be evaluated is a party to the litigation.

7.08. Competency to Be Sentenced and Executed

CASE STUDY 7.4

Assume that you are a psychologist employed by the Department of Corrections. George Brown is scheduled to be executed within 48 hours. You have heard via the prison grapevine that in the past two weeks Mr. Brown occasionally has lapsed into spells of wailing and talking in tongues. Having evaluated Mr. Brown previously as part of the system's classification program, you believe that he has a borderline personality and may decompensate under stress. On the other hand, the correctional officers are virtually unanimous in the view that Mr. brown is faking a mental disorder. The consulting psychiatrist has supported the latter assessment. You are assigned to give another opinion about Mr. Brown's competency to be executed.

QUESTIONS: (1) Will you conduct the evaluation? Why or why not? (2) Assume that you decide to conduct the evaluation. How will you go about it?

The prohibition against sentencing and executing those adjudged incompetent to understand what is being done to them has its origins in the common law.[225] Most states have since codified the rule that an incompetent individual may not be sentenced to prison or executed.[226] Foremost among the reasons advanced for this stance are the following: (1) an incompetent individual cannot assist counsel in challenging the sentence imposed, (2) it is inhumane to imprison or execute such a person, and (3) neither the deterrence nor retributive rationales of punishment are served by punishing an "insane" person [see § 8.02].[227]

As these rationales suggest, there are two stages at which competency may be relevant after conviction. The first is at the sentencing proceeding itself (which often occurs well after trial). The second is while punishment is being carried out. This section examines both stages.

(a) Competency at the Sentencing Proceeding

The most common standard utilized at this stage parallels the competency-to-stand-trial standard [see § 6.02(b)]. In *Saddler v. United States*,[228] for instance, the Second Circuit held that sentencing must be postponed if the judge has "reasonable grounds to believe that the defendant may not have a level of awareness sufficient to understand the nature of the proceeding or to exercise his right of allocution." (The right of allocution—analogous to the right to confrontation, upon which competency to stand trial is based [see § 6.02(a)]—provides the defendant with an opportunity to speak in his or her behalf and offer information in mitigation of punishment but—unlike the right to confront—is not constitutionally based.[229]) The Ninth Circuit, per *Chavez v. United States*,[230] even more closely follows the competency-to-stand-trial test by requiring that, to be sentenced, the offender must understand the nature of proceedings and be able to "participate intelligently to the extent that participation is called for."

Despite their similarity, the competency-to-be-sentenced standard is probably easier to meet than the competency-to-stand-trial test. First, although the convicted defendant does have a right to counsel, the sentencing proceeding is much more informal than trial and concern over accuracy much reduced [see § 9.03(b)]. Thus, the defendant's ability to consult with counsel or understand the proceedings is not perceived to be as crucial as in the trial context. Second, as a corollary of this fact, the right to allocution is often not taken seriously; therefore, unless allocution is considered important in the particular case and the defendant's disability makes allocution impossible, a finding of incompetency is unlikely.[231] As one court has pointed out, unlike other contexts in which competency is considered significant, the defendant at sentencing has no *constitutional* rights to waive.[232]

If a bona fide doubt as to competency is raised, many states require an evaluation by experts and a hearing to determine whether the standard is met.[233] If the individual is found incompetent, he or she is usually committed to a hospital for treatment until the proper authorities believe competency to be regained. Thus, hospitalization takes the place of imprisonment. In some states, time spent in the hospital does not count against time to be served under sentence.[234]

The American Bar Association (ABA) Criminal Justice Mental Health Standards take a different approach. The standards recommend that, at least in noncapital cases, a provisional sentence be imposed despite incompetency, as long as the judge indicates on the record the extent to which the incompetency affected the sentencing proceeding.[235] The fact that the defendant cannot exercise the right to allocution is not considered important, given the other safeguards at sentencing designed to elicit information about the defendant, including the presentence report, submissions by defense counsel, and the sentencing hearing itself. However, after imposition of sentence the standards would permit the defendant who has regained competency to present any evidence in mitigation; if given credence, this showing could then lead to reduction of sentence.[236]

(b)   Competency to Be Imprisoned or Executed

Virtually every state provides some mechanism for treating prison inmates who are "incompetent to serve sentence." In the typical sentencing context, the determination as to whether an individual is incompetent in this sense is in reality merely a decision as to whether the person is so mentally disturbed that transfer from prison to a mental health or mental retardation facility is necessary. Because this matter has more to do with commitment for treatment than with competency to understand or waive rights, it is considered in Chapter 10 on involuntary hospitalization [see in particular § 10.10(b)(1)].

The only issue covered here, therefore, is the decision as to whether a person who has received the death penalty is "competent" to be executed. For reasons suggested earlier, no state allows the execution of one deemed incompetent. Constitutionalizing this centuries-old common-law rule, the Supreme Court's 1986 decision in *Ford v. Wainwright*[237] held that the Eight Amendment (banning cruel and unusual punishment) prohibits the execution of an "insane" person. While the Court did not formulate a definition of competency to be executed, Justice Powell, in a concurring opinion, suggested that the Eighth Amendment "forbids the execution only of those who are

unaware of the punishment they are about to suffer and why they are to suffer it." He also felt that the state could properly presume the prisoner's competency at the time sentence is to be carried out and that it could require "a substantial threshold showing of insanity merely to trigger [a] hearing process."

Although the Court has yet to act on these suggestions, most states have adopted execution competency standards similar to Powell's. In Florida, for instance, it must be shown that the defendant understands the nature and effect of the death penalty and why it is to be imposed before execution may take place.[238] In contrast, the ABA's provisional standard on the issue is broader. Combining the rule for competency to be sentenced with that for competency to be executed, it defines incompetence in death penalty cases as an inability on the part of the defendant to "understand the nature of the proceedings against him, what he was tried for, the purpose of the punishment, or the nature of the punishment," as well an inability to "recognize or understand any fact which might exist which would make his punishment unjust or unlawful, or . . . to convey such information to counsel or the court."[239]

Although *Ford* did not directly define execution competency, it did address the procedures for determining competency in that context. Five members of the Court found Florida's procedure (which relied on the governor's assessment of clinical reports) unconstitutional, on three grounds: (1) it provided no opportunity for the prisoner or his or her counsel to be heard; (2) it did not permit challenge of the state-employed mental health professionals' findings on the competency issue; and (3) it left the final decision as to competency to the executive, rather than the judicial, branch. Although thus ruling Florida's statute unconstitutional, the Court did not explicitly establish a right to counsel at competency proceedings, nor did it require that the prisoner have a formal opportunity to cross-examine opposing experts or be provided funds for an independent expert.

Justice Marshall, who wrote the Court's opinion, suggested that Florida might want to create a competency procedure similar to that used in the competency-to-stand-trial or civil-commitment contexts. But he was unable to obtain a majority on this point; further, several members of the Court cautioned against requiring, as a constitutional ruling, a full-blown "sanity trial." The ABA's standards, adopting an intermediate position, recommend that the indigent prisoner be entitled to an independent evaluation of competency, that the prisoner be represented by counsel at the competency hearing, and that the burden be on the prisoner to show incompetence by a preponderance of the evidence standard (thus, in effect, establishing a presumption of competence).[240]

(c) Evaluation Issues

The principal focus of a competency evaluation in the sentencing context will be the individual's cognitive functioning, specifically whether the individual has the capacity to understand in a general way the penalty that could or will be imposed and the reason for its imposition. If competency at the sentencing *proceeding* is at issue, a second issue is whether the defendant can communicate relevant facts in mitigation to the attorney [see generally § 9.05(a) for factors relevant in mitigation]. Although the problematic voluntariness concept will normally not be a major issue in such evaluations, it also may arise. For instance, in *Gilmore v. Utah*,[241] the defendant waived his right to appeal his death sentence. The Supreme Court held that he could do so as long as the waiver was "knowing and intelligent." Although the word "voluntary" is missing from this formulation [see §§ 7.03, 7.04 on waiver of the right to remain silent and waiver of counsel], implicit in this ruling is a requirement that neither the state nor another third party somehow coerced the waiver.[242]

At least one court has imposed certain conditions on the competency evaluation in the death penalty situation. In *Hays v. Murphy*,[243] the Tenth Circuit required that evaluations be performed somewhere other than on death row and be "the type of extended close observation in a proper setting which is generally recognized as essential for all psychiatric and psychological evaluations." Although the court's concern for thoroughness is understandable given the stakes involved, it is not necessarily the case that an evaluation of this type, focused on a very specific competency, requires

"extended" observation. From a clinical standpoint, at least, the evaluation in this situation is one of the least complex discussed in this volume.

This last comment should not lead clinicians to the conclusion that evaluations of competency to be executed are "easy," however. As Brodsky has pointed out,[244] such evaluations may raise ambiguities. For instance, Brodsky asks, how does one evaluate the competence and voluntariness of a prisoner's decision to forgo further appeals when the reason for doing so is that the prisoner wants to appear "tough?" And how does one evaluate these issues when the person's decision is based on the belief that he or she cannot tolerate the thought of life without parole, yet this decision seems based on experience on death row, whereas a life sentence would usually be served in the general prison setting? Although, as we have suggested throughout this volume, the clinician should merely provide information in such situations and let the tribunal wrestle with the difficult moral issues, the courts are likely to press clinicians for their views when the stakes are this high [see § 18.05].

Furthermore, of course, sensitive ethical issues arise any time an evaluation that could lead to the subject's execution is performed. Some argue that mental health professionals should play only a limited role in such evaluations. For instance, one board of the American Psychological Association has opposed the participation of psychologists in "routine certification of competency for execution." In the board's view, "[j]ustification for participation in such evaluations should be based solely on the possibility of bringing new information which might change the legal verdict and subsequent death sentence."[245]

We think a more contextual stance is in order. As discussed in § 4.05(b)(1), mental health professionals should determine, before conducting an evaluation, whether their personal beliefs will make an objective assessment difficult. Under this standard, clinicians who find the death penalty morally repugnant may decide they cannot participate in *any* evaluation connected with a capital case, not just evaluations of execution competency. Or, the clinician may distinguish between capital-case evaluations of competency to stand trial and insanity, on the one hand, and competency to be executed evaluations on the other, on the ground that the latter are closer in time to the pending execution, or more closely connected to the issue whether or not execution will occur. Finally, a clinician could decide that objectivity can be maintained despite the high stakes involved in capital cases; in this instance, involvement in a competency to be executed evaluation would be ethical. As Bonnie stated:

> Although pleas of conscience (and likely bias, as a result) should be respected, I see no categorical objection to execution competency assessments. Indeed, in light of the fact that a significant proportion of death sentences are eventually set aside, enhanced sensitivity to this issue by correctional authorities actually could be *beneficial* to the interests of condemned prisoners as a class. Prisoners living for prolonged periods under the shadow of the executioner are at high risk for developing emotional and behavioral problems, especially in light of their tortured emotional histories. To the extent that prospective concern about execution competency provides an incentive for correctional authorities to assure that adequate clinical resources are available for ongoing monitoring and treatment, it might enhance the opportunities for healing.[246]

(d)   Treatment Issues

As this last statement suggests, *treatment* of the person on death row involves another difficult ethical decision; although technically beyond the scope of this book, a few words on this topic are useful because of its relationship to the evaluation issue. The National Medical Association (NMA) has adopted the position that the physician should always provide needed treatment, regardless of the prisoner's legal situation.[247] Bonnie, on the other hand, would condition treatment on whether prisoners state they want treatment at a time that they are competent to make that decision.[248] If so, Bonnie believes, along with the NMA, that the clinician is ethically obligated to provide treatment even if it will lead to the prisoner's restoration of competence to be executed. On the other hand, if the person's desires are unclear, or the person is incompetent to make treatment decisions, Bonnie believes, contrary to the NMA, that treatment would be unethical: In this situation "the clinician

would be serving a role that is ethically indistinguishable from the physician who administers the lethal injection of barbiturates."[249]

Of course, if all clinicians accepted this latter ethical tenet, it would be impossible to execute many of those found incompetent to be executed, or at least many of those whose incompetence can only be restored through psychiatric treatment. One response to this dilemma would be to commute the death sentences of these people[250]; the problem with this approach is that it might increase the incentive on the part of prisoners and clinicians to "manufacture" incompetence as a last-line defense against the death penalty. Another "solution" would be to allow execution of the incompetent, but *Ford* has apparently foreclosed that option.

In this regard, the litigation in *Perry v. Louisiana* is of interest.[251] After sentencing Perry to death, the trial court found him incompetent to be executed unless maintained on medication and ordered that he be forcibly medicated to ensure his competence. After the state appellate courts affirmed the trial court's order, Perry sought relief from the United States Supreme Court. That court vacated the trial court order and remanded for reconsideration in light of its decision in *Washington v. Harper*,[252] which was decided after the state court litigation in *Perry* and allowed forcible medication considered "medically appropriate" for a prisoner who was dangerous to others [see § 11.03(b)(1)].

On remand, the Louisiana Supreme Court concluded, somewhat surprisingly given the decision in *Harper* and the previous rulings of the Louisiana courts, that forcibly medicating individuals to render them competent to be executed is impermissible. It distinguished *Harper* by concluding that forcing drugs merely "to facilitate . . . execution does not constitute medical treatment but is antithetical to the basic principles of the healing arts."[253] Ultimately, however, the court's analysis of *Harper* was unnecessary to its decision because the court found two independent *state* law bases for its holding. First, it found that medicating an objecting individual to facilitate execution constituted cruel and unusual punishment under the state constitution because it "fails to measurably contribute to the social goals of capital punishment," "would add severity and indignity to the prisoner's punishment beyond that required for the mere extinguishment of life," and "is apt to be administered erroneously, arbitrarily or capriciously."[254] Second, the court held that such medication violated the right to privacy guaranteed in the Louisiana Constitution because, given the inhumaneness of the situation, the state's interest in executing such an individual was not compelling. If other courts follow the lead of the Louisiana Supreme Court, the treatment dilemma posed above would disappear.

Bibliography

Frendak v. United States, 408 A.2d 364 (D.C. 1975) (competency to waive insanity defense).

Godinez v. Moran, 509 U.S. 389 (1993) (competency to plead guilty and waive attorney).

Joseph Grano, *Voluntariness, Free Will, and the Law of Confessions*, 65 Virginia Law Review 581 (1979).

Thomas Grisso, Juveniles' Waiver of Rights; Legal and Psychological Competence (1981).

Dorothy Kagehiro, *Psycholegal Research on the Fourth Amendment,* 1 Psychological Science 187 (1990).

Gary B. Melton, Gail S. Goodman, Seth C. Kalichman, Murray Levine, Karen J. Saywitz, & Gerald P. Koocher, *Empirical Research on Child Maltreatment and the Law,* 24 Journal of Clinical Child Psychology 47 (1995).

Maria Zaragoza, John R. Graham, Gordon C.N. Hall, Richard Hirschman, & Yossef S. Ben-Porath (eds.), Memory and Testimony in the Child Witness (1995).

John E.B. Myers, *The Testimonial Competence of Children,* 25 Journal of Family Law 287 (1986).

Barbara Ward, *Competency for Execution: Problems in Law and Psychiatry,* 14 Florida State University Law Review 35 (1986).

Welsh White, *Police Trickery in Inducing Confessions,* 127 University Pennsylvania Law Review 581 (1979).

Charles Whitebread & Christopher Slobogin, Criminal Procedure chs. 12, 16, 26, & 31 (3d ed. 1993) (consent searches, confessions, guilty pleas, and counsel).

CHAPTER EIGHT

Mental State at the Time of the Offense

8.01. Introduction

This chapter discusses a number of defenses that can be raised by the criminal defendant at the guilt determination phase of the criminal process. Specifically, it addresses the insanity defense; the "automatism" defense; the "diminished capacity" defense; the so-called character defenses; "affirmative defenses" such as self-defense, provocation, duress, and entrapment; defenses associated with psychoactive substance use; and the guilty but mentally ill verdict. Although each of these defenses has different attributes, they all have one thing in common: When they are invoked, they require an investigation of the defendant's "mental state at the time of the offense" (MSO)—a reconstruction of the defendant's thought processes and behavior before and during the alleged crime.

Not all states recognize each of these defenses (for instance, only about half recognize the diminished capacity defense, and three states do not have an insanity defense). Moreover, each defense comes in various guises (e.g., there are at least five different insanity tests currently in use among the states). To ensure that the proper legal question is addressed, the lawyer and the mental health professional need to understand the various MSO doctrines.

This chapter outlines for each defense the majority approach and the most significant compet-

ing approaches. It also provides some guidance regarding the clinical syndromes most likely to form the bases for these defenses. Finally, it provides suggestions on the best way to evaluate and formulate an opinion about a person considering an MSO defense.

8.02. The Insanity Defense

The bulk of this chapter focuses on the insanity defense because it is the most commonly invoked doctrine relating to MSO. The premise of the defense is as follows: Most criminal offenders choose to commit crime for rational reasons and of their own "free will" and are therefore deserving of punishment; some mentally disturbed offenders, however, are so irrational in their behavior, or so unable to control it—that is, so unlike "us"—that we feel uncomfortable imposing criminal liability on them. To put it in terms of criminal law doctrine, these individuals are not properly punishable as criminals because the principal grounds for such punishment—retribution and deterrence—are not applicable to them. Society should not feel vengeful toward persons who, at the time of the offense, "did not know what they were doing" or "could not help themselves"; such individuals should be treated with compassion, not branded as criminals. Nor can society hope either to deter such persons from committing other crimes or to deter others like them from crime, because "crazy" people are oblivious to the constraints of the real world. Such people may need treatment, and perhaps restraint, but these two objectives are most properly met through hospitalization, not imprisonment.

The defense of insanity is probably the most controversial issue in all criminal law. Thousands of pages have been written debating the value of a defense that provides an excuse for one's antisocial actions.[1] Some have argued that the theoretical assumptions underlying the defense are unfounded—that very few, if any, individuals are completely nondeterrable or undeserving of punishment.[2] From a practical viewpoint, some contend that treatment of dangerous mentally ill persons can be better accomplished through alternative methods,[3] that the terms used to define "insanity" are unconscionably yet inevitably vague,[4] and that mental health professionals are unable to provide meaningful testimony on the issue.[5] Other commentators, the clear majority, have just as vigorously rejected the abolitionist stance.[6] They see the defense not only as a moral necessity for the sake of the individual but as the sole vehicle society possesses for publicly debating the meaning of "criminal responsibility"—for examining the assumption, basic to the criminal law and our notions of personhood generally, that by far the majority of those who commit crime could have acted otherwise.[7] To proponents of the defense, those criminal defendants who are afflicted by severe mental disorder at the time of the offense— and who are therefore intuitively, if not demonstrably, less able to control or appreciate their behavior—must be afforded the opportunity to argue their lack of blameworthiness or the moral integrity of the law will suffer.

(a) Common Misperceptions about the Defense

At the same time the academic battle has raged, the public has increasingly expressed its dissatisfaction with the defense.[8] Popular opinion about the insanity plea appears to be based largely on impressions gained from the extensive media coverage that inevitably accompanies insanity trials such as that of John Hinckley, charged with attempting to assassinate the President; Lorena Bobbitt, charged with cutting off her husband's penis; and Jeffrey Dahmer, charged with killing 13 people. (Hinckley and Bobbitt were acquitted by reason of insanity, Dahmer was convicted.) In one sense, this publicity may be desirable; it tends to encourage public examination of the moral premises underlying the criminal justice system. But it also appears to have given the public a somewhat distorted view of the nature of the defense. For example, many appear to believe that (1) a large number of defendants use the defense, and (2) most are successful (in part because defendants and their expert witnesses are able to deceive gullible juries). It also seems to be commonly assumed that (3) those acquitted by reason of insanity are released upon acquittal or shortly thereafter, even though (4) they are extremely dangerous. These perceptions, if accurate, would understandably lead to antipathy toward the defense. Yet, based on available data, they appear to be unsupportable.

(1) How Often Is the Plea of Insanity Made?

A study conducted in Wyoming between 1970 and 1972 indicated that the "average" community resident in that state believed the insanity defense was raised in 43% of all criminal cases in Wyoming during those years.[9] In fact, fewer than half of 1% (.47%) of all criminal defendants arrested in Wyoming during the period of the study raised the plea.[10] Similar statistics come from studies conducted in the 1970s or early 1980s in Michigan, New York, St. Louis, Richmond, Virginia, and New Jersey, all of which found insanity plea rates in felony cases ranging from 0.1% to 0.5%.[11] A multistate study by Steadman et al.,[12] examining insanity pleas from the late 1970s through the mid-1980s, found slightly higher rates in some states but for the most part replicated earlier studies. According to Steadman, the percentage of pleas in felony cases was highest in Montana: There the insanity plea rate ranged from 5.5% to 8% between 1976 and 1979 (the year the defense was abolished). In California, on the other hand, the rate declined 1% in 1979 to 0.3% in 1984, and in Georgia it hovered between

1.5% and 2.5% between 1976 and 1985.[13] Other studies show similar results.[14] Thus, available data appear to counter effectively the belief that the plea is an everyday occurrence in the criminal courts.

(2) How Often Is the Plea Successful?

Data on the success rate of the insanity defense are less uniform, but they suggest that the defense usually fails. The Wyoming study cited earlier found that although the "average" citizen in that state thought the defense was successful 38% of the time, in reality only one person (or 0.99%) of the 102 who pleaded insanity during the period of the study was acquitted.[15] Other states show significantly higher acquittal rates but typically still well below the 38% figure assumed by Wyoming residents. In Hawaii, between the years 1969 and 1976, approximately 19% of those who pleaded insanity were acquitted[16]; in Erie County, New York, roughly 25% of those who pleaded insanity were successful[17]; and in New Jersey the analogous figure for 1982 was 30%.[18] Steadman et al.'s multistate study found that the annual acquittal rate fluctuated considerably in each state: 40–50% in California from 1979 and 1984, 10–20% in Georgia from 1976 and 1980, 25–60% in New York from 1982 and 1987, and 15–35% in Montana from 1976 to 1979.[19] Obviously, the success of the defense varies from jurisdiction to jurisdiction. But Steadman, Pantle, and Pasewark have estimated that, nationally, the defense prevails one out of every four times it is raised.[20] As a general statement, it is probably not inaccurate to say that when the defense is challenged, it fails more often than it succeeds.

It can also be said that the absolute number of individuals found not guilty by reason of insanity (NGRI) is very low. In five state jurisdictions where relatively recent data are available, the annual number of NGRI verdicts ranged between 1 case (in Wyoming) and 259 cases (in California), representing an average well below 1% of all felony arrests in those states.[21] Nationwide statistics from 1978 indicate that only 8.1% (or 1,625) of the 1,971 admissions to mental hospitals in the United States were defendants found NGRI, representing fewer than 0.3% of all felony cases for that year.[22] Since then, the number of acquittals apparently has not grown, despite the increase in population.[23]

Finally, and perhaps most important, it appears that well over 70% of these insanity acquittals resulted from a plea-bargaining or quasi-plea-bargaining arrangement rather than a full-fledged jury trial.[24] In these cases, the prosecution agreed that the defendants were so "crazy" they should be hospitalized rather than convicted and imprisoned. Thus, the number of cases in which there is any potential for the defendant to somehow "fool" a trial jury is extremely small to begin with. Even if there is some abuse of the defense in such trials [see, e.g., § 8.04(a)], it would seem that the total number of "valid" acquittals far outweighs the number of "invalid" ones. This point is substantiated by evidence that most insanity acquittees (60–90%) continue to be diagnosed as "psychotic after acquittal" [see § 8.04(a)].[25]

(3) What Happens to Those Found NGRI?

A commonly held and not illogical assumption about defendants found NGRI is that they are treated like the typical acquitted defendant and permitted to "walk" after they are found "not guilty" by reason of insanity.[26] In reality, this disposition is the exception. One commentator who surveyed the laws of the 50 states in 1981 concluded that "[a]n acquittal by reason of insanity is rarely a ticket to freedom."[27] Since that year commitment laws in many states have been tightened even further.[28]

Many states require automatic commitment of those acquitted on insanity grounds, usually for a minimum averaging 60 days. Those states that do not have automatic commitment permit confinement for an initial period of up to a year upon relatively meager evidence of mental illness, dangerousness, or both. As § 10.10(c) discusses in more detail, the statutory criteria for releasing persons found NGRI after this initial detention period (which typically focus on the individual's mental illness and potential for endangering others) are more restrictive on their face or "as applied" than similar criteria used in the civil commitment process. Moreover, the release of NGRI individuals usually depends on judicial approval, in contrast to the typical discharge from civil commitment, which only requires the hospital director's authorization.[29] Finally, most states place no limit on the length of time NGRI individuals may spend in confinement, as long as they continue to meet the commitment criteria, and the acquittee usually bears the burden of showing the criteria are not met.[30] These facts substantiate the observation of Katz and Goldstein that the insanity defense is as much a method for restraining persons seen as "crazy" and "dangerous" as it is a means of airing the moral issues discussed earlier.[31]

How long does the typical NGRI individual spend in the mental institution? Data on this subject are available from at least four states. The most comprehensive information comes in Pasewark, Pantle, and Steadman's study of New York. Of the 178 persons found NGRI between 1965 and 1976 in that state, 40% were still hospitalized in 1978. The average length of stay for these individuals by the end of the study period in 1978 was three and a half years.[32] A study of New Jersey NGRIs over an eight-year period found that by the end of that time, 35% were still in custody and 47% were on conditional release.[33] In apparent contrast, in Michigan, a state that significantly relaxed its release criteria in 1975, the average confinement for those released after that date was only nine and a half months. However, 25% of those acquitted were still confined five years after passage of the liberal release provisions.[34]

Furthermore, a study of persons found NGRI in Illinois, conducted in 1979,[35] suggests that data about length of hospitalization may be somewhat of an underestimate. The Illinois study found the average stay in the hospital for those acquittees who were released to be 17.1 months. But it also found that 71% of all NGRI individuals had previously been found incompetent to stand trial, and that the average length of institutionalization between the finding of incompetency and the NGRI finding was 38.4 months. As there is nothing to indicate that the Illinois experience is unique, these data suggest that the bare postinsanity acquittal figures for New York and Michigan may have seriously underestimated the total duration of confinement for many of those ultimately found NGRI.

An interesting perspective on the confinement issue is provided by studies that compare length of hospitalization for persons found NGRI to length of imprisonment for felons matched with the NGRI individuals according to the nature of the crime charged and demographic variables. Three studies of this nature were conducted in New York during different periods. The first found no appreciable differential in confinement duration, the second discovered a 10-month differential (with NGRI individuals being released earlier), and the third (and most recent) found, like the first, a rough similarity between NGRI and felon incarceration for those charged with murder, but nearly twice as long for NGRIs when the charge was not murder.[36] Similar findings came from a comparison of inmates and acquittees in California and New Jersey in the early 1980s[37] and a more recent study involving several states.[38] On the other hand, a Georgia study found the ratio reversed (i.e., felons were confined twice as long as NGRIs) when nonmurder charges were involved,[39] and a study conducted in Connecticut found that NGRI individuals were released an average of 19 months earlier than the felons with whom they were paired.[40]

The second New York study, the Georgia study, and the Connecticut study do indicate that in some jurisdictions during some periods persons found NGRI spent a significantly shorter time in confinement than did felons. However, as the other studies indicate, the differential obviously does not exist everywhere and at all times, nor does it take into account the possibly longer pretrial rates experienced by NGRIs. Most important, any differential that does exist does not by itself signify that there is a problem with either the insanity defense or the disposition of insanity acquittees. Only if NGRI individuals *need* to be confined for longer periods would these data merit such a conclusion. This point anticipates the fourth and final perception of the insanity defense that will be discussed here.

(4)   How Dangerous Are Those Found NGRI?

An interesting study conducted in New York asked 417 randomly selected citizens to name offenders they believed to be "criminally insane."[41] Of those offenders named by more than one of those interviewed, none could be classified as insane, incompetent to stand trial, or prisoners who had become mentally ill. In fact, all had been convicted of murder, kidnapping, or bombings. The term "insanity" seems to attach itself to notorious individuals, whether or not they actually plead the defense and are successful with it.

There are no studies examining the "dangerousness" of persons found NGRI at the time of acquittal, because, as indicated earlier, these individuals are almost always automatically institutionalized and subjected to treatment. However, there are several studies comparing the recidivism rates of NGRI individuals who have been released from the hospital with those of released felons convicted on similar offenses. Most studies found that NGRI individuals as a group are less likely to have recidivating members than felons as a group, or that the two groups are about even in the rate of recidivism,[42] although a few have reached less clear results.[43] As with research comparing the recidivism rates of those who are civilly committed to those of the general population,[44] these studies tentatively suggest that the most accurate predictor of violence is the number and nature of prior offenses, not mental illness. They also suggest that the treatment provided to those found NGRI is not particularly effective at removing criminal tendencies. What they do not support is the contention that typical released insanity acquittees are "abnormally" dangerous or that such persons should be confined longer than felons because they are more likely to recidivate than their convicted counterparts.[45]

More data need to be collected on all these issues. But the available research suggests that support for abolishing the defense is misguided inasmuch as it is based on the belief that the insanity defense is frequently raised and usually successful, or on the impression that the insanity acquittee is a dangerous "monster" who is let loose once acquitted or at the whim of unmonitored hospital staff. It should also be noted that the last two subjects discussed—the duration of confinement for persons found NGRI and their potential dangerousness—have more to do with the correct *disposition* of NGRI cases than with the insanity defense itself. The defense, and what is done with those who successfully assert it, are two separate issues. The latter subject is discussed in more detail in § 10.09(c).

Over time, the defense of insanity has shown remarkable resiliency. Despite recent intense public hostility toward the doctrine and the introduction of scores of bills proposing its elimination, only three states (Montana, Idaho, and Utah) have abolished it as of this writing.[46] For better or for worse, the lawyer and the mental health professional must continue to grapple with both the evolution and the scope of the defense.

(b) History of the Defense

The idea of a defense to criminal responsibility based on mental disability goes back as far as the ancient Greek and Hebrew civilizations.[47] English case law, which heavily influenced early American courts, has long recognized the concept. At least as early as the 13th century, records show that English kings were pardoning murderers because their crimes were committed "while suffering from madness."[48] Over the next several centuries, many different formulations of the defense emerged. Sir Edward Coke, a famous legal scholar of the late 16th and early 17th centuries, felt that "idiots" and "madmen" who "wholly loseth their memory and understanding" should be found insane.[49] Sir Matthew Hale, Chief Justice of the King's Bench in the 17th century, concluded in his private papers that the "best measure" for determining insanity was whether the accused had "as great understanding as ordinarily a child of fourteen hath."[50] In 1723 Justice Tracy, refining a concept introduced five centuries before,[51] held that to be found insane "a man must be totally deprived of his understanding and memory so as not to know what he is doing, no more than an infant, brute or a wild beast."[52] At about the same time, other English courts were excusing those who lacked the capacity to distinguish "good from evil" or "right from wrong."[53]

It was this latter approach that, in slightly modified form, became the so-called "*M'Naghten* test" of insanity. In response to controversy surrounding the insanity acquittal of Daniel M'Naghten for killing the private secretary of Prime Minister Robert Peel, the House of Lords announced the following rule:

> To establish a defense on the ground of insanity, it must be clearly proved that, at the time of the

committing of the act, the party accused was la-boring under such a defect of reason, from dis-ease of the mind, as not to know the nature and quality of the act he was doing; or, if he did know it, that he did not know he was doing what was wrong.[54]

This formulation, announced in 1843, became the accepted rule in both England and the United States.

Criticism of the test was vigorous, especially from the medical community. Indeed, five years before the House of Lords' pronouncement, Sir Isaac Ray, a noted American physician, had argued that the "insane mind" is often "perfectly rational, and displays the exercise of a sound and well-bal-anced mind."[55] Thus, according to Ray, a defense based on mental illness that focuses merely on cognitive impairment is incomplete; the defen-dant's ability to control his or her acts must also be considered.[56] Although directed at the law as it existed in 1838, Ray's comments applied with equal force to the *M'Naghten* test, which varied only slightly from its predecessors.

A second criticism of the rule was its rigidity. Even if one accepts the premise that cognitive dysfunction is the only appropriate focus of the insanity defense, the *M'Naghten* rule, it was claimed, did not fairly pose the question; a literal interpretation of the *M'Naghten* test would sel-dom, if ever, lead to exculpation. In the words of one psychiatrist, "[if the test language were taken seriously,] it would excuse only those totally de-teriorated, drooling hopeless psychotics of long-standing, and congenital idiots."[57]

In the United States, the legal response to the first criticism came in the form of a supplemen-tary test for insanity, which eventually came to be called the "irresistible impulse" rule. One of the first courts to adopt the rule described it as fol-lows:

[The defendant is not] legally responsible if the two following conditions concur: (1) If, by rea-son of the duress of . . . mental disease he had so far lost the power to choose between the right and wrong, and to avoid doing the act in question, as that his free agency was at the time destroyed; (2) and if, at the same time, the al-leged crime was so connected with such mental disease, in the relation of cause and effect, as to have been the product of it solely.[58]

The adoption of the test was usually justified on the ground that those offenders who could not control their behavior at the time of the offense were not deterrable by criminal sanctions; there-fore, no legitimate moral or policy purpose was served by convicting them.[59]

The "irresistible impulse" test met resistance from several fronts. Many in the legal community believed that impulsivity could easily be feigned and feared that the test would lead to numerous invalid insanity acquittals.[60] From the medical side came the criticism that a separate "control" test furthered the mistaken impression that the human psyche is compartmentalized into cogni-tive and volitional components.[61] And, like *M'Naghten,* the test was seen as too rigid, excus-ing only those who were totally unable to prevent their unlawful behavior.[62]

In 1954, partly in response to the latter two contentions and the criticisms of *M'Naghten,* the federal District of Columbia Court of Appeals adopted the "product test" for insanity—a rule originally devised by the New Hampshire Supreme Court in 1870,[63] but one that had re-ceived little notice until this time. As set forth in *Durham v. United States,*[64] the test stated simply that "an accused is not criminally responsible if his unlawful act was the product of mental disease or defect." Judge Bazelon, the author of the *Durham* opinion, hoped that by removing legal strictures on clinical testimony and allowing explanation of all aspects of a defendant's personality and func-tioning, the rule would encourage mental health professionals to "help reform the criminal law" and "humanize" it.[65]

In time, however, this lack of guidance became a problem in itself. The product test asked essen-tially two questions: (1) Did mental disease or de-fect exist at the time of the offense? (2) Was the of-fense the product of this disease or defect? The *Durham* court failed to define either "mental dis-ease" or "product." Trial courts had particular dif-ficulty dealing with the meaning of the former term, as it was no longer modified by functional criteria, as it had been in earlier tests.[66] The prob-lem surfaced dramatically in 1957 when staff members at St. Elizabeths Hospital, which pro-vides the District of Columbia courts with most of their experts on the insanity issue, suddenly voted to incorporate the personality disorders, including the so-called sociopathic personality, within the definition of "mental disease" for purposes of the insanity defense.[67] Because many criminal offenders have some type of personality disorder, this well-known weekend change in hospital policy had a major impact on the courts. Not surprisingly, the insanity acquittal rate in the District of Columbia rose precipitously in the following years.[68]

In the 1962 decision *MacDonald v. United States*,[69] the District of Columbia Court of Appeals finally conceded that trial courts required some guidelines in implementing the product test and declared that henceforth "the jury should be told that a mental disease or defect includes any abnormal condition of the mind which substantially affects mental or emotional processes and substantially impairs behavior controls."[70] With the judicial gloss added by *MacDonald*, the difference between the product test and a test combining *M'Naghten* and the "irresistible impulse" rule was reduced substantially. Even so, definitional problems persisted, and *Durham* was finally overruled in 1972.[71] Maine, the only state besides New Hampshire to adopt the product test, later abandoned it as well.[72]

In place of the product test, the District of Columbia Court of Appeals adopted still another version of the insanity test, which was first proposed a year after *Durham*. This test, drafted by the American Law Institute (ALI), was an attempt to deal with most of the problems associated with previous tests by avoiding the "all-or-nothing" language of the *M'Naghten* and "irresistible impulse" formulations, while retaining some specific guidelines for the jury. The rule reads as follows:

> A person is not responsible for criminal conduct if at the time of such conduct as a result of mental disease or defect he lacks substantial capacity either to appreciate the criminality [wrongfulness] of his conduct or to conform his conduct to the requirements of the law.[73]

This language combines the notions underlying both the *M'Naghten* and irresistible impulse formulations but makes it clear that a defendant's cognitive or volitional impairment at the time of the offense need only be "substantial," rather than total, to merit an insanity defense.

The ALI's proposal also included a second paragraph, which, according to its drafters, was designed specifically "to exclude from the concept of 'mental disease or defect' the case of so called 'psychopathic personality.'"[74] It states: "As used in this Article, the terms mental disease or defect do not include an abnormality manifested only by repeated criminal or otherwise antisocial conduct."[75] Interestingly, this proposal was published two years before the St. Elizabeths vote on sociopathy.

The ALI test proved to be a popular one: Over the next two decades, a majority of the country's jurisdictions adopted the first paragraph, and many of these also adopted the second. Nonetheless, the ALI test came under attack by a new wave of critics, who felt that it and all of the tests that preceded it relied too heavily on the so-called medical model. Among these critics was Judge Bazelon, who came to believe that the *Durham* rule's emphasis on mental disease gave the psychiatric profession too much control over the insanity finding.[76] Thus, he formulated a new test: A person should be found insane "if at the time of his unlawful conduct his mental or emotional processes or behavior controls were impaired to such an extent that he cannot justly be held responsible for his act."[77] This test does away with the "mental disease or defect" requirement, as well as any specific requirement of functional impairment. It gives the factfinder virtually limitless discretion to decide what types of "impairment" merit excusing one for one's behavior. Legal scholars such as Moore and Morse have proposed other tests that abandon the medical model.[78] But the "justly responsible" test and similar formulations have not received widespread acceptance. Indeed, no state has rejected the medical model predicate for the insanity defense.[79]

A more popular (and the most recent) trend in insanity jurisprudence has been to attack the volitional prong of the defense. During the debates over the defense occasioned by the Hinckley verdict, both the American Bar Association (ABA) and the American Psychiatric Association recommended the elimination of the so-called control inquiry, although they continued to support the "appreciation" prong of the ALI's test (thereby indicating an unwillingness to return to *M'Naghten's* "knowledge" formulation).[80] The ABA's test reads as follows: "[A] person is not responsible for criminal conduct if, at the time of such conduct, and as a result of mental disease or defect, that person was unable to appreciate the wrongfulness of such conduct." Echoing past criticism, both the ABA and the American Psychiatric Association reasoned that if mistakes do occur in the administration of the insanity defense, they are most likely to result from utilizing a volitional test.[81] As the commentary to the ABA's standard states: "Clinicians can be more precise and arrive at more reliable conclusions about a person's awareness, perceptions and understanding of an event, than about the 'causes' of a person's behavior, especially when the determinants of behavior are felt to be unconscious."[82] In addition, Bonnie, who played an instrumental role in formulating both the ABA and American Psychiatric Association tests, argued that an "appreciation" test was sufficient to capture the universe of people who should be excused. As he put it:

> The most clinically compelling cases of volitional impairment involve the so-called impulse disorders—pyromania, kleptomania, and the like. These disorders involve severely abnormal compulsions that ought to be taken into account in sentencing, but the exculpation of pyromaniacs would be out of touch with commonly shared moral intuitions.[83]

Influenced by such arguments, in 1984 the United States Congress adopted an insanity test that essentially tracked the ABA proposal.[84] A number of states followed suit. Thus, as of 1995, the full ALI test was being used in only about 20 states, down from its peak of more than 25 states in the early 1980s. Some variation of the *M'Naghten*/cognitive-impairment-only test held sway in about half the states. New Hampshire continued to use the "product" test; Rhode Island relied on a variation of the "justly responsible" formulation; and, as noted earlier, three states, Idaho, Montana, and Utah, had abolished the defense, although expert testimony is still admissible on *mens rea* [see § 8.03(b)].[85]

A topic subjected to much research has been whether differences in test language produce any difference in outcome. The results are equivocal, regardless of the methodology used. Relying on mock juries, Simon found a small but statistically significant difference between verdicts from juries given the *Durham* instruction and juries given the

M'Naghten instruction, with the latter group finding fewer people insane.[86] But in a second mock jury study, Finkel and colleagues found no significant differences between five versions of the insanity test.[87] A vignette study asking forensic psychiatrists whether 164 defendants were insane under four different insanity tests found significantly different results depending on the test, especially between the volitional and cognitive prongs (with the former producing more insanity findings).[88] Another study that relied on the conclusions of clinicians (who, unlike the above study, were required to use a structured interview format) also found a difference between the volitional and cognitive formulations, but in the opposite direction.[89] A review of studies looking at the actual effect of changes in the insanity standard in five states concluded that, despite methodological flaws, there were differences in acquittal rates when the *M'Naghten* test was replaced by the ALI test.[90] Steadman and colleagues reported, on the other hand, that verdict outcomes in California probably did not depend on whether the factfinder was using the *M'Naghten* or the ALI test.[91]

Regardless of whether the test language affects jury verdicts, the following comment by the ABA bears repeating:

> [T]he impact of particular language on decisions made *before* a jury retires to deliberate also must be considered—the decisions of experts whether or not to testify and, if so, the formulation of their testimony; the strategic decisions by defense counsel relating to the insanity defense, direct and cross-examination, and summation; and trial court rulings on the legal sufficiency of the evidence to raise a jury question.[92]

(c)   A Closer Look at the Insanity Defense

CASE STUDY 8.1

Davidson, a person diagnosed with chronic schizophrenia, killed his employer. For 20 years he had experienced trances accompanied by hallucinations, including seeing and hearing devils committing abnormal sexual acts, sometimes upon Davidson himself. These experiences intensified in the weeks before the crime. On the day of the shooting, Davidson had been drinking at work. As a result, his supervisor told him to go home, and a fight ensued. Davidson then went home, got a gun, returned to work, and shot the victim.

Davidson later explained his action as follows: "I forgot about my family, I forgot about God's laws and human's laws and everything else. The only thing was to get that guy, get that guy, get that guy, like a hammer in the head." The expert at trial testified that Davidson's rage during the fight was a desperate attempt to ward off the imminent and total disintegration of his personality that would occur through regression into a schizophrenic relapse. As the expert put it: "[A]n individual in this state of crisis will do anything to avoid the threatened insanity."

QUESTIONS: As a mental health professional, what could you say about the role of mental illness in this case? The role of intoxication? Is the person's impairment cognitive, volitional, or both? What more would you want to know to answer these questions? As a lawyer, would you assert an insanity defense, or some other type of defense? [The case study is based on *People v. Gorshen*, 51 Cal. 2d 716, 336 P.2d 492 (1959), which recognized that the expert's testimony could be relevant to a "diminished capacity" defense; is this the right label for such testimony?]

CASE STUDY 8.2

Jacobs, a policeman, robbed or attempted to rob a series of banks and other businesses. Two years earlier, his wife and small daughter were brutally murdered by a drunken neighbor. He says he felt guilty about not being there to protect them. After this incident, he was often depressed; he was frequently overcome by fatigue and burst into tears for considerable periods. He also repeatedly threatened to commit suicide. At work, although much of the time Jacobs acted normally, at times he exhibited bizarre behavior. Occasionally when asked a question by a fellow officer he would fail to answer for ten minutes and then answer as if he had just been asked. Once while driving a scout car he constantly beat on the steering wheel with his fist for approximately a half hour. On the other hand, his superiors stated that his performance record was as good or better than before the murder of his wife and child.

The first robbery was unsuccessful because, after obtaining a bag full of money, Jacobs allowed a bank official to get behind him and throw his arms around him; Jacobs dropped the bag of money and ran. Later the same day, he went to a second bank and pointed a gun at a teller, who sounded the alarm; Jacobs again escaped. The same day he checked out a third bank but decided it was "too

wide open." During the next three weeks, he robbed or attempted to rob 12 other businesses, apparently on impulse, rarely scoping out the premises before he did so. He was caught when he attempted to hold up a grocery market. The proprietor screamed and Jacobs fled, leaving his car near the market. Police arrested him when he came back later to pick it up.

Jacobs was not in serious need of money; testimony indicated he was in better financial condition than most police. Three psychiatrists testified that Jacobs committed the robberies because he unconsciously wanted to be punished for not protecting his family.

QUESTIONS: As a mental health professional, how would you diagnose Jacobs? Is his impairment cognitive, volitional, or both? What "caused" his crimes? As a lawyer, would you try to assert an insanity defense in a jurisdiction that recognized only the *M'Naghten* test? [The case study is based on *United States v. Pollard*, 282 F.2d 450 (6th Cir. 1960), which reversed the trial court's decision to exclude the expert testimony, stating that the testimony was relevant to an "irresistible impulse" defense.]

CASE STUDY 8.3

Sorenson killed her husband, J.D. She had been beaten by J.D. for years. He would demand that she bark like a dog, eat dog or cat food, and sleep on the cold concrete floor. If she refused he would hit her with whatever was handy: his fist, a flyswatter, a baseball bat, a shoe, an ashtray, all of which left scars up and down her body. Two days before the shooting, J.D. took Sorenson to a truck stop and forced her to prostitute herself, something he had done on numerous other occasions. He also assaulted her, for which he was arrested. Upon returning from jail the next day, he beat her continuously, and Sorenson, apparently in distress, took an overdose of nerve pills. When emergency personnel arrived to treat her, J.D. tried to interfere, stating, "Let the bitch die. . . . She ain't nothing but a dog. She don't deserve to live."

The next day, the day of the shooting, J.D. again beat Sorenson all day, kicking her in the head, smashing food in her face, and putting a cigarette out on her chest. When he decided to take a nap, Sorenson took her daughter's baby, whom she had been babysitting, to her mother's house so J.D. would not wake up from the crying. At her mother's Sorenson picked up a gun, returned home, and shot her husband while he lay sleeping.

QUESTIONS: As a mental health professional,

how would you describe Sorenson's mental condition at the time of the offense? Do you have any expertise that can assist the factfinder in a case like this? As a lawyer, what type of defense might you assert in a case like this? [The case study is based on *State v. Norman,* 366 S.E.2d 586 (N.C. Ct. App. 1988), *rev'd,* 378 S.E.2d (1989), where the defendant's self-defense defense was unsuccessful.]

With the exception of the "justly responsible" test, each of the insanity tests described earlier incorporates the notion that to be excused on the basis of insanity the defendant must have been suffering from a "mental disease or defect." In addition, each test requires that this mental disease or defect "cause" some type of dysfunction at the time of the offense. Finally, except for the *Durham* rule, each test indicates in more specific terms the type of dysfunction that must occur in order to justify a finding of insanity. (Under *Durham,* the offense itself is sufficient evidence of dysfunction.)

This section focuses on these three components of the tests in more detail. It also looks at the issues of burden and standard of proof, because a jurisdiction's rules concerning how much evidence each party must produce in order to prevail may have a significant substantive impact. Although the discussion attempts to delineate the major legal trends in each area discussed, it cannot provide definitive answers for any given case because of the inevitable ambiguity of legal terminology. Whether an individual meets the legal criteria associated with insanity is ultimately a legal–moral question to be decided by the judge or jury on a case-by-case basis. The observations below are offered merely as guideposts to the clinician performing evaluations or testifying for the courts and to the lawyer making tactical decisions.

(1)   Mental Disease or Defect

From its inception, the insanity defense has been available only to those individuals who suffer from some sort of "mental disorder." It has been argued that because environmental and sociological factors, such as poverty and cultural "proclivities," can have as significant an impact on an individual's functioning as psychological ones, they too should have exculpatory effect.[93] But, as detailed above,

the law has continued to adhere to the so-called medical model of insanity. This tenacity is certainly due in part to the desire, noted earlier, to focus on those who lack free will, who are not rational enough to understand and obey the commands of the law. But it also stems from the belief that "exogenous" factors such as one's environment are more subject to an individual's control and therefore less deserving of consideration for purposes of assessing criminal responsibility.[94]

This is not to say that an insanity defense cannot be based on behavior that is "caused" by the environment, but only that some internal, more "proximate" cause must also be identified. For instance, Vietnam veterans have successfully attributed exculpatory effect to their experiences in Vietnam, but only when they can also show that those experiences led to trauma and confused thinking which contributed to the offense [see Wertz report, § 19.04(a)]. The focus in insanity analysis is whether the person is abnormal; the direct effect of abnormal *situations* is more commonly the province of other legal doctrines discussed later [see, in particular, § 8.03(d)].

Accordingly, every currently accepted test for insanity establishes "mental disease or defect" as a threshold consideration. The term "mental disease" has usually been equated with "mental illness," whereas the term "mental defect" is usually thought to be synonymous with "mental retardation," although some courts have indicated that "defect" refers to any condition that is incapable of improving.[95]

Can these terms be defined any more precisely? Written opinions grappling with the mental disease or defect threshold for purposes of the insanity defense are rare, but those that do exist construe the concept narrowly. It will be remembered, for instance, that the District of Columbia Circuit Court of Appeals, in defining the term for purposes of the *Durham* rule, stated that it only "includes any abnormal condition of the mind which *substantially* affects mental or emotional processes and *substantially* impairs behavior controls" [Emphasis added]. Other courts have emphasized that mild symptomatology will not support a defense, presumably even if the individual is psychotic.[96] A few have expressed some distaste for "temporary insanity"—pleas based on nonpsychotic disorders such as "dissociative states," which appear to take hold of the defendant at the time of the offense but at no other time.[97] A number have also indicated that alcohol- or drug-induced "insanity" is rarely a successful claim, at least when the dysfunction is caused by short-term or one-time use of the psychoactive substance[98]; usually only in cases involving "settled insanity" from prolonged alcohol or drug abuse (resulting in significant organic damage) are the courts willing to recognize an insanity defense [see § 8.03(e)].

Some states have also passed statutory provisions narrowing the content of the mental disease or defect threshold. A number of states have adopted the second paragraph of the ALI test which, it will be recalled, tends to exclude the antisocial personality disorder from this threshold [see § 8.02(b)]. Other state statutes exclude all personality disorders.[99] Connecticut has provided that pathological gambling cannot form the basis for an insanity defense.[100] And some states have equated the definition of mental disorder in insanity cases with the definition of mental disorder used in commitment statutes, which arguably requires a severe degree of impairment.[101] Similarly, both the American Psychiatric Association and the ABA have proposed definitions of mental disease and mental defect that would adopt a narrow threshold.[102] For example, the American Psychiatric Association's definition reads: "[T]he terms mental disease and mental retardation include only those severely abnormal mental conditions that grossly and demonstrably impair a person's perception or understanding of reality and that are not attributable primarily to the voluntary ingestion of alcohol or other psychoactive substances."[103]

Analysis of trial outcomes affirms the judicial and statutory law. In historical fact, most successful insanity defenses are based on the presence of one of two mental conditions: psychosis or mental retardation.[104] As noted earlier,[105] virtually all studies of the subject indicate that the majority (60–90%) of defendants acquitted by reason of insanity are diagnosed as psychotic [see also § 8.04(a)]. To judges, lawyers, and juries, then, these individuals are the most likely to appear sick rather than "evil" and the least likely to seem deserving of criminal punishment.[106]

Equating "mental disease or defect" with psychosis and retardation would be too simplistic a summary of the law, however, especially as it has developed in modern times. For example, some courts faced with statutory adoption of the ALI's second paragraph have been unwilling to conclude that antisocial personality disorder is thereby barred as a basis for the insanity defense.[107] In Michigan, one of the states which by statute has equated mental disease or defect with the definition of mental disorder in civil commitment, courts have nonetheless refused to conclude that the insanity defense is limited solely to those conditions that can form the basis for commitment.[108] As an empirical matter, individuals who are neither psychotic nor retarded have been found insane. The data described in § 8.04(a) show that in some jurisdictions, up to 25% of those acquitted by reason of insanity are classified as having personality disorders.[109] Furthermore, a number of new "syndromes," many of which are described in § 8.04, have led to successful insanity defenses.

Indeed, one well-known criminal law text has gone so far as to suggest that the mental disease or defect threshold adds nothing to the test for insanity beyond the previously described preference for endogenous causes. As the authors state: "[I]t would seem that any mental abnormality, be it psychosis, neurosis, organic brain disorder, or congenital intellectual deficiency . . . will suffice if it has caused the consequences described in the second part of the test."[110] They assert, in other words, that any mental disability that results in significant cognitive or volitional impairment should meet the threshold.

In short, legal definitions of the mental disease or defect threshold, if they exist at all, are extremely vague and will vary from jurisdiction to jurisdiction. Thus, it would be unwise to assume that a particular diagnosis can be equated with insanity or its threshold. The drafters of the American Psychiatric Association's *Diagnostic and Statistical Manual of Mental Disorders* (DSM) recognized this latter point with the following language:

> When the DSM-IV categories, criteria, and textual descriptions are employed for forensic purposes, there are significant risks that diagnostic information will be misused or misunderstood. These dangers arise because of the imperfect fit between the questions of ultimate concern to the law and the information contained in a clinical diagnosis. In most situations, the clinical diagno-

sis of a DSM-IV mental disorder is not sufficient to establish the existence for legal purposes of a "mental disorder," "mental disability," "mental disease," or "mental defect." In determining whether an individual meets a specified legal standard (e.g., for competence, criminal responsibility, or disability), additional information is usually required beyond that contained in the DSM-IV diagnosis. This might include information about the individual's functional impairments and how these impairments affect the particular abilities in question. It is precisely because impairments, abilities, and disabilities vary widely within each diagnostic category that assignment of a particular diagnosis does not imply a specific level of impairment or disability.[111]

Accordingly, the clinician preparing a report or testifying about insanity may be best advised, in the usual case, to focus on describing symptomatology, perhaps resorting to a diagnostic label only if it will help the factfinder understand the relative severity of the person's mental condition. The latter situation might occur if, for instance, the clinician concludes that the person has a schizoid personality disorder and that telling the legal system this fact, together with a description of symptoms associated with schizophrenia, will get across the comparative magnitude of the person's mental problems [see § 8.07(a) for further discussion of this point].

At the same time, it must be recognized that this fact-oriented approach to the mental disease or defect issue will probably meet with resistance from the legal profession. As § 18.05 discusses in more detail, lawyers and judges often ignore DSM-IV's cautionary injunction and demand that an expert give a diagnosis even when it is not particularly helpful, in the belief that, without one, no "mental disease or defect" exists. In such cases, the clinician may find it advisable to provide the diagnosis and defend it, for what it is worth. But the clinician (and lawyers conducting direct or cross-examination) should also keep in mind that succumbing to this pressure might well result in a confusing and largely irrelevant battle over whether a person fits the criteria of a particular diagnosis.

(2)   Causation

Every test of insanity requires that the mental disease or defect "cause" either the offense itself

(*Durham*) or a dysfunction that in turn impairs the individual's appreciation or control of the acts constituting the offense (as with the *M'Naghten*, "irresistible impulse," ALI, and ABA/American Psychiatric Association tests). To put it simply, there must be a link between the mental disease or defect and the crime.

One might assume that proving the defendant was suffering from significant impairment at the time of the offense would be sufficient to meet this element of the defense. But, in fact, the few courts that have addressed this issue (in particular, the District of Columbia Court of Appeals during the *Durham* era) have emphasized that if the disorder does not directly affect the defendant's actions at the time in question, it is irrelevant. One's illness is not presumed to cause all of one's acts; as the District of Columbia Court put it, the evidence must show that "but for" the disorder, the criminal act would not have occurred.[112] Thus, for instance, in Case Study 8.1 it might be important to tease apart the extent to which intoxication, rather than mental illness, played a role in the offense.

Furthermore, some have contended that merely establishing a link between a certain mental or physical state and the crime should not be enough. Moore has argued, for instance, that showing a crime was caused by factors such as the unconscious or biology (e.g., an extra "Y" chromosome) is generally *irrelevant* to criminal responsibility; the law typically should be interested only in the effect of the actor's conscious reasons on behavior.[113] Moore arrives at this conclusion by distinguishing, on the basis of linguistic philosophy, between "responsibility" and "causation": while the language of "causation" refers to events occurring because of antecedent events, the language of "responsibility" refers to persons acting for reasons. According to Moore, if the latter concept is *not* kept distinct from the former, one would have to adopt the untenable position that no one is responsible for his or her actions because all behavior can be said to be "caused" by factors other than an individual's reasons for the behavior—factors such as physiological processes or the unconscious. Thus, he states, even if one assumes that a particular person's behavior is "caused" by one of these other factors, that person is nonetheless "responsible" for his or her behavior whenever it is done for reasons that are rational (i.e., intelligible and relatively consistent with one another). Only if the person's conscious reasons for acting are irrational should exculpation result.

Moore's argument, which is of course much more elaborate than summarized above, has been criticized on a number of grounds,[114] most notably on the ground that it provides "an unduly thin account of the essential attributes for moral agency."[115] But it is probably the best effort to date at reinforcing the contentions summarized in § 1.03(a): namely, that the determinism of the behavioral sciences is inappropriate in the criminal context because it threatens the central premise of the criminal law—that "free will" exists and people are generally responsible for their behavior. Unless the defendant's own reasons for acting are seen as the "proximate cause" of his or her actions, *every* case is potentially open to deterministic claims that the actions were predestined by upbringing or biology. Moore's reasoning suggests that, in insanity cases, testimony describing unconscious motivation, physiological evidence, or environmental factors should generally be either excluded or minimized.[116]

Whatever the cogency of Moore's argument, however, the law's penchant for seeking explanations of human behavior is likely to lead to continued reliance on any competent evidence offered by mental health professionals, including that delving into the unconscious; the deterministic influence will be hard to dispel. Assume, for example, that a woman with schizophrenia states that she shoplifted from a grocery store because she needed the food, and that it was discovered that she in fact had no money with which to buy such food. Assume also, however, that the manner in which she states her reason for the theft is somewhat loose and flippant, as if she were kidding the interviewer, and that she makes occasional nonsensical comments. Under these circumstances, the woman's explanation of why she shoplifted (i.e., her conscious reasons for shoplifting) might not be taken at face value. At the least, the factfinder will want to know whether the explanation is "credible." To answer this question, it will be hard to avoid speculation about this woman's personality, perhaps based in part on hypotheses about her "psychodynamics." Indeed, as the cases upon which Case Studies 8.1 and 8.2 are based demonstrate, courts routinely permit testimony based on psychodynamic theories.

What are the implications of the foregoing discussion for the mental health professional and the lawyer? Perhaps this: When evaluating whether a defendant's mental problems "caused" the criminal behavior at issue, the primary focus should be on his or her conscious reasoning at the time of the offense. Only if the conscious reasons do not seem to explain a person's true motivation for acting (i.e., when they are not credible in some way) should other data (e.g., unconscious motivation) be sought out and relied on. As should become clear from the following discussion, the latter step is most likely to be necessary when volitional, as opposed to cognitive, impairment is the suspected culprit.

(3)   Cognitive Impairment

The *M'Naghten* test, the first prong of the ALI test, and the ABA/American Psychiatric Association formulation permit a defense of insanity only if a mental disease or defect causes cognitive impairment at the time of the offense. The *M'Naghten* test actually permits exculpation on either of two grounds: (1) when the defendant did not know the nature and quality of the criminal act, or (2) when the defendant did not know that the act was wrong. Typically an accused who does not meet the first test will not meet the second. The ALI and ABA/American Psychiatric Association formulations, on the other hand, focus on the single standard of whether the defendant "substantially" lacked the ability to "appreciate" the "criminality" of the act or, in the alternative, the "wrongfulness" of the act.

Looking solely at the language of the two different formulations, it is clear that *M'Naghten* is the more restrictive. Whereas *M'Naghten* speaks in terms of whether the offender did or did not know, the ALI refers to a lack of substantial capacity to appreciate. In justifying their approach, the drafters of the ALI test stated that whether an offender possessed "substantial capacity" is all "that candid witnesses, called on to infer the nature of the situation at a time that they did not observe, can ever confidently say, even when they know that the disorder was extreme."[117] In the same liberal spirit, they explained, use of the word "appreciate" is designed to permit testimony about defendants' emotional and affective attitude toward their offenses as well as their perceptions and memory of the crimes.[118] The language and intent of the ALI test, then, indicates it is significantly broader than *M'Naghten*. In theory, for instance, a person with a personality disorder might never have a defense under a literal construction of *M'Naghten* (because such a person will always "know" crime is wrong) but may have a defense under the ALI test (because such a person may not "emotionally appreciate" the wrongness of the crime).

Yet, according to Goldstein, who studied evidence presented and instructions given in jurisdictions that use the *M'Naghten* rule, most courts interpret *M'Naghten* liberally, in a manner that makes it equivalent to the ALI test.[119] Thus, the word "know," when it is defined at all, is usually given broad construction to encompass defendants' ability to "understand" or "appreciate" the nature and consequences of their actions. The phrase "nature and quality of the act" is either eliminated altogether from the jury's instructions or, in Goldstein's words, "treated as [if it added] nothing to the requirement that the accused know his act was wrong."[120] As indicated earlier [see § 8.02(b)], the little empirical evidence that exists is inconclusive with respect to whether the ALI test leads to more pleas of insanity and more successful defenses than *M'Naghten*.[121]

If there is any difference between existing formulations of the cognitive impairment necessary for insanity, it is likely to arise in connection with the "wrongness" issue rather than the know/appreciation language. According to Goldstein, under *M'Naghten* some courts have interpreted the word "wrong" restrictively, holding that defendants are sane if they knew their offenses were prohibited by law. Other courts, however, have taken the position that "wrong" should be read to mean "morally wrong."[122] Thus, to use Goldstein's example, these latter courts would find legally insane a man who thinks God ordered him to kill an individual even if he knew it was legally wrong to take another's life. The ALI options described earlier were meant to reflect this dichotomy. If the word "criminality" is adopted, the test is meant to apply only to those who did not appreciate that their act was legally wrong. If the word

"wrongfulness" is adopted, individuals who know that their acts were illegal but whose mental disorder nonetheless led them to feel morally justified in committing these acts (e.g., the individuals in Case Studies 8.1 or 8.3?) may be excused by reason of insanity.[123]

Some formulations of the cognitive prong attempt to stake out a position somewhere *between* the criminality and wrongfulness approaches. For instance, a second rule adopted by the House of Lords in the *M'Naghten* case was that if the defendant suffered from "partial delusions" he would not have an insanity defense unless his delusion would justify his crime. As the House of Lords explained it:

> For example, if, under the influence of his delusion, he supposes another man to be in the act of attempting to take away his life, and he kills that man, as he supposes, in self-defense, he would be exempt from punishment. If his delusion was that the deceased had inflicted a serious injury to his character and fortune, and he killed him in revenge for such supposed injury, he would be liable to punishment.

This modification of *M'Naghten,* which only a few states explicitly follow today, narrows the scope of the "wrongfulness" approach by providing that, of those defendants whose mental illness made them believe their crime was morally permissible, only those who would have been justified had their delusions been true will have a defense.

The Washington Supreme Court has limited the "moral wrong" approach even further by holding that it applies only when the defendant feels justified as a result of a "deific decree" of the type referred to earlier (where God orders the crime committed).[124] To adopt the full-blown moral wrong approach, or even the *M'Naghten* limitation on it, the Washington court reasoned, "would seriously undermine the criminal law, for it would allow one who violated the law to be excused from criminal responsibility solely because, in his own conscience, his act was not morally wrong." This analysis leaves out the fact that the person alleging insanity must also show a "mental disease or defect"—not any person who feels his or her act is justified will be excused. As Judge Cardozo stated in *People v. Schmidt*[125]—the first case to recognize the "deific decree" notion of insanity—" [t]he anarchist is not at liberty to break the law because he reasons that all government is wrong. The devotee of a religious cult that enjoins polygamy or human sacrifice as a duty is not thereby relieved from responsibility before the law." Nonetheless, the Washington court's fear that terrorists and similar routinely antisocial individuals would benefit from the broad "moral justification" formulation is understandable and could lead other jurisdictions to limit the defense in a similar fashion.

Again, however, it is important not to make too much of differences in legal language. The *M'Naghten* case itself provides an illustration of the degree of "stretch" in even that seemingly narrow test. Daniel M'Naghten shot Edward Drummond, private secretary to Prime Minister Peel, apparently under the mistaken impression that Drummond was the Prime Minister. The defense attorneys introduced evidence tending to show that M'Naghten felt persecuted by a Tory "system" of spies that followed him, allowed him no peace of mind, and was out to kill him; the defense also claimed that M'Naghten thought the person he shot was part of this system. However, there is little doubt that M'Naghten knew the nature and quality of his act in the literal sense: He knew he was firing a pistol, knew he was shooting a human being, and had every intention of killing that human being. It also appears that he knew, in the abstract sense, that it was unlawful to shoot another.[126] Yet he was acquitted under instructions that were very similar to the rules subsequently pronounced by the House of Lords.[127]

Furthermore, whatever the applicable test, the type of expert evidence submitted is not likely to vary. The basic issue under any of these tests—degree of cognitive impairment—is the same. Later in this chapter, we suggest some specific areas that can be investigated in this regard [see §§ 8.06, 8.07(a)].

(4) Volitional Impairment

The "irresistible impulse" test and the second prong of the ALI test excuse individuals whose mental disease or defect causes a loss of control over their actions at the time of their offenses. The former standard is popularly characterized as the "policeman at the elbow" test, under which

offenders will be found insane only if they would have committed their offenses in the presence of an officer[128]; the latter test, as with the ALI's cognitive prong, focuses on whether the defendant lacked "substantial capacity" to conform to the requirements of the law. Nonetheless, similar to experience with the cognitive tests, the irresistible impulse formulation has not led to less testimony on the impulsivity issue than is offered in ALI jurisdictions.[129]

Whatever language is used to encapsulate it, the lack-of-control defense clearly is not as favored as the cognition-based excuses. As noted earlier, as of 1995, only about 20 states use one of the two control formulations, and several states have specifically rejected the defense.[130] Recall also that the principal criticism of the control tests is the lack of objective basis for determining whether an impulse is irresistible. According to the American Psychiatric Association:

> The line between an irresistible impulse and an impulse not resisted is probably no sharper than that between twilight and dusk. . . . The concept of volition is the subject of some disagreement among psychiatrists. Many psychiatrists therefore believe that psychiatric testimony (particularly that of a conclusory nature) about volition is more likely to produce confusion for jurors than is psychiatric testimony relevant to a defendant's appreciation or understanding.[131]

Some question exists, however, as to whether these assertions of potential abuse are correct. At least one study suggests that volitional impairment is just as easily gauged as cognitive impairment, at least when a structured instrument is used.[132] Moreover, the courts in jurisdictions that maintain a loss-of-control defense have usually been careful to restrict its scope in two ways. First, many have narrowly defined the type of mental disease or defect that can form the predicate for this type of defense. As one court put it, the irresistible impulse "is to be distinguished from mere passion or overwhelming emotion not growing out of and connected with, a disease of the mind. Frenzy arising solely from the passion of anger and jealousy, regardless of how furious, is not insanity."[133] Illustrative is a decision that denied a volitional impairment defense to a woman with a "passive–aggressive personality" who concededly killed her husband in the heat of the moment, but at the same time acted merely on the basis of "sudden anger produced by the pain of his kick."[134] In another case, the court upheld a conviction for bail jumping of a defendant who claimed he was insane because he suffered from something called a "judgment disorder with mixed disturbances of emotions and conduct."[135]

A second way courts cabin the volitional impairment defense is through requiring a significant degree of impulsivity. For instance, Virginia courts have held that, under the irresistible impulse test, any indication of planning preceding the criminal act will prevent an insanity finding.[136] An old Pennsylvania decision, not yet overruled, held that an irresistible impulse defense is permitted only when the defendant can show that the same impairment had caused a similar act on another occasion.[137] Many jurisdictions using the ALI's volitional test or its equivalent have been similarly restrictive. For instance, one federal appellate court held, before abolition of the volitional prong in federal jurisdictions, that expert evidence that the defendant's embezzlement was due to his pathological need to gamble did not even overcome the "presumption of sanity" [see § 8.02(c)(5) for discussion of this term], much less make a case for insanity.[138]

On the other hand, it must be admitted that these types of restrictions are not uniformly applied. As the trial of Lorena Bobbitt (charged with severing her husband's penis) illustrated, insanity acquittals for "crimes of passion" have occurred despite an absence of significant mental disorder. As the case underlying Case Study 8.2 demonstrates, courts in other jurisdictions have been willing to let the volitional impairment issue go to the jury despite considerable evidence of planning.[139] And some courts have quoted with favor a comment made by Warren Burger before he rose to the Supreme Court that the irresistible impulse label "has always been a misleading concept because it has connotations of some sudden outburst of impulse and completely overlooks the fact that people do a lot of weird and strange and unlawful things as a result of not just sudden impulse but long brooding and disturbed emotional makeup."[140] In short, the scope of the volitional prong is extremely vague. Whether this vagueness leads to more "abuse" than occurs under the

cognitive impairment-only approach is still not proven, however.

The practical arguments against the volitional prong do not directly address whether volitional impairment—*if* it can be proven and *if* it is significant—should be given exculpatory effect. There is a long philosophical tradition suggesting that it should be.[141] Bonnie's assertion [described in § 8.02(b)] that it would violate our "shared moral intuitions" to find insane those people who have been diagnosed as having pedophilia or kleptomania may be correct. But these are not the only types of disorders that might cause volitional impairment with little or no cognitive ramifications. For instance, one study concluded that manic patients are often severely impaired in their capacity to control behavior, while their cognitive impairment is less striking. As a result, the authors of the study asserted, elimination of the volitional prong could lead to conviction of "a class of psychotic patients whose illness is clearest in symptomatology, most likely biologic in origin, most eminently treatable and potentially most disruptive in penal detention."[142] Even Moore, whose focus on the rationality of one's reasons for acting [see § 8.02(c)(2)] significantly diminishes the role volitional impairment would play in insanity analysis,[143] is unwilling to conclude that compelled behavior cannot form the basis of an exculpatory defense [for an example of a case in which volitional impairment might be relevant to insanity, see the Hedges report, § 19.04(c)].[144]

The lack-of-control tests are still viable in many states and may even make a comeback. Although appellate courts have interpreted the control tests somewhat restrictively, juries still seem willing to acquit on lack of control grounds, even when there is some evidence of planning. Later in this chapter, we attempt to pinpoint those factors that seem most relevant to the impulsivity inquiry [see §§ 8.04(g), 8.06, 8.07].

(5) Burden and Standard of Proof

In those cases that go to trial, neither side may be able to present evidence that is overwhelmingly convincing to the factfinder. The law has developed the "burden of proof" and "standard of proof" concepts to deal with this probability. If the party with the burden of proof does not meet the standard of proof established by law, that party loses. The outcome of an insanity case could depend as much on a jurisdiction's approach to these proof issues as on its substantive test of insanity.

There are two major competing approaches to proof issues in the insanity context. One-third of the states require the prosecution to prove sanity "beyond a reasonable doubt" (which translates to perhaps a 90–95% degree of certainty). If the factfinder is not convinced beyond a reasonable doubt that the defendant was sane at the time of the offense, the prosecution loses. Most of the remaining states, on the other hand, place the burden of proof on the defendant to show by a "preponderance of the evidence" (or with a 51% degree of certainty) that he or she was insane at the time of the offense. If the defendant's evidence does not meet this standard, the prosecution wins.[145] Arizona and the federal courts require the defendant to prove insanity by "clear and convincing" evidence (or with approximately a 75% degree of certainty).[146]

The courts that follow the first approach appear to treat sanity as if it were an element of every crime, just as some type of unlawful act is an element of every crime.[147] These courts reason that just as the prosecution must prove beyond a reasonable doubt that the act associated with a given crime was in fact committed by the defendant, it must also prove beyond a reasonable doubt that the defendant was sane at that time. Courts and legislatures that have adopted the second approach do not consider sanity a formal element of every crime, or they disregard the elements analysis entirely; their principal concern is that the "reasonable doubt" standard of proof might unfairly hinder the prosecution in cases involving the ambiguous matters raised by an insanity plea.[148] In fact, the data that exist do not suggest any consistent relationship between the burden of proof and the acquittal rate.[149]

Interestingly, the ABA proposed that while the burden of proof should be on the prosecution under its cognitive impairment-only test, the burden should be on the defendant if the ALI combined cognitive-volitional test is retained.[150] The ABA drafters felt that the prosecution should normally bear the burden of proving sanity beyond a reasonable doubt but that the difficulty in proving

lack of impulsivity should permit shifting the burden to the defendant when the control test is relied on.

A final proof issue deserving of mention is the so-called presumption of sanity. This evidentiary doctrine, which exists in all jurisdictions, does not affect the burden of proof just discussed; it merely requires the defendant to "get the ball rolling" on the insanity issue by presenting some evidence of insanity. Most state courts hold that a "scintilla" (or very minimal amount) of evidence satisfactorily rebuts this presumption[151]; other jurisdictions require that the defendant present a *prima facie* case of insanity,[152] which means that the evidence standing alone must be sufficient to support an insanity verdict. If the judge decides the presumption has not been rebutted, the defendant is not entitled to argue the insanity defense. If the judge decides the presumption has been rebutted, the evidence goes to the jury and the jury decides, under the appropriate burden and standard of proof, who wins. Unlike the burden and standard of proof, the presumption is never mentioned to the jury; it is merely a judicial device for ensuring the defendant does not waste the jury's time with a frivolous argument.

8.03.   Exculpatory and Mitigating Doctrines Other Than Insanity

Except for strict liability offenses, which are not relevant to the topic of this chapter, every crime consists of at least two elements: (1) the physical conduct associated with the crime (known as the *actus reus*); and (2) the mental state, or level of intent, associated with the crime (known as the *mens rea*). To convict an individual of a particular crime, the state must prove beyond a reasonable doubt that the defendant committed the *actus reus* with the requisite *mens rea* for the crime (e.g., murder is the unlawful killing of another human being—the *actus reus*—with intent to do so—the *mens rea*). Whether conviction also requires proof of a third element—sanity—has been discussed in the preceding subsection and is not reexamined here.

The law requires an act as a predicate for criminal liability because "evil thoughts" alone, however repugnant morally, have never been considered sufficient to justify the imposition of criminal sanctions. It has developed the *mens rea* requirement because proof that an individual has committed a given act is not viewed as a sufficient measure by itself of criminal culpability. All would agree, for example, that the unjustified killing of another is reprehensible. But we would all also probably agree that the driver who accidentally runs into a child, the husband who in a rage kills the man he finds sleeping with his wife, and the "cold-blooded" murderer should not be punished equally. Determining the individual's *mens rea* at the time of the offense provides a mechanism for deciding how much retribution is justifiable in such cases. Most of the legal doctrines to be discussed in the following subsections have developed out of the law's attempt to define the *actus reus* and *mens rea* concepts.

(a)   Automatism Defense

The *actus reus* contemplates a voluntary physical act. For instance, if *A* pushes *B*'s arm into *C, B* cannot be convicted of assault even though *B*'s arm committed the actual touching, because *B*'s act was not voluntary. It could also be said that *B* did not intend to commit the assault and thus did not have the *mens rea* for the crime. But a distinction is usually made between an act over which there is no conscious control and a conscious action with unintended consequences. The assault described here is an example of the first type of act and has traditionally been analyzed under the voluntariness requirement of the *actus reus*. An example of the latter situation would be if *B* meant to tap *C* but instead killed *C; B*'s act would be voluntary, but *B* would not have the *mens rea* for murder.

The automatism (or "unconsciousness") defense recognizes that some criminal acts may be committed "involuntarily," even though no third party (like *A* in the previous example) is involved. The classic example of the "automaton" is the person who commits an offense while sleeping; courts have held that such an individual does not have conscious control of his or her physical actions and therefore acts involuntarily.[153] Other more "clinical" situations in which the defense might be implicated arise when a crime occurs

during a state of unconsciousness induced by a head injury, hypnotic suggestion, shock created by bullet wounds, or metabolic disorders such as anoxia, hypoglycemia, or the involuntary ingestion of alcohol or drugs.[154] As discussed in more detail later, events caused by epilepsy and dissociation are probably best placed in this category as well.

Several courts have limited the automatism defense by holding that a person claiming to have been affected by one of the above-named conditions at the time of the offense cannot prevail if the disability has been experienced on previous occasions and steps reasonably could have been taken to prevent the criminal occurrence.[155] Thus, if a man knows he is subject to epileptic seizures, loses control of a car because of a seizure, and kills someone in the process, he may not be able to take advantage of the defense.

Conceptually, the automatism defense differs from the insanity defense in three ways. First, insane persons, unlike automatons, generally have conscious control of their acts but either do not understand the true nature of the acts or cannot stop themselves from performing them. Second, although there is some dispute over whether sanity is an element that must be proven for each offense, the prosecution clearly bears the burden of establishing the *actus reus* and thus bears the burden of negating an automatism claim beyond a reasonable doubt. Finally, to prevail, a person alleging insanity must be found to have a mental disease or defect; there is no such requirement when automatism is involved.

Partly because the automaton is not perceived to be as "sick" as the insane person, and partly because cases raising the issue of legal unconsciousness are rare, there are no special commitment statutes, analogous to those used in the insanity context, governing those who are acquitted on automatism grounds. But occasionally, of course, a person suffering from a condition that causes involuntary behavior in the legal sense may be both in need of treatment and quite dangerous. Thus, many courts confronted with an automatism defense have glossed over the theoretical distinctions between insanity and automatism in order to ensure the commitment of violent offenders. For example, most commentators agree that an epileptic seizure is best characterized as an involuntary act rather than an "irresistible impulse" because the seizure is not triggered by the individual's conscious, or even unconscious, processes.[156] Yet courts in Britain, where the law of automatism is well developed, have rejected automatism defenses based on epilepsy and instead have permitted only claims of insanity in such cases, on the explicit ground that to do otherwise would result in immediate release of dangerous individuals.[157] Rather than distorting the insanity doctrine in such a fashion, it would probably make more sense to subject those acquitted on automatism grounds to commitment provisions similar to those applicable in the insanity context.

The automatism defense is infrequent in the United States, even in cases in which it is most likely to be successful. Cases involving dissociation illustrates this point. Conduct committed by a person who is in a dissociative or fugue state is probably best described as activity that, although purposive in nature, is no longer subject to the conscious constraints of the superego or conscience[158] and is therefore "involuntary" or "automatic." Yet American defendants claiming to have experienced dissociation at the time of the offense usually rely on the insanity defense rather than the automatism doctrine. Moreover, they are usually convicted; as discussed in § 8.02(c), courts and juries tend to reject an insanity defense based on a dissociative incident because of their dislike for the notion of temporary insanity.[159]

Another example of the conceptual confusion between automatism and insanity involves defenses based on multiple personality disorder. According to DSM-IV, which uses the label "dissociative identity disorder," this diagnosis requires "the presence of two or more distinct identities or personality traits (each with its own relatively enduring pattern of perceiving, relating to, and thinking about the environment and self)" and an "[i]nability to recall important personal information that is too extensive to be explained by ordinary forgetfulness" [see § 8.04(d) for further clinical discussion of multiple personality disorder]. In most cases in which the diagnosis is involved, the issue has been whether the personality in control at the time of the offense was insane.[160] An arguably better analysis, suggested by automatism doctrine, is to determine "who" was in control at the time of the offense, the "host" personality or one of the alters.[161] If the latter, acquittal should result, given the defendant's lack of conscious control over his or her actions. If the former, then, and only then, should insanity become an issue. Admittedly, identifying the "host" may sometimes be difficult. In such a situation, Saks has argued that the defendant should be found nonresponsible, except under two conditions: (1) when "all of a multiple's alters know about and acquiesce in the crime," or (2) when there is a "ringleader alter in addition to well-established lines of responsibility for different tasks [such that] each alter has sufficient knowledge and control over the others that group liability makes sense."[162]

In any event, this discussion suggests that automatism may be a more appropriate defense than insanity in some types of cases. In light of its conceptual advantages and the fact that the prosecution bears the burden of disproving involuntariness, its relative dearth in the case law is somewhat surprising.

(b) Mens Rea *Testimony* (*Diminished Capacity*)

As noted in the beginning of this section, the principal device the law uses to grade culpability is mental state. A person who deliberately plans a crime is more culpable than one who accidentally commits one. Under the common law, courts developed literally scores of *mens rea* terms to describe various levels of culpability. Unfortunately, these terms—"willful and wanton," "with a depraved heart," and so on—were more colorful than descriptive. Over the years, two generic categories were created to help categorize these diverse mental states, although they were only partially successful in doing so. "Specific intent" was meant to designate the *mens rea* of those crimes that require a further intention beyond that identified with the physical act connected with the offense (e.g., "premeditated" murder, "aggravated" assault, and assault "with intent to rape"). "General intent" crimes, on the other hand, only require proof that the perpetrator was conscious or should have been conscious of his or her physical actions and their consequences (e.g., manslaughter, battery, and rape).

Because neither the original *mens rea* terms nor the concepts of specific and general intent were necessarily self-defining, modern statutory codes have attempted to be more precise on issues relating to mental state. Most influential in this regard has been the ALI's Model Penal Code formulation, which attempts to simplify the *mens rea* inquiry by specifying four different mental state "levels." In descending order of culpability, they are (1) "purpose," when the criminal conduct is the offender's conscious object; (2) "knowledge," when the offender is aware of the circumstances that make the conduct criminal but does not intend them; (3) "recklessness," when the offender "consciously disregards a substantial and unjustifiable risk" that the conduct will produce a given result; and (4) "negligence," when the offender, although not actually aware of such a risk, should have been aware of it.[163]

The first two mental states (purpose and knowledge) focus on subjective mental state (i.e., what the defendant was thinking), while negligence is objectively defined (i.e., what a reasonable person should have thought). Recklessness falls somewhere in between the two. Although the common-law terms are so amorphous that equating them with Model Penal Code mental states is a somewhat risky venture, it is probably fair to say that "specific intent" most closely coincides with the subjective mental states of "purpose" and "knowledge," while "general intent" can be equated with "recklessness" and "negligence." As will become clear later, distinguishing between subjective mental states (purpose, knowledge, and specific intent) and objectively defined mental states (negligence, general intent) is important in understanding the courts' approach to clinical input on *mens rea*.

It is also important to recognize that the *mens rea* inquiry described above is quite distinct from the insanity inquiry. Although a person who meets the *M'Naghten* test may also be incapable of forming the requisite intent for an offense, it is theoretically and practically possible for an insane person to have the appropriate *mens rea*. To use the *M'Naghten* case as an example once again, Daniel M'Naghten probably met the *mens rea* requirements for the crime charged (i.e., knowingly shooting at another with the purpose of killing him), but he was nonetheless found insane.

Out of this distinction has developed the so-called diminished capacity concept. In its broadest sense, this "doctrine"[164] permits the accused to introduce clinical testimony focusing directly on the *mens rea* for the crime charged, without having to assert an insanity defense. For example, in a murder case, the doctrine would allow clinical evidence relevant to whether the defendant purposely or knowingly committed the killing. If the charge is assault with intent to rape, mental health professionals would be permitted to address whether the defendant acted with the purpose of committing rape at the time of the offense. In contrast to the disposition when insanity is the defense, when the *mens rea* for a crime is negated by clinical testimony the defendant is acquitted only of that charge. Thus, in the homicide example, conviction might still be sought on a manslaughter charge (requiring a reckless or negligent *mens rea*). In the rape case, prosecution on assault charges is still an option. Showing the absence of *mens rea* for these lesser included offenses is unlikely, because these crimes are either partially or wholly objective (i.e., dependent on whether a "reasonable" person have known his or her conduct would cause the harm), and thus evidence of subjective mental state is relevant.

The diminished capacity doctrine should be distinguished from the "diminished" or "partial" responsibility doctrine. The latter doctrine is a "mini-insanity defense," which gives mitigating effect to mental disorder that causes cognitive or volitional impairment but produces neither insanity nor an inability to form the *mens rea* for the offense. For instance, in *People v. Poddar*[165] the defendant, a student from India who was accustomed to arranged marriages, tried to introduce testimony by an anthropologist that he killed his girlfriend because of the stress created by American-style relationships. This testimony, which was not permitted, would not have negated *mens rea*; Poddar clearly intended to kill his girlfriend. Nor was it evidence of insanity. Rather, it would have merely suggested that cultural differences impaired Poddar's reasoning and volitional capacities. A similar example comes from *United States v. Alexander and Murdock*,[166] in which the defendant, a black man, wanted to present evidence of his "rotten social background" and experience with racial oppression to explain why he shot two

Marines who had responded to his taunts with racial epithets. Again, this testimony, which the court excluded, would merely have suggested a reduction in impulse control in certain situations, not shown a lack of *mens rea* or the presence of insanity.

As the holdings in these two cases indicate, the doctrine of diminished responsibility has rarely enjoyed support in the courts. For a time in California, the doctrine appeared to flourish (although it was often confusingly called "diminished capacity," which explains the result in Case Study 8.1).[167] But in 1981 the California legislature abolished it.[168] Today, evidence of diminished responsibility might occasionally be permitted in first-degree murder cases and is considered very relevant at sentencing, especially in death penalty cases.[169] But except in these situations, it is likely to remain dormant, if only because it is so difficult to implement: How does one sensibly define "partial responsibility" for the jury, and of what crime is the partially responsible defendant guilty?[170]

On the other hand, the diminished *capacity* doctrine, focused solely on whether the defendant had the *mens rea* for the crime, has found increasing acceptance. A sizable number of states,[171] as well as the federal courts,[172] prohibit clinical testimony on any issue other than insanity, generally on the ground that such testimony is too speculative or comes too close to diminished responsibility testimony.[173] But many other states, perhaps 25 all told, permit clinical testimony on *mens rea* as well as on insanity, at least under certain circumstances.[174] Indeed, several courts have found it unconstitutional to hold otherwise. Some of these courts merely state that principles of fairness and due process require that defendants be permitted to introduce any competent relevant evidence, including psychiatric testimony, in their defense.[175] It could also be argued that because the prosecution is entitled to an inference that accused persons intend the natural consequences of their acts,[176] denying defendants the opportunity to present competent clinical evidence when such evidence is the only means of overcoming the inference would in effect permit the prosecution to convict when there is a reasonable doubt as to guilt.[177]

It should also be noted, however, that many of the states that permit clinical testimony on *mens rea* do so grudgingly. There are three types of limitations on such evidence. First, to prevent clinicians from testifying on the "ultimate issue" of whether defendants possessed the requisite *mens rea* at the time of their offenses, many courts permit clinicians to testify only as to the "capacity" of the defendant to form the requisite mental state (thus one reason for the name "diminished capacity").[178] Second, courts may require proof that some severe "mental disease or defect," analogous to that required in the insanity context, caused the lack of capacity.[179] Finally, most states restrict the admissibility of clinical evidence to certain types of crimes.

This third limitation on *mens rea* evidence is itself of two types. One approach, apparently followed by about a third of the states that recognize the doctrine, permits clinical testimony only when defendants are charged with some type of intentional homicide.[180] A second approach, taken by most other states that allow clinical testimony on *mens rea,* admits clinical testimony for any crime involving "specific intent" (in common-law jurisdictions), or for which intent is subjectively defined (in Model Penal Code jurisdictions), but does not admit such evidence for crimes involving "general intent" (in common-law states), or for which intent is defined objectively (in Model Penal Code states).[181]

The "capacity" and "severe mental abnormality" limitations represent an attempt by the courts to ensure that any opinions proffered by mental health professionals on *mens rea* are in fact clinical in nature. They are also motivated by a fear that without such restrictions every case will turn into a psychiatric one, as there is always something "expert" to be said about the psychological processes of criminals. Limiting *mens rea* evidence to certain types of crimes is directed toward another concern: that some mentally ill defendants (including those who ordinarily would have pleaded insanity and thus been committed) will otherwise be able to use clinical evidence to elude confinement completely.[182] The public is protected in states limiting testimony on *mens rea* to homicide cases by the fact that a defendant who has killed another can almost always be convicted of at least negligent homicide (involuntary manslaughter), no matter how mentally ill; as noted earlier, the *mens rea* for that crime is objectively defined in terms of what a reasonable person would do, making clinical evidence of the defendant's subjective state of mind irrelevant. Similarly, in those states in which the defense is available only for crimes involving specific intent, the mentally ill defendant can usually be convicted of some lesser included offense involving general intent.

The limitations on *mens rea* evidence thus grew from practical concerns. However, none of these limitations is conceptually justified. If, as many courts have held, due process prohibits barring competent evidence on *mens rea,* the sole requirement for clinical testimony relevant to that subject should be whether it is admissible as expert opinion [see § 1.04]. If a clinician's opinion is based on specialized knowledge and can assist the trier of fact in reaching a conclusion on the issue, it should be admissible whether it is phrased in terms of capacity or actual intent, whether it is based on a finding of significant mental abnormality or mere "quirkiness," and regardless of the offense charged.[183] Admittedly, deciding when a particular opinion is based on "specialized knowledge" may be difficult in certain cases. But this problem is alleviated somewhat by the narrow confines of the *mens rea* concept. As the example using the *M'Naghten* case illustrated, mere proof of "craziness" is insufficient for purposes of negating *mens rea*; it must be shown that because of mental aberration the defendant was actually unable to formulate the requisite intent. If *A,* a person with schizophrenia, intends to kill *B, A* has the *mens rea* for some type of intentional homicide; only if *A's* illness negates intent—for example, *A* thinks that *B* is a tree or that the gun is a toy—would *A* be able to benefit from a diminished capacity defense. Volitional impairment of the type evidenced in Case Studies 8.1 and 8.2 is also usually irrelevant to the *mens rea* issue.

The fear that the public will be endangered unless the doctrine is limited in scope is also exaggerated. Because most mentally ill defendants are conscious of their actions, they will often be guilty of some crime involving general intent, objectively defined, even without the technical restriction rigidly limiting clinical evidence to offenses involving specific intent. And there is no obstacle to adopting special-commitment statutes for the dangerously mentally ill who somehow do escape conviction altogether.

A description of a federal case may help illustrate why clinical testimony about *mens rea* should generally be admissible. In *Bright v. United States,*[184] the defendant was charged with possession of stolen checks—a crime requiring proof that the accused knew the checks were stolen. The defendant in the case received six checks under circumstances that would have suggested to most people that they were stolen. However, the defendant offered testimony by a psychiatrist suggesting that she had in fact not known they were stolen. According to the psychiatrist, the defendant had a "passive–dependent" personality and possessed a "childlike character structure," which led her to trust implicitly those close to her; because the person who gave her the checks was a good friend of her boyfriend and told her the checks were legitimate, she did not think they had been stolen. One may question whether the clinician's testimony was based on specialized knowledge (which is, in essence, the reason the court gave for excluding it). But his testimony, if accepted as competent, was clearly *relevant* to the issue whether the defendant knew the checks were stolen, even though it was neither phrased in terms of capacity nor based on a finding of severe mental illness. To exclude it on irrelevance grounds would permit conviction of a person who may not have been guilty of the crime as defined by the legislature.

Even in jurisdictions that do not recognize the diminished capacity defense, the testimony in *Bright* might possibly have been admitted as "character evidence." An increasing number of courts allow psychiatric opinion evidence about the defendant's character independent of their stand on the diminished capacity issue.[185] This trend is an outgrowth of the rule, found in the Federal Rules of Evidence and the evidence rules in most states, that opinion evidence of a "pertinent" trait of an accused's character is admissible to show the accused "acted in conformity therewith on a particular occasion."[186] The previously described limitations on diminished capacity testimony (i.e., the capacity, mental disease, and crime limitations) do not apply to character evidence. Such evidence *is* evidence of capacity, so that particular limitation is meaningless in this context. And, under the evidentiary rules, if character evidence tends to show the accused acted a certain way on the day of the offense, it is generally admissible regardless of the degree of disability or the crime involved.

The only limitation that does apply to psychiatric opinion evidence on character, aside from the obvious one that it must be acceptable as expert opinion based on specialized knowledge, is that it cannot be introduced unless the defendant chooses to open the door on that topic.[187] The prosecution is not permitted to introduce evidence of the defendant's bad character unilaterally, out of fear that the factfinder will convict based on the character evidence, not the evidence related to the crime in question. Once the defendant opens the door on character, on the other hand, the prosecution may rebut with opinion evidence on character, or evidence of specific acts that tend to show the defendant does not have the asserted character. Thus, in *Bright,* the expert testimony could have been admitted as character evidence because it showed a propensity on the part of the defendant to believe what those close to her said, a propensity that was relevant to whether she had the *mens rea* for the crime charged. The prosecution could have rebutted this testimony with expert testimony showing Bright was not a passive–dependent personality, or by proving specific instances in which she did *not* believe those who were close to her.

Although the character evidence issue was not raised in *Bright,* a number of other cases have addressed the issue. For instance, in *United States v. Staggs,*[188] the defendant argued that when he picked up a gun upon arrival of the arresting agents, he intended to turn it on himself rather than the agents (an argument which, if believed, would prevent conviction on assault charges, which require a specific intent to harm). In support of this position, the court permitted a psychologist's testimony that the defendant was the type of person who is more likely to be aggressive toward himself than toward others. In other cases, the character evidence has sought to "reduce" the level of *mens rea* rather than negate criminal intent completely. For instance, in *State v. Hallman,*[189] the court held that expert testimony describing the defendant's "impulsive personality"

was admissible because it tended to disprove the premeditation necessary for conviction on first-degree murder charges (but did not prevent conviction on lesser homicide charges which did not require proof of premeditation). These cases illustrate the breadth of situations in which character evidence relevant to *mens rea* might be introduced. They also illustrate how the character evidence rules can be used to circumvent a jurisdiction's limitations on, or rejection of, the diminished capacity doctrine.

It should also be noted that, in addition to negating or reducing *mens rea,* character evidence can be used to suggest that because the defendant is a certain way (e.g., passive or violent), he or she could not have (or could have) committed the offense in question. It can also be used to suggest that a person who admits committing the act with the requisite *mens rea* nonetheless acted "reasonably" given the type of person the defendant is (e.g., a person who cannot bear slights to his manhood). Character evidence used in the first way is meant to address whether the *actus reus* occurred and will be discussed in the next subsection. Character evidence used in the second way is used to support an "affirmative defense," such as self-defense, and will be discussed in the following subsection.

(c)   Actus Reus *Testimony*

In asserting any of the defenses discussed to this point—the insanity defense, the automatism defense, and the diminished capacity doctrine—the defendant is conceding that he or she committed the conduct connected with the crime but argues full or partial nonresponsibility due to mental disability. In some cases, however, the defendant may want to use psychological evidence to suggest that he or she was not even physically involved in the offense. Increasingly, clinicians are providing character testimony to the effect that the accused could not have been the perpetrator. By the same token, the prosecution has often used psychological evidence to suggest that the defendant could have committed (and therefore did commit) the act. Finally, in a growing number of cases, evidence from clinicians has been proffered to show that a criminal act (e.g., rape or child molestation) occurred—proof which, in conjunction with evidence that the defendant had the opportunity to commit such an act, is meant to suggest that the defendant is a criminal. These three uses of clinical testimony on the *actus reus* issue are discussed here.

A number of cases illustrate the first type of case, in which the defendant denies being the perpetrator. For instance, in *O'Kon v. Roland*[190] the court permitted psychiatric testimony that the defendant, charged with murder, was a passive person and unlikely to commit a violent act. In other cases, the courts have permitted expert opinion tending to show that a person with the defendant's personality would not have molested a child.[191] In still other cases, expert testimony to the effect that the defendant was not a violent person has been permitted to show he could not have committed rape.[192]

However, most courts confronted with this type of character evidence have excluded it, usually on the plausible ground that the scientific basis for such testimony is weak.[193] Probably the most famous case in this regard is *New Jersey v. Cavallo*,[194] in which the court affirmed the trial court's exclusion of expert testimony suggesting that Cavallo was "a nonviolent, nonaggressive person" who did not "fit within [the] mold" of a rapist. Applying the *Frye* "general acceptance" test [see § 1.04(c)], the court concluded that the defendants

> have not met their burden of showing that the scientific community generally accepts the existence of identifiable character traits common to rapists. They also have not demonstrated that psychiatrists possess any special ability to discern whether an individual is likely to be a rapist. Until the scientific reliability of this type of evidence is established, it is not admissible.

The second type of *actus reus* testimony, proof of character to show the defendant committed the crime, is limited by the rule, described above, barring prosecution expert evidence on character except in rebuttal to the defendant's character evidence. For instance, in *Minnesota v. Loebach,*[195] the prosecution in a child molestation case attempted to show that the defendant was the one who abused the child victim by presenting testimony that he fit a battering-parent syndrome. The

court reversed the defendant's subsequent conviction, stating that such testimony would not be admissible unless the defendant first argued he did not fit the syndrome. Most courts have followed this lead.[196] In at least one case, however, the court erroneously permitted prosecution character evidence when the defendant had not opened the door on the issue. In *State v. Hickman,*[197] the defendant, charged with rape, testified that the intercourse had been consensual; he did not testify to his own character or present any other type of character evidence. Nonetheless, the prosecution was permitted to present expert rebuttal evidence to the effect that the defendant fit in "the class of aggressive, antisocial or sociopathic, hatred rapists." The court's holding can be faulted not only for permitting questionable expert testimony but also for allowing prosecution character evidence in violation of the "defendant-first" orientation of the character evidence rule.

The final category of cases in which clinical testimony may provide information about the *actus reus* is when there is some doubt as to whether a crime has occurred. Here, the focus of the expert testimony is on the victim rather than the defendant. For instance, some courts have allowed expert opinion on whether a child who is suspected of having been abused fits the battered-child syndrome.[198] Others have permitted testimony that the alleged victim of rape is suffering from rape-trauma syndrome.[199] In both types of cases, nonclinical evidence of the crime is often weak (i.e., in the first type of case because a child is usually the only witness against the accused, in the second because there may be no physical evidence of rape). The syndrome evidence, which usually focuses on whether psychological symptoms associated with trauma are present, is introduced to support the victim's story. One problem with evidence of this type is that the symptoms reported may have resulted from a traumatic event other than the abuse or rape that is alleged. Most courts have not considered this fact sufficient to exclude syndrome evidence in cases involving the battered-child syndrome because there is usually physical evidence of trauma and the key question is whether it was due to human agency. On the other hand, many courts are more reticent about admitting rape-trauma syndrome evidence and its close relative—evidence that a child has been sexually abused (as opposed to battered).[200] As the court pointed out in *People v. Bledsoe*,[201] the studies relied on by experts who present rape-trauma syndrome evidence are based on reports from counselors who are trying to help rape victims, not probe the accuracy of the victim's account of the alleged rape. In contrast, the battered-child syndrome derives from studies of children known to be abused. Given its potential unreliability, the *Bledsoe* court rejected use of rape-trauma syndrome evidence in the case before it. However, it also stated that such evidence would be admissible to help dispel myths about rape victims, as in cases in which juries might assume that a delay in reporting an incident means the rape did not occur, when in fact it may have been due to postrape fears of reprisal, exposure, or shame.

This latter "dispelling-of-myths" concept is one that judges, lawyers, and mental health professionals might do well to consider in analyzing the admissibility of clinical testimony based on theories that are not well accepted or are based on shaky data. If such testimony only confirms what most laypeople would assume, given the facts, then it should not be permitted (unless it is offered in rebuttal of other expert testimony) [see § 1.04(b)]. Such testimony is likely to undercut the fairness of the adjudication because it will add the imprimatur of expertise to a concept the jury is already very willing to endorse, and because such testimony is unlikely to be treated with the skepticism it deserves. If, on the other hand, the opinion seems to lead to counterintuitive conclusions (e.g., that the defendant did not intend the obvious consequences of his acts—as in the *Bright* case described in the last subsection—or that women with no visible signs of sexual battery can still have been raped), admission should be seriously considered. Such testimony is unlikely to be accepted unquestioningly by the factfinder but at the same time may serve to counterbalance inaccurate lay preconceptions.[202]

(d)   Self-Defense, Provocation, Duress, and Entrapment

In many cases, defendants admit they voluntarily committed the crime, with the relevant mental state, but still assert they are not "guilty," based on what has traditionally been called an "affirmative defense." An affirmative defense—such as self-defense, provocation, duress, or entrapment—concedes that the prosecution has proven its case on the *actus reus* and *mens rea* elements but asserts that some justification or mitigating factor should lead to acquittal on the offense charged. Traditionally, the defendant bore the burden of proving an affirmative defense by a preponderance of the evidence. However, with respect to an increasing number of such defenses, since the Supreme Court's decision in *In re Winship* (holding that the prosecution must prove each element of its case beyond a reasonable doubt),[203] the state must disprove the defendant's claim beyond a reasonable doubt.[204]

Until recently, psychiatric testimony was seldom proffered in support of such defense claims. But as the criminal law has moved toward a subjective definition of culpability, the courts' willingness to hear expert clinical testimony on such issues has increased. To illustrate this development and its ramifications, we will first look at self-defense, provocation, and duress. Given its different origins, entrapment is discussed separately.

The traditional approach to self-defense, as summarized by LaFave and Scott,[205] is as follows: "One who is not the aggressor in an encounter is justified in using a reasonable amount of force against his adversary when he reasonably believes that he is in immediate danger of unlawful bodily harm from his adversary and that the use of such force is necessary to avoid this danger." In a majority of jurisdictions, a person may use deadly force to repel an attack that is reasonably believed to be deadly even if he or she could safely retreat from the attack; however, in a "strong minority" of jurisdictions, one must retreat before using deadly force if the retreat can be accomplished safely. Even in the minority jurisdictions, one need not retreat if the attack takes place in the defendant's house, on the theory that one is entitled to stand firm in one's home. A valid self-defense claim leads to acquittal on any charge.

The provocation "defense," on the other hand, is available only in homicide cases and, rather than acquittal, leads to reduction of the charge from murder to voluntary manslaughter. In most jurisdictions, this reduction occurs when the defendant can show that (1) the killing was in reaction to provocation that would cause the "reasonable person" to lose control, (2) this provocation in fact provoked the defendant, (3) a "reasonable person" so provoked would not have cooled off in the interval between the provocation and the delivery of the final blow, and (4) the defendant did not in fact cool off. The provocation defense has sometimes been characterized as "imperfect" self-defense because it recognizes that some types of provocation, although they do not justify the use of deadly force in return, might make a "reasonable" person impulsively kill someone and thus should be given mitigating (but not exculpatory) effect. The common law identified a number of situations in which such provocation might occur (e.g., use of serious but not deadly force against the defendant, serious assault, mutual combat not involving deadly force, and discovery of adultery by the offended spouse).[206]

Finally, the defense of duress is usually recognized for conduct produced by an unlawful threat that causes the defendant to have a reasonable belief that the only way to avoid imminent death or serious bodily injury (to him- or herself or to another) is to engage in conduct that violates the criminal law. The classic example of duress is a person who commits robbery because someone else has threatened to kill him or a member of his family if he does not. Duress is not normally a defense, however, to intentional homicide, since the rationale for the defense is generally thought to be that acquittal should be permitted only when the defendant, faced with a choice of evils, chooses the lesser evil.[207]

It should be clear even from this brief description that, under the common law, "reasonableness" language dominates the definition of these defenses. Use of such language presumably renders mental abnormality irrelevant because the reasonable person is the "normal" person as defined by the judge or members of the jury, a hypothetical actor who cannot, by definition, be mentally disordered. Thus with respect to the provocation doctrine, for instance, in most jurisdictions "the defendant's special mental qualities . . . are not to be considered."[208]

Modern developments in these three areas demonstrate an increasing willingness to consider the personal characteristics of the accused in deciding whether a defense is available. The Model Penal Code is representative of the trend, as indicated by the italicized language that follows. With respect to self-defense, the Code permits "the use of force upon or toward another person . . . *when the actor believes* that such force is immediately necessary for the purpose of protecting himself against the use of unlawful force by such person on the present occasion."[209] This formulation makes the actor's beliefs relevant to a self-defense claim regardless of how "unreasonable" they are. The provision of the Code that is analogous to the common-law provocation doctrine is somewhat more objectively defined but still incorporates subjective elements. It states that a homicide that would otherwise be murder is manslaughter if it "is committed under the influence of extreme mental or emotional disturbance for which there is reasonable explanation or excuse[,] . . . the reasonableness of such explanation or excuse [to] be determined *from the viewpoint of a person in the actor's situation under the circumstances as he believes them to be*."[210] Similarly, with respect to duress, the Code provides for an affirmative defense when a person commits a crime "because he was coerced to do so by the use of, or a threat to use, unlawful force against his person or the person of another, which a person of reasonable firmness *in his situation* would have been unable to resist." The defense is not available when the "actor recklessly placed himself in a situation in which it was probable that he would be subjected to duress."[211]

To the extent criminal law defenses are defined subjectively, they increase the potential for clinical testimony. Consider, for example, the fate of testimony about the "battered spouse syndrome,"[212] at issue in Case Study 8.3. Such testimony is "character evidence" (see the discussion in the previous subsections) which attempts to explain why a woman who has suffered repeated beatings from her spouse nonetheless finds it difficult to leave him; if accepted, this conclusion, combined with the obvious fact that women have difficulty responding to physical attacks by men at the time they occur, explains why a woman might kill her spouse even when she is not "imminently" threatened by him. Most courts that follow traditional self-defense doctrine are reluctant to allow such testimony, much less affirm a self-defense verdict based on it, because they believe that a "reasonable person" under the woman's circumstances would not kill her husband but rather would leave the home.[213] But courts following a more subjective approach usually permit testimony about the battered-spouse syndrome in homicide cases because it supports the woman's assertion that, in the words of the Model Penal Code, "the actor believe[d] that such force [was] immediately necessary for the purpose of protecting [her]self against the use of unlawful force by such person on the present occasion."[214] In other words, the subjective approach allows testimony that explains how a reasonable *battered spouse* would react in the given situation.

Similarly, subjectifying provocation and duress can expand the mental health professional's role as expert. Two examples will suffice. In *Bedder v. Director of Public Prosecutions,*[215] an English case, the defendant was an 18-year-old boy who was impotent and apparently emotionally distressed about his condition. On the night of the offense, he attempted in vain to have sex with a prostitute, who then taunted him and tried to leave. He grabbed her shoulders, at which point she kicked him in the groin. The defendant then knifed her twice in the abdomen. The court instructed the jury that it could find provocation only if a "reasonable person, an ordinary person," not one who "is sexually impotent," might react in this way, and the defendant was convicted of murder. Under a more subjective approach (as provided in the Model Penal Code, for instance), looking at the "reasonableness of the [actor's] explanation or excuse . . . from the viewpoint of a person in the actor's *situation* under the circumstances as he believes them to be" might have produced a different result. In *United States v. Hearst,*[216] the defendant (who had been kidnapped and forced, under threat of death, to participate in a robbery) explained that she continued to participate in criminal activities after the robbery, despite the absence of further direct threats, because she had been "brainwashed" by the kidnappers. Although the common-law definition of duress would not countenance the latter claim, one could construct an argument under the Model Penal Code formulation that "a person of reasonable firmness *in [Hearst's] situation*" might have been coerced by

the kidnappers' blandishments. In short, in contrast to the insanity defense and related defenses—where the assertion is that mental abnormality should lead to exculpation—duress permits a "normal" person to argue that an abnormal situation should lead to exculpation.

From the clinical perspective, the entrapment defense raises an issue similar to duress, except that the third party who induces the crime must be a government agent and the coercion need not be as significant. Unlike the three doctrines already discussed, entrapment doctrine in most jurisdictions has always been subjectively defined; specifically, the issue has been whether the defendant was "predisposed" to commit the crime. If the individual is predisposed, the entrapment defense fails. But if the defendant can show an absence of predisposition, the defense may be successful, at least when it can also be shown that the government's actions induced the defendant to commit crime.[217] Here again, clinical testimony about the defendant's "character" might be viewed as relevant to culpability, and many courts have so held.[218]

As these cases illustrate, subjectification of the defenses, whatever its justification on moral grounds, creates the potential for turning virtually every criminal case into a psychiatric one, replete with battles of the experts and confusing psychojargon. Some courts have resisted this development, usually by concluding, as described in the discussion about the diminished capacity doctrine, that clinical testimony is relevant only on the insanity issue. In those jurisdictions that have not taken this tack, clinicians have an ethical obligation to ensure that their testimony is based on solid ground. As already suggested in the discussion concerning *actus reus* testimony, one consideration clinicians might take into account in assessing this obligation is whether their testimony helps to dispel "myths" likely to be held by laypeople (e.g., that battered women find it no more difficult than other people to leave their spouses). Another consideration, treated in more detail in § 7.07(d)(1), is whether the clinical testimony is merely an endorsement of the defendant's claim (e.g., about how his impotence affected his reaction) rather than an "expert" opinion based on specialized knowledge independent of the claim.

(e) Defenses Based on Intoxication

Like mental illness and mental retardation, intoxication—either by alcohol or by narcotic drugs—can form the basis for an insanity defense, an automatism defense, or a mens rea defense. Whether it supports any of these defenses, and the particular one it supports, depends on whether the intoxication is "voluntary," "involuntary," or the result of long-term addiction or use.

Voluntary intoxication is intoxication of a non-addicted individual produced by drinking on one occasion. Because it is self-induced and temporary, it is seldom given complete exculpatory effect. It is well established that unless substance abuse has been prolonged to the point where it has produced "settled insanity" (i.e., a bona fide organic mental disease or defect), the insanity defense will not be an option.[219] This stance is generally taken even when the intoxicant is a drug that produces psychotic-like effects. For instance, in State v. Hall[220] the court upheld the trial court's refusal to give an insanity instruction even though the testimony indicated that the defendant's ingestion of LSD caused him to believe his driving companion, whom he shot, was a rabid dog. The majority adhered to the traditional rule that "a temporary mental condition caused by voluntary intoxication . . . does not constitute a complete defense." Similarly, proof that alcohol rendered a person "unconscious" at the time of the offense is likely to receive a hostile reaction from the courts.

Although voluntary intoxication seldom supports either an insanity or automatism defense, it can often support a defense analogous to a diminished capacity claim. In virtually every state, evidence of voluntary intoxication is considered relevant on the issue of whether a defendant charged with first-degree murder premeditated the crime. Most states also permit such evidence if offered to prove that a defendant did not possess the mens rea for other crimes involving specific intent.[221]

Some might wonder why voluntary intoxication should be given any mitigating effect; after all, the defendant intentionally chooses to drink, knowing that drinking can loosen inhibitions and self-control. Robinson has articulated a theory that tries to explain the common-law approach.[222] He analogizes the voluntary intoxication scenario to accomplice liability, with the "accomplice" being the defendant at the time he decides to drink and the "principal" being the defendant at the time of the crime: Just as a person is not considered an accomplice to a crime unless he or she aids and abets its perpetrator, a person who drinks without intending the consequences of the drinking is not culpable for those consequences. Under this approach, a man who drinks in order to fortify himself for a murder is liable for homicide. But the more typical person who is not aware of the risk that the drinking will contribute to crime should not be denied the appropriate defense if and when the drinking results in a lack of mens rea or conscious control of one's behavior. Note that this analysis might also be applicable to situations in which a person with a mental disability fails to take medication or a person subject to seizures drives a car. If their decisions (to forgo medication or to drive) result in harm, at most they should be guilty of "general intent" (i.e., objectively defined) crimes unless they intended or foresaw the eventual consequences of their decision.

To these arguments could be added the claim that prohibiting evidence tending to show a lack of mens rea is a violation of due process [see § 8.03(b)]. Nonetheless, in Montana v. Egelhoff,[223] a plurality of the Supreme Court held that because the defense of voluntary intoxication was of relatively "recent vintage," it is not so fundamental that a state statute prohibiting it is unconstitutional. The plurality also noted that elimination of the defense might serve as a deterrent to drunkeness and associated irresponsible behavior and was supported by recent research indicating that drunks are violent in part because they believe that they should be, not because they lack the requisite mens rea.

Courts are much more lenient in the relatively rare cases involving "involuntary" intoxication. Such intoxication occurs when a defendant is tricked into ingesting drugs or alcohol, or otherwise unknowingly takes the substance. Also conceivably falling in this category are cases of "pathological intoxication," where a defendant knows what has been taken but where the substance produces an atypical and excessive reaction that the defendant could not have foreseen.[224] If involuntary intoxication produces psychotic symptoms, makes it impossible for the defendant to form the *mens rea* for the crime, or renders the defendant's criminal act "automatic," courts will generally require acquittal of the crime charged[225]; the limitations imposed on evidence of intoxication that is voluntary do not apply in such a situation, apparently due to the accused's underlying innocence with respect to the initial ingestion of the substance.

A final type of intoxication, which may be seen as either voluntary or involuntary, is that resulting from chronic use of psychoactive substances. Some courts have held that alcohol or drug addicts are impelled to drink or use drugs, and that any use of such substances is thus "involuntary" in nature.[226] If this is true, then chronic users of psychoactive substances who can show that, due to intoxication, they did not appreciate the consequences of their act, lacked conscious control of their conduct, or lacked the *mens rea* for the crimes charged will be acquitted of those crimes, as in other cases of involuntary intoxication. Most courts, however, have been reluctant to accept this interpretation of addiction, with the result that these cases are most often analyzed as situations involving voluntary intoxication.[227] Even in these jurisdictions, however, severely chronic alcohol or drug users may be able to prove that their substance abuse has caused a "mental disease or defect" that in turn resulted in significant cognitive or volitional impairment at the time of their offenses. It is in these cases that a claim of "settled insanity" is most likely to be accepted.

(f)   "Guilty But Mentally Ill" Plea

Since 1976, at least 12 states have passed statutes authorizing the factfinder to return a verdict of "guilty but mentally ill" (GBMI).[228] Although there are many different versions of the GBMI concept, most proposals work basically as follows: A defendant who pleads NGRI may be found not guilty, guilty, insane, or, in the alternative, GBMI at the time of the offense. If the jury makes the last-mentioned finding, the defendant may be sentenced to any term appropriate for the offense. Thus, jurors in insanity cases are given three sets of instructions with respect to the ultimate verdict they may reach: One explains under what circumstances a defendant may be found guilty of the crime charged, one describes the state's test for insanity, and one informs the jury when a defendant who is guilty beyond a reasonable doubt and not insane may be found GBMI. The definition of mental illness found in the last of these instructions varies from state to state but usually borrows heavily from the definition of mental illness in the state's civil commitment statute. In Michigan, for instance, the definition is taken directly from the mental health code and states that mental illness is "[a] substantial disorder of thought or mood which significantly impairs judgment, behavior, capacity to recognize reality, or ability to cope with the ordinary demands of life."[229]

The GBMI verdict is to be distinguished from proposals for substituting a "guilty but insane" verdict for the insanity defense and other clinical defenses.[230] This proposal, which prohibits evidence of clinical testimony on *any* issue until the second phase of trial, has not been adopted by any state. As noted in § 8.02(b), three states have abolished the insanity defense. But in each of these states, clinical testimony relevant to *mens rea* (i.e., diminished capacity) is still admissible.[231] The *mens rea*-only approach has been upheld against constitutional challenge by at least two courts.[232] But the guilty but insane proposal, to the extent it would give *no* mitigating effect to evidence of mental illness, is probably unconstitutional [see § 8.03(b)].

Proponents of GBMI statutes do not wish to eliminate the insanity defense. However, by offering jurors a compromise verdict that ensures prolonged incarceration of people who are dangerous and mentally ill, they do hope both to reduce insanity acquittals and to provide greater protection to the public. Whether the verdict is any better than the traditional system at accomplishing these goals remains unclear. Research suggests that the verdict may actually increase insanity acquittals by encouraging defendants to raise the plea in the hope of at least obtaining a GBMI verdict.[233] Nor is the duration of a given individual's confinement likely to be increased by a GBMI verdict: As noted previously, a person found

GBMI receives the same sentence as a person convicted outright of the same crime, a term of confinement which in turn is usually equivalent to the detention received by a person found NGRI for the same crime [see research described in § 8.02(a)(3)].[234]

Even assuming that the GBMI verdict reduces insanity acquittals and results in longer confinement, however, it is a questionable reform for two reasons. First, the verdict creates a significant potential for jury confusion and abuse, given the similarity between its definition of mental illness and the definition of insanity (compare, for instance, the definition of mental illness under Michigan's GBMI statute set out above with the language of the ALI rule, which is the test for insanity in Michigan). Jurors who see little difference between the competing terminologies may choose the GBMI verdict solely because they think it results in longer confinement or better treatment or both. Even if these two assumptions about the effect of the verdict were true (which, as discussed above and below, they are not), this reasoning might well result in improper conviction of a person with a valid insanity defense.[235] Unfortunately, there is probably no way to define mental illness so as to avoid this result and still meaningfully distinguish between "normal" offenders and noninsane but mentally ill offenders.

Second, and more important, the GBMI verdict is deficient because it is not a proper "verdict" at all. It is neither a device for assessing criminal responsibility, as is the insanity defense, nor a method of grading culpability, as is the doctrine of diminished capacity. Thus, as noted, those found GBMI receive sentences similar to those found "guilty" of the same crime; indeed, several defendants found GBMI have been sentenced to death.[236] At the same time, because the finding of mental illness associated with the verdict relates to the time of the crime rather than the time of disposition, the GBMI verdict generally should not have (and in fact usually does not have) any effect on conditions of confinement either; indeed, only one state *requires* that the GBMI offender be put in a hospital.[237] Judicial instructions, found in some states,[238] telling the jury that those found GBMI are guaranteed treatment not afforded those found guilty are misleading for two reasons. First, in reality many GBMI offenders who need treatment

do not receive it,[239] and courts and legislatures have been unwilling, usually for financial reasons, to rectify this situation.[240] Second, providing treatment to GBMI offenders that is not provided other mentally ill offenders would raise serious equal protection concerns; indeed, virtually every state, including those with GBMI statutes, already has a statute providing for the hospitalization of *all* prisoners who require inpatient care.[241]

In short, the GBMI verdict is conceptually flawed, has significant potential for misleading the factfinder, and does not appear to achieve its goals of reducing insanity acquittals or prolonging confinement of offenders who are mentally ill and dangerous. The one goal it may achieve is relieving the anxiety of jurors and judges who otherwise would have difficulty deciding between a guilty verdict and a verdict of not guilty by reason of insanity.[242] It is doubtful this goal is a proper one or worth the price. Furthermore, to the extent the difficulty of the decision results from a fear that those found insane will "walk," instructions to the effect that a person found insane is confined indeterminately until no longer insane or dangerous would alleviate the factfinder's burden.[243] Perhaps for these reasons, interest in the GBMI verdict appears to have waned.[244]

8.04. Research on the Relationship of Diagnosis to MSO Defenses

CASE STUDY 8.4

The defendant is charged with the murder of his girlfriend. The defense attorney admits his client killed the victim but intends to assert a defense of insanity based on epileptic seizure. The defendant reports amnesia for his behavior during the time of the incident, and EEG (electroencephalogram) testing is interpreted as displaying some "mild abnormality." The victim was shot one time at close range in her home. After being shot in the dining room, her body was stashed under the basement stairs and covered with a blanket. The telephone in her hallway had been ripped out of the wall. There is third-party social data to indicate that the defendant was intensely jealous that she had been seeing a married man; a week before the murder the defendant had reported this affair by phone to the man's wife.

QUESTIONS: (1) What third-party information would be valuable in a case such as this? (2) How long do seizures typically last, and what does violence manifested during a seizure usually look like? (3) What are the implications of the fact that only a single bullet was fired?

CASE STUDY 8.5

You have been appointed by the court to evaluate Susan Tonlam, who has been accused of second-degree murder. Specifically, Ms. Tonlam has been accused of murdering her longtime boyfriend, Jack Blake, while he was asleep. Mr. Blake was found shot to death in bed, in the motel room that he shared with the defendant for three weeks. Ms. Tonlam was found walking aimlessly along the beach approximately two hours after the motel maid found the body. When initially questioned by the police, Ms. Tonlam neither denied nor admitted to the offense but instead reported that she had little memory for the event. She also claimed to be in a fog for a good deal of the time preceding and following the death of her boyfriend. When informed about the death of the boyfriend, Ms. Tonlam became hysterical and was admitted to the local Crisis Stabilization Unit. A gun with her fingerprints was found in a trash can on the beach and she was later charged. The public defender is considering an insanity defense; you have been appointed by the court to conduct the evaluation of mental state at the time of the offense. There is some indication of a psychiatric history on Ms. Tonlam's part. Specifically, at one point while being treated in a university-based psychiatric hospital, Ms. Tonlam received a diagnosis of multiple personality disorder (MPD).

QUESTIONS: (1) How will you go about the evaluation? (2) What kind of third-party information will you seek? List, in order of importance, the types of third-party information you think are most necessary or will be most helpful. (3) How will you structure your interview and evaluation with Ms. Tonlam? Will you follow a certain plan? (4) Will you request that any diagnostic testing (neurological, psychological) be completed? If so, what would you request and how do you think this will be helpful? What do you expect to find? (5) If you establish the MPD diagnosis, and it appears that an "alter personality" committed the offense, what are the implications for the clinical opinion?

This section looks at the types of clinical phenomena that have been associated with the insanity defense and other MSO defenses. It first examines research that describes the correlation between various well-known diagnoses and the insanity defense. It then looks at research on a number of relatively novel disorders or syndromes that, although relatively unlikely to form the basis for a defense, have been raised as exculpatory conditions often enough to merit close analysis of their relevance.[245]

(a) Psychoses and Personality Disorders

Table 8.1 displays various characteristics of individuals found NGRI in Michigan (two samples), New York (two samples), California, and Georgia.[246] The "typical" NGRI patient is a male charged with a violent offense who, as likely as not, has a record of prior psychiatric hospitalization. In four of the five samples for which racial breakdowns were available, the NGRI acquittees were more often Caucasian; however, when population base rates are taken into consideration, blacks are overrepresented in these samples.

Of most relevance to our purposes here, these data also suggest that the presence of a major psychosis is usually required for the insanity defense to succeed. This conclusion is especially valid in more recent years; the proportion of successful NGRIs diagnosed with major psychosis has increased over time across the six samples, as well as within Michigan and New York where data from two different periods are available.[247] Along with the relatively low success rate for the insanity defense even on those few occasions when it gets to a jury [see § 8.02(a)(2)], this information provides some comfort to skeptics who view the defense as a scam allowing criminals to "get away with murder."[248]

However, as Table 8.1 indicates, a substantial percentage of persons with nonpsychotic diagnoses have been found NGRI in various states at different times. Of interest in this regard is a study by Howard and Clark,[249] who gathered data on four groups of patients (n = 20 per group) who had been referred from various courts in Michigan for pretrial examination. Most important to this discussion are the 20 defendants recommended and acquitted NGRI (NGRI/NGRI) and the 20 defendants recommended as criminally responsible (CR) but adjudicated NGRI (CR/NGRI). The NGRI/NGRI and CR/NGRI groups did not differ

Table 8.1
NGRI Characteristics: Findings from Six Studies

Variables	Michigan 1967–72	Michigan 1975–79	New York 1971–76	New York 1982–87	California 1982–87	Georgia 1979–85
Gender						
Male	87	85	87	76–88[a]	91	81–87
Female	13	15	13	24–12	9	19–13
Race						
Caucasian	68	54	65	*	54	22–27
Nonwhite	32	46	35	*	46	78–73
Type of offense[b]						
Violent	87	75	81	73–92	74	53–58
Other	13	25	19	27–8	26	47–42
Victim a female	*	*	*	48–54	52	32–49
Victim a relative	*	*	*	31–38	20	41–59
Prior history						
Hospitalization	46	66	42	*	*	*
Criminal record	26	33	44	*	*	*
IST[c]	40	45	*	*	*	*
Diagnosis						
Major psychosis	68	73	67	82–97	84	85–86
Other	32	27	33	18–3	16	15–14

Note. All figures are percentages. * = data not available.

[a]Ranges are given where the study examined different NGRI samples pre- and post- some NGRI reform.

[b]For the first three studies, "violent" includes murder and other assault. For the last three studies, "violent" includes murder, physical assault, rape, arson, and kidnapping.

[c]Defendant was incompetent for trial for the NGRI offense.

significantly in terms of frequency of prior hospitalization or type of offense charged, nor did they differ in the frequency of a pretrial finding of incompetent to stand trial (eight and seven cases, respectively). However, diagnosis was significantly different across groups: The NGRI/NGRI group includes 19 persons diagnosed as psychotic and 1 diagnosed as having a personality disorder; the CR/NGRI group included 4 defendants diagnosed as psychotic and 10 as having personality disorders. Furthermore, the offenses committed by the latter group appeared to be less bizarre than those committed by the former group: Using a three-point offense classification system ("Rational," "Intermediate," or "Irrational") found to be reliable, Howard and Clark discovered that the NGRI/NGRI group had committed crimes classified as predominately Irrational (75%) or Intermediate (25%), while the CR/NGRI group committed mostly Intermediate offenses (65%). The

CR/NGRI group was also distinguished by a more extensive arrest history (13 vs. 6) and more frequent reports of intoxication at the time of the alleged crime (9 vs. 3).

Why were members of CR/NGRI group found insane in light of their diagnosis, type of crime, antisocial history, and intoxication at the time of the offense? One possible clue is that this group had a greater propensity for claimed amnesia (7 vs. 1) than the NGRI/NGRI group. Further, those members of the CR/NGRI group adjudicated incompetent to stand trial, although eventually diagnosed with a personality disorder, were initially diagnosed as suffering from psychosis, with malingering suspected. The presentation of questionable symptoms and amnesia, together with involvement in ambiguously irrational offenses and a history of prior hospitalization, may make these types of MSO cases difficult to decipher. With supportive psychiatric testimony (which for the

Michigan study came from privately retained clinicians), they are able to obtain an NGRI acquittal.

It was suggested earlier [see § 8.02(a)(2)] that most insanity acquittals are valid. The study described above indicates, although far from conclusively, that *some* acquittals may be bogus. Another Michigan study provides similarly ambiguous data. In that state all defendants found NGRI are sent to the Center for Forensic Psychiatry, the same facility that conducts the pretrial examination, for a 60-day diagnostic commitment to determine whether they are committable as mentally ill and dangerous. Criss and Racine reported differential rates for release from the 60-day commitment, depending on whether the Center's pretrial examiner had recommended the defendant as CR or NGRI.[250] Although patients in the NGRI/NGRI category were released at the end of this period 43% of the time, this figure escalated to 72.3% for patients in the CR/NGRI category, suggesting that the latter's adjudications of insanity may have been contrived. However, alternative explanations are possible: Those making the release decision may have been influenced by their staff's earlier recommendation about responsibility, the NGRI/NGRI group may have been more dangerous (thus necessitating more detentions) and, most plausibly, many of the acquittees in the CR/NGRI group may have been individuals with personality disorders who suffered a "break" at the time of the offense but eventually recovered.

To date, there are no studies relating diagnoses to automatism, diminished capacity, or the other defenses described earlier in this chapter, presumably because these defenses are relatively seldom asserted. There are, however, some studies that examine correlations between the GBMI verdict and diagnosis. It appears that most of those found GBMI have personality disorders,[251] reaffirming the assertion made earlier that the verdict probably does little to reduce insanity acquittals but instead merely provides another label for those who are guilty of the offense charged.

(b)   Epilepsy

Occasionally defendants will assert an MSO defense on the basis of epilepsy, particularly in cases involving assaultive crimes. Epilepsy is a neurological disorder "characterized by a tendency for recurrent seizures (two or three or more) unprovoked by any known proximate insult."[252] During a seizure, abnormal and uncontrolled electrical impulses are discharged across all or some parts of the brain. Generalized seizures are those in which the electrical discharge begins simultaneously throughout the brain; partial, or focal, seizures are those that begin in a relatively circumscribed region.

Clinically, the primary classifications of seizures are three in number: grand mal, petit mal, and complex partial.[253] Grand mal seizures involve massive, generalized electrical discharge in the brain. The person suffers a complete loss of consciousness during the seizure and displays massive convulsions throughout. Following the seizure, the person typically appears lethargic and drowsy and may sleep for a lengthy period, having no memory for the seizure upon awakening.[254] Petit mal seizures, in contrast, are the least disruptive general class of seizures. They are also called "absence seizures," because the person simply appears to "tune out" for a few moments before resuming normal functioning. The behavioral components of absence seizures are minimal, and most patients with such seizures are unaware of their seizure activity.[255]

Potentially most significant for legal purposes are the complex partial seizures (CPS), particularly those that originate in the temporal lobe area of the brain.[256] Unlike grand mal seizures, the person experiencing CPS does not lose complete consciousness during the seizure. Consciousness is partially impaired, however, and normal functioning is disrupted. A CPS

> usually begins with a cessation in verbal and motor activity associated with a motionless stare. The patient may not respond to normal auditory or visual information. Automatisms that are gestural (picking movements with the fingers) or oralalimentary (lip smacking) may be observed. They represent involuntary, automatic movements that occur with an alteration in consciousness.[257]

Following the ictus (seizure proper), which typically lasts from a few seconds to one and a half minutes, is a postictal phase which typically lasts from several minutes to an hour. The latter is often characterized by confusion and disorientation, although the person may perform some fairly complex behaviors in a stereotyped, automatic fashion.[258] Among such seizures, temporal lobe epilepsy (TLE) has received the most attention in the legal literature because of linkages to the limbic system, which is integral to the control and expression of emotion.[259]

A close look at the research, however, suggests that the relationship between aggression or "directed" violence and most forms of epilepsy is tenuous at best, especially during the ictus (the seizure proper). Although "aggressive behavior has been extensively reported in association with temporal lobe epilepsy,"[260] a major review of clinical case reports and systematic studies concluded that "there is no remotely persuasive evidence linking epilepsy to violence/aggression."[261] When potentially confounding variables are controlled for, studies of epilepsy or abnormal EEG activity in offender populations do not reveal an association between epilepsy and violence.[262] Nor do evaluations of persons referred specifically because of a history of unprovoked violence or outbursts of anger implicate seizure activity as contributory.[263] Similarly, clinical observations of persons experiencing either spontaneous[264] or chemically induced seizures[265] have failed to reveal evidence of directed violence. Indeed, Blumer reports that patients typically present an expressionless stare and are *passive* during seizures, generally not relating to the environment around them.[266] Another prominent study noted the "extreme rarity of directed aggression during seizures and the near impossibility of committing murder or manslaughter during random and unsustained automatisms."[267] Most researchers believe that aggressive behavior during a seizure is most likely to be "the unintended consequence of nonpurposeful movements such as swinging the arms wildly or kicking."[268] In short, violence generally occurs spontaneously, without provocation or evidence of planning; complex, sustained sequences of assaultive behavior are extremely unlikely.

Violent behavior is perhaps somewhat more likely during the postictal period that follows immediately after the ictus of a CPS. During this period, the individual is confused but is interactive with the environment. Amnesia for this period is common and may extend beyond the confusional stage to include periods of coherent responding and appropriate behavior. However, violent behavior during this phase is also extremely rare and is most likely to arise out of misinterpretations of efforts by others to render medical assistance.[269]

Directed violence toward others is most likely to occur during the period *between* seizures (the "interictal period"), often associated with psychotic symptoms in patients who experience epileptiform psychosis or a concomitant disorder such as schizophrenia.[270] Identifying valid claims of this nature requires knowing the characteristic features of psychoses associated with epilepsy, including the long delay between onset of the psychosis relative to onset of seizures (11 to 15 years)[271] and the distinct affective presentation of those with epilepsy/psychosis.[272] EEG data is not useful in such cases, as the association between EEG activity and psychotic symptomatology is generally not reliable.[273]

A number of researchers have also hypothesized the existence of a nonpsychotic personality disorder that characterizes some persons during the interictal period. The research identifying this "interictal syndrome" is inconsistent, however.[274] More important, although a wide variety of features are said to characterize the disorder,[275] those that have received the most empirical support (e.g., clinging behavior, excessive writing, and reduced sexual interest) would seem to have, at best, marginal relevance to the development of MSO formulations.[276] Other studies of persons with TLE and other neurological disorders have not confirmed a greater risk for aggression during the interictal phase compared to controls,[277] and qualitative descriptions of interictal "rage"[278] and aggression[279] suggest further caution in attributing interictal aggression to the effects of seizure disorder rather than some more conscious phenomenon. Although people with TLE might be moody and irritable,[280] most incidents of violence committed by this group during the interictal period are associated with provocation, planning, and otherwise undisturbed cognitive functioning.[281]

In short, epilepsy will rarely give rise to a mental state defense. When it does, it is most likely to do so in one of three ways. An assault that resulted from the uncontrollable flailing of arms or legs during a grand mal seizure might be excused on either insanity, automatism, or *mens rea* grounds (with automatism being the best fit conceptually, given the lack of conscious control over the body [see § 8.03(a)]). A crime might also result from the automatisms during the postictal phase of CPS; although partially conscious, the defendant during this phase may exhibit robot-like behavior (volitional impairment) and experience transient deficits in processing or meaningfully reflecting on incoming stimuli (cognitive impairment), thus possibly raising an insanity or automatism defense. Finally, aggression during the interictal period might be attributed to any of the three forms of epilepsy (grand, petit, or CPS) but is particularly likely in individuals who experience a CPS and also experience episodes of psychosis that might provide a basis for an MSO defense along more conventional lines.

In performing evaluations of those alleged to have epilepsy, clinicians will want to guard against unwarranted attributions of violence to an epileptic state. In this regard, clinicians should consider the criteria suggested by Walker:

1. Confirm that the individual was previously subject to bona fide epileptic attacks.
2. Confirm that the spontaneous attacks of the individual are similar to the one which allegedly occurred at the time of the crime.
3. Confirm that the loss of awareness alleged to have been present is commensurate with the types of epileptic attack the individual had.
4. Confirm that the degree of assumed unconsciousness is consistent with that reported from previous attacks.
5. Confirm that EEG findings are compatible with the type of disorder assumed to be present; repeated normal EEG's should be construed as decreasing to a one-to-twenty chance the possibility of epilepsy.
6. Confirm that the circumstances of the crime are compatible with the assumption of lack of awareness at the time—obvious motives are absent, the crime appears senseless, the mutilation was unnecessarily violent and extensive, there was no evidence of premeditation, and the offender did not attempt to escape.[282]

Clinicians must also be wary of overselling laboratory findings, such as an abnormal EEG obtained some time after the alleged crime occurred. Attempts to infer the presence of insanity or automatism solely on the basis of belated laboratory findings betray a mistaken emphasis on psychophysiological measures; it is the associated psychological conditions—thoughts, feelings, motivational states—that constitute the proper focus of these determinations.

(c)   Hypoglycemic Syndrome

Another defense theory occasionally encountered in court (e.g., in Dan White's "Twinkie defense" murder trial in San Francisco) is based on mental aberrations secondary to hypoglycemia, a condition stemming from shortage of blood sugar. Unlike other organs of the body, the brain obtains its energy solely from the combustion of carbohydrates. The brain itself has such small carbohydrate stores that it is "uniquely dependent on a constant supply through the blood stream."[283] When the blood sugar level drops substantially, the brain has no alternative energy source. As one commentator puts it, "The brain's metabolism must naturally slow down and cerebral function will suffer . . . the cerebral hemisphere and parts of the cerebellum metabolize at the highest rate and therefore are the first to suffer."[284] Lyle, who reviewed numerous case studies of psychological disturbance associated with low blood sugar, states the potential consequences of this slowed functioning most dramatically: "At the lower levels of blood sugar, humans are effectively decerebrated and are capable of nearly anything they have ever thought of or seen out of others in fiction or elsewhere."[285]

Whether this conclusion stands up under close scrutiny is not clear. Hall and his colleagues suggest that "chronic confusional states and anxiety are the symptoms most frequently seen" in people with hypoglycemia, although they also indicate that more severe cases may involve paranoia, hallucinations and delirium, seizures, or coma.[286] Other features include amnesia for the hypoglycemic episode, as well as a transitory nature (i.e., recovery from the episode quickly follows the ingestion of appropriate nutrients).[287] The potential role of alcohol ingestion in hypoglycemic episodes is also discussed in the literature. Some researchers have postulated the existence of a "low serotonin syndrome" based on research evidence linking cerebrospinal fluid metabolite levels, blood glucose regulation, and alcohol consumption.[288] Individuals with low serotonin levels may experience disruption in circadian rhythms (e.g., day–night functioning) and glucose metabolism, resulting in low-grade dysphoria or dysthymia. Alcohol intake elicits an acute release of serotonin, which may result in temporary relief of dysphoric mood. Chronic alcohol ingestion, however, exacerbates serotonin deficit and further disrupts glucose metabolism. Evidence for this syndrome has been found in a subgroup of violent offenders with a history of early onset for impulsive violent behavior and alcohol abuse and a family history of Type II alcoholism.[289]

Claims of hypoglycemic dysfunction can be tested in a number of ways. First, glucose tolerance or other appropriate laboratory tests can help the clinician judge whether hypoglycemia is a possible precipitant of violent behavior.[290] Second, because blood sugar levels may be inversely related to the recency of ingestion of carbohydrates, episodes should tend to occur early in the morning, late at night, or before mealtimes; reported episodes that occur at other times may be somewhat suspect. Third, Hall and colleagues suggest that endocrine disorders are most common in persons between ages of 30 and 40; thus, any "psychiatric" presentation with onset before that time is less likely to be associated with hypoglycemia.[291]

Further, although claims of amnesia are congruent with hypoglycemia, claims of impaired physical control may not be: Controlled laboratory tests have demonstrated that acute hypoglycemia causes more substantial impairment in cognitive spheres than in motor functioning.[292] Finally, individuals with hypoglycemia tend to have "episodic and repetitive" symptoms; thus, "although the tempo and severity of attacks may vary, the same patient will most often experience the same symptom complex[, and] recognition of the episodic nature of the patient's symptoms is of diagnostic significance."[293]

The coincidence of criminal behavior with hypoglycemic states is unknown. But it is known that crimes committed by persons with hypoglycemia often tend to show poor motivation and

no planning; further, the behaviors are atypical for these individuals, and amnesia follows the episode. These features—as well as the other characteristics of hypoglycemia described earlier—suggest that Walker's guidelines for attributing crime to seizure states could be applied, with minor modification, to the investigation of crimes allegedly committed in a hypoglycemic condition. The examiner should look for the following:

1. A documented history of prior episodes with symptoms similar to those displayed at the time of the alleged crime;
2. A crime scenario bereft of obvious motive, and lacking in evidence of planning or preparation;
3. Lack of escape attempt; and
4. Amnesia for the crime.

The clinician should also remember that the symptoms tend to be transient and may bear a relationship to eating schedule, fasting, and/or alcohol ingestion. As stated previously, glucose tolerance tests can also be useful. However, as with positive EEG findings in the case of epilepsy, the clinician should be careful not to overstate the importance of laboratory evidence of hypoglycemia obtained several weeks after the alleged crime. Lyle's review[294] (particularly of the work of Wilder) documents that the degree of mental abnormality varies from mild to severe according to blood sugar level, which can change radically in a relatively short time; it is the degree of mental disturbance, not the mere presence of a metabolic etiological component, that is dispositive in an MSO defense.

(d)   Dissociative States

Among those psychiatric conditions having potential legal relevance in reconstructive defenses, none are more perplexing or poorly understood than those falling under the heading of dissociative disorders. The ambiguity of the clinical criteria for these disorders makes application of legal doctrine particularly difficult.

According to DSM-IV, "The essential feature of these disorders is a disruption in the usually integrated functions of consciousness, memory, identity, or perception of the environment. The disturbance may be sudden or gradual, transient or chronic." Four dissociative diagnoses are listed, of which the most thoroughly researched and discussed is dissociative identity disorder (DID), known previously as multiple personality disorder (MPD). The three others are dissociative amnesia, characterized by an inability to recall important personal information, usually of a traumatic or stressful nature; dissociative fugue, marked by sudden, unexpected travel away from home or one's customary place of work, accompanied by amnesia for one's past and identity confusion or the assumption of a new identity; and depersonalization disorder, characterized by a persistent or recurrent feeling of being detached from one's mental processes or body.[295]

The quality of consciousness during dissociative episodes may vary considerably. Some dissociated individuals may be capable of complex sequences of behavior that are purposeful and goal-directed. For instance, many who suffer from a temporary alteration of identity of the type associated with multiple personalities are fully alert and aware of their surroundings, with good reality testing (save for their unawareness that they have assumed an alternate identity). Others with the same diagnosis, however, may experience serious disruption in their processing of information. Although hallucinations and delusions are not characteristically present,[296] in some cases perceptual aberrations such as "tunnel vision" have been reported. Similarly, those who experience depersonalization episodes describe them as akin to being "in a dream state" or as if they were third-person observers, watching themselves act, while observers of such people report disruptions in the executive and organizing functions of thought, as well as behavior of a mechanical quality.

Although studies conducted in the past decade suggest that dissociative disorders, particularly MPD/DID, may be much more prevalent than previously thought,[297] the existence (and therefore the prevalence) of MPD/DID remains controversial.[298] Research has been hampered by the lack of valid clinical and research instruments for diagnosing the disorder. In the latter regard, however, forensic clinicians should be aware of a relatively new measure for assessing MPD/DID that

has shown some promise as a screening device,[299] as well as the development of more comprehensive, structured interviews for the diagnosis of MPD/DID.[300]

In deciding whether a MPD/DID claim is valid, a few criteria are worth emphasizing. The diagnosis is more common in individuals who are emotionally immature, self-centered, and dependent.[301] The diagnosis is also empirically correlated with gender (with a substantially higher prevalence in women),[302] reports of physical and/or sexual abuse during childhood,[303] and the presence of multiple alter personalities.[304] Further, most persons diagnosed with MPD/DID report that their first alter appeared during childhood or adolescence.[305] Thus, MPD/DID in adults is a chronic or recurring condition, indications of which will usually have been observed over time by third parties close to the individual.

Clinicians should also be aware of the theoretical basis for the development of MPD/DID. According to psychodynamic theory, dissociative phenomena serve a primary function of reducing anxiety—originally, the fear associated with abuse or other trauma. Thus, the clinician might be more inclined to consider as valid reports of dissociative symptoms by individuals whose lives are interpersonally conflicted and to be more suspicious of such claims from individuals who are anxiety-free and unconcerned with the evaluative judgments of others. Similarly, MPD/DID as a basis for a mental state formulation will be more appropriate in scenarios involving acute situational stress than in scenarios that reveal careful preparation or extensive cooperation and planning with coperpetrators.

More problematic for the forensic examiner are the brief, transient episodes of depersonalization or dissociation, for which little evidence other than the individual's subjective recall or claim of amnesia may exist. In such cases, some experts have advocated the use of hypnosis,[306] although testimony based on hypnotic suggestion may have admissibility problems [see § 3.08(c)]. Dissociative states should also be distinguished from the effects of drug and alcohol use. Gathering and reporting third-party data describing any past "blackouts" and the defendant's behavior immediately prior to and during the period of the offense will be of considerable assistance in this regard.

In reporting and testifying about MPD/DID, clinicians should take care to avoid philosophical and moral judgments about responsibility. Consider, for example, a crime that was committed by an individual who presents two identifies (e.g., a person with a fugue state or MPD/DID). The clinician may describe the relevant behavior and dynamics of the two personalities and perhaps even measure their presence psychometrically or with other laboratory devices; it remains for the legal system, however, to determine whether the focus should be on the functioning of a particular personality (e.g., the one in "control" at the time of the offense), or whether instead the mere fact of having more than one personality is a sufficient ground to mitigate guilt.[307] Furthermore, it remains up to the trier of fact and the attorneys and judge to decide whether mitigation, when it is merited, should come under the automatism rubric [as discussed in § 8.03(a)], the insanity defense, or some other MSO doctrine.

(e)   Posttraumatic Stress Disorder

The possibility that stressful life events such as combat, rape, or earthquakes and other disasters might cause significant psychological symptoms reminiscent of the stressful event has long been recognized.[308] The formal diagnosis of posttraumatic stress disorder (PTSD) is a relatively new one, however, not appearing in the DSM until the third edition.[309] The DSM-IV requires as a predicate for the diagnosis "exposure to an extreme traumatic stressor,"[310] followed by symptoms that must persist longer than one month in each of three domains: reexperiencing of the traumatic event, especially when exposed to cues that resemble the event[311]; avoidance of stimuli associated with the trauma and a general numbing of affect[312]; and increased "arousal."[313]

PTSD has achieved considerable notoriety as a potential basis for mental state defenses to criminal behavior, particularly insanity.[314] Most of the attention has focused on the complex of symptoms identified as "reexperiencing" the trauma. Under this scenario, the defendant, confronted with events reminiscent of the traumatic event, suffers a dissociative "flashback," believes the previously experienced trauma to be presently ongoing, and acts accordingly. Thus, the theory goes, a Vietnam veteran may violently attack a home believing he is assaulting enemy troops, or a rape victim may harm someone believing she is fighting her assailant. The PTSD trait of arousal or hypervigilance may also contribute to reliving scenarios. Persons with PTSD may defensively scan and construe their environment in terms of threat cues, thus increasing the risk of acting out.[315]

The MSO evaluation of a person claiming to be suffering from PTSD poses several difficulties for forensic examiners. One is establishing the validity of the diagnosis; although a number of structured measures have been developed to assess PTSD,[316] most are based on self-report and are therefore susceptible to manipulation, especially as the most important factor may be the person's *interpretation* of the event rather than its objective impact.[317] In addition, the effects of "secondary disasters" (e.g., financial setbacks after an earthquake) are hard to tease out.[318]

Second, establishing retrospectively that a reliving "flashback" occurred is complicated by the fact that flashbacks are supposedly unconscious occurrences.[319] Thus, obtaining reliable accounts of the defendant's thoughts, feelings, and perceptions during the episode may be difficult, particularly in the absence of detailed third-party accounts of his or her actions. Identifying triggering stimuli in the crime scene reminiscent of the original trauma could be helpful in this regard. But the problem here is that because such stimuli in theory need only be symbolic of the original trauma, clinicians may be tempted to find triggering "stimuli" where none actually existed.[320]

A final difficulty concerns the interaction of drugs with PTSD. One investigator found that among Vietnam veterans with PTSD, flashbacks with disorientation were more common for those who also suffered from alcoholism (72%) than for those who were nonalcoholics (16%).[321] These data suggest that clinicians and courts may further have to wrestle with the possibility (and certainly the prosecution's assertions) that the effects of alcohol, commonly proscribed as a basis for an insanity defense, may have played a prominent role in producing the defendant's flashback.

Although PTSD has been associated with a wide variety of traumatic experiences, its use in criminal cases has been discussed primarily in connection with combat-related trauma. In this context, the following criteria have been suggested by Sparr and his colleagues for use in forensic evaluations:

1. the "flashback" behavior appears to have been sudden and unpremeditated;
2. the "flashback" behavior is uncharacteristic of the person in normal circumstances;
3. there is a retrievable history of one or more traumatic combat events that are reasonably reenacted by the "flashback" behavior;
4. the defendant is amnesic for all or part of the episode;
5. there is lack of any current motivation for the "flashback" behavior;
6. there are identifiable stimuli in the current environment which are reminiscent of environmental features in Vietnam;
7. the defendant is unaware of the specific ways in which he has reenacted prior experiences;
8. the victim may be fortuitous or accidental; and
9. the patient has, or has had, other symptoms of PTSD.[322]

(f)   Genetic Aberrations: The XYY Syndrome

The existence of a chromosomal abnormality involving an extra male sex chromosome—XYY—has been discussed in the literature since the early 1960s.[323] A number of physical and behavioral markers have been associated with this unusual genotype, including tallness, lower intelligence, and a tendency toward aggressive or violent behavior. Initially, the legal implications of this genotype were also thought to be significant. As Craft's review noted:

> Initial studies tended to concentrate on institutionalized populations for ease of access, and showed . . . sex chromosome abnormalities to be relatively common in prisons and hospitals treating criminals. These early surveys . . . suggested that XYY men tended to be over 180 centimeters tall, and to be more determined, aggressive and sexually active than their peers. Thus, courts as far apart as Melbourne and Lyons were assured, according to Kessler, that "every cell in (the defendant's) brain is abnormal," resulting in verdicts of legal insanity.[324]

Notwithstanding these early studies, our review of court decisions indicates that an MSO defense on the basis of the XYY chromosomal abnormality is quite rare.[325] However, for those who might consider or encounter such a defense theory, a brief summary from some recent reviews may be instructive.

Epidemiological studies confirm that the XYY genotype does appear more frequently in mental or penal groups than in newborn or adult normals. Studies reviewed by Jarvik, Klodin, and Matsuyama indicated incidence estimates in the normal/newborn populations to be 13–20 per 1,000 or 0.13–0.20%,[326] whereas samples from mental institutions revealed incidence estimates of 0.7% (5.3 times greater), and samples from penal institutions revealed an incidence of 1.9% (approximately 15 times greater). Although somewhat different figures were reported in a review by Walzer, Gerald, and Shah,[327] the relatively higher estimates for mental and penal populations were affirmed: 0.001% in newborns or the adult populations; approximately 3 times that in studies from mental settings, 4 times that in penal settings, and 20 times that in mental–penal settings.

Reservations regarding the accuracy or importance of such figures are widespread. For instance, Craft has criticized the methodology of epidemiological studies and the purported relationship between the XYY genotype and aggressive behavior on a number of grounds, noting that (1) different laboratories used different criteria for determining the presence of the genotype, deriving markedly different incidence rates and thus suggesting experimenter bias; and (2) "aggressive tendencies" had been poorly defined in many studies, resulting in unreliable or invalid dependent measures.[328] Walzer and colleagues also noted the inadequacies in classifying human aggressive behaviors and concluded, "[W]e cannot state definitely whether there is an increase in aggressive behavior associated with the genotype."[329] Similarly, Jarvik's group concluded:

> Whatever incidence may eventually be determined, it is safe to predict that persons with an extra Y chromosome will constitute but an insignificant proportion of the perpetrators of violent crime. . . . [Furthermore, whatever the predisposing effect of the extra Y chromosome,] external factors, [such as] home environment, early upbringing, and a host of socio-

cultural factors have either reinforcing or in-hibiting effects.[330]

Finally, Craft cited findings from European twin studies comparing the coincidence of XYY geno-type with criminality in either monozygotic (MZ) or dizygotic (DZ) twin pairs and concluded: "It seems that similarity of upbringing is more asso-ciated with criminality than genetic endowment, for in the most recent twin register studies the differences between MZ (23%) and DZ (18%) are statistically not significant."[331]

In summary, the reviews of the XYY genotype suggest that these individuals may, at worst, be weakly disposed toward criminal activity. A host of environmental factors seem to contribute to their criminal activities. Further, no reliable clus-ter of psychological characteristics has been asso-ciated with this genotype, making its association with a bona fide syndrome unlikely.[332]

(g)   Impulse Disorders

Although Bonnie and others have argued that im-pulse disorders normally should not form the ba-sis for an insanity defense [see § 8.02(c)(4)], lawyers recurrently contend that a defendant whose cognition was relatively unimpaired nonetheless should be acquitted because of voli-tional impairment. Thus, information about the disorders most often associated with such impair-ment may be useful, especially for those in juris-dictions that retain both prongs of the ALI test or have adopted the irresistible-impulse test. Here we review the sparse evidence related to three impulse disorders, pyromania, kleptomania, and pathological gambling, as well as research dealing with the urges created by psychoactive substance addiction.

In the contemporary psychiatric nosology found in DSM-IV the first three disorders are characterized as "impulse-control disorders not elsewhere classified."[333] The unifying characteris-tic of these disorders is "the failure to resist an im-pulse, drive, or temptation to perform an act that is harmful to the person or to others."[334] Further, none of these diagnoses are appropriate if the per-son's misconduct stems from significant cognitive or perceptual distortions (delusions, hallucina-tions), meaning that they will rarely if ever sup-port an MSO defense based on cognitive impair-ment.

The specific criteria for these three disorders are similar. In the instances of pyromania and kleptomania, diagnostic criteria require the clini-cian to rule out other more common or "rational" motives for the problem behavior. The criteria for pyromania require a conclusion that "fire setting is not done for monetary gain, as an expression of sociopolitical ideology, to conceal criminal activi-ty, to express anger or vengeance, [or] to improve one's living circumstances."[335] Similarly, the diag-nosis of kleptomania may only be made if the stolen objects "are not needed for personal use or their monetary value"[336] and the stealing "is not committed to express anger or vengeance."[337] Nor can these behaviors be "better accounted for by Conduct Disorder, a Manic Episode, or Anti-social Personality Disorder."[338] Rather, internal motivations involving arousal and reduction of tension are required for these diagnoses.[339]

Pathological gambling also involves affective components of this type. To fit this diagnosis, the person must gamble "in order to achieve the de-sired excitement" and must be "restless or irrita-ble when attempting to cut down or stop gam-bling," or gamble "as a way of . . . relieving a dys-phoric mood (e.g., feelings of helplessness, guilt, anxiety, depression)."[340] The subjective experi-ence of the pathological gambler includes obses-sive–compulsive features, in the sense that the in-dividual "is preoccupied with gambling" and "has repeated unsuccessful efforts to control, cut back, or stop gambling."[341] The diagnosis also in-volves ruling out gambling behavior attributable to a manic episode.[342]

Despite the presence of these disorders in the DSM, little systematic study of any of the impulse disorders exists.[343] With respect to pyromania and kleptomania, a wealth of clinical anecdotes, self-descriptions, and psychoanalytical specula-tions about unconscious motives is available, but little rigorous research can be found. In part, this paucity of data is probably due to the rarity of these disorders. One recent article reported that a comprehensive review of the English-language literature on kleptomania yielded a total of 26 case reports of persons diagnosed with this disor-der[344]; a more extensive review that scanned literature published in English, German, and French languages yielded a total of 56 case reports.[345] Similarly, recent efforts to examine the prevalence of fire setting in the histories of persons hospitalized for psychiatric disorder have yielded few if any cases that meet operational criteria for pyromania.[346] Perhaps because it is more common, pathological gambling has been studied more than either kleptomania or pyromania, despite the fact that it was the last of the three to be recognized as a disorder. There have been efforts to develop interview guides or assessment instruments to aid in the diagnosis of pathological gambling,[347] as well as some preliminary epidemiological studies.[348]

The few studies about these disorders that do exist are of little help to the forensic clinician. With respect to kleptomania, one study reporting data on a modest size sample ($n = 20$) found a mean age of 36 years and a mean frequency of 27–33 episodes per month of stealing.[349] Interestingly, however, 100% of this sample also met diagnostic criteria for mood disorder. Among reported cases, the disorder is more prevalent among women than men.[350] Few persons arrested for shoplifting meet diagnostic criteria for this disorder.[351]

With respect to pyromania, two separate studies on the lifetime prevalence of fire setting in the histories of state hospital psychiatric patients have been conducted, obtaining figures of 26%[352] and 27.2%.[353] However, these figures are *not* prevalence figures for pyromania. For many of these individuals the occurrence of illegal fire setting was limited to a single event,[354] and the diagnosis of pyromania was therefore rare within the sample.[355] Fire setting among psychiatric patients appears to cut across a wide variety of diagnoses, and "there appear to be no data on the salient features that would distinguish psychiatric patients with a history of fire setting from those without such a history."[356] Despite the proliferation of articles with titles suggesting the existence of discrete psychological profiles for fire setters,[357] the consensus of contemporary writers suggests substantial agreement that no distinct profiles or syndromes exist.[358]

In contrast, prevalence data are available for pathological gambling. One review of surveys conducted in the United States found prevalence

estimates ranging from 1.4% to 3.4%.[359] Studies from Canada have yielded lower estimates, from .42% to 1.2%.[360] Diagnostic studies of persons with pathological gambling have failed to reveal significant cognitive or functional impairment apart from the gambling behavior itself. IQ estimates of pathological gamblers in treatment have yielded above-average mean scores,[361] and comorbidity for alcohol abuse/dependence, affective disorders (e.g., depression), and antisocial personality has been reported in some studies.[362]

Given the lack of solid research on the three impulse disorders considered here, much remains unknown about them. Given the coexistence of cognitive intactness with "irrational" conduct that characterizes the criminal behavior, much of the early writing about kleptomania and pyromania utilized a psychoanalytical framework for analysis.[363] However, the constructs of psychoanalytical theory are difficult to test empirically because of the unconscious and unobservable nature of the key elements. At the same time, the adequacy of the medical model of pathological gambling (positing some organic cause) has also been challenged.[364] As a result, other theoretical models have been set forth to try to capture these diverse impulse disorders. Noting the comorbidity of some of these disorders with alcohol abuse/dependence, some have postulated a general "addictive personality" construct.[365] Others, noting the obsessive–compulsive qualities of these disorders and their comorbidity with mood disorders, particularly depression, have hypothesized an "affective disorder spectrum" meant to incorporate them.[366] Beyond differences in theoretical approach, concerns remain about the validity of the diagnoses themselves.[367]

In contrast to the various impulse disorders described above, addiction to psychoactive substances might support a defense of *cognitive* impairment as well as one based on volitional impairment. The connection between psychotic-like symptoms and abuse of various psychoactive substances is well documented.[368] When not associated with hallucinations and similar symptoms, however, proof of addiction, like a showing that an impulse disorder exists, is most likely to surface in a criminal trial in support of an argument that the defendant's criminal act (whether it involved obtaining the addicting substance or money with which to buy it) was either the result of an "irresistible impulse" or "involuntary." Research on the nature of addiction is relevant to both these issues.

After a comprehensive review of studies conducted prior to 1974,[369] Fingarette and Hasse concluded that the person who chronically abuses alcohol is "one who for any of a variety of other reasons, often rooted in his past or current patterns of life, has increasingly used drinking as a way of adapting to his life-problems." Even though the impulse to drink is intense, the addict's life is "so very distressing and so very difficult, both physically and mentally," that he or she is likely to seek help "entirely on his own initiative [or] with the aid of special encouragement, professional guidance, and/or coercive influence."[370] From this premise, the authors concluded that addiction should generally not support a defense. As they put it, "The threat of the criminal sanction may be a factor in controlling such drinking as is likely to lead to criminal offenses,"[371] and thus, for legal purposes, alcoholics do not suffer from complete "loss of control" but, rather, have some volition. They also admitted, however, that "the alcoholic is one who faces a choice that is (increasingly) more difficult than for most people."[372]

Similarly with narcotic addicts, Fingarette and Hasse pointed to several studies suggesting that the craving for such drugs as heroin and morphine is not overpowering.[373] They noted that "only a small fraction of the many millions of patients who receive morphine ever attempt to take the drug again, and only an exceedingly small proportion of addicts owe their dependence to medically initiated narcotic use."[374] They also pointed to a study of 13,240 Army enlisted men returning from Vietnam in 1971, which found that although almost half had tried heroin or opium while in Vietnam, only about 20% had developed signs of physical or psychological dependence, and of those, only 5% experienced such signs at any time after their return to the United States.[374] Finally, Fingarette and Hasse noted that "cold turkey" withdrawal from narcotics "is apparently never fatal; its effects are temporary, continuing at worst for no more than several days."[376]

When the narcotic substance is cocaine, withdrawal may be more difficult to weather. According to one source, "The positive reinforcing actions of cocaine may be more intense than those of other drugs of abuse, and as a result the withdrawal effect may share not only the intensity but also the motivational selectivity."[377] According to another, "Cocaine and the amphetamines are the most potent reinforcing agents known."[378] On the other hand, people are able to resist cocaine, at least initially. Estimates from the National Institute of Drug Abuse suggest that only about 10–15% of those who try cocaine intranasally end up abusing the drug.[379] It generally takes from two to four years to develop an addiction.[380]

The available evidence indicates that the longer a person uses alcohol or drugs to produce an intoxicated state, the harder it is to stop and the more likely it is that the addict will engage in behavior that will bring about intoxication. In evaluating addicted individuals, the mental health professional should attempt to ascertain facts that cast light on the difficulty the individual experiences in choosing between satisfying his or her craving (through criminal action) and suffering the consequences of not being able to ingest the sought-after substance. Information from the studies alluded to above may also be useful to the factfinder. As always, the clinician should decline from stating whether the choice was so hard as to mitigate responsibility.

(h) Other Novel Defenses

Many other novel defenses have been raised in selected cases; some of these have achieved considerable notoriety through extended media coverage. For instance, there was the "television intoxication" defense of Ronnie Zamora,[381] the "brainwashing" defense of Patricia Hearst,[382] and the battered-child defense of the Menendez brothers[383] (all of which were unsuccessful, it should be noted). Premenstrual syndrome, unusual plasma androgen levels, fetal alcohol syndrome, black rage, and coercive hypnosis are also among the diverse subjects found in current literature or popular culture that might be creatively argued as "causes" of criminal activity in support of an MSO defense. An attorney might contend, for example, that the physiological changes associated with the menstrual cycle create alterations in mood which reduce the capacity of a female offender to control her conduct[384]; similarly, "raging hormones" might be offered as an explanation for illegal sexual behavior by individuals whose androgen levels exceed the physiological norm.[385] An individual's volitional and cognitive impairments associated with exposure to drugs or alcohol while a fetus might bolster an insanity defense[386]; anger at a racist world could produce an "irresistible" impulse or irrational plan to avenge[387]; and Hollywood, at least, has been willing to sell to the public the notion that individuals under hypnosis gives up their free will to the hypnotist and can be coerced through suggestion to the most heinous of offenses.[388] The possibilities are seemingly endless, bounded only by the creativity of the attorney and the availability of data or theory from the social sciences that may be brought to bear on some aspect of criminal behavior.[389]

There may be few, if any, data on some of these topics, and alleged theoretical bases for the phenomena may be conflicting. We would not advise mental health professionals against use of social science data or theory in MSO cases simply on the basis that such defenses are "usually" not presented. However, when data and theory are weak, missing, or poorly understood, testimony should be ventured with considerable caution, if at all. Factors that may be contributory or weakly predisposing should be explained for what they are, and poorly understood relationships, such as that between viewing television and actual criminal behavior, should not be elevated to the status of syndromes, as with "television intoxication." The more unfamiliar or poorly understood the phenomenon, the more restrained clinicians should be in their advocacy of its potential relevance.

When contemplating a "novel" defense, it might be useful not only to consider its scientific basis but also to recall Moore's conceptualization of responsibility. Under his formulation, the fact that behavior is "caused" by a particular physiological mechanism or a peculiar situation is irrelevant unless it also renders the person's reasoning process irrational [see § 8.02(c)(2)]. To the extent the law does or should adopt this approach, at least some of the "defenses" described previously would not be recognized. For instance, the thought processes of a person with an extra Y chromosome are not typically irrational or even particularly distorted. Similarly, the fact that the war (or racism, television, or beating by the victim) caused or helped cause the crime would not, according to Moore, absolve a defendant on insanity grounds unless it also significantly compromised the defendant's thought process. The distinction between causation and explanation on the one hand and irrationality and excuse on the other may turn out to be a crucial one as science and popular belief add to the already long list of conditions that might contribute to criminal conduct.[390]

8.05.   Reliability and Validity of MSO Opinions

Though mental health professionals have long been involved in reconstructing mental state at the time of the offense, relatively little systematic research exists on the reliability and validity of their judgments in such cases. Thus, public perception on this issue has been shaped almost exclusively by a few highly publicized cases in which opposing expert witnesses have offered inconsistent or contradictory testimony.[391] Indeed, one caustic observer has noted, "For every Ph.D. there is an equal and opposite Ph.D."[392] An understanding of the research that does exist might help counteract this type of attitude or at least provide a more realistic perspective. Thus we briefly review here studies on reliability (interrater agreement) and validity (agreement with external criterion) of clinicians' opinions in insanity defense cases.

(a)   Reliability Studies

Table 8.2 summarizes the findings from seven studies of interrater agreement in insanity evaluations. The first study was reported by Stock and Poythress,[393] who examined the reliability of insanity opinions formulated by 12 Ph.D. psychologists at Michigan's Center for Forensic Psychiatry. In each of 33 cases, a pair of psychologists simultaneously interviewed the defendant and had equal access to relevant third-party information

Table 8.2
Reliability of Forensic Examiners' Opinions Regarding Insanity: Summary of Findings from Seven Studies

Study	Number of cases	Statistic reported	Level of agreement
Stock & Poythress	33	% agreement	97
Fukunaga, Pasewark, Hawkins, & Gudeman	355	% agreement	92
Raifman	214	% agreement	64
Rogers, Dollmetsch, & Cavenaugh	25	Correlation coefficient	.82[a]
Rogers, Wasyliw, & Cavanaugh	25	Kappa	.93[b]
Rogers, Seman, & Wasyliw	30	Kappa	1.00
Phillips, Wolf, & Coons	66	% agreement	76
		Kappa	.45

[a]Correlation coefficient is defined in § 20.02(b). The correlation of +.82 indicates fairly high agreement between the clinicians.

[b]Kappa is a statistic for measuring agreement between examiners on nominal categories, such as diagnosis or, in the present context, legal sanity–insanity. It is considered to be a conservative statistic because agreement between examiners is corrected to eliminate the effects of chance agreement. A kappa of +1.00 reflects perfect interrater agreement, while a kappa of .00 indicates that examiners agree at the level obtainable by chance alone (negative values indicate less than chance agreement).

such as police reports or prior medical records. Without conferring with each other, they provided the investigators their opinions regarding insanity. As the table shows, the pairs agreed in 97% of the cases.

Fukunaga, Pasewark, Hawkins, and Gudeman obtained a similar reliability estimate in a much larger study of defendants in Hawaii who were examined by a pair of psychiatrists.[394] However, in this study the examiners were not prevented from conferring with one another prior to forming their opinions. Thus, the rate of agreement may have been inflated by examiner efforts to iron out their differences.

The third study was conducted by Raifman,[395] who reported reliability estimates for psychiatrists performing insanity evaluations in Arizona. A total of four psychiatrists were involved in the study, with two involved in any one case. In each case, one psychiatrist was selected from a list provided by the prosecutor, the other from a list provided by the defense. Overall agreement here was much lower, with considerable variation among the pairs.

The following three studies listed in Table 8.2 were conducted by Rogers and his colleagues.[396] They reported interrater agreement between experienced clinicians (either psychologists or psychiatrists) using the Rogers Criminal Responsibility Assessment Scales (RCRAS),[397] a series of explicit rating scales described in more detail below. The agreement rate was consistent with the rate found in the first two studies.

The final study was reported by Phillips and colleagues,[398] who reported findings from insanity evaluations conducted in Alaska between 1977 and 1981. Their review of close to 1,000 state hospital, community mental health clinic, and private clinic files revealed 66 cases in which two or more clinicians had examined the defendant for MSO. As in the study by Fukunaga and colleagues, evaluators' opinions regarding insanity were not necessarily independent; even so, the agreement rate was relatively low.[399]

These studies differed in a number of important ways, which renders comparability among them or generalization of findings quite limited. First, the studies used examiners of different professional disciplines—psychiatrists (Raifman) versus psychologists (Stock and Poythress) versus both psychiatrists and psychologists (Rogers and colleagues). Second, the examiners may have differed in terms of their forensic training, a factor shown to influence output[400]: The psychologists in the Stock and Poythress study had received several months of supervised training in performing insanity evaluations, but the specific training of the clinicians in the other studies is not known. Third, there may have been differences attributable to examination settings—some occurred in private offices (Raifman), others in a hospital setting (Stock and Poythress). Different legal tests were also applied—ALI (Phillips et al.) versus *M'Naghten* (Raifman). Finally, the examiners may have differed in terms of allegiances—court-appointed (Stock and Poythress) versus retention by a particular party (Raifman).

Thus, no broad conclusions can be drawn concerning the reliability of mental health professionals' opinions on the insanity question. But the higher reliability figures reported by Stock and Poythress and by Rogers and colleagues suggest that the reliability of insanity opinions may be quite respectable under certain conditions—namely, among clinicians with forensic training, working in a hospital or clinic setting where similar concepts and approaches may be shared, with no *a priori* allegiance to either party. This conclusion is supported by research showing that clinicians working in state hospitals overwhelmingly agree that personality disorders should not form the basis for an insanity defense.[401] The substantially lower figure reported by Raifman and Phillips and colleagues paints a different portrait and leaves open to question (and, we hope, further empirical study) which factor or factors contribute to low agreement between examiners.

To our knowledge, there are no published reliability studies involving clinicians' judgments on MSO defenses other than insanity. It might be expected, however, that interrater agreement for issues such as GBMI, diminished capacity, or automatism would be somewhat lower than for insanity opinions, as the former issues are usually raised in connection with mental conditions that are less conspicuous than those required for consideration of an insanity acquittal.

There are also no studies looking at the reliability of judgments and inferences that stop short of ultimate conclusions about sanity, *mens rea,* and other mental state issues. Since we discourage forensic examiners from addressing ultimate legal issues [see § 1.04], this latter type of research would be the most useful from our perspective. There is some research about this topic conducted in nonforensic settings, however, and it has not

been encouraging. Staller and Geertsma asked 27 psychiatrists who were faculty members at a major medical school to view a 30-minute videotaped interview of a patient and then rate the applicability, on a scale from 0 to 5, of each of 565 descriptive statements that the investigators had prepared.[402] The mean correlation coefficient over all pairs of clinicians was only 0.37. The investigators had hoped to use the procedure to develop a device for assessing student's clinical skills; instead, they concluded:

> [E]xperts with the highest credentials did not agree on a sufficient number of the 565 items. . . given them to make up an examination. . . . [I]nstead of reporting here on a new device for assessing clinical skill in psychiatry, we are presenting these sobering findings on the failure of psychiatric experts to agree in their clinical judgments.[403]

Morse's review of the literature addressing the reliability of psychodynamic formulations led to a similar conclusion: "The very few studies of the reliability of dynamic formulations that exist are mostly impressionistic and suggest that these formulations are unreliable."[404]

Clearly, more than a few "impressionistic" studies need to be conducted; in the interim, theory-based formulations should be prefaced with appropriate qualifiers and caveats regarding scientific robustness. We can only speculate at this point that, given the abstract and flexible nature of personality theory constructs, it is unlikely that examiner agreement on symptoms and psychodynamics would approach the levels presently obtained in assigning criminal defendants to discrete (albeit moral rather than psychological) categories of "sane" versus "insane."

(b)   Validity Studies

While studies of the reliability of clinicians' MSO opinions are rare, good validity studies are almost nonexistent. We have found four such studies, all of which look at the concordance between clinical opinion and court decision. In the first such study, Daniel and Harris reported the results of pretrial examinations of female criminal defendants ($n = 66$) conducted at a large state hospital

in Missouri from 1974 to 1979.[405] Of the 25 recommended NGRI, the court returned an NGRI
verdict in 22 (88%).

Similarly, Fukunaga and colleagues reported
an overall clinician–court agreement rate of 93%
in their study of 315 cases in Hawaii; the court
disagreed with only 11 of the clinicians' 105 insanity findings and only 10 of the clinicians' 210
sanity conclusions.[406] This validity estimate is
probably inflated, however, as the investigators
excluded, among others, 44 cases in which the
examining psychiatrist did not state a definite
opinion. Although it is to the psychiatrists' credit
that they refused to offer an opinion when none
could be formed, exclusion of these cases probably biased the sample by excluding the more difficult cases.

Even using a more careful methodology, however, Poythress obtained impressive results.[407] In
each of the 139 cases studied, a Ph.D. clinical psychologist from Michigan's Center for Forensic
Psychiatry completed an insanity evaluation and
testified in court, usually with opposing testimony by a psychiatrist from the private sector. The
overall agreement rate between the opinion of
the center's psychologist and the ultimate verdict
was 93% (only 3 of the 41 defendants recommended insane by clinicians were found sane by
the courts, and only 6 of the 98 defendants recommended sane by the clinicians were found insane by the courts).

A fourth concordance study was published by
Rogers, Cavanaugh, Seman, and Harris,[408] who
compared court opinions to those of forensic psychiatrists and psychologists in Illinois and Ohio
using the RCRAs. The courts agreed with the
clinicians in 93 of 104 cases (88%). However, because the study looked at all cases referred for
evaluation, and some of those cases undoubtedly
did not result in assertion of an insanity defense,
the criterion variable for many of the "sane" cases
was, in effect, a defense attorney's or defendant's
decision not to raise the defense rather than judicial or jury review of the clinical opinion.

Although these studies report fairly respectable concordance rates, they are all bedev-
iled by still another significant methodological
problem. As we have already made clear, defining
an adequate criterion for a "correct" judgment on
issues such as insanity and automatism is virtually

impossible. Thus, the investigators in the studies
reported above compromised by using court decision as the criterion. This criterion may serve as
well as any other when the basis for the verdict is
developed through an adversarial proceeding.[409]
But when, as is often the case [see § 8.02(a)(2)],
the insanity determination occurs in a relatively
nonadversarial, bench-trial setting in which the
clinical opinion is uncontested and usually dispositive, the court's decision may well be contaminated by the very dependent measure being studied. Unfortunately, with the exception of
Poythress's study, the research reported above appears to depend at least in part on court decisions
of the latter variety.

Even when the verdict does come from an adversarial proceeding, a further problem with all
the studies is the fact that the examiners used
were employed at state or private facilities as
"court" evaluators, nominally without allegiance
to either party in the litigation. The parties calling these clinicians probably portrayed them in
court as "neutral," while characterizing the opposing clinicians as "hired guns." As a result, the
judges or jurors may well have viewed the studied
examiners as less biased or more objective, and
their verdicts may have been based on trust rather
than on a critical, independent assessment of the
evidence. In short, like the reliability studies,
these studies suffer from methodological problems that make it difficult to compare them or to
place much confidence in them as true validity estimates.

(c)   Formal Assessment of Insanity:
The RCRAS

Previously we mentioned the Rogers Criminal
Responsibility Assessment Scales (RCRAS), a series of explicit scales designed to measure variables pertinent to legal insanity. These scales are
available for general use in the forensic community[410] and represent the first serious attempt by
mental health professionals to formalize clinical
inquiry and decisionmaking on the issue of legal
insanity. A closer look at the construct and face
validity of this instrument is thus worthwhile.

The RCRAS test manual makes clear that the
major concern motivating its creation was the

lack of scientific respectability associated with clinicians' judgments on insanity. In the overview of the scales, Rogers noted:

> The scientific basis of such judgments remains practically unresearched. This absence of empirical data, compounded with problems of perceived financial self-interest, has led authors addressing this issue to conclude that psychiatric testimony lacks the requisite scientific precision for rendering expert opinions regarding sanity. . . . The purpose of the RCRAS is to provide a systematic and empirically based approach to evaluations of criminal responsibility. . . . The RCRAS is designed to quantify essential psychological and situational variables at the time of the crime and to implement criterion based decision models for criminal responsibility. This allows the clinician to quantify the impairment at the time of the crime, to conceptualize this impairment with respect to the appropriate legal standards and to render an expert opinion with respect to that standard.[411]

The RCRAS, in other words, is intended to correct perceived deficiencies in the scientific rigor of insanity evaluations and opinions. It seeks to accomplish this goal by allowing the clinician to "quantify" such aspects of human behavior as (1) the relative severity, for legal purposes, of disordered behavior; and (2) the relative contribution, for legal purposes, of symptoms of disordered mental states to the criminal behavior itself.

The mechanism by which this transformation is accomplished is the translation of an insanity standard (the ALI test) into a "testable psychological construct":

> The psychological construct for legal insanity developed in the RCRAS validation research paradigm is the presence, at the time of the crime, of (1) a severe mental disorder which results in (2) a substantial impairment of the individual's cognitive and/or behavioral control. . . . The first element of the construct, the mental disorder, is operationalized as a major psychiatric disorder (which parallels the ALI "mental disease or defect"). With regards to the second element, cognitive control (ALI, "ability to appreciate") is defined as the individual's awareness, knowledge, and comprehension of the criminal act while it was occurring. Further, behavioral control (ALI, "ability to conform conduct") is defined as the deliberateness and self-control that the individual was able to exert over the criminal behavior.[412]

The 25 individual scales that comprise the RCRAS address a number of different factors, including the reliability of the defendant's narrative and possible malingering (#1 and #2), possible organic conditions (#4), mental retardation (#5), and the possible presence of symptoms of functional disturbance such as anxiety (#9), hallucinations (#12), and thought or language disturbance (#15, #17). The clinician's ratings on these 25 scales are assimilated and translated into six summary "psycholegal criteria" which address the presence of malingering (A1), the presence of organicity (A2), the presence of major psychiatric disorder (A3), loss of cognitive controls (i.e., whether the person "lacked the ability to comprehend the criminality of his behavior") (A4), loss of behavioral control (i.e., whether the person "was unable to change, monitor, or control his criminal behavior") (A5), and a judgment (A6) of whether the assessed loss of control (A4, A5) was a direct result of the organic (A2) or psychiatric (A3) disturbance. Regarding these six crucial judgments, the RCRAS test manual states:

> Based on the standard of medical and scientific certainty, each decision model requires that individual psychological criteria be met with either a definite "yes" or a definite "no." Judgments of "more likely than not" (i.e., preponderance) or based on personal unvalidated judgments are excluded from the decision models.[413]

The conclusions with respect to the six psycholegal criteria are then plugged into a decision tree that produces the clinical opinion—sane, insane, or no opinion.

A casual reading of the RCRAS test manual and of the research published thus far by Rogers and his colleagues instills a sense of optimism that a degree of scientific rigor and precision is possible in insanity evaluation. Interrater reliability is good, and concordance between opinions based on RCRAS ratings and court verdict is respectable [see § 8.05(a)(b)]. A closer look, however, suggests that the RCRAS promises more than it delivers.

To begin with, an inspection of the individual scales uncovers numerous, and familiar, problems for the clinician. Each of the individual scales calls for the examiner to assign a number from 0 to 5 (or in some cases 6) to reflect the relative severity of the factor being rated; it is presumably this assignment of numbers that constitutes the RCRAS's ability to "quantify" the impairment at the time of the crime. However, almost all these ratings are *ordinal*. In a few instances the scale points are anchored to objective or normative measures of behavior; for example, scale #6, "mental retardation," anchors the higher scale points to "mild" (3), "moderate" (4), "severe" (5), or "profound" (6) retardation, as supported by scores on recognized intelligence tests. Typically, however, the numbers reflect a continuum or gradient of severity for recording the examiner's global judgment. For example, scale #9 purports to measure "anxiety present at the time of the alleged crime" and includes anchor statements such as "(2) Slight. Felt apprehensive for a few minutes; (3) Mild. Felt a little anxious; (4) Moderate. Was fairly anxious . . ."; and so on.

Other scales "quantify" the relationship, if any, between a symptom or diagnostic condition and the criminal act. For example, scale #5 addresses "relationship of brain damage to the commission of the alleged crime." To assign a score of 5 on this scale, the examiner must find that "the patient lacked intentionality, could not comprehend the criminality of what he was doing, or lacked control over his behavior." It is no surprise that the manual provides no instructions on how to *measure* intentionality, comprehension of criminality, or self-control. Simply assigning ordinal numbers to a continuum of conclusions of this type does not disguise the fact that these are the same philosophical and commonsensical judgments that mental health professionals have previously been criticized for passing off as scientific appraisal based on "reasonable certainty."[414]

The questionable value of ordinal numbers as true quantifiers becomes even more dubious when the clinician proceeds to the important summary decisions, A1 through A6 (the "psycholegal criteria"). The clinician must review and consider the ordinal ratings assigned to a subset of the basic 25 scales in reaching each of these six summary decisions. For example, summary decision A4—"definite loss of cognitive controls"—requires a review of basic ratings assigned to scales #15 ("patient's level of verbal coherence at the time of the alleged crime . . ."), #17 ("evi-

dence of formal thought disorder"), #18 ("planning and preparation for the alleged crime"), and #19 ("awareness of criminality during the commission of the alleged crime . . ."). However, in reviewing the numerical ratings (e.g., 0–5) assigned to each of the basic scales, the clinician is not required by the test manual to treat them in any arithmetical way (e.g., by adding them together). Rather, a global or intuitive judgment about "loss of cognitive control" is all that is called for. Thus, even assuming ordinal quantification on the scales makes sense, the ultimate judgments involved in the RCRAS are not based on truly quantitative measurement.

Rogers attempted to deflect these types of criticisms by testing his psychological constructs through a series of derived hypotheses. Specifically, he hypothesized, defendants evaluated as insane using the RCRAS should, compared to their criminally responsible counterparts, demonstrate (1) a relative absence of malingering, (2) more severe psychopathology associated with major mental disorder, and (3) a greater loss of cognitive and/or behavioral control. He and his colleagues then conducted a number of studies that supported these hypotheses.[415] However, the criterion classification of "sane" or "insane" in these studies was derived from the RCRAS decision tree itself, making their findings something of a foregone conclusion. For example, if the clinician assigns low ratings to scales that address malingering (hypothesis 1), high ratings to scales that address psychopathology (hypothesis 2), and high ratings to scales that address loss of control (hypothesis 3), a psycholegal finding of "insane" is virtually assured; conversely, if the opposite pattern of ratings is assigned (high malingering, low pathology, low loss of control), the clinician would be hard pressed to develop a psycholegal finding other than "sane" without violating the logic of the scales. The "findings" of the studies on the three hypotheses are thus tautological and relatively trivial.

The RCRAS has been criticized by others as well.[416] This criticism should not obscure its strengths. Rogers has identified and presented in an organized fashion many of the factors that an examiner must consider in an insanity evaluation (as well as other MSO assessments): malingering, amnesia, degree and type of pathology present, and third-party information about the defendant's behavior at the crime. The RCRAS may help clinicians organize their interviews or their thoughts about the data gathered in investigation. But the weaknesses of the RCRAS should also be recognized: its misplaced emphasis on addressing ultimate-issue questions, its claims to quantify areas of judgment that are logical and/or intuitive in nature, and its assertion of scientific rigor (e.g., the statement in the manual that assures that RCRAS-based opinions have "reasonable medical and scientific certainty"). The major risk involved in its use is that clinicians or courts may, in light of the unsubstantiated claims in the manual, attribute undeserved scientific status to judgments that remain—ordinal ratings notwithstanding—logical and commonsensical in nature.

8.06   MSO Investigation

The clinical evaluation of MSO is one of the more difficult assessments in forensic work, for a number of reasons. First, as the foregoing discussion makes clear, the governing legal doctrine is amorphous, which means that virtually any aspect of an individual's personality may assume legal relevance. Second, unlike most other forensic assessments, the focus of the evaluation is retrospective. Having to ascertain the inner workings of an individual weeks or months prior to the evaluation limits the applicability of many traditional clinical procedures and creates concern about the possible impact of intervening events. Added to these concerns are problems generic to forensic evaluations but which seemingly are encountered more frequently with MSO evaluations: the unavailability of desired third-party information and uncooperative or dishonest subjects.

We thus use the term "investigation" intentionally. In complex MSO cases, forensic examiners function more as investigative reporters than as traditional clinicians.[417] They often spend as much effort outside the interview room gathering and reviewing third-party information as they spend inside with the defendants. In addition, the time they do spend with the defendant is likely to be much more confrontive and inquisitive than is

typical in therapy or many other types of forensic evaluations. Chapter 3 detailed the many differences between forensic and therapeutic assessments; a typical MSO examination illustrates the forensic evaluation *par excellence*.

This section discusses the component parts of this evaluation: the types of third-party information that must be collected, the proper approach to examining defendants, and special techniques that may be useful in MSO assessments. Before looking at these attributes of "comprehensive" MSO investigation, however, we will first consider the feasibility of a brief screening evaluation as a preliminary approach.

(a)   Preliminary Screening for MSO Defense

That a brief screening evaluation for insanity might be feasible is suggested by the relatively high percentage of defendants evaluated who are not diagnosed as seriously disturbed [see § 8.04(a)], the large proportion of "obvious" cases among those that are successful [see § 8.02(a)(2)], and the infrequency with which the insanity defense is raised [see § 8.02(a)(1)]. If a screening mechanism could identify those who will not have a viable defense, substantial savings might result at no legal cost to defendants.

A study by Slobogin, Melton, and Showalter suggested that such a screening procedure may be possible.[418] These investigators developed a brief mental status examination (MSE) consisting of three phases: questions about the alleged offense, questions about the defendant's general psychohistory, and an examination of present mental state. Twenty-four mental health professionals were instructed in the use of the MSE and then worked in pairs to conduct brief (i.e., 30-minute) evaluations of criminal defendants (n = 36). Each team had available a limited amount of third-party data, including a description of the charges and, in some cases, a preliminary hearing transcript. Trainees were asked to conclude whether or not significant abnormality may have affected the defendants' actions at the time of the offense but were asked to err on the positive side so as to avoid prematurely screening out a defendant with a possible legal defense.

Table 8.3
Concordance of Hospital Staff MSO Examination Opinion and Screening Examiners' Opinions

MSO screening opinion	Hospital staff opinion	
	Potential legal defense	No legal defense
Might have significant abnormality (20)	10 (27.7%)	10 (27.7%)
No significant abnormality (16)	0 (0%)	16 (44.4%)

Note. From Slobogin et al., *The Feasibility of a Brief Evaluation of Mental State at the Time of the Offense*, 8 LAW & HUM. BEHAV. 305 (1984).

The criterion judgment regarding mental state at the time of the offense was that of an interdisciplinary team at a state hospital, which conducted comprehensive inpatient MSO examinations on each of the 36 defendants. The cross-tabulation of trainees' recommendations and hospital staff findings is shown in Table 8.3. The trainees successfully screened out 44% of the referrals and had zero false negatives.

Although replication of the results is necessary, these data suggest that a brief interview can identify cases in which no MSO defense is present. Moreover, though clinicians in this study were not asked to do so, the MSE may be able to detect the obviously insane individual for whom a more comprehensive evaluation is unnecessary. It might be particularly useful for the clinician performing outpatient evaluations at the initial stages of the criminal process.

(b)   Comprehensive MSO Investigation Procedures

When a screening procedure fails to exclude the possibility of an available MSO defense, the clinician should conduct a comprehensive inquiry utilizing information from a wide variety of sources. As suggested previously, this inquiry can be divided into collection of third-party information, interviewing the defendant, and use of other techniques for acquiring information from the defendant.

(1)   Third-Party Information

As Morse has stated, "In determining whether a defendant is crazy, there is simply no substitute for the fullest possible account from all sources of the defendant's behavior at the time of the alleged crime."[419] Third-party information is essential to a good MSO evaluation. Which third-party information to pursue, and how best to pursue it, will depend on the complexity of the evaluation [see generally § 3.05].

Table 8.4 identifies five categories of potential information. Information regarding the referral

Table 8.4
Sources of Third-Party Information

1. Information regarding evaluation itself
   a. Referral source
   b. Referral questions
   c. Why evaluation is requested (i.e., what behavior triggered the evaluation?)
   d. Who is report going to?
   e. When is report to be used?

2. Offense-related information
   a. From attorney's notes
   b. From witnesses, victim(s)
   c. From confession, preliminary hearing transcript, etc.
   d. Autopsy reports
   e. Newspaper accounts

3. Developmental/historical information
   a. Personal data (traumatic life events, unusual habits or fears, places lived)
   b. Early childhood illnesses (if organic deficit suspected)
   c. Family history (especially if young and/or still living with family)
   d. Marital history (especially in spousal homicide cases)
   e. Educational, employment, and military history
   f. Social relationships
   g. Psychosexual history (especially if sex offense)
   h. Medical and psychiatric records

4. "Signs of trouble"
   a. Juvenile and criminal court records
   b. Probation reports

5. Statistical information (i.e., studies of the behavior of individuals with the defendant's characteristics)

itself is crucial in defining the scope of the evaluation and ethical obligations [see § 4.05(b)(1)]. Reports about the crime scenario are also obviously essential, both for purposes of comparison with the defendant's narrative and for developing leads for further investigation. Developmental and historical information provides corroboration of mental state and diagnosis and helps in formulating alternative "causation" hypotheses. Within this category, recent hospital records in particular may contain a wealth of descriptive information regarding the frequency and duration of symptoms, response to medication or other intervention, and prior displays of legally relevant behavior. Records of treatment in the hospital or jail following arrest may also be important, particularly if the examiner suspects that a defendant's mental condition has changed significantly since the arrest. The fourth category, records of prior criminal activity, will suggest patterns of behavior, or types of triggering events, that can help the clinician gain insight into reasons for the individual's current criminal act. Finally, relevant statistical data about antisocial tendencies of people with similar personalities can form a baseline for the evaluation.

More difficult than determining what type of information is needed is obtaining it. Problems can occur with respect to each of the five types of information described in Table 8.4. Referral information should come from the initial consultation with the referral source, the court order, or both, but as discussed in Chapter 3, it is occasionally not forthcoming without considerable effort on the part of the clinician. Crime information is usually available from the police and the attorneys; because these sources may not be attuned to various psychological clues, however, the examiner may occasionally feel compelled to seek corroboration from complainants, witnesses, co-defendants or others who may help to reconstruct defendants' MSO. If so, allegations of "witness tampering" should be avoided by contacting the source through the referring party. Records regarding treatment, criminal history, juvenile history (to the extent it is not "expunged"), education, military service, and so on should be obtained by the defendant's attorney and given to the clinician; again, however, the adversarial nature of the criminal process may inhibit free ex-

change of information. Further, if the defendant's attorney does not provide the information, a release from the client will probably also need to be obtained, at least for psychiatric and medical records; even though the privilege associated with this material is probably waived once a defense is raised [see § 4.04(c)], when the defense has not been raised, or when there is any doubt as to the relevance of the sought-after records, a valid privilege claim may exist without such consent. Finally, as the preceding sections of this chapter made clear, to date useful statistical information about crime and mental disability is rare or so general as to be of little use.

Despite these difficulties, the evidence-gathering effort is usually worth it. Consider a case in which Poythress was involved, the data for which are found in Table 8.5. The defendant, a successful insurance saleswoman, was charged with the murder of her estranged husband while he was visiting with the family to celebrate the birthday of their teenage son. She claimed she was insane at the time of the killing. Hospital records indicated that she had suffered three manic episodes in the past. Other information accompanying the referral revealed that she had been taken directly from the scene of the shooting to the hospital, that she had been admitted in an "angry and disorganized state," and that she had subsequently received treatment for depression and grief reaction over a several-month period. Her usual attending psychiatrist had evaluated her at the request of the defense and prepared a report supportive of an insanity defense based on her bipolar disorder. As Table 8.5 reveals, however, the defendant's assertions regarding her mental state at the time of the shooting, her motivation, and her rationale for having a loaded gun in the home were all at odds with one or more pieces of third-party data gathered through investigative interviewing. These data were pivotal in supporting a formulation that the shooting was primarily a product of anger and jealousy rather than a relapse into a manic episode.

Assuming the appropriate information is sought and obtained, the clinician must still exercise caution about the degree to which the information is relied on. One concern is *admissibility* [see § 3.08]. For instance, a police file may contain an illegally obtained confession which may

Table 8.5
The Usefulness of Third-Party Information: An Illustration

Defendant assertion	Third-party source	Third-party data	Implication
		Cause of the shooting	
Experienced a manic episode that "caused" the murder.	Treating psychiatrist	Patient "religiously" took her medications; lithium levels well within the therapeutic range for past 3 months	Inconsistent with defendant claim of manic episode.
	Individual therapist	Therapy notes and verbal report of weekly sessions, including observations 2 days prior to shooting. No sign of manic/hypomanic symptoms; primary therapy issue is anger toward husband for separation.	Inconsistent with decompensation into psychotic state.
	Teenage child, age 18, living at home	Observations of defendant at/near time of shooting. No behaviors noted that were similar to symptoms at times of previous acute manic episodes.	Inconsistent with decompensation into psychotic state.
	Supervisor at work	Defendant described as a highly competent, effective insurance sales person. No behaviors noted that were similar to symptoms at times of previous acute episodes.	Inconsistent with decompensation into psychotic state.
		Feelings toward victim and motivation	
"Loved husband" despite separation; no reason to act aggressively toward husband.	Individual therapist	Repeated theme in therapy, especially in session 2 days prior to shooting, is anger over separation; much verbal hostility, but no explicit threats or plans of action toward him	Inconsistent with feeling/affect recalled by defendant at time of forensic evaluation.
	Teenage child, age 18, living at home	Observations on evening of shooting include that defendant and victim argued about family obligations moments before the shooting.	Confrontation and disagreement over family obligations may have provoked defendant's anger and behavior.
		Role, if any, of alcohol	
Episode may have been triggered by alcohol.	Bartender at lounge where defendant went some evenings to meet men	Defendant usually drank 1–2 glasses of wine; behavior described as reserved, controlled, and quiet.	Inconsistent with "pathological intoxication" or other explanation based on triggering effects of alcohol.
	Teenage child, age 18	Mother drinks infrequently and small quantities; no pattern of volatile or aggressive behavior noted when drinking.	No indication of history of radical reaction to alcohol consumption.

(continued)

Table 8.5. Continued

Defendant assertion	Third-party source	Third-party data	Implication
		Rationales for availability of loaded weapon	
Loaded rifle kept in home "since my husband moved out" (6 weeks ago) in order to protect family in high-crime neighborhood	Teenage child, age 18	Defendant asked him to load gun 2 weeks ago and leave in hall closet.	Inconsistent with defendant's rationales for keeping loaded gun.
—Radio had been stolen from son's car.	Teenage child, age 18	Radio had in fact been stolen, but while car was parked at school, 7 miles away.	Not a criminal incident in the vicinity of the home.
—Neighbors had had prowlers recently.	Interview neighbors	Next-door neighbor reports one incident of school kids marking car/house windows with bar of soap. Nine other neighbors deny any recent crime problems; some view neighborhood as "safe enough to leave your door unlocked."	Neighbors do not describe neighborhood as high-crime area, which is inconsistent with defendant's account and rationale for having rifle loaded.
—Police frequently called to area due to high crime.	Police dispatch log	No patrol cars dispatched to defendant's street in prior 4 months.	Inconsistent with defendant's characterization of needing to defend family against high-crime in the neighborhood.

not be admissible in the prosecution's case-in-chief. We do not suggest that mental health professionals acquire the habit of "playing lawyer" by trying to guess whether or not various items of evidence are, or will be, admissible. We do suggest, however, that clinicians initially refuse to consider any third-party information that is *known* to be inadmissible, as the ethical rules seem to require [see § 4.05(e)(2)]. Only after completing their usual investigation and arriving at a formulation should they decide whether to review the evidence known to be inadmissible. In this way, they can assure the court that they have developed a formulation that has not been contaminated by exposure to the inadmissible evidence.

A second concern is *validity* [see § 3.02(d)]. For instance, the statement of a co-defendant or a relative of the defendant may be suspect; the co-defendant may duplicitously want to place the entire blame on the defendant while the family member may want to absolve a loved one he or she knows is

guilty. Clinicians should also be circumspect about relying on statements by defendants whose intelligence is low or who may be suffering from mental disorder; the police method of obtaining and recording such defendant's statements may significantly influence the validity (in the clinical sense) of the information gathered. Examiners should be particularly careful with confessions written in formal, stilted, first-person language (e.g., "I, John Doe, on the evening of November 4, did break and enter . . ."). Such "confessions" may actually be police summaries of the defendant's words which consciously or unconsciously screen out important diagnostic information, such as language reflecting a formal thought disturbance.

One such confession, for instance, described the defendant's robbery of a liquor store and subsequent escape on foot, during which he hid under a front porch from pursuing police officers. Because the defendant had been in psychiatric treatment during the nine-month period after charges were filed, suspicion developed that this relatively straightforward account misrepresented the defendant's true state at the time of the confession. Accordingly, a concerted effort was made to obtain a transcript of the defendant's actual words. Obtained from the prosecutor's office, the confession read:

> Got a drink of water gas station with the dog walked through the blocks store opened, sign out of window walked in dog layed on step a car drove up near by asked 4 matches sorry eyed, didn't use them till bottle of brew was put in the bag with the money and out the door dogs noticed by passerby. Drove away crossed street other lawnway "south" of first house cut into block and lawns path took behind to porch and beneath I hide opened bottle left prints on door and bottle 2 cigarette butts. I knew a brunt check bag cover policeman shot a definite three times, as leaving porch space after asking questions to the house owner of the dog, and demanding me to leave out of there. I ran when crossed the first set of tracks hid again till rain ceased search of men Margarette not anywhere still cursing went over to vacant building and slept without change. Awoke to noon had a beer when met the old lady. Left to foot doctors office and received warranted arrest there.

Clearly, the defendant's "word salad" confession produces a different impression regarding his mental state near the time of the offense than could be gleaned from the cleaned-up version that the police had induced him to sign.

Even a verbatim transcript may not ensure a good accounting of the defendant's behavior at the time of the confession, however. For example, in an attempt to lead defendants to admit to certain facts about a case, officers will often ask yes–no questions. A transcript consisting solely of such responses is of diminished value to the clinician. It may be particularly suspect if the responses are of the "yes" variety and come from defendants of low intelligence, who have a tendency to acquiesce to persons in authority.[420] In short, the clinician performing an MSO evaluation must constantly be alert to validity problems.

(2)   Phases and Tone of the Defendant Interview

Currently there is no widely used standard interview procedure for MSO evaluations. It is possible to outline a relatively typical interview process, however, consisting of six phases.

The first phase involves orientation. The examiner first introduces those participating in the interview. The purpose of the interview is then explained, as well as any limitations on confidentiality (e.g., the fact that a report of the evaluation will go to the prosecution [see § 4.05(d)]). The examiner also explains any special equipment in use, such as a one-way mirror, recording devices, and the like. The defendant is asked to state his or her perception of the purpose and potential uses of the evaluation and is also invited to ask questions when uncertainties exist.

The second phase involves obtaining a developmental and sociocultural history from the defendant. At this stage many of the questions are relatively innocuous, and the interchange helps establish rapport and give the examiner a feel for how the individual functions in society. A third, related phase involves an assessment of present mental status, including current or recent symptoms of thought, mood, perception, or behavioral disturbance. Such information is suggestive of past mental state, although, of course, one cannot assume that the defendant's status has remained constant.

At the fourth phase the examiner focuses on the crime itself, inquiring about the defendant's recall of thoughts, feelings, and behavior at the time of the alleged crime. The examiner also seeks information regarding situational variables (e.g., intoxicants and actions of others) that may have contributed to the criminal act. Table 8.6 identifies specific areas of concentration at this point in the interview. At the end of this stage, the examiner should have developed a preliminary judgment about the degree and type of disturbance present at the time of the offense as well as at the time of the interview.

If other professionals are participating in the MSO examination, the fifth phase involves conferring with them outside the presence of the defendant and comparing impressions. In addition, if third-party data have been gathered, comparison of the defendant's narrative with others' reports about the crime scenario may give leads to further inquiries. At the sixth phase, if required, the examiner reviews with the client any areas of inconsistent or contradictory information and ex-

Table 8.6
Offense-Related Information from the Defendant

1. Defendant's present "general" response to offense—for example:
   a. Cognitive perception of offense
   b. Emotional response

2. Detailed account of offense
   a. Evidence of intrapsychic stressors—for example:
      1. Delusions
      2. Hallucinations
   b Evidence of external stressors—for example:
      1. Provoking events
      2. Fear or panic stimulants
   c. Evidence of altered state of consciousness—for example:
      1. Alcohol-induced
      2. Drug-induced
   d. Claimed amnesia
      1. Partial
      2. Complete

3. Events leading up to offense
   a. Evidence of major changes in environment—for example:
      1. Change in job status
      2. Change in family status
   b. Relationship with victim
   c. Preparation for offense

4. Postoffense response
   a. Behavior following act
   b. Emotional response to act
   c. Attempts to explain or justify act

plores any potentially important areas that the defendant was initially reluctant to discuss.

The examiner's interviewing style may vary, depending on the phase of the interview, the attitude or mental state of the defendant, and the consistency of the information received. If the client is depressed, guarded, or of low intelligence, the examiner may have to be more active throughout the interview; with clients who are cooperative and verbal, the examiner may be fairly low key while obtaining general or historical information. At the fourth and sixth phases—reconstruction of MSO—the examiner will be most active, soliciting details involving actions, feelings, perceptions, reactions, and memories of the alleged criminal act. The examiner may also

ask for repeated narratives from the defendant, looking for inconsistencies across versions or internal inconsistencies in a version. Often, one sees use of the "spiraling" approach; the examiner first elicits a brief general account of the offense, but subsequent queries focus to an increasingly greater extent on detail.

The examiner's tone may vary significantly as well: It can be receptive and supportive or skeptical and confrontive, depending on perceptions of the defendant's honesty and candor [see § 3.07 for discussion of various techniques for detecting malingering]. Suspected malingering should not always trigger confrontation, however. The approaches to be employed will depend on a variety of factors, including the nature of the suspect's symptoms (e.g., cognitive versus functional impairment), the client's level of cooperation with less confrontive structured testing procedures, and the availability of third-party sources which can be used to challenge the defendant. Furthermore, clinicians should be aware that some defendants will have a psychological need to "save face" in the process of admitting their feigning. Therefore, we recommend that when confrontation *is* used, clinicians adopt an "understanding" posture, perhaps prefacing the confrontation with acknowledgment of the defendant's legal situation and an expression of appreciation that such circumstances might reasonably induce people to exaggerate their symptoms. This tack is more likely than others (e.g., hostile, accusatory confrontation) to convince defendants to confess their feigning and subsequently interact in a more candid and forthright manner.

In summary, the examiner's style and tone of interviewing in an MSO evaluation may vary, depending on a number of factors. Significantly, the examination process may call for the clinician to be active and directive, confrontive, and accusatory—in stark contrast to a therapeutic session.

(3)   Testing, Hypnosis, and Other Special Procedures

As Chapter 3 indicated, forensic clinicians have at their disposal several specialized procedures that may assist in eliciting information from the defendant. Most of these procedures should be used sparingly in the MSO context, however. Although they can be very useful under specific circumstances, virtually none of them should be seen as having routine forensic application.

Probably the most controversial implementation of this stance is in connection with psychological testing. In the minds of many practitioners, such testing should be an integral part of all MSO evaluations. Cameron's comments are representative:

> Clinical psychologists generally utilize a standardized, self-report personality inventory in conjunction with one or two other tests usually of the projective type; however, any reliable psychological evaluation of a defendant should consist of an extensive battery of tests, both of the self-report personality inventory nature and projective techniques.[421]

Despite this apparently common practice, however, we suggest a much more limited role for testing in the MSO evaluation. The reasons for this position, discussed in full in § 3.03(b), can be summarized briefly here. First, psychological tests provide information about *current* functioning, whereas an MSO examination seeks to reconstruct the defendant's *prior* mental state. Some aspects of personality and behavior may be relatively stable over time (e.g., intelligence), but most conditions of interest in the MSO examination change naturally (the cyclical nature of some disorders, spontaneous remission, reactions to situational factors or to medication, etc.). Unless the testing takes place soon after the time of the offense, it will often provide information that is only marginally relevant. Second, and perhaps even more important, tests tap a general level of functioning, whereas the behaviors of interest in the MSO evaluation are relatively specific (e.g., thoughts or feelings about the particular victim or situation). Third, the professional literature is barren in terms of sound empirical studies demonstrating either that psychological test data are useful as a means of establishing a link between particular diagnostic conditions and legally relevant behavior in individual cases or that they are useful for assigning individuals to discrete legal categories (e.g., sane vs. insane).[422] Although testing can certainly perform a corroborative function [see § 3.07(b)], it generally should not play a primary role in MSO evaluations.

This analysis applies to other laboratory procedures as well. As noted in the discussions about MSO and epilepsy [see § 8.04(b)],[423] for instance, knowing that a defendant may produce an abnormal EEG in the laboratory gives no particular assurance that seizure activity was present at some past point in time. Furthermore, at best such tests can suggest what a person's behavior *may* have been like; they provide no certain information about the specific thoughts, feelings, motives, or behaviors that constituted the mental state sought to be reconstructed. Similar logic applies to more contemporary procedures, such as brain-imaging techniques that identify physical characteristics of the brain which may be correlated with a diagnosis such as schizophrenia. Although such data may be supportive of a general diagnosis, they are not likely to be informative regarding the specific thoughts, beliefs, or feelings that may have been contributory to the alleged crime.

Hypnosis and narcoanalysis are other fairly commonly used forensic techniques, at least when amnesia is claimed. If the various interview approaches alluded to in the previous section do not provide sufficient information to determine whether the amnesia is feigned, an interview of the defendant under the influence of hypnosis or a general anesthetic may indeed by indicated [see, e.g., the Wertz report, §19.04(a)]. Before using these techniques, however, the clinician should be satisfied that the type of amnesia present is potentially recoverable, make clear to the parties that information that is recovered may be suspect, and adhere to procedures that guard against fabrication or confabulation [see generally § 3.06].

In summary, we suggest that laboratory tests of present mental state, particularly psychological tests, have much less relevance to the MSO evaluation than has previously been claimed. We regard these procedures as supplementary to interview and investigative procedures, and we urge forensic examiners to admit candidly the limited use of these techniques for reconstructing MSO. Expert witnesses should be prepared to concede the modest reliability and validity of most tests for purposes of diagnosis and to make other appropriate qualifications as needed to ensure that the trier of fact is not misled regarding the power or precision of these techniques.

8.07. Formulating an Opinion

As a result of the investigation and reconstruction of a defendant's MSO, clinicians should have a wealth of information that is potentially useful to the judge and jury. How best should they assimilate and present the findings?

In Chapter 1, a seven-level typology of inferences about mental state was discussed in some detail [see § 1.04(a)]. It ranged from straightforward observations about behavior (e.g., wringing of hands) to opinions on the ultimate legal issue (e.g., the defendant was sane at the time of the offense). As we stress throughout this volume, mental health professionals should generally be reluctant to offer inferences at levels 6 and 7, which require a social and moral judgment or a legal interpretation that is usually not within the realm of mental health expertise. As the data permit, however, inferences at other levels are defensible if based on specialized knowledge that will help factfinders or on a specialized skill that can produce otherwise inaccessible knowledge.

Generally, as we suggested in § 8.02(c)(2), the most relevant inferences will be those based on the defendant's conscious reasons for committing the offense (which may be ascertained from the defendant or inferred from other information). However, there may be cases in which a person's unconscious "reasons" appear to explain the person's behavior best. The following two subsections look at both types of formulations.

(a) Behavioral Formulations

In reporting on defendants' conscious reasons for acting, forensic examiners can usually offer, at a minimum, extensive descriptive information (levels 1 and 2) based on their own observations and those of their investigative sources. When they observe a pattern of behavior over time (e.g., through the social history study) or a complex of behaviors recognizable as a clinical syndrome, constructs or diagnoses can also be provided; with appropriate caution, examiners may even elaborate on behaviors often associated with the syndrome or diagnosis—for example, type and degree of cognitive impairment, perceptual

disturbances, range and control of emotional expression, and so on (levels 3 and 4).

With respect to the role of diagnosis (level 4), a few words are in order. The importance of diagnosis to reconstructive evaluations has been both overstated and understated. Its importance has been overstated by those mental health professionals who have fashioned crude diagnostic decision rules for formulating their opinions on legal insanity[424]; as the empirical data in § 8.04 illustrate, psychosis does not equal insanity. The position at the other extreme is that of Morse,[425] who argues that diagnoses are not only not dispositive in legal cases but are *irrelevant*. He avers that diagnoses are abstractions that tell the trier of fact nothing about a defendant's specific legally relevant behavior and are not even translatable (at least by mental health witnesses) into legal terms such as "mental disease or defect."

Our position is closer to that of Morse. But we think he somewhat understates the utility of diagnosis to clinicians, lawyers, and factfinders. First, determining which diagnoses are present may help forensic examiners calibrate their sights. For instance, as a legal matter, certain diagnoses rarely support an insanity defense; indeed, as noted in § 8.02(c)(1), some jurisdictions explicitly limit the applicability of specific diagnoses to certain mental state defenses (e.g., drug or alcohol intoxication may be excluded as a basis for legal insanity). Knowledge of these diagnostically based legal limitations should help keep speculative tendencies in check.

Similarly, a diagnosis may provide the *lawyer* with a shorthand device for assessing the probable legal relevance of the findings. It may also help determine the particular legal doctrine (e.g., insanity vs. automatism) that will be the focus of the defense's case.

Finally, clinicians' knowledge of different disorders can be of help to factfinders. Contrary to Morse's assertion, for instance, it may assist in determining the presence of a legally sufficient "mental disease or defect." Although we agree with Morse that diagnoses are generally not translatable into this legal concept, they may nonetheless provide the factfinder with information about the fit between a defendant's mental state and the "disease model" underlying the predicate for the insanity defense. For example, factfinders may find useful the fact that disorders such as schizophrenia or major affective disorder—which appear to emanate from biological substrata, remit in response to medication, have a predictable course if left untreated, and can be "chemically induced"[426]—conform to this model better than do disorders that have none of these features. Put another way, psychiatric diagnosis may facilitate discussion of etiological issues that the factfinder might consider important (e.g., was the defendant's behavior biologically, characterologically, or situationally caused?). Along the same lines, as noted in § 8.02(c)(1), testimony about diagnosis may help the factfinder assess the relevant severity of a disorder by allowing reference to the nosological hierarchy of impairment (psychoses, borderline personalities, personality disorders).[427]

Diagnostic information may also be of some value to the factfinder in evaluating the type of impairment caused by the mental disorder. For instance, the small amount of clinical research on legally relevant behavior that does exist, such as the incidence of violence in different diagnostic groups, may interest judges and juries; to make such information relevant to a particular case, the diagnosis of the defendant must be mentioned.[428] It may also help the factfinder (as it does the clinician) to assess the defendant's credibility (e.g., is X's assertion that he did not develop multiple personalities until age 40 consistent with the MPD/DID diagnosis?).

Despite all these potential uses of diagnoses, however, we reiterate that a diagnosis, standing alone, is virtually useless to the legal system. The most relevant information is that specifically focused on the accused's characteristic thoughts, feelings, and beliefs. Put in clinical terms, symptoms are more important than diagnoses to resolution of legal issues.

The same sort of approach is recommended if and when the clinician proceeds to level 5—the relationship of the clinically relevant behavior to the alleged criminal act. Clinical testimony can be useful here, but only to the extent the clinician sticks to providing informed speculation about the defendant's judgment, concentration, focus of attention, interpersonal functioning, and other aspects of experience at this particular point in time. In this regard, it should be recalled that the legal doctrines discussed earlier in this chapter tend to sort into defenses based on either cognitive impairment (e.g., *M'Naghten,* first prong of ALI, and diminished capacity) or volitional impairment (e.g., irresistible impulse, second prong of ALI, and automatism). Cognitive impairment may be reflected in a variety of ways, but most typically through perceptual distortions (e.g., hallucinations), deviant thought content (e.g., delusions or idiosyncratic interpretations of ordinary events), or disruptions in the thought process (e.g., confused thoughts, disorganized thoughts, or illogical thoughts). Volitional impairment is most obviously reflected in states in which cognitive control mechanisms appear to be functionally disengaged, as in dissociative or depersonalization episodes and confusional states following head trauma or epileptic seizure (the postictal phase), or in cases in which criminal behavior occurs *despite* a desire not to commit it (consider Case Study 8.2).

Ultimately, however, forensic examiners should not be overly concerned with which particular MSO theory is being pursued in a given case. That issue should be left to the lawyers. This differentiation of role is most likely to occur if experts adhere to the ethical admonition to avoid ultimate-issue testimony and keep their statements at the descriptive and inferential levels (1 through 5). When they do not, they can be dragged into semantic battles over the language of the legal test (e.g., whether the defendant lacked "substantial capacity") or about legally defined mental states that cannot be directly assessed (e.g., "malice").[429] In short, we suggest that clinicians follow Morse's recommendation that they simply explain the ways in which clinical symptoms impair defendants' ability to act in the legally prescribed manner.[430] The following cases give illustrations of possible formulations relating symptoms of psychopathology to legally relevant behavior.

Case 1: Delusional Beliefs. A defendant charged with unlawfully driving away a bus was diagnosed as suffering from paranoid schizophrenia, with symptoms including delusions of grandeur at the time of the offense. Believing that he was a high government official, he commandeered a bus from a Greyhound Terminal at 6:00 in the morning. The clinical formulation included the following:

> Mr. Doe knew that he needed to return to his home city. While he indicated to me that he knew that the Greyhound bus did not literally belong to him, he stated that he felt entitled to take it. Mr. Doe described the strong belief, which was of course erroneous, that he was an important law enforcement official—specifically, the FBI director. It should be noted that records from several prior psychiatric hospitalizations describe similar exaggerated and erroneous beliefs of this type by Mr. Doe in the past. Thus it appears feasible that his delusional belief may have contributed to his unlawfully taking the bus, as he reported reasoning that he had the discretionary authority to commandeer public transportation vehicles in the execution of his official duties. It appears that Mr. Doe may have had some difficulty distinguishing between his legitimate authority, and the authority he imagined himself to have as a result of his illness.

Case 2: Mental Retardation. A mildly retarded young man was charged with third-degree sexual misconduct after approaching a woman outside the lion's cage at the city zoo, grabbing her from behind and briefly fondling her breasts before running away. The clinical formulation included the following:

> Mr. Roe is a mildly retarded young man who functions, intellectually, in the lower 1–2% of the population of persons his age. During psychological testing he was presented with hypothetical social situations involving two or more people and asked to describe what might be going on between them. In most instances his responses were brief, poorly articulated, and reflected a poor understanding of how social relationships are developed and appropriately maintained. This is consistent with the information provided by family members, who indicated that Mr. Roe does not know how to approach other people or make friends; significantly, he is described as shy and uncomfortable around women, having had no dating or courting experience to speak of.
>
> When asked to describe what happened at the zoo, Mr. Roe provided a factual account which, consistent with what I have already described regarding his limited social skills, reflects his naiveté in these matters. He reported that he had seen his cousin and girlfriend "hugging" on each other as they walked through the zoo with him, and he noted "It didn't seem like she minded it at all." He also indicated that dur-

ing recess at school, "The boys chase the girls around the playground and grab them. They usually just laugh and giggle. . . . I figured she [the victim] would too."

In summary, Mr. Roe is a mildly retarded individual who has extremely poor social skills and very minimal ability to discern appropriate behavior in social contexts, particularly when relationships with women are involved. His intellectual and social impairment appears to make it difficult for him to distinguish between, for example, what is appropriate conduct with classmates on the school playground, and what would be appropriate contact with a stranger in a public place. This difficulty appears to have contributed to the present offense.

Case 3: Dissociation. A young man was charged with second-degree murder. The victim was a woman who had been his date on the evening in question; she died as a result of extensive internal bleeding and ruptured internal organs secondary to a severe vaginal assault. The defendant was amnesic for the incident. The examiner located another woman, the defendant's usual girlfriend, who described a similar but substantially less serious assault on her approximately a week before the crime. She reported:

> While we were making love, he suddenly changed. It was like he was a different person—like he wasn't really there. He looked off to the side, his eyes were half closed and he had this strange look on his face. He kept saying, "You've wanted this for all these years . . . now you're going to get it." And then he shoved his whole hand in me. I don't know who he thought I was, because I've only known him a few months. It didn't matter, because he was off in another world. I yelled and told him to stop, that it hurt, but it was like he didn't even hear me. No response, no recognition, no nothing. Then suddenly he quit, he just changed back into himself. He didn't even know what had happened.

In the clinical formulation, the examiner relied heavily on this witness's account of the assault, offering that the present offense could feasibly have occurred during a similar episode. The examiner suggested that the defendant "may have experienced a brief dissociative episode during which he was unaware of or unresponsive to others in his presence or his impact on them. This impairment in his ability to receive and critically process information, including feedback about his own behavior, would have made it difficult for him to modulate his actions."

These examples illustrate how clinicians might provide descriptive accounts and logical links between symptoms (and diagnoses) associated with conventional psychiatric disturbance and alleged criminal behavior. Similar accounts could be developed to explain the possible impact of hallucinations, the effects of drugs and/or alcohol, or other symptom patterns determined to have been present at the time of an offense [see, e.g., the Wertz and Hedges reports, § 19.04].

(b)   Psychodynamic Formulations

Occasionally, a clinician may feel that a person's recitation of his or her motives for a criminal offense, even though completely "honest," does not provide a convincing explanation for the event. Or perhaps reference to diagnostic concepts and syndromes simply does not adequately describe why the defendant committed the criminal act. Psychodynamic formulations[431] are most often found when the usual constructs (conscious reasons for acting, mental "diseases and defects") do not appear to apply yet the defendant's behavior nevertheless seems illogical or inscrutable. They provide an *interpretation* of defendants' behavior by suggesting unconscious motives for their actions, theoretically originating in their psychosexual development, that are not obvious from their behavior or statements.

Are such interpretations legally relevant? If a person consciously chooses to commit a criminal act, the fact that it was motivated by unconscious "feelings" or "beliefs" does not change its voluntary nature or its intentionality; neither an automatism defense nor a diminished capacity defense would seem to lie in such a case. Yet one could argue that a defendant cannot know about, and therefore cannot control, unconscious motivations and thus cannot be held accountable for actions so motivated. As such, psychodynamic formulations might be offered as the basis for an insanity defense (Was there true "appreciation" of the act? Was there difficulty in "conforming to the requirements of the law?").[432]

Case 4: Unresolved Conflicts. Without resolving this issue, we offer the case of F.N. as an illustration of the potential usefulness of psychodynamic explanations in a legal setting. F.N. was a divorced white male in his mid-20s. One evening he went to the apartment of a woman whom he had known only as an acquaintance of his ex-wife. She recognized him and allowed him to enter the apartment, whereupon he commenced a lengthy and brutal sexual assault involving verbal and physical sadistic acts, including the forcing of various foreign objects into the victim's anal cavity. The case appeared on the surface to be a typical rape; the defendant did not have a documented history of any major psychiatric disorder, and from the victim's account he very clearly knew what he was doing at the time of the offense. However, certain peculiarities in his behavior, as described by the victim, suggested a psychodynamic explanation for the crime. She described him as speaking throughout the ordeal in an unusual voice, and on several occasions he stated to her rhetorically, "How do you like getting it from a big stud Mexican?" Because the defendant was Caucasian, the comment made no sense. The comment, plus the severity of the attack, suggested that the defendant was symbolically acting out hatred that was intended for someone else.

When the defendant was interviewed by the forensic examiner, he recalled little of the assault. Exploration of the defendant's psychosexual history, however, revealed some startling information. He recalled how his mother had physically coddled and caressed him well into late adolescence, and he intimated that he might have had intimate sexual contact with her at the age of 18. Long after they were living apart, she would continue to call him on the phone and describe in graphic detail her latest sexual encounters. One such occasion that stuck particularly firmly in his memory was his mother's account of her escapades with a "big stud Mexican." In light of these findings and the defendant's amnesia for the assault, a psychodynamic explanation based on repressed anger toward a seducing mother was developed, providing a feasible explanation (although not necessarily a legal excuse) for the crime—one that might otherwise have been unavailable to the factfinder.

Theory-based formulations such as the one just described provide plausible "stories" about unusual defendant behavior when organic-model formulations and commonsensical inferences fail to provide a complete accounting of the available data. In F.N.'s case, the defendant's behavior could be construed as simply a sadistic rape, but such an accounting would not have explained his altered voice quality and repeated (and peculiar) reference to "getting it from a big stud Mexican." Other cases, such as sexually motivated burglaries,[433] also invite a theoretical explanation when the ordinary and preferred models of comprehension leave unanswered questions.

In spite of their intuitive appeal and apparent usefulness, however, psychodynamic formulations carry considerable risks when applied to criminal behavior.[434] One problem is that psychodynamic explanations can be generated to explain virtually every human behavior—criminal or noncriminal, normal or "crazy." The same theoretical constructs and explanatory devices that seem to make sense of unusual behavior also apply to behaviors we would consider perfectly ordinary. In short, psychodynamic theory "overexplains." Thus, at least in jurisdictions where the mental disease or defect threshold is not rigidly applied, virtually every criminal case—including those in which obvious criminal motives appear conscious and controlling—is susceptible to psychodynamic theorizing.

A second problem with such theorizing is that it is usually highly speculative. The main constructs and explanatory devices of the theory are so abstract and flexible that two practitioners from the same school might offer strikingly different formulations; furthermore, neither formulation might be valid by external criteria. A case study reported by Ayllon, Haughton, and Hughes demonstrated these potential foibles of psychodynamic interpretations.[435] Through a one-way mirror, two board-certified psychiatrists observed a woman suffering from chronic schizophrenia compulsively carry a broom with her around the hospital ward. Both confirmed this odd behavior as a symptom of disturbed behavior, but their explanations for so concluding were considerably different:

Dr. X: The broom represents to this patient some essential perceptual element in her field of consciousness . . . it is clearly a stereotyped form of behavior such as is commonly seen in rather regressed schizophrenics and is rather analogous to the way small children or infants refuse to be parted from some favorite toy, piece of rag, etc.

Dr. Y: Her constant and compulsive pacing, holding a broom in the manner she does, could be seen as a ritualistic procedure, a magical action. . . . Her broom would be then (1) a child that gives her love and she gives him in return her devotion, (2) a phallic symbol, (3) the scepter of an omnipotent queen

. . . this is a magical procedure in which the patient carries out her wishes expressed in a way that is far beyond our solid, rational and conventional way of thinking and acting.[436]

With apparent ease, the two psychiatrists generated four at least somewhat conflicting symbolic meanings for the peculiar behavior. Moreover, their psychodynamic insights appeared to have no validity: In fact, the broom-carrying behavior had been acquired and maintained in response to a carefully controlled schedule of reinforcements using cigarettes and was easily extinguished by altering the contingency schedule; the "symptom" was a learned behavior and nothing more.[437] This example also illustrates that because theory-based formulations are speculative, the particular explanation chosen may be more a function of the values and training of the practitioner than of the data in the case at hand.[438]

Given the problems associated with such formulations, we restate our recommendation that psychodynamic opinions that attempt to explain behavior be advanced only when an analysis of a defendant's conscious reasons and motivations for a criminal act, including the possible effects of major psychiatric disorders, fails to provide a satisfactory understanding of the crime scenario. In such cases, the clinician should be prepared to identify the specific features of the case that invite theory-based analysis. He or she should also weigh the applicability of alternative theories, and willingly concede that theory-based formulations other than the one chosen may offer other feasible explanations. Finally, the clinician should be candid about the reasons for selecting the particular theory chosen and should be prepared to discuss the research, if any, on the reliability and validity of formulations based on that theory.

8.08.   Conclusion

As a way of synthesizing the various points made concerning the clinical evaluation of MSO, Figure 8.1 is offered. Note that once the MSO investigation is completed, the clinician can focus on five different types of dysfunction (in the left-hand column of the "Logic Tree") in determining whether the defendant's MSO was legally relevant. As pointed out earlier, the actual MSO de-

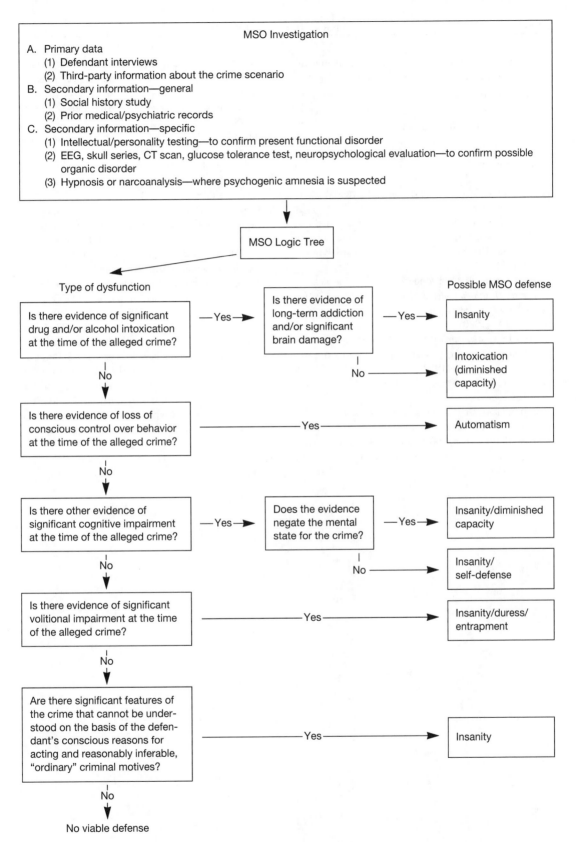

Figure 8.1. *The MSO evaluation.*

fense the defendant presents is not a concern of the clinician's; the figure lists the defense or defenses most probably related to each type of dysfunction merely to tie together the points made in the first half of this chapter.

Bibliography

AMERICAN BAR ASSOCIATION, CRIMINAL JUSTICE MENTAL HEALTH STANDARDS IV (1984).

Loftus T. Becker, Durham *Revisited: Psychiatry and the Problem of Crime,* in PSYCHIATRISTS IN THE LEGAL PROCESS: DIAGNOSIS AND DEBATE (Richard Bonnie ed. 1977).

Richard Bonnie & Christopher Slobogin, *The Role of Mental Health Professionals in the Criminal Process: The Case for Informed Speculation,* 66 VIRGINIA LAW REVIEW 427 (1980).

Charles R. Clark, *Clinical Limits of Expert Testimony on Diminished Capacity,* 5 INTERNATIONAL JOURNAL LAW & PSYCHIATRY 155 (1982).

Durham v. United States, 214 F.2d 862 (D.C. Cir. 1954).

ABRAHAM GOLDSTEIN, THE INSANITY DEFENSE (1967).

HENRY HART, PUNISHMENT AND RESPONSIBILITY (1968) (see particularly pp. 90–112 on unconsciousness).

M'Naghten's Case, 10 Cl. F. 200, 8 Eng. Rep. 718 (H.L. 1843).

MICHAEL MOORE, LAW AND PSYCHIATRY: RETHINKING THE RELATIONSHIP (1984) (see in particular chs. 6, 10).

NORVAL MORRIS, MADNESS AND THE CRIMINAL LAW (1982).

Stephen Morse, *Failed Explanations and Criminal Responsibility: Experts and the Unconscious,* 68 VIRGINIA LAW REVIEW 971 (1982).

MICHAEL PERLIN, THE JURISPRUDENCE OF THE INSANITY DEFENSE (1994).

Norman G. Poythress & Christopher Slobogin, *Psychological Constructs Relevant to Defenses of Insanity and Diminished Capacity,* in SCIENTIFIC REFERENCE MANUAL (David L. Faigman, David Kaye, Michael J. Saks, & Joseph Sanders eds. 1997).

Christopher Slobogin, *The Guilty But Mentally Ill Verdict: An Idea Whose Time Should Not Have Come,* 53 GEORGE WASHINGTON LAW REVIEW 494 (1985).

Landy F. Sparr, Michael E. Reaves, & Roland M. Atkinson, *Military Combat, Posttraumatic Stress Disorder, and Criminal Behavior in Vietnam Veterans,* 15 BULLETIN AMERICAN ACADEMY PSYCHIATRY & LAW 141 (1987).

HENRY STEADMAN, MARGARET A. MCGREEVY, JOSEPH P. MORRISSEY, LISA A. CALLAHAN, PAMELA CLARK ROBBINS, & CARMEN CIRCINCIONE, BEFORE AND AFTER HINCKLEY: EVALUATING INSANITY DEFENSE REFORM (1993).

United States v. Brawner, 471 F.2d 969 (D.C. Cir. 1972).

CHAPTER NINE

Sentencing

9.01. Introduction

"Sentencing" is the dispositional phase of the criminal process. A sentence may be imposed only after conviction. In the Anglo-American system, sentencing practices have been governed by one or more of the following goals: retribution, deterrence, incapacitation, and rehabilitation.[1]

The retributive approach to punishment focuses on ensuring that the offender receives the punishment that is "deserved." The only consideration is the culpability of the offender as measured by the nature of the crimes that have been committed and the mental state of the offender at the time they were committed. The more blameworthy the crime, the more punishment the offender should receive.

Deterrence as a goal of punishment is usually divided into general and specific types. Like the retributive principle, general deterrence focuses on the nature of the offense that has been committed. Rather than measuring punishment according to its relative culpability, however, general deterrence looks at how much punishment is needed to inhibit people from committing the type of crime in question. The empirical basis for assuming that a particular term of imprisonment will "deter" the commission of a particular crime more or less than another term is weak.[2] But it is obvious that, in general, punishment of offenders provides some disincentive to the rest of the population to commit crimes. Many commentators, from Jeremy Bentham onward,[3] have considered deterrence to be the sole or principal goal of punishment.

Specific deterrence, on the other hand, aims at deterring not society at large but the person being punished. Implementing this principle requires assessing the amount of punishment necessary to teach the *particular offender* a lesson. As such, it is closely related to both the incapacitation and the rehabilitation goals of punishment.[4]

Incapacitation is designed to prevent further crimes by the offender. Like specific deterrence, and unlike the retributive and general deterrence principles, it focuses on what the offender *will* do (if not punished) rather than on what the offender has already done.[5] The predictions the incapacitation model requires can often be very difficult to make [see § 9.09(c)], producing a great likelihood that punishment could be imposed erroneously. Nonetheless, incapacitative goals have played a prominent role in sentencing policy.

Punishment based on rehabilitation also requires a difficult prediction: Is the offender treatable? Further, it is based on the shaky assumption that offenders can be "cured" of their criminal tendencies through treatment programs [see § 9.07(b)].[6] Like the specific deterrence and incapacitation concepts, the rehabilitative approach to punishment is more oriented to the particular offender and less attuned to the nature of his or her offense than either the retributive or general deterrence goals.

Of the five goals described, only general deterrence does not raise clinical issues. The culpability assessment required for retributive punishment can involve psychological inquiries similar to those connected with the insanity defense and related doctrines. The specific deterrence and incapacitation goals could involve a clinician in an assessment of dangerousness or the related evaluation of whether particular treatment will curtail antisocial behavior. And the rehabilitation goal obviously even more directly asks treatment questions.

Since mental health professionals have been involved in the criminal process (i.e., since the end of the last century), the influence of these various punishment goals has varied considerably, and with it the role of mental health professionals at sentencing. At times the offender-driven, forward-looking rehabilitative and incapacitative goals prevailed, not coincidentally when faith in the behavioral sciences was at its height. At such times, mental health professionals have been heavily involved in correctional schemes. At other times, the offense-focused, backward-looking retributive and deterrence goals have dominated, and the role of mental health professionals has been more circumscribed.

This chapter begins with a brief overview of the history of sentencing. It then compares the rehabilitative/incapacitative model of sentencing (sometimes called the "therapeutic" model) with the retributive/deterrent model (sometimes called the "just deserts" model) in terms of premises, the roles of the various participants, and the typical procedures used. There follows a discussion of "special" sentencing statutes, including those for repeat or habitual offenders, sex offenders, youthful offenders, and those addicted to narcotics. A separate section on capital sentencing, which raises special issues for forensic evaluators, is included. Finally, the chapter discusses, from both the research and evaluation perspectives, the three issues that mental health professionals are most likely to confront during the sentencing phase: treatment needs assessment, cul-

pability determinations, and predictions of future risk.

9.02.   A Brief History of Sentencing

PROBLEM 9.1

The legislature has decided to revamp its sentencing scheme. A criminal justice subcommittee has been appointed the task of drafting legislation on the use of psychiatric information in the sentencing process. It has asked you to testify on this issue. Specifically, you are to address (1) whether you prefer indeterminate or determinate sentencing (or perhaps both, depending on the type of person being sentenced); (2) under the scheme you prefer, what role mental health professionals should play; and (3) under either scheme, what type of procedures should be followed for making clinical determinations relevant to sentencing.

The United States utilizes imprisonment at a higher rate per capita and has longer prison terms than any other Western country.[7] But imprisonment has not always been the norm in Anglo-American law. In England, early common law made death the penalty for all offenses except petty larceny and mayhem.[8] Even for the latter crimes, imprisonment was not common; the stocks and corporal punishments were the usual sanction. The same held true in colonial America, where incarceration was rare. Corporal punishment and banishment from the community were frequent for crimes of violence, while fines and restitution were imposed for economic crimes.[9]

By the middle of the 19th century, however, imprisonment had become commonplace. Antipathy toward execution and physical punishment as routine penalties played a role in this change, as did the disappearance of places of exile. In addition, a belief emerged that one purpose of sentencing was reformation of the offender. Criminality came to be explained as "a function of defective moral training, a byproduct of rapid urbanization and industrialization. The proposed solution was programs of moral training . . ." which could best take place in an enclosed environment, separate from the criminalizing influences of modern society.[10]

As this comment indicates, retributive and deterrence principles, which had dominated sentencing policy up to this time, began to give way to rehabilitative concerns. After the Civil War, the rehabilitative goal exerted an even stronger influence. Rooted in the philosophy of "positivism," it promised that the causes of crime could be identified and cured.[11] It found formal expression in 1870 in the enunciation of a Declaration of Principles by the National Prison Congress, which asserted that crime is

> a moral disease, of which punishment is the remedy. The efficiency of the remedy is a question of social therapeutics, a question of the fitness and the nature of the dose. . . . *[P]unishment is directed not to the crime but the criminal.* . . . The supreme aim of the prison discipline is the reformation of criminals, not the infliction of vindictive suffering.[12] [Emphasis added]

Probably the single most important consequence of this philosophy was not the move toward imprisonment, which undoubtedly would have occurred in any event, but the notion of indefinite sentences. The National Prison Congress recommended that such "indeterminate" terms be imposed to allow reformation to occur on an individual basis, unhampered by artificial time constraints. In the Congress's view, the ultimate length of a sentence should be determined by the success of the rehabilitation effort in a particular case. This approach was quite different from early sentencing practices, where the penalty imposed depended on the offense rather than the offender, and little discretion was left either to the sentencing judge or to prison authorities.[13]

The positivist movement resulted in the revision of sentencing laws in almost every state. By 1922, 37 states had enacted indeterminate sentencing statutes, and most of the rest had parole systems functionally similar to the indeterminate sentence.[14] Increased confidence in the efficacy of psychiatric treatment also gave rise to indeterminate sentencing provisions for "special populations" (e.g., "sex offenders" and "youthful offenders") thought to be particularly amenable to clinical treatment [see § 9.04(b), (c)]. By 1948, the United States Supreme Court was able to describe the rehabilitative model as the

prevalent modern philosophy of penology that the punishment should fit the offender and not merely the crime. The belief no longer prevails that every offense in a like legal category calls for an identical punishment without regard to the past life and particular habits of a particular offender. . . . Retribution is no longer the dominant objective of the criminal law. Reformation and rehabilitation of offenders have become important goals of criminal jurisprudence.[15]

Not surprisingly, the rehabilitation model's focus on the attributes of the individual offender and on "curing" offenders so that they would not offend again resulted in an infusion of psychiatric terminology and methodology into the prison system: An inmate was "classified," the functional equivalent of diagnosis; treatment plans were established; and the inmate's progress was closely monitored.[16] It also led to the employment of an array of clinicians and administrative personnel (on parole boards) who decided when an offender had been rehabilitated sufficiently to warrant release from prison.

The rehabilitative/incapacitative model enjoyed primacy until the mid-1970s. At that time, however, it came under serious attack, on a number of grounds. One such ground was the perceived failure of mental health professionals to implement the goals of the model successfully.[17] Studies showed, for example, that prison rehabilitation was simply not occurring,[18] and that clinicians could not reliably predict future behavior based on the rehabilitative efforts that were attempted.[19] Indeed, in 1980 two commentators suggested that the move away from the rehabilitative model was in part an effort to "empty the basket of what is perceived to be its psychological and psychiatric refuse."[20]

But the perceived failings of the clinical professions were only partially responsible for the hostile reaction to indeterminate sentencing. The political left complained that such sentencing "legitimated the expansion of powers used in practice to discriminate against disadvantaged groups and to achieve covert organizational goals (such as alleviating court backlogs and repressing political opposition),"[21] while the political right favored determinate sentencing primarily as a means of ensuring more certain punishment. Others speculated that the rehabilitative model might actually be countertherapeutic:

> The principal practical effect of an emphasis on "cure" has been to encourage convicts to view their time in prison as an exercise in theatre. They "volunteer" for group therapy and other rehabilitative programs, say the right things about the help that they have received, and even find Christ and become guinea pigs for medical experimentation in hypocritical efforts to curry favor with parole boards. In addition, it has become increasingly apparent that the very indeterminacy of indeterminate sentences is a form of psychological torture.[22]

Along the same lines, Hogarth asserted that "[i]t can be demonstrated that the rehabilitative ideal has led to neither humane nor effective sentencing decisions. Rather, it has led to massive disparity in the name of individualization, and longer sentences in the name of treatment."[23]

The suggested antidote for all these ills was to make sentencing more predictable to the offender and to the community, by once again focusing on the offense rather than the offender and by limiting judicial and prison official discretion.[24] So-called determinate sentencing has gained increasing popularity since Maine enacted the first statute endorsing its philosophy in 1976. By the mid-1990s, at least 20 states had passed major revisions of their sentencing laws aimed at narrowing the permissible range of sentence.[25] In addition, in 1984, the federal government required determinate sentencing in the federal courts.[26]

Yet determinate sentencing has been criticized as well. Both initial studies and more recent research on the impact of revised state statutes have echoed the same concerns: (1) most determinate sentencing schemes have done nothing to curb prosecutorial discretion with respect to selection of charges; (2) sentencing disparities still exist across jurisdictions, with minority groups and the unemployed receiving proportionately harsher sentences; (3) the reduction of judicial discretion in considering individual characteristics has led to unjust results; (4) many of the schemes result in unduly harsh penalties independent of any mitigating individual characteristics.[27] More recently, particular attention has focused on federal sentencing, with a number of symposia devoted to the topic.[28] For many of the reasons given above, critics have characterized the federal guidelines as "disastrous" and a "debacle."[29]

Analyzing these various claims about the rehabilitative/indeterminate sentencing model and the retributive/determinate sentencing model requires a more in-depth understanding of the two models. We undertake this task in the next section.

9.03   A Comparison of Rehabilitative and Retributive Sentencing

Today any sentencing scheme can be described along a spectrum ranging from one that wholeheartedly endorses the rehabilitative ideal to one that implements the retributive model. To summarize the import of the foregoing discussion, the primary goal of rehabilitative sentencing is the reform or "cure" of offenders. Sentencing

> is premised on the assumption that a sentencing judge, armed with an intimate knowledge of the offender's character and background and aided by scientific and clinical evaluations, can determine an appropriate sentence and treatment program that will rehabilitate the offender. Under this model, the sentencing judge seeks to define the offender's exact personality and social situations, and then prescribes an "individualized" sentence and treatment program. Because rehabilitation is the primary concern, the sentencing judge theoretically is less concerned with deterring future crime or achieving retribution for society.[30]

In contrast, the retributive model assumes that "those whose criminal actions are equally reprehensible deserve like amounts of punishment."[31] Rehabilitation is a secondary goal, or perhaps not a goal at all. Rather, the objective of exacting "just deserts" for the offense predominates,[32] with the severity of the sentence to be proportionate to the gravity of the defendant's criminal conduct. A related objective is to reduce the disparity of sentences received for conviction of the same offense. The implications of these differing premises in terms of the role of legal decisionmakers, the procedure used, and the role of mental health professionals is explored below.

(a) The Role of Legal Decisionmakers

There are potentially four groups that influence the type and duration of punishment: legislatures, prosecutors, courts, and parole boards. Each sentencing model has different consequences for these decisionmakers.

(1) The Legislature

In nearly all jurisdictions, the legislature establishes the statutory scheme for sentencing. It does this first by defining what constitutes a criminal offense and then by fixing the penalties for each offense or, more commonly, each category of offense. As outlined in § 2.04(a), there are two generic categories of offenses, felonies and misdemeanors, with the former typically carrying penalties of over one year to be served in prison, and the latter bringing penalties of less than one year, served in jail. There are also different classes of felonies and misdemeanors, representing different severity of punishment. For example, in New York there are five major classes of felonies.

Under the rehabilitative/incapacitative model, the sentence for these different classes of crimes is kept relatively open-ended. Thus, for instance, a legislature might provide that for the most serious, "Class A" felonies (e.g., first-degree murder) the minimum penalty ranges from 15 to 25 years and the maximum penalty might be life imprisonment. For a Class B felony the authorized penalty might range from 5 years to 30 years, and so on. As discussed previously, the wide ranges are provided to permit individualization of the sentence by the other decisionmakers, particularly the court and the parole board.[33] The criteria to be used in individualizing are typically unspecified and could relate to the offenders' culpability, treatability, or dangerousness, as well as less legitimate factors.

Under determinate sentencing, on the other hand, sentencing ranges are much more restricted, and individualized variations within the range are permitted only under narrow circumstances having to do with the culpability of the offender, rather than treatability or dangerousness. This notion can be implemented in a number of ways. Under the "presumptive" approach, the legislature establishes three possible terms for each offense, with the middle term to be imposed unless the court specifically finds the existence of statutorily created aggravating circumstances (in which case the higher sentence will be given) or mitigating circumstances (in which case the lower sentence will be assessed).[34] For example, the legislature might establish five years' imprisonment as the presumptive term for armed robbery, but allow a four-year sentence if the defendant can prove a legislatively created mitigating circumstance (e.g., age or mental disturbance), and permit a six-year penalty if the prosecution shows a legislatively created circumstance that allows the more stringent penalty (e.g., multiple counts or prior convictions).

A second type of determinate sentencing scheme is the "definite" sentence approach which, similar to an indeterminate sentencing scheme, involves setting a range of penalties within which the court imposes a sentence.[35] However, unlike an indeterminate sentence, a definite sentence is fixed at the time of sentencing, so the defendant knows the time to be served when the sentence is imposed. Furthermore, judicial discretion is limited because the court may consider only the factors (usually offense-related) set forth by the legislature.

In an effort to develop a third, sophisticated version of determinate sentencing, some legislatures have vested their penalty creation authority in a sentencing commission. By 1993, at least 12 states and the federal government used such commissions.[36] A sentencing commission sets sentencing guidelines by developing an actuarial-like table of penalties, using as criteria the severity of the offense and a prediction factor based primarily on prior criminal record.[37] The table establishes a recommended sentence, which becomes the "tariff" for that particular category of offense. The matrix established by the Minnesota commission is set out in Figure 9.1.

As this discussion suggests, there are many variations of determinate sentencing. A comparative analysis of the first determinate sentencing statutes (Maine, California, Illinois, and Indiana) revealed "vast differences" in the following:

- The constraints on judicial discretion to choose or reject incarceration.
- The degree of judicial discretion in setting the sentence.

CRIMINAL HISTORY SCORE

SEVERITY LEVELS OF CONVICTION OFFENSE		0	1	2	3	4	5	6 or more
Unauthorized Use of Motor Vehicle Possession of Marijuana	I	12*	12*	12*	15	18	21	24
Theft-related Crimes ($150-$2500) Sale of Marijuana	II	12*	12*	14	17	20	23	27 25-29
Theft Crimes ($150-$2500)	III	12*	13	16	19	22 21-23	27 25-29	32 30-34
Burglary - Felony Intent Receiving Stolen Goods ($150-$2500)	IV	12*	15	18	21	25 24-26	32 30-34	41 37-45
Simple Robbery	V	18	23	27	30 29-31	38 36-40	46 43-49	54 50-58
Assault, 2nd Degree	VI	21	26	30	34 33-35	44 42-46	54 50-58	65 60-70
Aggravated Robbery	VII	24 23-25	32 30-34	41 38-44	49 45-53	65 60-70	81 75-87	97 90-104
Assault, 1st Degree Criminal Sexual Conduct, 1st Degree	VIII	43 41-45	54 50-58	65 60-70	76 71-81	95 89-101	113 106-120	132 124-140
Murder, 3rd Degree	IX	97 94-100	119 116-122	127 124-130	149 143-155	176 168-184	205 195-215	230 218-242
Murder, 2nd Degree	X	116 111-121	140 133-147	162 153-171	203 192-214	243 231-255	284 270-298	324 309-339

1st Degree Murder is excluded from the guidelines by law and continues to have a mandatory life sentence.

*   one year and one day

Source: Minnesota Sentencing Guidelines Commission, Report to the Legislature 14 (1980)

Figure 9.1. *Minnesota Sentencing Matrix: Sentencing by severity of offense and criminal history.* [From Michael Tonry, *Real Offense Sentencing: The Model Sentencing and Correction Act,* 72 J. CRIM. L. & CRIMINOLOGY 1550, 1558 (1981). Reprinted by permission.]

- The specificity of aggravating and mitigating factors.
- The use of "good time" to reduce the length of incarceration.
- The range of possible penalties for a given offense.
- The degree to which determinate sentencing as practiced in the particular jurisdiction resembled indeterminate sentencing.[38]

In short, as indicated at the beginning of this section, sentencing schemes are probably best evaluated along a spectrum of indeterminate to determinate rather than rigidly categorized as one or the other.

(2)   The Prosecutor

The prosecutor exerts tremendous influence over the sentence in two ways: through selecting the charge and through plea bargaining. The initial charge against a suspect is wholly within the prosecutor's discretion, discretion that is enhanced by the fact that the same conduct may constitute several offenses, each falling within a different offense category and therefore carrying different potential penalties. In New York, for example, a prosecutor could charge a man who assaults and chokes his spouse with several offenses, including attempted murder, a Class A-II felony punishable by a maximum of life imprisonment; assault in the first degree, a Class C felony punishable by a maximum of 15 years' imprisonment; assault in the third degree, a Class A misdemeanor, punishable by no more than one year's imprisonment; or menacing, a Class B misdemeanor punishable by no more than three months' imprisonment. The prosecutor also enjoys similar discretion in disposing of cases through plea bargaining, a process that historically has resolved approximately 90% of all criminal cases short of trial.[39] As discussed in § 2.04(a)(1), there are two types of plea bargaining. In the first, "charge bargaining," the defendant pleads guilty or *nolo contendere* to one charge, while the prosecutor in return agrees to dismiss or reduce other charges. In the second, "sentence bargaining," the defendant pleads guilty to the original charge in exchange for the prosecutor's recommendation of a reduced sentence. In both cases, the court must approve the agreement, but this is usually a formality.

Under the rehabilitative/incapacitative model, this indirect ability to individualize punishment on the part of the prosecutor is not necessarily inappropriate. Even under a retributive approach, this discretion would not be anathema if the criteria used by the prosecutor related solely to an assessment of the offender's blameworthiness. But most determinate sentencing reforms do not address prosecutorial power, meaning that discretion remains unbounded. In fact, studies of federal practice suggest that prosecutorial control over sentencing has increased since enactment of the federal sentencing guidelines.[40] Although efforts have been made in some jurisdictions to reduce or eliminate plea bargaining, they have had little impact upon sentencing.[41] At least one commentator has argued that determinate sentencing statutes will not achieve their objective of eliminating disparity until the prosecutor's power to formulate charges and to bargain for guilty pleas is checked.[42]

(3) The Court

The trial judge imposes sentence in the vast majority of jurisdictions. In a few jurisdictions, however, the jury has sentencing authority,[43] and jury sentencing is the preferred method of sentencing in capital cases [see § 9.05(b)]. In those states in which the jury sentences, the jury will either return a sentence with the verdict or, if the statute calls for a bifurcated proceeding, return its verdict first and then consider sentence. Whether the judge or the jury imposes sentence, a defendant convicted of more than one offense may have the sentences imposed consecutively or concurrently. If the sentences are consecutive, one begins on completion of the other. If the sentences are concurrent they run simultaneously.

Under the rehabilitative/incapacitative model, the court, like the prosecutor, has broad discretion. The court must set a sentence falling within the range set by the legislature; if that is done, the appellate courts as a rule will refuse to disturb the punishment.[44] In shaping the sentence to individual characteristics, the court has a wide variety of options.

1. The court may incarcerate the individual for any term of years within the range established by the legislature.
2. The court may suspend all or part of the sentence.
3. In conjunction with a suspended sentence, the court may require that certain conditions be met to avoid reimposition of sentence; these "probation" conditions can include attendance in treatment programs, "work release," and restrictions on travel.
4. In lieu of sentence, the court may order the payment of a fine to the court or restitution to the victim, or the court may order forfeiture of property, such as contraband or property used in criminal activity. It may also order the offender to engage in work that benefits the community.

In a determinate sentencing scheme, many or all of these options (i.e., sentence suspension, probation, and restitution) may continue to exist. But judicial discretion is much reduced. In addition to having a narrower durational range to work with, the court usually must state in writing the reasons for any deviation from the legislated norm. Further, the typical sentence is readily appealable by either side. Finally, because rehabilitation is no longer the primary goal, and because the statute lists the only aggravating and mitigating circumstances that may be considered, a court in a determinate sentencing jurisdiction must narrow its focus. Rather than looking at the "total" offender, only those offense and offender traits deemed relevant by the sentencing commission or legislature may be considered.

(4)   The Parole Board

The parole board is an independent administrative body, usually composed of a mix of citizens and correctional officials. As noted earlier, in indeterminate sentencing states the parole board controls the length of the imprisonment once an inmate becomes eligible for parole (typically after serving one-third of the sentence). The parole decision is usually based on the seriousness of the inmate's crime, previous offenses, and behavior in prison, with the overall issue being whether the individual is sufficiently rehabilitated to warrant supervised return to the community. In 1972, near the height of the rehabilitative trend, the Supreme Court described parole in the following manner:

> During the past 60 years, the practice of releasing prisoners on parole before the end of their sentences has become an integral part of the penological system. . . . Rather than being an *ad hoc* exercise of clemency, parole is an established variation on imprisonment of convicted criminals. Its purpose is to help individuals reintegrate into society as constructive individuals as soon as they are able, without being confined for the full term of the sentence imposed. It also serves to alleviate the costs to society of keeping an individual in prison. The essence of parole is release from prison, before the completion of sentence, on the condition that the prisoner abide by certain rules during the balance of the sentence.[45]

As the last statement suggests, when parole is granted, it is often accompanied by a set of conditions, similar to those imposed on probationers. For example, parolees may be forbidden to use alcohol or drugs or to associate or correspond with certain individuals; parolees may also be required to seek permission from their parole officers before traveling, changing employment, or operating a motor vehicle. In addition, they are required to report on a regular basis to their parole officers. Violation of any of these conditions may result in revocation of parole and the reinstitution of sentence. Like the court's sentencing decision,

the board's decision on the merits and conditions of parole is generally unreviewable.

The role of the parole board changes significantly in a determinate sentencing scheme. In a few determinate sentencing states, parole has been abolished.[46] In most, the parole board's authority to fix the length of a sentence is drastically diminished by specific guidelines.[47] As in indeterminate states, however, it continues to monitor inmates after release.[48]

(b)   Procedures

Under the Sixth Amendment, the defendant has a right to counsel at the sentencing hearing.[49] But most other rights associated with trial (e.g., adherence to the rules of evidence and a right to cross-examine adverse witnesses) are not constitutionally mandated. Indeed, after reviewing the Supreme Court's decisions addressing the procedures constitutionally required for sentencing, Dix concluded in 1981 that the cases "provide no consistent pattern except perhaps to demonstrate sympathy for the state's interest in preserving flexible and minimally restricted sentencing procedures."[50] More recent Court cases, if anything, reinforce this lax approach to sentencing procedure.[51] The only explicit limitation imposed by the Court is that "misinformation of constitutional magnitude" may not be considered by the sentencing court,[52] and this exception in practice does very little to limit the general rule permitting wide-open inquiry.[53]

As a result, the degree of formality at sentencing is principally a matter for the individual states. With the exception of some special and determinate sentencing schemes, the rights accorded convicted offenders at the sentencing hearing do not approach those due a defendant at trial.[54] Similarly, parole board hearings, whether to decide about release[55] or revocation,[56] are subject to relatively few procedural constraints, and almost always less process than at sentencing.

(1)   The Degree of Formality

The sentencing process is particularly informal under the rehabilitative model, for three reasons. First, the success of individualized sentencing assumes the ability of the judge to "know" the defendant. When this model is operational, the Supreme Court has found "highly relevant . . . if not essential . . . to [the judge's] selection of an appropriate sentence . . . the possession of the fullest information possible concerning the defendant's life and characteristics."[57] Because obtaining information about the defendant is so important, courts have resisted arguments that the legal protections that might diminish access to this information (e.g., the Fifth Amendment's privilege against self-incrimination or the hearsay rules) should apply to sentencing. As the Supreme Court itself has stated, "Modern concepts of individualizing punishment have made it all the more necessary that the sentencing judge not be denied an opportunity to obtain pertinent information by a requirement of rigid adherence to restrictive rules of evidence properly applicable to trial."[58]

Informality is also based, in part, on the assumption that society has "earned" the right to punish a convicted individual. The due process protections associated with trial are in place to reduce error in determining guilt to a permissible level. Once guilt is determined, defendants, because of their convicted status, are thought to have forfeited the right to strict due process protection.

Finally, informality under a rehabilitative model is justified on the ground that the state is acting in the individual's interest in constructing a plan for rehabilitation. Adherence to strict principles of due process, which are applied when the interests of the state and the individual are in conflict, is deemed unnecessary.

Procedures under determinate sentencing schemes are often no more formal than under indeterminate approaches, perhaps because there is still a need for information about the defendant and because the belief persists that a convict is not as deserving of procedural protection. But some have argued that determinate sentencing inherently requires a more formal process. First, recall that under a determinate scheme a judicial finding that an aggravating or mitigating circumstance exists leads to an enhanced or reduced penalty. The traditional response of the legal system when a decisionmaker must determine the existence of a particular fact, especially when there are consequences for individual liberty, is to formalize the

process by adopting an adversarial proceeding in which each party presents evidence and has the right of cross-examination.

Second, as noted above, determinate sentencing schemes usually provide for an appeal of the sentence. To make such review possible, the appellate court needs to examine the reasons for the court's action. Thus, for instance, at least one federal court of appeals has told district courts to "elicit fully articulated objections" by the defendant to the court's factual and legal conclusions.[59]

Third, and most important, an informal process may be conceptually antithetical to sentencing once the rehabilitative ideal has been abandoned for a more punitive sentencing philosophy. As one commentator has argued, "The relaxed practices associated with rehabilitative sentencing cannot be reconciled with a [determinate] sentencing model that does not emphasize values of individualization and treatment"[60]; as sentencing moves from an "inquisitorial" to an "accusatorial" model, it must become more formal to protect individual interests adequately.[61] Such a transformation would not be without precedent. In both civil commitment and juvenile law, more safeguards were applied to the decisionmaking process as the courts rejected the notion that the state's interest was benevolent and defined the primary area of concern as the individual's liberty interests [see §§ 10.02(c), 14.02(d)].

(2) The Presentence Report

If a court rather than a jury imposes sentence, it normally first orders preparation of a presentence report. In federal courts, as is true in many states, the court *must* order preparation of a report unless the defendant, with the court's permission, waives the report or the court finds that the record before it contains information sufficient to enable it to properly exercise its sentencing discretion.[62]

If one is ordered, the report is prepared by a probation officer. Under the rehabilitative model, it is likely to follow a standardized format composed of five core categories[63]: (1) offense information, which includes both the official version and the defendant's version of the facts, information about any co-defendants, and statements of witnesses and victims; (2) prior record, including juvenile adjudications; (3) personal and family data, including the defendant's educational history and physical and mental health; (4) an evaluation section, which consists of alternative sentencing plans and data; and (5) a recommendation for sentencing. In determinate sentencing jurisdictions, on the other hand, the report is much more likely to stick to factors relevant to the offense and prior offenses and to specified aggravating and mitigating circumstances. One observer has noted that, since the advent of determinate sentencing, the federal probation officer has much greater influence over sentencing because of the reliance by the prosecutor and the court on the probation officer's report in deciding the offense category which should control sentencing.[64]

Once this report is submitted to the court, the judge typically holds a conference with the probation officer,[65] followed by the hearing itself. Because hearsay evidence is admissible and often included in presentence reports, the ability of the defendant to obtain a copy of the report is critical. However, in both indeterminate and determinate jurisdictions, the extent to which disclosure is mandated is still debated, and it is less than total in even the most disclosure-oriented jurisdictions [see § 9.06(c)].

(c)   The Role of Mental Health Professionals

Under the rehabilitative/incapacitative model of sentencing, the general role of the mental health professional is obvious. Making treatment assessments, providing information relevant to culpability, and making predictions about future actions all are functions that might be fulfilled by experts in the behavioral sciences. Although some have concluded that providing this type of information inappropriately leads clinicians into "the business of attempting to control people,"[66] mental health professionals have clearly played a prominent role at sentencing when this model holds sway.

Some have predicted that changes toward determinate sentencing will result in greatly decreased clinical participation in the sentencing phase.[67] Because treatability and dangerousness are deemphasized in determinate sentencing

schemes, there is no doubt the clinical role will be different. But to say it will greatly decrease may be an overstatement; even sentencing limited to implementing retributive principles requires input related to culpability. As Monahan and Ruggiero noted early in the determinate sentencing movement,

> [T]o the extent predictions by physicians and psychologists of future criminal behavior are eliminated from the sentencing process, these disciplines will assume a correspondingly larger role as experts on "culpability" during the trial itself, at sentencing, or in post trial "diversionary" commitments imposed in lieu of imprisonment.[68]

In fact, most determinate sentencing statutes invite clinical participation, primarily through the use of mitigating circumstances, proof of which may result in a reduced sentence. For example, the Minnesota guidelines include the following as mitigating circumstances:

(1) the offender played a minor or *passive* role in the crime or participated under circumstances of coercion or *duress.*
(2) The offender, because of physical or *mental impairment*, lacked *substantial capacity* for judgment when the offense was committed.
(3) Other substantial grounds exist which tend to excuse or *mitigate the offender's culpability*, although not amounting to a defense.[69] [Emphasis added]

In other determinate sentencing states, mitigating factors are unspecified but judges continue to rely on "psychiatric reasons" for setting sentences below the presumptive level. Thus, even in jurisdictions in which the court is bound to reduce the presumptive sentence by the same amount for everyone proving a mitigating circumstance, the potential for significant clinical input continues to exist.

9.04.   Special Sentencing Provisions

Most jurisdictions have experimented with special sentencing statutes for discrete populations thought to be significantly different from the mass of criminal defendants. The populations most frequently singled out for special sentencing are repeat offenders, those who have committed or may commit sexual offenses, youthful offenders, and certain types of drug users. As the discussion that follows suggests, some of these statutes have been eliminated or substantially modified as the rehabilitative model has fallen into disfavor.

(a)   Repeat Offender Statutes

By the early 1990s, nearly all jurisdictions had statutes allowing or mandating increased sentencing for those convicted of multiple felonies.[70] These statutes—traditionally called "repeat" or "habitual" offender statutes and more recently labeled "three-strikes-and-you're-out" laws—typically prescribe enhanced sentencing upon conviction of a third or fourth felony. For example, Indiana law defines an habitual offender as a person convicted of two prior unrelated felonies who, on conviction of a third felony, can receive a 30-year term in addition to the usual penalty.[71] A more recent habitual offender law, approved by California voters in 1994, doubles the sentence of felons with one prior conviction for a serious felony and imposes a 25-year-to-life sentence on felons with two prior convictions for violent felonies (even if the third conviction is for a nonviolent offense).[72]

Although these statutes could be justified on retributive grounds (e.g., people who commit three felonies are particularly "evil"), they are most often based on an incapacitative rationale. Fueled by public concern over crime, they assume that "the effect of imprisonment on street crime is a direct function of the rate at which incarcerated offenders would have committed crimes if they were not confined."[73] They have also been criticized, however, both as impractical and for falling most heavily on petty criminals and older offenders who may be approaching the end of their criminal careers.[74] For example, a study of the first 11 months of operation under the California three-strikes law indicated that the plea bargain rate dropped from 94% to 6% for offenders charged with their "third strike"; apparently, most defendants opted to go to through trial (at state expense) rather than suffer the mandatory sentence that would ensue after a third felony conviction.[75] In addition, the vast majority of those facing third-strike charges under the California law were charged with nonviolent offenses.[76]

Despite the harshness of the penalties available under these statutes, they have survived constitutional scrutiny. Indeed, in *Rummel v. Estelle*[77] the Supreme Court upheld a Texas habitual offender statute providing mandatory life imprisonment upon conviction of *any* three felonies, not just serious ones. Rummel was sentenced to life imprisonment under this statute after being convicted of fraudulently using a credit card to obtain $80 worth of goods, and after the prosecutor had shown that he had previously been convicted of forging a check for $28.36 and of obtaining $120.75 by false pretenses. Rummel's argument that the sentence violated the Eighth Amendment prohibition against cruel and unusual punishment was rejected by the Court, which concluded that the penalty was neither disproportionate nor "cruel." The Court later held, in *Solem v. Helm*,[78] that the imposition of a life sentence on a multiple offender may be unconstitutional when, unlike in *Rummel*, there is no possibility of parole. But *Solem* vigorously reaffirmed the general principle that habitual offender statutes are constitutional and that individual sentences will be overturned only in extreme circumstances. The court has thus placed its imprimatur on virtually unlimited legislative discretion in sentencing repeat offenders.[79]

Because habitual offender statutes are not rehabilitative in intent and operate primarily on the basis of accumulated convictions, an objective measure, clinical involvement will be minimal. The only clinical input is likely to be indirect, as defense attorneys try to find ameliorative evidence to avoid conviction for a third felony. Knowledge of these statutes is nonetheless useful as background for the discussion which follows.

(b)   Sexual Offender Statutes

Special sentencing provisions for sexual offenders date back to 1937, when Michigan passed the first "sexual psychopath" law.[80] Within 40 years, 28 states had enacted what came to be known as "mentally disordered sex offender" (MDSO) statutes, designed to divert individuals charged

with multiple sexual offenses to treatment programs of indeterminate length.[81] Similar statutes
aimed at younger offenders—so-called defective
delinquent statutes—were also passed in a number of states.[82] Not surprisingly, however, the rejection of the rehabilitative model in regular sentencing spilled over into this area as well. By
1990, the number of MDSO and defective delinquent laws had dwindled to about a dozen.[83] Recently, however, there appears to be a resurgence
of interest in such statutes, so they are worth
looking at in detail.

The indeterminate sentences authorized by
MDSO laws have two primary goals: the protection of society from sex offenders thought to be
dangerous and the rehabilitation of those offenders.[84] These twin objectives, involving prediction
and treatment, invite clinical participation as
forthrightly as any area of criminal law. In fact,
these statutes "were meant to be harbingers of a
future in which all criminals would be 'treated'
under similar provisions."[85]

The statutes come in a "criminal" and a "civil"
form. The criminal version provides for special
commitment procedures after conviction, whereas the civil version is triggered after a charge for a
sex offense has been filed but *before* conviction.[86]
Despite this difference and the different legal labels, the two types of statutes share several attributes:

- Commission of a sexual offense is required.
- The conduct generally must involve force or
  aggression or involve minors.
- The conduct must be repetitive. Unlike repeat
  offender statutes, however, demonstration of
  specific past offenses is not always required,
  and the idea of repetition may be satisfied by a
  prediction of future conduct.
- The offender must have a mental illness,
  though the term is broad enough to include
  many types of character disorders.
- The individual, once labeled, is to be treated,
  though a finding that the offender is treatable
  is typically not required.
- As indicated above, commitment is indeterminate, based on the individual's continued
  "need for treatment."[87]

Procedures under the two statutes are similar

as well, and are generally more formal than the
usual sentencing proceeding. The additional procedural rigor is the result of *Specht v. Patterson*,[88] a
United States Supreme Court decision holding
that because designating a person a "sexual offender" can lead to significant enhancement of the
normal sentence for the crime, the defendant is
entitled to an adversary proceeding, including notice, a right to a hearing, cross-examination and
presentation of evidence, and a right to counsel.
Although *Specht* dealt with a criminal MDSO
statute, it probably applies to the civil version as
well.[89] At the same time, the Supreme Court has
indicated that the Fifth Amendment's privilege
against self-incrimination does not apply in
MDSO proceedings.[90]

Beginning in the 1970s, MDSO statutes came
under heavy attack. As early as 1977, the Group
for the Advancement of Psychiatry (GAP), originally a proponent of the laws, came to believe
that "sex psychopath and sexual offender statutes
can best be described as approaches that have
failed"[91] and called for repeal of all sexual psychopath statutes. In the mid-1980s, the American
Bar Association (ABA) recommended repeal as
well.[92]

This antipathy toward MDSO statutes was
based on perceived flaws in the assumptions underlying sexual offender legislation, which the
ABA identified as follows:

> (1) there is a specific mental disability call sexu-
> al psychopathy, psychopathy, or defective delin-
> quency; (2) persons suffering from such a dis-
> ability are more likely to commit serious
> crimes, especially dangerous sex offenses, than
> normal criminals; (3) such persons are easily
> identified by mental health professionals; (4)
> the dangerousness of these offenders can be
> predicted by mental health professionals; (5)
> treatment is available for the condition; (6)
> large numbers of persons afflicted with the des-
> ignated disabilities can be cured.[93]

The GAP report and the ABA contested each
assumption. For example, according to GAP, the
categorization process created by sexual psychopath statutes lacks clinical validity. The assumption that a "hybrid amalgam of law and psychiatry can validly label a person a 'sex psychopath' or 'sex offender' and then treat him is
rejected as analogous to creating special cate-

gories of 'burglary offender' statutes or 'white collar' offender statutes."[94] Both the ABA and the GAP also noted the difficulty of predicting sexual dangerousness and asserted that although the statutes promise therapy, they are more means of reassuring the community of its own safety than providing treatment.[95]

Building on the latter point, the GAP also asserted that these statutes compromise clinicians in two ways. First, clinicians may be asked to make "generalizations about sex offenders not grounded in empirical data from the individual case which often do more harm to the individual and society than no statements at all."[96] Second, the absence of meaningful treatment programs for the condition diagnosed raises an ethical as well as practical dilemma for clinicians: "[P]erhaps the worst thing a psychiatrist can do is tailor his opinion to whatever compromised versions of treatment are currently being offered, thus putting himself in the role of sanctioning treatments in which he does not believe."[97]

Although these arguments appeared to persuade many state legislatures to repeal their MDSO laws in the 1970s and 1980s, they did not deter a new wave of MDSO statutes in the 1990s.[98] Indeed, the attack on treatment efficacy may have even lent support to the more recent MDSO statutes, which go well beyond earlier legislation in two ways. First, at least 37 states now require the registration of recidivistic sex offenders with local authorities following their release from prison,[99] with five also providing for the release of identifying information to the public (e.g., the name and address of the offender and the crime resulting in conviction).[100] This type of statute, which has been upheld by at least one state supreme court,[101] reflects not only public concern regarding safety but also doubt that treatment interventions result in reduced recidivism.

More significantly, several states have also enacted statutes that provide for coerced confinement of sex offenders *not* as an alternative to incarceration (as traditional sexual offender statutes provide) but *subsequent* to completion of incarceration. Under Washington's law, for instance, persons found to be "sexually violent predators" can be involuntarily committed for an indeterminate term after serving their sentences.[102] Under the

statute, a sexually violent predator is someone "who has been convicted of or charged with a crime of sexual violence and who suffers from mental abnormality or personality disorder which makes the person likely to engage in predatory acts of sexual violence."[103] The law's "legislative history" asserts that these persons can be subjected to special incarceration terms because they "generally have antisocial personality features which are unamenable to existing mental illness treatment modalities. [Therefore,] the prognosis for curing [them] is poor, [and] the treatment needs of this population are very long term."[104]

These newer statutes can be criticized on the same practical grounds as the original MDSO statutes: "Sexual predators" may be no more dangerous than other types of offenders and, in any event, determining who is a dangerous sexual predator can be very difficult.[105] Because the newer laws do not apply until after a sex offender has served his sentence, they also squarely raise a conceptual problem that was rarely considered in connection with the older statutes (although they share the problem): whether incarceration based solely on dangerousness/incapacitation grounds is permissible.

This last issue requires further comment. Based on the assumption of free will, the law traditionally has required an act before confinement may occur; incarceration based on what a person might do has been considered illegitimate.[106] There are generally thought to be only three exceptions to this general rule: (1) when a person is lacking in free will (i.e., is mentally ill) and thus can be confined without violating the free-will paradigm (as with civil commitment),[107] (2) when confinement based on dangerousness is not long term (as with pretrial detention),[108] and (3) when confinement based on dangerousness is limited by retributive principles (as is true with most indeterminate sentencing schemes, where a sentence range is set according to "just deserts" within which the court and parole board may impose a sentence based in whole or in part on dangerousness concerns).[109]

This tradition appeared to be reaffirmed in the Supreme Court's 1992 decision in *Foucha v. Louisiana*.[110] There the Court ordered the release of a person acquitted by reason of insanity who had since been diagnosed as an antisocial personality and, at least according to the state's doctors, was no longer "mentally ill."[111] The four-member plurality of the Court reasoned that because Foucha had not been convicted and could not be committed (due to the absence of mental illness), he had to be released. As the plurality put it, allowing indeterminate confinement of Foucha "would . . . be only a step away from substituting confinements for dangerousness for our present system which, with only narrow exceptions and aside from permissible confinements for mental illness, incarcerates only those who are proved beyond reasonable doubt to have violated a criminal law."

MDSO statutes may run afoul of the tradition summarized by the plurality in *Foucha*. Given the length and indeterminacy of the confinement they authorize, they clearly do not fit either the second or third exceptions outlined above. The newer statutes are particularly blatant in this regard. At least with the older statutes, incarceration would occur soon after the criminal act and as an "alternative" to a "sentence." With the newer postsentence statutes, however, indeterminate confinement incarceration is permitted *after* the retributive aims of the criminal justice system have been met. Of course, both types of statutes could still be said to fit under the first, "commitment" exception. However, as the Washington legislature candidly admitted in the legislative history quoted earlier, most of the people committed under its statute are likely to be diagnosed as antisocial personalities, the same diagnosis assigned to Foucha, and not one normally associated with "mental illness" or a lack of "free will."[112]

Nonetheless, in *In re Young*[113] the Washington Supreme Court upheld the sexual predator statute against constitutional attack. The state court noted that *Foucha* had never directly held that antisocial personality disorder was not a mental illness but, rather, merely assumed the validity of the state's concession in this regard. It also pointed out that Justice O'Connor, who provided the fifth and deciding vote in *Foucha*, had stressed that if "the nature and duration of detention were tailored to reflect pressing public safety concerns related to the acquittee's continuing dangerousness," then prolonged confinement based on dangerousness might be constitutional. What the state court did not mention is that Jus-

tice O'Connor conditioned this conclusion on the existence of "some medical justification" for the detention. Although elsewhere in its opinion the state court noted the statute's requirement of a treatment plan for every sexual predator, the "medical justification" for such statutes seems weak as long as the GAP's critique of treatment efficacy remains valid [see § 9.07(b)]; indeed, the *Young* court itself emphasized that a person does not have to be treatable to be "ill" for purposes of the statute.[114] In short, it seems fair to say that *Young* recognized a fourth "pressing public concern" exception to the general rule that dangerousness alone cannot form the basis for confinement—an exception that in effect swallows the rule. Nonetheless, in a decision handed down as this book went to press, the United States Supreme Court agreed with the reasoning of the *Young* majority,[115] upholding a statute that permits indeterminate detention of any dangerous sex offender who has a "mental abnormality" or "personality disorder," even if untreatable.

A more insightful approach to the MDSO issue was provided by the Minnesota Supreme Court. That court also upheld an MDSO law[116] but limited the scope of the statute to those who exhibit (1) an habitual course of misconduct in sexual matters, and (2) "an utter lack of power to control sexual impulses," in addition to (3) proof that the person will attack or otherwise injure others.[117] Criterion (2), if applied conscientiously, would restrict sex offender confinement to those cases in which the offender *is* lacking in free will and thus is a legitimate candidate for commitment. The first criterion is also noteworthy in that proof of recidivism should bolster the prediction of dangerousness and gives the extended confinement more of a retributive cast.

That the Minnesota court is serious about these limitations was demonstrated in its subsequent decision in *In re Linehan*.[118] There the court found that because expert testimony on the issue of whether Linehan could control his behavior was inconsistent,[119] the state had failed to demonstrate by clear and convincing evidence that Linehan had "an utter lack of power" to control his sexual impulses. The court also gave careful attention to the practical issue of prediction. Although the court did not address Linehan's argument that the state had failed to prove he would offend again (because of its finding on controllability), it did direct trial courts to consider the following factors when determining dangerousness: (1) relevant demographic characteristics (e.g., age and education); (2) the individual's history of violent behavior, focusing on recency, severity, and frequency of violent acts; (3) base-rate statistics for violent behavior among individuals of the defendant's particular background; (4) environmental stressors (defined by the court as cognitive and affective factors which indicate that the person may be predisposed to respond to stress in a violent or nonviolent manner); (5) the similarity of the present or future context to those contexts in which the person had engaged in past violence; and (6) the person's record in sex therapy programs.[120] In effect, the Court established a legal framework, borrowed principally from the work of John Monahan [see § 10.08(d)], for making the prediction of dangerousness required by the Minnesota statute. Although the courts are unwilling to bar prediction testimony,[121] *Linehan* suggests that arguments that seek to structure such testimony and anchor it in social science literature may have some success.

(c) Youthful Offenders

Special sentencing procedures for "youthful" offenders were pioneered by the federal government with the enactment of the federal Youth Correction Act (YCA) of 1950.[122] Although the statute was repealed in 1984,[123] it is briefly described here as an example of the rehabilitative model at its peak.

Congress enacted the YCA because of perceptions that youthful offenders committed a disproportionate amount of crime and that the penitentiary system had failed in rehabilitating these offenders.[124] Its goal was to "cure" offenders whose youth made them more amenable to treatment than older criminals.[125] The YCA defined a "youth offender" as a "person under the age of 22 years at the time of conviction."[126] An individual between the ages of 22 and up to but not including 26 at the time of conviction could also be sentenced under the YCA if the court found "reasonable grounds" to believe that the defendant would benefit from treatment. The court was to make

this decision after considering the previous record of the defendant as to delinquency or criminal experience; the defendant's social background, capabilities, and mental and physical health; and other pertinent factors.[127]

An offender sentenced under this law was given an "indeterminate" term generally not to exceed six years, with actual confinement not to exceed four years.[128] The parole commission set the length of sentence within these bounds, as it did with adult offenders.[129] If the youthful offender was unconditionally discharged prior to the expiration of the maximum sentence imposed, the conviction was automatically "set aside" and the individual given a certificate to that effect.[130]

The YCA was a pristine example of the rehabilitative model of sentencing. Its repeal is another illustration of the general shift in sentencing ideology and philosophy that transformed the adult and juvenile justice systems from the mid-1980s through the 1990s. Although there has been a resurgence of youthful offender statutes in recent years, their motivation differs from the premise of the YCA. Consistent with the ideological shift to the determinate sentencing model, these newer laws are meant to provide a means of holding juvenile offenders past the age of juvenile jurisdiction, not to provide a flexible treatment disposition [see § 14.02(e)].

(d) Drug-Dependent Offenders

In the mid-20th century, Congress enacted special sentencing provisions for drug-dependent offenders. These provisions called for confinement of an addicted convict for an indeterminate period of treatment for the addiction.[131] Like the YCA, however, they have been repealed.[132] Today, there is no explicit provision in federal law granting special consideration for the addicted offender. In fact, the federal sentencing guidelines explicitly prohibit consideration of addiction as a mitigating factor.[133]

However, federal law still permits the prosecutor to recommend civil commitment of individuals *charged* with a federal criminal offense and who acknowledge an addiction; if the individual successfully completes up to 36 months of treatment, the criminal charge may be dismissed.[134]

Further, a number of state courts have experimented with innovative "drug courts" which divert criminal offenders to treatment programs that are closely monitored by the court and require strict adherence to treatment goals and behavioral objectives. As described by one commentator:

> These court-initiated efforts attempt to break the cycle in which defendants are arrested, spend a short time in jail and are released only to be arrested once again by ensuring that defendants receive treatment for their substance abuse problems. These programs emphasize a "team approach" in which the judge, prosecutor, public defender and treatment provider work together to develop, implement, and monitor a treatment plan for each defendant.[135]

In this area, at least, the rehabilitative ideal has enjoyed some success, perhaps because the retributive model is so clearly ineffective.

9.05.   Capital Sentencing

CASE STUDY 9.1

On the morning of the murder, Miller was released from county jail, where he had been incarcerated for possession of a concealed weapon (a fishing knife). He wandered around town and bought a fishing knife similar to the one that had been taken from him by the police. An employee in the store where the weapon was purchased stated that Miller was "wild looking" and was mumbling angrily to himself. This employee called the police and followed Miller to two nearby bars. Finally the employee saw Miller leaving in a taxicab with a woman driver and contacted the taxi company to inform it of the apparent danger. The woman taxi driver was found murdered a short while later, having been stabbed nine times. Miller had apparently raped her when she was dead or dying. When Miller was arrested at the substation that evening, his pants were still covered with blood. Blood-soaked money, some of which had been taken from the taxi driver, was found in his pockets.

After Miller was charged with this crime, he was found incompetent to stand trial and was committed to a state mental hospital. Two and a half years later, after being heavily medicated, he was found to be competent to stand trial and was convicted of capital murder. At the sentencing hearing psychiatric testimony suggested that Miller was suffering from paranoid schizophrenia and hallucinations. He had been committed to mental hospitals on several previous occasions and had a long history of drug abuse. Testimony also indicated that Miller had a severe hatred of his mother, and that he had planned to kill her after his release from the jail. Apparently this hatred arose in part from the fact that his mother, who had been married four times, had refused any contact with her son for several years. On several previous occasions, Miller suffered hallucinations in which he saw his mother in other persons, in a "yellow haze." On at least one previous occasion, he had senselessly assaulted another woman during such hallucinations. Miller testified that at the time of the capital murder, he saw his mother's face on the 56-year-old woman taxi driver, in a "yellow haze," and proceeded to stab her to death.

QUESTIONS: Assume that the death penalty statute under which Miller is sentenced includes as mitigating circumstances (1) that the offender was under extreme mental or emotional distress at the time of the offense and (2) that the offender was substantially unable to appreciate the wrongfulness of his act or conform his act to the requirements of the law. Assume also that the statute includes as aggravating circumstances (1) that the crime was committed in a wanton, atrocious, and cruel manner; and (2) that the offender has a probability of committing criminal acts in the future. As a mental health professional, which, if any, of these issues would you address and what could you say about them? [Readers may want to review § 7.08 on ethical issues connected with capital sentencing.] As a lawyer for Miller, what arguments might you make to exclude clinical testimony about Miller's dangerousness?

Clinical opinion will be sought in most capital cases. Because the stakes are so high in such cases, defense attorneys want all the help they can get. In addition, the hostility toward the rehabilitative/incapacitative model in regular sentencing has not affected capital sentencing; because the penalty is death, the courts have allowed the defense to present almost any information that might put the defendant in a better light, including testimony about treatability and nondangerousness. This section describes the substantive and procedural requirements imposed by the United States Supreme Court in connection with death penalty proceedings. [See §§ 7.08(c),

9.09(c)(4) for a discussion on ethical problems that clinicians may confront when participating in such a process.]

(a)　Substantive Criteria

The modern death penalty process has been shaped by a long series of United States Supreme Court decisions, beginning in 1972 with *Furman v. Georgia*.[136] Prior to *Furman* most states had the death penalty. But in *Furman*, the Court signaled it would strictly scrutinize use of this punishment when it declared the capital punishment statutes of Texas and Georgia unconstitutional. Each of the nine Justices wrote separately in *Furman*, making it fruitless to describe the "Court's opinion." However, Justice Brennan perhaps best articulated a theme running through the opinions of the five Justices who voted to invalidate the statutes:

> [W]hen a country of over 200 million people inflicts an unusually severe punishment no more than 50 times a year, the inference is strong that the punishment is not being regularly and fairly applied. To dispel it would indeed require a clear showing of nonarbitrary infliction; . . . [otherwise] it smacks of little more than a lottery system.[137]

Justice Douglas described the populations arbitrarily singled out for those rare occasions when death was imposed: "It is the poor, the sick, the ignorant, the powerless and the hated that are executed."[138] To both Justices, the death penalty was a violation of the Eighth Amendment's prohibition against cruel and unusual punishment, as well as a violation of the equal protection guarantee.

Since 1972, the Court has attempted to make imposition of the death penalty less arbitrary. It has started with the premise that the death penalty is unique in the criminal justice system. As the Court stated in *Woodson v. North Carolina*: "The penalty of death is qualitatively different from a sentence of imprisonment, however long. Death, in its finality, differs more from life imprisonment than a 100-year prison term differs from one of only a year or two."[139]

Accordingly, the Court has emphasized that whatever might be permissible in noncapital sentencing, the substantive criteria for determining the appropriateness of the death penalty must give the judge or jury the opportunity to consider all relevant mitigating evidence about the individual capital offender. It has banned statutes making execution mandatory for certain types of offenses,[140] as well as statutes that somehow limit the individualization process. For example, in *Lockett v. Ohio*, it struck down an Ohio law that "did not permit the sentencing judge to consider as mitigating factors, [the defendant's] character, prior record, age, lack of specific intent to cause death, and her relatively minor part in the crime."[141] The Court reiterated its observation in *Woodson* that "in capital cases the fundamental respect for humanity underlying the Eighth Amendment . . . requires consideration of the character and record of the individual offender and the circumstances of the particular offense as a constitutionally indispensable part of the process of inflicting the penalty of death."

In an effort to meet these guidelines, the typical modern capital sentencing statute sets out a list of both aggravating and mitigating factors. The prosecution must prove the existence of at least one of the aggravating factors before the death penalty may be imposed. In most states, this proof must be beyond a reasonable doubt, although in some states the statute is silent on this point.[142] The defendant, on the other hand, is not required to prove any mitigating circumstances, although doing so obviously is better than remaining mute. Virtually none of the statutes tells the factfinder how to balance aggravating and mitigating circumstances once they are proven.[143] In theory, then, the jury may treat an offender with only one aggravating trait and six mitigating traits in the same way as an offender who meets two aggravating factors and is unable to produce any evidence in mitigation. As a result, although discretion has been limited somewhat, considerable potential for arbitrariness still exists.

The specific aggravating and mitigating factors vary among jurisdictions. A few general comments can be made about them, however. First, most mitigators are phrased in terms that invite clinical participation. For example, roughly half the states provide that facts in mitigation may include proof of the following:

- The defendant was under the influence of extreme mental or emotional distress.
- The capacity of the defendant to appreciate the criminality of his conduct or to conform his conduct to the requirements of law was significantly impaired.[144]

Other common statutory mitigators include mental retardation, "extenuating circumstances" at the time of the offense, "domination of another" during the offense, a belief that the act was "morally justified," and proof that the defendant is not dangerous.[145]

As this list indicates, a second aspect of mitigating circumstances is that they are broadly framed. Note that the language of the first mitigating circumstance listed above, although similar to that used to define provocation for manslaughter purposes [see § 8.03(d)], does not require that the emotional distress be "reasonable." Similarly, the language of the second listed mitigating circumstance, although similar to the ALI test for insanity [see § 8.02(b)(1)], does not include a mental disease or defect predicate. These differences emphasize the fact that, at the sentencing phase, the degree of mental disability necessary to establish mitigation need not be as serious as at the trial stage. Indeed, as already noted, *Lockett* established as a constitutional matter that *any* mitigating evidence relevant to the defendant's character and offense must be admitted during a capital sentencing proceeding. Thus, the mitigating circumstances found in typical death penalty statutes are not exclusive. Some of the nonstatutory mitigating factors that have been recognized by courts include whether the defendant was "contrite and remorseful," had a low IQ, suffered from organic brain damage, was under the influence of alcohol at the time of the offense, was abused or battered as a child or had an otherwise deprived childhood, suffered from "mental health problems," had a history of commitment to mental institutions, and is treatable.[146]

On the other hand, the statutory *aggravating* circumstances are usually considered exclusive.[147] That is, the prosecution must prove one of the listed aggravating circumstances to have a chance at the death penalty; other types of aggravation are irrelevant. Most of the aggravating circumstances listed in the typical statute (e.g., whether the crime was particularly cruel and atrocious . . . the offender's prior criminal history) do not call for clinical participation. But, in the roughly eight states with statutes that make dangerousness a legitimate aggravating circumstance,[148] such participation may occur. In Virginia, for instance, clinicians have testified about violence proneness under a statute that makes an offender eligible for the death penalty if "there is a probability . . . that he would commit criminal acts of violence that would constitute a continuing serious threat to society."[149]

This latter type of testimony has been of particular concern for mental health professionals on substantive and ethical grounds, but it is clear it will continue to be sought. Despite the difficulty of predicting violent behavior, the Supreme Court has upheld the constitutional validity of statutes permitting a death sentence based on a prediction of future dangerousness.[150] It has also explicitly found, in *Barefoot v. Estelle*,[151] that the Constitution does not bar clinical testimony on the subject. To the American Psychiatric Association's argument that long-term predictions of dangerousness are so unreliable that they should be proscribed at capital sentencing, the Court rather glibly responded: "The suggestion that no psychiatrist's testimony may be presented with regard to dangerousness is somewhat like asking us to disinvent the wheel." [See § 9.09(b)(2) for more about *Barefoot*.]

Two other capital sentencing issues that might be relevant to mental health professionals should be noted. First, in a state in which dangerousness is not an aggravating circumstance, certain types of mitigating information about an offender's *postcrime* behavior may be considered irrelevant. In *Skipper v. South Carolina*,[152] three members of the United States Supreme Court suggested that unless it is necessary to rebut the prosecution's assertion that the offender is dangerous, testimony that the offender has made a "good adjustment" in prison could be barred. It is unclear whether testimony about postoffense remorse on the part of the offender would also be prohibited by this reasoning.

Second, in many cases an offender's mental illness, although presumptively mitigating, might also be directly connected with an aggravating circumstance. For instance, an offender's dangerousness might be the result of mental illness. Similarly, the "atrociousness" of the murder might be due to mental disorder. In the case on which Case Study 9.1 is based, the Florida Supreme Court made clear that when an aggravating circumstance is the "direct consequence" of mental illness, a death sentence based on it is invalid.[153] In other words, when mental illness could form the basis for both an aggravating and mitigating circumstance, it may be considered only in connection with the latter. Although the United States Supreme Court has not yet addressed this issue, it has intimated it might agree with the Florida Supreme Court.[154]

(b) Procedural Criteria

In contrast to normal sentencing, the process when death is the potential sentence is very formal, providing the defendant with many of the procedural protections normally associated with trial. As Justice Blackmun has observed:

> In ensuring that the death penalty is not meted out arbitrarily or capriciously, the Court's principal concern has been more with the procedure by which the State imposes the death penalty than with the substantive factors the state lays before the jury as a basis for imposing death, once it has been determined that the defendant falls within the category of persons eligible for the death penalty.[155]

Accordingly, the typical death penalty statute provides the following procedural protection[156]:

- The determination of guilt or innocence and sentencing is bifurcated—that is, it occurs at two separate proceedings.
- The defendant must have access to all information to be relied on by the decisionmaker prior to trial, and if information is withheld, it must be made available in the record for appeal.[157]
- The reasons for the sentence must be stated in writing.
- Automatic appellate review by the state's highest court must be available.

- Rules of evidence usually apply (though their application is not constitutionally compelled).[158]

In addition, in practice, any obstacles to obtaining expert assistance are normally relaxed in capital cases. Indeed, in *Ake v. Oklahoma*,[159] the Supreme Court held that a capital defendant is entitled to psychiatric assistance when dangerousness is an issue in capital sentencing, although it also limited this assistance to one clinician and made clear that defendants are not entitled to the clinician of their choice [see § 4.03(b)(1)].

9.06. Factors Influencing Sentencing

From the foregoing, it should be apparent that mental health professionals could provide input on a variety of issues relevant to sentencing. But what is the impact of such input? Before examining in more detail the information the clinician can provide at sentencing, and to put its usefulness in perspective, we review briefly some of the nonclinical influences on the sentences assigned by judges and juries.

(a) Judicial Philosophy

An obvious influence on sentencing comes from the judge's own predilections. Indeed, one study that examined sentencing disparity in the federal courts prior to adoption of the federal sentencing guidelines concluded that "more variance in sentences is explained by differences among individual judges than by any other single factor."[160] Similarly, in her discussion of factors that contribute to sentencing disparity, Diamond identified varying judicial sentencing goals as a crucial important factor.[161] Some judges seem more attuned to retributive considerations, whereas others are prone to seek dispositions that further rehabilitative ends. Diamond hypothesized that cases in which individual philosophies play the most important role are probably those in which conflicting information (e.g., both aggravating and mitigating) is present.

(b) System- and Defendant-Based Factors

A variety of other factors have been shown to be related to sentencing decisions.[162] Several studies have found, for instance, that offenders who go to trial receive harsher sentences than offenders found guilty through plea bargaining[163]; the implication is that judges penalize defendants for exercising their constitutional right to a trial by jury. Another study found that individuals who are denied bail and who have appointed, as opposed to retained, counsel are subject to more severe sentences.[164]

Not surprisingly, factors related to characteristics of the offender also play a role in sentencing. In the study just noted, it was also shown that, for offenders with the same charge, those who threatened physical harm and had prior felony convictions tended to receive harsher sentences. Among demographic variables considered (age, marital status, educational level, race, etc.), gender was the most important variable, with women receiving less severe sentences.[165]

These various findings help explain the impetus for determinate sentencing designed to remove the influence of factors considered irrelevant to punishment (judicial preferences, type of counsel, gender) and to focus the issue on retribution (e.g., prior offenses and degree of harm caused). To the extent sentencing does become determinate, the influence of many of the factors described above should disappear.

(c) Presentence Reports

The probation officer's presentence report [see § 9.03(b)(2)] is generally conceded to be the most influential tangible factor on the ultimate sentence.[166] Indeed, in some determinate sentencing jurisdictions, including the federal courts, the report's calculation of guideline categories is often close to dispositive.[167] The clinician and lawyer need to be aware of these facts, if for no other reason than to avoid the assumption that the clinical report is the sole or primary source of information available to the court.

The presentence report also plays a critical role in the life of the offender after sentencing. For example, in the federal system, the Bureau of Prisons uses the report for the following purposes: to prepare the classification study that identifies the particular offender's needs and assists in assigning him or her to a particular institution and a particular level of security within the institution, to determine the conditions of the inmate's confinement (e.g., visitation rights, work-study release, and transfer to another institution), to make decisions on granting or withholding goodtime credits, and to assist the parole commission in determining the appropriateness of granting parole.[168]

Because of the importance attached to the presentence report both during and after sentencing, its accuracy is a paramount concern. Unfortunately, more than one study has concluded that there are "numerous instances of serious inaccuracies in presentence reports."[169] One way of correcting this inaccuracy would be to permit defendant perusal of the report before its use. Traditionally, however, full disclosure has not been required, out of fear the defendant would somehow misuse the information.

A more sensible approach is found in Rule 32 of the Federal Rules of Criminal Procedure, which, since 1974, has permitted greater disclosure in federal court. The rule provides that before imposing sentence the court, on request, "shall permit the defendant or counsel to read the presentence report, exclusive of any sentence recommendation."[170] In addition to excising the sentence recommendation, the court may limit disclosure if in the court's opinion "the report contains diagnostic opinion which might seriously disrupt a program of rehabilitation, sources of information obtained upon a promise of confidentiality, or any other information which, if disclosed, might result in harm."[171] At the same time, the court is to summarize deleted information and provide the summary to the defendant; the defendant may comment on both the report and the summary of deleted information and may introduce information relating to any alleged factual inaccuracy in the presentence report.[172]

The federal rule represents a reasonable attempt to balance the court's interest in obtaining and relying on all information about the defendant and the defendant's interest in having sentencing based on accurate information. A study of the impact of this rule concluded that, despite fears to the contrary, disclosure had not had a negative impact on the sentencing process.[173] However, the manner in which some courts utilized the exceptions to disclosure had potentially troubling consequences for the expressed aim of the rule. For instance, some courts withheld disclosure of law enforcement information under the rubric of "diagnostic information."[174] Since this information is notoriously unreliable, and may have a significant impact on sentencing, these courts were undercutting the purpose of disclosure.

Clearly, clinicians should try to gain access to the presentence report. Its impact on sentencing will be substantial and its recommendations should be taken into account in formulating a clinical opinion.

(d)   The Impact of Clinical Recommendations

In light of the foregoing, it is probably no surprise that despite the widespread use of clinicians at sentencing and the law's traditional acceptance of mental disorder as a mitigating factor at disposition, the impact of clinical opinion is insignificant in many cases—either in the sense that the judge pays no attention to it or in the sense that the judge merely uses it to justify "scientifically" a decision he or she has already made. Although a high concordance rate between psychiatric recommendations and court disposition has been found in many studies, it seems to reflect the influence of nonclinical factors on the clinician rather than the effect of clinical factors on the judge. Further, a second group of studies that focused on the effect of *clinical* factors found a relatively low concordance rate.

In the first category of studies are those that focus on the influence of psychiatric classifications of "defective delinquent" and "mentally disordered sex offender" (MDSO). In two separate 10-year samples, research conducted when Maryland's "defective delinquent" statute was in force revealed 82% and 91% concordance between the staff's recommendations for commitment and courts' dispositions.[175] A study in California involving offenders evaluated for MDSO status resulted in a similar finding: At least 91% of the courts' placements were consistent with the clinicians' recommendations.[176] But the numerical suggestion that clinicians held considerable power in the disposition of these cases is misleading. For example, the investigators in California concluded that both the clinicians' classifications (MDSO/not MDSO) and the judge's dispositions were highly influenced by a single variable—prior convictions for sexual offenses.[177] The information in the psychiatrists' reports thus added little discriminating power to the judge's decisions. Further, their judgments were highly predictable from information that requires no particular clinical skill or acuity either to gather or to interpret. As others have contended, psychiatric involvement in these kinds of decisions may serve primarily to pacify the public and policymakers by providing a humanistic facade to what is primarily a social control function.[178]

In a similar vein are studies from other countries, reviewed by Campbell, which revealed psychiatrist–court concordance rates of 93% in Tasmania and 77–95% in England.[179] Rates of agreement varied, however, with the specific type of disposition recommended: 17% when the recommendation was for discharge from court custody, 77% when probation was recommended, and 91% when incarceration was advised.[180] Furthermore, Campbell noted that agreement estimates may have been high in part because in some cases the disposition is "obvious," and in others the courts and the clinicians use common criteria in their decisionmaking (e.g., number of prior offenses).

When the offense is less serious, clinical participation may have a decidedly greater independent effect. For example, Smith's study of North Carolina sentencing practices reported overall significant agreement in cases involving minor offenders even when the recommendations were for probation (87%) or treatment (70%).[181] In studies in which more serious offenders were referred, however, as in Bohmer's study of sex offenders in Philadelphia,[182] agreement rates on these nonincarcerative types of dispositions are often substantially lower.[183]

One reason clinical input may not have much independent impact in many types of cases is the priority many judges assign to the presentence report. For instance, Bohmer found that recommendations contained in presentence reports received considerably more attention than psychiatric reports, which had a "low rate of acceptance" by the courts.[184] A related reason may be that many judges view mental health professionals as "bleeding hearts" who too often find pathology as an excuse for criminal behavior and are unrealistic about the true rehabilitative potential in a given case. A third reason—and one that mental health professionals may be prone to forget—is that even under an indeterminate sentencing scheme, rehabilitation is only one of many factors the judge must consider. In particular, retributive, incapacitative, and deterrence concerns may become paramount, especially as the seriousness of the crime escalates.

Despite this rather grim assessment of clinical participation at sentencing, mental health professionals do have a role to play at this stage of the criminal process, although one that is perhaps more restricted than the role envisioned by those who most avidly support the rehabilitative model. In our view, the mental health professional can best serve the sentencing process by carefully developing material about the individual that helps explain the way in which the offender differs from stereotypical notions the court might have about those convicted of a particular offense. That is, the clinician should try, in those cases in which it is appropriate, to answer the judicial question: "How is this offender different from any of the hundreds of others I've seen?"

Responses to this overarching question will be shaped by the type of sentencing scheme (indeterminate or determinate) that exists in the clinician's jurisdiction and the specific issues the referral source wants the clinician to address. As already indicated, one or more of the following assessments will usually be involved: (1) the offender's need for treatment (relevant under indeterminate sentencing), (2) information bearing on the offender's personal culpability (relevant under determinate and indeterminate sentencing), and (3) future dangerousness (relevant under indeterminate sentencing). The next three sections focus in turn on each of these issues. We give greatest emphasis to the issue of clinical involvement in the determination of future dangerousness. Assessment of treatability needs requires relatively little coverage in light of the significant

overlap with concerns common in ordinary clinical practice; similarly, much of what can be said about presentence evaluations on culpability overlaps both conceptually and practically with the clinical portions of Chapter 8.

9.07.   Assessment of Treatment Needs

Arguably, the most appropriate role for the mental health professional in sentencing is in the assessment of the offender's need for treatment. This role is the most consistent with the clinician's training and technical expertise in the identification of psychopathology and in the development of treatment planning. After briefly describing the types of offenders a treatment evaluation is likely to involve, this section discusses the areas of inquiry a typical evaluation might explore and problems connected with making treatment recommendations.

(a)   Characteristics of Offenders Evaluated for Treatment

Theoretically, most seriously disordered offenders should have been diverted before sentencing—either through civil commitment, adjudication as incompetent to proceed, or acquittal by reason of insanity. However, a substantial percentage of convicted offenders do exhibit serious mental illness.[185] Furthermore, even when not seriously ill, offenders referred for presentence examination are likely to display some level of impaired functioning. A referral is likely to stem from a judge's or attorney's perception that there is "something wrong" or "different" about an offender.

In our experience, the types of offenders most often referred for treatment evaluation, in descending order of frequency, are as follows:

- Youthful adult offenders "at a crossroad."
- Persons charged with offenses (not necessarily serious) that are intuitively associated with psychological aberration (e.g., exhibitionism, fire setting, and conduct associated with drug or alcohol use).

- Persons charged with serious crimes who do not have a significant history of prior criminality.
- Persons with an obvious serious mental disorder.

(b)   Conducting the Treatment Evaluation

Given its focus and the potential subjects, the typical treatment evaluation at sentencing will be very wide-ranging. This fact is reflected in an evaluation guide published by the National Institute of Corrections, which recommends determining the status of an offender in a number of areas, including:

- Serious psychological abnormality (e.g., acute functional disturbance).
- Drug/alcohol abuse or addiction.
- Deficits in intelligence and/or adaptive behavior.
- Academic training.
- Vocational skills.
- Interpersonal/social skills.[186]

In investigating these areas, clinicians should be able to make use of their usual array of structured and unstructured interviews, objective and projective psychological tests, laboratory testing procedures, or the collateral input of various consultants (e.g., educational or vocational counselors). One source that clinicians may find particularly useful is the manual on the assessment of offenders' needs, developed by Clements and his colleagues for the National Institute of Corrections.[187] For each of the areas of needs assessment listed above, this manual identifies formal psychological tests and/or structured questionnaires that assist in evaluation of offenders. Although the manual is aimed primarily at clinicians working within corrections, a number of the needs-assessment concerns are the same for clinicians who see clients prior to sentencing; thus, this manual may serve as an excellent tool for this purpose.

The clinician can also take advantage of empirical information on the efficacy of various treatment programs. Prior to the 1990s, the predominant view of these programs came from Martinson's assessment of the outcome research conducted before 1967,[188] which was construed to stand for the proposition that "nothing works."[189] In fact, however, few of the studies Martinson reviewed were based on sound theoretical premises, used valid criterion variables, or even ensured the treatment being evaluated was effectively implemented.[190]

More recent assessments are somewhat more optimistic, at least when criminal recidivism is the outcome variable. Meta-analyses by Andrews and colleagues[191] and by Lipsey[192] of large numbers of corrections treatment studies have yielded support for the position that at least certain types of "appropriate" treatments *do* work to reduce recidivism.[193] "Appropriate" treatments are those that are consistent with three theoretical principles: (1) the interventions are applied primarily to high-risk (i.e., relatively dangerous) individuals; (2) targets of treatment are *criminogenic* factors (e.g., antisocial attitudes or peer relationships, promoting identification with anticriminal role models, and training in prosocial skill development) rather than vague personal/emotional problems (e.g., poor self-esteem); and (3) the interventions focus on developing skills that offenders are capable of applying, which are more likely to come from cognitive and behavioral approaches rather than "nondirective" or "insight" approaches. The meta-analysis by Andrews and his colleagues found that "appropriate" treatments, so defined, may reduce criminal recidivism by as much as 50% compared to recidivism rates from those subjected to criminal sanctions alone (e.g., probation and incarceration), "inappropriate" treatment, or treatment that does not clearly meet the three theoretical criteria. Lipsey obtained similar findings.[194]

Although these studies suggest that "treatment" dispositions may reduce recidivism, some caveats are in order. First, these studies found that positive results were most likely to be obtained when the treatment was provided in the community to higher-risk clients,[195] not a disposition that courts are likely to endorse enthusiastically, especially to the extent retribution is favored by the public. Second, in both of these meta-analyses, the majority of studies examined dealt with juvenile as opposed to adult offenders; the implementation of treatment programs may be easier in the juvenile system, given its traditional emphasis on rehabilitation [see § 14.02(c)].

Notably, research focusing on the efficacy of sex offender treatment suffers from neither of these problems; these studies often look at the efficacy of in-prison treatment of adults. Unfortunately, however, this research is also less conclusive about what works and what does not.[196]

When summarizing the results of the wide-ranging inquiry suggested by the foregoing discussion, it may help to keep in mind the types of "data" courts especially focus on in evaluating the treatment recommendations in clinical reports. In our experience, the information that the courts find most relevant fall into five categories:

- The offender's motivation. (Does the offender express remorse about the act and express a desire to be treated?)
- Family/environmental situation. (Would it be beneficial or harmful to the offender and his or her associates if the offender returned to it?)
- Past treatment attempts. (If there have been successes, can they be repeated? If not, is there a treatment modality that has not been tried with this offender and that has demonstrated—preferably empirically—its efficacy?)
- Past offense record. (Is there a pattern that treatment might affect?)
- Need for external control. (Can treatment safely take place in an unsecure environment?)

Obviously, some of these issues, especially the last two, are related to dangerousness assessments—the subject of § 9.09. As developed in that section, "treatability" and "dangerousness" are two sides of the same coin to many courts and can be subsumed within the concept of "risk management."

(c) Formulating the Treatment Recommendation

As just indicated, a treatment recommendation often involves a risk assessment instead of a pure opinion about amenability to treatment. Even in a straightforward needs assessment, however, there are particular problem areas to keep in mind

when formulating a recommendation. These include treatment bias, unrealistic recommendations, "forced" treatment, and trenching on the ultimate issue.

(1) Treatment Bias

Because of their training in the medical model, many mental health professionals are inclined to see problem behavior as stemming primarily from personal pathology. Thus, they may be prone to conclude that every referral is a treatment case. One author reported that "[p]rominent forensic psychiatrists almost uniformly express the view that presentence reports ought to advocate lenient, individualized treatment."[197] Indeed, it appears that psychiatric recommendations for treatment are made in a substantial number of sentencing cases that are referred to clinicians. Caravello, Ginnetti, Ford, and Lawall reviewed studies reporting a frequency of treatment recommendations ranging from "more than half the cases" to as many as 90%.[198]

Perhaps this tendency is justifiable. Of particular concern in this regard is research that suggests that mentally ill offenders are especially prone to victimization in prison settings.[199] But it is also possible that clinicians may underestimate the role of learning factors or social/environmental conditions in the offender's illegal behavior and may be inclined to suggest treatment-oriented dispositions in cases in which negative reinforcement (e.g., fine and incarceration) might be more appropriate. In short, clinicians need to guard against overdiagnosing and against the pathologizing of criminal behavior.[200]

(2) Unrealistic Recommendations

Also mentioned in the literature is the problem of recommending treatment that either is not available or is available at a facility that may be under no obligation to accept the offender as a client.[201] The problem of recommending nonexistent treatment may be the greatest when evaluations are conducted by staff members at a remote state hospital who are not familiar with the treatment programs actually available. At the same time, Bartholomew's recommendation that presentence evaluations be conducted by local clinicians who will ultimately provide any treatment ordered by the court is unrealistic and possibly unethical.[202] It is unrealistic because careful diagnosis and treatment planning will frequently lead clinicians to advise treatments that they themselves are unable to provide. For example, a psychologist may recommend that a person suffering from chronic schizophrenia receive a maintenance dosage of medication or consideration for placement in a day-treatment program, neither of which the psychologist could provide through a private practice. Similarly, a dynamically oriented psychiatrist might diagnose a social-skills deficit best remedied by group therapy which is not offered in his or her practice, or the need for long-term drug rehabilitation, which is ideally offered in a residential setting. As to the ethical propriety of Bartholomew's recommendation, as § 4.05(c)(2) indicates, a routine practice of evaluating potential patients may create conflicts of interest.

The best way to avoid an unrealistic recommendation is for the evaluating clinician, whether at a hospital or in the local community, to be thoroughly familiar with available programs. Given the importance of matching clients' problems with specific treatment approaches for those problems, the most reasonable approach would be for clinicians to extend their investigative efforts to include inquiries in the state or region regarding available treatment programs (state agencies are often helpful in this regard). They may also be able to use defendants' attorneys; even if clinicians do not know of the available treatment programs statewide, they can describe clients' diagnoses to their attorneys, who can then use their own resources to seek out possible placements. Finally, there are various reviews that describe programs available in the mental health system, as well as within psychiatric facilities of the correctional system.[203]

Connected to the tendency to make unrealistic recommendations is the failure to provide sound information to the court as to whether a given treatment will "work" (i.e., reduce recidivism). To the extent that good research studies are available (of the type described by Andrews and Lipsey [see § 9.07(b)]), they should be reviewed by the clinician and provided to the court, lest unrealistic assumptions concerning program efficacy or inefficacy be made.

(3) "Forced Treatment"

The clinician should also be sensitive to potential problems that arise if the duration of a sentence or the potential for diversion from adjudication or incarceration is linked to the offender's participation in a treatment program (as may be true with sex offender and drug user treatment programs, for instance). First, clients who know that leniency may be gained by participating in such a program may exaggerate their true problems or interest in treatment to gain a less punitive disposition. Second, once in treatment, an offender may be motivated by the ulterior goal of obtaining a favorable recommendation for early release rather than a desire to be "cured"; thus, shamming is a real possibility.[204] Finally, because the treating clinician may be required to report progress (or other aspects of treatment), the usual guarantees of confidentiality considered of paramount importance to successful therapy may be abrogated, thereby threatening the therapist–client relationship with the individual who truly *wants* to be treated; indeed, individuals may be deterred from treatment because of the perception that therapists may not really be on their side.

Accordingly, when feasible, the clinician should recommend that dispositions that address the offender's need for treatment not entangle the degree of participation or success in therapy with the criteria for termination of sentence. If that is not possible, the clinician should at least try to minimize the personal information about the client that he or she must report to the court, and ensure that the client knows about the degree of disclosure which will occur [see § 4.05(b)(1)].

(4) Scope of Recommendations

As is true in every other context discussed in this book, the clinician's job in assessing treatment needs is to provide the data, not the ultimate decision. Thus, although a clinician may feel that an offender "needs" treatment in the sense that it will improve the individual's mental condition or behavioral skills, the clinician should not go further and conclude that the offender "needs," in the sense of "requires," a particular disposition. As indicated above, clinicians might advise the court of what is likely to happen if a particular treatment is provided or not provided—for example, whether a person with a psychosis is likely to become severely dysfunctional if imprisoned rather than hospitalized, or whether a person with limited vocational skills is likely to continue to function at the current level if vocational rehabilitation is not provided. Taking the next step, however, and recommending the precise disposition involves the contemplation of contrasting moral goals of sentencing and of current social and political pressures beyond the responsibility and clinical expertise of the mental health professional. In short, diagnosing a problem that might be the appropriate focus for a treatment intervention is not dispositive of whether treatment for the problem should be ordered.

Consistent with this posture, we advise against direct recommendations for disposition or placement, such as, "This patient should be sent to place X to receive treatment Y." Rather, we recommend that clinicians provide the court with a series of "If . . . , then . . ." statements that provide the court with alternatives, depending on what dispositional action is taken. For example, "If the court is inclined to a disposition such as probation, then Mr. Doe's inadequate social skills may be the focus of treatment through group therapy at the Westside Mental Health Center. If the decision is to place Mr. Doe in the state prison, then his limited social skills are not likely to improve, as the clinical staff members at the prison inform me that they presently have no active therapy that focuses on social skills training." The court can then decide whether to afford Mr. Doe that opportunity for group therapy in light of competing concerns, such as retribution or the need for preventive detention.

9.08.   Assessment of Culpability

Unlike treatment needs, offenders' culpability is an issue considered in every sentencing scheme, whether it is indeterminate, determinate, or some mix thereof. From the defendants' perspec-

tive, clinicians may contribute to the culpability assessment in any of three ways. The most conventional role would be to advise the judge or jury about situational factors that contributed to the occurrence of the crime; enhanced awareness of these factors may undermine the factfinder's presumption that the crime was a function of the offender's free choice. A closely related way in which the clinician may affect the culpability assessment would be to make the judge or jury aware of the offender's life generally; an offender who has suffered greatly may arouse more sympathy than one who has not. Finally, the clinician may serve in a consultative capacity to assist in overcoming misunderstandings about the victim's perception of the event. These three roles are discussed here in turn.

(a)   Understanding the Offense

"The jury and judge must be made to understand what caused a crime, particularly in homicides. . . . It is the role of psychiatry and related professions to provide that understanding so a rational approach to a penalty can be taken."[205] To set punishment, the sentencing judge or jury must determine the seriousness of the crime committed. This objective requires that they consider both the harm done and the culpability of the offender. Lay assessments of the harm factor have been shown to be reliable: For example, people can agree, when contemplating different crimes in the abstract, that armed robbery is more serious than shoplifting but less serious than murder. The same is not true, however, of judgments in the area of personal culpability; "attributions of culpability or blame are highly influenced by factors having little relevance to notions of justice."[206] As Bonnie has noted in discussing culpability in the context of capital sentencing, the law is seeking to make the difficult moral distinction between "a person who has chosen evil" and "the person whose homicidal behavior arose from significant impairment in his normal psychological controls."[207]

The clinical explanations for "how" or "why" a crime occurred that are offered at sentencing are similar to those described in Chapter 8, which discusses mental state defenses.[208] The significant difference is that to be admissible at the sentencing stage, explanatory formulations do not have to be so compelling as to constitute a possible defense. At sentencing, the door is open to a much wider range of clinical input and explanatory formulations than is true at trial. For example, as noted in § 9.05(a), in capital sentencing there is generally no requirement that the examiner be constrained by a threshold finding of mental disease or defect.[209] The possible influence of chronological youth, psychological immaturity, unstable family background, lack of adequate role models, physical or neurological impairment, chemical intoxicants, stress due to situational factors, or psychodynamic factors might all be woven into a clinical formulation that permits the judge or jury to attribute the crime, in part, to influences other than the offender's free choice.

(b)　Understanding the Offender

Even when *not* integrated into an explanatory theme, a description of the offender's life may arouse the judge's or jury's sympathy sufficiently to lead to a reduced sentence. Kalven and Zeisel noted that extraneous suffering by the offender sometimes influenced jury decisions.[210] Similarly, a study by Cooke and Pogany illustrated that merely having a history of psychiatric problems might affect punishment.[211] They examined sentences given to a group of 130 defendants who had been evaluated regarding competency to stand trial prior to being found guilty. The sentences given to this group were compared with those given to a control group of offenders who had not been referred for pretrial evaluation. Although no significant difference between the two groups was found in terms of the overall severity of sentences, significantly shorter sentences were given to offenders who had earlier (1) been diagnosed as having schizophrenia, or (2) been found incompetent for trial. Though the record contained no presentence report relating mental state to culpability issues, the sentencing courts apparently gave consideration to the offenders' psychiatric histories.

However, efforts that revolve around sympathy arousal are likely to less successful as the severity of the crime increases. This relationship has been demonstrated in laboratory research using simulated sentencing exercises. Austin varied the amount of extraneous offender suffering (none, moderate, excessive) in each of three cases involving increasingly more harm done (i.e., purse snatching, purse snatching plus assault, or rape).[212] Undergraduate students acting as jurors were asked to impose the most appropriate sentence, given the circumstances of each case. Results indicated that for the minor offense of shoplifting, sentences decreased as a function of offender suffering. With crimes of moderate or high severity, however, information that the offender had suffered moderate physical injuries had no sentence reducing impact; only when the offender's suffering was excessive was the sentence reduced.

Austin interpreted these findings to mean that jurors will sentence according to "just deserts" principles for offenses of low severity, but that other considerations (e.g., vengeance for harm caused to the victim) affect sentences for offenses that are more severe. His findings are consistent with Dix's finding in Ohio that potentially mitigating information offered in capital sentencing hearings was generally ineffective in persuading sentencing juries to forgo the death penalty.[213] Dix also speculated that this ineffectiveness may have been due to the expert witnesses' failure to relate the mitigating information to the offenses by using an explanatory theme.

Mitigating information submitted purely to arouse sympathy may also have lessened impact in certain types of sentencing schemes. Indeed, as indicated earlier, in many determinate sentencing jurisdictions such mitigating information may be inadmissible because it is not directly tied to the offender's mental state at the time of the offense.

(c)　Understanding the Victim

One of the factors that may heavily influence the court's sentence is the victim(s)' perception of a "just" sentence. This information is usually provided to the court in the presentence report through what is called a "victim impact statement," which includes the investigating officer's summary of the victim's stated desires regarding sentencing. It may also come from states' attorneys arguing for severe punishment to vindicate the victim's sense of justice.

Henderson and Gitchoff have suggested that this information about the victim may induce a retributivist "set" that unjustly operates against an offender being sentenced in two ways.[214] First, they noted that the way in which probation officers interview the victims to get victim impact information may influence the responses they receive. Officers typically asked, "What do you think the punishment should be?", without providing the victims with a menu of possible sentences or other information about sentencing (e.g., the cost of incarceration). When Henderson and Gitchoff approached the victims and described the various sentencing options available, they found that the victims were often quite willing to vacate vengeful positions and select alternatives. Second, the researchers noted that victims seemed to "mellow" with time and were more amenable to less severe punishment when the presentence interviews were conducted a longer period after the trial.

Henderson and Gitchoff's study suggests two possible roles for the mental health professional in situations in which the victim's perception may be influential. First, as the authors suggest, the mental health expert might obtain a victim impact statement independent of that obtained by the probation department. At first blush this would appear to be an unconventional use of the clinician at sentencing. However, the investigative model we have suggested for use in reconstructive defenses [see § 8.06] contemplates clinician–victim contact if appropriate legal procedures (including respect for victim privacy) are followed; a similar investigative effort is thus not out of the question in developing mitigating information regarding sentencing. Second, even if the clinician does not obtain an independent victim impact statement, he or she may be able to testify regarding the influence of the probation officer's style of questioning on the answers obtained from the victim, thus enlightening the court about the influence of methodology on the probation report's portrayal of the victim's desires.[215]

(d)   Evaluating Culpability

The presentence evaluation that focuses on possible mitigating factors at the time of the crime should be, in large part, similar to the investigative inquiry involved in reconstructive mental state defenses. Many of the same tools and techniques, including close attention to a variety of third-party information, may be helpful in this evaluation. At the same time, because the clinical investigation at presentencing is not constrained by threshold tests such as the presence of mental disease or defect, the door is open to a wider range of descriptive and theoretical formulations, such as those discussed in § 8.07(b). Any information that helps the judge or jury understand limitations in the development of an offender's psychological controls or that identifies factors that may have undermined the offender's controls may be of use in their determination of the individual's culpability.

In jurisdictions that have statutes explicitly identifying mitigating factors to be considered, clinicians should also be aware of the law's possible implications for the evaluation. For example, as noted in § 9.05(a), a number of state capital sentencing statutes include this mitigating factor: "The defendant acted under extreme duress or under the substantial domination of another person."[216] Depending on the facts of the case, clinical inquiry into the issue of the "domination of another person" might entail interviewing accomplices to the crime and developing some judgments as to the relative strengths of the various personalities involved and the dependencies among them.

As elsewhere, clinicians should be candid about reliability and validity with respect to their data and inferences and should be clear in advising the court of the theoretical nature of their formulations. They should also avoid moral conclusions regarding whether the developmental deficits, environmental stresses, or functional pathology assessed are of sufficient magnitude to meet the discretionary legal test. The clinician's responsibility in this capacity is limited to the development of the explanatory formulations. Whether, and to what degree, leniency should be accorded an offender should be left to the attorney to argue and to the judge or jury to decide.

9.09.   Violence Prediction and Risk Assessment

Regardless of the theoretical bases underlying sentencing structures, the offender's potential for future violence is almost always an explicit or implicit consideration. Forward-looking indeterminate schemes—exemplified by special-track provisions such as those for sex offenders—forthrightly gauge violence potential as part of the problem to be treated and reduced. Similarly, in many jurisdictions the judge or jury may be required to consider evidence on future dangerousness in deciding whether to impose the death penalty.[217] Although the backward-looking "just deserts" model is less accommodating to such concerns on its face, perceptions of violence-proneness may nonetheless implicitly affect where within the range set by retributive principles a sentence falls; one also suspects that the sentence enhancements for prior crimes that take place under these schemes is more of a proxy for a dangerousness assessment than a determination that the offender is more culpable than a first-time offender [see, e.g., discussion of *Rummel* in § 9.05(a)].

Clinicians' involvement in violence prediction is extremely controversial. With years of confinement or possibly the offender's life hanging in the balance, there is no other area of the law in which expert testimony may exert so significant an impact. At the same time, as we discuss below, myriad factors limit clinicians' abilities in this area; many have questioned whether mental health professionals' predictions of violent behavior are sufficiently accurate to meet acceptable scientific or legal standards.

This section discusses the literature on the assessment and prediction of dangerous behavior related to *long-range* risk assessment/violence prediction. (Readers will find a somewhat parallel discussion relating to short-term predictions in the chapter on civil commitment [see § 10.08(d)] and briefer references to prediction literature in many other parts of this book.[218]) We first review a variety of factors that can affect the accuracy of clinicians' judgments about violence potential. We then discuss empirical studies evaluating those judgments, as well as important criticisms of that body of literature. In the final sec-

tion, we suggest particular factors to which clinicians should attend and strategies that they might employ in developing and presenting formulations regarding violence potential.

(a)   Factors That Influence Judgments about Dangerousness

There are at least four separate aspects of dangerousness prediction that make the clinician's task difficult: definitional problems, the dearth of useful research on prediction, unconscious and conscious judgment errors and biases, and the political consequences of an erroneous prediction.

(1)   Variability in the Legal Definition

The definition of dangerousness varies extensively from context to context.[219] In civil commitment, the potential for causing emotional harm or harm to property may be sufficient to affix the label, whereas in death penalty cases serious violence against a person must usually be predicted. In other contexts, still other definitions may apply. In *Jones v. United States*,[220] dealing with the "criminal" commitment of an insanity acquittee, the United States Supreme Court construed the attempted theft of a windbreaker from a department store as sufficient evidence of dangerous behavior. In other courts and other situations, adequate evidence of dangerousness has ranged from the discovery, in somewhat dated records of prior treatment, that the patient has expressed anger toward others[221] to the notation in a psychological testing report that some testing indices suggested "explosive and infantile features."[222] Some statutes require proof of an overt act within a particular period, whereas other jurisdictions do not require proof of any act to find a person dangerous.[223]

The clinicians' task is obviously made more difficult by this lack of clear and consistent guidelines regarding what constitutes legally relevant risk. Absent such guidelines, clinicians may turn to definitions in other areas of statutory or case law, or they may apply their own value judgments as to what constitutes dangerous behavior.[224] In either case, they risk failing to address the question the court wants answered.

(2) Complexity of the Literature

There is a vast literature examining the relationship of a variety of factors to violence recidivism. Discussed in detail in § 9.09(c), this literature includes clinical anecdotes, theoretical analyses, experimental and quasi-experimental research studies, epidemiological studies, and program evaluation studies. It has yielded guidance that includes clinical and demographic markers, developmental indicators, psychodynamic formulations, empirically determined correlates of violence recidivism, and multivariate equations yielding actuarial classifications of risk.

The availability of this literature is both a blessing and a curse. On the one hand, many potentially relevant factors have been identified and their empirical relationship to some measure of violence or aggression has been established. On the other hand, as detailed below, many studies suffer from one or more methodological limitations, and their sheer number is daunting even to the conscientious professional. As Mulvey and Lidz have noted, "No consensus exists about the best way to assess dangerousness. . . . The problem, of course, is that this voluminous literature is both overwhelming and disjointed."[225]

(3) Judgment Errors and Biases

In the absence of systematic guidelines for synthesizing the prediction literature and for applying it to individual cases, mental health professionals have adopted varying approaches to the development of opinions on future violence. Noted here are a few of the common pitfalls encountered by clinicians who have done so.

One significant conceptual problem is the tendency to view dangerousness solely as a trait. Traditionally, clinicians have looked for explanations of violence in the personal pathology of the individual; situational contributors to violence, or the possible interactions between person and situation variables, have received less attention. This practice may be in part the result of training in and commitment to the medical model; inclined toward dispositional explanations for violent behavior, clinicians typically focus on clinical signs, symptoms, or diagnostic labels as predictors.[226] It is also fostered, however, by the context in which

evaluations of dangerousness typically occur. Clinicians see their subjects in jails, prisons, or hospital settings that are often far removed from the social environment in which the persons typically function. This discourages clinicians from going beyond the familiar assessment techniques of interview and psychological testing, despite (or in ignorance of) the fact that such techniques have limited utility for purposes of violence prediction.[227]

Clinicians' judgments may also be affected by cognitive heuristics that influence the selection and weighting given to particular predictor variables.[228] Steadman and his colleagues examined the dangerousness evaluations of 257 incompetent criminal defendants in New York.[229] Although the examining psychiatrists offered a variety of factors as the basis for predictions of future violence,[230] statistical analysis revealed that a single factor was given overriding significance: "Psychiatrists seem to be making recommendations as to dangerousness based almost exclusively on the defendants' charges, with little additional discrimination evident."[231] Other studies, noted earlier in this chapter in connection with the discussion of sex offender sentencing, reported similar results [see § 9.06(d)]. This research illustrates how a particular piece of data, because of its *recency* (current arrest) or its *salience* (crime severity), may disproportionately affect judgments.

Another potential source of error in clinical judgments is reliance on "illusory correlations," a belief that a relationship between two variables exists despite empirical demonstration that it does not (or not to the degree believed).[232] Illusory correlations exist in the clinical lore and are maintained by selective attention to and recall of individual cases in which the relationship appeared to be present. In the prediction area, for instance, Dinwiddie and Yutzy suggest that clinicians' perceptions that dangerousness is highly associated with misidentification syndromes (an individual's belief that he or she has changed identity) is an example of illusory correlation, given the lack of epidemiological data illustrating such a relationship in an unselected sample.[233] More generally, a person may be thought to be dangerous simply because he or she is mentally ill, an opinion that stems from a common but erroneous belief that violence and mental disorder are generally correlated.[234]

Along the same lines are personal biases or attitudes that distort the predictive endeavor. For instance, Levinson and Ramsay note that cultural differences between the examining clinician and the person being assessed may contribute to errors in judgments about dangerousness.[235] Clinicians are typically white male psychiatrists from middle- to high-income families, while the offender population is composed predominantly of low-income, low-socioeconomic-status males. Resentment over cultural or racial differences may inhibit rapport between the examiner and the client; even when rapport is established and the client talks freely, the client's experiences may be foreign to the clinician and their relevance for violence potential poorly understood.

(4) Political Consequences for the Predictor

Finally, it must be recognized that "politics" can influence a prediction. If the client is released on the basis of the clinician's prediction and subsequently commits a violent act, the clinician can expect extensive negative publicity in connection with media coverage of the crime,[236] as well as possible legal action for negligent release.[237] In contrast, there are typically no legal or reputational consequences if a client is predicted to be dangerous, whether the client is subsequently confined *or* released (at least if it is a *court* that ignores the clinical prediction). The obvious incentive created by these facts is to lean in the direction of a "dangerous" finding in borderline cases.[238]

(b) Accuracy of Clinical Predictions of Dangerousness

In any area of the law, a relevant concern is the quality of the evidence offered to inform judgments reached by the trier of fact. Regarding psychiatric judgments about future dangerousness, discussions of the quality of evidence have been dominated—perhaps even consumed—by analyses of research studies examining the accuracy of clinicians' categorical predictions of violent behavior (i.e., conclusions that a person is, or is not,

"dangerous"). As we discuss in greater detail in § 9.09(c)(4), this emphasis is misplaced. However, both clinicians and attorneys may benefit from a review of this literature, given its major impact on the role of mental health professionals in risk assessment.

(1) Types of Errors and Base Rates

Research findings have typically been evaluated using a 2 × 2 contingency table that arrays clinical predictions on one dimension and observed outcomes on the other. Table 9.1 illustrates such an array.

From this table a number of potentially informative statistics can be computed. The professional literature in the three decades prior to the mid-1990s was dominated by concerns with the *percentage of false positives*, calculated by dividing the number of people predicted to be violent who were not ("false positives") by the total number of people predicted to be violent—a calculus that can be represented as $B/(A + B)$ using the lettering in Table 9.1. This number represents the percentage of people erroneously found to be "dangerous" and thereby exposed to inappropriate government intervention. Although this percentage has been the focus of much of the literature described below, another type of error is worth noting: *false-negative error*, in which a person is predicted to be nonviolent but subsequently commits a violent act. This second type of er-

Table 9.1

Typical Structure of a 2 × 2 Contingency Table Illustrating the Accuracy of Violence Predictions

		Outcome at follow-up	
		Violent	Nonviolent
Prediction	Violent	*A* True positives	*B* False positives
	Nonviolent	*C* False negatives	*D* True negatives

ror exposes the community to the risk of harm by truly violent individuals. A full consideration of the policy implications of prediction research should consider the potential frequency of each type of error and the outcomes associated with each.

Further, a particular type of error may be viewed from different policy perspectives. For example, another way to examine the false-positive error, and one that may place the "accuracy" issue in a different light, is to ask what proportion of *nonviolent persons* are erroneously classified as "dangerous," an equation that can be expressed as $B/(B + D)$. Because violence is not a particularly frequent event in most studies ($A < D$), this percentage, the *false-positive error rate*, will typically be smaller than the false-positive index. If one is more concerned with the absolute accuracy of positive predictions, the percent-false-positive rate is more important; however, if one is primarily concerned that proportionately few of the citizenry be falsely labeled as dangerous, the false-positive error rate might be the statistic of choice.[239] Because the law has done so, our focus throughout the rest of this chapter will be on the former statistic.

In evaluating these error rates, it should also be recognized that when, as is usually the case, the truly violent population is quite small compared to the nonviolent population (i.e., when there is a low "base rate" for violence), even prediction methods that are highly valid will generate large numbers of false-positive errors. A brief example illustrates this phenomenon. Assume that in a population of 1,000 subjects, 15% ($n = 150$) will commit a violent act and 85% ($n = 850$) will not. Assume also that the clinician can accurately classify 90% of each group. In this example, the clinician will accurately label as violent 135 (150 × 0.90) truly violent individuals, whereas only 85 cases labeled "violent" (850 × 0.10) will be persons who on follow-up in fact will not be violent. Thus, the percent-false-positive figure will be a relatively respectable 39% [85/(135 + 85)]. As the incidence of violence gets smaller, however, this error rate increases. If, for instance, the incidence of violence in the 1,000-person population is only 5%, the same clinician (with the same accuracy rate of 90%) will have a false-positive rate of 68% (95/(45 + 95)).

(2)　First-Generation Prediction Studies

From the 1960s through the early 1980s, a number of studies addressed long-term predictions of dangerous behavior. These studies, collectively the "first-generation" violence prediction studies, took place in a political climate characterized by considerable concern regarding psychiatric control over the lives of persons with mental disorder.[240] Consequently, researchers' and policymakers' attention focused on the percent-false-positive index.

Table 9.2 summarizes the essential findings from a number of these prediction studies, organized according to the populations about whom the predictions were made. These studies varied considerably in methodology, which renders direct comparisons among them difficult (we encourage readers to review them). However, all of them focused on long-term prediction, and most utilized formal records—rearrest or rehospitalization—as dependent measures of violent recidivism. As the third column of Table 9.2 reveals, most of the studies obtained a false-positive percentage over 50%. Reviews of this literature, conducted a decade apart, concluded that when mental health professionals make affirmative predictions of violence, they will likely be accurate in no more than one-third of the cases.[241]

During the same period that these data were produced, other information casting a negative light on psychiatric assessments of violence emerged from studies of the predictive process and from case law. Pfohl studied the decisionmaking process of 12 teams of mental health professionals at the Lima State Hospital in Ohio.[242] These teams were charged with the responsibility of reviewing the dangerousness of all clients who had been involuntarily committed. Pfohl noted that the various teams periodically used differing and idiosyncratic criteria, including (1) a client's past record, (2) the client's ability to express insight into past deeds of violence, (3) the client's dreams and fantasies, (4) the results of psychological tests, or (5) signs of "repressed anger." One team reportedly considered "how they would feel having this man as (their) next door neighbor."[243] Pfohl also found that the ultimate impression of a patient's dangerousness was the outgrowth of compromise and negotiation among various team

Table 9.2
Summary of First-Generation Violence Prediction Studies

Study	Criterion behavior	False positives	Follow-up
	Studies of Department of Correction parolees		
Wenk, Robison, & Smith[a]			
Study 1	Documented act of violence	86%	?
Study 2	Crime involving violence	99.7%	1 year
Study 3	Documented violent act	93.8%	15 months
	Studies of maximum security forensic patients		
Steadman & Cocozza[b]	Rearrest or rehospitalized for an assaultive act	85%	3½ years
Thornberry & Jacoby[c]	Arrest or rehospitalization for a violent act	85.5%	4 years
Mullen & Reinehr[d]	Arrest for violent crime	89%	1–2 years
	Studies of special-track offenders (dangerous sex offenders, defective delinquents)		
Kozol, Boucher, & Garofalo[e]	Committing a serious assaultive act	65%	5 years
Rappeport[f]	Rearrest for *any* offense, violent or nonviolent	19–61%	?
Sidley[g]	Commission of an "aggravated" crime	67–81%	?
	Studies of pretrial offenders (incompetent to stand trial)		
Steadman & Cocozza[h]	Assaultive behavior while in the hospital	44%	?
	Assaultive behavior in community (arrest or rehospitalization for assaultive crime)	84%	?
Cocozza & Steadman[i]	Rearrest for violent offense	86%	3 years
Sepajak, Menzies, Webster, & Jensen[j]	Criminal charges; behavior precipitating hospitalization; behavior in hospital and prison	44%	2 years
	Studies of community residents evaluated for dangerousness		
Levinson & Ramsay[k]	Threats or actions that endangered the well-being of others	47%	1 year
	Acts that endangered the well-being of others	71%	1 year

[a]Data from Ernst Wenk et al., *Can Violence Be Predicted?*, 18 CRIME & DELINQ. 393–402 (1972).

[b]Data from Henry J. Steadman & Joseph Cocozza, *The Prediction of Dangerousness—Baxstrom: A Case Study, in* THE ROLE OF THE FORENSIC PSYCHOLOGIST 204 (Gerald Cook ed. 1980).

[c]Data from TERENCE P. THORNBERRY & JOSEPH E. JACOBY, *supra* note 272.

[d]Data from James M. Mullen & Robert C. Reinehr, *Predicting Dangerousness of Maximum Security Forensic Patients*, 10 J. PSYCHIATRY & L. 223–31 (1982).

[e]Data from Harry L. Kozol et al., *The Diagnosis and Treatment of Dangerousness*, 18 CRIME & DELINQ. 371–92 (1972).

[f]Data from Jonas Rappeport, *Enforced Treatment: Is It Treatment?*, 2 BULL. AM. ACAD. PSYCHIATRY & L. 148–58 (1974).

[g]Sidley, *supra* note 175.

[h]Data from Steadman & Cocozza, *supra* note 229.

[i]Data from Cocozza & Steadman, *supra* note 229.

[j]Data from Diana S. Sepejak et al., *Clinical Prediction of Dangerousness: Two-Year Follow-Up of 408 Pretrial Forensic Cases*, 11 BULL. AM. ACAD. PSYCHIATRY & L. 171–81 (1983).

[k]Data from Levinson & Ramsay, *supra* note 235.

members, many of whom yielded to the most in-fluential team member, usually the psychiatrist. The written report, however, was couched in technical and diagnostic language that hid the compromise nature of the finding. This study il-lustrated the point made earlier—how factors such as clinicians' theoretical preferences and the social context in which such judgments are made may influence decisions regarding violence po-tential.

A Texas death penalty case that reached the United States Supreme Court, *Estelle v. Smith*,[244] was also influential in shaping opinion regarding psychiatric predictions of violence. On the basis of a brief "mental status examination," the state's psychiatric expert, Dr. James Grigson, testified that Smith was a "very severe sociopath"[245] who, if given the opportunity to do so, "is going to go ahead and commit other similar or same criminal acts given the opportunity to do so."[246] These conclusions apparently followed largely from the single clinical impression that the offender "lacked remorse," which is neither necessary nor sufficient to establish a sociopathic personality di-agnosis in any conventional nosology. The fact that Smith had not killed the victim in the case at hand (an accomplice had), combined with the ab-sence of any prior documented history of violent behavior (Smith's sole conviction was for posses-sion of marijuana), and the obviously flimsy basis for the conclusions offered the sentencing court, led Dix to conclude that the psychiatrist was op-erating "at the brink of quackery,"[247] a conclusion with which it is difficult to muster much dis-agreement.[248]

The research and observations about psychi-atric predictions of dangerousness led to several proposals for limitations on mental health in-volvement in this area. Characterizing psychiatric expertise in violence prediction as tantamount to "flipping coins in the courtroom," Ennis and Litwack argued that such opinion testimony should be barred from the courtroom, a recom-mendation echoed by many others.[249] Several commentators also recommended ethical guide-lines for such testimony.[250] For instance, noting that expert opinions are routinely prefaced by claims of "reasonable scientific certainty," Stone commented that "[t]he assertion of clinical cer-tainty about future dangerousness is problematic

and it is arguably unethical to claim such certainty in light of the empirical evidence."[251]

Despite these suggestions, however, clinical prediction testimony continues to be offered. It appears that Stone's ethical injunctions are not followed by most mental health professionals. In-deed, a fair reading of the contemporary litera-ture reveals a marked enthusiasm for engaging in categorical predictions (i.e., predictions that ex-press certainty about violence).[252] Furthermore, courts have not been reluctant to accept such tes-timony. Indeed, as noted in § 9.05, in 1983 the Supreme Court's decision in *Barefoot v. Estelle* per-mitted such testimony in *death penalty* cases. Ig-noring amicus briefs describing the first-genera-tion research and making the legal arguments presented by Ennis, Litwack, and others, the Court reasoned that prediction testimony was not *always* wrong and that the jury, aided by the adver-sarial system and rebuttal experts, could be trust-ed to separate "the wheat from the chaff."[253]

(3)   Critique of First-Generation Studies

One reason the implications of the first-genera-tion research have been resisted is the recogni-tion, by an increasing number of commenta-tors,[254] that much of it was flawed, in ways that would be expected to exaggerate false-positive predictions of violent behavior. First, in many of the studies the persons determined to be at high risk for violence were confined and never re-leased during the follow-up period or were treat-ed before they were released. As a result, the sample of persons studied (i.e., those who were released and followed up) was restricted in a way that reduced clinicians' "chances" of attaining higher accuracy rates. A second problem is that some studies did not examine predictions derived from careful clinical assessment; rather, a purely administrative decision or cursory clinical contact was used as a proxy for a clinical judgment. Even among studies that involved actual assessments, researchers often utilized as evidence that a pre-diction of dangerousness had been made gross measures (e.g., psychotic vs. nonpsychotic) seem-ingly selected more on the basis of convenience than from careful theoretical considerations.

A third methodological problem had to do with the dependent measures of violence. As revealed in the second column of Table 9.2, researchers commonly used official records of rehospitalization or rearrest as outcome measures. These measures are flawed both qualitatively and quantitatively.[255] Qualitatively, they tend to focus exclusively on serious aggressive acts. Although these acts are important, they may not reflect the only conduct that meets the threshold of legally relevant dangerousness. The exclusion of relevant but less serious instances of aggression from the dependent measure may therefore fail to identify correctly all those who were "violent" during follow-up. Even more important, records of arrest and rehospitalization are weak measures of violence from a quantitative perspective. Rather than accurately reflecting the actions of the study subjects, these measures probably capture only the efficiency and behavior of the police and other social control agents. To the degree that the subjects perform violent acts that go unreported or commit reported acts these agents do not resolve through arrest or hospitalization, "true positives" are incorrectly coded as not violent during follow-up.

It is impossible to determine how much violent behavior has gone undetected in prior studies due to restricted samples, inadequate predictor variables, and inadequate outcome measures. However, the magnitude of the problem is suggested by the results of more recent research projects that followed subjects released shortly after the prediction, utilized more comprehensive definitions of violence, and relied on both official records and follow-up interviews with research subjects and collateral informants. In prior research investigating violence in the community by discharged mental patients, arrest rates during an average follow-up period of one year have been in the 2–5% range.[256] In a more recent study looking at emergency-room patients discharged into the community, Mulvey similarly reported a 3% rehospitalization and arrest rate, but he found a *40% incidence of violence* when relying on self- and collateral reports.[257] Steadman and colleagues also found substantially higher base rates (33.6%) using self- and collateral reports of violence in the community.[258] For the reasons explained earlier [see § 9.09(b)(1)], a 30–40% increase in base rates will have an inverse effect on the false-positive rate (i.e., it will be lower) even when predictive abilities remain unchanged.

(4) Risk Assessment and Management: A Second Generation of Research

In light of concerns with the earlier violence prediction studies, what conclusions can be drawn about the capacity of mental health professionals to assist in determinations of dangerousness? One is that the conventional reading of this body of studies—that clinical predictions of violence are likely to be wrong two out of three times—is too harsh a conclusion. Methodological limitations have probably combined to result in overestimates of the percent-false-positive statistic. Monahan suggested as early as 1984 that "there may . . . be a ceiling on the level of accuracy that can ever be expected of clinical prediction of violent behavior. That ceiling, however, may be closer to 50% . . . among some groups of clinical interest."[259]

Indeed, even some of the older studies suggested as much (see Table 9.2). Newer data also support this conclusion.[260] For instance, a study by Lidz, Mulvey, and Gardner,[261] described as "surely the most sophisticated study ever done of the clinical prediction of violence,"[262] yielded a false-positive percentage of 47%.

A second, and obvious, conclusion is the need for better research.[263] In the article quoted from above, Monahan called for a "second generation" of studies using research designs that corrected for the flaws in earlier studies. In this regard, there are at least two major study programs of note. One is funded by the National Institute of Mental Health through grants to Lidz and Mulvey at the Western Psychiatric Institute at the University of Pittsburgh, which resulted in the data referred to in the preceding paragraph.[264] The other is the MacArthur Risk Study, funded by the John D. and Catherine T. MacArthur Foundation through grants to Monahan and discussed in more detail later.[265]

A final observation is that the earlier research's fixation on percentage of false positives is not a particularly productive way to evaluate the utility of clinical input to legal decisions about dangerousness. Our view, developed in more detail below, is that rather than studying categorical judgments, the research should focus on providing clinical, descriptive, and empirical information that informs legal judgments about *risk assessment* (i.e., under what circumstances will violence occur?) and *risk management* (i.e., under what circumstances can risk be minimized?).

(c) Assessment of (Long-Term) Risk for Violence

PROBLEM 9.2

Read the report on Lester Thomas in § 19.05(c), up to the section on risk assessment. Draft the risk assessment part of the report. Compare it to the actual draft.

With due regard to the difficulty of the enterprise, this discussion attempts to provide guidelines for ensuring the best possible evaluation of violence-proneness. It starts by conceptualizing the evaluation and then offers specific suggestions, derived from the research, for performing an evaluation and presenting the results.

(1) Three Approaches to the Assessment of Risk

Miller and Morris describe three approaches to risk assessment, which they label "clinical," "actuarial," and "anamnestic."[266] The clinical method relies on unsystematic and widely differing approaches to data gathering and synthesis. As such, it is difficult to describe, although some flavor of the endeavor should have been obtained from reading the foregoing research descriptions of the typical prediction process. In contrast to clinical prediction, actuarial prediction explicitly identifies the criteria used and the weights assigned to each; the choice of data categories is driven by empirical research that demonstrates which groups of individuals, because of specific characteristics that determine group membership, are at relatively higher risk. A rigorously actuarial approach would also involve the mathematical combination of these variables to generate the prediction.[267] Finally, the anamnestic approach depends on the identification of factors that have distinguished a particular subject's prior displays of aggressive behavior. The clinician attempts to reconstruct vignettes through archival information detailing specific prior incidents of violence and through direct clinical interview of the individual and collateral sources. Analysis of these vignettes should yield insights about repetitive themes that

cut across violent events, revealing person or situational factors, or person-situation interactions, that inform judgments of risk-level or risk-management strategies.

As should be clear from this brief description, these three approaches are not mutually exclusive. Keeping them separate for the moment, however, some comparisons of their advantages and disadvantages are possible. Clinical predictions of dangerousness have been faulted because the process for generating the prediction can be difficult to ferret out. Those using this method may indicate that they attend to a large number of variables, but the calculus applied to yield classifications of "dangerous" or "not dangerous" is unknown. In testimony, the clinical reasoning may be put forth in a fashion that is difficult to penetrate by cross-examination or other means; lawyers may find the obfuscation of labels and jargon too much to cope with.[268]

The actuarial approach also has shortcomings, however. Two such shortcomings are its inability to consider case-specific information and the practical problem of getting judges or jurors to understand and use it. With respect to the first, once the specific predictors in an actuarial technique are set, all other information is irrelevant. Thus, an offender who has unique violence-reducing characteristics or situations that are not recognized in the literature may still be classified as "dangerous" by an actuarial procedure—equations tend to be inflexible. With respect to the second criticism, research has shown that persons in decisionmaking positions who receive both clinical case material and statistical information tend to prefer the former and to ignore the latter, even though the latter information may be highly relevant.[269] Given this possibility of misunderstanding statistics, and the attendant potential for intentional manipulation of them, some have proposed special procedures for the admission of this type of evidence.[270]

Most important, although actuarial prediction has been shown to be superior to clinical prediction in virtually every area of behavior that researchers have studied, only the promise, and not the practicality, of the former has been demonstrated in the area of risk assessment and violence prediction.[271] Few studies have contrasted clinical versus statistical predictions of violence, and the advantage of statistical prediction in these studies has been meager.[272] Further, most research in this area has involved single sites and small samples, which, along with failure to cross-validate the actuarial techniques, severely limits the generalizability of findings. The bottom line is that the research has not delivered an actuarial equation suitable for clinical application in the area of violence prediction.

Absent a proven formula we must continue, in Meehl's words, to "use our heads."[273] With this in mind, we encourage clinicians to use a combination of the "actuarial" and "anamnestic" approaches defined by Miller and Morris. By reading the published literature, clinicians can identify factors from a variety of domains (e.g., demographics and clinical features) that have established empirical correlations with violence. Depending on the features present and the strength of their associations with violence recidivism, the presence of more, or fewer, such factors in an individual case may then guide judgments about that person's relative risk for violence.[274] As do Miller and Morris, however, we stop short of recommending the more rigorously statistical approach of mathematically combining the data. Further, as developed below, added to the consideration of cues that have been correlated empirically with violence should be case-specific clinical judgment.

(2)   Empirical Correlates of Dangerousness

As noted earlier, the research on correlates of violence and recidivism is extensive. It indicates that a wide variety of factors are associated with violence, although few can be said to be strong

Table 9.3
Factors Related to Risk Assessment

1. **Dispositional factors**	C. History of crime and violence
A. Demographic	1. Arrests
1. Age	2. Incarcerations
2. Gender	3. Self-reported violence
3. Race	4. Violence toward self
4. Social class	
	3. **Contextual factors**
B. Personality	A. Perceived stress
1. Personality style	
2. Anger	B. Social support
3. Impulsiveness	1. Living arrangements
4. Psychopathy	2. Activities of daily living
	3. Perceived support
C. Cognitive	4. Social networks
1. IQ	C. Means for violence (i.e., guns)
2. Neurological impairment	
	4. **Clinical factors**
2. **Historical cues**	A. Axis I diagnosis
A. Social history	
1. Family history	B. Symptoms
Child rearing	1. Delusions
Child abuse	2. Hallucinations
Family deviance	3. Symptom severity
2. Work history	4. Violent fantasies
Employment	
Job perceptions	C. Axis II diagnosis
3. Educational history	
	D. Functioning
B. Mental hospitalization history	
1. Prior hospitalizations	E. Substance abuse
2. Treatment compliance	1. Alcohol
	2. Other drugs

predictors. Table 9.3, developed in the MacArthur Risk Assessment Study,[275] provides an organizational scheme for the major categories that might be considered potential risk factors.

Even with this table as an organizing heuristic, the number of general risk factors available for investigation is intimidating. The clinician's task is even more daunting considering the variability in state-of-the-art of measurement across domains and the absence of any accepted calculus for weighting and combining data that the clinician is able to measure. Indeed, the wealth of information in this table and the difficulty of accumulating and interpreting it may actually detract from the validity of an examination. As Monahan, one of the preeminent scholars in this area, has stated, "[F]ocusing on a limited number of *relevant valid* predictor items is . . . more important than an exhaustive examination that yields much irrelevant and ultimately confusing information."[276]

The recent research on risk assessment suggests that in fact there is a subset of factors that are more relevant and/or better supported by the research literature than are others. As comprehensive reviews of the literature reveal, some factors have been derived from studies using weak designs or that have not been replicated.[277] Others have been studied in relative isolation, without consideration given to how their relationship to violence may be influenced by other factors. For example, among demographic factors race has often been identified as a potentially important predictor, with African American status indicating higher risk for violence. However, the explanatory or predictive power of race as a correlate of violence has often been reduced to nonsignificance when the effect of factors such as socioeconomic status have been considered.[278]

At the same time, certain factors have been relatively rigorously tested and their relevance is supported by a more impressive body of research. Although we encourage mental health professionals to read the violence prediction/risk assessment literature for themselves, we offer in Table 9.4 a list of factors we think fall into the latter category, organized in terms of dispositional characteristics (gender, age, and personality characteristics such as antisocial personality disorder and psychopathy), historical facts (adult and juvenile arrest history, age of onset), contextual factors (weapon and victim availability, social support), and clinical factors (psychoses and substance abuse disorders).

Note that some of these factors are likely to be relevant to risk assessment only, while others are relevant to both risk assessment and risk management.[279] For example, dispositional factors and historical factors represent elements that are, in large part, inflexible and not subject to direct manipulation or control. Demographic features (e.g., gender and age) are fixed, and certain personality characteristics (e.g., basic personality style and IQ level) may not be changeable to any significant degree; similarly, prior events that may correlate with violence recidivism, such as arrest record or history of victimization as a child, cannot be undone. These factors may inform the fundamental judgment about baseline level of risk, but to address risk management issues clinicians will ordinarily have to focus on situational and contextual factors that may be subject to manipulation or on changeable clinical conditions.

In the first *dispositional* category, demographic factors, the literature generally reveals a positive association with criminality for younger persons and males. Although not as firmly established (and therefore not noted in the table), lower socioeconomic status is also sometimes implicated as a predictor and, as noted previously, may significantly account for the association sometimes found between race (nonwhite) and criminality.

As for personality factors, perhaps the single most promising recent development in risk assessment of correctional and forensic populations has been the Psychopathy Checklist—Revised (PCL-R). The PCL-R is a clinical instrument that yields ratings on 20 scales which load on two factors.[280] These scales tap a number of behavioral traits and historical features, including impulsivity, delinquency, and adult criminal behavior, that have been identified in research as associated with violence, criminality, or aggression. Although use of conventional psychological tests for purposes of violence prediction/risk assessment generally has significant drawbacks,[281] studies have consistently shown PCL-R scores to be helpful in identifying persons at greater risk for criminal recidivism and to have good interrater reliability (see Table 9.4, footnotes e–h). In addition to informing judgments about violence recidivism, PCL-R

Table 9.4
Factors Associated with Violence Recidivism

Dispositional factors	
Demographics	
Gender	Males are higher risk than females.
	Comments: Males at higher risk is a more robust finding in studies limited to serious expressions of violence (e.g., felony arrest reports). Some studies using collateral and self-report measures have reported a higher incidence of lesser violence among women.[a]
	Studies of domestic violence often find that women are more likely to be violent than are men.[b]
Age	Youth is associated with higher risk.
	Comments: Greatest risk is late adolescence to early adulthood.
	Some studies suggest a drop in aggressive behavior after age 40. This "burn out" phenomenon may not hold for male psychopaths.[c]
Personality disorders	
Antisocial personality disorder	APD is significantly associated with criminality in adults.
	Comments: The presence of APD mediates the association between major psychoses and crime; APD and substance abuse disorders together explain the association between crime and psychoses.[d]
Psychopathy	Psychopathy, as measured by the Psychopathy Checklist—Revised (PCL-R), is positively associated with parole failure[e] and violence recidivism in correctional/forensic populations.[f]
	Comments: Psychopathy (PCL-R) is related to, but distinguishable from, APD as defined by the DSM.[g] PCL-R may be a better predictor of violence recidivism than is APD.[h]

Historical factors	
Arrest history	The single most robust predictor of future violence is a history of multiple prior offenses. Some studies suggest that recidivism risk exceeds 50% for persons with more than five prior offenses.[i]
Conduct disorder and delinquency	Conduct disorder (CD) is associated with adult criminality. Its primary effect is through its association with delinquency and adult disorders (APD, substance abuse).[j]
	Comments: Childhood history of comorbid problems (CD with ADHD or aggressivity) is risk factor for delinquency/adult criminal behavior.[k] Childhood psychopathy, measured separately from conduct disorder, may be an important factor underlying delinquency.[l]
Age of onset	Early onset (age ≤ 13) is a significant predictor of delinquency careers and adult criminal activity.[m]

Contextual factors	
Weapon availability	Risk enhanced, particularly for more lethal forms of violence, when weapons are readily available.
	Comments: Clinical factors associated with increased propensity for weapons accumulation include (1) paranoid features and (2) use of stimulants (speed).[n]
Social support	Social networks can serve as a buffer against life stresses, thus aiding in adjustment/coping. Due in part to increased availability, family members may be at increased risk for violent victimization, especially where there is a prior history of domestic violence.[o]
	Comments: Risk for violence toward significant others may be enhanced when those persons are involved in setting limits[p] or are perceived by the individual to be threatening or hostile.[q]
Victim availability	Higher risk for persons with history of violence toward a broad range of victims, or multiple assaults on narrow class of victims who remain available (e.g., significant others).

(continued)

Table 9.4. Continued

Clinical factors	
Major psychoses	There is a modest association between *current diagnosis* of major psychoses (manic–depressive illness, schizophrenia) and violence in the community. Data from the ECA studies suggest a risk multiplier of about six compared to undiagnosed persons.[r]
	Comments: Having been diagnosed previously for major mental illness or having been hospitalized for same is *not* an indicator for increased risk.[s] The presence of current active symptoms explains the relationship between psychosis and violence.[t]
	Specific psychotic symptoms associated with enhanced risk include persecutory delusions (inducing perceived threat) and thought insertion/control (inducing perceived loss of internal controls).[u]
Substance abuse	Association between substance abuse diagnoses and violent behavior suggests a risk multiplier of 12–16 compared to the risk level of undiagnosed persons.[v]

[a]In the MacArthur Risk Study, incidence of violence during the initial follow-up period was 22.4% (males) versus 32.8% (females). Steadman et al., *supra* note 256, at 310. Lidz et al. reported rates of 42% (males) versus 49% (females), *supra* note 261, at 1010.

[b]R. Bland & H. Orn, *Family Violence and Psychiatric Disorder*, 31 CAN. J. PSYCHIATRY 129– 37 (1986). K. D. O'Leary et al., *Prevalence and Stability of Physical Aggression between Spouses: A Longitudinal Analysis*, 57 J. CONSULTING & CLINICAL PSYCHOL. 263 (1989).

[c]ROBERT D. HARE, THE HARE PSYCHOPATHY CHECKLIST—REVISED, 1991. *See* Robert Hare et al. *Male Psychopaths and Their Criminal Careers*, 56 J. CONSULTING & CLINICAL PSYCHOL. 710 (1988); age-related decreases in criminal behavior among psychopaths were accounted for largely by reduction in nonviolent offenses.

[d]Lee N. Robins, *Childhood Conduct Problems, Adult Psychopathology, and Crime*, in MENTAL DISORDER AND CRIME, *supra* note 226, at 183.

[e]Stephen D. Hart et al., *Performance of Male Psychopaths Following Conditional Release from Prison*, 56 J. CONSULTING & CLINICAL PSYCHOL. 227–32 (1988). Ralph C. Serin et al., *Predictors of Psychopathy and Release Outcome in a Criminal Population*, 2 PSYCHOL. ASSESSMENT: J. CONSULTING & CLINICAL PSYCHOL. 419–22 (1990).

[f]Robert D. Hare & Stephen D. Hart, *Psychopathy Mental Disorder, and Crime*, in MENTAL DISORDER AND CRIME, *supra* note 226, at 104–18.

[g]Robert D. Hare et al., *Psychopathy and the DSM-IV Criteria for Antisocial Personality Disorder*, 100 J. CONSULTING & CLINICAL PSYCHOLOGY 391–98 (1991).

[h]Grant T. Harris et al., *Psychopathy and Violence Recidivism*, 15 LAW & HUM. BEHAV. 625–37 (1991).

[i]Steadman & Cocozza, *supra* note 229.

[j]Robins, *supra* note d, at 188 (this table).

[k]Maughan, *supra* note 285.

[l]Paul Frick, *Psychopathy and Conduct Problems in Children*, 103 J. ABNORMAL PSYCHOLOGY 700 (1994).

[m]Gerald R. Patterson & Karen Yoerger, *Developmental Models for Delinquent Behavior*, in MENTAL DISORDER AND CRIME, *supra* note 226, at 140–72; Patrick H. Tolan, *Implications of Age of Onset for Delinquency Risk*, 15 J. ABNORMAL PSYCHOLOGY 47–65 (1987).

[n]REID MELOY, ASSESSMENT OF VIOLENCE POTENTIAL (1993).

[o]Edward W. Gondolf et al., *Characteristics of Family and Nonfamily Assaults*, 41 HOSP. & COMMUNITY PSYCHIATRY 191–93 (1990).

[p]Katherine A. Straznickas, *Violence Toward Family Caregivers*, 44 HOSP. & COMMUNITY PSYCHIATRY 385–87, 387 (1993).

[q]Sue E. Estroff & Catherine Zimmer, *Social Networks, Social Support, and Violence among Persons with Severe, Persistent Mental Illness*, in VIOLENCE AND MENTAL DISORDER, *supra* note 256, at 280.

[r]Jeffrey W. Swanson et al., *Violence and Psychiatric Disorder in the Community: Evidence from the Epidemiologic Catchment Area Surveys*, 41 HOSP. & COMMUNITY PSYCHIATRY 761–70 (1990).

[s]Swanson, in VIOLENCE AND MENTAL DISORDER *supra* note 256, at 132.

[t]Bruce G. Link et al., *The Violent and Illegal Behavior of Mental Patients Reconsidered*, 57 AM. SOC. REV. 275–92 (1992).

[u]Bruce G. Link & Ann Stueve, *Psychotic Symptoms and the Violent/Illegal Behavior of Mental Patients Compared to Community Controls*, in VIOLENCE AND MENTAL DISORDER, *supra* note 256.

[v]Swanson et al., *supra* note p (this table). Substance abuse diagnosis moderates the relationship between major mental disorder and crime. See also Robins, *supra* note d (this table).

scores may also inform judgments about the appropriateness of certain treatment programs for individuals being considered for therapeutic placements.[282] Note also that, as indicated in Table 9.4, psychopathy as measured by the PCL-R is distinguishable from the DSM diagnosis of antisocial personality disorder (APD), which is *not* as useful a predictor.[283]

For assessing baseline level of risk, *historical* factors such as adult criminal record and delinquency history are among the most important factors that may inform clinical judgments. Several recent papers describe well the developmental pathways to delinquency careers and adult violent behavior, including the linkages between childhood disorders such as conduct disorder (CD) and attention-deficit hyperactivity disorder (ADHD), parenting style or effectiveness, school/socialization failures, and affiliation with delinquent peer groups.[284] One caveat is that the impact of these developmental factors may be largely indirect, having greater influence through their association with APD/psychopathy in adulthood.[285] Absent APD/psychopathy or a clear adult arrest record, the prognostic value of a history of CD/delinquency or hyperactivity is more difficult to determine.[286]

Contextual factors have been less frequently and systematically examined for their relationship to violence recidivism. Further, as noted earlier, their changeability probably has greater implications for risk management than for evaluating baseline risk level. One of the important contextual factors is the degree of social support. Many mental health professionals have failed to appreciate the complexities of this construct.[287] Although it has generally been believed that having a support network is more favorable prognostically than having none, it is no longer a safe assumption that "objective" social support is benign. Investigators have come to recognize that qualitative differences in the type(s) of support offered (emotional, instrumental, information, and appraisal or feedback) and the recipient's point of view (*perceived* social support) may be important determinants of whether the proffered support is experienced by the person as a buffer or as just another source of stress.[288] Further, a comprehensive review by Estroff and Morrissey found little pertinent research bearing on the relationship of social support systems to violence recidivism. Clinicians should continue to evaluate whether, and what type(s) of, social support is potentially available; rather than assuming that available support is beneficial, they should be more detailed in their inquiries about prior interactions between the person being evaluated and the support network [see Table 9.4, note a].

Contextual factors also interact with factors related to violence potential. For instance, the effect of a diagnosis indicating substance abuse, one of the clinical predictors, must be tempered with information about alcohol or drug availability. Persons with a history of aggression may be more likely to recidivate if previous aggression has been directed toward both family and nonfamily victims than at one of these two classes of victims.[289] In the same vein, a history of involvement with delinquent or criminal peer groups accentuates the significance of prior aggression. These kinds of factors may all be important considerations that inform judgments about community placement and the type/level of supervision needed in that setting.

With respect to *clinical* factors, probably the most controversial issue has been whether a connection exists between serious mental disorder and violence. In the last decade epidemiological studies have established a positive, although modest, link between mental disorder and violence.[290] In the studies that have confirmed this relationship, however, most persons with mental disorder were *not* violent during the evaluation period; thus, it is relative risk level rather than absolute risk level that has been established.[291] It is also evident from the research that persons who suffer from both substance abuse and major psychosis are at greater risk than those who suffer either type of disorder, although the greater concern from a public health perspective is substance abuse, given the greater prevalence of that disorder.[292]

As Table 9.4 indicates, there may also be a connection between violence and particular symptoms of psychosis—that is, threat-inducing symptoms (e.g., paranoid delusions) and control override symptoms (e.g., feeling controlled by external forces or thoughts not your own). Most of the evidence supporting this correlation comes from *post hoc* analyses. However, the finding is consistent with clinical insights and anecdotal data about the potential role of these symptoms.[293] (There are also complementary findings in other research suggesting that certain other acute psychotic symptoms, such as mental confusion[294] or formal thought disorder,[295] may be associated with a *reduced* risk for violence.) At the same time, as Link and his colleagues note, many persons who experience threat/control override symptoms do not act violently. Therefore, rather than thinking of these latter symptoms as discrete predictors of violence, it is probably better to treat them as factors that place the person at increased risk.[296]

In conclusion, other things being equal, research establishes that the factors in Table 9.4, if present, are likely to be associated with poorer outcomes (violence recidivism). Although there is no empirically established calculus for combining these factors, we offer the flow chart in Table 9.5 as one rational way of developing initial baseline judgments of relative risk.

Dispositional and historical factors whose associations with violence in the community have been most reliably established—psychopathy (APD) and history of criminality (delinquency/adult criminal record)—appear earliest in the table. Weaker factors (clinical diagnoses) appear later in the sequence. Two aspects of the table require elaboration. With respect to psychopathy, for reasons suggested above we recommend as the criterion measure the use of the PCL-R rather than the DSM diagnosis of APD, at least with males (the PCL-R has not been validated for use with females, so the DSM diagnosis of APD will have to be utilized in evaluation of the latter group). With respect to criminal history, a general guideline for a positive rating in that column is more than two convictions for serious or felonious crimes.[297]

Readers should *not* construe this table as representing an absolutely linear set of outcomes. Judgments about the risk levels associated with different paths may be modified by consideration of other variables not represented in the table. Among persons with a history of violent episodes, for instance, the risk may be greater for males (except where that history is exclusively family assaults), especially young males. Similarly, some individuals who are assessed as presenting a lesser risk will behave aggressively because of variables not included in the table.[298] Other things being equal, however, relatively higher risk for violence recidivism should be associated with the upper paths of the chart. These baseline judgments may provide a starting point for evaluating and considering individualized violence histories.

(3)   Individualized (Anamnestic) Risk Appraisal

Although risk assessments may be guided to a significant degree by research findings of the type reported above, the limited utility of these kinds of correlational data was expressed well by Shah: "[B]ecause what is classified are the *disorders* that people have—not the people—there typically are many within-category variations among individuals given the same diagnosis (e.g., with respect to the particular patterns, severity, fluctuation of symptoms, etc.)."[299]

Shah was speaking specifically to clinical diagnosis as a risk factor, but the same observation applies to all types of variables. There are many individual differences that may provide important information about the risk for violence in particular cases. Clinicians cannot rely solely on actuarial information but must also examine data from the person's violence history for themes or indicators as to that individual's expressions of violence. Although this anamnestic analysis may explore many of the same factors discussed in the previous section, its focus on the individual may often uncover violence-related factors not characteristically associated with violence in group studies.

The anamnestic evaluation should involve a detailed reconstruction of the client's prior violent actions, much as one might undertake in an insanity evaluation [see § 8.06]. The most commonly available information about such events will usually be that provided by the client, who may even be willing to disclose prior incidents that have not led to apprehension by the authorities. This information can be augmented by available police reports, transcribed witness statements, telephone interviews with family members or other collaterals, and other archival information.

The attempt to discover repeated themes of violence can be facilitated if mental health profes-

Table 9.5
Combining Factors to Estimate Relative Baseline Risk

PCL/APD score	CD/delinq. and age of onset	Adult criminal record	Clinical diagnosis	Relative risk
High	Early	Yes	Substance abuse / Major psychosis / No diagnosis	Higher risk
		No	Substance abuse / Major psychosis / No diagnosis	
	Late	Yes	Substance abuse / Major psychosis / No diagnosis	
		No	Substance abuse / Major psychosis / No diagnosis	
	None	Yes	Substance abuse / Major psychosis / No diagnosis	
		No	Substance abuse / Major psychosis / No diagnosis	
Low	Early	Yes	Substance abuse / Major psychosis / No diagnosis	
		No	Substance abuse / Major psychosis / No diagnosis	
	Late	Yes	Substance abuse / Major psychosis / No diagnosis	
		No	Substance abuse / Major psychosis / No diagnosis	
	None	Yes	Substance abuse / Major psychosis / No diagnosis	
		No	Substance abuse / Major psychosis / No diagnosis	Lower risk

sionals systematically record the relevant information. For each violent incident in the person's history, narrative information can be coded to indicate categories of behavior from different domains (Table 9.3) or along theoretically relevant dimensions. Coding should include apparent motivation and perpetrator–victim dynamics in addition to historical and descriptive variables. Factors that recur across vignettes may then form the basis for hypotheses about particular themes or triggers of violence for that individual. The identification of these features (e.g., threat/control override symptoms) can then serve as the starting point for recommendations regarding management and control.

(4) Formulations Regarding Risk

Many mental health professionals testify in conclusory terms about whether or not individuals are "dangerous." Our review of the issues in risk assessment and our interpretation of ethical considerations lead us to counsel against developing such categorical formulations. Although the literature on violence prediction by mental health professionals is perhaps not as dismal as once thought, the field has yet to demonstrate that such predictions are likely to be highly accurate. In addition, the ambiguity of legal definitions of violence and the general concern regarding ultimate-issue testimony make conclusory testimony problematic.

We recommend instead that clinicians formulate their judgments in *relative* risk terms. Based on a rational integration of actuarial risk factors such as the model in Table 9.5, modified as appropriate based on careful anamnestic analysis, clinicians can use descriptors such as "relatively low" or "moderately high" when talking about risk for future violence. Reports or testimony explaining these risk assessments should include, of course, reference to relevant empirical correlates of violence and descriptive clinical information (attitudes, threats, violence fantasies, symptoms, etc.). With this information, the court can then decide the appropriate level of correctional control (regular vs. intensively supervised probation or incarceration), taking into account other important sentencing considerations such as retribution and general deterrence.

When the court is considering a lenient disposition (e.g., community placement), reports should also make recommendations about ways to reduce risk. For instance, for individuals whose violence appears to be the product of serious mental disorder, recommendations about management will require information about treatment adherence and treatment efficacy. If personal control is compromised by frequent use of alcohol or drugs, the efficacy of substance abuse treatment programs (including antiabuse therapy), as well as more intensive supervision (e.g.,

urine screens or other monitoring), may need to be considered. If placement in the community is an option, consideration about the likely living arrangements for the individual is necessary; the clinician may need to be prepared to indicate whether the court should consider imposing environmental constraints that limit access to certain individuals (e.g., potential victims and aggressive peers) or items (e.g., removal of weapons or alcohol from the home). Generally, recommendations about relative risk level should vary depending on the anticipated level of treatment and supervision or other external controls applied to the defendant. Thus, clinicians might be well advised to think and to recommend in terms of "conditional" risk, rather than offering static appraisals of risk level.[300]

Consistent with our admonition in connection with testimony about treatment [see § 9.07(a)], clinicians should formulate these types of recommendations in the form of "If . . . , then . . ." statements. The need for an outpatient substance abuse program or anger management counseling to curb domestic violence will obviously be less salient if the judge's decision, based on other considerations (past record, retribution), is going to be long-term confinement.

The approach recommended here, based on assessments that are informed by a careful reading of the empirical literature, firmly grounds clinical testimony about "dangerousness" on a specialized body of knowledge that stands outside the ken of laypersons and should incrementally assist the trier of fact. Some critics might argue that much of the empirical and clinical analysis described above relies on "face valid" factors that lay decisionmakers, applying common sense, could use to reach the same judgments. We disagree. Although the implications of some factors are evident on their face (e.g., multiple prior felony convictions suggests higher risk), laypersons will not be as familiar with or be able to interpret as well other types of factors, such as developmental deficits (e.g., when and whether ADHD is a cue to adult criminality), historical factors (e.g., age of onset for delinquency) and clinical factors (e.g., the relative risk associated with psychosis vs. substance abuse disorders and the particular psychotic symptoms associated with increased, or decreased, risk). Such informed testimony can help prevent the courts from reaching inappropriate conclusions based on stereotypical views of "psychopaths" or "schizophrenics" and may thus facilitate more disciplined and humane dispositions by judges and juries.

Bibliography

Barefoot v. Estelle, 463 U.S. 880 (1983).

Gray Cavender & Michael Muschenko, *The Adoption and Implementation of Determinate-based Sanctioning Policies: A Critical Perspective*, 17 GEORGETOWN LAW REVIEW 425 (1983).

Gerald Heaney, *The Reality of Sentencing Guidelines: No End to Disparity*, 28 AMERICAN CRIMINAL LAW REVIEW 161 (1991).

John Hogarth, *Can Psychiatry Aid Sentencing?* 2 INTERNATIONAL JOURNAL OF LAW & PSYCHIATRY 499 (1979).

Thomas R. Litwack, Stuart M. Kirschner, & Renate Wack, *The Assessment of Dangerousness and Prediction of Violence: Recent Research and Future Prospects*, 64 PSYCHIATRIC QUARTERLY 245 (1993).

Marc Miller & Norval Morris, *Predictions of Dangerousness: An Argument for Limited Use*, 3 VIOLENCE & VICTIMS 263 (1988).

John Monahan & Mary Ruggiero, *Psychological and Psychiatric Aspects of Determinate Criminal Sentencing*, 3 INTERNATIONAL JOURNAL OF LAW & PSYCHIATRY 143 (1980).

JOHN MONAHAN & HENRY STEADMAN, VIOLENCE AND MENTAL DISORDER: DEVELOPMENTS IN RISK ASSESSMENT (1994).

NATIONAL INSTITUTE OF CORRECTIONS, OFFENDER NEEDS ASSESSMENT: MODELS AND APPROACHES (1984).

Christopher Slobogin, *Dangerousness and Expertise*, 133 UNIVERSITY PENNSYLVANIA LAW REVIEW 97 (1984).

Symposium: Punishment, 101 YALE LAW JOURNAL 1681 (1992).

United States v. Grayson, 438 U.S. 586 (1978).

ANDRE VONHIRSCH, DOING JUSTICE (1976).

James Weismann, *Determinate Sentencing and Psychiatric Evidence: A Due Process Examination*, 27 ST. LOUIS UNIVERSITY LAW JOURNAL 343 (1983).

Robert Wettstein, *A Psychiatric Perspective on Washington's Sexually Violent Predators Statute*, 15 UNIVERSITY PUGET SOUND LAW REVIEW 597 (1992).

In re Young, 857 P.2d 989 (Wash. 1993).

PART III

Noncriminal Adjudication

CHAPTER TEN

Civil Commitment

10.01.   Introduction

The term "civil commitment" refers to the state-sanctioned involuntary hospitalization of mentally disordered individuals who are thought to need treatment, care, or incapacitation because of self-harming or antisocial tendencies. Like the criminal justice system, the civil commitment process authorizes institutionalization of an individual because of behavior deemed unacceptable to the community. There are at least four major differences between the two systems, however, including differences in the jurisprudential basis for the state's intervention, the definition of behavior that may trigger that intervention, the process by which the state accomplishes intervention, and the duration of the intervention.

The jurisprudential basis of criminal law is the "police power," which authorizes the state to protect the community and to "ensure domestic tranquility."[1] Although the criminal justice system may seek to rehabilitate offenders, it primarily serves other purposes, such as retribution and deterrence [see § 9.01]. In contrast, civil commitment has traditionally been justified under the state's *parens patriae* authority to act as the "general guardian of all infants, idiots and lunatics."[2] The grounds for intervention have focused on the needs of the individual, not society. Today, as a result of legal challenges making dangerousness to others an explicit criterion, the jurisprudential basis for commitment is an uneasy mixture of the *parens patriae and* police powers; however, this mixture still emphasizes treatment rather than punishment.

Similarly, although the behavior that precipitates intervention may be the same in either system, it is described differently. An act is not criminal unless the legislature has specifically defined it as such, in enough detail that the individual can fairly be said to have sufficient "notice" that the behavior is outlawed by society.[3] With civil commitment, on the other hand, the terms describing the grounds for intervention—"mental disorder," "need for treatment," "dangerousness"—have eluded precise definition. Furthermore, whereas criminal punishment is permissible only for conduct that has already occurred, commitment is designed to prevent a future occurrence. Thus, it would be difficult, and may in any event be counterproductive, to specify with the degree of detail required under the criminal law the type of behavior that will lead to commitment.

The process in criminal and commitment cases also differs. As described in § 2.04(a), the criminal process, because it may result in incarceration, affords a panoply of procedural protections, including the right to counsel, to cross-examination, and to an open hearing. Most important, from a symbolic standpoint at least, the state is forced to bear the burden of proving its case by proof "beyond a reasonable doubt." As the Supreme Court has noted, use of this highest standard of proof "manifests our concern that the risk of error to the individual must be minimized even at the risk that some who are guilty might go free."[4] In contrast, the civil commitment process, though more "legalized" now than it was prior to the 1970s, is still lax procedurally [see § 10.05(c)] and demands proof only by the lesser standard of "clear and convincing evidence,"[5] reflecting the notion that society is not as troubled by false commitment as it is by false conviction.

Finally, the duration of intervention varies in each system. In the criminal process, the length of sentence is fixed by the legislature, guided by retributive notions (as well as, perhaps, by rehabilitative, deterrence, and incapacitative concerns). Convicted offenders may be somewhat uncertain as to when they will be released, but the maximum length of their sentence is generally established by law and may not be altered.[6] With civil commitment, on the other hand, most jurisdictions impose no limits on the cumulative length of stay, as long as the individual continues to meet the statutory basis for commitment. The length of each discrete commitment is usually limited (e.g., an individual may be committed for a period not to exceed six months), but neither the legislature nor any other authority poses limits on the number of recommitments and, hence, on the total length of time the individual may spend hospitalized.

On the basis of these differences, the criminal system has been called an example of the "sanction model" of state intervention and the civil commitment process an example of the "control model."[7] The precise ways in which civil commitment controls behavior, rather than punishes it, are spelled out in Stone's summary of the four social goals to which commitment is responsive[8]: (1) By hospitalizing people with mental disorder, it provides care and treatment for those requiring it; (2) by removing the individual to a protective environment, it prevents allegedly irresponsible people from harming themselves; (3) by removing the individual from the community, it protects society from the anticipated dangerous acts of the person; and (4) by placing the individual in an environment providing basic needs in a setting isolated from the general community, it relieves society and the family from accommodating those who are bothersome though perhaps not dangerous.

The conflicted nature of the control model is evident from this enumeration. Commitment may be viewed as benevolent in intent because it facilitates the provision of treatment, but it also has protective functions generally associated with the criminal law. Moreover, it can potentially serve a political function by making possible the removal from society those considered nuisances or troublesome. Thus, while the need for a criminal justice system is generally accepted, questions about the underlying legitimacy of civil commitment persist. Some commentators, most prominently Szasz[9] and Morse,[10] have questioned whether the state should ever be permitted to confine an individual involuntarily except through the sanction model. Others, while conceding the propriety of intervention as a general principle, question its application to the facts of a given case.

Partly driven by these types of concerns, and also influenced by the generic civil rights movement of the time, a series of lawsuits beginning in the early 1970s sought to change drastically the institution of civil commitment. The suits were of three types: those challenging the substantive and procedural criteria of state commitment laws,[11] those attacking institutional conditions (e.g., "right to treatment" and "least restrictive alternative" suits),[12] and those addressing the administration of treatment (e.g., cases asserting a right to refuse treatment).[13] Although this litigation did not erase the differences between commitment and the criminal system, it did have a significant impact on the law of commitment.

After providing a brief history of commitment, the legal segment of this chapter focuses on the first type of litigation and the more recent trend dismantling some of its accomplishments. (The second—institutional—type of litigation is briefly discussed here as well, while § 11.03(b) examines the right to refuse treatment). There follows a section examining research on the impact of this civil rights litigation, most of which has concluded that changes in the law have had negligible effect and that, although conditions in hospitals have improved, community treatment is the best option in many cases. The chapter then discusses the proper commitment role for attorneys and mental health professionals in light of this empirical background, advocating that attorneys should generally assume an adversarial stance and that clinicians should proceed with caution. It also provides relatively detailed recommendations to clinicians concerning the substantive and procedural issues that arise in commitment evaluations. Finally, it briefly describes variations in the commitment law governing four specific populations: those acquitted by reason of insanity, those charged with criminal offenses, those with mental retardation, and those with substance abuse problems.

10.02.　History of Commitment Law

(a)　From Ancient Times to the 1970s

Ancient civilizations dealt with people with mental disorder by means of familiar-sounding methods. According to Brakel and Rock, Greek philosophers recommend that people with mental disability be cared for in a comfortable, sanitary, well-lighted place.[14] The Romans appointed a "curator" (guardian) to safeguard the property of these people and debated the legal effect of decisions made by the ward during lucid moments.[15]

During the Middle Ages, medical definitions of mental disorder were supplanted by theories of possession by demons, and exorcism and forms of torture became primary antidotes.[16] Nonetheless, the only significant change in the *law's* approach to mental disorder was a more refined effort to differentiate between people with mental retardation and those with mental illnesses. In England, the *De Praerogativa Regis* (literally, the "Prerogative of the King") was enacted between 1255 and 1290. It divided people with mental disability into two classes, "idiots" and "lunatics."[17] The King took custody of the lands of an idiot—defined as a person who "hath no understanding from his nativity"—and could retain any profits from the land.[18] In contrast, the King merely served as guardian of the lands of a lunatic, defined as "a person who hath had under-

standing, but hath lost the use of his reason"; any profits from such guardianships were not retained by the crown but were applied to the maintenance of the disordered persons and their households.[19] A procedure eventually developed whereby a jury determined whether an individual was an idiot or a lunatic. While the former were often confined in public houses, the latter were usually committed to the care of friends or relatives who received an allowance for the cost of care. Management of the person's estate went to an heir or the nearest relative to prevent its depletion.[20]

In colonial America, indigent people with mental disorders often formed bands, wandering the countryside.[21] Only occasionally did a community arrange for the sustenance of these individuals, utilizing a guardian or custodian. Typically, they were the subject of ridicule, harassment, and in some cases whipping from a society that equated a failure to work with immorality.[22] The first American hospital for the exclusive care of people with mental disorders was not established until 1773, in Williamsburg, Virginia; the second came in 1824 in Lexington, Kentucky.

These "asylums" turned out to be a mixed blessing themselves. Initially designed for the purpose of confining violent people with mental disorders,[23] they gradually became warehouses for other types of individuals, many of whom were placed there with little or no procedural safeguards.[24] For instance, an 1842 New York statute required the confinement of all at-large "lunatics," not just dangerous ones, and commissioned "assessors" to search for such people, two of whom could commit individuals for a *minimum* of six months.[25] In the latter half of the 19th century, reform efforts led by individuals who had been confined on flimsy authority[26] and by those concerned with the lack of adequate facilities for treating mental disability[27] stimulated cosmetic changes in commitment laws, some reformation of existing facilities, and the construction of new ones. But the movement toward a more legalized commitment process was relatively short-lived. During the first two-thirds of the 20th century, most changes in civil commitment law aimed at making commitment easier rather than more difficult, in large part due to medical advances that increased optimism about treatment efficacy.

Thus, by 1970, 31 states provided for hospitalization based simply on the certification of one or more physicians that the individual suffered from mental illness and needed treatment.[28] Even in jurisdictions in which judges were the principal decisionmakers, courts routinely deferred to medical opinion. For example, an American Bar Foundation study concluded:

> The judicial commitment procedure thus amounts to administrative monitoring, often cursory, or a medically oriented process upon which jural apparatus has been grafted . . . the court becomes essentially ministerial. . . . The medical treatment questions are determined by medical testimony from examiners whose opinions are rarely at variance and are rarely disputed.[29]

Nonetheless, beginning in the 1950s, the hospital population began dropping drastically. Between 1955 and 1975, the population of those confined in public institutions due to mental illness appears to have dropped from over 550,000 to under 200,000, a 65% decrease.[30] Today there are probably only about 90,000 people in state and county psychiatric hospitals.[31] Several events may explain these changes. First, the mid-1950s saw the first wide-scale use of psychotropic medication, seemingly allowing the stabilization and return to the community of thousands of formerly overtly psychotic patients.[32] Second, in 1963 President Kennedy called for the development of community services for people with mental disability, and the subsequent passage of the Community Mental Health Centers Act promised the development of a capacity to treat individuals on an outpatient basis.[33] Third, in the 1970s Congress enacted changes in the Medicare, Medicaid, and Social Security laws which created a financial basis for community-based care. Finally, beginning in the early 1970s the legal profession began examining the institution of commitment in earnest—a subject to which we now turn.

(b)   The Reform Movement

As noted earlier, the *parens patriae* power, rooted in English law, enabled the King to act as "general guardian of incapacitated classes, including infants and the mentally disordered," whereas the state's police power authorizes the state to act as protector of the community—to make law for the protection of public health, safety, welfare, and morals.[34] Until the 1970s, most courts viewed civil commitment as an exercise of *parens patriae* power. For example, the Iowa Supreme Court characterized commitment as fundamentally and acceptably paternalistic in nature:

> It must be kept in mind that appellant is not charged with a crime and is not so incarcerated. He is being restrained of his liberty in that he is not free to come and go at will, *but such restraint is not in the way of punishment but for his own protection and welfare* as well as for the benefit of society.[35] [Emphasis added]

The end result of this perspective was a process decidedly less formal than that found in criminal trials. Wexler has summarized the traditional view:

> Where the state's aim is not to punish but to assist by providing therapy, there is no need for an adversary process because *all* parties have the best interest of the deviant at heart. And, the argument continues, the criminal law safeguards have no place in a therapeutic proceeding, for they serve only to "criminalize" the process and further stigmatize the subject, and they are simply unnecessary impediments to achieving the central goal, which is to help the deviant actor.[36]

The early 1970s saw multiple challenges to this point of view, representing the juxtaposition of three related strands of thought. The first questioned the validity of the medical model on which commitment law was based and its corollary assumption that commitment was properly a medical decision made for benevolent reasons; the second questioned whether the consequences of commitment were in fact humane, and the third asked whether the criteria for commitment and the process by which commitment occurred were inherently flawed. The underlying premise that unified these challenges was a belief that civil commitment resulted in a deprivation of rights at least as serious as that faced by a convicted criminal.

(1) Challenges to the Medical Model

Civil commitment is premised on a belief that "mental illness" is definable and treatable. The frontal assault on this concept, and on the credibility of the psychiatric profession generally, was critical in providing a conceptual basis for the reformation movement. Reformers, inspired in large part by the work of Szasz,[37] characterized the term as nothing more than a label the state used to legitimize the segregation of individuals who were unacceptable to the majority of citizens. The attack on the validity of mental illness was accompanied by an attack on its "high priests," the psychiatric profession. A variety of studies questioned the validity and reliability of psychiatric diagnosis,[38] and a consensus developed that psychiatrists were unable to predict dangerous behavior with any greater degree of accuracy than a layperson.[39]

This challenge to the medical model resulted in a fundamental redefinition by the courts of the values at stake in commitment. Perhaps unwittingly, the United States Supreme Court itself bolstered the movement with its 1982 decision in *Humphrey v. Cady*, which countered a century of judicial deference to medical opinion by declaring that commitment involved a "massive curtailment of liberty."[40] In the same term, the Court seemed, in *Jackson v. Indiana*,[41] to invite challenges to commitment laws, commenting that given the number of persons affected by commitment in its various forms, "it is perhaps remarkable that the substantive constitutional limitations on this power have not been more frequently litigated."[42]

The lower courts were quick to recognize the challenges to the credibility of psychiatric decisionmaking. In the leading lower court decision, *Lessard v. Schmidt*, the court quoted a law review article to this effect:

> Obviously, the definition of mental illness is left largely to the user and is dependent upon the norms of adjustment that he employs. Usually the use of the phrase "mental illness" effectively masks the actual norms being applied. And, because of the unavoidably ambiguous generalities in which the American Psychiatric Association describes its diagnostic categories, the diagnostician has the ability to shoehorn into the mentally diseased class almost any person he wishes, for whatever reason, to put there.[43]

Another court, expressing concern over the broad latitude given psychiatrists by statutes relying on the vaguely defined concept of mental illness as a basis for commitment, concluded that the courts were "blindly relying on the conclusion drawn by the examining psychiatrist."[44] Creation of stricter statutory terms was thought necessary to avoid commitment decisions "dependent upon the examining psychiatrist's personal conception of normal social behavior."[45]

(2) Challenges to the Consequences of Commitment

A second prong of the reform movement challenged the consequences of commitment, focusing both on the deficiencies of the physical conditions to which persons were committed and on the loss of collateral civil rights that often ensued as a result of commitment. With respect to the first issue, one group recapitulated the argument as follows:

> The loss of physical freedom resulting from civil commitment is, for all practical purposes, little different from that which results from a prison sentence. Depending upon the quality of the hospital, a person committed may be subject to overcrowding, unsanitary conditions, poor nutrition and even to brutality at the hands of attendants or other hospital residents. Commitment also infringes grossly upon privacy, and committed patients may be subjected to compulsory medication, electroconvulsive therapy and other potentially hazardous and intrusive procedures. . . . [46]

Even leading psychiatrists confirmed that "the megainstitutions presided over by the mental health professions are an acknowledged disaster."[47] The result was "right to treatment" litigation, epitomized by the seminal case of *Wyatt v. Stickney*,[48] which ordered sweeping reforms in Alabama's mental health facilities. This type of lawsuit, often the result of joint efforts by lawyers and mental health professionals, adopted the view that the state could not be assumed to be acting benevolently when it commits an individual.[49]

Critics also pointed to the collateral consequences of commitment. The most significant was (and is) the "stigma" attaching to the individual labeled "mentally ill" and committed to an institution; the latter term, like its predecessors, such as "lunacy," "insanity," and "pauper lunatic," was said to carry with it notions of "alienation, [and] banishment from society."[50] The conclusion that commitment stigmatized its subject fueled the argument that the act of diagnosis itself was an inherently destructive act.[51] A second collateral consequence of commitment was (and is) an increased risk of institutional dependency, which undercut the individual's ability to deal with the world outside the institution.[52] Finally, commitment often resulted in the loss of important civil rights, including the right to enter into a contract, the right to vote, the right to marry and to bear children, the right to obtain a driver's license, and the right to serve on juries.

These arguments elicited a sympathetic judicial response. The West Virginia Supreme Court of Appeals, considering a challenge to that state's commitment laws, found that "in determining whether there is any justification under the doctrine of *parens patriae* for deviation from established due process standards, it is appropriate for this court to consider that the State of West Virginia offers to those unfortunates who are incarcerated in mental institutions Dickensian squalor of unconscionable magnitudes."[53] The federal court that decided the seminal case of *Lessard v. Schmidt*,[54] noting the low number of physicians available in Wisconsin's public mental health facilities, observed that "perhaps the most serious possible effect of a decision to commit an individual lies in the statistics which indicate that an individual committed to a mental institution has a much greater chance of dying than if he were left at large."[55] It summarized its findings by observing.

> It is obvious that the commitment adjudication carries with it an enormous and devastating impact on an individual's civil rights. In some respects, such as the limitation on holding a driver's license, the civil deprivations which follow civil commitment are more serious than the deprivations which accompany a criminal conviction.[56]

The conclusion that commitment was largely deleterious to the individual shook the *parens patriae* basis of commitment to the core. The Court of Appeals for the District of Columbia Circuit held that "without some form of treatment the state justification for acting as *parens patriae* becomes a nullity,"[57] and the West Virginia Supreme Court concluded that "the ancient doctrine of *parens patriae* is in full retreat on all fronts except in those very narrow areas where the state can demonstrate, as a matter of fact, that its care and custody is superior to any available alternative."[58]

(3) Challenges to the Commitment Process and Criteria

Those hoping to abolish commitment relied on the foregoing contentions: that mental illness was a bankrupt term easily manipulated to effectuate political acts and that the "treatment" provided those so confined was more likely detrimental than beneficial. On the realistic assumption that the commitment system would continue to exist, however, reformers also used these two arguments as the basis for seeking to replace the medically dominated and informal judicial commitment process with legalized procedure designed to minimize error in decisionmaking and with criteria designed to narrow the scope of intervention.[59] Their overarching contention was that the state should not be able to deprive individuals of liberty without affording them due process of law.

On the procedural front, plaintiffs turned naturally to the criminal justice model (i.e., the right to counsel, to confront one's "accusers," and to notice) because it represented the ultimate use and refinement of the constitutional "due process" model of decisionmaking. The Supreme Court provided impetus for this approach with its 1967 decision *In re Gault*,[60] which imposed the adult criminal model on a juvenile court system that until that time had been grounded on the same therapeutic, *parens patriae* principle underlying civil commitment. In doing so, the Court explained, it was trying to redress the fact that juveniles confined in deficient facilities after informal proceedings received the "the worst of both worlds."[61] To the critics of the medical model of commitment decisionmaking, those sent to public mental health facilities based on little more than a doctor's order were in the same situation.

Specifically, these reformers argued that the criminal procedure approach would not only improve the accuracy of commitment decisions but would also alter the basic nature of the inquiry conducted at commitment. Dershowitz, for example, contended that if the commitment decision is perceived as primarily medical in nature, medical control of the inquiry is inevitable because the pertinent questions will be posed in medical terms (e.g., Does a physician believe that the individual needs "treatment"?), and assumptions about the validity and reliability of medical decisionmaking and the therapeutic intent underlying the state's intervention will go unchallenged.[62] However, when loss of liberty is seen as the chief consequence of commitment, courts will become the decisionmakers of choice, and the inquiry will ideally involve more formalized scrutiny of the state's interests in restricting the individual's liberty.

The critics also argued that the Constitution required changes in the substantive criteria of commitment. Once courts adopted the assumption that clinical decisionmaking was inherently flawed because of its inexact nature and because of the vague criteria for commitment, something more than clinical opinion on treatability was required. Again borrowing from the criminal law, the idea grew that the individual must be shown to have committed an "overt act" unacceptable to society—the equivalent of the *actus reus* in the criminal law [see § 8.03]—before commitment can occur.[63] More fundamentally, the mere existence of mental illness and need for treatment was no longer deemed sufficient to commit an individual. Following the analogy with criminal law, plaintiffs argued that the state's *parens patriae* power should be strictly curtailed, and that commitment should be viewed primarily as an exercise of the police power. Thus, some argued that it should be permitted only when the individual was found dangerous to others. Others would permit commitments on "dangerousness to self" grounds as well, but strictly defined to exclude nonsuicidal behavior.

The judiciary accepted many of these arguments. The courts ordered state legislatures to change civil commitment statutes to incorporate a more legalistic process for commitment and more specific substantive criteria.[64] These statutes, largely products of the 1970s, are discussed later in this chapter [see § 10.03]. But first, to complete the historical picture, we trace the legal developments of the late 1970s and beyond. They appear to signal a retreat from the reform movement's efforts to equate civil commitment with the criminal model and may well augur a new generation of statutes.

(c) Supreme Court Retrenchment

As the 1970s drew to a close, the medical model of commitment stood largely discredited and the "legalistic" model held sway. While the lower courts were almost unanimous in their view of civil commitment, however, the United States Supreme Court, primarily through the opinions of Chief Justice Burger, began to encourage the emergence of a less "legalistic" approach to commitment issues. In a series of cases, the Court reasserted the legitimacy of the state's *parens patriae* authority and, more important, began rehabilitating the medical administrative model as a constitutionally permissible method of decisionmaking.

In doing so, the Court did not retreat from its earlier statement that commitment involved a "massive curtailment of liberty." For instance, in *O'Connor v. Donaldson,*[65] involving the lengthy coerced confinement of an individual who had repeatedly sought his freedom, the court defined the issue as a "single, relatively simple, but nonetheless important question concerning every man's constitutional right to liberty"[66] and went on to rule that "the State cannot constitutionally confine without more a nondangerous individual who is capable of surviving safely in freedom by himself or with the help of willing and responsible family members or friends."[67] Although the meaning of this rather conservative and ambiguous holding has been much debated,[68] it did at least emphasize the Court's belief that the civil commitment process must answer to the Constitution.

On the other hand, the majority opinion in *Donaldson* was studiously vague with respect to the limitations imposed by constitutional precepts and did not endorse explicitly any of the libertarian reforms adopted by the lower courts. Further, Chief Justice Burger, in a much less ambiguously worded concurring opinion, put forward a generous view of the *parens patriae* power which suggested a skeptical attitude toward these reforms. While acknowledging that involuntary commitment constituted a deprivation of liberty which the state could not accomplish without due process of law,[69] he rejected the contention, accepted by the lower court in *Donaldson*,[70] that the state could confine those who are not physically dangerous only if it provided treatment for them. Instead, he asserted, "custodial confinement" of those simply in need of care was a long recognized and legitimate purpose of commitment.[71] He concluded:

> [T]he idea that states may not confine the mentally ill except for the purpose of providing them with treatment is of very recent origin, and there is no historical basis for imposing such a limitation on state power. . . . [In addition to the police power] the states are vested with the historic *parens patriae* power. . . . The classic example of this role is when a state undertakes to act as "the general guardian of all infants, idiots, and lunatics."[72]

The Chief Justice wrote for a unanimous Court in its next major decision on civil commitment, *Addington v. Texas*,[73] a decision which some believed signaled an even more explicit retrenchment on the reform of the 1970s. There, the Court held that the Constitution permitted use of a "clear and convincing" standard of proof at a commitment hearing, a level of certainty falling between the "beyond a reasonable doubt" standard the Court had required in juvenile delinquency and in criminal cases[74] and the "preponderance of the evidence" standard typically used in civil proceedings [see § 2.04]. In so holding, the Supreme Court moved some distance from lower courts' pronouncements about the nature of involuntary commitment. While acknowledging that commitment involved a constitutionally significant loss of liberty, and noting that "stigma" could have a "very significant impact on the individual,"[75] the Court reiterated that the state had authority to commit both under its police power and under its *parens patriae* power. The Court also characterized the exercise of the latter power in decidedly less negative terms than many lower courts, stating explicitly that commitment and the criminal process were dissimilar: "In civil commitment state power is not exercised in a punitive sense. Unlike the delinquency proceed-

ing . . . a civil commitment proceeding can in no sense be equated to a criminal prosecution."[76]

The opinion also planted the seeds for recharacterizing the commitment process as primarily medical in nature. The Court asserted that "whether the individual is mentally ill and dangerous to himself or others and is in need of confined therapy turns on the meaning of the facts which must be interpreted by *expert psychiatrists and psychologists*"[77] [Emphasis added]. As indicated earlier, many other courts had assumed that it was for the judiciary to draw the necessary conclusions from the facts; *Addington* intimated that the Chief Justice and a majority of the Court did not accept that view.

The *Addington* opinion did emphasize the "lack of certainty and fallibility of psychiatric diagnosis,"[78] but it did so only to support its rejection of the reasonable doubt standard. It stated that because the art of psychiatry was insufficiently precise, the state could not meet the burden imposed by the criminal standard and therefore need meet only the less stringent clear-and-convincing-evidence test. However, Burger did not evidence any further willingness to question the preeminence of clinical expertise.

In fact, as he soon demonstrated, the Chief Justice could find significant rigor in clinical decisionmaking when it served the jurisprudence he was attempting to develop in the field of mental disability law. Within a year the Court, in a decision authored by Burger, took its most dramatic step toward rehabilitation of the medical model of commitment. *Parham v. J.R.*[79] involved a challenge to Georgia's voluntary commitment statute for children under the age of 18. Under this statute, a facility superintendent may admit a child for observation and diagnosis upon receipt of an application for hospitalization signed by a parent or guardian and, if observation reveals that the child suffers from mental illness and is suitable for treatment in the hospital, then can admit the child "for such period and under such conditions as may be authorized by law."[80] This statutory scheme had few of the elements that lower courts had found necessary to satisfy due process. It depended wholly on the judgment of the admitting parent or guardian (the latter including the state acting as custodian) and the facility medical staff. No judge was involved, no attorney was provided for the child, and there was no require-ment of a finding of "dangerousness." The lower federal court had found the statute unconstitu-tional because it failed to protect children's due process rights.[81]

Nonetheless, the Supreme Court reinstated the statutory scheme. The Court began by stating that, in determining whether the admission pro-cedures were constitutional, it had to consider three issues: the child's interest in not being com-mitted (which it considered "inextricably linked to the parents' interest in and obligation for the welfare and health of the child"), the state's inter-est in the procedures it had adopted for the com-mitment and treatment of children, and the need for protection against arbitrary commitment de-cisions.[82] In each of these three areas, the Court minimized or rejected outright assumptions that had been made in previous lower court rulings dealing with commitment.

The Court agreed that the child had a substan-tial and constitutionally protected liberty interest in not being confined unnecessarily. However, it rejected the notion that significant "stigma" at-tached in the case before it: The state, acting through its voluntary procedures, "does not 'la-bel' the child; it provides a diagnosis and treat-ment that medical specialists conclude the child requires."[83] It also concluded that the state's in-terest in avoiding "time-consuming procedural minuets" was "significant"; not only did Georgia's scheme give staff more time to treat patients but "the *parens patriae* interest in helping parents care for the mental health of their children" would be disrupted by an admission process that was "too onerous, too embarrassing, or too contentious."[84] Finally, it rejected the argument that the likeli-hood of parental abuse was so great that a formal adversary hearing had to be provided prior to commitment. It concluded that the affinity of in-terest between parent and child, long recognized by the law,[85] combined with the superintendent's review authority, were sufficient protection against such abuse.

Other courts had depicted commitment as a stigmatizing, negative experience, far removed from the realm of "normal" or usual medical deci-sions; to the Chief Justice, on the other hand, the decision to hospitalize a child was like a "tonsil-lectomy, appendectomy, or other medical proce-

dure."[86] Other courts viewed an adversary pro-ceeding as a necessary way of guarding against in-appropriate commitments; the Chief Justice con-cluded that, at least when commitment is initiat-ed by a parent or the state acting as guardian, it is a "time-consuming procedural minuet" that acted as an impediment to care.

As this last statement suggests, the Court also explicitly adhered to the medical decisionmaking model it had implicitly endorsed in *Addington*. The Court acknowledged that the risk of error inherent in parental decisionmaking was suffi-ciently great to require an inquiry by a "neutral factfinder" who would probe the child's back-ground using all available sources.[87] However, a judge would not be required because the decision to hospitalize was a medical decision and "neither judges nor administrative hearing officers are bet-ter qualified than psychiatrists to render psychi-atric judgments."[88] Lower courts had consistently characterized the decision to commit or not to commit as a *legal* decision informed by medical evidence. However, the Court thought the issue to be "essentially medical in character. . . . Even after a hearing, the nonspecialist decisionmaker must make a medical–psychiatric decision."[89] The Court also concluded that despite "the fallibility of medical and psychiatric diagnosis," a shift in the locus of decisionmaking from a "trained specialist to an untrained judge" would not remedy those shortcomings.[90]

The implication of these remarks is quite clear. To the Court, psychiatric decisionmaking in the commitment context is sufficiently refined that it deserves the type of deference generally reserved for judicial decisionmaking when constitutionally protected values are at stake. The fact that *Parham* involved the commitment of children should not obscure the fact that the decision represents a dis-tinct departure from the tone of earlier lower court decisions. Indeed, because those who seek to commit adults (e.g., family members or clini-cians) usually can be said to have the subjects' best interest at heart as well, the type of procedure permitted in *Parham* may well be sufficient to commit them.

The cases described above, plus a number of other Court decisions in the area of mental health,[91] have laid the groundwork for a new round in the debate over the legalization of the commitment process and the amount of deference that courts should properly pay to clinical decisionmakers. There is clear evidence that these decisions have had an impact on at least some lower courts,[92] despite criticism both within the Court[93] and from commentators.[94] It may be concluded, at a minimum, that it is highly unlikely that either the substantive or procedural criteria for civil commitment will be further legalized in the near future.

10.03.   Substantive Criteria for Commitment

CASE STUDY 10.1

Ms. Boggs, a.k.a. Ms. Joyce Brown, has lived on the public sidewalk in front of a restaurant in New York City for the past year. She uses this location as her bedroom, toilet, and living room. At a proceeding instituted to determine whether she should be committed, Ms. Putnam, a social worker who works for Project Help (an organization that attempts to assist the homeless), testifies that she observed Ms. Boggs scream racial epithets at delivery men who came near her on the sidewalk, to the point where she thought Ms. Boggs might be assaulted; Ms. Boggs seemed to believe black men treated her as a prostitute. Dr. Hess, a psychiatrist with Project Help, testifies that, a month after this incident, he saw Ms. Boggs for the first time; he also saw her on three subsequent occasions, on each of which he felt her condition had progressively worsened. On his first visit, she exhibited hostility to his staff's attempts to help her; wore disheveled clothing; twirled an open umbrella to avoid eye contact with him and the persons passing by; and spoke in rhymes, the content of which was sexual and related to his and her genitals. Five days later she had become more disheveled and was barefoot; cursed him; and flipped open her skirt and exposed her buttocks. Two months later, still at the same location, her clothes were torn to the point that large portions of her torso were exposed and her clothing was inadequate for the weather; her hair was matted; she smelled of urine and feces; she had torn up money and stuck its pieces in the sidewalk; and she shouted obscenities at him. A month later, she smelled strongly of feces and Dr. Hess saw more torn-up currency, which had been urinated upon; she repeatedly said, "What is my name?" At this point she was taken to the hospital.

At the hospital, another psychiatrist, Dr. Mahon, interviewed Ms. Boggs three times in the week before the hearing. He testifies that, on the first occasion, he could not speak with her because she was hostile and angry; on the second, she was less angry and he spoke with her for 30 minutes; on the third occasion, four days after her first interview, she was bright, verbal, and oriented. He diagnosed her as having chronic schizophrenia and said her improved condition might have been due to a dose of psychoactive medication. Dr. Gould, another psychiatrist, interviewed Ms. Boggs a few days after Dr. Mahon's first interview and found her to have no suicidal or homicidal ideation and no delusions or hallucinations. He testifies that "her insight was somewhat impaired" in terms of the "troubles [which] ensue from her behavior," but did not think she was suffering from schizophrenia. He says that she tore up the money because she found accepting it degrading; that she had no alternative to defecating in the street; that she had never been hurt and "has very good survival skills"; that she was congenial to those she liked; that the small amount of medication Ms. Boggs had been given could not account for the change in her behavior following hospitalization; and that he found no evidence of deterioration in Ms. Boggs's mental or physical condition, except for the state of her clothing.

Ms. Boggs testifies that she stays at the street location because there is a hot-air vent there; that she has never been cold; that she panhandles money for food, and makes eight to ten dollars a day, which is more than she needs for food; that she has friends who can supply her with clothes; that she uses profanity to make the state's staff go away; that she has no delusions about black persons giving her money for sex; and that she has never hurt or threatened anyone. She testifies that she would go back to the streets if released.

QUESTIONS: Should Ms. Boggs be forcibly treated? As a clinician, how would you address questions about the likelihood she will harm herself or harm others? If you were the commitment judge, would you commit her? Would it make a difference if you could commit her on an outpatient basis?

CASE STUDY 10.2

You are working in the emergency room. Police officers bring a 36-year-old man to the facility and report that he became irritated at a group of children and shook a small girl. Apparently, the children had been playing outside his apartment and he had rushed toward them screaming, among other things: "You've taken away my childhood. You'll go to hell." The children were upset, but a medical examination of the girl revealed no significant harm, and the officers reported that they would not charge the man. The man seems calm now. He states that he lives alone on social security, that he has never been on psychoactive medication, and that he hears voices from time to time telling him that he's getting old and will soon go to hell. He admits that the children made him very angry, but he cannot explain why, except that they reminded him of his past.

QUESTIONS: Should this man be forcibly treated? What else would you like to know? If he agrees to admit himself as a voluntary patient—apparently convinced, contrary to what the police tell him, that it is the only way to avoid jail—should he be allowed to do so?

Although the constitutional challenges to state commitment laws did not result in the abolition of commitment, they did bring significant change, which to date has been largely unaffected by the Supreme Court's retrenchment.[95] A description of each state's commitment law is impossible. However, certain key elements are incorporated in each law and are discussed in this section (on substantive criteria) and the next section (on procedural law).

With respect to substantive criteria, the starting point in all state commitment statutes is the existence of mental disorder. In defining mental disorder, some jurisdictions also inject what is in effect another substantive criterion by requiring that the disorder result in lack of capacity to recognize the need for treatment. Each statute also requires a finding that the individual is dangerous to self or others as a result of the mental disorder. This emphasis on dangerousness is the clearest legacy of the reform movement.

Further, most statutes allow commitment on the ground that the mental disorder renders the individual unable to care for one's basic needs. This latter criterion may be a part of the definition of danger to self, or it may stand as a separate justification for commitment. A few states also insist that there be a "need for treatment," although permitting commitment on this ground alone would probably be unconstitutional under *Donaldson*.

Finally, many statutes require consideration of

the place of treatment at the time of commitment. This criterion, the "least restrictive alternative" or "least restrictive environment" requirement, seeks to limit hospitalization to those cases in which no alternative (or less restrictive) locus for treatment exists. An outgrowth of this requirement has been a relatively recent movement toward authorizing outpatient commitment.

The content of each of these criteria is considered briefly here. Recall that, after *Addington*, the federal constitution requires that these criteria be shown by "clear and convincing evidence," although some states go beyond the constitutional minimum and require proof beyond a reasonable doubt.

(a)   Mental Disorder

The reform movement aimed to narrow the state's discretion in defining mental illness. It has been largely successful in doing so, at least on paper. Although as recently as 1982 Texas considered a "mentally ill person" to be "a person whose mental health is substantially impaired,"[96] today virtually every state defines mental illness in less tautological terms. Representative is Vermont's language: "'Mental illness' means a substantial disorder of thought, mood, perception, orientation or memory, any of which grossly impairs judgment, behavior, capacity to recognize reality, or ability to meet the ordinary demands of life, but shall not include mental retardation."[97] This definition gives notice that the "disorder" must be serious ("substantial") with significant consequences ("grossly impairs"). It also recognizes that the disorder must impair the person either cognitively ("judgment, capacity to recognize reality") or functionally ("behavior, ability to meet the ordinary demands of life").

Note that Vermont's definition also excludes mental retardation from the mental illness rubric. Several other jurisdictions exclude as well epilepsy and conditions resulting from alcohol or substance abuse (although individuals with these conditions can often be institutionalized under other commitment provisions [see § 10.10(d)(e)]). Some statutes also specifically exclude antisocial personality,[98] or even all personality disorders,[99] from the definition of mental illness, probably because these disorders are considered less treatable and apply to a class of people thought to be best handled through the criminal justice system.[100] Finally, a number of states exclude from commitment people whose primary diagnosis is organicity or dementia.[101]

(b) Capacity to Make Treatment Decisions

Although the typical definition of mental illness speaks of "impaired capacity," it does not directly focus on the extent to which the mental disorder affects one's competency to make treatment decisions. Yet a number of influential commentators, including Roth[102] and Stone,[103] have argued that individuals should not be subject to commitment unless their mental disorder impairs their capacity to make an informed decision concerning treatment. To the extent this threshold is limited to *parens patriae* commitments, it makes eminent sense. The state should have no authority to exercise this power over people who can make their own decisions [see §§ 7.01, 11.01]. On the other hand, when the state is committing someone as dangerous to others under the police power, the individual's ability to decide what he or she wants should probably not be determinative.[104]

Despite the logic of imposing an incapacity criterion on *parens patriae* commitments, only a handful of states do so, and none makes an effort to further define the competency concept.[105] This is unfortunate not only for the theoretical reasons just outlined but also because of two practical realities. First, as discussed in detail in § 11.03(b), a number of courts have recognized a constitutional right to refuse psychoactive medication for patients who are competent to make treatment decisions (at least if they are nondangerous). In these jurisdictions the issue of capacity will often have to be confronted in any event [see Marlar report in § 19.06(a)]; further, as Roth points out, "the risk is that the mental hospital will again become custodial" because competent patients will be able to refuse proffered treatment.[106] Second, as described in § 10.04(c), every state provides those subjected to commitment some sort of "voluntary" hospitalization option,[107] which can usually only be exercised if the person is competent to understand the conse-quences of the decision. Indeed, in *Zinermon v. Burch*,[108] the Supreme Court strongly suggested that "voluntary commitment" of an *incompetent* person is unconstitutional; as the Court put it, a state must either "comply with state procedures for admitting involuntary patients, or . . . determine whether a patient is competent to consent to voluntary admission."[109] If this requirement is taken seriously (which often is not the case[110]), some assessment of competency should be made preparatory to every commitment hearing in an effort to determine whether the voluntary option might be exercisable.

(c) Danger to Others

All states allow the commitment of individuals who present a danger to others. Indeed, given the Supreme Court's statements in *Donaldson* and *Addington*, dangerousness has firm support as a commitment criterion. Definitions of "dangerousness" vary widely, however. At one end of the spectrum are statutes like Alaska's, stating simply that a person with mental illness is committable if "likely to injure . . . others."[111] At the other end are laws such as Florida's, which requires a "substantial likelihood that in the near future [the person] will inflict serious bodily harm on . . . another person, as evidenced by recent behavior causing, attempting, or threatening such harm."[112]

Note that the Florida law requires proof of a substantial risk of "bodily" harm. Most states that define dangerousness do likewise. However, danger to property or other interests may occasionally form the basis for commitment. A federal court of appeals found that Hawaii's statute allowing commitment based on *any* type of harm to property was unconstitutionally broad but also noted that it need not decide "whether a state may ever commit one who is dangerous to property."[113] In addition, a few states allow commitment based on a prediction that the individual will cause emotional harm to others.[114]

A further refinement in the Florida statute is that there be some "recent" evidence of violent behavior or a threat of such behavior. A fair number of states explicitly require that some sort of "overt act" be proven to authorize commitment.

For example, Pennsylvania requires proof that the person poses a "clear and present danger" to self or others as shown by conduct that has occurred "within the past 30 days."[115] This type of requirement is designed both to minimize the risk of an erroneous prediction and to increase the likelihood that the danger is "imminent," as opposed to diffuse and distant.[116] However, a number of courts have held that proof of an overt act is not a necessary predicate for commitment, at least as long as the statute still requires proof that the dangerous behavior is reasonably foreseeable.[117]

Regardless of the definition, certain legal variables are always likely to be relevant in assessing danger to others. Brooks has helpfully conceptualized the analysis as focusing on four such variables: (1) the severity of the harm predicted, (2) the probability that the predicted harm will occur, (3) the frequency with which the harm might occur, and (4) how soon the harm will occur.[118] None of these factors are dispositive; rather, their relationship must be explored in each individual case to determine the extent of the "danger." For instance, one might be quite willing to confine a person who is predicted to be at risk of committing homicide within the next few weeks, even if the chance is a small one. By comparison, one might be less willing to commit a person who, like the woman in Case Study 10.1, is likely to hurl epithets at passers-by, even if on a routine basis, or a person who, like the man in Case Study 10.2, may occasionally cause slight physical injury (although the fact that the risk in this case is to children may affect the calculus somewhat).

(d)　Danger to Self

Each state also allows commitment of an individual presenting a danger to self. The definition of "danger to self" tends to mirror the definition of "danger to others." Thus, statutes providing little or no content in defining "danger to others" provide little or no content in defining "danger to self." Compare, for example, Alaska's statute (requiring a finding the person is "likely to injure himself"[119]) to Pennsylvania's (requiring a suicidal act within 30 days or an act of mutilation[120]).

Despite the variation in definition, every state statute appears to contemplate commitment for suicidal behavior. In addition, as the next subsection discusses in more detail, those states that do not have a "grave disability" criterion usually apply the "dangerous to self" criterion broadly enough to encompass nonsuicidal conduct that could cause serious harm to the person.

(e)　Grave Disability/Inability to Care for Self

To the reformers of the 1970s, attempts to commit penurious individuals with idiosyncratic lifestyles or solely because of a "need for treatment" were viewed as primary examples of the paternalistic use of state authority. Their position won partial support in *Donaldson*, where the Supreme Court firmly stated that the state could not hospitalize people simply to improve their living conditions or solely because they were mentally ill [see § 10.02(c)]. However, the majority opinion also stated that "the State may arguably confine a person to save him from harm,"[121] suggesting that the state's authority to commit the gravely disabled had continued vitality, a position Burger strongly endorsed in his concurring opinion.

In any event, today every state permits commitment of nonsuicidal persons who are "gravely disabled." At least three-quarters of the states do so explicitly,[122] whereas the rest allow their commitment under the danger-to-self rubric. The implementation of this criterion, as usual, varies among the states. Nevada defines the term "gravely disabled" to include a person who by reason of mental illness "is unable to maintain himself in his normal life situation without external support."[123] Other jurisdictions use an inability-to-care-for-basic-needs rubric and delineate the "needs" that the individual must be found incapable of meeting; the five usually listed are food, clothing, shelter, medical care, and the ability to secure personal safety.[124] A third variant, proposed by the American Psychiatric Association, would permit commitment if the person "will if not treated suffer or continue to suffer severe and abnormal mental, emotional or physical distress, and this distress is associated with significant impairment or judgment, reason, or behavior causing a substantial deterioration of his previous ability to function on his own."[125] This "predicted deterioration" standard, which a number of states have adopted,[126] is meant to be broader than the first two because it allows commitment based on predicted rather than present disability.

The problems perceived to be associated with the move toward deinstitutionalization,[127] combined with the call in some quarters for reinstitutionalizing the homeless mentally ill,[128] probably guarantee the continued vitality of the grave disability criterion. Yet commitment under this standard is the most problematic because, as Case Study 10.1 illustrates, it requires drawing a fine line between an individual living an impoverished existence and an individual living an existence impoverished because of treatable mental disorder. This criterion raises most starkly issues of state power, individual autonomy, and the multiplicity of causes for any specific living situation.

(f)   Need for Treatment

The majority of states also include as part of their commitment laws a requirement that the person need treatment.[129] This concept is frequently incorporated into the definition of mental illness. For example, Delaware defines a "mentally ill person" as "a person suffering from a mental disease or condition which requires such person to be observed and treated at a mental hospital for his own welfare."[130] It may also be included as part of another criterion, usually that having to do with "grave disability."

However, in no state is a need for treatment, by itself, a ground for commitment. Prior to the 1970s, need for treatment or care was the most common commitment criterion. However, since *Donaldson's* holding that the state cannot confine a person simply because he or she is mentally ill, it has been on shaky constitutional footing.[131] Conversely, as a conceptual matter, *lack* of treatability should not be a bar to commitment when the basis for commitment is the police power,[132] and perhaps not even for many types of *parens patriae* commitments.[133] The continued presence of the treatability criterion has thus been described as a "vestigial structure,"[134] and its relative unimportance in demonstrating the legal case for commit-

ment is another example of the focus on dangerousness that runs throughout civil commitment law.

Nonetheless, a number of commentators have proposed reinstituting this criterion as a primary basis for commitment.[135] The proposals of Stone and Roth alluded to earlier [see § 10.03(b)] are the most explicit in this regard. Although they run counter to the reform movement that is reflected in the emphasis on dangerousness in today's statutes, these proposals are discussed briefly here because, given the Supreme Court's retrenchment in mental health litigation, state legislatures have shown a renewed interest in more medically oriented commitment statutes.

The two models are similar in intent and in form. Each is intended to focus clinical attention and resources on the treatment of illness rather than on the patient's dangerousness. Each also seeks to limit the use of civil commitment only to the most seriously ill, and each attempts to ensure that treatment will be made available to the patient. The main features of these proposals are the following:

1. The individual must be reliably diagnosed as suffering from severe mental illness.[136]
2. In the absence of treatment, the prognosis for the individual is major distress.
3. The individual is incompetent; that is, the illness substantially impairs the person's ability to understand or communicate about the possibility of treatment.[137]
4. Treatment is available.
5. The risk–benefit ratio of treatment is such that a reasonable person would consent to it.[138]

If these conditions are met, as determined at a hearing at which the person has full procedural rights, a brief period (six weeks in Roth's proposal[139]) of treatment may occur. Because the patient has been found to lack capacity on the issue of treatment, a substitute decisionmaker is permitted to give or withhold informed consent to the proffered treatment.[140]

Roth would also allow limited use of commitment on dangerousness grounds,[141] while Stone would relegate the control of dangerousness to the criminal justice system.[142] The primary goal of each proposal, however, is to restore *parens patriae* as the primary source of civil commitment. Stone calls this the "Thank You Theory of Civil Commitment": "[I]t asks the psychiatrist to focus his inquiry on illness and treatment, and it asks the law to guarantee treatment before it intervenes in the name of *parens patriae*."[143] The proposals have been criticized on both theoretical and practical grounds,[144] and they have not been fully incorporated in any state statute. However, their existence demonstrates the continued vitality of the argument over the goals and substantive criteria for civil commitment.

(g)   The Least Restrictive Alternative

In at least two-thirds of the states, meeting the substantive criteria is not enough: Commitment to a hospital is still not permissible if a less restrictive alternative exists.[145] First recognized by Judge Bazelon as a right derived from statutory law,[146] the least-restrictive-alternative doctrine has since attained constitutional status in a number of cases.[147] The basis for the doctrine is the principle, developed in cases involving the First Amendment,[148] that the state may restrict the exercise of fundamental liberties only to the extent necessary to effectuate the state's interest. Because commitment infringes the fundamental interest of individual liberty, the argument goes, it may be used only to the extent necessary to achieve the interest in providing treatment and protecting the individual or community. Under this scheme, the state hospital is posited as the most restrictive environment, with community-based services and outpatient care seen as less restrictive.

The goal of the doctrine, which seeks to ensure that hospitalization is used only as a last resort, is laudable. However, as with the other criteria discussed, statutory guidelines in this area are not particularly precise. As Hoffman and Foust pointed out,[149] this ambiguity has led to a failure to resolve several critical issues. First, the doctrine is preoccupied with physical restrictiveness. It presumes that hospitals are the most restrictive environment, with other settings considered proportionately more preferable as they become less "hospital-like." This superficial analysis

fails to take into account the restrictive nature of the treatment modality itself; most important, it fails to recognize that certain physically restrictive treatments might be more efficacious and might therefore result in an overall reduction in the duration of state intervention. Second, it is not always clear who is responsible for the search for alternatives (the judge, the individual, or the state), or what the extent of that responsibility is. Even when the responsible party is identified, one study found that the responsibility was often ignored.[150] Third, alternative resources often simply do not exist. Is the inquiry limited to a search of available resources, or must it consider the most appropriate resource for the individual living in an ideal world? Several courts have found that the doctrine requires the development of community-based resources.[151] However, other courts have rejected this argument.[152] Further, the Supreme Court has expressed some distaste for the idea even when it is incorporated into federal legislation.[153]

In so doing, the Court may have weakened the constitutional validity of the doctrine.[154] But it remains an explicit statutory policy in most states, regardless of its constitutional underpinnings. That fact is demonstrated dramatically by the upsurge in statutes providing for outpatient commitment, discussed next.

(h)   Outpatient Commitment

To the extent the unit of measure is physical restrictiveness, the most obvious means of implementing the least restrictive alternative doctrine is to require, whenever feasible, commitment to a program in the community, preferably on an outpatient basis.[155] It must be recognized, however, that involuntary community treatment comes in at least three guises, two of which may not completely mesh with the doctrine's underlying policy.

The type of nonhospital treatment that most obviously implements the least restrictive alternative idea is straightforward *outpatient commitment*, an option authorized in approximately two-thirds of the states.[156] Commitment statutes endorsing this procedure purport to provide an alternative disposition to inpatient treatment for individuals who meet the usual commitment criteria.

A variation on outpatient commitment—which could be called *preventive commitment*—is a relatively new innovation that exists in only a handful of states; it permits commitment on an outpatient basis (and in some states, on an inpatient basis as well) of those who will *soon meet* the usual commitment criteria if intervention does not take place. The commitment criterion under these statutes is analogous to the American Psychiatric Association's "predicted deterioration" standard in the gravely disabled context. For instance, Hawaii allows outpatient commitment if the individual "has been imminently dangerous to self or others as a result of a severe mental disorder" and is now in need of treatment in order "to prevent a relapse or deterioration which would predictably result" in the person becoming "imminently dangerous."[157] Apparently, preventive commitment statutes were enacted not as an alternative to inpatient commitment (the purported reason for outpatient commitment) but for a number of other reasons, including

> concerns about . . . a growing number of mentally disordered people in shelters and on the streets, resistant to treatment and in various stages of decompensation, who cannot be hospitalized under the strict commitment criteria; a backlash among psychiatrists and mental health professionals to what is perceived as over-legalization of the mental health system; and advocacy by increasingly vocal parents' groups, particularly the National Alliance for the Mentally Ill, who are demanding treatment for their family members and increasingly allying themselves with mental health professionals to press for the easing of commitment standards.[158]

The third type of outpatient intervention, usually called *conditional release*, has been available for some time in about 40 states[159]; it involves continued supervision of a person who has been released from the hospital. Under this type of community program, the hospital or, in some jurisdictions, the court, informs the person of the release conditions (e.g., reporting to a clinic for medication); repeated violation of one or more of these conditions will usually trigger rehospitalization, either summarily or after some sort of hearing. In contrast to commitment at the front

end, the primary motivations here are to "test" the treated individual's ability to function in the community under supervision and to free up hospital beds.

The three legal mechanisms for treating people in the community thus stem from different policy goals. At the same time, they are similar in their salient substantive features. Technically, a person is not eligible for outpatient commitment unless he or she meets the usual commitment criteria, whereas preventive commitment and conditional release can be triggered on something less. But, practically, the substantive criteria as applied to people who are mentally ill and dangerous to self or others are probably not very different under any of these options. A person who is presently or "imminently" dangerous to self or others is not generally treatable on an outpatient basis.[160] On the latter assumption, the only type of "dangerous" person who is eligible for outpatient commitment is the person who will eventually harm others if certain treatment is not commenced or maintained. Presumably, this is the same type of "dangerous" person affected by preventive commitment and conditional release provisions. In other words, in practice the "predicted deterioration" standard applies in all three contexts.[161]

This standard may well violate the notion that the state may only intervene when danger is imminent,[162] but that fact may not render the standard unconstitutional, or even unwise. As § 10.03(c) points out, dangerousness is best conceptualized as a multifactor construct, involving the nature of the anticipated harm, its probability of occurrence, and the frequency with which it may occur, in addition to its imminence. Under this formulation, the imminence of the harm is only one of many factors considered in deciding whether a person is subject to involuntary state intervention for treatment or incapacitation purposes. Thus, assuming that the anticipated harm is significant and probable, or likely to occur frequently, it may not need to be imminent to justify commitment. Several courts have suggested as much, both when the predicted deterioration standard is used at the front end[163] and in connection with conditional release.[164] Bolstering this stance is the fact that, in the context at issue here, the predicted deterioration standard is being used solely to justify outpatient treatment, where the infringement on liberty interests is usually not as significant as is the case with institutionalization.

Although eliminating the imminence requirement may therefore be permissible, such a move might still have an unconstitutional impact unless certain precautions are taken. As research suggests,[165] the predicted deterioration standard could easily create a class of patients who never escape control by the state because their "dangerousness" is always just around the corner (consider, in this regard, Case Study 10.1). Consequently, commitment statutes using such a standard should perhaps be construed to provide that, unless their dangerousness does become imminent, those committed under this standard should be eligible for *automatic* release from outpatient commitment after a certain time period.[166]

10.04.   Procedural Due Process

The movement to reform civil commitment laws sought to "legalize" the commitment process. Because deprivation of liberty was at issue, the argument went, judges rather than clinicians should serve as primary decisionmakers, and the proposed patient should have procedural protections approaching those afforded a criminal defendant. The newly legalized process, combined with stricter and better defined substantive criteria, would improve the accuracy of the decisions made at commitment, eliminating inappropriate confinement.

The commitment process has in fact been legalized on paper (although perhaps not in practice [see § 10.05(c)]). Even those jurisdictions that, in substantive terms, are the most medically oriented grant a wide range of procedural rights; the primary difference between statutes appears to be when the judicial model for decisionmaking supplants the clinical. The first subsection that follows contrasts four representative statutes, which fall along a continuum from medically oriented (New York) to relatively legalistic (Washington and California) to primarily legalistic (Virginia). The procedures associated with outpatient and voluntary commitment are then discussed.

(a)   Inpatient Commitment Procedures

Each state provides for a least two stages of commitment. The first is emergency commitment, generally unencumbered by significant procedural trappings. The second, usually following soon after the first, is the formal commitment hearing, at which the full panoply of rights applies.

(1)   Emergency Admissions

Because of the frequent need to intervene immediately to prevent harm to self or others, even the most legalistic state commitment schemes allow emergency admission with a minimum of process. In California[167] and Washington[168] either a police officer or a clinician may authorize emergency admission of an individual. In New York,[169] the decision is made by a clinician at a facility or by the county director of mental health. By contrast, a judge or magistrate makes the emergency detention decision in Virginia,[170] although it is not necessary that he or she actually see the patient. In none of these states is the patient afforded a hearing, granted the right to contest the action at a formal proceeding, or entitled to counsel prior to hospitalization. Nor does the petitioner for emergency admission have to meet a high level of proof in establishing committability; no standard of proof is established in New York, Washington, or Virginia,[171] and California requires only that the decisionmaker state that "probable cause"[172] exists to believe that the person is mentally disordered and, as a result, gravely disabled or a danger to self or others.

Each state does require that the detained individual be given prompt notice of (1) the potential duration of the confinement, (2) when the right to counsel becomes available, and (3) when the patient becomes entitled to a hearing. In Virginia, these rights are related to the individual by a judge at a "probable cause" hearing held within 48 hours of detention,[173] in Washington they are announced either by the person taking the patient into custody or the facility at which the patient is detained,[174] and in New York[175] and California[176] the detaining facility provides the necessary notice. Counsel is theoretically made available immediately after notice except in California, where the right becomes available only if the individual is held longer than 72 hours.[177] In New York, patients automatically have the benefit of the Mental Hygiene Legal Service, a legal advocacy organization located on facility grounds.

In most states the period of emergency admission is sharply circumscribed (48 hours in Virginia[178]; 72 hours in California[179] and Washington[180]). However, in New York, the individual may be detained up to 15 days on an "emergency" basis if a second physician has examined the person within 48 hours of admission and finds that the individual is mentally ill and dangerous to self or others.[181] This provision is tempered somewhat by the monitoring of the aforementioned Mental Hygiene Legal Service and by a provision that the patient may request a judicial hearing at any time; if a hearing is requested, it must be held within five days of the request.[182]

A mechanism that may end up competing with the emergency admission procedures just outlined is the "prehearing screening." Beginning in the 1980s, a number of states established, by statute or local custom, "screening" organizations at the community level that are charged with referring mentally disabled people to the most effective treatment program available. In these jurisdictions, "the great majority of persons entering the mental health–judicial system never see the inside of a courthouse: many persons are screened and diverted to more suitable alternatives, many elect to enter mental health treatment and care programs voluntarily, and some are discharged shortly after arrival at the mental health facility."[183]

Most jurisdictions specifically exempt "emergency" cases from this screening procedure; even so, a significant number of individuals who would have been "emergency admissions" under the old system seem to avoid the involuntary commitment process altogether under this new scheme. In one study of the Arizona screening process, for instance, about three times as many individuals are diverted than proceed through the involuntary petition process.[184] The key ingredient to the screening process is knowledge of available services. As noted in one commentary:

> These early interventions should be based on knowledge of the mental health services delivery in the area and should take into account

such factors as the range of treatment and services available, the criteria for admission to various facilities, the security of particular mental health facilities, and the conditions within facilities. Good initial processing decisions also require an understanding of the linkages between the agencies.[185]

(2)   Long-Term Detention

In contrast to emergency admissions, which are designed to effectuate the state interest in confinement of acutely ill and presently dangerous persons, long-term detention requires judicial approval of continued confinement in an adversarial proceeding. In each of the four jurisdictions under consideration, the patient is entitled to the following rights before or during the hearing to determine long-term commitability:

1. Written notice of the fact that the patient faces a commitment proceeding, his or her rights therein, and with the possible exception of New York,[186] the underlying reasons for the proposed commitment.
2. A right to counsel, and to have counsel appointed if necessary.[187]
3. The right to call witnesses and cross-examine witnesses.
4. The right to request a jury trial, though in Virginia and New York this right does not attach unless the patient appeals the initial determination.[188]
5. The right to have a judge rather than a clinician make the ultimate decision.
6. The right to have the state prove its case by clear and convincing evidence.[189]

The states may differ on issues such as the admissibility of hearsay evidence [see § 3.08(a)],[190] the applicability of the privilege against self-incrimination [see §§ 4.02(e), 10.09(a)],[191] the right of the individual to an independent clinician to assist in the preparation of a "defense" [see § 4.03(b)(1)],[192] when the patient can waive the right to be present,[193] and the confidentiality of the commitment proceeding.[194] But the core procedural rights are fairly standardized throughout the country, whether the statute is "legalistic" or "medical" in general orientation. To a great extent, the criminal model has been adopted.

The procedural differences most revealing of a legislature's stance on the proper balance between individual and state interests involve the time at which the more formal adversary proceedings must occur and the duration of the resulting confinement. In Virginia, a full judicial hearing must occur within 48 hours of the initial detention.[195] If the court determines that the individual meets the commitment criteria, it may commit the person for a period of up to 180 days, at which time another full judicial hearing is required.[196] In contrast, Washington does not require a full hearing until over two weeks after the initial detention. Within 72 hours of that detention, a "probable cause" judicial hearing is held, which can result in 14 days of further detention if the state shows by a preponderance of the evidence that the criteria are met.[197] A full hearing takes place at the end of the 14 days; if the criteria are met, the person is committed for up to 90 days, with 180 day extensions thereafter.[198]

Similarly, in California, an individual may be confined for up to 7 days upon a written "certification" by two clinicians describing to the court the basis for continued hospitalization of the patient,[199] and for a total of 14 days from the time of hospitalization if a review hearing, presided over by a clinician, approves the certification.[200] If further care is required at the expiration of the 14 days, it may be obtained either through a second 14-day certification (for an "imminently suicidal" person),[201] "conservatorship" (guardianship) proceedings (if the person is gravely disabled),[202] or a full judicial hearing (for all others). Detention pursuant to the latter provision may last 180 days and may be renewed after a judicial hearing.

New York's scheme is quite different from the three just described. Confinement extending to 60 days after the 15 days of emergency detention may occur based on a certification by two physicians that the individual meets commitment standards.[203] Once hospitalized, a third physician at the institution must examine the patient and also consider alternatives to hospitalization,[204] and, as noted previously, the patient may also request a judicial hearing. But no such hearing is *required* until the expiration of the 75 days from the original detention.[205]

As with the substantive criteria for commitment, statutory procedural protections attempt to accommodate both the state's and the individual's interests. The balance struck, however, does make a difference. For example, New York's scheme, which does not require a judicial hearing for two and a half months, may vitiate the effect of procedural protections in checking unwarranted commitment, simply because of the delay after confinement in making the protections available. In contrast, Virginia's law, which requires a full hearing within 48 hours of the initial detention, may allow insufficient time for a complete clinical evaluation prior to hearing. Given insufficient data, the system may react by deciding close or undeveloped cases in favor of commitment. The balances struck by the Washington and California statutes seem more desirable. The California law in particular—which establishes clinical gatekeeping, an informal "probable cause" hearing before a 14-day confinement can occur, and a judicial hearing before longer detention—seems particularly suited to accommodate both individual and state interests.[206]

(b)   Outpatient Commitment Procedures

Whether the mechanism for implementing outpatient treatment is outpatient commitment, preventive commitment, or conditional release [see § 10.03(h)], three procedural components for ensuring compliance with the treatment regimen are necessary: a method for arranging the outpatient treatment program, some type of monitoring system, and some procedure for taking corrective action if the person committed does not adhere to the outpatient treatment plan. The laws of most states are extremely vague about these implementation issues.

The primary responsibility for developing a treatment plan rests on clinicians. In the conditional release context, once the plan is developed most states require that the committed person receive a copy of the conditions to be followed; some require a written agreement with the person.[207] Presumably, similar methods of informing the committed person are available under outpatient and preventive commitment statutes, although this is seldom made clear in the relevant statutes. The principal difference between the outpatient treatment mechanisms at this initial stage is that, in the latter two, commitment is to an outpatient facility, whereas under most conditional release regimes the person remains legally committed to the releasing institution.[208] Focusing solely on conditional release programs, another difference between states is that courts are not always involved in approving the treatment plan. Even when courts are involved, however, they rarely do more than rubber-stamp the treatment plan and order the committed person to follow it.[209]

Wexler has suggested a more sophisticated approach to arranging outpatient care.[210] Relying on health care compliance principles found to be efficacious in the clinical setting,[211] he proposes that judges closely scrutinize outpatient treatment plans (to ensure specificity of conditions); elicit a verbal, public agreement in court, in front of significant others, to abide by the treatment conditions; and engage the patient in "mild counterarguments" as to why the patient will not conform with the treatment plan, thus encouraging the patient to reaffirm his or her commitment to it. The judge is also to confirm with the patient that the judge will continue to monitor treatment progress through periodic hearings, the dates of which are specified. Although Wexler confines his proposal to conditional release of the insanity acquittee, it might work in the civil commitment, incompetency, and jail contexts as well [see generally § 10.10]. To date, no state has established this type of process.

Once the patient is placed in an outpatient program, some method for ensuring compliance with the treatment plan is usually necessary, especially if the person is thought to be dangerous without the treatment, Typically, in contrast to Wexler's suggestion, the monitoring is only nominally presided over by the committing court and in effect is controlled by the treatment facility. An alternative to the judicial model is the administrative model. This model is perhaps best represented by the Psychiatric Security Review Board in Oregon, which is composed of a psychiatrist, a psychologist, a lawyer, a parole expert, and a member of the public, and supervises conditional release of insanity acquittees.[212] In addition to making the initial release decision,[213] the Board is charged with intensively supervising the acquit-

tee's progress and appears to have performed well in this regard.[214] A number of legal issues could arise in terms of the appropriate intrusiveness of such monitoring,[215] but to date there are apparently no decisions addressing them.

From the legal perspective, the most controversial implementation issue concerns the procedure for "revoking" or terminating outpatient treatment and recommitting or committing the individual to an inpatient facility. Inevitably, courts analyzing this issue have focused on the analogy to revocation of parole [see § 9.03(a)(4)]. Here, the leading decision is *Morrissey v. Brewer*,[216] where the United States Supreme Court held that the "conditional liberty" of paroled criminals entitles them to preliminary and final revocation hearings, notice and confrontation rights and, in "complex" revocation proceedings, the right to counsel as well. Some lower courts, contrasting the therapeutic rationale of hospitalization with the punitive intent behind parole revocation, have held that *Morrissey* does not apply in the outpatient treatment context, at least to revocation of conditional release. These courts have thus upheld automatic (i.e., nonjudicial) rehospitalization of the outpatient who has violated a condition of treatment (although they also note that the person can always challenge a detention through a writ of habeas corpus).[217] Other courts have permitted emergency detention but then required a prompt *Morrissey*-type hearing to determine whether hospitalization was warranted.[218] Finally, a number of courts and state statutes permit rehospitalization only upon court order, although they differ as to whether a hearing must precede the order.[219] Some states also apply the latter procedures to attempts to hospitalize those *initially* committed on an outpatient basis.[220]

Analogizing revocation of parole with revocation of conditional release (or with hospitalization after an initial outpatient commitment), as most courts have, is problematic. In many cases, hospitalization will be less punitive and of shorter duration than imprisonment after parole revocation. At the same time, the state has clear authority to incarcerate the paroled criminal defendant for the period denominated by the uncompleted sentence; in contrast, the state does not have authority to confine the unconvicted mentally ill person unless he or she is dangerous to self or others.

Thus, in a sense, an erroneous determination in the latter situation is *more* consequential. At the least, a full hearing after a short emergency detention should be mandatory.

(c)　Voluntary Commitment Procedures

As noted earlier, every state allows competent adults to admit themselves voluntarily; a growing number of states permit juveniles over 14 or 16 to do so as well, without parental consent. Voluntary hospitalization has traditionally been preferred over involuntary commitment for a number of reasons, including the beliefs that the voluntary patient is more motivated to be treated and that voluntary treatment is less stigmatizing, demands less clinical staff time and resources, and is less likely to delay treatment than involuntary commitment.[221] As a result, about 50% of the population in public mental health hospitals is "voluntary."[222]

The quotation marks are necessary because many so-called voluntary admissions may not be. About one-fifth of the states allow "informal admission," which is triggered by an oral request for admission and can be terminated upon request as well, unless the hospital staff decides at the time of the discharge request that the person meets the involuntary commitment criteria. This type of admission can be seen as truly voluntary. Very few "voluntary" patients are in the hospital informally, however. Rather, they are there as a result of signing a written request for admission or because they were offered and accepted the voluntary option at a commitment hearing. Research indicates that many of the people in the latter categories either do not understand the consequences of their action or were "cajoled" into taking it by the threat of involuntary commitment.[223] Furthermore, a person hospitalized under the formal voluntary admission procedure may, depending on the state, be detained for 3 to 15 days even after a request to leave, to allow the staff to decide whether to initiate involuntary commitment proceedings.

As noted earlier, in *Zinermon v. Burch*,[224] the Supreme Court called into question the practice of "volunteering in" a person who is not competent to make treatment decisions. Instead, the Court suggested, an incompetent person should only be hospitalized if he or she is shown to meet the criteria for involuntary commitment at a full hearing. The *Zinermon* decision, which reinstated a damages suit challenging the volunteering-in practice, may be an important reinforcement of the due process reforms of the early 1970s. In particular, it may counteract economic and other pressures on clinicians to hospitalize unilaterally persons (like the man in Case Study 10.2?) who may not meet commitment criteria.

At the same time, *Zinermon* has been heavily criticized to the extent it requires involuntary commitment of clearly ill patients who express some willingness to be hospitalized.[225] The available empirical evidence suggests that many of these people do not understand most aspects of voluntary admission[226] and thus would require involuntary commitment hearings under *Zinermon*. Yet, as we discuss below, empirical studies of these hearings reveal that they are often *pro forma* exercises in which little effort is expended on the respondent's behalf. These facts, together with the perceived advantages of voluntary treatment listed above, led the American Psychiatric Association to recommend that an assenting patient be accepted as a voluntary admission if he or she understands two simple items of information: that he or she "is being admitted to a psychiatric hospital or ward for treatment, and . . . that release from the hospital may not be automatic."[227]

10.05.　The Effects of Commitment Laws and Commitment

Although reforms of commitment laws toward a more legalistic model were rampant in the 1960s and 1970s, it is important to acknowledge that these changes in the law were uniformly moderate. As noted in the preceding section, "medical" and "legalistic" statutes are typically more alike than they are different, with the major difference being in the point in the process at which judicial review is involved. More important, even the most legalistic statutes have generally been unsuccessful at "legalizing" civil commitment. This conclusion is based on an examination (undertaken below) of data regarding the frequency of hospitalization, the manner in which the new standards are applied, and the lack of adherence to procedural rules. When these data are combined with other data suggesting the general ineffectiveness of hospitalization as a treatment modality (also described below), one is led to the further conclusion that mental health professionals should be cautious when participating in the commitment process as it exists at present.

(a)   Frequency of Commitment

As noted in § 10.02(a), there has been a striking decrease in the number of people hospitalized in state facilities in the past two decades. In large part, financial incentives, the advent of new treatment techniques, and changing ideology in the mental health professions are responsible for this decrease.[228] One might conjecture that changes in civil commitment laws also have contributed to this decline. However, a number of studies suggest that they have not had much impact in this regard; at most, the research suggests, the typical legalistic change merely has a short-term effect.[229]

In one of the best-designed studies on this topic,[230] Luckey and Berman examined the effects of the Nebraska Mental Health Commitment Act.[231] Although the Nebraska law has some unusual provisions,[232] it is a particularly comprehensive "legalistic" statute. Using an interrupted time-series design,[233] Luckey and Berman found that the statute had merely a transitory effect on the number of commitments. Within 18 months after passage of the law, the total number of commitments had returned to the prereform level, based on admission trends prior to enactment of the law. Indeed, much of the initial observed decrease may have been the result simply of the time required to put the new commitment system into place. Corroborating this interpretation is the fact that the decrease was largely specific to rural counties, where the necessary professionals were in short supply.

Further evidence that changes in the law are not the primary reason for changes in commitment practices is provided by the fact that the frequency of institutionalizations, as opposed to the number hospitalized at a given time, actually increased between 1955 and 1980.[234] In view of mental health professionals' tendency to err on the side of overprediction ("false positives"),[235] one could assume that rigorous testing of their testimony in commitment proceedings would produce a drop in the number of commitments. That such a drop has not occurred suggests that the tighter standards and procedures required by the revised commitment statutes have not been applied in practice. Studies of commitment hearings themselves, to which we now turn, confirm this interpretation.

(b)   Commitment Criteria

The dangerousness standard was meant not only to narrow the scope of commitment but also to focus the commitment inquiry on the normative issue of when the state may deprive someone of liberty, rather than the clinical issue of whether a person needed treatment. Accordingly, one might predict, commitment decisions under the new laws would be based on moral considerations as well as on clinical information. Yet, in general, clinicians' opinions as to committability are dispositive, regardless of the legal standard to be applied. Studies indicate an agreement rate between clinicians' conclusions and factfinders' decisions of between 90% and 100%.[236] This evidence suggests, although it does not prove, that adherence to the supposedly narrower substantive criteria imposed by commitment has not been uniform.

Also supporting the proposition that the dangerousness criterion has had little restricting effect in practice is research suggesting that movement to a pure *parens patriae* model, using a need for treatment or predicted deterioration standard, would not substantially increase the size of the population subject to commitment.[237] Several studies show too that need for hospitalization is often assumed without critical application of the "least restrictive alternative" concept.[238] In short, the substantive criteria meant to limit unnecessary deprivation of liberty created by the reform legislation, far from "criminalizing" commitment,[239] appear to be neglected because of a *Parham*-like conceptualization of the civil commitment decision as medical or psychological rather than legal.

(c) Procedures

As a practical matter, this medical conceptualization is played out in a neglect of form as well as substance. Adversary procedures are especially well suited to enhancement of perceived justice.[240] Theoretically, such procedures are endorsed by all commitment statutes regardless of model, at least at the hearing stage. However, substantial empirical evidence demonstrates that informal, inquisitorial procedures are pervasive in civil commitment proceedings, no matter what the statutes say.[241]

Consider the following data, both self-report and observational, from the Iowa study cited previously.[242] Three-fourths of the referees and clerks of court surveyed acknowledged that commitment hearings were usually not conducted in an adversary manner. Defense attorneys were found to request an independent mental health evaluation (available by right under the statute) in fewer than 1% of cases, and they rarely called more than two witnesses (often none). The majority of the defense attorneys failed to put the respondents on the stand. One attorney even reasoned that to do so would risk respondents' persuading the referee that they had no mental illness! Consistent with their lack of active participation in the hearings, the attorneys uniformly spent less than two hours in preparation of these cases.

For their part, the referees encouraged passivity on the part of defense attorneys. Some referees expressly discouraged cross-examination of witnesses; if questions were to be asked, the referees themselves would ask them. The result was that commitment hearings were little more than a stamp of approval for the attending physician's opinion. In fact, a change in treatment plan from that which the hospital physician had recommended was observed to occur in fewer than 1% of cases. Referees and attorneys generally agreed that clinicians should decide whether the elements of the standard for civil commitment had been met, and, if so, what the conditions of treatment should be.

These types of findings are echoed in several other studies. Virtually all found that attorneys rarely act in an adversarial manner during commitment hearings and indeed often assist the state in its task of proving committability.[243]

(d) Why the Laws Have Failed: Pressures for Hospitalization

The primary reason the legalistic reforms have failed seems to be the intuition, of both clinicians and lawyers, that mental illness should result in hospitalization. Among clinicians, this attitude is particularly strong. Zwerling, Conte, Plutchik, and Karasu offered a dramatic example of this phenomenon.[244] As director of a major urban teaching hospital, Zwerling established a "No-Commitment Week." During that week, no commitments were to be made unless *absolutely* necessary. This judgment required corroboration by supervising clinicians. Yet during the experiment the commitment rate did not change at all. Each clinician thought that each case was the extraordinary one in which commitment was absolutely morally and clinically required. Other examples of the strong paternalistic, hospital-oriented bent of clinical testimony abound,[245] even under legalistic statutes and amid calls for cost containment.

As the previous evidence suggests, lawyers usually share the same views, encapsulated in the nostrum that "doctor knows best." Moreover, the bias toward hospitalization is remarkably resistant to change. Poythress trained mental health lawyers in cross-examining mental health professionals, but he found that the attorneys did not apply their new knowledge in commitment hearings.[246] Their reluctance stemmed most often from their conviction that their clients belonged in the hospital. When the attorneys did begin to act as adversaries, judges typically made clear that such advocacy would be to no avail if it controverted the experts' opinions.

Of course, legally suspect civil commitment is not simply the result of the conventional wisdom that doctors know best and that people with mental illness belong in the hospital. Indeed, clinicians themselves occasionally express discomfort about civil commitment.[247] Perhaps the best explanation for overcommitment is simply politics. Commitment is usually the safest course of action for clinicians and judges when a serious question of involuntary hospitalization is raised. No one hears about the persons who did not commit suicide or did not assault someone else. On the other hand, false-negative judgments may result in disastrous consequences for the patients themselves or their victims, public criticism of the professionals involved,[248] and perhaps feelings of personal guilt. Families may push to have their disturbed relatives "put away," and clinicians (and judges and lawyers as well) are likely to choose the most intrusive treatments for the most serious disorders.[249]

(e)   The Questionable Benefit of Hospitalization

The hospital orientation of the commitment process is unfortunate, for two reasons. First, community treatment can be equally, if not more, effective at providing treatment for many individuals. In the 1980s, Kiesler reviewed all the existing experimental comparisons of hospitalization and alternate care.[250] The ten studies made use of a multiplicity of interventions and outcome measures but came to consistent conclusions:

> It seems quite clear from these studies that for the vast majority of patients now being assigned to inpatient units in mental institutions, care of at least equal impact could be otherwise provided. There is not an instance in this array of studies in which hospitalization had any positive impact on the average patient care investigated in the study. In almost every case, the alternative care had more positive outcomes. There were significant and powerful effects on such life-related variables as employment, school attendance, and the like. There were significant and important effects on the probability of subsequent readmission. Not only did the patients in the alternative care not undergo the initial hospitalization but they were less likely to undergo hospitalization later, as well. There is clear evidence here for the causal sequence in the finding alluded to earlier that the best predictor of hospitalization is prior hospitalization. These data across these 10 studies suggest quite clearly that hospitalization of mental patients is self-perpetuating.[251]

Moreover, in no study was alternative care found to be more expensive than hospitalization.[252]

Kiesler was careful to point out that the available research does not prove that no one should be hospitalized.[253] Specifically, for those who are truly *imminently* dangerous to self or others,[254] a good inpatient unit may provide the most effective treatment, at least for the short term. Research also suggests that, for a small percentage of persons with chronic mental illness, hospitalization may be the best choice.[255] Nonetheless, Kiesler's research makes a persuasive case for a strong presumption against hospitalization. Only in a minority of cases will this most dramatic step be the least restrictive alternative for provision of treatment.

Furthermore, even when it is assumed that hospitalization is indicated, the necessary treatment may not be forthcoming in the state hospitals to which civilly committed patients are often sent. In theory hospitals can provide a structured environment that reduces overstimulation and allows stabilization on medication, but historically the care provided in many of these hospitals has been sadly deficient.[256] Moreover, even if state legislatures were willing, as they often have not been,[257] to provide sufficient funding for humane care, it is not clear that the quality of professional staff would improve substantially.[258] Although, nationwide, hospitals are better staffed than they were in the 1970s and 1980s,[259] in many jurisdictions geographically remote state hospitals continue to experience difficulties in recruiting and retaining staff. Finally, even in quality hospitals, the stigma and institutional dependency that accompany a history of psychiatric hospitalization may outweigh the benefits of treatment.[260]

(f)   The Need for Caution

When taken together with the literature on decisionmaking in civil commitment proceedings, research on the iatrogenic effects of hospitalization leads to the conclusion that mental health professionals should exercise care in evaluating persons for possible civil commitment.[261] Clinicians' opinions are likely to be dispositive, and the risk of harm resulting from these opinions (when the recommendation is for hospitalization) is substantial. At the least, it can be said with confidence that in the majority of cases, hospitalization is not likely to be the least restrictive alternative. In view of the great deference apt to be accorded their views in civil commitment proceedings, clinicians bear a special ethical obligation to ensure that factfinders are aware of possible alternatives to involuntary hospitalization and their relative efficacy.[262]

We do not intend to suggest by our review of how the civil commitment system typically works that legal reforms have had no effect at all. Particularly in states using a legalistic model of commitment, civil commitment reforms may have contributed to the enormous drop in the average length of stay in state hospitals[263] and to an increased appreciation of patients' human rights.[264] Moreover, reliance on hospitalization rather than other forms of treatment may have as much to do with financial incentives and disincentives[265] as with loose application of civil commitment laws.

There is also at least anecdotal evidence that civil commitment laws can work as intended when legal authorities take their obligations seriously.[266] Although such an orderly, responsible approach may require careful engineering of the civil commitment system as a whole,[267] it is clearly the appropriate goal, and most of the remainder of this chapter focuses on how the system should operate. At the same time, though, it is important for lawyers and clinicians to go into commitment proceedings with eyes fully open to both how the process is likely to work and what state and community hospitals realistically may offer.

PROBLEM 10.1

Construct an "ideal" civil commitment system in terms of (1) the substantive criteria, (2) procedural rules, and (3) the facilities needed.

10.06.   Attorney's Role

Perhaps the most important participant in civil commitment is the respondent's attorney. Deprivation of liberty, even with benevolent intent, is not a trivial matter, and the evidence supportive of such a disposition should be thoroughly tested for its reliability and probative value. In essence, justice demands that the respondent be able to put the best possible case forward and that state power does not go unchecked. Thus, whether the procedure is meaningful is likely to turn largely on whether the attorney assumes an adversarial stance; indeed, the research evidence is clear that

civil commitment procedures and standards will be just so many words unless attorneys behave adversarily.[268]

Yet significant difficulties inhere in adopting such a stance. As already noted, many lawyers do not appreciate the legal–moral aspects of civil commitment, and they may be mystified by clinical phenomena presented to them. Even when attorneys are neither naive nor lackadaisical, they may find judicial resistance to their doing their job.

Perhaps most problematic, the mental health attorney has no clear ethical mandate. It is cardinal in American jurisprudence that attorneys are "zealous advocates" of their clients' wishes.[269] Although this canon of professional responsibility may at times be a legal fiction,[270] it nonetheless provides a clear guide for lawyers in conceptualizing their role in most circumstances. Such clarity evaporates in mental health law, however. Does the lawyer zealously advocate the wishes of a client who seems to behave irrationally? What are such a client's interests? In this context, the American Bar Association's (ABA's) Model Code of Professional Responsibility does not endorse a pure adversarial stance. It recognizes that

> the responsibilities of a lawyer may vary according to the . . . mental conditions of a client. . . . Any mental or physical condition of a client that renders him incapable of making a considered judgment on his own behalf casts additional responsibilities upon his lawyer. . . . If a client under disability has no legal representative [a guardian], his lawyer may be compelled in court proceedings to make decisions on behalf of the client.[271]

However, the Model Code still retains a preference, albeit ambivalent, for an advocate's rather than a guardian's stance by the lawyer. If the client is capable of understanding the matter in question or of contributing to the advancement of his interests, regardless of whether he is legally disqualified from performing certain acts, the lawyer should obtain from him all possible aid. If the disability of a client and the lack of a legal representative (like a guardian) compel the lawyer to make decisions for his client, the lawyer should consider all circumstances then prevailing and act with care to safeguard and advance the interests of his client.[272]

In light, then, of both the stakes involved and ethical precepts, we believe the attorney should advocate the client's wishes and avoid acting as a guardian or an *amicus* (an attorney for the court) would. Only when the client is unable to express a preference, or expresses *clearly* irrational wishes, should the attorney consider what others perceive as the client's best interests, and even then these views should not be dispositive. Those authorities who have argued that attorneys for allegedly mentally disordered persons should always act as paternalists[273] have ignored the reality that the civil commitment system requires an advocate for the respondent if it is to work at all. They have also minimized the risk of harm resulting from inappropriate involuntary hospitalization, as well as the possibility that an adversarial process can be "therapeutic" for the respondent and the family in a number of ways.[274]

We do not mean to imply, however, that an attorney must necessarily pursue "getting the client off" with single-minded zeal (unless a competent client so directs). Rather, as with most legal issues,[275] the attorney's job lies in testing the case against his or client and bargaining for the best possible resolution in light of the client's desires. This process has different components prior to, during, and after the commitment hearing.

Wexler has provided a terse summary of minimal work required for effective representation by counsel prior to the hearing:

> The attorney should make a thorough study of the facts of the case, which should include court records, hospital records, and information available from social agencies. Communication with the patient is, in the ordinary case, a must. The family and friends of the patient should also be contacted to ascertain the true facts behind the petition. It is essential that the attorney have a full understanding of the events preceding the filing of the petition. An investigation of the financial condition of the patient and his family—including their hospitalization insurance—is necessary to determine if certain alternatives to hospitalization should be explored. Finally, the attorney should explore the treatment and custodial resources of the community, should understand the various services offered by social agencies, and should know the avenues by which these resources can be applied to meet the needs of the client as alternatives to involuntary commitment.[276]

Admittedly, these tasks will entail a considerable amount of time and effort on the part of the attorney. If time is needed, the attorney can ask for a continuance (assuming that the client will agree to delay). A vigorous pretrial effort will not only assure a well-prepared case but may also result in a "settlement," obviating the need for a hearing.

If a hearing is held, advocacy should also be vigorous. Cross-examining a psychiatrist may be difficult for one who is not trained in mental health, but not more so than in the criminal or tort context. In addition, relatively simple questions designed to elicit from the doctor why the subject is believed to be mentally ill or dangerous can have a surprising effect on the course of the hearing. In justifying the opinion, the doctor will have to divulge whether his or her conclusions are based on hearsay and to what degree they reflect a "gut reaction" to a given situation as opposed to a scientifically verifiable fact. Asking the expert to examine a list of outpatient facilities and explain why each is not a feasible treatment alternative may also prove beneficial.

Pursuing the case after the hearing—either through the occasional appeal or, if the court orders outpatient treatment, through monitoring the client's compliance—is a further important element of advocacy. When the judge and doctor know there is a possibility that their decision will be reviewed by a higher court, they may devote more effort to meeting their obligations under the commitment statute (although the appeal may be viewed as "moot" when the patient–client has been released pending the appeal). Follow-up of the client by the attorney is also useful to ensure that treatment is received and that a recommitment petition, based on noncompliance, is avoided.

A more detailed analysis of the commitment attorney's obligations can be found elsewhere.[277] What is needed is a means of alerting the legal community to these obligations. A forceful approach to the problem is through legislation. The state of Arizona, for example, has provided that counsel for a defendant in a commitment hearing must perform certain duties or be subject to a citation for contempt of court.[278] Legislation could also raise the fee of commitment attorneys and allow them to obtain funds for independent psychiatric evaluations and other expenses.

Underlying the foregoing discussion is the assumption that, by ensuring that the evidentiary bases for and against commitment are adequately developed, counsel can improve the fairness of the commitment process and reduce the factfinder's tendency to rely solely on the conclusory opinions of expert clinicians. This adversarial role of counsel is fundamental to ensuring that the "legalized" model of commitment process accomplishes the goals for which it was adopted.

10.07.   Clinician's Role

A general injunction to mental health professionals throughout this volume is to monitor, and to take care to avoid exceeding, the limits of their expertise. In particular, clinicians must be careful to refrain from invading the province of factfinders, and lawyers and judges must not delegate their responsibilities to the clinicians.

Nowhere is this theme more pertinent than in civil commitment. As noted in § 1.04(b), the moderate probative value of clinical testimony in commitment may not outweigh its prejudicial effect, especially if attorneys are not playing their role. Because of the great deference usually given to clinicians' opinions in this context, mental health professionals themselves bear much of the responsibility for staying within the boundaries of their expertise. Clinicians should resist giving ultimate-issue opinions. Whether a respondent is so ill and dangerous as to merit deprivation of liberty is a legal–moral decision, not a medical or psychological one. Specifically, the decision as to whether a respondent is "dangerous" subsumes a series of conclusions of law: the threshold probability of dangerous behavior, the range of behaviors that are "dangerous," the period to be covered by the prediction, and the necessary level of validity for the prediction.

Rather than articulating conclusions, mental health professionals should describe respondents' behaviors, their treatment needs, and alternatives for meeting these needs. When actuarial data relevant to the predictive questions are available, these should also be described. If the court insists on testimony about dangerousness, clinicians should only offer information about violence-en-hancing and violence-reducing factors [see § 9.09(c)(4) and the Marlar report, § 19.06(a)]. Regardless of the nature of the evidence being presented, it is incumbent upon clinicians to make clear the uncertainties of their opinion, especially in view of the weight likely to be given to those opinions.

Mental health professionals may also serve as consultants to attorneys in exploring alternatives to commitment and examining the reliability of evidence supporting commitment. Indeed, where legal aid programs are responsible for civil commitment representation, their effectiveness would probably be enhanced by having clinicians on their staffs assume such a consulting role.[279] When such "in house" professional consultation is not provided, attorneys for indigent respondents should be allowed to select independent mental health professionals to examine their clients and to assist in identifying possible alternative forms of treatment [see § 4.03(b)(1)].[280] The assistance of an independent expert may be very important in developing lines of defense against commitment (e.g., possible less restrictive alternatives). Perhaps most important, a "second opinion" might reduce the probability of an erroneous commitment based on unquestioning acceptance of a lone expert's opinion. In short, justice might well be served by a "battle of the experts" in commitment cases.

10.08.   Commitment Evaluation

As discussed in § 10.03, the typical commitment evaluation will require assessment of a person's disorder, treatment needs, dangerousness, and ability to survive outside the hospital or in some less restrictive alternative.

(a)   Mental Illness and Need for Treatment

This aspect of the evaluation resembles a "regular" clinical assessment; that is, a clinician must determine whether a respondent has a significant mental disorder, and, if so, how it might be treated. In making such judgments, clinicians will probably find their usually armamentarium of diagnostic techniques appropriate. Perhaps the key distinction between a regular evaluation for development of a traditional treatment plan and an evaluation of mental disorder for civil commitment arises from the fact that the latter involves *involuntary* treatment. In the latter context, there are special obligations for care and certainty in the invasion of liberty. Hence, the *content* of this part of the evaluation may be typical, but the *attitude* of clinicians should not be. As recommended earlier, clinicians should note the points of uncertainty in their diagnoses, the possible alternatives for treatment (including no treatment), and the probable levels of efficacy of each.

(b)   Dangerousness to Self

Several books review the literature regarding the risk of suicide and "parasuicide" (i.e., attempted suicide) and their clinical assessment.[281] In our description of the correlates of suicide and the clinical techniques for assessing suicide risk, we rely primarily on the work of Fremouw and colleagues[282] and Clark and Fawcett.[283] Further, the discussion that follows focuses on adults rather than children.[284]

(1)   Correlates of Risk for Suicide

Correlates of increased risk of suicide have been identified in several domains. In this section we briefly review some important demographic, diagnostic/clinical, and historical variables. In each area, the emphasis is on the *relative*, rather than absolute, risk posed by those with the identified traits.

With respect to the demographic correlates of suicide, Fremouw and colleagues suggest that a relatively higher risk for suicide is associated with the following demographic variables[285]:

- *Sex*: Males are at higher risk for suicide, by a factor of about 4:1.[286] However, the rate of suicide *attempts* shows quite a different pattern, with the rate for women about three times that for men.[287]
- *Age*: The risk for suicide increases with age for males, with elderly males being the highest age-risk group; females are at highest risk between the ages of 35 and 65.[288]

- *Race*: Suicide rates for whites are approximately twice those for nonwhites.
- *Marital status*: Married persons are at lower risk than are persons who are single, divorced, or widowed.[289]

These authors also note that relatively higher rates of suicide are associated with living alone, urban (vs. rural) residence, and being unemployed.

In contrast to violence toward others [see § 10.08(d)], suicide also correlates with major psychiatric illness. Data from numerous studies suggest that a recent major psychiatric illness is implicated in no less than 93% of suicides, with the diagnoses most often implicated being major depression (40–60% of cases), chronic alcoholism (20%), and schizophrenia (10%).[290] In contrast, parasuicide is more often associated with less severe forms of depression (dysthymic disorder) and personality disorder.[291] Perhaps even more important than the person's specific diagnosis is the dominant affect the person presents during the assessment. Numerous studies suggest that current symptoms of depression *with hopelessness* is an important indicator of increased risk; parasuicide, in contrast, may more often present with symptoms of depression accompanied by anger.[292]

Within each of the three diagnostic categories noted above, researchers have also identified clinical presentations that may be associated with relatively higher risk for short-term (i.e., within 6–12 months) suicidal behavior. For persons diagnosed with major depressive disorder, these presentations include severe psychic anxiety, severe anhedonia (loss of interest in activities that usually provide pleasure), global insomnia, diminished concentration, indecision, acute overuse of alcohol, panic attacks, obsessive–compulsive features, current cycling of affective illness, absence of children under age 18 years in the home, history of lacking friends during adolescence, and history of one to three prior depressive episodes.[293] For alcoholism, certain situational stressors are likely to increase suicide potential, including imprisonment (especially during the first 24 hours) and acute disruption of a major interpersonal relationship[294]; enhanced risk is also associated with *not* being currently hospitalized, with a simultaneous *drug* abuse/dependence, and with the presence of a supervening depressive episode.[295] For persons with schizophrenia, risk for suicide is enhanced in young, white males with good premorbid history and good intellectual functioning who are in the early course of their illness.[296] This increased risk stems from a "painful awareness of the discrepancies between the 'normal' future they once envisioned and the likely degree of chronic disability in the future."[297] In addition, these individuals experience frequent exacerbations and remissions, do not have florid psychosis, and also experience supervening depressive episodes and increased hopelessness.[298]

The third domain consists of historical factors. Most authorities agree that a history of prior suicide attempts places one at increased risk for suicide. The lifetime risk for suicide in the general population is about 1.4%, compared to a 7–10% risk for persons with a previous attempt.[299] Again, however, these figures represent only increased *relative* risk; although the risk for death by suicide for these individuals is five to six times that of the general population, clearly most people who attempt suicide do not eventually die by their own hand. A second historical factor about which there is more controversy is a family history of suicide. Fremouw and colleagues suggest that where such history is present "suicide has been modeled within the family and increases the probability of a family member attempting or completing suicide."[300] In contrast, a study funded by the National Institute of Mental Health of persons with affective disorders and their relatives found no such relationship during a five year follow-up period and suggested that the intergenerational risk of affective disorder, rather than modeling, explains increased risk for suicide.[301] Even if true, this interpretation should not lead a clinician to assume the family history of a person with an affective disorder is irrelevant.[302]

(2) Clinical Assessment of Suicidal Risk

Various authorities suggest that a direct, matter-of-fact approach is indicated when interviewing clients about suicidal thoughts and plans.[303] Typically, depressed clients are asked whether they have suicidal motives, plans, and means (e.g., presence of a weapon or legal doses of medicine). The adequacy of defenses—both internal (e.g.,

availability of rationalization) and external (e.g., whether someone is present as a monitor and a support)—is examined, along with any history (remote or recent) of self-destructive behavior. The history may be interpreted in purely clinical terms (e.g., patterns of precipitants) or in conjunction with actuarial data of the type described earlier. Such standard approaches are both intuitively and theoretically sound.

As one example of such an interview, Fremouw and colleagues provide 25 sample questions and encourage the use of the term "suicide" rather than euphemisms such as "ending it all" or "meeting your maker."[304] The examiner should seek to determine the extent and quality of the person's suicidal thoughts and plans by focusing on issues such as the following:

- Frequency and intensity of suicidal ideation.
- Whether the person's thinking has progressed beyond generalities (e.g., "I would be better off dead") to the consideration of specific methods.
- The lethality of those methods (e.g., relatively lower risk, such as cutting or pills, v. relatively higher risk, such as jumping or guns).
- Whether there has been rehearsal or preliminary steps taken to put a plan into action.
- Whether the person has engaged in making "final arrangements," such as recently making a will or disposing of valuable possessions.

Interviewing about suicide and related clinical factors may be augmented by the use of one or more structured measures. Recommended instruments include the Beck Depression Inventory, the Hopelessness Scale, the Suicide Probability Scale, and the Reasons for Living Inventory.[305] However, these measures are not shortcuts for the clinician and, their usefulness notwithstanding, no empirically determined cutoff scores on any of these measures has been demonstrated to predict, in an absolute sense, which clients will further attempt or commit suicide.

Another reason for avoiding overreliance on such inventories is that most do not require collection of third-party information. Yet corroboration from interested and available informants can be important in the assessment. Clark and Fawcett suggest:

[P]atients at risk for imminent suicide are much more likely to discuss suicidal impulses and plans openly with those closest, that is spouses, parents, children, lovers, and close friends. . . . Therefore we recommend that *the interviewer conducting a suicide risk assessment routinely contact and interview several family members and close friends,* inquiring specifically about examples of morbid preoccupations and suicidal thoughts.[306]

These third-party contacts may also be important as a means of identifying situational factors that contribute to suicide risk (such as job loss or loss of a loved one). Finally, they can be useful in discerning the context in which the client will operate if he or she is not hospitalized. For instance, Comstock notes that the risk for suicide varies with the availability of needed support systems outside the hospital.[307]

As just suggested, inpatient commitment normally provides the highest degree of supervision and treatment with the lowest morbidity. However, disadvantages of such placement include the reinforcement of dependency rather than autonomy, the potential for increased stigma, and the potential isolation of the client from contributing stressors that might more effectively be dealt with through outpatient therapy.[308] These considerations are pertinent in the civil commitment context, especially in light of the least-restrictive-alternative doctrine.

(3)   Suicide "Prediction" versus Risk Assessment

Empirical research indicates that mental health professionals' track record in the prediction of suicide is very poor. Pokorny, the leading investigator of the subject, reached the "inescapable" conclusion that "we do not possess any item of information or any combination of items that permit us to identify to a useful degree the particular persons who will commit suicide, in spite of the fact that we do have scores of items available, each of which is significantly related to suicide."[309] Pokorny noted, for instance, that on the basis of discriminant analyses of data derived from five-year follow-ups of 4,800 first admissions to a Veterans Administration psychiatric unit, one-fourth of the total sample (i.e., 1,2000) would have to be falsely identified to capture just one-half of the 63 actual suicides![310] Even if hospitalization of

this entire group is justified in order to prevent the deaths of some 30 people, it is impractical, as Pokorny himself noted: "[I]t is simply not feasible to maintain one fourth of psychiatric inpatients on 'suicidal precautions' indefinitely."[311]

Studies such as this one underscore our preference for assessments that identify features associated with enhanced relative risk rather than those that rely on categorical predictions. Fortunately, assessments conducted in the context of civil commitment will usually be precipitated by an event or set of events—often memorialized in a petition filed by a friend, family member, or law enforcement officer—that, on their face, make evident the potential for self-injury and the need for treatment. In such cases, the potential for a false-positive prediction may be reduced considerably. Nonetheless, a clinical opinion clarifying why (or why not) the person is at greater risk than the general population is more helpful and less prejudicial than a pronouncement that the person is or is not a danger to self.

(c)   Grave Disability / Inability to Care for Self

A logical extension of the criterion of dangerousness to self is inability to care for self: Inability to provide for one's basic needs is ultimately no less dangerous than active self-destructive behavior. As noted in § 10.03(e), some statutes combine these two factors into one prong of the civil commitment standard,[312] whereas others have adopted a separate provision, sometimes together with special procedures, for civil commitment based on "grave disability."[313] The latter standard requires identification of the particular survival skills the person has, as well as any means of protecting himself or herself that might be less restrictive than hospitalization.

Clinicians have limited "expertise" on this issue, at least as it arises in the commitment context. First, diagnostic information alone is not likely to offer much help; clients with the same or similar diagnoses may differ radically in their capacities to care for self and meet basic needs. Second, the context of the evaluation limits the data-gathering process. Researchers have developed standardized techniques for specifically assessing competency to live safely in the community [discussed in § 11.02(b)(2) in connection with guardianship, which raises issues virtually identical to the inability to care criterion[314]]. But the *commitment* assessment will often be conducted in a hospital or crisis stabilization unit, an environment radically different from that in which the respondent ordinarily functions (recall Case Study 10.1). Further, self-report on these issues from acutely symptomatic clients may be unreliable. Therefore, the key source of information about respondents' self-preservation and survival skills will usually be third-party informants from the community who have observed and can describe to the clinician (or preferably, to the court directly) the respondents' abilities in this regard.

Whether developed by the clinician or provided by third-party informants, some types of behaviors relevant to grave disability clearly "speak for themselves." Relevant, for instance, would be evidence that respondents have been unable to obtain (and properly store and preserve) food, cannot handle money in a fashion satisfactory to complete minimum self-maintenance transactions (e.g., cannot make correct change or balance a checkbook), have such confused and disordered speech that they cannot make their needs known or negotiate purchases, cannot successfully navigate in the community due to disorientation, or have been living in squalor. A thorough description of such impairments is usually all a clinician will have to offer on these matters; gratuitous opinions to the effect that these impairments meet the legal threshold justifying commitment should be avoided.

(d)   Dangerousness to Others

The assessment of danger to others in the civil commitment context is similar to the assessment of dangerousness made at sentencing [see § 9.09]. The clinician is referred to that portion of this book for a detailed discussion of the empirical correlates of violent behavior and the methods of evaluating danger to others. It should be emphasized, however, that there are several distinctions between the commitment context and other contexts in which danger to others assessments are made.

In particular, the time and resources available to clinicians are often more restricted in the commitment setting. In the presentencing or post-NGRI (not guilty by reason of insanity) acquittal evaluation, the defendant is likely to be in custody for a considerable period prior to disposition, allowing clinicians to obtain prior hospital records, pore over police reports related to current and/or prior offenses, examine presentencing reports, and track down potential third-party informants. In contrast, petitions in support of commitment must be completed within a short (usually 72-hour) time frame; even in these days of modern communication technology, obtaining and reviewing all of the desired archival documents may not be possible. Thus, in assessments for involuntary hospitalization, practical constraints may limit clinicians' ability to develop the optimal data base for risk assessment.

On the other hand, the legal issues at commitment are different in ways that facilitate and, arguably, simplify the risk assessment. Most notably, as noted in § 10.03(c), civil commitment is premised on *imminent* dangerousness; short-term, rather than long-term, danger to others is the focus. In this context, the extensive archival and historical information necessary in long-term risk assessments may not even be relevant. Insight into characterological contributors to aggression (e.g., psychopathy) will not be as important as understanding whether aggression can be reasonably attributed to current, active symptoms of mental disorder. Distant historical factors (e.g., multiple prior offenses) will not be as significant as recent overt acts, which in some states are the *required* focus of a commitment evaluation [see § 10.03(c)], and which will often be described in the commitment petition.

With this framework of short-term prediction in mind, the clinical inquiry in the typical case (such as Case Study 10.2) should assess feelings or attitudes toward persons in the respondent's usual social environment, along the lines suggested in § 9.09(c). Pertinent inquiries would include questions regarding (1) anger or revenge motives, (2) perceptions (particularly delusional ones) that someone in the community poses a threat to the respondent, and "plans" for a defensive or preemptive strike against such threats [see discussion of "threat/control override" symptoms in §

9.09(c)(2)], (3) grandiose beliefs of entitlement that might logically lead the respondent into conflict with others, and (4) other intentions to harm others for any reason. Although, as stated previously, archival data is not as important in this context, if accessible and available it should be reviewed to determine whether historic behavioral antecedents might be useful in offering a probability assessment of the individual's future behavior. Monahan's well-known series of questions, outlined in Table 10.1, can provide an organiza-

Table 10.1

Monahan's Recommended Approach to Assessment of Violence Potential

1. Is it a prediction of violent behavior that is being requested?
2. Am I professionally competent to offer an estimate of the probability of future violence?
3. Are any issues of personal or professional ethics involved in this case?
4. Given my answers to the above questions, is this case an appropriate one in which to offer a prediction?
5. What events precipitated the question of the person's potential for violence being raised, and in what context did these events take place?
6. What are the person's relevant demographic characteristics?
7. What is the person's history of violent behavior?
8. What is the base rate of violent behavior among individuals of this person's background?
9. What are the sources of stress in the person's current environment?
10. What cognitive and affective factors indicate that the person may be predisposed to cope with stress in a violent manner?
11. What cognitive and affective factors indicate that the person may be predisposed to cope with stress in a nonviolent manner?
12. How similar are the contexts in which the person has used violent coping mechanisms in the past to the contexts in which the person likely will function in the future?
13. In particular, who are the likely victims of the person's violent behavior, and how available are they?
14. What means does the person possess to commit violence?

Note. From J. MONAHAN, THE CLINICAL PREDICTION OF VIOLENT BEHAVIOR (1981). Reprinted by permission of the National Institute of Mental Health.

tional framework for all of these issues, as well as for some preliminary procedural and ethical issues that the examiner may need to consider.

Some have suggested that clinicians' short-term predictions of violent behavior are more accurate than long-term predictions.[315] However, even the best short-term prediction studies have false-positive rates that are troublesome.[316] Thus, as with long-term prediction, our position is that a focus on categorical prediction is misplaced. Instead, using information about risk-enhancing factors like that found in Table 9.4 and descriptions of the recent or intended behavior that suggests aggression, clinicians in the civil commitment context should merely provide descriptive formulations, analogous to the formulations of mental state at time of offense developed in insanity defense cases, that aid the judge in deciding whether the legal threshold for "danger to others" has been met.

10.09.   The Process of the Evaluation

In addition to understanding the content of the evaluation, the clinician should also be aware of certain factors that can affect the process of the evaluation. Some of these factors are legal and vary from jurisdiction to jurisdiction, whereas others are likely to affect any evaluation, regardless of location.

(a)   The Right to Silence

We have suggested that the civil commitment hearing should be adversarial. This assumption raises the question whether the respondent should be compelled to submit to an evaluation—in effect, to give "incriminating testimony." As noted in § 4.02(d), the majority view, now firmly supported by the Supreme Court, is that the Fifth Amendment is not applicable to civil commitment. Usually, however, this holding has been based on a conclusory statement that the Fifth Amendment is applicable only to criminal proceedings.[317] This pat conclusion is belied both by cases applying the Fifth Amendment in noncriminal proceedings[318] and by a more thoughtful analysis of the purpose of the privilege against self-incrimination. In a truly adversary system, the state should not be permitted to use "legal process to force from the lips of the accused the evidence necessary" to deprive him or her of liberty.[319]

Even if the Fifth Amendment is not applicable to civil commitment, both ethical and strategic issues should be considered in determining whether a respondent should be compelled to speak to a mental health professional. First, the clinician is ethically obligated to inform the respondent of the purpose of the evaluation and limits on confidentiality [see § 4.05(d)]. By its nature, such a requirement is based on the tenet that the privacy of the individual should not be invaded without the individual's permission. In a situation such as emergency detention for possible civil commitment, where the individual is in fact compelled to appear if not to talk, the clinician should also make clear any sanctions present in that jurisdiction for noncooperation [see § 4.02(d)].[320]

Second, under some circumstances counsel for the respondent may find it wise to advise the client not to talk even when there is no Fifth Amendment privilege in civil commitment proceedings. Particularly in jurisdictions with "overt act" requirements, the defense might want to force the state to develop the evidence from witnesses and other sources, because such evidence might later be used in criminal proceedings. However, the attorney considering such a tactic should be aware that, especially in jurisdictions in which no right to silence applies, silence itself may be perceived as indicative of pathological interpersonal relations. Also, when the client has been detained for observation, it is practically impossible to maintain silence over the course of the evaluation.

(b)   The Right to Assistance of Counsel

Although the presence of counsel for the respondent is required during the commitment hearing itself,[321] in some jurisdictions it will be late in the process before counsel is assigned.[322] This fact makes it especially important for mental health professionals to inform respondents about what is happening or potentially going to happen, their rights during the process,[323] and the means of obtaining counsel if it is desired. Even if not legally required,[324] taping clinical interviews may be advisable to provide the attorney eventually appointed with a basis for competent cross-examination of the examining mental health professionals [see § 4.03(a)].

(c)   The Context of Civil Commitment Evaluations

Forensic clinicians must always be aware of their double-agent status [see Chapter 4], a status starkly raised in civil commitment. Especially in the case of *parens patriae* commitments, clinicians may perceive their participation as being *for* the respondent, as part of treatment planning. Indeed, the clinician may have an ongoing therapeutic relationship with the respondent. At the same time, it is important for clinicians to remain mindful of the fact that they are also agents of the state, potentially instrumental in the deprivation of the respondent's liberty; accordingly, there is a need to keep some distance from the situation. Indeed, some have argued that one advantage of an adversarial proceeding is the honest exposure of this double-agent role; otherwise the therapist may not explain as fully the need for hospitalization and the proposed patient may feel a sense of betrayal.[325] In any event, as we have repeatedly noted in this chapter, the stance of *caution* should be maintained to a substantially greater degree in a commitment evaluation than it would be in a normal therapeutic relationship.

Mental health professionals involved in "prescreening" for civil commitment, a statutorily required step in some jurisdictions [see § 10.4(a)(1)], should also be mindful of their role as gatekeepers and should remain cognizant of community resources. "Prescreeners" may be crucial actors in ensuring continuity of care.[326] If a respondent is in fact committed, the prescreener should ensure that necessary background information is transmitted to the receiving hospital and that steps are taken for initiation of liaison with community clinics for eventual aftercare.

Finally, clinicians doing commitment evaluations should remember that they are often seeing respondents under especially strained circumstances. It may be, for example, that an irate family member has summoned the police after a domestic squabble and the police have forcibly brought the respondent to the emergency room. Thus, the situation is almost guaranteed to elicit disturbed behavior. Care should be taken to try to identify and reduce such stress-induced sequelae of the evaluation itself. Such thoughtfulness is necessary for maintaining the reliability and validity of assessments, as well as for providing humane care.

10.10.   Special Commitment Settings and Populations

Although the discussion thus far has broad applicability to evaluations for civil commitment, it is important to recognize that there are some special circumstances in which the prevailing standards, procedures, or both may differ from ordinary civil commitment. We briefly examine five such circumstances: (1) when the respondent is a minor, (2) when the respondent is a jail or prison inmate, (3) when the respondent has been acquitted of a crime by reason of insanity, (4) when the respondent is mentally retarded, and (5) when the primary diagnosis is substance abuse. Although commitment may not always be denominated "civil" when the respondent is a jail or prison inmate or has been acquitted of a crime by reason of insanity, we have included these situations here because the nature of the inquiry is usually similar to that in civil commitment, and because there is substantial interplay among the standards and procedures for civil and criminal commitment.[327]

(a)   Minors

At several points in this chapter, we have mentioned the Supreme Court's decision in *Parham v. J.R.*,[328] addressing the constitutional requirements when parents or guardians seek to "volunteer" their children or wards for admission to mental hospitals. In brief, the Court held that the only process due children in such situations is re-

view of the child's need for hospital treatment by the admitting physician, acting as a "neutral factfinder." It is important to recognize, however, that many states require more procedural protections than the constitutional minima announced in *Parham*.[329] Therefore, lawyers and mental health professionals involved in hospitalization of minors should take care to determine the law in their own jurisdictions.

As discussed in § 10.02(c), in determining that nonadversary, administrative procedures would adequately protect minors' constitutional interests, the Supreme Court relied on rather idyllic assumptions about the biological families of mentally disordered children (as well as the "families" provided by state social workers), the conditions of state hospitals, and the efficacy of administrative procedures. The questionable nature of these assumptions has been discussed elsewhere in detail.[330] Suffice it to say that the modal resident of state hospital facilities for minors is a troubled and troubling, but not crazy,[331] adolescent,[332] who is a ward of the state[333] and simply has nowhere else to go.

Much of what we have already said about the roles of lawyers and mental health professionals in civil commitment of adults applies also to civil commitment of minors, but perhaps with even more force. The populations of residential facilities in mental health, juvenile justice, social service, and special educational systems are to a large extent interchangeable.[334] There is no research establishing the efficacy of hospital-based treatment of minors,[335] especially the conduct-disordered youngsters who are often sent to psychiatric facilities in lieu of juvenile correction institutions.[336] For many of these youths, an approach that is more "educational" than "medical" may be the treatment of choice [see § 14.05(b)(3)]. Although hospitals are not per se the most restrictive or intrusive settings for treatment,[337] special care should be taken to ensure that minors are not being "dumped" into a hospital because it is the easiest—not necessarily the best or the least restrictive—thing to do with them[338] or simply because they have no advocates to watch out for them.[339] The "investigative" role of lawyers and clinicians in civil commitment thus assumes special importance in cases of minors.[340]

(b)   Jail and Prison Inmates

Within correctional facilities there are two distinct populations of people who may need mental health treatment. The first consists of those who have been convicted and are being housed in jail or prison for the duration of their sentence. The second consists of those who have not been subjected to adjudication.

(1)   Inmates Convicted of a Crime

The stigma and intrusions on privacy involved in mental hospitalization are sufficiently great that the Supreme Court held, in *Vitek v. Jones,*[341] that prisoners are entitled to an administrative hearing to determine the need for a transfer to a psychiatric facility. Inmates subjected to such hearings are also entitled to the services of a "qualified and independent" advocate, but not necessarily a licensed attorney, to assist them in the hearing.[342] *Vitek* thus recognizes residual liberty interests of prisoners in avoiding involuntary mental health treatment, but it suggests that those interests can be protected with less procedural rigor than required in civil commitment and with a mere showing of a need for treatment.[343]

Some commentators have suggested that the Court did not go far enough in *Vitek*. They argue that equal protection and due process demand that standards and procedures used in mental health commitment of prisoners should be largely indistinguishable from those used in civil commitment.[344] The ABA's Criminal Justice Mental Health Standards appear largely to endorse this view. The Standards provide for judicial commitment proceedings, with the prisoner having a right to legal counsel.[345] However, only the threshold prong of most civil commitment statutes (i.e., that the prisoner is "seriously mentally ill") need be met for transfer.[346]

It is not clear how broadly even the limited requirements of *Vitek* apply. For example, is a hearing necessary before transfer to a "hospital" run by the department of corrections or to a psychiatric wing of a regular prison?[347] What is clear is that *Vitek* is not being applied at all in many jurisdictions,[348] in part because prison transfers remain a largely hidden process. Indeed, it is probably true that less is known about the evaluation and treatment of prisoners than any other aspect of the forensic mental health system.[349]

Furthermore, as the ABA Standards recognize, ensuring that involuntary transfer is appropriate is a secondary problem compared to the difficulty in obtaining treatment for an inmate who wants and needs it.[350] Such treatment is probably required on both moral and constitutional grounds.[351] The Standards provide for administrative procedures and, if these are unsuccessful, for judicial proceedings to effect a transfer for an inmate in need of psychological treatment that cannot be obtained in the correctional facility.[352]

The inquiry for assessment purposes is similar, regardless of whether the proposed transfer is involuntary or voluntary. The clinician should determine whether the inmate has a bona fide mental disorder, what his or her needs for treatment are, and whether those needs can be met within the prison. The last element of this inquiry means that clinicians need to be aware of the services available within the correctional system (which are often woefully inadequate[353]) and the particular stresses and demands of prison life.[354] There is some controversy as to whether *any* nonorganic treatment can be effectively accomplished in prisons, given the incentive to malinger caused by inmates' desire to please whoever has input into a release or privileges decision.[355] Regardless, it should be recognized that the facilities receiving mentally disordered inmates may be little better.[356]

(2)   Inmates Awaiting Trial

If persons sentenced to prison still have an interest in avoiding involuntary mental health treatment, then surely persons who are in jail awaiting trial have an interest analogous to that of respondents who are living in freedom. Too frequently, however, jail management problems are dealt with by using relatively informal trial competency procedures to send prisoners to the state hospital even when there is no real question about their competency to stand trial.[357] As we have noted in § 6.03(c), in such instances the proper procedure would be to seek *civil commitment* rather than to apply a ruse that is more convenient to carry out. This recommendation is based not only on protection of the respondent's civil rights but also on the practical reality that the purpose of obtaining treatment may be frustrated by use of the mechanism for competency evaluations. The receiving facility may promptly return a clearly competent defendant, even if disturbed, because it lacks authority to treat such an individual.

Regardless, the clinician asked to evaluate a defendant in jail for possible treatment should view the assessment as a consultation in the strict sense. What might be done to stabilize the individual through the crisis engendered by arrest and incarceration? With the cooperation of the attorneys and the court, minor offenders might have their charges dismissed and be treated (involuntarily or voluntarily) in local facilities.[358] Serious offenders who cannot make bond may have to be treated in jail, either by jail staff or outside professionals. Whatever route is taken, mental health professionals and jail staff should have compatible goals.[359] Mental health interventions in jail should be directed toward diversion or stabilization of the defendant, which not only is effective treatment but has the effect of helping the jail to run more smoothly.

(c)   Insanity Acquittees

After a person is acquitted by reason of insanity, he or she is usually committed automatically to a forensic unit for evaluation, typically for 30 to 60 days. At the end of this period, a court must decide whether the acquittee is mentally ill and dangerous. If commitment occurs, the acquittee is confined anywhere from six months to two years after the original commitment until the next release hearing.[360]

In participating in these "criminal commitments," the clinician is asked to assess whether the acquittee is any longer mentally ill (e.g., "restored to reason") and/or dangerous.[361] Although these questions are similar, if not identical, to those posed in civil commitment, it is important to note that both standards and procedures for criminal commitment often differ significantly from those in civil commitment. For example, the state must prove by clear and convincing evidence that a civil respondent meets the commitment standard,[362] but the burden of proof may be shifted to

the defendant in postacquittal commitment.[363] Moreover, one study found that the standards, though identical, were more broadly applied to insanity acquittees than in the civil commitment context.[364] Further, the release decision was often made by a different process and in a different forum (e.g., by the judge who heard the insanity trial rather than by a hospital administrator).[365]

These differences are based on two assumptions: that defendants acquitted by reason of insanity are unusually dangerous (because they have committed a violent act, though not a technical crime) and that they are mentally ill (because of the insanity plea).[366] However, these assumptions may often be faulty. As to the first, the crime of which the defendant was accused may have been minor[367]; if so, that offense might not even qualify as the overt dangerous act necessary for civil commitment in many jurisdictions. Moreover, even a serious crime (e.g., murder of one's spouse) does not mean that the individual is likely to commit a similar act.[368] As to the assumption regarding "continuing" mental illness, in jurisdictions in which an insanity acquittal can be based on a reasonable doubt as to sanity,[369] mental disorder may not be proven to the requisite degree necessary for civil commitment. Also, it is quite possible that an acquittee's mental condition may have improved markedly since the offense, either spontaneously or because of the treatment necessary to render one competent to stand trial.

Nonetheless, in *Jones v. United States*,[370] the Supreme Court reaffirmed these assumptions about the dangerousness and illness of acquittees. It held that *any* criminal act by a defendant "certainly indicates dangerousness"[371]—even if, as in *Jones*, the act was attempted shoplifting of a jacket! The Court also maintained that "it comports with common sense to conclude that someone whose mental illness was sufficient to lead him to commit a criminal act is likely to remain ill and in need of treatment."[372] Based on these assumptions, the Court sanctioned the automatic posttrial evaluative commitment described earlier and strongly implied that placing the proof of burden on the acquittee at the initial review hearing would be constitutional. It also held that given the incapacitative and rehabilitative goals of criminal commitment, defendants may constitutionally be required to remain in confinement until they can prove that they no longer merit commitment, even though the maximum possible sentence for the offense of which a defendant was charged may have long since passed.[373]

Jones did not directly address another important issue: whether an acquittee should be released if *either* the mental illness or the danger have disappeared, or whether *both* must be shown to have been treated. In *Foucha v. Louisiana,*[374] discussed in detail in § 9.04(b), four members of the Court concluded that proof of dangerousness alone is insufficient to justify continued commitment; in other words, the state must show both mental disorder and dangerousness to keep the person confined. However, Justice O'Connor, who provided a fifth vote for this general proposition, also stated that she would be willing to create an exception to it in cases in which the acquittee has committed a violent offense and the state can demonstrate "some medical justification" for continued confinement. Further, in *Kansas v. Hendricks,*[375] the Court held that dangerous persons who have a "mental abnormality" or "personality disorder"—terms that are extremely elastic—may be confined indefinitely even if *not* treatable. Together, these holdings mean that, in practice, either mental illness or dangerousness may be sufficient for commitment.

Although it is likely that evaluation for commitment of acquittees will take place in a different setting from that of the civil commitment evaluation (e.g., a forensic hospital), and with different standards and different procedures, the scope of the evaluation itself is likely to be similar. We once again urge caution. The *Jones* definition of "dangerous" behavior exemplifies the need for clinicians to avoid conclusions as to ultimate legal issues. Although insanity acquittees as a group are not particularly prone to subsequent violent or criminal behavior, especially when compared to felons,[376] the legal meaning of a standard may easily depart from a clinician's understanding of the language.

(d)   People with Mental Retardation

Most states have enacted separate statutory provisions for commitment of the mentally retarded.

Traditionally, these statutes provided less procedural protection than commitment statutes for the mentally ill and were less explicit with respect to commitment criteria (often merely requiring a finding of mental retardation and need for treatment or habilitation).[377] In part, this was the result of historical accident. As noted in § 10.02(a), the law's approach to people with mental retardation, premised on the irreversibility of their condition, was less solicitous of their property and person than was the case with people suffering from mental illness. In addition, there may have been an underlying assumption that people with mental retardation require less legal protection because they are more easily identifiable than people with mental illness and thus are less likely to be committed arbitrarily.

Unfortunately, the Supreme Court has signaled a willingness to countenance these types of unjustified distinctions between the two groups. In *Heller v. Doe,*[378] the Court upheld a statutory scheme that allowed commitment of people with mental retardation under a lower standard of proof than is required for people with mental illness, primarily on the erroneous assumption that treatment for the former type of person is less intrusive.[379] It also upheld another statutory provision that granted party status to family members and guardians of people with mental retardation, even though the statute regarding commitment of people with mental illness did not do so. The reason given for the latter ruling was that, because people with mental retardation often live at their parents' home, the presence of family at their hearing is more likely to be useful and less likely to infringe privacy. Even if these assumptions are correct, the Court did not satisfactorily explain why, in light of a trial court's subpoena power, it is necessary to grant *party* status—which entitles a person to have an attorney present and appeal the commitment decision—to implement the state's goal of ensuring their presence.

In reality, there is no reason for treating individuals differently based on their diagnosis as far as the legal structure for commitment is concerned. The line between "mental retardation" and "normal" intellectual and adaptive functioning is as difficult to discern as that between "mental illness" and "mental health." Institutionalization is as much a deprivation of liberty for people with mental retardation as it is for people with mental illness and should only occur after appropriate due process has taken place. If dangerousness to self or others and grave disability are considered the proper criteria for commitment of those with mental illness, the same should be true of those with mental retardation. Those individuals who are not dangerous and can subsist on their own with or without help in the community should not be committable on the grounds of mental retardation and treatability alone. If anything, given the relatively stable nature of their condition, people with mental retardation should be entitled to more particularized attention than those with mental illness when it comes to the least restrictive alternative criterion and to periodic review provisions. Otherwise, hospitalization of such individuals could amount to confinement for life.[380]

Modern statutes, while still segregating the commitment provisions concerning the two groups, recognize these realities. In Florida, for instance, mental retardation is defined as "significant subaverage general intellectual functioning [meaning two standard deviations from the mean score on a standardized intelligence test specified by the mental health department] existing concurrently with deficits in adaptive behavior and manifested during the period from conception to age 18,"[381] thus signaling that IQ alone is not ground for meeting the disability threshold. Commitment may occur only if retardation, so defined, causes a propensity for violence toward others or a lack of sufficient capacity to give informed consent to treatment and a lack of basic survival and self-care skills that could lead to a "real and present threat of substantial harm to the person" if close supervision is not maintained.[382] Residential placement must be the least restrictive and most appropriate setting to meet the person's needs.[383] These criteria must be proven by clear and convincing evidence at a fully adversarial proceeding.[384]

Even this relatively sophisticated statute, however, fails to require, when commitment is on "danger to other" grounds, a recent act or threat and a prediction of *imminent* harm to others, provisions that are present in the statute governing commitment of people with mental illness.[385]

Moreover, discharge reviews are not automatic but depend on the initiation of the person, his or her guardian, or the hospital,[386] a framework that facilitates neglect.

In the criminal commitment context, people with mental retardation have traditionally received even less attention than they have in connection with civil commitment. Indeed, many state statutes fail to include provisions for commitment of the mentally retarded who have been acquitted by reason of insanity (although the courts, when confronted with this fact, construe the term "mentally ill" in these provisions to encompass mental retardation).[387] More important, given the permanence of their condition, those with mental retardation who are committed after an insanity acquittal are particularly disadvantaged in those states that permit continued confinement on the basis of *either* mental disability or dangerousness and that do not provide for *automatic* periodic review.[388] Whatever *Foucha* and *Hendricks* may allow as a matter of constitutional law, provisions such as those recommended by the ABA, permitting continued detention only on a finding of mental disability *and* dangerousness and establishing period review,[389] are necessary to ensure that individuals diagnosed as mentally retarded, whether in the civil or criminal system, are not warehoused or forgotten after commitment.

(e)   People Who Abuse Substances

Substance abuse continues to be one of the nation's most significant problems, both in terms of its effect on the abuser and because of its crimogenic impact. The predominant legal approach to this problem has been criminal prosecution. However, since the 1970s, states have begun to develop alternative approaches, including commitment. Although rarely used,[390] commitment may have advantages over criminalization.

Today, about two-thirds of the states have special statutes governing commitment of persons addicted to drugs or alcohol.[391] All these statutes require some proof of chronic or habitual lack of self-control as a result of substance abuse. As with commitment for mental illness, most also base involuntary hospitalization on proof of danger to others or self, although some require only a need for treatment. Related to the latter point, commitment statutes for addicts are more likely to require proof that treatment is available.

Procedurally, the statutes for commitment of substance abusers are generally similar to other commitment statutes. In some statutes, the initial period of commitment for people whose primary diagnosis is substance abuse is shorter than for those who are diagnosed as mentally ill. Another important practical difference stems from the fact that this type of commitment, on the infrequent occasions when it is used, often acts as a formal diversion mechanism for people who have been charged with crimes involving substance abuse.[392] In these cases, courts usually uphold the voluntariness of a person's "request" for treatment even though the request is driven by fear of prosecution and conviction or an alleged misunderstanding about the circumstances of the commitment.[393]

The development of special statutes for substance abusers may in part be due to the fact that some courts have been unwilling to label addiction a mental illness for purposes of commitment[394]; legislatures have thus had to devise separate laws to permit it. A second reason for these special statutes is that treatment for substance abuse often occurs in specialized programs outside the mental health system and may involve elements (e.g., detoxification, 12-Step groups) rarely found in mental health programs.

Some have questioned whether such treatment should ever be involuntarily imposed. Wexler has argued against police power commitment of addicts because they generally only commit property crimes and because, in a sense, their dangerousness is the fault of the state, which has intentionally prohibited their access to the intoxicant.[395] He has also criticized commitment of people who abuse substances on *parens patriae* grounds because, despite their lack of self-control, they are usually "competent" to make treatment decisions about their drug use (at least as competent as those who use cigarettes), and because treatment programs for addicts have not been particularly successful.[396]

Wexler also concedes, however, that using commitment as an alternative to the criminal process can encourage therapeutic progress, especially if the threat of prosecution is held over the committed person's head.[397] Further justification for this type of commitment may find support in new studies showing that drug and alcohol treatment is improving.[398]

Bibliography

Addington v. Texas, 441 U.S. 418 (1978).

AMERICAN BAR ASSOCIATION, CRIMINAL JUSTICE MENTAL HEALTH STANDARDS Pt. VII (1984) (commitment of insanity acquittees).

Michael Churgin, *The Transfer of Inmates to Mental Health Facilities: Developments in the Law,* in MENTALLY DISORDERED OFFENDERS; PERSPECTIVES FROM LAW AND SOCIAL SCIENCE (John Monahan & Henry Steadman eds. 1983).

Developments in the Law: Civil Commitment of the Mentally Ill, 87 HARVARD LAW REVIEW 1190 (1974).

Donaldson v. O'Connor, 422 U.S. 563 (1975).

James Ellis & Ruth Luckasson, *Mentally Retarded Criminal Defendants,* 53 GEORGE WASHINGTON LAW REVIEW 414 (1985).

Foucha v. Louisiana, 504 U.S. 71 (1992).

WILLIAM J. FREMOUW, MARIA DE PERCEL & THOMAS E. ELLIS, SUICIDE RISK: ASSESSMENT AND RESPONSE GUIDELINES (1990).

Thomas L. Hafemeister & Ali J. Amirshahi, *Civil Commitment for Drug Dependency: The Judicial Response,* 26 LOYOLA OF LOS ANGELES LAW REVIEW 39 (1992).

Donald Hermann, *Automatic Commitment and Release of Insanity Acquittees: Constitutional Dimensions,* 14 RUTGERS LAW JOURNAL 667 (1983).

Browning Hoffman & Larry Foust, *Least Restrictive Treatment of the Mentally Ill: A Doctrine in Search of Its Sense,* 14 SAN DIEGO LAW REVIEW 1100 (1977).

CHARLES KIESLER & A. SILBULKIN, MENTAL HOSPITALIZATION (1987).

Lessard v. Schmidt, 349 F. Supp. 1078 (E.D. Wis. 1972).

Gary B. Melton, *Family and Mental Hospital as Myths: Civil Commitment of Minors,* in CHILDREN, MENTAL HEALTH, AND THE LAW (N. Dickon Reppucci, Lois Weithorn, Edward Mulvey, and John Monahan eds. 1984).

Robert Miller, *Need-for-Treatment Criteria for Involuntary Civil Commitment: Impact in Practice,* 149 AMERICAN JOURNAL OF PSYCHIATRY 1380 (1992).

Stephen J. Morse, *A Preference for Liberty: The Case Against Involuntary Commitment of the Mentally Disordered,* 70 CALIFORNIA LAW REVIEW 54 (1982).

Parham v. J.R., 442 U.S. 584 (1979).

John Parry, *Involuntary Civil Commitment in the 90s: A Constitutional Perspective,* 18 MENTAL & PHYSICAL DISABILITY LAW REPORTER 320 (1994).

Loren Roth, *A Commitment Law for Patients, Doctors, and Lawyers,* 136 AMERICAN JOURNAL OF PSYCHIATRY 1121 (1979).

ALAN STONE, MENTAL HEALTH AND THE LAW: A SYSTEM IN TRANSITION (1975).

DAVID WEXLER, MENTAL HEALTH LAW: MAJOR ISSUES chs. 2, 3 (1981).

CHAPTER ELEVEN

Civil Competencies

11.01. Introduction

Chapters 6 and 7 considered the range of competencies that come into question when a criminal defendant is or may be mentally disordered. A theme throughout those chapters is that mental disability does not, in and of itself, equate with or even imply incompetency. Instead, mental health professionals and jurists should attend to whether there are specific *functional* incapacities that render a person incapable of making a particular kind of decision or performing a particular kind of task.

This principle is even more clearly applicable in the civil context. It requires answering questions such as the following: Should a person who is institutionalized because of mental disorder also lose the right to control property, the right to vote, or the right to marry? Do civilly committed persons have a residual right to privacy that permits them to decline intrusive treatments and, conversely, the right to consent to experimental treatment? If a person with mental retardation is unable to conceptualize large sums but does know what money is and can perform simple calculations, should that person be able to decide how to spend his or her money? These types of questions are considered in this chapter, in the context of evaluations for guardianship, competency to consent to treatment and research, and testamentary capacity (competency to make a will).

As noted in the introduction to Chapter 7, the underlying rationale for the idea that competency

is task-specific is that persons with mental disability, like other persons, have the right to self-determination absent compelling reasons to the contrary. As described by a presidential commission:

> More is involved in respect for self-determination than just the belief that each person knows what's best for him- or herself. . . . Even if it could be shown that an expert (or a computer) could do the job better, the worth of the individual, as acknowledged in Western ethical traditions and especially in Anglo-American law, provides an independent—and more important—ground for recognizing self-determination as a basic principle in human relations[.][1]

At the same time, the right to self-determination is not absolute. There are generally two broad exceptions to the principle that individuals should be allowed to do what they want: (1) when significant harm to others will result from their actions or (2) when they are incompetent to make the specific decision in question.[2] The dangerousness concept is explored elsewhere in this book [see §§ 9.09, 10.03(c)]. Here attention will be focused on the incompetence exception to self-determination.

Several different definitions of competency—ranging from the mere ability to indicate one's desires to a determination by an expert panel that one's decision is "reasonable"—are possible. These various levels are discussed further later in this chapter [see § 11.03(a)(2)]. What should be noted at this point is that the definition of "competence" may vary depending on the context. Assume, for instance, that doctors want to administer a treatment that is clearly beneficial, with minimal side effects for the patient in question. Some have argued that the competence required to consent to such a treatment should be lower than the competence required to refuse it, on the ground that the law should facilitate administration of beneficial treatment.[3] On the other hand, these commentators contend, if the proposed treatment is experimental, extremely intrusive, or likely to cause serious side effects, these competency requirements should be reversed, so as to make consent difficult and refusal easy. In a slightly different vein, it has been argued that as the consequences of a decision become more significant, the level of required competency should be increased.[4]

In response to the latter reasoning, Saks has argued that calibrating the level of competency according to the significance of the decision or its consequences is problematic because its significance or consequences may vary from individual to individual.[5] Further, she argues,

> if varying the level of competency based on the importance of decision made sense, a competency theorist might urge us to lower the level of competency for potentially consequential decisions. Because people care more about more consequential decisions, we should arguably permit them to choose what they will have to live with. Moreover, taking away consequential decisions may entail a greater assault on individual dignity. For example, telling a person that he can decide what kind of ice cream to have, but not where to live, may more seriously injure his self-esteem.[6]

Whether the nature of the decision to be made should influence the level of competency required is an issue that permeates this chapter.

11.02.   Guardianship

CASE STUDY 11.1

In a proceeding brought by a neighbor to determine whether Galvin should have a guardian of the estate and of the person appointed, the following testimony is adduced. A doctor testifies that he first treated Galvin three years earlier for "advanced multiple arthritis"; at that time, he noted that Galvin had also had a "cerebral vascular accident" or stroke. The doctor further testifies that Galvin was readmitted to the hospital the next year for treatment of his heart, cerebral, and arthritic conditions. Noting that Galvin was "a little bit confused at times and was a little bit agitated at times," the doctor requested a psychiatrist to interview Galvin; the psychiatrist observed that Galvin experienced "some delusions" and "hallucinations." Based on this evidence, the doctor diagnosed Galvin as having "organic brain syndrome" (i.e., an irreversible and progressive "behavioral disorder" that results from "degeneration or atrophy of the brain cells"). The doctor released Galvin from the hospital after about two months. According to the doctor, although Galvin's heart condition is currently stable, the condition is irreversible; further, failure to take his heart medication as prescribed could endanger his life. Although the doctor does not know how Galvin handles his finances, he believes Galvin is disabled and unable to manage his affairs. On cross-examination, however, the doctor testifies that Galvin has made some recent improvement. He states that Galvin is "more oriented and more realistic."

Galvin testifies that he owns the three-flat building in which he lives. He occupies the basement apartment with two men, John and Mike. They do not pay rent but Galvin does collect rent from the other two apartments. Galvin handles his own financial affairs and has a checking account, which currently has a balance of $350. He receives Social Security of about $500 per month. He does not believe he has a heart condition but he continues to take the medication prescribed by the doctor. On cross-examination, Galvin testifies that he invented the snowmobile, that at one time he had a pet black widow spider, and that he could produce fire by pointing his finger. He also testifies that John and Mike sometimes prepare his meals but that he can and sometimes does prepare his own meals. He says he can shop by himself and go to the laundromat with the use of his walker and can pull a shopping cart. He repeats that he is able to take care of himself and does not want a guardian.

John and Mike testify that Galvin has no concept of time relationship and believes he had been a coworker with the Shah of Iran. They state that they plan to move out of Galvin's apartment, meaning that Galvin will be left alone. The petitioner also testifies. She states that Galvin is "constantly" at her home, where she and her mother "take care of" him. In addition, she testified, Galvin goes outside "without shoes or stockings and wearing only slippers during subzero weather." Another neighbor testifies that when Galvin goes to the hospital his shopping and other needs are provided by the petitioner.

QUESTIONS: What other information, if any, would you want about Galvin to evaluate his decisionmaking ability and his ability to care for himself? Should a guardian be appointed for him, is some other method of monitoring him preferable, or should he be left alone? If a guardianship were considered advisable for Galvin, should it be a guardian of the estate, a guardian of the person, or both? Plenary or "limited"? If you were appointed guardian for Galvin, would you attempt to commit him? Use his money to have a nurse visit him?

(a)   Forms of Guardianship

Guardianship is the delegation, by the state, of authority over an individual's person or estate to another party. It is probably the most ancient aspect of mental health law. In both Roman and English common law, the sovereign possessed the power and duty to "guard" the estate of incompetent persons.[7] This power, which emanated from the state's interest in the preservation of its wealth, is the historic basis of the *parens patriae* authority, which has since been applied broadly—and perhaps illogically[8]—to the regulation by the state of many other aspects of decisionmaking by children and people with mental disability. In any event, it was this power that the state delegated to third parties (usually family members or members of the government) through the guardianship process.

Today guardianship comes in many forms. In some jurisdictions, there are separate provisions for appointment of a guardian of one's person (e.g., with authority over health care decisions) and a guardian of one's estate (e.g., with authority over contracts to sell one's property).[9] The latter type of guardian is often called a *conservator* or *committee,* although this nomenclature is not consistent across jurisdictions (with some, like California, using the former term to cover both person and property[10]). In addition to, or instead of,

this distinction, most jurisdictions also distinguish between *general (plenary)* and *specific* guardianship.[11] As the name implies, in the latter form of guardianship the guardian's powers are restricted to particular types of decisions. Thus, with respect to guardianship of the person, the guardian may have authority only to make a specific treatment decision (e.g., consent to a specific course of treatment that has been proposed) or "nonroutine" treatment decisions (e.g., consent to any major surgery); the ward would remain free to make other health care decisions. Similarly, a person with mental disorder under limited guardianship of the estate might be able to make decisions about the property except with respect to a particularly complicated business deal that has been proposed, or any purchase over $100. On the other hand, under general or plenary guardianship, the guardian has total control of the individual's person, estate, or both.

Clearly, limited guardianship schemes are more respectful of persons' autonomy than are plenary dispositions. But research has consistently shown that the limited guardianship option is rarely used.[12] Tor and Sales have suggested a number of reasons for this omission, including the vagueness of the implementing statutes, the biases of judges (who may presume or anticipate eventual total incompetency), the lack of resources to carry out a limited guardianship, and, most important to the subject of this book, a failure on the part of respondents (and their experts) to provide specific information on the respondent's limitations.[13] At the same time, widespread use of limited guardianship could have drawbacks. As some have argued with respect to outpatient commitment [see § 10.03(h)], limited guardianship could result in an inappropriate broadening of guardianship jurisdiction.

Beyond these distinctions about the *scope* of guardianship, it is also important to recognize disparate *bases* of guardianship. In most instances, individuals are found, on the basis of particularized evidence, to lack specific or general capacities. They are actually (or *de facto*) incompetent and in need of a guardian to make decisions for them. On the other hand, some people are *presumed* to require a guardian. Regardless of their *de facto* level of competency, they are incompetent in law (*de jure*).

For example, even though older minors are often as competent as adults to make decisions of various types,[14] they are *de jure* incompetent for most purposes and, as a result, lack legal authority to act on their own behalf.[15] Even in those instances in which the law permits some minors to make decisions independently,[16] they generally are presumed incompetent until they are able to rebut this presumption.[17] Because there is such a strong legal presumption of minors' incompetency, there usually is no need to adjudicate their need for guardianship. In most cases, there also is no need to determine who the guardian will be.[18] Children are generally subject to the wishes of their "natural" guardians—their parents—who are presumed, in the absence of strong evidence to the contrary, to act in their best interests.[19]

Civilly committed adults may also find themselves presumed incompetent to make many decisions. At one time, civil commitment often carried with it collateral loss of rights to marry, possess a driver's license, refuse intrusive treatments, manage one's property,[20] and so forth. Although most states now provide that commitment does not automatically render a person incompetent to perform such functions, vestiges of these practices remain, especially with respect to treatment refusal and management of one's property.[21] In such instances, there often is no need to appoint a guardian, in that state statutes assign authority to particular individuals (often state officials) to make decisions on behalf of the committed person.[22] Moreover, in some states, determination of general guardianship and civil commitment are coextensive. For example, in California, commitment as a "gravely disabled" person takes place through a conservatorship proceeding.[23]

Three separate issues arise in the guardianship context: determining whether someone needs a guardian; deciding, if a guardian is necessary, who that person shall be; and determining, once a guardian is appointed, what he or she should do. These issues are discussed below.

(b) Determining Need for Guardianship

(1) Legal Requirements

Because it is generally easy to determine who is *de jure* incompetent (i.e., by determining the person's age or whether civil commitment has occurred), proceedings to decide whether a guardian will be appointed generally occur only when an allegation of *de facto* incompetence is made. In most jurisdictions, any interested person can petition to have someone declared incompetent and subject to guardianship.[24] As a result, petitioners may not be acting with the person's interests in mind.[25] Nonetheless, as developed later, both the procedural and the substantive criteria in guardianship proceedings are less rigorous, on their face and as applied, than those found in civil commitment, which themselves have been subject to criticism [see §§ 10.03, 10.04].

Beginning with process issues, a common finding of researchers and commentators is that guardianship proceedings lack procedural rigor. Indeed, one commentator has asserted that "informality is the hallmark of incompetency proceedings,"[28] a situation explicitly endorsed by many courts on the questionable ground that the consequences of guardianship are not as onerous as those associated with other types of proceedings.[27] Typically, there is no requirement of specific allegations in the petition,[28] and notice to the respondent is limited to the fact that a hearing will be held.[29] At the hearing itself, the respondent often has no right to counsel[30] or trial by jury,[31] and in some jurisdictions the respondent is rarely present.[32] If counsel is appointed, he or she may well act like,[33] or is explicitly designated as,[34] a *guardian ad litem* who is free to pursue what he or she believes to be the respondent's best interests rather than the client's wishes.

If a guardian is appointed, the burden is usually on the incompetent person to initiate "restoration" proceedings.[35] This fact, combined with the reality that most guardianships are not actively monitored by the courts,[36] means that very few individuals receive such hearings.[37] If a hearing is held, the deck is often stacked against the petitioner by "the absence of specific information in the ward's file, a presumption of incompetence, judicial bias and overly broad discretion, and the absence of legal representation."[38]

This procedural laxity is commonly matched by ambiguity of standards. For general guardianship, many state statutes simply require findings of a threshold status (e.g., mental illness, idiocy, and senility) and incapacity "to care properly for oneself or one's estate."[39] As Alexander has noted, this vague standard leaves the door wide open for essentially arbitrary judicial decisions:

> The ambiguous standards of the substantive law in guardianship proceedings preclude effective application of procedural due process analysis to guardianship proceedings. In particular, the standard of what is an appropriate ability to manage property is unclear. Are persons who manage to meet the challenges of daily life with assistance from friends and families incompetent because they could not do it alone? Are they incompetent when they make decisions preventing the dissipation of their property but are noticeably less effective than those who managed it before? Are they incompetent if their property management skills are marginal, irrespective of their prior abilities? What does the word "properly" mean in the statutes relating to property management? Do persons whose survival is not in question manage "improperly" if they fail to live up to standards the trial court finds appropriate? How does the court decide on an appropriate standard?
>
> The statutory standards seem to allow definitions of functional ability ranging from simple improvidence in occasional transactions to incapacity to provide for food or medical care for extended periods of time. Since one can almost always find property managers who can improve on a particular owner's management, it is unclear when it becomes appropriate to impose such a manager on an unwilling recipient.[40]

Some modern guardianship statutes attempt to remedy these problems by focusing on the proposed ward's thought process rather than the capacity to care for self. The Uniform Probate Code, followed in a number of states, defines an incapacitated person as "any person who is impaired by reason of mental illness, mental deficiency, physical illness or disability, advanced age . . . or other cause (except minority) to the extent that he lacks sufficient understanding or capacity to make or communicate responsible decisions concerning his person."[41] However, this language is itself susceptible to many interpretations. Indeed, at least one court has held it to be unconstitutionally vague, unless it is interpreted to require a showing that the person is actually "unable to care for his personal safety or unable to attend to and provide for such necessities as food, shelter, clothing, and medical care, without which physical injury or illness may occur."[42]

Although this court-dictated definition returns the guardianship question to the inability-to-care inquiry that preexisted the Uniform Code, it does tighten that standard somewhat. A number of states are moving to this third, so-called functional approach to guardianship.[43] Note also that it is identical to the grave disability standard associated with civil commitment [see § 10.03(e)], which explains why some states, like California, appoint a guardian (called a conservator in California) to oversee the commitment.[44] Even this standard lends itself to significant value judgments, however. For instance, New Hampshire's statute defines functional limitations as "behavior or conditions . . . which impair [the person's] ability to participate in and perform *minimal* activities of daily living that secure and maintain *proper* food, clothing, shelter, health care or safety for himself or herself"[45] [Emphasis added].

As might be expected, given these ambiguities, there is considerable variation in the application of guardianship statutes. On the one hand, courts are sometimes prone to enter orders for guardianship on the basis of medical opinion alone or on the basis on what appears to the court to be the "reasonable" or "rational" course of action individuals should take (and whether they have taken, or plan to take, that action). For example, the Nebraska Supreme Court upheld appointment of a conservator for an elderly woman where the evidence showed that she had used most of the estate left by her husband (indeed, she had only $19.18 left in her checking account), that she had given much of it away, and that she had made some foolish real estate deals.[46] Apparently no evidence was taken as to her actual capacity to manage her property. Two members of the court entered an impassioned dissent:

> The fact that one has made bad investments or is inclined to give one's property away is not sufficient to justify the appointment of a conservator over the objections of the one for whom the conservator is being sought. Were it otherwise, a number of us would have conservators appointed for us. Often all that persons of advanced age have left is their dignity and the ability to dispose of their property as they may choose. We should not take that right away so quickly, absent evidence of mental incapacity.[47]

On the other hand, some courts have required considerable evidence of incompetency before entering an order for guardianship. For example, in the case giving rise to the facts of Case Study 11.1, the respondent's testimony about his financial dealings was enough evidence of competency to convince both the trial court and the appellate court that the individual did not need a guardian. Similarly, a California appellate court overturned a conservatorship for a man with schizophrenia who lived in his sister's backyard much of the time and who was described as dirty, disheveled, and incontinent.[48] The court held that it was reversible error for the trial judge to fail to admit evidence about, and to instruct the jury on, the availability of assistance by others that could meet the respondent's basic needs.

(2)   Clinical Evaluation

In contrast to laws dealing with the insanity defense, commitment, or entitlement laws, many states do not require evaluations prior to a guardianship proceeding.[49] As courts take a more due-process-oriented approach to guardianship, however, court-appointed lists and other methods for ensuring expert input are likely to burgeon.

Clinicians who are involved in such evaluations need to keep in mind several points. First, as already noted, the assessment should be focused on the range of *functions* that the respondent can perform, not the nature of any mental disorder per se. Such detailed evaluation will be especially useful in jurisdictions in which limited guardianship is an option. As pointed out earlier, one reason this option is not used often is because specific evidence about functional deficits, whether from an expert or a layperson, is simply not produced.[50] Thus, despite the difficulty of doing so, clinicians should try to pinpoint what the allegedly incompetent person can and cannot do.

Clinicians should also attend to whether weaknesses in the individual's performance are, or might be, alleviated by assistance from others. Of particular relevance in this regard are possible "less restrictive alternatives" to guardianship [cf. § 10.03(g)]. The most prominent such alternative, available in many states, comes under the rubric of "adult protective services," a legislatively mandated system of health and social services such as homemaker support, home health care, and alternate care arrangements, usually coordinated by a caseworker. Other alternatives that might be consider included "advanced directives" [discussed further in § 11.02(e)], representative payee arrangements (used for receipt of welfare benefits [see § 13.04(b)]), and trusts and joint tenancies which allow for transfers or sharing of specific property without the need for an overarching guardianship.

Finally, as in any evaluation context, the clinician should stay attuned to the newest strategies for performing guardianship evaluations. Despite the ancient basis of guardianship and the frequency with which the issue arises, until recently little attention was given to the reliability and validity of such evaluations, or even to formats for such assessments. One procedure for which there are promising data is the Community Competency Scale (CCS), developed by a group of researchers at St. Louis University.[51] Although its psychometric properties could be evaluated further,[52] it is a well-conceptualized instrument[53] that relies on behavior samples of "real-life" survival skills. There are 16 subscales: Judgment, Emergencies, Acquire Money, Compensate for Incapacities, Manage Money, Communication, Care of Medical Needs, Adequate Memory, Satisfactory Living Arrangements, Proper Diet, Mobility, Sensation, Personal Hygiene, Maintain Household, Utilize Transportation, and Verbal–Math Skills. The "apparatus" for the CCS is indicative of its attempt to address the kinds of tasks involved in basic independent living: telephone, blank checks, telephone book, envelope, and play money. In the Manage Money category, for instance, one question asks the person to fill out a check for $15, payable to the telephone company. In the Communication category, the person is asked to address an envelope to a close friend. A number of other competency protocols, of varying usefulness and reliability, have been developed as well.[54]

In the absence of a well-established format for evaluation, one strategy would be to have the person review a typical day and how everyday tasks (e.g., food preparation and payment of monthly bills) are accomplished. As suggested by the CCS items, the evaluator may want to request actual performance of some of these tasks during the interview. A home visit may also be useful to observe the individual's adaptation in that setting. Clearly, third-party information on the person's functioning can be crucial. Further, the examiner must be alert for biases about "quality of life" issues, as these may affect clinical judgment in situations like those described earlier in which the individual is not necessarily making the "best" decisions.

When complex estates are not involved, this type of evaluation should generally suffice whether the issue is guardianship of the estate or guardianship of the person; in these cases, everyday use of money will be highly correlated to general success in independent living.[55] For individuals with larger and more complex estates, however, competency in handling property will need to be discussed in detail. Areas that should be probed include respondents' knowledge of the nature and purpose of money, the extent of their wealth, the alternatives for disposing of the estate, their skills in everyday management (e.g., balancing of accounts and payment of bills), their plans for disposing of their estates, and the reasons underlying these plans. A comprehensive social history should also normally be taken, both to corroborate impressions from individual assessment and to determine the resources for assistance that may be available [see the Dyer report, § 19.07(a)].

Whether the evaluation involves complex or lesser estates, the clinician should always attempt to discern whether any gaps in knowledge are the result of inexperience or lack of education, rather than incapacity. Conversely, even the capacity to write checks, balance accounts, and the like may be insufficient evidence of survival skills, especially in those states which focus on the "responsibility" of one's actions. In particular, when the guardianship is being proposed because of a concern about the individual's *reasons* for making particular decisions (e.g., a decision about life-saving treatment or expenditure of certain funds), some assessment of "rationality" or "appreciation" of one's circumstances may also be necessary [a complex topic discussed in more detail in § 11.03(a)(2) in connection with treatment deci-

sionmaking]. In such situations, the clinician is well advised to simply report the reasons given by the individual (e.g., "the medicine will kill me"; a belief that keeping one's money is a sin) and provide any specialized information that will enable the decisionmaker to evaluate their validity (e.g., the nature of a medicine's side-effects).

(c) Determining Who Shall Be the Guardian

Several kinds of parties may be appointed as guardian (ranging from family members to government agencies to sheriffs).[56] There are pros and cons for each type of guardian. For instance, public guardians, available in approximately three-quarters of the states, provide services either free of charge or for a nominal fee, but because they generally are part of a bureaucratic structure with no relation to the ward they may be impersonal or overly casual about managing the person's affairs. Further, to the extent the public guardian is employed by an agency with the obligation to provide services to the ward, conflicts of interest can arise.[57] Although family members are likely to be less impersonal in approach, they too may have conflicts of interests, especially when the respondent's values or distribution of wealth are deemed improper by the rest of the family.[58]

Because the preference for one sort of guardian or another is likely to be a matter of policy or law, mental health professionals will generally have little involvement in this decision. However, they may become involved when conflicts are made manifest. Consider, for example, a situation in which a mentally retarded adult's parents are divorcing. In this instance, analogous to a custody battle, each parent may claim to be the potential guardian who would be most likely to meet the child's best interests. Another choice-of-guardian situation in which clinical assessment might be sought (albeit rarely) would be when there is an attempt to match an incompetent person with a guardian who would be especially attuned to the person's needs and able to communicate easily. Finally, there is the possibility that a clinician would be appointed guardian.[59] It should be obvious, however, that the clinician should not assume such a role if she or she is providing treatment to the ward [see § 4.05(c)].

(d)   Determining What the Guardian Shall Do

Once a guardian is appointed, two models guide decisionmaking. In one model, the guardian acts according to an objective test: What action will most effectively serve the ward's best interest? In the alternative model, exemplified by a series of cases in Massachusetts and New Jersey,[60] the guardian is instructed to rely on a subjective substituted judgment—that is, to act as he or she thinks the ward would have acted if the ward were competent.[61] The Supreme Court's decision in *Cruzan v. Missouri Deptartment of Health*,[62] discussed in the next subsection, suggests that the latter standard is required when the guardian must decide whether to terminate the life of a ward who is in a vegetative state. However, most courts have distinguished that situation from other situations, including provision of mental health treatment[63]; thus, the best-interests test prevails in the latter context.

In any event, the subjective test usually becomes a *de facto* best-interests test.[64] It may be easy to construct hypothetical cases in which the decision made by the guardian should differ depending on which of the two models is used.[65] But, in practice, the specific situation in which the guardian is required to act is often a novel one for the ward, leaving no basis for speculating what the ward would have done if competent except what the guardian believes is the best course of action after objectively weighing the merits. Indeed, when the ward is incompetent because of mental retardation, he or she may never have been competent.[66]

Thus, if the decision to be made by the guardian involves treatment of the ward and the mental health professional is asked to provide information to assist in the decision, the evaluation will typically be a traditional treatment-oriented assessment, focused on the ward's best interests. Given the individual's needs, what are the treatment plans available, their probable efficacy, and their probable side effects? To put it another way,

enough information needs to be generated for the guardian to give informed consent, a topic addressed in § 11.03.

(e)   Advanced Directives

A number of states have passed legislation that recognizes the legitimacy of so-called advanced directives. An advanced directive is an instruction from a competent individual that directs or authorizes certain action in the event the individual becomes unable to make a decision about the action. Such directives, if valid, are binding on the guardian; indeed, they are usually meant to eliminate the need for a court-appointed guardian in the specified situation.[67]

Advanced directives can take many forms. Most common is the so-called living will, used to indicate a person's desires should he or she become terminally ill and incompetent. A "durable" power of attorney,[68] available in all 50 states and the District of Columbia, can be used to cover other situations as well, including, at least in theory, decisions about treatment or property of a person who has become incompetent. Finally, as discussed below, some states have expressly provided for advanced directives in nonterminal situations. Also of note is the fact that, in 1991, Congress passed the Patient Self-Determination Act,[69] which requires that Medicare- and Medicaid-funded programs (including hospitals and nursing homes) provide patients with written information on the state law relevant to these issues.

As indicated above, most advanced directive legislation has focused on the procedure for indicating a person's wishes in the event he or she becomes terminally ill and incapable of making a decision as to whether to prolong treatment. But such directives can govern many other types of situations, including the treatment of a person who has since become mentally ill and incompetent to make treatment decisions. In Florida, a person (the "principal") can designate a "health care surrogate" through a simple, one-page "living will" document. The will must be witnessed by two persons, neither of whom is the designated surrogate. Subsequently, if two doctors certify that the principal has become incapacitated (meaning "physically or mentally unable to communicate a willful and knowing health care decision"), the surrogate is to make the necessary health care decisions in accordance with the principal's instructions in the living will. Although these decisions may be challenged judicially by the attending physician, the health care facility, the patient's family, or "any other interested person," they are presumptively valid.[70] Minnesota has a similar statute.[71]

In *Cruzan v. Missouri Dep't of Health*,[72] the United States Supreme Court appeared to give its imprimatur to this type of arrangement, even when the surrogate's decision is to end the patient's life. There, the parents of a 26-year-old woman who was in a permanent vegetative state sought to terminate procedures that were sustaining her life. The trial court approved the termination, finding that the daughter had been a "vivacious, active, outgoing, independent person who preferred to do for herself," and that a year prior to her death she had had "somewhat serious" conversations with a friend in which "she expressed the feeling that she would not wish to continue living if she couldn't be at least halfway normal." The Supreme Court found this evidence insufficient for determining the daughter's wishes and concluded that, under these circumstances, the state could require that her life be preserved:

> An erroneous decision not to terminate results in a maintenance of the status quo, the possibility of subsequent developments such as advancements in medical science, the discovery of new evidence regarding the patient's intent, changes in the law, or simply the unexpected death of the patient despite the administration of life-sustaining treatment, at least create the potential that a wrong decision will eventually be corrected or its impact mitigated. An erroneous decision to withdraw life-sustaining treatment, however, is not susceptible of correction.

On the other hand, the Court indicated, a formal written statement of intent to permit withdrawal of treatment—a "living will" of the type authorized by Florida law—would have sufficed to overcome the state's interest in preserving life.[73] Lower courts have echoed this holding in contexts involving mental health treatment.[74]

The evaluation of incapacity necessary to determine whether the advanced directive is triggered is in essence an evaluation of one's competency to make a treatment decision [which is described in § 11.03(d)]. Similar issues are also involved in evaluating the principal's capacity at the time the living will is drafted. However, in the latter situation, the clinician has the additional duty of sensitizing the principal to the kinds of eventualities noted in *Cruzan*—in particular, the possibility that medical advances or changed circumstances could affect one's intent at the time the decision by the surrogate must be made. In short, the clinician should ensure that the advance consent is informed.

11.03. Competency to Make Treatment Decisions

CASE STUDY 11.2

Mr. B, a 43-year-old man, has long-standing glaucoma in both eyes. In one eye, vision remains only for motion. In the other eye, vision is better but is getting worse despite medication. Mr. B's ophthalmologist has proposed a drainage procedure for the second eye which has a high chance of improving his vision for several months (at which time it could be undertaken again) and a negligible chance of damaging the eye. Although Mr. B expresses concern about the pressure in his eye and is fearful of going blind, he refuses the drainage procedure, explaining that his "voices" would be "angry with him" if he underwent the procedure. When his reasons for refusal are explored further, he notes that his mother had a similar drainage procedure which had not been helpful. He then discusses his attachment to his mother, stating that he feels that whatever happened to his mother will also happen to him.

QUESTIONS: How would you evaluate Mr. B's competency, under each of the five competency standards described below? What is the relevance of the fact that he gives at least two reasons for refusing the procedure? What is the relevance of the fact that without treatment Mr. B is very likely to go blind?

(a) Requirements for Informed Consent

Probably the most controversial competency issues arise in connection with decisionmaking about psychiatric and medical treatment. The doctrine of informed consent is designed to address this issue. A relatively recent development in tort law,[75] the doctrine may impose liability on the clinician for battery[76] or negligence[77] for treating patients whose consent is invalid [see § 4.04(d)(1)]. It has two primary purposes: "(1) to promote individual autonomy and (2) to encourage rational decision making."[78] The first purpose is probably the most important. As Katz has eloquently shown,[79] the interest in protecting autonomy in treatment decisions is not simply a reflection of a value placed on free agency for its own sake (which is not to imply that such value is in any way trivial). Protection of autonomy also ensures that the patient is respected as a person, rather than patronized, taken for granted, or treated as a dependent child or an object of treatment ("a case") by medical professionals.[80] As Stone has pointed out, the purely contractual model of health care may be naive today, given the intrusion of insurance companies and other third parties into that relationship.[81] Nonetheless, the informed consent doctrine serves to "humanize" the clinician–patient relationship and to restore the balance in authority between the clinician and the patient, on whose body or mind the proposed treatment would intrude.

Determining whether a consent is valid requires consideration of three elements: disclosure, competency, and voluntariness.[82] Although there is consensus about these elements, the tests to be used in determining their presence are far less settled.

(1)   Disclosure

In regard to disclosure, there have been two streams of thought. The first, essentially unchallenged until 1972,[83] examines the adequacy of disclosure from the point of view of the clinician—whether a reasonable clinician would disclose particular information under the same circumstances.[84] The second examines the adequacy of disclosure from the patient's perspective—whether the patient is given sufficient information to make a reasonable decision.[85] Courts adopting the second line of analysis have further divided as to whether to apply an objective test[86] (i.e., whether the patient is given the information

that a reasonable person would need to make an informed judgment) or, less commonly, a subjective test[87] (i.e., whether the patient is given the information that this *particular* patient would need to make an informed judgement). Under each of these tests, the elements of disclosure are commonly the same—the nature of the recommended treatment procedure, its risks and benefits, and its alternatives[88]—although the evaluation of the adequacy of disclosure obviously varies across tests.

Most states adhere to the first, malpractice standard of disclosure (i.e., viewing disclosure from a clinician's perspective).[89] There are at least two rationales for this approach: Only physicians can determine the effect that a risk might have on a particular patient, and negligence normally evaluates the conduct of a reasonable actor, not the expectations of a reasonable victim.[90] Yet, as one court that rejected this standard pointed out, it leaves disclosure "totally subject to the whim of the physicians in the particular community" and is "inconsistent with the patient's right to self-determination."[91] Katz adds that, under the malpractice standard,

> the objective of giving patients a greater voice in medical decisionmaking is well-nigh unattainable. For such disclosures do little to expand opportunities for meaningful consent, particularly in surrender-prone medical settings, in which a proposed treatment is zealously advocated despite its risks.[92]

For truly informed consent, he argues, not only must clinicians be empathetic with patients' needs for respect and information, but they must be willing to share authority and to engage in dialogue. Simply put, informed consent is a *process*, which cannot be one-way if the goals of the informed consent doctrine are to be met.

Whatever disclosure rule is adopted, its efficacy may be undermined by one of four exceptions to the rule, recognized in varying degrees in all jurisdictions. First, courts routinely hold that disclosure is not necessary in "emergencies," usually without defining that term further.[93] Regardless of its definition, however, this exception should seldom apply in the mental health context because in this setting disclosure can usually take place before treatment is administered.

Second, some case law suggests that the right to disclosure can be waived by the patient (e.g., "Doctor, don't tell me anything.").[94] Yet arguably a waiver is not valid if the patient does not know at least an outline of what is to be disclosed.

A related exception is the so-called therapeutic privilege, which permits withholding information that would "foreclose a rational decision, or complicate or hinder the treatment, or . . . pose psychological damage to the patient."[95] This third exception is potentially the broadest, so much so that it could swallow the rule. At the least, it should only apply when the *disclosure*, rather than any mental illness the person might have, would bring about an irrational decision; as one court put it, it should have effect only

> when a doctor can prove by a preponderance of the evidence he relied upon facts which would demonstrate to a reasonable man the disclosure would have so seriously upset the patient that the patient would not have been able to dispassionately weigh the risks of refusing to undergo the recommended treatment.[96]

A final exception recognized by the courts is when the person is incompetent, in which case the guardian rather than the putative patient is to receive the information. While plausible on the surface, this exception too can undermine the informed consent doctrine, particularly its purpose of promoting autonomy by insuring a collaborative relationship between treater and treated. Indeed, even when proxy decisionmaking is necessary, there are several related reasons for acting as a counselor[97] rather than a parent.[98] First, participation by the patient in the treatment plan is ethically mandated whenever possible.[99] Second, strong evidence exists that such collaboration is therapeutic in and of itself, often enhancing one's autonomous capacities.[100] Third, for reasons to be made clear below, reaching a definitive determination that someone is incompetent is often very difficult, thus suggesting that one should err on the side of treating the person as competent.

(2) Competency

Competence is usually assumed unless the case involves one of three classes of persons—those with mental disability, the elderly, and children.

Even within these groups of "uncertain competency," the competency issue is usually routinely raised only in certain situations. First, and perhaps most common, the issue is raised when a person of uncertain competency *refuses* the treatment prescribed. (Even if mentally ill, a person's consent to treatment is much less likely to be called into question unless the treatment is experimental or particularly intrusive.) Second, as just suggested, if an individual of uncertain competency is to undergo a major medical procedure, a physician may seek consultation to ensure that the patient can give informed consent, lest tort action be brought later for treatment without consent.[101] In this instance, evaluation is more oriented toward protection of the physician from liability than toward respect for the patient's autonomy. Third, evaluation may be sought in those instances in which a patient who is *de jure* incompetent for most purposes (e.g., a child) may, if *de facto* competent in a particular context, give informed consent in that limited, legally sanctioned context (e.g., sterilization).[102] Again, evaluation may be motivated as much by defensive practice as by concern about the limits of the patient's competent exercise of self-determination.[103] If the individual is found incompetent in any of these situations, surrogate decisionmaking, of the type described in the previous section, is usually in order.

Regardless of how the issue arises, the elements of competency to consent to treatment are rarely elaborated in law. The clinician is left, then, to a logical analysis of the scope of the evaluation. In that regard, Roth, Meisel, and Lidz have made a useful initial contribution to such a conceptualization, identifying five types of competency tests: expression of a preference, understanding, appreciation, reasonable decisionmaking process, and reasonable outcome.[104] These constructs, with some modification, have withstood the test of time and critical review.[105]

The simplest of these standards, and the one most respectful of autonomy, is *expression of a preference*. Under this standard, as long as the patient can indicate a decision, that decision is considered competently made. Generally, determination of competency under this standard is straightforward: The patient says yes (competent), no (competent), or nothing (incompetent). There are times, however, when consent under this standard is not so clear. Patients may be very ambivalent and may waver in their preferences. Consider, for example, a man who is brought to a psychiatric emergency room and, after disclosure of risks and benefits, is advised to take an injection of antipsychotic medication. He says "no" but holds out his arm. Should his clear verbal expression of a preference be accepted when his nonverbal behavior implies a different decision?

Of course, a policy of accepting *any* preference creates the possibility that individuals of uncertain competency may be permitted to make decisions without even knowing what they are doing and therefore are especially likely to make choices that are potentially harmful to themselves. The standard of *understanding* is intended to reduce this risk. Generally, it is aimed at ensuring that individuals have a reasonable knowledge of the major information disclosed. The danger is that the legal threshold for understanding will be set so high that most laypersons could not pass it. In such cases, individuals whose competency is brought into question (e.g., those with mental illness) will be held to a higher standard than persons whose competency is unquestioned.

Understanding is also sometimes transformed into *appreciation*, which takes into account the affective meaning to the individual of the information disclosed.[106] In that regard, a particularly thorny problem is presented by those persons who understand the nature, risks, and benefits of a procedure in the abstract, but who deny that they have a mental disorder or offer patently "crazy" reasons for refusing the procedure, and thus may not appreciate the need for treatment. Some courts and commentators have argued that a finding of incompetency to make a treatment decision, at least about psychoactive medication, is inappropriate unless a person's reasons for refusing (or consenting to) treatment are truly out of touch with reality (e.g., "the medicine will make my head explode," a belief that the doctors are practicing witchcraft, or a belief that the medicine is poison).[107] Mere statements that the medication will not work, has harmful effects, or is unnecessary may be insufficient evidence of competency under this approach.

When the focus of the test shifts from understanding to the *reasonableness of the decisionmaking*

process, there is a requirement that patients not only understand or appreciate the major information that has been disclosed to them but also that they weigh the information rationally. According to one variant of this test, attention would be given to the cognitive process itself. That is, does the patient consider each aspect of the information and logically perform a calculation of the expected value of each possible alternative? The major problem with this standard is that it assumes a quality of reasoning that most people rarely exercise in treatment decisions.[108] Another variant, which is especially important because of its central place in Stone's model of civil commitment [see § 10.03(b)],[109] is a determination of incompetency whenever a decision to refuse treatment is "irrational and is based on or related to the diagnosed illness."[110] This determination is likewise not as easy as it may sound. Suppose, for example, that a patient declines medication because "it makes my mouth dry [a real side effect], and the doctor doesn't want me to tell the truth about the FBI." As mentioned in regard to the appreciation standard, denial may also be a problem. If individuals who appear floridly delusional but who also have a good understanding of a treatment refuse the treatment because they think that they are not in need of treatment, can their reason for refusing be said to be a product of their disorder?

The final type of test—*reasonable outcome*—is the least respectful of personal autonomy. Under that standard, a person is judged competent to consent if his or her decision, irrespective of its foundation, is the choice that a reasonable person would have made. Of course, most clinicians are likely to believe that a reasonable person would accept the treatment recommended. Thus, despite its being an "objective" test, assessment of competency under the standard of reasonable outcome is especially vulnerable to the evaluator's values. The test does not leave room for preferences that are idiosyncratic, even if they are "knowing" and "intelligent."

With these differing levels of competency in mind, we can revisit the argument, raised in the introduction to this chapter, that the legal definition of competency should vary with the circumstances. On this view, competency might be defined narrowly (e.g., the reasonable outcome or rational decisionmaking test) when a patient *seeks* a very intrusive treatment with questionable efficacy and negative or irreversible side effects (such as psychosurgery), or when a patient *refuses* a very unintrusive treatment the benefit of which is clear (such as insulin shots when the patient has diabetes). On the other hand, competency might be defined as a mere ability to express a preference when a patient is refusing psychosurgery or consenting to insulin shots. For treatments that fall in between, the understanding or appreciation tests may make more sense. For instance, one might argue that, given its multiple side effects and only moderate efficacy, psychoactive medication should be refusable by a person who is competent at the understanding level, or at least one who is competent at that level and has no grossly delusional beliefs about the treatment or its efficacy.[111] Unfortunately, as the discussion on the right to refuse medication (in the next subsection) points out, the courts have yet to articulate clear standards in this area.

(3)   Voluntariness

As we have noted in other contexts [see §§ 1.03(a), 7.03], the assessment of voluntariness does not fit within the paradigm familiar to most mental health professionals and thus is especially difficult to approach clinically. Exacerbating this problem is the fact that the law's use of the concept in the informed consent context has lacked coherence. For instance, one court has worried that institutionalized patients' consent to particularly intrusive kinds of treatment (i.e., psychosurgery) may be rendered involuntary by the condition of institutionalization.[112] Although institutionalized persons are in an especially powerless position [see § 11.03(c)(3)], there is usually no reason to believe that their dependency would make consent to one form of treatment less voluntary than consent to others.[113] As a second example, courts have consistently considered voluntary hospitalization to be voluntary in fact, despite the reality that many "voluntary" patients are either unaware of their legal status or "choose" voluntary status to avoid involuntary commitment [see § 10.04(c)].

As these examples illustrate, separation of competency and voluntariness may also not be sound. As a conceptual matter, one can imagine a

person who has a thorough understanding of the pros and cons of a proposed treatment and who has the capacity to reason quite logically but who makes a decision under duress. In clinical situations, though, there is rarely such a clear distinction between competency and voluntariness. The same immaturity in social and moral development that may make some children and people with mental retardation incapable of perceiving rights as applicable to themselves (a cognitive deficit relevant to competency) may also render them especially vulnerable to influence by authorities (a volitional deficit relevant to voluntariness).[114] Similarly, competency itself is an *interactive* construct; the quality of one's reasoning is likely to be affected by the degree of support and strain in the social context.[115]

(b)   The Right to Refuse Psychoactive Medication

CASE STUDY 11.3

Jones, who tried to commit suicide after threatening to kill his girlfriend, has been committed to the state hospital as dangerous to self and others. His diagnosis is schizophrenia. The treatment staff believes that the best treatment for him at this time is 200 mg of Thorazine a day. At first Jones consents to the medication, and his psychotic symptoms disappear. After a few weeks, however, Jones complains of drowsiness, nausea, constipation, dry mouth, headaches, and irritation, and he refuses to take any more Thorazine. He says he is not mentally ill and that he would "rather die than take the medication." When pressed, he says he would rather stay in the hospital longer than be forced to take medication and be released sooner. His condition deteriorates to the point where he believes that all the blond patients on the ward are "Nazis" who are out to kill him and his "pet" dogs. There are in fact no dogs on the ward.

QUESTIONS: What can be said about Jones' decisionmaking capacity? His dangerousness? In arriving at answers to these questions, what other information would you want? What procedures, clinical and legal, should be followed? Based on what you know, can Jones be forcibly medicated?

Beyond the general legal requirements for consent to treatment, a special body of law has developed as to whether mental patients may refuse psychoactive medication. Well into the 1970s it was assumed that hospitals could administer such medication without consulting the patient or the family. It was not until such cases as *Rennie v. Klein*[116] and *Rogers v. Commissioner of Mental Health*[117] in the early 1980s that civil rights litigators shifted their focus from the criteria for commitment to the manner in which hospital staff treated those who were committed.[118] These and other cases not only recognized a right to refuse treatment but, in contrast to the common-law-based informed consent doctrine, derived it from the *Constitution*, relying on a host of theories including, as discussed further below, First Amendment freedom of thought and the penumbral right of privacy to control one's body.[119]

Although these cases are often referred to as "right to refuse treatment" cases, they generally focused not just on the right to refuse medication but on the right to refuse a particular subcategory of medication—the major tranquilizers (also called phenothiazines or neuroleptics) that are primarily used in the treatment of schizophrenia.[120] This relatively narrow scope is not surprising given the fact that such medication is the most prevalent form of treatment in the public mental health system. Moreover, although less so with some of the newer drugs (e.g., Clozaril), the side effects of the major tranquilizers are generally more significant than with other medications. These side effects often include akathesia, dystonia, fatigue, headache, and constipation, and sometimes include tardive dyskinesia (a serious nervous disorder which affects perhaps 20% of those on medication and which is irreversible once it reaches a certain point) and neuroleptic malignant syndrome (which is rare but results in death 30% of the time).[121] Furthermore, the drugs can be used purely as "chemical restraints," in which case treatment becomes either a secondary goal or is no longer a goal at all.[122] Finally, even when medication eliminates psychotic or other symptoms of mental disorder, it may achieve its results by suppressing other, "normal" types of behavior as well,[123] or it may be administered in inappropriately large dosages or with other drugs which are not compatible.[124]

There is fairly widespread agreement that mental health patients have *some* right to refuse such treatment.[125] The center of the controversy concerns instead (1) the breadth of situations in which state interests are sufficiently compelling to overcome the individual's right to refuse and (2) the rigor of procedures used to determine whether patients meet this standard. To a large extent, this debate is analogous to the ongoing dispute over the appropriate scheme to be used in civil commitment [see Chapter 10]. That is, most persons interested in the issue are willing to acknowledge that patients have at least some interest in avoiding involuntary treatment, but most are also willing to acknowledge some circumstances in which involuntary treatment is justified.

The differences that exist seem to turn to a large extent on whether the issue is conceptualized as a *medical* or a *legal* question. Those who take the medical perspective tend to perceive refusals of treatment as a product of mental illness and to emphasize the harm to the patient and others that could arise from lack of medication and from the ensuing need to pursue alternatives such as long-term hospitalization or restraints. They also advocate deference to clinical judgment, in part because of the belief that the decision is a clinical one and in part due to concern about the time and energy that will be diverted by court hearings.[126] In contrast, the legal perspective emphasizes the significance of intrusion on individual autonomy and privacy—interests that are believed to be as applicable to mentally disordered persons as to other persons. Advocates of the latter perspective understand the question whether treatment should be administered involuntarily to be a legal–moral issue that should be decided by a judge or jury.

The United States Supreme Court appears most comfortable with the first, medically oriented stance, although it has yet to resolve several important points. At issue in *Washington v. Harper*[127] was a state prison policy that permitted involuntary medication if a three-person committee, composed of two mental health professionals and the associate superintendent of the prison, concluded that the refusing prisoner suffered from a "mental disorder" and was either "gravely disabled" or likely to pose a "substantial risk" of "serious harm" to self or to others. Harper argued that this policy was unconstitutional because it deprived him of liberty without due process; instead, he contended, forcible medication should be allowed only after a finding of *incompetence* by a *court* and a further finding that the medication was in the person's best interests under the "substituted judgment" standard. Six members of the Court disagreed with both the substantive standard and the procedures put forward by Harper and upheld the prison policy.

Noting the potential side effects of psychiatric medication, the majority had "no doubt" that citizens have "a significant liberty interest in avoiding the unwanted administration of antipsychotic drugs under the Due Process Clause of the Fourteenth Amendment." But it concluded that the state has an even stronger interest in ensuring the safety of prisoners and prison staff. According to the majority, as long as antipsychotic medication is administered "for no purpose other than treatment" designed to further these objectives, a prisoner, even a competent one, cannot refuse it. On the procedural issue, the Court followed its precedent permitting informality in civil commitment proceedings and other mental health contexts.[128] It concluded that, in light of the variable nature of competency, the expense of judicial proceedings, and the state's requirement that the treatment refusal board not be composed of staff currently treating the prisoner, the state's review procedure was constitutional. It also found that counsel need not be provided during the hearing.

Some have argued that, given its focus on the prison setting, *Harper* has few or no implications for individuals who have been civilly committed, committed after an insanity acquittal, or hospitalized after a finding of incompetency.[128] But the state's interest in protecting confinees and staff is just as strong in these settings, and the individual's interest in avoiding medication is no stronger. Another way of distinguishing *Harper* in subsequent cases would be to ground the right to refuse on constitutional provisions other than the due process clause (the provision relied on in *Harper*). But this maneuver is unlikely to be of much help either. The right could be said to stem from the First Amendment right to freedom of speech (and thought),[130] the right to avoid cruel and unusual punishment, the equal protection clause (given the right of the non-mentally ill to avoid treatment absent informed consent),[132] or

the "penumbral" right to privacy and bodily integrity (which appears to come closest to the Court's approach).[133] But regardless of the source of the right, the state interest in avoiding behavior harmful to others or self, identified in *Harper*, could always be said to override it.

On the other hand, if the medication is for a "purpose other than treatment," or if it is administered for treatment purposes but to a person who is not dangerous or gravely disabled, *Harper* suggests that a competent individual should be able to refuse.[134] The Court seemed to reinforce this point in its second right-to-refuse case, *Riggins v. Nevada*.[135] There, a defendant being tried for capital murder was medicated with 800 mg of Mellaril a day, ostensibly to ensure his competence for trial. Noting that this dosage was extremely high and may have impaired Riggins's ability to communicate with his attorney,[136] a seven-member majority held that the state had failed to show the drug treatment "was medically appropriate and, considering less intrusive alternatives, essential [either to] Riggins' own safety or the safety of others" or to "obtain an adjudication of Riggins' guilt or innocence" [Emphasis added]. The Court remanded the case for a determination as to whether the medication dosage affected Riggins's ability to testify and interact with counsel.

Riggins is important not only because it emphasized *Harper*'s requirement that involuntary medication be a medically appropriate means of implementing an important state objective but also because it stressed, in the language quoted above, that the medication be the least intrusive means of achieving this objective. Whether this latter aspect of the decision applies beyond the trial context at issue in *Riggins* is unclear, however; the Court may have thought that because trial defendants have an interest not only in avoiding medication side effects per se but also in retaining a clear head to consult with counsel, they are entitled to greater constitutional deference than those who are civilly or criminally committed.

After *Harper* and *Riggins,* it is important to identify which state interests are implicated by a person's refusal of drugs and, at least when the refusal is in the context of trial, the scope of the least-intrusive-means idea. In all likelihood, courts will construe both of these elements in a fashion favoring administration of medication.

For instance, *Harper* seemed to contemplate a broad definition of state interest with its willingness to uphold a policy that permitted involuntary medication both of "gravely disabled" persons and of persons for whom there is no proof of "imminent" dangerousness. Similarly, *Riggins* said only that medication must be the least intrusive way of achieving the state's goal of ensuring defendants' competence, not that the latter goal can never be achieved through involuntary medication. And even if it is applied outside the trial context, the least-intrusive-means requirement is likely to be given narrow scope there as well. In *Harper*, the Court responded to the prisoner's argument that physical restraints were a less drastic way of achieving the state's goal of preventing harm simply by stating that this suggestion was "in no way responsive to the state's legitimate interests." Other Court decisions, in particular *Youngberg v. Romeo*,[137] suggest that the Court will view the state's "professional judgment" as dispositive on the issue of whether medication is the least intrusive method for achieving its goals.[138] Many lower courts appear already to have adopted this view.[139]

With respect to procedure, which is at least as important as the substantive standard, the courts also tend to eschew restrictions on clinical decisionmaking. Although *Harper* approved an administrative procedure, it did not *require* even that amount of process as a constitutional matter; Supreme Court cases in related contexts suggest that something less may be sufficient.[140] Some lower courts have required a judicial determination of incompetence or dangerousness in nonemergency situations,[141] but the majority either permit an administrative procedure such as that sanctioned by *Harper* or allow the treating professional's decision to go unreviewed.[142] There is something to be said for avoiding judicial involvement, given the inefficiency and cost of such a process.[143] At the same time, research indicates that a procedure like that endorsed in *Harper*, where the review board is staffed by people from the same ward as those who make the initial recommendation for medication, is likely to be biased.[144] Probably the best balance between independence and efficiency is to require, in nonemergency situations, a review of the refusing person's situation by a panel composed of staff

from a different ward or, where possible, a different institution.[145] The proportion of refusals (normally well under 15%),[146] is typically not so great that this requirement would be unduly burdensome, and the individual's interest in an accurate, relatively unbiased decision on complex issues such as incompetence, dangerousness, and medical appropriateness is significant.

Of course, *Harper* and *Riggins* only address the constitutional minima under the *federal* constitution for a right to refuse *psychotropic medication*. State courts can and have been more protective of individual interests in this regard.[147] And a number of cases have indicated that, when the treatment is perceived to be even more intrusive (psychosurgery, electroconvulsive therapy, aversive conditioning using anectine), patients may have a greater right to refuse (as well as a more constrained right to consent).[148]

(c)   Research on Informed Consent

(1)   Disclosure

The most general thing that can be said about disclosure in health and mental health settings is that there is rarely adherence to the spirit of informed consent.[149] Consent forms are often lengthy,[150] written in vocabulary beyond the comprehension of many or even most patients,[151] and presented as a mere formality.[152] Information about alternative treatments is often omitted, or patients may be given only the option to refuse treatment, not the option to decide which treatment will be administered.[153] Negative information (e.g., a stigmatizing diagnosis, the risk of tardive dyskinesia) also is often omitted.[154] Such omissions may occur because the clinician wants to avoid bad news, fears admitting professional weaknesses, or consciously invokes the "therapeutic privilege."[155]

More needs to said about the latter doctrine which, it will be recalled, permits withholding information that the doctor believes will so upset the patient that it would hinder "rational" decisionmaking or cause "psychological damage." Although we argued previously that this practice should be rare, empirical evidence clouds the issue sufficiently to caution against a rigid stance in this regard. It has been asserted that there is virtually no proof of harm arising from disclosure of risk information to patients, whether in medical or mental health units.[156] Yet research does suggest that mere mention of a risk or benefit may cause exaggerated concern or hope; information designed to convince people that various "disaster scenarios" are unlikely often backfires and makes people more alarmed.[157] Thus, people who receive information supporting the safety of technology sometimes *increase* their estimates of its hazards,[158] and people who hear about the low risk from such things as prescription drugs sometimes attribute more weight to those risks than experts think they should.[159] These kinds of effects are apparently particularly likely if the negative consequence is "easy to imagine."[160] As a result of these heuristic problems, one commentator has concluded:

> Subjects' autonomy is arguably only protected if they are given all of the information that would make a difference to their decision to participate. But if certain pieces of information make a difference by inducing an inaccurate picture of the risks and benefits of an experiment, disclosing such information may lead people to act in a manner contrary to their best interests. In other words, fully preserving subjects' autonomy may require sacrificing their welfare, and vice versa.[161]

In light of this information, disclosure obligations may become somewhat murky. For instance, one might wonder whether a patient considering psychoactive medication should be told of the possibility of neuroleptic malignant syndrome, which, as noted previously, is rare but results in death 30% of the time. Does the possibility that a patient would "irrationally" fixate on the "easily imagined" consequence (death) to the exclusion of its low probability mean the therapeutic exception to the informed consent doctrine may be invoked? Or is the fact that the patient might "fixate" on the consequence rather than the probability irrelevant, because respect for autonomy mandates that it is precisely this exercise of one's desires, however irrational it may seem to others, that must be honored? Perhaps a compromise is to withhold such information only if there is a good indication that this particular person's delusional system would treat the fact as dispositive.

As to the format for disclosing information,

besides the obvious point that easily understandable language should be used, data from the MacArthur Foundation Research Network on Mental Health and Law group suggests that repetition and staged disclosure is advisable.[162] The group's research indicates that all persons, whether hospitalized or not, "manifested considerably better understanding of the treatment information after it was disclosed to them part by part the second time (element disclosure) than when disclosed as a whole the first time (uninterrupted disclosure)."[163] In other words, after an initial full disclosure, a second disclosure, following a step-by-step process in which the patient is allowed to feed back each element of information (e.g., alternatives, risks, and benefits) after each step, is likely to improve "competency" significantly.[164]

(2)   Competency

The effects of varying disclosure levels, just described, make many of the studies on competency suspect. A majority of the naturalistic studies of patients' competency to consent, whether of medical or psychiatric patients, report substantial gaps in relevant knowledge.[165] But these studies usually fail to document the information that was disclosed,[166] thus leaving unclear whether the findings are the result of lack of disclosure or incompetency.

Studies that remedy this problem, conducted in mental health settings, have yielded inconsistent results. Soskis found that, relative to medical patients, people with schizophrenia tended to have a good understanding of the risks of their medication.[167] Similarly, Jaffe found no differences in understanding between two groups of 16 outpatients, one treated for mental disorder and the other for a physical condition,[168] and another study obtained like results comparing elderly depressed persons with nonpsychiatrically ill older persons.[169] On the other hand, a number of studies found that poor understanding correlated significantly with thought disorder, organic impairment, psychosis and schizophrenia (as opposed to depression).[170] Along the same lines, Munetz and colleagues were able to teach only 3 of 13 patients with tardive dyskinesia that their movement disorder was related to their medication.[171]

The best-constructed study to date tends to confirm both points of view: although the incidence of incompetence in persons with significant mental illness is probably below 50%, severely mentally ill individuals, particularly those with thought disorders, are clearly more likely to be incompetent to make treatment decisions than other groups.[172] Using the step-by-step disclosure of information described earlier and well-conceptualized instruments that measure understanding, appreciation, and reasoning ability,[173] the MacArthur research group compared the competency of six groups: three groups of hospitalized patients and three control groups of non-hospitalized persons taken from the same communities as the patients. One of the hospital groups was composed of patients whose admitting and confirmed diagnosis was schizophrenia or schizoaffective disorder, the second hospital group consisted of those whose admitting and confirmed diagnosis was major depression, and the third hospital group was from a medical hospital unit which treated heart disease. The summary results are worth reporting in full:

> There were three main findings in this study. *First,* on the measures of understanding, appreciation, and reasoning, as a group, patients with mental illness more often manifested deficits in performance than did medically ill patients and their non-ill control groups. Indeed, when the most highly impaired subgroups were identified on each measure, they were composed almost entirely of patients with mental illness.
>
> *Second,* despite overall lower levels of performance in the groups with mental illness, there was considerable heterogeneity within and across the schizophrenia and depression groups. Impairments in performance were more pronounced and more consistent across measures for the schizophrenia patients than for patients with depression. This finding is consistent with a large body of research establishing the poorer performance of patients with schizophrenia, compared to normal controls, on a wide array of cognitive tasks.[174] Even so, on any given measure of decisional abilities, the majority of patients with schizophrenia did not perform more poorly than other patients and nonpatients. The poorer mean performance of the schizophrenia group for any particular measure was due to a minority within that group.
>
> *Third,* among patients with schizophrenia, the minority with poorer performance on the measures of understanding and reasoning tend-

ed to manifest greater severity of psychiatric symptoms, especially those of thought disturbance (e.g., conceptual disorganization, unusual thoughts). These results are in keeping with both theory and empirical findings regarding cognitive deficits associated with schizophrenia.[175] Apart from this difference, however, this poorer-functioning subgroup was not distinguishable on the basis of other demographic, mental status, or patienthood variables used in this study.[176]

As the authors suggest, based on these data, "the justification for a blanket denial of the right to consent to or refuse treatment for persons hospitalized because of mental illness cannot be based on the assumption that they uniformly lack decision-making capacity."[177] Even those with thought disorders should not be considered automatically incompetent. At the same time, between 23% and 52% of those patients hospitalized with schizophrenia and between 5% and 24% hospitalized with major depression had substantially impaired decisionmaking, compared to much smaller percentages with the control groups.[178] Thus, persons with these diagnoses are more "at risk" of incompetence than people with no such diagnosis. Further, given these percentages, to the extent competency assessment focuses solely on patients who refuse treatment (who, as noted above, normally comprise at most 15% of those who receive treatment), it may miss patients whose treatment competency should be questioned (although it is likely that any proxy decisionmaker appointed for this latter group would authorize the treatment being proposed in any event).

There is also extensive research literature on *developmental* factors in competency to consent to treatment, although it primarily (but not exclusively) involves nonclinical samples.[179] In the most widely cited study, Weithorn and Campbell asked 9-, 14-, and 18-year-olds to decide several hypothetical situations involving physical or mental health problems.[180] In general, the 14-year-olds were as competent as adults in making treatment decisions, not just in terms of outcome but in terms of understanding the alternative treatments and their risks and benefits and in terms of rationally weighing such information. Even the 9-year-olds, although deficient in reasoning capacity, did not differ from adults in their ability to express a preference or reach a reasonable outcome (i.e., the choice that a panel of experts would have made). These findings from the laboratory have been validated by studies of real-life treatment decisionmaking suggesting that, at least for *routine* medical and mental health decisions, even elementary-school-age children tend to make "good" (i.e., adultlike) choices and give reasons approximating those used by adults.[181] This research also indicates that involving children in the process tends to facilitate treatment.

(3)　Voluntariness

The available research raises doubt as to whether most consent in mental health care settings is truly voluntary ("voluntary" is used in this context to mean behavior that *appears* to be the product of free choice rather than the result of overbearing third-party influence). First, there is the effect of institutionalization. Relying on Kelman's work,[182] Grisso has suggested that those in institutions may have a "power deficiency" that results from their being drawn from the relatively powerless segments of society and the fact that the hospital is the doctor's, not the patient's, "turf."[183] He also points to Goffman's work on asylums,[184] which found that members of institutions assume a group identity and an allegiance to officially controlled rules and customs. Finally, he notes research suggesting that hospital patients come to believe noncompliance with doctors' requests can mean that other services will be withheld.[185]

Exacerbating this possible institutionalization effect are two other phenomena that can affect noninstitutionalized patients as well. As already noted, medical professionals typically treat consent requirements in a *pro forma* fashion. They seldom make an effort to involve a patient in a truly collaborative relationship, and they often cajole agreement to accept a particular treatment.[186] (It is noteworthy in this regard that obviously nonconsensual treatment is common on general medical wards as well as psychiatric wards.[187]) There is also the "white-coat phenomenon"—the trust and acceptance of authority that patients sometimes place in their doctors, whether or not they are in an institution.[188] Although the occasionally observed psychological attempts to salvage freedom, described by Brehm,[189] may make patients'

compliance with medical regimens less than doctors desire, direct refusal of "doctor's orders" is rare.

(d)　Evaluation of Competency to Make Treatment Decisions

When competency to consent to a *particular* proposed treatment is at issue, the task is to determine whether the elements of informed consent are present. It is important to find out first (usually by talking with the patient's physician or social worker) what the patient has been told about the treatment. If it becomes apparent that the patient has misunderstandings or points of ignorance about the treatment, it is usually a good idea to try to teach the relevant information to him or her, using the "element," step-by-step approach noted previously, to ensure that these problems are not simply the result of inadequate disclosure. To carry out this sort of interview, the clinician obviously needs to have at least a basic knowledge of the treatment. Unless there is reason to believe that the physician (or other treating professional) is intimidating to the patient, it is sometimes useful to have the physician present for at least part of the interview to answer questions that the patient may have and to try to clear up misunderstandings.

After such disclosure, the person's competency can be assessed. At a minimum the clinician will want to learn the patient's understanding of the nature and purpose of the treatment; its risks and benefits; and the nature, risks, and benefits of alternative treatments. Under the "appreciation" and "reasonable process" test of competency, it will also be important to determine the patient's reasons for consenting or refusing consent.

The latter information may also be relevant to determining the voluntariness of consent. In addition, the clinician may be able to rely on basic social psychology to identify situational factors which may affect voluntariness. For example, according to Saks's study of procedures for children's consent to organ and tissue transplants,[190] consent was typically obtained to a succession of procedures (e.g., blood samples to test donor compatibility, counseling) before consent was finally sought for the transplant. By that time, there had been so many affirmative steps consented to that the probability of consent to the transplant was increased significantly.[191] Other research confirms that individuals can be induced to comply with requests of increasing demand if they have first been induced to comply with a relatively small, "easy" request.[192] The effects of institutionalization can be investigated by asking whether the individual believes receipt of other benefits is conditioned upon agreeing to the treatment and stressing that the decision is up to the patient, rather than the treating physician.

If the issue is competency to consent to treatment as a general matter (i.e., outside the context of considering a specific treatment), presenting hypothetical treatment decisions and then probing as described above can be a useful strategy. In that regard, some vignettes have been developed for research purposes, complete with uncomplicated scoring systems that are potentially adaptable for clinical evaluation.[193]

There may be additional evaluation questions when the issue is whether psychoactive medication should be administered involuntarily. First, depending on the relevant state law, the clinician may need to evaluate the degree to which the individual is dangerous or likely to deteriorate without the medication. Second, some assessment of whether the medication is the only effective option must be made to obtain information relevant to the least-restrictive-alternative issue.[194] In jurisdictions using a medical model, the clinician will then have to make the ultimate decision on the competency, dangerousness, and intrusiveness issues, often with very little direction as to how to weight these variables. For example, in what was almost a "nonopinion" as to the standard to be used, the Court of Appeals for the First Circuit held that the federal Constitution requires only that clinicians do an idiosyncratic "*ad hoc* balancing" of "the varying interests of particular patients in refusing antipsychotic medication against the equally varying interests of patients— and the state—in preventing violence," with "neither . . . allowed necessarily to override the other in a blanket fashion."[195] In more legalized jurisdictions, the evaluator should provide the relevant information, without reaching such conclusions.

A few instruments have been developed for evaluating treatment competency.[196] The best appears to be the MacArthur Competence Assessment Tool for Treatment Decisions (MacCAT-T), which uses features of the three research instruments alluded to earlier: the Understanding Treatment Disclosures (UTD) instrument, the Perceptions of Disorder (POD) instrument, and the Thinking Rationally about Treatment (TRAT) instrument. The UDT assesses understanding of disclosed information, with each of its five paragraphs corresponding to an element of informed consent (i.e., the nature of the patient's disorder, the nature of the treatment, the probable benefits of the treatment, the probable risks and discomforts of the treatment, and alternative treatments and their benefits and risks). The POD has two parts, measuring nonacknowledgment of one's disorder and nonacknowledgment of the potential value of treatment even when successful treatment is likely. The TRAT assesses the quality of a person's cognitive functions by giving the person vignettes, responses to which are scored to provide data about the person's skills at information seeking, consequential thinking, comparative thinking, complex thinking, and generating consequences; other parts of the TRAT assess weighing of consequences, transitive thinking, and probabilistic thinking.[197] Research on these instruments indicates they can be reliably scored and are internally consistent.[198] However, it should also be noted that criticism has been directed at the conceptual basis of these instruments, especially the POD.[199] The latter instrument may conceptualize the appreciation construct too broadly, allowing a finding of impairment merely because a patient disagrees with the doctor's judgment that the patient is "sick."[200] The MacCAT-T, which is a shorter combination of these instruments, is now available but is still being tested for its psychometric properties.

11.04.   Competency to Consent to Research

A subcategory of informed consent doctrine has to do with consent to participate in research. For obvious reasons, research about new medical and psychiatric treatment modalities is important and thus, within limits, is to be encouraged. Furthermore, most human research in the social and behavioral sciences is innocuous and has rarely resulted in "malresearch" litigation.[201] Nonetheless, such research still presents serious ethical problems when practiced on persons of dubious competency; the usual tension in mental health law between autonomy (patients' rights to decide for themselves about participation) and paternalism (clinicians or researchers making this decision) is heightened because experimental treatment is rarely intended for the participants' direct benefit. It is also important to note that some human research, especially in biomedical areas, *does* necessarily present significant—albeit often unknown—risk to the participants.[202] Thus, some knowledge of the special rules for obtaining consent in this situation is important.

(a)   Legal Requirements

The Nuremburg Code established the legal framework in this area by prohibiting any research using persons who are not in a position to give valid informed consent.[203] Today in the United States, however, such research is regulated primarily by rules promulgated by the Department of Health and Human Services[204] and adopted by most other federal agencies.[205] Procedurally, these regulations provide for administrative review of all human research by local institutional review boards (IRBs). Substantively, they require that researchers inform potential participants of the nature and purpose of the research, its risks and benefits, alternative treatments (in treatment-oriented research), the limits of confidentiality,[206] compensation and treatment for any injuries (in research involving more than "minimal risk"), whom to contact with questions, the choice of participating, and the freedom to withdraw at any time.[207] However, the IRB may waive the full-disclosure requirement when the research cannot be undertaken without deception or withholding of information,[208] no more than "minimal risk" exists, and the participants will be fully informed during "debriefing."[209] Minimal risk "means that the risks of harm anticipated in the proposed research are not greater, considering probability and magnitude, than those ordinarily encountered in daily life or during the performance of routine physical or psychological examinations or tests."[210]

Drawing from discussions by a national commission,[211] the regulations also provide special requirements for research involving participants of uncertain competency.[212] Research on prisoners, for example, is forbidden (because of the potential for coercion) unless the research (1) is directly related to the special aspects of criminal behavior or incarceration[213] and (2) does not involve incentives for participation that would unduly influence decisions whether to participate.[214] Research on children generally requires the *assent* of the children themselves and the *permission* of their parents.[215] Additional review is required when the research involves more than minimal risk[216] or the potential participants are wards of the state.[217] The requirement of parental consent may be waived by the IRB if it is found that parental involvement will harm, or at least not protect, the potential child participants (e.g., neglected or abused children).[218]

On the other hand, the Department of Health and Human Services has never implemented proposed regulations for research involving the "institutionalized mentally infirm."[219] These would have paralleled the regulations for children, with requirements for assent to minimal-risk research, increased supervision, and various forms of substituted consent in risky research. Critics of the proposed regulations regarded them as insufficiently respectful of patients' autonomy.[220] Presumably, in the absence of special regulations, research involving mental patients would follow the general regulations on human research. If so, such research requires the informed consent of the patients themselves or their legal representatives (e.g., a guardian). IRBs would, of course, remain free to require more protection than do the regulations themselves.

(b)   Research

In all likelihood, much of the literature on consent to treatment is generalizable to consent to research, especially consent to treatment-oriented research.[221] If so, those with mental illness should not automatically be considered incompetent to consent to research, and children 14 and older should generally be considered competent to do so. At the same time, mentally ill individuals with serious thought disorders and younger children are significantly more likely to be incompetent.

The few studies that have focused specifically on the competency-to-consent-to-research issue have reached similar, if not entirely confirmatory, results. Some research has suggested that elementary-school-age children are not significantly less competent than adults at assessing proposed research.[222] Abramovitch and her colleagues found, however, that although children between the ages of 7 and 12 "were quite competent with respect to knowing why the studies were being done," even with probing they "had difficulty describing benefits and risks" when compared to adults.[223] Furthermore, children were much more likely to stop their participation in research if they were told the experimenter would not be upset if they stopped.[224] Research focusing on people with mental disability, on the other hand, tentatively suggests that they are not significantly different in their ability to distinguish risks and benefits of research.[225] Furthermore, the fear that mental patients may be more vulnerable in the research setting because their lack of understanding leads them to agree to risky experiments is somewhat allayed by findings that understanding is correlated with consent (i.e., psychiatric patients who understand more of the information disclosed are more likely to agree to the proposed procedures).[226]

Much more empirical work on this issue is necessary because some aspects of treatment research are not analogous to ordinary treatment. First, participants in research must comprehend the concept of "research," which even professionals have difficulty doing. Of particular concern is the finding that participants in experimental treatment studies often do not understand that they are part of a research project[227]; rather, their perception is primarily the provision of *treatment* to which they have consented.

Second, the nature of a rational risk assessment for consent to research is inherently different from that for consent to treatment. For the latter, the provision of actuarial tables concerning treatment success or their equivalent is at least theoretically possible, although patients may find it difficult to apply such base-rate information to their own cases.[228] On the other hand, many of the risks in research are generally unknown. The best that can be done is to generalize from analogous situations and to speculate on the basis of theory. For example, the first humans to be administered an experimental drug can be told the effects the drug has had in animal studies and the theories about the drug's action, but the precise risks cannot be known until the research has been performed.

Third, the motivations for consent to research are presumably different from those for consent to treatment. It is conceivable that the desire to be altruistic or to receive compensation might dwarf other factors in the calculus of whether to participate. Nonetheless, at least for minimal-risk research, there appears to be little reason not to honor the preferences of many who are mentally ill or in their teenage years.

(c) Evaluation

The evaluation of competency to consent to research will mirror the evaluation of competency to consent to treatment to a large extent. The clinician should be careful, however, to evaluate the elements of informed consent that are specific to research (e.g., the nature of research as opposed to treatment; freedom to withdraw or set limits, including the fact that the experimenter will not be upset if withdrawal or limit-setting occurs; and, when relevant, the lack of benefit to the participant). To determine understanding of the nature of research, use of hypothetical situations, derived from the few studies of competency to consent to research,[228] may be a good strategy.

11.05. Testamentary Capacity

CASE STUDY 11.4

Ms. K died, leaving only one dollar of a sizable estate to her only child, Ms. R, with the rest going to a church. Testimony at a will contest proceeding reveals that, when asked why she wanted to distribute her estate in this way, Ms. K stated that she had not gotten along well with R, that while living with the R family she had been required to do things which she did not want to do, that Mr. R had made a derogatory remark concerning Germans (K was of German descent), that the R family was lacking in religious spirit, and that Ms. R had tried to kill her by putting glass in her pudding. She also stated that she (Ms. K) had failed to contribute enough in support of the church. Independent evidence discloses that the daughter had prepared the pudding with the glass in it but that the glass was there accidentally. Furthermore, Ms. K had been assured by many people that such was the case, but she persisted in believing that her daughter wanted to harm her.

QUESTIONS: As a clinician, how would you evaluate Ms. K's testamentary capacity? Do you think your evaluation would be of any assistance to the court?

Another type of competency that the clinician may be asked to evaluate is whether an individual is (or, more commonly, was) competent at the time of executing a will. This type of "competency," like those referred to throughout this chapter, does not refer to the individual's general competency but rather the capacity to meet the legal threshold required to perform a particular act—in this case, the writing of a will. If the individual (the "testator") is judged to have lacked competency (referred to in this context as "testamentary capacity") at the time of the writing of the will, the will is not "admitted to probate" and its provisions have no effect. In such cases, distribution of the estate will proceed under the terms of any valid will that exists or, in the absence of a will, under the rules of "intestate succession," which favor the immediate family.

(a)　Legal Requirements

The requirement that testators be competent is most often expressed by the simple admonition that they be "of sound mind."[230] The courts have interpreted this phrase to encompass the following four attributes:

1. Testators must know at the time of making their wills that they are making their wills.
2. They must know the nature and extent of their property.
3. They must know the "natural objects of [their] bounty."
4. They must know the manner in which the wills they are making distribute their property.[231]

In determining whether testamentary capacity exists under these standards, the law is not interested in "perfect" capacity or knowledge. As with many competencies, only a low threshold of functioning is required: "Capacity" in this context means testators' ability to understand in a general way the nature and extent of their property, their relation to those who may naturally claim to benefit from the property they leave, and the practical effect of their wills.[232] For example, testators need not know every detail concerning their property. Similarly, mere forgetfulness is not equivalent to a lack of capacity: If a testator has forgotten about a cousin who lives 3,000 miles away and, as a result, has not included that cousin as a beneficiary, the will is not automatically invalidated.

Most relevant for present purposes, the simple existence of mental illness is not equivalent to testamentary incapacity. A person with mental illness may make a valid will, as may an individual addicted to narcotics or alcohol.[233] The question to be addressed is the functional abilities such an individual possesses at the time the will is made with respect to each of the four attributes noted above. Thus, for instance, if the will of a person with florid mental illness has been executed during a "lucid interval," it will be deemed valid.[234] Similarly, a testator's prejudice against a particular individual, no matter how ill-founded, is not the same as a lack of capacity, nor is a belief on the part of a testator that another party has been attempting to injure him or her. The issue in a case such as Ms. K's (in Case Study 11.4) is not the existence of such beliefs but their cause; the court, and clinicians called on to assist it, must distinguish between beliefs that might be mistaken and actual delusions. The latter will not be found to exist unless the testator's belief "has no basis in reason, cannot be dispelled by reason and can be accounted for only as the product of mental disorder."[235]

As may be surmised from the foregoing, the competency requirement creates a tension between the principle, well-established in Western society, that persons should have control over their property and the natural inclination to question atypical distribution patterns. Suppose a man leaves his property to an animal shelter rather than to his family. The competency paradigm allows the family members to question this bequest and may lead to invalidation of the will. A valid question, raised by Szasz,[236] among others, is why such challenges should be allowed; even if the man is psychotic, he has expressed a desire through the will that arguably should be honored to the same extent a bequest based on "reasonable" mistake should be. But, as in other areas, of the law [see § 8.02(c)(1)], the medical model has provided the dividing line. Correcting for all "mistakes" would violate libertarian notions; allowing "irrational" ones would insult those same notions. The difficulty, of course, is separating the rational from the irrational bequests. Again, as always, the clinician's task is to gather information that informs the judgment of those required to perform this separation—the judge and jury.

(b) Clinical Evaluation of Testamentary Capacity

One obvious difference between the evaluation of testamentary capacity and the assessment of other capacities is that in most instances the subject of the evaluation is dead. This fact ensures that in the vast majority of cases, "the best evidence of capacity—the testator himself"[237]—will be unavailable to the clinician.

In at least some cases, however, the testator will be available. A few states, for example, have adopted antemortem probate statutes, which allow a will to be probated prior to the testator's death,[238] and in other jurisdictions attorneys may advise their clients to seek an evaluation of capacity at the time of execution of the will in an attempt to reduce the possibility of a contest later.

The areas of inquiry will be similar, whether or not a testator is alive. The primary difference will be in the source of information—obviously, the testator will be the primary source if alive. In such cases, we recommend videotaping the evaluation, as the tape may be persuasive in demonstrating the reasons for clinical conclusions on the subject's mental state and functioning. If the testator is not alive, the information will have to be obtained from friends, acquaintances, family, available medical records, and any other source that might shed light on the testator at the time of making the will.

As a general rule, clinicians should remember that the question of testamentary capacity is best conceptualized as a functional one, focusing on the testator at the time the will was made. Thus, they may want to structure their evaluation and report to conform with the legal elements of the capacity test.

(1) Testator Knowledge That Will Is Being Made

When testators are available for interview, they should be asked about their conception of a will, what it is intended to do, and why they are preparing theirs at this time. The last piece of information is important in part because it may provide a key to any delusional system that might exist (e.g., "I'm writing a will because the television tells me my death is near") and in part because it will enable clinicians to ascertain that individuals are, in fact, aware that they are preparing their wills. In some cases, the question may also be useful in determining whether individuals are writing wills of their own volition, rather than as the result of coercion from others. Virtually every jurisdiction invalidates an otherwise valid will that is the result of "undue influence" by a third party.[239]

If the testator is not alive, the fact that a will exists may often be considered sufficient to demonstrate he or she had a basic understanding of what a will does, as long as the will purports to distribute the testator's property. Spaulding suggests that the question of whether a testator knew he or she was making a will should be left to the commonsense of the factfinder[240]; in the case of a retrospective inquiry into capacity, we concur that an expert generally will have little to offer on this prong of the test.

(2) Testator Knowledge of Nature and Extent of Property

If the testator is alive, questions designed to elicit information about his or her property holdings are appropriate. These might include questions on occupation, salary, living accommodations, personal possessions, intangibles (e.g., bank accounts or notes), and any other possessions. Questioning should be open-ended and designed to let subjects describe their property in their own words. Again, clinicians are interested in this material primarily to determine whether subjects' assessments of their possessions are realistic or are instead wholly at odds with the facts. In this regard, clinicians obviously need to obtain corroborative information about the estates in question.

If the testator is dead, the determination as to knowledge of the nature and extent of the property will be determined by the factfinder, relying on objective evidence found in the will: Does the disposition made by the testator match the estate, or does the will attempt to bequeath items that the testator does not possess? For example, if a will states that "I give the one million dollars in my State Bank account to the Society for the Preservation of Prince Philip's Ponies," and neither the bank account, the one million dollars, nor the society exists, the factfinder may reach reasonable judgments about the testator's capacity solely from this provision. Accordingly, clinical opinion on the issue whether testators knew the nature and extent of their property may add little to what can reasonably be inferred from the degree of "match" between property bequeathed and actual possessions.

(3) Testator Knowledge of Natural Objects of Bounty

Spaulding has pointed out that clinicians will probably be most useful in this area of inquiry because they can help ascertain testators' actual values and preferences, thus inhibiting application of an objective "reasonable person" test that might not reflect a testator's intent.[241] If testators are alive, they should be asked to identify family, friends, and those who might have played a major role in their lives and then ask about relations

with them, to assist the factfinder in answering the following sorts of questions: Is a particular relationship a close and loving one? If not, why not? Does a testator believe that the other party is "out to get" him or her? If so, what is the basis of the belief? The clinician should remember that prejudice or hostility held by a testator against another does not automatically render the testator incapable.

This part of the inquiry obviously will be much more difficult when testators are dead. In many cases, disputes over a will's validity will have arisen because one or more individuals who believe themselves the "natural object" of the testator's "bounty" will have been excluded. In such cases, clinicians will have to attempt to reconstruct the testator's relationships with these significant others by relying on extrinsic sources— including, quite probably, the individuals embroiled in contesting the wills. Therefore, clinicians must take particular care to corroborate the information relied on, and to keep in mind that information may be suspect because of the source. Archival records that document frequency of contact or communication with the testator or provide evidence of the quality of the relationship (e.g., close and caring vs. remote or distant) may offer further clues as to the testator's awareness of and intentions toward family members.

(4) Testator Knowledge of the Manner in Which Property Is Disposed

If the testator is alive, clinicians should ask questions about the general consequences of the property disposition made. For example, if a woman intends to leave her only daughter a few dollars a month out of a considerably greater fortune, does the testator know the likely impact on the daughter's life? Does she believe that a greater sum is unnecessary because the daughter has independent means of her own? If so, is that true, or is the daughter in fact living an impoverished existence that will be unchanged by the disposition? If the latter situation obtains, is the testator's belief a product of delusion, personal pique, or simply mistake? The clinician should keep in mind, of course, that the testator may simply value the designated recipient(s) of the balance of her wealth more highly than her daughter.

If the testator is dead, inquiry into his or her understanding of the dispositions made by the will is problematic. In a case such as the one just described, a question as to capacity would probably be raised because the disposition is "unnatural." As when the testator is alive, the focus of clinical inquiry would then be on any material that would reveal why the testator made the disposition. The difficulty lies, of course, in finding and assessing the material. As before, the role of the clinician should not be to evaluate the wisdom of the choices made by the testator but rather to discover the factors leading to those choices.

(c)   Conclusion

Clinical opinion about testamentary capacity has often been denigrated and ignored[242]; Bromberg attributes this to a suspicion that clinicians testifying for a particular side, like others involved in a will contest, have an "undiluted interest in the money involved."[243] A second reason that clinical testimony may have negligible impact is that it is often superfluous. As should be clear from this discussion, the inquiry into testamentary capacity is largely a commonsense one. In such cases, clinicians will often have little or nothing to add to the bare facts, and should not participate.

In some cases, however, clinicians may be able to provide useful information to the probate court. Senility, psychosis, or mental retardation may have some impact on capacity, and clinicians —through physical and neurological examinations, intelligence tests, and interviews if the testator is alive and through careful information collection if the testator is dead—may be able to cast light on the extent of these conditions and the thought processes they engendered. At the same time, assuming that the clinician can assist the factfinder, opinion testimony should still avoid the ultimate question as to whether a person lacked testamentary capacity. This admonition is stressed here because of the pressures that can come to bear in probate contests where considerable money is involved, and thus, to put it bluntly, where greed can become an overriding motivation for those contesting the will.

Bibliography

Paul Appelbaum, Thomas Grisso, Edward P. Mulvey, & Kenneth Fletcher, *The MacArthur Treatment Competence Study. I. II. III.*, 19 Law & Human Behavior 105, 127, 149 (1995).

Alexander Brooks, *The Right to Refuse Medication: Law and Policy*, 39 Rutgers Law Review 339 (1987).

Children's Competence to Consent (Gary Melton, Gerald Koocher, & Michael Saks eds. 1983).

Lawrence Frolik, *Plenary Guardianship: An Analysis, a Critique and a Proposal for Reform*, 23 Arizona Law Review 599 (1981).

Harper v. Washington, 494 U.S. 210 (1990).

Jay Katz, The Silent World of Doctor and Patient (1984).

Charles W. Lidz, Alan Meisel, Eviatar Zerubavel, Mary Carter, Regina M. Sestak, & Loren H. Roth, Informed Consent: A Study of Decisionmaking in Psychiatry (1984).

Mark Munetz, Loren Roth, & Cleon Cornes, *Tardive Dyskinesia and Informed Consent: Myths and Realities*, 10 Bulletin of the American Academy of Psychiatry & Law 77 (1982).

Research Ethics: A Psychological Approach (Barbara H. Stanley, J. E. Sieber, & Gary Melton eds. 1996).

Willis Spaulding, *Testamentary Competency: Reconciling Doctrine with the Role of the Expert Witness*, 9 Law & Human Behavior 113 (1985).

Phillip B. Tor & Bruce D. Sales. *A Social Science Perspective on the Law of Guardianship: Directions for Improving the Process and Practice*, 18 Law & Psychology Review 1 (1994).

20 C.F.R. §§ 404.1501 *et seq.* (1985) (regulations governing consent to research).

CHAPTER TWELVE

Compensating Mental Injuries: Workers' Compensation and Torts

12.01. Introduction

Society has long been concerned with compensating those injured by others. Although the criminal justice system helps fulfill this objective by exacting vengeance, it exists primarily for the benefit of society. Individual monetary compensation is most directly achieved through the civil justice system, primarily via "tort" law—the law of civil wrongs. Thus, the same act can trigger both systems. An assault, for example, may be punished by the state in criminal court and also lead to damages for the victim in a tort action. In the first instance the state will be the "complainant"; in the second it merely provides the forum for resolution of a dispute between private parties [see § 2.04].

The separation between the criminal law and civil compensation law was not always so distinct. In medieval England, the idea of compensating injured parties developed as an alternative to the warfare that traditionally occurred when the honor of one clan was affronted by another.[1] The Anglo-Saxons ranked individuals in terms of relative worth and assigned a tariff, known as the *wer*, which established the official money worth of each person. When a clan caused injury to a member of another clan, fighting was avoided by offering the *wer*, which was distributed in prescribed allowances to the paternal and maternal

kin of the injured party. Over time, however, penalties also became due the King when the transgression disturbed the King's peace; this payment became known as the *wite*. Eventually, the functions of appeasing the family and atoning for the breach of the King's peace separated: The latter emerged as the criminal law, and the former became the law of "torts."[2]

As tort law developed, it came to incorporate a broad universe of harms. Today, the American Law Institute's Restatement (Second) of the Law of Torts defines the word "tortious" as

> appropriate to describe not only an act which is intended to cause an invasion of an interest legally protected against intentional invasion, or conduct which is negligent in creating an unreasonable risk of invasion of such an interest, but also conduct which is carried on at the risk that the actor shall be subject to liability for harm caused thereby, although no such harm is intended and the harm cannot be prevented by any precautions or care which is practicable to require.[3]

As this definition suggests, tortious conduct may result from intentional conduct, from negligent conduct, or in some instances from conduct in which the actor's motivation is not at issue and for which strict liability is imposed. At the same time, in determining the compensability of an injury, the law not only considers the actor's conduct but may consider that of the injured party as well. For example, if the injured party has consented explicitly or implicitly to the invasion of the protected interest (i.e., has "assumed the risk"), or has been negligent as well, damages may not be assessed at all, or at least may be apportioned according to the relative "fault" of the parties.[4]

Because of the complex, fault-oriented nature of the present tort system, other systems of compensation have developed over the years.[5] The most extensive such system is workers' compensation, which is designed to provide compensation to injured workers for the loss or impairment of their wage-earning power.[6] The "workers' comp" system came into being in the early 20th century, largely because the various defenses available to employers in tort suits left employees injured on the job grossly undercompensated.[7] In contrast, workers' compensation ignores the potential fault of the injured party and instead provides compensation for all injuries arising out of employment.

Both the tort system and the workers' compensation system were initially reluctant to accept claims of "mental injury."[8] However, this reluctance has gradually given way to expanded coverage, at least in part because of an increased willingness by courts to accept diagnosis and prognosis as legitimate skills. Thus, under each system of compensation, the clinician may be asked to assess the impact of conduct or events on an individual's mental status, functioning, and prognosis for recovery.

This chapter discusses the workers' compensation system first and then examines compensability for mental injury under tort law. In the latter area, we focus particularly on the tort of infliction of emotional distress because it most clearly raises the issue of "mental suffering." Differences between the workers' compensation and tort systems are noted throughout. We conclude with a discussion of clinical evaluation techniques relevant to each.

CASE STUDY 12.1

Ms. Friend, a longtime employee of Big Sound, a manufacturer of stereo equipment, had a spotless employment history. She rarely missed work either for vacations or because of illness, and was well liked by other employees. Her job was to drive a fork-lift on the floor, moving cartons of materials. One morning, as she was moving material, she heard a loud noise. She looked to her left, and saw hundreds of cartons falling from shelving directly onto a coworker who was driving another lift. The other employee's neck was broken in the accident and he died instantly.

Ms. Friend brought a workers' compensation claim against her company for the emotional injury sustained as a result of witnessing the fatal accident. You are asked to evaluate Ms. Friend. She states that since the accident she has been unable to sleep and has lost her appetite. She also has had difficulty at work because when she gets on her fork-lift she begins shaking so badly she has difficulty driving. She complains of stomach and neck pains as well. You also discover that one month before the accident Ms. Friend's young son died in a home accident. After returning from a two-week paid leave to attend to funeral arrangements, she seemed depressed, according to coworkers. She has one small daughter remaining at home, who is watched by a nanny (Ms. Friend's husband works full-time as well). She has told her coworkers that she feels guilty about leaving her son at home and wants to spend more time with her daughter.

QUESTIONS: Based on what is known at this point, if you are a lawyer representing Ms. Friend how do you respond to her question as to whether she can recover monetarily from the workers' compensation system? Assume her employer is not governed by a workers' compensation plan. Could she recover damages in a tort suit? In either case, what information would you want from a clinician in trying to determine the amount of compensation? As a clinician how would you answer the lawyer's queries?

12.02. Workers' Compensation Law

Before the development of workers' compensation law, an employee injured at work could only be compensated through tort law. In these tort actions, the employer could raise several defenses, including *contributory negligence* (asserting that the employee's negligence contributed to the injury), *assumption of the risk* (asserting that the employee assumed the risk of injury by taking the job), and the *fellow servant* rule (asserting that the worker's injuries resulted from the negligence of another worker).[9] These defenses effectively barred many workers or their families from recovering any compensation for workers' injuries or deaths and subsequent loss of employment. Furthermore, even when no defense applied, proving fault was often a long, involved process that "frequently worked an injustice on the worker,"[10] who could ill-afford waiting for compensation. An Illinois study at the turn of the century found that of 614 work-related death cases, 214 families had received no compensation and 111 cases were in pending litigation. In New York City in 1908, there had been no compensation for 43.2% of those accidents in which disposition was known.[11] As one commentator put it, this state of affairs was "a complete failure [which], in most serious cases, left the workers' family destitute."[12]

The workers' compensation system was designed to change this situation. By entering into this system, which is compulsory in most states,[13] both employers and employees give up rights possessed in tort law. Employers have to insure employees against work-related injury and, except in a few limited circumstances, waive the various defenses available in tort.[14] Employees, for their part, forfeit the potentially unlimited compensation available in a tort case (assuming the requisite proof of tortious conduct and damages) but obtain more certain recovery, based on a fixed schedule derived from the degree and duration of the disability and the workers' preinjury salary. Generally paid over a fixed period on a weekly basis, this compensation is not designed to "make the person whole" as is the case with tort damages but is meant to replace some meaningful degree (typically two-thirds) of lost earning capacity.[15] In addition, the disabled worker receives payment for medical care, surgery, nursing, and burial services.[16] Today, all states and the federal government have workers' compensation laws,[17] and the vast majority of all civilian employees are covered.[18]

(a) The Claims Process

One of the primary goals of workers' compensation is the expeditious adjustment of claims for compensation.[19] Therefore, nearly all jurisdictions provide for summary and generally informal proceedings before an administrative agency, as well as for appeal to the courts.

As a first step, the worker must give notice of injury to the employer and, in some jurisdictions, to the workers' compensation board. The notice must provide general information regarding the circumstances of the accident and the nature and extent of the injury.[20] Once notice is given, the employee may be required to submit to a medical or physical examination to determine whether there is an injury and, if so, its extent.[21] In such situations, the patient–physician privilege is considered inapplicable [see §4.04(c)].[22]

The statutes generally provide an opportunity for the parties to reach a voluntary settlement. If adjudication becomes necessary, the proceeding is normally administrative in nature; the case is tried before a hearing officer (who may be called a "commissioner") rather than a judge in the court system. Technical rules of pleading are not followed (although the claim must set forth facts adequate to establish the case for compensation[23]), and the rules of evidence may not apply either, in which case hearsay will be admissible.[24] The adjudication is informal in character; the parties may not even be represented by counsel.

The claimant has the burden of making out a case for recovery. The standard of proof, which courts have described in various ways, is equivalent to the preponderance of the evidence test, which means that the claimant must show it is "more probable than not" that the employment caused the injury.[25] Expert testimony is allowed at the hearing, though in at least some jurisdictions the expert is (and in our opinion should be) barred from testifying on the ultimate issue as to the percentage of loss of earning power suffered by the claimant.[26] The hearing officer determines questions of both law and fact and is often required to write out express findings of fact. Thus, the hearing officer determines whether an injury has occurred, its extent, and its compensability. Compensation can be for permanent total disability (paid out for the worker's life or for some large number of weeks, such as 500), permanent partial disability (often paid out as a percentage of total impairment), or temporary total or temporary partial disability (paid weekly for the duration of the disability).[27]

These findings, and any award given, are conclusive as to the parties' interests in the case, unless reversed on appeal. As noted, workers' compensation was designed to replace tort law in adjudicating work-related injuries, so as a general rule the employee cannot go to court under a tort theory in the hope of supplementing the compensation award. However, the administrative outcome may be appealed to a court if a party questions the manner in which the law has been applied to the particular case.

(b) Substantive Criteria for Compensation

Although workers' compensation laws vary in some respects, they all contain certain common features. Typically the worker—or in the case of death, the beneficiary[28]—must demonstrate (1) an injury or disability, (2) arising out of and in the course of employment, (3) which is "accidental," as that term has come to be used in workers' compensation laws.

(1) Injury or Disability

The first substantive criterion for compensation is the requirement that the worker show that he or she has suffered an injury or disability that affects earning power.[29] Because of the requirement that injury and earning power be related, certain types of injuries that might be compensable in tort have been held noncompensable under workers' compensation. Examples include facial disfigurement, loss of sexual potency, and pain and suffering.[30] Despite this substantive limitation, the types of injuries and disabilities found compensable are legion; they encompass nearly every other type of disability imaginable, including, as discussed later, various types of mental injury.[31]

(2) In the Course of Employment

Assuming a compensable injury is involved, the employee must also demonstrate that it arose "out of and in the course of employment." This criterion is generally considered to contain two separate ideas. The first, arising "out of" employment, involves determining the causal relationship between the employment and the injury—that is, whether the disability resulted from a risk faced by the employee as a condition of employment.[32] In the past, courts required a showing that the injury resulted from an increased risk that the worker, as distinct from the general public, faced as a result of employment.[33] Thus, a worker who contracted lung cancer because of coworkers' smoking might not recover, whereas a construction worker injured from falling off a building would. In many jurisdictions, however, this stance has since been modified to permit recovery for injury resulting from any risk of employment, even if it is a common risk to the public as well.[34] Adopting an even broader interpretation, a growing number of courts have endorsed the "positional risk" test. Under this test, an injury is compensable if it occurred because the conditions or obligations of the employment placed the claimant in the position in which the injury occurred.[35] The effect of this modification has been to make more types of injuries compensable; it means, according to one commentator, that "the only connection of the employment with the injury is that its obligations placed the employee in the particular place at the particular time."[36]

The second causal requirement—that the injury arise "in the course of employment"—focuses on whether the injury occurred within the period of employment, at the place of employment, and where the employee might reasonably be expected to be while fulfilling duties associated with employment.[37] In jurisdictions that adopt the positional-risk approach, this determination may often be congruent with the arising-out-of inquiry.

A difficult issue connected with determining causation in workers' compensation cases is the relevance of a preexisting condition [see, e.g., the Cates report, § 19.08]. As a general rule, employers are said to take employees as they find them; a history of either physical or mental problems or a preexisting sensitivity to them will not in itself result in a denial of compensation.[38] Thus, if a workplace injury aggravates or accelerates the existing disease or infirmity, compensation is due.[39] "Aggravation" of a disease might include situations in which cancer that existed prior to employment spread as a result of the employee's work.[40] Examples of "acceleration" include failure of an already weak heart due to work-related excitement or exertion and the "lighting up" of tuberculosis because of exposure.[41] However, if injury was not caused, aggravated, or accelerated by the workplace, but existed or worsened independently of work, the claimant is not entitled to compensation.

(3) Injury Arising "by Accident"

The cause of the injury must usually be "accidental"—that is, an unanticipated event that occurs at the work site. However, "nonaccidents" in the lay sense may also be compensable. For example, if a worker who is routinely expected to lift heavy objects in the course of employment one day collapses during the course of these exertions, the result of the job performance is unexpected (or "accidental"), and therefore the injury is compensable.[42] In short, in most instances, either an event that accidentally causes injury or an accidental result of normal job performance will satisfy the test.

Although "usual exertion" with an unexpected result generally suffices for compensability, courts have been reluctant to apply this principle when heart disease is involved. Rather, a number of courts have required "unusual exertion" before awarding compensation.[43] This type of holding flows from a concern alluded to in the discussion about causation—the difficulty in proving that deaths resulting from heart failure actually arise out of employment.[44] It is noted here because it is similar to limits courts have placed on recovery for mental injuries, again because of concern over difficulties in proving etiology and causation.

(c) Mental Injury

In the early days of workers' compensation, compensation for mental injury was much more difficult to obtain than compensation for physical injury. This reluctance stemmed from a number of concerns. Courts rejecting such claims often relied on findings that the mental disorder could not have been caused by an "accident," or that the mental disorder was not an "injury" within the statutory meaning. But, at bottom, the hostility to compensation for mental injury reflected inherent distrust of such claims, including a fear of ma-

lingering,[45] and concern over the problem of objectively linking employment with mental injuries whose etiology is uncertain or unknown.[46]

In more recent times several states have been more generous in compensating mental injury.[47] One commentator has noted that workers' compensation cases today involve mental disorders of "almost every conceivable kind of neurotic, psychotic, depressive, or hysterical symptom, functional overlay, or personality disorder."[48] Nonetheless, the success of a modern mental injury claim is still relatively tenuous, depending on its character. Most commentators divide such claims into three categories: physical trauma causing mental injury, mental stimulus causing physical injury, and mental stimulus causing mental injury.[49] Although the first two categories are usually compensable, the latter category continues to be greeted with relative hostility.

(1) Physical Trauma Causing Mental Injury

In a situation in which a physical stimulus or trauma either causes a mental injury or causes a physical injury resulting in a mental disorder, the mental injury is usually compensable.[50] In such cases, the courts have little difficulty with the causation issue (i.e., the linking of employment with the injury); the usual reasoning is that "the existence of an objective, traumatic, work-connected physical impact or injury provides an intuitive guarantee that the mental disorder is genuine and that the employment genuinely caused it."[51] Although such an analysis may overstate the case in clinical terms (e.g., by ignoring the multiple causative factors that may underlay the now discernible mental disorder), the reliance on the presence of physical impact is not confined to workers' compensation. As will be seen, it is also the case in torts law.

There are myriad physical situations that have given rise to compensable mental injury. The following provide some idea of the variety: emotional trauma caused by rape at gunpoint; mental injury resulting from a pulled muscle sustained while swinging a sledgehammer; a "posttraumatic neurosis" resulting from an employee's fall from a scaffold; a "conversion reaction" caused when a 20-pound steel weight struck an employee; a neurosis that developed without any discernible physical cause, but that arose after several work-related accidents; a mental disorder resulting nine years after a work-related amputation of an arm; traumatic neurosis that developed from the loss of an employee's eye, suffered while removing the cap of a fire extinguisher; and a "fear complex" that prevented an employee from working after suffering severe finger fractures from operation of a power press.[52]

(2)　Mental Stimulus Causing Physical Injury

Just as mental injury caused by physical trauma is usually compensable, *physical* injury as a result of a *mental* stimulus is generally compensable as well,[53] whether the mental stimulus is sudden (e.g., extreme fright resulting in physical injury) or more protracted. For example, heart failure resulting from a long period of emotional strain arising out of work will often be compensable. Courts have also upheld awards for a claims adjuster who suffered angina pectoris due to exhaustion, a negotiator who after 65 days of work-related tension suffered a stroke and paralysis, an insurance administrator who had a cerebral thrombosis as a result of job pressures, an employee who suffered a heart attack after becoming emotionally upset over office clerical errors, and an employee who suffered a stroke while arguing over the amount of his paycheck.[54] Perhaps some of the symptoms experienced by Ms. Friend in Case Study 12.1 would fall in this category as well; however, most would probably fall in the third and final category of injury, discussed below.

(3)　Mental Stimulus Causing Mental Injury

The most controversial of the three categories is the last, in which a claimant seeks compensation for a mental injury caused by mental stimulus. Courts initially resisted compensating injuries that fell into this category because there was no "physical" evidence (i.e., a definable event or observable bodily changes). As medical science convinced the courts that physical indicia were not necessary to ensure the genuineness of a mental injury claim, that view has changed,[55] with the result that today a "distinct majority" of American jurisdictions find such injuries compensable.[56]

However, in many American jurisdictions, as well as in Canada,[57] recovery for "mental–mental" injury is limited in ways that recovery for physically related injury is not.[58]

For instance, some states limit compensation to a sudden stimulus (e.g., fright or shock)—a limitation much like the "physical" limitation formerly imposed by courts uncertain of the genuineness of injuries without a physical etiology.[59] While this limitation has existed in some states for years, in others it is relatively new. For example, in 1989, the Louisiana Supreme Court ruled that a claimant could recover for mental injury suffered after a period of harassment by other employees.[60] Two years later the Louisiana legislature amended the workers' compensation statute to permit recover for mental injury only if it "was the result of a sudden, unexpected, or extraordinary stress related to the employment and is demonstrated by clear and convincing evidence."[61]

Although most other jurisdictions allow compensation for mental injuries arising from "gradual" stress, they typically impose a requirement that the stimulus complained of "exceeds in intensity the emotional strain and tension normally encountered by employees on a daily basis."[62] In other words, the stress or strain that culminates in the mental injury cannot simply be the routine stress associated with the job. One court put the matter succinctly when, in rejecting a claim resulting from "a tremendous amount of pressures and tensions," it observed that the concept of a compensable injury "still does not embrace every stress or strain of daily living or every undesirable experience" presented by employment.[63]

A final tack used to limit compensability of mental injury claims, whether arising from mental or physical causes, is to require more "causation" than in other types of cases. For instance, California provides that compensation for mental injury is available only if the employee demonstrates that "actual events of employment were predominant as to all causes combined of the psychiatric injury." Further, when the injury results from being a victim of a violent act or from witnessing one, the event must be responsible for "at least 35 to 40 percent of the causation from all causes combined."[64]

To some extent, these various limitations reflect a distrust of such claims.[65] But they also stem from concern about financial resources. By the early 1990s, the costs of workers' compensation had escalated dramatically, at a rate 50% greater than the inflation in total health care spending during the 1980s; in absolute terms, the total cost of the system was $70 billion in 1992, a tripling in costs since 1982.[66] Commentators cited three reasons for this escalation: the rising cost of medical care,[67] the increased litigiousness associated with the workers' compensation system,[68] and, most important for present purposes, the expanding definition of "compensable injury," particularly with respect to job-related stress and emotional or mental injury.[69] In California, for instance, claims of mental injury without a physical injury rose from 1178 claims in 1978 to more than 9,000 claims in 1988. Nationally, the percentage of claims for stress or mental injury doubled between 1980 and 1988.[70]

These trends may have since reversed[71]; in any event, mental injury claims appear to have been unfairly singled out as a major source of problems in the workers' compensation system.[72] Nonetheless, *concern* over such claims clearly increased in the late 1980s and early 1990s. Thus, among the many reforms proposed or adopted in the workers' compensation area,[73] redefining the compensability of mental injury is likely to rank high in priority. As Pryor has stated, such limitations will probably continue to be imposed on the theory that "employees should bear the risk and loss of ordinary nonphysical features of the worksite."[74]

(4)   Preexisting Mental Disorder

A difficult issue which can arise in all three of the categories discussed above is the extent to which the mental injury preceded the work-related incident or stress. As noted earlier, the core question is whether the employment "aggravated" or "accelerated" the course or severity of the preexisting disorder. If this inquiry is answered affirmatively, the employee may receive compensation even for mental injury.[75] Note, however, that the presence of a preexisting disorder will make proof of a casual connection between the employment and the mental injury more difficult, given the somewhat ephemeral quality of the concepts of acceleration and aggravation. The implications

of this point for mental health professionals performing evaluations of mental injury are discussed further later in this chapter [see §§ 12.04, 12.05(d)].

12.03.   The Tort of Emotional Distress

Like the workers' compensation system, the tort system is designed to provide monetary compensation for certain types of injuries. However, tort law differs from workers' compensation in several critical respects. First, in nearly all jurisdictions, workers' compensation depends on administrative decisionmaking whereas tort law relies on judicial proceedings. Second, the guidelines for compensability under workers' compensation are statutorily created by the legislature (though judicial interpretation is important), whereas tort law generally is developed by the courts (though legislatures increasingly have sought to address cost inflation, particularly in medical malpractice). Finally, the two systems differ in terms of objective. Workers' compensation is based on a fixed schedule and primarily seeks to redress impairment in earning capacity; only a few of the associated costs (medical care, nursing care, etc.) may be covered. In contrast, damages in tort law are set by a jury, subject only to review by the presiding judge for reasonableness in light of the facts, and seek to compensate *all* damages resulting from the tortious conduct, including ephemeral categories such as "pain and suffering," "loss of consortium," and mental anguish.

(a)   Substantive Criteria

As noted at the beginning of this chapter, the primary purpose of tort law is to provide compensation for private wrongs. Thus, a tort is not the same thing as a crime and does not normally contemplate an evil intent or motive.[76] Nor is it an action for breach of contract, which is based on violation of an explicit understanding about the duties between parties.[77] Conversely, an action that might be a "moral" wrong to most is not necessarily tortious conduct if the actor's conduct is "within the rules."[78] Thus, for instance, failure to save a drowning child will not be considered a tort unless one has an affirmative obligation to act, as would be true of parents of the child.

There are many separate torts for which one party may be held liable to another. Examples include assault, battery, false imprisonment, defamation, libel, slander, invasion of privacy, and malicious prosecution. Although the definitional criteria differ for individual torts, certain core concepts define whether an actionable wrong has been committed in each case: (1) the defendant must owe a "duty" to the plaintiff, which (2) the defendant "breaches" or violates, (3) thereby "proximately" causing (4) a type of injury that is recognized as compensable.[79]

(1) Duty

Prosser defines the first prong of a tort as "an obligation, to which the law will give recognition and effect, to conform to a particular standard of conduct toward another."[80] He acknowledges the vague quality of the concept, concluding that "no better statement can be made, that the courts will find a duty where, in general, reasonable men would recognize it and agree that it exists."[81]

"Duty" is probably best understood by considering certain principles that govern relationships between individuals. For example, an individual has a "duty" to refrain from going uninvited on the property of another; if the individual nevertheless does so, he or she may have violated that duty and may be subject to damages for the tort of trespass. A physician has a "duty" to treat patients according to accepted professional standards; a failure to perform this duty may result in a claim for damages based on the tort of malpractice. An individual has a "duty" to avoid engaging in uninvited physical contact with another individual; to strike the other person violates the duty and may make the actor liable for the torts of assault and battery. And, to repeat an example given above, parents have a duty to prevent their children from dying if they can reasonably do so. Duties may be created by the legislature, by the courts, or by a jury ruling in a case in which neither legislative nor judicial guidelines exist.

(2) Breach of Duty

An individual may violate a duty either by act or by omission. To use the parent–child example again, an omission likely to lead to tort liability is a parent's failure to save a child. Another example more relevant to clinicians is a mental health professional's failure to take steps to protect a third party endangered by the clinician's patient, recognized as actionable in jurisdictions that follow *Tarasoff v. Board of Regents*[82] [discussed in § 4.04(b)].

Violation of a duty, whether by act or omission, may be intentional, negligent, or, in some cases, neither. An example of an intentional tort is the intentional infliction of emotional distress, discussed below. A second intentional tort is assault and battery. The central issue in intentional tort cases is whether the actor intended the *result* of the act, not the act itself.[83]

"Negligence," in contrast, does not describe a state of mind but, rather, is defined as "conduct which falls below the standard established by law for the protection of others against unreasonable risk of harm."[84] The standard against which the actor's conduct is measured is commonly known as the "reasonable person" standard. In other words, the question is, "Would a reasonable person have acted as did the defendant in similar circumstances?"[85] If the jury finds that a reasonable person would not have acted as the defendant did, the defendant will be found negligent.

Finally, in some cases liability will be imposed regardless of whether the defendant intended harm or acted reasonably. The best examples of this so-called strict liability come from product liability cases. For instance, a manufacturer of pharmaceuticals may be held liable merely on proof that it manufactured defective drugs and that the defect caused injuries. Imposition of strict liability represents a policy judgment that certain entities owe a heightened duty to society, as well as a practical judgment that proof of actual intent or negligence in such cases often would be difficult.

It should be clear from this brief discussion that distinguishing between duty on the one hand and its violation on the other is somewhat artificial. Both concepts aim at defining the type of conduct that society wishes to regulate when it causes foreseeable injury.

(3) Proximate Cause

Whether conduct is intentional, negligent, or governed by strict liability rules, it will not lead to liability unless it "proximately" causes injury. The concept of proximate cause is elusive. The traditional method of determining whether one event is the proximate cause of another is to ask whether one could "reasonably foresee" that the former would lead to the latter. The concept has also been defined as "the conduct or thing, which, in the ordinary unbroken sequence of events, without a new factor intervening, produces injury, and but for which that injury would not have occurred."[86] Thus, for example, if a driver strikes a child while speeding but the child was shoved into the driver's path at the last minute by a third party, the driver may not be the proximate cause of the child's injury. Slovenko calls proximate cause

> legal cause, a pragmatic view, and not . . . the "first cause" of philosophy or "field theory" of science. . . . As one judge put it, "What we do mean by the word proximate is that because of convenience, public policy, or a rough sense of justice, the law arbitrarily declines to trace a series of events beyond a certain point."[87]

The concept has also been characterized as "the near issue, not the remote one,"[88] and "the straw that broke the camel's back."[89] In short, tort law, like worker's compensation law, attempts to conceptualize causation as a series of events, with the most recent event or events being the only legally relevant one(s).

(4) Compensable Damages

Not every harm or injury proximately caused by violation of a duty is compensable. "Damages" or "injury" in the tort context means that there has been "an invasion of a legally protected interest."[90] In other words, even though the individual may feel harmed, that harm is not compensable unless the law defines it as sufficiently important or worthy of protection to hold the person caus-

ing the harm liable. For example, as discussed in more detail below, some jurisdictions do not provide compensation for emotional distress: Harm may have occurred, but it is not compensable because of a policy decision that broadening the scope of liability to include "bruised feelings" would make the conduct of daily life intolerable.

(b) Mental Injury

It has been claimed that "in every case of personal injury, there will be some accompanying mental damage."[91] The question addressed here is when the law of torts will compensate that damage (variously referred to as "psychic trauma," "emotional distress," or "emotional harm"). Traditionally, tort compensation was denied for mental injury unless it resulted from another, independently recognized, tort.[92] For example, if an individual was slandered and suffered emotional distress as a result, the harm was compensable because it was a consequence of an independent tort, that of slander. If an individual could not trace a mental injury to the tortious conduct of another, compensation was unavailable.

Recognition of emotional injury as an *independent* tort was slow in coming for a number of reasons: a fear of false claims, a concern that quantifying and proving emotional injury would be too difficult, a belief that emotional injury was "too removed" from the claimed source of an injury, and a fear that compensation would "open the floodgates" to litigation.[93] Those jurisdictions that did allow recovery for mental injury unassociated with another tort generally insisted that the plaintiff show physical as well as mental effects of the defendant's conduct,[94] just as a physical predicate was traditionally required in workers' compensation cases.

However, many jurisdictions have departed from this traditional view; according to one commentator, the trend "has been to give accelerated, increasing and extensive protection to feelings and emotions and to enlarge and redress reparation for psychic injuries."[95] The most concrete illustration of this trend is the recognition in the past several decades of the independent torts of intentional infliction of emotional distress and negligent infliction of emotional distress. While our discussion here is limited to these torts, the elements identified below are likely to be the focus of any tort case where mental injury is alleged.

(1)   Intentional Infliction of Emotional Distress

Recognition that an individual could engage in tortious conduct by attempting to cause emotional harm to another first came in 1948, in the Restatement of Torts. Today, at least 43 jurisdiction recognize the tort.[96] As described by one review of state law, the tort "provides that liability may be imposed where a wrongdoer's extreme and outrageous conduct, intended to inflict severe emotional distress in another, in fact proximately causes that result."[97] To prove a case, the plaintiff must show the following elements: (1) the defendant acted intentionally or recklessly, (2) the conduct was "extreme and outrageous," (3) the conduct caused the plaintiff's emotional distress, and (4) the emotional distress was severe.[98]

Note that the first element of the tort is met not only when an intention to produce emotional distress exists but also when the defendant is reckless with respect to that result.[99] Recklessness does not require a conscious purpose to produce harm but instead refers to a deliberate disregard of a high probability that harm will occur; thus, even if the harm was not intended, if the defendant foresaw it was likely, liability can attach.[100] If the defendant knows that the plaintiff is particularly susceptible to emotional distress, the requisite intent or recklessness may be inferred.[101]

The requirement of "outrageousness" recognizes that not all intentional or reckless conduct resulting in distress is tortious. This element of the tort is sometimes described as an assessment of whether the defendant's conduct would greatly offend the community's sense of decency.[102] A wide variety of conduct has been labeled "extreme and outrageous" in past cases.[103] For example, although the courts have been reluctant to impose liability for harm caused by an individual's words—in part because of concern for the constitutional right of free speech[104]—numerous exceptions to this rule have been recognized.[105] Thus, a majority of jurisdictions hold racial or re-

ligious epithets actionable if they result in emotional harm.[106] In addition, innkeepers, common carriers, and others in a business relationship with an individual may be subjected to liability for insulting or abusive language.[107]

The third requirement is the familiar one that the conduct must have been the "proximate cause" of the injury, a requirement discussed in more detail below [see § 12.04]. Finally, the fourth requirement for the tort bars compensation unless the injury is severe. In attempting to provide content to this concept, one authority suggests that the distress must be extremely severe:

> Complete emotional tranquility is seldom attainable in this world, and some degree of transient and trivial emotional distress is a part of the price of living among people. The law intervenes only where the distress inflicted is so severe that no reasonable man could be expected to endure it. The intensity and duration of the distress are factors to be considered in determining its severity.[108]

Compensation may result if the plaintiff suffers fright, grief, humiliation or shame, embarrassment, anger, chagrin, worry, or disappointment,[109] but only if it is demonstrated by substantial evidence and is significant in nature.

(2)   Negligent Infliction of Emotional Distress

The courts have been even more reluctant to impose liability when mental injury was caused by the simple negligence of another party. However, nearly one-third of jurisdictions today recognize a tort of negligent infliction of mental or emotional distress.[110] The elements of this tort are the traditional ones necessary to establish an action for negligence: that is, a duty on the part of the defendant to protect the plaintiff from injury, violation of which proximately causes compensable injury.[111]

The tort arises most frequently in two types of situations: bystander recovery cases and product liability cases. As an illustration of the former type of case, a mother who sees her child struck and killed by a negligently driven automobile and suffers distress as a result may be able to recover under the tort of negligent infliction of emotional distress, even though she was a bystander to the central action. In most states, the plaintiff/bystander and the victim must be related and the bystander must be within the "zone of danger" created by the defendant.[112] In a few states, however, the plaintiff need not even see the injury (e.g., as when the mother comes upon the injured child minutes after the accident),[113] and in others the bystander need not be related.[114] In every state the distress must be severe, and generally must be manifested by objective symptomatology (e.g., vomiting, loss of sleep, or nervousness).[115] Consider the relevance of these various approaches to Case Study 12.1.

Courts have also shown increased willingness to compensate individuals who suffer emotional distress as a result of manufacturers' negligence. For example, a baby food manufacturer was liable to a mother for emotional distress suffered as a result of seeing her son gag and choke on foreign material contained in his food.[116] In another case,[117] an auto manufacturer was liable for the emotional distress a couple felt watching their children thrown out of the defective rear door of their van after it was struck by another car.[118]

(c)   The Predisposed Plaintiff

With respect to plaintiffs who are predisposed to mental injury, the rule applied in torts cases is the same as that found in workers' compensation cases. A plaintiff's preexisting condition or susceptibility does not per se bar compensation. However, if the emotional distress would have resulted without the defendant's intervening act, the defendant should prevail.[119] The subtle nature of this inquiry is discussed next.

12.04.   Causation in Mental Injury Cases: A Paradigm Clash?

Although the terminology may be different in workers' compensation cases, both workers' compensation and tort law refuse to hold a defendant liable unless the defendant "proximately caused" the victim's injury. As noted earlier, for practical reasons, the concept of proximate cause

has come to mean "recent" cause—"the straw that broke the camel's back." Events further back in the causal chain are considered irrelevant.

Several commentators have recognized the divergence between this legal definition of causation and the behavioral sciences' view of the concept. As Blinder states:

> Speaking medically, the true cause of the . . . illness lies within [the claimant's] personality structure—who he was at the time of the injury rather than what happened to him. This deviant personality was not less immediate—no less proximate as it were—than the physical injury (leading to the injury).[120]

Sheeley puts the matter slightly differently:

> The syllogism, "The patient had no pain and he was working before the industrial incident; he now has pain and is not working: ergo, the industrial incident produced the psychiatric disorder or at least aggravated it," may be false. The danger of such conceptual error is magnified by the patient's characteristically denying evidence of a pre-existing disorder and by his exaggerating current symptoms that he ascribes to the industrial incident and that may themselves be suggested by the very psychiatric procedure itself.[121]

Similarly, Marcus asserts that the issue of causation is "exceedingly complex" but is in large part a "chicken or the egg" question that "cannot be determined with any degree of 'reasonable medical probability.'"[122] In short, the concept of proximate cause may not make sense in a deterministic paradigm [see § 1.03(a)].

For these reasons, in addressing the causation issue (in, for instance, the situation presented by Case Study 12.1), the clinician should merely indicate whether the legally relevant incident (the employment injury or the negligent act by the defendant) appears to have played a role in the claimant's current mental injury; other contributing factors should also be identified. Pronouncements to the effect that the work-related event or the tort "caused" the claimants' mental state, or is the sole, "predominant" or primary cause of it, should generally be avoided, as should attempts to quantify the degree to which an incident caused the injury, statutory provisions notwithstanding.

This approach best reflects the clinical view of causation and the extent of clinical knowledge.

It has another significant benefit as well. Perhaps because of the conceptual difficulty surrounding causation, in practice resolution of this issue has become "primarily the function of the subjective value judgments of the examining psychiatrist."[123] A more circumspect, less conclusory opinion by the clinician should deter any tendency on the part of the legal decisionmaker to abdicate responsibility for analyzing the causation issue and applying the relevant legal construct.

12.05. Clinical Evaluation of Mental Injury

The evaluation of mental injury is similar in workers' compensation and tort cases. Each type of evaluation requires an understanding of the context of the evaluation, extensive information gathering, and a determination of whether mental injury has in fact occurred. If mental injury is found, the evaluation also requires assessing whether the injury was work-related (in workers' compensation cases) or a result of action by the defendant (in a tort case); the causation investigation will inevitably involve the corollary question of whether there are any preexisting disorders. Finally, assuming that there is an injury and that it is connected with the defendant, the impact of the mental injury on the individual's ability to function at the time of the evaluation and in the foreseeable future must be examined. These facets of the evaluation are discussed below.

(a) Context of Evaluation

The first issue in any evaluation is whether the clinician is qualified to perform it [see § 4.05(a)]. In workers' compensation cases, many states require that physicians be involved; thus, the role of psychologists and other mental health professionals in such cases may vary depending on the state.[124] Although such restrictions generally do not apply in tort suits, one commentator has suggested that examinations of mental injury be conducted jointly by a psychiatrist and a psychologist, regardless of the relevant law on qualifications, because each brings skills that will be particularly useful in conducting the comprehensive inquiry that such evaluations require.[125] As we make clear elsewhere [see § 1.05], as a general rule we favor competency-based rather than degree-based criteria for identifying forensic examiners. In the context of mental injury exams, however, we concur that in many mental injury cases an examination drawing on both psychiatric and psychological skills is preferred. For example, as will become clear later, both neurological and psychological testing can be an important component of a mental injury examination.

Assuming one has the educational and experiential qualifications necessary, other ethical concerns should be considered. Davidson has observed that a psychiatrist who "does much medical–legal work soon acquires a personal philosophy with respect to psychoneuroses following injury." He asserts that many clinicians believe "either, (a) that most of these patients are motivated primarily by greed; or (b) that they have a genuine illness in which the money-motivation factor is of minor importance."[126] Before conducting an evaluation, a clinician should attempt to assess whether either of these descriptions fits his or her views and the effect they may have on the evaluation; if the effect would be substantial, the clinician should withdraw.

It should also be recognized that a clinician's posture relative to a case may affect the attitude of the claimant. Davidson has observed:

> In a sense, the opposing doctors are examining different patients. The plaintiff-selected physician starts off with a good rapport. He is the helping doctor. The claimant trusts him—but sees the defense physician as the enemy. The first physician gets the picture of a sincere, trusting, and friendly soul. The defense examiner sees a surly and suspicious one. These differences obviously affect the examination technique, as well as the credibility of the history and subjective symptoms.[127]

A related point is that participation in the legal process may exacerbate certain personal traits of the claimant. Bromberg notes that "emotional tensions stimulated by the legal process tend to support a suspicion of exaggeration, malingering, or excess interest in remuneration."[128] The clinician will have to sort out these myriad "causative" factors in forming a picture of the individual—a task discussed more fully below.

(b) Scope of Evaluation

An evaluation in a mental injury case has been likened to an inquiry into mental status at the time of the offense,[129] another retrospective inquiry fraught with difficulty [see § 8.06]. Yet the mental injury evaluation in some respects is even more difficult: Not only is a retrospective construction of the claimant's mental functioning necessary (to determine the extent, if any, to which past events "caused" the injury), but a prospective inquiry is also required. In workers' compensation cases, this latter inquiry involves assessing the effect the injury will have on the claimant's wage-earning capacity. In tort law, it is the effect on the claimant's continued ability to function as the "person he or she was" prior to the defendant's tortious conduct.

Because the issues are so broad, these evaluations require the clinician to come to know and to explain the claimant's life much more thoroughly than do most of the evaluations discussed elsewhere in this book. A complete history must be gathered, with emphasis not only on the events surrounding the alleged injury but also on the period before, extending into the past as far as the clinician deems relevant in understanding why the injury may have occurred. Since the issue of the claimant's predisposition to mental injury or possible preexistence of the mental injury is certain to be raised, particular attention must be paid to the gathering of clinical and medical histories, evidence of behavioral or emotional disorder that did not reach the stage of formal clinical interventions, and any other social history that might shed light on the claimant's condition. If the evaluation is being performed for a workers' compensation case, the clinician must also obtain in as much detail as possible a description of the claimant's employment, place of work, conditions of employment, and all other work-related information.

In addition to clinical interviews, other techniques may be useful. Psychological testing, particularly the personality inventories, may be more relevant here than in other forensic areas, especially if their results can be compared to tests taken before the legally relevant event [see § 12.05(d)].[130] It will also be important to investigate the extent of physical injury, if any, using neurological testing if necessary. The "total person" of the claimant will be considered when the claim for damages is adjudicated, and a clinical picture given without reference to other possible explanations for and consequences of the claimed injury will not only be less useful than it might otherwise be to the legal system but may expose the clinician to personal embarrassment. As one commentator has stated, for example, a clinician who testifies only to the emotional effects of trauma, while failing to address its effects upon physical functioning, "is asking to have his or her testimony impeached."[131]

Given the broad reach of a mental injury evaluation, some attempt to organize the inquiry is essential. A number of structured evaluation formats concerning mental injury exist, the most prominent of which is the American Medical Association's *Guides to the Evaluation of Permanent Impairment* (hereafter AMA *Guides*).[132] According to a 1990 survey, 36 states require by statute or by administrative policy that workers' compensation examiners use these guidelines.[133] Other states, while not adopting the AMA *Guides,* have endorsed similar criteria.[134] Although the AMA guidelines are meant for use in workers' compensation cases, they help provide a structure for any examination of mental injury, including one triggered by a tort lawsuit. The *Guides* are referred to throughout the following discussion.

(c) Ascertaining Mental Injury

The law requires some objective indicia of mental injury to make out a compensable claim. The touchstone for this inquiry generally is the *Diagnostic and Statistical Manual of Mental Disorders* (DSM). Some states (e.g., California) *require* the use of the DSM in determining whether a mental disorder exists. However, appellate courts in California have also reversed compensation awards that are based primarily on conclusory labels rather than on more detailed data.[135] It is important to remember that diagnosis and mental injury are not necessarily synonymous. As one observer notes, a diagnosis indicates that a mental disorder exists but does not always clarify the degree of dys- function.[136] In evaluating mental injuries, establishing the former is useful, but it is the latter that is most critical. The AMA *Guides* make the same point.[137] Modeled explicitly on the Social Security Administration rules for determining disability [see § 13.04(c)], these guidelines emphasize two issues: (1) Does the individual suffer from an impairment (the mental injury)? and (2) What is the impact of that impairment upon the areas of functioning relevant in the particular case?[138]

Nonetheless, there are several typical "conditions" that the clinician might rule in or out in determining whether injury exists and what its significance may be. These are explored in some detail below.

(1) Traumatic Neurosis / Posttraumatic Stress

The constellation of mental effects most frequently reported in workers' compensation or emotional distress cases is usually termed "traumatic neurosis," although it has been called by a variety of other names as well.[139] The concept posits a reaction to some "trauma," but beyond this no clear definition seems to exist. Keiser has admitted, "The traumatic neurosis can take many forms, including all of the known psychiatric illnesses."[140] Perhaps partly because of the lack of definitional clarity, he states, the "concept of a nervous reaction of some kind after trauma remains suspect in many quarters."[141]

The "trauma"-based diagnosis most likely to be involved in mental injury cases is posttraumatic stress disorder (PTSD). PTSD is almost "made to order" for personal injury and worker compensation plaintiffs because the diagnostic criteria explicitly include an etiological stressor[142]; PTSD is defined in DSM-IV as

> the development of characteristic symptoms following exposure to an extreme traumatic stressor involving direct personal experience of

an event that involves actual or threatened death or serious injury, or other threat to one's physical integrity; or witnessing an event that involves death, injury, or a threat to the physical integrity of another person; or learning about unexpected or violent death, serious harm, or threat of death or injury experienced by a family member or other close associate.[143]

Previous editions of the DSM required that the traumatic event be one that is ". . . generally outside the realm of human experience."[144] With the removal of this limiting criterion in DSM-IV, it is reasonable to expect that the prevalence of this diagnosis, and its use in litigation, will increase.

Still, the requirement that the event be one that involves death, serious injury, or a threat to physical integrity, or the witnessing of same, does limit the applicability of this diagnosis in mental injury cases. While a relationship between stress and psychopathology has been documented in studies of released prisoners of war,[145] concentration camp survivors,[146] victims of stressful crimes,[147] and a wide range of natural and civil disasters,[148] research focusing on more mundane stressors is less impressive. Thus, the PTSD diagnosis may be difficult to establish in some workers' compensation cases when the claimed stressor is, say, a tedious job that gradually affects the individual over time.[149]

As discussed in detail in § 8.04(e) (dealing with PTSD in connection with evaluations of mental state at time of offense), there are a number of other reasons to be cautious about concluding that a person has incurred sustained or permanent emotional injury after exposure to stressful situations. First, many of the studies concerning PTSD have been anecdotal case reports of individuals or groups experiencing trauma[150]; rarely have investigators concerned themselves with the presence of preexisting symptoms or the need for a group of control subjects in documenting the psychological responses that characterize the disorder. Second, research indicates that when evaluations are made retrospectively (which is always the case in workers' comp and emotional injury cases), estimates of pathology are inflated (compared to prospective studies or studies using nondisaster control groups).[151] Third, despite its presence in DSM-IV, controversy continues regarding the validity of the PTSD diagnosis; persons who meet PTSD criteria often meet criteria for other diagnoses as well,[152] and the high correlation of PTSD with general measures of psychopathology ($r = .50–.60$) suggest that general psychological stress, not a tight set of symptoms, define the response to traumatic events.[153] Finally, many studies of disaster victims reveal that few or no symptoms remain after a few months time has passed.[154]

As PTSD has increased in popularity, special instruments for diagnosing it have been developed.[155] Clinicians may want to familiarize themselves with these measures and consider their use in diagnostic evaluations. Alternatively, Wilkinson has developed a checklist, a generalized version of which is presented here, that may serve as a convenient inventory for the clinician conducting an examination regarding stress-related disturbance.[156]

- Repeated recollections of the incident
- Sadness
- Fatigue
- Recurrent feelings, usually anxiety and depression
- Sleep disturbance
- Loss of appetite
- Loss of enthusiasm
- Ease of startle
- Difficulty concentrating
- Guilt
- Avoidance of situations that cause recollection of the incident
- Reminders of the incident leading to worse feelings
- Inability to feel deeply about anything
- Anger
- Loss of interest (in general activities)
- Feelings of detachment
- Memory difficulties
- Psychosomatic complaints
- Diminished sexual interest

All these symptoms need not be present; the existence of one or more may be compensable if the requisite "causation" element is met and if wage-earning capacity is affected (workers' compensation) or the jury finds that damages should be awarded (torts). The legal system seems both accustomed to and curious about the "traumatic neurosis." Despite its amorphous nature, it is reported that "more lawyers and physicians attend programs on the legal aspects of traumatic neurosis than on the subject of sex."[157]

(2) Other Conditions

Although "traumatic neurosis" is the most commonly observed mental injury, many other "disorders" have led to compensation. One example of such a disorder is "post-physical-injury trauma,"[158] which involves a change in the injured person's "body image" or self-perception in the aftermath of physical injury.[159] This phenomenon is particularly prevalent (at least in the eyes of plaintiffs' lawyers) when the person has suffered disfigurement or trauma to the head and spinal cord.[160]

Other compensable conditions the clinician may encounter include grief or sorrow.[161] These conditions will of course be particularly likely in cases involving death of a loved one or in cases asserting intentional or negligent infliction of emotional distress, where the survivors may claim damages for "sorrow, mental anguish and solace which may include society, companionship, comfort, guidance, kindly offices, and advice of the decedent."[162] In addition, the claimant may present evidence of the symptoms and sequelae of concussion and postconcussion syndrome,[163] various neurotic reactions to spinal injuries,[164] and (on occasion) psychosis following trauma,[165] as well as posttraumatic epilepsy[166] and deficits in intellectual functioning.[167]

Finally, given the broad nature of the compensability of mental injury and the fact that the constellation of symptoms for which the claimant seeks relief normally need not fit into formal diagnostic nomenclature, the clinician may be asked to evaluate the existence or impact of a host of vaguely defined "symptoms," such as irritability and headache. These may not readily lend themselves to diagnostic labels, but compensation may nonetheless be sought.

(3) Malingering

Most if not all of the previously described conditions can be "faked" or exaggerated. It is nearly certain that a clinician performing a mental injury evaluation will be asked whether the claimant is malingering. Bromberg defines *malingering* as "an assumed state which feigns illness but may be built on an historical event preceding it, i.e., an actual injury."[168] In his view, it is synonymous with *simulation,* which he defines as "an assumed state of pain and disability, an imitation of illness without any etiological or organic basis."[169] The clinician may also confront *exaggeration,* which is defined as a "magnification of pain and disability"; *overevaluation,* an "individual reaction to pain which may appear feigned but is not"; *functional overlay,* an "emotional superimposition on the original symptoms of an injury or illness"; and *hysteria,* "a physical representation of an emotional conflict."[170]

None of these latter reactions is automatically noncompensable. However, the label that is ultimately attached to the individual (i.e., simulator vs. exaggerator vs. credible victim) will have an impact on whether an award is made and, if so, its amount. For this reason, the clinician should seek to describe the etiology of the alleged injury, backing up each inference with behavioral observations, and let the factfinder decide whether it merits compensation. Some techniques for detecting malingering have been discussed elsewhere in this book [see § 3.07]. In this specific context, probably the best single device is corroboration through third-party information of the symptoms reported by the plaintiff.

(d)   Assessing the Relationship between Injury and Event

Of course, the mere fact of mental injury will not lead to liability. The defendant/workplace must have proximately caused the injury. The conceptual problems attending this issue have been discussed in § 12.04. Here we attempt to provide some techniques that will help in assessing and reporting this difficult aspect of mental injury cases.

To begin with, the clinician should be familiar with the literature on the relationship between particular life events (e.g., an accident) and both precedent and subsequent psychological adjustment. Some studies have suggested that psychological maladjustment can *lead* to accidents.[171]

Numerous other studies have demonstrated a positive relationship between life change *other* than accidents and later psychiatric illness.[172]

In addition, several structured questionnaires have been developed to help assess the frequency and/or impact of life changes. The most comprehensive questionnaire is the Life Events Scale,[173] which contains 102 items inquiring about change in 11 different areas: School, Work, Love and Marriage, Having Children, Family, Residence, Crime and Legal Matters, Finances, Social Activities, Health, and Miscellaneous.[174] A life change questionnaire may be useful in discovering events or changes that may have contributed to psychological distress or decompensation in the client (e.g., loss of a spouse, change in job performance ratings, change in attendance at church, and social activities). Typically, the clinician specifies a particular time frame (e.g., six weeks or six months) prior to the incident and has the individual (as well as, ideally, a close friend or family member) complete the survey regarding changes that occurred during that preincident period. In this manner, the clinician can pinpoint areas of further inquiry and try to establish some "baseline" data regarding the client's prior condition against which to compare the posttrauma presentation [see, e.g., Cates report, § 19.08].

The creative examiner may also make use of other measures of preincident adjustment when available. Pre- and postincident psychological testing could be particularly useful, as might be other relevant records from medical, military, and education sources. The more objectively and systematically the clinician can document change before and after the legally relevant incident, the more complete and compelling will be the clinical formulation regarding the relative contributions of various factors to the client's distress.

Once these data have been accumulated, the clinician may find useful the following analytical structure proposed by Ebaugh and Benjamin, designed to help sort out alternative conclusions on causation:

> 1. The trauma (or event or accident) was the sole cause of the psychoneurosis (or mental injury). This would be the case when there were neither manifest or latent signs of mental disorder before the trauma; when the mental injury,

in the clinician's best opinion, would not have occurred now or later, had there been no trauma. These criteria can be met only in head injury cases, and not in many of them.

2. The trauma was a major precipitating factor. For example, this would be the case in head injuries where the emotional disorder was present in latent or potential form, but where it is reasonable to suppose that, but for the accident, the symptoms would not have occurred at this time.

3. The trauma was an aggravating factor. In these cases, some emotional disorder was clinically manifest prior to the trauma, but the cause of the condition was materially affected by the injury.

4. The trauma was a minor factor. In these cases, the emotional disorder was well-developed before the trauma, but the psychologic or mechanical effects of the claimed precipitating event contributed somewhat to the intensity of the present symptoms.

5. The trauma is unrelated to the emotional disorder.[175]

Another commentator, who served as the presiding judge for the Los Angeles Workers' Compensation Appeals Board, has opined that there are three principal causation issues in workers' compensation cases: (1) whether the industrial stress contributed substantially to the mental injury or whether other, non-work-related events were the precipitating factors; (2) whether the mental disorder is the type for which the particular industrial stress could be the precipitating event; and (3) whether there was a preexisting disability.[176]

Whatever analytical structure the clinician adopts on the issue of causation, it is important to remember, as noted in § 12.04, that the factfinder decides where, if anywhere, along the spectrum of causation "proximate cause" is found. The clinician's job is to report the data and distinguish between speculation and behavioral observation. As Ebaugh and Benjamin point out, the conclusion that a given incident is the sole or primary cause of emotional injury should be rare.

(e) Ascertaining Effects of Mental Injury

The core of the inquiry in a mental injury case is the functional impact of the injury. In workers' compensation cases, where the examination is increasingly structured by statute or state policy, the AMA *Guides* or alternative sources provide detailed guidelines on this issue. The AMA *Guides* adopt the format utilized by the Social Security Administration in disability determinations,[177] which focuses on activities of daily living; social functioning; concentration, persistence, and pace; and ability to adapt to stressful circumstances in work or work-like settings [for further discussion of these capacities, see § 13.04(a) on Social Security determinations]. A slightly different format is found in the California workers' compensation rules, which require that the examiner assess the impact of mental injury on eight areas of functioning: (1) the ability to comprehend and follow instructions; (2) the ability to perform simple and repetitive tasks, including the ability to manage concrete activities and to make decisions based on simple sensory data; (3) the ability to maintain work pace appropriate to workload, including the ability to perform activities on schedule, to be punctual, and to have regular attendance and to complete a regular workweek; (4) the ability to perform more complex and varied tasks (e.g., to analyze and synthesize material); (5) the ability to relate to other people beyond giving and receiving instructions (e.g., the ability of the examinee to interact with coworkers and peers); (6) the ability to influence people effectively and consistently; (7) the ability to make generalizations and decisions without immediate supervision (i.e., higher-order reasoning); and (8) the ability to accept and carry out responsibility for direction, control, and planning (i.e., skills relevant to supervision if the examinee is in a supervisory position).[178]

The techniques used in evaluating these functional capacities will vary. In connection with the California criteria, for instance, Enslow suggests that cognitive psychological testing (e.g., the WAIS) will be useful in evaluating the first function (the ability to comprehend and follow instructions) whereas a psychiatric assessment may be more helpful than cognitive testing in evaluating factors five through eight (the more complex functional skills of relating to people, etc.).[179]

In workers' compensation cases, the examiner will also usually be asked to rate the *degree* of impairment in each function. In some jurisdictions, the examiner may be asked to fix a percentage to the amount of deterioration (e.g., "the ability to comprehend has been impaired 50 percent by the mental injury"). In those jurisdictions following the AMA *Guides*, this type of conclusion is required only in cases involving physical injury, whereas cases involving mental and behavioral disorders involve rating the degree of impairment from class 1 (no impairment) through class 5 (extreme impairment). Regardless of the system used, an assessment of degree of impairment is necessarily arbitrary. Earlier versions of the AMA *Guides* seemed to deny this fact, claiming that "[i]f the protocols and tables have been followed, the clinical findings may be compared directly to the criteria and related as a percentage of impairment with confidence in the validity and acceptability of the determination."[180] Fortunately, the fourth edition of *Guides* is much more circumspect in this regard, stating that "[i]t should be understood that the *Guides* does not and cannot provide answers about every type and degree of impairment,"[181] and that "an impairment percentage is an informed estimate."[182]

In tort law, the examination will generally not be as structured, and the clinician may consider issues of broader impact, as all injury is potentially compensable (assuming that the other substantive criteria for tort liability are met). However, the clinician must still focus on ways in which the individual is "diminished" from the person he or she was prior to the trauma or accident. For example, the mere presence of increased irritability, depression, or constant headache will probably be insufficient to convince a jury that such problems substantially alter the individual's life from what it had been previously. Again, the AMA *Guides*, though focused on work-related injury, provide a point of reference for the examiner in tort cases because they stress linking the injury to the activities in which the claimant normally engages.

(f) Prognosis

The clinician not only must gather information relevant to whether the mental injury is severe at the present time but must attempt to predict its likely impact in the future and whether treatment might alleviate its debilitating effects. In tort cases this information is extremely relevant to the amount of damages the plaintiff will receive, assuming that liability is found. In workers' compensation cases, prognosis is important because it will be useful in determining the likely duration of the impairment caused by the injury. As the AMA *Guides* stress, a key component of this inquiry is the injured person's motivation to recover and participate in rehabilitation programs.

This kind of prognosis is similar to those clinicians often make in traditional practice. However, one problem area of specific concern in mental injury cases should be noted—the possibility of "secondary gain," or the unconscious desire for the "fringe benefits" from appearing disabled. As Blinder states:

> Though not causative (in that secondary gain arises as an issue following injury), such secondary gain factors as financial compensation, the solicitude of others, freedom from responsibility and/or restitution for real or imagined past exploitation may greatly prolong convalescence and prevent recovery.[183]

Another author concludes that "one of the peculiar aspects of 'treatment' and 'compensation' is that both these supposedly reparative procedures can themselves further complicate the problems they address."[184]

The extent of secondary gain behavior in mental injury cases is unclear. One author, after reviewing whether and when workers' compensation claimants recover sufficiently to return to work, was only able to state that "almost any conclusion drawn from a group of industrially-injured patients is valid for some and invalid for others."[185] If behavior related to secondary gain appears to be present, this fact should be communicated to the factfinder, which is ultimately responsible for judging its impact on any award.

The evaluator should also be aware that early intervention and attentive case management may curtail secondary-gain behavior.[186] The evaluator's report might not only address the types of issues discussed above, but also make recommendations as to the timing and type of treatment that would most effectively deal with the claimant's mental problems.

12.06. Conclusion: Reports and Testimony

Detailed guidelines for writing reports and testifying are found in Chapter 18 of this book; other sources also provide helpful hints on these topics.[187] As a way of summing up the various aspects of the clinical evaluation of mental injury, however, three general points about communicating with the court system are made here, based in large part of principles found in the AMA *Guides.*

First, the clinician should avoid overreliance on diagnosis. The inquiry in workers' compensation and tort cases seeks ultimately to explain why a particular individual reacted in a particular way to a particular event or series of events. A diagnostic label may provide an organizing principle for the constellation of symptoms demonstrated by the claimant but does not provide sufficient information as to how the claimant has been affected. If a diagnosis is given, its relative lack of importance to the questions posed by the legal system should be noted explicitly, or implicitly, through a more detailed narrative in which the clinician provides the substantive bases for his or her opinion.

Second, a complete assessment of mental injury requires a longitudinal history of the impairment, its treatment, and attempts at rehabilitation, including the claimant's motivation to recover. Reports and testimony must canvass the period before and after the legally relevant incident, as well as predict the future, relying on multiple sources of information. It bears repeating in this regard that the clinician must be sensitive to the causation issue. He or she should note the presence of any preexisting condition or predisposition and explain why it may or may not be relevant to the claimant's current condition. The clinician should also make clear that he or she is describing causation from a clinical point of view, and that, from that perspective, multiple causation is the rule rather than the exception.

Third, consonant with the first two points, conclusory information should be avoided. Because of the amorphous nature of concepts such as mental injury, causation, and degree of impairment, clinicians bear a special responsibility to provide descriptive reports and testimony in these cases. On a systemic level, the failure to ex-ercise this responsibility may have had significant consequences. Although written in 1979—before some of the aforementioned retrenchment in the workers' compensation system had taken place—these words from Blinder assessing the legal system's treatment of mental injury cases are still worth considering:

> There is probably never a physical injury without some measurable psychic trauma or functional overlay. The past 30 years, and particularly the last decade, however, have seen the exploitation of this truism in workers' compensation and personal injury litigation coupled with ever broader interpretations of the concepts of proximate cause, predisposition, work-connection, and secondary gain, resulting in a staggering number of physically fit, mentally competent individuals forever being relieved of responsibility for earning a living—on psychiatric grounds. The medicolegal system as it is presently construed not only drains away funds necessary for the sustenance of those truly disabled but may foster or even increase disability where one otherwise would not have occurred . . . resulting in intolerable financial burdens for compensation funds, employers and carriers alike, substantially higher costs to the consumer, and ultimately, loss of coverage.[188]

This view is not universally shared, of course, and expansion of recovery for serious mental injury is probably, on the whole, a good thing.[189] But to the extent Blinder's critique is a response to the fact that legal decisionmakers have often accepted, at face value, conclusory statements by mental health professionals about causation and degree of impairment, we agree with it. Both the legal system and mental health professionals have more than occasionally forgotten that the clinician should be a disseminator of information, not benefits.

Bibliography

American Medical Association, *Guides to the Evaluation of Permanent Impairment* (4th ed. rev. 1993).

Marc Antonetti, *Labor Law: Workers' Compensation Statutes and the Recovery of Emotional Distress Damages in the Absence of Physical Injury,* 1990 ANNUAL SURVEY OF AMERICAN LAW 671 (1990).

Martin Blinder, *The Abuse of Psychiatric Disability Determinations,* 1979 MEDICAL TRIAL TECHNIQUES QUARTERLY 84 (1979).

Lawrence Joseph, *The Causation Issue in Workers' Compensation Mental Disability Cases: An Analysis, Solutions, and Perspective,* 36 VANDERBILT LAW REVIEW 263 (1983).

LARSON'S WORKMEN'S COMPENSATION LAW (rev. ed. by Matthew Bender 1993).

Eric H. Marcus, *Causation in Psychiatry: Realities and Speculations,* 1983 MEDICAL TRIAL TECHNIQUES QUARTERLY 424 (1983).

MARILYN MINZER, JEROME H. NATES, CLARK D. KIMBALL, DIANA T. AXELROD, & RICHARD P. GOLDSTEIN, 1 DAMAGES IN TORT ACTIONS (1991).

JEFFREY O'CONNELL & R. HENDERSON, TORT LAW: NO-FAULT AND BEYOND (1975).

Willis J. Spaulding, *A Look at the AMA Guides to the Evaluation of Permanent Impairment: Problems in Workers' Compensation Claims Involving Mental Disability,* 8 BEHAVIORAL SCIENCE & THE LAW 361 (1990).

CHAPTER THIRTEEN

Federal Antidiscrimination and Entitlement Laws

13.01. Introduction

Although state law governs most areas of forensic practice, certain provisions of federal law may also call for significant clinical participation in at least three areas. First, several federal civil rights statutes (most prominently, the Americans with Disabilities Act of 1990 and the Fair Housing Amendments Act of 1988) make discrimination against an individual with a mental disability illegal in a number of contexts, such as employment and housing. Under these statutes, testimony from a mental health professional may be needed to determine whether a mental disability exists and, if so, whether employers or housing authorities have made reasonable efforts to accommodate the disability. Second, Congress has enacted entitlement statutes (e.g., the Social Security Act) designed to ensure minimum levels of financial support for individuals with a disability. Here clinical input is also important because entitlement to financial assistance turns on whether an individual has a serious disability and the extent to which that disability affects the ability to work. Third, the federal Individuals with Disabilities Education Act requires handicapped children to be given a free appropriate education in the public school environment whenever possible, a goal that also encourages expert evidence concerning

the nature of disability, as well as information about the best way to ameliorate it.

This chapter discusses the first two types of statute (the Education Act is discussed in Chapter 17, in connection with children's issues). At the outset, it is important to note a number of differences between evaluations performed under these statutes and most other types of forensic evaluations. First, although court adjudication is available, these statutes generally are enforced initially through administrative proceedings. As discussed in § 2.04(c) and elaborated on in this chapter, these proceedings differ in important respects from the court process that triggers nearly every other type of evaluation discussed in this book. Second, the evaluation issues that arise under these federal statutes are usually spelled out explicitly in statute or regulation; for example, examinations performed pursuant to the Social Security Act must address specific issues delineated in federal law. Therefore, the clinician engaged in such work must be aware of considerably more "law" than in many other forensic contexts, where awareness of one or two general notions may provide adequate substantive knowledge. Third, many of the examinations performed under these statutes will require specialized clinical knowledge which may (or at least should) make examiners without such knowledge hesitant to accept a referral. For example, in conducting examinations under the Americans with Disabilities Act, determining possible "accommodations" for a person with a mental disability may be difficult without some grasp of industrial occupational psychology or at least an appreciation of the particular employment situation at issue.

The first section of this chapter examines the Americans with Disabilities Act, the second looks at the Fair Housing Act, and the third describes Social Security statutes and regulations. Each section discusses the pertinent statutory and regulatory base, the forensic issues that may arise under each statute, research that may be relevant to the examination, and the examination process itself. Because the Americans with Disabilities Act and the Fair Housing Act are more recent statutes than the Social Security laws, the role of the forensic examiner under the former statutes is only beginning to emerge; discussion of that role is thus less complete than treatment of the examiner's role under entitlement law.

CASE STUDY 13.1

Fred Phantom is a 32-year-old individual who works for Better Plastics. His job is to test new forms of plastic that the company's engineers develop; if he performs these tests incompetently, products made with the plastic might shatter or melt when they are not supposed to. He has recently been transferred to the night shift. He has been treated in a private hospital in the past for schizophrenia and still takes psychotropic medication in low dosages. He has a good work history but since his transfer to the night shift has had increased difficulty sleeping during the day. At the same time, he has fallen asleep twice while at work, and was reprimanded the second time it happened. He is becoming increasingly uneasy about his work status and is concerned that he may have to increase his medication in an effort to reduce stress. He has never revealed his psychiatric history because of a concern that his employer will terminate him. He is uncertain how to proceed and has the following questions: Can he be fired from his job because of his diagnosis or past or present psychiatric treatment? Can he request a transfer back to the day shift, using his disability as a reason, without getting fired or hurting his chances for promotion?

Assume that Fred is transferred back to the day shift but that a few years later he begins experiencing panic attacks, which for brief periods of time leave him unable to speak and feeling as if his body is covered with bee stings. He is diagnosed as having posttraumatic stress disorder as well as a panic disorder by the company doctor, who is also his treating physician. As a result of these problems, he is unable to carry out his job at Better Plastics. Based on the recommendation of the doctor, the company offers him a job as a janitor (characterizing it as an accommodation to his mental problems), but he rejects this offer in part because he views it as demeaning and he is fired. He becomes extremely fearful of other people and buys a Great Dane to protect himself, despite his apartment complex's no-pet policy. He now has three more questions. Can he get his old job back, or some other job better than a janitor? If he can't, can he collect Social Security Disability Insurance payments now that he has no job? Can he enjoin his landlord's attempts to evict him because of his violation of the no-pet policy?

QUESTIONS: As a lawyer or mental health professional what information would you like to have before answering Fred's questions? How would you answer them based on what you know?

13.02.   Americans with Disabilities Act

The Americans with Disabilities Act (ADA)[1] was enacted in 1990 and became effective in 1992. The motivation for the statute was Congress's conclusion that 43 million Americans had one or more disabilities,[2] and that many of these people suffered discrimination in gaining access to services, employment, and other aspects of society most Americans take for granted.[3] The statute attempts to end such discrimination by requiring that people who have a disability be treated like other people unless it can be demonstrated, on an individual basis, that the person's disability creates substantial barriers to his or her participation. It imposes this prohibition in connection with a wide variety of activities: employment (addressed in Title I of the Act), public services (Title II), public accommodations and services operated by private entities (Title III), and access to telecommunications (Title IV).

This chapter focuses on Title I of the Act, barring discrimination in employment, because it appears to be the part of the ADA most likely to create issues for the forensic examiner; it can thus serve as a paradigm for evaluations under any other title of the Act. Title I stemmed from congressional findings that approximately two-thirds of people with disabilities are unemployed,[4] and that one reason for this situation is discrimination. According to the preamble of the ADA:

> [I]ndividuals with disabilities continually encounter various forms of discrimination, including outright intentional exclusion, the discriminatory effects of architectural, transportation, and communication barriers, overprotective rules and policies, failure to make modifications to existing facilities and practices, exclusionary qualification standards and criteria, segregation, and relegation to lesser services, programs, activities, benefits, jobs, or other opportunities.[5]

Congress also noted that discrimination has a significant economic impact, "cost[ing] the United States billions of dollars in unnecessary expenses resulting from dependency and nonproductivity."[6] Additional support for Title I came from research showing a clear relationship between employment status and mental health[7] and other empirical evidence indicating that only a few companies antidiscrimination had policies in place that addressed the needs of people with mental disabilities.[8]

Title I applies to any business with more than 15 employees. The ADA was preceded by the Rehabilitation Act of 1973,[9] which barred employment discrimination in language virtually identical to that subsequently found in the ADA, but which applied only to federal agencies and entities receiving federal assistance. Because the ADA is relatively new, much of the case law discussed in this chapter involves construal of the Rehabilitation Act. Given the similarity in language, the courts are likely to treat cases under the latter statute as precedent for the ADA.

(a)   Overview of Title I

Title I of the ADA establishes the general principle that

> no covered entity shall discriminate against a qualified individual with a disability because of

the disability of such individual in regard to job application procedures, the hiring, advancement, or discharge of employees, employee compensation, job training, and other terms, conditions, and privileges of employment.[10]

In contrast to many statutes, which use vague language intended to be refined through regulation or judicial decision, Title I is very detailed,[11] defining a number of activities that constitute employment discrimination. These include:

1. limiting, segregating, or classifying a job applicant or employee in a way that affects the opportunities or status of that individual because of his or her disability;

2. subjecting an applicant or employee with a disability to discrimination by participating in a contractual or other relationship with an employment or referral agency, union, or training program [which discriminates against the individual];

3. utilizing standards, criteria, or methods of administration that either have the effect of discriminating based on disability or perpetuate the discrimination of others;

4. excluding or otherwise denying equal jobs or benefits to an individual because of a known disability of an individual with whom the applicant or employee has a relationship or association;

5. not making reasonable accommodations to the known physical or mental limitations of an otherwise qualified individual with a disability who is an applicant or employee, unless it can be shown that the accommodation would impose an undue hardship on the operation of the business of the covered entity; or denying employment opportunities to an applicant or employee if the denial is based on the need to make a reasonable accommodation;

6. using qualification standards, employment tests or other selection criteria that screen out or tend to screen out an individual with a disability or class of individuals with disabilities unless the standard, test or other selection criteria as used by the covered entity is shown to be job-related for the position in question and is consistent with business necessity; and

7. failing to select and administer tests concerning employment in the most effective manner to ensure that, when the test is administered to an applicant or employee with a disability that impairs sensory, manual, or speaking skills, such test results accurately reflect the skills, aptitude, or whatever other factor of the applicant or employee that the test purports to measure, rather than reflecting the impaired sensory,

manual, or speaking skills of the employee or applicant (except where such skills are what the test purports to measure).[12]

To ensure that these types of discrimination do not occur, the ADA sets out a detailed analytical structure for determining who is covered by the ADA, provides for an administrative enforcement procedure, and specifies remedies for violations, all of which are described below.

(b) Coverage

The ADA only protects a "qualified individual with a disability," which is further defined as "an individual with a disability who, with or without reasonable accommodation, can perform the essential functions of the employment position that such individual holds or desires."[13] This definition contains three separate criteria: "disability," "qualified individual," and "reasonable accommodation."

(1) Disability

"Disability" is defined broadly to include either "(1) a physical or mental impairment that substantially limits one or more of the major life activities of such individual; (2) a record of such an impairment; or (3) being regarded as having such an impairment."[14] This definition creates three separate categories of "disability." The first covers individuals with current impairments. The second covers individuals with a history of having an impairment but who may at present be unaffected by their disability. The third covers individuals who may not be and may never have been impaired but who are perceived as having an impairment. The latter two categories were included in the ADA to ensure that discrimination based on past history, stereotyping, or false assumptions about an individual does not occur.[15]

Mental impairment is defined further, in terms that give it a broad reach, despite arguments in Congress that it should not be covered at all.[16] It includes "any mental or psychological disorder, such as mental retardation, organic brain syndrome, emotional or mental illness, and specific learning disabilities."[17] As applied, courts and the

Equal Employment Opportunity Commission (EEOC) seem to have given this definition even more extensive scope in that they tend to rely on the *Diagnostic and Statistical Manual of Mental Disorders* (DSM) in deciding whether an impairment exists for purposes of the ADA.[18] Further, as presumably should be the case given the goals of the ADA, "[t]he existence of a mental disorder is determined without regard to medication or other mitigating measures that eliminate or control the symptoms of the disorder."[19]

However, the law also specifically excludes several conditions from coverage. Alcoholism is a covered condition, but on-the-job drinking and illegal drug use is not (although former addicts who have been successfully rehabilitated may be covered).[20] Nor does the ADA protect against discrimination on the basis of homosexuality, bisexuality,[21] or other types of sexual orientation or various types of criminal pathology, such as pyromania and kleptomania.[22] It is also worth noting that such personality traits as poor judgment or quick temper are not impairments for purposes of the ADA.[23]

Other conditions may or may not be a mental impairment, depending on the context and etiology. For instance, the EEOC has observed that general stress resulting from job pressures would not come under the definition of impairment, but that a psychiatric diagnosis of stress disorder would constitute an impairment.[24] Similarly, a court has found that although poor judgment alone is not an impairment under the ADA, poor judgment caused by a "mental disorder" is.[25] Given this expansive approach, much may depend on the willingness and ability of mental health professionals to assign a diagnosis to a particular problem.

A person with an impairment does not automatically meet the threshold requirement of the ADA, however. The impairment must also *substantially limit* one or more *major life activities*. Whether a limitation is substantial depends on its severity and permanence.[26] One commentator has suggested, for instance, that short-term depression following loss of a spouse will probably not be considered a disability and that conditions that are episodic in nature are less likely to be viewed as disabling even if they periodically affect major life activities.[27]

As to which activities are considered "major," EEOC rules specifically list walking, speaking, breathing, performing manual tasks, seeing, hearing, learning, caring for oneself, working, sitting, and standing.[28] Activities more relevant to those with mental disorder, such as interpersonal skills, concentration, and cognitive processing, were initially specifically excluded from this list during the rulemaking process out of fear that impairment in these areas is widespread and would lead to too many ADA claims.[29] Nonetheless, the EEOC list is not meant to be exclusive; it specifically states that "other activities that an average person can perform with little or no difficulty" should also be included. Thus, one commentator has argued that as applied to individuals with mental disability, the term "major life activities" encompasses working, thinking, communicating, and perceiving.[30]

Note that there is an inherent tension between this definition of disability and the "qualification" requirement that is discussed further below: A person whose mental disorder substantially impairs major life activities, including work, may often be unqualified for most positions. But such a person can still be qualified for certain types of jobs, especially if the disorder is under treatment; as noted previously, a substantially limited impairment that is masked by medication is generally still considered an impairment.[31] Moreover, the ADA does not just bar discrimination against those who are currently "disabled." Recall that the ADA's definition of disability also includes having a record of, or being regarded as having, the type of impairment defined above.

The EEOC illustrates the "record" category of impairment as follows: "A job applicant, formerly a patient at a state psychiatric institution, was misdiagnosed as psychopathic and the diagnosis was never removed from her records. If she is otherwise qualified for the job, but is not hired based on this record, the employer has violated the ADA."[32] In such a case, although the employee is not presently disabled, the protection of the ADA is triggered because the employee's history of impairment was the basis for an employment decision.

The "perception" category of impairment may be implicated in one of three ways, according to the EEOC. First, an employer may perceive an employee's impairment to be substantial when in fact it is not. The EEOC uses as an example a person who has controlled high blood pressure but who is reassigned to a less strenuous job because her employer fears, without cause, that the employee might suffer a heart attack in her current position.[33] Second, the discriminatory attitudes of others (e.g., customers) may impermissibly affect an employer's treatment of the employee. For example, an employer may pass over for promotion an individual who suffers from a manic–depressive condition because of a concern that customers will react negatively to someone who is mentally ill, even though the employee's illness is controlled by lithium. Third, an employee may have no impairment at all but still be regarded by the employer as having a substantially limiting impairment. The EEOC illustrates this situation with the example of an employee discharged based on an incorrect rumor that the person was HIV positive.[34] In short, under the perception category, the ADA prohibits an employer from taking adverse action against an employee based on the employer's unsubstantiated fears that the person has an impairment that will affect productivity, safety, liability, attendance, or other types of job performance.[35]

(2) Qualified Individual

A person who has a disability as defined by the ADA does not automatically benefit from the statute. He or she also must be a "qualified individual." The ADA defines this term as a person who, "with or without reasonable accommodation, can perform the essential functions of the employment position that such individual holds or desires."[36] The EEOC has broken down the term further, into two separate factors. First, it must be determined that the person meets the "necessary prerequisites" for the job in terms of education, work experience, training, skills, licenses and certificates, and other job-related requirements such as good judgment or the ability to work with other people.[37] Second, if the person meets the general qualifications for the job, he or she must be able to perform the "essential functions" of the job with or without "reasonable accommodation."[38]

Determining the "essential functions" of a particular job is often difficult. The EEOC regulations define the term as "the fundamental job duties of the employment position the individual with a disability holds or desires"[39] and provide several illustrations of this concept. A function may be essential because the position exists to perform the function; for example, if a person is hired to proofread documents, the ability to proofread would be an essential function because the only reason the position exists is to proofread.[40] A function also may be essential because only a limited number of employees are available to perform the function.[41] Finally, a function may be essential because it is so highly specialized that the employee has been hired for his or her expertise in performing a particular function.[42] In addition, the scope of a job's "essential" functions may be based on (1) written job descriptions prepared before interviewing for a position, (2) the amount of time spent on the function, (3) the consequences of not having the function performed, (4) the terms of a collective bargaining agreement, (5) the work experience of past employees in a particular job, and (6) the experience of employees in similar jobs.[43]

In deciding whether a function is "essential," deference is to be given to the employer's judgment.[44] An example of how courts have interpreted the concept is found in *Guice-Mills v. Derwinski*.[45] There a federal court of appeals ruled that working the morning shift was an "essential function" of the job of a head nurse in a Veteran's Administration hospital because the head nurse was the only "management" employee available to consult with the night supervisor about modifications to treatment and staff attendance at meetings. Thus, the court found that a well-qualified nurse was nonetheless not entitled to relief under the ADA because she suffered from a depressive condition that required early-morning medication with significant side effects. Similarly, in *Altman v. New York City Health and Hospitals Corporation*,[46] the court decided that the plaintiff, who had been Chief of the Department of Internal Medicine at one of the defendant's hospitals before alcoholism led to his removal, could no longer carry out the essential functions of that job despite intervening treatment for his condition. Although the hospital had concluded that Altman could be reinstated, on a trial basis, as a physician

in a high-level position, it also concluded that he still needed supervision and that such supervision would be lacking in the chief of the department position, a view in which the court concurred. As a final example, the EEOC concluded in *Stocketta v. Runyon*[47] that a postal clerk with posttraumatic stress disorder was not otherwise qualified to perform the essential duties of his position, which involved computer data entry, because the stress accompanying heavy computer work triggered Stocketta's memories of military experiences and debilitated him from working.

(3) Reasonable Accommodation

Even if an impaired person is not qualified for a job as it is presently constituted, he or she may come under the protection of the ADA if the employer can reasonably accommodate the impairment and fails to do so. The ADA prohibits

> not making reasonable accommodations to the known physical or mental limitations of an otherwise qualified individual with a disability who is an applicant or employee, unless such covered entity can demonstrate that the accommodation would impose an undue hardship on the operation of the business of the covered entity.[48]

It is also illegal discrimination for an employer to deny employment to an otherwise qualified individual if the denial is based on its anticipated need to make a reasonable accommodation.[49]

The reasonable accommodation principle has a long history in civil rights statutes and litigation.[50] It is designed to eliminate unnecessary barriers in the workplace.[51] The ADA refines the concept by providing that it be used to promote three objectives: (1) ensuring equal opportunity in the application process (e.g., prolonging the time in which to take a test and assisting a person with limited manual dexterity in completing an application form), (2) enabling a qualified individual with a disability to perform the essential functions of the job (e.g., providing modified work schedules and flexible leave policies), and (3) enabling an employee with a disability to enjoy equal benefits and privileges of employment (e.g., providing equal pay and pension benefits).[52]

However, the EEOC also recognizes several limitations on the reasonable accommodation goal. First, the employer is obligated to make an accommodation only to the *known* limitations of the individual (thus requiring the employee to disclose the disability). Second, the reasonable accommodation obligation applies only to the removal of barriers to employment, not those related to nonemployment goals. Third, a reasonable accommodation, if it is effective, does not need to be the best possible accommodation. Most important, as noted earlier, an accommodation need not be made if it causes the employer "undue hardship." The ADA lists a number of factors to be considered in determining whether a proposed accommodation would work undue hardship: the nature and cost of the accommodation; the overall financial resources of the covered entity; the size of the business and number of persons employed; the impact of the accommodation upon the operation of the business; the number, type, and location of its facilities; and the composition, structure, and functions of the work force.[53] The EEOC admonishes, however, that an employer may not claim undue hardship solely because an accommodation "has a negative impact on the *morale* of other employees."[54]

Application of the reasonable accommodation principle to individuals with a mental disability may be more difficult than in cases of physical disability, for a number of reasons. First, employees or applicants with a mental disability may be reluctant to disclose the existence of the disability because of the stigma associated with mental disability (like Phantom in Case Study 13.1).[55] Second, employers may be less familiar with mental disability and its impact on the ability to work. Similarly, employers may be less certain about how to provide accommodation for people with a mental disability.[56] Finally, as the debates in Congress attest, there may simply be more resistance to accommodating those with mental, as opposed to physical, disability.

Nonetheless, accommodations can be and have been made for persons with mental disability. One guide to the ADA provides a number of suggestions for such accommodations, in four areas: (1) changes in the physical environment, (2) flexible scheduling, (3) restructuring of jobs and training, and (4) improved communication and support.[57] In the first area, the authors suggest that if necessary to provide quiet, the employer

can build partitions and place people in enclosed offices. In connection with providing flexible scheduling, the authors' recommendations include not only obvious adjustments, such as shift changes and split time, but also longer work breaks and leaves, which may be the most important type of accommodation for those with mental disability.[58] The third area—job restructuring and training—is probably the most controversial, because it is likely to require the biggest and most expensive changes, and thus trigger claims of unfair "affirmative action" for people with disabilities. The suggestions here include restructuring jobs to focus on their primary functions, providing part-time opportunities and special training, allowing additional time to learn new jobs, breaking the duties of a job into discrete steps, and the use of clear job descriptions. Finally, in the area of improved communications and support, suggestions include regular meetings with a supervisor to establish clear goals, sensitizing other employees to the nature of the disability, allowing the use of a job coach and other peer supports, providing health insurance that covers the cost of mental illness treatment, and establishing on-site services or access to such services as employee assistance programs and crisis intervention services. Although not all these suggestions might be supported by the courts in a given fact situation, a number of them have been followed by employers, as Table 13.1 attests.[59]

A number of decisions have found proposed accommodations to be unreasonable, however. For instance, in *Gore v. Shalala*,[60] the EEOC concluded that the agency sufficiently accommodated an employee with an alcoholism problem by rescinding its removal proceedings against him and giving him leave without pay to receive treatment. The agency did not need to grant the employee's requests for advanced sick leave to cover the treatment period and for a transfer during his recovery to a place closer to his family. *Gore* illustrates the precept noted earlier that the ADA does not require that an accommodation be the best possible one. In other decisions, the court or the EEOC have simply found that the employee could under no circumstances carry out the essential functions of the job and that accommodation was therefore impossible or unnecessary. *Guice-Mills* (the depressed nurse case), *Altman* (the

Table 13.1
Examples of Reasonable Accommodation

- Time off for weekly therapy sessions, or schedule adjustments to accommodate these sessions
- Time-management training
- A mentor or job coach for employees with mental retardation to demonstrate and discuss tasks, the organization of work, or specific on-the-job problems
- Special supervision at the beginning and end of the shift to organize work and review lists of tasks to see that they have been completed
- A quiet environment free of background noise or distractions
- Telecommuting
- A modified schedule that permits an employee with narcolepsy to nap, or place in an empty office or other location in which an employee may take a nap
- Allowing a person who has bipolar disorder to work in bright light or near a window
- Allowing an individual with a learning disability to dictate work, instead of writing it or typing it
- Obtaining a spell-checker or furnishing software with spell-check and grammar-check capabilities for an employee with a learning disability
- Allowing an individual more time to complete certain tasks
- Using descriptions with an employee other than "right" or "left"
- Providing extra or specialized training to an employee
- Allowing an employee to trade marginal job functions with a coworker
- Educating coworkers and supervisors about the special needs of a particular employee, including behaviors, how to handle seizures, and appropriate terminology
- Allowing the use of company facilities for self-help or support groups
- Providing instructions in written form instead of oral form, or vice versa, to accomodate specific learning disabilities
- Allowing an individual to tape-record interviews or meetings and to have transcripts prepared
- Color-coding objects or files
- Having supervisors explain inappropriate behaviors in the workplace and why they are inappropriate
- Having supervisors provide unusually specific instructions

Note. From Margaret Hart Edwards, *The ADA and the Employment of People with Mental Disabilities,* 18 EMPLOYEE RELATIONS L.J. 347, 381–82 (1992–93). Reprinted by permission.

alcoholic physician case), and *Stocketta* (the traumatized postal worker case), discussed earlier, are all illustrative of this line of cases.[61] These cases echo EEOC guidelines, which state that "employees with disabilities should not be evaluated on a lower standard or disciplined less severely than any other employee. This is not equal employment opportunity."[62] Fred Phantom's request for the day shift and his subsequent request for a job other than janitor (in Case Study 13.1) need to be considered against this backdrop.

Several other limitations on the reasonable accommodation rule may exist. For example, earlier decisions under the Rehabilitation Act held that the reasonable accommodation requirement did not contemplate either efforts to reassign the employee to an entirely different job within the organization[63] or job assignments that would constitute breaches of seniority clauses within collec-

tive bargaining agreements.[64] Although, in contrast, the ADA explicitly permits reassignments to another "position" within the company,[65] and also seems to provide that the provisions of the ADA take priority over agreements with unions,[66] these issues await further resolution through the EEOC and the courts. Similarly, the EEOC has yet to decide whether coworker sensitivity training, which research indicates decreases fear of people with mental disorders,[67] is a reasonable accommodation.[68] It has also stated that supported employment (e.g., modified training materials, restructuring of essential functions, or hiring a job coach) "is not synonymous with reasonable accommodation,"[69] despite its apparent efficacy.[70] At least one commentator has also suggested that changing supervisors or paying for or monitoring medication for those with mental disability would be considered too disruptive to be a "reasonable" accommodation.[71] These various limitations may explain why mental illness has been associated with only about 1% of the accommodations made under the ADA and the Rehabilitation Act through the early 1990s.[72]

(4)   Employees Who Pose a Threat to Others

An aspect of the ADA's coverage deserving of special mention is its provision permitting employers to condition a job on a showing that the individual "not pose a direct threat to the health or safety of other individuals in the workplace."[73] The term "direct threat" is defined as a "significant risk to the health or safety of others that cannot be eliminated by a reasonable accommodation."[74] The regulation implementing this statutory exclusion provides that the determination as to whether an individual poses a "direct threat"

> shall be based on an individualized assessment of the individual's present ability to safely perform the essential functions of the job. This assessment shall be based on a reasonable medical judgment that relies on the most current medical knowledge and/or on the best available objective evidence. In determining whether an individual would pose a direct threat, the factors to be considered include: (1) The duration of the risk; (2) The nature and the severity of the potential harm; (3) The likelihood that the potential harm will occur; and (4) The imminence of the potential harm.[75]

The EEOC's interpretive guidelines flesh out the meaning of this regulation with three principles.[76] First, the risk must be significant (i.e., represent a high probability of substantial harm rather than being speculative or remote). Second, the determination must be made on a case-by-case basis. It is illegal to assume that a category of individuals—for example, people with a particular diagnosis of mental illness—represents a "direct threat." Third, the determination must rely on "objective, factual evidence—not on subjective perceptions, irrational fears, patronizing attitudes, or stereotypes—about the nature or effect of a particular disability, or of disability generally." As an illustration, the EEOC notes that a law firm may not reject an applicant with a history of mental illness based on a generalized fear that the stress of attempting to make partner might cause

a relapse of the illness and somehow harm others. In short, the ADA seeks to deter judgments based on stereotypes about groups of people with disabilities.

Despite these admonitions, the "direct threat" provision in the ADA has the potential for significantly undercutting its thrust where people with mental disabilities are concerned. As one review of decisions under the Rehabilitation Act indicated, the employer usually will be required to do little by way of accommodation when an employee's mental disability leads to disruptive or dangerous behavior.[77] Some decisions under the ADA seem to continue this trend. In *Scofield v. Bentsen*,[78] for example, the plaintiff, an acknowledged alcoholic working for the Bureau of Alcohol, Tobacco, and Firearms, had been involved in a car accident while driving a government vehicle under the influence. Although the EEOC found plausible the plaintiff's assertion that his continued employment could be accommodated by providing him a "firm choice" between alcohol treatment and termination, it found this option to be an undue burden on the government because it would compromise "public confidence" and, given the plaintiff's need to carry firearms, perhaps endanger the public as well. The danger in this case seemed to be of the "generalized" type the EEOC guidelines indicate should not prevent accommodation, but it was nonetheless of sufficient concern to convince the EEOC that the ADA did not cover the plaintiff.[79] The implication of this type of decision for people who, like Phantom in Case Study 13.1, desire jobs that could endanger others if inadequately performed, may be greater difficulty in obtaining accommodations.

Other decisions more clearly represent the direct threat scenario. For instance, in *Franklin v. U.S. Postal Service*,[80] decided under the Rehabilitation Act, the court upheld the discharge of an individual with schizophrenia who periodically refused her medication and had a history of carrying a concealed weapon into the office of the state's governor and attempting to force entry into the White House. The court found that the employee was not "otherwise qualified" for her job; even if she were qualified, the court asked rhetorically, "how many times must violence be overlooked before a 'reasonable accommodation' has been achieved?" *Franklin* is also interesting because it suggests that an employer may consider, without violating federal law, the impact of an employee's failure to adhere to a treatment regimen, at least when that failure may result in violence.

(c) Applicant Testing

As noted previously, the ADA not only regulates decisions to fire, or not to hire, particular people but also governs application procedures for all persons. In contrast to the hiring and firing contexts, proof of discrimination in the application process does not require a showing that the applicant is qualified for the job, because that is what the process should be designed to test. Rather, this aspect of the ADA is violated when an employer uses

> qualification standards, employment tests or other selection criteria that screen out or tend to screen out an individual with a disability or a class of individuals with disabilities, unless the standard, test or other selection criteria . . . is shown to be job-related for the position in question and is consistent with business necessity.[81]

This provision is designed to ensure that employer-created job qualifications do not routinely screen out individuals whose disability does not interfere with their ability to perform the job.[82]

As a result of this aspect of the ADA, the application process is regulated in three significant respects: questions about personal information, the substance of screening tests, and the way in which such tests are administered. In the first area, the employer may no longer ask certain types of questions during the application process, even if such questions are asked routinely of all potential employees. Prohibited questions include asking whether the person has a disability, asking for a list of diseases or conditions for which treatment has been received, asking whether work has been missed because of illness or treatment, asking whether the applicant is being treated or has been treated by a psychiatrist or psychologist, and asking whether the applicant is taking medication.[83] On the other hand, the employer may ask applicants whether they will be able to get to work on time and work the hours of the shift for the job, whether they will require accommodation to per-

form the essential functions of the job, and how they would go about performing the job.

The ADA's principal limitation on the substance of applicant testing is an obvious one given the underlying premise of the ADA: To the extent they tend to screen out persons with a disability, such tests may only do so using exclusion criteria that are job-related and consistent with business necessity.[84] This requirement applies to all tests, including medical examinations (which may only be conducted once the employer has decided to hire the person), aptitude tests, psychological tests, tests of knowledge and skill, intelligence tests, agility tests, and job demonstrations.[85]

The one exception to this rule is tests for illegal drugs, which may be given at any time. Note also that, to the extent a test does not single out people with an impairment as defined by the ADA, it may be permissible even if it screens applicants using criteria that are not job-related. For instance, because personality traits (e.g., the ability to handle stress) are not in and of themselves impairments under the ADA, tests designed to elicit their existence may continue to be permitted as long as they do not have the effect of disadvantaging people with impairments that *are* covered by the ADA.[86]

The ADA will also affect the manner in which tests are administered. If a test is given to an individual with impaired sensory, speaking, or manual skills, it must be administered in a format and manner that does not require use of that skill unless the test is designed to measure the skill and the skill is job-related.[87] In illustrating this principle, the EEOC uses the example of a person with dyslexia. According to the EEOC, such a person should be given the opportunity to take a written test orally unless the ability to read is a job-related function that the test is designed to measure, and even then the EEOC suggests that a reader be made available unless the ability to read *unaided* is an essential function of the job.[88] Similarly, the EEOC suggests providing extra time for people with visual or learning disabilities or mental retardation unless a timed test is necessary to measure the speed crucial to performing an essential function of the job.[89] Other types of test-related accommodations might include permitting people with visual or learning disabilities or with limited use of their hands to record test answers by computer, dictation, or tape recorder; scheduling breaks for people with mental or other disabilities who require such breaks; permitting a person with a disability who is easily distracted to take a test in a separate room; or, if no alternative formats are available, evaluation of the individual's skills and ability through another means such as a job interview, work experience, or a trial job demonstration.[90]

(d)   Enforcement

The employment provisions of the ADA are implemented in the same manner as the employment provisions of the Civil Rights Acts of 1964,[91] meaning that the EEOC is principally responsible for the ADA's enforcement. The ordinary process for resolving a complaint under this section of the ADA has several steps.[92]

First, an individual who believes that he or she has been discriminated against files a charge with one of the EEOC's regional offices, either in person, by telephone, or by mail. The charge must be filed within 180 days of the alleged discriminatory act and must contain information identifying the parties, the nature of the discrimination, the nature of the disability, details of the purported discrimination, and any witnesses. Within ten days of the charge being brought, the EEOC must notify the party that allegedly has violated the ADA.

Once notification occurs, the EEOC may contact witnesses, seek additional information, and make preliminary findings regarding the charge. After it completes its investigation, the EEOC issues a "letter of determination," which states whether or not it has found "reasonable cause" to believe that discrimination has occurred. If the EEOC finds no cause, it will take no further action but will issue a "right to sue" letter to the charging party; at that point, but not before, the charging party may initiate a lawsuit. If the EEOC finds reasonable cause to believe that discrimination has occurred, it will attempt to resolve the matter through conciliation and negotiation, which it prefers to adversarial litigation. If these efforts fail, however, the EEOC may initiate litigation on its own, or issue a right-to-sue letter to the charging party.

The EEOC may utilize a number of remedies in resolving discrimination cases. These include directing the employer to hire, reinstate or promote the individual, award back pay, fashion a reasonable accommodation, and pay the party's attorney fees, costs, and expert witness fees. If intentional discrimination is found, compensatory and punitive damages may be awarded as well.[93]

Although the enforcement mechanisms for the ADA are elaborate, the EEOC's capacity to use them is suspect because of the high volume of cases it is called upon to handle and its simultaneous staffing shortages. In the first year the ADA was in effect, nearly 12,000 complaints were filed with the EEOC, a figure that far surpassed the number of complaints filed by women and minorities in the year after enactment of the Civil Rights Act of 1964.[94] Claims based on mental disability (nearly 10% of the total) represented the second highest percentage of claims in the first year of the ADA (back impairments were first, with approximately 18% of the total).[95] However, the EEOC was given no new staff to administer the ADA, and investigations were taking between one and five years to complete.[96] An important question for the future will be whether the agencies and courts charged with enforcement of the ADA are able to handle cases in an expeditious and efficient manner.

(e)   Forensic Evaluation

The forensic examiner might be asked to examine four issues under Title I of the ADA: whether the job applicant or employee has a "mental impairment," whether the person with such an impairment is a "qualified individual," whether a proposed "accommodation" is "reasonable" given the person's disability, and whether a person constitutes a "direct threat to the health or safety of others."

(1)   Mental Impairment

As noted in § 13.02(b)(1), the threshold determination on the issue of mental impairment under the ADA is whether the individual being evaluated has "any mental or psychological disorder, such as mental retardation, organic brain syndrome, emotional or mental illness, and specific learning disabilities," but not including certain sexual disorders, conditions resulting from illegal drug use, and symptoms that are mere "personality traits." Therefore, in evaluating this issue, the examiner should draw on customary diagnostic and evaluative tools. Recall, however, that the ADA also protects people who are discriminated against because of a history of an impairment. Thus, an examiner may be asked to conduct a retrospective inquiry as well. In such cases, the examiner will need to document the past existence of an impairment which may not be evident at the point of the examination. The clinical task in such a case should nonetheless be comparatively simple: Presumably, if the employer has engaged in this type of discriminatory conduct it has done so based on knowledge of the person's previous impairment, and evidence (e.g., medical records) should be available to document the existence of any impairment that existed.

Even if a person has a "mental impairment," the impairment does not fall within the ADA's coverage unless it substantially limits one or more of the major life activities of the person. Although such activities are broadly defined, it will be necessary to examine the manner in which the impairment is limiting. For example, if a woman is diagnosed as having depression and anxiety,[97] the examiner must then determine the functional limitations created by the impairment. Does the person's illness substantially limit her capacity to work, or her ability to interact with other people? Does the impairment result in increased sensitivity to stress in a way that is disabling or reduces her ability to "cope" with life? Proof that doctors have recommended hospitalization for the condition would presumably meet this criterion of the ADA. But evidence of less significant impairment might be sufficient as well.

In short, a simple diagnosis does not end the inquiry. Ideally, the examiner will take pains to situate the diagnosis in the nosological hierarchy and to explain the severity of the symptoms. Legal decisionmakers should then decide whether the condition substantially limits the person's ability to engage in major life activities.

(2)   Qualified to Perform Essential Functions

If the examiner concludes that a "substantial limitation" due to mental impairment exists or might

exist, the next question is whether the person is qualified to perform the job [see § 13.02(b)(2)]. The person must be qualified at two levels. First, he or she must meet the general qualifications for the job. Assessing this issue generally involves looking at objective criteria (e.g., educational level and possession of specified licenses), and therefore is not normally within the province of the forensic examiner. Beyond meeting general qualifications, however, the person must also be able to perform the "essential functions" of the job. Here a clinician may be of some help, but only after first understanding what the job's essential functions are. The examiner should review written materials describing the job, including descriptions in personnel manuals, advertisements, and other published sources, and should also obtain what is known as a "job analysis" if the employer has prepared one.

Once the examiner has understood the essential functions of the job, he or she should inquire into the relationship between the mental impairment and the person's ability to perform those functions. For example, suppose the depressed woman noted earlier is normally competent at her job as a therapist in a clinic but occasionally misses work because of bouts with depression and is obsessed with thoughts of suicide. Further, the employer fears that her patients will be traumatized if she does commit suicide, or expresses her suicidal ideation to them. Do these facts indicate that the woman is unable to perform an "essential function" of her job as therapist? Although the answer to this question is ultimately legal, the clinician may be able to give the decisionmaker useful information on the extent to which the disability undermines the person's ability to relate to patients, establish long-term relationships with them, and carry out other functions associated with being a therapist.

(3)   Reasonable Accommodation

If the person can perform the essential function of the job but is not considered qualified for the job as it is presently constituted, the next question is whether the employer can implement a reasonable accommodation that ameliorates the impact of the disability. In the example provided in the preceding subsection, the inquiry would be whether there is an accommodation that would enable the therapist, despite suffering from depression and anxiety, to fulfill her job. Perhaps such an accommodation would include a paid or unpaid leave during which the woman could be stabilized on antidepressant medication and seek therapy. Or, perhaps reassignment to a diagnostic position that did not involve prolonged contact with patients would be advisable.

As with the qualification issue, it is not the role of the forensic examiner to determine whether a proposed accommodation is reasonable or instead imposes an undue hardship on the employer. That is a legal question that lies beyond the responsibility of the examiner. However, the examiner may be useful in evaluating the impact of providing an accommodation upon the person's ability to perform the job. If the woman did undergo medication therapy, how long would it take to be successful? What would be her reaction to a reassignment, especially if she believes that her contact with patients is what sustains her? The clinician may also be able to provide accounts of research on the efficacy of various types of accommodations.[98]

(4) Direct Threat

As indicated in § 13.02(b)(4), the inquiry into whether an individual is a "direct threat" is rigidly structured by law. First, the assessment is to be based on "the most current medical knowledge and/or the best available objective evidence." Although the direct threat provision was written primarily with medical conditions, specifically AIDS, in mind, one can also read the phrase to require familiarity with the current state of knowledge on risk assessment [see §§ 9.09(c), 10.08(d)]. In addition, the "best available objective evidence" language suggests that the examiner must look for corroborating evidence of dangerousness from sources other than the person being evaluated.

Second, the regulatory structure directs that four factors be considered in assessing risk under the ADA: the duration of the risk, and the severity, likelihood, and imminence of the harm. These factors are comparable to the examination of dangerousness in the context of civil commitment [see § 10.08(d)]. Recall also that the regulations prohibit employment decisionmaking based on speculative or remote threats. In the hypothetical

case involving the therapist, the employer's fear of harm to patients is an issue that must be addressed by the legal decisionmaker, who might be aided by a clinician's assessment of the likelihood the woman will commit suicide or express the idea of suicide to her patients and the harm either event may cause her patients.

13.03. Fair Housing Amendments Act

The Fair Housing Amendments Act of 1988 (FHAA)[99] prohibits discrimination in the sale or rental of housing on the basis of "handicap" or familial status. It is similar in structure to the ADA but is treated separately here because of the importance of housing in the lives of people diagnosed as mentally ill and because it occasionally raises different types of issues than the ADA. To avoid redundancy, the reader is referred to relevant sections of the ADA discussion for more detailed discussion of concepts that appear in both statutes.

(a) Purposes of the Act

The FHAA of 1988 was designed to amend the Fair Housing Act of 1968, in two ways. First, Congress intended to strengthen enforcement of the 1968 Act.[100] Many observers and members of Congress believed the original Fair Housing Act did not provide adequate protection against housing discrimination. As one commentator noted, under that Act the Department of Housing and Urban Development (HUD) received fewer than 5,000 complaints each year, a figure estimated to represent less than 1% of housing discrimination incidents occurring annually.[101] To correct this problem, the FHAA grants HUD additional enforcement powers.

The second change wrought by the FHAA, of more importance to this book, was an extension of the 1968 Act's prohibition on housing discrimination to situations involving "handicaps" and familial status, in addition to those involving race, color, religion, or national origin.[102] With respect to people with mental disability in particular, Congress intended to achieve two specific goals through the FHAA. The first was to enable such people to obtain housing in the communities of their choice. The second was to use access to housing as a vehicle for integrating people with disabilities into the mainstream of American life.[103]

These goals stemmed from the belief that such people have often been denied access to housing because of discrimination,[104] a phenomenon which is not only problematic in itself[105] but also increases the risk of rehospitalization and further mental disability.[106] Congress was also undoubtedly influenced by the United States Supreme Court's 1985 decision in *City of Cleburne v. Cleburne Living Center*,[107] which found that the defendant city violated the equal protection clause when it required a group home for people with mental retardation to obtain a special permit that private clubs and fraternities, apartment hotels, and homes for the elderly did not need to obtain. Although *Cleburne* purported to be a narrow decision, applying only to the facts before the Court, it squarely rejected housing decisions based on "an irrational prejudice against the mentally retarded"; it stated that "mere negative attitudes, or fear, unsubstantiated by factors which are properly cognizable in a zoning proceeding, are not permissible bases for treating a home for the mentally retarded differently from apartment houses, multiple dwellings and the like." This language could be applied to discriminatory actions against people with mental disabilities other than mental retardation as well.

To stymie this and other types of discrimination, the FHAA makes it illegal

> to discriminate in the sale or rental, or to otherwise make unavailable or deny, a dwelling to any buyer or renter because of a handicap of: (A) that buyer or renter; (B) a person residing in or intending to reside in that dwelling after it is so sold, rented, or made available; or (C) any person associated with that buyer or renter.[108]

Note that the FHAA bars discrimination based not only on the disability of an individual buyer or renter but also discrimination based on an *association* with an individual with a disability.[109] For example, assume that a landlord refuses to rent to an organization providing housing for people with disability. Although technically the landlord's re-fusal may have been conveyed to a person without a handicap, the statute will apply because the refusal is motivated by a desire to avoid renting to individuals with a handicap who are "associated" with the organizational representative.[110]

(b)   Coverage of the Act

As noted above, the structure of the FHAA is similar to that of the ADA. To show discrimination under the FHAA, there must be proof of (1) a handicap, which (2) does not disqualify the person for access to the housing in question, at least when (3) reasonable accommodation can be made, and (4) the person does not pose a direct threat to others.

Although the FHAA uses the word "handicap" instead of "disability" (the latter a term Congress believed to be more acceptable when it enacted the ADA two years later[111]), the FHAA's definition of handicap is virtually identical to that used by the ADA in defining disability. Under the FHAA, a "handicap" is either (1) a physical or mental impairment that substantially limits one or more of such person's major life activities, (2) a record of having such an impairment, or (3) being regarded as having such an impairment.[112] As with the ADA, mental impairment includes most major mental disorders but excludes the "current, illegal use of or addiction to a controlled substance" and conditions associated with sexual orientation.[113]

Similarly, just as the ADA requires that a person with a disability be "otherwise qualified" for the job, the FHAA creates a "qualified-for-tenancy" requirement. For example, in announcing the rules implementing the FHAA, HUD regulations observe that although alcoholism is a handicap within the FHAA, a landlord is not obligated to make a dwelling available to an individual who suffers from this problem unless the individual can follow rules of the tenancy:

> [T]he fact that alcoholism may be a handicap does not mean that housing providers must ignore this condition in determining whether an applicant for housing is qualified. On the contrary, a housing provider may hold an alcoholic to the same standard of performance and behavior (e.g., tenant selection criteria) to which it

holds others. . . . In other words, while an alcoholic may not be rejected by a housing provider because of his or her alcoholism, the behavioral manifestations of the condition may be taken into consideration in determining whether or not he or she is qualified.[114]

As with the ADA, the FHAA also circumscribes the questions that may be asked of applicants to see if they are "qualified"; as a general rule, for instance, a landlord (or property seller) may not ask whether a potential tenant has a handicap. However, the landlord may ask whether (1) the applicant can meet the conditions of tenancy (i.e., abide by the rules imposed on tenants), (2) the tenant is qualified for housing that carries a priority for, or is exclusively designed for, people with handicap, and (3) the applicant is currently taking illegal drugs, is addicted to a controlled substance, or has been convicted of the illegal manufacture or sale of a controlled substance.[115]

The FHAA also includes a reasonable accommodation requirement similar to that found in the ADA. For instance, the FHAA labels as discriminatory a refusal to permit, at the expense of the person with a handicap, reasonable modifications of the premises if the modifications are necessary to afford the person full enjoyment of the premises.[116] It is also discriminatory to refuse to make reasonable accommodation in rules, policies, practices, or services when the accommodation may be necessary to enable the person to enjoy the premises fully.[117] In addition, the law requires compliance with several statutory provisions requiring physical accessibility to the premises of multifamily dwellings.[118]

Finally, similar to the ADA, the FHAA exempts from its coverage "an individual whose tenancy would constitute a direct threat to the health or safety of other individuals or whose tenancy would result in substantial physical damage to the property of others."[119] In its proposed regulations implementing this provision of the statute, HUD observed that it was the intent of Congress

> to require that the landlord or property owner establish a nexus between the fact of the particular individual's tenancy and the asserted direct threat. Any claim that an individual's tenancy poses a direct threat and substantial risk of harm must be established on the basis of objective evidence, e.g., a history of overt acts or current conduct. Generalized assumptions, subjective fears, and speculation are insufficient to prove the requisite direct threat . . . the landlord may not infer that a history of physical or mental illness or disability, or treatment for such illnesses or disabilities, constitutes proof that an applicant will be unable to fulfill his or her tenancy obligations.[120]

Congressional history makes the same point, noting that "there must be objective evidence from the person's prior behavior that the person has committed overt acts which caused harm or which directly threatened harm."[121] This insistence on objective evidence of dangerousness resonates with the analogous ADA regulations [see § 13.02(b)(4)].

(c)   Judicial Interpretation

A recent review by Petrila suggests that the courts have generally enforced the congressional intent behind the FHAA,[122] holding a variety of restrictions to be discriminatory. Examples of these cases can be divided into several categories.

(1)   Zoning and Building Requirements

The FHAA is not meant to prohibit typical zoning ordinances that may affect group homes or other accommodations for those with mental disability. For instance, the FHAA states that "nothing in this title limits the applicability of any reasonable local, State, or Federal restrictions regarding the maximum number of occupants permitted to occupy a dwelling."[123] At the same time, it was the intent of Congress to prohibit the application of special restrictive covenants and conditional or special-use permits that have the effect of limiting the ability of individuals with disability to live in the residence and community of their choice.[124] Thus, in *City of Edmonds v. Oxford House*,[125] the United States Supreme Court held that a city ordinance that limited the number of unrelated people in a single-family dwelling to five was not necessarily exempt from challenge under the FHAA by a group home that housed 10 to 12 addicts recovering from addiction. Although the Court avoided specifically deciding whether the FHAA prevented the city from prohibiting operation of the Oxford House, it indicated that, on remand, the group home should prevail if the city could not point to "reasonable" health and safety considerations that explained the ordinance's distinction between such a home and a dwelling housing single families larger than five people.

Another type of municipal ordinance that might be challenged under the FHAA is one creating safety requirements for housing used by people with mental disabilities. Even assuming good faith, such requirements are discriminatory if they are not based on empirically derived findings that the individuals in question require the equipment. For example, in *Marbrunak, Inc. v. City of Stow*[126] the city advised operators of a home for people with mental disability that a permit would not be issued unless the home was equipped with special sprinkling systems and with special doors to make access and egress easier. The provider challenged the requirements because they were not imposed on the operators of group homes for other types of clients and also argued that the extra cost associated with the requirements made opening the home more difficult. The court agreed, finding the requirements discriminatory.[127]

(2)   Notice and Hearing Requirements

Some states and municipalities require public notice and an opportunity for a public hearing prior to the issuance of a permit for group homes for those with mental disability. These laws are subject to attack under the FHAA because such requirements typically are not imposed on other individuals or groups as a condition of obtaining a housing permit. Thus, for example, in *Potomac Group Home Corporation v. Montgomery County*,[128] a federal district court declared illegal a notice-and-hearing requirement prior to obtaining a permit for a home for four elderly handicapped individuals, observing that "this requirement on its face creates an explicit classification based upon disability and is not supported by any justification of the County. . . . [It] is not imposed upon any family residential unit nor on any other properly

zoned residential unit in the County besides group homes for the disabled."[129]

(3)   Reasonable Accommodation

The reasonable accommodation requirement of the FHAA has supported challenges both to tenancy rules and to restrictions on the siting of residences for people with disability. An unusual example of the first type of case is *Crossroads Apartments Associates v Lebo*.[130] There, as in Case Study 13.1, the landlord sought to evict a long-term tenant soon after he bought a pet (in this case a cat), on the ground that he was in violation of the landlord's no-pet policy. The tenant responded by bringing suit under the FHAA, arguing that he had a mental disability and that the cat was therapeutically necessary for his continued enjoyment of the apartment. The landlord moved for a summary judgment, but the court ruled that there were issues of fact that had to be litigated regarding whether the tenant had a disability and whether the cat was so necessary to his continued tenancy that the landlord would have to waive the no-pet rule as a reasonable accommodation. Eventually, the case was settled; the tenant agreed to move out because the tenant's expert mental health witnesses could testify only that the cat was therapeutically helpful, not that it was necessary to his continued tenancy (as suggested by the fact that he had lived in the apartments for years without a pet). This case demonstrates how the FHAA can convert an otherwise routine eviction into a "mental health" issue, complete with affidavits from experts for both sides concerning the presence of disability and how best to ameliorate its consequences.

A more common application of the reasonable accommodation test involves judicial review of state and municipal laws prescribing a minimum space between residences for people with a mental disability. For example, in *United States v. Village of Marshall*,[131] a federal court ruled that, as a reasonable accommodation, the village had to permit two such homes within 1,600 feet from one another despite a state law requiring them to be at least 2,500 feet apart. The court found that the law in question had been enacted to ensure that such homes would not be clustered in one location and ruled that waiving the requirement in this case would not violate this legislative intent.[132]

(4)   Direct Threat

One type of case applying the "direct threat" criterion under the FHAA involves consideration of whether housing decisions are based on stereotypical views of people with disability. For example, in *Baxter v. City of Belleville*[133] a federal court overturned a denial of a permit to a provider who wished to open a home for people with AIDS, despite arguments that the proposed residents of the home posed a danger to the community. The court observed that "the scientific and medical authority is that HIV-positive persons pose no risk of transmission to the community at large."[134]

Other cases pose the more traditional forensic question of whether a particular individual is dangerous enough to evict from public housing. In *Roe v. Sugar River Associates,*.[135] the plaintiff brought suit under the FHAA to stop his eviction. The landlord responded by alleging that the plaintiff had threatened an 82-year-old resident of the complex with physical harm on several occasions, using obscene and threatening language. Another tenant alleged in a supporting affidavit that as a result of witnessing these confrontations she had become very fearful of the plaintiff and sick to her stomach. The plaintiff claimed that his behavior was the result of an unspecified mental handicap, and that the defendant was obligated to create an (also unspecified) accommodation that would ameliorate the potential behavioral consequences of his handicap. The court denied the landlord's motion for summary judgment, ruling that disputed issues of fact existed regarding whether the plaintiff had a protected handicap and that the landlord had to demonstrate that no reasonable accommodation could acceptably minimize or eliminate the risk posed by the plaintiff to other tenants. In reaching its decision, the court cited congressional committee language that noted that although

> a dwelling need not be made available to an individual whose tenancy can be shown to constitute a direct threat and a significant risk of harm

to the health or safety of others. . . . If a reasonable accommodation could eliminate the risk, entities covered under this Act are required to engage in such accommodation.

As a result, the landlord could not summarily evict the tenant without factual inquiry into these issues.

The decision in *Roe* can be questioned. The congressional language to which it refers was written in an attempt to ensure that people suffering from contagious diseases, specifically AIDS, were not automatically excluded from housing. *Roe*, on the other hand, involved apparently credible claims of threatened physical violence that would be difficult if not impossible to accommodate. Indeed, as under the ADA, other cases suggest less willingness to engage in protracted inquiries like the one mandated by the *Roe* decision.[136]

(d)   Enforcement

As noted at the beginning of this section, Congress passed the FHAA in part to improve enforcement of the original Fair Housing Act. Primary responsibility for enforcement of these laws rests with HUD. The enforcement provisions enacted in 1988 contain a mixture of administrative and judicial remedies for violations of the statute.

A person claiming discrimination must file a complaint with the Secretary of HUD within a year of the alleged discrimination.[137] Upon receiving a complaint, HUD is to attempt to mediate the dispute in a fashion similar to the conciliatory role the EEOC plays after the filing of a complaint under the ADA. If HUD finds reasonable cause that discrimination has occurred, it may charge the party engaging in the discriminatory practice and hold an administrative hearing. Available relief includes issuance of an injunction and financial penalties.

A person may also file a complaint in federal or state court within two years of the alleged discriminatory practice. However, if HUD is already conducting an administrative proceeding, the court must stay its proceedings (i.e., hold the case in abeyance). HUD also has the right to go to court on its own, as does the United States Attorney General.

(e)   Role of the Forensic Examiner

As the previous discussion suggests, at least three types of issues raised by the FHAA may result in the involvement of mental health professionals. First are challenges to special physical requirements for housing for people with mental disability. In a case contesting such requirements, a clinician might be able to provide useful information about (1) the existence of a handicap, (2) its impact on functioning in the areas in question (e.g., in a case like *Marbrunak*, whether the handicap interferes with the person's ability to become aware of danger and to exit the residence in the event of danger), and (3) whether the special requirements are *necessary* to enable the person to protect him or herself. To address the latter issue, the examiner will need to learn as much as possible about the characteristics of the residence in which the person or persons will live and will need to explain whether the handicap (if one exists) substantially limits the person's ability to live in the residence. In a case such as *Oxford House*, the evaluator may be able to provide information about the effect on health and safety of housing more than five people with mental disability in the same dwelling.

The opinion of a mental health professional may also be sought regarding the appropriateness of a reasonable accommodation in a particular case. Recall that in *Lebo*, for example, mental health professionals were asked by both parties to assess whether having a pet was therapeutically necessary for the tenant to continue to live successfully within his apartment complex. In such a case the examiner is not to determine whether an accommodation (in this case, waiving the no-pet rule) is appropriate, because that is the ultimate legal issue. Rather, the examiner should (1) provide information on whether the person has a handicap within the meaning of the statute, (2) discuss the effect of that handicap on the capacity of the person to live according to the rules of tenancy, and (3) determine, if possible, whether the accommodation proposed is necessary to ameliorate the behavioral consequences that might ensue without the accommodation.

As the *Roe* case suggests, a third question that might be raised under the FHAA is the more traditional issue of dangerousness. Under the applicable law, the direct threat criterion is only met on production of objective evidence, based on previous behavior. The discussion of this issue in connection with the ADA is relevant here [see § 13.02(e)(4)].

13.04.   Social Security Laws

Since the 1930s, the federal government has funded "income maintenance" programs for persons who, because of physical or mental disability, are unable to engage in substantial gainful employment. In contrast to Title I of the ADA, which protects those who are able to work, these programs are meant to provide financial aid for people whose mental disability prevents them from functioning at a self-sustaining level. The most significant modern programs in this regard are the Social Security Disability Insurance (SSDI) program[138] and the Supplemental Security Income (SSI) program.[139] Since 1972, these programs have been administered solely by the federal government.[140] Together, they comprise the bulk of the federal government's effort to aid those who lack the capacity to work.

The Social Security Disability Act is found in Title II of the Social Security Act. SSDI functions as an insurance program, providing benefits for disabled people who have worked and paid into the Social Security Trust Fund in 20 of the 40 calendar quarters prior to the beginning of a disability.[141] In contrast, the SSI program, found at Title XVI of the Social Security Act, is available to anyone meeting the eligibility criteria, regardless of work history or payment of Social Security taxes[142]; thus, it is need-based rather than insurance-based. Benefits may be sought under either SSI or SSDI, or both; if the latter, applications are processed simultaneously.

Although the two programs differ in other ways,[143] further discussion will not differentiate between the two, because other than the distinction noted above their eligibility criteria are identical. This section begins with a detailed examination of these criteria. The regulations setting them out are complex and change with some frequency. At the same time, they are bottomed on certain core principles that can profitably be discussed here. After looking at these principles, we examine the process by which disability determinations are made and conclude with suggestions concerning clinical involvement in this process.

(a) Eligibility Criteria

This discussion of eligibility criteria first addresses those pertaining to adults and then discusses those pertaining to children. For many years, the criteria for the latter differed significantly from those applicable to adults. A Supreme Court ruling forced the adult and juvenile criteria into greater alignment, but as a result of statutory changes in 1996 the differences are as great as ever.

(1) Adults

In the late 1970s and early 1980s the disability criteria for adults were the focus of much controversy, brought on by executive branch efforts to reduce the costs of Social Security through narrow interpretation of statutory coverage. By 1983, the congressional watchdog agency, the General Accounting Office (GAO), had concluded that the Social Security Administration (SSA) was "overly restrictive" in making disability determinations.[144] Yet efforts to eliminate people with disability from the program continued, until a series of lawsuits culminated in a 1986 ruling by the United States Supreme Court that the SSA had applied eligibility criteria inappropriately.[145] The current statutory and regulatory structure is a result of these court decisions, subsequent direction from Congress,[146] and regulatory changes enacted by SSA.

The key question under these laws is whether the individual has a "disability," defined in the statute as an inability "to engage in any substantial gainful activity by reason of any medically determinable physical or mental impairment which can

be expected to result in death or which has lasted or can be expected to last for a continuous period of not less than 12 months."[147] As this wording suggests, the degree of impairment required by the Social Security laws is significant. According to another provision in the statute, an individual will not be eligible for benefits unless the impairment is

> of such severity that [the claimant] is not only unable to do his previous work but cannot, considering his age, education, and work experience, engage in any other kind of substantial gainful work which exists in the national economy, regardless of whether such work exists in the immediate area in which he lives, or whether a specific job vacancy exists for him, or whether he would be hired if he applied for work.[148]

In interpreting these statutory requirements, the SSA has developed a five-step process, summarized in Figure 13.1.[149] First, the SSA determines whether the individual is ineligible because he or she is engaged in "substantial gainful activity," which it defines as work that involves significant and productive physical or mental duties and is carried out for pay or profit.[150] In the 1980s this term was broadly interpreted; one commentator has noted that even some types of sheltered workshop activity were found to meet this test.[151] Whether the spirit of the liberal "reforms" in the late 1980s has changed this interpretation is not clear.

If the individual is not gainfully employed, the second step is to determine whether he or she has a "severe" impairment, that is, one that results in a significant limitation on the person's physical or mental abilities to perform basic work activities.[152] The regulations define basic work activities to include physical functions such as walking, standing, sitting, lifting, pushing, pulling, reaching, carrying, or handling; capacities for seeing, hearing, and speaking; understanding, carrying out, and remembering simple instructions; use of judgment; responding appropriately to supervision, coworkers, and usual work situations; and dealing with changes in a routine work setting.[153] In evaluating the functional loss from *mental* impairment, the SSA divides these inquiries into four areas: restriction of activities of daily living,

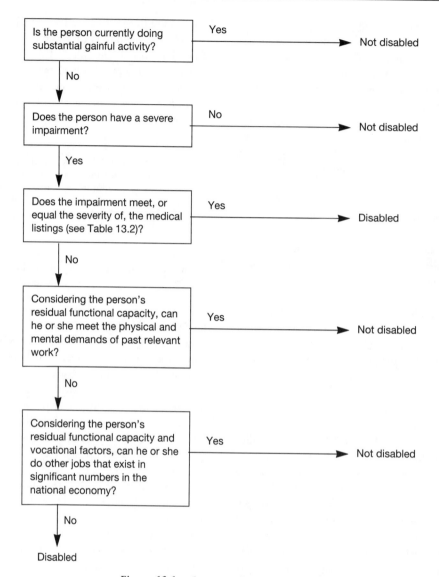

Figure 13.1.   *Logic tree: Competency to work.*

difficulties in maintaining social functioning, deficiencies of concentration and persistence resulting in failure to complete tasks, and episodes of deterioration or decompensation in work or work-like situations that cause the individual to withdraw from that situation and/or experience exacerbation of signs and symptoms. Recall that the assessment of severity also requires a determination as to whether the impairment has or will last for a continuous period of at least 12 months. However, the fact that a "severe" impairment has been in remission occasionally during the 12-month period will not automatically disqualify the individual for eligibility.[154]

If the person's impairment is severe, the third step is to determine whether the impairment meets or equals a "listed" impairment, that is, an impairment listed in the regulations; if so, the person is eligible for benefits on "medical grounds alone."[155] The "listed" mental impairments are found in the appendix to Chapter 12.00 of the federal regulations[156] and are eight in number: organic mental disorders (12.02); schizophrenic, paranoid, and other psychotic disorders (12.03);

Table 13.2
Mental Impairments Resulting in Disability Finding on "Medical Grounds Alone"

12.02 *Organic Mental Disorders* (Psychological or behavioral abnormalities associated with a dysfunction of the brain. History and physical examination or laboratory tests demonstrate the presence of a specific organic factor judged to be etiologically related to the abnormal mental state and loss of previously acquired functional abilities.)

The required level of severity for these disorders is met when the requirements in both A and B are satisfied.

A. Demonstration of a loss of specific cognitive abilities or affective changes and the medically documented persistence of at least one of the following:

1. Disorientation to time and place; or
2. Memory impairment, either short-term (inability to learn new information), intermediate, or long-term (inability to remember information that was known sometime in the past); or
3. Perceptual or thinking disturbances (e.g., hallucinations, delusions); or
4. Change in personality; or
5. Disturbance in mood; or
6. Emotional liability (e.g., explosive temper outbursts, sudden crying, etc.) and impairment in impulse control; or
7. Dementia involving loss of measured intellectual ability of at least 15 IQ points from premorbid levels or overall impairment index clearly within the severely impaired range on the Luria–Nebraska or Halstead–Reitan; and

B. Resulting in at least two of the following:

1. Marked restriction of activities of daily living; or
2. Marked difficulties in maintaining social functioning; or
3. Deficiencies of concentration and persistence resulting in frequent failure to complete tasks (in work settings or elsewhere); or
4. Repeated episodes of deterioration or decompensation in work or work-like situations which cause the individual to withdraw from that situation and/or to experience exacerbation of signs and syptoms.

12.03 *Schizophrenic, Paranoid, and Other Psychotic Disorders* (Characterized by the onset of psychotic features with deterioration from a previous level of functioning.)

The required level of severity for these disorders is met when the requirements in both A and B are satisfied, or when the requirements in C are satisfied.

A. Medically documented persistence, either continuous of intermittent, of one or more of the following:

1. Delusions or hallucinations; or
2. Catatonic or other grossly disorganized behavior; or
3. Incoherence, loosening of associations, illogical thinking, or poverty of content of speech if associated with one of the following:

   a. Blunt affect; or
   b. Flat affect; or,
   c. Inappropriate affect; or

4. Emotional withdrawal and/or isolation; and

B. Resulting in at least two of the following:
1. Marked restriction of activities of daily living; or
2. Marked difficulties in maintaining social functioning; or
3. Deficiencies of concentration and persistence resulting in frequent failure to complete tasks (in work settings or elsewhere); or

(*continued*)

Table 13.2. Continued

4. Repeated episodes of deterioration or decompensation in work or work-like situations which cause the individual to withdraw from that situation and/or to experience exacerbation of signs and symptoms; or

C. Medically documented history of one or more episodes of acute symptoms, signs and functional limitations described in A and B of this listing, although these symptoms or signs are currently attenuated by medication or psychosocial support, and one of the following:

1. Repeated deterioration with increased mental demands requiring substantial increases in mental health services and withdrawal from the stressful environment; or
2. Documented current history of two or more years of inability to function outside of a highly supportive living situation.

12.04 *Affective Disorders* (Characterized by a disturbance of mood, accompanied by a full or partial manic or depressive syndrome. Mood refers to a prolonged emotion that colors the whole psychic life; it generally involves either depression or elation.)

The required level of severity for these disorders is met when the requirements in both A and B are satisfied.

A. Medically documented persistence, either continuing or intermittent, of one of the following:

1. Depressive syndrome characterized by at least four of the following:
   a. Anhedonia; or
   b. Appetite disturbance with change in weight; or
   c. Sleep disturbance; or
   d. Psychomotor agitation or retardation; or
   e. Decreased energy; or
   f. Feelings of guilt or worthlessness; or
   g. Difficulty concentrating or thinking; or
   h. Thoughts of suicide; or

2. Manic syndrome characterized by at least three of the following:
   a. Hyperactivity; or
   b. Pressure of speech; or
   c. Flight of ideas; or
   d. Inflated self-esteem; or
   e. Decreased need for sleep; or
   f. Easy distractibility; or
   g. Involvement in activities that have a high probability of painful consequences which are not recognized; or

3. Bipolar syndrome with episodic periods manifested by the full symptomatic picture of either or both manic and depressive syndromes; and

B. Resulting in at least two of the following:

1. Marked restriction of activities of daily living; or
2. Marked difficulties in maintaining social functioning; or
3. Deficiencies of concentration and persistence resulting in frequent failure to complete tasks (in work settings or elsewhere); or
4. Repeated episodes of deterioration or decompensation in work or work-like situations which cause the individual to withdraw from that situation and/or to experience exacerbation of signs and symptoms

Note. Taken from 20 C.F.R. § 404, subpt. P., App. 1, ch. 12 (1993).

affective disorders (12.04); mental retardation and autism (12.05); anxiety related disorders (12.06); somatoform disorders (12.07); personality disorders (12.08); and substance addiction disorders (12.09).[157] Table 13.2 provides the first three mental disorders from the listing.

If a person not currently engaged in substantial gainful activity is found to have a severe impairment but not one that is listed (or its equivalent), the fourth step is an individualized determination of whether the claimant has a nonlisted impairment that prevents him or her from doing any work that the claimant has done in the past.[158] If the SSA finds that the claimant can perform such work despite impairment, the claimant will not be considered disabled.

If the individual is unable to do any work done in the past (as might be the case with Fred Phantom, in Case Study 13.1), the fifth and final step involves an analysis of the person's "residual functional capacity," together with his or her age, education, and past work experience, to determine whether the person can do any *other* job that exists in significant numbers in the national economy[159]; if so, the individual is still denied benefits. Residual functional capacity (RFC) is defined as "what [the claimant] can still do despite . . . limitations."[160] To help determine whether RFC exists, the SSA has developed Medical Vocation Guidelines that set out, based on age, education, skill, and exertional abilities, when a person can engage in substantial gainful employment. Although these guidelines are not dispositive of the issue,[161] they often heavily influence SSA determinations.

Three points about this five-step analysis should be emphasized. First, note that the SSA requires evidence of functional impairment, not just clinical evidence of diagnosis. For example, note from Table 13.2 that a claimant who seeks to show he or she is suffering from schizophrenia (12.03) must prove not only the presence of relevant symptomatology under Part A (e.g., "1. delusions or hallucinations") but also that the symptoms resulted in at least two types of dysfunction from Part B (e.g., marked restrictions of activities of daily living and marked difficulties in the maintaining of social functioning), as well as a history of continuing dysfunction and deteriora-

tion despite treatment and support efforts, pursuant to Part C.

Second, impairment must be shown by external evidence; according to the statute, it must result "from anatomical, physiological, or psychological abnormalities which are demonstrable by medically acceptable clinical and laboratory diagnostic techniques."[162] Simple statements from an individual that he or she suffers from depression, for example, are insufficient to establish eligibility without corroborating evidence. However, in this regard the courts have been sensitive to the relative imprecision of psychiatric as opposed to physical diagnosis. As one court noted:

> Courts have recognized that a psychiatric impairment is not as readily amenable to substantiation by objective laboratory testing as a medical impairment and that consequently, the diagnostic techniques employed in the field of psychiatry may be somewhat less tangible than those in the field of medicine. . . . A strict reading of the statutory requirement that an impairment be "demonstrable by acceptable clinical and laboratory diagnostic techniques" is inappropriate in the context of mental illness. Rather, when mental illness is the basis of a disability claim, clinical and laboratory data may consist of the diagnoses and observations of professionals trained in the field of psychopathology. The report of a psychologist should not be rejected simply because of the relative imprecision of the psychiatric methodology or the absence of substantial documentation, unless there are other reasons to question the diagnostic technique.[163]

A third observation worth making about application of these criteria is their similarity to the impairment inquiry under the American with Disabilities Act [see § 13.02(b)]. Both inquiries require a showing that mental impairment will significantly affect a major life activity, such as work. The difference, presumably, is that under the ADA the impairment must be treated or in remission; otherwise, the person is unlikely to be qualified to perform the "essential functions" of the job. In theory, then, the impact of the Social Security laws and the ADA should dovetail; a person with a severe mental disability who can work will be allowed to do so, whereas a person who cannot work will receive benefits. At least one commentator, however, has suggested that to the extent the ADA transforms society's image of those with mental disability "from one of inability to one of some ability," they will be expected to work. In his words, "[t]here is a risk that the disability rights model [of the ADA] may replace the benefits model [of the social security laws] not only with respect to those individuals who are capable of working in spite of disability but also with respect to those who are not."[164]

(2)   Children

In 1996, as part of an overall reform of the welfare system, Congress dramatically changed the scope of the Social Security program for children.[165] To understand these changes, it is important to understand the legal approaches to juvenile Social Security that preceded them.

Until 1996, the Social Security statute's definition of disability did not appreciably differentiate between adults and children, merely stating that, "in the case of a child under the age of 18," eligibility depends on the existence of "any medically determinable physical or mental impairment of comparable severity" to that required for adult eligibility.[166] Despite this language, prior to 1990 the SSA required only the first three steps of the five-stage process for adults. Advocates argued that this truncated procedure resulted in inappropriate denial of benefits to children. SSA, on the other hand, contended that steps four and five of the adult process were a vocational assessment, which was not feasible with children.

These conflicting positions were eventually reviewed by the United States Supreme Court in *Sullivan v. Zebley*.[167] There, the Court held that the SSA regulations for children were illegal because they applied different and more restrictive criteria than the regulations for adults. In reaching its decision, the Court cited a congressional study showing that 25% of the adults found to be eligible for benefits were found eligible during the last two steps of the five-stage process.[168] As a result, the Court concluded, the regulations had the effect of denying to children a process that should have made at least some of them eligible for benefits.[169] The Court also rejected the SSA's argument that it could not perform a vocational as-

sessment of children, noting that the additional steps used with adults involved a functional as well as vocational assessment. In the Court's words:

> [A]n inquiry into the impact of an impairment on the normal daily activities of a child of the claimant's age—speaking, walking, washing, dressing, and feeding oneself, going to school, playing, etc.—is, in our view, no more amorphous or unmanageable than an inquiry into the impact of an adult's impairment on an ability to perform "any other kind of substantial gainful work which exists in the national economy."[170]

After the Court's decision in *Zebley*, the SSA revised its regulations for children to make the eligibility process comparable to that used for adults.[171] While it retained the three-step process that had existed prior to *Zebley*, it added two more steps. Thus, as a fourth step, the regulations stated that if the impairment was severe but did not match a listed impairment, the SSA "will assess the impact of [the] impairment(s) on . . . overall ability to function independently, appropriately, and effectively in an age-appropriate manner."[172] In evaluating this criterion, the SSA used an "individualized functional assessment" (akin to RFC analysis for adults) to determine whether the individual had an impairment of comparable severity to an impairment that would prevent an adult from engaging in substantial gainful activity.[173] As a fifth step, the SSA recognized five distinct developmental categories (e.g., from birth to attainment of age one; from age one to attainment of age three)[174] and looked at five domains within each: cognition, communication skills, motor skills, social abilities, and personal/behavioral patterns.[175] In addition, the SSA looked at two behaviors it associated with specific age groups: the physical and emotional response of an infant to stimuli and the capacity in children over age three for concentration, persistence, and pace in the completion of tasks.[176] As one commentator noted, the post-*Zebley* rules inquired into "the broader contexts of developmental domains and age specific behaviors."[177]

In 1996, however, Congress significantly amended the Social Security laws as they apply to children, in effect changing the law back to its pre-*Zebley* state. First, the law amends the definition of "eligible mental disability" from a disability of a severity that is "comparable" to that triggering adult eligibility to a "medically determinable physical or mental impairment which results in marked and severe functional limitations" of substantial duration.[178] This change is designed to avoid the import of *Zebley* by removing the "comparability" language. Second, the statute explicitly eliminates the Individual Functional Assessment (IFA)[179] and thus renders irrelevant the fourth and fifth steps of the SSA's post-*Zebley* regulations.

Apparently, the primary reason for these amendments was the concern that parents were coaching their children to fake mental disorders. Yet studies by the SSA, the Health and Human Services Office of Inspector General, and the GAO failed to discover evidence of widespread fraud.[180] The Congressional Budget Office estimated that, as a result of the IFA's elimination, 267,000 children would lose access to benefits over the six years following enactment of the amendments.[181]

Under the new law, the SSA evaluation for children is once again a three-step process. First, it must be determined whether the child is engaging in "substantial gainful activity." If so, the child is not considered disabled.[182] If not, the second step is to determine whether the child has a severe impairment; if the child does "not have any impairment or combination of impairments that causes more than a minimal limitation in [his or her] ability to function in an age-appropriate manner" he or she is not considered disabled.[183] If the individual has a severe impairment, the third step is to determine whether it "meets or equals" a listed impairment; that is, whether it is an impairment that "precludes any gainful activity or that is comparable in severity to an impairment that would preclude an adult from engaging in any gainful activity."[184]

The list for children differs somewhat from the adult list because it contains impairments that apply only to children. The 11 listed impairments for children are organic mental disorders; schizophrenic, delusional (paranoid), schizoaffective, and other psychotic disorders; mood disorders; mental retardation; anxiety disorders; somatoform, eating, and tic disorders; personality disorders; psychoactive substance dependence disor-

ders; autistic disorder and other pervasive developmental disorders; attention-deficit/hyperactivity disorder; and developmental and emotional disorders of newborn and younger infants.[185] As with adults, the definition of each impairment includes a paragraph A, which describes the characteristics necessary to substantiate the existence of the disorder, and a paragraph B, which describes the social and personal functional limitations that must result from the disorder for the child to be considered disabled. As a result of the 1996 amendments, however, the types of maladaptive behaviors that will support a medical listing have been significantly reduced, again on the theory that they are too easily faked.

(b)   The Process for Decisionmaking

A Social Security claim is initiated by filing an application for benefits at the local Social Security district office. The application form asks for work and medical history, the identity of any doctors consulted, and a description of the basis for the disability claim.[186] The initial determination of disability rests with a state agency, acting on behalf of the Secretary of Health and Human Services (although the state may decline this function if it desires, in which case the federal government fulfills the role[187]). In cases involving claims of mental disability, the initial determination is made by a "disability analyst" (who is not supposed to be a physician) and a psychiatrist or clinical psychologist.[188] No hearing occurs at this point, and the claimant is advised by letter of the outcome of the claim. If the state agency decides in favor of the claimant, benefits typically will be paid.[189] If benefits are denied, the claimant may seek reconsideration of the decision by the program administrators.

If the claim is denied by the program administrators as well, the claimant may request a hearing before an administrative law judge. This hearing is governed by administrative law rules [see § 2.04(c)]; rules of evidence do not apply, the hearing officer may consider written as well as oral submissions, and the hearing is not adversarial. The conduct of the hearing is almost wholly within the control of the law judge[190]; one administrative law judge described his role in these cases as "unique" within the American judicial system because of the broad powers the judge has over the conduct of the hearing and the fact that the government is not represented by counsel.[191]

Two sources of information are particularly important in case determinations. One is a "vocational expert," who may help the judge determine whether there is a job in the "national economy" that fits the claimant's skills.[192] Testimony from such an expert is not mandatory, although some courts take the position that "[t]here should be a per se rule . . . requiring outright reversal of the Secretary's 'finding' where no vocational expert testified."[193] Second, in an effort to rebut the claimant's evidence, the government will often require the claimant to undergo a medical examination at government expense (a consultative examination, or "CE").[194] In some jurisdictions, the results of this examination heavily influence the administrative law judge. Other jurisdictions, however, have adopted the "treating physician rule," which "provides that a treating physician's opinion on the subject of medical disability, i.e., diagnosis and nature and degree of impairment is . . . binding on the fact-finder unless contradicted by substantial evidence. . . ."[195] In these jurisdictions, a presumption exists in favor of the treating physician's (as opposed to the CE's) conclusions about dysfunction. Of course, the treating physician rule benefits only those claimants who had a clinician prior to the claim, a relatively rare phenomenon.

After considering these various types of evidence, the law judge must render a written decision, including findings of fact and conclusions of law. The judge may reach one of several decisions.[196] First, the judge may find that the claimant became disabled on the date claimed and that the disability continues (a "fully favorable allowance" finding). Second, the judge may find that the claimant was at one time disabled but has since improved to the point where the disability has ended (a "closed period of disability"). Finally, the judge may find that the claimant was not disabled and is not entitled to benefits (a "denial"). Administrative appeal is available from the decision of the administrative law judge, and judicial appeal of the administrative decision is also authorized.[197]

It is evident from this brief description that establishing disability requires negotiating a many-tiered administrative structure. Because most applicants will suffer from some impairment (whether or not it turns out to be severe enough to show disability), and many have also been recently hospitalized for psychiatric disorders, a large proportion of applicants have difficulty in maneuvering through the process. Many have difficulty even getting past the first stage of the process, meaning that they do not ever receive a hearing on their claims.[198]

(c) Evaluation of Adults

As should be clear from the foregoing, without clinical information a Social Security determination cannot be made. The agency and the administrative law judge require information about whether a mental impairment meets or equals one of the listed impairments and, if not, information about the residual functioning capacity of the claimant. Clinicians who provide this information may be the claimant's treating clinician, an evaluator hired by the claimant, a "consultant" hired by the government, or a member of the agency's panel making the disability decision.

The first major task of the examiner in Social Security cases is determining whether a listed impairment or its equivalent exists. In doing so, it is important to remember that the criteria require a finding both of enumerated clinical signs and symptoms (the Part A criteria) and the limitations on functioning caused by the impairment (the Part B criteria). In addition, in evaluating the presence of schizophrenia and of anxiety-related disorders, the regulations establish a third set of criteria (the Part C criteria) which consider the impact of structured settings and of medication on the person's functioning. The examiner should also remember the durational requirement that an impairment has existed or will exist continuously for a period of at least 12 months. In evaluating whether the person has a listed impairment, the American Psychiatric Association urges reference to its DSM because of the manual's emphasis on objective and observable criteria.[199]

Whether or not the individual has a listed impairment, the examiner should also determine whether the impairment has a significant impact on the activities of the person, with specific reference to its impact on the person's ability to work. As noted, the SSA regulations focus on four types of activities in addressing this issue: activities of daily living; social functioning; concentration, persistence, and pace; and deterioration or decompensation in work or work-like settings. The regulations also provide examples of each.[200] *Activities of daily living* include such adaptive activities as shopping, cleaning, or taking public transportation, with the focus being on the appropriateness and effectiveness of these activities, and the individual's ability to undertake them independently of others. *Social functioning* refers to the ability to get along with others (e.g., neighbors, family, and friends). In work situations it may involve interactions with the public, or responding appropriately to supervisors; impaired social functioning is illustrated by a history of altercations, evictions, firings, fear of strangers, or other interactions. *Concentration, persistence, and pace* refer to the ability to sustain focused attention long enough to ensure the timely completion of tasks (e.g., in everyday household routines). *Deterioration or decompensation in work or work-like settings* refers to the repeated failure of the individual to adapt to stressful circumstances, which causes the individual either to withdraw from the situation or to experience exacerbated symptoms. In the work environment, common stresses include adherence to work schedules, completing tasks, and interacting with supervisors and coworkers.[201]

In performing these assessments, the clinician may use forms developed by the SSA to structure the inquiry. For instance, to "facilitate uniform and accurate application of listings at all levels of administrative review," the SSA has developed a Psychiatric Review Technique Form (PRTF), which is used in evaluating whether an individual has a mental impairment that meets or equals the medical listings illustrated by Table 13.3.[202] The PRTF is divided into three sections: a medical summary (indicating the severity of the disability and the category or categories into which the individual may fit), a checklist designed to help the evaluator assess the presence or absence of each of the disorders, and a checklist designed to assist the evaluator in judging the severity of functional impairment caused by the disorder. Table 13.3

displays the two checklists for the category of organic mental disorder. Note that the bottom half of the form tracks the four areas of functioning described earlier. If a claimant is rated "none" or "slight" in the first two areas, "never" or "seldom" in the third, and "never" in the fourth, the SSA generally will find that the impairment is not severe.[203]

The clinician may also use a Residual Functional Capacity Assessment Form to measure the capacity of the individual to perform work if he or she does not have a listed impairment. This form asks the rater to rate certain restrictions and limitations as mild, moderate, marked, or extreme. Areas of inquiry include but are not limited to "estimated restriction of activities of daily living," "estimated degree of difficulty in maintaining social functioning," and "estimated impairment of ability to respond to customary work pressure."[204]

Although these forms probably do help structure the inquiry, overreliance on them has undermined the quality of evaluations. For example, one survey found that many Social Security reports drew conclusions without evidence of disabling illness or impairments, rarely described individual behaviors, presumed disability from evidence of episodic psychosis, and ignored data on psychosocial stressors and adaptive functioning.[205] Similarly, a GAO report found that use of a previous version of these checklists led to reliance on the conclusions reached rather than the facts underlying the judgment.[206] The American Psychiatric Association has also noted that many disability reports provide poor descriptions of the level of functioning: "Common conclusions that a claimant 'is not able to take care of himself' or is 'never able to get along with anyone' or 'has no interests' lack the specificity required to substantiate a conclusion that the person is disabled."[207]

Thus, in undertaking Social Security evaluations, the examiner should remember several points. First, diagnosis is important but alone is not enough to prove that an impairment exists. As stressed previously, the examination must explore the impact of an impairment upon the functional areas spelled out in the regulations. In using the PRTF and other forms, therefore, the clinician should take full advantage of their provision for a "narrative summary" of findings focused on

Table 13.3
PRTF Checklists for Rating Organic Mental Disorders

12.02 Organic Mental Disorders

A. *Documentation of Factors That Evidence the Disorder*

☐ No evidence of a sign or symptom CLUSTER or SYNDROME which appropriately fits with this diagnostic category. (Some features appearing below may be present in the case but they are presumed to belong in another disorder and are rated in that category.)

☐ Psychological or behavioral abnormalities associated with a dysfunction of the brain . . . as evidenced by at least one of the following:

Present–Absent–Insufficient Evidence

1.	☐	☐	☐	Disorientation to time and place
2.	☐	☐	☐	Memory Impairment
3.	☐	☐	☐	Perceptual or thinking disturbances
4.	☐	☐	☐	Change in personality
5.	☐	☐	☐	Disturbance in mood
6.	☐	☐	☐	Emotional lability and impairment in impulse control
7.	☐	☐	☐	Dementia involving loss of measured intellectual ability of at least 15 IQ points from premorbid levels or overall impairment index clearly within the severely impaired range on the Luria–Nebraska or Halstead–Reitan
8.	☐	☐	☐	Other _____

B. *Rating of Impairment Severity*

Functional limitation   Degree of limitation

Functional limitation	None	Slight	Mild	Moderate	Marked*	Insufficient evidence
1. Restriction of activities of daily living	☐	☐	☐	☐	☐	☐
2. Difficulties in maintaining social functioning	☐	☐	☐	☐	☐	☐

Functional limitation	Never	Seldom	Occas.	Often	Frequent*	Insufficient evidence
3. Deficiencies of concentration and persistence resulting in failure to complete tasks	☐	☐	☐	☐	☐	☐

Functional limitation	Never	Once	Twice	Repeated* (three or more)	Insufficient evidence
4. Episodes of deterioration or decompensation in work or work-like situations which cause the individual to withdraw from that situation and/or experience exacerbation of signs and symptoms	☐	☐	☐	☐	☐

*Degree of limitation required by the listings.

the effect of the individual's disorder. Relatedly, the examiner should always conduct a mental status examination; indeed, such an examination is required under the regulations and failure to conduct it is the most common error in cases reversed on review.[208] Third, according to the SSA, "in psychiatric claims, perhaps more so than in any other [area], a detailed longitudinal history is needed."[209] Thus, the clinician should evaluate and describe the length and history of the impairment, points of exacerbation and remission, any history of hospitalization and/or outpatient treatment, and modalities of treatment used in the past.

Fourth, collateral sources of information are very important, both because functional limitations cannot be assessed without knowledge of the person's daily activities and because of the durational requirement for the impairment. For example, in assessing how a person interacts at home or at work, the mental health professional necessarily will have to rely on the reports of others—information made available through the clinical interview will not be sufficient. In many instances, the regulations indicate that such collateral information is required. For example, according to the regulations, assessing concentration, persistence, and pace with a psychiatric examination or psychological testing alone will be insufficient.[210]

Finally, the clinician should consider the claimant's treatability, which in this context means the extent to which treatment will restore the person's capacity to work. According to the regulations, a claimant will receive benefits only if he or she follows treatment prescribed by a doctor,[211] so the treatment recommendation made by the examiner may have a significant impact on the eligibility determination. In addition, prognosis is important in determining the duration of the disability.

In an effort to create a useful format for evaluations and report writing in this area, the American Psychiatric Association created model guidelines in 1983.[212] The report format, similar to the general format for report writing endorsed in this book [see § 19.01], has several elements[213]:

An *introduction,* providing basic identifying and demographic information;

A *history of present illness,* including its course, treatment, and important clinical changes, as well as an "explicit description" of the claimant's functioning over a period of time with examples of that functioning;

Past history, including a description of the claimant's history prior to the onset of the current illness, and relevant family and developmental history;

Mental status exam report, designed to clearly establish the presence or absence of a current mental illness, organized in a logical fashion with "actual descriptions of behavior and direct quotations from the claimant";

A *summary of information,* which ties together the information from the previous sections;

Diagnosis;

Prognosis, which is important in assessing whether the disability will be considered lasting enough in duration to meet statutory requirements; and

Ability to handle funds, often required as part of the report when the referral for evaluation is made.

Note that the American Psychiatric Association's report format does not include a section concluding whether the person is disabled or deserving of compensation. This conforms with our usual injunction against reaching the ultimate issue. As the tumultuous history of the Social Security laws indicates, politics can play a significant role in determining the scope of the disability rules. It is not up to the clinician to determine how much impairment means compensation.

(d) Evaluation of Children

At the time this chapter was written, the SSA had not promulgated its regulations implementing the 1996 amendments to the Social Security laws. Thus, the following discussion of necessity speculates as to the likely contours of the Social Security evaluation for children. It seems likely, however, that the evaluation will track the first three stages of the pre-1996 evaluation process. If so, the above discussion of the first three stages of the adult disability examination would generally be applicable to disability evaluations of children as well. However, several likely distinctions between the two inquiries should be noted.

First, some of the listed impairments are different for children. As indicated previously, under the pre-1996 regulations a few of the diagnostic categories diverge (e.g., the childrens' listing includes attention-deficit/hyperactivity disorder, whereas the adults' listings do not). In addition, within diagnostic categories, the definitions may vary, primarily in the Part B criteria defining the functional limitations created by the symptoms of the impairment. Instead of focusing on deficiencies in the areas of daily living, social functioning, concentration, and work settings, as is the case with adults, these criteria are expressed in terms of age-appropriate behaviors in the areas of cognitive/communication functions, social functions, personal/behavioral functions, and concentration.

Second, and more important, although both sorts of evaluation focus on the interrelationship between the impairment and functioning, the functional areas at issue vary depending on the age of the examinee. Recall that under the pre-1996 regulations there were five different age groupings; the intent was to incorporate developmental principles generally used in assessing children and adolescents. Whether or not the specific structure is maintained under the new regulations, the examiner must be knowledgeable about child developmental theory as a predicate to any evaluative work with children.

Third, although collateral information is important in both types of evaluation, the sources will vary from those relied on in performing an evaluation of an adult. With a child, school records will be important, as will communications with parents or those acting in that role. Other informants may include friends or others in a position of authority. The pre-1996 SSA rules required use of multiple sources of information in making its determinations, stressing in particular "the importance of parents and others as sources of information about a child's day-to-day functioning in medical evaluations of mental disorders and in our adjudications of the cases."[214] They also emphasized the need for third-party information "to establish the consistency of the medical evaluation and longitudinality of impairment severity."[215] These types of admonitions are likely to be found in the new regulations.

Finally, the evaluation of a child or adolescent must consider the impact of both hospitalization (or placement in other structured settings) and medications. As the pre-1996 regulations recognized, "the reduced mental demands of . . . structured settings may attenuate overt symptomatology and superficially make the child's level of adaptive functioning appear better than it is."[216] Therefore, the degree to which the child can function outside of the structured setting should be determined. At the same time, the regulations made clear that the fact of placement in such a setting does not alone permit a conclusion that the child or adolescent has an impairment. Similar cautions were made in connection with the impact of medication, particularly psychoactive medications.[217]

13.05.   Conclusion

It is worth summarizing the way in which the three federal statutes described in this chapter attempt to create a "safety net" for people with mental disability. The Social Security laws are meant to ensure a minimal degree of financial sustenance for those people who, because of disability, are unable to perform a job. The ADA attempts to assist those who can perform a job by prohibiting discrimination on the basis of disability, perceived as well as actual, in the employment context. The ADA also bans such discrimination in the transportation, telecommunications, and public accommodation contexts, while the Fair Housing Act does so in connection with housing. Although, as applied, these statutes provide only imperfect protection for those with mental disability, together they represent a pioneering attempt to ensure that this group of people is a functioning part of the community rather than ignored or shunned. This overraching purpose behind the laws should inform both the lawyer and the mental health professional working in this area.

Bibliography

RICHARD J. BONNIE & JOHN MONAHAN, MENTAL DISORDER, WORK DISABILITY AND THE LAW (1996).

Robert Burgdorf, *The Americans with Disabilities Act: Analysis and Implications of a Second-Generation Civil Rights Statute,* 26 HARVARD CIVIL RIGHTS–CIVIL LIBERTIES LAW REVIEW 413 (1991).

Julie Clark, *Determining Disability for Children: Implementation of* Sullivan v. Zebley, *Part I: The New Sequential Evaluation Process—An Overview,* CLEARINGHOUSE REVIEW 246 (July, 1991).

Margaret H. Edwards, *The ADA and the Employment of Individuals with Mental Disabilities,* 18 EMPLOYEE RELATIONS LAW JOURNAL 347 (1992–93).

Rachelle Lombardi, *Note: The Evaluation of Children's Impairments in Determining Disability under the Supplemental Security Income Program,* 57 FORDHAM LAW REVIEW 1107 (1989).

LAURA L. MANCUSO, CASE STUDIES ON REASONABLE ACCOMMODATION FOR WORKERS WITH PSYCHIATRIC DISABILITIES (1993).

John Petrila, *Enforcing the Fair Housing Amendments Act to Benefit People with Mental Disability,* 45 HOSPITAL & COMMUNITY PSYCHIATRY 156 (1994).

Special Report: Guidelines for Psychiatric Evaluation of Social Security Disability Claimants, 34 HOSPITAL & COMMUNITY PSYCHIATRY 1044 (1983).

BONNIE TUCKER & BRUCE A. GOLDSTEIN, LEGAL RIGHTS OF PERSONS WITH DISABILITIES: AN ANALYSIS OF FEDERAL LAW (1992).

U.S. Equal Employment Opportunity Commission, *A Technical Assistance Manual on the Employment Provisions (Title 1) of the Americans with Disabilities Act* (1992).

DEBORAH ZUCKERMAN, KATHLEEN DEBENHAM & KENNETH MOORE, THE ADA AND PEOPLE WITH MENTAL ILLNESS: A RESOURCE MANUAL FOR EMPLOYERS (1993).

PART IV

Children and Families

CHAPTER FOURTEEN

Juvenile Delinquency

14.01.   Introduction

In the first edition of this book, this chapter began:

> Perhaps nowhere in the legal system is there as much deference to mental health professionals as in the juvenile court. Indeed, the child mental health and social service professions have grown up with the juvenile court to a large extent. Although this symbiosis has been under attack in the last two decades, it persists and shows no sign of disappearing.[1]

Now the situation is somewhat different. Although the outright abolition of the juvenile court does not appear likely in the near future, the attack on the court and its rehabilitative mission has accelerated in the past decade, from both the left and the right. Those on the left continue to worry about the watered-down version of due process that is a vestige of the original highly paternalistic juvenile court,[2] and those on the right lament the coddling of juvenile offenders, which they believe is at least partially responsible for an epidemic of serious juvenile crime. The right's assumptions about the record of the juvenile court and the prevalence of serious juvenile crime, although largely contrary to empirical evidence,[3] are widely shared by the general public.[4] Nearly everyone doubts the efficacy of the existing juve-

nile justice system in rehabilitating offenders—ironically, at the same time that the state of the art (if not the state of the practice) of treating juvenile delinquents has improved significantly [see § 14.05(b)(3)].

The result of these perceptions has been a steady erosion of the juvenile court in most states through reduction of the court's jurisdiction, increased *transfer* (or *waiver*) of juveniles to criminal courts,[5] and deemphasis of its historic rehabilitative purpose [see § 14.02(e)]. Nonetheless, the rehabilitative goal typically has not been eliminated altogether. Indeed, the transfer decision itself usually requires mental evaluation to determine whether the juvenile is amenable to treatment in the juvenile system [see § 14.04(b)]. The increased complexity of the juvenile court's roles and functions gives new weight to the conclusion to the introduction to this chapter in the first edition:

> In view of the special role of mental health professionals in the juvenile process, it is particularly important for child clinicians and juvenile attorneys to have an appreciation of the situations in which clinical opinions are likely to be significant in juvenile court, as well as of the limits of expertise on these questions.[6]

To obtain such an appreciation, it is useful to begin by examining the evolution of the juvenile

417

court. The chapter then discusses the modern process of adjudicating delinquency and some directions for reform, including those that have been advanced in the international arena. Finally, it provides recommendations for mental health evaluations in the delinquency context, together with relevant recent research concerning the causes and patterns of delinquency and the most effective ways of treating juveniles with mental and behavioral problems.

PROBLEM 14.1

A juvenile court clinic is involved in a long-term planning process. You are asked to (1) advise clinic staff about ways that trends in legal policy and research on serious delinquency are apt to affect their work and (2) make recommendations about changes that may be needed in their program. In preparing your response, consider (1) the shrinking jurisdiction of the juvenile court, (2) the expectation in international human rights law that procedures will comport with a child's sense of dignity, and (3) knowledge about the causes and treatment of delinquency.

14.02.   The Rise and Fall of the "Therapeutic" Juvenile Court

(a)   Juvenile Justice in the Common Law

The juvenile court is a relatively recent jurisprudential invention. The first juvenile code (in Illinois) did not appear until 1899. Prior to that time, juveniles' indiscretions were considered within the general body of criminal law. There was, however, an assumption that immaturity might reduce or even exculpate the blameworthiness of errant youth. Specifically, in the common law, infancy[7] was an absolute defense against criminal charges until age 7 (or 10, depending on the jurisdiction); for children ages 7 to 14, the presumption of capacity to form criminal intent was rebuttable by a showing of immaturity.[8]

Two points are noteworthy about the common-law heritage. First, the age at which children were held fully responsible for adhering to adult standards of conduct was quite young in comparison with current social and moral standards. Second, when charges were brought against children

and youths, the action was indeed *against* them. The question was whether the juveniles had engaged in conduct deserving of criminal punishment, not whether the state might assist the youths in their socialization.

(b)   The Social and Legal Segregation of Youth

The prevailing ethos with respect to both of these points began to change late in the 19th century. First, the industrial age brought the need both to socialize the immigrant class and to lengthen the period of immaturity so that it was long enough for skills to be acquired to meet the increasingly complex demands of the workplace. These social needs led to the "invention" of adolescence and the postponement of adult responsibilities.[9] For the first time, there was clear demarcation of youth as a special time of life, an identifiable stage of development.

Second, with the invention of adolescence came demands for age-grading of responsibilities and increasing segregation of youth from the adult world.[10] This policy trend was endorsed by the leading social reformers and scholars in the social sciences. For example, starting from the premise that ontogeny (the development of the individual) recapitulates phylogeny (the development of the species), G. Stanley Hall, the father of developmental psychology, conceptualized adolescence as an evolutionary way station between primitive savagery and civilization.[11] In the view of Hall and his contemporaries, special legal and social structures for youth were necessary to ensure their socialization as rational contributors to the commonweal. Less elegantly, "child saving" became the rubric for protecting middle-class, small-town youth from the threats that the lifestyle of working-class immigrants allegedly posed to the American way.[12] Age-graded institutions were thus perceived as highly compatible with the interests of *both* the state and the juvenile. Paternalistic social structures for youths would protect society from an immature social class and would assist in their acculturation; it would also "save" youths from both the "lower" elements of the culture and their own baser instincts.

(c)   The Invention of the Juvenile Court

Around the turn of the century, a number of age-graded legal structures were developed in response to these beliefs; one of these structures was the juvenile court.[13] These legal reforms all were founded on a philosophical assumption that the interests of the state and the juvenile were co-extensive. In the juvenile court, unlike the criminal court, the state as *parens patriae*[14] would act *on behalf of* youths and provide them with the treatment needed to ensure that they overcame their youthful indiscretions and adopted civilized mores.

The overriding *raison d'être* of the juvenile court was, therefore, rehabilitation. Because it did not subject youths to punishment, this court had no need for formal protections of due process. Indeed, there was nothing adversary about the proceeding (the state, after all, was acting *for* the juvenile); furthermore, the reasoning went, the trappings of criminal procedure and formal rules of evidence might interfere with the treatment that the court would initiate.

Several additional features followed from this philosophy. To avoid stigma (and resulting self-fulfilling prophecies of criminal behavior) and to promote the beneficent appearance of the juvenile court, proceedings would be closed and records would be sealed. The proceeding would be "civil," and terminology derived from civil procedure would be used.[15] Because the focus was on rehabilitation rather than retribution, the disposition would fit the offender and not the offense. A remorseful, troubled juvenile murderer might be treated by a social worker in freedom, whereas another, more streetwise youth might be incarcerated for several years for engaging in behavior that was neither clearly defined nor illegal for an adult (e.g., "incorrigibility"). As this latter example illustrates, because the aim was reform of errant youth, a whole new category of offenses based on *status* was invented to provide the courts with the authority to implement this reform. Typical "offenses" included incorrigibility, unruliness, and truancy, today all lumped together under the rubric *children (or persons) in need of supervision (or services)* (CHINS; also known as PINS).

Perhaps most important, the key actors in the juvenile court would be social workers, mental health professionals, and probation officers. There was, after all, very little law and even less need for lawyers. Indeed, many of the juvenile court *judges* were untrained legally.[16] From intake to release, the key questions were need for, and amenability to, treatment, and the experts on these questions were clinicians and caseworkers, not lawyers.

(d)   The Fall of the Rehabilitative Ideal

In the view of the reformers, the juvenile court was the paragon of legal realism,[17] the ideal marriage of "science"[18] and law for the social good. Even as late as 1950, Dean Roscoe Pound, an illustrious proponent of "sociological jurisprudence,"[19] lauded the juvenile court as "the greatest step forward in Anglo-American jurisprudence since the Magna Carta."[20]

In fact, however, there was very little science in the juvenile court. Although clinicians were invited to diagnose the psychopathology of wayward youth, to design dispositions, and in effect to adjudicate cases, there was little attention to the assumptions of social fact[21] that were fundamental to the court's work. The malleability of youth, the incompetency (and, therefore, lack of responsibility) of youth, the desirability of informal proceedings for juveniles, and the rehabilitative potential of the court were all taken for granted rather than empirically tested.

Gradually, however, it became clear that the juvenile court had failed to match its promise. As Justice Fortas wrote in the majority opinion in *Kent v. United States* in 1966, "[T]here may be grounds for concerns that the child [brought before juvenile court] gets the worst of both worlds: that he gets neither the protections accorded to adults nor the solicitous care and regenerative treatment postulated for children."[22] The criticism was even more strident a year later in Justice Fortas's opinion for the Court in *In re Gault,*[23] doubtless the most important case in juvenile law specifically and children's rights generally. In *Gault,* Justice Fortas described juvenile courts as "kangaroo court[s]"[24] characterized by arbitrariness,[25] ineffectiveness,[26] and the appearance of injustice.[27]

The *Gault* case had two major effects. First it

made clear for the first time that children are "persons" within the meaning of the Constitution; in the words of the Court, "neither the Fourteenth Amendment nor the Bill of Rights is for adults alone."[28] These dicta opened the door to a whole series of questions about the extent of constitutional rights for minors and their competence in exercising these rights.[29] Second, *Gault* "legalized" the juvenile court by establishing that juveniles were owed at least those elements of the due process essential to fundamental fairness (e.g., the rights to counsel, written and timely notice of the charges, and the privilege against self-incrimination).[30] The Court made clear that a trade-off between fair procedures and the provision of "treatment" or custody would no longer be tolerated.[31]

It is indisputable that *Gault* has had a profound effect on the juvenile court system. Lawyers and law-trained judges in juvenile courts are now commonplace, and in many jurisdictions juvenile courts have the same trappings and most of the same procedures as criminal courts. At the same time, though, it is noteworthy that ambivalence— less charitably, false hope—about the juvenile court has persisted since *Gault*. The *Gault* Court itself seemed to suggest that the failures of the juvenile court were, to a large extent, the result of inadequate resources rather than inherent flaws.[32]

Four years after *Gault*, the Supreme Court clearly enunciated that belief in denying juveniles the right to a jury trial:

> The juvenile concept held high promise. We are reluctant to say that, despite disappointments of grave dimensions, it still does not hold promise, and we are particularly reluctant to say . . . that the system cannot accomplish its rehabilitation goals. So much depends on the availability of resources, on the interest and commitment of the public, on willingness to learn, and on understanding as to cause and effect and cure. In this field, as in so many others, one perhaps learns best by doing. We are reluctant to disallow the States to experiment further and to seek in new and different ways the elusive answers to the problems of the young, and we feel that we would be impeding that experimentation by imposing the jury trial. . . .
>
> If the formalities of the criminal adjudicative process are to be superimposed upon the juvenile court system, there is little need for its separate existence. Perhaps that ultimate disillusionment will come one day, but for the moment we are disinclined to give impetus to it.[33]

Consistent with this ambivalence, some juvenile courts still are not "*Gault* courts" in that they are loath to permit full adversariness and strict application of the rules of evidence.[34] Analogously, there is a continuing controversy about the proper role of defense attorneys in juvenile court [see § 14.04(c)].[35] In short, there is a persistent debate about how to reconcile the promise of the juvenile court as a therapeutic instrument with requirements for due process. Increasingly, this debate has merged with controversies about ways to accommodate the desire to hold juvenile offenders—especially violent juveniles and repeat offenders— accountable for their behavior. Policymakers are searching for a court form that vindicates the public's interests in retribution against and protection from serious offenders at the same time it provides justice tempered by the offenders' immaturity. In effect, there has been open recognition of the long-present but formerly denied reality that punitive impulses exist side by side with altruistic aims in the juvenile justice system.[36]

A 1991 national survey revealed the public's support for *all* these positions.[37] With a level of unanimity rarely present in public opinion, 99% favored punishment of serious violent offenders, and 97% supported punishment of drug dealers and serious property offenders. At the same time, almost two-thirds opposed incarceration of juveniles in adult prisons for serious property offenses, and the majority opposed such incarceration even for serious violent crimes. More than three-fourths favored providing juvenile respondents with the due process rights accorded to adult defendants. Almost three-fourths supported primary reliance on community-based programs rather than training schools, and nearly all favored rehabilitative programs even for serious offenders.

(e)   The Shrinking of the Juvenile Court

Although the public has conflicting attitudes about appropriate measures to take, there is little disagreement that *something* needs to be done to reform juvenile justice. Despite contrary empirical evidence,[38] most people believe that an epidemic of juvenile crime has been under way in the 1990s.[39] Responding to this perception, 20 state legislatures toughened their juvenile codes between 1992 and 1994, and there is little sign that the trend is abating.[40] This trend is an extension in many ways of the legalistic reforms that took place in the 1980s when legislators began to try to bring juvenile codes into full conformance with *Gault*.[41]

The challenge for legislators has been to arrive at solutions that accommodate the widespread public support both for maintenance of a rehabilitative regime and for a more punitive response to serious juvenile crime. Although there may be other ways of reconciling these conflicting goals,[42] the primary legislative response has been to shrink rather than abolish the juvenile court.[43] The new juvenile court laws appear to grow from an effort to limit juvenile court jurisdiction to those youth who "deserve" that court's presumably less punitive approach.

Legislatures have followed several kinds of strategies in reducing the juvenile court's jurisdiction.[44] Least commonly, they have lowered the upper age for juvenile jurisdiction (e.g., from 18 to 16). More commonly, legislatures have made certain kinds of serious offenses subject to concurrent jurisdiction with adult criminal court, so that prosecutors are able to choose where to file cases. Still more states, as well as the federal government, now have statutes requiring criminal filing of certain kinds of cases when older youth are involved, and many have expanded the range of ages (e.g., down to 13) and offenses (e.g., possession of a handgun) in which transfer is possible.[45] Other states have established classes of juvenile offenders subject to special provisions, an approach illustrated by statutes that extend juvenile commitments into criminal sentences for older youth and for those charged with especially serious offenses.

14.03. The Nature of the Juvenile Process

(a) A Typical Statute

As the new transfer statutes illustrate, most state juvenile codes now are an uneasy mixture of the old "therapeutic" approach and the new "criminalized" approach. Responding to constitutional dic-

tates and public opinion, state legislatures have uniformly rejected the pure *parens patriae* model, but almost all have been reluctant to discard a beneficent approach altogether. The current hybrid model has emerged in waves of legislation responding to the Supreme Court's decisions in the late 1960s and early 1970s, the American Bar Association's (ABA) Juvenile Justice Standards Project in the late 1970s and the early 1980s, and the public concern about violent juvenile crime in the 1990s. To provide a concrete picture of the resulting legislative framework, we will examine Virginia's juvenile code,[46] which is typical.

(1) Purpose

The Virginia juvenile code exemplifies the attempt to accommodate simultaneously rehabilitative, incapacitative, and retributive goals. Virginia proclaims that "in all [juvenile] proceedings the welfare of the child and the family is the paramount concern of the Commonwealth."[47] At the same time, it requires juvenile courts to act "[t]o protect the community against those acts of its citizens which are harmful to others and to reduce the incidence of delinquent behavior."[48] Although it is not as explicit as some laws in establishing a retributive or just desert purpose [see § 9.02], the Virginia statute also provides, consistent with such a purpose, for determinate commitment of two classes of juveniles: those 14 years of age or older who have a recent history of a previous felony and those 14 or older who are convicted of an offense that would carry a penalty of at least 20 years' imprisonment if it were committed by an adult.

An even more recent change in this latter provision also illustrates the tendency to get "tough" on juvenile delinquents. Prior to 1994, this provision had allowed commitment for a maximum of one year. In 1994, it was amended to permit commitment of up to seven years.[49]

(2) Jurisdiction

Several types of jurisdiction are connected with the juvenile court.[50] *Act* jurisdiction concerns the types of conduct that trigger juvenile court adjudication. In Virginia, the juvenile court has jurisdiction over cases involving delinquency, CHINS, domestic relations, and civil commitment. Delinquency jurisdiction, which is the primary subject of this chapter, may be exerted over any act that would be a crime if committed by an adult, including traffic offenses. CHINS jurisdiction, which is a secondary topic of this and the following chapters, encompasses habitual truancy, habitual running away, and illegal acts commitable only by children (e.g., violation of curfew); in Virginia, as is true in most other states, it may be exercised only if these acts present a substantial danger to the child's health, or the child or family is in need of services not presently received and court intervention is necessary to provide them. Domestic relations adjudications—which include neglect, abuse, abandonment, and custody determinations—are discussed in Chapters 15 and 16. Finally, civil commitment jurisdiction, discussed in § 10.10(a), allows the juvenile court to hospitalize involuntarily children found to be mentally disordered and dangerous to themselves or others.

The retention of CHINS jurisdiction illustrates the continued resistance toward completely criminalizing the juvenile court system. It may be that Virginia and other states that recognize status offenses see them as mechanisms for protecting the child from unpleasant family situations rather than as disciplinary devices. However, to the extent that this is the case, CHINS jurisdiction overlaps with domestic relations jurisdiction and is unnecessary [see Chapters 15 and 16].

Age jurisdiction determines the point in a child's life when the court loses control over him or her. In Virginia, the juvenile court has authority to adjudicate claims against any child who has not yet reached the age of 18 at the time the act complained of was committed but has dispositional control over a youth through the age of 20. This means, for instance, that a 17-year-old who is found delinquent may be detained in a juvenile facility for three years. The court also has jurisdiction over adults in abuse, neglect, and CHINS cases.

A final type of jurisdiction possessed by the juvenile court in Virginia as well as most other states is transfer or waiver jurisdiction. As noted previously, this type of jurisdiction gives the court authority to decide whether a child charged with delinquency should be tried in criminal court. If transfer occurs, the juvenile court loses jurisdiction over the child.

As in the majority of other states in recent years, Virginia has expanded transfer jurisdiction and made such action easier for prosecutors to undertake.[51] In 1994, the minimum age for transfer was lowered from 15 to 14. For the most serious offenses, transfer can take place simply upon a probable cause finding that the offense has been committed and a showing that the juvenile is competent to stand trial. Telegraphing that promoting rehabilitation is no longer necessarily paramount, Virginia also revised the standard for transfer of older youth charged with less serious felonies, from *amenability to treatment* to being a *proper person to remain within the jurisdiction of the juvenile court* (language borrowed from the Juvenile Justice Standards). In making the latter determination, the court is directed to consider the seriousness and number of alleged offenses, the services available in both the criminal and juvenile justice systems, and the juvenile's age, prior offenses, history of escapes from juvenile facilities, mental retardation, mental illness, school record, emotional and physical maturity, and physical condition. Thus, the criteria for determining whether a youth is appropriately retained in the juvenile system are a complex set of factors bearing on culpability, rehabilitative potential, and public safety.

(3)   Procedure

The stages of a juvenile delinquency or CHINS proceeding parallel those in adult criminal court [see § 2.04(a)]. However, the terminology used to describe these stages continues to reflect the desire to avoid equating delinquency with criminality and thus to minimize the stigma associated with the juvenile process.

In Virginia, after arrest (in most other states called *apprehension*[52]) the juvenile has the right to a *detention hearing* to determine whether release is appropriate (analogous to an adult defendant's bail hearing). The juvenile may be detained if there is no suitable person to whom he or she can be discharged or if release would endanger the juvenile or the public. A second preliminary hearing (*intake*) is held within a few days (or weeks) and is presided over by an *intake officer* (a specialized probation officer). The purpose of intake is to determine whether there is probable cause to believe an offense has been committed and, if so, whether it would nonetheless be in the best interest of the child to be diverted out of the juvenile court system. If diversion is found to be inappropriate, the probation officer files a *petition,*[53] and an *adjudicatory hearing* (trial) is held, at which a judge determines whether the petition is "true" or "not true." At the hearing, the juvenile is entitled to counsel and all other rights of adult defendants, except the right to a trial by jury.

If the juvenile is found to be a delinquent or a child in need of services or supervision, a *dispositional hearing* (sentencing) takes place. The judge usually depends heavily on the probation officer's *social study* (presentence) report. Appeal may be made to the circuit court (a trial court of general jurisdiction); if so, the trial is de novo (in other words, the circuit court need not show deference to the juvenile court's findings of fact).

Although this description depicts the law in a single state, it can fairly be said to represent the typical juvenile code. The Virginia statute reflects public ambivalence about the juvenile court, especially in regard to adjudication and disposition of serious offenses. At the same time, it retains much of the historic juvenile process focused on the youth's best interest.

(b)   Directions for Reform

(1)   Community-Based Systems

The public's mixed attitudes about the stance that the juvenile court should take are further reflected in the fact that the "get-tough" response to the perceived increase in serious juvenile crime has not been uniform. Indeed, legislatures and administrators in some of the most conservative states have been among the leaders in progressive juvenile justice reform.[54] Recognizing that traditional training schools are ill-suited to modify the multiple determinants of juvenile crime, policymakers in some states have substantially reduced their use of incarceration and substantially expanded their community-based alternatives to incarceration. The motivation for this shift has not been a desire to "go easy" on vulnerable juveniles.

Rather, policymakers in such states—often with a nudge from the courts[55]—have concluded that large institutions are both expensive and ineffective relative to well-conceptualized community alternatives. From such a perspective, the growth of noninstitutional programs is closely linked to the public's clamor for a reduction of juvenile crime.

Idaho is an example of a politically conservative state with an increasingly expansive juvenile justice policy. Consider the list of principles found in a three-page intent section that was adopted by the Idaho legislature in 1995 and that describes critical elements of a "coordinated program of rehabilitation":

> It is the . . . intent of the legislature that the primary purpose of this act is to provide a continuum of supervision and rehabilitation programs which meet the needs of the youthful offender in a manner consistent with public safety. These services and programs will individualize treatment and control the youthful offender for the benefit of the youth and the protection of society. It is legislative intent that the department of health and welfare be operated within the framework of the following principles to accomplish this mission:
>
> 1. Provide the least restrictive and most appropriate setting for the youthful offender while adequately protecting the community.
> 2. Provide humane, secure and therapeutic confinement to a youth who has demonstrated that he or she presents a danger to the community.
> 3. Provide a diversity of community-based and secure correctional programs which, whenever possible and appropriate, would be in close proximity to the youth's community and family.
> 4. Strengthen rehabilitative opportunities by expanding linkages to human service programs and community resources.
> 5. Hold youth accountable for their criminal behavior in a manner consistent with their long-term individual needs through such means as victim restitution, community service programs and the sharing of correctional costs.
> 6. Promote a functional relationship between a youth and his or her family.
> 7. Provide assistance to the magistrate division of the district courts in development of and implementation of appropriate juvenile offender dispositions.
> 8. Provide for efficient and effective juvenile

correctional programs within the framework of professional correctional standards, legislative intent and available resources.

9. Provide for a diversity of innovative and effective programs through research on delinquent behavior and the continuous evaluation of correctional programs.

10. Provide assistance to counties in establishing meaningful programs for juveniles who have come into the juvenile justice system but who have not been committed to the custody of the department of health and welfare.

11. Provide programs to increase public awareness and participation in the juvenile justice system of the state.[56]

Note that although the tenor of this statutory language is well within the rehabilitative tradition, it is tempered by the beliefs that the juvenile justice system sometimes does more harm than good, that careful evaluation and planning are needed to avoid such a result, and that juveniles should be held accountable for their behavior. The approach adopted by Idaho also entails a multiplicity of responses (e.g., "humane, secure and therapeutic confinement" for dangerous youth) matched to community resources as well as offender risk and needs.[57]

(2)   Juvenile Justice Standards

The values and beliefs underlying the Idaho juvenile code, as recently revised, bear considerable resemblance to those grounding the Juvenile Justice Standards adopted 15 years earlier. The products of the Juvenile Justice Standards Project, a mammoth interdisciplinary undertaking sponsored by the Institute of Judicial Administration and the ABA in the late 1970s and early 1980s, the Standards remain the most influential scholarship in the debate about the proper form of the juvenile justice system. The Project generated 23 volumes of standards and commentary on various topics of juvenile court administration, procedure, and substance. Most of these volumes have been adopted as official ABA policy.[58]

The Standards are important not simply because of their official status and the stature of the panels that composed them. They are also significant because they present a well-thought-out model for the post-*Gault* juvenile court. Indeed,

the Standards go well beyond *Gault* in the limits that they would place on discretion and in their rejection of the assumption that juvenile courts are primarily agencies for treatment.

In terms of procedure, the Standards emphasize the appearance and reality of fairness through adherence to the sorts of procedures that have been linked in the Constitution and the common law with due process (including the right to public jury trial).[59] With respect to substantive provisions,[60] the most significant (and most controversial) provisions replace offender-based dispositions with determinate sentences proportionate to the offenses in question (the *just deserts* approach discussed in § 9.02). On the theory that the juvenile justice system is usually more debilitative than rehabilitative, they provide for a presumption at intake in favor of referrals to community agencies in lieu of filing charges and require that postadjudicative dispositions be to the least restrictive alternatives. Status offenses are "decriminalized" and removed from the jurisdiction of the juvenile court.[61]

In short, the Standards reject rehabilitation as a feasible and fair primary basis for a justice system and provide for the "five D's": due process, deserts, diversion, deinstitutionalization, and decriminalization. Even if the philosophical foundations are not fully compatible, the systemic reforms attempted under the Idaho code described in the previous section are thus progeny of the reforms that attracted widespread attention from both scholars and policymakers nearly two decades earlier.

(3)   Abolition or Reform?

Given the extraordinary scope of the Standards Project, its most remarkable aspect may be that it nearly completely avoided the question of whether the juvenile court could be justified at all.[62] By contrast, a number of law professors have recently advocated abolition. They believe that *Gault*, if taken seriously, would result in courts so close in form to adult criminal courts as to be indistinguishable; at the same time, they note that adult courts still could administer punitive sanctions that were less harsh for juveniles than for adults. The most influential proponent of abolition has been Barry C. Feld, who has observed that "[t]he juvenile court has demonstrated a remarkable ability to deflect, co-opt, and absorb ameliorative reform virtually without institutional change."[63] Accordingly, Feld has questioned whether there is "any reason to maintain a separate court whose sole distinguishing characteristic is its persisting procedural deficiencies."[64]

Some other commentators acknowledge that the historic rationales for the juvenile court are bankrupt[65] but nonetheless assert that there still is a need for a court that combines rigorous protection of juveniles' rights with mild punitive sanctions (relative to criminal courts). Such commentators sometimes argue that the level of change needed to establish such a court is so great that functionally the result would be a new court.[66] They premise their begrudging support for a separate juvenile court on one or more of the following three arguments:

• The lesser culpability of juveniles (relative to adults) and the lower stigma associated with juvenile delinquency (relative to adult convictions).[67]
• The lack of adherence to ideals of due process and humane treatment in criminal courts and adult corrections.[68]
• The difficulty that many juvenile respondents have in using adult due process protections.[69]

Neither abolition nor radical reform has made much headway, however. The fact that legislatures have focused on shrinking the jurisdiction of the juvenile court rather than eradicating or significantly changing it suggests that—however dissatisfied lawmakers may be with the court's response to serious juvenile crime—they desire a variant of the historic juvenile court. The modal view thus appears still to be that fairness and rehabilitation can be achieved in the juvenile justice system for most juveniles who come before the court.

Even the staunchest defenders of the juvenile court generally concede, however, that the level of reform needed is substantial. Common "mainstream" proposals include:

• Greater judicial leadership than has been common.

• Development and vigorous implementation of court rules to improve the quality of advocacy for juveniles.
• Community action to increase the availability of high-quality preventive and rehabilitative services.
• Changes in policy to accomplish sufficient diversion that the court's caseload can be managed effectively.[70]

In general, moderate reformers must address the following impression that is widely shared by commentators on juvenile justice:

Although juvenile courts increasingly converge with criminal courts, most states do not provide youths with either procedural safeguards equivalent to those of adult criminal defendants, or with special procedures that more adequately protect them from their own immaturity. Instead, states place juveniles on an equal footing with adult criminal defendants when formal equality acts to their detriment, and employ less effective juvenile court procedures when they provide the state with an advantage. Allowing juveniles to "waive" their right to counsel under the adult standard of "knowing and intelligent" is an example of formal equality producing practical inequality, while denying them the right to a jury trial is an example of the less adequate juvenile court procedures that confer an advantage to the state. Young people know what "real" trials are like from viewing courtroom dramas or highly publicized criminal trials. The contrast between the idealized adult proceedings in which defense attorneys aggressively represent their clients before a jury, and the reality of a juvenile bench trial often conducted without the effective assistance of counsel undermines the legitimacy of the justice process.[71]

As the global community has recognized through its *Convention on the Rights of the Child*, the challenge is to create a juvenile legal system that treats every child within it "in a manner consistent with the child's sense of dignity and worth, which reinforces the child's respect for the human rights and fundamental freedoms of others and which takes into account the child's age and the desirability of promoting the child's reintegration and the child's assuming a constructive role in society."[72] Accomplishment of this goal will require law reform,[73] probably including a reduction of cases coming before the court so that adequate attention can be given to the cases that are heard.[74] It will probably also require changes in mental health professionals' role in the court.

14.04.   The Mental Health Professional's Role in Juvenile Court[75]

(a)   Criminal Forensic Questions

Before we discuss the role of mental health professionals in juvenile court, it is useful to consider the ways that the recent evolution of the court may be reshaping forensic evaluation in juvenile proceedings. One result of changes designed to tie juvenile law more closely to precepts of the adult criminal law is that forensic questions commonly raised in the criminal process [see Chapters 6 through 8] may now arise in juvenile cases.

For example, if the proceedings are truly adversary, the question of juveniles' ability to assist in their defense is enlivened. Consistent with that logic, several states have amended their statutes to give express authority for preadjudicatory evaluation of competency to stand trial,[76] and the few appellate opinions on the subject have all included a holding that the issue of a defendant's competency is relevant to delinquency proceedings.[77] However, the reported cases generally have involved older juveniles, usually when they were at risk for transfer to criminal court.[78] Therefore, the difficult practical questions arising from a finding of incompetency in juvenile court have yet to be confronted. Suppose, for example, a seven-year-old accused of shoplifting is found to be too immature to understand the nature of the proceedings or to assist counsel in preparing a defense. Is the adjudicatory hearing to be postponed until the juvenile is, say, 14 years old and "restored" to competency? If so, what is to be done with the juvenile in the interim?

The case law is also divided about the applicability of the insanity defense in juvenile cases. Those courts holding that the defense is unavailable have usually argued that, because juvenile respondents are not subject to criminal penalties, there is no need for exculpation of those who are

mentally disordered, and that in any event there is already provision for adequate care and treatment under the juvenile code.[79] Such a conclusion flies in the face of the logic underlying *Gault* and its progeny. As Chief Justice Burger wrote for the Supreme Court in *Breed v. Jones,* "it is simply too late in the day to conclude . . . that a juvenile is not put in jeopardy at a proceeding whose object is to determine whether he has committed acts that violate a criminal law and whose potential consequences include both the stigma inherent in such a determination and the deprivation of liberty for many years."[80] If criminal conduct is to be excused because of insanity, it is hard to understand why the same defense should not also be available to juveniles whose conduct is mitigated not just by mental disorder but by immaturity.

Regardless of the law's approach to these issues, however, the only situation in which clinicians are likely to be asked to evaluate juveniles with respect to either competency to stand trial or insanity is when the juvenile may be transferred to an adult court. When the juvenile remains in juvenile court, defense attorneys are apt to conclude that the disposition after a finding of incompetency or insanity is likely to be nearly identical to the result of an adjudication of not innocent. Clinicians are even less likely to encounter a defense of diminished capacity [see § 8.03(b)] in juvenile court. When, as is true in most jurisdictions, the disposition is linked to the offender's needs rather than to the offense, there is little strategic advantage to reducing guilt from, for example, first-degree to second-degree murder.[81]

(b)   Amenability to Treatment

In contrast to the infrequency with which they assess competency and culpability issues, forensic child clinicians are likely to spend considerable time in the evaluation of respondents' amenability to treatment. Indeed, it may be fairly stated that amenability to treatment remains the overriding question in the juvenile process. In many states it is typically the key question at every pre- and postadjudicatory stage of the proceeding, and it remains important, although less so, even under the just deserts model underlying the Juvenile Justice Standards.[82]

At intake, as noted earlier, a probation officer must decide whether to release the juvenile outright, to release with conditions, or to pursue delinquency proceedings (i.e., to file a *petition*). Some of the issues at this point are analogous to those presented in a criminal preliminary hearing (e.g., legal sufficiency of the complaint). The most significant question, though, is usually whether the juvenile is amenable to treatment by a community agency other than the court. Theoretically, this phase of the proceeding is designed to minimize the number of youths who come before the juvenile court. However, there is substantial research evidence suggesting that the development of special programs for diversion often tends to "widen the net" of the juvenile court.[83] The same youths who would have been adjudicated still are, and juveniles who would have been released through police, prosecutorial, or court discretion are coerced into special treatment programs under the aegis of the juvenile court.

Amenability to treatment is also likely to arise in the context of "dispositional bargaining," the juvenile equivalent of plea bargaining. Indeed, "for the attorney who represents accused delinquents, often the most critical issue is devising an appropriate disposition."[84] As we noted in the discussion of diminished capacity, the specific charge of which a juvenile is eventually convicted typically makes little difference in most jurisdictions, if the juvenile is guilty of *something* and the case is not transferred to the criminal court. Unlike the situation in criminal court, a defense attorney has won little if he or she bargains successfully for reduction of an aggravated assault charge to simple assault in exchange for a juvenile's plea of not innocent. Therefore, whether at the formal intake conference or in negotiation with the prosecutor, bargaining in juvenile court is likely to focus on the intrusiveness of the disposition. Will the prosecutor accept a relatively unrestrictive treatment plan in exchange for a plea of not innocent? To have a strong hand in negotiation, the defense attorney may need a clinical opinion as to the respondent's amenability to treatment using alternatives other than incarceration. It is likely that clinicians' involvement (at least indirectly) in preadjudicatory dispositional bargaining is very frequent.[85]

For some juveniles, the next point in the process at which amenability to treatment is at issue is at the transfer or waiver proceeding. As noted previously, juveniles above a certain age and/or charged with a serious felony may be transferred (waived) to criminal court, provided that certain findings are made. Some of these findings are not within the expertise of mental health professionals (e.g., whether probable cause exists to believe that the juvenile has committed the felony and whether transfer would serve the public interest). Commonly, however, transfer hearings ultimately focus on general questions of the juvenile's "best interest" or "amenability to treatment" as a juvenile.[86] As Standard 2.2 of the Juvenile Justice Standards frame the issue, the ultimate question is whether the juvenile is "a proper person to be handled by the juvenile court." To reach such a conclusion, the court must find, by clear and convincing evidence, "[1] the likely inefficiency of the dispositions available to the juvenile court as demonstrated by previous dispositions; and [2] the appropriateness of the services and dispositional alternatives available in the criminal justice system for dealing with the juvenile's problems."

If the juvenile is not transferred and is found to be delinquent at the adjudicatory hearing, amenability to treatment also always arises as an issue at the dispositional hearing. Because most jurisdictions still insist upon rehabilitation as a primary basis for the juvenile justice system, amenability to treatment is ostensibly the primary question in determining the disposition.[87]

Finally, if the juvenile is found not amenable to treatment in the community (as part of probation) and is committed to a juvenile correctional facility or "training school," in most jurisdictions the period of incarceration will depend once again on a treatment assessment. Disposition is usually indeterminate (at least as long as the individual remains young enough to be subject to juvenile jurisdiction), so that release will be contingent upon the juvenile's progressing to a point where he or she is found to be amenable to treatment in the community.

In short, dispositional issues arise at every phase of the juvenile process except adjudication.[88] Because amenability to treatment remains the ubiquitous, practically dispositive issue in juvenile court, clinicians tend to play an important role in the process.

(c) Consultation

Beyond their role as evaluator on specific forensic questions, clinicians potentially can be especially useful to the legal system as consultants in juvenile court. We have already noted the potential usefulness of clinicians in assisting attorneys in the development of treatment plans that may be used as negotiating chips. Forensic clinicians often may be of even more help to attorneys in the process of "lawyering" with juveniles than with the substance of the case itself. Such a role is likely to become especially important if courts begin to be restructured along the adversarial lines that we discussed in § 14.03(b)(3) and thus become more concerned with ensuring that juveniles have the opportunity to assist actively in their defense.

The role of defense attorneys in juvenile court—not unlike their role in civil commitment [see § 10.06]—is ambiguous and controversial.[89] How much weight should an attorney give to the wishes of a 12-year-old client in "zealously" defending the client's interests? Still more basically, is it really the juvenile who is the client? Should the attorney's primary allegiance be to the juvenile or the juvenile's parents (who may be paying the bill for the attorney's services)? To the extent that a true adversary system applies in juvenile court, the answer is superficially clear: The attorney zealously advocates the wishes of the juvenile respondent. However, there is presumably some point of cognitive and social immaturity in the client, such that even the most adversarial attorney begins to shift into a guardian-like role in which decisions about defense strategy are made independent of the client's wishes.[90]

Obviously, the less attuned attorneys are to their clients' concerns and the less able the attorneys are to communicate with youths, the more problematic their representation of juveniles becomes. The research literature strongly suggests that such communication is a substantial problem in juvenile cases. Although there is little evidence concerning what actually happens between attorneys and juvenile clients,[91] it is well substantiated

that on average, juveniles' understanding of the legal process is substantially less complete and accurate than that of adult defendants.[92] Juveniles are less likely to conceptualize rights as entitlements applicable to their own cases,[93] and they tend—perhaps realistically—to perceive the juvenile court as inquisitory rather than adversary.[94] Consistent with that view, juveniles frequently do not appreciate the meaning of the attorney–client privilege.[95] Moreover, juveniles often have trouble comprehending the vocabulary in *Miranda* warnings and other legal contexts.[96] These misunderstandings are not alleviated by previous experience with the law,[97] contrary to the assumption of many courts.[98]

When juveniles' understanding of the process is so likely to be at least partially incorrect, it would certainly be unsurprising to find that attorneys fail to appreciate their clients' concerns fully and that juvenile clients fail to make good use of their attorneys. In such a situation, mental health professionals who are knowledgeable about children's and adolescents' understanding of the legal system could be very helpful in consulting with attorneys about communication with their clients, and even in acting as "interpreters" or "legal educators" for the juveniles.

Mental health professionals may also be useful adjuncts to attorneys in preparing juveniles for intake hearings and court appearances. For example, the proportion of juvenile delinquents who have diagnosable learning disabilities is known to be very high.[99] It has often been suggested that learning disabilities in some way predispose juveniles to delinquency. Learning-disabled youths, it is said, might be more likely to behave impulsively, or their delinquency might be responsive to frustration resulting from repeated school failure. However, a study conducted by the National Center for State Courts[100] suggests that neither explanation is valid. Learning-disabled youths are in fact no more likely to *commit* delinquent offenses than are other youths, as measured by both self-report and police contacts. The difference comes in the proportion actually *adjudicated* for delinquency. Presumably, the learning-disabled youths appear less amenable to treatment (perhaps realistically), or they are simply not very adept at appearing appropriately remorseful and respectful. In other words, they are not skilled in manipulating the system. In such cases, clinicians acting as consultants might be very helpful to attorneys in preparation of clients for the legal process.

Finally, mental health professionals may take a consultant's role more typical among expert witnesses: evaluation of the evidence of the opposing side. In particular, clinicians may be able to assist in supporting (or rebutting) assessments of amenability to treatment through discussion of the treatment outcome research on juveniles with particular characteristics and presentation of the literature on clinical prediction. Similarly, in transfer hearings, the conclusions as to a juvenile's amenability to treatment often turn on findings about the reason for failure of previous treatments. Therefore, clinicians may often be very helpful in evaluating the adequacy and appropriateness of previous efforts to rehabilitate the juvenile.

14.05. The Nature of the Evaluation

(a) The Process of the Evaluation

If mental health professionals do act as clinical evaluators of juveniles, they should be cognizant of the difficulty of the enterprise, in particular in terms of eliciting meaningful communication from a child charged with an act of deliquency. This difficulty can arise for any number of reasons. First, juveniles whose understanding of the legal process is inaccurate—which, as discussed previously, is a relatively common phenomenon—may be suspicious about the purpose of an evaluation. Second, in our experience, although adult defendants often wish to appear "sick" in the hope of facilitating less aversive dispositions of their cases, adolescents almost never adopt such a stance. Indeed, a far more common problem is that juveniles "clam up," or, alternatively, try to present themselves as streetwise "tough guys," lest clinicians conclude that they are crazy. For many adolescents, including those whose misbehavior is more neurotic or impulsive than characterological, the label of "delinquent" or "troublemaker" is less threatening to their self-esteem than being considered "crazy" or "weird."[101] Finally, it must be acknowledged that the conse-

quences of being found amenable to treatment, particularly for those juveniles charged with minor offenses, may well be more intrusive—even if necessary or desirable—than a contrary finding. Thus, juveniles may be *realistically* unmotivated to cooperate with evaluations.

For these reasons, juveniles referred for evaluation typically require more "warming up" than adult defendants, and it is especially important to spend a substantial amount of time going over the purpose of an evaluation and the limits of confidentiality. Although allowance must be made for individual differences, it is usually true that juveniles reveal more when the interviews are low key and conversational rather than confrontational. Moreover, juveniles are more likely to require "patching up" and reassurance at the end of the interviews, especially when their offenses are masked symptoms of depression or concurrent with such a disorder,[102] and their evaluations touch, therefore, on especially painful and conflict-laden memories. In part because more time usually must be given to establishing rapport and ending evaluations supportively, it is our experience that juvenile assessments often take longer (e.g., require more interviews) than evaluations of adult defendants on comparable questions.

(b) The Scope of the Evaluation

The greater typical length of juvenile assessments is not simply a matter of clinical technique. It also reflects the greater typical scope of juvenile forensic evaluations. The evaluator may occasionally be asked to focus on competency or insanity issues alone (in which case we refer the reader to Chapters 6, 7, and 8). But as we have discussed earlier in this chapter [see § 14.04(b)], evaluations in juvenile cases are usually focused on amenability to treatment. Thus, the juvenile court evaluator should be particularly aware of the scope of this type of evaluation, which is defined by the legal meaning of treatment, the dispositions available, and the dispositions most likely to work.

(1) The Meaning of "Treatment"

Amenability to treatment should not be read as "amenability to psychotherapy"; rather, it refers to amenability to *any* treatments available, or even potentially available, in the juvenile court.[103] As detailed later, because the range of dispositions open to juvenile judges in most jurisdictions is very broad, the evaluation of amenability to treatment should also be very broad. A thorough assessment of a juvenile's amenability to treatment should usually include an evaluation not only of personality functioning but also of cognitive, educational, vocational, and social needs in the context of the various systems (e.g., family, school, and neighborhood) of which he or she is a part. As already noted, the assessment may also require evaluation of previous treatment efforts.

A qualifier to this broad conceptualization of treatment is that the meaning of amenability to treatment may vary, depending on the stage of the proceeding. Mulvey has articulated this point well:

> Each different proceeding presents potentially different factors weighing on the amenability judgment, and no single decision equation applies to all hearings where amenability is at issue. In the transfer decision, for example, the consideration of amenability is explicit (usually defined by statute), and must be documented in the judge's written decision. Also, the consequences of a judgment of nonamenability in this hearing is that the juvenile is processed through the adult system. For transfer, the question for the clinical profession is, thus, usually one whether the youth is treatable at all. In contrast, the diversion and disposition decisions present a much more implicit amenability question, often framed by its interaction with several unstated but influential variables (e.g., concern for public safety and court philosophy). Clinical information in these situations is deemed valuable for matching a juvenile with an appropriate service. The point is that, while pervasive, the amenability determination and the clinical question related to it are far from uniform. Different court proceedings frame the decision differently.[104]

Mulvey's point notwithstanding, the clinician asked to assess a juvenile's amenability to treatment should consider *all* the alternatives: those that are easily available (e.g., a local court diversion program), those that are available but require extraordinary efforts (e.g., fashioning an individualized program from the offerings of several agencies) or expense, and those that might work but are not presently available (i.e., a particular kind of program that is matched to the offender's needs but is unavailable in the community or the state). It is true that the factfinder—whether a judge or an intake officer—may choose to consider only certain kinds of alternatives at particular points in the proceeding. However, the clinician should recognize that the possibilities for treatment at all stages of the proceeding are typically very broad and should permit the factfinder to make the legal judgment of whether the level of effort or expense required for a particular plan of treatment is justifiable. Such a stance is especially appropriate in jurisdictions in which the juvenile court exercises judicial oversight over public agencies (or private agencies receiving public funds) serving youths and their families; in these jurisdictions, the clinician may be very helpful to the court in identifying gaps in services to troubled youths.

In short, the more specificity that is present in the conclusions to a report about the sort of program that would aid a juvenile, the better. The seemingly ubiquitous recommendation for a "structured treatment program" is practically worthless to a court trying to make a transfer or dispositional decision. Clinicians should be similarly straightforward in reporting the *level* of juveniles' amenability to particular treatments and the level of confidence they attach to these opinions.

On the other hand, the probability of success required to warrant a finding of amenability at various stages of the juvenile process is a legal judgment that should be vested with the factfinder. A related qualifier is that the *definition* of success implicit in the judgment of amenability should also be left to the factfinder. It has been our experience that, in the minds of legal authorities, there is usually an implicit clause in the standard: amenability to treatment, *such that the juvenile will be less likely to recidivate*. That is, as is true in the adult context as well [see § 9.07], the court tends to be most interested in treatment as it affects legally relevant behavior, and predictions should be made in that regard if there are data available on which to base a valid prediction. Nonetheless, given the historic child-centered approach of the juvenile court, clinicians should also feel free to make assessment of amenability to treatment in the context of juveniles' treatment needs even if there is no clear connection to the juveniles' offenses [see the Young report, § 19.10(a)]. The factfinder can then decide whether it is appropriate to consider such treatment options in its findings about the juveniles' amenability.

(2)   Dispositional Alternatives

To reinforce the point about breadth of treatment available to the juvenile court, it may be useful to consider in some detail the range of dispositions at the disposal of a creative juvenile court. The juvenile court in Virginia, for example, may (1) order state and municipal agencies to provide services to the juvenile; (2) order the parent(s) of the juvenile to participate in treatment or "be subject to such conditions and limitations as the court may order and as are designed for the rehabilitation of the juvenile"; (3) place the juvenile on probation "under such conditions and limitations as the court may prescribe"; (4) levy a fine; (5) suspend the juvenile's driver's license; (6) transfer custody of the juvenile to an individual, a private agency, or the department of welfare; (7) if the juvenile is at least age ten, commit him to the juvenile justice system; and (8) order restitution or public service.[105]

Even when there is no explicit authority for creative dispositions, juvenile judges generally have wide-open discretion for establishing special conditions of probation for juveniles and/or their parents, as long as the conditions are believed to be in the juveniles' best interest. Indeed, juvenile judges' authority over probationers may be limited only by a lack of power to order them to go to church![106] As in Virginia, judges may even be able to order agencies to produce for approval the treatment plans they construct.[107] In some sense, the juvenile court's dispositional authority is limited only by a judge's imagination and the finite nature of human and economic resources.

Moreover, in the transfer context, even finite resources may not be a permissible consideration in the determination of amenability to treatment. Although the issue is unsettled, unavailability of resources may be a constitutionally indefensible basis for a finding of unamenability to treatment when such a finding subjects a juvenile to possible criminal penalties.[108] The explicit purpose of re-

habilitation in many state juvenile codes may create a right to treatment requiring that some rehabilitation effort be made for *all* delinquents.[109]

(3)   What Works

To be meaningful, evaluation of amenability to treatment requires delineation of the context. As already noted, the clinician needs to have an appreciation of the range of treatments actually or potentially available to the court. A prediction of the outcome of treatment obviously also requires a knowledge of which treatments work, and for whom.

Less than two decades ago, a panel of the National Academy of Sciences lamented that no research had persuasively refuted the hypothesis that "nothing works" in both juvenile and adult corrections.[110] Just a few years ago, one of us acerbically summarized the literature as indicating that "[t]he most well-validated treatment for delinquent behavior remains getting older!"[111]

Fortunately, the state of knowledge about the *potential* efficacy of treatment is substantially more positive today, even if the state of practice remains seldom matched to the state of the art. The most extensive meta-analysis of delinquency treatment programs was conducted by Lipsey, who reviewed nearly 500 studies through 1987.[112] In nearly two-thirds of the studies (all of which were experimental or quasi-experimental), the results favored the experimental group.

Two caveats are noteworthy, however. First, overall the magnitude of the positive results was quite modest. Nonetheless, even a modest effect of treatment can have substantial social and economic benefits. The South Carolina Department of Youth Services has estimated, for example, that a reduction in adult recidivism by juvenile probationers from 29% to 25% would result in savings equivalent to one-half of the entire budget of the state's juvenile justice system.[113]

A second important observation about Lipsey's findings is that forms of treatment that were single-faceted and ill-matched to the development of skills in the natural environment (e.g., traditional counseling and social skills training) generally were unsuccessful.[114] Further, those that relied on deterrence (e.g., "shock" approaches) typically had *negative* effects.[115] In other words, nothing works that nobody should expect to work.

By contrast, the programs that consistently had at least moderately positive effects on recidivism were multimodal and skill-oriented. Designers of intervention studies have become more creative in addressing the multiplicity of factors involved in juvenile delinquency (especially serious and chronic offending [see § 14.06]). In so doing, researchers have been able to demonstrate positive effects—sometimes substantial effects—on recidivism even by "deep-end" populations.[116]

Perhaps the best validated program is *multisystemic* treatment, which has been evaluated in a series of true experiments by Henggeler and his colleagues.[117] Multisystemic treatment is a relatively short-term (approximately three-month) intensive treatment delivered in home and community settings. Relying on research on the multiple personal, familial, educational, and socioeconomic factors involved in delinquency, therapists work to put a self-sustaining system into place in which families are empowered to solve their own problems but ongoing supports are also available in the extended family and community.

Multisystemic treatment is perhaps best summarized by its guiding principles:

1. The primary purpose of assessment is to understand the "fit" between the identified problems and their broader systemic context.
2. Interactions should be present-focused and action-oriented.
3. Interventions should target sequences of behavior within or between multiple systems.
4. Interventions should be developmentally appropriate and should fit the developmental needs of the youth.
5. Interventions should be designed to require daily or weekly effort by family members.
6. Intervention efficacy is evaluated continuously from multiple perspectives.
7. Interventions should be designed to promote treatment generalization and long-term maintenance of therapeutic change.
8. Therapeutic contacts should emphasize the positive and should use systemic strengths as levers for change.
9. Interventions should be designed to promote

responsible behavior and decrease irresponsible behavior among family members.[118]

This approach [the application of which is fleshed out in greater detail in § 14.06] has shown remarkable efficacy even with chronic serious offenders. In one clinical trial based in a community mental health center, recidivism in the first year was reduced by approximately one-half relative to the usual juvenile justice services—a difference that sustained itself across at least three years.[119] Even more positive results were obtained in a second trial in which graduate students in clinical psychology served as therapists. In that study, after four years of follow-up, the overall recidivism for adolescents who completed multisystemic treatment (22.1%) was less than one-third of that for those who completed individual treatment (71.4%), dropped out of individual treatment (71.4%), or refused treatment altogether (87.5%), and less than one-half of that for those who dropped out of multisystemic treatment (46.6%).[120]

Although the work on multisystemic treatment provides perhaps the most extensive evidence that an intensive, individualized home- and community-based treatment can substantially reduce delinquent behavior, even among chronic, serious offenders, there are other, similar examples in the literature. In an early example, Massimo and Shore demonstrated change sustained across 15 years among delinquents who received vocationally oriented psychotherapy (a program that was similar to multisystemic treatment in intensity and scope but focused on getting and keeping a job).[121] Another series of experiments showed a substantial reduction in recidivism among delinquent youth who, with their families, were the recipient of several hours of volunteer service per week by undergraduates trained in empathic listening, behavioral contracting, and family advocacy.[122] Similarly, a Norwegian school-based secondary prevention program that focused on changes in the school itself as well as individual children and their families showed marked and sustained reduction of school aggression (bullying), fighting and victimization, vandalism, alcohol abuse, and truancy, as well as marked improvement in school order, peer relationships, and attitudes toward school and schoolwork.[123]

14.06.   Specific Areas of Evaluation

Given the range of dispositions available to the juvenile court and the outcome research showing that well-conceived treatment often does work to prevent recidivism, what sorts of things should a clinician who is asked to evaluate amenability to treatment examine? The general answer, which should be obvious by now, is anything relevant to determination of interventions (including interventions outside the mental health system) that would assist in the adaptation of the juvenile to the community. The clinician will need to adopt a broad, ecological perspective for evaluation. Therefore, the evaluation will often require an interdisciplinary approach, or at least a thorough investigation of a juvenile's behavior in home, school, workplace, and neighborhood. It will often be helpful to enlist the assistance of the defense attorney or court staff (depending on the stage of the proceeding and the source of the referral) in the gathering of information for the evaluation.

The specific content of the evaluation will obviously vary, depending on the issues that seem to be presented by the case and upon the orientation and style of the evaluation. However, we present some areas that are common considerations: family, peers, community, vocational skills, and personality functioning.

(a)   Family

(1)   Reasons for Assessment

There are three major reasons for conducting a thorough family evaluation. First, evaluation of the family is often important in formulating the causes of the delinquent behavior, just as such an evaluation is usually helpful or perhaps even necessary in nonforensic assessment of an adolescent. Family assessment becomes central if the offense itself is familial—for example, if the juvenile is charged with violence against another family member,[124] if a family member is a prosecuting witness,[125] or if the offense may have been perpetrated by multiple family members. Second, parents and other family members can provide historical information to supplement or corroborate the juvenile's own account. Third, as we have not-

ed in the preceding section, the juvenile court has authority in many jurisdictions to order a family disposition.[126] It also has the power to remove the juvenile from the home. Accordingly, the clinician should be alert to the possibility of treatment of the juvenile through family therapy or parent counseling.

The clinician's assessment of the emotional supports available or potentially available in the family may also inform the judge's determination of the juvenile's amenability to treatment while living at home. Such an assessment may also provide ideas about external supports that would enable the parents to provide necessary supervision and nurturance for their child. As noted in the preceding section, the most effective approaches do not rely solely on traditional counseling or therapy but instead integrate such techniques into a more comprehensive intervention.

(2)   Clinical Issues

Generally, there are two themes in the literature about families of aggressive children. First, aggressive children tend to come from families in which there are high levels of hostility and aggression.[127] This principle was vividly illustrated by data gathered from the Rochester site of the Causes and Correlates study, a landmark three-site, large-scale longitudinal study of the development of delinquency.[128] A history of child maltreatment increased by 24% the likelihood that a youth would report violent behavior at some point during adolescence. If partner abuse and a general climate of hostility (e.g., general conflict or physical fighting) in the family also existed, the risk of violent delinquency was two times greater than among nonviolent families.

In short, aggressive children often live in homes in which there are high levels of conflict, with aggression being a common mode of dispute resolution among family members.[129] There are frequently cycles of coercive behavior (e.g., parents are targets as well as instigators of coercive behavior)[130] and high levels of parental rejection and punitiveness, especially physical punitiveness.[131] There is sometimes direct parental reinforcement of aggression, especially aggression directed toward people outside the family.[132]

Second, aggressiveness in children is related to

parental ineffectiveness and family disorganization. Generational role boundaries are commonly blurred,[133] and parents are relatively likely to respond positively to deviant behavior and aversively to appropriate behavior.[134] There are also high levels of father absence[135] and, when both parents are present, conflict between spouses.[136]

The significance of father absence apparently lies largely in the associated level of supervision and the consistency of discipline and not in father absence per se. The time that parents spend with their children is negatively related to incidence of almost all forms of antisocial behavior.[137] Time that parents spend with their children decreases time spent with delinquent peers, increases availability of positive models, and diminishes acquisition of delinquent peers.[138]

To summarize, families of delinquents frequently benefit from measures that enhance the warmth of relationships, provide nonaggressive models and clear, consistent norms for behavior, and increase parental monitoring of children's behavior. Such efforts are important to prevent the effects of other risk factors as well as to diminish family problems themselves. A strong attachment to parents and close supervision by them are the strongest correlates of "resilience" (i.e., avoidance of delinquency while at high risk for it).[139]

Nonetheless, clinicians should be careful not to limit their assessment to the domains most familiar to mental health professionals (i.e., to personal and familial factors) and, by so doing, to circumscribe dispositional planning. Although some phenomena of family structure and process have been consistently shown to be correlates of delinquency, such variables by themselves are only modest correlates of delinquency.[140] What may be more notable than the family factors in delinquency is how weak they are. Contrary to what is probably popular belief as well as clinical intuition, family interventions, without more, are unlikely to turn the tide in development of a pattern of chronic offending.

(b)   Peer Relations

By contrast, association with delinquents and drug users may be the most potent correlate of delinquency.[141] Indeed, delinquency is normative

behavior among adolescents in some communities.[142]

Given that group delinquent behavior need not represent an antisocial personality structure, the prognosis is better for delinquent youth who only co-offend (rather than instigate the offense),[143] as is often the case when antisocial behavior begins in adolescence.[144] That is not to say, of course, that group delinquency is benign. Notably, gang crime accounts for a substantial proportion of youthful offending in many metropolitan centers, especially among minority youth in their teens and early 20s.[145] Much of the public fear of juvenile crime probably stems from the marked increase in gang violence that has occurred in recent years, in part because of increasing availability of guns.[146]

Nonetheless, the image of well-organized gangs establishing "franchises" in multiple locations does not match reality. Family migration, not gang relocation, and local genesis are the primary causes of growth of gangs outside major metropolitan areas. Most gangs are poorly organized and transient; membership is "not simply a matter of rational choice by career criminals."[147] Offending does tend to increase substantially while an adolescent is a gang member, but membership is generally very unstable. Membership for a few months is much more common than membership across a number of years. Accordingly, long-term membership in a gang is an especially bad prognostic sign.[148]

In short, treatment programs that do not conscientiously promote relationships with nondelinquents are setting an uphill course in attempting to prevent recidivism.[149] Conversely, as the literature on gangs illustrates, delinquent peer networks often can be disrupted; establishment of more positive peer relationships can be a powerful factor in preventing recidivism.

(c)   Community

The reasons for evaluating the community (as it interacts with the juvenile) parallel the reasons for assessing the family. First, consideration of support systems (or lack thereof) in the community may suggest both reasons for the delinquent behavior and resources for changing it. Neighbors, youth group leaders, and teachers can be valuable informants about the juvenile's behavior.

Moreover, long-term change in the juvenile's behavior is unlikely to result without there also being change in the community. Some creativity may be necessary in identifying and making use of both natural helpers and formal programs that might assist the juvenile and prevent further delinquency. Even if the juvenile is going to be removed from the home or incarcerated, ultimately there must be attention to the preparation of the community for his or her return. There needs to be sufficient assessment of the community to construct such plans.

Finally, as noted previously, in some jurisdictions the juvenile court has authority over public agencies. The court may order agencies to provide services that might contribute to the rehabilitation of the juvenile. Therefore, some assessment of the match between the juvenile and the community's resources is useful.

It is known that neighborhood cohesion is negatively related to the prevalence of delinquency.[150] Increasing concentration of poverty in particular neighborhoods and weakening of social networks supportive of families throughout society—what might be described as "social poverty"—have coalesced into dangerous situations in many American communities.[151] With a level of alarm rarely found in such reports, a panel of the National Academy of Sciences summarized in 1993 the socially toxic condition of many neighborhoods:

> Over the past two decades, the major settings of adolescent life have become increasingly beleaguered, especially where the number of families living in poverty has expanded and where their concentration in the inner cities of large urban areas has increased. Schools in such areas do not have the resources needed to sustain their mission, school buildings are in disrepair, and there is often the threat of violence in classrooms and corridors; neighborhoods are more dilapidated, and streets often physically dangerous; communities are also fraying as ever-rising mobility destroys personal ties and traditional institutions, such as churches, and local businesses suffer from disinvestment; families are more frequently headed by a single parent, often a working mother unable to obtain competent child care or by two working parents with less time for childrearing because they are striving to main-

tain their standard of living in the midst of a general decline in wages. Such settings have become the crucible in which the lives of increasing numbers of America's youth are being shaped.[152]

Obviously, the courts' ability to deal with such problems is limited. The limitation is not simply one of the boundaries of technology. It is also a problem of paradigm: It is difficult to change *communities* when the disposition is necessarily fashioned around the individual.[153] Nonetheless, there has been some success with juvenile advocacy programs in reducing recidivism.[154] Broad assessment will be necessary to construct programs to reshape the social context in which particular juveniles live and to promote community responsibility for the well-being of youth.[155] Judicial leadership can be important in that process.[156]

One issue that is noteworthy in the assessment of community resources is that the use of an amenability-to-treatment standard is likely to result in more restrictive dispositions for juveniles from lower-class communities. We do not mean to imply that poor people are untreatable. Indeed, there is substantial evidence to the contrary, even with traditional verbal therapies.[157] However, it is doubtless true that the resources for significant change—or simply for elaborate, if not necessarily effective, treatment plans—are increasingly less likely to be available as the socioeconomic ladder is descended. At the same time, the level of drain on the resources that are available is likely to be higher. Although the inequities of disposition arising from use of the amenability-to-treatment standard may not be an immediate concern of forensic evaluators, they should be considered by policymakers in the analysis of the proper bases for punitive interventions.[158]

(d) Academic and Vocational Skills

It is especially important to identify a juvenile's academic and vocational skills because such skills enable a youth to adapt to the environment. That is not to say that improving achievement level will prevent violent recidivism; obviously, academic and vocational skill levels on their face have little to do with such a crime. On the other hand, it can be said with some confidence that, without sufficient skills, the probability of a juvenile's getting into some kind of trouble is increased substantially. Whether treatment gains will be maintained over time appears to be highly related to the seriousness of academic deficits that remain.[159] As already noted [see § 14.05(b)(3)], the programs that have demonstrated some success in treatment delinquency have had a strong educational/vocational component. Analogously, the only adult correctional programs that have shown evidence of effectiveness are those that have combined work and financial support.

The power of school failure in setting a course for delinquency was illustrated by the finding in the Causes and Correlates study that reading performance and retention grade are both related to delinquency *even for first-graders*.[160] In that connection, it is important to note that the relationship between commitment to school and delinquency is reciprocal.[161] In other words, low commitment to school increases the likelihood of delinquency in the subsequent year, and vice versa.

Beyond their obvious implications for establishing a niche in the community and particularly the school itself, vocational and educational skill levels are likely to be significant in design of dispositional plans for several other reasons. First, such skills are important in establishing a sense of self-esteem and active mastery of conflicts.[162] Second, the ability to verbalize conflicts (which can come from educational attainments) contributes to delay in expression of impulses and probably to less reliance on physical aggression.[163] Third, a carefully designed educational treatment program may increase social skills and accuracy of social perceptions, which may in turn improve interpersonal relationships and the ability to navigate through the juvenile justice system itself.[164] The ability to conceptualize behavioral alternatives and to plan accordingly may be a bridge between cognitive development and personality functioning.[165]

To reach conclusions sufficiently refined to base an individualized educational program on them, it will generally be necessary to perform a formal psychoeducational assessment—one of the few situations in which we believe psycho-

logical testing to be an efficient means of gathering data to answer a forensic question. It is important in that regard not to stop with vocational interest scores, grade levels, and IQs but to develop a full picture of a juvenile's learning style and the interaction of that style with the juvenile's emotional development and behavior.[166] Such a profile will be more useful than global scores in both understanding the juvenile's fit with the environment and developing a specific treatment program.

In most cases, the attorney should see not only that the broad evaluation recommended here is used for assessing the juvenile's amenability to treatment and developing a dispositional plan in juvenile court but also that it is transmitted directly to the local school system. Under the Individuals with Disabilities Education Act [see Chapter 17], an individualized educational plan (IEP) paves a procedural avenue for ensuring that a juvenile receives appropriate educational treatment, whether he or she remains in the local school system or is institutionalized. Official identification as a pupil with special needs may also substantially reduce the juvenile's future vulnerability to suspension or expulsion for school misbehavior.[167]

(e) Personality Functioning

It is, of course, in the area of personality functioning that the assessment of a juvenile is most likely to resemble a traditional mental health evaluation. We need not prescribe the format for such an evaluation, but we do wish to offer several notes of caution. First and most important, it should be emphasized that the same behavior may have multiple etiologies even excluding environmental considerations. It has been our experience that clinicians often generalize from preconceptions about delinquent behavior without really examining the environmental and intrapsychic determinants of the behavior in a particular juvenile. Even from a psychodynamic perspective, serious delinquent behavior may be the product of group norms (i.e., "sociosyntonic" or "socialized aggressive" behavior), a "pure" character disorder, "overdetermined" neurotic motivation (e.g., when the delinquent behavior is a depressive equivalent), or truly crazy thinking. There may be substantial differences in the mental health treatment of choice, given these various etiologies.

Second, clinicians need to be attuned to base rates of behavior. In that regard, it is useful to note that mental health professionals tend to ascribe more disturbance to *normal* adolescents than even *clinical* groups of adolescents themselves report[168]—a point that bears special emphasis given that delinquent "careers" are usually short-lived adolescent phenomena.[169]

Third, at the risk of rekindling the classical debate about the relative validity of clinical and actuarial prediction, we remind clinicians that the best predictor of adolescent behavior—like adults' behavior—is simply past behavior.[170] As delinquent records accumulate, so does the risk.[171]

Fourth, although we have noted that well-conceptualized treatment has a good track record even in cases of serious delinquency, it must also be acknowledged that such a conclusion does not extend to traditional psychotherapy. Furthermore, conclusions about *particular* juveniles' amenability to treatment may have little empirical basis. In short, the clinician must remember that the need for modesty about the limits of expertise are no less present here than in other legal contexts. This admonition is especially important given the likelihood that juvenile courts may be unusually receptive to mental health professionals' theorizing about the causes of a particular's youth transgressions and about the avenues that treatment might take.

Although there needs to be an individualized assessment given the multiple specific causes of delinquent behavior, some directions are especially likely to be fruitful. In particular, certain social–cognitive distortions (notably, a tendency to perceive hostile intent) have been shown to be common in aggressive youth.[172] Focused cognitive-behavioral treatments are available to remediate such distortions and to facilitate thoughtful problem solving. However, their efficacy in reducing aggressive behavior is not yet established,[173] and attempts to establish constellations of personality traits that cause delinquency have been "fraught with conceptual and methodological difficulties and have generally yielded few meaningful findings."[174]

14.07. Special Juvenile Populations

(a) Very Young Offenders

Some populations of juvenile offenders present special issues. One such group is preadolescent offenders. Age of onset of chronic antisocial behavior is sufficiently prognostic that the fourth edition of the *Diagnostic and Statistical Manual of Mental Disorders* differentiates between conduct disorders that develop during childhood (prior to age ten) and that have adolescent onset.[175] The earlier that children come into the juvenile justice system, the more frequent their involvement with the courts tends to be.[176]

At the same time, these correlations should not be used to "write off" children prematurely. Most juveniles appear in court only once, and it is difficult to differentiate at first offense who will become chronic offenders. The nature of the initial offense has little validity as a predictor of recidivism, in regard to either future court involvement at all or the nature of the offense if recidivism does occur.[177] Moreover, epidemiological research suggests that early intervention has good promise to interrupt budding delinquent careers and that very young offenders should receive special attention to avert development of a chronic pattern of offending:

> [R]esults reported here suggest that if problems in the family or school, or initial delinquency itself, are left unattended, a behavioral trajectory is established that increases considerably the likelihood of a delinquent career. After some initial impetus is provided, the reciprocal nature of the causal system tends to be self-perpetuating, and delinquency becomes more and more likely. On the other hand, however, if early problems are successfully treated, then the same reciprocal quality of the system works to decrease the chances of delinquency and increase the chances for conformity. For example, successful family intervention should both reduce delinquency and increase commitment to school, which should begin a set of mutually reinforcing relationships that make delinquency less and less likely. The most important point from an interactional perspective is that all of the causes of delinquency need to be identified and dealt with in a coordinated fashion to take advantage of the reciprocal quality of the system, thereby establishing a behavioral trajectory that makes delinquency increasingly less likely.[178]

Therefore, clinicians making an assessment of very young offenders for diversion or disposition should be especially careful, so that they address the family, peer, school, and community characteristics that may be conducive to development of a chronic offending pattern. Just as multiple problems can feed on each other to build a context in which delinquent behavior is difficult to change, multiple positive changes can have a multiplicative effect to enable resilient responses.

(b) Sex Offenders

Although considerable programmatic attention has been given in recent years to juvenile sex offenders, little research with appropriate comparison groups is available. Evidence thus far, however, shows juvenile sex offenders to have particularly pronounced emotional and interpersonal deficits, with sex offenders often being loners with high levels of anxiety and especially troubled, often abusive families.[179]

The dominant approach to treatment of juvenile sex offenders consists of group therapy with a cognitive-behavioral orientation and foci on development of skills in building relationships, differentiation and management of emotions, and correction of myths about sexuality.[180] The only clinical trial of treatment of juvenile sex offenders suggests, however, that this approach is too limited in scope, given the multiple serious problems common within that group. In that study, 16 adolescents were randomly assigned either to individual psychotherapy or to multisystemic treatment that included not only cognitive-behavioral interventions but also work directly on peer relations, school performance, and family relations.[181] Within three years, six (75%) of the individual treatment group but only one (12.5%) of the multisystemic treatment group had been arrested for another sex offense. Also, although this study did not include a group therapy condition, it is probable, as in other contexts in juvenile justice, that promotion of prosocial peer relations would be more effective than requiring interaction with groups of antisocial or asocial youth.[182]

Accordingly, although evaluations of juvenile sex offenders should include a focus on attributions, beliefs, and attitudes about sexuality, and

indeed relationships in general, clinicians should not overlook other domains of life. To be effective, a dispositional plan probably must include attention to the youth's family and community.

(c) Status Offenders

When Melton testified on behalf of the American Psychological Association to a Senate subcommittee in 1991, he noted that a search of the PsychLit data base failed to uncover a single article on status offenses or status offenders published after 1988.[183] With the attention given by federal agencies to serious offenders, concern about status offenders had evaporated, notwithstanding the huge number of youth involved. Discussing the links between status offense jurisdiction and child maltreatment, Melton concluded:

> [T]he topic of status offenses . . . presents exemplars of state-inflicted harm on children and youth. It is only slightly overstated to say that, however noble public officials' intent may be, *status offense jurisdiction often is de facto punishment for being maltreated.*
> [Several facts underlie this harsh conclusion.] . . . First, research shows that status offenders do "look different" from juvenile delinquents. The notion that status offense jurisdiction is a wise exercise in early intervention among antisocial youth is simply untrue. Research shows that status offending is typically *not* a stepping-stone to delinquency. Adolescent girls, many of whom have been subjected to sexual abuse, enter the juvenile justice system much more often, proportionately, under status offense jurisdiction than as a result of delinquency petitions. Moreover, they tend to be subjected to harsher dispositions than male status offenders.
> Second, as illustrated by the examples of girls who run away from home as a defense against incest and of youth who are classified legally as runaways but who really are "throwaways," juvenile court jurisdiction in status-offense cases often could be sought instead on the basis of child protection petitions. As one well-known scholar on juvenile justice and child welfare has succinctly stated, "One of the most problematic aspects of the juvenile justice system is its failure to distinguish offenders from victims. Nowhere is this more true than in the case of sexual abuse and sexual behavior."
> Indeed, the most striking commonality of status-offense cases is serious family dysfunction. Although the proportion varies across ju-

risdictions, in many communities the majority of status offense petitions—in some cities, the vast majority—are filed by parents against their children as "ungovernable" or "incorrigible." Research shows that such petitions are especially likely to result in detention and restrictive dispositions. It is hard to imagine how a quasi-punitive response to an individual child in the face of such serious family conflict can be either fair or effective. The ineffectiveness of such an approach is confirmed by available evaluation research, which shows that services based in juvenile justice often fail even in inducing youth to keep their appointments.

Third, the Children in Custody survey shows that thousands of children and youth charged with status offenses are confined each day without even the pretense of a status offense. They are acknowledged to be incarcerated simply because they are victims, and an alternative emergency placement is unavailable. . . .

Fourth, just as child protective jurisdiction has become the entry point for overburdened child welfare agencies in some communities, status offense petitions often are misused as a means of obtaining services for troubled youth and families. In some communities, the court is the first rather than the last resort for families desiring services. . . . Families should not have to resort to a stigmatizing determination of their child's "guilt" in a juvenile court proceeding in order to obtain help when they are having serious problems. . . .

[S]tatus offense petitions often are signs of failure of, or at least dissatisfaction with, the service system more than indicators of culpable behavior of the individual youth. Such petitions are clear exemplars of blaming the victim—subjecting a child who already may have a traumatic history to a quasi-punitive process because of a lack of adequate services.[184]

In short, evaluations for diversion or disposition of status offenders should include a special focus on family issues. That assessment should incorporate an analysis of resources outside the family that might be useful in reducing the youth's conflict with his or her family and (especially in truancy) school [see Chapter 15].

14.08. Do the Mental Health and Juvenile Systems Belong Together?

Although this volume focuses primarily on *evaluation* in the legal system, it is appropriate in this chapter to discuss the *initiation* of forensic evaluations. As we noted in § 10.10(a), the populations of youth in juvenile justice facilities and in mental hospitals are to a large extent interchangeable. Indeed, in many jurisdictions, juvenile courts are the primary referral agents for hospitalization of children and adolescents[185]; the specific route that difficult youths travel depends largely on the ease of entry into one system or the other,[186] and on other criteria that are unrelated to the juveniles' treatment needs or the nature of their behavior disorders.[187]

Even in less serious cases, though, there is often such movement back and forth between the mental health and juvenile justice systems. In particular, mental health and social service personnel sometimes use the juvenile court—especially status-offense jurisdiction—as a means of obtaining treatment for youths.[188] There may be various motives for this strategy: (1) the juvenile, the juvenile's parents, or the whole family may be refusing treatment; (2) public agencies may be slow to respond for bureaucratic reasons, in the absence of a court order; or (3) the court may be perceived as an avenue for integrating services for a multiproblem family.

The practice of invoking juvenile court jurisdiction as a means of obtaining treatment is mistaken, albeit benevolently motivated. Pragmatically, the experience of the juvenile court over the past century certainly reveals the necessity of reasonable goals for the court. As Mulvey has pointed out,[189] courts are ill-equipped to deal with family problems; the juvenile court is not in fact structured as a crisis intervention or mental health agency. If the need is to make treatment available, it would be more effective and more efficient to focus advocacy on the systems designed to provide human services, rather than to try to deflect courts from their central purposes. Expansion of juvenile court jurisdiction will not result in a substantial increase of services to children, youths, and families, but it will transform them into *coercive* services,[190] and it will subject them to added stigma from the label of "delinquent."[191]

We concur with Morse and Whitebread that mental health professionals (and legal authorities) should welcome the trend toward an increasingly legalistic model in juvenile law:

Although the [Juvenile Justice Standards] clearly have shifted from the traditional discretionary, medical model of juvenile justice, it is apparent nonetheless that mental health service providers will continue to play a substantial if considerably more modest role. The opinions of mental health professionals will be sought regularly and they will be asked to provide services in both institutions and community programs. Although informed consent will be required for most mental health services, we suspect that many juveniles will accept such services if their benefits are patiently and clearly explained. Moreover, treatment under such conditions is not only more likely to be successful, it is also more respectful of the juvenile's autonomy and privacy than coerced treatment. Mental health professionals are vitally concerned with respect for the individual and should therefore applaud a model that enhances autonomous, contractual relations between helping professionals and their patients or clients. It is true, of course, that some juveniles who might have been helped by coerced treatment will refuse such treatment. But, again, we suspect that such cases will be few in number and it is a price worth paying in order to develop a freer and more respectful treatment regime. Mental health professionals will lose some power, but they are still charged with performing those services they are trained best to provide—evaluating and treating patients who want and need such services.[19]

Bibliography

BARRY C. FELD, JUSTICE FOR CHILDREN: THE RIGHT TO COUNSEL AND THE JUVENILE COURTS (1993).

SCOTT W. HENGGELER, DELINQUENCY IN ADOLESCENCE (1989).

MICHAEL A. JONES & BARRY KRISBERG, IMAGES AND REALITY: JUVENILE CRIME, YOUTH VIOLENCE AND PUBLIC POLICY (1994) (available from the National Council on Crime and Delinquency, 685 Market Street # 620, San Francisco, CA 94105).

JUVENILE JUSTICE AND PUBLIC POLICY: TOWARD A NATIONAL AGENDA (Ira M. Schwartz ed. 1992).

THE JUVENILE SEX OFFENDER (Howard E. Barbaree et al. eds. 1993).

Gary B. Melton, *Children as Legal Actors,* in HANDBOOK OF PSYCHOLOGY AND LAW 275 (Dorothy K. Kagehiro & William S. Laufer eds. 1991).

Gary B. Melton, *Taking* Gault *Seriously: Toward a New Juvenile Court,* 68 NEBRASKA LAW REVIEW 146 (1989).

NATIONAL RESEARCH COUNCIL, LOSING GENERATIONS: ADOLESCENTS IN HIGH-RISK SETTINGS (1993).

REASON TO HOPE: A PSYCHOSOCIAL PERSPECTIVE ON VIOLENCE AND YOUTH (Leonard D. Eron et al. eds. 1994).

SERIOUS, VIOLENT, AND CHRONIC JUVENILE OFFENDERS: A SOURCEBOOK (James C. Howell et al. eds. 1995).

HOWARD N. SNYDER & MELISSA SICKMUND, JUVENILE OFFENDERS AND VICTIMS: A NATIONAL REPORT (Aug. 1995) (compendium of data on juvenile justice; published by the Office of Juvenile Justice and Delinquency Prevention and available from the Juvenile Justice Clearinghouse, P.O. Box 6000, Rockville, MD 20849-6000; 800-638-8736).

David C. Tate et al., *Violent Juvenile Delinquents: Treatment Efficacy and Implications for Future Action,* 50 AMERICAN PSYCHOLOGIST 777 (1995).

CHAPTER FIFTEEN

Child Abuse and Neglect

15.01. The Nature of Abuse and Neglect Proceedings

(a) Philosophical Dilemmas

As discussed in Chapter 14, the separate system of juvenile justice has its roots in *parens patriae* doctrine; it was intended to reflect state interests in the socialization of children. An even more direct reflection of the state's interest and duty in protecting children is found in the invocation of state power on behalf of abused and neglected children, an issue that is usually considered by the same specialized court that has jurisdiction over delinquency cases. State action in cases of child maltreatment represents a direct conflict with family privacy and parental liberty; as such, it is an area of the law in which the complex and sometimes confusing mixture of interests among child, family, and state is starkly presented.[1] For example, the state has an interest in the socialization of the child to be a productive citizen, but it also has an interest in the preservation of the family as a basic social institution and a buffer between the state and the individual. Similarly, parents are usually assumed to act on behalf of the child, but their interests may be demonstrably in conflict with, or at least different from, the child's. The child has an interest in preserving his or her care and relationships (and, therefore in parental autonomy), but he or she may also have independent interests in liberty and privacy. These philosophical issues, combined with difficulties in clearly and narrowly defining abuse and neglect,[2] have made the question of the proper breadth of state jurisdiction and intervention in cases of child maltreatment a hotly debated one in recent years.

The attempt to balance the state's interest in protecting children with the parents' interest in family privacy is especially troublesome because of questions about the state's ability to fulfill its interest. The documented lack of stability in foster care in most jurisdictions[3] frames the balancing of interests in terms of a dreadful dilemma: Are children worse off in the care of abusing and neglecting parents or in that of the state?[4] Although there are no clear answers to this question yet, the fact that it is seriously posed indicates both the depth of controversy about policies concerning child maltreatment and the widespread skepticism about the ability of social service and mental health professionals to evaluate possible maltreatment validly and to treat parents and children successfully.

(b) Stages of the Legal Process

These issues permeate each stage of abuse and neglect proceedings. The first such stage is the identification of "abuse." The most important development here are the abuse reporting statutes that now exist in every state.[5] These laws usually require certain categories of professionals, most prominently mental health professionals, to report any case in which they have reasonable cause to suspect that child abuse or neglect has occurred. Therefore, initial state intervention, in the form of investigation and any emergency action, often takes place on the basis of an assessment by a professional. This process has been subject to numerous criticisms. First, it may disrupt ongoing services by requiring a breach of confidentiality.[6] Second, although there can be no doubt that reporting laws have "worked" in the sense that they have greatly increased the incidence of reported cases,[7] the magnitude of the increase has so overloaded protective caseworkers that it is questionable whether any substantial degree of protection is added.[8] Finally, it is unlikely that the law has been applied uniformly, because of some professionals' resistance to reporting, uncertainty about the behavior that should be reported, and differences among demographic groups in the degree to which they are subject to scrutiny by mandated reporters.[9]

Once possible child maltreatment has been reported and investigated, there may be a second stage, in which a petition is filed by a state attorney or social worker alleging that the child is in fact abused or neglected.[10] At the hearing that results, there is an adjudication of whether the allegation is valid—that is, whether there is a legally sufficient basis for the state to assume jurisdiction over the child and family. It is at this phase that definitional problems and questions of the proper balance between state and parental authority are most directly presented.

If the child is found to be abused or neglected, there is a third phase, in which disposition is determined. There are two sorts of dispositional questions that may be posed. The first concerns temporary or time-limited dispositions. The inquiry in that regard typically follows a best-interests standard, in which the court has broad authority to require the parents to meet conditions designed to improve the quality of their care of the child (e.g., to attend parent-education classes to obtain vocational training) and to ensure the safety and welfare of the child (e.g., the court

may transfer custody to the department of social services). The second kind of dispositional question, typically not raised until a later hearing, concerns permanent termination of the parental rights. Besides consideration of the best interests of the child, termination typically requires specific findings of parents' lack of amenability to treatment, and sometimes requires documentation that the state has made diligent efforts to remediate the parents' propensity to maltreat the child. If rights are terminated, the parents become strangers to the child from the point of view of the law. The child becomes available for adoption, and the parents lose even visitation rights. Both kinds of questions demand difficult predictions of future parental behavior and the efficacy of treatment, and both again present issues concerning the proper reach of the state and the proper deference to parents. The latter issue is acutely presented in cases in which children are in foster care for extended periods of time but are unavailable for adoption (because parental termination has not yet occurred) or are even returned to parents with whom they have lived for little, if any, of their lives.

(c)   General Policy Perspectives

(1)   Perspectives on State Intervention

As the preceding discussion shows, the general problem of balancing state and parental interests and the corollary problem of the proper level of involvement of mental health professionals arise at several points in the process. There is no consensus on these questions,[11] and different answers may be given for different stages of the proceedings.

Historically, for example, "child savers" have preferred to err on the side of ensuring protection for the child.[12] They would, therefore, establish low standards for invoking state jurisdiction, and they would prefer high levels of intervention once that threshold is crossed. In its modern version, proponents of this perspective argue that deference to family privacy is ultimately destructive of families and is certainly not in the best interests of children.[13] The child savers advocate broad discretion and considerable resources for state social workers so that they can fashion and implement a comprehensive plan for rehabilitation of the family.

A second perspective emphasizes the potential harm (at least the lack of clear benefit) of state intervention in many cases, the often arbitrary grounds for intervention, and the limits of available resources. Advocates of this perspective argue for clearly defined, limited bases for state intervention, and they state a preference for minimal intrusions upon family privacy once jurisdiction is taken.

Although the latter view now dominates among scholarly commentators, its leading proponent probably remains Michael Wald,[14] whose arguments heavily influenced the relevant volume of the Juvenile Justice Standards.[15] The fact that the Standards Relating to Abuse and Neglect have never been adopted as policy by the American Bar Association (unlike almost every other volume of the Juvenile Justice Standards) is illustrative of the deep and long-standing divisions about child protection policy. Nonetheless, the Standards remain important authority for the advocates of limited state intervention in cases of child maltreatment.

State intervention under the Standards generally would be limited to situations in which there are findings that a child has suffered, or is at substantial risk of suffering, serious harm, and that intervention is necessary to protect the child from being endangered in the future [see § 15.02]. If this high standard is crossed, the court would be required to choose the disposition that, while protecting the child from the harm justifying intervention, is least invasive of familial privacy.

A third perspective was offered by Goldstein, Freud, and Solnit,[16] who argued for a very high threshold for state intervention (significantly higher than that of the Standards) but, once that threshold had been crossed, would have made it very easy to terminate parental rights. Relying on psychoanalytical theory, Goldstein and his colleagues argued that the prime considerations in family policy should be preservation of continuity in the child's "psychological parent" and respect for the authority of that parent. They claimed that children need the security of a parent who is perceived as omnipotent, and that the state is not equipped to meet the emotional needs of the

child. Therefore, they would have permitted state intervention only under circumstances of the direst and clearest harm to the child, with no prospective inquiry. That is, serious harm, or an attempt to do such harm, must already have occurred before jurisdiction could be invoked.

When the child did enter foster care, foster parents could assume parental rights just by showing that they were now the "longtime caretakers" of the child (i.e., they had cared for the child for at least one year if the child was placed at less than three years of age, or two years if the child had been placed at a later age).[17] If the basis for removal had been sexual abuse or serious physical abuse, the natural parents would not even have a right to a hearing on the matter.[18]

Of course, the three perspectives presented are not necessarily ideologically pure, and similar policies in regard to the threshold and intensity of state intervention can be advocated for different reasons. For example, Goldstein, Freud, and Solnit's preference for a high threshold for *any* state intervention into family life but a low threshold for termination of parental rights if the first threshold is crossed was derived from a child-centered belief about the nature of children's relationships. Some conservatives now advocate a similar policy on the bases of their strong "family values" and a corollary general distrust of government intervention into family life, coupled with the belief that the behavior of some parents (e.g., drug abusers) deviates so much from such values that those parents do not deserve the state's respect for their authority.[19]

Child protection policy thus rests on a complex set of normative and empirical assumptions, many of which remain unsettled.[20] Development of coherent policy is further complicated by often competing policy goals. For example, policy and practice in regard to spouse abuse—a context that is in many ways analogous to child maltreatment—have been guided in recent years by the belief that there is a perpetrator and a victim and that the perpetrator must be controlled through, for example, protective orders prohibiting the perpetrator from access to the family. Although this model is sometimes applicable in cases of child maltreatment[21] (notably when a family member is sexually exploitive), the more common situation is that there is not a clear "bad guy."

Others may view particular parents as inept, un-motivated, or cruel (indeed so cruel that retribution may be justifiable),[22] but the child's welfare may still demand that attention be given to strengthening the parent–child relationship.

(2)   "Neighbors Helping Neighbors": The New Paradigm in Child Protection

The historic perspectives on child protection policy have focused for the most part on the coercive application of state power to prevent harm to individual children. Accordingly, the policy debate has rested largely on questions about the circumstances justifying such intrusion, the scope of mandated reporting, and the adequacy of the investigations triggered by such reports. All too often, public attention has been directed to exposés of tragedies purportedly resulting from incompetence or sloth of workers in Child Protective Services (CPS), the program in state and county social service agencies that is charged with investigating reports of suspected child maltreatment and developing related case plans. The "answers" thus have been framed as (1) a refined threshold for reporting so that the "right" cases come to CPS and (2) an enlarged and better trained work force so that caseworkers will competently and diligently investigate the reports and respond accordingly.

In recent years, these answers have themselves come into question, at least in part as a result of the arguments raised by the United States Advisory Board on Child Abuse and Neglect (ABCAN) in several reports published between 1990 and 1995.[23] Noting the stunning incidence of child maltreatment, the catastrophic failure of the child protection system in all its elements, and the costly consequences of this failure, ABCAN drew extraordinary media attention with its declaration of a national emergency.[24] ABCAN described the combination of child maltreatment with an ineffective societal response as a "moral disaster."[25]

Although ABCAN's stark description of the problem's scope helped focus the issue, its biggest contribution was its analysis of the roots of the emergency. Noting that the failure to protect children goes far beyond CPS, ABCAN traced the emergency not to inadequate resources for CPS but instead to intrinsic problems in the system's design:

The most serious shortcoming of the nation's system of intervention on behalf of children is that it depends upon a reporting and response process that has punitive connotations, and requires massive resources dedicated to the investigation of allegations. State and County child welfare programs have *not* been designed to get immediate help to families based on voluntary requests for assistance. As a result it has become far easier to pick up the telephone [and report abuse than] to request and receive help before the abuse happens. If the nation ultimately is to reduce the dollars and personnel needed for investigating reports, more resources must be allocated to establishing voluntary, non-punitive access to help.[26]

ABCAN contended that even if policymakers patched the existing child protection system, the emergency would recur unless the question facing caseworkers was transformed from "What happened?" to "What can we do to help?" Similarly, ABCAN argued, policymakers must shift their primary focus from the question of the grounds for coercive state intervention to the fundamental concern: What can society do to prevent or ameliorate harm to children?[27]

To achieve such a shift, ABCAN recommended a radical solution: "Once the emergency is brought under control, the Board believes that the nation should commit itself to an equally important goal: *the replacement of the existing child protection system with a new, national, child-centered, neighborhood-based child protection strategy.*"[28] To effect this strategy, ABCAN advocated a new national child protection policy[29] and a corollary shift in the nature of government's involvement in the protection of children to facilitation of "comprehensive community efforts to ensure the safe and healthy development of children."[30]

The cornerstone of ABCAN's proposed strategy was signaled in the title of the report presenting it: *Neighbors Helping Neighbors.*[31] ABCAN argued that, whether for prevention or treatment, a strong emphasis should be placed on the design of communities to promote mutual assistance—neighbors watching out for each other's families. ABCAN was influenced by research showing the potency of both economic and social support—neighborhood quality—in preventing child maltreatment [see § 15.03(d)(2)].

The adoption of this new policy framework

has several important implications for forensic clinicians. First, in many instances, decisionmaking about help for families in which child maltreatment is suspected to have occurred is apt to shift away from formal legal processes [see § 15.04(f)]. Evaluators may find themselves in new roles in which they collaborate with families to understand the risks that may be present and to design ways to mitigate the danger. Second, mental health professionals will be involved with new community structures for assessment, planning, and implementation of voluntary service plans [see, e.g., § 15.04(a), describing new state requirements for community child protection teams]. Third, the menu of services is likely to expand, with a particular focus on design of sustainable informal support networks. Accordingly, clinicians will be challenged to develop alternatives that are truly ecological—that integrate psychological and social strategies in the design of everyday settings to ensure safety for particular children [see § 15.03(c)].

15.02. Legal Definitions of Child Maltreatment

Although it is clear that the *Zeitgeist* is shifting in the field of child protection, it is also clear that there still is no consensus among authorities about even the overall framework that should guide legal policies on child maltreatment. There is basic disagreement over the proper balance among interests at both the invocation of state authority and the dispositional phases. This philosophical disagreement—in combination with conceptual unclarity among mental health professionals about the nature and etiology of child maltreatment [see § 15.03]—has led to often vague and disparate standards for the type of "abuse" and "neglect" that can lead to state intervention.

(a)   Physical Abuse

All jurisdictions provide for state intervention to protect physically abused children. They differ substantially, however, in terms of the degree to which the finding of abuse is based on value judg-

ments about what behavior is abusive and the nature of the proof required. In view of the ubiquity of corporal punishment as a disciplinary technique in American families,[32] and the perception that it is relatively more common in particular social groups,[33] there is the possibility of arbitrariness and the probability of unreliability in the application of broad standards.

Recognizing this problem, the drafters of the Juvenile Justice Standards proposed a standard that is much stricter than in most state statutes (although not as limited as Goldstein and colleagues advocated): Intervention is permitted in this context only if "a child has suffered, or there is a substantial risk that a child will imminently suffer, a physical harm, inflicted nonaccidentally upon him/her by his/her parents, which causes, or creates a substantial risk of causing disfigurement, impairment of bodily functioning, or other serious physical injury."[34] The commentary to the standard indicates that its "intent . . . is to prevent injuries such as broken bones, burns, internal injuries, loss of hearing, sight, etc. It is not intended to cover cases of minor bruises or black and blue marks, unless the child was treated in a way that indicates that more serious injury is likely to occur in the future."[35] In making that judgment, the drafters emphasized that it "does not imply acceptance of corporal punishment as a means of discipline. Rather, it reflects the judgment that even in cases of physical injury, unless the actual or potential injury is serious, the detriment from coercive intervention is likely to be greater than the benefit."[36]

Like the Standards, many state statutes require a finding of "harm" or at least "danger of harm" as a result of intentional infliction of physical injury; the abuse act alone is not enough. In some of these states, the *level* of harm required is also similar to that of the Standards. Florida, for example, defines physical injury to include "death, permanent or temporary disfigurement, or impairment of any bodily part."[37] However, a separate section of the Florida statute also seems to include any physical abuse resulting in mental injury.[38] There is a similar open-ended quality to some of the other statutes that, at first glance, seem to conceptualize physical abuse in terms of intentional action resulting in serious bodily harm. Wyoming, for example, defines physical injury as "death or *any harm* to a child *including but not limit-ed to* disfigurement, impairment of any bodily or-gan, skin bruising, bleeding, burns, fracture of any bone, subdural hematoma or substantial mal-nutrition"[39] [Emphasis added].

Most problematic, however, are those statutes that expressly call for a value judgment about the limits of acceptable physical punishment indepen-dent of its actual or probable harm. Some states include "excessive corporal punishment" in the definition of abuse[40] or even in the definition of neglect (as discussed further below).[41] Others define abuse in terms of "cruel or inhumane" parental practices.[42] Courts are divided as to whether such standards are so vague as to be vi-olative of due process.[43]

(b)   Physical Neglect

Every state also permits intervention if there has been "neglect" of the child. Here the variations are even greater.

As in the standard defining abuse, the Juvenile Justice Standards require a finding of serious physical harm before a child can be adjudicated to be neglected. That is, it must be found that

> a child has suffered, or . . . there is a substantial risk that the child will imminently suffer, physi-cal harm causing disfigurement, impairment of bodily functioning, or other serious physical in-jury as a result of conditions created by his/her parents or by the failure of the parents to ade-quately supervise or protect him/her.[44]

The drafters of the standard made clear that they opposed state intervention on the basis of "inade-quate" parental behavior, which they viewed as both too vague and too likely to result in overin-tervention.[45] But state neglect statutes frequently require only that the state show that the parents have failed to provide "proper supervision."[46] Some states even invoke jurisdiction if there is sufficient "immorality" to make the home unfit.[47]

(c)   Sexual Abuse

Sexual abuse of the child by a parent is also a typ-ical basis for intervention. Child sexual abuse was "discovered" in the early 1980s,[48] and reporting of sexual abuse increased dramatically.[49] The con-ceptualization of sexual abuse also changed, so that criminal prosecution became common and even routine in some jurisdictions.[50]

Reflecting the "prediscovery" *Zeitgeist,* howev-er, the drafters of the Juvenile Justice Standards Relating to Abuse and Neglect (who did their work in the mid-1970s) were ambivalent about application of *family court* jurisdiction. Although the Standards would permit coercive intervention in all cases of sexual abuse,[51] an alternative stan-dard was offered to require a finding of serious harm, on the theory that the legal-system inter-vention might often engender more distress than the sexual abuse itself.[52] Furthermore, sexual abuse was not defined in the Standards because of a preference for using the definition of the term found in a state's *penal* code.[53] Although some states do define the term in their criminal statutes,[54] others do not,[55] and some of the states that specifically include sexual abuse in their *civil* child abuse statutes do not define it there or in any other law.[56]

(d)   Emotional Abuse and Neglect

Emotional abuse—also known as psychological maltreatment[57]—is the most controversial aspect of child protection jurisdiction, probably because it is so difficult to define. Although one can imag-ine cases in which most people would agree that there was emotional abuse (e.g., locking a child in a dark closet for prolonged periods of time), there is no such consensus for most questionable parental practices. It is probably also true that in many, perhaps most, circumstances where there is a consensus that emotional abuse is present, there would be other grounds for invocation of jurisdiction.

Another problem is that establishing the basis for emotional harm presents difficult problems of proof. How does one really know whether a child's maladjustment is the result of parental practices? It is clear in this regard that many chil-dren develop appropriately in spite of growing up with parents who are relatively unresponsive or who have what may be mistaken ideas about chil-dren's needs [see § 15.05]. Moreover, given the myriad parental behaviors that may adversely affect child development, do we really want to expand jurisdiction to the range of situations that may be psychologically unhealthy?[58] If not, what is to be the decision rule for determining whether an unwise practice is also an abusive practice that warrants state intervention to protect the child?

For these reasons, the Juvenile Justice Standards would permit invocation of state authority in cases of emotional abuse and neglect in only a single narrow situation:

> [when] a child is suffering serious emotional damage [not necessarily as a result of parental actions], evidenced by severe anxiety, depression, or withdrawal, or untoward aggressive behavior toward self or others, *and* the child's parents are not willing to provide treatment for him/her.[59] [Emphasis added]

In contrast, those states providing for intervention in cases of emotional abuse and neglect tend to use broad definitions of "mental injury" that offer little guidance. Wyoming, for example, permits state intervention when parental action results in "an injury to the psychological capacity or emotional stability of a child as evidenced by an observable or substantial impairment in his ability to function within a normal range of performance and behavior with due regard to his culture."[60]

(e)   Conclusions

Clearly there is great diversity in statutory definitions of abuse and neglect. Also, there is often sufficient vagueness in state statutes to raise constitutional questions.[61] Vague or value-laden definitions unfortunately do often result in arbitrary application. There is solid empirical evidence of gross unreliability in perceptions of child maltreatment, with the groups most likely to be involved in initial investigations (i.e., social workers and the police) being those that tend to have the most expansive concepts of child abuse and neglect.[62] Even within the social work profession, though, there is substantial variation in understanding of the definition of child maltreatment, as a result of difference in the setting in which social workers are employed and in their theoretical

orientation.[63] We turn now to examination of these clinical concepts.

15.03.   Child Maltreatment as a Clinical Phenomenon

(a)   The "Discovery" of Child Abuse

Although the juvenile court has had jurisdiction over poorly supervised children since its inception, the development of the special system of legal regulation and social services for abused and neglected children is a rather recent phenomenon. The major impetus for this development came from an article published in the *Journal of the American Medical Association* in 1962.[64] In that article, Henry Kempe and his colleagues identified the existence of "battered-child syndrome" as a clinical condition. There was a considerable hue and cry thereafter, and all states enacted mandatory reporting laws over a four-year period in the mid-1960s.[65]

Since then, not only has the number of reported and substantiated cases grown at an astronomical rate,[66] but the range of parental behavior at issue has steadily expanded. New public concern with sexual abuse added an additional spurt of cases in the 1980s and led to many new laws and programs as criminal prosecution became more frequent.[67]

Today, as elaborated in the remainder of this section, the typical child protection case does not comport with the image of the battered child. Rather than being victims of malicious beatings or even of sexual exploitation, at least half the children entering the child protection system are believed to have been neglected.[68] Although the risk to their health and welfare often is substantial, they typically live in families with multiple complex and serious problems. Solving those problems is a substantially more difficult matter than "just" ensuring that they are safe from a brutal parent. Meanwhile, as already noted, a "backlash" has arisen in which many critics argue that the child protection system is prone to overreaching, sometimes with life-shattering results.[69]

We emphasize these shifts in scope here because the "eye-of-the-beholder" problem is as real for the social welfare and mental health professions as it is for the law. Child maltreatment is certainly not new; indeed, trends across generations have been toward more humane treatment of children and more recognition of children as persons.[70] However, the identification of child maltreatment as a clinical entity *is* relatively new. We do not wish to minimize the realities of abuse of children, but it is important to recognize that child abuse and neglect are *social constructs* that have entered the behavioral sciences only in the past generation.

(b)   Social Science Definitions

Definitions of child maltreatment used by social scientists tend to be substantially broader than those in law, at least in the more carefully drafted statutes, and even more diverse. Parke and Collmer advocated a culturally relative definition: "non-accidental physical injury (or injuries) that are the result of acts (or omissions) on the part of parents or guardians that violate the community standards concerning the treatment of children."[71] Also using a culturally relative but still broader definition, the Garbarinos defined child maltreatment as including "acts of omission or commission by a parent or guardian that are judged by a mixture of community values and professional expertise to be inappropriate and damaging."[72] They further defined emotional abuse to include parental behavior that hampers the development of social competence by penalizing a child for normal exploration and expression of affect, discouraging attachment, lowering self-esteem, or discouraging relationships outside the family.[73] Another well-known pioneer in research on child maltreatment, sociologist David Gil, defined physical abuse as "the intentional, non-accidental use of physical force, or intentional non-accidental acts of omission, on the part of a parent or caretaker interacting with a child in his care, aimed at hurting, injuring, or destroying that child."[74] Gil's definition would appear to include all corporal punishment.

More recent definitions are generally just as broad and culturally relative. A 1989 consensus conference of the National Institute of Child Health and Human Development recommended that maltreatment be defined as "behavior towards another person, which (a) is outside the norms of conduct, and (b) entails a substantial risk of causing physical or emotional harm. Behaviors included will consist of actions and omissions, ones that are intentional and ones that are unintentional."[75]

The broad and inconsistent definitions used by social scientists are problematic not only because of the difficulty in applying vague definitions. They are troublesome also because of their potential influence on helping professionals, who may apply even broader standards than the law permits. Inconsistent definitions also make comparisons across studies difficult, and overly broad definitions render research questionably applicable to legal policy. The National Research Council's Panel on Research on Child Abuse and Neglect was so disturbed by such issues that it devoted a full chapter to definitional issues,[76] and its first recommendations were for development of a consensus on research definitions and corollary "reliable and valid clinical–diagnostic and research instruments for the measurement of child maltreatment."[77]

(c)   Social Science Perspectives

Probably of even more consequence than the specific *definitions* used by social scientists are the overall *perspectives* adopted, which tend to shape both the standards for intervention and the kinds of interventions employed. Psychodynamic theorists emphasize the significance of the personality traits and personal histories of parents who neglect or abuse their children. Policy grounded in such a perspective is likely to rest on a determination of their treatability, and interventions are apt to be individually focused counseling or psychotherapy programs aimed at the parents. Professionals with a social learning orientation are likely to give principal attention to parental skill deficits and maladaptive attributions and to organize behavioral training programs ("parent education") and therapies designed to correct erroneous beliefs and expectancies that parents may have. Sociologically oriented theorists regard child maltreatment as a societal problem reflecting the level of violence in the society, the status of children and women, and the unequal distribution of wealth. They are apt to place most of their energy in the development of large-scale preventive programs.

Practitioners and policymakers are still likely to view child maltreatment from one of these perspectives. However, the evidence is now clear that child maltreatment is multiply determined.[78] There is a need to understand the social factors *in interaction with* individual differences in psychological traits. Ecological theorists offer such a complex perspective.[79]

Ecological theorists emphasize the fit between the person and the environment. The environment itself is recognized to consist of several levels, each in interaction with the other: (1) the "microsystem," the immediate social context of the child (e.g., the family); (2) the "mesosystem," the connections among microsystems of which the child is a part (e.g., an older sibling's accompanying the child to school); (3) the "exosystem," external influences on the life of the child (e.g., the flexibility of the father's place of employment enabling him to set aside time for the family); and (4) the "macrosystem," the broad cultural blueprint influencing the structure and processes of lower-level systems (e.g., the overall concept and status of childhood). Thus, although ecological theorists do not deny the effects of individual differences in personality and skills, they look to diverse and complex social factors to determine how those individual differences will be expressed.

For example, the effects of unemployment on a family might be expected to vary with the following factors, among others: (1) the parents' ability to respond to frustration (microsystem), (2) the degree of interaction between the family and social resources (e.g., friendly teachers) that might help to alleviate stress (mesosystem), (3) the availability of help in finding jobs (exosystem), and (4) the national economic policy in regard to tolerable levels of unemployment (macrosystem). Therefore, to say that unemployment—or poor impulse control—is the cause of child maltreatment is to oversimplify a complex social phenomenon. Assessment of only one level or aspect of the situation will be shortsighted, and intervention directed at only one level or aspect is unlikely to have substantial effects.

Ecological theorists also recognize that cause–effect relationships are rarely unidirectional, although differentials in power may make effects in one direction stronger than the other. For example, it is obvious that in most families most of the time, parents have more effect on children than the converse. Parents generally have greater control over reinforcements and greater physical strength, cognitive skills, social experience, and behavioral repertoire.[80] However, it is also clear that the presence of children changes the life of adults, and that the care of some children is much more demanding and stressful than the care of others.[81] Moreover, these effects are likely to be mediated by external influences (e.g., the parents' support system) that may not be directly involved with the child.[82]

It is noteworthy in that regard that the antecedents of neglect and physical abuse appear to be largely the same.[83] Both neglect and physical abuse commonly take place in socially toxic situations in which economic and social poverty combine with parental inadequacy and child vulnerability.

The relationship of sexual abuse to risk factors is not as strong,[84] probably because of the dynamics of exploitive or predatory behavior, a dimension that generally is not present in other forms of child maltreatment. Nonetheless, the situation in sexual abuse cases often also is noteworthy for its complexity:

> Empirical studies have found that families of both incest and nonincest sexual abuse victims are reported as less cohesive, more disorganized, and generally more dysfunctional than families of nonabused individuals. The areas most often identified as problematic in incest cases are problems with communication, a lack of emotional closeness and flexibility, and social isolation.[85]

Although reviewers commonly conclude that socioeconomic status is unrelated to sexual abuse,[86] there is also evidence that this conclusion is erroneous, at least in regard to severe abuse. When epidemiological surveys in broad, reasonably representative populations have focused on genital contact (thus, e.g., excluding being "flashed"), researchers have found sexual abuse to be strongly related to poverty.[87]

(d)   Factors in the Etiology of Child Maltreatment

(1)   Psychological Factors

The dominant early view of child maltreatment (perhaps still the dominant view among the general public and the courts) was that it is a reflection of psychiatric dysfunction—a "syndrome"—in the parent. Wolfe has succinctly described the history and logic of this perspective:

> Because pediatricians and other medical personnel brought the problem of abuse to worldwide attention, early attempts to explain this phenomenon were couched predominantly in terms of the individual psychopathology of the offender. Child abuse was a deviant act; therefore, it was reasoned that the perpetrators of such acts were themselves deviant. The search began for the identification of the psychiatric symptoms or psychopathological processes that were responsible for such inhumane behavior toward one's offspring, and that would respond to psychiatric treatment.[88]

The literature resulting from this search long consisted largely of clinical impressions based on case reports and other uncontrolled clinical studies. The result was inconclusive. In a review published in 1973, Gelles found that at least two or more authorities had agreed on only 4 of 19 traits reported in the literature.[89] A largely uncritical review published by Spinetta and Rigler a year earlier reached a similar conclusion:

> A review of opinions on parental personality and motivational variables leads to a conglomerate picture. While the authors generally agree that there is a defect in the abusing parent's personality that allows aggressive impulses to be expressed too freely, disagreement comes in describing the source of the aggressive impulses.[90]

Simply saying that an abusive parent has trouble controlling aggression is, of course, tautological. Such an "insight" offers no help in understanding the phenomenon.

More systematic studies in recent years have shown a variety of mental health problems—but not severe mental illness—to be common among abusive and neglecting parents: hostility, depression, anxiety, dependency, and general inadequacy, often accompanied by substance abuse.[91]

However, the search for a child abuser syndrome has remained elusive. As a panel of the National Research Council concluded in 1993, a "consistent profile of parental psychopathology or a significant level of mental disturbance has not been supported."[92]

More conceptually based research has suggested some psychological problems that may relate directly to parents' maltreatment of their children. Abusive and neglecting parents have often been shown to be low in empathy and understanding and acceptance of the nuances of behavior.[93]

Even this conclusion, however, must be qualified. The evidence that maltreating parents have inappropriate expectations—at least in terms of expectation for their children—is equivocal. Rosenburg and Reppucci reported data from a study that cast doubt on this hypothesis, although their findings did raise other possible explanations.[94] In presenting abusive and matched nonabusive parents with vignettes about childrearing, the abusive group actually perceived *more* alternative reasons for their children's behavior (e.g., they more often saw misbehavior as possibly accidental as opposed to purposeful), and there were no group differences in attribution of intentionality. The abusive mothers tended to be much more self-critical, however. Rather than misperceiving the children's behavior, they seemed to experience behavior management problems as threats to their own self-esteem. The more alternatives that they could generate for their children's difficulties, the more responsible—and the more out of control—they felt. Thus, the mothers may have had expectations that were too high for *themselves,* not for their children. The abusive mothers also indicated significantly more sources of stress on them in the past year than did the nonabusive parents. Therefore, there was the suggestion of a lethal combination of high stress, self-reproach (perhaps abusive parents blame themselves not just for childrearing problems but for other sources of stress as well), and displacement of anger onto children.

Indeed, a low sense of competence as a parent, accompanied by affect (e.g., depression) appropriate to that self-perception, seems to be the most well-validated personality attribute of abusive and neglecting parents.[95] As Pelton has argued, such a trait is even apt to mediate the effects of poverty and, therefore, to distinguish between poor families in which maltreatment occurs and poor families that adapt to their circumstances.[96]

(2)   Social and Economic Factors

The evidence that social and economic factors play a role in the etiology of child abuse and neglect—especially neglect—is far stronger than it is for psychological factors. To summarize the discussion to follow, when social poverty (i.e., isolation and lack of social support) combines with economic poverty, the result is significant danger for children.

Neighborhood Quality.   A dysfunctional neighborhood is clearly one aspect of social poverty that contributes to neglect and abuse. Particularly strong evidence for this conclusion has come from the studies that James Garbarino and his colleagues have conducted over the past two decades.[97] In one study they conducted, it was found that although economic factors alone accounted for 52% of the variance in the rate of child maltreatment across communities, variables related to neighborhood stability were also very significant correlates.[98]

Examining the latter finding in more detail, Garbarino and Sherman studied two low-income neighborhoods that had dramatically different reported rates of child maltreatment.[99] The two neighborhoods had identical proportions of low-income families living in them (72%), but child maltreatment was eight times more prevalent in one neighborhood than in the other. Interviews with expert informants (ranging from scout leaders to school principals to letter carriers) gave contrasting pictures of the two neighborhoods as places to live—impressions confirmed by interviews with residents. One-third of the families in the high-risk neighborhood, compared with just 8% of the families in the low-risk neighborhood, played regularly with children in the neighborhood. Parents in the high-risk neighborhood were much less likely to be available for their children after school, much more likely to have experienced multiple major stressors in the previous year, and likely to have fewer other adults whom they considered to be interested in their children.

The general picture of the high-risk neighborhood was of a community in which there were great emotional drains and few social supports to replace the depleted human resources. In such a situation, regardless of the personal inadequacies of parents, intervention must take into account the need to build the community as a whole if it is to be successful.

Social Support.   Social isolation has long been known to be related to child maltreatment. Abusive and neglectful parents have been found to be less likely than other parents to belong to organizations, to have a telephone, to have relationships outside the home, and so forth.[100] However, the direction of causality has been unclear. Have maltreating parents been excluded from supportive social networks, are such networks unavailable to them, do they lack the skills to enter into networks, or have they withdrawn from social interaction?

Moreover, until recently, little effort has been made to understand the elements of social support that are important in preventing child maltreatment. It is not self-evident that having increased social contacts with significant others should be an objective in treatment plans for abusive and neglectful parents. Consider, for example, situations in which relatives are hostile toward one another[101] or friends were made in the process of sharing illicit drugs.

Coohey's research is illustrative of recent work designed to identify the critical elements of social support in prevention and treatment of child abuse and neglect:

> To summarize, *neglectful mothers* had fewer members in their networks, had fewer total contacts, had less contact with the members they did have, perceived their members to be less supportive, and received fewer instrumental and emotional resources from their network members compared to mothers who did not abuse their children. Thus, the neglectful mother's perception of support was consistent with the actual receipt of fewer resources. . . .
>
> In retrospect, the finding that neglect is related to fewer instrumental resources seems obvious, since close family members and friends provide instrumental resources that may, in

part, prevent some types of neglect. For example, children being left alone is by far the largest group of neglected children in Illinois, and family members and friends are the major source[s] of short-notice or emergency assistance (especially baby sitting). If a mother has only a few people she can turn to when she needs to go out, she may under certain circumstances (e.g., cannot reciprocate the favor) leave her children alone.[102]

Thompson has contributed the most extensive analysis of the relation of social support to child maltreatment.[103] He noted that there are several benefits to social support for high-risk families: "appropriate models of parenting behavior; a buffer against the effects of socioeconomic or other life stresses; enhanced access to skills, services, or information; counseling; or other kinds of assistance," as well as ongoing monitoring and social control.[104] However, such support is only offered, accepted, and sustained if it is perceived as noncontingent (as in kin relations) and reciprocal.[105] Thompson argued, therefore, that dispositional plans should be tailored to extend the latter type of resources:

> [A] program of social support intervention, especially one emphasizing informal social networks, must extend significantly beyond neighborhoods to encompass extended kin; workplace social networks; friends who live outside local neighborhoods; associates through churches, unions, and other broader community groups; school-based associates; and other potentially valuable social resources to parents and their offspring.[106]

As Coohey's findings illustrate,[107] these "natural" networks must be constructed (the paradox embedded in this language is noteworthy) so that not only emotional but also instrumental support is provided. Child care appears to be a particularly important contribution that friends and relatives can make to prevent neglect of a child.[108]

Material Support.   Research on the etiology of child abuse and neglect suggests that concrete assistance (such as child care) ought to be a central feature of most dispositional plans. Pelton began a background paper for ABCAN with this stark conclusion: "After years of study and research, there is no single fact about child abuse and ne-

glect that has been better documented and established than their strong relationship to poverty and low income."[109] Elaborating, Pelton noted:

> The great majority of families to which child abuse and neglect have been attributed live in poverty or near-poverty circumstances. The finding that poor children are vastly overrepresented among incidents of child abuse and neglect has been obtained across a range of methodologies and definitions, forms of abuse and neglect, and levels of severity.[110]

Moreover, there is evidence that the risk of child maltreatment is related to the severity and intractability of the deprivation that a family experiences. For example, among families receiving Aid to Families with Dependent Children (AFDC), families known to be abusive or neglectful were living in more crowded and dilapidated conditions, more likely to have gone hungry, and in general experiencing a worse standard of living.[111] Similarly, unemployment is most strongly related to child maltreatment in the poorest communities.[112]

Inadequate housing appears to be a particularly potent risk factor.[113] ABCAN identified five reasons for this relationship:

> First, parents who lack adequate housing—or *any* housing—face an unusually difficult task to keep their children safe, because the hazards of everyday life become more frequent and more serious. . . .
>   Second, poor housing itself is a stressor that may make coping with the demands that children pose more difficult. Notably, when homes are overcrowded, conflicts may escalate faster, because physical confrontation may be inevitable.
>   Third, housing costs account for a sufficiently large proportion of household budgets, especially for families in poverty, that housing policy may have a direct effect on the level of poverty that disadvantaged families experience and, therefore, the prevalence of child maltreatment.
>   Fourth, housing is a major marker of social status and community integration. People living in dilapidated housing may be especially prone to regard themselves as unworthy. High levels of absentee ownership and building vacancies may be important factors in residents' feelings of loss of control and their unwillingness to invest their energy in caring for their neighborhood and the children within it. . . .

Fifth, regardless of the particular state of repair of the homes in a neighborhood, housing patterns can promote or inhibit interaction and watchfulness among neighbors. Accordingly, housing designed in a manner that impedes such interaction may increase social isolation and foster zones of violence.

In short, inadequate housing can result both directly and indirectly in increased risk of child maltreatment. . . .[114]

In general, the relationship between child maltreatment and poverty is valid across forms of maltreatment (including sexual abuse), but it is especially applicable to neglect.[115] The relationship with neglect is almost by definition, because the most common allegation in neglect cases is "deprivation of necessities."[116] Similarly, poverty substantially raises the risk associated with "inadequate supervision," a particularly common specific allegation.[117] The problem of inadequacy of care typically involves the interaction of personal problems, social isolation, and economic deprivation:

> Impoverished families tend to live, though not by choice, in neighborhoods with the highest crime rates, in apartments that are not secure, and in homes made dangerous by lack of heating, poor wiring, and exposed lead paint, to name only a few of the health and safety hazards associated with poverty. These conditions, the same ones that may cause indirect danger to children by generating stressful experiences for the parents, cause direct danger as well, for which it becomes possible to implicate the parents for not preventing. Moreover, in the presence of these conditions, impoverished parents have little leeway for lapses in responsibility, whereas in middle-class families, there is some leeway for irresponsibility, a luxury that poverty does not afford.[118]

(e) Prognosis and Treatment

(1) Treatment of Abusive and Neglecting Parents

Ultimately, good dispositional planning rests on a sound body of research showing what works for whom. Unfortunately, this data base is largely lacking. Treatment research is remarkably scarce,[119] especially for neglect cases,[120] and most of what is available does not meet basic methodological requirements.[121]

Moreover, the evidence at this point is largely discouraging.[122] For instance, the attendance by parents at counseling sessions is low, notwithstanding court orders.[123] Even federally funded demonstration projects have failed to produce convincing evidence of success in ensuring safety for children who have a history of maltreatment:

> Child abuse and neglect continue despite early, thoughtful, and often costly intervention. Treatment programs have been relatively ineffective in initially halting abusive and neglectful behavior or in reducing the future likelihood of maltreatment in the most severe cases of physical abuse, chronic neglect, and emotional maltreatment. One-third or more of the parents served by these intensive demonstration efforts maltreated their children while in treatment, and over one-half of the families served continued to be judged by staff as likely to mistreat their children following termination.[124]

At least in part, this dismal record is the product of insufficient attention to the complexity and severity of needs of families in which child maltreatment occurs. Traditional parent-focused casework, including psychodynamic treatment, is largely ineffective.[125] In contrast, better success has been obtained in programs that have incorporated material supports (e.g., emergency cash) and featured intensive multifaceted interventions.[126]

(2) Treatment of Abused and Neglected Children

One point on which research is clear is that maltreated children—especially those who are neglected—are at high risk of psychological, educational, health, and social problems.[127] The ordinarily circumspect General Accounting Office (GAO; the auditing office of the U.S. Congress) began a report on the health needs of young children in foster care with the following stark reminder: "Foster children are among the most vulnerable individuals in the welfare population. As a group, they are sicker than homeless children and children living in the poorest sections of inner cities."[128]

Tragically, however, the fact that maltreated children are unlikely to receive adequate therapeutic services is just as clear as the fact that they are likely to have special health, mental health, and educational needs. In the report of its task panel on child maltreatment, the National Research Council lamented: "Despite the large literature on the detrimental effects of child maltreatment . . . the majority of treatment programs do not provide services directed at the psychosocial problems of the abused child."[129]

Even more starkly, maltreated children—even those in the care of the state—are unlikely in many communities even to receive basic services that should be available to all children.[130] In its study of young foster children in three major cities with excellent health care facilities (Los Angeles, New York, and Philadelphia), the GAO found that

> [d]espite state and county foster care agency regulations requiring comprehensive routine health care, an estimated 12 percent of young foster children received no routine health care, 34 percent received no immunizations, and 32 percent had at least some identified health needs that were not met.[131]

Only 1% of the sample received early and periodic screening, diagnosis, and treatment services to which they were entitled under Medicaid.[132]

Given the dearth of services, it is perhaps unsurprising that research on treatment of abused and neglected children is very limited. The best evidence concerns efficacy of therapeutic daycare programs for physically abused preschoolers.[133] Lacking a substantial body of knowledge about treatment of older abused and neglected children, therapists are left to develop treatment plans and methods that are theoretically grounded.[134]

15.04.   Clinicians' Involvement in the Legal Process

CASE STUDY 15.1

You are therapist for Joan McIntyre, a single mother who is being treated for depression. Ms. McIntyre works as a housekeeper in a local motel and ekes out a living for her two children, ages 8 and 4. In the context of the treatment, you learned that there have been times that Joan has been so short on energy as well as funds for child care that she has left the children alone for hours at a time and that she sometimes has been psychologically unavailable

even when physically present. You became sufficiently concerned that, with Ms. McIntyre's knowledge but over her objection, you reported your suspicion of child neglect to Child Protective Services (CPS).

After conducting a home visit in which it was determined that the neglect had occurred but that the children were not in immediate danger, the CPS caseworker called you to ask you to conduct an evaluation so that a dispositional plan could be developed. The plan may ultimately be submitted to juvenile court.

QUESTIONS: Should you agree to conduct the evaluation? Would your answer change if you were the children's therapist, or the therapist for the whole family? Suppose that CPS does assume jurisdiction and that the children remain in the home but that CPS and Ms. McIntyre cannot come to an agreement about the specific steps to be taken to ensure the children's safety. Would you accept a request to mediate the dispute? To provide an evaluation for use by the mediator? What types of issues would you want to raise in conducting such a mediation or evaluation?

(a)   Investigation

Historically, mental health professionals rarely became involved in addressing forensic issues in child maltreatment cases before the cases were adjudicated. In recent years, however, clinicians' involvement has begun increasingly earlier in the process. In that regard, child protection bears some resemblance to civil commitment in that a forensic clinician may assume the role of decision-maker and even initiator (i.e., mandated reporter) of the process in its early phases but then return to the role of neutral expert at the adjudication and disposition.

The potential role confusion is even more likely to be present, however, because of the nature of the questions posed in child protection cases. After a report is made, state authorities—most often, CPS workers—have two kinds of questions that they are legally obligated to answer. First, did child maltreatment occur? This question actually is in two forms: Did child abuse or neglect, as defined in the criminal *and* the family codes, occur? Second, if child maltreatment did occur, what disposition would alleviate the danger? The latter question potentially involves immediate (emergency), short-term, and long-term predictions and decisions. Note that a positive answer to the first question necessarily triggers an inquiry in regard to the second—in effect, an exploration of the coercive steps that the state might take to ensure the child's safety. However, even when CPS fails to substantiate that legally cognizable abuse or neglect has occurred, the state may pose the second question (or an even broader question about a plan to meet the needs of the child and family) in regard to *voluntary* services.

Unfortunately, the former question (What happened?) so dominates the inquiry in most states that the latter question (What can we do about it?) often is addressed minimally if at all. Even when maltreatment is substantiated, often no services at all are delivered; as noted in the preceding section, children's own needs for services are especially unlikely to be addressed.[135] As ABCAN [see § 15.01(c)(2)] concluded:

> Investigation now drives the child protection system. Stated differently, *the system acts in response to allegations—not needs for help. . . . The result of the current design of the child protection system is that investigation often seems to occur for its own sake, without any realistic hope of meaningful treatment to prevent the recurrence of maltreatment or to ameliorate its effects, even if the report of suspected maltreatment is validated.* Obviously investigation cannot be removed altogether, but it should no longer be the centerpiece of child protection.[136]

In most states, the inquiry in regard to both questions (What happened? What can we do about it?) is labeled an "investigation." That term connotes, however, an emphasis on the answer to the former question. To try to reorient the child protection system, some CPS agencies are now differentiating between an *investigation* (the former inquiry) and an *assessment* (the latter inquiry). Some states no longer require an investigation (distinguished from an assessment) in cases that are unlikely to require judicial intervention,[137] and others now try to separate the investigatory and therapeutic roles by placing primary responsibility for the former work on law enforcement agencies, at least in cases in which criminal charges may be invoked.[138]

Such differentiation is likely to reduce the role confusion—and related ethical problems [see § 15.06(c)]—of mental health professionals. The determination of whether abuse or neglect oc-

curred is a judgment requiring common sense and legal acumen, but it is outside the specialized knowledge of mental health professionals [see § 15.04(c)(4)]. On the other hand, dispositional planning is well within the province of clinicians. Even on the latter issue, however, clinicians should avoid giving ultimate-issue opinions about dispositions (e.g., whether the risk to the child's safety is so egregious that it warrants placement of the child in foster care).

These attempts to increase the clarity of various professionals' roles in child protection cases are laudable. But clarity in concept does not necessarily translate into clarity in practice. Three points are noteworthy here. First, clinicians must remain mindful that although dispositional issues are *conceptually* within their province, their expertise on such issues may still be limited. In particular, the scientific foundation for risk assessment[139] and treatment planning in cases of child maltreatment is quite weak [see § 15.03(e)].

Second, as this last point implies, determination of the circumstances in which maltreatment has occurred may be highly relevant in assessing the risk to the child and developing a plan to mitigate it. Therefore, drawing a bright line between "investigation" and "assessment" may be quite difficult.[140]

Third, states increasingly are establishing multidisciplinary teams for investigation, assessment, and intervention.[141] Thus, responsibility for decisionmaking about civil child protection petitions, corollary dispositional matters, and even the filing of criminal charges may be diffused across the justice, health, mental health, and social service systems, including mental health professionals practicing in any of these settings. Although the clinicians' roles may primarily be to plan and implement treatment, they are likely to be involved as team members in at least an advisory capacity in decisionmaking about the pursuit of legal matters. In that connection, the clinicians' role may be especially ambiguous because they may be regarded as the team's experts in interviewing children. In such a capacity, they may substitute not only for CPS workers but also for police officers in conducting part of the investigation.[142] In such a circumstance, the clinicians may remain information gatherers without becoming decisionmakers. Nonetheless, when clinicians have an explicit role of eliciting information that may be used in a prosecution, the possibilities for confusion not only of the clinicians themselves but also of the individuals whom they are interviewing are obvious.

(b)   Emergency Decisions

The first step in the investigation and assessment precipitated by a report of suspected maltreatment is to obtain the information needed to stabilize the situation. Analogous to an emergency-room physician, the caseworker or child protection team must determine the level of imminent risk and, if necessary, take emergency action to protect the child.

State statutes permit removal of a child from parental custody as one of the options in emergency situations. The specific circumstances justifying such action vary, but they typically include, for example, a caseworker's or law enforcement officer's belief that a child is in imminent danger or in need of immediate medical attention, or that the child has been sexually abused. The criteria specified in the Alaska statute are illustrative:

(1) the minor has been abandoned;

(2) the minor has been grossly neglected . . . and immediate removal . . . is necessary to protect the minor's life or provide immediate necessary medical attention;

(3) the minor has been subjected to child abuse or neglect by a person responsible for the minor's welfare . . . and the department determines that immediate removal . . . is necessary to protect the minor's life or that immediate medical attention is necessary; or

(4) the minor has been sexually abused [under certain circumstances].[143]

In most states, the authority for taking a child into emergency custody rests with CPS, the local law enforcement agency, or both. Under such a statutory structure, a mental health professional may become involved in decisionmaking as a consultant assisting the CPS worker in analyzing the level of imminent risk to the child and considering steps that might be taken to mitigate that risk. Alternatively, in the course of an evaluation or treatment, the mental health professional may become alarmed at the apparent level of risk and

may recommend—and thereby precipitate—emergency action to protect the child.

In some states, clinicians may also act directly to initiate emergency protective action. For example, Arkansas permits

any person in charge of a hospital or similar institution or any physician treating a child [to] keep that child in his custody without the consent of the parent or the guardian, whether or not additional medical treatment is required, if . . . continuing in his place of residence or in the care and custody of the parent, guardian, custodian, or caretaker presents an immediate danger of severe maltreatment.[144]

If the physician or the hospital makes this decision, a court with jurisdiction over juvenile matters and the responsible human services agency must be notified immediately, and custody is generally limited to 72 hours. The burden for showing a continuing need for custody then rests with the state.[145]

Whether the assessment relates to an initial clinical or a later judicial determination of danger to the child, the clinician should remember that the question is not simply whether the child's safety demands placement outside the home. If a less intrusive action (e.g., periodic monitoring) can mitigate the risk sufficiently for the short term, that plan should be followed.

(c)   Adjudication

Several issues arise in connection with the adjudication of neglect and abuse. Some are procedural, such as the appropriate manner of taking a child's testimony in the highly charged context of an abuse proceeding where the accused and the accuser are related. Others are evidentiary, including when an out-of-court statement by a child is admissible. A third series of issues concerns a child's competency to testify in abuse cases. Finally, there are a host of issues associated with identifying whether abuse has occurred and who committed it.

(1)   Procedural Issues

In the 1980s, as reporting and criminal prosecution of sexual abuse cases began to increase dramatically, legislators and courts began to be more concerned about removing barriers to children's testimony (given the common lack of eyewitnesses and corroborative physical evidence in sexual abuse cases) and diminishing the emotional trauma that many believed the legal process inflicted on child witnesses. Accordingly, most states adopted new statutes and court rules that changed the procedural and evidentiary rules governing children's testimony, at least in abuse cases.[146] Typically, these new legal rules limit the defendant's confrontation of the child (e.g., though close-circuit TV), minimize public access to the child's testimony (e.g., through courtroom closure), and change the way in which the jury hears the child's evidence. Although the specific issues vary, the new rules typically raise questions about attenuation of the defendant's rights to confrontation and a fair, public jury trial and the public's right, through the press, to access to the trial process.

Apparently because of prosecutors' preference for live testimony by the witnesses they call, their reluctance to open doors to appeal of convictions, and concern over costs, the special procedures are applied in relatively few cases in most jurisdictions.[147] Nonetheless, the number of sexual abuse cases reaching the courts is now so vast and the issues regarding special procedures so controversial that appellate courts decide questions of law in approximately 1,500 sexual abuse cases each year.[148]

A state-by-state, law-by-law review of the status of special procedures in child abuse cases is beyond the scope of this book. The overarching principle of federal constitutional law governing testimony by child witnesses in abuse cases can be described, however. In a series of such cases decided between 1982 and 1990,[149] the United States Supreme Court repeatedly applied the well-settled constitutional principle that intrusions on fundamental rights must be narrowly drawn to meet a compelling state interest.[150] Specifically, the Court held that although access to evidence and protection of children's welfare are compelling state interests sometimes justifying intrusions on the rights of defendants and the public, states cannot establish blanket rules to infringe on such rights in cases involving child victims. Relying heavily on amicus briefs filed by the

American Psychological Association,[151] the Court emphasized the need for case-by-case determination of the need for special procedures.

This principle was elaborated most forcefully in *Maryland v. Craig*.[152] The Court held that only

> if the State makes an adequate showing of necessity [will] the state interest in protecting child witnesses from the trauma of testifying in a child abuse case [be] sufficiently important to justify the use of a special procedure that permits a child witness . . . to testify at trial against a defendant in the absence of face-to-face confrontation with the defendant.[153]

To reach a conclusion of "necessity" for testimony outside the physical presence of the defendant (for instance, via one-way closed-circuit television), the trial court has to make three findings to satisfy *Craig*. First, "the requisite finding of necessity must of course be a case-specific one: the trial court must hear evidence and determine whether use of the . . . procedure is necessary to protect the welfare of the particular child witness who seeks to testify."[154] Second, "the trial court must also find that the child witness would be traumatized, not by the courtroom generally, but by the presence of the defendant."[155] Third, "the trial court must find that the emotional distress suffered by the child witness in the presence of the defendant is more than de minimis, i.e., more than 'mere nervousness or excitement or some reluctance to testify.'"[156] The Supreme Court also held, however, that such findings could be made without the trial judge's direct observation of how the child behaves in the presence of the defendant:

> The trial court in this case, for example, could well have found, *on the basis of expert testimony* before it, that testimony by the child witnesses in the courtroom in the defendant's presence "will result in [each] child suffering serious emotional distress such that the child cannot reasonably communicate."[157] [Emphasis added]

In short, the Supreme Court encouraged trial courts to consider means of mitigating children's distress without limiting confrontation by the defendant. For example, if the trial process itself is found to be traumatic, "the child could be permitted to testify in less intimidating surroundings, albeit with the defendant present."[158] The Court declined to specify the level of disturbance required for a "more than de minimis" showing that confrontation would be traumatic because the Maryland statute at issue in *Craig* established a threshold that "clearly suffices to meet constitutional standards."[159] Specifically, the Maryland statute required a finding that the child would suffer such emotional distress that he or she would be unable to communicate reasonably—in effect, that the court would be deprived of the child's testimony and that justice would be stymied.[160] It is unclear whether the Supreme Court would sanction statutes, present in some states,[161] that condition use of special procedures on protection of the child from mere "psychological" harm.[162]

Craig opened the door to testimony by mental health professionals in hearings to determine whether there is a necessity for special procedures to protect particular child witnesses. The Maryland statute and others like it appear on their face to require a type of evaluation that will be familiar to forensic mental health professionals specialized in work with children. As one commentator stated:

> [T]he Maryland procedures seem to require a focus on expectable cognitive–linguistic–social performance when faced with a particular stressor. This focus is not unlike that of an evaluation of competency to testify, one element of which is a child's ability to relate a story accurately.[163]

In contrast, in states that base their use of special procedures on their desire to protect children from psychological harm,[164] "[t]he focus is on the potential injury to the child of testimony in front of the defendant, regardless of whether the child can communicate sufficiently to offer useful testimony."[165] Thus, the type of evaluation demanded in these jurisdictions, whether involving use of special procedures in a criminal court or a family court, may overlap with a dispositional evaluation in child protection proceedings in the family court. It is narrower than that type of evaluation, however, in the sense that it requires consideration of the emotional consequences of the child's interaction with a *particular* adult in a specific context.

Although the nature of the inquiry may be fa-

miliar under either type of statute, the information needed to make the necessary predictions is sparse, and it is unlikely that the necessary scientific foundation will be available soon. A working group of the American Psychological Association concluded:

> Although there are reasons to believe that some children need special procedures in order to avoid trauma and provide full and accurate testimony, identification of these children is complicated by the infrequent use of such procedures. The sample sizes for testimony under different conditions are so small that it is unlikely that an actuarial risk–benefit assessment soon will be available for determination of the particular cases requiring procedural modification.[166]

The knowledge that is now available provides additional foundation for the need for caution in such evaluations. Although research on the emotional sequelae of child victims' testimony in criminal proceedings "lends credence to the case-by-case approach, it also suggests the difficulty of implementing it"[167]:

> Interestingly, the children who most want to have their day in court are those who are in some of the most negative circumstances (e.g., who have a history of previous abuse; whose caretaker is poorly adjusted) and thus are at high risk for negative effects of testimony. This finding has important policy implications. First, it suggests the need for special procedures in some cases so that children who, in a sense, have the most to tell are able to do so without undue risk. Second, when combined with other findings, it indicates the complexity of determining who is most at risk. Bright-line rules (e.g., age) will not validly discriminate children at high risk of negative effects of testimony. Assessments of overall clinical risk will be overbroad because some children who may be in especially difficult circumstances will benefit from the opportunity to testify. In either instance, assessment of probable effects of *testimony* may not be informative about probable effects of *testimony under special procedures* [the question posed by *Craig* and the preceding cases].[168]

Moreover, the scant research available on the general effects of use of special procedures raises some questions about their efficacy. Notably, research conducted in two Australian jurisdictions showed that, contrary to the beliefs of parents and the professionals involved, use of closed-circuit television for children's testimony affected neither their emotional well-being nor their perceptions of their court experience.[169] On the other hand, having a *choice* about whether to use closed circuit (regardless of the choice made) did make a difference. This finding is paralleled by British research showing that having a choice about the site for an investigative interview diminished the emotional sequelae of the process.[170]

Thus, although research and theory on the dynamics of child abuse[171] and the nature of children's experience in the legal process[172] may be helpful in suggesting the possible effects of alternative procedures, there is little research directly on point, and that which is available gives more reason for caution in predictions. Amid such uncertainty, there is special significance in our usual injunctions to avoid the ultimate issue (in this instance, in regard to whether there is a necessity for use of a particular procedure) and to illuminate the level of uncertainty in the foundation for one's opinions.

(2)   Reliability of Hearsay

Another potential side issue for forensic evaluation at the adjudicatory stage is the reliability of hearsay statements [see § 3.08(a) for a general treatment of hearsay]. In their zeal to minimize child victims' direct confrontation of defendants and to preserve evidence that inculpates defendants, prosecutors frequently desire to admit statements that children made out of court. Moreover, many state legislatures have adopted special hearsay exceptions for use in cases involving child abuse.[173] While the various grounds for admission of children's hearsay statements are diverse,[174] the important point for present purposes is that because such statements by their nature affect a defendant's right to confront the witness, the proffer of such hearsay statements in a *criminal* child abuse case implicates the Sixth Amendment's Confrontation Clause. In construing the scope of the Sixth Amendment in this context, the Supreme Court's rulings have opened the door to expert testimony on the admissibility of such statements.

The leading case on point is *Idaho v. Wright,*[175] which was announced by the Supreme Court at

the same time the decision in *Craig* was released.[176] Drawing on the Court's decision a decade earlier in *Ohio v. Roberts,*[177] the Court reaffirmed two criteria for determination of the admissibility of hearsay statements in prosecution of a criminal defendant. First, the use of hearsay without the opportunity for cross-examining the person who made the hearsay statement is permissible only when it is necessary; the state must produce the witness or demonstrate his or her unavailability. (In *Wright,* the Court assumed without deciding that the child witness's incompetence to testify at the time of trial rendered her unavailable.[178]) Second, if the witness is shown to be unavailable, the statement can be admitted if it is shown to have sufficient "indicia of reliability." Reliability can be presumed if the hearsay statement meets the criteria of a "firmly rooted" exception to the hearsay prohibition; otherwise, there must be a showing of "particularized guarantees of trustworthiness." In *Wright,* the state relied on the "residual" hearsay exception,[179] which in essence states that hearsay that does not meet other exceptions may nonetheless be admissible if certain requirements are met. The Court held that "almost by definition," this exception does not "share the same tradition of reliability that supports the admissibility of statements under a firmly rooted hearsay exception."[180] This logic would also appear to bar admission of hearsay statements under the special child abuse exceptions mentioned above (unless particularized guarantees of reliability are provided) because such statutes were enacted in recent years.

As to when "guarantees of reliability" are present, no clear rule exists. For instance, in *Wright* the Court held that there is no "preconceived and artificial litmus test for the procedural propriety of professional interviews,"[181] and overruled the Idaho Supreme Court's holding that interviews must be videotaped and avoid leading questions. Indeed, the Court noted that such procedures "may in many instances be inappropriate or unnecessary to a determination whether a given statement is sufficiently trustworthy for Confrontation Clause purposes."[182]

At the same time, the Court barred use of corroborative evidence (e.g., physical evidence) as an indicator of reliability; rather, the statement must stand on its own.[183] Specifically, a hearsay statement is only to be admitted against a defendant when "the declarant's truthfulness is so clear from the surrounding circumstances that the test of cross-examination would be of marginal utility."[184] Although the Court emphasized that this judgment must be individualized—not a "mechanical test"[185]—the Court did note several factors that should be considered in sexual abuse cases: the spontaneity and consistency of the statement, the child's emotional state at the time of the statement, the child's use of language (whether it appears to be beyond the child's developmental level and, therefore, perhaps to have been coached), and the lack of a motive to fabricate.[186]

In short, the Court appeared to impose a requirement that the hearsay statement be so trustworthy as to render cross-examination virtually unnecessary. This stance was reinforced by the Court's language explaining the nature of the "firmly rooted" exceptions:

> The basis for the "excited utterance" exception, for example, is that such statements are given under circumstances that eliminate the possibility of fabrication, coaching, or confabulation, and that therefore the circumstances surrounding the making of the statement provide sufficient assurance that the statement is trustworthy and that cross-examination would be superfluous. Likewise, the "dying declaration" and "medical treatment" exceptions to the hearsay rule are based on the belief that persons making such statements are highly unlikely to lie.[187]

Clinicians asked to determine the trustworthiness of children's hearsay statements should consider two points about the Court's analysis in *Wright*. First, it is not self-evident that the historic assumptions about the circumstances of trustworthiness apply to children, and research on such points is essentially nonexistent.[188] For example, do children being subjected to medical exams as part of a sexual abuse evaluation uniformly regard physicians as beneficent individuals solely concerned with guarding children's health and planning their treatment? If so, is such a belief by a child sufficient to prevent the child from lying about whether abuse has occurred and, if it occurred, about the circumstances of the offense? Second, the factors that the Court urged trial courts to consider in determining the trustwor-

thiness of a child's statement are largely matters of common sense.

Given these facts, there is good reason to doubt whether mental health professionals bear specialized knowledge justifying admission of their opinions about the reliability of a child's hearsay statements, although there may be some specific factors about which psychological knowledge is relevant (e.g., the sophistication of vocabulary and grammar that is common among children of a given age and the specific child whose statement is in question, the range of emotion that children may display when they initially disclose abuse). Even in these instances, however, there clearly is no foundation in psychological research for the ultimate conclusion about whether a child's statement is trustworthy.

(3)   Competence to Testify

The criteria for competency to testify are elaborated in § 7.07. Children are competent to testify when they have the capacity to observe and remember events and to communicate about them, when they can distinguish reality from fantasy, and when they understand the obligation to tell the truth.[189] The majority of states now presume children to be competent witnesses, whether in general or in child abuse cases specifically.[190] Although the presumption is typically rebuttable, there are questions about whether the inquiry in regard to competence to testify should remain at all, given that time will be consumed in any event by a competence hearing and that juries are probably capable of assessing the reliability of most testimony.

The clinician who is invited to evaluate a child's competency to testify should be aware of the large body of research on children's skills as witnesses [see § 7.07(b)].[191] Much of this research may actually speak more to the child's credibility than to his or her competence as a witness. *Credibility* is a continuum; *competence* is a dichotomy. As long as the competency threshold is passed, developmental differences in children's cognitive, linguistic, or social skills or their moral judgment are irrelevant to the latter determination. As indicated in the preceding paragraph, that threshold can be quite low; in any event, it is based at least as much on jurors' competence in weighing children's testimony as it is on children's skill in presenting it.

One last point has to do with the distinction between competency to testify and the confrontation issue addressed in the previous section. Recall that in *Wright,* the child was found incompetent to testify. One might justifiably ask how an out-of-court statement by such an individual could be reliable enough to pass *Wright's* test. The Supreme Court in *Wright* accepted the trial court's reasoning that the absence of one element of competence to testify (i.e., ability to communicate to a jury) does not necessarily imply the absence of another element (i.e., capacity to "receiv[e] just impression of the facts"), only the latter of which is germane to the trustworthiness of a hearsay statement.[192] As Myers has pointed out, the reliability determination involved in hearsay confrontation analysis is different from the ability-to-communicate determination involved in competency to testify analysis.[193] Interviewers conducting investigations or dispositional assessments should be mindful of the need to document children's ability to relate facts in different contexts (e.g., to social workers vs. jurors).[194]

(4)   The Case in Chief: Proving Injury and Abuse

The most controversial uses of clinicians' testimony in child maltreatment cases relate to the questions "What happened?" and "Who did it?" There may be no other context in which evidentiary and professional issues of the sort discussed in Chapter 1 are as frequently and acutely raised. When, if at all, may group data be used as evidence about whether a particular individual perpetrated or experienced abuse or neglect? What level of inference should mental health professionals be permitted to reach in their opinion testimony?

Use of mental health professionals' testimony to prove elements of the prosecution's case in chief—whether in a family court adjudication or a criminal trial—is a relatively new and highly debated phenomenon. It is possible to identify several different kinds of questions that clinicians might be asked and that are directly germane to proof of elements of the offense.

Admission of a Child's Statements through a Mental Health Professional.   In one scenario, the clini-cian's *opinions* are not at issue; rather, the clinician is asked to testify as a voice for the child, a reporter of statements that the child made about the maltreatment that he or she experienced. As noted earlier, because of a child's unavailability, a desire to avoid the necessity of his or her testimony, or simply a wish to corroborate testimony that is given, attorneys often wish to admit statements made by the child outside the courtroom. One potential source of such hearsay evidence is a health professional (possibly a mental health clinician) to whom the child confided about maltreatment. Attempts to follow this avenue have met with mixed results.

If statements are made in the course of a medical exam unrelated to a legal proceeding, many states provide that the health care professional[195] may testify as to those statements. As noted earlier, this exception to the hearsay rule is often referred to as the "medical diagnosis and treatment" exception. In *White v. Illinois,*[196] the Supreme Court held that admission of hearsay statements by a four-year-old under this exception did not violate the Confrontation Clause because the exception was "firmly rooted" and because "a statement made in the course of procuring medical services, where the declarant knows that a false statement may cause misdiagnosis or mistreatment, carries special guarantees of credibility that a trier of fact may not think replicated by courtroom testimony."

As noted earlier [see § 15.04(c)(2)], there are reasons for disputing the Court's assumptions in *White,* at least as applied to children. And some lower courts have refused to construe the exception broadly. For example, in *United States v. Tome,*[197] a federal court of appeals rejected efforts to admit a caseworker's account of the statements of a child who had been sexually abused by her father. The court ruled that because the caseworker had neither diagnosed nor treated the child but instead had acted in an investigative capacity, the testimony did not fall within the "medical diagnosis and treatment" exception. In addition, the court found the child's statements insufficiently reliable to allow admission, in part because they occurred more than a year after the allegation of abuse.[198] In a somewhat similar case, a federal court of appeals refused to allow the admission of a videotaped interview conducted by a social worker with a child victim on the ground that there was insufficient evidence of the trustworthiness of the statements.[199] The tape was not prepared as part of the medical exam of the child and so was not admissible under that exception. In addition, the court found that the spontaneity of the child's statements had been compromised by repeated prior questioning.

In short, mental health professionals' descriptions of out-of-court statements by children are not admissible under the medical-diagnosis exception unless made for the purpose of treatment planning. As discussed earlier, under *Wright* they may still be admissible if sufficiently trustworthy, but this outcome requires overcoming judicial skepticism about the circumstances under which such statements often are made, doubts about their spontaneity, and concerns about the possible suggestive effects of prior and leading questions.

Expert Testimony about Whether an Injury Has Occurred.   The most common use of mental health professional's testimony is not simply to repeat statements made by children but to testify as an expert—an approach that may also permit admission of the child's statements but as foundation for the expert's opinions rather than for their factual value. This type of testimony is much more controversial.

Perhaps least controversial, testimony by a mental health professional may be sought when the child protection statute requires proof of harm as an element of abuse or neglect [see § 15.02]. In such a case, the clinician will usually be asked to determine whether a "mental injury" has resulted from maltreatment of the child. Thus, the evaluation and testimony will be focused on the child's mental status and, if significant disturbance is present, whether it may have been caused by abuse or neglect. The nature of the inquiry in this context is similar to that in tort cases in which mental injury is alleged [see § 12.05(c), (d)]. The problem for mental health professionals is most likely to be the question of causation.

In that regard, it is important to remember that child maltreatment commonly occurs in a context in which children face many psychosocial challenges [see § 15.03], each of which might cause disturbance. Moreover, at the time that a clinician is asked to evaluate a child believed to have been maltreated, the child is likely to be ex-

periencing stress as a result of the child protection proceedings themselves. If the child has been placed in foster care as a protective measure prior to adjudication, the child also may be experiencing trauma as a result of separation from the family of origin, placement with strangers, a change of schools, and disruption of other daily routines.

Expert Testimony about Whether Abuse or Neglect Has Occurred.   Another instance in which clinicians may be asked to testify about the particular alleged victim is when they are asked to address whether a child has been abused (as opposed to harmed from acknowledged abuse). When this question is framed in terms of the child's truthfulness ("I believed her, because . . .") or of the truthfulness of abused children in general ("children don't lie about sexual abuse"), courts and commentators are virtually unanimous in their view that such opinions usurp the role of the trier of fact and should not be admitted.[200] Some appellate courts have been vociferous in their rejection of such testimony. For example, the Oregon Supreme Court wrote: "We have said before, and we will say it again, but this time with emphasis—we really mean it—*no psychotherapist may render an opinion on whether a witness is credible in any trial conducted in this state.* The assessment of credibility is for the trier of fact and not for psychotherapists."[201] Also bemoaning the intrusion on the factfinder's role, a Texas appellate court observed that "experts on child abuse are not human lie detectors. Nor are they clairvoyant. Nothing in this literature suggests that experts can or should replace the jury as the ultimate arbiters of credibility."[202]

Some commentators distinguish the admissibility of an opinion about whether a purportedly abused child is believable from that of a "diagnosis" of a child as abused.[203] In our view (and that of most appellate courts[204]), this is a distinction without a difference. Many clinicians are convinced that assessment of whether abuse has occurred is a matter in which they are skilled and about which they should be permitted to testify.[205] Such a belief is understandable when the law not only permits but requires a clinician's report of his or her mere suspicion that a child has been abused or neglected, although the point should not be lost that this duty extends in most jurisdictions to many more people than those who have professional training in the mental health disciplines.[206] There is no reason to believe that clinicians' skill in determining whether a child has been abused is the product of specialized knowledge.[207] The conclusions to be drawn from a child's graphic description of a sexual encounter, for example, are a matter of common sense, not scientific knowledge or even clinical acumen.

Because testimony as an expert involves an implicit representation that the opinions presented are grounded in specialized knowledge, a mental health professional should decline on ethical grounds to offer an opinion about whether a child told the truth or has been "abused." By the same token, under the rules of evidence, such as opinion should never be admitted.

Expert Testimony about Characteristics of Maltreated Children. The question is harder and the case law is divided about the admissibility of a mental health professional's opinion concerning the typical characteristics of abused or neglected children (as opposed to whether a particular child is abused).[208] If such an opinion is grounded in hard data, its careful presentation does not violate professional ethics. However, we are leery of such testimony as substantive evidence. In the current state of knowledge, such testimony is likely to be so misleading and prejudicial that it will not assist the trier of fact.

Too often, clinical impressions about child abuse "syndromes" are presented without regard to the lack of a systematic empirical foundation for such opinions. Although clinical intuition may be useful in guiding treatment planning, it is insufficient as a basis for determining whether maltreatment may have occurred. Furthermore, when statistical data are available, they provide acute evidence of a serious base-rate problem. As a recent consensus conference concluded: "No specific behavioral syndromes characterize victims of sexual abuse. Sexual abuse involves a wide range of possible behaviors which appear to have widely varying effects on its victims."[209] Many sexually abused children show no symptoms at all, and most of the symptoms that are disproportionately common among sexually abused children are quite common among children in general.[210] The probability is that children showing behavior said to be indicative of sexual abuse—even

those that most strikingly differentiate sexually abused children—have *not* been abused [see § 1.03(c)(3)].[211]

Of course, these issues apply in both directions. One cannot assume, for example, that a purported victim without obvious emotional distress lacks credibility. Presentation of scientific *rebuttal* evidence thus may assist the trier of fact to weigh the evidence without prejudicing the factfinder toward conviction. Accordingly, courts that have been skeptical about admission of syndrome evidence in the case in chief still often have permitted use of such evidence for rebuttal purposes.[212]

Also, the problems with *psychological* syndrome evidence may not apply to *physical* evidence.[213] Alternative explanations for particular physical injuries (e.g., shaken-baby syndrome and spinal fractures) may be hard to generate.[214]

Expert Testimony about Characteristics of Child Abusers. An early illustration of the use of testimony about the characteristics of child abusers came in the Minnesota case of *State v. Loebach,*[215] an appeal of the conviction of Robert Loebach for the third-degree murder of his three-month-old son, Michael. Although *Loebach* was a criminal case, the evidentiary issue presented in it is equally applicable to civil adjudication of child abuse and neglect. In *Loebach,* Dr. Robert ten Bensel, an expert on battered-child syndrome, first testified that the pattern of injuries that Michael had sustained was consistent with the syndrome. As noted above, this medical testimony about *physical* injuries presumably fell well within the boundaries of acceptable expert testimony in terms of assisting the jury to determine whether the death of Michael was the product of nonaccidental injury. However, Dr. ten Bensel also described the psychosocial characteristics of "battering parents": a history of abuse in their own childhoods, role reversal, low empathy, a "short fuse" and a "low boiling point," high blood pressure, strict authoritarianism, uncommunicativeness, low self-esteem, isolation, and lack of trust. The prosecution then called two caseworkers who had known Loebach since he was a child to testify that he did in fact possess many of those characteristics.

The Minnesota Supreme Court ruled that Dr. ten Bensel's testimony about the characteristics of battering parents and the related testimony by the caseworkers should have been excluded. The court seemed to rely initially on the fact that the evidence was admitted essentially to establish that the defendant's *character* was such that he was prone to child abuse. Under traditional evidence law, such evidence is not admissible unless the *defendant* places his or her character at issue, which the defendant in *Loebach* did not. Ultimately, however, the court's decision did not rest on the bar against gratuitous prosecution use of character evidence.[216] Rather, the holding was said to be "required until further evidence of the scientific accuracy and reliability of syndrome or profile diagnoses can be established."[217]

We have no quarrel with the result in *Loebach*, a result unanimously reached by the courts that considered the same issue subsequently.[218] The review of the literature in § 15.03(d)(1) shows that the scientific basis for the battering-parent syndrome is very weak. When used in combination with medical evidence as to the cause of physical injuries, it is likely to be highly prejudicial and misleading.[219] Although the low validity of the syndrome could have been elicited through skillful cross-examination and rebuttal testimony by other experts, it is unlikely that Dr. ten Bensel's testimony on the syndrome could have assisted the jury.

However, the *Loebach* court's ultimate reliance on scientific invalidity may have been a ruse. The court apparently did not review the scientific evidence on the battering-parent syndrome, and it avoided the more basic and harder question of when group data should be used in individual cases [see § 1.03(b)]. Suppose that Dr. ten Bensel had given a scholarly, comprehensive review of the literature in terms comprehensible to a lay jury. Suppose further that he had indicated the proportion of abusers possessing each of the characteristics, the proportions in other groups in the population, and the methodological strengths and weaknesses of the literature. This information would have provided the jury with base rates that might have assisted it in weighing the evidence.

The critical point, however, is that a description of the general characteristics of many child abusers is only tangentially relevant to the question of whether a *particular* defendant abused a child. It is fundamentally unfair to require the defendant, in effect, to disprove that he or she is a battering parent in the absence of direct evidence of the parent having abused the child.[220] Defendants should be convicted and respondents' parental rights should be infringed on the basis of what they did, not who they are [see also, § 8.03(c) on the admissibility of character evidence].

In the unlikely event that behavioral scientists are called to testify about the characteristics of abusive parents, they would certainly be ethically obligated to indicate the limitations of the literature and the overlap among populations. To prevent misuse of the evidence, they also should make clear to the factfinder the difficulties in drawing inferences about individual events on the basis of group data.

(d) Disposition and Postdispositional Review

Although much of the debate about use of mental health professionals in child protection cases focuses on their involvement in generating and presenting evidence about the case in chief, the most common use of mental health professionals is in the development of information that may be used in crafting dispositional plans. This role may first arise in emergency decisionmaking soon after a report of suspected child maltreatment is made to CPS or a law enforcement agency [see § 15.04(b)]. It usually continues at the dispositional hearing that follows a family court's adjudication that child maltreatment has occurred or the sentencing hearing that follows a criminal conviction for such behavior. Indeed, dispositional questions may continue to arise even after the disposition is settled. Federal law specifically requires a postdispositional review of the child and parents at least semiannually if a child is placed in out-of-home care.[221] Of course, the prospect of long-term placement of this type may stimulate questions about possible termination of parental rights [see § 15.04(e)] or, conversely, eventual reunification of children with their biological parents.[222] In short, as long as the court maintains jurisdiction over the family—in effect, as long as CPS has an open case—dispositional questions are apt to arise.

This process is analogous to juvenile delinquency proceedings in several respects. First, no matter what the specific point in the process,[223] the court is able to undertake a far-ranging inquiry about the child's best interests, and the range of potential specific dispositions (e.g., conditions placed on parents in either retaining or regaining custody of their children) is broad.[224] Second, in consideration of a child's best interests, an overarching predictive question (analogous to "amenability to treatment" in juvenile justice) dominates the process: What is the level of risk to a child's safety associated with each dispositional option?

Third, notwithstanding this commonality across proceedings, each point in the process brings different specific issues (analogous to the variations in meaning of "amenability to treatment" at various points of delinquency proceedings [see § 14.04(b)]). For example, emergency decisions and subsequent hearings on temporary disposition are apt to focus on *imminent* risk that may justify *immediate* removal [see § 15.04(b)]. Postadjudication hearings are likely to focus instead on long-term risk and actions that could be taken to reduce it. Because of a federal statutory requirement[225] and corollary statutes in many states,[226] postdispositional hearings (whether conducted by a juvenile or family court, a foster-care review board, or both) typically include an inquiry about whether the state has made reasonable efforts "to prevent or eliminate the need for removal of the child from his home, and [when placement occurs,] to make it possible for the child to return to his home."[227] Proceedings in which termination of parental rights is under consideration typically require other specific findings about the long-term prognosis [see § 15.04(e)].

For the clinician, the second point made above is probably the most important. Regardless of the specific point in the process, mental health professionals are apt to be most helpful to the court and other decisionmakers (e.g., CPS workers and foster-care review boards) by conducting and reporting clinical assessments focused on prevention of further maltreatment and alleviation of the psychological harm that may already have occurred. Drawing from research and theory about the nature, causes, and sequelae of child abuse

and neglect [see § 15.03], clinicians may be able to ask the "right" questions to identify the precipitants of abuse and neglect, the particular needs of the family as a whole and as individuals, and the nature of relationships within the family.

The nature of this inquiry is closely analogous not just to delinquency assessments but also adult sentencing evaluations [see §§ 9.07, 9.09] in that the clinician is charged with identifying the level of risk and the nature and relative efficacy of interventions that may increase safety. The sentencing analogy is also an apt reminder of the problems with such dangerousness assessments. Although the existence of mandatory reporting and central registries potentially provides the foundation for precise actuarial determination of risk, the data analyses that would enable empirically based predictions generally have not been performed.[228] Moreover, research on the effectiveness of various dispositional alternatives is woefully thin [see § 15.03(e)]. A panel of the National Research Council concluded in 1993 that "[a] coherent base of research information on the effectiveness of treatment is not available at this time to guide the decisions of case workers, probation officers, health professionals, family counselors, and judges."[229] In short, although enough is known about child maltreatment to provide some foundation for informed speculation about possible dispositional alternatives, the more striking impression about the literature is how much is *not* known. Therefore, even when experts are involved in the relatively uncontroversial context of dispositional decisionmaking, they should have great humility in making predictions and offering other opinions.

Moreover, because many of the determinations that courts make in the dispositional phases of child maltreatment cases are similar to the judgments that mental health professionals make in treatment planning, we repeat that clinicians need to exercise special care in avoiding ultimate-issue opinions [see § 1.04]. The level of risk to children that society should and will tolerate, the question whether children should be removed from their home against their parents' will, and the circumstances justifying involuntary family treatment are not "clinical" or "scientific" matters. Although clinicians may guide courts in identifying dispositional options, mental health professionals do not have specialized knowledge about the embedded legal and moral issues.

(e) Termination of Parental Rights

Although the question whether parental rights should be terminated sometimes arises at the initial dispositional phase,[230] that issue more commonly arises at a later hearing to review disposition. In some states, the question will automatically arise if the child has been in foster care for a particular period of time, although a more common procedure is to consider the question only if the state moves for termination.[231] Termination itself occurs in a single proceeding in most states, although the proceeding is bifurcated in some jurisdictions.[232] In the bifurcated procedure, there is an initial "factfinding" proceeding to determine whether particular threshold conditions (e.g., parental unfitness) exist. If the threshold questions are answered in the affirmative, a second "dispositional" hearing considers whether termination of parental rights would be in the best interests of the child.

Termination of parental rights may be one of the most difficult decisions a court is required to make.[233] On the one hand, permanent severance of family ties is recognized as an especially grave step, perhaps even more severe than imprisonment.[234] On the other hand, authorities are increasingly mindful of the history of "legal abuse" of children by bouncing them among foster homes because the children are unavailable for adoption. Amid this profound conflict, there is concern about the high risk of error, in view of both vagueness of standards and unreliability of assessment. This risk is compounded by the fact that mental health and social service evaluations are usually crucial evidence in termination proceedings. The deck is usually stacked against the parents in that regard in that they typically have substantially less access to these professionals than the state has.[235]

In § 15.02, we noted the common problems of vagueness of standards for abuse and neglect and reliance in the standards on individual value judgments as to proper childrearing practices. These problems are often compounded at the termination phase. Although some standards rely on rela-

tively objective determinations of fact (e.g., whether the parents abandoned the child or whether the parents failed to maintain contact with the child or to comply with orders of the court after the child was placed in foster care), even in these instances termination typically is discretionary, based on the judge's conclusion as to the child's best interests.

More troublesome are statutes that permit termination if the parents are found to be "unfit," usually without further explication of the standards. Often these broad, value-laden grounds for termination are accompanied by an express or implicit presumption of unfitness on the part of parents who are mentally ill, mentally retarded, or dependent on drugs or alcohol. Nebraska, for example, permits termination if "the parents are unfit because of debauchery, habitual use of intoxicating liquor or narcotic drugs, or repeated lewd and lascivious behavior, which conduct is found by the court to be seriously detrimental to the health, morals, or well-being of the juvenile."[236] Termination may also occur if "the parents are unable to discharge parental responsibilities because of mental illness or mental deficiency and there are reasonable grounds to believe that such condition will continue for a prolonged indefinite period."[237]

The model statute recommended by the National Council of Juvenile Court Judges also permits termination based on a broad inquiry leading to a finding that "the parent [is] unfit or that the conduct or condition of the parent is such as to render him/her unable to properly care for the child and that such conduct or condition is unlikely to change in the foreseeable future."[238] The model statute directs the court to consider a number of factors (e.g., parental mental disorder, "excessive use of intoxicating liquors or narcotic or dangerous drugs," and "conduct towards a child of a physically, emotionally or sexually cruel or abusive nature"), but it permits discretion as to the weight accorded these and any other relevant factors.[239] When the child has been in foster care, the court is also required to consider the child's relationship with the foster family and the family's suitability as a permanent home.[240]

Concern about the risk of error arising from such broad discretion has led to a trend toward more clearly limited inquiry. This limitation takes two forms. One approach is to move the focus somewhat away from the failings of the parents to the adequacy of the services offered, and procedures followed, by the state. It is increasingly common to require a showing of "reasonable"[241] or even "diligent"[242] efforts by the state to rehabilitate the parents.

A second approach, exemplified by the Juvenile Justice Standards, is to rely on relatively narrow and objective standards. The Standards would permit termination at the initial disposition only if the child has been abandoned; the child has been previously removed because of maltreatment, then returned to the parent, and now requires removal again; or another child in the family has been abused and the parent has received treatment thereafter. At the review phase, termination would occur if the child has been in foster care for six months (if placed under age three), or one year (if placed when over age three) and cannot be returned to the home.

Moreover the Standards recognize several exeptions to automatic termination, many of which call for a more psychological (albeit limited) inquiry. Termination would not occur in any of the following circumstances:

A. Because of the closeness of the parent–child relationship, it would be detrimental to the child to terminate parental rights.
B. The child is placed with a relative who does not wish to adopt the child.
C. Because of the nature of the child's problems, the child is placed in a residential treatment facility, and continuation of parental rights will not prevent finding the child a permanent family placement if the parents cannot resume custody when residential care is no longer needed.
D. The child cannot be placed permanently in a family environment and failure to terminate will not impair the child's opportunity for a permanent placement in a family setting.
E. A child over age ten objects to termination.

Under the Standards, if termination is ordered, the court would be directed to consider whether the foster home is suitable and whether "the child has substantial psychological ties to the foster parents." If so, the child would remain in the foster home even if the foster parents are unable or unwilling to adopt the child. Unlike the Juvenile Court Judges' model statute, the Standards do not require consideration of this factor in the termination decision itself, except insofar as it arises in paragraph D above.

Under the Standards, the involvement of mental health professionals in a termination proceeding would be similar to that in a temporary dispositional assessment in that the key question would generally be whether the child could be safely returned home. There would be additional special evaluation questions relating to the intensity of the parent–child relationship (paragraph A) and the adoptability of the child (paragraphs C and D).

Under the Juvenile Court Judges' model statute and the statutes prevailing in most jurisdictions, the nature of questions posed to mental health professionals in a termination proceeding is also likely to be very similar to that in any dispositional review. The focus of the inquiry is likely to be slightly different, however, in that the prognosis for successful treatment of the parent is the key question. The mental health professional might also be asked to evaluate the adequacy of efforts to treat the parent and the nature of the child's relationship with the foster parents.

(f) Mediation and Other Alternative Processes

In § 16.01(b)(1), we review the issues involved in mental health professionals' assumption of dual roles as evaluator and mediator in child custody disputes arising in divorce. Although the issues involved in such duality of roles in child protection cases are at least as serious, they have received little attention in that context from other commentators. The reason is simple. Until recently, programs for alternative dispute resolution (ADR) in child protection cases were virtually nonexistent. The conventional wisdom has been that mediation is inappropriate in cases in which one party has been subjected to abuse. Even more fundamentally, the adversary model is seen as optimal for child protection cases—on this view, the state *ought* to prosecute parents who abuse or neglect their children (although the prosecution may be civil rather than criminal). Opponents of ADR in child protection cases argue that a compromise is apt to threaten the child's safety and that rehabilitation will occur only if the state exercises coercive authority.

These assumptions have begun to be widely questioned among professionals involved in child protection. In the report of a symposium convened by several national legal organizations, Davidson noted several scenarios in which mediation might be helpful in child protection cases: (1) conflict between caseworkers and parents about the dispositional plan; (2) conflict between parents and relatives, when such conflict is interfering with implementation of the dispositional plan; (3) conflict among foster parents, the child welfare agency, and biological or adoptive parents; and (4) conflict among the professionals involved in the case.[243] In each instance, the goal would be to facilitate the prompt establishment or implementation of a workable plan to protect the child and to do so in a manner that minimizes trauma to the child and the family.[244] There may even be instances in which ADR is useful prior to adjudication in reaching an agreement between the family and neighbors or professionals about the range of behaviors that constitute a threat to the child and about some means of reducing or preventing them.[245]

Responding to these possibilities and attempting to develop a helping and cooperative approach rather than a prosecutorial and adversarial stance, programs for ADR in child protection cases have begun to appear, although still typically on a demonstration basis.[246] Research on these innovations is scant, but that which is available is encouraging. In a true experiment (with random assignment of cases) involving child protection cases in Denver (omitting those in which an immediate threat to the child was identified or parents were perceived as incompetent to negotiate), parents who participated in mediation were more likely to "own" the resulting plan and to be less alienated.[247] Legal-system professionals in Connecticut have expressed a high degree of satisfaction with mediation of child protection cases, although parents (in contrast with their attorneys) are not present in about one-fourth of the conferences.[248]

Some new forms of ADR show promise as means to build community and extended-family responsibility and thus to diminish families' isolation.[249] Perhaps the foremost example is the family group conference, a procedure pioneered in New Zealand in 1989 in its overhaul of its juvenile justice and child protection systems.[250] Drawing from Maori traditions, New Zealand began relying on meetings of family groups—extended families and others, such as football coaches and family friends, who are important people in the lives of the family—rather than courts to create and confirm dispositional plans. This concept now is being piloted in a number of North American jurisdictions, although typically as a mechanism for diversion rather than disposition.[251]

In light of these developments, three points are noteworthy. First, the audience for information generated in dispositional evaluations is increasingly likely to be a nonjudicial decisionmaker. Second, as the emphasis on voluntary dispositions (including dispositions involving private parties outside the family) increases, the range of possibilities to consider expands. Third, clinicians must guard against inadvertently being drawn into a decisionmaker or advocate role when they have represented themselves as investigators or evaluators.

15.05.   Special Populations

(a)   Parents with Mental Illness

The various special provisions for termination of the rights of parents with mental disabilities noted in § 15.04(e) have been subject to considerable litigation in recent years. There are two broad constitutional challenges to these provisions. First, it is argued that the statutes violate equal protection because there is no compelling basis for discrimination on the basis of a parent's mental condition. Second, particularly when the statutes do not expressly require a finding that a parent's condition is directly and adversely related to his or her competence as a parent, there is a claim that due process is violated. Relatedly, there may be an argument that provisions for termination of the parental rights of parents with mental illness are so vague as to violate due process.[252] Nonetheless, in recent cases considering termination of parental rights of parents with mental illness or substance abuse problems, appellate courts have almost uniformly upheld the order to terminate.[253]

In the recent reported cases, the state has generally taken at least some care to relate the parents' disorder to childrearing practices, and the results of the various cases may have been proper. However, the rationality of a lower threshold for termination of the parental rights of parents with mental disabilities is questionable. Perhaps contrary to intuition, having a parent with mental illness—even serious mental illness—is in fact not very predictive of inadequate adjustment in the child. Although children of parents with mental illness are at relatively high risk for significant developmental problems, most develop normally.[254] Insofar as children of disordered parents are prone to disorders themselves, there is still a question whether the developmental risk is a result of parental incompetence (rather than genetic factors, for example).[255] The state would have no interest in termination of parental rights unless a child's welfare would be substantially improved in another home. Moreover, given that parental *physical* illness understandably also increases children's stress and corollary symptoms,[256] questions remain (on equal protection grounds) why stress resulting from parental mental illness should be given heightened consideration in intrusions on family integrity.

In the meantime, the problem of support for parents with serious mental illness and their families deserves greater attention. The majority of women with serious mental illness marry,[257] and their birth rate approaches that in the general population.[258] Yet adult mental health programs generally give insufficient attention to parental issues. In fact, the programs' management information systems typically do not even provide for recording information about parental status.[259]

The research that has been conducted on parenting by individuals with serious mental illness is scant, and much of what is available is arguably inapplicable to an understanding of ongoing parenting in the community. Much of the research on infant care by mothers with serious mental illness has been conducted on small samples in specialized inpatient programs outside the United States.[260] That research shows that some mothers with severe mental illness apparently care for their babies normally, even when they are in the most acute phase of psychosis.[261] Combined with evidence about child outcomes, such a finding runs against presumptions present in many states for termination of parental rights of parents with mental illness. However, clearly there is a need for research on parenting by individuals with mental illness in families living in the community and containing children of various ages.[262] Similarly, as psychopharmacological advances permit greater and greater independence of adults with serious mental illness, there is a need for parallel development of supports for them as parents and for their children.[263]

Absent an extensive literature on such programs, clinicians conducting dispositional evaluations are left to their general knowledge of social support and mental health services in suggesting alternatives that might enable families of parents with serious mental illness to live together with safety for the children. In the meantime, neither clinicians nor legal authorities should infer from a diagnosis that a parent is unfit. To guard against such inferences, clinicians should make clear in their reports and testimony that conclusions as to parental difficulties based on the presence of a mental illness per se are at present scientifically unsupportable.

(b) Parents with Mental Retardation

There is also weak empirical support for special provisions for terminating the parental rights of mentally retarded persons. It is true that a high proportion of mothers who are in the child protection system for neglect have mental retardation.[264] But it is not clear that this *should* be so. Most parents with mental retardation are *mildly* retarded and people with mild mental retardation are typically capable of holding jobs and living independently under reasonably normal conditions.[265]

Moreover, mild mental retardation is heavily related to social class.[266] Thus, as with mental illness, it is unclear whether any heightened risk of neglect that does occur results from parental incompetence, apart from the well-documented effects of poverty [see § 15.03(d)(2)]. This fact also means that a heightened review of the competence of parents with mental retardation is in effect a heightened review of parental competence of lower-class persons. The risk of capriciousness in application of the policy is obvious.

That being said, mental retardation is often one of the many challenges faced by the neglectful families that now predominate in the child protection system, and that fact needs to be considered in the design of dispositional plans. In this regard, it may be useful to know that although parents with mild mental retardation are more likely than nonretarded parents to bear children with mental retardation, most of the children of parents with mental retardation are not identified as mentally retarded. The risk in such instances is only about 10%,[267] although it rises substantially if both parents have mental retardation *and* they have already had a child with mental retardation.[268]

(c)   Parents Who Abuse Alcohol

Although parental use of illegal drugs, especially cocaine, has attracted the attention of policymakers in recent years, the far greater problem in incidence rate in child protection caseloads is alcoholism.[269] Alcohol abuse is also a common factor in sexual abuse cases.[270]

Notwithstanding that parental alcohol abuse and alcohol dependence have long been known to be common problems that may be plausibly hypothesized to have serious effects on parent–child relations, there is limited research from which to draw conclusions about the risks incurred by children of alcoholic parents. In a review of the literature in 1978, Jacob et al. uncovered only 16 studies of children of alcoholics, and only one of those studies included appropriate comparison groups.[271] Most of the studies on the effects of mothers with alcoholism on their children have looked at toxic effects on drinking during pregnancy, not the adequacy of childrearing. The childrearing outcome literature that does exist gives reason for caution in assuming that alcoholism in a parent is often related to poor socialization of a child. In a comprehensive review of the literature

in 1983, Vaillant concluded: "Perhaps for every child who becomes alcoholic in response to an alcoholic environment, another eschews alcohol in response to the same environment."[272]

In a recent review,[273] Rotunda et al. reached similar conclusions. They noted that relative to families in which parents are not dependent on alcohol, families of alcoholics are characterized by higher levels of negativity, conflict, and competitiveness and lower levels of cohesion, expressiveness, and problem-solving capacity.[274] However, there is no family pattern that is unique to families of alcoholics; similar problems are experienced in families facing other challenges.[275] Most important for legal policy and forensic assessment, there is great variation among children of alcoholics. Adult children of alcoholics do not differ from other adults on personality measures, although they are more likely to have alcohol-related and physical problems.[276] Of course, the greater risk of alcohol abuse and dependence may be the product of genetic predisposition.

Although parental alcoholism is undoubtedly a factor that should be considered when designing dispositional plans, there again is good reason not to jump from a diagnosis of alcoholism to a conclusion about parental unfitness. One specific dynamic that ought to be considered in dispositional planning, however, is the sense of isolation commonly experienced by families of alcoholics, especially when the parents are "wet" (in an episode of active drinking).[277] In view of the relation of this variable to child maltreatment [see § 15.03(d)(2)], there is special reason to make enhancement of social support an element of dispositional plans when parental alcoholism is an issue. Research also suggests a particular need to consider mechanisms to monitor child supervision, especially when both parents have alcohol problems.[278]

(d)   Parents Who Use Illegal Drugs

In recent years, there has been extraordinary attention by policymakers to the problem of parental use of illegal drugs.[279] Although this debate has focused in large part on prenatal exposure and related policy responses,[280] research thus far suggests that the bigger issue concerns parental behavior per se.[281] Although prenatal cocaine exposure may have some subtle developmental effects (notably, impaired ability to organize behavior and temperament problems), the majority of cocaine-exposed infants are not significantly developmentally delayed, and the quality of early caregiving is important in mediating whatever direct effects that the prenatal toxic exposure may have.[282]

Thus, the core problem is the care that children receive from drug-abusing parents, not the prenatal toxic effects. For example, a study comparing mothers in a substance abuse treatment program with mothers in Head Start programs in southeastern Michigan found substantially more frequent moves, less contact with the fathers, and less adequate housing, child care, and toys.[283] Nearly half the children of the substance-abusing mothers had been in foster care; none of the children in Head Start programs had had such an experience.[284] Substance-abusing mothers commonly reported periods of psychological unavailability and physical neglect of their children.[285] Similar findings have been reported by other researchers.[286]

Such research findings indicate the level of the challenge that is involved in treating families in which parents are using illegal drugs. It is not clear, however, how special the challenge is. Drug abuse commonly occurs in a context in which there are other impulsive and antisocial behaviors and a panoply of social and economic problems.[287] Similarly, child maltreatment, especially neglect, typically occurs in a complex situation in which there are many serious problems. Accordingly, in cases of parental drug abuse, like other instances of child maltreatment, an integrated multifaceted dispositional plan usually is needed.

For example, Magura and Laudet recommended that programs for substance-abusing parents and their families include the following elements:

> access to physical necessities including food, housing, and transportation; life skills training including parenting, financial management, assertiveness training, stress management and coping skills; educational and vocational assessment, counseling, training and opportunities, including language and literacy competency; counseling on topical issues including substance abuse and family therapy; health education and

medical care; child care; social services, social support, psychological assessment and mental health care; family planning services; and planned, continuing care after program completion.[288]

Similarly, a review of the scores of demonstration programs that were funded by the Pregnant and Postpartum Women and Infants Program of the Center for Substance Abuse Prevention (CSAP) showed that the best programs looked like well-conceptualized family service programs in other agencies. The typical CSAP-funded demonstration program for substance-abusing women and their families included the following elements:

- an array . . . [of] services that includes education and services to meet the diverse and complex needs of families;
- practical help, including transportation, child care, job seeking, emergency assistance, housing, food, and fun;
- recognition and use of extended family, neighbors, friends, and tribal members who seem to have natural ability to understand and help;
- locations (and times) that are convenient for participants;
- novel approaches to education and counseling tailored to special needs and usually developed from earlier efforts that were less successful than was hoped;
- support, being there, even after program services are complete, an ongoing network of help, support, and advice;
- collaboration across boundaries that previously had not been crossed, whether between a tribal community and a dominantly European-American town or businesses, human services [or] law enforcement.[289]

A final note is that, although the challenge should not be minimized, it should not be assumed that the fact of parental drug use necessarily means that the situation cannot be made safe for the child or that the parent cannot recover. In a report to Congress, the General Accounting Office recently summarized research and clinical experience on treatment of cocaine-dependent individuals:

> [T]hree cognitive/behavioral treatment approaches—relapse prevention, community reinforcement/contingency management, and

neurobehavioral therapy—have shown early promise with cocaine-abusing and cocaine-dependent clients, many of whom are classified as "hardcore" users. Clients treated with these approaches have demonstrated prolonged periods of cocaine abstinence and high rates of retention in treatment programs. For example, more than 60 percent of the cocaine-addicted clients who attended a relapse-prevention program in New York were continuously abstinent from cocaine during the 6- to 24-month follow-up period; more than 70 percent completed the relapse prevention program. About half the cocaine-dependent clients receiving community reinforcement/contingency management in a Vermont outpatient program remained continuously abstinent through 4 months of treatment; 58 percent completed the entire 6-month course of therapy. And 36 percent of the cocaine-using clients enrolled in a California neurobehavioral therapy program were abstinent from cocaine 6 months after entering treatment; the average length of stay in the program was 18 weeks.[290]

(e)   Biologically Related Foster Parents

Evaluators may be asked to address not only what might be done to increase safety for a child but also who might do it. A particularly common question concerns the optimal involvement of relatives, particularly whether they might provide appropriate supplementary or substitute care. Such involvement has become known as "kinship care."

In part because of the phenomenon of grandparents assuming responsibility for care of their grandchildren because their daughters are drug abusers,[291] there has been an extraordinary increase in kinship care, especially in urban states. The exact magnitude of the increase is not known because most states do not track kinship care cases separately.[292] However, there are some striking examples. For example, the prevalence of kinship care in New York City grew from 1,000 children in 1986 to 24,000 in 1992.[293] The majority of states now have an explicit policy preference for use of kinship care rather than foster care outside the extended family, and most of the remaining states frequently use kinship care.[294]

Recent congressional action seems sure to increase the frequency of use of kinship care and the frequency with which the question of kinship care is raised in dispositional hearings. Adding a new section to Title IV-E of the Social Security Act (the title providing for funds to states for foster care), the federal welfare reform bill enacted in 1996 appeared to create a presumption in favor of kinship care.[295] Specifically, Congress required states to "consider" giving preference to an adult relative over nonrelative caregivers when a child is placed outside the home, provided that the relative meets relevant state standards.

A number of potential advantages of kinship care underlie these developments:

- Enabling children to live with persons whom they know and trust;
- Reducing the trauma children may experience when they are placed with persons who initially are unknown to them;
- Reinforcing children's sense of identity and self-esteem, which flows from knowing their family history and culture;
- Facilitating children's connections to their siblings;
- Encouraging families to consider and rely on their own family members as resources;
- Enhancing children's opportunities to stay connected to their own communities and promoting community responsibility for children and families; and
- Strengthening the ability of families to give children the support they need.[296]

On the other hand, skeptics about the increasing use of kinship care worry whether relatives will exercise sufficient control over parents' access to the children, whether the relatives' own parental skills are likely to be adequate, and whether the often elderly caregivers will have the energy and resources[297] to provide care to children with great needs. These concerns are heightened by the fact that licensing and supervision for relative caregivers are typically less stringent than for nonrelative foster parents.[298]

Research on kinship care is just beginning, and its relation to developmental outcomes for children is still unknown. However, a number of clear facts have emerged from the work thus far, although their meaning is not so certain.

First, *clearly there is more stability in kinship care than in other foster care.* Children in kinship care remain in care longer than do children in other forms of out-of-home placement, but they are much less likely to require multiple placements.[299] A study of relative caregivers in Baltimore graphically illustrated the stability in kinship care.[300] Almost all the relative caregivers indicated that they would care for the child as long as necessary,[301] and three-fourths of the children had in fact been moved only a single time (from their parents to the caregiver).[302] About three-fourths had not moved in the past year.[303]

The lack of disruption in placement is probably desirable in itself, and it is likely to facilitate a smooth transition into adult roles for adolescents in care.[304] However, caseworkers may use the stability as a basis for avoidance of case planning and services. For instance, most caseworkers (81%) had worked with the family for less than a year before moving to other cases.[305] This avoidance is inconsistent with public policy but may or may not be inconsistent with the child's interests and his or her sense of permanence:

> [Q]uestions have arisen about the extent to which permanency planning is actually being carried out with children in kinship care and the appropriateness of these provisions for children in kinship care. What "reasonable efforts" are required to reunite children in kinship care with parents? Are the alternative permanency planning options, particularly adoption, appropriate? When the placement with kin is stable, safe, and likely to last until the child reaches adulthood, what is the appropriate ongoing role of the state in the lives of the child and the family?[308]

Second, *children in kinship care tend to have needs at least as great as children in nonrelative foster care.* The Baltimore group found that children in kinship care had low levels of immunizations and dental care but that they were at high risk of hypertension, uncorrected vision and hearing problems, anemia, asthma, dental problems, stunted growth, obesity, psychosomatic problems, behavioral problems, depression, poor school achievement, and poor attention.[307]

Third, *kinship-care providers typically do not have the same level of resources available to them that nonrelative foster parents do.* Kinship-care providers tend to be much less affluent than nonrelative foster parents.[308] Kinship-care providers are generally older, often single, and often poorly educated,[309] and they almost never receive training.[310] They rarely have access to support groups for fos-

ter parents,[311] as well as other services such as respite care, which are often inadequate but nonetheless more often available to nonrelative foster parents.[312]

Fourth, *although kinship-care providers often have grave doubts about the parental ability or motivation of the biological parents, they are more likely than nonrelative caregivers to facilitate a continuing relationship between the child and the parents, as well as other family members.* In a substantial proportion of kinship-care cases (the majority in some jurisdictions), the relative volunteered to provide foster care; indeed, she often was the reporter of suspected child maltreatment.[313] Accordingly, kinship-care providers are substantially less likely than caseworkers to support reunification.[314] However, they also are more likely than nonrelative foster parents to perceive themselves as responsible for maintaining the child's relationship with the biological parents and responding to the child's sense of loss.[315] Therefore, visitation occurs more frequently and naturally in kinship care than in nonrelative care.[318]

Fifth, perhaps reflecting cultural norms of care by extended families,[317] *kinship care is much more often the disposition in cases arising in African American families than in other ethnic groups.*[318] In California, for example, half the children in kinship care are African American, a proportion twice as large as in foster care overall.[319]

In short, kinship care shows promise as a way of meeting foster children's right to a family environment,[320] but questions remain about its implementation:

> If kin can be prepared to assume their new role, if they can be assisted or trained in advocating for health, mental health, and educational services for these children, and if they can provide suitable protection for children in homes where boundaries may be blurred by relationship and history, kinship foster care may uniquely meet the best interests of many (perhaps the majority of) foster children. If, however, we view kinship care as a cheap alternative to foster family care and provide little to bolster the significant work involved in caregiving, we will create a two-tiered system. Given the striking differences found in several of these studies in the services and supports kinship caregivers—largely single women of color—received from their child welfare agency, this two-tiered system already appears to be in place.[321]

Thus, evaluators need to be aware of presumptions in many states in favor of kinship care, and they should consider the support that may be available to the family (with or without a change of residence for the children) from within the kin network. At the same time, as with other living arrangements, clinicians conducting dispositional evaluations should consider the nature of the supports that will best facilitate healing, safety, and healthy development for the child.

15.06.   The Technique of Abuse/Neglect Evaluations

(a)   Content of the Evaluation

Two points should be given special attention in planning dispositional evaluations in child protection cases. First, the evaluation should be functional. It should focus on the parent's competence *as a parent,* as well as the ways in which the child's safety can be enhanced. Conclusions about adequacy as a parent should not be based on general mental status evaluations; diagnosis tells little about the individual's parental abilities, motivation, and practices. Indeed, ultimately the question should shift from parental competence as a personal characteristic because the critical problem is one of *relationships.*

Second, given what is known about the multiplicity of factors involved in child maltreatment [see § 15.03], the evaluation should be wide-ranging. Of course, both the parent(s) and the child(ren) should be interviewed. Whenever possible, the child and the parent should be observed together [see § 19.11(a) for an illustrative report], preferably in natural settings. But the evaluation should go beyond this dyad and beyond psychology. There should be assessment of relationships outside the immediate family that might be used, perhaps with some enhancement by professional support, to ensure social support (sometimes including monitoring) for the family. In considering such alternatives, thought should be given to ways that the potency of social support could be maximized by making it reciprocal. Similarly, attention should be given to the family's need for material support and steps that

might be taken to resolve the family's practical problems.

Collection of records of the family's involvement with helping agencies is especially important in dispositional evaluations. At a dispositional review, the degree of improvement in the situation, the adjustment of the child, and the adequacy of services are typically all at issue, and agency records (often followed by interviews of service providers) will usually be necessary to address these issues fully. Of course, knowledge of past treatment and its outcome is helpful in developing recommendations about possible interventions and reaching conclusions about prognosis. Social service and police reports, in combination with interviews of the parent, may also be useful in identifying possible precipitants of maltreatment—information that is often helpful for both designing interventions and determining prognosis.

Although clinicians should take a broad approach to dispositional assessment in child protection cases, they should do so humbly. As the review in § 15.03(e) indicated, the scientific foundation is weak for predictions about threats to the child's safety as well as the likely efficacy of various interventions, alone and in combination. Although enough is known about the factors that cause and maintain child maltreatment to provide the foundation for thoughtful dispositional planning (at least in regard to issues that should be addressed), it must be acknowledged that the selection of interventions is more art than science. There is little basis for confidence. Predictions, whether implicitly or explicitly made, should be framed accordingly.

(b)   Interviewing the Child

With some ambivalence, we are including a section on interviewing the child. As discussed in §§ 15.04(a) and 15.06(c), we believe that the increasing reliance on mental health professionals as investigative interviewers (in effect, as law enforcement agents) in child protection cases is unfortunate. However, we are including a brief discussion of the subject both because of the interest in it (clinicians may reasonably act as consultants to investigative interviewers even if the clinicians do not assume such a role themselves) and because of the need for child interviews as part of dispositional assessments. Even if the clinician does not assume the job of determining whether a violation of law occurred, finding out the child's perception of events may be quite useful in determining precipitants for incidents of abuse and assessing the nature and strength of the child's relationships. Of course, interview of the child is also important for assessment of the child's individual needs for treatment and social support.

In that regard, it is important not simply to *assume* what the child must feel and what he or she has experienced. The field of child protection has been rampant over the years with unstudied assumptions about what "everybody knows" that ultimately have proven to be distorted or simply incorrect. Notably, the "trauma" approach to sexual abuse and related legal involvement simply cannot be taken for granted. For example, the fact that the average severity of demonstrable harm resulting from sexual abuse is less than that resulting from some other forms of maltreatment that rarely elicit criminal prosecution[322] negates neither the wrongfulness of such violations of personal integrity nor the severe harm experienced by some sexually abused children. Similarly, there is evidence that conventional clinical wisdom about the way that disclosure of sexual abuse typically unfolds is incorrect.[323]

We turn then to some general comments about interviewing children in child protection cases. Since the mid-1980s, there has been extraordinary attention by researchers to issues related to children's ability as witnesses,[324] especially their suggestibility [see § 7.07(b)(2)].[325] In our view, this concern has been overblown.[326] Research shows that most children are resistant to suggestion for salient events, although the risk of inaccurate reports in response to direct questions is highest among very young children (e.g., three-year-olds).[327]

Further, much of what is known about ways to minimize distortions in children's memory (as in that of adults) and to maximize the quantity and accuracy of information reported borders on common sense. Consider, for example, the recommendations of two distinguished scholars on children's statements and testimony:

To bolster the reliability of preschoolers' reports, the following methods are indicated by the available research: (a) Misunderstandings can be minimized by keeping questions short, grammatical constructions simple, and vocabulary familiar. (b) Accuracy is promoted when questions concern events that are salient and meaningful to children and when question content is matched closely to children's knowledge and experience. (c) Accuracy can be facilitated when hesitant preschoolers are not pressured, coerced, or bullied into answering questions by authority figures. Inconsistencies can be probed by professing confusion, not by challenging children. (d) Suggestibility may be reduced when interviewers are neutral or supportive of children's efforts but do not praise them for providing specific content. (e) Interviewer bias can be reduced when interviewers take an objective, nonjudgmental stance on both nonverbal and verbal levels (e.g., tone of voice, facial expression, wording of questions). This does not preclude empathic comments to overcome children's anxiety. It does imply that an accusatory climate must be avoided—for example, one in which suspects are labeled as "bad" and assumed to have done "bad things" based on uncorroborated information provided by someone other than the child.[328]

Although adults who know better still often use difficult vocabulary and complex grammar in questions to children,[329] such linguistic lapses may be the most common inhibitors of effective communication between interviewers and children. Linguistic complexity lowers the accuracy of statements and testimony by witnesses of all ages, but it especially does so in communication with children.[330] Good practical guides are available, however, to prompt adults to avoid such miscommunication. A particularly useful brief manual, including a model voir dire for determination of a child's competence to testify, has been prepared by Anne Graffam Walker, a forensic linguist.[331]

Specific techniques to enhance communication also are becoming available. The most extensively studied may be the *cognitive interview,* which relies on mnemonic principles to increase the amount of information provided. A summary of the procedures follows:

First, have the child reconstruct the circumstances of the crime by encouraging her to put herself in the place and time that the abuse occurred—e.g., "picture it as if you were there right now." To ensure the child focuses on actual events, do not use the words "imagine," "pretend" or "story." Second, report everything the child says. Ask her to tell you as much information as possible, even seemingly unimportant details. After the child finishes her narrative description, follow with questions to clarify what was said. Third, go through the incident from beginning to end, then reverse the order and go through it again. Finally, encourage the child to recount events from different perspectives—e.g., "if you were sitting in the corner of the room, what would you have seen?"[332]

Designed originally for use in interviews of adult eyewitnesses, the cognitive interview increases elementary-school-age children's recall of facts without a decrease in accuracy, especially when the children have an opportunity to practice the technique.[333] However, again, children's level of performance depends on adults' skill in communication. In the above-described study, for instance, problems were observed with interviewers' (in that instance, sheriff's deputies') adherence to the protocol.

Other techniques that have been shown to improve elementary-school-age children's recall include training in comprehension monitoring[334] and narrative elaboration (i.e., thinking about the elements of a story—the participants, the setting, the action, and the conversation by and feelings of the participants).[335] Encouraging elementary-school-age children to indicate when they don't know the answer to an adult's questions also increases resistance to leading questions but sometimes at the cost of overcaution in reporting information that the child does know.[336]

(c) Psychometric Instruments

On occasion, specialized instruments for assessment of parental competence, parental attitudes, and family relations may help suggest dispositional issues in child protection cases. Detailed attention to the merits of such instruments has been given in reviews by Grisso[337] and, more recently, Budd and Holdsworth.[338] There are a number of structured instruments for assessment of parental competence, parental attitudes, and family relationships. These instruments may be very helpful

in clinical evaluation, although the fact that most have not been validated for use in child protection dispositions should make clinicians cautious in interpreting observations drawn from them.

There also are several instruments for assessment of "abuse potential," of which the best validated is the Child Abuse Potential (CAP) Inventory.[339] As one reviewer put it, "the CAP's hit rate in identifying known abusers *in highly selected samples* is simply uncanny. It is hard to imagine another instrument of similar age with better established psychometric properties"[340] [Emphasis added]. Nonetheless, we do not recommend the CAP for clinical use in screening CPS cases; rather, it shows most promise as a research instrument.[341] As the italicized language indicates, the success of the CAP in identifying *past* abusers came largely in validation samples in which half of the participants were known to have physically abused their children—a base rate that is obviously far higher than in the general population. CAP scores also tend to be elevated among parents of children with disabilities, especially when other stressors or possible support deficits (e.g., single parenthood) are present. Therefore, incorrect inferences can be drawn from CAP scores when parents are in situations in which they have especially difficult problems of child care. Perhaps most seriously, the false-positive rate rises substantially when the CAP is used predictively. Also, we remain concerned that judges and CPS workers will misinterpret CAP validation data to indicate the odds that a parent actually abused his or her child.

(d) Anatomically Detailed Dolls

Undoubtedly, the most controversial evaluation technique is the use of anatomically detailed dolls. Much of the debate rests on the use of doll play as a projective exercise to indicate whether a child has been sexually abused. There is evidence that such interpretation is common,[342] even though it obviously embraces the ultimate issue and thus is inconsistent with our general view about the proper bounds of expert testimony. Apart from our general recommendation, professional authorities are united in their view that play with anatomically detailed dolls cannot be used as a test to determine whether child mal-treatment has occurred.[343]

The question remains whether the dolls are so suggestive that they should not be used even as demonstration aids to clarify a child's statements. Wolfner and his colleagues reached a number of factual conclusions from a careful review of 20 studies on anatomically detailed dolls, including the following:

- Anatomically detailed dolls "do not evoke a large base rate of sexualized play among those who have not been sexually abused."

- There appear to be group differences in the frequency of sexualized doll play when abused and nonabused children are compared.

- At the same time, sample size and nonequivalence of comparison groups on other variables reduce confidence that the null hypothesis can be validly rejected.

- It is unknown whether the use of anatomically detailed dolls increases the validity of either investigation or clinical assessment when sexual abuse is suspected.[344]

In similar fashion, a working group on doll use established by the American Psychological Association urged caution in "interpreting the results of children ages 4 years and under, at least so far as when affirmations to leading questions about 'being touched' are concerned and when repeated misleading questioning has been used."[345] The working group also noted, however, that "using AD [anatomically detailed] dolls in evaluations does not inherently distress or overstimulate children," that "using the dolls can clearly assist in identifying children's preferred or idiosyncratic names for body parts," and that "using AD dolls often results in increased verbal productions during standardized research interviews."[346]

(e) Avoiding Ethical Problems

In his book of maxims for expert witnesses, Brodsky began one chapter with the following assertion: "Of all mental health legal procedures, termination of parental rights and child custody decisions probably produce the most heat and greatest hazards for the professionals doing the assessments."[347] Brodsky concluded his discussion of termination proceedings with the following maxim: "The heated emotionality of termination of parental rights hearings calls for exceptionally well-prepared and constructive testimony."[348] Because of the desire to "save" maltreated children and to preserve the family relationships of clients, there may be special pulls, both psychologically and socially, on mental health professionals to reach beyond their specialized knowledge in child protection proceedings and to act as advocates rather than neutral experts.

Moreover, the mixed civil–criminal system heightens the possibilities of mental health professionals becoming de facto law enforcement agents, sometimes without realizing that they are assuming such a role. Statements made in a civil child protection proceeding and a corollary treatment program might ultimately be used in a criminal proceeding or, of course, a civil hearing to infringe parental rights.[349]

Perhaps most acutely, the child protection system as presently structured invites conflicts between "doing justice" and "doing good."[350] As we discussed in § 15.04(a), mental health professionals are increasingly being used as investigators charged with gathering evidence about whether maltreatment has occurred. We are troubled by this development for three reasons. First, it encourages clinicians to reach conclusions outside their expertise. Second, it promotes confusion of the mental health professional's purpose in the minds of both the clinician and the interviewee, and thus raises ethical problems in regard to fidelity to role, a variant of the "white-coat" phenomenon in forensic mental health [see § 3.02(a)]. Indeed, it is increasingly common to link treatment services for abused children directly to the prosecutor's office.[351] Third, it may exacerbate the already pronounced tendency to sacrifice prevention and treatment of child maltreatment in the name of investigation.

We discussed the first two points at length earlier in this chapter [see §§ 15.04(a), 15.04(c)(4)]. The third point bears further discussion.[352] There is good reason to believe that clinicians' involvement as investigators will directly and indirectly impede the provision of treatment. The framing of child protection services as adjunctive to investigation and prosecution inevitably leads to conflicts between the mental health professions' emphasis (on behalf of their clients) on confidentiality and the prosecution's need for inculpatory evidence—conflicts that may prevent the treatment programs' further development. Apart from role conflicts, the need for mental health professionals to deal with legal issues; to prepare reports for attorneys, courts, and probation officers; and to interrupt clinical practices for court dates may distract clinicians from providing the scarce treatment services now available and may deter or distract them from serving maltreated children and their families. Moreover, although there is little direct evidence about public perceptions of mental health professionals' involvement in child maltreatment cases, it is possible that increasing involvement in contested cases (or at least the perception of increasing involvement) will diminish public confidence in the mental health professions. Certainly high publicized forensic work has had such an effect before.[353] The phenomenon may be occurring again in sexual abuse cases as clinicians appear on nationally televised talk shows to debate false-memory syndrome (an issue discussed below).

Whether or not public perceptions about these issues are accurate, they tend to defeat the most fundamental purpose of child protection; they deter people from seeking or fully using treatment to prevent child maltreatment or ameliorate its harm. Note that although more traditional forensic child protection work (i.e., conducting postinvestigation assessment as a step toward development of a treatment plan) does not completely obviate such issues, it presents them much less acutely. In dispositional assessment (especially when the court is not necessarily looming in the background), the inquiry is oriented toward development of help for the child and the family, and the clinician's mind is in fact likely to be focused on service provision.[354]

15.07.   Adult Cases Related to Abuse and Neglect

(a)   Elder Abuse

The legal architecture for responses to abuse and neglect of elderly and disabled adults is closely analogous to that for responses to child abuse and neglect, and thus is discussed here. For example, California's Adult Civil Protection Act[355] provides for mandated reporting of abuse of a dependent adult[356] to a social services agency (Adult Protective Services), law enforcement, or a state agency regulating institutional settings. The definition of reportable situations is even broader than the analogous provisions in the child protection context. Elder abuse must be reported if a professional suspects that the dependent adult has been subjected to "physical abuse, neglect, fiduciary abuse, abandonment, isolation, or other treatment with resulting physical harm or pain or mental suffering, or the deprivation by a care custodian of goods or services that are necessary to avoid physical harm or mental suffering."[357] The breadth appears to reflect concerns that disabled and elderly adults often have some conflict of interest with their caretakers, a circumstance that may be less likely in parent–child relations.[358]

As in other states and as is the case in child protection matters, California also has a mixed civil–criminal system to handle adult protection issues. Criminal sanctions may be applied if one willfully causes or permits an elder or dependent adult to suffer "unjustifiable physical pain or mental suffering" or to be "placed in a situation such that his or her person or health is endangered."[359]

Clinically, there also are striking parallels between child and elder maltreatment. The demographic correlates and perhaps even the prevalence rate in elder abuse and neglect also closely relate to those in child maltreatment.[360] Beyond the epidemiological similarity, the questions and dynamics often are similar. Victims often have ambivalent responses to state intervention, and many are unwilling to acknowledge that a loved one could mistreat them.[361] Moreover, it often is unclear whether elders are objectively better off following an investigation. Notably, about one-half of reports result in placement of the victim in a nursing home or other institutional placement.[362]

Perpetrators themselves often are enmeshed in multiple problems that make their blameworthiness unclear. In the typical case, the abused elder is very old (over 75) and frail, with great needs for personal care to remain clean, oriented, well nourished, and safe.[363] In such a situation, it is easy for care even by a well-meaning family member to lapse, especially when the caregiver is poorly educated and facing many life challenges (e.g., divorce, unemployment, and substance abuse):

> It is common to receive a referral that describes an elder as confused, incontinent, dehydrated, or malnourished, and there may also be evidence of skin breakdown, fractured bones from falls, and drug toxicity from improper prescriptions. The person reporting elder abuse must determine abuse or neglect based upon many factors, including the nature and extent of the trauma, the likelihood of abuse or neglect given the care provider's resources, and the level of accountability the care provider can be held to. In cases of intentional physical abuse that results in trauma to the elderly, few professionals would argue against the validity of the label "elder abuse." However, many responsible adults are not educated to prevent or detect risk factors for subsequent neglect. When an elderly individual, cared for at home by well-intentioned family members, presents with symptoms of neglect such as urine burns and decubitus ulcers, the determination of abuse is not so clear.[364]

In short, the issues presented in elder abuse and neglect cases are closely related to those in child maltreatment cases. Evaluators should address many of the same domains in dispositional evaluation, and they should be alert to many of the same potential ethical problems and role confusion. In that regard, the clinician needs to remain sensitive to the problem of mixed and sometimes conflicting purposes of adult protective action (e.g., retribution and treatment).

There are two obvious differences in the nature and scope of the evaluation, however. First, clinicians conducting dispositional evaluations in cases involving elders or other dependent adults need to be aware of the service alternatives for adults with disabilities, and they need to have a realistic view of the care needs that the victim presents. In that sense, the scope of an evaluation in an elder maltreatment case may have much in common with an evaluation for limited guardianship [see § 11.02(b)].

Second, in the adult protection context (unlike child protection cases), the victim is presumed to be competent until there is a legal determination otherwise. About one-fourth of the complainants

in adult protection cases are the victims themselves.[365] As in guardianship cases, there may also be questions of financial conflicts of interest, especially as they may relate to issues about expenditure of assets, in that caregivers are often financially dependent on the victim.[366] Although resolution of possible conflicts of interest is not within the evaluator's role, the clinician needs to be sensitive to the ways in which complex relationships may complicate the elder's care and to consider alternative sources of care and support for him or her, including autonomous action by the elder himself or herself (perhaps with facilitation by others).

(b)   Adult Survivors of Child Abuse and Neglect

The other "adult" issue in abuse and neglect is actually a problem of child maltreatment: legal and clinical issues that arise when a history of child maltreatment is identified in adulthood. There has been a pointed and sometimes heated controversy about the recollection of child abuse in adulthood,[367] complete with establishment of a foundation for study of cases of false-memory syndrome.[368]

Building on the belief that children are sometimes so traumatized and/or dependent that child abuse is not remembered and disclosed until many years later, many state legislatures have explicitly made the delayed discovery rule applicable in such instances.[369] "Delayed discovery" is a common-law principle in tort law that enables a victim of tortious conduct to be compensated contrary to the statute of limitations (the maximum time in law between a violation of law and the initiation of legal action) when the victimization was not promptly discovered. For example, that surgical instruments were left in a patient's abdomen may not be discovered until sometime later when symptoms appear and are correctly diagnosed, but the patient should be able to recover for the damages experienced as a result of the surgeon's negligence even if the statute of limitations has been exceeded. By establishing a special exception to the statute of limitations for child abuse cases, legislatures are establishing an assumption in law that victims of child abuse sometimes are unable to disclose the abuse before they reach adulthood.

Two studies have formed the foci for the debate about the frequency of delayed discovery in sexual abuse cases. In the first, Briere and Conte reported that about three-fifths of adult survivors then in treatment indicated that they had experienced periods in which they could not remember the abuse.[370] Amnesia was particularly likely to be reported when the abuse was violent (i.e., it involved physical force, multiple perpetrators, or fears of death) or occurred over a long period of time, or when *current* mental health symptoms were relatively severe.

In the second study, Williams interviewed women who, as girls, had been seen in an urban emergency room 15 to 18 years earlier as victims of sexual offenses.[371] In three-hour interviews that included a broad assessment of psychosocial functioning and history (including sexual history), more than one-third did not report the incident that had brought them to the emergency room or any other abuse by the perpetrator identified at that time, although two-thirds of these individuals did report other incidents involving other perpetrators. Whether the index events were recalled was unrelated to whether the individuals reported other embarrassing or traumatic events. Even among those women who were age seven or older at the time of the incident, 28% did not recall it.

As in Briere and Conte's research, the women in Williams's study who were least likely to recall their childhood victimization were those whom clinical theory would suggest were most traumatized and those who were most likely to have been pressured into silence:

> For example, the records from 1973 show that Maria was abused by her father at least six times. The last time was when she was 12. She now reports no memory of it. June was abused by three of her cousins over a two-year period. She was 7 years old at the time of the last abuse and now reports no memory of it. Contrary to skepticism about how someone could forget such abuse, there is reason to believe that the dynamics of incestuous abuse—which may include grooming the child to accept the advances of the perpetrator, the use of adult authority, and a progression (confusing to the child) from acts of affection to physically invasive sexual

penetration and rape—may be associated with memory problems. . . . [W]omen in my sample were more likely to forget abuse by someone to whom they were close.[372]

Skeptics about the validity of repression or other forgetting among a high proportion of victims of child sexual abuse have made three primary counterarguments. First, they have argued that the purported frequency is an artifact of study designs. For example, Loftus criticized Briere and Conte's question asking research participants about any "time when you could not remember the forced sexual experience," because it could be interpreted to mean a time when one consciously (rather than unconsciously) suppressed the terrible memory.[373] Second, critics have pointed to experiments and anecdotes about circumstances in which demonstrably false memories for childhood traumatic events have been induced.[374] Third, they have argued that adult reports of child sexual abuse often are the products at least in part of therapists' suggestive interviewing.[375]

Some evidence that at least the most severe allegations by adults are often in part the product of suggestion (whether by peers, the media, or therapists) arose in a large-scale survey of therapists by Bottoms and her colleagues about ritualistic and religion-related abuse.[376] A very small proportion (2%) of the therapists surveyed accounted for most of the reports of ritualistic abuse,[377] and the majority of those who reported any such cases had been to workshops on the subject.[378] Allegations of ritualistic abuse, when made by adults about childhood experiences, were almost always initially disclosed in treatment,[379] and therapists almost always believed the stories, even when no corroboration was present.[380] The evidence for the ritualistic cases was much sketchier than in "religion-related" cases (e.g., cases of medical neglect or physical abuse based on religious beliefs or delusions with religious content, such as a belief that the child has been possessed by the devil).[381] Further, the most bizarre accounts of ritualistic abuse typically were alleged by or about adult survivors, not by children.[382]

Echoing law enforcement specialists who have been unable to find evidence supportive of vast satanic conspiracies,[383] Bottoms et al. reviewed the weak evidence for adults' graphic allegations that they had been subjected to ritualistic abuse in childhood:

> Believers in ritual abuse assert that it has been occurring in the same fashion for generations. If the intergenerational view is valid, current reports by child and adult survivors should be quite similar because they are simply two views of the same phenomenon. Our data challenge that premise. Child ritual cases shared some features with adult cases, but they also differed in important ways. In general, child ritual cases were not as extreme as adult ritual cases. There was more social service and legal investigation of child cases and more corroborative evidence of abuse. . . . Children were less likely than adults to have disclosed their alleged abuse in the context of psychotherapy.[384]

Such evidence does not negate the possibility—indeed, probability—that studies such as those by Briere and Conte and by Williams and related clinical observations reflect instances in which valid memories of child abuse are first revealed in adulthood because of the combination of repression or other forgetting and of real or perceived pressure not to tell. To a large extent, the academic debate about repressed memory for sexual abuse is about its frequency and mechanism, not its reality.

In any event, the repressed-memory debate need not be resolved in a book on forensic assessment because the assessment of truthfulness and validity of memory is not a matter for clinical opinion in the courtroom. Regardless of whether one accepts Loftus's assertions that many adult memories of child abuse may be distorted, it is difficult to argue with her conclusions about the stance that mental health professionals should take:

> What should therapists do . . . ? As a first step, it is worth recognizing that we do not yet have the tools for reliably distinguishing the signal of true repressed memories from the noise of false ones. . . . Zealous conviction is a dangerous substitute for an open mind. Psychotherapists, counselors, social service agencies, and law enforcement personnel would be wise to be careful how they probe for horrors on the other side of some presumed amnesic barrier. They need to be circumspect regarding uncorroborated repressed memories that return. Techniques that are less potentially dangerous would involve clarification, compassion, and gentle confronta-

tion along with a demonstration of empathy for the painful struggles these patients must endure as they come to terms with their personal truths.[385]

It is further noteworthy that even this advice really is aimed at therapists, not at forensic evaluators. In that regard, in adult as well as child cases, mental health professionals should resist attempts to induce them to assume the role of human lie detector. Nothing in the professional preparation of clinicians uniquely qualifies them to discern the validity of memories and the truthfulness of allegations that result.

Bibliography[386]

THE APSAC HANDBOOK ON CHILD MALTREATMENT (John Briere et al. Eds. 1996).

Karen S. Budd & Michelle J. Holdsworth, *Issues in Clinical Assessment of Minimal Parenting Competence*, 25 JOURNAL CLINICAL CHILD PSYCHOLOGY 2 (1996).

CHILD VICTIMS, CHILD WITNESSES: UNDERSTANDING AND IMPROVING TESTIMONY (Gail S. Goodman & Bette L. Bottoms eds. 1993).

THE EFFECTS OF CHILD ABUSE AND NEGLECT: ISSUES AND RESEARCH (Raymond H. Starr Jr. & David A. Wolfe eds. 1991).

Gail S. Goodman et al., *Testifying in Criminal Court*, 57 MONOGRAPHS OF THE SOCIETY FOR RESEARCH IN CHILD DEVELOPMENT (Serial No. 229), at 1 (1992).

JEFFREY J. HAUGAARD & N. DICKON REPPUCCI, THE SEXUAL ABUSE OF CHILDREN: A COMPREHENSIVE GUIDE TO CURRENT KNOWLEDGE AND INTERVENTION STRATEGIES (1988).

SETH C. KALICHMAN, MANDATED REPORTING OF SUSPECTED CHILD ABUSE: ETHICS, LAW, AND POLICY (1993).

MURRAY LEVINE & HOWARD J. DOUECK ET AL., THE IMPACT OF MANDATED REPORTING ON THE THERAPEUTIC PROCESS (1995).

Gary B. Melton & Susan Limber, *Psychologists' Involvement in Cases of Child Maltreatment: Limits of Role and Expertise*, 44 AMERICAN PSYCHOLOGIST 1225 (1989).

NATIONAL RESEARCH COUNCIL, UNDERSTANDING CHILD ABUSE AND NEGLECT (1993).

PROTECTING CHILDREN FROM ABUSE AND NEGLECT: FOUNDATIONS FOR A NEW NATIONAL STRATEGY (Gary B. Melton & Frank D. Barry eds. 1994).

Mark A. Small & Gary B. Melton, *Evaluation of Child Witnesses for Confrontation by Criminal Defendants*, 25 PROFESSIONAL PSYCHOLOGY: RESEARCH & PRACTICE 288 (1994).

Symposium, *Kinship Foster Care*, 16 CHILDREN & YOUTH SERVICES REVIEW 1 (1994).

Symposium, *Psychological Issues Related to Child Maltreatment: Working Group Reports of the American Psychological Association Coordinating Committee on Child Abuse and Neglect*, 24 JOURNAL OF CLINICAL CHILD PSYCHOLOGY 1 (Supp. 1995).

ROSS A. THOMPSON, PREVENTING CHILD MALTREATMENT THROUGH SOCIAL SUPPORT: A CRITICAL ANALYSIS (1995).

U.S. ADVISORY BOARD ON CHILD ABUSE AND NEGLECT, NEIGHBORS HELPING NEIGHBORS: A NEW NATIONAL STRATEGY FOR THE PROTECTION OF CHILDREN (1993).

ANNE GRAFFAM WALKER, HANDBOOK ON QUESTIONING CHILDREN: A LINGUISTIC PERSPECTIVE (1994).

CHAPTER SIXTEEN

Child Custody in Divorce

16.01. The Scope of Clinicians' Involvement in Custody Disputes

(a) Current Involvement

Although no studies have been conducted on the point, it would be unsurprising to find that clinicians believe that divorce involving children, a seemingly ubiquitous phenomenon in contemporary American families,[1] is the context in which the legal system is most likely to seek their expertise. Even general clinicians who try diligently to avoid forensic involvement can find themselves subpoenaed to give evidence about a family in which they treated one or more members. Clinicians probably also believe that they have more to offer in disputes about child custody than in most other contexts. After all, family dynamics are the stuff of which clinical work is often made,[2] and these dynamics surely are relevant to determining who shall retain legal authority over a child. Thus, one might assume, clinicians not only are, but should be, frequently involved in resolution of custody disputes.

However, it is our contention that both of these assumptions are mistaken. First, at present, *mental health professionals are directly involved in only a small fraction of custody cases in most jurisdictions.* Most custody decisions—perhaps 90%—are made during bargaining between the divorcing spouses.[3] Even in those instances in which cases make their way to trial, only a small proportion involve presentation of testimony or a report by a mental health professional. In a national sample of judges who hear such cases, 55% reported that such opinion evidence is presented in fewer than 10% of the custody cases they hear.[4] Only 25% said that such evidence is presented in the majority of contested custody cases in the courts, and none reported receiving such evidence in more than three-fourths of cases.[5] Similar findings were reported in surveys of attorneys and judges in a single northeastern state.[6] This lack of mental health involvement is perhaps less surprising when one recognizes that in most jurisdictions divorce cases are heard in general jurisdiction courts, unlike cases of delinquency and child maltreatment, which are heard in separate juvenile or family courts where there is a strong tradition of mental health or social services involvement.[7]

Second, *mental health professionals may have little expertise that is directly relevant to custody disputes.* Thus, there are probably substantive as well as structural impediments to mental health involvement. Some of the considerations most relevant to a determination of the child's best interests in law (e.g., parental "responsibility" and moral guidance) are ones that are arguably well within the province of the factfinder and about which clinicians have no special expertise.[8] Moreover, there is limited scientific basis for opinions about the kinds of questions that the courts must decide in divorce cases when children are involved. Although much is known about the effects of *divorce* on children [see § 16.03(a)], there has been remarkably little research meeting minimal standards of methodological rigor about the effects of various *custody arrangements* on children and families of different characteristics. Furthermore, it may be impossible to generate such data at a level that would be very helpful in determination of best interests in individual cases [see § 16.02(g)].

Thus, the state of the literature does not promote confidence about the validity of opinions concerning dispositions judges might consider in custody cases.[9] Indeed, there is probably no forensic question on which overreaching by mental health professionals has been so common and so egregious. Besides lacking scientific validity, such opinions have often been based on clinical data that are, on their face, irrelevant to the legal questions in dispute. As one distinguished commentator on forensic assessment has noted:

> Custody cases involving divorced or divorcing parents rarely involve questions of parental fitness, but rather the choice between two parents, neither of whom [is] summarily inadequate [as a parent]. . . . Mental health professionals do not have reason to be proud of their performance in this area of forensic assessment. Too often we still evaluate the parent but not the child, a practice that makes no sense when the child's own, individual needs are the basis for the legal decision. Too often we continue to rely on the assessment instruments and methods that were designed to address *clinical* questions, questions of psychiatric diagnosis, when clinical questions bear only secondarily upon the real issues in many child custody cases. Psychiatric interviews, Rorschachs, and MMPIs might have a role to play in child custody assessments. But these tools were *not* designed to assess parents' relationships to children . . . [or their] childrearing attitudes and capacities, and *these* are often the central questions in child custody cases.[10]

Problems associated with clinicians reaching beyond their expertise and data in custody disputes have become sufficiently visible and important that on several occasions since 1980 the Ethics Committee of the American Psychological Association has issued statements of concern about such cases.[11] Culminating in the adoption by the American Psychological Association's Council of Representatives of the *Guidelines for Child Custody Evaluations in Divorce Proceedings,*[12] discussions by several American Psychological Association committees focused on the pressures that lead to misuse of psychologists' influence in custody evaluations. The problem of managing these pressures is discussed later in this chapter [see § 16.04(a)]. For now, however, it is important to note that the most basic ethical issues for clinicians involved in custody disputes may be ones of monitoring the limits of competence and avoiding trespass across these limits. Although this forensic issue is not unique to custody evaluations, it is rendered especially acute in that context because of the small body of relevant specialized knowledge and the complex interests and relationships typically involved in custody disputes. The superficial relevance of everyday clinical practice to custody disputes, the shifting boundaries and allegiances within families (and the resulting pulls on clinicians), and even the related gender politics [see § 16.05] may sometimes seduce mental health professionals into reaching unwarranted opinions.

It is noteworthy that legal practitioners generally are quite skeptical about the usefulness of mental health involvement in child custody cases. Almost half the judges in the national study mentioned previously reported that clinicians' opinions in custody disputes were useful no more than occasionally—substantially less frequently than for other forensic issues.[13] Only 2% of the judges in the northeastern study ranked mental health professionals' opinions among the top five factors in their custody decisions,[14] and 86% cited no social science readings or workshops as influential in their thinking about child custody.[15]

(b)   Some Possible Roles

(1)   Evaluator and Investigator

Although we began this chapter by emphasizing the serious reservations that we—and apparently most attorneys and judges—have about mental health professionals' present and potential involvement in custody disputes, we do not wish to imply that clinicians have no proper role at all.

There are probably times when conventional clinical speculation about family dynamics will provide judges with some (albeit limited) assistance in making decisions about child custody. For example, although the opinions reached will probably have less scientific foundation than Morse would require [see § 1.04],[16] clinical impressions about alliances and conflicts within the family and their bases might present judges with a useful framework for consideration of which child goes where. Similarly, opinions about present and past intensity of marital conflict and its sources may provide the factfinder with some basis for prediction of the probable success of various conditions of custody and visitation. Certainly, it is conceivable that research will develop that will provide a basis beyond mere speculation for links between pre- and postdivorce behavior.

At present, however, we find ourselves close to Morse's position in regard to the proper roles of clinicians in custody evaluations. That is, mental health professionals are primarily helpful as *investigators* in custody disputes, particularly if they are sure to perform a thorough, wide-ranging evaluation of the type we recommend in § 16.04(c). Analogous to Morse's observation about clinicians' having more experience than laypersons in interviewing people with mental illness,[17] clinicians (at least those specialized in child or family practice) are trained in, and used to, talking with children and families under stress and gathering information from diverse sources about the life of the family. Therefore, child and family clinicians are likely to be efficient and effective gatherers of facts for the court, even when they are not able to add opinions based on specialized knowledge about the implications of those facts.

Unfortunately, given present practice, the courts often do not obtain the significant amount of relevant information clinicians can provide. Although, as we shall see, the legal standards in most jurisdictions would seem to demand such extensive evidence, current procedures inhibit it. Because only the parents have *standing*,[18] evidence about the *child's* best interests may not be presented unless it is clearly helpful to the case of one of the divorcing spouses. Even appointment of a guardian *ad litem* to represent the child's interests may not ensure development of this type of evidence, in part because of the ambiguities of the role. In § 16.04(a), we suggest ways of overcoming these obstacles to the mental health professional's fulfilling an investigative role.

Mental health professionals (and other behavioral scientists) may also assist the court by pointing out what is *not* known about the psychological effects of various custody arrangements. This honesty about the limits of knowledge serves dual purposes. It assists the factfinder in determining the degree of confidence to attach to any speculations about the import of psychological factors, and it deters the court from "psychologizing" and thus obscuring value preferences in the law. A good example of the potential for such a role came in the United States Supreme Court's consideration of *Palmore v. Sidoti*.[19] The trial court, affirmed by the Florida Circuit Court, had transferred custody of a white child from her mother to her father after her mother had married an African American man. The lower court relied on psychological assumptions (i.e., the "inevitable" vulnerability to "peer pressures" and "social stigmatization") to justify its decision.[20] Although the Supreme Court ultimately rejected this argument unanimously,[21] evidence as to the *lack* of psychological authority for the Florida courts' assumptions might have served to focus attention from the start on the constitutional values at stake.

(2)   Mediator and Intervenor

Mental health professionals often may be useful as adjuncts to the negotiation process in clarifying points of agreement and disagreement. In performing custody evaluations, we have been struck by the number of times the spouses' disagreements—on which they are expending substantial energy and money—are objectively rather insignificant (e.g., a difference of one or two hours a week in how much time each parent has the children). In an emotionally charged atmosphere, the availability of a third party to mediate the dispute might facilitate settlement.[22] Divorce lawyers often perceive their role to be one of moderating their clients' wishes[23]; thus, referrals for "evaluation" may actually be a thinly disguised request for information that might illuminate the foundation for a settlement or even for mediation, involving direct assistance by the clinician in bringing the parties to agreement.[24]

In such a circumstance, two important caveats should be remembered. First, when a clinician is employed as an *evaluator,* he or she should be careful not to slip into the role of *intervenor* unless the parties or the court so requests. Although the report might help clarify topics for potential negotiation (and, indeed, as already noted, one or both attorneys might request a report for just such a purpose), it would be presumptuous of a clinician as an evaluator to attempt to force a settlement. There are also potential ethical pitfalls associated with competence issues when clinicians begin skirting—or crossing—the bounds of legal practice. Although mental health professionals may be sensitive to the emotional fallout of separation and divorce, they are more often than not ignorant of the property and related matters. Analogous concerns are obviously present when attorneys begin acting like therapists. Even for those mental health professionals who are also trained as lawyers, there are serious problems of dual practice and dual representation.[25]

Second, even when the role conflicts can be resolved, mediation (especially when compulsory[26]) is not necessarily beneficial. It has been asserted that, relative to litigation, mediation will likely reduce competition between parents, improve children's adjustment, reduce relitigation, and increase compliance with agreements.[27] But even some proponents of mediation, noting the diversity in auspices, length, voluntariness, and scope of mediation programs, have indicated a lack of surprise at research showing that mediation does not consistently produce results superior to litigation.[28] Although the majority of studies on particular hypothesized benefits of mediation have confirmed the hypotheses, research to the contrary is also available on virtually every point.[29] No study has shown mediation, relative to litigation, to have the hypothesized ultimate benefit: better postdivorce adjustment by children.[30] Indeed, mediation—especially when conducted in a high-conflict divorce—may actually increase the strength of association between parental and child problems.[31]

These caveats notwithstanding, the movement toward compulsory mediation of custody disputes is likely to continue, because it undeniably

reduces courts' workloads.[32] Moreover, even without compulsory mediation, changes in the justice system are rapidly fostering a two-tiered, extrajudicial system.[33] Looking for a prompt resolution of their family disputes, affluent clients are engaging private mediators. And many states have established public mediation services, which permit poorer couples to avoid the court system and perhaps even obtain a resolution to their dispute without benefit of counsel.[34] Consequently, whether the service is framed as an intervention (e.g., mediation) or an evaluation, clinicians working in the public system and dealing with the vast number of divorces involving children will find themselves increasingly in a position in which they must educate parents about what is to come not only in their family life per se but also in the pending dispute resolution proceeding. The problems presented often are thorny ones that are both clinically and ethically challenging.[35]

(c)   The American Psychological Association Guidelines

Indeed, the challenges are sufficiently great that the American Psychological Association has taken the unusual step of promulgating the previously mentioned practice guidelines specific to child custody evaluations,[36] many of which coincide with admonitions we have already stated. Starting from the premise that the child's needs must be paramount,[37] the American Psychological Association's *Guidelines* advise clinicians (as do we) to undertake a functional assessment of the skills and values of the parents and their match to the needs of the child: In performing a custody evaluation, "[p]sychopathology [of the parents] may be relevant . . . insofar as it has impact on the child or the ability to parent, but it is not the primary focus."[38] This functional inquiry, the American Psychological Association's *Guidelines* state, necessarily requires a wide-ranging assessment using multiple sources of information and methods of data gathering (i.e., the investigator role we advocate).[39] Recognizing that the multiple lenses through which family members embroiled in a high-conflict divorce are apt to be clouded by emotion and that the scientific foundation for prediction of postdivorce behavior is thin, the

American Psychological Association also admonished clinicians to interpret clinical information "cautiously and conservatively, seeking convergent validity."[40]

The American Psychological Association's *Guidelines* further recognize that child custody evaluators are often pulled in conflicting directions by their concern for the various individuals involved [see §§ 16.04(a), 16.05]. They note that the psychologist's role is "that of a professional expert who strives to maintain an objective, impartial stance"[41]:

> The psychologist should be impartial regardless of whether he or she is retained by the court or by a party to the proceedings. If either the psychologist or the client cannot accept this neutral role, the psychologist should consider withdrawing from the case. If not permitted to withdraw, in such circumstances, the psychologist acknowledges past roles and other factors that could affect impartiality.[42]

To further maintain objectivity and avoid role conflicts, the American Psychological Association's *Guidelines* advise clinicians to refrain from testimony (other than as a fact witness) in any case in which the clinician has been a therapist for one of the family members (a topic to which we shall return).[43] For the same reason, the American Psychological Association also emphasized the need to obtain a picture of the family from all perspectives. Therefore, although noting some exceptional situations,[44] the American Psychological Association's *Guidelines* generally advised clinicians to interview all parents or guardians and children alone and together[45] and not to give an opinion about any individual whom the clinician had not directly evaluated.[46] This too we endorse, although our approach is even more "ecological" [see § 16.04].

16.02. Standards for Resolution of Custody Disputes

As in all forensic areas, mental health professionals conducting custody evaluations need to be knowledgeable about the standards for determining custody. The prevailing standard should define the scope of the evaluation. However, as we shall see, the most common standard gives clinicians—and, ultimately, the courts—little guidance.

(a)   Historic Preferences

Until relatively recently, there was rarely any real contest for custody of children following divorce. Until well into the 19th century, custody was routinely perceived as a concomitant of the father's power; children, like wives, were in effect the father's chattels.[47] However, late in the 19th century, the predominant view began to be that the determining factor in a child's custody should be the child's own best interests.[48] With that change in perspective also came a presumption that children of "tender years" are best served by remaining with their mothers.[49] Thus, although the best-interests standard is theoretically indeterminate,[50] in fact the question of custody was usually settled a priori by award of custody to the mother, unless the *tender-years presumption* could be rebutted by a showing of unfitness. When that event occurred, it was often *de facto* punishment for the mother's fault in the divorce (e.g., adultery) rather than a real concern with the mother–child relationship.[51]

Ironically, the women's movement has resulted in a weakening of the maternal preference. With new social and legal concern for the equality of the sexes, judges have applied equal-protection analysis[52] and legislatures have adopted clear statutory directives[53] to end legal preferences for maternal custody. Although it is important to recognize that maternal custody remains the norm and that the tender-years presumption is still given great weight in some jurisdictions,[54] in general the trend is toward determining the best interests of the child by examining the relationship with both parents. Therefore, the room for clinical input has increased substantially in recent years.

(b)   The Best-Interests Standard

Most jurisdictions now determine custody on the basis of the best interests of the child. The court is usually given some guidance as to the factors to be included in determining best interests, but the weight to be accorded them is left to judicial discretion. Thus, custody determinations will usually be reversed only if the judge refuses to consider a factor that the appellate court believes is, as a matter of law, a part of "best interests."[55] The calculus is necessarily idiosyncratic. Moreover, except for certain suspect classifications that are constitutionally or statutorily impermissible as basis for custody,[56] courts are free to weigh any factors that they believe are important in any particular case.[57]

This indeterminate approach is illustrated by the model standard incorporated in the Uniform Marriage and Divorce Act, which has been adopted in many states[58]:

The court shall determine custody in accordance with the best interest of the child. The court shall consider all relevant factors including:

(1) the wishes of the child's parent or parents as to his custody;
(2) the wishes of the child as to his custodian;
(3) the interaction and interrelationship of the child with his parent or parents, his siblings, and any other person who may significantly affect the child's best interest;
(4) the child's adjustment to his home, school, and community; and
(5) the mental and physical health of all individuals involved.

The court shall not consider conduct of a proposed custodian that does not affect his relationship to the child.[59]

Just as the implicit elements of the best-interests test are almost infinite (i.e., "all relevant factors"), the desired outcome against which the factors must be weighed is also indeterminate. There is usually no clear guideline, for example, as to whether the best-interests standard is present- or future-oriented. Should the court be concerned with the child's immediate welfare, or the child's well-being 10 or 20 years from now?

More broadly, the best-interests test seems to demand no less than a judicial determination of the desirable traits of a citizen. This principle was graphically illustrated by the often-cited opinion of the Iowa Supreme Court in *Painter v. Bannister*.[60] Custody of seven-year-old Mark Bannister was awarded to the parents of his deceased mother instead of his father, who was described as an agnos-

tic and a "political liberal" living in an unpainted house in northern California.[61] The court concluded that Mr. Bannister would provide Mark with an "unstable, unconventional, arty, Bohemian, and probably intellectually stimulating" home.[62] The grandparents were said to be church-going, "highly respected members of the community" who offered a "stable, dependable, conventional, middle-class mid-west background."[63] The court "unhesitatingly" believed the Painters' home to be more suitable for a child: "We believe security and stability in the home are more important than intellectual development in the proper development of a child."[64]

Cases rarely offer such dramatically different potential households, and courts rarely are as forthcoming about the values on which they have based their decisions. Nonetheless, the sort of situation presented by *Painter* is common. Contested custody determinations are easy only in those rare cases in which one and only one parent is obviously unfit, or one and only one parent is attached to the child.[65] More commonly, courts are faced with competing homes which, whether because of divergent personalities, educations, or social and financial resources, are likely to nurture somewhat different traits in the child but are unlikely to result in substantial differences in the ultimate well-being of the child. The case is likely to turn, then, on the judge's own view of the most desirable traits and his or her prediction as to the parent more likely to socialize them. While the judge may be guided by a sense of the values of the community, thus reducing arbitrariness, there is clearly an indeterminacy in the nature of "best interests" themselves.

For the same reason, clinicians have little objective basis for determining what to examine in a best-interests custody evaluation; the lack of statutory guidance may make subjective influences about the "best" outcome inevitable. Accordingly, clinicians should report their assumptions about the factors and outcomes to be considered (as they shape the scope of the evaluation and the opinion resulting from it), as well as the uncertainties of their opinion. Furthermore, given the fact that the ultimate conclusion as to best interests is at least as value-laden and unscientific as other legal determinations, it should clearly be preserved for the factfinder. A clinician should *never* reach a conclusion as to the parent who would better meet a child's interests.

(c)   The Least Detrimental Alternative

Another rule, suggested by three leading psycho-analysts (Joseph Goldstein, Anna Freud, and Albert Solnit)[66] has not been adopted in state statutes, but it has nonetheless been quite influen-tial in the thinking of many judges, lawyers, and mental health professionals.[67] Although the scien-tific foundation for their argument was dubious,[68] Goldstein and colleagues believed a child's prima-ry need is a seemingly omnipotent, omnipresent attachment figure.[69] Therefore, they advocated vesting total legal authority for a child in the *psy-chological parent*.[70] The psychological parent would not only have physical custody and authori-ty for medical and educational decisionmaking on behalf of the child but also would be able to regu-late how much involvement, including visitation, the noncustodial parent would have in the life of the child.[71] When both parents are equal psycho-logical parents[72]—a situation that is probably not unusual in divorce—the couple would draw straws for custody.[73]

Under the theory that the state is ill-equipped to regulate the lives of children and that, in any event, *any* determination of custody is likely to have an untoward effect on the child,[74] Goldstein and colleagues called their proposed standard the *least detrimental alternative*. However, the standard would likely have substantial undesirable effects. For example, the all-or-nothing custody decision would probably result in more custody fights by parents who wish to avoid the possible loss even of visitation.[75] It might also increase the possibili-ty of the custodial parent's using the child as a marble in "visitation roulette" to punish or manip-ulate the noncustodial parent.[76] Because the stan-dard includes a presumption that the parent who has custody is the psychological parent,[77] it could even increase the incidence of parental kidnap-ping.[78]

Nonetheless, Goldstein, Freud, and Solnit's emphasis on choosing a single parent represents important authority for foes of joint custody (which, as discussed later, has become popular in many jurisdictions). They also provide guideposts

for judges in best-interests jurisdictions who, in the absence of definitive standards, may seek to determine who the "psychological parent" is (al-though two or perhaps even multiple psychologi-cal parents may be the norm[79]).

(d)   The Primary-Caretaker Standard

A seemingly more objective alternative to the quest for a psychological parent is the *primary-caretaker* rule. This rule has received its greatest development in West Virginia, where it has been championed by Justice Neely,[80] but it has also been applied in some other jurisdictions.[81] Os-tensibly gender-neutral,[82] the primary-caretaker rule has a premise similar to the tender-years pre-sumption: that young children generally are bet-ter off when their primary attachment is pre-served.[83] Consequently, custody is awarded to the "natural or adoptive parent who, until the ini-tiation of divorce proceedings, has been primarily responsible for the caring and nurturing of the child."[84]

From courts' perspective, the major advantage of the primary-caretaker standard is that it is more easily susceptible to proof than is psycho-logical parenthood.[85] As defined by the West Vir-ginia Supreme Court, the primary caretaker is es-tablished by determining who has been principal-ly responsible for:

(1) preparing and planning of meals; (2) bathing, grooming and dressing; (3) purchasing, cleaning, and care of clothes; (4) medical care, including nursing and trips to physicians; (5) ar-ranging for social interaction among peers after school, i.e., transporting to friends' houses or, for example, to girl or boy scout meetings; (6) arranging alternative care, i.e., babysitting, day-care, etc.; (7) putting child to bed at night, at-tending to child in the middle of the night, wak-ing child in the morning; (8) disciplining, i.e., teaching general manners and toilet training; (9) educating, i.e., religious, cultural, social, etc.; and, (10) teaching elementary skills, i.e, reading, writing and arithmetic.[86]

Although more palatable as a practical matter than either the best-interests or psychological-parent standards, the primary-caretaker approach can be challenged on normative grounds. Its purely quantitative inquiry may offer little insight into the nature of the child-care arrangements that would "naturally" develop under various scenarios after a divorce. Although meal preparation may be correlated with the intensity of a child's relationship, it seems unlikely that cooking a child's food *causes* the development of such a relationship. The same argument can be made, for example, about washing a child's laundry. Nonetheless, the results under a primary-caretaker rule (as operationalized by the West Virginia judiciary) may appear fair from adults'—at least adult women's[87]—perspective. Custody is awarded to the parent who has invested the most time and energy in household management, including but not limited to direct care of the child.

Thus, although the conceptual foundation for the primary-caretaker rule is more explicitly psychological than the traditional best-interests standard, it calls for no psychological opinions. Instead, it invites evidence on who did what, and it starts from a presumption that more is better. In such a framework, mental health professionals are apt to be used most extensively as interviewers to gather and corroborate evidence, not as experts to offer opinions. In short, the primary-caretaker rule implicitly limits mental health testimony in a manner that is consistent with our own preference [see § 16.01(b)(1)].

(e)   Joint Custody

As with the primary-caretaker rule, joint-custody rules resulted in part from the difficulty in choosing between two fit parents.[88] In contrast to the former rule, however, joint custody has achieved widespread adoption. In 1975, only one state, North Carolina, had a joint-custody law. Spurred by California's enactment of a preference in favor of joint custody in 1979,[89] about 30 states enacted joint-custody statutes within the next five years.[90] The more recent statutes tend to have stronger presumptions in favor of joint custody.[91]

Technically, *joint custody* refers to shared parental authority to make decisions on behalf of children. It does not necessarily include joint physical custody; indeed, such an arrangement is far less common than joint legal custody.[92] However, it is clear that the initial proponents of joint

custody expected both shared legal authority and shared physical custody.[93]

In some "strong presumption" states,[94] joint custody must be ordered unless the court finds that such an arrangement would be harmful to the child, presumably even if both parents object.[95] Even among states with weaker presumptions, the preference for parental cooperation is often expressed in a *friendly-parent* rule, which provides that if joint custody is not awarded, sole custody should be granted to the parent more likely to facilitate the noncustodial parent's involvement with the child.[96] As Scott and Derdeyn have pointed out, this rule may diminish the presentation of evidence suggesting that joint custody will be detrimental.[97] Parents may be reluctant to describe continuing conflict or question the fitness of the other parent lest they be viewed as "unfriendly."[98]

(f)   Special Populations

The shifts in custody standards probably reflect changes in society.[99] The changing roles of women have provided the push for standards that are facially neutral in regard to gender, and the extraordinary increase in divorce during the past generation has increased the pressure on courts to resolve custody cases efficiently.

Other societal changes have had a more ambiguous impact on family law. The traditional family structure has been strained by relationships that formerly were "in the closet" socially and unrecognized legally.[100] Some of these relationships (e.g., heterosexual cohabitation and childbearing outside marriage) now are commonplace and substantially destigmatized, although many people continue to disapprove of them. Others have been more controversial.

(1)   Gay and Lesbian Parents

Societal and, therefore, judicial ambivalence may be most profound in cases involving gay and lesbian parents. Seeking to resolve the factual questions about the relationship between parental sexual orientation and child well-being [see § 16.03(e)], courts have been especially prone to look to the behavioral sciences—or their beliefs about behavioral science questions—for answers.[101] The results have been variable. Some courts have held that homosexuality is indeed a factor to be considered in custody decisions.[102] Others have applied restrictions on visitation to limit children's exposure to their gay or lesbian parent's relationships.[103] The trend, however, clearly is to reject such restrictions because they are regarded as unrelated to parenting.[104]

(2)   Grandparents and Other Third Parties

As households have become less likely to include extended family members and as non-work-related relationships have become less common and less intense, the law has more routinely had to deal with the extended family relationships that do remain and that might enhance the well-being of children. The general rule in most jurisdictions remains that biological parents may lose custody to a nonparent only when the parents are unfit.[105] This rule applies even when a stepparent seeks custody.[106] Moreover, even when states have opened the door to custody by someone other than a biological or adoptive parent, they generally have established a strong presumption in favor of custody by the parent.[107] In fact, when a biological parent asserts the right to custody, courts have been reluctant even to award visitation to nonparental individuals who have functioned as a child's parents.[108]

The major exception to the general rule is a by-product of the political influence of older Americans and, specifically, their success in convincing legislatures to recognize grandparents' rights. Although the strong presumption in favor of parental custody does generally apply when a grandparent seeks custody,[109] all 50 states now have statutes recognizing visitation rights for grandparents who wish to maintain contact with their grandchildren when their adult children no longer have custody.[110]

Such reforms reflect the changing roles of grandparents. Although the number of grandparents present in households with children has steadily declined during this century,[111] these family members—especially the parents of the custodial parent—can assume increased importance after separation and divorce.[112] In recognition of this fact, legislatures have enabled grand-

parents to obtain standing to assert their interests in divorce cases involving children.

Although not doubting the general desirability of strong grandparent–grandchild relationships, some commentators have hypothesized possible negative side effects of legal enforcement of such relationships in divorce cases. In particular, the new standing of grandparents may exacerbate family conflict by adding new parties to the fray in custody and visitation battles.[113] Thus, the legal recognition of grandparents' interests may complicate bargaining by the divorcing parents[114] and may even increase the likelihood of conflicts between the divorcing parents and their children.[115]

Regardless of the wisdom of the policy, clinicians may find themselves faced with new questions as grandparents seek visitation. At the same time, the underlying inquiry about extended family relationships should not be appreciably different from the traditional assessment aimed at arriving at custody and visitation arrangements most in keeping with a child's interests. In other words, grandparent–grandchild relations may well affect courts' parental custody and visitation decrees even when they are not the direct focus of a custody dispute.

(g)   Multiplicity of Issues

The example of grandparent visitation illustrates the fact that, under every standard except the least detrimental alternative, there are numerous issues at stake in custody disputes beyond the award of custody per se. Despite attempts to provide more precision (as with the primary-caretaker and joint-custody standards), the modal practice in child custody and visitation cases remains broad judicial discretion. Even in joint custody, the allocation of physical custody may be subject to the discretion of the court, as may be the arrangements for financial support of the children. In more traditional, sole-custody arrangements, there is a seemingly infinite array of possibilities for amount and conditions of visitation. Moreover, the court may make other determinations (e.g., whether Johnny and Susie will go to summer camp; if so, who will pay) if they are in dispute. Further, as Mnookin and Kornhauser have pointed out,[116] money issues may be inextricably intertwined with custody issues in divorce bargaining. For example, a father who values time with his children may not fight a property settlement that is generous to his wife and may not even resist her having custody if visitation arrangements are liberal.

The broad range of potential dispositions in custody disputes, particularly when a best-interests standard is employed, is important in the present context for two reasons. First, the breadth of possible dispositions suggests the need for a wide-ranging evaluation. Second, it creates inherent difficulty in ever generating an adequate research data base to be useful in charting specific dispositions in individual cases. The possibilities are simply too numerous to compare.

16.03.   What Do We Know?

(a)   Effects of Divorce on Children

Knowledge about the effects of divorce on children has increased substantially in the past two decades, primarily as a result of data gathered in two longitudinal studies[117]: the Virginia Longitudinal Study of Divorce by Mavis Hetherington, Martha Cox, and Roger Cox[118] and the California Children of Divorce Project by Judith Wallerstein and Joan Kelly.[119] Before discussing what has been learned from these projects,[120] it is useful to indicate their limitations. Hetherington, Cox, and Cox conducted a carefully designed quasi-experimental[121] study of 72 white, middle-class four- and five-year-old children and their divorced parents (maternal custody in all cases) and a matched control group. Thus, although conclusions from the Virginia study can be drawn with some confidence, the population to which they are applicable is limited.[122] The California project had some different limitations. The sample consisted of 60 white, middle-class divorcing families in northern California, including 131 children ranging in age from 3 to 18 years, which was recruited through an offer of counseling. Hence the sample was essentially a clinical sample, which might be expected to differ from a general sample of divorcing families in coping with marital breakup. There are also significant methodological problems with

the California data. Wallerstein and Kelly often did not report quantified data, and when they did there typically were no measures of interrater reliability.

The general findings of these studies were aptly summarized by Thompson:

> [T]hese investigations characterize divorce as a multistage process with multiple influences on family members. During the period immediately following the divorce, the family is in crisis, characterized by emotional turmoil in parents and children and impaired parent-child relationships. Most of these stresses were still evident one year following the divorce, with boys in mother-custody families displaying more acute difficulties in adjusting to divorce than girls. Following this, however, was a period of restabilization for the family and its individual members. Parents achieved greater personal stability and happiness, and this fostered improved interactions with their children. The children themselves also showed signs of growing adjustment to new family conditions, although persisting difficulties remained even at five years, especially for boys. Children's longterm divorce adjustment was a function of both their earlier success at coping and the growing stability and support of the home environment. But even long after the parents had separated, children and their families were still adjusting to the effects of this critical event on their lives. Divorce is, in short, a difficult transition for all concerned, and long-term outcomes vary considerably for parents and children.[123]

The crisis model suggested by the research must be qualified by the findings indicating that high conflict in *intact* families is even more deleterious for children than divorce.[124] Nonetheless, divorce obviously has a negative effect.[125] Both studies indicate that during the first year after the divorce, conflict typically escalates as both parents deal with the depression and anger engendered by the divorce as well as the practical problems resulting from separate households.[126] The crisis for the children is particularly exacerbated if there is very high conflict between the parents.[127] In such cases, children are worse off when their parents remain in contact. In an average, less conflicted divorce, however, postdivorce adjustment (especially for young boys) is apparently facilitated by frequent visitation by the father (assuming maternal custody).[128]

It should be remembered, however, that all these conclusions are based on correlational data, and the causal links are not clear. For example, paternal visitation is presumably more likely to occur if there is cooperation between the spouses. Is the enhanced well-being of children who are frequently visited the result primarily of their access to their fathers or the relative lack of acrimony in their homes? Moreover, the data from the Virginia study and the California project give bases only for speculation as to what the result would be of judicial interventions to increase visitation or to require parental cooperation (e.g., through imposition of joint custody). They provide no direct evidence on this point.

The Virginia and California studies do offer four more reasons to be cautious in drawing conclusions from custody evaluations. First, it was found that postdivorce relationships were largely unpredictable from predivorce behavior. For example, some fathers who had been largely uninvolved in child care prior to the divorce become "superdads" afterward. Others who were intensely attached to their children found the intermittent visitation relationship too painful and withdrew.[129]

Second, long-term effects may be very different from those during the first months or even years following the divorce. For example, preschoolers were the age group most traumatized by separation and divorce, but ten years later they were minimally affected by the experience.[130]

Third, at the time of divorce, both parents and children typically are experiencing acute and sometimes disorganizing stress. The general level of adjustment of parents and children, parent–child relationships, and parental skills are all likely to be atypical of usual functioning. Thus, the inferences that can be drawn from behavior samples taken during a custody evaluation (when the stress produced by divorce is likely to be at its most intense) are limited, although validity may be greater for families of older children and adolescents.[131]

Fourth, although both the Virginia and California studies were focused on parent–child relations, the glimpses they provided of extended-family[132] and extrafamilial influences suggest that the factors affecting the success or harm of a custody disposition are quite complex.[133] The warmth of schoolteachers and the level of structure in the school day both affect postdivorce adjustment,[134] especially for children with "difficult" temperaments[135] and presumably for children who must move to a new school or neighborhood (or even shuttle between neighborhoods[136]) as a result of divorce.[137] Similarly, the degree of economic downward mobility engendered by the divorce is likely to affect the probability of success of various dispositions.[138]

The significance of extrafamilial influences on adjustment after divorce is likely to be even greater for older children and adolescents[139]:

> With further advance into adolescence, many youngsters may find supports outside the home—in the neighborhood, school, work place, or peer groups—that are not available to younger children and that are able to buffer the experience of multiple family reorganizations or adverse family relationships. . . . [S]ocial and academic competencies can provide a positive counter to the negative effects of disruptive family relationships. Hence, the disengagement reported to occur in about one-third of adolescent children [of divorce] who are confronting their parents' marital transitions may be a constructive way of coping with a stressful family situation when other sources of social and emotional gratification are available. However, other research has indicated that involvement on the part of a caring adult is critical for children in high-risk situations. In the case of children who disengage from their divorced or remarried families, this role may be played by the noncustodial parent, a grandparent, a teacher, or a neighbor; becoming attached to the family of a friend can also have salutary effects. Disengagement accompanied by high involvement in peer activities with no concomitant adult monitoring is more likely to be associated with the development of deviant behavior.[140]

In short, the available literature on the effects of divorce gives little basis for either policy or individual case dispositions, even for the narrow (white, middle-class, predominantly preschool) population that has been studied thus far. We do not mean to denigrate the available studies. They offer important initial descriptions that may assist clinicians in recognizing, preventing, and alleviating the deleterious effects of divorce. At the same time, though, it is important to recognize that this literature gives little help in decisionmaking about custody. Indeed, if anything, it suggests the pitfalls in making predictions from clinical assessments at the time of divorce.

(b)   Father Custody

Although the law now is ostensibly gender-neutral, father custody remains a relatively rare event in law and an even more uncommon arrangement in practice. Only 10 to 15% of divorced fathers have physical custody of their children.[141] If children were living with their mother prior to divorce, a decree of joint or paternal custody is unlikely to be implemented.[142]

Given the limited literature available as to the aftermath of divorce under traditional arrangements (i.e., maternal custody with some parental visitation), it is hardly surprising that there is scant authority as to the effects of nontraditional dispositions. Thompson's summary of the available studies of father custody is instructive:

> Unfortunately, the research studies we have to draw upon in this area are scanty and somewhat qualified. First, with only one exception, all of these studies rely upon interviews with single fathers without direct observations of father–child interaction. Their portrayal of family life is thus inherently subjective and, quite likely, positively skewed. Second, the fathers who were interviewed included widowed and abandoned fathers as well as those who were divorced, although the large majority were the latter. Among the divorced group, most fathers received custody by mutual consent of both spouses, but some fought for custody in the courts. Thus the causes of the marital breakup and custody decision were varied, and this undoubtedly had an effect on subsequent family interaction. Third, nearly all of these studies report on single fathers who were interviewed long after making the adjustment to being the sole caregiver. Their descriptions of the transition were thus retrospective rather than direct, and it is sometimes difficult to know how they should be interpreted. Finally, these fathers were contacted through informal, word-of-mouth sources, advertisements or, on occasion, single-parent support groups (such as Parents Without Partners), and thus probably reflect a select, highly motivated, and involved sample. This final concern over unrepresentative sampling may be excused, in part, due to the rarity of single fathers in most Western cultures.[143]

Beyond the methodological issues raised by Thompson, there is an additional question whether findings derived from these studies of "pioneers" in father custody are informative as to the probable outcomes of father custody when it becomes more commonplace. In particular, father custody often has been the product of allegations of maternal unfitness or at least fault for the divorce.[144] Some confidence in ultimate generalizability of the results can be based, though, on the finding (albeit in a single study) that custodial fathers, compared with noncustodial fathers, typically show similar gender-related behavior and have a history of a similar level of child care.[145]

With these several caveats, the evidence from the available studies of father custody as well as of father–child relations in intact families gives almost no reason for a general gender-based preference.[146] Fathers who become principal caretakers of their children are able to become competent in "maternal" caregiving while maintaining the sort of physical, rough-housing style of relating to children common among men.[147] To the extent fathers do fail at caregiving, they are *least* likely to do so with infants (contrary to the intuition expressed in the tender-years presumption). In contrast, adolescent daughters of custodial fathers appear to have more adjustment problems than those in maternal custody, and adolescent children of custodial fathers are more likely to engage in delinquent behavior, perhaps because of less careful parental monitoring.[148]

Thompson has argued that paternal incompetence is the "least convincing" reason for maintenance of a *de facto* maternal preference:

> A large research literature examining the caretaking capabilities of fathers reveals extraordinary competence in child care, even of infants, for whom greatest doubt has traditionally existed concerning male caretaking competence. . . . [N]ot surprisingly, infants respond to paternal caretaking as they do to maternal care: infants develop deep emotional attachments to their fathers that do not depend on the security they derive from their attachments to mothers. As children mature, fathers are involved in the lives of offspring in increasingly more diverse ways as role models, teachers, homework consultants, and disciplinarians. In short, caretaking competence—defined narrowly or broadly—is not gender-specific.[149]

(c)   Same-Sex Custody

A study that compared observations of maternal-custody, paternal-custody, and two-parent, intact families (20 families per group) indicated that the social development of children ages 6 to 11 proceeds more smoothly when children live with the same-sex parent.[150] Indeed, boys in single-father homes were found to be more socially competent than boys in intact families.[151] These data are consistent with other research showing less frequent coercive cycles between custodial fathers and sons than custodial mothers and sons and greater self-perceived difficulty of fathers in dealing with adolescent daughters than with adolescent sons.[152] Behavior of the custodial parent also appears to be more directly related to the adjustment of same-sex than opposite-sex children.[153]

In theory, same-sex children would be likely to do better because of the availability of a model of gender-related behavior and because of the parent's own experience growing up as a boy (for fathers) or a girl (for mothers). The parent's own experience may be manifest not only in useful practical advice for the child but also in maintenance of emotional closeness and support as the child enters adolescence and sexuality becomes a greater issue. As already noted, for instance, there is some research suggesting that adolescent daughters have more adjustment problems in father-custody than mother-custody homes, perhaps reflecting the role strains in cross-gender family relations.[154]

A simple conclusion that children will do better with the parent of the same sex is inappropriate, however, because this study included only *single* parents. A general problem of both the research and the policy debate on various custody arrangements is that the possibility—indeed, probability—of remarriage is often ignored. The lack of a same-sex model would presumably be mitigated in a stepfamily, although remarriage presents other challenges for adaptation by parents, stepparents, and children.[155]

Moreover, the advantages of same-sex custody may be countered by its disadvantages. Children learn important lessons from the opposite-sex parent as well as from the same-sex parent.[156] For example, fathers may be more authoritative than mothers in teaching daughters about what to expect from boys, and gender is a sufficiently powerful independent variable that children are likely to learn somewhat different ways of relating to others and solving problems from their mothers and fathers (and same- and opposite-sex steppar-

ents). Moreover, a same-sex parent preference would require separating brothers from sisters. The conventional wisdom is that, all things being equal, children adjust better when the sibling group remains intact,[157] although we know of no research testing this assumption. Given this complex picture, it is unsurprising that the match between parental and child gender is not a consistently strong factor in children's adjustment.[158]

(d) Joint Custody

The gender of the custodial parent obviously is rendered irrelevant if both parents remain primary caregivers for their children after divorce. The desire for such a scenario fueled states' movement toward a preference for joint physical custody.

Whatever the wisdom of this legal preference, data from California in the mid-1980s indicate it is not the preference of divorcing parents, at least once the dust settles. Notwithstanding that state's strong presumption in favor of joint custody,[159] two-thirds of divorcing families in California reached at least a *de facto* maternal-custody arrangement.[160] In about half the cases in which dual residence was the initial arrangement, a change in physical custody took place at some point (compared with one-fifth of children initially in maternal physical custody).[161] Indeed, almost half the cases in which there was an *uncontested* request for joint physical custody eventually resulted in a different arrangement, usually maternal custody.[162]

Joint physical custody clearly requires diligent efforts by parents to make it work. It typically results from a significant commitment by both parents to the maintenance of strong parental relationships.[163] Although this dual commitment sometimes reflects a shared belief system about the importance of both parents' involvement, it more commonly reflects the father's insistence on a higher level of involvement than the mother had wished.[164]

Given the level of motivation required to sustain joint physical custody, even when the law supports such an arrangement, it is perhaps unsurprising to find that "[t]he superiority of . . . joint arrangements over sole physical custody measured in terms of positive child adjustment and parental satisfaction has not been clearly demonstrated."[165] The positive results that appeared in early studies of joint physical custody, conducted before legal presumptions favorable to such an arrangement were enacted, must be interpreted cautiously because the parents participating in the research were especially highly motivated to make joint physical custody work.[166]

Of course, parents who *choose* joint custody are apt to differ from those who simply accept a legal presumption and those who choose or accept single-parent (usually maternal) custody. In one small study, couples who chose joint custody differed from those who chose maternal custody in three ways.[167] First, the fathers in the former group were more likely to be perceived by both parents as having been actively involved in childrearing. Second, the parents who chose joint custody commonly placed relatively greater emphasis on the parent–child relationship itself than the responsibility to ensure that the child is fed and clothed. Third, the two groups of parents differed in their motivation to negotiate a custody arrangement. The fathers whose children were placed into joint custody were more interested in custody than those whose children were placed into sole custody, and the mothers who agreed to joint custody were relatively eager to obtain a divorce.

Given the continuing parental contact and negotiation required to sustain joint physical custody, it is associated with poor adjustment when it occurs in a high-conflict context.[168] Thus, it is particularly unfortunate that joint physical custody is a common compromise reached by courts faced with warring but apparently equally competent parents. In more than a third of the cases in California in which both parents requested sole physical custody, joint physical custody was the result.[169] When an evaluation or trial occurs— circumstances that usually reflect parents' inability to reach a compromise on their own—joint physical custody is almost as common as maternal custody.[170] In fact, more than one-third of the cases resulting in a decree of joint physical custody in California involve substantial or intense legal conflict—a higher proportion than among divorcing families in general.[171] At the same time, as alluded to earlier, in half of these high-conflict joint-custody cases maternal physical custody is still the ultimate *de facto* arrangement.[172] Cooperative parenting rarely is the ultimate result in such cases.[173]

Even in relatively favorable circumstances, joint physical custody is unlikely to bring sustained parental cooperation of the type proponents envisioned. Despite the advantages of cooperation, the disengaged (parallel) style of parenting is most common among joint-custody parents, with disengagement or conflict occurring ultimately even among cooperative parents when one or both parents enter new relationships.[174] Indeed, it is remarkable how little the parental relationship has to do with children's living and visitation arrangements.[175] As with other custody arrangements, practical considerations and extrafamilial support have as much to do with how well joint physical custody works: "Children who alternate between mother and father residences fare better when the parents live in close geographic proximity so that the children's school and peer group memberships remain stable. . . ."[176]

Although its import often is purely symbolic, joint legal custody is far more common than joint physical custody and far easier for parents to manage. When one parent requests joint legal custody, that is the usual disposition, at least in California.[177] It is almost always the result when both parents are represented by counsel. The overwhelming preference for maternal custody, at least on a *de facto* basis, is reflected, however, in the fact that even joint legal custody occurs only about half the time in California when neither parent has an attorney.[178]

(e)   Special Populations

Mental health professionals may be especially likely to become involved in cases in which there is an unusual circumstance that a court is apt to believe is unlikely to be illuminated by commonly shared knowledge of families.[179] Unfortunately, the existing literature is limited largely to samples of white, middle-class families. This gap is especially unfortunate when one considers that ethnicity and family structure (including, e.g., remarriage rates) are highly related[180] and that poverty or near-poverty substantially increases the risk of divorce.[181]

The small range of evidence that does exist in this area is mixed. For some specific topics (e.g., the visitation of parents in prison), the literature is virtually nil.[182] For some clinical populations (e.g., parents with serious mental disorders [see § 15.05]), however, there is at least some research on typical parental behavior and children's outcomes. These studies may be useful in determining the range of parental characteristics that are in fact related to success as a parent.

There has also been substantial commentary about custody and visitation by gay and lesbian parents. In a review in *American Psychologist*, Falk identified seven assumptions that have guided courts that have viewed a mother's lesbian orientation as contrary to her child's best interest:

- Homosexuality is associated with mental illness.
- Lesbian women are less maternal than heterosexual women.
- Children reared by lesbian mothers are at risk for mental health problems.
- Children reared by homosexual parents are more likely to be subjected to sexual molestation.
- Children reared by lesbian mothers may have difficulty in establishing a clear gender identity.
- Children reared by homosexual parents are more likely to become homosexual themselves than if they were cared for by heterosexual parents.
- Children living with lesbian mothers are likely to be stigmatized, especially by their peers, and teased and ostracized as a result.[183]

Although noting that research on these points is scant and fraught with methodological problems,[184] Falk—like subsequent commentators[185]—concluded that no studies thus far have supported any of the assumptions about adverse effects of having a lesbian mother.[186] (Perhaps unsurprisingly given the relative rarity of father custody, no studies have compared custodial gay fathers with custodial heterosexual fathers,[187] although a few studies are available on children born in the context of heterosexual relationships

to fathers who subsequently identified themselves as gay.[188]) Research addressing the variations among lesbian and gay families with children is especially sparse.[189] But the studies available have suggested that mothers' mental health and children's adjustment in families of lesbian mothers may be greater when there is openness about the mother's sexual orientation, cohabitation by the mother's partner, and acceptance by other key adults in the child's life (e.g., the child's father).[190] Therefore, at least insofar as courts' concern is focused on children's mental health, initial studies suggest that it is unwise to limit custody or visitation to periods in which gay and lesbian parents' partners are not present.[191]

(f) Children's Participation in Decisionmaking

(1) Law and Empirical Research

As noted in the discussion of the best-interests standard, the Uniform Marriage and Divorce Act considers the child's wishes as a determinant in best-interests analysis, but it does not indicate the weight to be given to the child's preference. Some states have provided statutory guidelines based on age, reasoning ability, or both.[192] Nebraska, for example, requires consideration of a child's wishes if he or she is at an "age of comprehension, regardless of chronological age, when desires are based on sound reasoning."[193]

Nonetheless, there is little research to guide evaluators or judges in determining a child's competence to participate in decisionmaking about divorce. The one study directly on point[194] found that even elementary-school-age children gave adult-like reasons, in response to hypothetical situations, for preferring a particular custody arrangement. The rationality of the responses was more highly related to the children's general cognitive competence than to their ages. The direct application of these results is limited somewhat by the fact that children whose parents were divorced or divorcing were removed from the sample.

There is also little research directly testing whether querying children about their preferences is psychologically harmful because of the bind in which it places them. There is, on the other hand, a general literature in social psychology, including developmental social psychology, indicating the positive effects of being permitted to have some control over one's fate and of reducing ambiguity about a strange situation through direct discussion of it.[195] Finally, there is no research on the effects of the *procedure* for involving a child (e.g., whether interviewing takes place in chambers or who does the interviewing). In sum, the psychological impact of involving children in custody proceedings has not yet been explored in any detail.

(2)   Professional Standards and Practices

Although in some quarters the direct involvement of children in matters pertaining to their family remains controversial, the conventional legal wisdom now seems to be that children's voices ought to be heard, at least when the child is beyond the infant stage. For instance, in one jurisdiction in which there was no legal obligation to elicit children's opinions, most judges indicated that they nonetheless did so in cases not involving preschoolers:

> The judges reported that children below the age of six were the subject of fifty percent of litigated custody disputes, and most agreed that children's wishes in this age group were irrelevant to the decision. In contrast, the vast majority of judges reported that they routinely attempted in some way to get information about older children's wishes. Even for children in the six-to nine-year age group, sixty-five percent of judges tried to obtain some information about the child's preference, although usually not directly from the child. For children over fourteen years of age, ninety-seven percent of judges considered the child's views.[196]

The judges reported that interviews typically were brief and conducted in chambers,[197] usually alone.[198] More than two-thirds reported that children fourteen and over are routinely interviewed, but fewer than one-fourth said that they commonly interviewed six- to nine-year-old children, and few ever interviewed preschoolers.[199]

The judges' behavior may have been based as much on practical considerations as it was on respect for older children's opinions. If a fifteen-year-old is refusing to live with one parent but not the other, the law may have few means (short of draconian measures) to enforce an order to grant custody to the parent with whom the adolescent is in conflict. Whatever judges' motivation, however, and notwithstanding the dearth of research on the effects of children's direct involvement in divorce proceedings, there is clearly ample opportunity for mental health professionals to assist lawyers and judges in structuring interviews of children who are the subjects of custody and visitation disputes.

A separate question is whether the child ought to be given a more formal voice, through a lawyer. In an analogous context (child protection cases), the American Bar Association (ABA) has adopted the position that an attorney should be provided for the allegedly abused child and, once so provided, generally should not stray from zealous advocacy: "The term 'child's attorney' means a lawyer who provides legal services for a child and who owes the same duties of undivided loyalty, confidentiality, and competent representation to the child as is due an adult client."[200]

According to the ABA Standards on child protection, if a conflict arises between the child's preferences and his or her interests, the attorney should continue to follow the former.[201] However, if "the child's expressed preference would be seriously injurious to the child (as opposed to merely being contrary to the lawyer's opinion of what would be in the child's interests)," the attorney also should request the appointment of a *guardian ad litem*[202] who would protect the child's interests without being bound by the child's expressed preferences.[203]

The ABA Standards further provide that, "irrespective of the child's age, the child's attorney should visit with the child prior to court hearings and when apprised of emergencies or significant events impacting on the child."[204] In those contexts, the attorney "should explain to the client, in a developmentally appropriate manner, what is expected to happen before, during and after each hearing."[205] "In most circumstances," the attorney should arrange for the child's presence at hearings (even when the child is not expected to testify)[206] and prepare the child for the experience.[207]

Building on a recommendation that children's lawyers receive specialized training,[208] the Standards also presume that a child's lawyer will undertake an extensive investigation of the child's history,[209] including interviews not only with the child but also with the child's parents, "school personnel, child welfare case workers, foster parents and other caretakers, neighbors, relatives, school personnel, coaches, clergy, mental health professionals, physicians, law enforcement officers, and other potential witnesses."[210]

Of course, the ABA Standards were designed to guide lawyers involved in child protection cases, and the specific provisions of the Standards may have been different if the focus were on custody in divorce cases. It seems unlikely, however, that the child protection standards and the hypothetical divorce standards would differ in more than their nuances. Surely it is no more aversive for children in a divorce case than for those who are believed to have been maltreated to hear about the details of their family life in an official forum. Similarly, although the state's interest may differ in degree in the two contexts, surely children's attorneys in contested custody cases ought to take due care in investigating potential conditions of custody for their clients. Indeed, the principal difference in the two contexts in regard to the child's role may simply be the child is much less likely to have his or her own legal representative (even a guardian *ad litem*) in the custody context.

Indeed the relative infrequency with which guardians *ad litem* are appointed in divorce cases may mean that some of the educative role normally assigened children's attorneys will fall on clinical evaluators, who are ethically obligated to inform their interviewees about the context for the evaluation. In such situations clinicians may even be tempted to act as advocate for the child, a difficult role discussed in the next section. When children do have their own attorneys, however, the clinician's role is more likely to consist of generating and communicating information that will assist the attorney in "developmentally appropriate" representation. Thus, in this context as in many others, forensic clinicians are likely to find themselves used as *consultants* as much as *evaluators*, in the narrow sense of the latter term.

16.04. The Technique of Custody Evaluations

CASE STUDY 16.1

In many cases, legal presumptions or practical reality make it likely that one particular parent will receive custody; in such situations, custody evaluations often center on the visitation issue. Contested visitation requests are often "messiest" because they typically involve at least implicit allegations of unfitness and extreme parental conflict. In essence, one parent is claiming that it would be detrimental for the child even to *see* the other, at least for any extended period of time. Visitation issues are also difficult because they involve potential *de facto* termination of parental rights, but with a low substantive standard (best interests) and standard of proof (preponderance of the evidence). When maltreatment is alleged, concurrent cases may be pending in three courts on three issues (i.e., postdivorce visitation; child abuse/neglect, and criminal abuse/neglect), all requiring different standards of proof. Consider the following hypothetical case, which illustrates (1) the difficulty of the ethical and evaluative questions that may be raised in such cases and (2) the number of parties who may be involved in and profoundly affected by evaluations:

John and Jane Doe are divorcing after a rather tumultuous marriage. Jane says that John's hostility toward her was so intense that she was often fearful for herself and their eight-year-old daughter, Jean. However, she admits that John never actually was abusive. (In your initial interview with John, he became enraged that he was having to defend himself. He raised his voice, turned red, gritted his teeth, leaned forward, and questioned your credentials.) When John and Jane separated six months ago, Jane was awarded temporary custody of Jean, and John was permitted visitation from eight to five on Saturdays. There is uncontroverted evidence that Jean has been having difficulty in school since the separation. Although Jean says that she wants to visit her father, Jane has observed that Jean becomes very anxious on Friday evening. She has begun wetting the bed frequently on Friday nights. Jane claims often to have difficulty managing Jean's behavior when she returns from visits.

After the Does filed for divorce, John's adult daughter from a previous marriage, Sue, came forward and alleged that John had molested her when she was about ten years old. John's denial has been vehement. He claims that Sue must have imagined the episode because of her emotional distress (which John acknowledges) after the first divorce and her anger at John, who admits having walked out on Sue and her mother. Regardless, there is no physical evidence that Jean has been molested, and she has made no such allegations.

John insists that it is important for both Jean and him to maintain a close relationship. Therefore, he is requesting that the court order weekend (overnight) visitation during the school year and alternate-week physical custody during the summer. He is willing to concede legal custody to Jane. On the other hand, Jane says that the visits are obviously upsetting to Jean, and she worries for Jean's safety. She has asked the court to bar any visitation. The court orders evaluation by a clinical psychologist to determine the visitation arrangement (if any) that would be in Jean's best interest. All parties are to cooperate in the evaluation.

QUESTIONS: (1) How would you conduct the evaluation? (2) What kinds of conclusions might you be able to reach? (3) You receive a phone call at home from Sue. She says that Jane has told her that you are conducting an evaluation of John. Sue is calling you because she fears that John will retaliate against her. She wants to know whether you think that John might in fact harm her. What do you say or do? (4) If you decide to interview Jean as part of the evaluation, what, if anything, should you tell her about the purpose of the evaluation and the limits of confidentiality? What feedback should you give her about your findings at the conclusion of the evaluation?

(a)   Auspices: Who Is the Client?

In other contexts (e.g., criminal evaluations), we have defended the practice of having the parties employ their own experts [see § 4.03(b)(1)]. In an adversary system justice normally is served by giving each side the chance to put its best case forward. However, we do not recommend this procedure in custody evaluations. First, it is the *child's* interests, not the parties' (i.e., the parents') interests, that are theoretically paramount; accordingly, some of the usual reasons for protecting the interests of the parties do not so readily apply. That is, there may be substantial reason for the court to seek its own evidence as to the interests of a third party (i.e., the child). Second, as a practical matter, it is difficult to do a credible custody evaluation without access to both parents. Yet, under a pure adversarial approach, the clinician would have no basis for rendering an opinion about the parent not employing the clinician. Even if the clinician is asked to address only the effects that might occur if custody is granted to the employing party, he or she is hampered by not hearing the other parent's side of things, because the family history and family process are likely to be perceived differently by each party. Accordingly, as a general rule, we suggest that clinicians seek to enter custody disputes as an expert for the court or the guardian *ad litem*,[211] although there may be some rare circumstances in which it is sufficient to have access to only one parent.

A clinician who already has an ongoing therapeutic relationship with one or both of the spouses should be especially careful to avoid giving opinions without adequate foundation. Opinions as to parental competence or parent–child relationships should never be offered unless there has been specific focus on these topics. As indicated earlier, an interview with the child, with the parent and child together, or both kinds of interviews will generally be necessary if there is to be any substantial basis for an opinion on custody issues. Thus, reliance on therapeutic encounters as the sole basis for evaluation and testimony is inappropriate.

Indeed, it may be that *any* opinion about custody given by the therapist of one or both parents is inappropriate [see generally § 4.05(c)(2)]. We have already noted [see § 16.01(c)] the American Psychological Association's recommendation that therapists refrain from offering custody opinions as an expert (as opposed to acting as a "fact" witness who recounts observations). The reasons for this position are numerous. There is often a temptation when an adult client is involved in a custody dispute to act to protect the client. After all, if the client is heavily invested in being a parent, an adverse ruling will be likely to take a substantial psychological toll. Even when a clinician is treating both parents, as in marriage counseling, there may be pulls to take sides.[213] One parent may feed information damaging to the other. And even if the clinician could maintain perfect objectivity, evaluation and testimony are likely to create an acute sense of betrayal on the part of one or both parents. There are similar issues when a clinician hired as a mediator begins to act like an evaluator [see § 16.01(b)(2)].

(b) Application of the Psychotherapist–Patient Privilege

There are other pitfalls in moving from the role of therapist to that of evaluator (which even cautious clinicians may be forced to do under subpoena). The applicability of psychotherapist privilege[214] in custody cases is unclear and is highly variable across jurisdictions.[215] Can one spouse waive privilege for both when they have been jointly involved in marriage counseling?[216] Can a child assert (or waive) privilege?[217] Or can privilege be claimed at all in custody disputes (given the fact that the contestants are implicitly, if not explicitly, making an issue of their mental state)?[218] In some jurisdictions these issues are unsettled. Clinicians involved in marital or family therapy should seek legal advice as to the limits of privilege in their jurisdiction [see generally § 4.04(c)]. In the meantime, the therapist should be aware that material from family, child, or marital treatment is often not protected by privilege in a custody case, even in jurisdictions recognizing a general psychotherapist privilege and even when a person involved in the treatment objects to the admission of evidence based on it.

(c) Scope of the Evaluation

In the past decade a number of books describing clinical assessment procedures in child custody cases have been published.[219] As they indicate, potential approaches to assessment in custody evaluations include (1) comprehensive observation and interviewing of the parents and children and gathering of interview and archival information from third-party sources, (2) the administration of traditional psychological tests, and (3) the administration of specialized tests. Our position is strongly in favor of the first of these approaches. For reasons discussed below, we recommend only a limited role for the use of traditional tests and caution against the use of the commercially available specialized tests for child custody assessments.

Investigative interviewing is the predominant model in custody assessments. In view of both the breadth of the best-interests concept and the multiplicity of factors potentially affecting the outcome of various custody and visitation arrangements, a child custody evaluation can be best summarized as *comprehensive* [see, e.g., the Gonz-Jones report, § 19.12(a), and Table 16.1]. Parents, stepparents, and children should all be interviewed as to their perceptions of relationships in the family (past, present, and future), their preferences to custody, and any special needs of the children. Because of the significance of interparental conflict in the literature on effects of divorce, special attention should be given to the parents' capacity for cooperation, the nature and intensity of disagreements about the children, and points of possible compromise. As a means of observing the parent–child relationship in a realistic environment, home visits may be advisable as well.

Nor should the evaluation stop with interviews of the immediate family. Contact with extended family, teachers, social services agencies, and even babysitters can illuminate potential sources of support (or the lack thereof) under various custody arrangements (e.g., switching between parental homes). Sources outside the nuclear family may also give important, relatively objective glimpses of children's responses to arrangements developed during separations and under temporary custody orders. In that regard, the existing and previous custody arrangements can be conceptualized as natural experiments of a sort. The clinician should be sure to elicit information as to the parties' attitudes and behavioral responses to those arrangements.

However, even these directly relevant data may have limited usefulness in predicting children's long-term responses to custody dispositions. The California and Virginia studies have made it clear that these responses shift substantially over time. We remind readers of the point we have made throughout this chapter: Careful attention must be paid to the limits of expertise in custody evaluations.

(d) Traditional Psychological Testing

One of the more controversial issues in the child custody literature is the proper role for traditional psychological tests in the assessment process.

Table 16.1
Clinical Inquiry in Custody Evaluations (for Each Parent and Child)

- Parent's description of marital relationship and family structure
- Parent's attitude and concerns regarding the other parent, his or her access to the children, nature of visitation, etc.
  —Discussion with children about the separation and divorce
  —The parent's communications with the children about the other parent
  —The parent's goals for visitation and decisionmaking should he or she be awarded custody
- Parent's prior and current relationship with the children and responsibility for caretaking
  —Reaction to pregnancy and childbirth, and impact of these on relationship and functioning outside the family
  —Early caretaking
  —Current caretaking
  —Punishment
  —Leisure and social activities
  —Interactional style
  —Allegations of abuse/neglect
- Parent's current, anticipated living and working arrangements
  —Who is living in the home
  —Significant others
  —Day care, babysitting
  —Schools and school districts
- Parent's emotional functioning and mental health
  —Prior or current substance abuse/dependence and treatment
  —Prior or current mental health problems and treatment
  —Emotional response to the divorce
- Child's attitude and preference regarding the parents, current living arrangement, visitation, and future placement
- Child's depictions and conceptualization of relationship with each parent
  —Punishment
  —Leisure and social activities
  —Interactional style
  —Allegations of abuse/neglect
- Child's emotional functioning and mental health
  —Prior or current substance abuse/dependence and treatment
  —Prior or current mental health problems and treatment
  —Emotional or behavioral responses (i.e., problem behaviors) to the divorce
- Child's social, academic, and vocational functioning prior to and after divorce

Note. Adapted from RANDY OTTO, OUTLINE ON CUSTODY EVALUATIONS, Florida Mental Health Institute (August 1996).

Grisso summarized the debate in his 1986 text on forensic assessment:

> Psychological testing of parents in custody cases (for intelligence, personality, and/or psychopathology) has been described variously as of no utility, of dubious value, potentially useful when performed selectively and only when a clear need is identified, and one of the better indications of a parent's true feelings and intentions. Rarely are opinions of this type offered with any empirical support or with reference to any particular psychological tests.[220]

The debate continued a decade later, with some authors offering an unbridled endorsement of psychological testing,[221] others expressing caution regarding their use,[222] and still others advocating against their use.[223]

The little data that exist concerning the practices of mental health professionals in custody assessments suggest that the use of conventional tests is routine. A survey of 302 mental health professionals reported use of 82 different protocols involving testing practices.[224] Respondents, 78.1% of whom were doctoral-level psychologists,[225] indicated that most used conventional tests in evaluating both the parents (75.6%) and the children (74.4%).[226]

Although the authors of this study concluded that many tests were selected for use only "when appropriate,"[227] they did not report any objective indicators of "appropriateness." It is our contention that such tests are often used inappropriately. Tests of intellectual capacity, achievement, personality style, and psychopathology are linked only indirectly, at best, to the key issues concerning custody and visitation. As Brodzinsky notes, such testing might occasionally be helpful, as when there is a possible impairment of the child that might influence special education needs (e.g., learning disability), or when there is a question of significant mental disorder (e.g., depression) in a parent previously so diagnosed.[228] However, like most other commentators,[229] he questions the routine use of testing in custody assessments and concludes that "psychologists routinely misuse test data in this type of forensic case."[230] Thus, apparent practices notwithstanding, we recommend the use of traditional psychological tests only when specific problems or issues that these tests were designed to measure appear salient in the case.

(e) Specialized Tests

A number of tests purport to provide a more focused determination regarding custody and visitation. Two such tests are the Ackerman–Schoendorf Scales for Parent Evaluation of Custody (ASPECT)[231] and scales developed by Barry Bricklin.[232] These approaches have been described as "promising" by one reviewer,[233] and another reviewer has endorsed one of the Bricklin scales as helpful in assessing the child in custody evaluations.[234] In our view, however, these measures suffer from serious conceptual flaws and in-

adequate psychometric construction. Pending the development of an adequate empirical research base for their use, we advise against including them in custody evaluations.

The ASPECT is essentially a battery of largely standard tests (e.g., the Wide Range Achievement Test and the Minnesota Multiphasic Personality Inventory). A review by Melton,[235] noted a panoply of problems with the ASPECT:

- The evidence for reliability and validity was scant. The "content validation" consisted exclusively of the test author's logical analysis. A highly unrepresentative small sample (clients of private practitioners) provided the only validation, and the outcome variable (agreement between clinicians' opinions and ultimate outcomes) was affected by the assessments themselves. Interrater reliablities were based on only two raters evaluating a small sample, and the internal consistency of two of the three ASPECT scales yielded an r of 0.

- The items (e.g., whether the parent's IQ is more than five points below that of the child; which parent the child is placed beside in the child's drawing) have not been shown to be related to parental competence or child outcomes.

- ASPECT reduces complex constructs to narrow behavior samples (e.g., bedtime rituals as indicators of family life).

- ASPECT ignores factors, such as support by third parties, that are probably highly related to the success of custody dispositions but that are not included in traditional psychological instruments.

- Clinicians must average ASPECT scores across children in a family (what does one do when there are dichotomous choices for an item—yes or no—and there are two children in the family?).

- Most fundamentally, "the ASPECT was ill-conceived: an instrument that results in a score showing the parent who should be preferred necessarily results in overreaching by experts who use it. Even if the idea had merit, though, the psychometric properties of the ASPECT remain essentially unknown, and the item selection and scoring procedures appear to pull for often irrelevant conclusions."[236]

Similar concerns about the ASPECT have been expressed by Arditti[237] and Nicholson.[238] Indeed, we found no methodologically sound research, published in refereed scientific journals, to support the use of the ASPECT in child custody decisionmaking.[239]

Bricklin's measures include the Bricklin Perceptual Scales (BPS), Perception-of-Relationships-Test (PORT), Parent Awareness Skills Survey (PASS), and the Parent Perception of Child Profile (PPCP).[240] The BPS is designed to tap children's perceptions of each parent's actions. Thirty-two questions (16 about the mother, 16 about the father) are posed to each child. The child provides both a verbal response about "how well" each parent performs with respect to each issue and a nonverbal response obtained by poking a stylus through a black line, the end points of which are anchored with descriptors of "very well" and "not so well."[241] The PORT is a measure based primarily on projective drawings made by the child and aspires to provide an index of the degree of closeness a child feels with a given parent. The PASS is designed to assess parent awareness of factors important in reacting to 18 dilemmas or situations that arise regarding child care. Scores of 0, 1, or 2 are assigned to a parent's initial responses to each situation and subsequent to a series of probes about each situation. Finally, the PPCP solicits information from each parent regarding his or her perceptions through 121 questions (with additional probes) about each child.

The same kinds of concerns expressed by reviewers of the ASPECT have appeared in critical reviews of the various Bricklin measures: the measures contain unrealistic or untested assumptions,[242] have been developed on inappropriately small, inadequately described, or inappropriate clinical samples,[243] lack adequate reliability and validity,[244] and so forth. As with the ASPECT, no methodologically sound research studies were found in refereed scientific journals to support the author's claims regarding the BPS or other Bricklin measures.[245]

In summary, we join with other reviewers who recommend caution in the use of these commercially available "child custody" measures.[246] Although some of these measures may facilitate gathering useful responses regarding parents' attitudes, knowledge, or values with respect to raising their children, the lack of adequate reliability and validity studies counsels against use of the formal indices they yield. Certainly these indices do not identify "scientifically" the parent of choice

or indicate other dispositional conclusions, matters which are properly reserved for the court.[247]

16.05.   The Politics of Divorce

We conclude this chapter as we began it—with caveats. Throughout this chapter, we noted that the relevant empirical knowledge is especially limited and that the prevailing legal standards are especially problematic. Making this combination of legal and clinical conundrums even more problematic is the fact that forensic clinicians involved in divorce cases work against a politically charged backdrop.

Consider, for example, the lead paragraphs from a full-page article in the *APA Monitor*:

> It used to be that a woman had to be considered a terrible mother to lose custody of her children in a divorce case. It usually took something like a serious mental illness, substance abuse or child abuse to convince a judge that keeping a mother and her children together was not in the children's best interests.
>
> But today, losing children through divorce is much easier. Something as seemingly innocent as working late hours or enrolling a child in day care can be used as evidence of bad mothering.[248]

The author went on to lament the "devastating" effects of loss of custody on mothers' mental health.[249]

Such mother-centered critiques of egalitarian custody policies assume special significance when viewed in the context of domestic violence cases because most such violence is perpetrated by men (as alleged in Case Study 16.1). Some states have created a rebuttable presumption that giving custody, including joint custody, to a parent who has perpetrated domestic violence is contrary to a child's best interest.[250] Others require that visitation by the parent with such a history be supervised unless the court determines that "the violent parent has successfully completed a treatment program, is not abusing alcohol and psychoactive drugs, [and] poses no danger to the child, and that such visitation is in the child's best interest."[251]

The politics of divorce is not simply a matter

of gender. Generational conflicts also are in the backdrop. As discussed in § 16.02(f)(2), such groups as the American Association of Retired Persons have been active in advocating the interests of grandparents. At the other end of the age spectrum, child advocates are disturbed that children's lack of standing in cases involving their own custody[252] often means their interests receive the least attention in divorce. Following similar logic, concern about the effects of divorce on children has led some commentators to argue that divorce has become too easy,[253] even if more stringent standards and onerous procedures would have troubling effects on the parents themselves.

Such a complex political context intensifies the potential ethical dilemmas for clinicians. Without providing elaboration about the ways that "biases" can influence child custody evaluations, the American Psychological Association's *Guidelines* indicate a concern about personal and political interests that may affect child custody evaluations:

> The psychologist is aware of personal and societal biases and engages in nondiscriminatory practice. The psychologist engaging in child custody evaluations is aware of how biases regarding age, gender, race, ethnicity, national origin, religion, sexual orientation, disability, language, culture, and socioeconomic status may interfere with an objective evaluation and recommendations. The psychologist recognizes and strives to overcome any such biases or withdraws from the evaluation.[254]

Although the issues typically are subtle, mental health professionals conducting custody evaluations should take special care to examine ways in which their own experiences and attitudes color their views about childrearing and "proper" roles—especially gender roles—of family members. They also need to be especially sensitive to ways that clinicians can be unwittingly drawn into taking sides with a family member.

Bibliography

Paul R. Amato & Bruce Keith, *Parental Divorce and Adult Well-being: A Meta Analysis,* 53 JOURNAL OF MARRIAGE & FAMILY 43 (1991).

Paul R. Amato & Bruce Keith, *Parental Divorce and the Well-being of Children: A Meta Analysis,* 100 PSYCHOLOGICAL BULLETIN 26 (1991).

AMERICAN PSYCHOLOGICAL ASSOCIATION, LESBIAN AND GAY PARENTING: A RESOURCE FOR PSYCHOLOGISTS (1995) (prepared by the American Psychological Association Committees on Women in Psychology, Lesbian and Gay Concerns, and Children, Youth, and Families).

ROBERT E. EMERY, RENEGOTIATING FAMILY RELATIONSHIPS: DIVORCE, CHILD CUSTODY, AND MEDIATION (1994).

ROBERT E. EMERY, MARRIAGE, DIVORCE, AND CHILDREN'S ADJUSTMENT (1988).

Guidelines for Child Custody Evaluations in Divorce Proceedings, 49 AMERICAN PSYCHOLOGIST 677 (1994).

E. Mavis Hetherington & W. Glenn Clingempeel, *Coping with Marital Transitions,* 57(2-3) MONOGRAPHS FROM THE SOCIETY FOR RESEARCH IN CHILD DEVELOPMENT (Serial No. 227) 1 (1992).

MIMI E. LYSTER, CHILD CUSTODY: BUILDING AGREEMENTS THAT WORK (1995) (practical guide for divorcing parents; includes self-administered questionnaires that may be useful in facilitating and structuring data gathering).

ELEANOR E. MACCOBY & ROBERT H. MNOOKIN, DIVIDING THE CHILD: SOCIAL AND LEGAL DILEMMAS OF CUSTODY (1992).

PSYCHOLOGY AND CHILD CUSTODY DETERMINATIONS: KNOWLEDGE, ROLES, AND EXPERTISE (Lois A. Weithorn ed. 1987).

Symposium, *Families in Transition,* 7 JOURNAL OF FAMILY PSYCHOLOGY 3 (1993).

Symposium, *Children and Divorce,* FUTURE OF CHILDREN, Spring 1994.

Judith S. Wallerstein, *The Long-term Effects of Divorce on Children: A Review,* 30 JOURNAL OF THE AMERICAN ACADEMY OF CHILD & ADOLESCENT PSYCHIATRY 349 (1991).

CHAPTER SEVENTEEN

Education and Habilitation

17.01. Introduction

Aside from Social Security, the most significant federal entitlement program for those with mental disability is the Individuals with Disabilities Education Act (IDEA) (originally the Education of All Handicapped Children Act when it was passed in 1975).[1] The IDEA is based on the principle that children with disabilities are entitled to the same education as their nondisabled peers. Thus, the IDEA seeks to provide a "free appropriate public education" in the "least restrictive environment" for all disabled children.[2] To the extent it accomplishes this ambitious goal, it provides a significant rehabilitative mechanism for disabled children, including those with legal or familial problems of the type discussed in the previous three chapters. It also creates a major forensic opportunity for clinicians who are versed in educational and developmental psychology.

For these reasons, we include this brief chapter on the IDEA in the discussion of children and families. After describing the genesis and structure of the IDEA, this chapter explores some of the ways in which an evaluation might proceed under the IDEA.

17.02. The Impetus for the IDEA

CASE STUDY 17.1

Bob, a 13-year-old, has become severely withdrawn in the last year. His grades have been declining steadily, he is starting to skip school, and when the teacher calls on him in class, he responds rudely or not at all. Most recently he pushed over a desk and stalked out of the room when disciplined by the teacher. The teacher is worried that he may have an emotional disorder. She makes a referral to the special education department. If you are called in as a consultant, how would you conduct an evaluation of Bob? What legal strictures might be placed on your evaluation? What would the objectives of such an evaluation be?

In the preamble to the 1975 Act, Congress stated that there were "more than eight million handicapped children in the United States," over half of whom were not receiving an appropriate education, and more than one million of whom were excluded from the public school system entirely.[3] Therefore, Congress concluded, it is "in the national interest . . . to provide programs to meet the educational needs of handicapped children."[4]

Behind this rather conclusory pronouncement lay at least three related influences. The first was clear evidence that many of the institutions in which disabled children were then being housed were abominations. Hearings before the United States Senate featured professionals, parents, and children describing overcrowding, lack of staff, and inadequate treatment, as well as abuse.[5] For example, one educational psychology professional described an institution she visited as follows:

> [t]he evidence was overwhelming that corporal punishment was inflicted upon the residents by the staff . . . that the employees and the staff would physically strike the residents, that various restraints were used by way of straps, sheets, et cetera, completely without medical authorization or direction, that residents would be tied to chairs or tied to their beds for lengthy periods of time. Residents would be forced to sit in their own feces or urine for long periods of time and it goes on and on.[6]

Complementing the desire to provide alternatives to these institutions was research suggesting that disabled children could benefit from education.[7] As Neal and Kirp put it, "Once it became arguable that such children were capable of being educated, it became virtually impossible to mount a politically palatable argument denying handicapped children's claim to education."[8] This research, along with other studies showing that testing designed to determine educational abilities was often racially discriminatory,[9] also suggested an analogy between disabled children and once powerless minority groups that had since benefited from federal legislation.[10]

A final influence on Congress was the more general push to "mainstream" into the community *all* those with mental disability. Beginning in the early 1960s, with the advent of federally funded community mental health centers, this "community-first" movement was premised on several assumptions: (1) that treatment in the community is less of a deprivation of liberty than placement in a segregated institution; (2) that integrated treatment, habilitation and education within the community is at least as effective, if not more so, than institutional services; (3) that community-oriented services places the disabled person closer to family and friends who provide emotional sustenance; (4) that community programs give

the disabled person practice at and "role models" for dealing with the rest of the world; and (5) that exposure of the disabled to the nondisabled accelerates the former group's acceptance by the latter.[11] By fostering education in the "least restrictive alternative," within the public school system, the IDEA was meant to accommodate these various goals.

17.03.   The Structure of the IDEA

The IDEA is implemented through provision of federal funds to those states that agree to abide by its essential provisions (by 1995, all 50 states had so agreed). As the United States Supreme Court stated in *Honig v. Doe*,[12] the IDEA "confers upon disabled students an enforceable substantive right to public education in participating States . . . and conditions federal financial assistance upon States' compliance with substantive and procedural goals of the Act." These substantive and procedural goals are the subject of this section.

(a)   Substantive Coverage

The IDEA guarantees to all children with disability a "free appropriate education," as well as "related services," in the "least restrictive environment." The following discussion fleshes out the meaning of these various phrases.

(1)   Disability

The original Education Act referred to "handicapped children." In 1990, along with changing the statute's name to the Individuals with Disabilities Education Act, Congress replaced statutory references to handicapped children with the term "children with disabilities." Under the Act as amended in 1990, children with the following disabilities are covered if, "by reason thereof" they require "special education and related services"[13]: mental retardation, autism, "serious emotional disturbance," learning disabilities (including perceptual handicaps, brain injury, minimal brain dysfunction, dyslexia, and development aphasia[14]), and a number of physical disabilities, including deafness, visual handicaps, and orthopedic handicaps. Serious emotional disturbance is defined in the federal regulations as a severe condition of long-term duration caused by (1) an inability to learn not explicable by intellectual, sensory, or health factors; (2) an inability to build or sustain satisfactory interpersonal relationships; (3) inappropriate behavior or feelings; (4) pervasive unhappiness or depression; or (5) a tendency to develop physical symptoms or fears associated with personal or school problems.[15]

From this definition of disability, it is clear that Congress sought to extend educational rights to a wide variety of disabled children. At the same time, learning problems that result from "conduct disorders," family dysfunction, or psychosocial stressors generally will not form the basis for eligibility under the IDEA. State and local regulations often elaborate on these somewhat vague categorizations.

(2)   Free and Appropriate Education

Congress defined free and appropriate education (FAPE) to mean "special education" and "related services" that are provided at "public expense, supervision and direction"; conform with the standards of the State educational agency; and "include an appropriate preschool, elementary, or secondary education in the State involved."[16] Case law has elaborated on this tautological definition, although not very helpfully. The leading case in this regard is *Board of Education v. Rowley*,[17] in which the Supreme Court rejected the lower court's definition of FAPE as "an opportunity to achieve full potential commensurate with the opportunity provided to other children."[18] Rather, the Court held, the statute merely requires free "personalized instruction with sufficient support services to permit the child to benefit educationally from that instruction."[19] According to the majority in *Rowley*, the special education need not maximize or try to maximize a disabled child's potential, or even provide resources sufficient to allow the child to reach a level proportionate to that reached by other children. Rather, in the Court's words, it need merely provide "some benefit" to the child.

Such a holding may seem narrow, but it reflects the reality of the school system. Tradition-

ally, the public schools have not been obligated to maximize the potential of nondisabled children or even ensure that they reach a certain proportion of their potential. Thus, requiring such goals for those with disability would undermine the normal approach to education, which places students in grades according to general criteria such as age and minimal performance rather than individualizing the learning experience.[20]

Furthermore, *Rowley* does require *some* effort at providing meaningful education. The lower courts have generally interpreted that decision liberally. For instance, in *Polk v. Central Susequehanna*,[21] the Third Circuit held that the "some" benefit language in *Rowley* "connotes an amount of benefit greater than mere trivial advancement." Similarly, other courts have concluded that, as construed in *Rowley*, the IDEA requires "satisfactory or meaningful progress" toward a child's individual educational goals.[22] Finally, some states seem to have gone beyond *Rowley* by requiring that disabled children obtain the same "educational opportunity" as nondisabled children, which may mean that the former group must be provided with resources sufficient to realize the same degree of their potential as is generally achieved by the latter group.[23]

(3)   Related Services

Children who are eligible to receive special education under the IDEA are also entitled to "related services." The IDEA includes under this rubric services "required to assist a child with a disability to benefit from special education," including "developmental, corrective, and other supportive services . . . psychological services . . . therapeutic recreation, social work services, counseling services [and] rehabilitation counseling and medical services" (the latter to be provided "for diagnostic and evaluation purposes only").[24] In *Irving Independent School District v. Tatro*,[25] the Supreme Court interpreted this provision to require "only those services necessary to aid a handicapped child to benefit from a special education." Thus, for instance, whether psychological services must be provided by the school district depends on whether they are "necessary" to allow the student to function in the classroom. At the same time, *Tatro* held that medical services that *are* "necessary" to provide an educational benefit must be provided even if they go beyond providing a diagnostic or evaluative function.

(4) Least Restrictive Environment: Mainstreaming

The most dramatic aspect of the IDEA is its command to educate disabled children with nondisabled children. The original Education Act stated that

> special classes, separate schooling or other removal of handicapped children from the regular educational environment [should] occur only when the nature or severity of the handicap is such that education in regular classes with the use of supplementary aids and services cannot be achieved satisfactorily."[26]

Although this language was already relatively strong, the 1990 amendments to the Act again emphasized that "mainstreaming" is a priority.[27] The drafters of the amendments probably were reacting to research showing that at least three-quarters of the children covered by the Act were still being educated in separate classes.[28] In a study of one school district, for instance, only between 3% and 7% of the students with disability were assigned to regular academic classes, with mainstreaming occurring only in such subjects as art, music, and physical education.[29]

While this resistance to mainstreaming may stem from prejudice and misunderstanding, it could also be the result of good-faith concerns on the part of school districts that placing children with disabilities in the classroom will disrupt both their education and the education of nondisabled students. Furthermore, of course, mainstreaming can be an expensive proposition to the extent it requires additional teaching staff in each regular classroom as well as teachers for special education classes. Finally, the "benefits" of mainstreaming are not always apparent; indeed, even commentators supportive of the IDEA have suggested that perhaps only those classrooms which are truly "integrated" can help overcome stereotyping and improve everyone's learning experience.[30]

The courts have been sensitive to the tension between these concerns and the statute's language to varying degrees. Although the Supreme Court has not yet addressed the issue, the lower courts

have produced two different tests for deciding whether the school district has complied with the IDEA's mainstreaming requirement. One test appears to lean toward favoring the school district's recommendations, whatever they may be, while the other seems more supportive of pro-mainstreaming decisions.

The first test was articulated by the Sixth Circuit in *Rockner v. Walter*.[31] Rockner involved a moderately mentally retarded nine-year-old boy with an IQ below 50 and a mental age of two to three. The school district sought to place him in a "segregated" county school exclusively for mentally disabled children because it believed that he would not receive any benefit from placement in a regular school. Although the parents agreed that their child could not be fully mainstreamed, they challenged the school district's recommendation because it provided *no* contact with the child's nondisabled peers.[32] The Sixth Circuit did not resolve this dispute (which was eventually settled out of court). It did, however, articulate a two-prong test for determining whether the mainstreaming requirement is met. The first question is whether the school district's proposed placement is "appropriate" under the Act, which merely requires, under *Rowley*, that the proposed placement provides "some educational benefit" to the disabled child. If so, and if the school district's proposal involves segregated placement, the second question is "whether the services which make that placement superior could be feasibly provided in a non-segregated setting."[33]

Although the second prong appears to support a mainstreaming argument, the court's discussion of "feasibility" emphasized that some children must be segregated, because they will not benefit from mainstreaming, will receive better education with segregation, or will be disruptive if mainstreamed. Furthermore, the court concluded that cost is a factor that may be considered because excessive spending on one child with disabilities can deprive other children with disabilities of a free appropriate education.

The second test for determining whether mainstreaming is required was first articulated by the Fifth Circuit in *Daniel R.R. v. State Board of Education*.[34] The child in the *Daniel* case had Down Syndrome; at the age of six his developmental age was between two and three years old. The parents wanted him to spend a half day in a segregated special education class and a half day in a regular prekindergarten class. The school district initially agreed to the placement. However, after a few months the school district decided that the child required too much constant individual attention by the teacher and her aide, to the detriment of the nondisabled students. Furthermore, the school district believed that the child was not benefitting from the regular classroom placement.

In resolving this case, the Fifth Circuit rejected the *Rockner* test as inimical to the policies underlying the IDEA. Instead, it adopted its own two-prong test. According to the *Daniel* test, the court must first determine whether education in a regular classroom, with supplemental aids and services, can be achieved satisfactorily. If so, the school district must mainstream the child in the regular classroom. If not, the school district may place the child in special classes or remove the child from regular education. Even in the latter situation, however, the school district must still mainstream the child to the maximum extent appropriate.

This test appears on its face to be more supportive of mainstreaming than the *Rockner* formulation because it starts from a presumption in favor of mainstreaming, whereas the latter test, in effect, puts the burden on the plaintiff to show that a segregated placement is inappropriate. Whether there is in fact a significant difference between the two tests is an open question, however. For instance, in construing the first prong of *Daniel's* test (as to whether a child can be educated satisfactorily in a regular classroom), a subsequent decision by another circuit held that school boards may consider the comparative benefits of "mainstreaming" versus separating the child, the effect of the child on the education of other children in the classroom, and the costs of the supplemental aids and services necessary to accommodate the "mainstreamed" child.[35] It may also be noteworthy that, in *Daniel* itself, the court refused to grant relief to the plaintiffs.

(b)   Procedures under the Act

The IDEA creates a several-stage process for deciding whether it applies. It begins with identify-

ing children who may have disabilities, proceeds with developing an education plan for those who are so identified, and establishes several mechanisms for reviewing the child's educational progress. The essential elements of this process are described below.

(1)   Identification of Children with Disability

Under the IDEA, a participating state and, in turn, each of its local education agencies (LEA) must identify, locate, and evaluate "all children residing in the state who are handicapped, regardless of the severity of their handicap, and who are in need of special education and related services."[36] If a child has been identified as being potentially handicapped,

> [a]n LEA must provide written notice to parents in each of the following situations: if it identifies their child as handicapped, evaluates the child for determination of a handicapping condition, proposes to change the child's identification or evaluation, refuses to initially identify and evaluate, or subsequently refuses to reidentify and reevaluate the child.[37]

In addition, each state must ensure that education agency personnel, as well as parents and volunteers, receive in-service training that will assist them in identifying and evaluating children with special educational needs.[38]

(2)   Evaluation of the Child: The Individual Education Plan

Once identified, each child is evaluated by a "multidisciplinary team," which must include at least one teacher or specialist knowledgable about the area of the child's suspected disability (e.g., an occupational or physical therapist, medical specialist, or school psychologist), as well as the child's teacher or potential teacher, the child's parents or guardians, and "whenever appropriate," the child.[39] Parents were included on this committee to act as a check on administrators and professionals who might overlook special needs of the child, but they often do not take advantage of this opportunity or are ignored by the rest of the team.[40]

The primary objective of the team and the evaluation is to develop an individual education plan (IEP) for the child. The IEP must contain the following elements:

(A) a statement of the present levels of educational performance of such child, (B) a statement of annual goals, including short-term instructional objectives, (C) a statement of the specific educational services to be provided to such child, and the extent to which such child will be able to participate in regular educational programs, (D) the projected date for initiation and anticipated duration of such services, and (E) appropriate objective criteria and evaluation procedures and schedules for determining, on at least an annual basis, whether instructional objectives are being achieved.[41]

Every child eligible under the IDEA must have an IEP.

The original Act covered only children between the ages of 6 and 21. In 1986, the Act was amended to extend coverage to children below the age of 6. For these children, participating states must set up a system of early intervention, including family counseling, home visits, and diagnostic and evaluative medical services. The state must also develop an individualized family service plan (IFSP), which is similar to an IEP but focuses more on the needs of the family as a whole rather than the individual child.[42]

The evaluation that produces the IEP or IFSP must conform to certain specifications. As already mentioned, the evaluation must be performed by a "multidisciplinary team." Further, evaluation materials and procedures must be selected and administered so as to avoid racial or cultural discrimination; thus, for instance, procedures must be administered in the child's native language, unless it clearly is not feasible to do so.[43] Finally, no single procedure can be the sole criterion for determining an appropriate educational program for the child[44]; the IDEA specifically provides that IQ tests may not form the only basis for an evaluation.[45] Thus, "[p]lacement decisions should not be based on tests alone, but should include at least one other evaluation source, such as a teacher's observation of the child's classroom performance."[46]

(3)   Review Procedures

There are several layers of review of the identification and evaluation process. First, if the parents

are dissatisfied with the evaluation, they can ask for an independent educational evaluation (IEE). The school can either pay for this evaluation or request a hearing from the LEA as to the adequacy of its initial evaluation. If it loses at this hearing, it must pay for an IEE. If it wins, the parents can still obtain an IEE at their expense.[47] This administrative procedure was designed to place "more systematic pressure on school systems, put handicapped children on an educational par with nonhandicapped students, and lead to uniformity of treatment among handicapped children."[48] Second, if the administrative process finds against them, parents are entitled to take the issue to the courts, and are awarded attorney's fees if they prevail.[49] Third, even if the parties agree on the IEP, the child "must be reevaluated at least every three years to insure that [he or she is] receiving the appropriate education resources."[50]

(4)   Disciplinary Procedures

After a disabled child has been placed in a regular classroom, the question arises as to whether the school's discipline code, established for all students, can be applied to that child. Specifically, if a disciplinary sanction conflicts with the IEP, how is the conflict to be resolved?[51] Three Supreme Court cases provide guidance on this issue.

The first two cases deal with minimum procedures in *any* disciplinary case. *Wood v. Strickland*[52] held that education is "a right of property and liberty," and thus is protected by the Fourteenth Amendment's prohibition of life, liberty or property "without due process of law." Accordingly, "a student who is to be expelled and deprived of an education, albeit temporarily, must be accorded due process." *Goss v. Lopez*[53] elaborated on the specific requirements of due process in this context by holding that "suspension," limited to ten days, may only be imposed after the student is given an oral or written notice of the charges, an explanation of the evidence that the authorities have, and an opportunity to present his or her side of the story. When expulsion (i.e., suspension of more than ten days) is involved, the student is entitled to an opportunity to secure counsel; the right to call, confront, and cross examine witnesses; and the right to have the case heard by an impartial hearing officer. Finally, when the suspended individual poses a threat to persons, property, or the education of others, the person may be immediately removed, but notice and an informal hearing should follow as soon as practicable.

Against the backdrop of these cases, the Supreme Court decided *Honig v. Doe*,[54] involving disciplinary action against two disabled children. One child was involved in a physical assault; the other was allegedly engaged in extortion. In both cases, the relevant school district first temporarily suspended the child, then proposed to exclude him permanently and extended the suspension pending the expulsion proceedings. The lower courts held that these latter actions violated the IDEA, specifically the provision that requires the school district to keep the child in his current placement pending review of its decisions on changes in placement (the "stay put" provision).[55] The Supreme Court agreed with this finding. It held that schools may use normal disciplinary procedures in temporarily suspending disabled students for up to 10 days. Further, longer removal of a student can be accomplished where the district and the parents can agree on an interim placement pending a review of the student's placement. In the absence of parental consent, however, the school district seeking expulsion and new placement must convince a court that the child's present placement is inappropriate under the IDEA and the child's IEP. In the meantime, the child is to remain in the school. According to the Court, the "stay put" provision "effectively creates a presumption in favor of the child's current placement which school officials can overcome only by showing that maintaining the child in his or her current placement is substantially likely to result in injury either to himself or herself, or to others."[56]

As a result of the latter holding, which contemplates a full-blown court hearing and a finding of dangerousness, disabled students may be accorded more due process than other students before they can be permanently removed from the school system (although recent changes to IDEA make the procedure more flexible). At the same time, when suspension for less than ten days is involved, the disabled student is not immune from ordinary disciplinary procedures. Ellis and Geller conclude that these rulings should encourage administrators to remain "in close contact with the group of people responsible for the student receiving an appropriate education," and to establish a code of behavior that is fair to both disabled and nondisabled students.[57]

17.04. Clinical Evaluation under the Act

The typical evaluation under the IDEA will need to address several issues: (1) Does the child have one of the listed disabilities that requires special educational efforts? (2) If so, what would be an appropriate education (i.e., what instructional methods would provide some benefit to the child by promoting educational progress)? (3) What related services are necessary to ensure this education occurs? and (4) To what extent can it be carried out in a regular classroom without endangering or disrupting the other students?

Answering these types of questions involves a wide-ranging assessment. As noted earlier, the IDEA imposes several strictures on the evaluation process: It must be multidisciplinary, it must use more than one procedure, and it must avoid racially or culturally discriminatory practices. The regulations implementing the statute also mandate that test and other evaluation materials be validated for the specific purpose for which they are used and administered by a person trained to do so.[58] In cases involving a specific learning disability, they also provide for additional team members, classroom observations, a special written report, and a specific finding that the child's disability is not in fact another type of disability.[59] Beyond these minimum requirements imposed by statutes and regulations, an evaluation under the IDEA should include assessment of several specific skills areas, comprehensive information gathering, and testing.[60] These components of the evaluation are discussed below, followed by suggestions about reports and testimony called for by the IDEA.

(a) Specific Skills to Assess

One review of the assessment process under IDEA lists the following factors that should be considered in devising an IEP:

- In what physical environment does the child learn best?

- What is useful, debilitating, or neutral about the way the child approaches the task?
- Can the student hold multiple pieces of information in memory and then act upon them?
- How does increasing or slowing the speed of instruction impact upon the child's accuracy?
- What processing mechanisms are being taxed in any given task?
- How does this student interact with a certain teacher style?
- With whom has the child been successful? What about the person seems to have contributed to the child's success?
- What is encouraging to the child? What is discouraging?
- How does manipulating the mode of teaching (e.g., visual or auditory presentation) affect the child's performance?[61]

Generally, there are at least five traits or skills that the evaluator should consider assessing in any evaluation under the IDEA. The most obvious evaluation area is intelligence. As noted previously and discussed further below, the IDEA makes clear that this trait cannot be assessed solely by a standardized test and that if such a test is used, it must be appropriately normed. A second area that requires assessment is language and communication skills. These can also be evaluated with various standardized tests. Again, however, such tests may not be sensitive to everyday communication problems, which are better explored through direct conversation with the child. Third, perceptual abilities—visual, auditory, motor, and "attentional"—should be examined, using tests or interviews. Fourth, academic achievement, in terms of reading, writing, and mathematics, may need to be examined. Finally, of particular relevance to readers of this book, behavioral and emotional deficits and their causes need to be assessed using the usual techniques. Addressing all these issues should provide the examiner with sufficient information to answer the questions posed by the IDEA.

(b) Information Gathering

Given the wide-ranging nature of the skills to be assessed, several sources of information may be important to an evaluation under the IDEA. One

such source is school records, if they exist. These records might describe changes in behavior, attendance, or grades that help identify emotional problems. At the same time, it should be remembered that *most* students experience difficulties at particular times in their educational careers; for instance, changes in class performance may merely stem from beginning middle school, which is often accompanied by differences in length and intensity of assignments.

A second source of information is student work, both on paper and in the classroom. Many teachers maintain portfolios for each student which can be skimmed by the evaluator. Observation of the student in the classroom is crucial. It is important to make such observations at different times and in different classes. If the observer is interested in monitoring certain behavior, he or she may simply keep a log of occurrences, look for specific behavioral events and tally their frequency, or use checklists or rating scales developed for the purpose.[62] Generally, it is important to study the student's "ecology," a construct to which we referred in previous chapters [see, e.g., § 14.06, which provides a discussion, in the context of delinquency evaluations, that is very relevant here]. As Wallace, Larsen, and Elksinin state: "[a]n evaluation that fails to consider a student's ecology as a potential causative factor in reported academic or behavioral disorders may be ignoring the very elements that require modification before we can realistically expect changes in that student's behavior."[63]

Of course, interviewing the relevant parties is crucial (indeed, as noted earlier, involving the parents in the evaluation process is required by law). Teachers and parents should probably be consulted before interviewing the child, to help pinpoint specific learning deficits or cultural differences. Hoy and Gregg suggest that the viewpoints of these various individuals be compared in a number of domains, including (1) perception of the primary problem and its cause, (2) the attempts that have been made to solve or address the problem, (3) recent changes in the problem's severity, and (4) student strengths and weaknesses.[64]

Interviews with the child can be conducted in a number of different ways, times, and places. If the child's ability to perform certain tasks is at issue, it can be directly assessed through asking the child to perform the task, in small steps or all at once. Or the assessment can be more "dynamic," involving

> modeling the task for the student, giving the student prompts or cues as he or she tries to solve a given problem, asking what the student is thinking while working on the problem, sharing on the part of the examiner to establish the task's relevance to experience and concepts beyond the test situation, and giving praise or encouragement.[65]

This interaction not only provides information about how the student thinks but also gives clues as to how the student learns best (e.g., with praise or criticism, in crowded or empty rooms, visually or tactilely). Various methods of interviewing the child are discussed in more detail elsewhere.[66]

(c)   Testing

Testing may be more useful in this context than in many of the other situations described in this book because the forensic issue centers on present functioning (rather than past or future functioning) and requires an assessment of specific dysfunctions that such tests can often provide. At the same time, many educators object to standardized tests that are not normed for the target population, a concern that, as noted previously, has found its way into the regulations implementing the IDEA. Along the same lines, it is well-known that obtaining "correct" answers on some tests requires having specific culturally based knowledge to which some members of society are not privy.[67]

Thus, tests much be carefully selected. The skill areas to be assessed, the similarity between the test's tasks and classroom tasks, the reliability and the validity of the test, and (when the test is norm-referenced) the norm group's resemblance to the student are all important considerations. Even when these and other considerations are taken into account, testing may be better at identifying deficits than at providing information relevant to instructional strategies. As one review put it, parents and teachers are often frustrated by "assessment . . . information that more or less states, 'The student is having problems.'"[68] They

are interested in an educational plan, not a diagnosis.

(d)   Report and Testimony

Recall the four questions raised by the IDEA. The first issue, whether the child is disabled, will depend on whether the child is diagnosable with one of the disorders identified in the IDEA. The clinician or team writing a report or testifying in support of special education should attend to these diagnoses and distinguish the child's problems from "conduct disorders" and other problems arising solely from social maladjustment. The "appropriate education" issue is even more amorphous because legally it merely requires a plan that provides the child with "some benefit" or "satisfactory progress." Perhaps the best approach is to identify the best possible educational plan and then indicate variations of this plan that are feasible and will still promote progress. Similarly, defining "related services" and which of these are "necessary" to make the educational plan work is probably best accomplished through identifying the ideal situation and backup plans. Addressing the "appropriate education" and "related services" issues may make clear whether education in a regular classroom will work, but this point too needs to be specifically addressed given the Act's preference for mainstreaming. Finally, given *Honig,* the clinician or multisciplinary team should address the extent to which education in the classroom will be disruptive or dangerous to other students.

It would no doubt be tempting, after a comprehensive evaluation such as that described above, to pronounce in the evaluation report that the child is (or is not) "disabled," and if the former, that the child "needs" a particular type of education, that a given array of services are "necessary" to ensure the education will take place, and that the educational and related services can (or cannot) be "satisfactorily" provided in the regular classroom. Indeed, it is likely that schools and parents will exert considerable pressure on the evaluation team to produce just such a report. Thus, our usual injunction against giving into the lure of ultimate-issue conclusions is important here as well. If such conclusory language is considered important, perhaps because local regulations demand it, it should only be used after the evaluation's results, and alternative interpretations of those results, are canvassed. Phrases such as "some benefit," "necessary," and "satisfactory" are legal terms susceptible to multiple interpretations, and the clinician should not pretend that he or she knows what they mean.

Bibliography

Board of Education v. Rowley, 458 U.S. 176 (1982).

C. Hoy & N. Gregg, Assessment: The Special Educator's Role 46 (1994).

48(1) Law and Contemporary Problems (1985) (this issue consists solely of articles about the Education Act).

Christopher Slobogin, *Treatment of the Mentally Disabled: Rethinking the Community-First Idea,* 69 Nebraska Law Review 413 (1990).

H. Lee Swanson & Billy L. Watson, Education and Psychological Assessment of Exceptional Children (2d ed. 1989).

Gerald Wallace, Steven C. Larsen, & Linoa K. Elksinin, Educational Assessment of Learning Problems: Testing for Teaching (1992).

Betsy B. Waterman, *Assessing Children for the Presence of A Disability,* NICHCY News Digest 1 (1994) (disseminated by the National Information Center for Children and Youth with Disabilities, P.O. Box 1492, Washington, DC 20013-1492).

PART V

Communicating with the Courts

CHAPTER EIGHTEEN

Consultation, Report Writing, and Expert Testimony

18.01. Introduction

The legal system's use of reports and testimony from mental health expert witnesses dates back to well before the beginning of the 20th century.[1] Since that time the courts' reliance on such witnesses has steadily increased. Today, according to one estimate,[2] psychiatrists, psychologists, and social workers are involved in as many as one million legal cases a year. Further, there is every indication that this trend will continue for the foreseeable future.

As Chapter 1 indicated, the influx of mental health professionals in the courtroom is viewed with cynicism and doubt by a considerable number of detractors. To some extent, this antipathy stems from the belief that mental health professionals too often try to answer legal questions for which there are no good behavioral science answers[3] or, worse, are merely selling their testimony to the highest bidder.[4] But it also flows from the fact that even when clinicians have something useful to say and are eager to maintain their integrity, their message is often obscured or confused. Their reports are perceived as conclusory and filled with jargon, their testimony as hard to follow (on direct) and befuddled (on cross).[5]

Forensic knowledge of the type provided in the previous chapters will be virtually useless if it is not organized and presented in a manner that will be helpful to legal consumers (lawyers, judges, jurors) and if its purveyors are not prepared to endure the sometimes harsh scrutiny that the adversary process demands. Accordingly, the forensic clinician needs to develop skills in consultation, forensic report writing, and delivery of oral testimony. Lawyers too need to develop skills, parallel to those the clinician must have. As Bonnie has noted:

> The bench and the bar are ultimately responsible for improving the administration of justice. If judges and juries are confused or misled by expert testimony, this usually means there has been poor lawyering. If experts give conclusory testimony, encompassing so-called ultimate issue issues—and fail to explain the bases for their opinions—the fault lies with the bench and bar, not with the experts. If forensic evaluators do not have access to the same information and reach different opinions for this reason, the fault lies with the legal system, not with the experts.[6]

In short, both clinicians and lawyers need to do better at translating clinical knowledge into legally useful form.

In this chapter, we explore formal and informal communications between the clinician and agents of the court, in particular examining the social psychology of the courtroom and the mechanics for presenting testimony.[7] The first two sections below deal with the preliminary contacts between the clinician and the legal system. The following section provides suggestions for the preparation of written reports. The final two sections deal with various aspects of testimony in court.

A principal theme of this chapter is that, above all, *clinicians should be effective advocates for their data,* whether or not that makes them effective advocates for the party that calls them to court. Because much of the content of this chapter deals with ways of coping with the courtroom and the adversarial system, readers may be misled into thinking we are simply coaching clinicians on how to "win" for their side. That is not our intention. For instance, throughout this chapter we recommend full disclosure of data (including that which limits or may be inconsistent with primary formulations) and discourage testifying in terms of ultimate legal issues. Both of these postures stem from the belief that clinicians should endeavor to remain neutral with respect to the policy objectives of the party who calls them to testify. At the same time, effective communication requires knowing the "system." Defending one's data in any forum requires familiarity with the rules, roles, and procedures that one can expect to encounter, and that is what we purport to address here.

PROBLEM 18.1

Read the Timmy Gonz-Jones custody report in § 19.12. Assume you are participating in a pretrial conference as either the psychologist who wrote the report or the lawyer representing Mr. Jones, who has called the psychologist as an expert in that case. How would you prepare for testimony? How should direct examination proceed? What should the lawyer tell the mental health professional? What should the mental health professional tell the lawyer?

Now assume the mental health professional has testified on direct examination. How should he or she respond to the following questions on cross-examination? Should the lawyer object to any questions?

"Doctor, I'd like to start with some questions about your qualifications and evaluation procedure. You are not a medical doctor, correct? Isn't it true that Dr. Cowan prescribed Ritalin for Timmy? And isn't it true that you would have no way of knowing whether this was the correct treatment for Timmy? Even if you have some idea, the fact remains that, if medication rather than therapy is the best treatment for Timmy, you don't have the expertise to tell us, correct? Thus, your ability to tell us what is in Timmy's best interests is somewhat circumscribed, correct?

"As to your evaluation procedure, you stated during *voir dire* that you interviewed several people, including all the parties, and conducted testing, specifically the Minnesota Multiphasic Personality Inventory [MMPI]. Did you do a Thematic Apperception Test? A Rorschach? A Wechsler Adult Intelligence Scale [WAIS]? A Bender–Gestalt? And you call this evaluation comprehensive? Nor did you do a home visit, which is a standard part of any custody evaluation, did you? So you never really saw Timmy in his everyday environment did you?

"Doctor, I'd now like to turn to your suggestion that Mr. Jones is the best parent for Timmy. Isn't it true that, all else being equal, fathers are generally not the best parent? Do you have any research to back up the belief that fathers are, all else being equal, as good parents as mothers? Doctor do you recognize this book? [Shows witness this book.] Is it an authority in the field? In § 16.03(b), Melton et al. state that the studies that tend to show fathers are good parents 'all . . . rely upon interviews with single fathers without direct observation of father–child interaction. Their protrayal of family life is thus inherently subjective and, quite likely, positively skewed.' Further, the book says, the fathers in these studies 'were contacted through informal, word-of-mouth sources, advertisements or, on occasion, single-parent support groups (such as Parents without Partners), and thus probably reflect a select, highly motivated and involved sample.' Thus, the research is highly flawed, is it not?

"Turning to Mr. Jones in particular, let's look at how good a parent he would be compared to Ms. Gonz. First, isn't it true he was arrested for stealing from his employer? Was Ms. Gonz ever arrested for a criminal offense?

"Second, isn't it true that Mr. Jones is an alcoholic? Does Ms. Gonz have a drinking problem? Isn't it true that once an alcoholic, always an alcoholic—that these people must fight to keep from drinking? And isn't it true that Mr. Jones has never sought help for this problem until recently, indeed after this custody battle began? Would you be surprised to learn that Mr. Jones is drinking again?

"Third, isn't it true that Mr. Jones faked his answers on the MMPI? I read from your report: 'Mr. Jones may have minimized his difficulties or shortcomings, in an attempt to portray himself in a positive way.' That means he faked his answers, right? At the same time, did you not describe Ms. Gonz's responses as 'honest and straightforward?'

"Fourth, isn't it true that Mr. Jones thinks that a major reason his marriage with Ms. Gonz failed was the fact that they married after only knowing each other for ten weeks? Yet isn't it also true that Mr. Jones become engaged to his current wife after only one month? Do you think Mr. Jones learns from his mistakes?

"Now let's talk about Ms. Gonz's strengths and her supposed problems. First, you don't think Ms. Gonz is a bad parent, correct? Indeed, you state that she is creative and loving, correct? She has never abused the child, correct? Timmy has always lived with her, correct? And it would be wrenching to take him away from her at this point, correct? Especially, now that he has a baby brother whom he loves, correct?

"Doctor, it appears that you think her biggest problem is her inability to follow through and get things done, correct? One reason for that conclusion is her MMPI test, correct? Could you show me the scale that led to your conclusion in this regard? [The Ma scale, on which Ms. Gonz received a 27.] Now isn't it true that Mr. Jones's performance on this scale looks pretty similar? [Mr. Jones received a 25 on this scale.] We're talking a difference of two points on a 50-point scale right? Doctor, do you recognize this book as an authority? [Showing the witness Jim Butcher et al., THE MMPI IN COURT (1994).] On page 269 of this book, there is a table that seems to state that Ms. Gonz's results means she is less able to follow through than 92% of those tested, but it also indicates that, based on his test results, Mr. Jones is less able to follow through than 85% of those tested. There's not much difference between the two, is there?

"Another reason you seem to think Ms. Gonz has difficulty in getting things done is that she hasn't followed through on appointments and therapy, correct? Yet she has never been late for an appointment with you, has she doctor? As to these appointments with the three therapists, isn't it true that one encounter ended because Mr. Jones, not Ms. Gonz, wanted to terminate the relationship? And isn't it true that one of the other encounters was terminated by Ms. Gonz because no one had told her that Timmy was getting Ritalin? Doesn't this show concern, rather than inattention, on her part?

"As to Ms. Gonz's failure to keep appointments with the last therapist, and with Timmy's teachers, isn't it true that one reason for this could be the fact that Ms. Gonz is a single mother, with a job? Isn't it true that, since the last therapist, her mother has moved in with her? This is likely to mean Ms. Gonz will have fewer child-care burdens, correct?

"Doctor, would you like to change your opinion at this time?"

18.02.   Preliminary Consultations

Ideally, the groundwork for a forensic evaluation, report, or testimony is laid through a series of consultations between the clinician and the attorney (or court) responsible for the referral. The primary tasks during the initial contact are clarification of issues [discussed in detail in § 4.05(b)], and sharing of information [see § 3.04(b)]. As the evaluation proceeds and once it is completed, the clinician has various options in terms of reporting results and providing consultation on other types of issues. These various stages are discussed here.

(a)   Clarification of Issues

When a forensic evaluation is requested, the clinician must make sure to verify the legal issues to be addressed. Too often, a brief, informal call from a court clerk is followed by a written court order for evaluation that is unclear. Or a court routinely uses dated order forms that are overly restrictive or vague in light of what the referring judge intends. In either case, amended orders may need to be requested. An initial referral from a private attorney can be just as ambiguous. Brodsky and Poythress have noted:

> As elementary as it may seem to do so, attorneys do not always tell the mental health professional in clear terms the focus of the examination and testimony to be provided. Attorneys may confuse the different legal issues, or they may mistakenly assume that one examination will suffice for a variety of purposes.[8]

There are several reasons for clarifying the issues. The most fundamental one is to make sure the clinician has the clinical and forensic skills necessary to undertake the referral. Assuming so, a second obvious reason for ascertaining the evaluation's scope is to ensure that the proper topics are probed during the evaluation. Third, the type of evaluation determines the type of notification that must be given the client; failure to give proper notification may trigger legal or ethical rules restricting the admissibility of the information gathered [see §§ 4.02(f), 4.05(d)]. Fourth, even apparently clear referrals may have hidden agendas. For example, an order for an inpatient examination of competency to stand trial may actually have been requested because (1) the sheriff wants to reduce overcrowding in the jail, (2) the defendant is considered a suicide risk and is thought to require civil commitment, (3) the defendant has medical problems for which the county does not wish to pay, or (4) the attorney is using the referral for tactical delay. Careful clarification of the bases for the referral may save time in the evaluation process or obviate it altogether.

The clinician also needs to clarify other matters. Even if competent to perform the evaluation, the clinician should alert the attorney to the limits of his or her expertise on the referral questions. Legal professionals may approach mental health professionals with mistaken assumptions about what is possible in a clinical evaluation. To avoid any misunderstandings, the clinician should discuss the possible range of outcomes, as well as the procedures that will be used.

Finally, clinicians should indicate their posture with respect to testifying on ultimate legal issues. Based on prior experience, attorneys will probably expect clinicians to readily offer opinions or conclusions couched in ultimate legal language. Clinicians who intend (as we encourage in § 18.05) to deviate from the traditional posture should so advise lawyers, who can then decide whether to make another referral.

(b)   Sharing Information

Assuming the referral is accepted, information exchange becomes crucial. At the initial contact, most of the information will be in the referring party's possession. What current behavior or background information has prompted the referral? What prior records have been obtained or requested? Where is the client residing, and what

special arrangements, if any, must be made for the clinical evaluation? What other information sources should be contacted? What time constraints, if any, exist? Is a written report requested regardless of the outcome, or only if the clinical data are favorable to the attorney's case? Generally, these questions should all be answered at the initial contact stage.

Also at this stage, the clinician may begin to compile a list of information which the attorney or court can obtain for the evaluation. Criminal, psychiatric, medical, educational, and employment records are usually more easily obtained by the attorney (as personal representative of the client) or the court than by the clinician. Furthermore, some potentially useful information might be available only through discovery, subpoena, or private investigation, procedures only the attorney or court can initiate. If there appear to be time constraints for the examination, the clinician should suggest that the attorney request a continuance so that a proper evaluation can be completed.

Finally, it is also prudent at this point to discuss various practical issues. One is the clinician's availability in light of existing court schedules. Another, discussed in detail in § 5.05(a), is manner of payment.

(c)   Preliminary Report of Findings

Throughout, the clinician should keep the referring agency informed about the progress of the evaluation and whether additional information is needed. When the evaluation is completed, the next step depends on the referring agency. When the assessment is for an attorney, the examiner should generally offer an oral summary and let the attorney decide whether a written report is needed. When the referral originated with the court, on the other hand, usually a written report is prepared without preliminary oral communication of the findings.

Not uncommonly, the clinical evaluation will result in findings that suggest legal strategies other than those considered at the initial contact. For example, an evaluation of competency to stand trial may reveal that the individual has a chronic mental impairment that affected his or her competency to waive *Miranda* warnings [see § 7.03]. Similarly, an evaluation in a divorce/custody case may conclude that both partners are amenable to a mediated settlement, which would be less costly, both emotionally and financially, than proceeding to an adversary hearing [see § 16.02(b)(2)]. When alternative uses of the data appear viable, and the client agrees to them after proper explanation, the clinical findings may be revised to address the new legal issues.

At this preliminary stage, clinicians may also be able to give feedback that will assist attorneys in working more effectively with their clients.[9] Such advice can be particularly helpful when clients appear somewhat mentally disordered; attorneys may not be accustomed to working with such individuals and may feel frightened or uncomfortable around them. For example, clients with manic symptoms such as elated affect and pressured speech are sometimes extremely difficult to interview, given their rapid speech, poor transitions between topics, excessive emotionality, and movement that may be intimidating. In such cases, the attorney can be advised to impose structure during the interviews (e.g., ask brief, focused questions) and avoid showing fear of the clients' outbursts. Similarly, in cases in which intellectual impairment is mild but perhaps not obvious, clinicians can recommend the use of closed questions and simplistic language or the use of analogy (e.g., "The judge is like a referee or an umpire") to facilitate communication with the client about the case. Clinicians can also offer advice about the appropriate precautionary measures to be taken for recurring disturbances, such as epileptic seizures, and can warn attorneys or the court of the probable extent of trial delay should a seizure occur. Finally, examiners might comment on interactions between the client and the social–legal environment (e.g., relationships to family members, to the court, or to jail personnel) and suggest ways to improve the clients' coping skills while awaiting the resolutions of their cases.

18.03. Report Writing

Virtually all cases referred from a court and most referred from attorneys will result in the preparation of written reports. Reports of forensic evaluations differ in a number of important ways from reports prepared for use in traditional clinical settings. First, the recipients of the report will not be other mental health professionals but legal personnel and laypersons who are unfamiliar with clinical shortcuts in report writing; therefore, jargon should be kept to a minimum or explained. Second, the substance of the report is more likely to become public knowledge, as part of a court record, through word-of-mouth statements of courtroom spectators or through media coverage of court proceedings. Thus, special care must be taken to minimize any infringement on the privacy rights of persons mentioned in the report. Finally, and most important, the report and the clinician who writes it will, or at least should, receive close scrutiny during adversary negotiations or proceedings. A well-written report may obviate courtroom testimony. A poorly written report may become, in the hands of a skillful lawyer, an instrument to discredit and embarrass its author. Therefore, attention to detail and to the accuracy of information is required. All these issues are elucidated further below.

(a) Functions of a Forensic Report

The written report serves several important functions. It is, first of all, a professional record documenting that an evaluation has taken place. The nature of the evaluation and the extent of professional contacts with the client are memorialized through a summary of the contacts, investigative methods, and referrals to other professionals. Findings and limitations in the clinical data are also preserved in written form.

In addition, the act of creating the report forces the clinician to impose some organization on his or her data. Data are often gathered from widely diverse sources and may often be inconsistent. Drafting a report requires the examiner to weigh this information, find a theme that best integrates the various findings, consider alternatives, and recognize vulnerabilities. Organizing data and thoughts for the report also helps the mental health professional covertly prepare and rehearse the essence of any direct and cross-examination testimony that may be given.

A third function of the report, as noted previously, is to permit disposition without formal proceedings. A well-written, articulate report may satisfy both parties to the degree that stipulations to the written findings and conclusions are entered. It may also serve as a basis for informal negotiations, as in plea bargaining or out-of-court settlements in civil cases.

(b)   General Guidelines for Report Writing

There are no hard-and-fast rules for writing forensic reports, and substance and organization may vary, depending on the type of referral. However, several general guidelines appear applicable across many contexts.[10]

(1)   Separate Facts from Inferences

Factual information and descriptive material based on clinical observations should be presented separately from the theoretical and inferential formulations that link the clinical data to the legal referral question, with the former presented first. This organization allows the clinician to "build" a case, organizing the investigative data in a manner that invites the reader to reason along with the author. Furthermore, if the judge or jury wishes to consider and assimilate the examiner's data independently, this segregation facilitates the effort.

Regardless of the forensic issue it addresses, a report should always include certain items of information. In the order we usually follow, they are:

1. *Circumstances of the referral.* Identify the referral source, legal issues addressed, and circumstances leading to the clinical evaluation (e.g., a description of ongoing litigation in custody/divorce or criminal proceedings).
2. *Date and nature of clinical contacts.* This section would list chronologically the examiner's contacts with the person and describe the nature of the contact (e.g., interview, psychological testing, and family observation).
3. *Collateral data sources.* In this section, the clinician would identify sources of information other than the individual who was examined (e.g., third-party interviews; written material

such as academic, medical, or employment records; etc.).
4. *Relevant personal background information.* Historical information about the client relevant to the clinical formulation would be summarized here. This section might be extensive in some kinds of cases (e.g., a lengthy history of illness and treatment in a disability case) and extremely brief in others (e.g., an evaluation of competency to stand trial).
5. *Clinical findings.* This section would summarize the clinician's own observations, test results, and so forth. Observations about present mental functioning, or, when appropriate, statements of diagnosis, would be included here.
6. *Psychological–legal formulation.* In this section, the examiner would draw on information reported in the previous sections and integrate the data, using a logical or theoretical theme to indicate the possible relevance of the clinical material to the legal issue being decided.

Chapter 19 presents model reports in several forensic areas, each of which reflects variations in the use of this general format.

Some sections of the report may, on occasion, include two or more alternate summaries. Situations that would warrant this approach include (1) reports based on evaluations by a team (rather than an individual examiner), in which two or more team members have significantly different views about the data or the meaning of the data; and (2) evaluations in which there is conflicting factual information, such that assuming one set of facts leads to one formulation and assuming a different set of facts leads to a different one. In each of these situations, the report should carefully spell out the data and assumptions associated with each of the formulations or opinions presented. When appropriate, the examiner(s) may also address the level of confidence associated with each formulation. Generally, clinicians should avoid becoming embroiled over which of two or more factual situations is the "real" one; they should leave that controversy to the trier of fact.

(2)   Stay within the Scope of the Referral Question

As discussed in § 4.05(e), a referral for forensic evaluation is not a license to inquire into any aspect of the client's life or behavior. Admittedly, clinicians privately retained by counsel may have somewhat greater latitude in their examinations than mental health professionals working for the court, where a court order may specify limits of inquiry. In either case, however, examiners should confine themselves to inquiries legitimately raised by the referral source and should restrict the substance of their reports accordingly.

As obvious as this recommendation may seem, mental health professionals occasionally err by either (1) failing to address issues that have been raised in the referral or (2) offering gratuitous opinions on issues that have not been raised. McGarry's study of competency evaluations in Massachusetts documented the first type of error.[11] Of 106 reports audited, none spoke to the issue of the defendant's competency to stand trial, which was an explicit referral question in the court orders. We have anecdotally observed the second type of error. To provide just one example, a defendant was referred to a psychiatrist for evaluation of his mental state at the time of a crime. The following paraphrase fairly reproduces the examiner's written summary:

> It does not appear that Mr. S. was suffering from any psychosis at the time of the assault. He may have been under the influence of various drugs and alcoholic beverages, which he reported consuming at that time. There is no clinical basis for an insanity defense here. Mr. S. is one of the most dangerous persons I have ever examined; the only appropriate disposition would be a lengthy prison sentence.

Here the psychiatrist went beyond the referral question and made uninvited statements about disposition and sentencing. With these damning statements appended, it is unlikely that the defendant's attorney would have felt comfortable submitting the report to the court, even though parts of it (e.g., the defendant's drug history) would have been relevant in weighing culpability.

(3)   Avoid Information Over(and Under)kill

In preparing a written report, the clinician must make some decisions about the volume of information to be included. Any written report will be a distillation of essential material from a larger body of data. There are many schools of thought about this issue of data reduction, each of which has its costs and benefits. Individual preferences may dictate which philosophy a clinician will follow.

At one extreme are those who advocate very brief reports. These reports tend to be conclusory, with extensive data and justification excluded by design. The objective is to provide as little ammunition as possible for the cross-examining attorney. The problem with this approach is that the report cannot serve the documentation and organizational and efficiency objectives outlined in § 18.03(a). At the other extreme are those who encourage lengthy, overly detailed reports. Such reports "cover all bases" and usually leave the clinician an "out" from a tight situation in testimony. The problem with this type of report is that it may not be read or, if read, may not be understood.[12] Further, longer reports tend to include irrelevant detail, redundancies, or excessive equivocations, which may convey to the reader the impression of uncertainty or lack of self-confidence in the examiner.

For the written report to be useful, it should be brief enough that the attorney, judge, or juror is not intimidated by the mere magnitude of the document. At the same time, it should be comprehensive: relevance to the factfinder, not tactical considerations (such as minimizing information to be scrutinized for cross-examination), should guide the clinician in condensing the data. Indeed, the clinician is ethically obliged to make known all sources of data and to present a balanced account of the evaluation.[13] Thus, although extraneous social history data, overly technical accounts of formal testing results, and reference to dated and perhaps marginally relevant records of prior psychiatric involvement may be excluded (or at least deemphasized), findings essential to the clinical formulations advanced must be included.

To help determine which, and how much, information needs to be included in the written report, consultation with the attorney may help. Although the clinician must exercise independent judgment in deciding what is relevant to his or her findings, the attorney may assist in selecting the anecdotal or historical material that is most important in light of the legal arguments that will be pursued.

(4)   Minimize Clinical Jargon

In the clinical setting, mental health professionals' reports are replete with clinical jargon. A man who knows his identity and the date and place of the interview is "oriented times three"; a client who tenaciously holds to obviously mistaken beliefs, even in the face of good evidence to the contrary, is said to exhibit "delusional thinking"; a person who demonstrates no emotion has "blunted affect."

As useful as this shorthand may be to therapists, it can be confusing to the legal consumer and may even lead to erroneous impressions on the part of laypeople who assign the "generally accepted" meaning to a clinical phrase (e.g., the belief that schizophrenia means "split personality"). Unfortunately, many forensic clinicians do not seem to recognize this problem. For instance, in a study conducted by Petrella and Poythress,[14] judges and lawyers labeled "unclear" the following phrases from reports prepared by experienced forensic clinicians: "delusional ideation"; "affect"; "neologisms"; "loosening of associations"; "flight of ideas"; "blocking"; "his paranoid ideation is nonspecific, completely unsystematized"; "oriented to time, place, and person"; "lability"; "loose associations and tangentiality"; "flat affect"; "grandiosity"; "personality deficit"; "hysterical amnesia"; " 'lack of registration' amnesia"; and "psychotic mentation."

To say that clinical jargon is confusing to the legal consumer is not say that it is useless in the forensic context, however. In addition to serving as a convenient shorthand, it helps to establish that the clinician is dealing with a special body of knowledge. Psychological terms and constructs may also be useful in developing and explaining theoretical formulations of the type that would not be obvious to the trier of fact.

The obvious compromise is to explain the terms for the legal consumer when they are first used; this approach conveys the message that the clinician is an expert in a specialized field at the same time it ensures more effective communication with the legal system. Furthermore, once

explained, the terms acquire a "shorthand" function for the new audience as well. These explanations need not be elaborate. For example, a clinician might use such terms as "delusions" and "hallucinations" in the following manner: "During the clinical interview Mr. Jones voiced several delusional beliefs (i.e., strongly held but bizarre and obviously mistaken beliefs) and reported a history of auditory hallucinations (i.e., hearing imaginary voices)." The sample reports in Chapter 19 offer other examples of explaining jargon in written reports. In addition, the glossary of clinical and research terms in Chapter 20 may be of some aid to clinicians developing a lay "dictionary" (as well as assist lawyers attempting to decipher "clinicalese" that has not been explained).

18.04.   Expert Testimony and the Social Psychology of Persuasion

For many mental health professionals, going to court arouses considerable anxiety, fed by tales of colleagues who have been embarrassed by clever attorneys. To some extent, such trepidation is legitimate. Nowhere are the differences in training, philosophy, and objectives between lawyers and mental health professionals more clearly on display than in an adversarial proceeding. The clinician as scientist–practitioner is accustomed to the pursuit of truth through dispassionate examination of data; the attorneys on both sides are instead committed primarily to persuasion, and the "truth" as the clinician sees it is but one more piece of information subject to manipulation in service of the greater goal of achieving the desired verdict. Stated differently, attorneys are more interested in *credibility* than in truth per se; many of the questions posed in court by attorneys are aimed at enhancing (through direct questioning) or undermining (through cross-examination) a witness's credibility [see § 1.03(b)].

On the other hand, if the clinician understands the attorneys' agenda and adjusts to it, the courtroom appearance need not be traumatic. It is the exception rather than the rule that attorneys are truly malicious in their cross-examinations; as often as not, it is lack of preparation by witnesses or their inexperience in detecting or anticipating cross-examination gambits that leads to embarrassing moments in court. Once witnesses gain an appreciation for the tactics of direct and cross-examination and work out strategies for dealing with common ploys, courtroom testimony can be an enjoyable experience that is also informative to the factfinder.

The key to such appreciation is understanding the notion of "credibility." Research on the social psychology of persuasive communications deconstructs credibility into three components: expertise, trustworthiness, and dynamism.[15] "Expertise" pertains primarily to the formal aspects of the witness's experience and training, including such factors as degrees obtained, positions held, populations evaluated or treated, honors and awards, and so forth. "Trustworthiness" refers to perceptions that listeners (in this context, judges and jurors) form regarding the honesty of the witness; put another way, it has to do with their degree of confidence that testimony has been offered in good faith to inform rather than mislead. The third element, "dynamism," comprises a number of features related to style and charisma, including nonverbal aspects of presentation; sensitivity to this latter aspect of credibility has given rise to the well-worn adage that attorneys are often more interested in locating and retaining a good witness than a good doctor.[16]

This section is intended to assist clinicians in preparing for court by highlighting common tactics attorneys use to enhance or undermine the perceptions of judges and jurors regarding mental health experts' expertise, trustworthiness, and dynamism. We first look at how these tactics are used during the deposition, the pretrial conference and the three typical phases of testimony— *voir dire* (when the expert is qualified), direct examination, and cross-examination. As will be seen, expertise issues arise primarily during the *voir dire* phase of testimony, challenges to trustworthiness may be launched during either *voir dire* or testimony proper, and efforts to combat dynamism are most likely to occur during cross-examination. The section concludes with a general discussion of the procedural devices used by attorneys attempting to elicit or prevent testimony and the important issue of impression management.

(a) Deposition

In most civil cases involving money, and increasingly in criminal cases as well, opposing counsel files a motion to depose the expert witness prior to trial. As discussed in § 2.04(b), a deposition involves sworn testimony, given out of court but transcribed as a formal record. Depositions may take place in a conference room at one of the attorney's offices or even at the clinician's place of business.

Deposition procedures vary significantly from the courtroom procedures described below. While both attorneys and a court recorder are present, no judge or jury is involved. There is no formal "qualification" (*voir dire*) of the witness (although credentials may be examined), nor is there any direct testimony prior to questioning by opposing counsel. The rules governing questioning of the witness are also somewhat relaxed; the expert's counsel may "object" on the record to certain questions, but because no judge is present, there is typically no contemporaneous ruling on the objection.[17] The witness will usually be instructed to answer all questions, and the objections may be ruled on later by the judge based on review of the deposition transcript.

Depositions can serve several functions. First, they allow the opposing attorney to find out the gist of the expert's findings and the methods used to obtain them. Second, they might permit discovery of the other side's theory of the case, especially when the expert's deposition testimony indicates a particular rationale or line of reasoning. Third, opposing counsel has an opportunity to "size up" the expert, especially in terms of "dynamism"; questioning during deposition may reveal how adept the expert is at handling cross-examination and offer an indication as to how the witness will come across with a judge or jury. Fourth, depositions may be used to impeach the expert witness at trial; if answers to questions at trial are inconsistent with deposition testimony, the latter may be introduced to expose the contradiction, thus undermining trustworthiness. Alternatively, depositions sometimes help avoid trial because they persuade an opposing attorney to pursue a plea bargain or out-of-court settlement. Although not relevant to the current subject, a final purpose of depositions is to preserve the testimony of a witness who will be unavailable at trial.

Of course, clinicians should answer all deposition questions honestly and fairly. Because of their potential use as an impeachment weapon, however, depositions are not the best place to be overly elaborate. Information that goes beyond the scope of the question asked should not be volunteered because it may come back to haunt the witness. Specifically, clinicians should not be lulled by the seemingly less formal atmosphere of the deposition into accepting casual invitations to speculate beyond their data.

For the same reason, we advise clinicians to insist on reviewing the deposition transcript (usually the witness will be asked if he or she wants to do so). Review of the transcript allows identification of errors or misstatements that are best clarified prior to testimony in court. Furthermore, if court testimony does become necessary, clinicians should review the transcript of deposition testimony very carefully to minimize the possibility that their courtroom testimony will contain inconsistencies.

(b) Pretrial Conference

Although perhaps not always feasible, a pretrial conference with the referring attorney is highly recommended. This meeting is often invaluable in planning strategy on direct examination, in anticipating questions during cross-examination, and in learning about each other's attitudes toward the case beyond that which evolved during earlier telephone conferences and consultations. It is also the best mechanism for deciding how to enhance one's expertise, trustworthiness, and dynamism in the courtroom.

Specifically, during the conference the attorney should make clear to the clinician the theory of the case, what the opposing side will try to prove, how the clinician's data should be presented, and, if necessary, the nature of the courtroom process. The clinician should make sure the attorney knows his or her qualifications (for *voir dire*), describe the evaluation procedure, admit possible weaknesses in the opinion, provide assessment of the other side's opinion, and rehearse the data base so the attorney will know what types of background information will need to be introduced. The clinician should also critique the attorney's plans for presenting the clinical opinion. For example, the clinician may suggest that the more important findings or conclusions be presented very early or very late in the testimony to capitalize on "primacy" and "recency" effects.[18]

During the discussion of the clinician's data base, it may become clear that the witness feels ethically obliged to reveal information the attorney would prefer remain undisclosed (e.g., a prior offense or the results of an amytal interview). In such a situation, the clinician should ascertain whether the attorney intends to avoid eliciting the troublesome information; if so, the clinician may refuse to testify. An alternative solution, which may be superior not only from the clinician's but from the attorney's perspective, is to develop specific questions for direct testimony that allow the clinician to "explain away" the inconsistent data or provide alternative formulations. This latter strategy serves as a preemptive strike on facts or inferences the opposing attorney would probably bring out of the witness anyway, in an atmosphere that is likely to be less anxiety arousing for the clinician. Most important from the attorney's point of view, it increases the credibility of the witness by showing a willingness to admit weaknesses and inoculating the judge or jury against anticipated challenges to the clinician's ultimate formulation.[19]

Although the conference will probably focus on direct testimony, it may also be used to identify areas best reiterated on redirect testimony, after cross-examination. Some of these areas will be rescue points—topics on which it is known in advance that concessions will have to be made. In addition, a small number of major points should be identified for repetition on redirect, to capitalize on "recency" effects.

Finally, the witness and the attorney should be in agreement with each other on the clinician's posture with respect to ultimate-issue questions. As we discuss more fully in § 18.05, the attorney's inclination will probably be to ask the clinician questions that are couched in the explicit language of the statutory test or verdict. These questions will often be prefaced with inquiries about "reasonable medical certainty" or "reasonable scientific certainty." Although these terms may have some meaning when talking about confidence in the clinical diagnosis or assessment results, the questions will usually be asked so as to cast the desired legal conclusion in terms of rigorous medical or scientific validity. We recommend that the clinician take steps to avoid being misused in this fashion; to ensure that the flow or impact of direct testimony is not disrupted, these issues should be discussed and clarified prior to testimony.

Sometimes something more than general discussion about these various points might be advisable. For example, without overly rehearsing the specific responses to questions (so as to avoid mechanical presentation at trial), some minimal role playing of *voir dire*, direct, and redirect may be helpful at this stage. The attorney might even want to role play the cross-examiner, to give the expert a feel for the types of questions that the opposing side may use to challenge the expert's credibility.

(c)   Voir Dire: *Qualifying as an Expert*

Voir dire is the first stage of testimony—usually conducted while the jury is present—and consists of an examination by the attorneys, and perhaps the judge as well, designed to determine the qualifications of the witness. As discussed in § 1.04(a), under the rules of evidence, "lay" witnesses usually may offer only factual observations in testimony; "expert" witnesses, on the other hand, may offer inferences, conclusions, and opinions regarding matters in their fields of expertise. The *voir dire* establishes the extent and limits of this expertise.

In terms of the components of credibility noted earlier, the primary focus during *voir dire* is clearly "expertise," with trustworthiness and dynamism taking a back seat at this point. Accordingly, when a witness's credentials are particularly impressive, or at least are known to be sufficient, the side proffering the witness wants to put them on display, whereas the the opposing side attempts to downplay them. Indeed, in such instances the opposing side may often offer to stipulate to the expert's qualifications in an effort to avoid their psychological impact; if the other side agrees, and the judge accepts the stipulation, the

hearing will proceed to the next stage. Of course, the proffering party need not agree with the stipulation, in which case *voir dire* will proceed.

If *voir dire* does takes place, the side calling a witness to testify initially leads the witness through a fairly predictable series of questions designed to elicit for the judge and jury a history of the witness's education, training, and professional experience. As indicated in the previous section, in preparation for this process the clinician should meet with the attorney, who can rehearse the examination and discuss the substance of *voir dire* testimony. Brodsky and Poythress suggest that the following items be reviewed prior to trial:

- Formal education, including dates and places of degrees awarded, major areas of study, and title of thesis or dissertation if appropriate.
- Practical experience, including internship, residency, and professional positions held; type of work (teaching, research, administration, or service provision); and kinds of clients served (adult, adolescent, child; inpatient or outpatient).
- Professional certification or licensure; board certification, where applicable.
- Membership in professional organizations (e.g., American Psychiatric Association, American Psychology–Law Society).
- Professional publications—books, journal articles.
- Prior court experience as an expert and in what kinds of litigation.[20]

Questions dealing with substantive areas of expertise should be tailored to the particular case at hand—emphasizing, for example, experience or training with children and families in a custody case or experience with adult offenders in a sentencing hearing.

Clinicians and attorneys should also consider whether to include a brief discussion of discipline differences—the distinctions between a psychiatrist and a psychologist, a psychologist and a licensed family counselor, and so on—in terms of academic preparation, experience, and training.[21] Through such comparisons and contrasts of disciplines, the trier of fact may better understand the unique strengths and skills of the proffered expert. This understanding may be particularly important if the opposing side is planning to call an expert from a discipline traditionally perceived to be of higher status.[22] The *voir dire* questioning might even encourage the factfinder to view the disciplines as complementary rather than competing in terms of their contribution to the case at hand.[23]

Following the litany of credentials on direct questioning, the opposing attorney has an opportunity to question the witness further. The opposing attorney will usually focus on what the witness is not ("Doctor, as a psychologist you are not trained in administering and evaluating the effects of medications, are you?") and on what the witness did not/could not do ("Doctor, as your training is in psychiatry and medicine, you are not qualified to administer and interpret neuropsychological tests, are you?"). Predictable areas of emphasis include one's limited contact with particular populations, lack of training, or lack of prior court experience. Less common, but equally appropriate for exploration during *voir dire*, is an inquiry into the evaluation procedure and data relied on. Admissibility of expert testimony may be challenged if the clinician has used procedure(s) "not generally accepted in the field"[24] or if he or she has relied on data other than those on which experts in the field "reasonably rely"[25] [see generally § 3.08 for a discussion of these terms].

All the testimony described to this point is focused on the "expertise" component of credibility. However, attorneys on cross-examination may also try to attack the "trustworthiness" of the proffered expert. A common ploy is to inquire about the fees that the witness is collecting in the case, with the implication being that the clinician is a "hired gun" whose testimony has been bought.[26] In response, clinicians should assert that fees are paid on the basis of professional time, not for a particular outcome or finding in the forensic evaluation.

A second common ploy is to inquire about the frequency with which the witness has testified for a particular side ("Doctor, how many times have you testified for the plaintiff in personal injury cases?"). To a degree, the expert asked this type of question is at the mercy of his or her own history of involvement in the type of litigation in question. However, the innuendo of "bias" can be deflated to some extent if the witness can honestly state that his or her conclusions have favored the opposing side on several occasions and, for this reason, were never relied on by the referring party. For instance, a witness might state:

> "Although I have testified on behalf of plaintiffs in 11 cases, I have served as a consultant to plaintiff's attorneys in 36 cases. Thus, I have testified on behalf of plaintiffs in less than one-third of the cases in which I have been consulted by them."

Replies to challenges on expertise and trustworthiness grounds can also come on redirect examination, in which the attorney proffering the witness raises these issues again (e.g., fees and customary alignment with one party) in a way that allows the clinician to discuss them in a more favorable light. However, as noted earlier, we recommend that attorneys consider raising these issues during the initial *voir dire* direct examination rather than waiting for redirect. This approach can enhance trustworthiness by showing that the witness has "nothing to hide," thus inoculating the judge and jury from impressions of "bias" that are "uncovered" on cross-examination. Other approaches to establishing trustworthiness of the witness include noting membership in professional organizations that have ethical codes governing clinical/forensic practice and eliciting the witness' affirmation of an effort to conduct evaluations that are consistent with professional guidelines.

Mental health professionals occasionally attempt to bolster their credentials with claims or elaborations that come off as phony. One psychologist received his doctorate from a nonaccredited program but instead of modestly conceding the point during cross-examination, he launched into a defensive narrative that doctoral training at nonaccredited programs was widely regarded as superior to that provided at accredited programs. This same expert averred that he had worked in the "field of psychology" for 15 years, an assertion that was technically true but appeared at best to be a distortion when the cross-examiner brought out that for 12 of these years he had worked as a nonprofessional, as a paraprofessional, or as a student. In a similar illustration of deceit, a psychiatrist who had attended and audited some classes at Harvard Law School but had not earned a law degree was asked on *voir dire* about having a law degree. He responded, "Well, I attended Harvard Law School, but I never took the bar exam to practice law." He thus avoided the true confession that he did not have a law degree and left hanging a possible erroneous impression.

We strongly discourage any such efforts to enhance perceived expertise through fabricated or contrived credentials or half-truths. Mental health professionals have an ethical responsibility to avoid misrepresentation, no matter how cleverly disguised. Moreover, judges and jurors will probably see through such contrivances and attribute them to lack of confidence or, worse, to dishonesty in the witness. Trustworthiness is perhaps the most important component of credibility,[27] and to compromise personal or professional integrity is probably the single greatest error a witness can make in court.

Following *voir dire*, the attorney calling the witness to testify will make a motion to the judge requesting that the court acknowledge on the record that the clinician is an expert witness. This decision is generally entirely within the discretion of the trial court; as noted earlier, judicial preferences concerning clinicians of different training may be influenced not only by the clinicians' credentials but also by the type of litigation involved. If designated an expert, the witness is allowed to offer inferences, opinions, and conclusions that go beyond the data. If not, the clinician may still, it is important to note, testify about observations and descriptive data. Not infrequently, judges will take an intermediate position, allowing clinicians whose credentials have been challenged to testify as experts but instructing the jury that the limits in training or experience should be considered in addressing the weight to give their testimony.

As the foregoing discussion illustrates, *voir dire* testimony is typically not particularly difficult or traumatic for the witness. The issues to be covered are prepared for in advance, and the challenges from opposing counsel are predictable. Clinicians should present themselves as confident and enthusiastic about their professional identities, matter-of-factly stating for the court what they are and what they are not, but they should remain nondefensive and detached during debate about their "expert" status, leaving that issue up to the attorneys and the court.

(d)　Direct Testimony

Following *voir dire*, the witness undergoes direct examination by the attorney who has called him or her to court. Direct testimony involves describing the evaluation procedures conducted, the data obtained, and the conclusions drawn by the clinician. As discussed previously, a pretrial conference can help immeasurably in preparing for this phase of the trial.

A popular way to structure the body of the testimony is modeled on an inverted pyramid: The expert begins by describing evaluation techniques and the data those techniques have produced; then proceeds to inferences; and ends with the "peak," the summary conclusion. If tests or laboratory procedures were used, the clinician should be prepared to discuss their validity and to describe the method of test development. As noted throughout this volume, the clinician should not hesitate to describe uncertainty in the process of opinion formation. Again, this latter recommendation is not only ethically mandated[28] but also tends to "steal the thunder" of the cross-examining attorney.

As to the style of the testimony, it is probably best to avoid staccato-like questions and answers that come across as rehearsed. The dynamism of the expert, as well as the information he or she possesses, is best displayed through a narrative style of testimony that enables the clinician to reference and synthesize various findings from the evaluation in a fluid manner. In general, the same suggestions we have made with respect to writing reports—avoiding information overkill, eschewing unexplained jargon, separating facts from inferences—are useful here as well.

When the fundamental facts of a case are in dispute, an attorney may wish to establish the credibility of a client by seeking to have the clinician affirm the honesty and candor of the client. Although clinicians may have something legitimate to say about deception [see § 3.07], they should generally avoid being used as "lie detectors" [see § 3.08]. The best tactic is to leave the credibility issue up to the trier of fact. However, that admonition does not prevent the clinician from alluding to third-party information corroborating that obtained from the client or offering feasible clinical explanations for contradictions or inconsistencies in the data base. In addition, analogous to the discussion of report writing, the clinician can assume hypothetically each of the competing factual situations and report formulations consistent with each.

With careful preparation, direct examination is usually the smoothest stage of testimony. The clinician can expect open-ended questions that allow considerable latitude in responding. The only interruptions will be the succession of questions from the attorney and, infrequently, objections from opposing counsel [the latter discussed in more detail in § 18.04(f)].

(e)   Cross-Examination

Cross-examination, which follows direct testimony, is the stage that is most trying for the inexperienced witness. Gone is the friendly, understanding expression of the attorney who has led direct testimony; in its place is the scowl or piercing stare of the opposing attorney, whose tone of voice and looks of astonishment convey to the jury the "unbelievable" nature of the clinician's testimony. A variety of verbal and nonverbal ploys are tried in an effort to confuse or discredit the witness, the testimony, or the witness's profession. In place of the logical progression of open-ended questions are narrow, constricting inquiries that emphasize vulnerable points in the clinical findings and attempt to distort the very message the witness is trying to convey. The attorney will stress that whatever the witness did in the evaluation was insufficient, and that whatever the witness did not do was essential. Also emphasized will be what the witness does not know.

In general, the most important way of coping with this type of attack is careful preparation. As indicated earlier, conducting a careful evaluation, becoming familiar with the reliability and/or validity of tests used, going over one's deposition testimony, and consulting with the referral attorney should be part and parcel of the witness's pretrial work. Once on the stand, a second important response, also noted earlier, is to acknowledge controversial points and concede minor or indefensible ones, although not at the expense of a balanced presentation that includes positive support for the witness's position.

Following these general recommendations may not be enough to protect one's credibility, however, particularly from the expertise and trustworthiness perspectives. The art of cross-examining the mental health expert witness has been the subject of considerable writing.[29] Thus, the attorney has numerous sources to call on in preparing an attack on witness credibility. At the same time, there is a significant literature suggesting responses to specific cross-examination ploys.[30] It is beyond the scope of this chapter to review the full range of such ploys, but this section describes several of the more common ones and indicates appropriate responses by the mental health witness. Readers who anticipate appearing frequently in court as expert witnesses may wish to become more intimately familiar with the literature.

(1)   The "Infallibility Complex" and "God Only Knows" Gambits

To overcome any perception the jury may have of the witness as infallible, the cross-examining attorney may ask a question designed to suggest fallibility. For instance, the attorney may ask the witness about the relevance of some very new, or very obscure, research that the witness will probably have not seen; this ruse, the attorney hopes, will result in an "I don't know" response. Or the attorney may ask questions to which there is not a sure, easy, or precise answer (e.g., "What really causes schizophrenia?").

When confronted with these "infallibility complex" or "God only knows" gambits, the witness can use an admit–deny response. With this response, the witness concedes the attorney's narrower point yet does so in a way that demonstrates some knowledge or mastery of the subject. Here is an example:

Q: Doctor, do you think that the new research by Smith and Jones might be relevant here?

A: The studies having the most direct bearing on this issue are those by Holmes, Dawson, and Wortman. I don't recall seeing citations to Smith and Jones. If you have the paper, perhaps I could look it over during a recess.

Rather than simply conceding ignorance of the Smith and Jones study (which would be, of course, an acceptable response), the witness answered in such a way as to affirm expertise in the area generally. Further, the witness's final statement—the offer to review the paper during a court recess—shows an openness to new information that may enhance the witness's trustworthiness in the eyes of the jury; it will also force the attorney to withdraw if he or she has simply posed a misleading citation for purposes of confrontation.

Here is a similar response to the "God only knows" gambit:

Q: Doctor, what really causes schizophrenia?
A: Research has implicated a number of factors that contribute to schizophrenia. There is some evidence for a genetic contribution, as biological relatives of people with schizophrenia are at much greater risk for the illness than are persons selected randomly. Pathological family relationships may also contribute. Unfortunately, the state of the science at present does not permit us to determine what has caused schizophrenia in a particular case.

Again, the witness admits ignorance in such a way as to appear well informed and to make the jury aware of the complex nature of the subject.

(2) "Yes–No" Questioning

With this gambit, the attorney attempts to box the witness in by phrasing questions in such a way as to force a "yes" or "no" answer. For instance, the attorney might ask: "Isn't it true that predictions of dangerousness are very inaccurate?"; then, when the clinician attempts to answer in an explanatory fashion, the attorney will cut off the answer with, "Doctor, a simple yes or no would suffice." In response to this type of questioning, the clinician should be assertive and state, when true, that a "yes" or "no" response would be inappropriate or misleading. If the attorney presses for a yes–no answer, the witness may appeal to the judge ("Your Honor, I believe that an answer of "yes" or "no" without explanation would be misleading"), who will either instruct the witness to answer the question or instruct the attorney to rephrase it. In any event, the other attorney will be alerted to clear up this matter with clarifying questions on redirect examination.

(3) The "Unreliable Examination" Gambit

Often the attorney will question the witness about the uncertainty of his or her findings (low reliability/validity of individual tests or diagnosis, low accuracy of predictions, etc.). This gambit can be dealt with in numerous ways. As noted previously, the witness can simply concede the degree of inaccuracy or unreliability that exists; such concessions, if made nondefensively, convey a sense of honesty and candor that the judge or jury will appreciate. Although ideally they would be made during direct examination, they can often be used to the witness's advantage even on cross, through what is known as the "push–pull" response. With this response, the witness does not simply concede the point; rather, he or she concedes even more than the attorney asked for, so that it appears to be a point the witness wants to impress on the jury, not one the attorney has forced the witness to make. In other words, the witness concedes substantive ground but reclaims territory in the area of trustworthiness. For example:

Q: Doctor, isn't it true that the validity of the Rorschach test has been seriously questioned by some psychologists?
A: No psychological test, the Rorschach included, is a perfectly valid test. It is important that you [the jury] not place undue weight on any one of the particular test results I've described but consider all of the information as a whole.

Conceding the substantive point about the Rorschach, the witness recaptures the possible loss of credibility by extending the point to other findings as well.

However, simple concessions and push–pull should be used only when the substantive concessions being sought are reasonable. When the attorney asks for too much, the appropriate response is to correct him or her.

Q: Doctor, isn't it true that psychiatric diagnosis is generally unreliable? Isn't it true that you psychiatrists rarely agree on when somebody is, or is not, suffering from schizophrenia?
A: No, that is not true. The reliability of a diagnosis of schizophrenia is quite good, at least if DSM criteria are used [explaining DSM if it hasn't already been explained]. Agreement

among trained clinicians may be as high as 80–90%.

(4)   The "Subjective Opinion" Ploy

The cross-examining attorney sometimes asks whether the witness has personally been involved in systematic research to investigate the reliability and/or validity of his or her own clinical opinions and judgments. This "subjective opinion" ploy attempts to impress upon the jury that the clinician's formulations and opinions are simply "what the witness thinks" rather than findings with scientific or clinical legitimacy.

Responses to this ploy should include a brief statement of the scientific underpinnings of the clinician's training and a modest statement of personal and professional integrity to this effect: "Because I am a person with a particular personal set of values, I am careful in the collection and analysis of data to ascertain that my clinical formulations are consistent with known data or widely accepted theory," which should then be described. Of course, if in fact the witness's clinical judgments have been the subject of systematic study, the results of such study should be described.

(5)   The "Loaded Question" and "Lawyer as Expert" Ploys

Occasionally an attorney may intentionally distort information, especially if he or she is desperate. For instance, the attorney may misstate what the witness has said or agreed to in an earlier response, usually by "loading" the prior statement with additional information. If a witness has previously agreed to assertions X, Y, and Z, a later question by the attorney might be, "Doctor, you earlier testified that W, X, Y, and Z were true. Doesn't that mean that . . . ?" Or the lawyer might graciously volunteer to testify for the clinician regarding the clinician's own field (e.g., "Doctor, doesn't a standard psychological evaluation consist of . . . ?"); this gambit sets up the clinician for later questions that depend on the attorney's definition of what is "standard."

The "loaded question" and "lawyer as expert" ploys primarily require good listening by the witness. If clinicians are familiar with their written reports (as they should be) and are careful in their own testimony, they will be able to pick up on the gratuitous "findings" or concessions that such attorneys may attribute to them when they load their questions. At such points, clinicians should clarify what they do or do not agree with or what they have or have not stated in their reports.

In particular, under no circumstances should clinicians take the "lawyer as expert" ploy casually. Leading questions regarding what is "standard," "acceptable," or "proper" clinical practice should be scrutinized carefully. The safest response to such questions is never to answer them with a "yes." By avoiding simply agreeing with attorneys' definitions of standard or proper procedure, clinicians will ultimately force the attorneys to ask them to define such terms themselves. Then they are on safe ground, for they can offer definitions of the terms that are broad or qualified enough to encompass procedures they have used. In short, clinicians should jealously guard their area of expertise and should not cede it to the clever phrases of cross-examining attorneys.

(6)   The "Learned Treatise" Assault

One additional cross-examination tactic worthy of special attention is the "learned treatise" assault. Here the attorney attempts to undermine the clinician's testimony by showing that it is contradicted by findings in the published literature. Typically, the attorney first produces copies of published research or clinical commentary, such as journal articles or books, and attempts to establish that these documents are by authorities in the field. Once the credibility of the documents is established, the attorney then reads, or requires the witness to read aloud in court, excerpts that contradict the oral testimony of the clinician, thus raising questions in the jurors' minds about the credibility of the witness.

Clinicians may employ different tactics to combat this assault.[31] One approach is to prevent the treatise from being declared authoritative. In many jurisdictions, the rules of evidence governing learned treatises require that the witness acknowledge the authority of the source before it can be used as impeachment evidence. In others, evidentiary rules require further that the document must have been relied on by the witness.[32]

Both variations of the "refuse to acknowledge" response carry substantial risks, however: If the witness refuses to acknowledge the authority of the source or admits being ignorant of much of the published research, he or she may appear uninformed (lacking "expertise") or even dishonest (not "trustworthy"). Furthermore, in most jurisdictions the judge or another witness can declare a treatise authoritative independently of the witness.[33]

An alternative response tactic is for the clinician to accept the proposed document as authoritative and deal with its alleged contradictions directly. In this way, the clinician can parry the "learned treatise" assault without resorting to avoidance tactics. Of course, this response is most effectively carried out if the clinician has anticipated the major issues to be debated. If so, the clinician not only can acknowledge or criticize the findings as appropriate but also can provide specific citations to support the position taken.[34] Note further that when a treatise is used to impeach, the witness is always entitled to ask to see it, a move that can facilitate a reasoned response.

The witness should also be alert to misuse of an authoritative source. Two anecdotes from our experience illustrate this concern. In one case, Poythress testified that a defendant's WAIS Full Scale IQ score of 67 placed him in the lower 2% of the population of persons his age. The attorney then produced a well-known psychology text book, which the witness acknowledged as an authoritative source. At this point the attorney queried, "Doctor, would it surprise you to learn that this authoritative text indicates that an IQ of 67 is not at the 2nd percentile, but in fact is at the 22nd percentile?" With this question, the attorney implied that the book asserted that an IQ of 67 is at the 22nd percentile (and that the doctor either made a mistake or is lying). But the attorney had not actually said the book made that assertion, because the question began with *"Would you be surprised to learn that . . . ?"*

The lesson here is that witnesses must pay close attention to the phrasing of attorneys' questions. Two responses to such questions are appropriate. The first is to ask to see the book, which, as noted previously, the witness is entitled to do. The other is to answer the question that was asked; in this instance the response was, "Not only

would I be surprised, I would be amazed if an eminent scholar such as Professor *X* allowed an error of that magnitude in his book." Because the WAIS is constructed to obtain a normal distribution of scores with a standard deviation of 15 (around a mean of 100), such a statement would be unlikely from any credible source.

The second anecdote involved questioning of Poythress about the side effects of a certain drug that the defendant had taken the evening prior to committing a murder. The attorney produced the *Physicians' Desk Reference* (PDR), which was acknowledged as an authoritative text on medication actions and side effects. The attorney then queried, "Doctor, isn't it true according to the PDR that drug *X* 'produces hallucinations, disorientation, confusion . . . (and a litany of other drastic psychological reactions)'?" Here the proper response was to ask to review the reference, which the attorney permitted, albeit while holding on to the book. The attorney then asked the witness to read the list of side effects verbatim from the PDR. The witness alertly noted that the attorney's finger was covering up the first word of the sentence, which turned out to be "Rarely." Bringing this out when reading from the PDR exposed the attorney's effort to misrepresent what the PDR actually said about reasonably expected side effects.

(f) Objections and Hypotheticals

An objection is a motion, usually made by the attorney who is not questioning the witness, to have a question or answer stricken from the record or modified in some respect. When an objection is made, the clinician should either not answer the question or, if the objection comes in the middle of an answer, stop testifying. If the objection is "overruled," the testimony may proceed. If the objection is "sustained," the questioning attorney either rephrases the question or goes on to something different (although the judge or lawyer may request an answer for the record, out of the presence of the jury, to preserve the objection on appeal).

Typical objections during cross-examination, made by the clinician's own attorney, might include "badgering the witness," "asked and answered" (suggesting that the cross-examiner has already obtained one answer and is now fishing for a better one), and "irrelevant" (suggesting that the cross-examiner is asking for information that is not legally material to the case). Often, objections by the witness's own attorney are strategic moves designed to allow the witness to catch his or her breath and think through a good answer.

During direct examination, a prominent objection by opposing counsel is designed to prevent the direct examiner from asking leading questions (i.e., questions that suggest the answer, often in the format of "Isn't it true that . . . ?"). The leading-question objection is often sustained because the direct examiner is supposed to let witnesses speak for themselves rather than put words in their mouths (leading questions are permitted, however, during the more adversarial cross-examination, and indeed they are the principal mode of interrogation). A second type of objection during direct examination is a challenge to the basis of the expert's statements. Such objections come in many varieties; as discussed in § 3.08, they range from objections on "hearsay" grounds to complaints based on the Constitution and objections that the information forming the basis for the testimony is not "reasonably relied" on or is not "generally accepted."

Clinicians should also be alert to the potential use of hypothetical questions by attorneys for either side. Such questions are usually prefaced by a clear signal (e.g., "Doctor, I'm going to ask you a hypothetical question") and consist of a statement of several assumptions, followed by an inquiry as to the clinician's opinion about them. For example:

Q: Doctor, I am going to ask you to assume certain facts, and then I want you to tell the jury what you would conclude about the defendant's mental condition if all of these facts were true. I want you to assume that W, X, Y, and Z are true. Given these facts, what would you conclude about the defendant's mental state at the time of the murder?

Such hypothetical questions are generally permitted,[35] but clinicians should be careful in answering them. The attorney will usually have arranged the assumed facts in such a way as to force a conclusion or opinion that supports the theory or verdict being pursued. In doing so, the attorney may (1) exclude factual information that the clinician knows to exist, (2) include factual information of which the clinician is unaware, or (3) include as information to be assumed facts not in evidence in the case. In the third of these instances, the other attorney may successfully object, and the hypothetical question may have to be rephrased. In the first two instances, the clinician should answer the question but may wish to qualify the opinion or conclusion, if only to remind the jury that the response is tailored exclusively to the hypothetical and is not based on his or her entire information base. Thus, the witness might respond to the question above as follows:

A: Assuming only W, X, Y, and Z is difficult for me, because in my own investigation I found A and B, as well as C, which contradicts W. However, if I assume only what you stated and disregard what else I know, a reasonable inference would be R.

The clinician might also appropriately avoid drawing a conclusion or inference if the information to be assumed is not clear, as in the following response:

A: You have asked me to assume that a neighbor testified that Mr. Doe was acting crazy before the shooting. Without knowing more about what the neighbor meant by "crazy" behavior, I am not sure what inferences or conclusions I would draw.

Finally, if the hypothetical is so long and convoluted that a sensible answer would be difficult, the clinician can ask for clarification or—especially deadly when the question has gone on for ten minutes or so—politely ask: "Could you repeat the question, please?"

It is worth noting that hypothetical conclusions and inferences not only may be offered in response to limited questions constructed by the attorney but may also be volunteered by the clinician on either direct examination or cross-examination. Situations in which this might be appropriate have previously been described both in the discussion on report writing and in the discussion of direct testimony.

(g)   Impression Management

Up to this point, we have discussed primarily substantive features of expert testimony. Another important consideration, and one to which many mental health professionals pay insufficient attention, is the image that clinicians convey through their nonverbal behavior. For better or worse, "dynamism" or charisma is an element in the structure of credibility. Dress, posture, tone of voice, and a variety of other factors may have a considerable impact on the impression jurors form of the witness; perceived expertise is not determined simply by the litany of credentials recited on *voir dire*. Thus, we devote a few words to "impression management."

(1)   Style of Dress

The clinician's attire should be selected so as to conform to the judge's or juror's stereotype of a professional person. Thus, clinicians are advised to dress conservatively when going to court. Dress does not have to be expensive, but it should be neat. Blue jeans and a sweater may be fine in the private office for conveying a "low-key" image and making therapy clients feel comfortable, but they are not suitable for the courtroom. Similarly, bright or flashy colors, short skirts, excessive makeup or jewelry, or "mod" attire are not consistent with the professional image and are likely to distract courtroom personnel from thinking of the clinician as an expert.

(2)   Familiarity with Courtroom Protocol

The courtroom is not the place to appear timid, passive, or unsure. Clinicians should learn in advance how the courtroom is set up and what is expected of them and should execute the legally appropriate behaviors in a manner that reflects comfort and familiarity.

For example, the clinician should not wait to be ushered around the courtroom like a lost child. When called to testify, he or she should stride forward confidently, stopping at the witness stand to face the judge or bailiff and be sworn in. In giving testimony, the clinician should take time to think through a question, pause reflectively if necessary, and respond in a clear, even

tone. Information should not be volunteered from the witness stand but should be provided only in response to questions. The clinician should also know about typical "objections" made during direct and cross-examination and how to react when an objection is made [see discussion in § 18.04(f)].

(3)   Speaking to the Jury

The witness should face the factfinder (i.e., the jury or the judge) when answering questions. Good eye contact should be maintained. This advice is important at all times but perhaps most important during cross-examination. Opposing attorneys may attempt to interrupt the channel of nonverbal communication between the witness and the jury in either of two ways. The attorney may approach the witness stand, almost to the point of invading the witness's personal space, in order to become a physical obstruction between the witness and the jury. More subtly, the attorney may wander across the room away from the jury box, speaking in such a low voice that the witness must look away from the jury to hear the question. The witness will occasionally forget to turn back to face the jury, and the nonverbal communication will have been severed.

In testimony, as in report writing, the clinician should use language that the jury members can easily understand. A limited amount of clinical jargon may reaffirm the clinician's expertise, but any jargon used should be explained to ensure the jurors' comprehension.

(4)   Powerful Speech

Clinicians who are going to be testifying in court should cultivate a style of speech that enhances their credibility. They should develop a fluid, conversational tone and a clear, even, and confident voice. Dramatics are to be avoided, but the witness should be sufficiently personable and animated to maintain the audience's attention. Also important is the ability to communicate with relatively few hesitations, "qualifiers," or "intensifiers," phenomena that tend to diminish the force of one's presentation.[36] Finally, although reports and records should be available, credibility is likely to be enhanced when testimony is delivered with little or no reliance on written materials.

(5)   Maintaining Composure

The importance of maintaining composure cannot be overstated. Apart from any substantive concessions made in testimony, the most damaging thing that can happen to a witness is to become angry, defensive, or flustered. If the witness can be confused or flustered to the point that a powerful speech style is abandoned or composure is lost, the third component of credibility (dynamism/charisma) will have been undermined.

As indicated earlier, one technique that cross-examining attorneys use to frustrate witnesses is to ask complex questions to which no simple response can be given. Rather than becoming frustrated and grasping for an adequate response when none is possible, clinicians should ask the attorneys to repeat or simplify the questions, thus placing the responsibility on them for clarifying confusing situations of their own creation.

Attorneys may also engage in argumentative or harassing tactics simply to destroy clinicians' demeanor, caring little for substantive points gained or lost. A witness should endeavor to maintain a polite, respectful posture toward a hostile lawyer, even in the face of a personal attack. Not only will this composed response maintain credibility, it may well leave the jury with the impression that the lawyer is a "bully," thereby hurting *his* (or her) credibility. Another response is humor. Though the witness should never become flippant in tone, the use of wit can be effective in judiciously selected situations. One colleague reported being badgered about her inability to clinically distinguish between an "irresistible impulse" and an "impulse that was not resisted." Noting (to herself) that the hostile attorney was noticeably overweight, she answered with an analogy to a person on a diet who succumbed to the temptation of a double chocolate sundae—was the temptation irresistible or simply not resisted? The line of questioning abruptly ended.

A final cross-examination technique, used when the witness is conceding a point, is to induce the witness to adopt an apologetic tone. Unless a witness is admitting an error, however, there is no need for such a tone. Limits in the technology, data, or precision are not a clinician's fault; they are simply the way things are. The clinician may explain limitations in his or her knowledge or formulation, but apologies for the state of the art and science of behavior are uncalled for.

(6)   Conclusion

The import of what has been said about impression management is captured in this passage by Brodsky:

> [C]redibility is dependent upon the perception of the witnesses by judges and jurors as likeable, honest, and confident. Note that these three personality attributes are unrelated to accuracy of the witnesses' specific observations. However, these attributes are vitally important in being believed. People believe individuals they like, people believe individuals they see as honest, and people believe individuals who are confident. The implication of such attributions is that presentation of self in these ways greatly enhances effectiveness on the witness stand.[37]

As this passage indicates, mental health professionals who engage in forensic work must develop skills for effective testifying. In part these skills involve simply being at ease with oneself. But they also can be honed in various ways. One way to do so is to go to court and watch expert witnesses testify; observing various models can be an educational vicarious experience. Another good learning exercise is to rehearse expert testimony with colleagues who play the parts of judge and attorneys; videotaping the exercise should even further enhance feedback from such a role-playing experience. Although impression management should never take priority over clinical acuity, we encourage mental health professionals to develop a calm, friendly, and professional manner for testifying to maximize the chances the factfinder will attend to their testimony.

(h)   Lay Attitudes toward Experts

Recent research on the criteria that lay people use to evaluate expert testimony provides helpful hints to would-be experts that supplement the foregoing comments. One particularly interesting study in this vein looked at the effect of experts in capital trial and sentencing proceedings.[38] Although anecdotal in nature (152 jurors from 36 different trials were interviewed for an average of 3 hours about their trial experience), the study provides some interesting insights into juror perceptions and decisionmaking that may be very relevant to mental health professionals and lawyers preparing for trial.

The first series of comments made by the capital jurors who were interviewed had to do with their general perceptions of expert witnesses, both clinical and nonclinical. On the whole, the jurors tended to remember defense experts as less credible than prosecution experts, lay witnesses, or even family members of the defendant (who obviously have a motivation to shade the truth on the stand). Defense experts were seen as hired guns, especially when they disclosed they had received large sums of money (e.g., $200/hour) for their evaluation and testimony. Explanations that this money was for time actually spent on the case did not impress many of the jurors, who knew that the prosecution experts were on salary and who probably did not make nearly that hourly amount themselves. Especially when, as was usually the case, the defense expert was paid by the state, jurors were galled at the "waste of taxpayer money."

Other factors that led jurors to distrust or discount expert testimony, whether defense or prosecution, centered on practical concerns having little to do with the content of the testimony. Jurors were critical of experts who did not spend much time investigating the case, had seen the defendant only shortly before trial, destroyed recordings and notes, and appeared to be pompous and self-centered. Another common thread in juror comments was the criticism of experts who seemed to have made no effort to relate their testimony to the rest of the evidence being presented. Those experts who wove the physical evidence and the testimony of other witnesses into their testimony were perceived as more credible than experts who appeared to be popping into the courtroom from their busy schedule and were isolated from the rest of the defense (or prosecution) "team."

Finally, whether rightly or wrongly, some jurors felt they knew more about the expert's subject matter than the experts themselves. One recurring example of this phenomenon involved expert testimony about the negative effects of alcohol and drug use. Many jurors dismissed expert opinion on this issue based on their own knowledge or stories they had heard from friends or relatives. Similarly, some jurors were irritated by experts on eyewitness accuracy because of the latter's suggestion that people cannot trust their senses. To these jurors, such testimony was clearly erroneous. Indeed, in those cases in which the lay jurors felt more knowledgeable than the experts, the term "expert" was often used perjoratively and equated with quackery.

Again, this study is anecdotal. But recent research using more scientific methodology bolsters many of its conclusions. In a survey of participants in civil cases, Champagne, Shuman, and Whitaker found that clarity of presentation, familiarity with the facts of the case, and impartiality (as connoted by reliance on third-party information and source of payment) were more important than educational credentials and appearance and personality,[39] although the latter were not unimportant.[40] In a related study using a different sample,[41] Shuman and his colleagues obtained similar results and also found that plaintiffs' experts were generally less believable than experts who testified for the defense (perhaps because, it was speculated, plaintiffs tend to raise novel claims or are associated with frivolous lawsuits).

These results provide interesting food for thought. The clinician who is going to court, and the lawyer who is presenting the expert, would do well to consider their implications.

18.05.   The Ultimate-Issue Issue

Throughout this volume, we have discouraged mental health professionals from offering opinions or conclusions couched in the language of the ultimate legal issue. As Chapter 1 showed, philosophical differences between the law and the behavioral sciences abound. Furthermore, analysis of forensic legal issues requires not only clinical information but reference to social and moral policy. Thus, the ultimate legal issue (e.g., Is this person legally sane, competent, dangerous, or fit to be a parent?) lies outside the province of scientific inquiry. Clinicians may provide useful information about the mental infirmities of an elderly person, but they have no barometer for determining when such infirmities are sufficient to warrant the appointment of a guardian or conservator who will infringe upon the individual's interest in autonomy. Clinicians may provide diagnostic and prognostic information about a criminal offender at sentencing, but their scientific expertise does not allow them to determine what a proper sentence would be in light of competing sentencing goals such as retribution, rehabilitation, and deterrence. Conclusions on such ultimate legal questions are the responsibility of the judge and jury, and clinicians should resist drawing them.

Our analysis and recommendation notwithstanding, contemporary practices often encourage, permit, and in some instances require mental health professionals to address ultimate legal issues in their reports and testimony. Thus, to appreciate the consequences of our position, several questions need to be addressed: From the courts' perspective, how important is ultimate-issue testimony from mental health professionals? What are the various pressures on mental health professionals to provide such testimony? How, in the context of actual testimony, can these pressures be resisted?

(a)   Perceived Importance of Opinions on Ultimate Legal Issues

Avoiding the ultimate legal issue in forensic reports or in testimony would be a relatively simple matter were it not for the fact that attorneys and trial court judges regard ultimate-issue opinions as very important. This fact is borne out by considerable anecdotal information.[42] It is also supported empirically by a survey of circuit court judges in Michigan.[43] In this survey, Poythress asked 30 judges to rate the importance of the following eight aspects of mental health expert testimony [which roughly correspond with the typology of levels of inference introduced in § 1.04(a)][44]:

A. *Statistical/actuarial data on diagnosis or clinical observation*. The clinician may refer to statistical

or actuarial data from experimental studies on the subject before the court (e.g., epidemiological data regarding the incidence of a disorder, normative data regarding scores on a test, and reliability of diagnosis).

B. *Statistical/actuarial data on the relationship between clinical findings and legally relevant behavior*. The clinician may refer to such research findings as the relationship between clinical diagnosis and relative probability of suicide, correlational data relating number of prior arrests to criminal recidivism, the relationship between chronological age and memory or susceptibility to leading questions, and the like.

C. *Descriptive testimony*. The clinician describes the clinical observations and test results of a particular individual who is the subject of the court hearing. The description may include physical appearance, nonverbal behavior, attitudes, affect, memory, mental status, historical data, and so on.

D. *Diagnosis*. Formal (e.g., from the fourth edition of *Diagnostic and Statistical Manual of Mental Disorders* [DSM-IV]) or informal diagnosis (e.g., "severely mentally ill") will be given in many instances. The clinician identifies the clinical data that meet the diagnostic criteria and conveys the message of having observed a recognized clinical syndrome.

E. *Theoretical accounts or explanations for legally relevant behavior*. The clinician offers an interpretation of the individual's behavior and an explanation for the legally relevant behavior by invoking the constructs of some formal or implicit personality theory. Most commonly, the medical ("mental illness") model is invoked, followed closely in popularity by the psychodynamic theory.

F. *Weighing the relative contribution of different motives or explanations for legally relevant behavior*. The clinician may voice an opinion on which of several contributory factors or conflicting theoretical explanations appears most applicable in a given case (e.g., "Although it is true that Ms. Doe suffered a severe loss of income following her separation from her husband, it is my opinion that her sense of failure as a woman and as a wife and an unconscious feeling of guilt and need to be punished were the primary factors contributing to her shoplifting").

G. *Interpreting the legal standard for mental disorder*. The clinician may attempt to relate a clinical diagnosis or condition to a legal standard or definition (e.g., "This person has below-average intelligence, though not to the degree that the legal term 'mental defect' would apply").

H. *Ultimate legal issue.* The testimony of the witness may embrace the ultimate legal issue, often including the specific language of the legal test that the judge or jury is to consider (e.g., "This person is unable to assist his attorney in a reasonable manner; in my opinion, he is incompetent to stand trial").

Judges indicated their ratings on the importance of these types of testimony on a 9-point scale, anchored as follows:

- Scale points 7, 8, and 9 should reflect that "you consider the element/item to be essential to dispensing justice; judgments by the trier-of-fact would be seriously hampered if this element/component were not included."
- Scale points 4, 5, and 6 should reflect that "you consider the element/item *desirable* for inclusion in expert testimony. Justice could be fairly dispensed without this particular feature having to be present, but its inclusion would perhaps allow for more fully informed decisions."
- Scale points 1, 2, and 3 should reflect that "you consider the element/item either unnecessary, uninformative, or *undesirable* as a feature of expert testimony. Its presence would add nothing of particular significance for the trier-of-fact, and possibly it might have negative impact by confusing or clouding the issue."

Table 18.1 lists the median ratings based on the responses of 30 judges; also shown are the relative rankings of probative value for each of the eight aspects of testimony (with item B, at 8, being the least probative and item C, at 1, being the most probative). Both aspects of testimony involving opinions on ultimate legal issues (G and H) were rated by the judges in the "essential" range and were outranked in importance by only one factor, descriptive testimony. These findings clearly support the conclusion that mental health professionals' opinions on ultimate legal issues are viewed as very important.

Table 8.1
Types of Testimony Presented in Court

Aspects of mental health testimony[a]	Judges' ratings of probative value	
	Median rating	Rank order
A. Statistical/actuarial data on diagnosis or clinical observations.	5.25	7
B. Statistical/actuarial data on the relationship between clinical and legally relevant behavior	3.20	8
C. Descriptive testimony	7.83	1
D. Diagnosis	5.83	5
E. Theoretical accounts or explanations for legally relevant behavior.	6.00	4
F. Weighing of different motives or explanations for legally relevant behavior.	5.50	6
G. Interpreting the legal standard for mental disorder.	6.83	3
H. Ultimate legal issue.	7.60	2

[a]From N. Poythress, *Conflicting Postures for Mental Health Expert Witnesses: Prevailing Attitudes of Trial Court Judges* (1981). Unpublished manuscript on file with the Department of Training and Research, Center for Forensic Psychiatry, P.O. Box 2060, Ann Arbor, MI 48106.

To delve more deeply into this issue, we assigned ordinal values of 1 through 8 to each of the eight aspects of testimony listed in Table 18.1; aspects in which the witness stays closest to the data were rated as most appropriate (A = 1, B = 2, and so forth), whereas those aspects that are more likely to involve the witness in addressing issues beyond the realm of clinical inquiry were rated as least appropriate (G = 7, H = 8). These rankings of "appropriateness" of testimony were then compared with the rankings based on the judges' ratings (see Figure 18.1). The inverse correlation we obtained (Spearman rank-order correlation $r = -.55$) again reflects the judges' preference for testimony of a more conclusory type and rejection of testimony based on the hardest scientific data (A and B) social scientists can muster.[45] It appears that judges do not want to

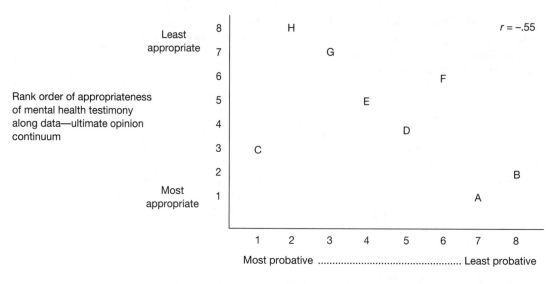

Figure 18.1. *Judicial perceptions of clinical opinions.* [From N. Poythress, *Conflicting Postures for Mental Health Expert Witnesses: Prevailing Attitudes of Trial Court Judges* (1981). Unpublished manuscript on file with the Department of Training and Research, Center for Forensic Psychiatry, P.O. Box 2060, Ann Arbor, MI 48106. Used by permission.]

struggle alone with the difficult moral issues raised in legal decisionmaking.

(b) Pressures to Address Ultimate Legal Issues

Numerous pressures, some subtle and some not so subtle, push mental health professionals in the direction of ultimate-issue testimony. The most prominent pressure is the one just described: the belief on the part of legal professionals that such testimony is one of the most important aspects of the expert's presentation. If judges, as reflected in the Michigan survey, are prone to prefer such testimony, attorneys who want a particular verdict are even more likely to do so. This pressure may be exacerbated if there is any type of positive relationship between the clinician and the attorney seeking clinical assistance. Brodsky and Poythress have noted:

> Mental health professionals who testify regularly find themselves subjected to pressures to join the attorney in the adversarial process. After all, the attorney who has engaged the experts is the

person with whom the personal relationship has been established. A sense of loyalty exists. . . . It is not unusual, therefore, for some experts to find themselves committed to defending "their" attorney's position in a fierce and vigorous manner.[46]

The legal profession's desire for conclusory testimony has other effects as well. In some jurisdictions, it has led to legal statutes and rules of evidence that permit or require the examining clinician to reach a conclusion on the ultimate legal issue.[47] Clinicians working at state forensic facilities may feel further pressure from department or facility policies dictating that such opinions be generated. These policies, which probably reflect explicit or implicit judicial preferences, might be resisted in rare cases but usually not without creating some subjective concern over job security.

Economic considerations might also affect clinicians in private practice. If their livelihood depends on attracting a certain amount of forensic evaluation business, they may feel that their market value will diminish if they too strenuously resist providing opinions and conclusions that may be easily obtained elsewhere.[48] This pressure might explain why one clinician was willing to diagnose a defendant, charged with property damage at an abortion clinic, with the non-DSM disorder of "abortion clinic mania," and why another, in the highly publicized trial of cannibalist Jeffrey Dahmer, was willing to state that the defendant suffered from "cancer of the mind." If clinicians are willing to make such pronouncements, they presumably would have no difficulty mouthing legal language.

The dynamics of the courtroom may also seduce the clinician into addressing questions that are properly beyond his or her expertise. The process of *voir dire* is a public statement of professional expertise by the witness, a statement subsequently endorsed by the trial judge's official proclamation that the witness is an expert on issues before the court. Thus, a clinician might feel it incongruent to demur with "I have no opinion" at just the point when the issues of greatest concern are raised. In fact, Bradley's research suggests that persons who have openly professed expertise will guess rather than admit ignorance in response to questions arguably related to their areas of expertise, even if the questions are virtually impossible to answer.[49]

Finally, of course, clinicians may be willing to offer ultimate-issue testimony because they believe there is no ethical or legal prohibition against doing so. Historically, clinicians have operated with crude and erroneous diagnostic decision rules (e.g., psychosis equals insanity), on occasion expressing exasperation that jurors might disagree with their professional judgments. One psychiatrist's commentary is illustrative: "[I]f a jury found that the accused was not insane, then it was a fact that he was not insane, no matter what any number of medical men might say! What a source of confusion."[50] More nuanced defenses of conclusory language have also been advanced,[51] including the view expressed by Slobogin that while ultimate-issue testimony should be barred, "penultimate" testimony (e.g., whether a person could "appreciate the wrongfulness of an act," as opposed to whether the person was "insane") should be permitted, at least if it has meaningful clinical content and is proffered in a truly adversarial proceeding.[52] These positions were canvassed in § 1.04(a) and will not be reviewed here.

In summary, there are a variety of inducements for the mental health professional to give ultimate testimony. The precedents for doing so come not just from lawyers but have been established by the past practices of psychologists and psychiatrists, who pass the tradition on to their proteges through the processes of socialization and training. Because of competition among the various disciplines, none can unilaterally impose a "gag" rule on its members without risking forfeiture of its share of the business. Thus, in spite of a growing number of hortatory appeals from legal and clinical academicians, there is little movement in the law toward imposing formal restrictions on these witnesses.[53]

(c)   Resisting the Ultimate-Issue Question

We suggest that such a movement should take place. "Since it is not within the professional competence of psychologists to offer conclusions on matters of law, psychologists should resist pressure to offer such conclusions."[54] This recommendation of the American Psychological Association's task force on the role of psychology in the criminal justice system is applicable, we feel, to all mental health professionals and in virtually all litigation. Mental health professionals do have considerable expertise in their own fields of study—for example, in identifying and describing abnormal behavior, providing information about etiology and prognosis, and offering theoretical formulations that provide the factfinder with feasible psychological explanations for complex human behavior. However, as we have already pointed out, they do not have the expertise, nor are they charged with the responsibility, to make truly ultimate legal judgments such as whether someone is incompetent or insane—judgments that involve moral values and the weighing of competing social interests.

Because we are encouraging a posture that is unconventional by current standards, and one not likely to be well received by the court, it is incumbent upon us to suggest practical methods of implementation. As a predicate for doing so, it should first be noted that the position advocated here requires only that the mental health professional make openly and candidly the same concessions that a good attorney could extract through careful cross-examination: Few knowledgeable clinicians would maintain, under close questioning, that they are experts in moral decisionmaking or that such decisions can be made scientifically.

Moreover, a careful analysis reveals that this posture may be used to advantage. For instance, a denial that ultimate opinions are within the province of the mental health sciences can be an effective rebuttal to ultimate opinions from the opposition's witness. Indeed, if one witness tries to defend the indefensible position (that clinicians *are* experts in drawing legal conclusions) but the other witness readily concedes otherwise, an advantage in trust goes to the second witness. If, on the other hand, both sides concede the point, ultimate-issue opinions may be discarded without loss, leaving the experts free to develop their data, observations, and theoretical formulations and leaving arguments and persuasion to the attorneys. Under this arrangement, cross-examination will go more smoothly as well. With no straw figures to knock down, the opposing attorney is more likely to focus on the data.

Consider the following hypothetical civil commitment proceeding, in which the state attempts to prove that the subject should be involuntarily committed. If the clinician is acting as a witness for the state, testimony might proceed as follows:

Attorney: Doctor, is Mr. Doe presently suffering from any mental disorder, and, if so, what symptoms does he display?

Doctor: Mr. Doe is presently diagnosed as suffering from schizophrenia, paranoid type. His primary symptoms include excessive distrust of family members, to the point that he has nailed boards over the doors and windows to his room to keep others from looking in or entering. He also reported excessive fears that his parents are trying to hurt him, to the degree that he no longer eats with other family members for fear of poisoning; he also reported that he sleeps with a knife and loaded gun under his bed. Research examining the relation of specific symptoms of mental illness to risk for violence suggests that persons who perceive themselves as imminently threatened by others may be at increased risk for aggressive behavior.

Attorney: Have there been prior incidents of actual violent behavior?

Doctor: None to my knowledge, though Mr. Doe admitted to prior threats and the intent to protect himself by whatever means necessary.

Attorney: What kind of treatment is needed for this disorder, and in what setting might it be appropriately given?

Doctor: Psychotropic medication with supportive verbal therapy would provide the best chance for remission of symptoms and the restoration of more normal functioning. However, Mr. Doe adamantly denies that he is ill in any way; thus, I doubt that he would take medication or attend therapy sessions voluntarily. Thus, if the treatment I have suggested is going to be effective, it may have to be administered on a locked hospital ward.

Attorney: Doctor, are you saying that Mr. Doe should be committed to the state hospital for treatment?

Doctor: Whether he *should* be committed is a decision the judge must make. It is beyond my skills as a psychiatrist to say that Mr. Doe is mentally ill and dangerous *enough* that his freedom should be restricted and treatment provided involuntarily. However, if it is the court's decision that he does need involuntary treatment, then I consider the most appropriate treatment setting to be a locked hospital ward.

Alternatively, suppose that our hypothetical clinician has been called by the prospective patient's attorney and has testified that the subject has grudgingly admitted a willingness to go to the community mental health center for outpatient treatment if it will mean avoiding commitment to the state hospital. Assume also, contrary to the previous hypothetical, that the state's clinician has offered the conclusion that "Mr. Doe is so mentally ill and so dangerous that he should be committed to the hospital for involuntary treatment." Cross-examination of the first clinician might go as follows:

Attorney: Doctor Smith, you seem to be suggesting that Mr. Doe *might* be treatable on an outpatient basis, but you're not sure.

Your colleague, Dr. Jones, testified with reasonable medical certainty that Mr. Doe was *too dangerous* to remain at liberty and *required* involuntary treatment on a locked hospital ward. You don't seem very confident in your opinion, Dr. Smith.

Doctor: I have not offered an opinion, counselor. Dr. Jones and I have both described the threats that Mr. Doe has made to family members, but neither he, nor I, nor any other psychiatrist has any way of determining whether those threats are sufficient cause to legally restrict his freedom. That is a decision the judge must make weighing the risks to Mr. Doe's family against his rights as a free citizen. As to whether or not Mr. Doe will actually follow through with outpatient treatment if it is offered, again, no one can say with certainty. This is Mr. Doe's first episode of acute symptoms, thus there is no prior history of treatment or medication compliance to draw on. Although he denies that he is ill, he stated that he would go the health center if necessary in order to avoid being locked up. Dr. Jones has no more scientific basis for saying that Mr. Doe won't keep outpatient appointments than I would have for asserting that he will.

As these examples illustrate, no matter which party calls them, clinicians can avoid being dragged into a "battle of the experts" revolving around ultimate-issue opinions by modestly asserting the limits of mental health expertise. In casting the ultimate issue as a moral and legal judgment outside the realm of scientific inquiry clinicians can maintain the integrity of their testimony and force the trier of fact to focus on the clinical data and formulations that make up the substance of mental health testimony.

Although the posture we propose thus has practical advantages, it also clearly has disadvantages. As already noted, pressure to form and provide ultimate-issue opinions will come from judges who do not want the responsibility for making tough moral decisions alone, from attorneys who are accustomed to using "expert opinions" to sway the jury, and from statutes or hospital policy dictating that opinions on legal issues be

developed. Recognizing that there may be situations in which clinicians will not be able to resist these pressures, we strongly recommend the following tactics.

First, clinicians should try to define exactly what they mean when they use legal language. Thus, for instance, if the word "sane" must be used, clinicians should link it to the appropriate test and then explain how they understand each component of the test. Or, if the lawyer wants the clinician to tell the jury whether the defendant could "appreciate" the wrongfulness of his or her conduct (the test language found in the American Law Institute's formulation for insanity [see § 8.02(b)]), the clinician can explain what he or she means by the word "appreciate"; if that word has been defined by case law in the jurisdiction, the clinician can point out how his or her definition of "appreciate" differs, if at all, from the court's. In this way, the clinical nature of the testimony will be driven home to the factfinder.

Similarly, clinicians should make clear that ultimate opinions are not derived from scientific inquiry. In reports and testimony, they can state that their "opinions" are not scientific determinations and that the evidence they have to offer should be considered advisory only.[55] In testimony, clinicians should also be careful in responding to questions about "reasonable medical certainty" or "reasonable scientific certainty" and perhaps volunteer that such statements relate more to the clinician's subjective confidence in his or her findings than to a firm basis in science for the opinions that follow.[56] In short, it should be clear that such opinions, if given, will not be offered for more than they really are—judgments based in common sense and personal moral values. These steps, we believe, will encourage more ethically sound testimony by mental health professionals and more independent decisionmaking by the trier of fact.

On the question of the ultimate legal issue, the relationship between the law and the mental health sciences invokes the analogy of a couple in psychotherapy who are locked in an overly dependent relationship. The legal system resists dealing with problems of its own by demanding that mental health professionals accept responsibility for them, conferring special status as an inducement. For their part, mental health professionals experience an increasing awareness of the unreasonable demands being made but are unsure how to break the bond. Although both feel ambivalence, it is a relationship with old roots and considerable inertia. Change, when attempted, is slow to take effect and is usually resisted. It is our hope that suggestions in this volume for changes in the relationship will contribute to a weaning that is long overdue.

Bibliography

STANLEY L. BRODSKY, TESTIFYING IN COURT: GUIDELINES & MAXIMS FOR THE EXPERT WITNESS (1991).

Stanley Brodsky & Norman Poythress, *Expertise on the Witness Stand: A Practitioner's Guide,* in PSYCHOLOGY, PSYCHIATRY AND THE LAW: A CLINICAL AND FORENSIC HANDBOOK (Charles Ewing ed. 1985).

HAROLD A. FEDER, SUCCEEDING AS AN EXPERT WITNESS: INCREASING YOUR IMPACT AND INCOME (1991).

GROUP FOR THE ADVANCEMENT OF PSYCHIATRY, THE MENTAL HEALTH PROFESSIONAL AND THE LEGAL SYSTEM (GAP Report No. 131, 1991).

W. O'BARR, LINGUISTIC EVIDENCE: LANGUAGE, POWER AND STRATEGY IN THE COURTROOM (1982).

Norman Poythress, *Coping on the Witness Stand: Learned Responses to "Learned Treatises,"* 11 PROFESSIONAL PSYCHOLOGY 139 (1980).

Christopher Slobogin, *The Ultimate Issue Issue,* 7 BEHAVIORAL SCIENCES & LAW 259 (1989).

GERALD H. VANDENBERG, COURT TESTIMONY IN MENTAL HEALTH: A GUIDE FOR MENTAL HEALTH PROFESSIONALS AND ATTORNEYS (1993).

Andrew Watson, *On the Preparation and Use of Expert Testimony: Some Suggestions in an Ongoing Controversy,* 6 BULLETIN AMERICAN ACADEMY PSYCHIATRY & LAW 226 (1978).

JAY ZISKIN & DAVID FAUST, COPING WITH PSYCHIATRIC AND PSYCHOLOGICAL TESTIMONY (4th ed. 1988).

CHAPTER NINETEEN

Sample Reports

19.01.   Introduction

This chapter contains 16 sample reports, many of them based on actual cases. They are included in this book primarily for two reasons. First, they provide concrete illustrations of the type of information we think should be communicated to the courts in the subject areas covered in this book. Second, they demonstrate application of the report-writing guidelines set out in the previous chapter [§18.03(b)]. The editorial comments that follow each report highlight the ways in which it illustrates these substantive and communicative objectives; they also note other interesting legal and clinical issues raised by the reports.

We do not offer a report on each of the subjects covered in this book, both because of space considerations and because reports on some subjects (e.g., the various competencies) will be similar in tone even if the specific legal issue addressed varies. However, we do provide at least one sample report for each of the chapters on substantive legal issues (Chapters 6 through 17). The reports address the following topics: competency to stand trial; competency to plead guilty, to confess, and to waive an insanity defense; mental state at the time of the offense; sentencing under a sexual offender statute; long-term dangerousness in the criminal context; short-term dangerousness in the civil commitment context;

competency to handle finances; employment-related mental injury; reasonable accommodation under the Americans with Disabilities Act; transferability of a juvenile; review of disposition in an abuse case; custody and visitation rights; and the educational needs of a child who may be eligible under the Individuals with Disabilities Education Act.

Before presenting the reports, a brief summary of what has been said in this book about communicating with the courts—whether the communication is written or oral—may be helpful. Above all, it should be remembered that forensic reports and testimony are for a lay audience interested in information relevant to specific legal questions. The clinician should either avoid clinical jargon or explain it if it is used. The expert should also avoid giving gratuitous opinions on questions that have not been asked (although there are exceptions to this rule, as the first report in this chapter illustrates). Throughout, the expert should strive for clarity and conciseness.

It also bears emphasizing that writing a report and giving testimony require thought and preparation. Regardless of the legal issue presented, the clinician should develop an outline to make sure that the presentation of the information will be organized, addresses each issue raised by the referral source, and informs the reader of the underlying bases for each conclusion. When possible, "facts" or "data" should be separated from "inference" and "opinion." Sources should always be attributed.

Finally, clinicians should always be sensitive to the limits of their expertise. Speculation should be identified. Most important, conclusions as to whether a legal test or standard is met should be avoided because of their nonscientific nature.

The reports below attempt to achieve these objectives, although they may not always be successful at doing so. They follow a similar sequential format: subject name, date of birth, date of referral, referral issues, data sources for the evaluation, relevant personal history, presentation of clinical data, and discussion of the legal issues (in those reports based on actual cases, identifying information has been changed to ensure confidentiality). Aside from this similarity in structure, however, the format varies considerably. The clinician will soon develop a report-writing style suited to his or her personal needs; we would only reemphasize the importance of organization, both to assure that the report is understandable to the nonclinicians who are its primary audience, and to assist the clinician in assuring that all relevant issues have been addressed.

19.02.   Competency to Stand Trial [Chapter 6]

(a)   Harry Mills Report

NAME: Harry Mills
D.O.B.:   August 6, 1962
DATE INTERVIEWED: November 4, 1995
SUBJECT: Competency to stand trial

SOURCES OF DATA: Interview of defendant by Harry P. Nelson, Ph.D.; interview of defendant's attorney by Dr. Nelson; indictment; police report

REFERRAL AND BACKGROUND INFORMATION: Mr. Mills was referred to the Clinic by his court-appointed attorney, Mr. Hahnemann, of Luther, Minnesota, for evaluation of his competency to stand trial on a charge of rape. Mr. Hahnemann also indicated concern that Mr. Mills appeared to be experiencing a significant degree of depression, although he has no history of psychiatric problems.

MENTAL STATUS: Mr. Mills communicated effectively throughout his interview and did not hesitate to answer questions. However, his affect (emotional demeanor) was sad, and on several occasions he described suicidal thoughts. In particular, he stated he would commit suicide if sent to jail. (These statements are discussed in more detail below.)

While no formal assessment of Mr. Mills's intellectual ability was conducted, he appeared to be of grossly normal (perhaps low-average) intelligence. He appeared to have no significant problems with either recent or remote memory. However, at several points during the interview, he described himself as "dumb about things." These statements appear to reflect both an accurate assessment of his low fund of general information and his low self-esteem at present.

UNDERSTANDING OF LEGAL SITUATION: Mr. Mills can state the charge against him, describe its elements (he defined it as "nonconsensual intercourse"), and describe the possible sentence he'll receive if convicted. He is able to give a coherent description of the circumstances surrounding the alleged offense. He is able to describe in a basic way the actors in the court process. For instance, he stated that the prosecutor "is the attorney who presents the evidence against me," and that the judge "runs the trial and decides what to do with me." He can describe the process of testimony and cross-examination. He knows that he has a right to remain silent when asked questions by the judge. He describes the jury as a "group of citizens who decide whether you're guilty." When asked to describe "plea bargaining," he stated, "It's when the two attorneys agree on a charge for me."

Mr. Mills understands his attorney is supposed to "represent" him in court and states he has no difficulty conferring with him (a statement Mr. Hahnemann confirms). Mr. Mills also stated, however, that one of Mr. Hahnemann's jobs is "to decide if I'm guilty or innocent." It might be helpful if Mr. Hahnemann clarified the exact nature of his role to Mr. Mills.

CONCLUSIONS CONCERNING COMPETENCY TO STAND TRIAL: As indicated above, Mr. Mills has no difficulty describing the charges against him, nor does he appear to have significant difficulty communicating in general or with his attorney in particular. He does have some misconceptions about the legal process—specifically about the role of his attorney, which Mr. Hahnemann should be able to clear up. Whether Mr. Mills accepts a plea-bargaining agreement or decides to go to trial may be influenced by his expressed dislike for jail, discussed more fully below.

COMMENTS CONCERNING TREATMENT:
During the course of this evaluation, it became obvious that Mr. Mills is suffering from an acute depression. The most notable consideration is his clearly stated suggestion that the notion of self-destruction is not foreign to him and that in fact he has considered killing himself on a number of occasions. Mr. Mills stated that upon his release from an earlier prison sentence, he vowed that he would "never be placed in prison again." Today Mr. Mills reiterated several times that he had made this promise to himself; this suggests that he would at least consider self-destruction as an alternative to serving further time in prison.

The scope of the examination today did not allow for a thorough review of this man's history of covert, if not overt, suicidal ideation and/or intent. It is my recommendation at this time that he seek immediate psychotherapeutic follow-up, specifically for the purpose of establishing an appropriate treatment program for the depression that he currently experiences. In this regard, it should be noted that he is not particularly introspective and finds it difficult to verbalize a number of the strong emotions that he is experiencing. These feelings may only surface through this type of treatment.

Harry P. Nelson, Ph.D.

(b) Discussion

Except for the last section, the Mills report is fairly typical of many reports on the issue of competency to stand trial. As is true in many such cases [see § 6.05(a)], there was not much room for doubt as to the defendant's competency, although Mr. Mills was obviously experiencing some mental difficulties.

When competency (criminal or civil) is the issue, the forensic report should be very focused. For example, the writer of the Mills report presented virtually none of the individual's personal history. Historical material may be critical in the evaluation of certain issues (e.g., in sentencing), but it has little utility in most evaluations of competency to stand trial.

Note that details of the offense were not given. The writer observed that Mr. Mills could describe the offense, which was relevant to whether he was competent [see § 6.02(b)]. However, the *details* of the offense are usually irrelevant in reporting on competency to stand trial and, in any event, should not be included given Fifth Amendment concerns [see § 4.02(a)].

Note also that the writer dealt with each of the functional elements of the competency test in describing Mr. Mills's abilities [see § 6.02(b)]. He observed that Mr. Mills could describe the court process and the roles of the participants and gave specific examples using the defendant's own words. He then described Mr. Mills's relationship with this attorney, using information from both Mr. Mills and the attorney. Whether these statements in fact indicated sufficient knowledge about the legal process to merit a finding of competency was a question the writer left to the factfinder (although in this case the answer seems to have been clear). In addition, the descriptive details demonstrated clinical awareness of the competency standard and may have saved the writer a trip to court.

Finally, this case presents three examples of situations in which the clinician appropriately included in the report material somewhat beyond the narrow issue of the person's competence. First, the report writer, in delineating the various elements of competency, noted that Mr. Mills was unclear about the role of his own lawyer and suggested that a conversation between the two should alleviate this problem. Second, the writer highlighted a clinical concern (Mr. Mills's fear of jail) and its possible impact on the legal process (i.e., Mr. Mills's fears could influence a plea-bargaining decision). This concern was more directly relevant to Mr. Mills's competency to plead but also had ramifications for the extent to which Mr. Mills would cooperate with his attorney. Third, the writer strongly suggested further clinical evaluation and treatment of Mr. Mills's depression. Comments on treatment may not always be appropriate in a competency evaluation, but in this case the combination of possible acute depression on the client's part with a strong aversion to jail raised legitimate questions about the issue of harm to self. The oblique reference to Mr. Mills's previous prison term, although "prejudicial," was probably unavoidable if the writer was to give a complete clinical picture of Mr. Mills's suicidal thought patterns.

It is possible that Mr. Mills's attorney was more concerned about the treatment issue than about Mr. Mills's competency when he asked for the evaluation. Ideally, in such cases the attorney would communicate this interest via the court order rather than leave its assessment to the discretion of the examiner.

(c)   Warner Premington Report

NAME: Warner Premington
D.O.B.:   November 18, 1940
DATE INTERVIEWED: October 24, 1997
SUBJECT: Competency to stand trial

SOURCES OF DATA: Interview by Samuel Tatum, M.D., and Guy C. Harris, Ph.D.; interview of Mrs. Premington by Drs. Tatum and Harris; Competency Screening Test; University of Virginia Hospital Chart.

REFERRAL INFORMATION: Mr. Premington was referred to the Forensic Psychiatry Clinic for evaluation of competency to stand trial by his attorney, Mr. Smith of Fairfax, Virginia. Specifically, the clinic was asked to determine whether Mr. Premington has substantial mental capacity to understand the proceedings against him, whether he has the mental capacity to aid and assist his counsel in his defense, and whether more extensive evaluation and observation are required. The present evaluation concerns Mr. Premington's charges of "driving after having been adjudged an habitual offender." These charges result from incidents in Fairfax County on April 25, 1997, and in Loudoun County on May 19, 1997. Also pending is an appeal in Loudoun County General District Court on a related charge of driving under the influence.

Mr. Smith has represented Mr. Premington for a number of years, and he was concerned about a steady deterioration that he has observed in Mr. Premington's ability to understand and orient himself to present events. Particular precipitants of the current evaluation were Mr. Premington's tendency to confuse the Loudoun County charge with the incident in Fairfax County and his disorientation at the time of a preliminary hearing in Loudoun County, according to Mr. Smith.

BACKGROUND INFORMATION: Mr. Premington has a lengthy history of psychiatric problems. He was hospitalized on several occasions for paranoid schizophrenia at the Salem Veterans Administration Hospital after a psychiatric discharge from military service in World War II. He was evaluated here at the Forensic Psychiatric Clinic in December 1988, subsequent to charges of breaking and entering. At that time, he was apparently actively delusional and hallucinating. Of most relevance to the current situation, Mr. Premington suffered rather severe damage to the cortical area of the brain as a result of head trauma in-

curred in a motorcycle accident in July 1995. Since that time he has had serious memory deficits and, according to his wife, periodic rage reactions. He has been hospitalized for these problems on occasion at the University of Virginia Hospital. He is currently being maintained on Haldol (an antipsychotic medication) at 2 mg per day. It is also noteworthy that Mr. Premington has a history of chronic alcohol abuse.

MENTAL STATUS EXAMINATION: Mr. Premington presented as a rather tense, anxious man who appeared somewhat bewildered by the evaluation process. It was immediately apparent that he has some difficulty in recalling life events. He stated that his memory "has really gone downhill" since the accident of July 1995. The problems in recall were somewhat diffuse but appeared to be more pronounced when he was attempting to relate events in the recent past. On examination, Mr. Premington was able to retain and recall a series of three digits; when four digits were given, his sequential recall deteriorated significantly. He had very inconsistent recall when asked to repeat several series of three and four digits in reverse order. He could recall his own telephone number but claimed no recall for the telephone numbers of his children (who live in the area). He also stated he cannot remember the extent of his extended family (he is not sure how many grandchildren he has).

Mr. Premington was unable to engage in abstract thinking in the evaluation. This was tested through the presentation of a series of items, one of which does not belong to the set (i.e., "Which one does not belong to the series: apple, orange, pear, ice cream cone?").

The client was fully oriented to time, person, place (i.e., his awareness of his whereabouts and identity was intact), and his situation (i.e., being evaluated by physicians), although it cannot be assumed that he understood the actual medical–legal significance of this examination. It is noteworthy also that Mr. Premington had a marked tendency to perseverate. That is, he would make an appropriate verbal response but then would continue to repeat that response in contexts in which it no longer made any sense. He was apparently unable to shift his understanding of the situation when the situation had in fact changed. For example, on a sentence completion task (the Competency Screening Test), Mr. Premington repeatedly responded, "I'd tell the truth" when that answer was not relevant to the sentence stems presented. An originally appropriate response was thus repeated in inappropriate contexts. Largely because of this confusion, Mr. Premington scored below the cutoff point for competency on the Competency Screening Test, an instrument that has been found to discriminate validly between defendants later found incompetent to stand trial and those found competent. As a screening instrument, however, the Competency Screening Test slightly overpredicts incompetency, so it should not be relied on as the sole factor in a determination.

UNDERSTANDING OF THE LEGAL SITUATION: Mr. Premington is aware that he was not supposed to be driving because he did not have a driver's license. He apparently does not understand the reason why his permit was revoked, though. He defined "habitual offender" as "driving the car more than once." He does understand the meaning of "driving under the influence" and its illegality. Mr. Premington was able to give a reasonably cogent description of the circumstances surrounding the offense in Fairfax County. However, when asked about other charges, Mr. Premington stated several times that he had no other charges pending. During the second interview, Mr. Premington did recall the Loudoun County offense, although he did not seem to realize that he was still liable for it. At best, he confuses the two events and has a clear awareness only of the Fairfax County charge. He was aware of no current charges of driving under the influence. He also had no memory of any recent court appearances.

Mr. Premington has some limited understanding of the process of a trial. He knows that a judge "gives you time" or "dismisses the case if you're not guilty." He observed that police are often present at the court, but he was unable to describe why. He also had no idea how an attorney might help him. Mr. Premington claimed to have no memory of what had happened in previous trials in which he had been a defendant. He described a jury as "three or four people together saying that you're guilty." He defined "guilty" as meaning that one is "charged with a crime." It was not clear if he understood that one could be charged but actually found not guilty; that is, it was unclear if he really knew what "being charged" means.

Mr. Premington does not understand his rights in a trial. He said that the right to remain silent means that one is "not guilty" and later said it meant "telling the truth." A third definition he gave was that, if a policeman says it, "he don't believe that you're guilty." He also does not understand the process of confrontation of witnesses. When asked what he would do if a witness lied about him, he reasoned that "I'd just feel bad" and that "I wouldn't do nothing."

CONCLUSIONS CONCERNING COMPETENCY TO STAND TRIAL: Subsequent to head trauma, Mr. Premington has suffered a significant memory loss. In the current context, he confuses the offenses with which he is charged, and it is questionable whether he would be able to keep the events of a trial in sequence in his mind. Because of his tendency to perseverate, it is also questionable whether he would be able to follow the trial as it progresses. Mr. Premington does understand that it was against the law for him to drive, and he remembers the Fairfax County incident reasonably well. Although he does understand a trial as possibly resulting in "giving him time," Mr. Premington has numerous misconceptions and gaps in knowledge about the process of a trial. Mr. Premington's ability to engage in abstract thinking is so minimal that he is unable to conceptualize the roles of various participants in the trial. It is not likely that Mr. Premington would be able to give his attorney relevant facts as the trial progresses, because he could not be expected to understand the implications of testimony. He is compliant, though, and he would probably assist his attorney as much as he could, which realistically would be on an extremely limited basis.

CONCLUSIONS CONCERNING TREATMENT: We believe that Mr. Premington's lapses are largely related to brain damage. These lesions are permanent, and, as a result, he cannot be expected to become more competent, even with treatment. In our opinion, he does not require hospitalization at this time. Continued supervision by Mrs. Premington at home with medication would be a "less restrictive alternative" for his care than a hospital.

> Samuel Tatum, M.D.
> Guy C. Harris, Ph.D.

(d)   Discussion

The Premington report is more complicated than the Mills report because Mr. Premington's competency was much more in doubt. Several things about the report are worth noting.

First, in contrast to Mr. Mills's case, historical information was relevant to a determination of Mr. Premington's competency. Most significant in this regard was his history of brain damage. Some of this background information was received from the attorney; a form such as that found in Figure 6.1 can help focus the attorney (or other informant) on the relevant considerations.

Second, note the cautious manner in which clinical information was offered. Instead of bald assertions of "poor memory," examples were given of Mr. Premington's problems with memory and abstract thinking. By providing the court with the basis for their clinical judgments, the report writers enhanced the court's ability to judge the validity of their conclusions. Toward the same end, clinical terms (e.g., "perseverate") were explained in lay terms. Note also the explanation of the Competency Screening Test, and the qualification that it tends to overpredict incompetency slightly [see § 6.06(a)].

Third, as in the Mills report, the writers focused on the specific functional elements of competency. They described Mr. Premington's understanding of court process and of the roles of the various participants, using concrete examples from his statements at the interview and other sources. Although the court might not have given credence to the information (e.g., the court might have asked whether other individuals—say, Mr. Premington's wife—could corroborate what appeared to be his extremely hazy notion of court process), these examples would at least have made the court aware of the reasons for the clinical opinion.

Fourth, note that although on balance, the writers appeared to suggest that Mr. Premington was not competent, they avoided the ultimate issue, as we suggest they should. Leaving this judgment to the legal system might frustrate the court and counsel. But competency is a legal issue and its determination often involves considerations that are not clinical in nature. In this case, for instance, the state needed only to prove that Mr. Premington had a previous driving offense and was "behind the wheel" on this occasion to obtain a conviction under the "habitual offender" statute. The court might have decided that Mr. Premington was competent to understand his relatively simple charges and to confer with his attorney about them.

Finally, the report noted the permanency of Mr. Premington's condition. This fact would be relevant to the issue of restoration of competency if the court found Mr. Premington incompetent [see §§ 6.04(a), 6.07(c)].

(e)   Fordham Rhodes Report

NAME: Fordham Rhodes
D.O.B.:   April 26, 1972
DATE OF REPORT: January 3, 1995
SUBJECT: Competency review

DATE OF INTERVIEW: January 2, 1996, by Walt Allman, M.D.

PURPOSE OF REPORT: Mr. Rhodes has been housed here at the South Florida Treatment and Evaluation Center since August 1993, after a Dade County court found him incompetent to proceed on charges of aggravated assault (a felony), credit card theft (a misdemeanor), and fraudulent use of a credit card (a felony). As mandated by statute, he is to be evaluated every six months to determine whether he remains incompetent to proceed. This report addresses that issue.

NOTIFICATION: Mr. Rhodes was told that he was being evaluated for his competency to proceed and that the results of the evaluation would go to the court, the prosecution, and his lawyer. He signed a form indicating his understanding of these points and indicating his agreement to participate in the evaluation.

BACKGROUND: Mr. Rhodes is a 34-year-old black male. He entered the Navy at the age of 18, serving as an aircraft mechanic on an aircraft carrier. He also claims he was a Navy Seal during his enlistment, but this cannot be verified. After eight years of service, he left the Navy and worked at various jobs, including a radio and television tuner repairman. In 1989 he was arrested for unauthorized use of a vehicle but charges were dismissed. In 1992, he was charged with assault with intent to cause serious bodily harm, possessing a hypodermic needle, resisting arrest, and disorderly conduct, but again charges were dismissed, on "grounds of mental disorder." The current charges arose out of an incident on August 2, 1993, at the Miami International Airport.

PSYCHIATRIC HISTORY: Mr. Rhodes has spent most of his adult life hospitalized for psychiatric problems. His consistent diagnosis is schizophrenia (paranoid type) with polysubstance dependence. His first experience with treatment was in the Navy, where he reported hallucinations (i.e., seeing persons or things that were not there) which were treated with Haldol (an antipsychotic medication) and Cogentin (a medicine that relieves the side effects of Haldol). Since then, he has been in mental hospitals on three other occasions, including his current hospitalization here, for a total of almost six years out of the past nine years. As his diagnosis indicates, he has a history of alcohol and drug abuse as well. Cocaine is his drug of preference, although he has reported using marijuana, LSD, and mushrooms.

COMPETENCY CRITERIA: In his initial evaluation, as well as in previous reviews, Mr. Rhodes has done poorly on all six of the competency criteria listed in the Florida Rules of Criminal Procedure. My assessment of these factors indicates that he has improved significantly in all six areas.

1. *Capacity to appreciate the charges or allegations.* Mr. Rhodes can state with confidence what his charges are and can explain, in abstract terms, what aggravated assault and credit card theft mean. For example, he knew that assault means hitting someone and that theft means taking away someone's property. He also understands that "aggravated" assault is more serious than nonaggravated assault.

2. *Capacity to appreciate the range and nature of possible penalties.* Mr. Rhodes states, accurately, that he can receive up to seven years for his offenses under the Florida sentencing guidelines. He also understands that a person who is sent to prison can get time off for good behavior. However, he also says, "I'll never go to prison." When asked why, he says, "I'm a hospital man. I'm going to spend the rest of my life in a hospital. They can't send me to prison." When pressed with the possibility that he might be convicted and sentenced, at least technically, to a prison, he persists in his statement that he will never be sent to prison. He also states that he likes the hospital environment and would not like prison. Thus, although he appears capable of describing the penalties he faces, he appears emotionally or affectively somewhat indifferent about them. This attitude might lead him to misassess any bargains that might be offered or the consequence of a conviction.

3. *Capacity to understand the adversary nature of the legal process.* Mr. Rhodes's previous experience with the criminal justice system appears to have made him well acquainted with its attributes. Specifically, he stated that the role of his attorney is to "take the case to court (trial) and fight for me"; he also acknowledged that the attorney can arrange a plea in place of a trial. He was aware of the responsibility of the judge (bench trial) or jury to "listen to both sides" and render a decision of guilty or not guilty. He gave a rudimentary description of the role of witnesses in criminal proceedings and was able to identify potential witnesses both for him and against him. For example, he was aware that this examiner or other mental health professionals who have treated him in the past might be witnesses regarding his mental condition; he also recognized, in the abstract, that a person who is assaulted or whose credit card is stolen might be a witness in a trial involving his type of charges. He knows that the right to remain silent means he does not have to talk even if the judge asks him questions.

4. *Capacity to disclose to counsel facts pertinent to the proceedings at issue.* The police reports state that, at the time of the offense, Mr. Rhodes was trying to purchase a $2,500 ticket to Australia with four credit cards belonging to other people. When confronted with this fact, he became belligerent and struck an airport guard. There is no information in the report about how he obtained the credit cards, although it is conjectured that he bought them from somebody on the street. Mr. Rhodes claims that he met someone on the street who took him to a bank vault full of gold. Somehow during this visit to the vault he came away with the credit cards. He says the names on the cards represent various names he has had throughout his life. As to the alleged assault, Mr. Rhodes says, "You'd hit someone too if they were in your face and calling you names." He became very agitated at this point and the interview was delayed for a short time. When the interview resumed, he stated he would never plead guilty to the charges, again because he belongs in the hospital.

Perhaps also relevant to this criterion, and his ability to relate to his attorney generally, is his delusional system. Mr. Rhodes will often talk about an experience in the Navy, when he somehow fell in the water, or was in the water during his work as a Seal, and ended up as a tooth in a shark who was really his dead stepfather. The delusions are much more elaborate but will not be described further here. They are mentioned because Mr. Rhodes often begins describing them in response to questions about his prior life and criminal offenses.

5. *Capacity to manifest appropriate courtroom behavior.* Mr. Rhodes is generally relaxed and even happy. Although he did become agitated when asked questions about the assault, he did not become violent; rather, he was allowed to smoke a cigarette and he calmed down immediately. He did not raise his voice and stayed seated throughout the interview, which in many ways simulated a mild cross-examination. He is currently on Haldol. He states, and this evaluator can confirm, that this medication "shades" his hallucinations but does not relieve them totally. He also reports that he does not have significant side effects from his current dosage. As noted previously, when focused and not talking about his delusions, he appears to be able to describe with lucidity various aspects of the system, his current situation, and his everyday behavior. There were four or five occasions during our two-hour interview when Mr. Rhodes interjected somewhat bizarre and inappropriate material; however, he could rather easily be directed to contain this material until a later and more appropriate time for discussion. The hospital ward staff reports that he has

been relatively cooperative and appropriate during this period of confinement. Thus, although it is clear that Mr. Rhodes suffers from some symptoms of mental disorder, the likelihood of substantial disruption as a result of those symptoms is considered relatively low.

6. *Capacity to testify relevantly.* The above information is relevant to this criterion as well. If Mr. Rhodes took the stand, he would probably be able to provide information "relevant" to an insanity defense and the assault charge but would not be particularly helpful to a jury trying to find out precisely how he obtained the credit cards. He would probably be able to recount other aspects of his history with the same clarity that he did during this evaluation (described above). Again, any digressions on his part can easily be halted; thus, should he be called on to testify, only minimal difficulties or disruptions should occur.

7. *Other relevant factors.* Mr. Rhodes understands, in the abstract, that if he pleads guilty he gives up his right to jury trial and to confront his accusers. Again, however, he states he would never plead guilty.

CONCLUSIONS REGARDING COMPETENCY:
In summarizing his performance in connection with the six factors, Mr. Rhodes is most likely to have difficulty with respect to appreciating the consequences of a conviction. On the other hand, he may be correct in believing that even if he were convicted he would end up in a hospital, given his need for medication and his history. Mr. Rhodes also is not able to provide accurate information about the credit card charge, although his description might bolster an insanity defense. Whether these or other mental problems described previously make him incompetent is beyond the expertise of this examiner.

TREATMENT CONSIDERATIONS: If Mr. Rhodes is found competent to stand trial, he should be maintained on his current dosage of Haldol pending the trial proceeding. If found incompetent to proceed, the chances of his mental status further improving are very low. In an effort to minimize his hallucinations, this hospital has tried a number of medications, including lithium (usually given to those with manic–depressive psychosis) and Clozaril (a newer antipsychotic drug that has fewer side effects than Haldol). The lithium did not work, however, and the Clozaril turned out to affect Mr. Rhodes's blood pressure and was discontinued. Thus, given our current medical resources, Mr. Rhodes mental state is the "best" it can be at the present time.

Walt Allman, M.D.

(f)   Discussion

A few differences between this report and the two other competency-to-stand-trial reports should be noted. First, this evaluation was not at the "front end" of the process. Rather, it was a review procedure, mandated in virtually all states, of a person who has already been found incompetent to proceed. Note that Mr. Rhodes has already been in the hospital for well over two years. Although this might seem to be a violation of *Jackson v. Indiana* [see § 6.04(a)], in Florida, the state in which this evaluation took place, the relevant rules provide that charges against a person found incompetent do not have to be dismissed until five years after arrest on a felony charge and one year after arrest on a misdemeanor charge.

Second, Florida law dictates that certain specific criteria be assessed, in contrast to many states where the competency standard consists solely of the *Dusky* test. These criteria help focus the evaluator and the court. But they may not be adequate. For instance, note that despite the fact that most defendants plead guilty rather than go to trial, the six criteria do not directly assess one's understanding of rights waived by a guilty plea, an issue the evaluator therefore had to discuss under the "basket" category of "other relevant factors."

As to application of the criteria, probably the most interesting issues are raised by criteria 2 (appreciation of consequences) and 4 (recounting facts). Mr. Rhodes has the capacity to understand that a person charged with his offenses could receive seven years, but he does not appreciate (in the sense of believe) that this consequence could happen to him. It is not clear whether this lack of appreciation mean the person is incompetent (an issue the evaluator wisely avoided). In this regard, note that some of the newer assessment instruments, including the Mac-CAT-CA, specifically try to assess not only the individual's understanding of the situation but also his or her "appreciation" of the legal facts as they apply in his or her case [see § 6.06(g)].

With respect to criterion 4, note that in contrast to the previous two reports, this report recounts Mr. Rhodes's own account of the offense in some detail. Because this report is court-ordered, this detail may present a Fifth Amendment issue, especially when the defense attorney is asserting that his or her client did not commit the crime (although those jurisdictions that prevent use of the competency results at trial minimize this problem [see § 4.02(a)]). In any event, an interesting issue is whether Mr. Rhodes's capacity to give his presumably delusional version of the offense is sufficient to meet criterion 4. The answer to that question may depend on whether he raises an insanity defense. Or a court may decide that the attorney's ability to represent this client is inevitably compromised until the attorney gets a "coherent" account from his client about the manner in which the credit card was obtained and the alleged assault. Similar issues arise in connection with factor 6, having to do with the capacity to testify. Note the hints the evaluator gives as to how to handle Mr. Rhodes should he take the stand or be interviewed.

Third, this individual, unlike Mr. Mills or Mr. Premington, is heavily dependent on antipsychotic medication (the various types of which are explained rather than merely named). Note how the report addresses the "*Riggins* treatment refusal issue" [see § 6.02(d)] in that it describes the effects of the medication on Mr. Rhodes's ability to communicate. The report also tries to predict whether the medication, or any other treatment, will improve Mr. Rhodes's condition, an inquiry necessitated by *Jackson*.

19.03.   Competency to Plead and Confess [Chapter 5]

(a)   Carl Bates Report

NAME: Carl Bates
D.O.B.:   March 28, 1927
DATE OF REPORT: June 22, 1984

DATES OF INTERVIEWS: Social history by John Waggoner, M.S.W., on June 6, 1984; psychiatric evaluation by George Fordham, M.D., on June 13, 1984.

REFERRAL INFORMATION: Mr. Bates is a 57-year-old white male charged with one count of felonious attempted shooting. The charge arose out of an incident that occurred on March 19, 1984, in which Mr. Bates allegedly shot an airplane as it flew over his

property. The plane, a crop duster, was hit five times, but no one was injured. Mr. Bates has signed a confession stating that he did shoot at the plane.

Mr. Bates was referred to the clinic pursuant to an agreement between the Commonwealth's Attorney of Columbia County, Charles Daniels, and Mr. Bates's attorney, Sam James, of Columbia, Maryland. The Clinic was asked to address the following questions:

1. Was Mr. Bates's confession voluntary and intelligent?
2. Is Mr. Bates competent to plead guilty?

The clinic has the following sources of information available to it: a summary of the police investigation relating to Mr. Bates's charge, prepared on March 13, 1984, by Trooper G.W. Jones; a summary of a psychiatric report on Mr. Bates from Brisbane Hospital in Jessup, Maryland, prepared by Dr. Lester Oldes Jr., psychiatrist at the Columbia County Family Guidance Center; a copy of Mr. Bates's indictment; and the clinic's own evaluation, consisting of a two-hour social history interview, a two-and-a-half-hour psychiatric evaluation, and the administration of the Comprehension of *Miranda* Rights and Comprehension of *Miranda* Vocabulary tests.

PERSONAL HISTORY: Mr. Bates has been admitted to a psychiatric facility on only one occasion. In 1968, he was hospitalized at Columbia General Hospital and then transferred to Brisbane Hospital, a mental health institution. Mr. Bates is not sure why he was hospitalized, though he suspects it may have had something to do with his drinking. (He told the clinic that prior to his hospitalization he would often consume a fifth of whiskey while watching a baseball game on TV.) The clinic does not have access to the final report from Brisbane, but a summary of the report prepared by Dr. Oldes indicates that the hospital staff believed Mr. Bates was manifesting "paranoid delusions of a great variety" on his admission to Brisbane. His condition was diagnosed as "chronic undifferentiated schizophrenia with organic features." Signs of heavy drinking were also noted. Mr. Bates told the clinic that he received no treatment at Brisbane. He was apparently released after approximately six months.

According to Mr. Bates, his admission to Brisbane marked a time of significant change in his life. He stated that although he had enjoyed an active sex life before his admission, afterward he did not engage in sex at all. He began having trouble sleeping; he said that this was the result of loud pounding noises originating from rooms adjacent to his. Most significantly, it was at this time that Mr. Bates began to believe that government officials were attempting to harass him. He eventually came to believe that the noises were made by these government agents, whom he alternatively characterized as the "Law," the "Metropolitan Police," the "Government," or "plainclothesmen."

Mr. Bates reported other manifestations of government harassment over the years since 1968. He stated that even though he changed residences several times in the years between 1968 and 1979, the night noises continued. The "Law" allegedly placed bugging devices in his bed and kept him under constant surveillance with cameras and other electronic equipment. Automobiles with Washington, D.C. plates (perceived as indicating a connection with the government) would be waiting outside his door to tail him. He said that the government even began making use of his neighbors and family in its attempt to harass him. He reported that although he used to have a close relationship with his family, he no longer trusts them because they have been "turning to the Law."

From Mr. Bates's description, it appears that the government's scheming increased after he moved to his present location in Archer, Maryland, which happens to be near a military training center. He claimed that eavesdropping devices were planted all over his house and that government cameras were set up in his elder brother's home across the street. Neighbors' children were supposedly employed by the "Law" to observe his activities. The ploy that most annoyed Mr. Bates was the alleged use of planes and helicopters by the "Law" to conduct surveillance and bombard his home with electronic weapons. According to Mr. Bates, the latter action resulted in damage to his house and the death of one of his dogs.

In his confession to the police, Mr. Bates admitted to the shooting incident that led to the current charges. In the confession, he justified his act as an effort on his part to retaliate against the long years of government surveillance and to bring attention to government methods. Though asked at several points during the clinic interview why he thought the government was conducting this campaign against him, he could recite no reason other than the possibility of "some sort of grudge." When confronted with the suggestion that perhaps the cameras and bugging devices did not exist (he admitted to not being able to find them) and that the planes were engaged in legitimate enterprises, he rejected the notion vigorously. He appears to be convinced that the government is "out to get him" and that the plane he shot at was just another indication of this plot.

Since his arrest, Mr. Bates has been living at home. He reported that he has not observed any government-sponsored plane flying over his house, though he believes the cameras are still in place. He stated that he is not concerned about the outcome of the pending proceedings because he has "everything in his hands"; this appears to mean that he has caught the government in the act and it will eventually suffer for it. He believes that his trial and incarceration, if they take place, will be the "match to the gasoline barrel" that will highlight the misdeeds of the "Law" and its officials. He compared himself in this regard to Jack Anderson, the columnist.

Mr. Bates also believes that the "Law" has been behind the delay in having his case heard. He stated that if he is sent to jail he would not be surprised if it was because the judge and the lawyers had been bribed.

MENTAL STATUS: Mr. Bates is a 57-year-old white male with a ruddy complexion. He rarely smiled during the interview and assumed a belligerent tone during most of it; however, his irritation was directed toward those he believed to be harassing him and not toward the interviewers. Mr. Bates was oriented to time, place, and person; that is, he knew what time of the year and day it was, where he was, who he was, and who the interviewers were. He did seem somewhat confused as to the purpose of the interview, at one point stating that he felt his evaluation at the clinic was another attempt at delay by the "Law." He understood, however, that the interview was somehow connected with his pending criminal proceeding.

Mr. Bates exhibited significant signs of delusion when discussing the "Law's" involvement in his life. On other topics he did not exhibit such delusional symptoms; he was able to discuss rationally such subjects as his weight, gardening, different types of guns, and the weather.

Clinically, there is some evidence of incipient organicity (i.e., damage to brain tissue, which often manifests itself through deficits in memory and orientation). Mr. Bates could have done damage to his brain through his heavy drinking in the past. Such damage could also result from deterioration due to the aging process. Mr. Bates's thought content was often tangential (i.e., divergent from the topic under discussion). When confronted with the assertion that some of his statements contradicted reality, he answered with seemingly irrelevant pronouncements. For instance, when it was noted that he had never been able to discover any bugging devices in his home, he responded, "I don't have to find it because I know just what I'm looking for." Clinically, Mr. Bates is estimated to be of average intelligence.

Mr. Bates's affect (his emotional response to the content of the interview) also appeared abnormal. He exhibited little emotion other than anger or irritation throughout most of the interview.

**OBSERVATIONS ABOUT MR. BATES'S COMPE-
TENCY TO CONFESS:** Mr. Bates could coherently
describe the events leading up to his confession, the important aspects of which are corroborated by the police
account. Mr. Bates stated that he was arrested by three
policemen shortly after the alleged offense and was tak-
en to the station house. He was not asked any questions
on the ride to the station, and he did not volunteer any
information, other than exclaiming, "You'll pay for this"
from time to time. After booking, he was given *Miranda*
warnings and was asked several questions about the offense; the session took about an hour and took place in
a windowless room on the second floor of the police
station, with three plainclothes officers and a tape
recorder present. About one hour after the questioning
ended, he was asked to sign a document purporting to
summarize his statements, which he did.

When asked during the interview, Mr. Bates could
state with reasonable precision the *Miranda* warnings.
However, he did forget the fourth prong of the warnings (i.e., that if the person cannot afford an attorney,
one will be appointed for him). He was given two tests
developed by Grisso to examine understanding of *Miranda* rights. *See* T. GRISSO, JUVENILES' WAIVER OF
RIGHTS: LEGAL AND PSYCHOLOGICAL COMPETENCE
(1981). He scored 7 (out of a possible 8) on the Comprehension of *Miranda* Rights Test, and 10 (out of a
possible 12) on the Comprehension of *Miranda* Vocabulary Test, both of which represent scores in the upper
60% of the 203 defendants evaluated by Grisso using
the same tests. Of course, these scores are relevant
primarily to Mr. Bates's present understanding of *Miranda*, not his understanding at the time of the arrest.

Mr. Bates stated that he had not felt physically
threatened by the police at the time of the confession,
nor was he under the influence of drugs or alcohol at
that time. As evidenced during his interview, he does
not seem particularly suggestible, particularly when an
aspect of his delusional system is challenged (see
above).

**OBSERVATIONS ABOUT MR. BATES'S COM-
PETENCY TO PLEAD GUILTY:** In the state of
Maryland, to be competent to plead one must be competent to stand trial plus understand the various rights
that are waived through a guilty plea; in addition, the
plea must be voluntary.

Thus, competency to plead guilty first requires a
capacity to communicate with one's lawyer. Mr. Bates's
mental condition, which demonstrates clear evidence
of paranoia, distorts his perception of reality. However, he is able to communicate verbally with relative
ease. He can recite the events leading up to his arrest
and what occurred thereafter. Although his interpreta-

tion of these events is somewhat abnormal, he is able
to describe them in sufficient detail to give an attorney
a factual basis on which to work.

Mr. Bates stated that he does not believe his attorney is part of the plot to harass him and in fact told the
clinic interviewers that he "trusts" Mr. James. There is
a possibility that Mr. Bates could change his opinion of
Mr. James as the trial date approaches or after he sees
how the trial progresses. However, at present he appears willing to cooperate with his attorney in his own
defense.

The other prong of the test of competency to plead
guilty is whether the defendant possesses a rational and
factual understanding of the proceedings against him.
As noted previously, Mr. Bates's perception of the legal
process is distorted by his belief that if he is found
guilty it will be because the court has been corrupted
and not because he has done something illegal. This
belief is not "rational" in the sense that it does not comport with reality (though it is "rational" if one accepts
Mr. Bates's premise that the "Law" is determined to
martyr him). The important point here, however, is
that Mr. Bates's delusion does not obscure his understanding of the functions of various court personnel,
nor does it hinder his grasp of the purpose of trial. He
was able to explain adequately what the judge and
lawyers are expected to do in and out of the courtroom. For instance, he said that the judge "makes the
decision about the case" and lawyers "help him do it, by
showing him both sides of the case."

Mr. Bates also was able to demonstrate a minimal
understanding of what it means to plead guilty. When
asked if he would receive a trial after pleading guilty,
Mr. Bates stated "no." When asked what he would
plead guilty to, he stated, "Shooting an airplane." As
noted previously, he understands that a plea of guilty
could potentially result in incarceration, although he
did not know the maximum penalty. (As it turns out,
no one knows the maximum penalty for "shooting an
airplane," because technically it is not a crime in Maryland. Mr. Daniels states he will probably eventually
charge Mr. Bates with some type of assault.) Whatever
the charge, it seems probable that Mr. Bates, on a cognitive level, would understand the implications of
pleading guilty to it.

It is noteworthy in this regard that if Mr. Bates did
plead guilty, he would still in all likelihood believe that
his acts were totally justified and that he is not "guilty"
in the moral sense. He would probably admit to shooting the airplane but would never admit that he was
"wrong" in doing so.

The Clinic has no opinion as to the voluntariness
prong of the guilty plea test, as that will presumably depend on the circumstances surrounding the occasion of

the plea. Our observations with reference to Mr. Bates's suggestibility in a general sense are stated above.

George Fordham, M.D.
John Waggoner, M.S.W.

(b)   Discussion

The Bates report is interesting from a number of perspectives. First, it demonstrates a point made in all the chapters dealing with competency [Chapters 6, 7, and 11] that psychosis or delusions do not automatically render a person incompetent. A competency evaluation must focus on the individual's understanding of the specific functions considered relevant by the law; even if the person is "out of touch with reality" in a general sense, he or she may still be able to grasp the narrow notions encompassed by the legal test. Here, the data presented in the report suggest that Mr. Bates was competent to stand trial and plead guilty (and that his confession was valid as well), despite his paranoid delusions. Of course, a judge might have decided that Mr. Bates's delusional system, and specifically his refusal to admit any moral wrongdoing, rendered his confession or guilty plea "unintelligent" or "unknowing"; such a possibility illustrates the importance of avoiding the ultimate issue, as the examiners did.

With respect to the portion of the report concerning competency to confess, it is worth noting the use of Grisso's assessment instruments to gauge present understanding of the *Miranda* litany and the careful recitation of the events surrounding the confession. Both these aspects of the report, together with the observation about Mr. Bates's suggestibility (or lack thereof), would be relevant to the voluntariness determination required in such cases [see § 7.03(b)]. However, it should be stressed that data such as Grisso's must be used with care. His instruments do not "establish" competency or incompetency; they merely give the factfinder some feel for the comparative extent to which the typical defendant understands the *Miranda* warnings.

With respect to the portion of the report concerning competency to plead guilty, note that the writers first set out their understanding of the legal test (and their formulation is still accurate even after *Godinez v. Moran* [see § 7.04]). They

then addressed each aspect of it—including the important issues of whether Mr. Bates's paranoia would affect his relationship with his attorney, the extent to which he would in fact believe he was guilty if and when he pled guilty, and the voluntariness of such a plea. On the latter issue, as the report noted, a prospective assessment such as the one required here could not be made because the examiners had no knowledge of the circumstances surrounding the plea arrangement.

Because of the complicated nature of Mr. Bates's delusional system and its possible relevance to the competency issues, the report spent more time recounting Mr. Bates's personal history than many competency reports do. Given Mr. Bates's history, and his apparent perception of the offense, it is interesting to speculate whether Mr. Bates should have been found "insane" at the time of the offense. Under the *Durham* rule [see § 8.02(b)], he would probably have been found insane because the shooting was the "product" of his paranoia. Under the American Law Institute or *M'Naghten* formulations, on the other hand, whether he would have been found insane might have depended on whether the "appreciation of wrongfulness" notion incorporated in each referred to awareness that the offense was legally wrong or morally wrong [see § 8.02(c)(3)]. Mr. Bates clearly knew his act was wrong in the first sense but just as clearly believed it was "right" in the second sense. Because, for him, the "Law" was in essence breaking the law by gratuitously attacking his home, killing his pets, and monitoring his every move, he might have been justified in retaliating. On the other hand, if what he believed to be happening had actually been happening, it might still have been wrong (morally as well as legally) to react in the way he did, rather than, for instance, contacting other authorities.

19.04.   Mental State at the Time of the Offense [Chapter 8]

(a)   Ed Wertz Report

NAME: Ed Wertz
D.O.B.:   July 27, 1950
DATE OF REPORT: July 20, 1988

REFERRAL INFORMATION: Mr. Wertz is a 37-year-old, married white male who is charged with armed robbery. The offense occurred on or about March 3, 1988, when Mr. Wertz allegedly entered the K & K Gun Shop and robbed the owner at gunpoint, leaving the scene with two semiautomatic rifles and ammunition. Mr. Wertz was referred to the clinic by his attorney, Mr. Ed Whitley, who requested an assessment of Mr. Wertz's mental state at the time of the offense.

INTERVIEW DATES AND INFORMATION SOURCES: First interview (two hours) by Sally Patton, Ph.D., on June 19, 1988; second interview (one hour) and sodium brevital interview (one hour, 15 minutes) performed by Louis Beck, M.D., on July 3, 1988.

Third-party information reviewed by the examiners included: (1) a summary of the investigation report describing the crime scenario, prepared by Detective Warren Bond of the Columbia police department; (2) two transcripts of statements given by Mr. Wertz to police officers on March 4 and 5, 1988; (3) photocopies of handwritten statements prepared by each of three witnesses present at the scene of the crime and by the arresting officer; and (4) a telephone interview with Jane Wertz (defendant's wife) on June 22, 1988.

Professional literature pertinent to the present clinical findings includes the following:

Atkinson et al., *Diagnosis of Post-Traumatic Stress Disorder in Vietnam Veterans: Preliminary Findings,* 114 AMERICAN JOURNAL OF PSYCHIATRY 694 (1984).

Behar, *Flashbacks and Posttraumatic Stress Symptoms in Combat Veterans,* 28 COMPREHENSIVE PSYCHIATRY 459, 463 (1987).

Hendin et al., *The Reliving Experience in Vietnam Veterans with Post-Traumatic Stress Disorder,* 25 COMPREHENSIVE PSYCHIATRY 165 (1984).

Spyker, *The Acute Toxicity of Ethanol: Dosages and Kinetic Monograms* (1984) (manuscript submitted to JOURNAL OF THE AMERICAN MEDICAL ASSOCIATION).

Sparr et al., *Military Combat, Posttraumatic Stress Disorder, and Criminal Behavior in Vietnam Veterans,* 15 BULLETIN AMERICAN ACADEMY PSYCHIATRY & LAW 141, 152 (1987).

Williams, *The Mental Foxhole: The Vietnam Veteran's Search for Meaning,* 53 AMERICAN JOURNAL OF ORTHOPSYCHIATRY 4 (1983).

PERSONAL BACKGROUND: Mr. Wertz was born in Minnesota and lived there until the age of four,

at which time his parents separated and he moved to Texas and continued living with his mother. He described both parents as heavy drinkers and reported that at approximately age 12 he ran away from home because "my mom was an alcoholic. . . . I was tired of her drinking and the constant parade of men she brought into the house." He was subsequently picked up and placed in a foster care home, where he remained until age 18.

At age 21 he entered the U.S. Army and served a two-year tour of duty in Vietnam. It was considered clinically noteworthy that Mr. Wertz had significant difficulty discussing his Vietnam experiences; with persistent questioning, however, he gave a brief summary of his combat experiences, including one occasion on which he used a .50-caliber machine gun to kill approximately 31 North Vietnamese soldiers holed up in a concrete bunker.

In 1976 he married his present wife, Jane (Decker) Wertz. Also at that time he began working at the Columbia City Hospital as a maintenance mechanic, a job that he held continuously until his arrest on the present charge. Mr. Wertz's feelings about his job appear quite mixed. On the one hand he reported, in an almost boastful tone, that when on duty he had the maintenance responsibility for the entire hospital and additional duties as a security person; with respect to the latter duties, he seemed quite concerned that the examiners understand the importance of his role. He repeatedly stressed the value in having a "nonviolent person" responsible for calming agitated patients. On the other hand, he also described considerable anxiety associated with his job, primarily in relation to concerns of how workers on other shifts might perceive him (and his competence) if he passed uncompleted projects to them at the end of his shift. He also admitted feeling chronically dissatisfied with the lack of opportunity for advancement.

Mr. Wertz denied any current use of illicit drugs, though he admitted that he had smoked marijuana while in Vietnam. He reported that he occasionally drinks alcoholic beverages (usually beer) but not to the point of feeling intoxicated.

Mr. Wertz denied any prior contact with the mental health professions. However, he did describe one prior episode of behavior that is regarded as clinically significant. In September 1986, he was packing his car to leave for a hunting trip. As he was doing so, he began ruminating about the anxiety and dissatisfaction associated with his employment, and he considered that he might be forced to desert his family and "run away" to escape the situation. His next memory of the event is waking up at the hunting cabin, initially quite disorganized because he could not recall having driven up there (a drive of over four hours). He reported feeling even more perplexed after inspecting his automobile, which was packed with virtually all his personal possessions (e.g., tools, clothing); further, he had apparently acquired a powerful rifle (30.06) but had no recollection of having purchased it. Feeling quite upset, he returned home to his family the next day. Jane Wertz remembers her husband telling her about the experience on the day he returned, describing it essentially in the same terms just reported.

There was no indication of prior criminal behavior, either in the police files or in the self-report from Mr. Wertz.

CIRCUMSTANCES OF THE OFFENSE: At the June 19 interview, Mr. Wertz provided the following information regarding the alleged crime. After having worked the midnight shift on his job at the hospital, he arrived home in the morning in time to see his wife off to work and his daughter off to school. He then drove to a nearby store, purchased some beer, and returned home, where he began working in his garage. He reported that he was building a lawn cart for a friend, and his last memory of the morning was of standing in the garage, staring at the blueprints.

His next memory was of "being in the gun shop with a shotgun in my hand. . . . I can see John [owner], and I remember pointing the gun at him." He also recalled leaving the gun shop with two automatic rifles and "starting heading west on a dirt road, back toward Winford County." He could recall no other details regarding the robbery, nor could he recall the route he took after "heading west." Mr. Wertz could not recall stopping his jeep, nor could he explain why he stopped where he did. His next memory was of standing in a field, shooting one of the automatic rifles at an abandoned farm building. He recalled that a deputy sheriff approached and asked, "Why are you shooting at that building?" Mr. Wertz recalled feeling very exasperated by the question, for he had no idea why he was standing in the field and firing the weapon. He reported that he readily put the weapon down and agreed to talk with the officer after receiving his *Miranda* warnings. Initially he could not recall the robbery and could not explain how the automatic rifles came to be in his possession. When the officer mentioned a robbery at the K & K Gun Shop, Mr. Wertz's memory was jogged, and he reported the sketchy memories summarized above.

Because of Mr. Wertz's memory at the time of the first interview was quite sketchy, the examiners elected to conduct a subsequent interview with the defendant under the influence of sodium brevital. Sodium brevital is a general anesthetic that can be administered intravenously to create an altered state of consciousness in the subject. Although such chemicals have no proven validity as "truth serums," they may be useful in relaxing the subject's psychological defenses and may permit repressed memories to surface into consciousness. The brevital interview was conducted on July 3, 1988, and Mr. Wertz's memory was somewhat enhanced by this procedure. He recalled working in his garage on the morning in question and stated that his cousin, David, dropped in for a visit. He estimated that he consumed ten beers before leaving home around 11:30 A.M. He reported entering the K & K Gun Shop two times, the first time simply to use the men's room. Before entering the second time, he removed the shotgun from his jeep and loaded it as he walked toward the door. He described feeling "nervous, scared, hurt. . . . I wanted to give the butt end of the gun to them . . . so they could stop me from what I was doing." After driving away from the gun shop, he stopped the jeep and loaded the automatic rifles. He then proceeded to a deserted farm and began firing on a concrete outbuilding. He stated that the building reminded him of concrete bunkers he had assaulted in Vietnam, and he recalled having been bothered by ruminations of Vietnam earlier that day.

PRESENT MENTAL STATUS: Mr. Wertz was on bond at the time of the clinical evaluation. He was on time for both appointments and presented as a tall, slender white male who was dressed in casual but neat clothing. He was a cooperative informant who responded to all questions from the staff; he responded without undue delay and discussed positive and negative aspects of his background without becoming guarded or defensive. This, along with the consistency between his account of his behavior and the account distilled from third-party sources, led the staff to view him as a candid respondent. There was no evidence of bizarre or peculiar thought patterns or perceptual distortions (e.g., hearing imaginary voices), nor did Mr. Wertz report having previously experienced such symptoms. His mood was variable and appropriate to the topic of conversation, though he was predominately serious and somber and appeared to have difficulty relaxing. He admitted to some chronic feelings of depression and dissatisfaction associated with his employment situation, and to transient periods of increased anxiety and depression associated with memories of combat experiences in Vietnam. He reported that he tries to cope with these disturbing memories by "not thinking about it." He otherwise presented himself as a conscientious and responsible member of the community, a characterization that appears consistent with the available prior history.

MENTAL STATE AT THE TIME OF THE OFFENSE:

In the opinion of the clinic staff, Mr. Wertz was suffering from a significant psychological disturbance at the time of the offense. As noted previously, this defendant is a Vietnam veteran. He reported extremely stressful events during the war, including witnessing the gruesome deaths of many fellow soldiers who fought next to him in the field. He recalled ambivalent feelings about his role as a soldier, feeling guilt about having killed other human beings, but also feeling anger and hatred sparked by his desire to avenge the deaths of his own comrades. Since his discharge, he has experienced anxiety and depression associated with ruminations about Vietnam; he reported such ruminations on the day of the offense.

Mr. Wertz's behavior on the day of the crime is, in the staff's opinion, reasonably viewed as a response to the recurring stress associated with painful memories of combat in Vietnam, a phenomenon recognized in the American Psychiatric Association's *Diagnostic and Statistical Manual of Mental Disorders* (DSM) as posttraumatic stress disorder (PTSD). Delayed responses to wartime stress are well documented in Vietnam veterans (see studies cited). One characteristic stress response is for individuals to "relive" through their own thoughts and fantasies the original stressful episodes in an apparent effort to bring about more successful (i.e., psychologically acceptable) solutions. Such "reliving" episodes are sometimes referred to as "flashbacks"; during these episodes the individuals' behavior is marked by feelings of detachment or estrangement from the present-day world around them, and they act "as if" they are back in time when the stressful event occurred. One study reported that such reliving episodes occur in as many as 20% of Vietnam veterans suffering from delayed stress response syndrome (Hendin et al., 1984).

Several features of Mr. Wertz's behavior and recollection of March 3, 1988, suggest that he may have been in an altered state of consciousness in which he was reliving Vietnam experiences. Most obvious is the choice of a target for assault with the semiautomatic weapons taken from the gun shop—a concrete building on a deserted farm, which visually reminded him of concrete bunkers he had assaulted during the war. It should also be mentioned that Mr. Wertz admits owning several rifles and handguns, but no semiautomatic weapons such as those he used in the war. Thus, a special purpose in obtaining the semiautomatic weapons is implied. His sketchy memory and reported subjective feelings of ambivalence during the robbery ("I wanted to give them the butt end of the gun . . . so they could stop me . . .") are also consistent with the kind of altered state associated with reliving prior experiences, during which the experience of self-control is diminished. In the opinion of the clinic staff, the absence of evidence of careful planning of the offense, the lack of resistance at the time of arrest, and the absence of other apparent motive for obtaining these particular weapons lends further credence to this psychological explanation.

Sparr and his colleagues (1987) have developed criteria for evaluating the credibility of a "Vietnam flashback" that might also be relevant here: (1) the flashback behavior appears to have been sudden and unpremeditated, (2) the flashback behavior is uncharacteristic of the person in normal circumstances, (3) the flashback reasonably reenacts one or more traumatic combat events, (4) the person is amnesic for all or part of the episode, (5) there is no apparent motivation for the flashback behavior, (6) the offense environment was reminiscent of environmental features in Vietnam, (7) the person is unaware of the specific ways in which he has reenacted prior experiences, and (8) the victim may be fortuitous or accidental. Virtually all these criteria appear to be met in this case.

It should also be noted that other research, from Behar (1987), indicates that, among Vietnam veterans with PTSD, flashbacks with disorientation are more common for those who also suffer from alcoholism (72%) than for those who are nonalcoholics (16%). In other words, drinking may play a role in producing a flashback. Mr. Wertz reported consuming as many as ten cans of beer on the morning of the offense. The effect of the alcohol may have been to weaken the elements of self-control he normally uses to control or repress these recurring feelings about his Vietnam experience. The alcohol alone would probably not have been sufficient to account for his behavior but may have contributed by lowering Mr. Wertz's usual inhibitions or psychological mechanisms of self-control.

A computer program developed by Dr. Daniel Spyker (see Spyker, 1984) provides data on this issue that might be useful. The program makes use of several variables that the literature considers essential in computing the blood alcohol level of humans and the impact of alcoholic intoxication on their functioning. These variables include the age and weight of the subject, which both relate to the individual's "tolerance" level and to the volume of alcohol distribution within the blood, the quantity of alcohol ingested, and whether or not the subject has recently consumed food (a variable that affects the absorption rate of the alcohol). The program combines information concerning these variables with a constant ("V_{max}" = 230 mg/ml/hr), which expresses the rate at which an "average" male drinker (i.e., one who has developed some tolerance for alcohol but who is not an alcoholic) "eliminates" alcohol from his system over time. The result is a relatively accurate blood ethanol concentration (BEC), expressing the amount of alcohol within the individual's blood stream at the given time. (Under this program, it should be noted, it is assumed that 99% of the alcohol consumed is eventually absorbed by the blood. The program does not account for the possible variances in the "natural" genetic alcohol tolerance level of particular individuals, as this variable is essentially impossible to measure. Nor is the V_{max} figure—the elimination rate—fine-tuned for each individual measured.)

Assuming that Mr. Wertz is telling the truth with respect to his consumption of alcohol, and assuming further that, as he told us, he did not eat before the offense was committed and that the drinking took place approximately three hours before the offense, and factoring in Mr. Wertz's age and weight, the program would produce a BEC in Mr. Wertz at the time of the offense of 139 mg/dl (milligrams per decaliter). "Legal intoxication" in this state is a BEC of 100 mg/dl. In many individuals, "ataxia," or severely impaired leg and arm coordination, sets in at a BEC of 200 mg/dl.

Sally Patton, Ph.D.
Louis Beck, M.D.

(b)   Discussion

The Wertz report is an evaluation of mental state at the time of the offense (MSO) in a case presenting an unusual clinical picture. Several points are worth making.

First, note the detailed list of sources of information used in the evaluation. Although this type of list should appear in any report, it is particularly important with an MSO exam, where credibility is likely to be an important issue. Of special significance are those sources describing the offense. This information will assist the legal system in assessing the credibility of the report's offense description.

Second, note the amount of historical material in the report. Compared to the typical competency report, much more history is presented in an MSO report, particularly that relevant to the individual's status at the time of the offense. For example, in this report Mr. Wertz's Vietnam experience and his attitude toward employment (i.e., his "chronic dissatisfaction" with a lack of advancement opportunities) were discussed because they were directly related to the clinical formulation of the offense.

Third, the evaluators describe the offense, Mr. Wertz's feelings while committing it, and his later recall of it in some detail. In contrast to a competency report, such a discussion is crucial to an MSO evaluation, for the obvious reason that it is highly relevant to insanity and related issues. It also enables the legal system to "see" an offense through a clinician's eyes and thereby to evaluate more effectively the clinical explanation of the offense. For example, if the clinician describes the offense in a manner wholly at variance with the eventual determination by the legal system as to how the offense actually occurred, clinical explanations of behavior will become less compelling. Conversely, if the explanation of the offense is generally consistent with the legal system's views (or at least those of one side of the controversy), the clinical conclusions may be more persuasive. In this regard, it should be noted that the writers carefully gave reasons why they believed Mr. Wertz to be credible about the offense, an issue of paramount importance to an MSO report.

Fourth, the writers sought and relied on a wide range of data outside of the clinical interview to support their opinion. Relevant literature about post-wartime stress was cited, a brevital interview was conducted, and a sophisticated assessment of Mr. Wertz's ability to withstand the impact of the alcohol he said he consumed was made. In each case, the report tried to make clear the extent to which the data were relied on and the possible problems with their use. For instance, the writers were careful to avoid equating sodium brevital with "truth serum," and they specified the methodological qualifications connected with the computer analysis of Mr. Wertz's BEC at the time of the offense. Such caution is important, as these techniques might otherwise assume undue importance for the unknowledgeable factfinder.

Indeed, given the relatively untested theories and procedures on which it relies, all or parts of the report (as well as testimony based on the excluded portions) might be excluded. For instance, the trial court might decide, under *Frye,* that the posttraumatic stress syndrome is not generally accepted (despite its inclusion in DSM-IV) or that the brevital and BEC procedures are not sufficiently established in the field. If in a *Daubert* jurisdiction, the court might reach the same ultimate conclusions, but based on a finding that the scientific validity of these clinical devices has not been proven [see § 1.04(c)].

Finally, note that although the clinical conclusions were given in detail and with an absence of jargon, the report did not give an opinion on the ultimate legal issue of insanity. The report— properly, in our view—left to the legal system the legal significance of the clinical material, which may or may not have established insanity, automatism, diminished capacity, or some other defense [see §§ 8.02, 8.03].

Consonant with our recommendations in § 4.02(b), a report of this type should not be sent to the prosecution prior to notice of an intent to raise a defense of mental abnormality. Instead, unless the court orders otherwise, we recommend that only a short summary containing no incriminating material be sent to the prosecutor prior to such notice.

(c) Seth Hedges Report

NAME: Seth Hedges
D.O.B: January 6, 1966
DATE OF REPORT: June 2, 1987

IDENTIFYING DATA: Mr. Seth Hedges is a 22-year-old, who has received a G.E.D. He was committed to the Department of Health and Rehabilitative Services on February 1, 1988, by the Honorable John Shell Jr., Circuit Court Judge in the Circuit Court of the Fourth Judicial Circuit, in and for Clay County, Florida, as incompetent to stand trial. He was charged with kidnapping to facilitate a felony and attempted sexual battery with some force or violence, allegedly occurring on January 26, 1987. He was admitted to the Forensic Service of Florida State Hospital on April 23, 1987.

PROCEDURES: To assess Mr. Hedges's sanity at the time of the alleged offense as set forth in the Florida Standard Jury Instructions (the *M'Naghten* test), the following was done. Mr. Hedges was interviewed on May 11, May 17, and June 2, 1987. He also received a standard psychological test, the Minnesota Multiphasic Personality Inventory (May 20, 1987). His medical record and ward chart were reviewed; these records include documents received from the court concern-

ing the alleged offense, an admission summary and social history, reports on treatment progress, and descriptions of current behavior. Interviews were also conducted with Mr. Hedges's parents, Ken and Sarah Hedges (April 28, 1987), with Detective Fox, who transported Mr. Hedges to the Clay County Jail following his arrest, and with Ms. Diane Shorty, the victim of the alleged offense. Before the evaluation began, Mr. Hedges was informed of its purpose and the associated limits on confidentiality. Specifically, he was told that he was being evaluated as a result of a court order requiring assessment of his mental state at the time of the offense, and that the results of the evaluation would be sent to the court, the prosecutor, and the defense attorney. He appeared to understand this notification and agreed to participate.

RELEVANT HISTORY: Mr. Hedges was born in Reno, Nevada, and was adopted at the age of five by Mr. and Mrs. Hedges. He has a younger brother who was also adopted. The family moved from Nevada to Tuscaloosa and then to Melbourne when he was about 12 years old. Mr. Hedges appeared to do well in school up until approximately the fifth grade, when he started to have disciplinary problems. He was suspended from high school twice for skipping and being "the class clown." He has had various types of labor jobs including construction and fast-food restaurants, but no job has lasted for any longer than one or two months, with many lasting only a few days. His criminal history includes two DWI charges, one that involved an accident while drinking, resulting in loss of his driver's license for five years. He has also been arrested for forgery and uttering, trespassing, and failure to appear on a charge of indecent exposure. Mr. Hedges began to drink and eventually abuse alcohol beginning at age 14, and began to use marijuana heavily at approximately age 13. He reports that he has tried speed and cocaine but not on a consistent basis. His previous psychiatric history includes a year stay at Florida State Hospital, as well as two admissions to PATH (the local receiving unit for civil commitments), and he also completed a month-long residential treatment program through Gateway Services in Jacksonville. His previous diagnosis has been bipolar affective disorder, manic type (a diagnosis explained further below) and mixed substance abuse, as well as antisocial personality and alcohol abuse. According to past history records, the patient responds well to lithium and antipsychotic medications.

The bipolar affective disorder was apparently diagnosed for the first time in 1985, when he was committed to PATH (where he stayed one month). There followed a commitment to Florida State Hospital (admitted September 5, 1985; discharged June 20, 1986 after two four-day leaves of absence in March and April 1986, respectively). Following his discharge from Florida State Hospital, he returned home to live with his parents. At first, according to his parents, he "lay around the house, shaved badly, didn't work, and had to be helped with simple jobs." He went through vocational rehabilitation and subsequently obtained a job at Goodwill, from which he was reportedly fired for sleeping on the job. After attending day treatment at Forest County Mental Health Services (FCMHS) for three weeks in July 1986, he boarded there briefly in their halfway house. He then began working a series of jobs (Calico Jack's Oyster Bar, Perkins, Western Sizzlin', Lorenzo's) which lasted anywhere from three days to two months. He also bought some very expensive ($1,600) musical equipment and worked in yards as well as at the previously noted jobs to keep up his payments. He joined a band as well that fall, but the band "let him go" after six weeks, reportedly because of his mental difficulties. During this period he continued to keep his scheduled medication appointments at FCMHS, being prescribed mood-stabilizing (Lithium) and antipsychotic (Navane) medications by Dr. Mark Fisher.

It was also during this period that he first met Diane Shorty, who was eventually the victim of the alleged offense. She was the general manager of Perkins, where Mr. Hedges began working in late August/early September 1986. Although she saw little of him during that time (she worked day shift, he was on night shift in the kitchen), she did report interviewing him and hiring him for the job. She stated that she saw "nothing unusual or untoward" about him, particularly in terms of behavior toward her, during this time. They overlapped for three weeks, at which time she left to establish her own business. She said the leaving was not related in any way to him; she had already given notice before he was even hired.

She next saw him "around Thanksgiving," when he came into her store in the Tallahassee Mall. She reported that he complimented her on her appearance, saying something like "you sure look gorgeous" or "you look a lot better in those clothes than in your Perkins uniform." Mr. Hedges stated that he did not remember this meeting. Several weeks later, according to Ms. Shorty, she was getting gas in an Exxon Station on Loganville Road when Mr. Hedges pulled up to the pump next to her. He then leaned out of the passenger side of the truck (driven by another man) and "asked me to get in the car and go get married." Ms. Shorty did not know whether he was joking, but said, "he wasn't smiling." She immediately walked over and notified the station manager, and Mr. Hedges appar-

ently drove off. Mr. Hedges did recall riding in a truck with a friend ("Chester") that day and said he "might have" made that comment but added, "I say that to all the girls."

Ms. Shorty reported that Mr. Hedges was "in and out of the store quite a bit over Christmas." On one occasion, he reportedly asked her whether she had plans for New Year's. She replied, "Yes, I do." He then said, "My band's playing; why don't you come watch?" She repeated, "I have plans." She added that she was as direct as she could be in discouraging his advance "without having him thrown out of the store." Mr. Hedges's recollection was vaguer but somewhat different. He recalled asking her to come watch his band play but said it would not be a "date"; "she'd just be coming with a friend." When asked how she responded to his invitation, he replied, "she probably said, 'I'll try to.'"

Their last meeting before the day of the alleged offense took place on Saturday (January 23, 1987), when Mr. Hedges was in the store and made several comments such as "you sure look pretty today" and "are you still dating the same guy?" Ms. Shorty, who felt uncomfortable around him at this point, asked another customer in the store (a neighbor of hers) to stay until he left.

MENTAL STATE AND COURSE OF HOSPITALIZATION: Prior to hospitalization, Mr. Hedges was evaluated by Feather Dorn, Ph.D. (February 17, 1987), and Melissa Cortez, M.D. (January 29, 1987). Dr. Dorn indicated that Mr. Hedges appeared "agitated and restless. Speech was rambling and disorganized. Paranoid ideation was present, with delusional content." She also stated that he was "hyperverbal and psychotic." Finally, Dr. Dorn stated that Mr. Hedges "appears to be in an acute manic phase of bipolar disorder, although his history of drug usage means I cannot not rule out some sort of drug induced psychosis." Dr. Cortez stated that Mr. Hedges spent most of his time in seclusion and in and out of restraints. She stated that "he is grossly psychotic, constantly banging his hands and/or his head on the wall, which is the reason he has to be restrained. He is confused, appears terrified, states that they want to kill him. They want to shoot him in the desert." Dr. Cortez also stated: "This is a twenty-two-year-old white male who, in examination and per history, carries a diagnosis of bipolar disorder, manic. He also carries a diagnosis of mixed substance abuse and antisocial personality disorder." Both Dr. Dorn and Dr. Cortez recommended that Mr. Hedges be found incompetent to stand trial and involuntarily hospitalized.

Following admission to Florida State Hospital, Mr.

Hedges was evaluated by the admitting psychiatrist, Frank Boz, M.D. Dr. Boz found Mr. Hedges to be "agitated but cooperative with very poor eye contact and also flat affect (emotional content). He was also quite easily distracted." Dr. Boz also noted that Mr. Hedges reported that he was hearing voices, "both male and female which seemed to be in pain but did not state why they were in pain." Dr. Boz also reported that Mr. Hedges stated "he saw a vision in which he saw Jesus and that he got messages from TV. He further felt that people frequently talked about him." Dr. Boz offered a diagnosis of bipolar disorder, manic phase, mixed substance abuse, and antisocial personality. Mr. Hedges was continued on medication, and he is currently being maintained on 1,200 mg of lithium and 40 mg of Prolixin, daily.

For the first month of his hospitalization, Mr. Hedges appeared agitated and suspicious. He also attempted to escape on one occasion by hiding in the back of the Coca-Cola truck. This agitation and suspiciousness required that he be secluded and restrained on several occasions. Following his transfer to another pod (or unit) approximately one month after admission, however, his agitation and suspiciousness seemed notably diminished. He attended group and adjunctive therapies on an irregular basis, and was also described as passive and withdrawn.

During the present interviews, Mr. Hedges presented as appropriately, although somewhat carelessly, dressed and groomed. Mood appeared markedly anxious, with affect blunted (i.e., with very little emotional expression). He was oriented correctly as to time, place, and person. Overall level of intellectual functioning was not formally measured but appeared to be in the dull normal to normal range. His speech was largely coherent and relevant, although occasionally tangential (digressing from the topic on hand). There were no indications of currently held delusions, although Mr. Hedges acknowledged having had bizarre beliefs (such as getting messages from the TV and having "special powers") at previous times. Results obtained from the MMPI, a diagnostic personality inventory (or test), were consistent with the impression that Mr. Hedges's thinking disorder was currently in remission. It also suggested that he continued to experience significant depression, although some of that appeared related to his present situation. Individuals with MMPI profiles of the type produced by Mr. Hedges are often described as excitable, tense, and anxiety-prone. Strong emotional reactivity (an inability to modulate behavior) is often seen in these types of individuals. Exaggerated needs for affection and basic insecurity are often noted as well, as are argumentativeness, irritable rebelliousness, and egocentricity.

SANITY AT THE TIME OF THE ALLEGED OFFENSE: Mr. Hedges was arrested on January 26, 1987. The ten days prior to the arrest he was described by his parents as follows. On January 17, Mr. Hedges attempted to have himself admitted to PATH, as he felt "way up" and was having trouble sleeping. On January 18, he was advised by Dr. Fisher to continue on his medication but not to enter PATH. After attending a Narcotics Anonymous meeting at PATH on January 19, Mr. Hedges again asked to stay at PATH, which he was permitted to do for one night. On January 21, Mrs. Hedges spoke with Dr. Cortez, describing Mr. Hedges as "manipulative and obnoxious." On January 23, Mr. Hedges was taken by a friend to Day Treatment and appeared to his mother "still way up." He arose at 3:30 A.M. on January 23 and seemed to his parents to be "irrational and argumentative," demanding money. He again awoke and dressed at 3:30 A.M. on January 25, and "wanted to go looking for a job right then." He "called 30 minutes later from a phone on Capital Circle, saying there were packs of dogs after him."

Later that morning he was taken to PATH but apparently could not be seen by Dr. Fisher. He did not appear for a yard job that afternoon which his mother had arranged. On January 26, the day of the alleged offense, he again awoke at 3:30 A.M. and wanted to go to the mall. His mother took him to Tallahassee Mall at about 8:00 A.M., telling him, "Son, be careful, you're awfully manic today."

Mr. Hedges's own account of his thinking and behavior on the day of the alleged offense began as quite vague. He initially stated that he "blacked out" and remembered nothing about the entire day. Upon questioning based on the accounts of others, he reported recalling some of the details. Frequently during our interviews, however, he would stop and say something like, "don't remember, I was sick, I was insane, I didn't know what I was doing." While some of the vagueness is probably a function of his manic condition, it is noteworthy that his account of his thinking would become considerably vaguer when he was asked about potentially damaging information. At the same time, the more he was questioned about the events, the more forthcoming he was about them, suggesting that his claimed "lack of memory" was malingered.

He reported that he arrived at the mall "about 10:00" on January 26 and stopped in Ms. Shorty's store "for cigarettes." According to her account, he was waiting outside the store when it opened at 10:00. When it was opened by a male colleague (Mr. Hooper) rather than Ms. Shorty, Mr. Hedges reportedly walked away. He returned at 10:30, "walking in quickly right after I arrived." He left several minutes later when Mr.

Hooper, still in the store, came out from the back room with a customer. At about 10:30, Mr. Hedges returned to the store for a third time. Ms. Shorty, feeling uncomfortable, left to get stamps and a book. When she returned five minutes later, she saw that Mr. Hooper, who had been talking with Mr. Hedges, had a "horrified look" on his face. Apparently, Mr. Hedges had been asking how she was "in bed." At this point, Mr. Hedges reportedly stuck out his hand to Mr. Hooper, said, "I'm Seth Hedges," and left the store. Mall Security was then notified, and they said they would look for Mr. Hedges and watch the store.

Mr. Hedges's own account included only one stop in the store that morning, "for cigarettes." He could not (or would not) describe further details of this visit or the other visits before the offense, even when prompted with others' accounts. He did report going into the New Life Health Club in the mall sometime that morning, and thinking there were girls in the spa having sex. He reportedly took off his clothes in a room with exercise equipment and was asked by club staff to put them back on.

Mr. Hedges next remembered being outside the store at about 2:00, which coincides with Ms. Shorty's recollection of the approximate time. He then recalled going in the store and taking off his clothes. He remembered that she was screaming and that he was trying to have sex with her but stated that they were not fighting. He also recalled having a sheriff's deputy come into the store, point a gun at them, and threaten to "blow my head off" unless he released her. He stated that he released her immediately. Ms. Shorty indicated that Mr. Hedges disrobed immediately upon entering the store, saying "let's make out" or "I've been working out." He then grabbed her as she attempted to reach a metal pipe she had put behind the cash register. At this point, he was saying, "Be quiet, Ms. Shorty, let's do it just a little, fuck me, fuck me." She reported that he had an erection. He then pushed her into the stockroom and tried to push her face to his penis; shortly after that Detective Joe Fox arrived. All parties (Hedges, Shorty, and Fox) agree that Fox identified himself as a police officer and said, "Let her go or I'll blow your head off." According to Shorty and Fox, however, Mr. Hedges did not immediately release her (as he reports) but said "no" and held her body between himself and the weapon. Fox then cocked the weapon and Ms. Shorty bent over, exposing Mr. Hedges to the line of fire. At that point, he released her.

As he was being transported to Clay County Jail by Detective Fox, Mr. Hedges appeared "fairly calm." He put on a jumpsuit Fox had brought with "no resistance or comments." During their drive to the jail, Mr.

Hedges reportedly told Fox that he had gone "door to door" in the mall, looking for a girl "to have fun with." He also stated, regarding Ms. Shorty, that "I always wanted to get some of her" and that "all I wanted was a little pussy—there's nothing wrong with that."

It is clear that Mr. Hedges was experiencing some active symptoms of a bipolar affective disorder on January 26, notably impulsivity and a highly sexualized manic "high." He also reported that he thought he had "special powers to heal," so he may have been experiencing some grandiose thinking as well (this is more difficult to judge, as none of the descriptions of him that day contain accounts of speech that would clearly reflect the presence of such delusions, and Mr. Hedges himself appeared at times to exaggerate the symptoms he experienced). Impulsive behavior, grandiosity (i.e., beliefs about one's powers that are not based in reality), and manic (i.e., hyperactive) behavior are typical of people diagnosed with a bipolar disorder. All these features could have affected Mr. Hedges's knowledge of the wrongfulness of his conduct with Ms. Shorty. In answer to a direct question about the wrongfulness of his actions, he stated: "Hell, I know it's wrong to rape. But she wanted it. It was the way she looked at me. Girls always go for me. She wanted me bad, which is why I still don't understand why that cop came at me with the gun." When asked whether he thought it was strange to approach a woman in a public place he stated, "Hell, we were behind the counter. No one would have bothered us if it hadn't been for the stupid cop."

On the other hand, there is also clear evidence of a long-standing social and sexual attraction to Ms. Shorty, which was not reciprocated. Having seen her at her store on a number of previous occasions, and (in another setting) suggested they get married (jokingly or not) would all suggest a pattern of persistence in the face of refusal and increasingly intimate advances that are more characteristic of personality disorder (i.e., antisocial personality disorder) than affective disorder (i.e., bipolar disorder). Mr. Hedges's previous diagnosis of antisocial personality cannot be definitively confirmed by this evaluator, but he does have a history of antisocial behavior and an apparent inability to feel remorse for or appreciate the harm his acts can cause others, two hallmarks of that diagnosis.

CONCLUSIONS: In the opinion of the undersigned, based on all of the above:

1. Seth Hedges was experiencing some active symptoms of a bipolar affective disorder on January 26 1987, most notably impulsivity, diminished judgment, and a highly sexualized manic "high."

2. These symptoms interfered with his ability to con-

trol his sexual attraction to Ms. Shorty. His choice of her as a victim, however, appeared strongly influenced by his prior knowledge of her. He appeared to retain some limited sense of the nature and wrongfulness of his conduct, as evidenced by his repeated brief visits to her shop that morning, leaving when Mr. Hooper appeared, telling her to be quiet, and releasing her when exposed to the line of fire.

Zebulon Fike, M.D.

(d) Discussion

Note again how, as in the Wertz report, the evaluator carefully laid out the differing descriptions of the alleged offense. Crucial in such cases is the account of the victim and any other eyewitnesses. When such accounts are available, relying solely on the defendant's version (unfortunately a common occurrence) borders on "evaluation malpractice." Also important is the "triangulation" carried out by this evaluator; that is, elicitation of information about the defendant's mental state, both before *and* after the offense, from the defendant *and* other sources (family, victim, and professionals). This information helps in understanding and corroborating accounts of mental state at the time of the offense.

One question that might arise in a case like this is that posed by Morse [see § 1.04(a)]: If this wealth of descriptive information is provided to the factfinder (by a mental health professional or, alternatively, by the parents, the other doctors, the victim, and the detective), are the opinions provided by Dr. Fike "helpful" to the factfinder or merely superfluous personal judgment? Do the diagnoses provide useful information?

As to the legal issues involved, in contrast to the Wertz case, the evidence that this defendant suffers from a serious mental disorder is unquestionable; the diagnosis of bipolar disorder clearly applies to him, is well-accepted and considered "valid," presumably sufficiently so for legal purposes under *Frye* and *Daubert* [see § 1.04(c)]. What is uncertain is the effect the disorder had on the defendant's behavior at the time of the offense. Recall that the coexistence of mental disorder and a criminal offense does not prove insanity; even under the *Durham,* or product, test some

proof that the former caused or at least contributed to the latter must be shown [see § 8.02(c)(2)]. Further, even if such a link exists, there must also be proof of the specific dysfunction required by law. Here the relevant doctrine is the *M'Naghten* test, which is a "cognitive" test and thus does not countenance insanity based solely on volitional impairment of the type often manifested by those with bipolar disorder. In this case the evaluator points out that Mr. Hedges's criminal behavior could have been influenced by either the bipolar disorder or his antisocial tendencies and notes that, in any event, the degree of cognitive distortion was unclear. Left to the trier of fact are the ultimate issues (whether the manic behavior or the antisocial tendencies were the most significant contributors to the action; whether a lack of remorse due to the latter equates with an inability to know that his actions were wrong; whether his attempts to obtain help prior to the offense mitigate his responsibility in any way).

Another interesting legal issue posed by this case is whether Mr. Hedges had the "intent" to commit rape. Generally, rape requires only an intent to have intercourse with a woman under circumstances that would lead a reasonable person to know she was not consenting; in some jurisdictions, however, conviction may occur only if the defendant *knew* the victim was not consenting [see § 8.03(b) for discussion of the objective and subjective definitions of *mens rea*].

19.05. Sentencing [Chapter 9]

(a) George Sanders Report

NAME: George Sanders
D.O.B.:   July 5, 1958
DATE OF REPORT: June 26, 1982

REFERRAL AND SOURCES OF INFORMATION: Mr. Sanders, who recently pled guilty to one count of first-degree sexual assault committed while on escape from a work-release center, was referred by the Hon. John Lamb of Middlesex County District Court for evaluation and possible sentencing as a mentally disordered sex offender (MDSO). The statutory definition of such a person is "any person who has a mental disorder and who, because of the mental disorder, has been determined to be disposed to repeated commission of sexual offenses (sexual assault or debauching a minor) which are likely to cause substantial injury to the health of others." If an individual is found to meet this statutory standard, the court must then determine where the individual should be confined (either in prison or a hospital), with the decision turning upon the person's treatability within facilities available within the state. Evaluation was requested as to whether Mr. Sanders meets the statutory definition of an MDSO, and, if so, if he is treatable and if the appropriate treatment is available in Massachusetts.

Mr. Sanders was previously evaluated by this examiner as to his competency to stand trial, mental state at the time of the offense, and need for treatment. When material from that evaluation is pertinent to the MDSO questions, it is included herein.

In the current evaluation, Mr. Sanders was interviewed for approximately one and a half hours on June 21, 1982. In addition, the county attorney made available police reports, including accounts of their investigation and interviews of the victim and the defendant.

In the previous evaluation, Mr. Sanders was interviewed on August 3, 7, and 21, 1981 (a total of approximately three and a half hours). Psychological testing was also conducted (i.e., Wechsler Adult Intelligence Scale—Revised [WAIS-R] and Competency Screening Test on August 7, 1981; Thematic Apperception Test, Rorschach, and Draw-a-Person on August 21, 1981). Also available at that time were the following: a statement written by Mr. Sanders on August 6, 1981; the affidavit for the warrant for his arrest; and notes from an interview of Mr. Sanders by his attorney (Ronald Jones) on July 27, 1981. Correctional evaluation and treatment records were requested but not received.

HISTORY: Mr. Sanders is the oldest of three sons of Edward Sanders and Wendy Martin. His parents divorced when Mr. Sanders was about age 12 or 13, and he lived with his mother and her second husband thereafter. Mr. Sanders was in high school (about ninth grade) when they moved from Springfield to Boston. Mr. Sanders's father has also remarried; he now lives in Framingham. Brothers are named Adam, 21, and Carl, 17; Mr. Sanders thinks that they still live at home, but he is not sure.

Mr. Sanders described considerable conflict with his stepfather. He said that they never got along and that they never really talked to each other. When Mr. Sanders tries to call him, Mr. Martin is said to hang up on him. At the time of his escape from the work-release center (the present offense was committed while he was absent without leave), Mr. Sanders was worried that he had no place to go and that, therefore, he would be denied parole because Mr. Martin had refused to allow him to come home after his release. Prior to going to prison, Mr. Sanders had moved out and was living in motels because of conflicts with his stepfather. Mr. Sanders stated that his stepfather may have gone to Hartford at one point for inpatient alcoholism treatment. He could not be sure, however, because Mrs. Martin would not confirm his stepfather's whereabouts at that time. Most recently, Mr. Sanders claimed that he wrote his stepfather's employer earlier this month with an allegation that Mr. Martin had been stealing from the company; this allegation was designed to retaliate against him.

Mr. Sanders seemed not to be able to say very much about his mother, but he insisted that relations with her had been pleasant until she remarried. Until then, Mr. Sanders said that he felt that he could talk with her about his problems (many of which apparently were school-related). It is not clear, however, that there was much active interaction. Mr. Sanders indicated that "Mom always left me alone when I had problems." He would then go into his room and lock the door. Mrs. Martin did visit him when he was in the work-release center; she has not visited him in prison, however, although she is said to write about one time per month. Mr. Sanders claimed to find female counselors easier to talk to than male counselors; he related this greater ease of interaction to his relationship with his mother.

Mr. Sanders had minimal contact with his natural father after the divorce. Some years thereafter, they did resume occasional contact. Mr. Sanders said that he was the only member of the family who ever spoke to his father. He denied knowing the reason for the divorce or even having any ideas about it.

Relationships between Mr. Sanders and his brothers are also strained. He knows virtually nothing about their current circumstances. He said that he read in the newspaper that Carl had been arrested for assault. Mr. Sanders speculated that the reason his brothers do not talk to him is "because I'm heavyset." In his opinion, both brothers were more favored than he by his parents because they were more successful in school.

Mr. Sanders described himself as having always been "quiet" and isolated. In fact, his greatest wish was and is "to be alone by myself somewhere." He described himself as having been a loner as long as he can remember. For recreation, he eschewed organized sports and instead went fishing by himself. Mr. Sanders reported being overwhelmed by anxiety and becoming tongue-tied when he is in large groups of people or in the center of a group of people. When asked what he needed to change about himself, he could think of only his "fear of people"—a fear that he said he has not divulged to his counselor in the prison mental health unit, where he is currently incarcerated.

Mr. Sanders's general lack of relationships carries over to relationships with women. He reported never having had a real date. In the August 1981 interviews, he said that his only close relationship was with Joan, a woman who was said to have died a few months prior to the escape from the work-release center. However, in the June 1982 interview, he stated that her relatives lied about her "going away" so as to end their relationship. In the more recent interviews, Mr. Sanders blamed Joan for all of his problems, and he said that he would not want another girlfriend because it "would make me depressed." It is important to note that Mr. Sanders never actually met Joan. She was the sister of a fellow inmate, and they corresponded and had phone conversations. Mr. Sanders said that he and Joan had planned to be married. He also thought that his mother liked her, although he was not sure why. Mr. Sanders said that his only other girlfriend was Susan, whom he met while he was in school. Susan was a drinking buddy, but they never dated formally. However, police records of an interview with her suggest that Mr. Sanders had sent her love letters on occasions.

Although he graduated from Southern High, Mr. Sanders's school career apparently consisted almost exclusively of special education classes. Upon graduation, he went to work as a laborer on sewers for the city of Boston. This job lasted about one and a half years. Mr. Sanders quit because of conflicts with his supervisor, who said that he was not a good driver. Thereafter, he worked for about six months as a security guard for Acme Security Company. He was fired from that job for being out of uniform.

While unemployed, Mr. Sanders turned to criminal activity (check forgeries, burglaries) to support himself. The burglaries were all in his neighborhood. For example, he broke into the house of one man who he knew collected coins. Mr. Sanders was apprehended and convicted of two burglaries. On April 6, 1981, he was sentenced to two to four years. At the time of his escape, he had only 75 days remaining in his term. Most of Mr. Sanders's incarceration has been in the prison mental health unit. He spent seven months there during his incarceration for the burglaries, and he is currently on that unit.

Mr. Sanders seemed not to be able to identify why he was on the prison mental health unit for so long, except that "I cracked up." He said that he had asked to go to the state hospital during his previous stay at the mental health unit and that he wished that he could go there now. In his opinion, the counseling there would be better than in the correctional system. Mr. Sanders said that his most recent counselor at the mental health center, Harold Nevins, had indicated that he was ready to leave the mental health unit and enter the medium-security portion of the prison. However, Mr. Sanders said that he had resisted a transfer because he would only stay in his room at the medium-security prison; in the mental health unit, on the other hand, he felt comfortable enough to mix among people a bit. He also said that he has difficulty controlling his temper when he is amid the general inmate population, and that several inmates had assaulted him during his three-month stay at the medium-security prison before his escape. In fact, as he told it, he was sent to the work-release center essentially for protective reasons. Unfortunately, that option may be foreclosed this time because his offense may result in a tightening of admission into work release.

Mr. Sanders became introduced to amphetamines while at the work-release center. He said that "some kid gave me two to lose weight." He began using them more frequently to suppress his appetite and to keep from becoming nervous. He claimed that he had in fact taken 24 pills on the day that he was apprehended. Mr. Sanders said that his only drug use prior to going to prison was of marijuana on a couple of occasions. He did admit to drinking binges on the weekends, with occasional consumption of several six-packs of beer.

Except for his stay in the prison mental health unit, Mr. Sanders has had no psychiatric hospitalization. He reported having had an evaluation at a community mental health center in 1979. He said that when he was younger, his mother had taken him to "another place across the street from Boston Garden" (Family Services?). He is uncertain what the reasons were for these evaluations.

As far as Mr. Sanders knows, the only psychiatric history in his family was that his paternal grandfather "went crazy" when he was very old.

ACCOUNT OF THE CURRENT OFFENSE:

Mr. Sanders's account of the offense for which he is currently awaiting sentencing matched the victim's report as well as his own confession to the police. He claimed that he did not know that anyone might be in the apartment; he entered in search of food. When someone did come home, he hid in the closet and became increasingly panicky. Mr. Sanders claimed not to remember when he got the idea to assault the woman, or what any of his thoughts or feelings were at the time of the assault itself. He also claimed not to know why he committed the assault. All that he could say is that he took advantage of the situation to "find out what it was like. I thought that I could get away with it." His motivation to "find out what it was like" is consistent with the victim's report that he stated initially that "he just wanted to look." In addition, in the August 1981 interviews, Mr. Sanders did recall being mad at the victim "for coming home. She wasn't supposed to do that." He said that he was mostly just scared, though. Mr. Sanders claimed in the June 1982 interview that he had given the matter little more thought. Although he related this lack of preoccupation with bravado ("I couldn't care less about that broad"), further questioning suggested that Mr. Sanders avoided thinking about the incident to avoid depression.

OBSERVATIONS: Mr. Sanders is a tall, somewhat obese man. He impresses one almost immediately as being a rather schizoid (withdrawn, isolated) man. Verbal productions were terse, and affect (expression of emotion) was generally flattened. In the August 1981 interviews, Mr. Sanders did seem quite depressed, however. He expressed sadness directly at times and in fact became tearful at one point in the first interview. In the June 1982 interview, although his facial expression seemed never to change, there was considerable anger in his voice. He seemed to be attempting to master the situation by being a tough guy (e.g., "I'm not a rapist; I'm a burglar") and to be indicating that he did not care about other people because no one cared about him. In none of the interviews was there evidence of delusions or hallucinations.

IMPRESSIONS FROM INTERVIEWS AND TESTING: Mr. Sanders is of borderline intelligence. His poorest performance on the WAIS-R was on a subtest in which the task is to arrange pictures into order to tell a story. Mr. Sanders seemed generally to miss the point of the picture stories. Although his ideation was not bizarre, he seemed to lack a sense of the course of social relationships.

Indeed, such social ineptitude and isolation from people seem to constitute a persistent theme throughout Mr. Sanders's history and the material presented in the evaluations, in both interviews and psychological testing. For example, Mr. Sanders was unable to find people in a Rorschach stimulus on a card on which they are commonly seen, even after it was suggested that most people perceive people on that card. Similarly, his human figure drawings were distorted and suggested serious isolation from people.

Mr. Sanders seems generally to expect interactions with people to be frustrating and typified by a lack of reward and loss. He may occasionally act impulsively

in response to frustration or as a way of dealing with loss (i.e., hurting other people before they hurt him).

Mr. Sanders had difficulty in integrating affect (in other words, he had difficulty talking about his feelings). Indeed, he displayed some difficulty identifying or labeling feelings he had experienced in a wide variety of social situations. His defenses (i.e., his ways of dealing with reality) seem to be limited largely to simple withdrawal and denial, and he has difficulty in responding to feelings and conflict. He probably presents some suicidal risk. Mr. Sanders left a suicide note when he escaped, and he claimed that his original reason for escaping was to commit suicide. He said that a combination of not having a girlfriend, being rejected by his parents, facing parole with no place to go, and having taken a number of amphetamines had become too much. Mr. Sanders claimed that he tied weights around himself and that he planned to jump in the lake. He saw a police car, though, and threw the weights away and "just ran." He said in the June 1982 interview that he now wishes that he had jumped into the lake. At the time of the August 1981 evaluation, Mr. Sanders was obviously depressed. He complained of headaches, and he wrote that "I'm dieing [sic] slowly and god is helping me." When asked to clarify, Mr. Sanders said that his medication had been switched to a liquid base because he had been saving pills for the purpose of a suicidal attempt. (According to Mr. Sanders, he is currently taking Atarax 50 mg q.i.d. and Elavil 25 mg b.i.d.) He said at the more recent interview that if his sentence is more than 10 years, he will definitely commit suicide. He said that he "couldn't care less about anybody," and that if he committed suicide, his mother "would not have to worry about me."

Although there may be slips at times in Mr. Sanders's reality testing (i.e., his ability to differentiate reality from fantasy), and his judgment is poor, he seems generally to be in contact with reality. His range of ideation is constricted, but its quality is not bizarre.

In summary, Mr. Sanders presents generally as a person with inadequate social skills who has severe difficulty in the formation and continuation of relationships. He is subject to depression, but he has little capacity to integrate affect, and he may present some suicidal risk.

CONCLUSIONS: In response to the specific issues raised by the MDSO statute, the following impressions are offered.

Presence of a Mental Disorder.   Although Mr. Sanders is not psychotic, he is seriously disturbed. He is suffering from a schizoid personality disorder, a disorder typified by social isolation and detachment and difficulty in the integration and expression of affect. In addition, he is subject to recurrent depression, and he requires support and monitoring to avoid expression of self-destructive impulses.

Predisposition to Sexual Offense.   With respect to the offense for which Mr. Sanders is currently awaiting sentencing, he apparently entered the victim's apartment for the purpose of obtaining food. His motivation for the sexual assault that ultimately occurred is unclear. It is possible that he tried to master the anxiety created by the situation by assuming a power stance vis-à-vis his victim. It is also possible that he simply took advantage of the victim's vulnerability to satisfy his sexual curiosity, and to do so within a context in which he was in control. Regardless of which explanation (or combination of explanations) is true, it is clear that Mr. Sanders has little, if any, appreciation of the impact of the offense upon the victim, and that he has few skills either for development of a normal relationship with a woman or for social expression of hostile feelings.

Whether, if freed, Mr. Sanders would repeat sexual offenses is a difficult question. The accuracy of mental health professionals' predictions of assaultive behavior is quite low. [See generally J. Monahan, The Clinical Prediction of Violent Behavior (1981).] However, research suggests that the best predictor of future behavior is simply past behavior. There is no evidence to suggest that Mr. Sanders will experience less anxiety and anger related to women, or that he will react to these emotions in a more adaptive, integrated fashion than he has in the past. However, it should also be noted that he is known to have committed a sexual assault on only one occasion and that on this occasion he did not seek a woman with the idea of assaulting her; rather, as noted above, the assault apparently occurred when he was "surprised" by the victim.

Treatability.   Mr. Sanders's chronic problems relate primarily to his severe difficulty in forming and sustaining relationships (described in detail in earlier portions of this report). These difficulties are characterological (i.e., reflective of general personality structure) and consequently resistant to change. Mr. Sanders's limited verbal skills and poor capacity for insight also make traditional (insight-oriented) forms of psychotherapy unlikely to result in substantial change. One approach that might be taken would be to do relatively concrete social skills training (i.e., to have Mr. Sanders practice specific social situations, particularly those involving women)—a common form of treatment that should be available in the state hospital and also at Northwestern Clinic Sevices here in town. Even here, however, the range of skills to be addressed is both basic and pervasive. Consequently, any signifi-

cant change is likely to require arduous, long-term work, although such an approach might give him sufficient concrete skills for at least minimal maintenance of relationships.

With respect to his depression and possible self-destructive behavior, Mr. Sanders requires supportive counseling and monitoring at times of personal crisis, which could be provided on an outpatient basis if Mr. Sanders is not incarcerated. Mr. Sanders appears to depend to a certain extent on the availability of such external supports and controls. Although such counseling is unlikely to result in basic personality change, it does offer some short-term alleviation of distress and management of impulses. It may also be that continued use of an antidepressant is advisable; such a determination should be made through psychiatric consultation, however.

Harriet A. Wilson, Ph.D.

(b) Discussion

As noted in Chapter 9, a "normal" sentencing referral allows the clinician to explore the client's clinical needs more freely than any other type of criminal court evaluation. The author of the Sanders report was responding to a specific statutory standard, which narrowed the scope of the report relative to a general sentencing report. Yet even within this somewhat narrower context, the author presented a rather detailed history.

Of particular importance were the descriptions concerning Mr. Sanders's social relationships—with men as well as women—and his past violent behavior. This historical material was necessary to establish the foundation for the later clinical conclusions concerning the existence of a "mental disorder" and was also obviously useful in setting the context for the discussion of dangerousness and treatability at the end of the report.

Note also that the writer observed that Mr. Sanders's account of the offenses matched those of the victims, as well as that contained in his confession. This was a useful point for the examiner to make: Her clinical conclusions drew heavily from the manner in which the offense was committed, and an apparent consensus concerning those facts would make it less likely that the foundation of her conclusions would be shaken. If the versions of the offense were dramatically different, it is not inconceivable that the writer would have presented alternative clinical explanations, allowing the factfinder to determine which version of the offense was "true."

In addition, the author broke down the statutory definition governing the referral into its individual components and discussed each in turn. This approach is useful, not only because it enables the legal system to better understand the clinical observations but also because it facilitates organization of one's thoughts. At the same time, opinion on the ultimate issue was avoided. Specifically, no statement that Mr. Sanders *required* a certain disposition (e.g., incarceration, behavior modification, outpatient treatment) was made [see § 9.07(c)(4)].

The report also qualified the validity of long-term dangerousness predictions. The court was essentially told that very little can be said on this subject. Thus, no statement as to the likelihood of "dangerousness" was made. Rather, the report only identified situations that tend to enhance or inhibit violence, as suggested in § 9.09(c)(4). (Note that this report was written in 1982, and cited to the relevant literature at the time. A report based on more recent research is found below.)

Finally, the proposals for treatment were fairly concrete (although less so than in the next report). Discussions of treatability are of little utility to the court system unless they are offered in the context of available resources, or, if resources are presently unavailable, are accompanied by realistic proposals for obtaining the necessary resources [see § 9.07(c)(2)]. Note again that the ultimate issue of whether Mr. Sanders should be incarcerated was avoided.

(c) Lester Thomas Report

DEFENDANT: Lester Thomas
D.O.B.: October 14, 1953
DATE OF REPORT: January 15, 1995

REFERRAL: Lester Thomas is a 42-year-old, single, white male referred for an evaluation by his attorney, Jim Scott. Mr. Thomas is currently charged with two counts of misdemeanor stalking. An evaluation was requested on the following issues: (1) competence to proceed, (2) mental state at the time of the offenses, and (3) risk assessment for purposes of informing the court's decision at disposition.

NOTIFICATION: Prior to the evaluation Mr. Thomas was advised of the purpose of the evaluation, this examiner's status as a confidential expert for his attorney, the probable evaluation procedures, and the potential uses of the evaluation at subsequent stages of his case. Mr. Thomas indicated that he understood the notification and he agreed to participate in the evaluation.

EVALUATION PROCEDURES: The following records were reviewed during the evaluation:

A. Criminal Justice Records/Documents Reviewed
   1. Criminal Report Affidavit dated June 1, 1994, completed in conjunction with present charge of stalking.
   2. Walker County Sheriff's Office Incident Report (Case No. 96-000331) dated June 1, 1994 related to charge of stalking.
   3. Walker County Sheriff's Office Incident Report (Case No. 96-078891) dated June 6, 1994 related to charge of stalking, and supplemental investigation report dated 6-06-94.
   4. Walker County Sheriff's Office Incident Reports dated 1990–1991 related to prior charges involving harassing phone calls, trespassing, and trespass after warning.
   5. Pretrial forensic evaluation reports for the current case prepared by Dr. Boris Cutler (November 18, 1994), Dr. Ervin Johns (November 21, 1994), and Dr. Fred Cox (December 15, 1994).

B. Records of Psychiatric Treatment Reviewed
   1. Mountain View Community Mental Health Center (selected records from 1984–1986, including termination noted).
   2. Premium Health Care, Inc., various records 1985, 1988, 1989–1992, and 1994.
   3. Missouri Mental Health Institute, 1989–1990.
   4. Walker County Jail, Tyson Road, medical record 1994.

C. Third-Party Interviews
   1. Defendant's brother, John Thomas (January 9, 1995, by phone).
   2. Hans Rabel, Discharge Coordinator, Premium Mental Health Care, Inc. (regarding community placement options).
   3. Adam Nester, Case Management Supervisor, Mountain View Health Centers (regarding community placement options).

D. Clinical Procedures
   1. December 30, 1994 interview of Mr. Thomas at the Tyson Road Jail (2:10) including administration of the Psychopathy Checklist—Revised (PCL-R).
   2. January 7, 1995 interview of Mr. Thomas at the Tyson Road Jail (3:00) including administration of the Competency to Stand Trial Assessment Instrument (CAI) and the Structured Interview of Reported Symptoms (SIRS).

PERTINENT HISTORY: The history summarized here represents a synthesis of self-report information from Mr. Thomas, information gleaned from prior medical records, and information obtained from an interview with the defendant's brother.

Mr. Thomas is a 42-year-old white male, born and raised in St. Louis by his natural parents. His history is relatively benign until approximately age 27. He attended school in St. Louis where he reported making "average and above" grades. Neither the defendant nor his brother reports any significant history of delinquency or acting out behavior when Mr. Thomas was a child or during adolescence. Mr. Thomas attended college at the University of Kansas from (approximately) 1969–1971, was out of school for two years, then continued his education at the University of Arkansas (1973–1978), where he graduated with a degree in biology. He reported studying theater for approximately two years. During his college years he experimented briefly with drugs, having tried heroin (perhaps 2–3 times), cocaine (6–7 times), and marijuana. He denies having used illicit drugs in the past 15–20 years.

Despite his intelligence and academic accomplishment, Mr. Thomas's work history and social history suggest marginal achievements during his adult life. He has held jobs as a painter, plumber's apprentice, private security guard, and pizza delivery man. He has never been married and apparently has had only one serious relationship. It is clear that his adjustment has been variable, depending on his fluctuating psychiatric condition.

His first psychiatric "break" occurred in approximately 1978, when he reported being seen at the University of Arkansas Counseling Center and then at Walker County Hospital and Premium Health Care, Inc. Mr. Thomas reported that he was diagnosed as suffering from schizophrenia and was treated with major tranquilizing medications (Haldol); symptoms he recalled included bizarre and unrealistic beliefs (delusions) that "hit men from the Mafia were out to get me." He received transitional services and aftercare but his compliance with treatment was variable and he at one point discontinued treatment against medical advice.

A second major psychotic episode occurred around 1984. Records suggest that he became unrealistically preoccupied with a female acquaintance and contacted local authorities, reporting his (delusional) belief that she had been kidnapped by his neighbors. Because of his bizarre behavior, he was committed involuntarily for treatment to the Mountain View Community Mental Health Center. He was diagnosed as suffering from schizophrenia, paranoid type, and was treated with psychotropic medications. He received outpatient follow-up care until his termination from the Mountain View case load on July 7, 1986. During aftercare his medication (Navane) was gradually lowered, then discontinued, and he remained psychiatrically stable until termination. In contrast to his prior treatment experience, Mr. Thomas was described as "quite dependable about keeping his appointments. . . . Made progress on all goals."

In 1989 Mr. Thomas came to the attention of the criminal justice system for charges of harassing phone calls and trespassing. He again developed a preoccupation with a woman who, records suggest, was no more than a casual or social acquaintance from his church. He came to hold the (inaccurate and delusional) belief that she was interested in developing a relationship with him. He also reported attempting to communicate with her by "sending mind waves." These problems led to recommitment to Premium Health Care and transfer to the Missouri Mental Health Institute and subsequent follow-up outpatient care with Premium Health Care. As before, his psychotropic medication was discontinued by the psychiatrist during follow-up treatment (May 26, 1992) and he remained psychiatrically stable until termination in September, 1992.

In September 1994, Mr. Thomas was readmitted to Premium Health Care on a voluntary basis as his current legal difficulties came to a head. Records note his "pathological obsession with a woman [a different one from the two previous occasions] prior to coming in." During this brief admission Mr. Thomas was compliant with treatment and notes indicate "client has been treated before for this illness. . . . Client benefitted from outpatient counseling and would benefit again. . . . Client responds to medication."

CURRENT CLINICAL PRESENTATION: Mr. Thomas was interviewed on two occasions at the Tyson Road Jail. Dressed in standard jail clothing, he appeared to be mildly anxious and somewhat self-conscious during the first interview, but attentive and cooperative. According to jail medical records, Mr.

Thomas was receiving medication (Navane) for "delusional disorder" at the time of this evaluation. The sedating effects of this medication may have contributed to the lack of animation and emotion in Mr. Thomas's presentation. Although he was cooperative and responsive throughout two lengthy interviews, his emotional expression was judged to be somewhat flat or muted. His memory was intact and he neither reported nor presented with obvious symptoms of mental disorder throughout much of the interview. He was able to remain on topic, to elaborate his responses to questions, and to provide a detailed history that appears reasonably reliable in light of available records and other third-party information.

The PCL-R (published by Multi-Health Systems, Toronto, Canada) was administered as one piece of information to inform clinical judgment regarding risk for aggressive behavior. In contemporary research with forensic and correctional populations, this instrument is the best clinical instrument for the prediction of recidivism or violent recidivism. [See Robert Hare et al., *The Revised Psychopathy Checklist: Reliability and Factor Structure*, 2 PSYCHOLOGICAL ASSESSMENT: JOURNAL OF CONSULTING & CLINICAL PSYCHOLOGY 338 (1990).] Clinical ratings on 20 scales yield a PCL-R score that ranges from 0–40. The manual recommends a score of 30 as probably indicative of psychopathy, although scores 25 and higher have been noted in research to raise concerns regarding increased risk. Mr. Thomas's PCL-R score, however, is only 5 and therefore well below the range conventionally associated with increased risk.

The SIRS is a psychological inventory used to assess malingering—the exaggeration or assertion of false symptoms. Again, Mr. Thomas's responses were in the benign range on all subtests of the SIRS; if anything, his responses suggested a tendency to understate symptoms or personal problems.

Despite his overall benign presentation during clinical interview and on formal testing, serious psychopathology was clearly evident in his remarks concerning his history with and perceptions about the complainant in his current stalking cases. Mr. Thomas described chronologically and in considerable detail his feelings toward and perceptions regarding the complainant. It is clear from Mr. Thomas's account that during the lengthy period of time that his behavior gave rise to concerns of stalking, he was suffering from bizarre and unrealistic beliefs (delusions), as well as perceptional distortions (hallucinations). For example, he described numerous occasions when he was able to "hear her speaking to me" when he was not physically close enough for this to have realistically occurred. He also

asserted that she "led me on" by a sophisticated and intricate set of "coded" behaviors that, per Mr. Thomas's (delusional) interpretations, gave him signals as to when and where he might expect to meet with her.

Although he is presently forced by the salience of his legal difficulties to consider that his previous experiences and encounters with the complainant may have been colored by his symptoms, Mr. Thomas insists that he experienced the events as described above. The array of delusional thinking, perceptual distortions, and idiosyncratic interpretations of events all in support of his heightened focus on a casual female acquaintance are reminiscent of at least two of his prior psychotic episodes. Thus, the diagnosis of schizophrenia, paranoid type, appears appropriate.

EVALUATION OF COMPETENCE TO PROCEED (DELETED)

EVALUATION OF MENTAL STATE AT THE TIME OF THE OFFENSE: Mr. Thomas admits that "objectively" he never had a formal, serious relationship with the complainant, that they never really "dated," and that there were few if any occasions in which they were actually in close physical proximity with one another during which they could communicate. Nevertheless, he asserts that she "led me on" by communicating with him over considerable distances, although his description of specific instances of such communications defy credibility and, in this examiner's opinion, give evidence of how his stalking behavior was driven by misperceptions and hallucinations that are part and parcel of his illness. For example, he asserted that while he observed the complainant dance on one occasion at the St. Louis Performing Arts Center, she singled him out from a crowd of 200–300 people to tell him, from the stage, that she wanted to "go to bed with me." This refueled his interest in a relationship with her and increased the attention he gave to her at her work setting. Although no actual face-to-face conversations were held, he asserted that he "heard" her make aside comments as she worked on her job at Taco Bell to the effect that "in the end, it will all work out. We'll get married and move to Chicago." After being instructed not to return to her place of work, he monitored her from across a busy boulevard and asserted that she set up a series of special codes (e.g., focusing her eyes in one direction and shaking her head) as she walked into work in order to tell him whether or not "I'll see you after work tonight." Similar "messages" were "received" from patrons who entered and exited her place of work, with whom Mr. Thomas believed he was communicating from afar.

These claims by the defendant appear incredible on their face and, in light of the complaints filed, almost certainly false. Yet they are not unlike prior symptoms experienced by the defendant, also during times of intense and inappropriate focus on developing an amorous relationship with women who had not expressed any real interest in him. Mr. Thomas had not been taking psychotropic medications for quite some time (since May 26, 1992) when his preoccupation with the complainant developed and flourished. In this examiner's opinion, Mr. Thomas's actions toward the complainant are reasonably attributed to the difficulty he experienced accurately perceiving the reality of his (non)relationship with her. Hallucinated voices and idiosyncratic interpretations of ordinary, meaningless, and innocuous events (e.g., a change in posture or shaking of her hair) formed the "encouragement" that fueled his attention to and monitoring of the complainant. Thus, Mr. Thomas, during this period of heightened psychotic symptoms, would have had difficulty correctly determining that his attentions were unwanted and inappropriate—in a word, wrong.

RISK ASSESSMENT: Whether Mr. Thomas is found guilty of the present charges or is found not guilty by reason of insanity, consideration as to appropriate placement and disposition will have to weigh the potential risk for violence that he poses to the community. Consistently accurate predictions of future instances of violence cannot be made by mental health professionals; whether a person will behave aggressively is a function of a variety of factors that include history, personal disposition, and situational variables (e.g., provocation) that cannot all be known in advance. However, it is possible to consider the available historical data and the anticipated placement/situational factors to estimate relative risk. This is the basis for the current risk assessment.

Among historical factors most strongly correlated with aggression or violence recidivism, a history of serious aggressive behavior during adolescence, particular with early onset (below age 12) is a primary concern. There is no such history in the case of Mr. Thomas.

In terms of psychological/psychiatric factors, the best clinical instrument for the assessment of risk is the PCL-R. As noted previously, Mr. Thomas scores well below the critical range for concern to be raised about increased risk for violence.

Recent epidemiological studies suggest some level of increased risk for persons with certain psychiatric diagnoses. [See Saleem A. Shah, *Recent Research on Crime and Mental Disorder: Some Implications for Programs and Policies,* in MENTAL DISORDER AND CRIME 303 (Sheilah Hodgins ed. 1993).] Schizophrenia, from which Mr. Thomas suffers, is one such illness. However, two caveats are in order. First, although persons with schizophrenia are at increased risk relative to persons with no diagnosis, their risk level is relatively low compared to some other disorders (e.g., persons with drug/alcohol abuse/dependence diagnoses). Second, among persons who suffer from schizophrenia, those who are at greater risk usually show one or both of the following symptoms: persecutory delusions (unrealistic beliefs that others are trying to harm them) or perceptions that others are controlling their thoughts (e.g., inserting or removing their thoughts). Importantly, Mr. Thomas displays *neither* of these symptoms and thus, among persons with schizophrenia, should be considered at relatively lower risk.

A third important historical factor is adult history of violent behavior. Although no "bright line" indicators exist, the literature suggests that a history of less than three felony arrests involving crimes against person is a favorable prognostic sign; Mr. Thomas has zero prior felony arrests, according to information made available to me.

A fourth consideration is the individual's current thoughts, feelings, and attitudes toward others. This can and should include fantasies that he has about possible interactions with others. In interviews with this examiner, Mr. Thomas denied any prior or current intentions or fantasies of harming others. He denied any history of owning/using firearms or other weapons, and no angry/aggressive feelings other than "frustration" that his desired relationship with women did not eventuate. He described that his intentions and fantasies have always been benign/amorous, which is corroborated by reports from the defendant's brother who has discussed these matters with Mr. Thomas on occasion.

A fifth consideration is the availability of support and supervision to ensure that behaviors of concern (e.g., taking medication and avoiding further "stalking") can be monitored. As noted previously, Mr. Thomas has a history of compliance with and success in outpatient psychiatric treatment. A number of community-based placements may be available, ranging from living at home with day-care activities and medication monitoring to residential or supervised living situations (group homes, apartments, adult congregate living facilities) that have overlay mental health and case management services. In light of Mr. Thomas's excellent recent history of compliance with and success in outpatient care, these options should be explored should the court be willing to consider supervised probation as a disposition. I have spoken with

Mr. Adam Nester, Case Management Supervisor at Mountain View Mental Health Center, who would be able to arrange for a screening evaluation of Mr. Thomas should the court determine that to be appropriate. Mountain View is capable of providing virtually the full range of options noted here.

Although Mr. Thomas should be considered, on the analyses provided here, to be a relatively low risk for violent or aggressive behavior in the community, the recurrent pattern of his symptoms suggests that, absent medication and periodic outpatient follow-up, he should be considered a relatively high risk for the recurrence of hallucinations and misinterpretations of the behavior of others, most likely in the context of a sought-after relationship with a woman who becomes the focus of his attention. Thus, suppression and deterrence of the kinds of behavior that led to his current charges may be dependent on the reliability of external controls (medication, counseling); although Mr. Thomas has attained sufficient remission following two prior treatment episodes that his doctors have voluntarily discontinued his treatment, the longer view of his history suggests that this discontinuation should not happen again.

Jefferson Dodge, Ph.D.

(d)   Discussion

This report is included primarily as an example of the more sophisticated analysis of dangerousness that research conducted in the late 1980s and the 1990s suggests is possible [see § 9.09(c)]. In this regard it can be contrasted to the Sanders report (above) and the Marlar report (next). Note the reference to the various empirically validated predictors (the actuarial approach) as well as the close analysis of Mr. Thomas's behavior and mental state during past stalking episodes (the anamnestic approach). Some of the evaluation techniques are also worth nothing. The SIRS has been shown to be a useful way of detecting malingering [see § 3.07(a)], and the PCL-R is considered a useful test for evaluating violence-proneness [see § 9.09(c)(2)].

Finally, note that the evaluator follows the recommendation in § 9.07(c)(4) that treatment recommendations should follow the "if–then" format. He makes his observations about outpatient services only after noting that they are relevant solely if probation is a consideration.

19.06.   Civil Commitment [Chapter 10]

(a)   J. Marlar Report

Judge Jane Doe
County Court House

Dear Judge Doe:

This letter reports my evaluation of Mr. J. Marlar (Case No. 1234) under the state commitment law. That law authorizes involuntary commitment if the individual (1) is mentally ill, defined as "a substantial disorder of thought or mood which significantly impairs judgment, behavior, capacity to recognize reality, or ability to cope with the ordinary demands of life," and (2) the mental illness causes the person to be "likely to inflict serious bodily harm on self or others within the near future, or causes the person to be unable to survive safely in freedom with the help of friends or others."

Mr. Marlar is a 37-year-old single male. He was arrested yesterday, March 2, 1995, on charges of trespassing upon property other than a structure. Rather than being brought to a judge, he was brought here, to the Receiving Unit, on the same day. My evaluation, which consisted of a one-hour interview of Mr. Marlar, a brief conversation with the arresting officer, and a perusal of his arrest and psychiatric records (received by fax), took place on that day as well.

Information from Interview and Records. When I interviewed him, Mr. Marlar was dirty and disheveled. He apparently had been living on the streets for some time. He was arrested while sitting on a bench in front of a restaurant. When asked to leave by the owners of the restaurant he refused, stating that he had a right to sit and sleep on the bench. The police were called and he was arrested.

Mr. Marlar denies having hallucinations and has refused all medication (although, given his emergency status, the hospital staff has medicated him with Prolixin, Trilafon and Cogentin). This medication had had little effect at the time I interviewed him. During the interview he asked that the TV be turned down when in fact no TV was on. He claims to be a prophet and a savior. Although he says his parents knew he was an important religious figure from the time of his birth, he also claims that they paid his landlord to have him evicted and are setting him up to be killed by federal agents in response to his political and religious writings. He also reports that he is named in the "real" bible, which is found in the basement of Buckingham Palace. He claims that the current Bible is a fake, orchestrated by the Jews, who were originally aliens from another planet. He also feels that the police officer who arrested him was not a real officer. He claims to have extraordinary healing powers. He carries a "pendulum" which he uses to heal himself and others of diseases like exposure to Agent Orange, AIDS and broken vertebrae.

He has one prior month-long admission to a psychiatric facility, in December 1994. There he was diagnosed as suffering from schizophrenia, paranoid type. Apparently, the admission was voluntary on his part. He also has a history of drug and alcohol abuse dating back to his teenage years. He was arrested for possession in 1982 and arrested for DUI [driving under the influence] in 1984.

Mental Illness. I confirm Mr. Marlar's diagnosis as schizophrenia. As reported above, this disorder substantially impairs his ability to recognize reality.

Danger to Others. Mr. Marlar has no record of physical harm to others. His delusions are predominately focused on healing and prophesy rather than paranoia. He states he would not harm his parents, despite their efforts to have him evicted and killed, because he is a "healer," not a "killer." Further, his parents live in another state. However, when arrested he did struggle with police and take a swing at one of the two officers; he also insists that if released he will return to the bench, because it is public property (a belief this evaluator cannot disconfirm). Further, his DUI arrest indicates that he may engage in behavior resulting from drug abuse that could harm others. However, there is no current evidence of psychoactive substance use and driving is unlikely in any event given his current inability to purchase or rent a vehicle. Mr. Marlar also may be a "nuisance" to those around him in that he appears quite willing to walk alongside people and tell them about his healing prowess.

Danger to Self. Research shows that young people with worsening schizophrenic symptoms, such as Mr. Marlar, are at relatively high risk for suicide [see Melton et al. § 10.08(b)(1)]. However, Mr. Marlar does not appear depressed generally but only bothered by his present hospitalization and his feeling that he is powerless in this setting.

Ability to Survive. As stated above, Mr. Marlar was dirty and disheveled when I talked to him. His clothing was smelly and he was very thin. He claimed that he was able to get food from handouts and from the homeless shelter, and that he lived in a box under the Massif Bridge. According to his records, he was at one time a landscaper. However, in his current condition, it is unlikely he could obtain employment in that capacity (or in any other).

Competence to Make Treatment Decisions. If Mr. Marlar

is committed, he will probably continue to refuse medication. Under state law, such a refusal must be honored in nonemergency situations if he is found competent to make a treatment decision by the court. Mr. Marlar understands the diagnosis of schizophrenia, and that medications can remove delusional and hallucinatory systems. He also understands the side effects of that medication. He denies that he is suffering from schizophrenia or that he has hallucinations or delusions and, consistent with the latter view, he also denies that medication could eliminate these symptoms in him. He says he does not feel sick and that "mental illness" and schizophrenia are labels doctors use to oppress people. He also does not like the side effects of his current medication. He adamantly states that he does not want the medication and wants to return to the streets. If he becomes sick, he says, he can heal himself, using the pendulum.

Conclusion. It is the opinion of this evaluator that if [he is] released without treatment, Mr. Marlar's condition will continue to deteriorate. However, he will probably be able to survive the way he has in the past, especially if Social Services checks on his "box" and ensures he receives food from the homeless shelter; he may also be eligible for SSI or SSDI. These might be "less restrictive alternatives" to hospitalization. However, his delusional system will probably again lead to a confrontation with others of the type that precipitated this admission; further his physical condition will deteriorate along with his mental condition. At the present time, he has the cognitive ability to understand the risks and benefits of treatment but clearly does not appreciate his own condition.

Martha Questin, M.D.

(b) Discussion

Typically, no written report is prepared in civil commitment cases. When the evaluation is at the front end of this process, as was the case here, there may be no time to do so, because in many jurisdictions judicial review takes place within 48 hours of admission [see § 10.04(a)(1)]. For the same reason, the evaluator seldom has access to the type and amount of information available in criminal cases and most other civil cases, as this report illustrates.

Note that the evaluator addressed each statutory question. Only the first issue (mental illness) is addressed with any confidence, however. Whether Mr. Marlar is dangerous to self or others or unable to survive are difficult legal questions that require balancing liberty interests against the interests of society under the police power and *parens patriae* power. Relevant to this question are the degree and probability of the risk and its imminence [see § 10.03(c)]. The evaluator provided information on these various points without performing the ultimate calculus. Note also that given Mr. Marlar's refusal of medication, the evaluator addressed the competence issue but left it up to the judge to decide whether a lack of "appreciation" of one's illness constitutes incompetence [see § 11.03(a)(2)].

Finally note that the evaluator addressed least-restrictive-alternative issues [see § 10.03(g)], although somewhat tentatively. Ideally, the evaluator would have a firmer grasp of institutional and noninstitutional community options and could provide a fuller description of them to the judge. Of course, if Mr. Marlar were entitled to an independent expert (as is the case in a few jurisdictions [see § 10.04(a)(2)]), this information could come from that source.

19.07. Competency to Handle Finances [Chapter 11]

(a) Dorothy Dyer Report*

NAME: Dorothy Dyer
D.O.B.:   September 3, 1952
DATE OF REPORT: September 4, 1984

CIRCUMSTANCES OF REFERRAL: Dorothy Dyer, a 32-year-old white female, was referred to the Elk County Clinic for evaluation by her attorney, Sally Hudson of the Elk County Legal Aid Society. On March 9, 1974, Ms. Dyer was found incapable of handling business matters due to "retarded physical and mental condition, as a result of congenital deficiency." Richard Perkins, an attorney from Athens, Arizona, who had handled her family's legal affairs, was appointed as her guardian at that time. At the present time, Ms. Dyer would like to have the guardianship dissolved because she believes she is able to handle her own financial affairs. As a result, she has procured the

*This report was provided the authors by Lois Weithorn, Ph.D.

counsel of Ms. Hudson in the hope of restoring her legal competency. Ms. Hudson has requested the clinic to assess Ms. Dyer's present competency as it pertains to the management of her financial affairs.

SOURCES OF INFORMATION: In conducting its evaluation, the clinic had available to it information from the following sources:

1. Court order appointing Guardian from the Corporation Court of the City of Athens, Arizona, dated March 9, 1974.
2. Medical records from the Elk County General Hospital regarding Ms. Dyer's treatment immediately after birth, dated September 4, 1952, through September 20, 1952.
3. Medical records from the Neuropsychiatry Department at the Elk County General Hospital regarding outpatient speech and play therapy with Ms. Dyer dated December 1, 1958, through June 1, 1959.
4. Medical records from the Neurology Clinic at the Elk County General Hospital regarding an evaluation of Ms. Dyer, dated April 10, 1968.
5. A report of psychological testing of Ms. Dyer, performed at age 12, from the file of the Social Security District Office, Athens.
6. A telephone interview with Mr. Perkins, the Guardian, by Janet Higham, Ph.D., conducted on August 30, 1984.
7. A telephone interview with Sarah Smith, Ms. Dyer's supervisor at the Frost Diner, by Lisa Madding, D.S.W., conducted on August 27, 1984.
8. A telephone interview with Jean Smart, the babysitter for Ms. Dyer's two-year-old son, by Lisa Madding, D.S.W., conducted on August 27, 1984.
9. A telephone interview with Farah James, a Health Department nurse who has treated Ms. Dyer's son, by Lisa Madding, D.S.W., conducted on August 27, 1984.
10. A psychosocial interview by Lisa Madding, D.S.W., with Ms. Dyer, conducted on August 30, 1984.
11. A psychosocial interview by Lisa Madding, D.S.W., with Mr. John Daniels, Ms. Dyer's boyfriend (and father of her child), conducted on August 30, 1984.
12. Psychological testing of Ms. Dyer by Marci Levin, M.S., a clinical psychology resident supervised by Janet Higham, Ph.D., conducted on August 30, 1984.
13. A competency assessment interview of Ms. Dyer

by Janet Higham, Ph.D., conducted on August 30, 1984.

PERSONAL/FAMILY BACKGROUND: Ms. Dorothy Dyer was born on September 3, 1952, and has lived all her life in Athens, Arizona. According to Ms. Dyer, she was the youngest of the six children born to the Dyer family. She reported that her father supported the family by working in a garage, while her mother supplemented the family income by doing laundry. She stated that her father died in 1972 and her mother in 1975, and that her grandparents also died around this time—"They all went one after another." Ms. Dyer indicated that she does not get along well with her three brothers and two sisters (the oldest of whom is 53 years of age) because of their chronic use of alcohol. Related to this point, she noted that the guardianship was initially established because her mother was afraid that Ms. Dyer's sister would "use up all my money drinking."

Ms. Dyer explained that she attended school in Athens through the fourth grade. She remarked that she "liked it one time" but quit because "I couldn't talk." (In this respect, she referred to a pronounced speech impediment from which she suffers.) She reported that she had been living with her parents, and following her mother's death moved in to live with a sister. In 1979, she moved out of her sister's home and established her own residence. She described the move as "hard at first," stating that "at first I was lonely, but then I enjoyed myself." She remarked that she wanted her own place "because all my friends got one." This seemed very important to her.

Ms. Dyer stated that she met her first and current boyfriend, John Daniels, in late 1980 at her aunt's home. Mr. Daniels reported in this regard: "We watched each other for a couple of weeks and then decided to go out." The couple began dating steadily at this point; in December 1981, one year later, Ms. Dyer gave birth to a male child, whom she named Larry. Following the birth of the child, she and John began living together and have resided together since that time. The relationship has lasted four years, and they both speak of it in positive terms. Ms. Dyer reported that she loves John and hopes to marry him some day but also indicated that she's "not quite ready yet." Mr. Daniels described Ms. Dyer as a "good and understanding person." He explained that they "just took to each other." During the last year, Mr. Daniels was in Nevada for 12 months between April 1982 and April 1983. According to Ms. Dyer, he sent her about $250 during that time and called on a regular basis. He explained that he was involved in a one-year training program to become a mechanic but indicated that he had to withdraw from the program when Ms. Dyer asked him to come home.

Larry, their son, is presently two and a half years old. Ms. Dyer and Mr. Daniels spoke of him with apparent affection, and both agreed that "he's real smart for a two-year-old." Ms. Dyer explained that he "loves McDonald's" and reported that he even "jogs" with the two of them. She stated that she hopes to have one more child but commented, "I'm going to wait until Larry's a little older. Then, I'm going to stop—two's enough." Farah James, a public health nurse, reported that Ms. Dyer is very regular with her appointments at the Care-Baby Clinic and apparently devotes considerable energy to being a good mother. She stated that Larry is developing normally and suffers from no observable impediments.

Ms. Dyer stated that she works as a dishwasher at the Frost Diner in Athens. She stated that she "likes my job," where she has been working for ten years. She stated that she works from 7:30 A.M. to 2:30 P.M. daily during the winters and is free to spend the summers at home with her son.

Her supervisor, Sarah Smith, reported that Ms. Dyer is very responsible in her work and gets along well with the other employees. She stated that she follows instructions well and never misses work unless she is taking her son to an appointment.

DETERMINATION OF INCOMPETENCY: On March 9, 1974, Ms. Dyer was deemed incompetent in the Corporation Court of the City of Athens. Donald Siegle, the guardian *ad litem,* reported that as a result of "some congenital deficiency," Ms. Dyer is a "person of retarded physical and mental condition." Thus, Ms. Dyer was considered "incapable of handling business affairs." The court order provided no further elaboration regarding the reasons for the ruling of incompetency. At that time, Richard Perkins (an attorney for the Dyer family prior to the death of Ms. Dyer's mother) was appointed guardian of the estate.

BEHAVIORAL OBSERVATION: Ms. Dyer was neatly and casually dressed for her sessions at the Elk County Clinic. She made good eye contact and was cooperative throughout the sessions. She seemed well aware of the nature and purpose of the evaluation and clearly understood the clinic's role in providing her attorney with information about her need, or lack thereof, for a guardian. She responded to questions directly.

Ms. Dyer has a severe speech impediment, which made it difficult to understand her speech most of the time. She patiently repeated responses to items until she was certain she was understood. She was aware of this deficit and was able to discuss her impairment openly and nondefensively. Similarly, Ms. Dyer worked patiently and conscientiously on difficult test items. Although she was aware that she was unable to respond correctly to many items, she continued patiently and methodically to attempt new items.

Ms. Dyer also appeared to have some gait disturbance; however, she was able to walk without assistance. She reported poor fine motor coordination. Her fingers appeared stiff.

In general, Ms. Dyer appeared friendly and motivated to perform well on tasks. In spite of speech, motor, and intellectual deficits, she was able to relate in an effective way to others.

ASSESSMENT OF INTELLECTUAL FUNCTIONING:

In 1964, Ms. Dyer was administered Form 1 of the revised Stanford–Binet intelligence test by a Dr. D.T. Fletcher. At that time, she was 12 years of age and in the fourth grade. Ms. Dyer's mental age was calculated as five years, eight months, giving her an IQ of 47. Dr. Fletcher suggested that she be referred to a class for the trainable mentally retarded.

On August 30, 1984, at the Elk County Clinic, Ms. Dyer was administered the Wechsler Adult Intelligence Scale—Revised (WAIS-R) and the Peabody Individual Achievement Test (PIAT) to identify specific strengths and deficits that characterize her present intellectual and neuropsychological functioning. Neuropsychological assessment involves the evaluation of the behavioral expression of brain dysfunction.

Ms. Dyer is currently functioning in the upper end of the mild mental retardation range of intellectual functioning. Her scores on the Verbal and Performance scales of the WAIS-R did not differ significantly from one another. The Verbal scale includes subtests that focus primarily on skills related to fund of general information, vocabulary, abstract reasoning, social judgment, auditory memory, concentration, attention, and mathematical skills. The Performance scale subtests measure perceptual–motor integration and motor coordination, ability to perceive visual details, ability to solve visual and spatial problems, and sense of the appropriate sequences of social interactions.

Relative to her overall functioning, Ms. Dyer evidenced particular strength in her social judgment skill (the ability to use facts in a pertinent, meaningful, and emotionally relevant manner). Ms. Dyer also performed relatively well on the Block Design subtest. This subtest assesses visual organization skills of analysis (breaking down a pattern) and synthesis (building the pattern up again with blocks). She performed relatively poorly on a subtest (i.e., the Object Assembly subtest) measuring perceptual organization skills. The

subtest requires a person to arrange parts into a meaningful whole.

On the PIAT, Ms. Dyer performed relatively well on the subtest measuring spelling ability. Her poorest performance was on a subtest measuring general fund of information. This latter score can be explained in part by her limited schooling. The other subtests measured reading and mathematics skills. Ms. Dyer's achievement scores all fell in the lower-elementary-grade range.

ASSESSMENT OF ADAPTIVE FUNCTIONING:

Ms. Dyer was administered subscales of the American Association of Mental Deficiency (AAMD) Adaptive Behavior Scale. Information provided by Jean Smart, the babysitter for Ms. Dyer's child, and Farah James, a Health Department nurse, as well as information obtained from Ms. Dyer and clinic staff's observations, were also used to determine the level of Ms. Dyer's adaptive functioning. According to reports from Ms. Smart and Ms. James, Ms. Dyer is able to care adequately for her child. In addition, Ms. Dyer's supervisor at work, Sarah Smith, reported that Ms. Dyer is capable of functioning well at her job. In general, Ms. Dyer appears capable of self-care skills required in independent functioning. These skills include the ability to eat, clean, and dress herself and maintain an appropriate appearance. Moreover, she indicated that she is able to ride a bus or call a taxi to travel places locally by herself. She reported an awareness of how to use the telephone and find a phone number. She maintains her own phone notebook and can use a directory in some instances. She stated that she shops for herself and is able to make simple purchases. She also reported knowledge of how to use a bank.

COMPETENCY TO MANAGE HER FINANCIAL AFFAIRS:

An assessment of Ms. Dyer's competency to manage her financial affairs was performed. The accuracy of her understanding of her financial assets and the practicality and soundness of logic underlying her financial planning were assessed.

Ms. Dyer was asked a series of specific questions about her financial assets. Her responses were compared with information provided by Mr. Perkins. Mr. Perkins had reported to Ms. Hudson that Ms. Dyer receives her weekly paychecks directly from her employer. However, according to Mr. Perkins Supplemental Security Income checks for both herself and her child are sent to Mr. Perkins, who deposits the money in bank accounts, drawing upon these funds when Ms. Dyer's or the child's expenses are greater than her salary. In addition, Ms. Dyer has a savings account including money left to her by her family, as well as a savings certificate from her father. The various accounts currently total more than $7,000. Mr. Perkins stated that he was not certain whether Ms. Dyer had been informed as to the specific amount and nature of her assets.

When asked to do so, Ms. Dyer was able to describe her assets only partially. She knew that her salary check was $101 weekly. However, she only knew the approximate amount of her Supplemental Security Income checks and did not know how much money she had in the bank. She was aware of the existence of a large sum of money left to her by her family. She reported that it was her understanding that her father left her enough money in the bank to live the rest of her life. It appears that someone told Ms. Dyer that this was the case because she was not aware of the specific amount of money.

Ms. Dyer was able to provide a fairly detailed description of her bills and how she pays each bill. For example, she reported that she receives a $101 check at work, which she cashes at work. Groceries cost approximately $30, which she pays in cash. She pays the babysitter $20 in cash each week. She stated that she puts aside the remainder of each week's money to pay the monthly utility bills and other expenses (such as shoes). Although she plans ahead by saving this money, she does not appear to budget systematically specific amounts of money for each expense. Rather, she saves what is left over and pays her bills. If she requires additional funds—for clothing, for instance—she contacts Mr. Perkins, who writes her a check, or arranges payment for such items directly with the merchant. She states that she obtains a money order at the post office to pay phone and electric bills. Although she does not write checks, she stated that she knows how to do this. Ms. Dyer demonstrated her ability to work with money during the sessions. She was given coins and bills and could "pay for" hypothetical items. She also would calculate—in her head in some instances—how many bills of specific types would be needed to pay for an item costing $30, for example. However, whereas she knew that three $10 bills or a $20 bill and a $10 bill could pay for the item, she was unable to estimate how many $5 bills would equal $30. In contrast, she could count out $30 in $5 bills. This differentiation of skills suggest that whereas Ms. Dyer is able to work with actual money, her ability to work abstractly with monetary concepts is somewhat limited. This appears to be the case when she is asked to consider larger sums of money. She could not *fully* comprehend, for example, the difference between $500 and $5,000. She could only say the latter sum was "bigger" than the former. She did not have a clear idea as to what could be bought (e.g., a car, a house) with the latter sum.

Although Ms. Dyer demonstrated a working knowledge of how to buy items and could provide a detailed account of her regular daily expenses, she was not able to grasp more complex concepts that would be necessary in the administration of large sums of money. For example, she could not comprehend the difference between a checking and a savings account. When these concepts were explained to her, she did state that if she had control of all of her money, she'd "put it away in a bank."

CONCLUSIONS AND RECOMMENDATIONS: Ms. Dyer demonstrated several strengths and weaknesses related to her ability to manage her financial affairs. She is currently functioning in the upper end of the mild mental retardation level of intelligence. She also has a severe speech impediment. Despite her speech impediment and impaired intellectual functioning, she has adapted well to her environment. She is able to work effectively and care for herself and her child. She is also able to travel within this local environment using the public transit systems. She responsibly manages the money to which she has access, successfully paying her bills and shopping to meet food and clothing needs. She currently sets aside money to pay bills that are due at the end of the month. Clearly, she has learned to adjust to her environment in an adaptive and productive manner. However, her intellectual deficits limit her ability to deal with abstract and symbolic concepts, including monetary concepts. She is most adept when dealing with the concrete physical reality of a situation rather than theoretical concepts requiring her to plan for the future. She is not able to specify how much money should be set aside each week to ensure a total amount at the end of the month to cover her bills. She cannot perform the arithmetic necessary to handle large sums of money. Although this inability does not currently interfere with her management of money, it would likely pose a problem with transferring larger sums of money, to the extent that this requires "paper transactions" rather than direct use of the money itself. Moreover, her ability to conceptualize the actual value of large sums is limited.

Janet Higham, Ph.D.
Clinical and Supervising Psychologist

Marci Levin, M.S.
Clinical Psychology Resident

(b)   Discussion

This report was triggered by Ms. Dyer's desire to have her guardianship dissolved. As noted in §

11.01, a competency report must zero in on the specific function the law has made relevant. The writers of this report painstakingly obtained information from Ms. Dyer about her ability to handle various sums of money. She was asked to describe her assets and the bills she paid, was given hypothetical situations requiring her to use money to pay for different items, and was quizzed about other aspects of financial dealings, including banks and checking accounts. Of particular note is the examiners' use of hypothetical situations: What better way to determine whether a person will be able to perform a task than to have her perform it in front of an examiner?

The examiners also attempted to gather information relative to Ms. Dyer's general ability to deal with abstract, as well as concrete, notions. Several sources were consulted (her guardian, her employer, her nurse, her boyfriend, and even her babysitter) in an effort to derive useful data on this point. In addition, performance-oriented psychological tests were administered that focused on organizational and social judgment skills. This kind of information might have been very relevant to the court attempting to determine the extent, if any, to which Ms. Dyer should be given control of her affairs.

On the central question presented by this case—whether Ms. Dyer should be allowed to control the $7,000 managed by her guardian—the examiners suggested that although Ms. Dyer appeared capable of handling small sums of money, larger sums were difficult for her to fathom. Whether this fact should deny her control of the money was a legal–moral issue that the examiners left to the judge. The Dyer report does illustrate, however, that in competency cases (as opposed to most of the other types of cases discussed in this book), the gap between clinical data and the ultimate issue is often minuscule.

19.08.   Workers' Compensation for Mental Injury [Chapter 12]

(a)   Lane Cates Report

NAME: Lane Cates
D.O.B.:   April 1, 1957

REFERRAL INFORMATION: Lane Cates is a 27-year-old, married white male who was referred for a clinical evaluation regarding possible psychiatric or psychological disturbance secondary to injuries received due to an accident on his job.

CLINICAL CONTACTS AND SOURCES OF INFORMATION: Mr. Cates was interviewed at my office on the following dates: April 11, 1984 (two hours); April 30, 1984 (one-hour interview and administration of the Minnesota Multiphasic Personality Inventory [MMPI]); and May 16, 1984 (one-and-a-half-hour joint interview of Mr. Cates and his wife and administration of Life Experiences Survey).

Additional information received included the following: records of hospitalization and treatment associated with the surgical removal of Mr. Cates's right testicle in October 1983; records of attendance and disciplinary actions from Mr. Cates's employer, the Acme Machine Shop, from February 1980 through March 1984; brief interviews with two of Mr. Cates's fellow workers, Mr. Jones and Mr. Smithers.

CIRCUMSTANCES OF THE REFERRAL: Mr. Cates reported that he has worked at the Acme Machine Shop since February 1980. His duties have included operating various power tools, including a lathe, a table saw, and a grinding machine. He reported that in late September 1983 he was struck in the groin while operating the grinding machine. He developed an abscess, which resulted in the surgical removal of his right testicle on October 4, 1983. He returned to work in December 1983 but was assigned primarily to janitorial and "clean-up" duties. He reported that he continues to experience periodic "nagging" pain in the right groin area and occasional sharp or shooting pain extending to his right pelvic region. A lawsuit against the manufacturer of the machine is pending.

PRESENT CLINIC FINDINGS: Lane Cates is a slender white male of medium build. He was on time for each of the three interviews I had with him and was accompanied by his wife on each occasion. Mr. Cates has been married for six years and has one child, a daughter two years old. He indicated that he comes from a big family (three brothers and four sisters) and that he and his wife had also planned to have a large family.

In presenting his current problems, Mr. Cates began by stating that "it all happened as a result of my accident" (referring to the groin injury and subsequent surgery). He complained of occasional difficulty in maintaining an erection (corroborated by his wife's statements) and a fear of pain during sexual intercourse; he indicated that since his operation he has been occasionally fearful of having relations with his wife, who has at times responded with anger and frustration. He voiced the fear that his "sexual problems" might lead to further problems in their marriage, and his wife stated that they had talked about going to their minister for counseling. Both Mr. Cates and his wife voiced concerns that they may not be able to have any more children; laboratory findings from tests conducted at Harper Heights Clinic indicated that a February 1984 sperm count from his left testicle was zero.

During the interviews Mr. Cates appeared alert and oriented to his surroundings; he neither complained of physical pain nor displayed pain response behavior. His speech was relevant, organized, and coherent, and there was no interview behavior suggestive of major thought disturbance. Mr. Cates did, however, appear both anxious and depressed. Anxiety was manifest in nervous movements of his hands (e.g., picking at his skin or clothing) and face (e.g., grimaces) and in his frequently averting his eyes from the examiner's, particularly when discussing his groin injury and diminished sexual activity. He also reported feeling fatigued, unhappy, and self-conscious, particularly around other men at work who know the nature of his injury. Transient sleep disturbance was also noted. His wife corroborated that he had had trouble sleeping for the past several months and that he had become progressively "more nervous-acting."

The results of the MMPI, a self-report objective personality measure, were consistent with the interview impression of mild to moderate depression. The validity scales suggest that Mr. Cates may have mildly exaggerated his current symptomatology, though there is no indication of outright feigning or malingering, and the elevation on the clinical scales measuring anxiety and depression is at a level consistent with interview presentation.

I also interviewed two men who work with Mr. Cates, Mr. Jones and Mr. Smithers. They both stated that Mr. Cates seemed more withdrawn and nervous "lately."

OTHER PSYCHOLOGICALLY IMPORTANT EVENTS: An examination of Mr. Cates's attendance record at the Acme Machine Shop revealed almost perfect attendance (except for approved vacation time off) until July 1983, two months *before* his accident. In July Mr. Cates took four days' sick leave; two additional days of sick leave were taken in August, and three sick days were taken in September *before* his accident. When questioned about this, Mr. Cates responded that his father passed away in July and that "it hit me pretty hard." He indicated that he had been very close to his

father when he was younger but had felt more distant from him in recent years. He had intended to try to "mend the fences between us"; he indicated that his father had always been quietly dissatisfied with Mr. Cates's choice of a wife, and, later, with the way he was raising his child. His father's sudden and unexpected death in July precluded any possibility of restoring their relationship. As a result, Mr. Cates felt guilty about not having made up with his father and was described by Mrs. Cates as "all torn up" following the funeral. The subsequent absences from work in late July, August, and September were a result of continued mourning for his deceased father and "difficulty getting going again" after the father's death.

Partly as a result of this information, I administered the Life Experiences Survey to Mr. Cates and his wife in the course of interviewing them. The inventory surveys the occurrence and perceived impact of potentially stressful life events during a given period; Mr. and Mrs. Cates were each asked to complete the survey for the six-month period preceding Mr. Cates's accident at work. Mr. Cates identified the loss of his father as one stressful event, though he tended to minimize its impact on him; the only other stressful events identified by Mr. Cates were receiving a traffic ticket for running a red light and decreased attendance at church.

Mrs. Cates, however, identified several other life changes during that period, including "trouble with in-laws" (Mr. Cates's parents, prior to Mr. Cates's father's death) and changes in social activities for the family generally. Further inquiry into these areas revealed that Mr. Cates had been openly criticized by his father at a family reunion approximately six weeks before the father's death, primarily about the way he was raising his child and his failure to be more financially successful. Mrs. Cates indicated that her husband could never stand up to his father face to face but later at home ruminated excessively about the confrontation and defended himself to her against his father's accusations. She indicated that he became preoccupied with proving himself to his father and was subsequently distant from her and other family members for a period. It was during this period that he received his traffic ticket for running a red light—an incident that Mrs. Cates described as resulting from her husband's "driving around in a daze . . . like he was lost in a fog." She also reported other incidents—for example, $1,200 damage to the family car; this was never fully explained, though she clearly suspected that Mr. Cates was at fault. During Mrs. Cates's narrative, Mr. Cates was noticeably uncomfortable and appeared embarrassed, though he never mustered the initiative to defend himself except to assert meekly that the car had been "sideswiped" while parked on the street. Mrs. Cates described her husband as periodically "absent-minded" and possibly accident-prone, though she could recall no other specific events in their recent history to illustrate this impression.

This description was corroborated by Mr. Jones and Mr. Smithers, both of whom said Mr. Cates had begun to "stare into space" during work hours beginning over a year ago and that on several occasions prior to the accident had forgotten to turn off the machine he was using after he was through with it.

CLINICAL FORMULATION: Lane Cates is a 27-year-old, married white male who presently reports residual, transient pain secondary to an injury that necessitated the removal of his right testicle and mild to moderate anxiety and depression of approximately four months' duration. He complains that his sexual relationship with his wife has been unsatisfactory since his surgery, and his wife confirms this. Both appear disappointed at the prospect of not being able to have any more children.

Given the medical evidence available regarding the nature of Mr. Cates's surgery and the subsequent laboratory sperm count, it appears reasonable to infer that Mr. Cates's present anxiety and depression is, in part, an emotional reaction to the effects of his job-related injury. Other factors, however, must be considered in weighing the relationship between Mr. Cates's accident and his emotional state.

Most particularly, assuming that the above reconstruction of events concerning his father is accurate, it appears reasonable to infer that Mr. Cates may have been clinically depressed prior to the accident that led to his subsequent surgery. Having not had the opportunity to examine Mr. Cates at that time, I cannot describe in detail the symptoms associated with the probable grief reaction and depression or comment in any precise way about their possible contribution to his job-related accident. However, it is probable that the death of his father contributes to his current depression and loss of self-esteem, though there is no precise way to tease apart the relative impact of this loss and that of the accident on his present emotional state.

Finally, a key facet of Mr. Cates's personality may have had a role to play. The information gleaned from individual and family interviews suggests that Mr. Cates is a somewhat passive individual who avoids confrontation with others and may deal with conflict by excessive ruminating and preoccupation. It is possible that this increased mental activity results in reduced attention to the external environment and may thus contribute to inefficient performance or minor incidents such as, for example, running a red light. Although it cannot be confirmed whether such inatten-tion contributed to his accident at work and thus to his current mental state, this history may have to be considered as a possible contributory factor.

I cannot say whether Mr. Cates will be "mentally" able to return to the type of work he performed in the past. Certainly, from the evidence, it appears that his nervous and distracted state has increased rather than decreased since the accident. I have recommended to Mr. Cates that he consider seeking professional help to counsel him through his current problems (specifically, his reaction to his father's death and to his injury). This type of therapeutic intervention may reduce his anxiety level.

Leslie Dean, Ph.D.

(b) Discussion

This workers' compensation report attempted to evaluate whether Mr. Cates suffered "mental injury" and the extent to which it was the result of a work-related incident. The compensability of mental injury in workers' compensation cases varies considerably from state to state [see § 12.02(b)]. Several aspects of the report should be noted.

First, the organization of the report tracked the legal analysis. After, as always, listing the sources of information, the examiner described the incident that allegedly precipitated the mental injury, then reported the evidence relevant to whether that injury existed, and finally tried to discern the extent to which the present clinical findings concerning Mr. Cates's mental problems related to the incident.

Second, the examiner attempted to seek corroboration of Mr. Cates's statements whenever possible. An MMPI was administered to seek verification of his present mental state. Mr. Cates's wife and fellow workers were consulted about both the present and past state of his mental health. Mr. Cates was interviewed on three separate occasions (given typical expert fee schedules, three interviews may be viewed as a luxury by many forensic clinicians, however).

Third, an extensive historical review was conducted. Because the examiner took the time to develop Mr. Cates's work history, she became aware of the death of Mr. Cates's father. Through use of the Life Experiences Survey, she discovered the occurrence of other events that suggested an accident-prone person. Without these aids, the picture of Mr. Cates's mental injury and what "caused" it would have been incomplete.

Fourth, the examiner was extremely cautious in discussing the issue of causation. As discussed in § 12.04, she avoided labeling any one factor as the cause of Mr. Cates's current state and made it clear that his basic personality structure was a relevant consideration. Whether the work-related injury or some other phenomenon was the "proximate" cause of his current problems was left up to the factfinder. In this regard, however, it should be noted that, as pointed out in § 12.02(c)(4), the law generally holds that employers take employees as they find them. Thus, it is unlikely that compensation would be withheld merely upon proof that Mr. Cates's grief over his father's death or his absent-mindedness contributed to the physical injury. There is no defense in workers' compensation law of "contributory personality." Even in a tort suit, it would have to be proven that the father's death, and not the work-related injury, was the proximate cause of Mr. Cates's mental state to deny compensation.

Finally, the report avoided the value judgment of whether the injury was "severe" and admitted the difficulty of predicting its future course. It did suggest, however, ways of remediating Mr. Cates's problem that might prove relevant, if compensation was to be awarded, to whether and how much money would be allocated to treatment.

19.09. Reasonable Accommodation under the Americans with Disabilities Act [Chapter 13]

(a) Mike Johnson Report*

DATE: July 8, 1994
SUBJECT: Mike Johnson

PURPOSE: The purpose of this assessment is to help determine whether a reasonable accommodation

*This report is adapted from a sample reasonable accommodation plan described in Peter David Blanck et al., *Implementing Reasonable Accommodations Using ADR under the ADA: The Case of a White-Collar Employee with Bipolar Mental Illness*, 18 MENTAL & PHYSICAL DISABILITY L. REP. 458 (1994).

for Mr. Johnson is necessary and feasible under the Americans with Disabilities Act (ADA). This evaluation is undertaken under a written contract with Perfect Technologies, Mr. Johnson's employer, under which I agreed to "stimulate a problem-solving dialogue" with respect to accommodations for Mr. Johnson. The contract states that Perfect does not have to accept any of my recommendations. The contract also makes clear that I am providing information only from my perspective as a clinical psychologist, and that I will not address financial or other nonclinical aspects of accommodating Mr. Johnson.

BACKGROUND: The following information was obtained from Mr. Johnson's psychiatric and employment records, a phone conversation with Dr. Jones, who is a psychiatrist treating Mr. Johnson, and an interview with Ms. Coltrane, Mr. Johnson's supervisor. Mr. Johnson is a 35-year-old senior account executive for Perfect Technologies, Inc., a large nationwide manufacturer and distributor of sophisticated communication systems. By 1993, Mr. Johnson had held this position for five years and, according to Ms. Coltrane, was considered an excellent employee. He consistently exceeded his sales goals and earned more than $80,000 annually in salary and commissions, largely by developing accounts with national clients.

After a recent sales campaign, Mr. Johnson checked himself into the Paradise mental health facility in Houston, where he was diagnosed as having bipolar mental illness (sometimes called manic–depression). Mr. Johnson immediately reported his illness to Ms. Coltrane and applied for short-term disability benefits. After a three-week period of hospitalization and rest, Mr. Johnson told Ms. Coltrane that he was "ready to return to work" and that he should "stay this way as long as he continued outpatient treatment." Mr. Johnson returned to work, and after one month on the job appeared to be performing satisfactorily. Indeed, he exceeded his sales quota for his first two months after returning to work.

Toward the end of this two-month period, however, Ms. Coltrane noticed that most evenings Mr. Johnson worked extremely late and that occasionally he did not arrive at work until lunchtime. Further, during this period it became clear that Mr. Johnson did not return phone calls he would normally be expected to return and that he missed a few appointments during his travels around the country. During the next six months (which led up to this evaluation), he failed to meet his sales quota in two successive months (although he was again ahead of the quota in the other four months). Ms. Coltrane indicates that until last year, Mr. Johnson "was my best salesperson." But lately, she states, he has overloaded his schedule, making impossible demands upon himself, and at other times he seems fatigued and doesn't schedule enough activity. She also remembers that, after being back on the job for two months, Mr. Johnson told her, "I feel stressed out again and wish there were an alternative."

Dr. Jones, Mr. Johnson's psychiatrist at Paradise, was contacted after Mr. Johnson signed a release form. Dr. Jones is currently prescribing a combination of medications and varying the levels of medication. Although Mr. Johnson's mental illness has stabilized somewhat over the past several months, Dr. Jones continues to monitor and adjust the drug therapy. According to Dr. Jones, this therapy will eliminate severe shifts between mania and depression, but Mr. Johnson will continue to experience a wider range of euphoria and depression than would persons without bipolar disorder. Mr. Johnson is also attending group therapy and individual counseling sessions twice each week to help him function with bipolar disorder. Dr. Jones also indicates that Mr. Johnson has a "minor" drinking problem, which can exacerbate the manic and depressive episodes.

INTERVIEW WITH MR. JOHNSON: Mr. Johnson arrived for his interview on time, well dressed and aware of the purpose and nature of the interview. When confronted with the above history, he corroborated all of it. He is aware that he has manic phases and depressed phases. Indeed, he stated that, at the time of the interview, he felt a "manic phase coming on," although his speech did not seem particularly pressured and his thought patterns were not delusional or grandiose. He states that he plans to continue taking his medication and seeing Dr. Jones, and that he plans to curtail his drinking, if only because it can exacerbate the negative side effects of Lithium. He admits to some tension with Ms. Coltrane, whom he describes as a "strict supervisor who wants everyone under her to meet their quotas or they're in trouble." When asked if he can work with Ms. Coltrane, he answered, "No problem, so long as she understands my situation and makes a little leeway for it." He feels confident that he can meet his quotas if he stays with his treatment and is provided with some "help" at work, in particular if Ms. Coltrane allows him a lighter schedule when he becomes depressed and monitors his work closely when he is more manic.

ADA ASSESSMENT: The ADA appears to require inquiry into four separate areas, discussed below.

Disability. Mr. Johnson is suffering from a bipolar illness, meaning that he has mood swings which alter-

nate between hyperactivity and grandiose thinking on the one hand and depression and relatively self-deprecating thoughts on the other. This condition can be moderated with treatment, as has been the case with Mr. Johnson, but it is "permanent" in the sense that it will probably be with Mr. Johnson for the foreseeable future. Furthermore, as indicated previously, the treatment will not remove all symptoms. Finally, if left untreated, Mr. Johnson's condition is likely to worsen and would probably disable him from carrying out any of the functions he currently fulfills at Perfect.

Mr. Johnson's moderate abuse of alcohol also contributes to his difficulties at work. This behavior does not amount to alcoholism as traditionally defined in that there appears to be no physiological addiction.

Qualified to Perform an Essential Function of the Job. According to Ms. Coltrane and Perfect's written job description for Mr. Johnson's position, Mr. Johnson's job requirements are cyclical, consisting of periods of intense performance and travel followed by periods of relative inaction. According to both Ms. Coltrane and Mr. Johnson, Mr. Johnson's work during the periods necessitating high performance is occasionally substantially limited by his tendency to create grandiose schemes, to overload his schedule, and to work late at night (when he is in his manic phase) or by his tendency to wake up late for work, miss appointments and project deadlines, and experience fatigue (when in his depressed phase). According to Dr. Jones, Mr. Johnson has experienced relatively mild manic and depressive cycles for the entire period after returning to work. At the same time, as noted previously, he has often exceeded his quotas and he recently landed a new national account.

What these behaviors mean with respect to Mr. Johnson's ability to carry out "essential functions" of his job would seem an issue best assessed by Ms. Coltrane and Perfect, in conjunction with Mr. Johnson. What this evaluator can assist with is advice as to how to accommodate Mr. Johnson's disability in his current work environment.

Reasonable Accommodation. The following steps might assist in improving Mr. Johnson's performance at Perfect:

(1) The company could, consistent with confidentiality concerns, provide to Ms. Coltrane and others who work closely with Mr. Johnson a description of bipolar mental illness written in lay terms, to dispel common myths associated with the illness. This description should include the facts that people with a bipolar disorder experience periods of mania and depression; that symptoms of mania include abundant energy, an unrealistic belief in one's abilities, increased

risk taking, and irritability or distractibility; and that symptoms of depression include pessimism, sleep problems, decreased energy, social withdrawal, and difficulty making decisions. It should also make clear that treatment for bipolar disorder is generally effective and that persons with this condition function for long periods free of debilitating symptoms.

(2) Probably no new staff support position is needed to accommodate Mr. Johnson's disability. In other words, Mr. Johnson does not need a full-time assistant to "shadow" him as he performs his duties. However, Mr. Johnson could benefit from peer support, because he travels for prolonged periods and could suffer a relapse while on the road caused by failing to eat or sleep regularly and by the increased stress of traveling. Ideally, during a six-week transitional period Perfect could send a coworker—preferably one of Mr. Johnson's choice—to accompany Mr. Johnson on extended national sales campaigns. This coworker would ensure that Mr. Johnson ate and slept and did not become overanxious due to stressful traveling. An assessment should be made at the end of this six-week period as to whether the coworker is needed further; if so, appropriate arrangements should be made.

(3) To the extent possible, the high performance periods required of Mr. Johnson should be correlated with periods during which his bipolar illness is at its lowest ebb. The latter periods can be ascertained by conferring with Mr. Johnson himself and Dr. Jones. To facilitate this inquiry, Mr. Johnson and Ms. Coltrane should meet weekly, at an established time, to discuss matters including sales calls, sales proposals, Mr. Johnson's new initiatives, and other essential tasks Mr. Johnson performs. The goal of these meetings, to which Ms. Coltrane appears amenable, is to permit the two to make adjustments to the accommodation plan when necessary.

(4) In addition, flexible scheduling should be permitted to enable Mr. Johnson to obtain appropriate medical care and attend group therapy sessions.

(5) Finally, Mr. Johnson should have a private office to minimize interruptions during his periods of stress.

Before the company decides to implement these accommodations, Ms. Coltrane should of course be consulted. As noted earlier, when asked whether she would mind meeting with Mr. Johnson on a weekly or more frequent basis to determine his needs, she stated she would not mind doing so if the meetings were not long and if they would guarantee high-quality work from Mr. Johnson. However, if friction does develop between the two, Mr. Johnson's stress could be exacer-bated. Thus, ensuring that Ms. Coltrane agrees with the preceding suggestions is important.

Threats to Others. At the present time, Mr. Johnson appears to pose absolutely no threat to others in the physical sense. Of course, if he fails to meet his quotas he could "threaten" his colleagues in a fiscal sense, but the above accommodations should prevent this from occurring.

Everett Sims, Ph.D.

(b)   Discussion

The type of report provided here might be requested by a company or by the employee of a company as an aid to implementing the ADA's command that employees with disabilities be afforded reasonable accommodation. Ideally, such a consultation would take place prior to any litigation, in an effort to reach agreement between the parties.

Confidentiality can often be a major concern in such cases. For instance, many employees may not be as forthcoming as Mr. Johnson was in providing consent to view and report on psychiatric records. (In this regard, note that the ADA does not require accommodation of someone who does not make known the limitations of his or her disability [see § 13.02(b)(3)].) Further, "evaluation" of the employee's coworkers, in an effort to determine their attitudes toward the employee, may become important. For instance, here the evaluator emphasized the need to involve Ms. Coltrane in the plan to ensure that it has a chance of succeeding.

As to the report's substance, note that at the beginning of the report the evaluator makes clear the areas of his expertise. Only an industrial psychologist is likely to have the specialized knowledge to analyze job requirements in detail, and even that type of professional is not necessarily equipped to provide information helpful to the financial and personnel decisions required by a reasonable accommodation plan under the ADA. Note further that the evaluator divides the report into the four substantive areas that are the focus of the ADA [see § 13.02(b)]. In all four areas, the evaluator avoids the ultimate legal issue, that is, whether it is permissible under the ADA to take action against Mr. Johnson for alcohol abuse (the relevant law states that alcohol use short of alcoholism is not a basis for protection under the ADA), whether Mr. Johnson is qualified for his job, whether any of the suggested accommodations are "reasonable," and what is meant by the "threat" exception to the ADA.

Like a treatment plan, an accommodation plan should be reduced to writing, after consultation with professionals and the relevant parties. A written accommodation plan, like a written treatment plan, can facilitate interaction between the employer and the employee and makes review and modification easier. To provide some idea of how such a plan might look, the following plan, based on the Johnson case and taking into account nonclinical as well as clinical factors, is set out below:

A.   Short-Term Accommodations

The following temporary accommodations will be accorded to Mike as support for an orderly resumption of the performance of all the responsibilities of a senior account executive and are not anticipated to be needed for more than six weeks.

1. A coworker will be designated as a peer support person for Mike. Mike's peer support person will accompany him on every trip that requires an overnight stay outside Mike's base city.

2. On average, the number of sales calls Mike will make will equal one-half of those required by his normal appointment schedule.

3. Mike's rate of pay will remain at his average for this period in the previous calendar year, including bonus income.

4. Mike's emergency calls and new customer calls will be minimized.

5. Mike's supervisor will continue to learn the characteristics of bipolar disorder so that she has an understanding of Mike's disability and will maintain an open-door policy for discussion.

6. Perfect will engage a neutral adviser to assist in the dialogue on evaluating and modifying the plan of accommodation and will make the adviser available to Mike and his supervisor in Mike's base city.

7. Although Perfect's company policies would permit it to apply Mike's paid vacation to his peri-

od of hospitalization, Perfect has chosen not to do this. Instead, Mike may retain his pool of vacation days so that he can draw on them to reduce stress.

B.   Long-Term Accommodations

1. Mike's supervisor will permit the flexible scheduling of hours to accommodate Mike's need to attend doctor appointments, therapy sessions, or other treatment.

2. Mike will have access to a private work office space so that he can regulate his environment and minimize interruptions during periods of stress.

3. During Mike's annual performance review, Mike's supervisor will not use any information gathered during Mike's period of hospitalization or the period of short-term accommodation or any information concerning bipolar mental illness in considering whether Mike qualifies for a promotion or raise.

C.   Assessment

1. Mike and his supervisor will meet at least weekly, and more often if necessary, to discuss whether Mike is performing tasks as expected.

2. Mike and his supervisor agree that Mike must return to the level of productivity consistent with a senior account executive. That level of productivity should be reached in six weeks.

3. At the end of six weeks, Mike and his supervisor will meet to discuss the removal of the short-term accommodations.

19.10.   Transfer to Adult Court [Chapter 14]

(a)   Tom Young Report

NAME: Tom Young
D.O.B.:   August 9, 1961

DATES OF INTERVIEWS:
1. Social history performed on October 13, 1978, by Theresa Rogers, M.S.W.
2. Psychological testing administered on October 13, 1978, and October 21, 1978, by Harvey A. Nichol-

son, Ph.D. Psychological tests included the Rorschach Inkblot Test, the Thematic Apperception Test (TAT), the Wechsler Adult Intelligence Scale (WAIS), the Stanford–Binet, the Bender–Gestalt, and the Competency Screening Test.

3. Psychiatric interviews conducted on October 21, 1978, by Patrick Roberts, M.D., and Harvey A. Nicholson, Ph.D., and on November 4, 1978, by Dr. Roberts.

CIRCUMSTANCES OF REFERRAL: Tom Young is a 17-year-old resident of Raleigh, who has been charged with breaking and entering and with rape. Tom was arrested on June 28, 1978, the day of the alleged rape, and has been held at the juvenile detention facility since his arrest.

Irving Jencks, Tom's attorney, referred Tom to the clinic for an evaluation of his competency to stand trial, his level of mental functioning and mental status, and his amenability to treatment. A hearing to consider transfer of the case from juvenile to adult court will be held after the clinic's evaluation is completed.

Information made available to the clinic includes Tom's juvenile court record; the police report on the current offenses; a neurological evaluation dated July 3, 1978, by Dr. Dennis Evans of the Piedmont Hospital in Durham, conducted after Tom experienced a *grand mal* seizure on July 2, 1978; a court-ordered transfer report by the juvenile probation department, dated July 20, 1978; a psychiatric evaluation from Dr. James Farson of the Greensboro Psychiatric Center, dated August 13, 1978; and medical records from the Raleigh city public school, including disciplinary records and psychological reports from 1969, 1970, and 1973.

SOCIAL HISTORY:

Family Background. Mr. Harvey Young, the client's father, is 60 years old and is employed at the tobacco plant in Durham as a warehouse laborer. He often works 14 to 16 hours per day and earns about $250 per week. Because of the many hours he puts into work, Mr. Young has less contact with Tom than his wife does. He described himself in good health and denied that he drinks excessively. Mrs. Debbie Young, age 45, has been employed as a maid at the Holiday Inn for the past 13 years and earns $80 per week. She has been in good health and has never experienced psychiatric problems or difficulties with substance abuse.

Mr. and Mrs. Young married soon after she became pregnant in ninth grade. They reported no marital problems. They have 11 children, ranging in age from 14 to 32. Tom is the fourth youngest child. It is interesting to note that a probation report indicates that

Mr. and Mrs. Young told the probation officer about only five of their children. Among the children whom they did not mention were two teenagers who have records with the Juvenile Court. Yet the Youngs had stated that besides Tom, none of their children had ever been before the Juvenile Court.

Mr. Young explained that he and his wife do not have frequent contact with the older children, because "they are married, have their own lives, and live all over the United States." Tom described his relationships with his siblings, primarily the three who live at home, as "fine, we have no problems." He elaborated somewhat on his relationship with his youngest brother, George, age 14. Tom explained, "I like to be around him. I take him everywhere I go." Tom stated that he has always enjoyed living at home and that he is anxious to return. He stated that he "liked growing up" with his brothers and sisters and recalled enjoying playing in the woods with them.

Tom emphasized that he "likes" his parents equally, is close to both of them, and has "never had any problems" with them. He stated that when his parents disapprove of his behavior they "talk" to him. He insisted that he has never been disciplined in a harsh manner. However, a psychiatric report from Dr. Farson, dated September 1978, indicates that Tom described his family as very unstable. He apparently reported to Dr. Farson that his father used to be a severe alcoholic who became violent at times and physically punished him.

Mr. and Mrs. Young reported to us that they never used physical punishment with any of their children. Mr. Young explained that they sometimes take away television viewing privileges as a form of discipline. It may be important to note that Mr. Young stated, "If you do anything else, they get you for child abuse."

Tom's father was so dominant in the interview that it was difficult for Mrs. Young to talk. He sometimes smiled (almost as though he was proud) when discussing Tom's rape charge. Mrs. Young sat quietly, looked very depressed, and seemed to be daydreaming at times. Also, it appears that Tom's parents reinforce his avoidance and denial of certain issues. They denied that Tom has any history of behavioral problems, arrests, or serious alcohol problems. They supported Tom's claims of innocence on the present charges.

Education and Work History. Tom has been in special education classes throughout most of his schooling. He explained, "I have always had trouble learning. It's hard for me." His parents seemed to have little understanding of Tom's learning problems and claimed that they were never called in to the school by a teacher or counselor. According to a probation report, in 1970 the client was evaluated and determined to be educable mentally retarded. It is important to note that the school system has always believed Tom to be one year older than he really is. His parents enrolled him early and lied about his age because he was "a big boy."

Records of Tom's grades for his last three years of school show that his work was significantly below average. He was absent more than 35 days every year. A school report in 1973 described the client as "immature but not a serious discipline problem" and commented on his short attention span in class. A probation report noted that later Tom was suspended eight times for truancy and showing disrespect to teachers. Tom's parents denied that the client had any behavioral problems in school and insisted, "He is a good, normal boy."

During tenth grade, Tom attended vocational–technical as well as special education academic classes. He learned bricklaying, and after he left school he worked for short periods as a bricklayer. He has also worked in a saw mill, and at the time of the offense he was employed by the rape victim's husband, Mr. Davis, as a farmworker. Tom has not had much experience in a structured work situation.

Social and Sexual Relationships. According to his parents, Tom has always been able to form and maintain friendships with peers. They explained that he has played on various sports teams even after leaving school; this gave the impression that he has been very socially active. In contrast, Tom explained that after he left school, he spent a great deal of time at home watching the "stories" on television by himself.

Tom claimed that he has had "ten girlfriends." He has had sexual intercourse with all of them, he said. The client had difficulty discussing sexual relationships openly. He did say that he broke up with one girlfriend after his arrest but was too embarrassed to tell her that he was charged with rape.

Tom first engaged in sexual intercourse at age 16. He stated that he does not really enjoy sexual activity, despite the fact that he claims to have had frequent sexual experiences, but would not explain why it is not satisfying. He stated, "Girls just come over to the house while I watch the stories and they want to have sex." His father also mentioned that girls frequently call Tom at home.

The client explained that he "misses" girls very much, but since he has been in the detention home, he has refused to participate in activities that include girls. For example, sometimes boys and girls are allowed to sit together in the evenings. Tom claimed that he goes to his room during these times. He explained that he does not want to be with girls since his rape charge, and "they'll bust you even if you touch a girl."

Tom appeared to be very embarrassed, somewhat immature, and confused about sexual matters. It was very difficult for him to discuss the topic with women. Also, he stated that he could not look at the interviewer during the social history interview, regardless of the subject, because she was a "girl" and "I haven't talked to one for so long." Tom expressed difficulty in relating to girls at the detention facility. He seemed quite embarrassed about the charge of rape.

Tom was unable to describe relationships in detail and provided only brief answers to questions about interpersonal relationships. Although he seems to be emotionally impoverished or shallow, it should be noted that his vocabulary is probably limited, making it difficult for him to accurately describe his feelings.

Juvenile Record. Tom's previous juvenile record includes prior arrests for cruelty to animals, trespassing, and destruction of property (1972); five counts of destruction of property and trespassing (1974); and one runaway report (1977). None of these charges resulted in commitment to any juvenile detention program.

Health. Tom has suffered from head injuries and seizures. His first head injury occurred in 1974, when he was struck in the head by a swinging door while at school. He was knocked unconscious for three or four hours and was hospitalized. He was transferred to the Raleigh General Hospital for observation.

Last year Tom was hit in the head with a tree branch while cutting wood with his father. Mr. Young explained that for a period of ten minutes Tom was unconscious and "shaking hard all over." He was not taken to a physician at that time. In 1976, a local rescue squad was called to the Youngs' home when Tom arrived home from school in an "apparent deep sleep" and was confused and dazed. Tom was not hospitalized.

Last July, while in the detention facility, Tom experienced an episode that was diagnosed as a *grand mal* seizure (the most serious type of epileptic seizure). He was then evaluated by Dr. Evans, who reported that his electroencephalogram (EEG) was normal, meaning that no sign of brain lesions was evident. He prescribed Tegretol, an anticonvulsant, for Tom. The "cause" of the seizure has not been determined. The client has been taking the medication and having follow-up medical appointments.

Although all written reports indicate that Tom does not suffer from headaches or dizziness, he reported that he has headaches "every week or every month." In fact, Mrs. Young stated that Tom complained of a headache the day before he was arrested. She stated that he came home early from work to lie down. According to the client's mother, aspirin relieved Tom's headache that day, as it generally does. Tom noted that besides headaches, he has frequent nosebleeds. He does not have a history of other health problems.

Psychiatric and Behavioral Information. Tom was evaluated by Dr. Farson of Greensboro Psychiatric Center in August 1978, in response to forensic questions asked by the Juvenile Court. Dr. Farson noted that Tom had been a bedwetter until age eight and had a history of lying, breaking and entering, stealing, truancy, and running away from home. Tom was described as displaying anxiety, shallow affect, and emotional detachment. Although Tom was oriented to place and person, he was disoriented as to time. His memory of recent and remote events was poor. Tom's problems with concepts of time were apparent. It seemed that he often could not remember when a past event occurred (months ago? years ago?). Dr. Farson concluded that Tom had a serious personality disorder but that he was not psychotic. Recommendations for Tom included referral to a state hospital with behavioral therapy and chemotherapy and the later possibility of transfer to the rehabilitation center for training in vocational skills.

In reference to his current situation, Tom explained that being "locked up" is becoming emotionally intolerable for him. He described feeling tense and frustrated and "when someone gets on my case, I blow, I act too fast." He has had disagreements with staff members in which he was physically restrained and was forced to remain in his room or in "solitary" as a result of his behavior. Tom claimed that recently when he was left alone in his room he contemplated suicide and started to tie sheets together to hang himself. Tom's weekly visits from his mother are the only activities that help him "feel better."

Tom and his parents were reluctant to admit his past offenses. They explained Tom's charge of cruelty to an animal as his feeding a neighbor's hungry horse without first asking the owner. Also, his parents insisted that Tom had no other arrests and never ran away from home, even though our records indicate otherwise. Tom denied use of drugs but stated that he sometimes drinks beer.

DESCRIPTION OF THE OFFENSE: During the interviews at the clinic, Tom steadfastly denied any involvement in the break-in at the Davis home and the rape of Mrs. Davis, his employer's wife. Tom said that he rarely saw Mrs. Davis, although he and his brothers had been employed by Mr. Davis for some time.

According to police reports, Mrs. Davis was attacked at about 6:45 A.M. on June 28, 1978, shortly after her husband left home to pick up the Young boys for work in his fields. After the rape, the attacker threatened Mrs. Davis and tied her up. He then fled, but she was able to escape in time to see him riding away from her house on a bicycle. Tom was arrested at his home a short time later.

PRESENT MENTAL STATUS AND PSYCHODYNAMIC FUNCTIONING:

Cognitive Functioning. Most noteworthy on both interviews and psychological testing were Tom's serious cognitive limitations. Tom scored in the moderately retarded range on standardized intelligence tests. His actual educational achievement is consistent with this finding: Tom is unable to read or to do simple arithmetic computations. He was able to remember only three digits at a time. He was also unable to perform simple abstractions, such as determining the item in a series that is different (e.g., shoes, shirt, car, and pants). Tom is able to tell time and to count at least through the teens.

There were indications that the intelligence tests may be an underestimate of Tom's adaptive behavior and that his "true" intelligence may be somewhat higher than his measured intelligence—perhaps in the mildly retarded range. First, Tom scored lower on the present test than on previous assessments (1969–73). Essentially, he has not made any academic progress since then; this may be due to lack of adequate stimulation at home, coupled with his social and emotional withdrawal. Thus, it is probable that Tom's potential for cognitive growth is somewhat higher than his current test scores indicate.

Second, Tom did show some ability suggestive of higher potential and motivation to master new learning. For example, on the WAIS Block Design, Tom had severe difficulty in putting the puzzles together. However, with help from the examiner Tom was able to learn a trial-and-error strategy for assembling the puzzles—a feat in which he took considerable pride. Similarly, in the interview setting Tom was able to make some use of cues provided by the interviewers and within the environment. For example, when asked to count, Tom looked at the clock for cues. He was able to reach 16 before he stopped, apparently from frustration. Tom also was able to use words that he did not know (e.g., "feelings") after they were defined for him by the interviewers.

Third, Tom's social competence within his own community was unclear from our assessment. It may or may not reflect adaptive behavior higher than measured intelligence.

Not surprisingly, Tom's understanding of the legal process is limited. As he put it, "I don't know about the words." Tom did not know the meaning of the word "guilty," and he seemed to confuse being charged with crime with being guilty of it. He appeared to have no comprehension of the possibility of being found innocent at a trial. Trials, in Tom's view, are simply to set one's punishment. There were also suggestions of very limited trust in his lawyer or lawyers generally and of anticipation that a trial would, in some way, be stacked against him. At the same time, however, Tom also showed glimmers of sophistication about the process. He was aware of the purpose of a transfer hearing and of the distinction between juvenile and circuit court. He also knew that a lawyer's task is to "help you get out of trouble." Tom also understands the current charges against him.

Personality Functioning. On the bases of both projective testing and interviews, Tom appeared to have a limited capacity for relationships. He is somewhat negativistic (i.e., prone to resist friendly approaches), and he is unable to establish trust easily. He reported never having had a best friend. Tom withdraws, particularly in contexts in which he is frustrated or feels accused. Thus, Tom would turn away and become increasingly nonverbal if presented with questions to determine his knowledge or if questioned about topics related to his current charges (sexuality, relationships with his employer, etc.).

Tom recounted an incident exemplary of this style. He had a teacher who was "nice" and who he felt was trying to help him. However, the teacher mistakenly accused Tom of banging on the building one day. Tom decided on the basis of this incident alone that the teacher was "not on my side no more" and left school. Apparently, Tom has acquired what is sometimes called "learned helplessness." That is, he has come to expect failure and, when frustrated, he responds quickly and in a passive–aggressive manner. However, Tom did respond positively when the interview style became informal, "street-wise," and concrete. He may be able to make use of an empathic, nonthreatening relationship. In fact, with continued help and support, Tom was able to sustain attention through lengthy, frustrating testing sessions.

Tom's impulse control may often be tenuous, at least partially because of his poor verbal skills and resulting inability to label feelings. There may be a self-destructive element to his acting out. He noted that he seems to "hurt myself" by getting into trouble. Tom expressed suicidal ideation several times, but it is our opinion that he is not an active suicidal risk. Rather, these threats seemed to be an attention-getting device reflective of his immaturity.

Tom clearly has limited skills in the expression of feelings. For example, he said that when he became angry one time recently (while in detention), he went into his room and started eating soap. Furthermore, he tends to lash out if he feels that someone cannot be trusted or may be taking advantage of him. This may indicate difficulty in social perceptions (perceiving intentions and feelings of others). For example, Tom said that sometimes someone will play with him and that

Tom will "accidentally" hit him. At the same time, Tom told of some fights with a degree of bravado, and some aggressive behavior appears congruent with his value system. As he put it, "I gotta do what I gotta do." Furthermore, in the present context, he claimed to be ready to "do my time and get out."

Tom steadfastly claimed innocence of the charges against him. Consequently, we were unable to construct a formulation of the dynamics underlying the offense if it in fact occurred. He refused to discuss personal information that might have illuminated intrapsychic or interpersonal conflicts. As noted in the social history, Tom's discussion of sexuality seemed to have the primary purpose of presenting a "macho" image ("ten girlfriends"), which was not credible. His discussion of sexuality in the psychiatric interviews was even more limited and in the same vein. He presented himself as dropping girls at a whim or whenever they do not please him ("I'm famous for that"). Similarly, Tom would not go beyond a vague description in talking about his family.

Third, Tom's social competence within his own community was unclear from our assessment. It may or may not reflect adaptive behavior higher than measured intelligence.

CONCLUSIONS AND RECOMMENDATIONS:

Competency to Stand Trial. Tom clearly understands the nature of the charges against him, and he has a general understanding of the possible consequences of these charges. His understanding of the general nature of the proceedings against him and of his attorney's role is recounted above. Because of vocabulary deficits and difficulty in conceptualization, he will require careful, simple, and repeated explanations of procedure and strategy as they progress. Tom can be expected to give his attorney basic facts to aid in his defense, but (because of his general distrust of people) he will require patient, relaxed questioning by his attorney.

Transfer. The transfer statute requires consideration of Tom's "mental retardation" and "criminal insanity" but these terms are not defined. It is clear, however, that Tom is clinically mentally retarded, probably in the range of moderate to mild retardation. On the "insanity" issue, while Tom's range of ideation is quite limited, it is generally reality-based and not psychotic (i.e., out of touch with reality) or bizarre. He is capable of understanding that rape is wrong and does not evidence serious impulse disorder.

Amenability to Treatment. We were unable to construct a formulation of the dynamics underlying the alleged offense. Thus, it is not possible to determine amenability to treatment in terms of the alleged rape. However, in terms of Tom's general personality and cognitive deficits, it is our impression that Tom would profit from a specialized treatment program. Specifically, without acquisition of more vocational and social skills, Tom cannot be expected to manage an independent or semi-independent, productive lifestyle. Tom has some mastery of simple skills and appears to be motivated to work within a prevocational training program. Within such a context, a counselor (preferably a black male) could informally assist him in labeling feelings, understanding intentions, and developing social skills. In short, there should be an educational focus rather than formal psychotherapy.

We would in fact recommend development of an educational plan for Tom, as required under Public Law 94-142 (the federal special education law), as a first step, regardless of the trial's outcome. Tom will require patience and informality initially, given his low frustration tolerance and limited capacity for relationships. It is important to note that a structured educational–treatment program would be included in our recommendation, whether or not Tom actually committed the rape. We do not feel there are sufficient general or actuarial data to predict the likelihood of recidivism in Tom's case. However, the plan described would most likely increase his impulse control, especially as he becomes more comfortable and has some successes.

Project Adventure in Asheville may be an appropriate treatment program for Tom. Besides providing individualized counseling, a recreation program based on skill building is offered in which learning takes place in the community rather than in a traditional classroom. Funding could be made available through Public Law 94-142. However, if Tom is accepted, he may be placed on a waiting list. Also, an intake interview must first be arranged for Tom before a decision on admission would be made.

Patrick Roberts, M.D.
Harvey A. Nicholson, Ph.D.

(b)   Discussion

This was a juvenile case in which the referral source sought evaluation for the purpose of considering whether Tom Young should be transferred from juvenile to adult court [see §§ 14.03(a)(2), 14.04(b)]. At the time the report was written, the question of transfer in Virginia turned on a defendant's "amenability to treatment." In addition, transfer was prohibited if the client was "mentally retarded," "criminally insane," or incompetent to stand trial.

Note first that the writers of this report discussed Tom's personality in considerable detail, including his family, education, and work history; his social and sexual relationships; his court record; and his health and psychiatric history. This is to be expected when the primary issue is the client's amenability to treatment. As noted throughout this chapter, the amount of historical material and discussion of personality and mental state will vary, depending on the legal issue to be addressed.

Second, the writers discussed Tom's intellectual ability very carefully, concluding that estimates of intelligence derived from test results might have been too low. This information was important because part of the legal test for transfer in this jurisdiction involved the presence or absence of mental retardation; in addition, the level of Tom's intelligence was presumably relevant to the question of his amenability to treatment.

Third, the writers offered concrete suggestions for improving the attorney–client relationship and thereby for enhancing the client's competency to stand trial, another issue that is relevant to the transfer decision under Virginia law.

Fourth, note that the writers took care to distinguish between the statutory terms "mental retardation" and "criminal insanity" in making clinical observations as to Young's mental state. They pointed out that the statutory terms are not defined (e.g., does "insanity" refer to the insanity defense or simply to mental illness?), and then discussed "mental retardation" and "insanity" in the context of their clinical meaning. It was left to the legal system to determine whether the statutory definitions applied to Tom.

Fifth, on the amenability to treatment issue, the writers specifically stated that they were unable to explain why the offense was committed or whether Tom would recidivate. If clinicians do not have sufficient data or sufficiently solid opinion based on the data, they should not offer an opinion. The writers did offer concrete treatment suggestions. Such recommendations are much more useful to the legal system than conclusory statements that an individual is or is not amenable to treatment. Ideally, however, the treatment plan would be more "multi-systemic" in approach [see § 14.05(b)(3)].

19.11. Dispositional Review [Chapter 15]

(a) George and Gerald Jones Report

NAME: George and Gerald Jones
D.O.B.:   George—December 5, 1976
          Gerald—October 20, 1980
MOTHER: Suzanne Jones
FOSTER PARENTS: George—David and Jane
                  Williams
                  Gerald—Molly Davidson

SOURCES OF INFORMATION:

1. Referral letter and notes from Sue Jacobson, Department of Social Services; predispositional report from Ms. Jacobson, dated August 1, 1982.
2. Records regarding Ms. Jones from North State Hospital (NSH) (including admission and discharge summaries).
3. Report of evaluation of Ms. Jones by Jack Henderson, M.D., on August 30, 1982.
4. Report of evaluation of Ms. Jones by James Johnson, Ph.D., on October 31, 1982.
5. Letter regarding Ms. Jones from Marian Disney, R.N., Community Mental Health Center (CMHC) of Johnstone County, dated May 1, 1983; phone conversation with Ms. Disney on May 18, 1983.
6. Intake evaluation report by Susan Hilton, M.S.W., CMHC of Johnstone County, dated January 10, 1978.
7. Phone conversation with Lynn Nelson, Broadview School (George's teacher), March 1, 1983, and face-to-face conversation, April 5, 1983.
8. Notes on visits between Ms. Jones and her children by Jeannette Sterling, December 30, 1982, through April 10, 1983; conversation with Ms. Sterling on March 15, 1983.
9. Interviews with Ms. Jones on March 1, May 1, and May 3, 1983, including administration of Shure–Spivack Problem-Solving Childrearing Style Interview on May 3.
10. Observation of Ms. Jones with George and Gerald on March 20, 1983.
11. Interview with Jane and David Williams on March 15, 1983.
12. Interview with George, including administration of the Vocabulary subtest of the Wechsler Intelligence Scale for Children—Revised (WISC-R), on March 15, 1983.
13. Classroom observation of George on May 5, 1983.
14. Interview with Molly Davidson on March 20, 1983.
15. Play interview with Gerald on March 20, 1983.

Records were requested from Stone Ridge Workshop at NSH, where Ms. Jones is now employed, but they have not been received.

REFERRAL: The Jones family, consisting of Suzanne (the mother), and George and Gerald (the children), was referred for evaluation by Sue Jacobson, Social Services caseworker. Suzanne Jones, age 26, has a history of hospitalization at NSH with a diagnosis of paranoid schizophrenia. At the time of the first hospitalization (1978), George was placed in foster care for about four months. He reentered foster care in August 1979, and he returned to his mother about two months later. After Ms. Jones became pregnant with Gerald in February 1980, she was unable to take her psychotropic medication and her mental health deteriorated. After several instances of reported abuse, George was returned to foster care in June 1980. A few days later Ms. Jones was readmitted to NSH. The Williams home, where George has lived since July 1982, is his sixth foster home. Gerald was born in October 1980 while Ms. Jones was in NSH. He was immediately placed in foster care with Molly Davidson, with whom he has lived continuously.

Ms. Jones's visits with the children have been supervised under court order since an incident in Spring 1982 when she experienced auditory hallucinations (i.e., hearing voices that were not present), lost control, and destroyed some property during a visit with George. She now has visits with George alone once a week and with George and Gerald together once a week. These visits are supervised by a Social Services worker.

The present evaluation is intended to assist Social Services in developing a permanent plan for the Jones children. The evaluation was ordered by Johnstone County Separate Juvenile Court in August 1982. According to Ms. Jacobson, the court sought assistance as to the probable effect of Ms. Jones's mental disorder on her ability to function as a parent and the effect of Ms. Jones herself on the mental health of the children. Ms. Jacobson also requested an opinion as to George's needs for treatment or preventive services. An opinion was also sought as to the Williamses' and Ms. Davidson's attachment to George and Gerald, respectively, and their ability to meet the children's special needs in the future.

EVALUATION OF MS. JONES:

History. Ms. Jones reported that her mother died when she was about two years old. She never knew her father. Following her mother's death, she went to live with her uncle and aunt and their four children (all four to ten years older than Ms. Jones). Ms. Jones's uncle worked in a factory and her aunt, who died when Ms. Jones was 14, was a domestic worker. Ms. Jones reported that each of her cousins has made a satisfactory adjustment as an adult. She indicated that she sometimes thinks she is an embarrassment to the family because of her history of mental disorder. Sean, age 36, is married and owns a small business. Jennie, age 34, is married and living in Georgia. Kathryn, who is about age 32, is recently divorced and a secretary. Joan, age 30, is living with a dentist, and she owns a clothing shop. Ms. Jones has four older natural siblings, who live around the country, and one younger sister, who was adopted and whom she does not know. Ms. Jones was unable or unwilling to describe her childhood in much detail, but she said it was unremarkable.

Before dropping out of school, Ms. Jones obtained a tenth-grade education. She then went to live with a sister in Cleveland. She worked briefly as a secretary at a large company before becoming a dancer at about age 19. The latter occupation was apparently embarrassing to Ms. Jones, and she declined to discuss it except to say that the auditory hallucinations she experienced in the past sometimes consisted of voices making accusations about her conduct as a dancer. Apparently Ms. Jones began to become quite paranoid during her last months in Cleveland, and she obtained some mental health care there.

Ms. Jones met the father of both boys, Elton Jones, in 1976, when she left Cleveland and came to Johnstone County. When she was not in the hospital, she lived with him, on and off, until 1980, when Gerald was born. He has since disappeared. Ms. Jones was married to John Morton in June 1982. The marriage was short-lived, however, and the divorce is currently being finalized. Ms. Jones had known Mr. Morton for about two years prior to their marriage. She said that they separated because of differences in religious beliefs and Mr. Morton's unreliability (drinking and unemployment). Mr. Morton has no contact with the children, and pays no child support.

Ms. Jones was hospitalized at NSH from December 28, 1977, to January 5, 1978, and from June 5, 1980, to May 7, 1981. Since then she has been attending a vocational rehabilitation program at Stone Ridge and therapy at CMHC of Johnstone County. Ms. Jones sees Marian Disney, R.N., every other week for therapy. She is also involved in social activities at the CMHC, and her medications (Prolixin, Artane, and Halcion) are monitored there.

Ms. Disney reported that Ms. Jones has been reliable in keeping appointments and has been cooperative as well. Since August 1982, Ms. Jones has reported no hallucinations, and Ms. Disney said that she has no reason to dispute that report. Ms. Disney has worked with Ms. Jones in maintaining cognitive control over her feelings and ideation. However, Ms. Disney is not sure that Ms. Jones would be able to apply these skills when under stress (e.g., to know what to say to herself if she began to hear voices). She sometimes does not remember things discussed and skills learned several sessions previously. Ms. Disney indicated that Ms. Jones has reported no episodes of aggression or inappropriate temper outbursts in recent months. However, she added that Ms. Jones has been under no particularly stressful situations other than the current legal proceedings concerning her children. Ms. Jones gave a similar report of her recent mental status and stress level during her interviews with me.

Ms. Disney indicated that her current concern about Ms. Jones is "her tendency to withdraw and isolate herself." This impression was corroborated by history in the current evaluation. Ms. Jones said that there is no one inside or outside her family on whom she can really depend. However, she is closest to her cousin Kathryn, and she is sometimes able to use her as a sounding board. According to Ms. Disney, Ms. Jones has not joined an activity or group on her own, although she does participate in social activities at CMHC.

Ms. Jones reported that she is now seeking employment through Vocational Rehabilitation. She is looking for a job as a custodian; in the meantime, she is considering doing volunteer work at the Veterans Administration Hospital. At present, Ms. Jones is supported by Supplemental Security Income. She handles all of her own financial affairs and daily living skills.

Mental Status. Ms. Jones was cooperative for the evaluation and reliable in keeping appointments.

Ms. Jones's affect (expression of feelings) was generally flattened. Although she did show appropriate laughter at times, her access to affect appeared limited. Her demeanor was marked by a blank stare typical in chronic schizophrenia.

Ms. Jones's ideation was very concrete, although not bizarre. She was unable to solve common proverbs. She was not a very good historian, and she seemed to have some difficulty in remembering and describing her experiences. Some of her lack of fluency was probably attributable to guardedness about the nature of the evaluation, however. Ms. Jones gave no sign of attending to hallucinations (which she denied having experienced in recent months), although she may have been somewhat distracted by inner experiences. Her performance on digit spans (five digits forward, three digits reversed) was about two standard deviations below the mean (i.e., a level surpassed by well over 95% of persons her age). Such deficits in short-term memory are sometimes associated with difficulties in attention. Reports from Ms. Disney of her having had difficulty in retaining directions and lessons are consistent with such a picture as well.

Ms. Jones's insight and judgment appeared somewhat improved over previous evaluations. For example, she described her medication as designed to "stop me from hearing voices and having temper tantrums, help me relax, and get a good night's sleep," and she recognized the need to take the medication on a regular basis. However, she seemed to have little insight about the origins of her disorder or patterns in her behavior, although she is aware that she has gotten out of control when she has experienced hallucinations. She recognizes that she has not really been tested with respect to her ability to maintain control during hallucinations, although she says that she knows what to do if they would recur (e.g., "hit a beanbag" if the voices make her angry; "tell myself they're not real—use rational thinking").

As already noted, Ms. Jones reported very sparse relationships. She said that there had been "loneliness" since her separation from her husband but that she is "surviving." In view of her avoidant style, her capacity to form and maintain relationships may be limited.

Summary. Ms. Jones retains some of the symptoms of schizophrenia (e.g., social isolation and flattened affect), but she does not appear to be actively paranoid at this point. She apparently has made slow but steady progress over the past few months in her general mental status. Her insight and judgment have improved, but her thinking remains very concrete.

EVALUATION OF GEORGE:

Interview. On interview, George related appropriately and cooperatively. He did show some signs of anxiety (e.g., nails bitten to the quick), and he was very aware of (although somewhat reluctant to talk about) the instability of home life he has experienced. George said that the reason that he had been placed in foster care was that his mother had thrown him against the wall. Although he said that he enjoyed visiting his mother, he would prefer to live with someone else "just in case." As might be expected, given the proportion of his life spent in foster care, George's attachment to his mother is tenuous. When asked to draw a picture of his family, he drew the Williamses. Similarly, he drew a picture of a home (the one in which he currently lives) and pointed out where "Mommy" and "Daddy" (Rev. and Mrs. Williams) sleep. At the same time, though, he does not seem very attached to the Williamses. He said that he would most like to live

with Helen (a home from which George was removed because the foster father allegedly engaged in inappropriate sexual contact with a foster daughter), and Social Services notes indicate that he frequently telephones Helen during his visits to Ms. Jones.

Some of the content of George's interview material suggested that he may be preoccupied at times by concerns about aggression and his vulnerability. For example, when asked what animal he would most like to be, George replied that he would like to be an eagle, because "if somebody is going around killing animals, I could be an eagle to fly so they couldn't get me." These suggestions are corroborated by home and school observations indicating significant emotional disturbance. Rev. and Mrs. Williams reported that George has a short attention span, often stares off into space, sleeps deeply and frequently (he actually fell asleep in the waiting room while I was interviewing the Williamses), and has difficulty in shifting moods (e.g., when he becomes angry, he stays angry for a prolonged period of time).

Lynne Nelson, George's teacher, also noted his difficulty in shifting moods and, in particular, marked responses to frustration. Ms. Nelson said that he is also very sensitive to discipline and becomes obstinate and pouting after being corrected. She noted that George easily becomes angry, and then he becomes quite aggressive at times and hits and pinches the other children and shows no remorse for having done so. He also has a tendency to disrupt the class by being noisy and silly and refusing to do his work. Ms. Nelson added that his misbehavior is especially marked after even a single day's absence from school; he seems to have difficulty when routines are disrupted. Ms. Nelson indicated that George seems to crave attention from adults and that he does best in one-to-one work, a tendency that was apparent during my classroom observation. Ms. Nelson is sufficiently concerned about George that she has made a referral for school psychological services.

Academic Achievement and Testing. George's academic progress is mildly delayed (around beginning first-grade level). He is in low groups in both math and reading, although he has begun making rapid progress in math, which he enjoys. A screening for intelligence was performed using the Vocabulary subtest of the WISC-R, the subtest that correlates most highly with Full-Scale IQ and school performance. It is noteworthy in that regard that George scored just above the mean for his age group; this suggests, in light of his poor schoolwork, that he is not working to his potential, perhaps because of interference by emotional factors. Care should be taken not to overinterpret this single subtest score, however.

Summary and Recommendations. Although George does not show signs of severe psychological disorder, he is clearly a troubled and perhaps somewhat troubling youngster. He appears to have substantial concern about the instability in his life, and he has difficulty in managing his feelings, especially anger. I strongly recommend his becoming involved in psychotherapy, both to help him to deal with the traumatic events he has experienced and to give him skills in controlling his feelings. Such treatment would preferably be long-term to give him the possibility of exploring his feelings within a consistent relationship. My expectation is that it would take a number of sessions before he would begin to feel secure enough in the relationship to make good use of it therapeutically. Cognitive-behavioral work aimed at giving George skills in dealing with anger and increasing his attention span and tolerance for frustration would also be useful. In any case, some form of intervention would be especially important if there is a change of residence or custody.

EVALUATION OF GERALD:

Interview. Gerald appeared to be a remarkably bright, inquisitive 28-month-old boy. His play when with Molly Davidson (his foster mother) and me was structured and imaginative. He was highly verbal for a two-year-old. Gerald talked a great deal, and he did so in three-word sentences. With Ms. Davidson he was very polite (e.g., using "please" and "thank you" consistently), and his play was quite social for a child of his age. For example, he wanted to make sure that there were dolls to go with cars and other toys ("[Where are the] People, Mama?"). Ms. Davidson said that Gerald is close to his stepsister (an eight-year-old foster child whom Ms. Davidson is adopting). He gets up to tell her good-bye every morning when she leaves for school, and he plays violin with her sometimes. (Ms. Davidson has involved both children in Suzuki violin lessons.)

Gerald's developmental milestones have generally been appropriate. He walked at 11 months. Toilet training is just beginning.

Summary. Gerald is a bright two-year-old who shows appropriate cognitive and social development.

NATURE OF THE FOSTER HOMES:

Willamses. Rev. and Mrs. Williams appear on first impression to be caring people. They have, for example, endeavored to involve Ms. Jones in some of the activities of their church, and they have kept communication open (e.g., permitting holiday visits and frequent phone calls). They also appear to have reasonable sensitivity to George's emotional needs. They are committed to long-term foster care, if necessary, for George. However, they have not really discussed the possibility of adoption at some point, and they perceive the best option as eventually returning George to his natural mother.

The Williamses are Pentacostalists, and they may have unnecessarily strict expectations. For example, they will not allow their children to play with other children in the neighborhood because of the "bad mouths" of the neighbor children. They also forbid dancing and rock music. No mention was made, however, of any conflicts with George concerning the household rules per se.

At the same time that I met with the Williamses, I was just beginning my evaluation of George. Consequently, I have not broached the possibility of his receiving psychological help with them. Assuming that long-term care by the Williamses continues, Social Services workers might explore their willingness to cooperate with a treatment program.

Ms. Davidson. Ms. Davidson is a single foster parent who apparently pays special attention to the intellectual stimulation of her children. As has already been noted, she has enrolled the children in Suzuki lessons. She encourages Gerald to watch Sesame Street, Romper Room, etc., but she denies access to TV cartoons because of the violence in them. She does permit "classical cartoons" (e.g., library showings of animated versions of The Nutcracker), however.

Ms. Davidson is a graduate of Peace College, and for several years she worked as a media specialist in Peace's laboratory school. She has recently been a substitute teacher, and she is working on setting up a preschool with some friends. She has obtained an elementary-school teaching job in St. Louis, and she will be moving there in July. She would like to take Gerald with her and indeed to adopt him.

Ms. Davidson's mother, a widow who lives in St. Louis, is also in the process of adopting three foster children, and she has taken care of foster children for some time. Ms. Davidson herself seemed to minimize the realistic problems of being a single parent. However, she apparently has substantial social support at present in church groups, and she will have the support of her family when she moves to Missouri.

RELATIONSHIP BETWEEN MS. JONES AND HER CHILDREN:
On observation Ms. Jones seemed generally to be appropriately involved with the children, although Social Services notes suggest that she may be somewhat detached at times. During the play session, the children were, in her words, "hyperactive" and often somewhat out of control. She was generally slow to respond. When she did respond, she was not very effective. Gerald's behavior presented a

particular contrast to his behavior with Ms. Davidson. Although he had frequently shown toys to his foster mother and talked with her, he seldom engaged in that behavior with Ms. Jones. He was also markedly less well behaved and polite, although the presence of a second child may have contributed to his misbehavior. (Gerald's identifying most of the toys as his own whenever George wanted to play with something was the instigation of much of the rowdiness.)

Ms. Jones appears to be trying to be a good parent (at least as good as one can be without custody). According to the Williamses, she calls George about every other day. During the interviews, she seemed at times to be asking for the "answers" about how to handle childrearing situations. At the same time, though, her skills in problem solving as a parent need more development. The structured interview on parental problem solving developed by Shure and Spivack was administered. [See M. SHURE & G. SPIVACK, PROBLEM-SOLVING TECHNIQUES IN CHILDREARING (1978).] One aspect of the interview involves giving the respondent a series of vignettes about parent-child relations; the respondent is given the beginning of the story and the end (a positive outcome). The task then is to identify what the mother in the story might have said or done to achieve a positive result. Although Ms. Jones's answers were generally not bizarre or noticeably inappropriate, they were also sparse. That is, she sometimes seemed "stuck" in figuring out ways of getting from a problem to a successful resolution of the problem. It is likely that her concreteness of thought and limited relationships have adversely affected her ability to empathize with the children in a situation in which they are having difficulty.

Ms. Jones has made an effort to apply some of the childrearing concepts taught in the CARE program. For example, she describes "time out" as a primary disciplinary tool, and she apparently uses the technique on occasion during visits with the children (according to Social Services notes prepared by Ms. Sterling). However, there is an impression reported in the notes and in conversation with Ms. Sterling that she uses the technique somewhat arbitrarily without explanation to the children and without clear understanding of the concept. Ms. Sterling's impression that Ms. Jones may not fully understand the application of time out was corroborated during my own interviews with her. In response to one of the Shure–Spivack vignettes (about a child's shoplifting cookies from the grocery store), Ms. Jones initially talked only about how to get the cookies back to the grocery store. When pressed to identify the appropriate consequences for the child, she said, "The first time I'd just tell him. The second time he'd get a spanking. I don't think he should just go

on time out for stealing. I don't think he'd learn from it." However, she had also said that time out "*always* works."

Ms. Jones said that she would prefer to regain custody of both children. However, she added that having only one would be "OK." If it came to that, she thinks that George would be the child for whom she could better care. Besides the fact that Gerald has always lived in foster care, he requires more care because he is younger. Her first response was simply that George "helps me." There may be some role reversal with him, a tendency that has been commonly reported in clinical reports of abuse and neglect.

At the current time, Ms. Jones denied that her hallucinations that have occurred have contained content about the children. Although she was very reluctant to talk about the voices, she said that they made accusations about her having been a dancer (she refused to elaborate further) and her being unclean (e.g., "You smell"). Apparently, however, the hallucinations *have* often focused on the children, although without direct instructions of what to do to the children. The NSH records indicated that the hallucinations at the times of her hospitalizations often focused on accusations about her care of her children. More recently, Ms. Disney asked Ms. Jones to keep a log of hallucinations. Although, as already noted, she has not reported any for several months, prior to that time the content often involved the children (e.g., "You should give your baby to someone who loves him"; "Does Mommy want this baby?"; "You have to go back to the hospital so you can beat the boy"; "She's always hurting someone. Yaaa!"; "I can't wait until you lose the kid").

CONCLUSIONS: Although Ms. Jones's mental status appears to have improved in recent months, she continues to show residual signs of chronic schizophrenia (e.g., flattened affect/emotional response and social isolation), which are likely to persist. A major concern is the question of recurrence of hallucinations and Ms. Jones's ability to keep control if and when they return. It is clear that the probability of florid paranoid symptoms is substantially decreased while Ms. Jones remains on medication. However, it is unclear what the probability is of her again experiencing hallucinations and losing control. Apparently she has not been under great stress in recent months. Accordingly, one cannot make very strong inferences from the recent lack of active hallucinatory behavior as to the probability of her losing control in the future. Based on previous behavior, it is at such times that the children would be at physical risk.

For the time being, the general treatment plan being used by CMHC seems appropriate for Ms. Jones. It might be useful to add work on empathy and problem solving with respect to the children themselves. Continuing work by Social Services on application of parental skills would also be appropriate. However, Ms. Jones's concrete thinking style and low relatedness make such work difficult.

On the basis of the one-time interviews with them, I do not feel confident in making strong statements about the adequacy of the Williamses and Ms. Davidson as long-term foster parents or potential adoptive parents. Generally, however, the care given the children sounds appropriate. It is clear that Gerald is securely attached to Ms. Davidson (e.g., he uses her as "home base" for exploration of an unfamiliar setting). However, George appears not to be strongly attached to either Ms. Jones or any of the series of foster parents with whom he has lived.

George appears to have substantial concerns about his vulnerability and difficulty in managing affect, especially anger. He is also having both academic and social problems in school. I recommend his referral for psychotherapy, preferably long term. A full psychoeducational evaluation would also be advisable. Gerald, on the other hand, appears well adjusted for a child of his age.

A final point that should be made is that Ms. Jones's schizophrenia should not be viewed as an indicant per se of inability to function as an adequate parent. Recent research by Arnold Samaroff, Bertram Cohler, Norman Garmezy, and others indicates that, although children of mothers with schizophrenia are at greater risk for developmental difficulties than children of normals, most of these differences are erased when comparisons are made with other diagnostic groups (e.g., mothers with affective disorders), and many of the differences, at least for young children, disappear when proper controls are added for social class and stress level. Moreover, many children of mothers with schizophrenia appear to cope reasonably well. However, the risk level is related to the chronicity of the mother's condition. In general, the more serious and durable the condition, the more likely neglect or abuse will occur.

David P. Rodriguez, Ph.D.

(b) Discussion

The Jones report was prepared for a review of disposition in a child abuse case, which usually requires a very wide-ranging evaluation [see §15.06(a)]. In that regard, note that the clinician took care to obtain records that might illuminate the degree of change that had occurred since the last review. He also interviewed the natural mother, both sets of foster parents, and the children themselves, both by themselves and with their mother. There were also conversations with Ms. Jones's therapist, the social worker, and the social services aide, and the clinician did a school visit. The checks with other sources (e.g., Ms. Jones's therapist) were helpful as well; besides giving a baseline against which to measure change, they hinted at some relationships between Ms. Jones's mental disorder and her behavior with her children (e.g., child-related content of auditory hallucinations) that Ms. Jones had not disclosed. Exploration of these diverse sources of information was also essential in reaching conclusions about specific issues related to the children's adjustment and the adequacy of the foster homes. Both types of issues are ancillary to questions of a parent's fitness, but both frequently arise in dispositional reviews.

Substantial attention was given to Ms. Jones's mental status, but it is important to note that it was not scrutinized for its own sake. Rather, the clinician was interested in changes in Ms. Jones's condition and the relationship between Ms. Jones's psychiatric problems and her care for her children. In fact, one interview was devoted largely to the Shure–Spivack vignettes on child-drearing situations.

Note also that, in the conclusion to the report, the clinician informed the court and the social services department of the research showing little relationship between schizophrenia and parental incompetence [see § 15.05(a)]. Elsewhere in the report, there were indirect references to research literature (e.g., using an adult as "home base" for exploration as an indicator of a child's attachment), which may have illuminated behavioral science information unlikely to be known to the court.

Finally, note the care with which conclusory statements, particularly predictive statements, were made. The clinician indicated that abusive incidents in the past all occurred in the context of Ms. Jones's hallucinations. He reported the apparent lack of hallucinations over the previous months, but he also noted that Ms. Jones had not been under much stress in that time. Therefore, he concluded that he was unable to draw a firm conclusion as to the likelihood of Ms. Jones's experiencing hallucinations again or of being unable to control herself if they did recur. Similarly, the clinician emphasized the limited data base available to him for determining the suitability of the foster parents for long-term placement or adoption. In keeping with our usual injunction against ultimate-issue testimony, the clinician refrained from drawing conclusions as to whether Ms. Jones was an unfit parent and whether the children should be returned to her.

19.12.   Custody [Chapter 16]

(a)   The Gonz-Jones Report*

CHILD: Timmy Gonz-Jones
DATE OF BIRTH: October 31, 1986
PARENTS: Robert Jones and Mae Gonz
DATES OF INTERVIEWS: September 10, 1993; September 22, 1994; September 29, 1993; and October 16, 1993
DATE OF REPORT: November 20, 1993

REFERRAL/NOTIFICATION: Mr. Robert Jones and Ms. Mae Gonz were referred for a psychological evaluation to assist the court with respect to determining the custody and placement of their seven-year-old son, Timmy Gonz-Jones. Attorneys for Mr. Jones and Ms. Gonz agreed that this writer would be appointed by the court to evaluate both parties and submit a written report.

Mr. Jones and his fiance, Carol Wright (who has now married Mr. Jones), were interviewed on two occasions (see below). Ms. Mae Gonz also was interviewed on two occasions (see below), and her mother, Faye Diane Gonz, was interviewed on one occasion. Tim was seen on two occasions, during the course of the second interview with Mr. Jones and Ms. Wright and during the course of the second interview with Ms. Gonz. This writer was assisted with the evaluation by Barbie Owling, a clinical psychology intern at the Florida Mental Health Institute.

The nature and purpose of the evaluation were explained to Mr. Jones, Ms. Wright, and Ms. Gonz. They agreed to participate in the evaluation process. Mr. Jones and Ms. Gonz reviewed and signed consent

*This report was provided to the authors by Randy Otto, Ph.D.

forms describing the evaluation procedure in more detail. Mr. Jones, Ms. Wright, and Ms. Gonz all appeared to understand the nature of the evaluation process and agreed to participate in every aspect of it.

SOURCES OF INFORMATION: In conducting this evaluation the following sources of information were relied on:

1. Clinical interviews with Robert Jones and Carol Wright (September 22, 1993, 3.5 hours; September 29, 1993, 2.25 hours).
2. Clinical interviews with Mae Gonz (September 10, 1993, 3.2 hours; October 16, 1993, 1.5 hours).
3. Clinical interviews with Timmy Gonz-Jones (September 29, 1993, October 16, 1993)
4. Minnesota Multiphasic Personality Inventory—2 completed by Robert Jones.
5. Minnesota Multiphasic Personality Inventory—2 completed by Carol Wright.
6. Minnesota Multiphasic Personality Inventory—2 completed by Mae Gonz.
7. Review of psychological evaluation of Timmy Gonz-Jones completed by Vanessa Kandies, Ph.D., dated May, 1993.
8. Clinical treatment records describing interactions with Robert Jones, Mae Gonz, and Timmy Gonz-Jones compiled by Michael Johnson, Ph.D.
9. Telephone interview of Austin Cowan, M.D., treating psychiatrist for Timmy and parents, conducted on November 9, 1993.
10. Telephone interview of Mark Johnson, Ph.D., treating psychologist for Timmy and parents, conducted on October 1, 1993.
11. Telephone interview of Vanessa Kandies, Ph.D., evaluating psychologist for Timmy, conducted on October 20, 1993.
12. Telephone interview of Andrew Lane, Ph.D., treating psychologist for Timmy and parents, conducted on October 21, 1993.
13. Telephone interview of Francis George, owner and director of Children's World Learning Center, conducted on November 12, 1993.
14. Review of final judgment of dissolution of marriage of Robert Jones and Mae Gonz dated April 14, 1990.
15. Review of court order for psychological evaluation in the case of Robert Jones and Mae Gonz dated July 22, 1993.
16. Clinical interview with Faye Diane Gonz (December 9, 1993, 40 minutes).
17. Telephone contacts with Attorney Sara Giovanie, Timmy's guardian *ad litem*.

18. Copy of Timmy's first-grade report card for the first nine weeks of the 1993–94 school year.

EVALUATION OF ROBERT JONES:

1. *History and background information.* Mr. Jones was born in Washington and raised in Orlando, Florida; his parents remain married and live in the Orlando area today. Mr. Jones is the oldest of three children; he reported having a close relationship with his brothers and parents. Mr. Jones described his parents as doing a "great job."

Mr. Jones reported that he was an average student who, after graduating from high school, enlisted in the Army. While stationed in Delaware Mr. Jones met Mae Gonz. He reported that they dated for ten weeks prior to marrying in October 1984. In retrospect Mr. Jones described the short courtship and subsequent marriage as a mistake.

While Mr. Jones was stationed in Boston, Mae delivered Timmy. Shortly after Timmy's birth, Mr. Jones left the Army, and he, Mae, and Timmy returned to Florida. He described Mae as becoming significantly depressed after the birth of Timmy, and she refused to be treated for this depression. Mr. Jones described Mae as being somewhat neglectful of Timmy during the course of her alleged depression. For example, he reported that she did not change Timmy's diapers as frequently as necessary and sometimes forgot or neglected to feed him.

Mr. Jones reported that he and Mae eventually came to live with his parents because of financial difficulties. He reported that his separation from Mae was in response to her allegations that his brother sexually abused Timmy while he was asleep. Mr. Jones denied any knowledge of such an incident and doubted that it happened. Shortly after this incident Mae separated from Mr. Jones, apparently citing concerns about the safety of Timmy as well as the family's failure to address this issue. Mr. Jones saw Mae's allegations as an excuse to leave their difficult marriage.

Mr. Jones described his current relationship with Mae as "very touchy but civil." He described Mae as resenting him, partly as a result of allegations he made regarding the suspected sexual abuse of Timmy allegedly perpetrated by Mae's ex-boyfriend, Ralph.

Mr. Jones reported experiencing employment difficulties during the course of his marriage as a result of his alcohol abuse and dependence. He reported finding stable employment since he has abstained from alcohol (see below). He currently works for a hardware store.

At the time of the interviews, Mr. Jones was engaged to Carol Wright. By the time this report was written, Ms. Wright and Jones had married. Mr. Jones and Ms. Wright met in May 1992 and were engaged one month later. They married in September 1993. Mr. Jones and Ms. Wright have lived together since July 1992.

2. *Mental health history and current psychological functioning.* Mr. Jones arrived promptly for both of his appointments. He was well groomed and casually attired on both occasions. Mr. Jones cooperated throughout the evaluation process. His responses to questions were direct and to the point.

Mr. Jones denied any significant psychiatric history with the exception of a history of alcohol abuse and dependence. He reported that he first began drinking heavily after enlisting in the Army. He reported drinking alcohol on a daily basis while in the Army and afterwards. He reported experiencing a number of employment and marital difficulties as a result of his alcohol abuse and dependence.

Mr. Jones reported abstaining from alcohol since February, 1990. He reported that he stopped drinking without entering any treatment program. He reported being involved in Alcoholics Anonymous on a monthly basis for the past few months.

With the exception of the above, Mr. Jones denied experiencing any emotional or psychiatric difficulties in the past. He denied ever receiving any kind of mental health treatment. Jones has participated in therapy with three of Timmy's therapists (Drs. Lane, Cowan, and Johnson).

Mr. Jones communicated well during the course of the evaluation. His responses to questions were direct and on point. There were no indications of any major psychiatric disturbance or disorder. Mr. Jones displayed a range of emotions that were always in control and always appropriate to the content of his speech (i.e., when talking about serious issues he adopted a serious tone and when talking about less serious issues he was less serious).

Mr. Jones was administered the Minnesota Multiphasic Personality Inventory–2 (MMPI-2), a structured psychological instrument that assesses emotional functioning, psychological symptomatology, and behavioral patterns. Individuals with similar profiles are described as responding somewhat defensively to the inventory. Validity indices indicate that Mr. Jones may have minimized his difficulties or shortcomings in an attempt to portray himself in a positive way. Such an approach to testing, of course, is not uncommon among people completing the testing under such circumstances.

Individuals with similar MMPI-2 profiles are considered to be without significant mental health difficulties. They may have limited insight into their psychological functioning, however. People with similar MMPI-2 profiles are often overly sensitive to the criticism and disapproval of others, and are perhaps passive and overcompliant in interpersonal relationships as a result. They often have difficulty expressing anger directly because of their fear of disapproval. They also find it difficult to assert themselves with others and may express their anger indirectly as a result. Persons with similar MMPI-2 profiles are outgoing and enjoy interacting with others. They may have difficulty sustaining attention and remaining focused on particular issues.

3. *Mr. Jones's relationship with and concern for Timmy.* Mr. Jones portrayed himself as highly concerned about his son's adjustment at home, at day care, and at school for the past few years. He reported a history of behavioral and emotional difficulties that Timmy had displayed in his various day-care and school placements. These difficulties are not described in detail here as they have been documented by various mental health professionals (see, e.g., Dr. Kandies' report) and Timmy's teacher (see his report card). Mr. Jones reported that Timmy was almost expelled from day care on one occasion because of some of these difficulties. Mr. Jones believes that his ex-wife lied to day-care professionals in response to their suggestions that Timmy be treated for these difficulties.

Mr. Jones reported that, about one year ago, he and his ex-wife agreed that Timmy would live with him and Carol if he continued to show behavior problems. He reported that Mae later denied ever reaching such an agreement and refused to let Timmy move in with him.

Mr. Jones reported that he, his ex-wife, and Timmy first enrolled in treatment for Timmy's difficulties with Dr. Andrew Lane in December 1992. He reported that Dr. Lane met mostly with him and Mac over the course of their three to four sessions and that the sessions focused on communicating with each other and agreeing on how to treat and handle Timmy. Mr. Jones reported that he saw treatment of little help because of his ex-wife's unwillingness to engage in treatment and respond to Timmy's difficult behaviors. Thus, he discontinued treatment.

From March through May 1993, Mr. Jones and Ms. Gonz sought treatment with Dr. Austin Cowan. Mr. Jones reported that he "wanted somebody fresh." Dr. Cowan apparently diagnosed Timmy as suffering from attention deficit disorder and prescribed Ritalin, a psychostimulant often used with hyperactive children. Ritalin was apparently prescribed without Ms. Gonz's knowledge. The Ritalin was discontinued after two weeks because of increased aggression and no improvement in attention on Timmy's part. Treatment with Dr. Cowan was subsequently discontinued, in part because of Ms. Gonz's concern regarding Tim-

my's being administered the medication without her knowledge or approval.

Finally, Mr. Jones and Ms. Gonz initiated treatment with Dr. Mark Johnson in June 1993. Mr. Jones's understanding of the treatment was that he and his ex-wife were to work together to establish a stable, consistent, and supportive environment for Timmy. Dr. Johnson discontinued treatment in response to Ms. Gonz failing to keep a number of appointments and her inability to pay the bill for those missed appointments (see below). Further treatment has not been initiated.

In January 1993, Mr. Jones contacted Health and Rehabilitative Services (HRS) and alleged that Timmy might have been abused by Ralph, Ms. Gonz's ex-boyfriend. Mr. Jones reported that he was granted custody of Timmy until June 1993, at which time it was determined that the allegation of sexual abuse was unfounded, based on the evaluation by Dr. Kandies.

Mr. Jones was agreeable to Timmy's returning to his mother after reading Dr. Kandies's report. Between May 1993 and October 1993 Timmy alternately lived with his mother and father, moving back and forth between their households every two days or so. Mr. Jones reported that Timmy did not appear to be experiencing any difficulties as a result of this arrangement until he entered school. He reported, however, that this was sometimes confusing for Timmy.

Mr. Jones described himself as having a positive, happy, and loving relationship with his son. He described Timmy as affectionate and sometimes distant. He reported that Timmy always sought to do things with him on their visits. He reported paying more attention to Timmy now than he had in the past.

Mr. Jones described Timmy's and Carol's relationship in a positive way. He acknowledged that their relationship was somewhat tentative because Timmy was "still getting to know" Carol. Mr. Jones described his fiance/wife as adopting a parenting role with Timmy in a very natural way. He reported that Carol sometimes becomes frustrated because she has not been involved in Timmy's treatment in the past.

Mr. Jones reported that Timmy is very confused about his current living arrangement and what is and is not acceptable behavior. Mr. Jones attributed this confusion to differences he and his ex-wife have with respect to raising Timmy and responding to his inappropriate or problematic behaviors. Mr. Jones also identified Timmy as having problems with a short attention span and infrequent aggression. He sees these as secondary to other problems. For example, Mr. Jones reported that difficulties with attention and aggression appear to be mostly a problem at school, and he wondered whether Timmy's difficulties with bed-wetting in the past have contributed to teasing and frustration that resulted in him becoming aggressive with other children.

Mr. Jones believes that Timmy needs to establish a primary residence because of the consistency that would result. He also believes that placement in a smaller school, with more individualized attention, would be helpful to Timmy.

With respect to his strengths as a parent, Mr. Jones identified his love for Timmy and children in general and his devotion to his son. He identified as a potential weakness his tendency sometimes to act before thinking. He acknowledged that he sometimes "comes on stronger" than he realizes. Mr. Jones thinks that Mae believes that he is "too strict" and that she might be concerned about his history of alcohol abuse.

Mr. Jones described his ex-wife as highly creative and as easygoing and fun for Timmy to be around. He described his ex-wife as having an "explosive temper" and being too permissive with Timmy on some occasions. Mr. Jones sees some of Timmy's difficulties as resulting from his ex-wife's failure to appreciate the significance of Timmy's problems and/or her unwillingness to punish his problem behaviors.

With respect to responding to Timmy's problem behaviors, Mr. Jones and Carol provided examples of behavioral programs and strategies they had developed. For example, Mr. Jones and Carol developed and posted lists for Timmy to refer to in terms of identifying what kinds of responsibilities he has during the morning (e.g., using the bathroom, dressing, brushing his teeth, and turning off the bedroom light). Mr. Jones also described developing a behavioral program for Timmy whereby he was rewarded on those days that he did not wet his pants. Mr. Jones and Carol reported that these techniques have generally been successful although there have been some setbacks. They see the lack of consistency between their household and Mae's as responsible for the less than ideal improvement.

4. *Mr. Jones's preferred custody arrangement.* Mr. Jones sees the ideal custody arrangement as Timmy maintaining primary residence with him and Carol. He identified this as most appropriate for Timmy for a number of reasons. First, as indicated above, Mr. Jones sees Timmy as needing consistency and direction. He considers himself and Carol as most able to provide this. Mr. Jones sees one of his ex-wife's weaknesses as her difficulty in being firm and consistent with Timmy. Mr. Jones also cited Timmy as needing significant intervention as a result of his behavioral and emotional difficulties. He related numerous instances where he believed his ex-wife was lax in either responding to these difficulties or ensuring that Timmy received

some kind of treatment for these difficulties. Finally, Mr. Jones, who is anticipating a move to Pinellas County, reported that Timmy would benefit from the opportunity to attend a new school where he would not suffer because of his reputation for past difficulties. Mr. Jones made clear that he fully expected Timmy to remain involved with Mae, however.

EVALUATION OF MAE GONZ:

1. *History and background information.* Ms. Gonz was born and raised in Delaware. She is the oldest of three children. She was enrolled in college when she met Robert and dropped out of college to marry him. Ms. Gonz reported some positive experiences over the early course of her marriage but reported experiencing significant financial and relationship difficulties as a result of his alcohol abuse.

Ms. Gonz reported an uncomplicated pregnancy and delivery with Timmy but noted that Timmy endured some problems with his digestive tract after being born and that this was successfully treated. She described Robert as supportive and helpful during her pregnancy and delivery.

Shortly after Timmy's birth, Ms. Gonz and her ex-husband left the Army and moved in with Robert's parents in Orlando. Ms. Gonz reported experiencing some depression which she attributed to her mother-in-law's overcontrolling behavior and negative comments offered by Robert's family regarding her depression. She reported undergoing one or two counseling sessions for depression at the suggestion of her husband, but she could not remember the content of the sessions or why they ended.

Ms. Gonz obtained a job when Timmy was approximately three or four months old. She reported that her mood improved significantly and she attributed this to her increased self-esteem. Ms. Gonz reported experiencing ongoing financial problems over the course of her marriage as a result of Robert's alcohol abuse and job instability. She reported that her ex-husband was once jailed and fined after stealing approximately $1,000 from his employer. Both Ms. Gonz and Robert reported that he was not convicted after completing a pretrial intervention program.

Ms. Gonz reported that she and her ex-husband had to return to his parents' home after being evicted from their apartment because of his failure to pay their rent. It was at this time that the incident with Robert's brother allegedly occurred. Ms. Gonz's concerns about her ex-husband's failure to protect and intervene on Tim's behalf eventually led to her separation and eventual divorce.

Ms. Gonz reported that during the initial part of their separation she and her ex-husband did not develop specifics about visitation and custody. Ms. Gonz claimed that her ex-husband was less involved in decisionmaking about Timmy but that his interest in Timmy increased and appeared to coincide with his involvement with Ms. Wright.

At the time of the evaluation, Ms. Gonz had recently ended the relationship with Ralph, her boyfriend and the father of her second child, Ron, who was born in June 1993. Subsequent to completing the clinical interviews, Ms. Gonz reported via telephone that her mother had moved to Florida to live with her and help her raise her children.

2. *Mental health history and current psychological functioning.* Ms. Gonz arrived for her interviews promptly. There were no indications of a significant or serious psychiatric disorder. There were no indications of depression; Ms. Gonz reported adequate adjustment and no significant psychiatric difficulties. As indicated previously, Ms. Gonz did report experiencing some depression shortly after the birth of Timmy. She reported no similar difficulties subsequent to the birth of Ron, however.

Ms. Gonz cooperated with the evaluation process. Her responses to questions were direct and on point. She displayed a range of emotion that was always appropriate to the content of her speech. She denied any history of drug or alcohol abuse or dependence.

Ms. Gonz was administered the MMPI-2, a structured psychological instrument that assesses psychopathology, behavior patterns, and personality style. Individuals with similar validity configurations are described as responding to the items in an honest and straightforward manner. Thus, the profile is considered to accurately reflect her current level of psychological functioning.

Individuals with similar MMPI-2 profiles are described as experiencing some psychological difficulties. They are observed to drive themselves excessively and to be overextended as a result. They develop unrealistic plans and may fail to complete or reach their goals. Individuals with similar MMPI-2 profiles dislike having to deal with details and are somewhat disorganized. Individuals with similar MMPI-2 profiles are described as highly confident. They are highly focused on their own needs, and when things do not go their way they may become frustrated, irritable, and moody. Persons with similar MMPI-2 profiles sometimes act without considering the consequences of their behavior; this may create difficulties for themselves or others.

Individuals with similar MMPI-2 profiles may be manipulative and superficial in their relationships with others. They may experience strained interpersonal relationships as a result. Such persons are easily bored;

they are outgoing and sociable; they have a strong need to be around others.

3. *Ms. Gonz's relationship with and concern for Timmy.* Ms. Gonz described both Timmy and Ron in very positive terms. Her appraisal of Timmy's adjustment, however, suggested that she saw him as having fewer and less severe problems than her ex-husband does. She acknowledged problems with Timmy's school behavior, including decreased attention and difficulty following directions, and physical aggression directed toward other children. She stressed, however, Timmy's intelligence and ability to learn.

Ms. Gonz described herself as willing to do whatever was necessary to facilitate her son's adjustment. She reported meeting with teachers and intervening at home with respect to helping Timmy with his homework and directing him to take time to consider things before acting. She reported that she planned to meet with Timmy's teacher on a daily basis.

Ms. Gonz reported that Timmy's problems appeared to develop in kindergarten. She attributed this, in part, to the fact that Timmy had five teachers in two months. Ms. Gonz reported that it was about this time that Timmy began having difficulties with bedwetting. Unlike her ex-husband, Ms. Gonz felt Timmy's behavior improved somewhat in response to therapy with Dr. Lane. She saw the termination of treatment with Dr. Lane as resulting from her ex-husband's refusal to participate in treatment.

According to Ms. Gonz, it was shortly after this termination that her ex-husband alleged that her ex-boyfriend, Ralph, abused Timmy. Ms. Gonz reported that Timmy was evaluated by Dr. Kandies in response to these allegations.

Ms. Gonz reported that she, her ex-husband, and Timmy also entered treatment with Dr. Cowan. She reported that she became upset with Dr. Cowan after he prescribed Ritalin without her permission. Finally, Ms. Gonz and her ex-husband agreed to see Dr. Johnson this past spring. It was Ms. Gonz's understanding that she and her husband were to work together so that they would be more consistent in their interactions with Timmy. At the time of the evaluation Ms. Gonz reported having questions about whether therapy with Dr. Johnson would be successful; she attributed her concerns to her ex-husband's attitude.

4. *Ms. Gonz's preferred custody arrangement.* Ms. Gonz sees Timmy's behavior as partly a function of the lack of consistency and confusion that presumably results from his movement between two households. She believes that Timmy needs to identify one household as home. She would prefer that Timmy live with her during the week and live with her ex-husband on weekends. Ms. Gonz believes that placement with her ex-

husband would not be in Timmy's best interest for a number of reasons. Ms. Gonz thinks that entering a new school, rather than helping Timmy, would increase problems because of a lack of consistency and further change. She also sees the change of day-care centers that have occurred in the past as detrimental to Timmy. She reported that Timmy has been involved in three day-care centers and she saw her ex-husband as moving Timmy from one center with little justification. Ms. Gonz also sees her ex-husband as too strict with Timmy and this is yet another reason that placement would be better with her.

When asked about her strengths as a parent, Ms. Gonz described herself as a fair, honest, patient, loving parent who stressed independence. She identified as a weakness her need to increase her consistency in response to misbehavior on Timmy's part. She reported that she did not use corporal punishment and preferred to use "time out." She also identified as a weakness her tendency to be "scatterbrained." She described herself as having no concept of time and acknowledged that appointments had been missed as a result.

When asked to describe her ex-husband's strengths Ms. Gonz identified his love and concern for their son as well as some of the behavioral programs that he has developed for Timmy. Ms. Gonz identified her concerns regarding her ex-husband's parenting abilities as his "short fuse, his lack of patience, and his tendency to be too strict." She also described her ex-husband as not acting on his own but being easily led by those around him.

EVALUATION OF CAROL WRIGHT-JONES:

1. *History and background information.* Ms. Wright reported growing up in a military family and moving around frequently while a young child. She has lived in Florida since the age of 12. Ms. Wright has worked for a finance company for the past four years. This is Ms. Wright's first marriage.

2. *Mental health history and current psychological functioning.* Ms. Wright was seen on two occasions in the department clinic. She was cooperative with the evaluation process and appeared to make a sincere attempt to answer all questions that were presented to her.

Ms. Wright gave considerable thought to her responses and was able to express herself quite well. She displayed a range of emotion during the interviews and her expressed emotion was always appropriate to the content of her speech. At one point during the second interview she became tearful as she talked about Timmy's difficulties, and the frustration that she experiences as she feels left out of decisions made about Timmy.

Ms. Wright denied any history of involvement with the mental health system. She denied any history of drug or alcohol abuse. She reported significantly decreasing her alcohol use over the past one and half years, since meeting Robert. Ms. Wright denied having any need for mental health treatment in the past.

Ms. Wright was administered the MMPI-2. Validity indices of the MMPI-2 indicate that Ms. Wright portrayed herself in a positive manner, minimizing difficulties, faults, or shortcomings. Such an approach to testing is typical of persons who are trying to maintain an appearance of adequacy and self-control or who are completing psychological testing as part of a forensic evaluation. Individuals with similar validity configurations are also described as having somewhat limited insight. They may be inflexible in their approach to their problems and may not be open to psychological evaluation or interpretation.

Persons with similar MMPI-2 profiles are sometimes seen as intolerant of others' shortcomings. As a result of their approach and self-concept, such persons are unlikely to seek mental health treatment. Individuals with similar MMPI-2 profiles are described as having few difficulties. Persons with similar MMPI-2 profiles are generally outgoing and energetic. They enjoy being around and in the company of others.

3. *Ms. Wright's relationship with and concern for Timmy.* Ms. Wright expressed obvious concern and affection for Timmy. When asked to describe Timmy, Ms. Wright responded that Timmy is "physically attractive and very charming, he has a cuteness about him, which he sometimes uses to manipulate" others. Ms. Wright went on to note that she sometimes saw Timmy play his parents against one another. Like Robert, Ms. Wright sees Timmy as having significant behavioral and emotional difficulties that have not been ideally treated. She and her new husband are in general agreement regarding how to respond to Timmy's behavior, and their approach is more behaviorally focused than that which is offered by Ms. Gonz (see above and below).

Ms. Wright identified Timmy's main problems to be the instability and inconsistency in his life, due to the lack of a stable and structured environment. Ms. Wright sees Timmy as responsive to interventions and limits that are placed on him. She believes that if Timmy were placed with Robert and her, he would show improvement in his behavior and difficulties.

Ms. Wright identified her parenting strengths to include her stability and consistency. She described herself as loving Timmy "with all my heart" and expressed considerable concern about his future given his current difficulties. When asked to identify potential weaknesses, Ms. Wright reported that she needs to increase her patience. Ms. Wright stated that Timmy came into her life in an abrupt way as a six-year-old, and that she may have expected too much too soon from Timmy. She sees herself as making significant gains in this area, however. In contrast to herself, Ms. Wright sees her husband as having considerable patience and she sees them as "balancing each other out." She also sees her husband's love for his son and desire for involvement with him as strengths. Ms. Wright identified her husband's weaknesses with respect to parenting to be his fear of being seen as a "heavy" by Timmy and being less consistent as a result.

INTERVIEW WITH FAYE DIANE GONZ (MAE GONZ'S MOTHER): Ms. Gonz was interviewed after she had been living with her daughter for four weeks. She reported that she and Mae agreed that she would move to Tampa from Delaware to offer both financial and emotional support. She described her daughter as undergoing a number of stressors in the past year including questions about custody of Timmy, financial problems, the birth of a new son, and the dissolution of her relationship with Ralph. Ms. Gonz, however, noted that her daughter appeared to manage these stressors in a positive way. Ms. Gonz reported that although her plans were not fully crystallized, she hoped to remain in Tampa for at least one year to assist and support her daughter.

Ms. Gonz described Timmy as doing very well in terms of his adjustment at home. She described him as acting as she would expect most boys his age to act, with relatively few problems. However, she did acknowledge that Timmy was having some difficulties and also acknowledged some awareness of difficulties at school.

Ms. Gonz described her daughter as loving, creative, and consistent with respect to making rules. With respect to weaknesses, she reported that her daughter could be more organized and she believed that Timmy would benefit from this. Moreover, Ms. Gonz stated that the number of stressors her daughter was under in some ways negatively affected her parenting on a day-to-day basis.

EVALUATION OF TIMMY GONZ-JONES: Timmy was interviewed on two occasions, once accompanied by his father and stepmother and once accompanied by his mother. On both occasions, Timmy was quite energetic and distractible. In his interactions with this writer and Ms. Owling, he frequently had to be redirected and reinstructed regarding what was expected and asked of him. Timmy was quite fidgety and had difficulty sustaining attention for any length of time. He frequently left his chair and moved around

the room, sometimes ignoring the directions or instructions of Ms. Owling. However, Timmy eventually came to comply with almost all requests that were made of him.

Timmy spoke about his father, his mother, and Ms. Wright in positive terms. He indicated that his parents did not live together because "they are not happy together." He described himself as happy when spending time with both his mother and father. He reported not being able to spend as much time with his mother, however, because of his new baby brother, whom he also described in positive terms.

Timmy described his school experience in generally negative terms. He reported not having many friends, sometimes being teased, and not being liked by his teacher. Timmy reported that his mother helped him with his homework. He reported that his father and Ms. Wright did not do this because he did not take schoolwork to their house on weekends. Timmy was able to identify a number of friends that he has in his neighborhood.

Timmy reported having different responsibilities and schedules in both houses and acknowledged that this was sometimes confusing. When interviewed in the presence of his mother, father, and Ms. Wright, Timmy was somewhat better behaved and more compliant. He appeared to respond to the directions and requests of his mother, father, and Ms. Wright equally. Timmy was able to describe his daily routine and responsibilities in both homes with the assistance of his mother, father, and Ms. Wright. All three adults showed affection for and an ability to work with Timmy during these interactions.

Timmy's report card from the most recent term indicated that he was having difficulties in all areas of behavior. The guardian *ad litem,* Ms. Ciovanie, was informed by Timmy's teacher that he continues to show significant behavioral and emotional difficulties. She also informed Ms. Ciovanie that Timmy continued to fail to complete homework assignments and Ms. Gonz had not kept appointments with her or followed through with recommended interventions.

REPORTS OF EVALUATING AND TREATING MENTAL HEALTH PROFESSIONALS: In a telephone interview, Dr. Lane, the first psychologist to treat Timmy and his parents, reported that he considered Timmy's problems to largely be a result of parental conflict. It was Dr. Lane's impression that Mr. Jones chose not to continue their sessions. Dr. Lane believed that Mr. Jones was not fully invested in the treatment. He saw Ms. Gonz as more focused on Timmy's needs and more agreeable to treatment.

Dr. Cowan, the second psychologist who saw Timmy and his parents, believed that Mr. Jones and Ms. Gonz blamed each other for Timmy's difficulties. As compared to Dr. Lane, Dr. Cowan saw Mr. Jones as more involved in treatment. Dr. Cowan understood that treatment was discontinued because Ms. Gonz was upset by the fact that Timmy was started on psychostimulant medication without her knowledge.

Dr. Johnson was the last mental health professional to be involved with Timmy and his parents for treatment. Dr. Johnson reported that Ms. Gonz failed to make a number of scheduled appointments or call to cancel them. Dr. Johnson reported that he terminated treatment based on Ms. Gonz's inconsistency and her inability to pay for her missed sessions. Dr. Johnson stated that the parents appear to be unable to cooperate with each other and carry out an effective intervention for their son. He described Mr. Jones as "overprotective" and Ms. Gonz as unable to "follow through."

IMPRESSIONS AND RECOMMENDATIONS:
Interviews with Timmy, Timmy's parents, and treating mental health professionals indicate that Timmy is experiencing considerable emotional and behavioral difficulties. It is also the consensus of most, if not all, of those involved that Timmy's difficulties are largely related to confusion and inconsistency that he has experienced as a result of his parents' divorce. Compounding the general difficulties experienced by Timmy as a result of the dissolution of his parents marriage is his parents' inability to interact with each other in a reasonable way and consistently place the needs of their son before their own needs and desires.

It is also the general agreement of all those involved that Timmy will benefit from a more structured and consistent environment. It is agreed that finalization of the custody arrangement and placement in a "primary home" should lead to an improvement in terms of Timmy's adjustment. Such a placement, however, in and of itself, will not be enough to facilitate Timmy's adjustment. Therapy for Timmy, his custodial and noncustodial parents, and significant others who are involved (i.e., his maternal grandmother and his stepmother) is clearly indicated. Of some concern is the fact that Mr. Jones and Ms. Gonz have not been able to manage to make this work to any degree in the past.

The results of psychological testing, as well as impressions gained through clinical interviews, suggest that neither Mr. Jones nor Ms. Gonz is an "inadequate" parent. Both have strengths and weaknesses that they and treating mental health professionals have identified. If Timmy is to remain in the primary custody and residence with his mother, he will have access to his half-brother and maternal grandmother. These are important issues to be considered. Placement with his mother, however, does have drawbacks. Accounts of Ms. Gonz's behavior suggests that she has experienced some significant stressors that have affected Timmy in a negative way. Specifically, Ms. Gonz's mother sees these stressors as negatively affecting Ms. Gonz's ability to parent Timmy in some ways. A more significant concern perhaps is Ms. Gonz's apparent difficulties with organization and follow-through as evidenced by her difficulty maintaining contact with this examiner as well as withTimmy's most recent therapist. Moreover, school personnel reported that Timmy's schoolwork is suffering because of his mother's failure to supervise his homework or follow through adequately. It is disheartening to see that Timmy's most recent attempt at therapy was abandoned, in part, because of a lack of follow-through on his mother's part.

There are also strengths and limitations of placing Timmy with his father. Mr. Jones and Ms. Wright appear to have a greater awareness of, and are more focused on, Timmy's emotional and behavioral difficulties. They were able to describe, in detail, reasonable and organized attempts they made to work with Timmy at home to facilitate his adjustment. These attempts, if initiated on a regular and ongoing basis, in addition to therapy, should result in improvements in Timmy's adjustment and behavior. There are drawbacks to Timmy living with his father and stepmother, however. They include his removal from a half-brother with whom he has bonded and the lack of regular exposure to his mother, who is considered by all to be a very loving, creative, and stimulating parent.

Again, this writer would like to reiterate that it is apparent that both Ms. Gonz and Mr. Jones are very concerned about Timmy. Neither parent is "inadequate," but rather, each parent has relative strengths and weaknesses that may be more or less important to Timmy at this point in his life.

Respectfully submitted,
Raoul K. Osmond, Ph.D.
Licensed Psychologist

(b) Discussion

Note that the evaluator in this case is working for the court rather than for one of the parties. As suggested in § 16.04(a), this role is often advantageous in the custody setting because it reduces the adversarial pressures on the expert and facilitates gathering information. Although the expert appears to lean in the direction of the father and his new wife, the court-appointed role probably made it easier for him to ensure that the report recounted the strengths and weaknesses of both sides.

The evaluation is perhaps not as "ecological" as it could be [see § 16.04(c)]. For instance, the evaluator did not make a home visit. On the other hand, he did obtain information from multiple sources, including school records, standardized testing, interviews with other therapists, and interviews with Timmy's significant others. Note that the evaluator interviewed each parent with Timmy present so as to be able to observe their interaction. From each parent, he elicited descriptions of the family structure; the parent's attitudes toward the other parent; the parents' goals with respect to Timmy, custody, and visitation; and their prior, current, and anticipated caretaking procedures and lifestyle. From Timmy he elicited attitudes and preferences regarding the parents' current living arrangements, visitation, and placement and his conceptualization of the relationship with each parent. The mental and emotional functioning of each individual was also assessed.

After reading this report, consider how you would answer the questions posed in Problem 18.1 (in Chapter 18), assuming you are the court's witness.

19.13. Evaluation under the Individuals with Disabilities Education Act [Chapter 17]

(a)   Sam Shay Report*

PSYCHOEDUCATIONAL EVALUATION

NAME: Sam Shay
D.O.B: August 3, 1987
SEX: Male
DATE INTERVIEWED: May 28, 1995
CLINICIAN: Patti Barrett, Ph.D.
REFERRED BY: School psychologist

*This report was provided to the authors by Patti Slobogin, Ph.D.

REASON FOR REFERRAL: Sam was referred for a psychoeducational evaluation by the school psychologist, Ms. Thompson, to determine whether he has a learning disability. Sam has been having difficulties in school, both academic and behavioral. Ms. Thompson would like to understand what is causing Sam's difficulties and to obtain appropriate services for him under the Individuals with Disabilities Act.

BACKGROUND INFORMATION:

Current Functioning. Sam is currently in a general education third-grade class at school. His classroom teacher has suggested that he repeat third grade next year. A report card from the third grading period shows F's in mathematics, science and social studies, and D–'s in reading and language arts. Sam received a B in art and C's in music and physical education. Effort and behavioral grades are all Unsatisfactories or Needs Improvement. The teacher's comments from the first quarter describe poor reading and writing skills ("Sam does not know letters sounds . . . cannot pronounce new words . . . flubs directions . . . writes anything because he cannot read the directions"). The teacher also describes poor behavior and effort by the third quarter ("Sam has made no effort . . . doesn't seem to care . . .").

Sam receives additional academic support in the form of a small-group remedial reading class daily. A teacher report from this group in April 1995 says that Sam's behavior has improved as he has been learning word attack skills on the Macintosh computer. This teacher says that, "Despite his difficulties with the process of learning to read, he never gives up. He has a great attitude."

Ms. Thompson does not believe that Sam can receive adequate support for his academic difficulties in the large class, and that many of his behavioral problems stem from frustration and the low self-esteem that comes from failing in the large class. She notes that with appropriate support, like that in the remedial reading class, Sam is motivated and learns; however, she does feel that he has visual and learning problems that make many academic tasks difficult.

History. Sam was born after a pregnancy complicated by preeclampsia (high blood pressure and fluid retention) and toxemia (which can follow from preeclampsia and involves convulsions). He weighed 7 pounds, 11 ounces at birth and was a healthy baby. According to his mother, he met developmental milestones early.

Sam's medical history includes a bout of scarlet fever, for which he was not hospitalized. He has asthma and takes Ventolin (an antiasthmatic drug) as needed. Otherwise, he appears to be in good health.

Sam started school at St. Clemens Elementary School, where he is now. The report card from kindergarten indicates that Sam mastered most of the required skills, although even then he was having some difficulty learning letters and sounds and had some small muscle control difficulties. In first grade, he achieved "Good" in mathematics computation, science, social studies, art, and music, but his performance in other areas was inconsistent. In handwriting, he started the year with Unsatisfactory, but achieved a Good by the end of the year. In reading, although his comprehension was Good, he clearly struggled with phonetic analysis. Things changed significantly in second grade where, in the first quarter, Sam was described as below grade level across the board with weaknesses in mathematics and reading and as Unsatisfactory in most areas of behavior.

The school suggested that Sam repeat first grade at that time, but Mrs. Shay chose instead to transfer Sam to a private school, where there were smaller classes: In the smaller class, Sam continued to have academic difficulties, receiving a C+ in reading, and D+'s in mathematics, language arts, science, and social studies but receiving Satisfactory in behavior. At the end of second grade, Sam had to leave the private school for financial reasons and went to public school to repeat second grade. His report card shows Good work and study habits and Good achievement in mathematics, social studies, spelling, art, and music but continued difficulties (Needs improvement) in reading and language arts. This teacher described Sam as being cooperative and working well independently but also as being easily distracted. When Sam returned to St. Clemens, Mrs. Shay had him tested for a learning disability.

Sam was found to have average intellectual functioning on the WISC-III and average visual–motor integration skills as measured by the Bender–Gestalt test. The psychologist who conducted this testing described a number of specific behaviors on the part of Sam. These included some misinterpretations of what Sam heard, inordinate erasing on the Bender–Gestalt, use of verbal self-instruction on some Performance tasks, and needing considerable probing on some Verbal tasks. Despite Average intellectual abilities, Sam's performance on the Kaufman Tests of Educational Achievement fell somewhat below grade expectations, particularly in reading where he scored at the 21 percentile rank. More in-depth educational assessment was conducted by the educational evaluator, who described Sam as a hesitant reader who made many word recognition errors and reversed d's and b's. On rereading with a page mask, he was able to correct many reading errors. On the Slingerland (a test measuring learning disability which looks at visual processing of letters), he made many errors indicative of a learning

disability, including transpositions, substitutions and reversals; the evaluator described Sam as having weak visual and auditory perception and memory with poor sound–symbol associations. The speech and language evaluator described Low Average receptive language skills, with difficulty discerning phonological differences and an uneven vocabulary. Expressive language appeared to be Average.

Mrs. Shay independently had a visual evaluation conducted by Oscar Bing, who found that Sam was significantly far-sighted and astigmatic, a condition that could be corrected with glasses to only a limited extent. Dr. Bing noted that Sam was likely to have underlying visual–motor integration and spatial organization problems resulting in significant interference with learning, with concomitant loss of attention and motivation. The school recommended no special education supportive services for Sam but, according to Mrs. Shay, recommended that she work with him in phonics and read with him more. As stated earlier, Sam does participate in a small group remedial reading class daily.

TEST BEHAVIOR: Sam came to the assessment with his mother and chose to participate in an initial informational interview between the clinician and his mother rather than play with toys in the room. He participated in the 45-minute interview appropriately, clearly interested in the issues being discussed and contributing relevant information. He demonstrated good turn-taking skills, and both initiated and responded to conversation. His language appeared age-appropriate; his sentences were well organized and his vocabulary adequately developed for his age. He related well to the clinician and willingly turned to testing tasks when the interview ended.

Sam was very cooperative during both test sessions. He showed good concentration and attention across tasks and enjoyed the challenge of many of them. He was persistent even with difficult tasks but was able to appropriately assess what was too difficult for him. He was interested in the process of testing and asked appropriate questions about what the subtests were for, demonstrating a good understanding of some of the types of behavior being assessed.

Sam demonstrated some good test-taking strategies which, if applied in the classroom, would support classroom learning. He self-monitored, checking his work and frequently correcting errors. He had an ordered step-by-step approach to some familiar academic tasks, and he did not let failure upset his subsequent performance. He tried to relate unfamiliar tasks to familiar experiences, saying, "Oh, this is kind of like when I . . ." making appropriate analogies to his experience.

Sam understood the reason for testing but showed

limited insight into his behavioral difficulties. He tended to blame others for these problems, saying that the teacher and other kids picked on him and that he was never responsible for any problems. He had more insight into academic problems, saying that language arts was hardest for him in school because he couldn't always understand the tasks and that reading was often hard for him. He felt he behaved better in the reading class because the teacher there taught in a way that helped him learn better.

TESTING: The tests administered were the Woodcock–Johnson Tests of Cognitive Ability—Revised, Woodcock–Johnson Tests of Achievement—Revised, Bender–Gestalt Test, and some informal tests of academic functioning. The results of the cognitive tests are reported first, followed by an interpretation of those results. Achievement test results and interpretation follow.

Tests of Cognitive Ability: Results

Woodcock–Johnson Test of Cognitive Ability

Areas	SS	A–E	%ile for Age
Long-Term Retrieval	110	13–9	74
Short-Term Memory	91	7–9	27
Processing Speed	90	8–9	26
Auditory Processing	87	6–11	20
Visual Processing	118	13–5	89
Comprehension–Knowledge	79	7–1	8
Fluid Reasoning	93	8–2	33
BROAD COGNITIVE	86	8–2	17

Bender–Gestalt Test:
Age-equivalent: 7.0 to 7.5

Tests of Cognitive Ability: Interpretation

Age-appropriate scores on the Woodcock–Johnson test fall roughly between the 15th (Low Average) and 85th (High Average) percentiles. Sam's Broad Cognitive score (i.e., his overall score) of 17 fell in the Low Average range; however, this score is the result of significantly different domain scores, suggesting wide variability in his abilities. As the table shows, Sam's scores in the different cognitive areas assessed in this test ranged from the 8th percentile rank to the 89th percentile rank in relation to his age-peers, and his scores on the subtests varied even more widely (from the 5th to the 99th percentiles).

Sam has a number of processing strengths. He

processes and retains visual information accurately and he can demonstrate this ability as long as the assessment task requires recognition and not motoric reproduction of what he has seen. On two subtests, he accurately identified incomplete pictures (39th percentile rank) and easily recognized which pictures in a group of pictures he had seen before (99.7 percentile rank). This latter was an area of real strength and suggests that visual presentation of information could help enhance his recall of information.

Sam also has age-appropriate short-term auditory memory skills. On two memory subtests, he was able to attend to and recall sentences and lists of words he heard, accurately recalling sentences of up to nine words (27th percentile rank) and lists of five words (68th percentile rank). His score for the recall of sentences would have been higher but he made a number of minor grammatical errors when repeating sentences that lowered his score. On another subtest, he also could fill in missing auditory information, that is, sounds and identifying incomplete words he heard (46th percentile rank). Thus, he is clearly able to process and recall the content of verbal messages accurately.

Sam's strong performance on tasks that required making new auditory–visual associations shows that he is able to integrate information across these two modalities. On subtests, Sam easily recalled nonsense labels for unusual designs (72nd percentile rank) and meaningful labels for symbols (70th percentile rank). His recall of information presented in the two modalities was stronger than his recall of information presented only in the auditory modality.

However, Sam does have difficulties processing some types of auditory and visual information. He had great difficulty with the sound blending task subtest (11th percentile rank). He both added and omitted sounds and was unable to blend more than two sounds. This was an area of significant difficulty, which clearly underlies phonetic analysis and decoding skills.

Sam also had difficulty discriminating visual information, familiar and unfamiliar, when scanning small symbols or numbers was required (26th percentile rank). He could do this accurately, but the effort required resulted in slow speeds. To identify two matching numbers in a row of numbers he often had to scan the row of numbers more than once, and he sometimes skipped numbers in his scanning.

Sam also had difficulties that interfered with his expression of information, not just intake of information. On tasks requiring motor reproduction of what he saw, Sam consistently had integration difficulties; that is, he could not accurately copy two designs in relationship to each other. He knew that there were errors in his reproductions but was not able to correct them. When asked to reproduce the drawings from memory, he recalled seven of the nine designs, showing good visual memory, but persisted in his drawing errors. His performance on the Bender–Gestalt suggested a one-and-a-half- to two-year delay, somewhat worse than his performance in previous testing. However, an inordinate amount of erasing was noted in the previous testing, suggesting that attainment of an average score required significant effort to compensate for visual–motor difficulties.

The other expressive difficulty Sam had was a word-finding problem. He did relatively poorly in the Comprehension-Knowledge area, which tests expressive vocabulary. On one subtest, Sam had great difficulty naming pictures of familiar objects (5th percentile rank). However, it was clear that he often knew what the object was but could not recall the name on demand. So, for instance, he called a faucet a "pipe," a globe a "model of earth," and a thermostat a "heat-on."

Overall, the following was learned about Sam's learning style. He is motivated to perform in the one-to-one situation and, by teacher report, in small group instructional situations. He does well when he feels successful and he enjoys demonstrating his prowess and does not get thrown by failure. He has good reasoning skills and can follow an organized approach to problem solving. He learns new information best when information is presented simultaneously in the visual and auditory modalities because each compensates for difficulties in the other. Although he understands meaningful information presented in both modalities, he has difficulty scanning visual information and copying it, and he has difficulty blending sounds he has heard and retrieving words. These difficulties, if not remediated, would be expected to interfere with learning of phonetic analysis, mathematics computation, and written composition.

Test of Achievement: Results

Area	SS	G–E	%ile for Grade
Letter–Word Identification	76	2.0	6
Passage Comprehension	81	2.2	3
BROAD READING	77	2.0	6
Calculation	88	3.0	21
Applied Problems	103	4.0	58
BROAD MATH	96	3.4	38
Dictation	86	2.6	18
Writing Samples	97	3.3	42
BROAD WRITING	91	2.8	26

Test of Achievement: Interpretation

Reading. Sam scored at a beginning second-grade level in reading overall, placing him at the 6th percentile rank in relation to his grade-peers. Both comprehension and word recognition scores were consistent with this overall score. This suggests that Sam is ready for instruction in reading on second-grade-level texts.

Sam had great difficulty attacking words he did not know by sight and sometimes made errors on even simple words, which he was usually able to correct. These word identification difficulties seemed to be due to a number of different factors. He made a number of letter identification errors; for instance, he read "is" for "as" (he self-corrected this error) and "farest" for "fastest." In some instances he read the first part of the word but omitted or misread the ending; for instance, he read "shouldn't" for shoulder, and "person" for personal. These errors may well be due to visual scanning difficulties. He did not use a phonetic approach but tried to find known words within the unknown word, an approach that might help compensate for his sound blending difficulties but that was often not effective because of the inaccuracy of his visual scanning. Thus he read "cor-re-city" for correctly. When reading paragraphs, Sam used context, his good reasoning skills, and his knowledge of the world to guess what unknown words might be and was able to correctly read more difficult words. He still made many word recognition errors but he reread sentences that did not make sense and was then able to correct about one third of his errors.

Sam's comprehension of paragraphs was significantly impaired by his word recognition difficulties. He made so many errors when reading that, even after corrections, he could get little meaning out of texts above the early second-grade level. He has the reasoning and language skills to understand the concepts of higher-level text but his decoding difficulties are too great.

Mathematics. Sam scored at a 3.4 grade level overall in mathematics, or at the 38th percentile rank for grade. However, he was much better at applying mathematical concepts to solving daily living problems (58th percentile rank for grade) than at solving straight calculation problems (21st percentile rank). In large part, this was due to the fact that he made many errors in calculations that he was able to correct when told to check his work; with corrections he improved his calculation score to the 4.3 grade level. This level of performance suggests significant gains from the previous testing in mathematics.

When doing calculations, Sam demonstrated a

good understanding of the procedures involved in addition and subtraction. He knew how to carry and borrow and knew how to place decimal points. He has not yet memorized basic math facts but could count on his fingers to solve basic addition, subtraction, and multiplication facts. Sam initially scored at the 3.0 grade level in calculation because he misread four signs. When told to check his work, he independently corrected all the errors. Thus, Sam's difficulty in visual scanning appears to be interfering with his performance on calculation tasks.

On the Applied Problems subtest, Sam easily demonstrated basic knowledge about money, time, and measurement. He also was able to solve word problems, correctly identifying the appropriate operation to perform and which information was relevant to the solution of the problem. He was able to set up the correct calculations on his scrap paper and to line up and organize numbers correctly.

Writing. Sam scored at the 2.8 grade level in written language overall, or at the 26 percentile rank in relation to grade. Again, there was a significant difference between the two subtests comprising this area. In a test of the mechanics of writing and spelling, Sam scored at the 2.6 grade level, or the 18th percentile rank. In a test that looks at sentence organization but does not penalize the student for spelling or errors in writing mechanics, Sam scored at a 3.3 grade level, or at the 42nd percentile rank for grade.

Sam's handwriting was neat but he wrote somewhat awkwardly, pressing hard, writing small, and having some difficulty forming some letters. His letters tended to sink below the line, and he frequently erased or reinforced letters. Handwriting did not appear to be fluid but required some effort.

Sam knew how to spell some words correctly from memory but occasionally omitted letters. When he did not know a word from memory he tried a phonetic approach with little success. He spelled comb as "kome," which demonstrates a good understanding of the silent "e" rule, but other attempts at phonetic spelling showed limited knowledge of other phonetic principles.

Sam was able to write generally well-organized, complete sentences to describe pictures. He was able to communicate the central information about a picture, despite spelling and grammatical errors. He was willing to produce long sentences despite the effort it required.

Overall, Sam's academic achievement is significantly below grade level in reading and in some aspects of written language, including spelling and mechanics. He achieves at grade level in mathematics when he carefully checks his work, and in the communicative aspects of writing.

SUMMARY: Sam is a child of average intellectual ability who was held back in second grade and who is still achieving significantly below grade level in reading and some areas of writing. He has responded inconsistently to classroom demands over the years in terms of motivation and attention, but he has consistently had difficulties with reading tasks. While he can accurately understand and retain information presented both visually and auditorally, he has some specific basic psychological processing difficulties that are interfering with his learning. He has great difficulty with sequential auditory processing and thus has difficulty blending sounds, he has difficulty scanning sequences of visual symbols and thus is slow at processing letters and numbers and tends to make omission errors, and he has difficulty integrating visual and motor processes so that it is hard to accurately copy designs and symbols without effort. Sam has a learning disability that contributes to his academic problems and may be contributing to behavioral problems. He needs specialized instruction to compensate for his difficulties.

RECOMMENDATIONS: The following recommendations should be considered as a whole.

1. Sam needs specialized instruction in a small class setting of 15:1. He may also need other supportive services. As recommended in the report by Dr. Bernstein, further evaluation of Sam's visual difficulties should be conducted to determine appropriate interventions. Also, an occupational therapy evaluation should be conducted to determine need for intervention for visual–motor difficulties.

2. Sam would benefit from short-term individual counseling to help him understand the reasons for his academic difficulties and to help him take more responsibility for his behavior.

3. Sam would benefit from oral language development classroom activities to increase vocabulary and decrease word-finding difficulties. The classroom teacher should consult with the speech and language therapist to develop such activities.

4. Sam's ability to use good problem-solving strategies should be supported by recognition of them and direct instruction. When he self-monitors, self-corrects, accesses prior knowledge, and relates new information to his previous experience this should be acknowledged and reflected back to him to make his use of the skills more conscious. He also should be directly instructed in such techniques.

5. Sam learns best when new information is presented in multiple modalities. Whenever possible, graphics, demonstrations, written directions, and other visually perceived cues should accompany verbal instruction.

6. Sam needs to experience success in the classroom and should receive positive reinforcement whenever appropriate. Classroom tasks should initially be structured so that he can succeed and he should be given the opportunity to practice new skills. Immediate, informed, and supportive feedback should be given.

7. Sam learns well in small groups and small group learning experiences should be provided whenever possible.

8. In reading, Sam is currently ready to be instructed on second-grade-level texts. He should be directly instructed in areas of difficulty using a multimodality approach. Therefore, a technique such as Orton–Gillingham, Slingerland, or Fernald should be used to teach phonetic analysis of words. Sam's strength in comprehension monitoring should be supported, and he should also be taught new comprehension skills, such as predicting, self-questioning, and previewing texts.

9. In mathematics, Sam should be taught the second-grade-level curriculum. However, he needs to be directly taught strategies for checking his work and attending to signs.

10. In both mathematics and reading, Sam would benefit from aids for accurate visual scanning, such as page masks.

11. In writing, Sam might benefit from learning keyboarding to eventually reduce the problems caused by visual–motor difficulties. He should be allowed to write compositions on a voice output word processing program with spell-checking and auditory prompts for misspellings, such as Write OutLoud.

12. Given Sam's positive response to reading interventions on the Macintosh computer, Sam should continue to work with reading software as well.

Patti Barrett, Ph.D.
School Psychologist

(b) Discussion

The Individuals with Disabilities Education Act has made this type of evaluation relatively routine. One of the underlying premises of this type of evaluation is the idea that, to the extent feasible, children like Sam should be educated in regular classrooms rather than specially treated. Another, sometimes contradictory, premise is that the state has an obligation to the child to provide a meaningful education.

This evaluation made prolific use of school records and interviews with teachers to identify the precise perceived problems. Using interactive interviews and appropriately normed tests, the evaluator then explored the five areas outlined in § 17.05 (intelligence; language; perceptual abilities; academic achievement; and behavioral, emotional, and social development), although it did not track these categories in that order. The resulting recommendations are very specific. Of course, the school might decide not to follow all of them, at which point the parent can decide whether to pursue administrative or judicial remedies. As a practical matter, obtaining an "order" that these recommendations be followed is very time-consuming and perhaps useless. Ideally, a cooperative relationship can be developed, which the evaluator can facilitate by making as persuasive as possible the case for the recommendations, and being prepared to be flexible in this regard.

CHAPTER TWENTY

Glossary

The glossary is divided into two parts: legal terms, and clinical and research terms. References to other terms in the glossary are capitalized.

20.01. Legal Terms

No effort is made here to define specific crimes or torts, as their definition varies from jurisdiction to jurisdiction. For other definitions, see BLACK'S LAW DICTIONARY.

A

ABET. Aid; help.

AB INITIO. From the beginning; from the first act.

ABSTRACT OF RECORD. An abbreviated history of a legal case, from the initial filing to its resolution.

ACCESSORY. A person who contributes to or aids in the commission of a crime, either before or after its commission.

ACCOMPLICE. A person who knowingly aids the principal offender in the commission of a crime.

ACQUITTAL. Used in criminal cases to designate a finding, after trial, that a defendant is not guilty of the crime charged.

ACTUS REUS. The physical act or omission required for conviction of a particular crime; the act or omission must be one over which the person has conscious physical control.

AD LITEM. For the suit; for the purposes of the suit. A GUARDIAN *AD LITEM* is a GUARDIAN appointed to prosecute or defend a suit on behalf of a party incapacitated by infancy or otherwise.

ADJUDICATION. The judgment rendered in a criminal or civil case.

ADJUDICATORY HEARING. In juvenile court, the trial.

ADVERSARY SYSTEM. A procedural system found in the United States and some other countries, in which each party has an opportunity to present opposing views in front of a tribunal that is not itself responsible for conducting an investigation into the facts. To be distinguished from an INQUISITORIAL SYSTEM.

ADVERSE WITNESS. A witness for the opposing party.

ADVISORY OPINION. A formal opinion by a court provided at the request of a legislative body or governmental official, addressing an issue not yet raised in litigation.

AFFIDAVIT. A written declaration or statement of facts, confirmed by oath or affirmation.

A FORTIORI. With stronger reason; much more.

AGGRAVATING CIRCUMSTANCE. In capital or determinate sentencing, a factor that, if proven, tends to enhance the sentence. To be distinguished from MITIGATING CIRCUMSTANCE.

ALLOCUTION. Court's formal inquiry of a prisoner as to why sentence should not be pronounced.

AMICUS CURIAE. Literally, a "friend of the court"; a person or organization permitted by the court to provide information to the court relevant to the subject matter before it.

ANSWER.   A pleading in which the defendant in a civil case replies to the allegations made in the plaintiff's COMPLAINT.

APPELLANT.   The party appealing a decision or judgment.

APPELLATE COURT.   A court that reviews the decision of a lower court, focusing on that court's rulings on the proper law to apply to the case and the proper interpretation of that law. To be distinguished from a trial court.

APPELLEE.   The party against whom an appeal is taken.

APPREHENSION.   In juvenile court, arrest.

A PRIORI.   From the cause to the effect; from what goes before.

ARRAIGNMENT.   The stage of the criminal process at which a defendant is required to plead in court to a criminal charge.

ATTORNEY–CLIENT PRIVILEGE.   A legal doctrine that permits a person to refuse to disclose, and to prevent others from disclosing, communications between the person and his or her lawyer (or the lawyer's agent) that are made during the course of their professional relationship. The privilege is deemed waived by the client under circumstances described in § 4.02.

AUTOMATISM.   A defense to crime. Lack of conscious control of one's physical acts. See § 8.03(a).

B

BAIL.   The release of an arrested person in exchange for security, usually money provided by a bail bondsperson who thereby becomes responsible for the released person's return; designed to ensure the person will appear in court on a specified date.

BAILIFF.   A court official who keeps order in the courtroom and is "in custody" of the jury.

BENCH TRIAL.   A nonjury trial.

BENCH WARRANT.   A document issued by the court, or "bench," authorizing arrest of a person or seizure of property.

BEST INTERESTS.   An amorphous term, used particularly in the juvenile and guardianship contexts, connoting the optimal arrangement or action under the totality of the circumstances. See §§ 11.02(b), 16.02(b).

BEYOND A REASONABLE DOUBT.   A STANDARD OF PROOF required to be met by the prosecution in criminal trials for each element of the crime charged; normally defined as a belief to a moral certainty that does not exclude all possible or imaginary doubt but that is of such convincing character that a reasonable person would not hesitate to rely and act upon it in the most important of his or her own affairs.

BIFURCATED TRIAL.   A two-phase trial. One type of bifurcated trial is that in which guilt is determined in the first phase and sanity in the second phase. Another variant used, particularly in capital proceedings, is a first phase determining guilt and a second phase devoted to deciding what penalty should be imposed.

BIND OVER.   To certify that there is probable cause for grand jury or trial proceedings.

BONA FIDE.   In or with good faith; honestly.

BRANDEIS BRIEF.   A brief using social science research to buttress its arguments. So-called because the first Supreme Court case in which such a brief was submitted was drafted by Louis Brandeis, later a Supreme Court Justice.

BRIEF.   A written argument filed with the court by counsel, almost always required in appellate cases, occasionally at the trial level.

BURDEN OF PROOF.   The necessity of proving a fact or facts in dispute. It consists of both the "burden of production" (the obligation of a party to provide sufficient evidence on a certain issue to avoid a directed verdict by the judge on that issue) and the "burden of persuasion" (the obligation of a party to persuade the factfinder of the truth of an issue, to the degree of certainty required by the STANDARD OF PROOF).

C

CAPIAS.   Literally, "that you take"; a blanket term referring to several types of writs that require a state official to take the person of the defendant into custody.

CAUSE OF ACTION.   A legal claim.

CERTIORARI.   A writ issued by a court to a lower court requiring it to produce a certified record of a case the superior court wishes to review. This is the primary method the United States Supreme Court uses to review cases.

CLEAR AND CONVINCING PROOF.   A measure of persuasion greater than a mere PREPONDERANCE OF EVIDENCE but less than BEYOND A REASONABLE DOUBT; defined as proof that produces a firm belief or conviction as to the proposition sought to be established.

CIRCUIT COURTS OF APPEAL.   In the federal judicial system, the intermediate courts of appeal. See § 2.03(a).

COMMON LAW. Judge-made law, as opposed to constitutional, statutory, or administrative law. See generally § 2.02(d).

COMMUTATION. A reduction in punishment, as from a death sentence to life imprisonment.

COMPETENCY. The capacity to perform a given function with a degree of rationality, the requisite degree depending on the function to be performed. Chapters 6, 7, and 11 all deal with various types of competency.

COMPLAINT. A pleading in which the plaintiff in a civil case asserts allegations against a named defendant.

CONCURRENT SENTENCE. A sentence served simultaneously with sentences for other crimes. To be distinguished from consecutive or CUMULATIVE SENTENCE.

CONSERVATORSHIP. A guardianship (see GUARDIAN) which in some states is limited to control over the ward's fiscal affairs and in others (e.g., California) permits control over the ward's physical person. See § 11.02(a).

CONTEMPT. Willful disobedience to or disrespect of a court or legislative body, which may result in fines, incarceration, or other penalties designed to force the action desired by the condemning agency.

CONTINUANCE. A postponement, usually of trial.

CORAM NOBIS. A writ whose purpose is to correct a judgment made by the same court issuing the writ.

CORPUS DELICTI. The body (elements) of a crime; also, the material substance upon which a crime has been committed (e.g., a corpse, a burned-down house).

COUNT. A single allegation in a civil pleading, or a single charge in a criminal indictment or information.

COURT OF RECORD. A court whose proceedings are transcribed with a view toward appeal. To be distinguished from a court not of record, in which no transcription is taken.

CRIMINAL RESPONSIBILITY. One's accountability under the criminal law for one's acts; often equated with INSANITY, but including notions underlying the AUTOMATISM doctrine and other legal doctrines as well. See Chapter 8.

CROSS-EXAMINATION. The questioning of a witness by an opposing party.

CUMULATIVE SENTENCE. A sentence consisting of several sentences imposed against one offender for separate crimes, to be served consecutively.

D

DECREE. A decision or order of the court.

DE FACTO. In fact; actually. To be distinguished from DE JURE.

DEFAULT. When the defendant in a civil action fails to plead within the time allowed or fails to appear at trial.

DEFENDANT. The accused in a criminal case; the alleged tortfeasor (wrongdoer) in a TORT case.

DE JURE. Legitimate, lawful, but not necessarily in fact. To be distinguished from DE FACTO. De jure incompetency is incompetency as a matter of law (as with a child) even if the person may not be incompetent in fact.

DEMURRER. In a civil action, a defense to the effect that the opposing party has failed to state a claim that is recognized by the law.

DEPOSITION. A proceeding in which a witness is questioned or "deposed," out of court, usually by an opposing party. The deposition is transcribed for use both in preparation for trial and at the trial itself, where it may be entered in evidence in the witness's absence or used to impeach the witness if he or she testifies. See § 18.04(a).

DETENTION HEARING. In juvenile court, the bail hearing.

DETERMINATE SENTENCE. A sentence whose length is established at the time of sentencing. To be distinguished from an INDETERMINATE SENTENCE. See generally § 9.03.

DICTUM (pl. DICTA). A statement in a judicial decision that does not have the force of law or precedent because the court does not rely on it to decide the case.

DIMINISHED CAPACITY. A doctrine permitting clinical testimony relevant to MENS REA. See § 8.03(b).

DIMINISHED RESPONSIBILITY. Although sometimes confused with DIMINISHED CAPACITY, the term actually refers to a degree of mental impairment short of that necessary to meet the INSANITY test. It does not negate MENS REA, but it may be relevant at trial to reduce the grade of the offense, or, more likely, relevant at sentencing to mitigate the severity of punishment. Also known as "partial responsibility." See § 8.03(b).

DIRECTED VERDICT. A verdict entered by the trial judge in a jury trial after a determination that the jury could not rationally decide the case any other way.

DIRECT EXAMINATION. Questioning of a witness at trial by the party calling the witness.

DISCOVERY. The process through which parties to

an action find out, or "discover," facts known to each other or other relevant parties. Discovery devices include but are not limited to DEPOSITIONS, INTERROGATORIES, and physical and mental examinations.

DISPOSITIONAL HEARING. In juvenile court, the sentencing hearing.

DISSENT. An opinion in an appellate judicial decision that disagrees with the result in the court's, or majority, opinion.

DOUBLE JEOPARDY. The prohibition, found in common law and constitutional law, against multiple trials or punishments for the same offense.

DUE PROCESS. The constitutional guarantee found in the Fifth and Fourteenth Amendments that the government will act fairly when it attempts to deprive a person of life, liberty, or property.

DURHAM RULE. A test for INSANITY. See § 8.02(b).

E

EMANCIPATED MINOR. A minor who, as a result of exhibiting general control over his or her life, is found to be no longer in the care or custody of his or her parents or guardians and is thus accorded the rights of an adult.

ENJOIN. The act of requiring a person, by an injunction issued by a court, either to perform some act or to abstain or desist from some act.

EXCLUSIONARY RULE. A judicially created remedy designed to exclude illegally obtained evidence from a criminal trial.

EX PARTE. By or for one party; put another way, done in the absence of interested parties. For example, if the court issues an *ex parte* order, it is issuing an order without having heard argument from the party or parties directly affected.

EXPERT WITNESS. A witness who, by virtue of specialized knowledge or skill, can provide the factfinder with facts and inferences drawn from those facts that will assist the factfinder in reaching a conclusion on the issue addressed by the witness. A lay witness is not generally permitted to offer opinions about the evidence; an expert witness is. See generally § 1.04.

EX POST FACTO. After the fact.

F

FELONY. An offense punishable by death or imprisonment in the penitentiary. To be distinguished from a MISDEMEANOR.

FIDUCIARY. A person, such as a trustee or GUARDIAN, whose duty is to act in the BEST INTERESTS of those whose property or person is held to be in his or her care.

FRYE TEST. A test governing the admissibility of scientific evidence announced in Frye v. United States, 293 F. 1013 (D.C. Cir. 1923), stating that such evidence must be derived from theories or procedures that are "generally accepted" by the relevant scientific community before it may be admitted into evidence. See § 1.04(c).

G

GRAND JURY. See JURY.

GRAVAMEN. The substance of an allegation.

GUARDIAN. A person lawfully invested with the power to and charged with the duty of making personal and/or financial decisions for a person who, due to some deficiency, is considered incapable of doing so.

GUARDIAN *AD LITEM*. A person appointed by a court to represent the BEST INTERESTS of a minor or an incapacitated person who is involved in litigation.

GUILTY BUT MENTALLY ILL. A verdict in criminal cases that first enjoyed widespread popularity in the early 1980s, providing the jury with a compromise between a guilty verdict and a verdict of not guilty by reason of insanity. See § 8.03(f).

H

HABEAS CORPUS. Literally, "you have the body." Typically, a writ directing a state official in charge of detaining a person to produce that person in court so as to determine whether his or her liberty has been deprived in violation of due process.

HARMLESS ERROR. An error that does not require the reversal of judgment.

HEARSAY. Statements or acts described by a witness who did not directly perceive or hear them. Hearsay is presumptively inadmissible unless the maker of the statement (or the doer of the act) can be subjected to cross-examination about the circumstances under which the statement (or act) occurred. However, the rules of evidence recognize many exceptions to the hearsay prohibition, including the LEARNED TREATISE EXCEPTION, the business-records exception, the statement-against-interest exception, the dying-declaration exception, and the excited-utterance exception. Most of these exceptions represent situations in which the law has assumed that the out-of-court statements will be reliable, or that the information in the statement will not be available from another source, or both. See § 3.08(a).

HOLOGRAPHIC WILL. A will written and signed by the testator, but unwitnessed. Admitted to PROBATE in approximately half the states.

HOSTILE WITNESS. A witness who is subject to cross-examination by the party who called him or her because he or she has evidenced antagonism toward that party during direct examination.

HYPOTHETICAL QUESTION. A question composed of proven or assumed facts designed to elicit an opinion from an expert witness.

I

IMPEACHMENT. An attack on the credibility of a witness.

IN CAMERA. Literally, "in chambers"; thus, out of the presence of the jury.

INCOMPETENCY. See COMPETENCY.

INDETERMINATE SENTENCE. An indefinite sentence, with the minimum term usually set at the time of sentencing but the maximum term left up to parole authorities. To be distinguished from DETERMINATE SENTENCE. See generally § 9.03.

INDICTMENT. A document issued by the grand jury accusing the person named of a criminal act.

INFORMATION. A document issued in the absence of an INDICTMENT by a state official, usually the prosecutor, accusing the person named of a criminal act.

INFORMED CONSENT. Consent to a treatment that is based on adequate knowledge about the risks and benefits of the treatment, is not coerced, and is given while the individual is COMPETENT to do so. See § 11.03(a).

INJUNCTION. An order from a court requiring a person to act or to abstain or desist from acting.

IN PARI DELICTO. In equal fault.

IN PERSONAM. With reference to a person.

IN REM. With reference to things, property.

INQUISITORIAL SYSTEM. A procedural system in which the judge is the principal investigator as well as decisionmaker. To be distinguished from ADVERSARIAL SYSTEM.

INSANITY. A lack of responsibility for one's acts due to MENTAL DISEASE OR DEFECT. Incorrectly often used to designate INCOMPETENCY. The various tests for insanity are discussed in § 8.02(b).

INSTRUCTION. An explanation of the law by the judge to the jury, designed to guide the jury in its deliberations.

INTAKE HEARING. In juvenile court, a preliminary hearing for the purpose of determining what disposition of a child charged with a delinquency or status offense is appropriate; dispositions range from diversion from the juvenile court system to adjudication (trial). Usually initiated by a probation or "intake" officer. See § 14.03(a)(3).

INTENT. Mental state ranging, in the law, from purpose to awareness of the consequences or risks of one's actions. See *MENS REA.*

INTERROGATORIES. Written questions drafted by one party to a civil action and served on another party to the action, who then must answer the questions truthfully or state a valid reason why they cannot be answered.

INTESTATE. Without a will.

J

JOINT CUSTODY. Shared parental authority to make decisions about children. It does not necessarily include shared physical custody.

JUDICIAL NOTICE. Recognition by the court of a fact not proven by evidence.

JURY. A group of persons selected through *VOIR DIRE* to hear evidence. The "petit jury," composed of from 5 to 12 members, hears evidence at civil and criminal trials and returns a verdict. The "grand jury," composed of from 12 to 24 members in most states, investigates specific criminal charges brought to it by the prosecutor and issues an indictment if it finds probable cause.

JUVENILE. In most states, a person under the age of 18.

L

LEADING QUESTION. A question that suggests its answer; technically prohibited on direct examination.

LEARNED TREATISE EXCEPTION. An exception to the HEARSAY rule which permits an examining attorney to introduce into evidence the text of a book which is recognized as an authority, either by the court or by the witness being examined. See § 18.04(e)(6).

LEAST RESTRICTIVE ALTERNATIVE. The concept that when the government is authorized to infringe upon individual liberty, it must do so in the least drastic manner possible. See § 10.03(g).

LEGAL FICTION. An assumption known to be false

or of questionable validity but adopted by courts to further legal analysis or promote certain policies, as in the assumption that a corporation is a "person" for purposes of criminal law, or the assumption that a family always acts in a child's BEST INTERESTS.

LIABLE.   In a civil case, a finding by the factfinder that the plaintiff has met the BURDEN OF PROOF on his or her claim.

LITIGATION.   A lawsuit.

LIVING WILL.   Procedure by which competent persons can direct their doctors to treat them in a prescribed way if they become incompetent. See § 11.02(e).

M

MALPRACTICE.   The failure to exercise the degree of skill in treatment or diagnosis customarily expected of a professional.

MANDAMUS.   A writ commanding a government official to take action.

MANSLAUGHTER.   The unlawful killing of another without "malice." Voluntary manslaughter is reckless or impulsive, but still intentional, homicide; involuntary manslaughter is negligent homicide.

MATERIAL.   Relevant.

MENS REA.   The specific state of mind (e.g., purpose, knowledge, recklessness, or negligence) required for conviction of a crime; "guilty mind." See § 8.03(b).

MENTAL DISEASE OR DEFECT.   The threshold mental condition for the INSANITY defense and, in some states, for the DIMINISHED CAPACITY defense. See § 8.02(c)(1); § 8.03(b).

MENTAL STATE (CONDITION) AT THE TIME OF THE OFFENSE.   Those aspects of a criminal defendant's functioning that are relevant to INSANITY, *MENS REA,* AUTOMATISM, or DIMINISHED RESPONSIBILITY.

MISDEMEANOR.   A category of offense less serious than FELONY; generally punishable by fine or imprisonment in jail, as opposed to the penitentiary, for a year or less.

MITIGATING CIRCUMSTANCE.   In capital or determinate sentencing, a factor that, if proven, tends to reduce the sentence. More generally, any factor that tends to reduce culpability at trial or at sentencing.

MOOT.   Undecided; in judicial decisions, a moot question is one that does not arise under the existing facts of the case.

MOTION.   An application for a ruling or order from the court, either verbally or in writing.

MOTION *IN LIMINE*.   A motion to limit or prohibit the introduction of certain evidence, usually triggering a pretrial hearing or removal of the jury to determine the admissibility issue.

MURDER.   The unlawful killing of a human being with "malice" or purpose.

N

NEGLIGENCE.   An act or failure to act that the "reasonable person" would not have committed or have failed to commit.

NO BILL.   A finding by the grand jury that no indictment should be issued; also known as "not a true bill."

NOLLE PROSEQUI.   A formal entry upon the record by the plaintiff in a civil suit or the prosecutor in a criminal case declaring that he or she "will no[t] further prosecute" the case, but which, in criminal cases, does not prevent reprosecution at some later time.

NOLO CONTENDERE.   A pleading by a criminal defendant meaning "I will not contest" the charge. Unlike a plea of guilty, such a plea usually cannot be used against the person in subsequent proceedings.

NON COMPOS MENTIS.   Not of sound mind.

NUNC PRO TUNC.   Having retroactive effect.

O

OBITER DICTUM.   See DICTUM.

OBJECTION.   A formal exception to a statement made by a witness, lawyer, or judge or a procedure followed by a lawyer or judge, designed to have the statement of a witness or lawyer stricken from the record or the procedure aborted. If the objection is "overruled," as opposed to "sustained," it may be "preserved" by the objecting party in order to create a record for appellate review.

OPINION TESTIMONY.   Testimony as to what the witness infers with respect to facts in dispute, as distinguished from personal knowledge of the facts themselves. Generally, only expert witnesses may offer opinions.

P

PARENS PATRIAE.   The authority of the state to act as "parent"; traditionally exercised over children, the mentally ill, and the mentally retarded.

PAROLE.   Conditional release of a convict before the expiration of his or her sentence; failure to abide by conditions of parole will result in the convict's serving the remainder of the sentence.

PARTIES.   Those persons or entities involved in the litigation, as defined by the pleadings in civil cases and the INFORMATION or INDICTMENT in criminal cases.

PENDENTE LITE.   Pending the litigation of a case.

PEREMPTORY CHALLENGE.   The right, exercisable at VOIR DIRE, to remove a person from participation on the jury for no stated reason; each side to a dispute is limited to a certain number of peremptory challenges. To be distinguished from "for-cause" challenges, which are unlimited in number but which require a legally recognized reason (such as evidence that the potential juror has a personal relationship with the defendant) before it can be exercised.

PETIT JURY.   See JURY.

PLAINTIFF.   In civil cases, the person who initiates the litigation by filing a complaint.

PLEA BARGAINING.   The process by which a criminal defendant seeks a reduced charge or a recommended sentence from the prosecutor in exchange for a plea of guilty.

POLICE POWER.   The authority of the state to act to protect the public welfare; punishing criminal offenders is the primary exercise of this authority.

POLLING THE JURY.   Asking the individual members of the jury after its verdict has been announced how they voted.

POWER OF ATTORNEY.   An instrument authorizing another to act. Such an instrument expires when the delegator becomes incompetent, unless it is a "durable" power of attorney. See § 11.02(e).

PRECEDENT.   A judgment of a court that is viewed as authority for deciding similar cases similarly. See *STARE DECISIS.*

PRELIMINARY HEARING.   Any of a number of different pretrial hearings in the criminal process concerning issues such as probable cause to detain, bail, and whether a *PRIMA FACIE* case against the defendant exists. See § 2.04(a)(1).

PREPONDERANCE OF EVIDENCE.   The standard of proof in civil cases, requiring sufficient evidence to show that a given proposition is more probable than not.

PRESUMPTION.   An inference of fact or law that must be drawn by the factfinder upon proof of a predicate fact, unless other evidence rebuts the inference. An "irrebuttable presumption" is one that cannot be so rebutted once the predicate fact is shown. For example, under common law, there was an irrebuttable presumption that children under the age of 7 cannot be criminally responsible, and a rebuttable presumption that children between 7 and 14 are not responsible. In each case, age is the predicate fact that must be proven.

PRESUMPTION OF INNOCENCE.   A presumption that a person charged with an offense is innocent, which can be rebutted through adequate proof of guilt. Somewhat different from the normal PRESUMPTION, since no predicate fact need be proven in order to benefit from the "presumption."

PRIMA FACIE.   Sufficient proof to establish a claim before challenge by the opposing side.

PROBABLE CAUSE.   A reasonable ground for belief in the truthfulness of a proposition. Most commonly used in the criminal law to refer to the degree of certainty required for issuing an arrest or search warrant, or for detaining an arrested person.

PROBATE.   The process of certifying the validity of a will and distributing its bequests.

PROBATION.   The suspension of a sentence at the time of sentencing on the condition that the offender abide by conditions set by the court. If these conditions are violated, the offender may be required to serve the remainder of the sentence.

PROSECUTOR.   An official of the state responsible for charging persons with crime and representing the state against those so charged at pretrial and trial proceedings.

PROXIMATE CAUSE.   Legal cause; generally refers to the event or occurrence closest in time to the injury without which the injury would not have occurred. See § 12.03(a)(3).

PSYCHOTHERAPIST (PSYCHOLOGIST)–PATIENT PRIVILEGE.   A legal doctrine that permits, under limited circumstances, the patient to prevent disclosure of any communication between the patient and his or her treating clinician that was made during treatment. See § 4.04(c).

Q

QUANTUM MERUIT.   As much as is deserved.

QUASH.   To annul.

QUID PRO QUO.   Literally, what for what; in law, something for something.

R

RATIO DECIDENDI.   The principal reason for a court's opinion.

REBUTTAL.   The introduction of evidence attempting to contradict evidence presented by the opposing side.

RECROSS-EXAMINATION. Questioning of a witness by the party that cross-examined the witness; follows REDIRECT EXAMINATION.

REDIRECT EXAMINATION. Questioning of a witness by the party that questioned the witness on DIRECT EXAMINATION; follows CROSS-EXAMINATION. Often designed to "rehabilitate" the witness or to clarify his or her answers during cross-examination.

REGULATIONS. Rules of law promulgated by government agencies, as opposed to STATUTES, passed by legislatures.

RES IPSA LOQUITUR. The thing speaks for itself.

RES JUDICATA. A matter or case which has been decided. A final decision not subject to review.

RESPONDENT. In appellate practice, the party responding to the appeal. In civil commitment and delinquency proceedings, the party subject to commitment and thus analogous to DEFENDANT.

S

SCIENTER. Knowingly; having knowledge.

SEARCH WARRANT. A written order issued by a magistrate or judge authorizing search of the named premises for the named items.

SELF-DEFENSE. A justification for a criminal act when it is based on a (reasonable) belief that one is in danger of immediate harm and when it is in proportion to the perceived danger.

SEQUESTRATION. The act of barring from the courtroom a witness or the jury so as to prevent the witness or the jury from hearing evidence. Also, the act of prohibiting the jury from reading or observing media accounts of a trial.

SERVICE. The exhibition or delivery of a writ, notice, or injunction by an authorized individual to the person named in the document.

SINE QUA NON. An indispensable requirement.

SOCIAL AUTHORITY. A phrase coined by John Monahan and Laurens Walker to refer to social science used to make law, analogous to the phrase "legal authority." An example of social authority would be the use of research about clinical predictions of dangerousness to help determine whether the law ought to impose liability on therapists who do not take reasonable steps to prevent the harm caused by their patients.

SOCIAL FRAMEWORK. A phrase coined by John Monahan and Lauren Walker to refer to the use of general conclusions from social science research in determining factual issues in a specific case (e.g., syndrome evidence, profile evidence, and testimony based on research about eyewitness accuracy).

STANDARD OF PROOF. The measure of proof that the party with the BURDEN OF PROOF must meet, as in proof by a PREPONDERANCE OF EVIDENCE, proof by CLEAR AND CONVINCING EVIDENCE, or proof BEYOND A REASONABLE DOUBT.

STANDING. The right to litigate a given issue, usually dependent on having a property interest or some other substantial interest that might be affected by legal resolution of the issue.

STARE DECISIS. The legal principle stating that the legal rules expounded in decided cases govern subsequent cases; designed to ensure the consistency of legal rules.

STATUTE. Law passed by a legislature and codified; to be distinguished from REGULATIONS or COMMON LAW.

STAY. A stopping of a judicial proceeding by order of the court.

STIPULATION. An agreement by attorneys on opposing sides regarding a procedural or substantive matter involved in the litigation between the two sides. To be binding, it must be agreed to by the attorneys' clients.

SUA SPONTE. At the court's initiative.

SUBPOENA. A process, or document, requiring a witness to appear and give testimony.

SUBPOENA *DUCES TECUM.* A process, or document, requiring a witness or other person to produce named documents or records at trial or at another proceeding.

SUI GENERIS. Unique.

SUI JUDICE. Pending decision before a court.

SUMMONS. A writ directing the sheriff or other proper officer to notify the person named that an action has been commenced against him or her in the court that issued the writ, and that the person is required to appear there on the named day and answer the complaint made against him or her.

T

TARASOFF. A California court decision holding liable therapists who fail to take steps to prevent harm by patients they know or should have known are dangerous. See § 4.04(b).

TENDER-YEARS PRESUMPTION. The PRESUMPTION, still recognized in some jurisdictions, that custody of children of "tender years" (i.e., below two) is best given to the mother.

TESTAMENTARY CAPACITY.   Capacity to execute a will. See § 11.05.

TESTIMONIAL CAPACITY.   The capacity to testify, usually defined as the ability to observe and remember events and to understand the oath requiring that testimony be truthful. See § 7.07.

TESTIMONY.   Evidence given by a witness under oath, as distinguished from written or other tangible evidence.

TORT.   An injury or wrong, committed intentionally or negligently, to the person or property of another. The act constituting a tort may also be a crime. See § 12.03.

TRANSCRIPT.   The official record of judicial proceedings.

TRANSFER HEARING.   In juvenile court, the hearing to determine whether a juvenile should be tried in adult court. Also called a "waiver hearing." See § 14.04(b).

TRIAL *DE NOVO*.   A separate, totally "new" trial; most commonly applied to the trial held in a court of record when a criminal defendant appeals the result in a court not of record.

TRUE BILL.   The finding by a grand jury that a criminal indictment is warranted.

U

***ULTRA VIRES*.**   Beyond the scope of one's authority.

UNDUE INFLUENCE.   Influence that causes a person not to act of his or her own free will.

UTTER.   To circulate (e.g., a forged check).

V

***VENIRE*.**   The group of individuals from which jurors are selected.

VENUE.   The political division in which a court sits, and which thus determines which cases it may hear.

VERDICT.   The final judgment of the judge or jury in a criminal or civil case.

VICARIOUS LIABILITY.   Indirect legal liability for the acts of someone under one's control.   A doctor may be vicariously liable for the acts of his or her employees.

***VOIR DIRE*.**   An examination of a prospective juror to determine whether he or she should serve. Also, a pretrial examination of a witness to determine whether he or she is competent or possesses the qualifications to testify, or whether the information the witness has to offer is admissible.

W

WAIVER.   The relinquishment of a right. If the right is of constitutional dimensions, it generally may be waived only under circumstances that are shown to lead to a knowing, intelligent, and voluntary decision.

WAIVER HEARING.   See TRANSFER HEARING.

WARRANT.   A writ issued by a magistrate or judge in a criminal case authorizing an arrest or a search. See SEARCH WARRANT.

WITNESS.   One who testifies as to what he or she has seen or heard.

WRIT.   An order issuing from a court requiring the performance of a specified act, or giving authority to have it done.

20.02.   Clinical and Research Terms

Many of the definitions in the following glossary are adapted from the American Psychiatric Association's AMERICAN PSYCHIATRIC GLOSSARY (7th ed. 1994). Although some psychiatric diagnoses are defined, official definitions should be sought from the APA's DIAGNOSTIC AND STATISTICAL MANUAL OF MENTAL DISORDERS (4th ed. 1994), commonly called DSM-IV.   For more detailed description of statistical techniques, see D. W. BARNES, STATISTICS AS PROOF: FUNDAMENTALS OF QUANTITATIVE EVIDENCE (1983).

A

ABREACTION.   Emotional release or discharge after recalling a painful experience that has been repressed because it was consciously intolerable.

ABULIA.   A NEUROLOGICAL DEFICIT evidenced by lack of will or motivation, as with an inability to make decisions or set goals.

ACTING OUT.   Expressions of emotional conflicts or feelings in actions rather than words. The person is often not aware of the meaning of such acts.

ACUTE CONFUSIONAL STATE.   An acute stress reaction to new surroundings or new demands, common in adolescence; a loss of memory or orientation, usually associated with amnesia and clouding of consciousness.

ADDICTION.   Physiological dependence on a chemical substance, such as narcotics, alcohol, and most sedative drugs.

ADJUSTMENT DISORDER. Maladaptive reactions to identifiable life events or circumstances. The symptoms generally lessen as the stress diminishes or as the person adapts to the stress.

AFFECT. The outward manifestation of a person's feelings, tone, or mood. "Affect" and "emotion" are commonly used interchangeably. "Blunted" or "flat" affect means the absence or near absence of expression; "inappropriate" affect means discordance of voice and movements with the content of the person's speech or ideas; "labile" affect means repeated, rapid, or abrupt shifts in expression.

AGNOSIA. A NEUROLOGICAL DEFICIT evidenced by failure to recognize objects despite ability to see.

AKATHISIA. Motor restlessness ranging from a feeling of inner disquiet, often localized in the muscles, to inability to sit still or lie quietly. A side effect of some ANTIPSYCHOTIC DRUGS.

AKINESIA. A state of motor inhibition; reduced voluntary movement. A side effect of some ANTIPSYCHOTIC DRUGS.

ALIENATION. The estrangement felt in cultural settings one views as foreign, unpredictable, or unacceptable.

ALIENIST. Obsolete term for a psychiatrist who testifies in court about a person's sanity or mental competence.

ALOGIA. Literally, speechlessness. Most commonly used to refer to the lack of spontaneity in speech and diminished flow of conversation that occur in SCHIZOPHRENIA.

AMERICAN BOARD OF FORENSIC PSYCHIATRY. A group of professionals who administer and grade the certification examination in forensic psychiatry. Questions about the Board can be addressed to 819 Park Avenue, Baltimore, MD 21201. To be distinguished from the American Academy of Forensic Psychiatry, which conducts seminars and training programs.

AMERICAN BOARD OF FORENSIC PSYCHOLOGY. A group of professionals who administer and grade the certification examination in forensic psychology. Questions about the Board can be addressed to 2100 E. Broadway, Suite 313, Columbia, MO 65210-6082. To be distinguished from the American Academy of Forensic Psychology, which conducts seminars and training programs.

AMERICAN BOARD OF PSYCHIATRY AND NEUROLOGY (ABPN). A group of 16 physicians that arranges, controls, and conducts examinations to determine the competence of specialists in addiction psychiatry, PSYCHIATRY, child psychiatry, geropsychiatry, NEUROLOGY, and neurology with special competence in child neurology. The group consists of five physicians from the AMERICAN PSYCHIATRIC ASSOCIATION, four from the American Neurological Association, three from the Section Council on Psychiatry of the American Medical Association, two from the American Academy of Neurology, and two from the Section Council on Neurology of the American Medical Association.

AMERICAN PSYCHIATRIC ASSOCIATION. The leading national professional organization in the United States for physicians who specialize in PSYCHIATRY. Its headquarters are at 1400 K Street, N.W., Washington, DC 20005. Its forensic component is the American Academy of Psychiatry and Law, headquartered at 1 Regency Drive, Bloomfield, CT 06002.

AMERICAN PSYCHOLOGICAL ASSOCIATION. The leading national professional organization in the United States for individuals who specialize in PSYCHOLOGY. Its headquarters are at 750 First Street, N.E., Washington, DC 20002. Its forensic component is the American Psychology–Law Society, headquartered at the University of Nebraska, Burnett Hall, Room 309, Lincoln, NE 68588-0308.

AMNESIA. Partial or total loss of memory. Some subcategories of amnesia refer to the etiology of the memory loss. "Psychogenic" amnesia refers to memory failure secondary to stressful emotional experiences that "cause" the person to be unable to remember certain events; other causes of amnesia include physical trauma (e.g., a blow to the head), chemical intoxication (e.g., alcohol blackouts), or disease processes (e.g., amnesia associated with epileptic seizures). Other subcategories refer to the period in time for which memory is impaired relative to the occurrence of a significant event (e.g., head trauma; see ANTEROGRADE). Still other subcategories refer to the type of cognitive function that accounts for the memory impairment. "Registration" amnesia refers to memories not available because, at the time the events occurred, the individual's mental state would not permit the permanent registration and storing of memory traces (e.g., severe intoxication); "recall" amnesia implies that the memory traces are intact but that other factors interfere with their retrieval. Recall that is sketchy or patchy may be referred to as "partial" or "selective" amnesia.

AMPHETAMINES. A group of chemicals that stimulate the cerebral cortex of the brain; often misused by adults and adolescents to control normal fatigue and to induce euphoria.

ANALYSAND. A patient in psychoanalytic treatment.

ANALYSIS OF VARIANCE (ANOVA). A widely used statistical procedure for determining the significance of differences obtained on an experimental variable studied under two or more conditions. Differences are commonly assigned to three aspects: the individual differences among the subjects or patients studied; group differences, however classified (e.g., by sex); and differences according to the various treatments to which the subjects have been assigned. The method can assess both the main effects of a variable and its interaction with other variables that have been studied simultaneously.

ANAMNESIS. The developmental history of a patient and of his or her illness, especially recollections.

ANTABUSE (DISULFIRAM). A drug used in treatment of alcoholism to create an aversive response to alcohol.

ANTEROGRADE. Amnesia for events occurring after a significant point in time. To be distinguished from retrograde, which is defined as impairment in memory for events occurring prior to a significant point in time.

ANTIPARKINSONIAN DRUGS. Pharmacological agents that ameliorate PARKINSONIAN symptoms. These agents are used to combat the untoward Parkinson-like and EXTRAPYRAMIDAL effects that may be associated with treatment with PHENOTHIAZINE drugs and other ANTIPSYCHOTIC DRUGS.

ANTIPSYCHOTIC DRUGS. Drugs used to control psychosis. See PHENOTHIAZINE DERIVATIVES.

ANTISOCIAL PERSONALITY. See PERSONALITY DISORDERS.

APHASIA. A NEUROLOGICAL DEFICT evidenced by loss of a previously possessed facility of language comprehension or production that cannot be explained by sensory or motor defects or by diffuse cerebral dysfunction.

    ANOMIC OR AMNESTIC APHASIA. Loss of the ability to name objects.

    BROCA'S APHASIA. Loss of the ability to comprehend language coupled with production of inappropriate language.

    WERNICKE'S APHASIA. Loss of the ability to comprehend language coupled with production of inappropriate language.

APHONIA. An inability to produce normal speech sounds, due to either organic or psychological causes.

APPERCEPTION. Perception as modified and enhanced by one's own emotions, memories, and biases.

APRAXIA. A NEUROLOGICAL DEFICIT evidenced by loss of a previously possessed ability to perform skilled motor acts, not due to weakness, abnormal muscle tone, or elementary incoordination.

ATAXIA. A NEUROLOGICAL DEFICIT evidenced by failure of muscle coordination; irregularity of muscle action.

AUTISM. A DEVELOPMENTAL DISABILITY caused by a physical disorder of the brain appearing during the first three years of life. Symptoms include disturbances in physical, social, and language skills; abnormal responses to sensations; and abnormal ways of relating to people, objects, and events.

AUTOPLASTIC. Referring to adaptation by changing the self.

AVERSION THERAPY. A therapy in which undesirable behavior is paired with a painful or unpleasant stimulus, resulting in the suppression of the undesirable behavior.

B

BARBITURATES. Drugs that depress the activities of the central nervous system; primarily used for sedation, or treatment of EPILEPSY.

BASE RATE. The frequency of occurrence of a particular phenomenon in a specified time frame. For example, the base rate for suicide in the general population is approximately 12 cases per 100,000 persons annually.

BAYESIAN EQUATION. In probability theory, a mathematical relationship that defines the probability of an event A occurring, given that event B did occur, as a function of the independent probabilities that A might (or might not) occur and the joint probabilities of B occurring with or without A occurring. For example, let A be the event that a person will attempt suicide, and let B be the event that the person scored above some cutoff score on a suicide prediction test. Assume that the initial probability of a suicide attempt is 5% $p(A) = .05$, and that the probability of no attempt is 95% $p(\text{not } A) = .95$. Assume also that of those who attempt suicide, 80% will have scored above the cutoff point on test B; thus, $p(B/A) = .80$. Finally, assume that of those who do not attempt suicide, 30% score above the cutoff point on B; $p(B/\text{not } A) = .30$. Given these figures, we can then compute the probability that a person will attempt suicide, given that he or she scored above the cutoff point, using the following equation:

$$p(A/B) = \frac{p(B/A) \times p(A)}{[p(B/A) \times p(A)] + [p(B/\text{not } A) \times p(\text{not } A)]}$$

$$= \frac{.80 \times .05}{(.80 \times .05) + (.30 \times .95)}$$

$$= \frac{.04}{.04 + .29}$$

$$= .12$$

BEHAVIORAL SCIENCE(S).   The study of human development, interpersonal relationships, values, experiences, activities, and institutions; fields within the behavioral sciences include psychiatry, psychology, cultural anthropology, sociology, political science, and ethology.

BEHAVIORISM.   The school of psychological theory that holds that behavior is generally determined and explicable by principles of learning and conditioning.

BEHAVIOR THERAPY.   A mode of treatment that focuses on modifying observable and, at least in principle, quantifiable behavior by means of systematic manipulation of the environmental and behavioral variables thought to be functionally related to the behavior. Some behavior therapy techniques include OPERANT CONDITIONING, TOKEN ECONOMY, AVERSION THERAPY, and BIOFEEDBACK.

BENDER–GESTALT TEST.   A psychological assessment technique in which the subject is required to accurately copy relatively simple stimulus figures that are presented to him or her. The organization and accuracy of the drawings can be scored by the examiner in light of developmental norms for different age groups and may be useful in the gross screening for organic conditions that involve impairment in visual–motor areas.

BIOFEEDBACK.   The use of instrumentation to provide information (feedback) about variations in one or more of the subject's own physiological processes not ordinarily perceived (e.g., brain wave activity, muscle tension, or blood pressure). Such feedback over time can help the subject learn to control those processes, even though he or she is unable to articulate how the learning is achieved.

BIPOLAR DISORDER.   A MAJOR AFFECTIVE DISORDER in which there are episodes of both MANIA and DEPRESSION; formerly called "manic-depressive illness," circular or mixed type.

BLOCKING.   A sudden interruption of thinking or speaking, experienced as an absence of thought.

BLUNTED AFFECT.   See AFFECT.

BOARD-CERTIFIED PSYCHIATRIST.   A psychiatrist who has passed examinations administered by the AMERICAN BOARD OF PSYCHIATRY AND NEUROLOGY, and thus becomes certified as a medical specialist in psychiatry.

BOARD-ELIGIBLE PSYCHIATRIST.   A psychiatrist who is eligible to take the examinations of the AMERICAN BOARD OF PSYCHIATRY AND NEUROLOGY a psychiatrist who has completed an approved psychiatric residency training program.

BORDERLINE INTELLECTUAL FUNCTIONING.   An IQ in the range of 71 to 84. An "additional condition that may be a focus of clinical attention" (DSM-IV), especially when it coexists with a disorder such as SCHIZOPHRENIA.

BORDERLINE PERSONALITY.   See PERSONALITY DISORDERS.

C

CASE MANAGEMENT.   (1) A type of health care delivery with emphasis on the development of alternative treatment plans for the patients who have been identified (by preadmission certification, diagnosis, etc.) as potential high-cost cases. Once such a case has been identified, the case manager confers with the patient's physician to develop a less expensive treatment plan and aftercare. (2) The process of following a patient through various types of treatment and helping gain access to care and other social services and entitlements.

CATATONIA.   Immobility with muscular rigidity or inflexibility and at times excitability. See also SCHIZOPHRENIA.

CHARACTER DISORDER (CHARACTER NEUROSIS).   A PERSONALITY DISORDER manifested by a chronic, habitual, maladaptive pattern of reaction that is relatively inflexible; that limits the optimal use of potential; and that often provokes the responses from the environment that the subject wants to avoid. In contrast to symptoms of NEUROSIS, character traits are typically EGO-SYNTONIC.

CIRCUMSTANTIALITY.   Pattern of speech that is indirect and delayed in reaching its goal. Compare with TANGENTIALITY.

CLANGING.   A type of thinking in which the sound

of a word, rather than its meaning, gives the direction to subsequent associations; punning and rhyming may substitute for logic, and speech may become increasingly a senseless association of sounds and decreasingly a vehicle for communication.

CLOZAPINE. An ANTIPSYCHOTIC DRUG with fewer side effects than most.

COGNITIVE. Refers to the mental process of comprehension, judgment, memory, and reasoning, as contrasted with emotional and volitional processes. Contrast with CONATIVE.

COGNITIVE-BEHAVIORAL MODIFICATION. Form of treatment that uses principles of learning to modify the cognitions of the individual as well as his or her behavior. The underlying theory of the interaction between cognitions and environmental contingencies is often called "social learning theory."

COMMUNITY MENTAL HEALTH CENTER (CMHC). A mental health service delivery system first authorized by the federal Community Mental Health Centers Act of 1963 to provide a comprehensive program of mental health care to catchment area residents. The CMHC is typically a community facility or a network of affiliated agencies that serves as a locus for the delivery of the various services.

COMORBIDITY. The simultaneous existence of two or more illnesses, such as the co-occurrence of schizophrenia and substance abuse or of alcohol dependence and depression. The association may reflect a causal relationship between one disorder and another or an underlying vulnerability to both disorders. Also, the appearance of the illnesses may be unrelated to any common ETIOLOGY or vulnerability.

CONATIVE. Pertains to one's basic strivings as expressed in behavior and actions; volitional, as contrasted with COGNITIVE.

CONCRETE THINKING. Thinking characterized by immediate experience, rather than abstractions. It may occur as a primary, developmental defect, or it may develop secondary to ORGANIC BRAIN DISORDER or SCHIZOPHRENIA.

CONDENSATION. A psychological process, often present in dreams, in which two or more concepts are fused so that a single symbol represents the multiple components.

CONDITIONING. Establishing new behavior as a result of psychological modifications of responses to stimuli.

CONDUCT DISORDER. A disruptive behavior disorder of childhood characterized by repetitive and persistent violation of the rights of others or of age-appropriate social norms or rules. Symptoms may include bullying others, truancy or work absences, staying out at night despite parental prohibition before the age of 13, using alcohol or other substances before the age of 13, breaking into another's house or car, firesetting with the intent of causing serious damage, physical cruelty to people or animals, stealing, and use more than once of a weapon that could cause harm to others (e.g., brick, broken bottle, or gun).

CONFABULATION. Fabrication of stories in response to questions about situations or events that are not recalled.

CONFLICT. A mental struggle that arises from the simultaneous operation of opposing impulses, drives, external (environmental) demands, or internal demands; termed "intrapsychic" when the conflict is between forces within the personality, "extrapsychic" when it is between the self and the environment.

CONJOINT THERAPY. A form of marital therapy in which a therapist sees the partners together in joint sessions.

CONSCIOUS. The content of mind of which one is aware.

CONTROL. In research, the term is used in three contexts: (1) the process of keeping the relevant conditions of an experiment constant, (2) the process of causing an INDEPENDENT VARIABLE to vary in a specified and known manner, and (3) the use of a spontaneously occurring and discoverable fact as a check or standard of comparison to evaluate the facts obtained after the manipulation of the independent variable.

CONTROL GROUP. A randomly selected group of research participants exposed to the same treatments as an experimental group except the INDEPENDENT VARIABLE under investigation.

CONVERSION. A DEFENSE MECHANISM by which intrapsychic CONFLICTS that would otherwise give rise to anxiety are instead given symbolic external expression, including such symptoms as paralysis, pain, or loss of sensory function.

CORRELATION. The extent to which two measures vary together, or a measure of the strength of the relationship between two variables. It is usually expressed by r, a coefficient that varies between $+1.0$, perfect agreement, and -1.0, a perfect inverse relationship. A correlation coefficient of 0 would mean a perfectly random relationship. The correlation coefficient signifies the degree to which knowledge of one score or variable can predict the score on the other variable. A high correlation between two variables does not necessarily indicate a causal relationship between them: The correlation may follow because each of the variables is highly related to a third yet unmeasured factor.

COUNTERTRANSFERENCE.   The clinician's partly unconscious or conscious emotional reactions to the patient. See also TRANSFERENCE.

CRISIS INTERVENTION.   A form of brief clinical intervention that emphasizes identification of the specific event precipitating the emotional trauma and uses methods to neutralize that trauma.   Often used in hospital emergency rooms.

CRITERION VARIABLE.   Something to be predicted.

D

DECOMPENSATION.   The deterioration of existing defenses, leading to an increase in the behavior defended against. More generally, a reduction in levels of functioning.

DEFENSE MECHANISM.   Unconscious intrapsychic processes serving to provide relief from emotional CONFLICT and anxiety. Conscious efforts are frequently made for the same reasons, but true defense mechanisms are unconscious. Some of the common defense mechanisms are CONVERSION, DENIAL, DISPLACEMENT, DISSOCIATION, IDENTIFICATION, INTROJECTION, PROJECTION, RATIONALIZATION, REACTION FORMATION, REGRESSION, and SUBSTITUTION.

DEINSTITUTIONALIZATION.   Change in locus of mental health care from traditional, institutional settings to community-based services. Compare TRANSINSTITUTIONALIZATION.

DELIRIUM TREMENS.   An acute and sometimes fatal brain disorder (in 10–15% of untreated cases) caused by total or partial withdrawal from excessive alcohol intake. Usually develops in 24–96 hours after cessation of drinking. Symptoms include fever, tremors, and ATAXIA, and sometimes convulsions, frightening ILLUSIONS, DELUSIONS, and HALLUCINATIONS.

DELUSION.   A false belief based on an incorrect inference about external reality and firmly sustained despite clear evidence to the contrary. The belief is not part of a cultural tradition such as an article of religious faith.

DEMENTIA.   An ORGANIC MENTAL DISORDER in which there is a deterioration of previously acquired intellectual abilities of sufficient severity to interfere with social or occupational functioning. Memory disturbance is the most prominent symptom. In addition, there is impairment of abstract thinking, judgment, impulse control, and/or per-

sonality change. Dementia may be progressive, static, or reversible, depending on the pathology and on the availability of effective treatment.

DENIAL.   A DEFENSE MECHANISM used to resolve emotional conflict and allay anxiety by disavowing thoughts, feelings, wishes, needs, or external reality factors that are consciously intolerable.

DEPENDENT VARIABLE.   The aspect of the subject that is measured after the manipulation of the INDEPENDENT VARIABLE and is assumed to vary as a function of the independent variable.

DEPERSONALIZATION.   Feelings of unreality or strangeness concerning either the environment, the self, or both.

DEPRESSION.   A condition marked by a disturbance in mood or emotion, often associated with feelings of helplessness, hopelessness, and low self-esteem.

DETERMINISM.   The theory that one's emotional life and actions are determined by earlier events or physiological states.

DEVALUATION.   A mental mechanism in which one attributes exaggerated negative qualities to oneself or others. Contrast with IDEALIZATION.

DEVELOPMENTAL DISABILITY.   A substantial handicap or impairment originating before the age of 18 that may be expected to continue indefinitely. The disability may be attributable to MENTAL RETARDATION, cerebral palsy, EPILEPSY, or other neurological conditions, and may include AUTISM.

DIAGNOSTIC AND STATISTICAL MANUAL OF MENTAL DISORDERS (DSM).   The AMERICAN PSYCHIATRIC ASSOCIATION'S official classification of mental disorders, first published in 1952 and most recently published, in its fourth edition, in 1994.

DIATHESIS–STRESS HYPOTHESIS.   A theory that mental disorder is triggered by the interaction between environmental stressors and genetic predisposition.

DIPLOMATE.   One who has been certified as having special competence in a particular professional specialty (e.g., see BOARD-CERTIFIED PSYCHIATRIST). Diplomates in forensic mental health are recognized by the AMERICAN BOARD OF FORENSIC PSYCHIATRY, the AMERICAN BOARD OF FORENSIC PSYCHOLOGY, and the American Academy of Forensic Social Work.

DISCRIMINANT ANALYSIS.   A statistical classification procedure that selects from an initially large pool of predictor variables (e.g., test scores and demographic measures) a smaller number of measures, which, when mathematically combined, maximize the correct classification of individuals into nominal criterion groups (e.g., diagnoses).

DISORIENTATION. Loss of awareness of the relation of self to space, time, or other persons; confusion.

DISPLACEMENT. A DEFENSE MECHANISM in which emotions, ideas, or wishes are transferred from their original object to a more acceptable substitute.

DISSOCIATION. A DEFENSE MECHANISM through which emotional significance and affect are separated and detached from an idea, situation, or object. Dissociation may defer or postpone experiencing some emotional impact, as, for example, in selective AMNESIA.

DISSOCIATIVE DISORDER. Category of disorders in which there is a sudden, temporary alteration in normally integrated functions of consciousness, identity, or motor behavior, so that some part of one or more of these functions is lost. It can be associated with psychogenic AMNESIA, FUGUE, MULTIPLE PERSONALITY, and DEPERSONALIZATION.

DOUBLE-BLIND. A study in which a number of treatments—for instance, one or more drugs and a placebo—are compared in such a way that neither the patient/research participant nor the persons administering the treatment know which preparation is being administered.

DUAL DIAGNOSIS. The co-occurrence within one's lifetime of a psychiatric disorder and a SUBSTANCE ABUSE DISORDER. COMORBIDITY is the preferred term. The former term is most often used to describe the co-occurrence of major mental illness and mental retardation.

DUALISM. Philosophical belief in the separation of mind and body.

DYSPHORIA. Unpleasant mood.

DYSTONIA. Acute muscular spasms, often of the tongue, jaw, eyes, and neck, but sometimes of the whole body. Sometimes occurs during the first few days of ANTIPSYCHOTIC DRUG administration.

E

ECOLOGICAL THEORY. Perspective in psychology, identified with Urie Bronfenbrenner and others, which emphasizes the interaction among the individual and the various systems affecting the individual in determining behavior.

ECOLOGICAL VALIDITY. The extent to which controlled experimental results can be generalized beyond the confines of the particular experimental context to contexts in the real world.

EGO. In psychoanalytic theory, one of the three major divisions in the model of the psychic apparatus, the others being the ID and the SUPEREGO. The ego represents the sum of certain mental mechanisms, such as perception and memory, and specific DEFENSE MECHANISMS. It mediates between the demands of primitive instinctual drives (the id), of internalized parental and social prohibitions (the superego), and of reality. The compromises between these forces activated by the ego tend to resolve intrapsychic CONFLICT and to serve an adaptive and executive function. Psychiatric usage of the term should not be confused with common usage, which connotes self-love or selfishness.

EGO BOUNDARIES. Hypothesized lines of demarcation between the ego and (1) the external world (external ego boundary) and (2) the internal world, including the repressed UNCONSCIOUS, the ID, and much of the SUPEREGO (internal ego boundary).

EGO-DYSTONIC. Aspects of a person's behavior, thoughts, and attitudes viewed as repugnant or inconsistent with the total personality. Contrast with EGO-SYNTONIC.

EGO-SYNTONIC. Aspects of a person's behavior, thoughts, and attitudes viewed as acceptable and consistent with the total personality. Contrast with EGO-DYSTONIC.

ELECTROCONVULSIVE THERAPY (ECT). Use of electric current with anesthetics and muscle relaxants to induce convulsive seizures. Most effective in the treatment of DEPRESSION. Introduced in 1938. Modifications are electronarcosis, which produces sleeplike states, and electrostimulation, which avoids convulsions.

ELECTROENCEPHALOGRAM (EEG). A graphic (voltage vs. time) depiction of the brain's electrical potentials recorded by scalp electrodes. It is used for diagnosis in neurological and neuropsychiatric disorders and in neurophysiological research.

EMPIRICISM. A philosophical approach to knowledge maintaining that knowledge is acquired through observation and experience.

ENDOGENOUS. Originating or beginning within the organism.

EPILEPSY. A disorder characterized by periodic motor or sensory seizures or their equivalents, and sometimes accompanied by a loss of consciousness or by certain equivalent manifestations. May be "idiopathic" (no known organic cause) or "symptomatic" (due to organic lesions). Accompanied by abnormal electrical discharges, which may be shown by EEG.

MAJOR EPILEPSY (*GRAND MAL*). Gross convulsive seizures with loss of consciousness and of vegetative control.

MINOR EPILEPSY (*PETIT MAL*). Nonconvulsive epileptic seizures or equivalents; may be limited only to momentary lapses of consciousness.

PSYCHOMOTOR EPILEPSY. Recurrent periodic disturbances of behavior, usually originating in the temporal lobes, during which the patient carries out movements that are often repetitive and highly organized but semiautomatic in character.

ETIOLOGY. Causation, particularly with reference to disease.

EXHIBITIONISM. One of the PARAPHILIAS, characterized by marked distress over, or acting on, urges to expose one's genitals to an unsuspecting stranger.

EXOGENOUS. Originating or having to do with outside the body.

EXPERIMENTAL RESEARCH. A research approach that tests causal linkages among variables. The experimenter manipulates the INDEPENDENT VARIABLE, attempts to control extraneous conditions, and assesses the effect on a DEPENDENT VARIABLE by randomly assigning groups to various conditions.

EXPLOSIVE PERSONALITY. A disorder of impulse control in which several episodes of serious outbursts of relatively unprovoked aggression lead to assault on others or the destruction of property. There is no organic, epileptic, or any other personality disorder that might account for the behavior. Also called "intermittent explosive personality."

EXTERNAL VALIDITY. The degree to which results of a study can be generalized to the real world.

EXTRAPYRAMIDAL SYNDROME. A variety of signs and SYMPTOMS, including muscular rigidity, tremors, drooling, shuffling gait (PARKINSONISM), restlessness (AKATHISIA), and many other neurological disturbances. May occur as a reversible side effect of certain psychotropic drugs, particularly PHENOTHIAZINE DERIVATIVES. See also TARDIVE DYSKINESIA.

F

FACTITIOUS DISORDERS. A group of disorders characterized by intentional production or feigning of physical or psychological symptoms or signs related to a need to assume the sick role rather than

for obvious SECONDARY GAINS such as economic support or obtaining better care. The symptoms produced may be predominantly psychological, predominantly physical, or a combination of both. An example is MUNCHAUSEN SYNDROME.

FALSE NEGATIVE. An erroneous opinion that something is not present or will not be present (e.g., an opinion of normal behavior when a mental disorder is actually present).

FALSE POSITIVE. An erroneous opinion that something is or will be present (e.g., an inaccurate diagnosis of mental illness or prediction of violent behavior).

FETAL ALCOHOL SYNDROME. A congenital disorder resulting from alcohol use by the mother, with the following possible symptoms: central nervous system dysfunction, birth deficiencies (such as low birth weight), facial abnormalities, and variable major and minor malformations. A safe level of alcohol use during pregnancy has not been established, and it is generally advisable for women to refrain from alcohol use during pregnancy.

FIXATION. The arrest of psychosocial development at a particular stage.

FLIGHT OF IDEAS. Verbal skipping from one idea to another. The ideas appear to be continuous but are fragmentary and determined by chance or temporal associations.

FORMAL THOUGHT DISORDER. An inexact term referring to a disturbance in the form of thinking rather than to abnormality of content. Can consist of BLOCKING, incoherence, LOOSENING OF ASSOCIATIONS, and POVERTY OF SPEECH.

FREE ASSOCIATION. In psychoanalytical therapy, spontaneous, uncensored verbalization by the patient of whatever comes to mind.

FREE-FLOATING ANXIETY. Severe, generalized, persistent anxiety not specifically ascribed to a particular object or event and often a precursor of panic.

FUGUE. A DISSOCIATIVE DISORDER characterized by AMNESIA and involving actual physical flight from the customary environment or field of conflict.

FUNCTIONAL DISORDER. A disorder in which the performance or operation of an organ or organ system is abnormal, but not as a result of known changes in structure.

G

GANSER'S SYNDROME. Also called nonsense syndrome, syndrome of approximate answers, or prison psychosis; classified in DSM-IV as one of the DISSOCIATIVE DISORDERS. It is characterized by giving deviously relevant or approximate answers to questions. Asked what a 25-cent piece is, the person says it is a dime. The syndrome is commonly associated with dissociative AMNESIA or FUGUE. Other symptoms may include disorientation, perceptual disturbances, and CONVERSION symptoms. The syndrome is described most frequently in prison inmates, for whom it may represent an attempt to gain leniency from prison or court officials.

GENERALIZABILITY. The degree to which conclusions of a study may be applied in situations beyond the conditions of the study itself. See also EXTERNAL VALIDITY.

GRANDIOSITY. Exaggerated belief or claims of one's importance or identity, often manifested by DELUSIONS of great wealth, power, or fame. See BIPOLAR DISORDERS; MANIA.

GRAND MAL. See EPILEPSY.

H

HALLUCINATION. A sensory perception in the absence of an actual external stimulus. May occur in any of the senses.

HEALTH MAINTENANCE ORGANIZATION (HMO). A form of group practice (composed, e.g., of physicians and supporting personnel) to provide comprehensive health services to an enrolled group of subscribers who pay a fixed premium (capitation fee) to belong. Emphasis is on maintaining the health of the enrollees as well as treating their illnesses. HMOs must include psychiatric benefits to receive federal support.

HEURISTIC. Serving to encourage discovery of solutions to a problem, but otherwise unjustified or incapable of justification.

HUMANISM. The school of psychological theory that holds that human behavior is ultimately purposeful. Humanists, such as Abraham Maslow and Carl Rogers, have stood as a "third force" opposing the deterministic underpinnings of behaviorist and psychoanalytical theories. Humanistic theories are also distinguished by their phenomenological approach; they generally emphasize the significance of understanding an individual's here-and-now experience (as opposed, e.g., to the individual's childhood or history of reinforcement).

HYPERACTIVITY. Excessive motor activity, generally purposeful. It is frequently, but not necessarily, associated with internal tension or a neurological disorder. Usually the movements are more rapid than customary.

HYPOGLYCEMIA. Abnormally low level of blood sugar.

HYPOMANIC EPISODE. Characteristics are the same as in a MANIC episode but not so severe as to cause marked impairment in social or occupational functioning or to require hospitalization, even though the mood change is clearly different from the subject's usual nondepressed mood and is observable to others. See BIPOLAR DISORDERS.

HYSTERICAL PERSONALITY. See HISTRIONIC personality under PERSONALITY DISORDERS.

I

IATROGENIC ILLNESS. A disorder precipitated, aggravated, or induced by the physician's attitude, examination, comments, or treatment.

ID. In Freudian theory, the part of the personality structure that harbors the unconscious instinctual desires and strivings. See also EGO and SUPEREGO.

IDEALIZATION. A mental mechanism in which the person attributes exaggerated positive qualities to the self or others. Contrast with DEVALUATION.

IDEAS OF REFERENCE. Incorrect interpretation of casual incidents and external events as having direct reference to oneself. May reach sufficient intensity to constitute DELUSIONS.

IDENTIFICATION. A DEFENSE MECHANISM by which a person patterns himself or herself after some other person. Identification plays a major role in the development of one's personality, and specifically of the superego. To be differentiated from "imitation" or "role modeling," which is a conscious process.

IDIOGRAPHIC. Referring to an individual case.

IDIOPATHIC. Of unknown cause.

ILLUSIONS. A misperception of a real external stimulus. Example: the rustling of leaves is heard as the sound of voices. Contrast with HALLUCINATION.

ILLUSORY CORRELATION. An incorrect belief often resulting from selective attention to unrepresentative occurrences, that two variables are correlated in a particular fashion when in fact they are not. See CORRELATION.

IMPULSE DISORDERS. A varied group of nonpsychotic disorders in which impulse control is weak. The impulsive behavior is usually pleasurable, difficult to resist, and EGO-SYNTONIC.

INADEQUATE PERSONALITY.   See PERSONALITY DISORDERS.

INCIDENCE.   The number of cases of a disease that come into being during a specific period of time.

INDEPENDENT VARIABLE.   The variable under the experimenter's control.

INSANITY.   A vague term for PSYCHOSIS, now obsolete. Still used, however, in strictly legal contexts such as the insanity defense. See INSANITY [§ 20.01].

INTEGRATION.   The organization and incorporation of both new and old data, experience, and emotional capacities into the personality.

INTELLIGENCE QUOTIENT (IQ).   A numerical value, determined through psychological testing, that indicates a person's approximate level of intellectual functioning relative to either his or her chronological age or to other persons having similar demographic characteristics.

INTELLIGENCE TESTS.   Any of several psychological techniques for systematically assessing the cognitive functioning and general problem-solving ability of an individual relative to others of his or her own age or of similar demographic background. Intelligence tests typically result in an IQ score, which can be interpreted according to population norms to estimate a person's level of adaptive intelligence. Commonly used intelligence tests include the Wechsler Adult Intelligence Scale—Revised (WAIS—R), the Wechsler Intelligence Scale for Children (WISC—III), the Stanford–Binet, and the Peabody Picture Vocabulary Test.

INTERNAL VALIDITY.   The degree to which any effects of an experimental intervention can be logically attributed to the intervention and to which rival hypotheses may be ruled out. Internal validity can be affected by "history" (when an observed effect is due to an event that takes place between the pretest and posttest); "maturation" (i.e., aging); a "testing effect" (e.g., familiarity with a given test); "instrumentation" (e.g., a flaw in the instrument or observers); "selection bias" (resulting from differences in comparison groups, a validity problem pervasive in QUASI-EXPERIMENTAL designs); and "statistical regression" (where, to the extent an instrument does not accurately reflect the subjects' views or attitudes, etc., the inaccuracy will tend to be in the direction of, or "regress toward," the mean).

INTERVENING VARIABLE.   Something intervening between a circumstance and its consequent, modifying the relation between the two. For example, appetite can be an intervening variable determining whether or not a given food will be eaten.

INTRAPSYCHIC.   That which takes place within the psyche or mind.

INTROJECTION.   A DEFENSE MECHANISM whereby loved or hated external objects are symbolically absorbed within oneself. The converse of PROJECTION. May serve as a defense against conscious recognition of intolerable hostile impulses.

INVOLUTIONAL MELANCHOLIA.   A term formerly used to describe an agitated DEPRESSION in a person of climacteric age. Currently, such patients are not distinguished from depressed patients of other age groups.

IQ.   See INTELLIGENCE QUOTIENT.

K

KLEPTOMANIA.   See MANIA.

KORSAKOFF'S SYNDROME.   A disease associated with chronic alcoholism, resulting from a deficiency of vitamin B_1.   Patients sustain damage to part of the thalamus and cerebellum.   Symptoms include inflammation of nerves, muttering delirium, insomnia, ILLUSIONS, and HALLUCINATIONS.

L

LABILE.   Rapidly shifting, unstable (referring to emotions).

LEARNING DISABILITY.   Difficulty experienced by school-age children of normal or above-normal intelligence in learning to read ("dyslexia"), write ("dysgraphia"), and/or calculate ("dyscalculia"). The disorder is believed to be related to slow developmental progression of perceptual-motor skills. See also MINIMAL BRAIN DYSFUNCTION.

LIBIDO.   The psychic drive or energy usually associated with the sexual instinct. ("Sexual" is used here in the broad sense to include pleasure- and love-object seeking.)

LIMBIC SYSTEM.   An area in the brain associated with the control of emotion, eating, drinking, and sexual activity.

LITHIUM CARBONATE.   An alkali metal, the salt of which is used in the treatment of acute MANIA and as a maintenance medication to help reduce the duration, intensity, and frequency of recurrent affective episodes, especially in BIPOLAR DISORDER.

LOOSENING OF ASSOCIATIONS.   A disturbance of thinking in which ideas shift from one subject to another in an oblique or unrelated manner. When loosening of associations is severe, speech may be incoherent. Contrast with FLIGHT OF IDEAS.

M

MAJOR AFFECTIVE DISORDERS. A group of disorders in which there is a prominent and persistent disturbance of mood (DEPRESSION or MANIA). The disorder is usually episodic but may be chronic.

MALINGERING. Deliberate simulation or exaggeration of an illness or disability to avoid an unpleasant situation or to obtain some type of personal gain.

MANIA. A mood disorder characterized by excessive elation, hyperactivity, agitation, and accelerated thinking and speaking. Sometimes manifested as FLIGHT OF IDEAS.

MANIC–DEPRESSIVE ILLNESS. See BIPOLAR DISORDER.

MEAN. The arithmetic average of a set of observations; the sum of scores divided by the number of scores.

MEDIAN. The middle value in a set of values that have been arranged in order from highest to lowest.

MEDICAL MODEL. A perspective that views abnormal behavior as the product of an illness. The "illness" may be intrapsychic rather than organic.

MENTAL DISEASE. See MENTAL DISORDER.

MENTAL DISORDER. Impairment in functioning due to a social, psychological, genetic, physical/chemical, or biological disturbance.

MENTAL RETARDATION. Significantly subaverage general intellectual functioning, existing concurrently with deficits in adaptive behavior and manifested during youth. Four degrees of severity are recognized: Mild (IQ, 50–55 to 70); Moderate (IQ, 35–40 to 50–55); Severe (IQ, 20–25 to 35–40), and Profound (IQ, below 20 or 25).

MENTAL STATUS EXAMINATION. The process of estimating psychological and behavioral function by observing the patient, eliciting his or her description of self, and formally questioning him or her. The mental status is reported in a series of narrative statements describing such things as AFFECT, speech, thought content, perception, and COGNITIVE functions.

MILIEU THERAPY. Socioenvironmental therapy in which the attitudes and behavior of the staff of a treatment service and the activities prescribed for the patient are determined by the patient's emotional and interpersonal needs.

MINIMAL BRAIN DYSFUNCTION (MBD). A disturbance of children, adolescents, and perhaps adults, without signs of major neurological or psychiatric disturbance. Characterized by decreased attention span, distractibility, increased activity, impulsivity, emotional lability, poor motor integration, disturbances in perception, and disorders of language development. See also LEARNING DISABILITY.

MINNESOTA MULTIPHASIC PERSONALITY INVENTORY (MMPI/MMPI-2). An OBJECTIVE PERSONALITY TEST composed of items that the subject scores as "true–false" as applied to himself or herself. The test contains ten scales for clinical assessment and three "validity" scales to assess the person's test-taking attitude or candor. Other popular tests of this type include the California Psychological Inventory and the Millon Clinical Multiaxial Inventory.

MODE. The most frequently occurring observation in a set of observations.

MULTIPLE PERSONALITY DISORDER. In DSM-IV, this has been renamed dissociative identity disorder (multiple personality disorder). It consists of the existence within one person of two or more distinct personalities or personality states (alters or alter personalities). Each personality state has its own relatively enduring pattern of perceiving, relating to, and thinking about the environment and the self, and at least two of them alternate in taking control of the person's behavior. Characteristically, there is an amnesic barrier between personalities, which may be absolute or, more commonly, unilateral, denying one personality access to the memories of the other but allowing the other personality full access to the memory systems of both.

MUNCHAUSEN SYNDROME (PATHOMIMICRY). In DSM-IV, a chronic form of FACTITIOUS DISORDER with physical symptoms that may be totally fabricated, self-inflicted, or exaggerations of preexisting physical conditions. The subject's entire life may consist of seeking admission to or staying in hospitals (often under different names). Multiple invasive procedures and operations are eagerly solicited. The need is to assume the sick role rather than to reap any economic benefit or ensure better care or physical well-being.

N

NARCISSISM (NARCISM). Self-love as opposed to object love (love of another person). To be distinguished from "egotism," which carries the connotation of self-centeredness, selfishness, and conceit. Egotism is but one expression of narcissism.

NARCOTIC. Any opiate derivative drug, natural or synthetic, that relieves pain or alters mood. May cause ADDICTION.

NATIONAL ALLIANCE FOR THE MENTALLY ILL (NAMI). An organization whose members are parents and relatives of mentally ill patients and former patients whose main objective is for better and more sustained care. Its trustees and chapter officers engage in active lobbying and in education projects.

NATIONAL INSTITUTE OF MENTAL HEALTH (NIMH). An institute within the National Institutes of Health responsible for research on the causes and treatments of mental illnesses.

NEOLOGISM. A new word or condensed combination of several words coined by a person to express a highly complex idea not readily understood by others; seen in SCHIZOPHRENIA and ORGANIC MENTAL DISORDERS.

NEURASTHENIA. One of the SOMATOFORM DISORDERS, characterized by persisting complaints of mental or physical fatigue or weakness after performing daily activities and inability to recover with normal periods of rest or entertainment. Typical symptoms include muscular aches and pains, dizziness, tension headaches, sleep disturbance, and irritability.

NEUROLEPTIC. An ANTIPSYCHOTIC DRUG.

NEUROLOGICAL DEFICIT. An inability to perform because of some interference along the chain of neurophysiological or neurochemical events that lies between stimulus and response.

NEUROLOGIST. A physician with postgraduate training and experience in the field of organic diseases of the nervous system, whose professional work focuses primarily on this area. Neurologists also receive training in psychiatry.

NEUROLOGY. The branch of medical science devoted to the study, diagnosis, and treatment of organic diseases of the nervous system.

NEUROSIS. In common usage, emotional disturbances of all kinds other than PSYCHOSIS. It implies subjective psychological pain or discomfort beyond what is appropriate in the conditions of one's life. Common neuroses are as follows:

ANXIETY NEUROSIS. Chronic and persistent apprehension manifested by autonomic hyperactivity (sweating, palpitations, dizziness, etc.), musculoskeletal tension, and irritability. Somatic symptoms may be prominent.

DEPERSONALIZATION NEUROSIS. Feelings of unreality and of estrangement from the self, body, or surroundings. Different from the process of DEPERSONALIZATION, which may be a manifestation of anxiety or of another mental disorder.

DEPRESSIVE NEUROSIS. An outmoded term for excessive reaction of DEPRESSION due to an internal CONFLICT or to an identifiable event such as loss of a loved one or of a cherished possession.

HYSTERICAL NEUROSIS, CONVERSION TYPE. Disorders of the special senses or the voluntary nervous system, such as blindness, deafness, absence of sensation, PARATHESIA, pain, paralysis, and impaired muscle coordination.

HYSTERICAL NEUROSIS, DISSOCIATIVE TYPE. Alterations in the state of consciousness or in identity, producing such symptoms as AMNESIA.

OBSESSIVE–COMPULSIVE NEUROSIS. Persistent intrusion of unwanted and uncontrollable EGO-DYSTONIC thoughts, urges, or actions. The thoughts may consist of single words, ruminations, or trains of thought that are seen as nonsensical. The actions may vary from simple movements to complex rituals, such as repeated handwashing.

PHOBIC NEUROSIS. An intense fear of an object or situation that the person consciously recognizes as harmless. Apprehension may be experienced as faintness, fatigue, palpitations, perspiration, nausea, tremor, and even PANIC. See also PHOBIA.

NOMOTHETIC. Referring to comparisons between groups.

NORMS. In one usage, a set standard of development or achievement usually derived from the average or median achievement of a large group. In another sense, any pattern or trait taken to be typical in the behavior of a social group.

NOSOLOGY. The classification of diseases.

NULL HYPOTHESIS. Predicting that an experiment will show no difference between conditions or no relationship between variables. Statistical tests are then applied to the results of the experiment to try to disprove the null hypothesis. Testing requires a computation to determine the extent to which two groups (e.g., an experimental and a control group) may differ in their results even though if the experiment were often repeated or the groups were larger no difference would be found. The probability of the obtained difference being found if no true difference existed is commonly expressed as a p value (e.g., p less than .05 that the null hypothesis is true). See STATISTICAL SIG-NIFICANCE.

O

OBJECTIVE PERSONALITY TESTS. Psychological diagnostic tests that are highly structured and have a limited response format, usually one that can be reliably scored by a technician having little knowledge of the theoretical construction of the test or meaning of the responses obtained. Personality inventories consisting of "true–false" responses to series of descriptive statements are representative of this type of test. An example is the MINNESOTA MULTIPHASIC PERSONALITY INVENTORY (MMPI/MMPI-2).

OBJECT RELATIONS. The emotional bonds between one person and another, as contrasted with interest in and love for the self; usually described in terms of capacity for loving and reacting appropriately to others.

OCCUPATIONAL THERAPY. An adjunctive therapy that utilizes purposeful activities as a means of altering the course of illness. The patient's relationship to staff members and to other patients in the occupational therapy setting is often more therapeutic than the activity itself.

OPERANT CONDITIONING (INSTRUMENTAL CONDITIONING). A process of treatment by which, in theory, the results of the person's behavior determine or influence whether the behavior is more or less likely to occur in the future.

ORGANIC BRAIN SYNDROME. See ORGANIC MENTAL DISORDER.

ORGANIC MENTAL DISORDER. Transient or permanent dysfunction of the brain, caused by a disturbance of physiological functioning of brain tissue at any level of organization—structural, hormonal, biochemical, electrical, etc. Causes are associated with aging, toxic substances, or a variety of physical disorders.

ORIENTATION. Awareness of one's self in relation to time, place, and person (i.e., identity).

ORTHOPSYCHIATRY. An approach that involves the collaborative effort of psychiatry, psychology, psychiatric social work, and other behavioral, medical, and social sciences in the study and treatment of human behavior in the clinical setting. Emphasis is placed on preventive techniques to promote healthy emotional growth and development, particularly of children.

OUTPATIENT. A patient who is receiving ambulatory care at a hospital or a health facility without being admitted to the facility.

OVERCOMPENSATION. A conscious or unconscious process in which a real or imagined physical or psychological deficit generates exaggerated correction.

P

PANIC ATTACK. A period of intense fear or discomfort, with the abrupt development of a variety of symptoms and fears of dying, going crazy, or losing control that reach a crescendo within ten minutes. The symptoms may include shortness of breath or smothering sensations; dizziness, faintness, or feelings of unsteadiness; trembling or shaking; sweating, choking, nausea, or abdominal distress; flushes or chills; and chest pain or discomfort.

PARADIGM. A way of looking at the world; the set of philosophical assumptions that underlies a discipline or school of thought.

PARANOIA. A condition characterized by the gradual development of an intricate, complex, and elaborate system of thinking based on (and often proceeding logically from) misinterpretation of an actual event. A person with paranoia often considers himself or herself endowed with unique and superior ability. Despite its chronic course, this condition does not seem to interfere with thinking and personality. To be distinguished from SCHIZOPHRENIA, paranoid type, and paranoid PERSONALITY DISORDER, which are specific diagnoses of which paranoid ideation may be a part.

PARAPHILIAS. The paraphilias (also called perversions or sexual deviations) are recurrent, intense sexual urges and sexually arousing fantasies that involve nonhuman objects, children or other nonconsenting persons, or the suffering or humiliation of oneself or the sexual partner.

PARAPRAXIS. A faulty act, blunder, or lapse of memory, such as a slip of the tongue or misplacement of an article. According to Freud, these acts are caused by unconscious motives.

PARATHESIA. Abnormal tactile sensation, often described as burning, pricking, tickling, tingling, or creeping.

PARKINSONISM (PARKINSON'S DISEASE, PARALYSIS AGITANS). One of the medication-induced movement disorders, consisting of a rapid, coarse tremor; muscular rigidity; or AKINESIA developing within a few weeks of starting or raising the dose of neuroleptic medication or of reducing medication used to treat EXTRAPYRAMIDAL symptoms.

PASSIVE–AGGRESSIVE PERSONALITY. See PERSONALITY DISORDERS.

PASSIVE–DEPENDENT PERSONALITY. See DE-PENDENT personality under PERSONALITY DISORDERS.

PATHOGNOMONIC. A symptom or group of symptoms that are specifically diagnostic or typical of a disease.

PEDOPHILIA. Sexual activity of adults with children as the objects.

PERSEVERATION. Tendency to emit the same verbal or motor response again and again to varied stimuli.

PERSONALITY DISORDER. Enduring patterns of perceiving, relating to, and thinking about the environment and oneself that begin by early adulthood and are exhibited in a wide range of important social and personal contexts. These patterns are inflexible and maladaptive, causing either significant functional impairment or subjective distress. Many types of personality or personality disorder have been described. The following include those specified in DSM-IV:

ANTISOCIAL. In older literature called PSY-CHOPATHIC PERSONALITY. Among the more commonly cited descriptors are superficiality; lack of empathy and remorse, with callous unconcern for the feelings of others; disregard for social norms; poor behavioral controls, with irritability, impulsivity, and low frustration tolerance; and inability to feel guilt or to learn from experience or punishment. Often there is evidence of CONDUCT DISORDER in childhood or of overtly irresponsible and antisocial behavior in adulthood, such as inability to sustain consistent work behavior, conflicts with the law, repeated failure to meet financial obligations, and repeated lying or "conning" of others. Characteristic behavior appears before age 15, although the diagnosis may not be apparent until adulthood.

AVOIDANT. Characterized by social discomfort and reticence, low self-esteem, and hypersensitivity to negative evaluation. Manifestations may include avoiding activities that involve contact with others because of fears of criticism or disapproval, experiencing inhibited development of relationships with others because of fears of being foolish or being shamed, having few friends despite the desire to relate to others, or being unusually reluctant to take personal risks or engage in activities because they may prove embarrassing.

BORDERLINE. Instability in a variety of areas, including interpersonal relationships, behavior, mood, and self-image. Interpersonal relationships are often intense and unstable, with marked shifts of attitude, including inappropriate, intense, or uncontrolled anger. Frequently, there is impulsive and unpredictable behavior that is potentially physically self-damaging, including self-mutilation and suicide threats. There may be chronic feelings of emptiness and boredom or brief episodes of PSYCHOSIS.

DEPENDENT. Inducing others to assume responsibility for major areas of one's life, subordinating one's own needs to those of others on whom one is dependent to avoid any possibility of independence, lack of self-confidence, inability to express disagreement because of possible anger or lack of support from others, and preoccupation with fears of being left to take care of self.

HISTRIONIC. Excitability, emotional instability, overreactivity, and attention seeking, and often seductive self-dramatization, whether or not the person is aware of its purpose. People with this disorder are immature, self-centered, vain, and unusually dependent; there is overattention to physical attractiveness, rapidly shifting and shallow emotions; speech that is excessively impressionistic and lacking in detail; viewing of relationships as being more intimate then they actually are; and seeking immediate gratification. Sometimes referred to as "hysterical personality."

NARCISSISTIC. Characterized by a pervasive pattern of GRANDIOSITY. Manifestations may include an exaggerated sense of self-importance or uniqueness; preoccupation with fantasies of limitless success; need for constant attention and admiration; and disturbances in interpersonal relationships, such as lack of empathy, exploitativeness, and relationships that vacillate between the extremes of overIDEALIZATION and DEVALUATION.

OBSESSIVE–COMPULSIVE. Also compulsive personality; characterized by preoccupation with perfectionism, mental and interpersonal control, and orderliness, all at the expense of flexibility, openness, and efficiency. Some of the manifestations are preoccupation with rules, lists, or similar items; excessive devotion to work, with no attention paid to recreation and friendships; limited expression of warm emotions; reluctance to delegate work and the demand that others submit exactly to his or her way of doing things; and miserliness.

PARANOID. Pervasive and long-standing suspiciousness and mistrust of others; hypersensitivity and scanning of the environment for clues that selectively validate prejudices, attitudes, or biases. Stable psychotic features such as DELUSIONS and HALLUCINATIONS are absent.

PASSIVE–AGGRESSIVE. Aggressive behavior manifested in passive ways, such as obstructionism, pouting, procrastination, intentional inefficiency, and obstinacy. The aggression often arises from resentment at failing to find gratification in a relationship with an individual or institution on which the individual is overdependent.

SCHIZOID. Manifestations include shyness, oversensitivity, social withdrawal, frequent daydreaming, avoidance of close or competitive relationships, and eccentricity. Persons with this disorder often react to disturbing experiences with apparent detachment and are unable to express hostility and ordinary aggressive feelings.

SCHIZOTYPAL. Characterized by a combination of discomfort with and reduced capacity for close relationships and cognitive or perceptual distortions and eccentricities of behavior. Possible manifestations include odd beliefs or magical thinking inconsistent with cultural norms; unusual perceptual experiences including bodily ILLUSIONS; odd thinking and speech; no (or only one) close friends because of lack of desire, discomfort with others, or eccentricities; and persisting, excessive social anxiety that tends to be associated with paranoid fears rather than negative judgments about oneself. Some studies suggest that schizotypal personality disorder might more properly be considered a part of a schizophrenia spectrum disorder.

PERSONALITY TESTS. See OBJECTIVE PERSONALITY TEST.

PHENOTHIAZINE DERIVATIVES. A group of psychotropic drugs that include Thorazine, Stelazine, Haldol, Mellaril, and Prolixin and can cause side effects such as AKATHISIA, DYSTONIA, and TARDIVE DYSKINESIA. As a group of drugs, the phenothiazines are also known as ANTIPSYCHOTIC DRUGS.

PHOBIA. An obsessive, persistent, unrealistic, intense fear of an object or situation. The fear is believed to arise through a process of displacing an internal (unconscious) conflict to an external object symbolically related to the conflict. See also DISPLACEMENT.

POSTTRAUMATIC STRESS DISORDER (PTSD). A disorder in which exposure to a mental or physical stressor such as war, rape, or an accident is followed—sometimes immediately and sometimes not until three months or more after the stress—by persistent reexperiencing of the event, avoidance

of stimuli associated with the trauma or numbing of general responsiveness, and manifestations of increased arousal. The trauma typically includes experiencing, witnessing, or confronting an event that involves actual or threatened death or injury, or a threat to the physical integrity of oneself or others, with an immediate reaction of intense fear, helplessness, or horror. Reexperiencing the trauma may take several forms: recurrent, intrusive, and distressing recollections (images, thoughts, or perceptions) of the event; recurrent distressing dreams of the event; sudden feeling as if the event were recurring or being relived (including DISSOCIATIVE flashback episodes); or intense psychological distress or physiological reactivity if exposed to internal or external cues that symbolize or resemble some part of the event. The affected person tries to avoid thoughts or feelings associated with the event and anything that might arouse recollection of it; there may even be AMNESIA for an important aspect of the trauma. The person may lose interest in significant activities, feel detached or estranged from others, or have a sense of a foreshortened future. The person may also have difficulty falling or staying asleep, be irritable or have angry outbursts, experience problems concentrating, and have an exaggerated startle response.

POVERTY OF SPEECH. Restriction in the amount of speech. Spontaneous speech and replies to questions range from brief and unelaborated to monsyllabic or no response at all, or are vague, stereotyped, or obscure in content.

PRECONSCIOUS. Thoughts that are not in immediate awareness but that can be recalled by conscious effort.

PREDICTOR VARIABLE. The test or other form of performance that is used to predict the person's status on a CRITERION VARIABLE. For example, scores on the Scholastic Assessment Test might be used to predict the criterion "finishing college within the top 33% of graduating class." Scores on the Scholastic Assessment Test would be predictor variables.

PRESSURED SPEECH. Rapid, accelerated, frenzied speech. Sometimes it exceeds the ability of the vocal musculature to articulate, leading to jumbled and cluttered speech; at other times it exceeds the ability of the listener to comprehend, as the speech expresses a FLIGHT OF IDEAS (as in MANIA) or an unintelligible jargon.

PRIMACY EFFECT. The tendency to have better recall of events that occur at the beginning of a sequence. To be distinguished from RECENCY EFFECT.

PRIMARY PROCESS. In psychoanalytic theory, the generally unorganized mental activity characteristic of the UNCONSCIOUS. It is marked by the free discharge of energy and excitation without regard to the demands of environment, reality, or logic. See also SECONDARY PROCESS.

PROFESSIONAL STANDARDS REVIEW ORGANIZATION (PSRO). A physician-sponsored organization charged with comprehensive and ongoing review of services provided under Medicare, Medicaid, and maternal and child health programs. The object of this review is to determine for purposes of reimbursement under these programs whether services are medically necessary; provided in accordance with professional criteria, norms, and standards; and, in the case of institutional services, rendered in appropriate settings.

PROGNOSIS. The prediction of the future course of an illness.

PROJECTION. A DEFENSE MECHANISM in which what is emotionally unacceptable in the self is unconsciously rejected and attributed (projected) to others.

PROJECTIVE DRAWINGS. Any of several projective techniques requiring that the subject draw specific figures or objects. The clinician then draws inferences about the subject's personality, based on his or her interpretations of the style, manner, degree of detail, and other features of the drawings in light of the theoretical or empirically determined meaning of those features. Tests of this type include the Draw-a-Person test and the House–Tree–Person test.

PROJECTIVE TESTS. Psychological diagnostic tests that utilize ambiguous stimulus material to elicit the subject's responses, usually in a relatively unstructured procedure. Because the subject must impose his or her own meanings and organization on the ambiguous material, the responses are viewed as projections of the subject's own personality. Scoring of projective tests is typically complex and may involve a significant amount of interpretation by the clinician. See, for example, RORSCHACH TEST.

PSYCHIATRIC NURSE. Any nurse employed in a psychiatric hospital or other psychiatric setting who has special training and experience in the management of psychiatric patients. Sometimes the term is used to denote only those nurses who have a master's degree in psychiatric nursing.

PSYCHIATRIC SOCIAL WORKER. A social worker with specialized psychiatric training leading to a master's or doctoral degree. See SOCIAL WORK.

PSYCHIATRIST. A licensed physician who specializes in the diagnosis, treatment, and prevention of mental and emotional disorders. Training encompasses a medical degree and four years or more of approved residency training. For those who wish to enter a subspecialty, such as child psychiatry, psychoanalysis, administration, or the like, additional training is considered essential.

PSYCHOANALYST. A person, usually but not always a psychiatrist, who has had training in psychoanalysis and who employs the techniques of psychoanalytic theory.

PSYCHODYNAMICS. The systematized knowledge and theory of human behavior and its motivation, the study of which depends largely on the functional significance of emotion. Psychodynamics recognizes the role of unconscious motivation in human behavior. The theory of psychodynamics assumes that one's behavior is determined by past experience, genetic endowment, and current reality.

PSYCHOGENESIS. Production or causation of a symptom or illness by mental or psychic factors as opposed to organic ones.

PSYCHOLOGICAL TESTS. Any of a variety of systematic techniques for measuring human behavior, including personality, intelligence, attitudes, achievement, academic performance, or other aspects of behavior. See PROJECTIVE TESTS, PROJECTIVE DRAWINGS, THEMATIC APPERCEPTION TEST, OBJECTIVE PERSONALITY TESTS, and INTELLIGENCE TESTS.

PSYCHOLOGIST. A person who holds a master's degree or doctorate from an accredited graduate training program in psychology involving the study of mental processes and of the behavior of people and animals. A psychologist may be involved in teaching, in research, or in an applied position. Those who apply psychological knowledge and techniques in the assessment and amelioration of abnormal or disturbed human behavior are usually "clinical psychologists" and, in most states, must obtain licensing or certification to practice. Other applied practitioners include "counseling psychologists," who typically work with less severely disturbed populations than do clinical psychologists (though many of the same assessment techniques and therapy principles may be utilized), and "school psychologists," who work with problems that arise in school settings.

PSYCHOMOTOR EPILEPSY. See EPILEPSY.

PSYCHOPATHIC PERSONALITY. An early term for ANTISOCIAL personality. See PERSONALITY DISORDERS. Such persons are sometimes referred to as "psychopaths" or "SOCIOPATHS."

PSYCHOPATHOLOGY. The study of the significant causes and processes in the development of mental disorders. Also the manifestations of mental disorders.

PSYCHOSEXUAL DEVELOPMENT. A series of stages from infancy to adulthood, relatively fixed in time, determined by the interaction between a person's biological drives and the environment. With resolution of this interaction, a balanced, reality-oriented development takes place; with disturbance, FIXATION and CONFLICT ensue, which may result in characterological or behavioral disorders. The stages of development are (1) "oral," lasting from birth to 12 months or longer; (2) "anal," lasting usually from one to three years; (3) "phallic," occupying the period from about two and a half to six years; and (4) "Oedipal," overlapping somewhat with the phallic stage (ages four to six) and representing a time of inevitable conflict between the child and parents.

PSYCHOSIS. A major mental disorder of organic or emotional origin in which a person's ability to think, respond emotionally, remember, communicate, interpret reality, and behave appropriately is sufficiently impaired as to interfere grossly with the capacity to meet the ordinary demands of life. Often characterized by regressive behavior, inappropriate mood, diminished impulse control, and such abnormal mental content as DELUSIONS and HALLUCINATIONS. The term is also applicable to conditions having a wide range of severity and duration. See also SCHIZOPHRENIA, BIPOLAR DISORDER, DEPRESSION, ORGANIC MENTAL DISORDER, and REALITY TESTING.

PSYCHOSOMATIC. Referring to the constant and inseparable interaction of the psyche (mind) and the soma (body). Most commonly used to refer to illnesses in which the manifestations are primarily physical but with at least a partial emotional etiology.

PSYCHOSURGERY. Surgical intervention to sever fibers connecting one part of the brain with another or to remove or destroy brain tissue, with the intent of modifying or altering severe disturbances of behavior, thought content, or mood. Such surgery may also be undertaken for the relief of intractable pain.

PSYCHOTHERAPY. A therapeutic procedure involving verbal interaction between a mental health professional and a client. Also, the interpersonal relationship that develops between them; the objective is to help alleviate the client's suffering and/or to increase his or her coping skills.

PSYCHOTROPIC. A term used to describe drugs that have a special action upon the psyche. See PHENOTHIAZINE DERIVATIVE.

Q

QUANTITATIVE VARIABLE. An object of observation that varies in manner or degree in such a way that it may be measured.

QUASI-EXPERIMENT. Experimental design that uses a comparison group of subjects that is not randomly selected. Thus, the group differs not only in terms of the INDEPENDENT VARIABLES but, in contrast to the comparison group in a "true" experiment, also differs in some other systematic way. For instance, a before–after design is a quasi-experiment in that the comparison group (the "after" group) may have been affected not only by the intervention to be studied but also by other factors that can affect INTERNAL VALIDITY, such as aging of the subjects.

Q-SORT. A personality assessment technique in which an individual "sorts" a series of descriptive statements into categories along some ordinal dimension, to reflect the degree to which each statement applies to a target person (either himself or herself, or someone else specified by the examiner).

R

RANDOM SAMPLE. A group of subjects selected in such a way that each member of the population from which the sample is derived has an equal or known chance (probability) of being chosen for the sample.

RATIONALIZATION. A DEFENSE MECHANISM in which the person attempts to justify or make consciously tolerable by plausible means feelings, behavior, or motives that otherwise would be intolerable. Not to be confused with conscious evasion or dissimulation.

REACTION FORMATION. A DEFENSE MECHANISM in which a person adopts affects, ideas, attitudes, and behaviors that are the opposites of impulses he or she harbors either consciously or unconsciously (e.g., excessive moral zeal may be a reaction to strong but repressed asocial impulses).

REALITY TESTING. The ability to evaluate the external world objectively and to differentiate adequately between it and the internal world. Falsification of reality, as with massive DENIAL or PROJECTION, indicates a severe disturbance of ego functioning and/or the perceptual and memory processes upon which it is partly based.

RECALL. The process of bringing a memory into consciousness. "Recall" is often used to refer to the recollection of facts, events, and feelings that occurred in the immediate past.

RECENCY EFFECT. The tendency to have better recall of events that occur at the end of a sequence. To be distinguished from PRIMACY EFFECT.

REGRESSION. Partial or symbolic return to more infantile patterns of reacting or thinking. Manifested in a wide variety of circumstances, such as in patterns of sleep, play, and physical illness and in many mental disorders.

RELIABILITY. The extent to which a test or procedure will yield the same result either over time or with different observers. The most commonly reported reliabilities are (1) "test–retest reliability," the correlation between the first and second test of a number of subjects; (2) "split-half reliability," the correlation within a single test of two similar parts of the test; and (3) "interrater reliability," the agreement between different individuals scoring the same procedure or observations.

REMISSION. Abatement of an illness.

REPRESSION. A DEFENSE MECHANISM that banishes unacceptable ideas, fantasies, affects, or impulses from consciousness or that keeps out of consciousness what has never been conscious. Although not subject to voluntary recall, the repressed material may emerge in disguised form. Often confused with the conscious mechanism of SUPPRESSION.

RETARDATION, MENTAL. See MENTAL RETARDATION.

RETROGRADE AMNESIA. See AMNESIA.

RORSCHACH TEST. A PROJECTIVE TEST requiring that the subject free-associate to ambiguous ink blots. The manner and content of the subject's perceptions and verbalizations are scored and interpreted by a trained clinician to reveal hypotheses and insights about the person's general psychological functioning.

S

SCHIZOID. See PERSONALITY DISORDERS.

SCHIZOPHRENIA. A large group of disorders, usually of psychotic proportion, manifested by characteristic disturbances of language and communication, thought, perception, AFFECT, and behavior that last longer than six months. Thought disturbances are marked by alterations of concept forma-

tion that may lead to misinterpretation of reality, misperceptions, and sometimes DELUSIONS and HALLUCINATIONS. Mood changes include ambivalence, blunting, inappropriateness, and loss of empathy with others. Behavior may be withdrawn, regressive, and bizarre. The clinical picture is not explainable by any of the ORGANIC MENTAL DISORDERS.

SCHIZOPHRENIFORM DISORDER. Clinical features are the same as those seen in SCHIZOPHRENIA but the duration is less than that required for a diagnosis of schizophrenia.

SECONDARY GAIN. The external gain derived from any illness, such as personal attention and service, monetary gains, disability benefits, and release from unpleasant responsibility.

SECONDARY PROCESS. In psychoanalytical theory, mental activity and thinking characteristic of the EGO and influenced by the demands of the environment. Characterized by organization, systematization, intellectualization, and similar processes leading to logical thought and action in adult life. See also PRIMARY PROCESS.

SELECTION BIAS. The inadvertent selection of a nonrepresentative sample of subjects or observations. A classic example is a 1936 Literary Digest poll that predicted a victory for Landon over Roosevelt in the presidential election because telephone directories were used as a basis for selecting respondents. In 1936, telephones were owned primarily by persons in higher socioeconomic brackets.

SENSITIVITY. An indication of a test's capacity to select the individuals who possess the trait or exhibit the behavior that the test is designed to measure. Compare to SPECIFICITY.

SENSORIUM. Synonymous with "consciousness." Includes the special sensory perceptive powers and their central correlation and integration in the brain. A clear sensorium conveys the presence of a reasonably accurate memory, together with ORIENTATION for time, place, and person.

SOCIAL WORKER. A professional with a graduate degree whose primary concern is how human needs—both of individuals and of groups—can be met within society. Social and behavioral sciences provide its educational base. Practice methods are directed to fostering maximal growth in people and to influencing their environments to become more responsive to their needs. The services provided include general social services, such as health and education, and welfare services to targeted groups such as the economically disadvantaged, the disabled, the elderly, or victims of disasters.

SOCIOPATH. An unofficial term for ANTISOCIAL personality. See PERSONALITY DISORDERS.

SOMATIC THERAPY. In psychiatry, the biological treatment of mental disorders (e.g., electroconvulsive therapy, psychopharmacological treatment). Contrast with PSYCHOTHERAPY.

SPECIFICITY. An indication of a test's capacity to select only those individuals possessing the trait or expressing the behavior that the test is designed to detect. Compare SENSITIVITY.

SPLITTING. A mental mechanism in which the self or others are reviewed as all good or all bad, with failure to integrate the positive and negative qualities of self and others into cohesive images. Often the person alternately idealizes and devalues the same person.

STANDARD DEVIATION (SD). A mathematical measure of the dispersion or spread of scores clustered about the MEAN. In any distribution that approximates a normal curve in form, about 68% of the measurements will lie within one SD of the mean and about 95% will lie within two SDs of the mean.

STATISTICAL SIGNIFICANCE. A finding that an observed phenomenon (e.g., a difference between two groups) is unlikely to have occurred by chance. Conventionally, in the social and behavioral sciences, findings are held to be statistically significant when $p = .05$, that is, when a group difference of a given magnitude would be expected by chance fewer than 5 times in 100.

STRESS REACTION. An acute, maladaptive emotional response to industrial, domestic, civilian, or military disasters, and other calamitous life situations.

SUBCONSCIOUS. Obsolete term. Formerly used to include the PRECONSCIOUS and UNCONSCIOUS.

SUBLIMATION. A DEFENSE MECHANISM, operating unconsciously, by which instinctual drives, consciously unacceptable, are diverted into personally and socially acceptable channels.

SUBSTITUTION. A DEFENSE MECHANISM by which an unattainable or unacceptable goal, emotion, or object is replaced by one that is more attainable or acceptable.

SUGGESTIBILITY. Uncritical compliance or acceptance of an idea, belief, or attribute.

SUPEREGO. In psychoanalytical theory, that part of the personality structure associated with ethics, standards, and self-criticism. It is formed by identification with important and esteemed persons in early life, particularly parents. The supposed or actual wishes of these significant persons are taken over as part of the child's own standards to help form the conscience. See also EGO and ID.

SUPPRESSION. The conscious effort to control and conceal unacceptable impulses, thoughts, feelings, or acts.

SYMPTOM. A specific manifestation of a patient's condition indicative of an abnormal physical or mental state; a subjective perception of illness.

SYNDROME. A configuration of symptoms that occur together and constitute a recognizable condition. Examples are the battered-spouse syndrome, child abuse accommodation syndrome, and the rape-trauma syndrome.

T

TANGENTIALITY. Replying to a question in an oblique or irrelevant way. Compare with CIRCUMSTANTIALITY.

TARDIVE DYSKINESIA. Literally, "late-appearing abnormal movements"; a variable complex of movements developed in patients exposed to ANTIPSYCHOTIC DRUGS. Typical movements include writhing or protrusion of the tongue, chewing, puckering of the lips, finger movements, toe and ankle movements, jiggling of the legs, or movements of neck, trunk, and pelvis.

TEMPORAL LOBE EPILEPSY. PSYCHOMOTOR EPILEPSY; see EPILEPSY.

THEMATIC APPERCEPTION TEST (TAT). A PROJECTIVE TEST requiring that the subject create narrative stories in response to a series of pictured cards, usually portraying one or more persons. The subject's responses regarding the thoughts and feelings of the stimulus figures, the nature and quality of their relationship with each other, and techniques they employ in resolving personal or interpersonal problems are interpreted by the clinician to gain insight into the subject's own personality. For use with children, there is the Children's Apperception Test.

THOUGHT DISORDER. A disturbance of speech, communication, or content of thought, such as DELUSIONS, IDEAS OF REFERENCE, POVERTY OF THOUGHT, FLIGHT OF IDEAS, PERSEVERATION, LOOSENING OF ASSOCIATIONS, CLANGING, WORD SALAD, etc. See also FORMAL THOUGHT DISORDER.

TOKEN ECONOMY. A system involving the application of the principles and procedures of OPERANT CONDITIONING to the management of a social setting such as a ward, classroom, or halfway house. Tokens are given contingent upon completion of specified activities and are exchangeable for goods or privileges desired by the patient.

TRANSINSTITUTIONALIZATION. Moving a patient from one facility to another. Compare DEINSTITUTIONALIZATION.

TRANSFERENCE. The unconscious assignment to others of feelings and attitudes that were originally associated with important figures (parents, siblings, etc.) in one's early life. The clinician utilizes this phenomenon as a therapeutic tool to help the patient understand emotional problems and their origins. In the patient–clinician relationship, the transference may be negative (hostile) or positive (affectionate). See also COUNTERTRANSFERENCE.

TRUE NEGATIVE. An accurate opinion that something is not present or will not be present. Compare FALSE NEGATIVE.

TRUE POSITIVE. An accurate opinion that something is or will be present. Compare FALSE POSITIVE.

TYPE I ERROR. The error that is made when the NULL HYPOTHESIS is true but, as a result of the test of significance, is rejected or declared false.

TYPE II ERROR. The error that is made when the NULL HYPOTHESIS is false but, as a result of the test of significance, is not rejected or declared false.

U

UNCONSCIOUS. That part of the mind or mental functioning of which the content is only rarely subject to awareness. It is a repository for data that have never been conscious (primary repression) or that may have become conscious briefly and later repressed (secondary repression). See REPRESSION.

UNIPOLAR PSYCHOSES. Recurrent major depressions. See MAJOR AFFECTIVE DISORDERS.

V

VALIDITY. Accuracy. The degree to which a type of measurement is related to a construct or criterion; for example, the level of CORRELATION between a test score and a criterion (e.g., school performance) which the test is designed to predict.

VARIABLE. Any characteristic in any experiment that may assume different values. See INDEPENDENT VARIABLE and DEPENDENT VARIABLE.

VARIANCE. The square of the STANDARD DEVIATION. Also used interchangeable with "variability."

W

WORD SALAD. A rare form of speech disturbance, sometimes observed in persons suffering from SCHIZOPHRENIA, marked by a mixture of words and phrases that lack meaning or logical coherence.

Notes

In the following pages, references to materials are often made in abbreviated forms, some of which may not be familiar to the reader. To aid in using the notes, the most commonly abbreviated terms are listed below.

A—Atlantic Reporter
A.L.R.—American Law Reports
C.F.R.—Code of Federal Regulations
F.—Federal Reporter
FED. R. CIV. P.—Federal Rules of Civil Procedure
FED. R. CRIM. P.—Federal Rules of Criminal Procedure
FED. R. EVID.—Federal Rules of Evidence
F.R.D.—Federal Rules Decisions
F. Supp.—Federal Supplement
L. REV.—Law Review

N.E.—Northeastern Reporter
N.W.—Northwestern Reporter
P.—Pacific Reporter
S.Ct.—Supreme Court Reporter
S.E.—Southeastern Reporter
So.—Southern Reporter
S.W.—Southwestern Reporter
U.S.—United States Supreme Court Reports
U.S.C.—United States Code
U.S. CONST.—United States Constitution

Chapter 1

1. *See* PETER HUBER, GALILEO'S REVENGE: JUNK SCIENCE IN THE COURTROOM (1991); Sharon Begley, *The Meaning of Junk,* NEWSWEEK, Mar. 22, 1993, at 62; David E. Bernstein, *Junk Science in the Courtroom,* WALL ST. J., Mar. 24, 1993, at A15.

2. *See generally* Richard Bonnie, *Excusing and Punishing in Criminal Adjudication: A Reality Check,* 5 CORNELL J. L. & PUB. POL'Y 10 (1995). *See also* description of Osby trial, *infra* note 3.

3. The abuse excuse became infamous during the trial of Eric and Lyle Menendez (who argued, ultimately unsuccessfully, that their killing of their parents was provoked by years of mistreatment) and later in the trial of Lorena Bobbitt (who defended against charges of assault against her husband by claiming insanity resulting in part from his abuse of her). *Id.* The urban-survival-syndrome defense was raised in the trial of Daimian Osby, an African American who killed two men, also African American and both cousins of his. At his first trial Osby

contended that he acted in self-defense because the victims had threatened him with a shotgun a week earlier, in a year-old dispute about a $400 debt. To bolster the self-defense claim, an expert testified that young African American men are statistically more likely to commit violence or to be its victims than other groups. The attorney argued, based on this information, that men like Osby are afflicted by the "urban survival syndrome," a state, he alleged, in which the level of terror is increased when a young African American male is set upon by other young African American males. Osby's first trial ended in deadlock. At his second trial, the judge excluded the expert, as well as a supporting psychologist, and Osby was convicted. *See* Courtland Milloy, *Self-Defense Goes Insane in the City,* WASH. POST, May 18, 1994, at D1.

4. *See* Daniel Slater & Valerie P. Hans, *Public Opinion of Forensic Psychiatry Following the Hinckley Verdict,* 141 AM. J. PSYCHIATRY 675 (1984).

5. *See, e.g.,* George Will, *Insanity . . . and Success,*

WASH. POST, June 23, 1982, at A27, col. 1 (criticizing the *Hinckley* verdict); WALTER WINSLADE, THE INSANITY PLEA: THE USES AND ABUSES OF THE INSANITY DEFENSE (1983).

6. David Bazelon, *Veils, Values, and Social Responsibility*, 37 AM. PSYCHOLOGIST 115 (1982).

7. *See, e.g.*, JUDITH AREEN ET AL., LAW, SCIENCE AND MEDICINE (1984); JOHN MONAHAN & LAURENS WALKER, SOCIAL SCIENCE IN LAW (3d ed. 1994); John Monahan & Laurens Walker, *Teaching Social Science in Law: An Alternative to "Law and Society,"* 35 J. LEGAL EDUC. 478 (1985).

8. Much of the commentary has been in the form of debate. *Compare, e.g.*, Gerald V. Barrett & Scott B. Morris, *The American Psychological Association's Amicus Curiae Brief in* Price Waterhouse v. Hopkins: *The Values of Science versus the Values of the Law*, 17 LAW & HUM. BEHAV. 201 (1993), *and* Michael J. Saks, *Improving APA Science Translation Briefs*, 17 LAW & HUM. BEHAV. 235 (1993), *with* Susan T. Fiske et al., *What Constitutes a Scientific Review? A Majority Retort to Barrett and Morris*, 17 LAW & HUM. BEHAV. 217 (1993), *and* Jane Goodman, *Evaluating Psychological Expertise on Questions of Social Fact: The Case of* Price Waterhouse v. Hopkins, 17 LAW & HUM. BEHAV. 249 (1993); Rogers Elliott, *Social Science Data and the APA: The* Lockhart *Brief as a Case in Point*, 15 LAW & HUM. BEHAV. 59 (1991), *with* Phoebe C. Ellsworth, *To Tell What We Know or Wait for Godot?*, 15 LAW & HUM. BEHAV. 77 (1991); David Faust & Jay Ziskin, *The Expert Witness in Psychology and Psychiatry*, 241 SCI. 31 (1988), David Faust & Jay Ziskin, *Response to Fowler and Matarazzo*, 241 SCI. 1143 (1988), *and* Jay Ziskin & David Faust, *A Reply to Matarazzo*, 46 AM. PSYCHOLOGIST 881 (1991), *with* Raymond D. Fowler & Joseph D. Matarazzo, *Psychologists and Psychiatrists as Expert Witnesses*, 241 SCI. 1143 (1988), Joseph D. Matarazzo, *Psychological Assessment Versus Psychological Testing: Validation from Binet to the School, Clinic, and Courtroom*, 45 AM. PSYCHOLOGIST 999 (1990), *and* Joseph D. Matarazzo, *Psychological Assessment Is Reliable and Valid: Reply to Ziskin and Faust*, 46 AM. PSYCHOLOGIST 882 (1991); William Gardner et al., *Asserting Scientific Authority: Cognitive Development and Adolescent Legal Rights*, 44 AM. PSYCHOLOGIST 895 (1989), *with* Gary B. Melton, *Knowing What We Do Know: APA and Adolescent Abortion*, 45 AM. PSYCHOLOGIST 1171 (1990); Gail S. Goodman et al., *The Best Evidence Produces the Best Law*, 16 LAW & HUM. BEHAV. 244 (1992), *with* Ralph Underwager & Hollida Wakefield, *Poor Psychology Produces Poor Law*, 16 LAW & HUM. BEHAV. 233 (1992); Thomas Grisso & Paul S. Appelbaum, *Is It Unethical to Offer Predictions of Future Violence?*, 16 LAW & HUM. BEHAV. 621 (1992), *and* Thomas Grisso & Paul S. Appelbaum, *Structuring the Debate about Ethical Predictions of Future Violence*, 17 LAW & HUM. BEHAV. 482 (1993), *with* Thomas R. Litwack, *On the Ethics of Dangerousness Assessments*, 17 LAW & HUM. BEHAV. 479 (1993); Elizabeth F. Loftus, *Science Is Not Golden*, 38 AM. PSYCHOLOGIST 564 (1983), *with* Rogers Elliott, *Expert Testimony About Eyewitness Identification: A Critique*, 17 LAW & HUM. BEHAV. 423 (1993), *and* Michael McCloskey & Howard E. Egeth, *Eyewitness Identification: What Can a Psychologist Tell a Jury?*, 38 AM. PSYCHOLOGIST 564 (1983).

For discussions of the legitimate use of behavioral science in the legal process, *see, e.g.*, REFORMING THE LAW: IMPACT OF CHILD DEVELOPMENT RESEARCH (Gary B. Melton ed. 1987); Thomas Grisso & Michael J. Saks, *Psychology's Influence on Constitutional Interpretation*, 15 LAW & HUM. BEHAV. 205 (1991); Daniel E. Koshland Jr., *Get-Rich-Quick Science*, 259 SCI. 1103 (1993); Gary B. Melton, *Bringing Psychology to the Legal System: Opportunities, Obstacles and Efficacy*, 42 AM. PSYCHOLOGIST 488 (1987); Ronald Roesch, *Social Science and the Courts: The Role of Amicus Curiae Briefs*, 15 LAW & HUM. BEHAV. 146 (1991); Symposium, *The Ethics of Expert Testimony*, 10 LAW & HUM. BEHAV. 1 (1986); Symposium, *Expert Evidence*, 16 LAW & HUM. BEHAV. 253 (1992); Symposium, *Judgment and Decision Processes*, 7 BEHAV. SCI. & L. 429 (1989); Charles R. Tremper, *Organized Psychology's Efforts to Influence Judicial Policymaking*, 42 AM. PSYCHOLOGIST 496 (1987).

9. Faust & Ziskin, *The Expert Witness*, supra note 8; Faust & Ziskin, *Response*, supra note 8; Ziskin & Faust, *A Reply to Matarazzo*, 46 AM. PSYCHOLOGIST 881 (1991). These articles emanated from Ziskin and Faust's three-volume treatise, COPING WITH PSYCHIATRIC AND PSYCHOLOGICAL TESTIMONY (4th ed. 1988), which is designed to provide ammunition for attorneys attacking mental health testimony.

10. We devote considerable attention to the arguments made by Stephen Morse. *See* § 1.04(a).

11. Fowler & Matarazzo, *supra* note 8; Matarazzo, *Psychological Assessment versus Psychological Testing*, supra note 8; Matarazzo, *Psychological Assessment Is Reliable and Valid*, supra note 8.

12. With their potentially profound consequences for litigants, the conflicts of interest and of principle in forensic work are sufficiently common and thorny [see Chapter 4] that the most recent revision of the psychologists' ethical code includes a special section on forensic activities. American Psychological Association, *Ethical Principles of Psychologists and Code of Conduct*, 47 AM. PSYCHOLOGIST 1597 (1992), § 7. *See also* Kenneth S. Pope & Valerie A. Vettner, *Ethical Dilemmas Encountered by Members of the American Psychological Association: A National Survey*, 47 AM. PSYCHOLOGIST 397 (1992). *See generally* § 4.05.

13. United States v. Lewellyn, 723 F.2d 615 (1983). *See also* United States v. Shorter, 618 F. Supp. 255 (D.D.C. 1985); Alan J. Cunnien, *Pathological Gambling as an Insanity Defense*, 3 BEHAVIORAL SCI. & L. 85 (1985). The case study is based loosely on *Lewellyn* and on State v. Campanaro, Union County Indictment No. 632079 (N.J., Crim. Div. 1981), where expert testimony about pathological gambling was allowed. At the time of *Lewellyn*, DSM-III, the version of the American Psychiatric Association's *Diagnostic and Statistical Manual of Mental Disorders* then extant, included the diagnosis of pathological gambling and, according to expert witnesses at the trial, perhaps 20 to 25 mental health professionals had experience with pathological gambling. The study about criminal propensities of pathological gamblers is made up; the study about suicidal behavior, on the other hand, is mentioned in DSM-IV, albeit with no cite. AMERICAN PSYCHIATRIC ASSOCIATION, DIAGNOSTIC AND STATISTICAL MANUAL OF MENTAL DISORDERS 616 (4th ed. 1994).

14. *Durham* was finally overruled and replaced in the

District of Columbia by the test found in the American Law Institute's (ALI's) Model Penal Code, United States v. Brawner, 471 F.2d 969 (1972), and then, as in other federal jurisdictions (by congressional action), by a modified version of the cognitive prong of the ALI test. *See* § 8.02(b). Before *Brawner,* the D.C. Circuit court, then led by Chief Judge Bazelon, made several unsuccessful attempts to salvage the *Durham* rule by limiting its terms. *See, e.g.,* Carter v. United States, 252 F.2d 608 (1957) (defining "product"); McDonald v. United States, 312 F.2d 847 (1962) (defining "mental illness"). *See also* Bazelon, supra note 6.

15. Ideological conflicts may also be substantial within particular mental health professions, particularly when leaders of professional organizations rather than ordinary practitioners attempt to shape mental health policy. *See, e.g.,* Lynn Kahle & Bruce D. Sales, *Comment on "Civil Commitment,"* 2 MENTAL DISABILITY L. REP. 677 (1978); Gary B. Melton, *Organized Psychology and Legal Policymaking: Involvement in the Post-Hinckley Debate,* 16 PROF. PSYCHOL.: RESEARCH & PRAC. 810 (1985).

16. Such a division among the professions was observed, for example, in the amicus briefs submitted in Washington v. Harper, 494 U.S. 210 (1990) (whether prisoners have a constitutional right to refuse psychoactive medication), Mills v. Rogers, 457 U.S. 291 (1982) (whether mental patients have a constitutional right to refuse psychoactive medication), and Parham v. J.R., 442 U.S. 584 (1979) (whether parents may admit their child to a mental hospital without a hearing). In a concurring opinion in *Harper,* 494 U.S. at 178, Justice Blackmun noted his ambivalence in evaluating the conflicting briefs of the American Psychiatric Association and the American Psychological Association.

17. *See* Norman G. Poythress, *Psychiatric Expertise in Civil Commitment: Training Attorneys to Cope with Expert Testimony,* 2 LAW & HUM. BEHAV. 1 (1978).

18. Most correlation coefficients, when squared, indicate the proportion of variance in a given phenomenon (i.e., the proportion of individual or group differences) accounted for by a second variable.

19. The degree to which such control is achieved is called *internal validity.* Generally, the highest level of internal validity is achieved in an *experiment* (also known as a *clinical trial*), in which participants are randomly assigned to conditions that vary only with respect to one variable. Because of the appearance of unfairness attached to random assignment (e.g., it is difficult to imagine judges randomly assigning children to various custody arrangements), such a high level of control is rarely accomplished in research on problems of legal policy. *See* § 20.02, Glossary, Clinical and Research Terms.

20. The real-world generalizability of a study is called its *external validity.* In the leading case on use of scientific evidence, the Supreme Court noted that the question of experts' *assistance to the trier of fact* is primarily one of *relevance* or, in scientific terms, *generalizability.* Daubert v. Merrell Dow Pharmaceuticals, 509 U.S. 579, 591 (1993). *See* § 20.02.

21. Although there are a number of kinds of scientific reliability, in the present context *reliability* refers to the similarity of conclusion by two or more observers. Generally, it describes the degree of elimination of error in observation (i.e., the repeatability and stability of measurement). *See* § 20.02. As used in evidence law, reliability is synonymous with scientific *validity.* Daubert v. Merrell Dow Pharmaceuticals, 509 U.S. 590–591 n.9 (1993).

22. In scientific terms, *validity* refers to the degree to which an observation actually measures something; commonly, it is established by the strength of correlation between one form of observation and a criterion (e.g., the validity of an instrument to measure disability in a guardianship proceeding may be established in part by a strong correlation with demonstrated performance on various tasks in the community). *See* § 20.02.

23. Mental health professionals often have persisted in particular forms of practice even in the face of unfavorable scientific evidence. *See, e.g.,* CHARLES A. KIESLER & AMY E. SIBULKIN, MENTAL HOSPITALIZATION: MYTHS AND FACTS ABOUT A NATIONAL CRISIS (1987); Stephen J. Morse, *Failed Explanations and Criminal Responsibility: Experts and the Unconscious,* 68 VA. L. REV. 971, 991–1018 (1982). Moreover, mental health professionals are subject to the same cognitive biases that distort the decisionmaking of people in general. As two leading cognitive psychologists have summarized, "We hold a . . . view, [also] expressed by Amos Tversky [another eminent cognitive psychologist], that there is *no* inferential failure that can be demonstrated with untrained undergraduates that cannot also (at least with a little ingenuity) be demonstrated in somewhat more subtle form in the highly trained scientist." RICHARD NISBETT & LEE ROSS, HUM. INFERENCE: STRATEGIES AND SHORTCOMINGS OF SOCIAL JUDGMENT 14 (1980). Indeed, the detailed case-specific information available to clinicians is likely to build unduly both their own and legal authorities' confidence in the accuracy of clinical judgments. Hal R. Arkes, *Principles in Judgment/Decision Making Research Pertinent to Legal Proceedings,* 7 BEHAVIORAL SCI. & L. 429, 445–47 (1989) and citations therein; Baruch Fischoff et al., *Knowing with Certainty: The Appropriateness of Extreme Confidence,* 3 J. EXPERIMENTAL PSYCHOL.: HUM. PERCEPTION & PERFORMANCE 552 (1977); Gary Wells & Donna Murray, *Eyewitness Confidence,* in EYEWITNESS TESTIMONY: PSYCHOLOGICAL PERSPECTIVES 155, 161 (Gary Wells & Elizabeth Loftus eds. 1984); *cf.* Elizabeth Loftus & Willem Wagenaar, *Lawyers' Prediction of Success,* 28 JURIMETRICS J. 437 (1988).

24. *See, e.g., In re* Hayes, 93 Wash. 228, 608 P.2d 635 (1980).

25. *See* Michael Moore, *Mental Illness and Responsibility,* 39 BULL. MENNINGER CLIN. 308 (1975). For some legal tests that are strictly "cognitive," there is no need to consider problems of volition. The historic *M'Naghten* test of insanity does not require examination of voluntariness of action, *see* § 8.02(b), although it is arguable that it is rooted in assumptions about the class of persons for whom choices to avoid criminal behavior are too hard. In general, the competencies also are theoretically cognitive, although in most instances (e.g., competency to confess),

there is a prong of "voluntariness" in the test. *See* Chapters 7 & 11.

26. Joseph Grano, *Voluntariness, Free Will, and the Law of Confessions,* 65 VA. L. REV. 858, 886 (1979).

27. *See, e.g.,* BURRHUS F. SKINNER, SCIENCE AND HUM. BEHAVIOR (1953); BURRHUS F. SKINNER, BEYOND FREEDOM AND DIGNITY (1971).

28. Sigmund Freud, *Psychopathology of Everyday Life,* in 6 THE STANDARD EDITION OF THE COMPLETE PSYCHOLOGICAL WORKS (James Strachey ed., 1960) (orig. publ. 1901).

29. *See, e.g.,* HEINZ HARTMANN, THE EGO AND THE PROBLEM OF ADAPTATION (1958) (orig. publ. 1939).

30. In Freud's initial theory, psychic structures developed through the process of interaction between (1) the infant and his or her collection of instinctual drives and (2) the demands and limits of reality. Later psychoanalytic theorists, *e.g.,* HARTMANN, *id.,* argued that some aspects of cognition were determined by innate, adaptive structures rather than a history of conflict. For a readable discussion of these and other basic developments in psychoanalytic theory, *see* PHILIP HOLZMAN, PSYCHOANALYSIS AND PSYCHOPATHOLOGY (1970).

31. ROLLO MAY, LOVE AND WILL 199 (1969).

32. There really is no single medical model—a point that is sometimes ignored, with resulting confusion. For example, psychodynamic clinicians frequently focus on intrapsychic "pathology." Hence, the disorder is believed to be an underlying disease that presents behavioral symptoms; however, the disease is not viewed as a manifestation of *organic* pathology. Regardless, the well-known arguments by Szasz and others about the social and moral inferences required to determine that behavioral aberrations are products of a disease apply to both organic and nonorganic medical models. *See* THEODORE SARBIN & JAMES MANCUSO, SCHIZOPHRENIA: MEDICAL DIAGNOSIS OR MORAL VERDICT? (1980); THOMAS SZASZ, LAW, LIBERTY AND PSYCHIATRY (1963); THOMAS SZASZ, THE MYTH OF MENTAL ILLNESS (rev. ed. 1974).

33. An exception may occur when a defendant with epilepsy was aware of his condition and did not take proper precautions to ensure that no one is injured as a result of behavior caused by the illness. *See, e.g.,* People v. Decina, 2 N.Y.2d 133, 138 N.E.2d 799, 157 N.Y.S.2d 558 (1956). *See generally* § 8.03(a).

34. *See* DAVID ROSENTHAL, GENETICS OF PSYCHOPATHOLOGY (1971).

35. An extraordinary investment is being made in the Human Genome Project, a huge initiative sponsored by the U.S. Departments of Energy and of Health and Human Services. This initiative is directed toward "mapping" the human genome (i.e., identifying the functional significance of particular genetic patterns).

36. *See, e.g.,* MICHAEL MOORE, LAW AND PSYCHIATRY: RETHINKING THE RELATIONSHIP (1985)(discussed in more detail in § 8.02(c)(2); Stephen Morse, *Brain and Blame,* 84 GEO. L. J. 547 (1996).

37. For a discussion of the implications of this point for mental health professionals involved in child protection cases, *see* Gary B. Melton, *Doing Justice and Doing*

Good: Conflicts for Mental Health Professionals, FUTURE OF CHILDREN, Summer/Fall 1994, at 102.

38. There is, of course, the possibility that the expert will be subtly swayed by the attorney's "preparation" of him or her and by the desire simply to be helpful. *See* Michael J. Saks, *Opportunities Lost: The Theory and the Practice of Using Developmental Knowledge in the Adversary Trial,* in REFORMING THE LAW: IMPACT OF CHILD DEVELOPMENT RESEARCH 179 (Gary B. Melton ed. 1987).

39. Paul Freund, *Is the Law Ready for Human Experimentation?,* 22 AM. PSYCHOLOGIST 393, 394 (1967).

40. *E.g.,* H.L. v. Matheson, 450 U.S. 398 (1981); Parham v. J.R., 442 U.S. 584 (1979). *See* Gary B. Melton, *Developmental Psychology and the Law: The State of the Art,* 22 J. FAM. L. 445 (1984); *see also* Gail S. Perry & Gary B. Melton, *Precedential Value of Judicial Notice of Social Facts: Parham as an Example,* 22 J. FAM. L. 633 (1984) (judicially noticed social facts sometimes take on precedential value of their own and obscure the meaning of case holdings). Although there is some controversy about the confidence that one can have in conclusions about the relative competence of adolescents and adults, *see* Gardner et al., *supra* note 8, there is little disagreement that the foundation is lacking for judicial conclusions about widespread incompetence of adolescents. *See* Gary B. Melton, *APA and Adolescent Abortion: Knowing What We Do Know,* 45 AM. PSYCHOLOGIST 1171 (1990).

41. *See generally* Gary B. Melton, *The Law Is a Good Thing (Psychology Is, Too): Human Rights in Psychological Jurisprudence,* 16 LAW & HUM. BEHAV. 381 (1992) (discussing the relation of human rights to psychological evidence).

42. Craig Haney, *Psychology and Legal Change: On the Limits of a Factual Jurisprudence,* 4 LAW & HUM. BEHAV. 147, 165 (1980).

43. *See* § 18.05 and citations therein.

44. *See, e.g.,* United States v. Serna, 799 F.2d 842 (2d Cir. 1986); United States v. Amaral, 488 F.2d 1148 (9th Cir. 1973) (rejecting such testimony). Some evidence exists for a legal preference for testimony by clinicians even when basic research is being presented. *See* § 18.05(a).

45. Michael Martin, *The Uncertain Rule of Certainty: An Analysis and Proposal for a Federal Evidence Rule,* 20 WAYNE L. REV. 781, 804–05 (1974).

46. An amusing account of one psychologist's attempt to describe to a jury his reservations about the term "reasonable psychological certainty" is found in Norman G. Poythress, *Concerning Reform in Expert Testimony: An Open Letter from a Practicing Psychologist,* 6 LAW & HUM. BEHAV. 39 (1982); *see also* Stephen J. Morse, *Reforming Expert Testimony: An Open Response from the Tower (and Trenches),* 6 LAW & HUM. BEHAV. 45 (1982).

47. State v. Middleton, 668 P.2d 371 (Or. 1983). Similar testimony has been at issue in scores of appellate cases in recent years. *See* § 15.04(c)(4).

48. State v. Loebach, 310 N.W.2d (Minn. 1981).

49. *See* United States v. Mendenhall, 446 U.S. 544 (1980). In the surveillance campaign of which this case was a part, the stops were not solely the result of correlation between those stopped and the profile. Tips from in-

formants, information from ticket agents, and other sources all contributed.

50. This type of evidence has been called "social framework" evidence. *See* Laurens Walker and John Monahan, *Social Frameworks: A New Use of Social Science in Law,* 73 VA. L. REV. 559 (1987). The phrase refers to generalizable information that is presented to provide a framework with which to determine a factual issue (e.g., reliability of an eyewitness identification) in a particular case. Walker and Monahan argue that such information (like law) should be presented to the court through briefs and to the jury through instructions.

51. Laurence H. Tribe, *Trial by Mathematics: Precision and Ritual in the Legal Process,* 84 HARV. L. REV. 1329 (1971).

52. Tribe would permit mathematical evidence to be presented to negate a misleading impression that might be left by expert opinion. *Id.* at 1377.

53. A Bayesian analysis provides a method for determining the probability that a certain event or events influenced another event. *See* § 20.02, Glossary, Clinical and Research Terms.

54. Tribe, *supra* note 51, at 1368–72.

55. *Id.* at 1361–66.

56. *Id.* at 1372–75.

57. *Id.* at 1375–77.

58. Michael J. Saks & Robert Kidd, *Human Information Processing and Adjudication,* 15 LAW & SOC'Y REV. 123 (1980–81).

59. *See* Daniel Goodman, *Demographic Evidence in Capital Sentencing,* 39 STAN. L. REV. 499, 508–27 (1987).

60. *See, e.g.,* Goodman, *supra* note 59; Barbara Underwood, *Law and the Crystal Ball: Predicting Behavior with Statistical Inference and Individualized Judgment,* 88 YALE L.J. 1408 (1979).

61. Federal Rule of Evidence 401 states that all relevant evidence is admissible except as provided for in other rules. The principle rule limiting the admissibility of relevant evidence is Rule 403, which bars evidence whose "probative value is substantially outweighed by the danger of unfair prejudice, confusion of the issues, or misleading the jury, or by considerations of undue delay, waste of time, or needless presentation of cumulative evidence." All relevant evidence is "prejudicial" to one party or the other. When used in this chapter, "prejudice" refers to the "unfair prejudice" mentioned in Rule 403, meaning a tendency on the part of the evidence to mislead or "overpower" the jury.

62. *See* Morgan Cloud, *Search and Seizure by the Numbers: The Drug Courier Profile and Judicial Review of Investigative Formulas,* 65 B.U. L. REV. 843 (1985)(arguing that such profiles should not be used because they are not based on anything intrinsic to the particular individual stopped, often rely only on "innocent" facts, and are made up on an ad hoc basis).

63. *See* Christopher Slobogin, *The World Without a Fourth Amendment,* 39 U.C.L.A. L. REV. 1, 82–86 (1991)(conceding that such profiles are questionable statistically, but arguing that if a solid statistical foundation does exist, use of such profiles to stop individuals is little

different from traditional policework which relies on past experiences, and in any event is not inimical to the probability assessment at issue during the investigative phase).

64. FED. R. EVID. 404.

65. *See* Arkes, *supra* note 23, at 435–42 and citations therein.

66. *Cf.* Christopher Slobogin, *Dangerousness and Expertise,* 133 U. PA. L. REV. 97, 141–48 (1984).

67. FED. R. EVID. 704, advisory committee's note.

68. *See* Christopher Slobogin, *The "Ultimate Issue" Issue,* 7 BEHAVIORAL SCI. & L. 259, 259–60 (1989), and citations therein. *But see* Richard Rogers & Charles P. Ewing, *Ultimate Opinion Proscriptions: A Cosmetic Fix and a Plea for Empiricism,* 13 LAW & HUM. BEHAV. 357 (1989).

69. *See, e.g.,* American Psychological Association, *supra* note 12, especially Principle A & Standards. 1.04, 3.03, 7.01, & 7.04; Committee on Ethical Guidelines for Forensic Psychologists, *Specialty Guidelines for Forensic Psychologists,* 15 LAW & HUM. BEHAV. 655 (1991), Guideline III. These provisions are discussed in detail in § 18.05.

The qualifier in regard to role (i.e., that clinicians *acting as experts* should refrain from providing ultimate-issue opinions) relates to the fact that mental health professionals sometimes are in the role of legal decisionmaker. For example, mental health professionals often are empowered to issue emergency orders as the first step in civil commitment, and they always are required to report suspected child maltreatment. In such instances, a legal decision (e.g., whether a person with mental illness is so imminently dangerous that he or she should be immediately hospitalized involuntarily) is required; hence, an ultimate-issue opinion not only is permissible but necessary. On the other hand, when the clinician moves from decisionmaker to expert—for example, when the clinician testifies in a commitment hearing about the individual whom he or she hospitalized—then the ultimate-issue opinion formation should be reserved to the court.

70. *See* Stephen J. Morse, *Law and Mental Health Professionals: The Limits of Expertise,* 9 PROF. PSYCHOL. 389 (1978).

71. *Id.* at 392.

72. Diagnoses do not translate directly into "mental disease or defect," and certainly not into conclusions about the degree of impairment of certain functions. Indeed, DSM-IV recognizes as much. AMERICAN PSYCHIATRIC ASSOCIATION, DIAGNOSTIC AND STATISTICAL MANUAL OF MENTAL DISORDERS xxii (4th ed. 1994). Diagnosis may relate to relevant research, however, and it serves as a convenient shorthand. Thus, although we usually prefer omission of diagnoses from forensic reports, we would not bar them. *See* § 8.07(a).

73. *See generally* ZISKIN & FAUST, COPING WITH PSYCHIATRIC AND PSYCHOLOGICAL TESTIMONY, *supra* note 9.

74. *See, e.g.,* STANLEY L. BRODSKY, TESTIFYING IN COURT: GUIDELINES AND MAXIMS FOR THE EXPERT WITNESS 201–03 (1991); Stanley L. Brodsky, *Advocacy in the Guise of Scientific Objectivity: An Examination of Faust and Ziskin,* 5 COMPUTERS HUM. BEHAV. 261 (1989); Norman G. Poythress, *Coping on the Witness Stand: Learned Responses to Learned Treatises,* 11 PROF. PSYCHOL. 139 (1980) (providing

rebuttals to frequently cited assertions about the mental health professions).

75. Richard J. Bonnie & Christopher Slobogin, *The Role of Mental Health Professionals in the Criminal Process: The Case for Informed Speculation,* 66 VA. L. REV. 427 (1980).

76. It is important to note that a particular opinion, although equally relevant in two legal contexts, might be admissible in one context but not the other. Where the prejudicial import of evidence varies, so too would its admissibility. Hence, the standard of admissibility should be somewhat stricter in civil commitment proceedings, where experts' opinions typically go unchallenged, than in insanity cases, where jurors tend to be skeptical of experts' opinions. This point is developed further below in § 1.04(b).

77. Stephen J. Morse, *Failed Explanations and Criminal Responsibility: Experts and the Unconscious,* 68 VA. L. REV. 971 (1982).

78. *Id.* at 979–80.

79. JOSEPH PETERSON ET AL., CRIME LABORATORY PROFICIENCY TESTING RESEARCH PROGRAM: FINAL REPORT (1978).

80. Arthur Falek & Hanna Moser, *Classification in Schizophrenia,* 26 ARCHIVES GEN. PSYCHIATRY 59 (1975); Lorrin Koran, *The Reliability of Clinical Methods, Data and Judgments: Part I,* 293 NEW ENG. J. MED. 642 (1975); Lorrin Koran, *The Reliability of Clinical Methods, Data and Judgments: Part II,* 293 NEW ENG. J. MED. 695 (1975).

81. GARY B. MELTON ET AL., COMMUNITY MENTAL HEALTH CENTERS AND THE COURTS: AN EVALUATION OF COMMUNITY-BASED FORENSIC SERVICES 43–55 (1985).

82. Morse, *supra* note 77, at 1016–18.

83. It should be noted that we are not arguing that psychodynamic opinions should be admissible simply because they have achieved widespread scientific acceptance. As we discuss later, such a standard has been largely discredited legally. It is unlikely in any event to correspond completely with usefulness to the trier of fact. Our approval of admission of psychodynamic opinions in some contexts is based on the assumption that opinions derived from a coherent, if unproven, scientific theory may offer the factfinder some assistance in constructing the range of plausible explanations for particular behavior. For an argument developing this point of view in connection with equally "unscientific" character evidence, *see* Andrew Taslitz, *Myself Alone: Individualizing Justice Through Psychological Character Evidence,* 52 MD. L. REV. 1 (1993).

84. *Cf.* Slobogin, *supra* note 68 (arguing for this position). Fulero and Finkel found that the lack of rebuttal experts significantly affected outcome whether testimony was framed in ultimate, penultimate or diagnostic terms (levels 7, 6 and 5 in our schema). Solomon M. Fulero & Norman J. Finkel, *Barring Ultimate Issue Testimony: An "Insane" Rule?,* 15 LAW & HUM. BEHAV. 495 (1991).

85. An important empirical question is whether legal decisionmakers will accept such statements of caution, particularly when also faced with experts who, by contrast, overstep the bounds of expertise. *See* § 18.05.

86. This section is based in part on Gary B. Melton, *Expert Opinions: "Not for Cosmic Understanding,"* in PSYCHOL-

OGY IN LITIGATION AND LEGISLATION (Bruce D. Bales & Gary Van den Bos eds., 1994).

87. 392 F. 1013 (D.C. Cir. 1923).

88. Note that this language is very similar to that in Rule 703 (see Table 1–2). Some have wondered whether Rule 703 was meant to incorporate the *Frye* test. STEPHEN SALTZBURG & KENNETH REDDEN, FEDERAL RULES OF EVIDENCE MANUAL 452 (3d ed. 1982). However, the history of the rule suggests it was meant to get at another problem: the admissibility of expert testimony based on facts that are not otherwise admissible (e.g., hearsay). This issue is discussed at length in § 3.08.

89. *See, e.g.,* People v. Beckley, 456 N.W.2d 391, 404 (Mich. 1990)(recognizing a "fundamental difference between techniques and procedures based on chemical, biological, or other physical sciences as contrasted with theories and assumptions that are based on the behavioral sciences" and holding that *Frye* should not apply to the latter).

90. Indeed, even with respect to predictions of dangerousness, which are generally considerably relatively unreliable, courts have had no difficulty permitting clinical testimony from those who believe it is "accepted." *See* George Dix, *Expert Prediction Testimony in Capital Sentencing: Evidentiary and Constitutional Considerations,* 19 AM. CRIM. L. REV. 1. 19–21 (1986).

91. *See, e.g.,* Jahnke v. State, 682 P.2d 991 (Wyo. 1984 (rejecting battered child syndrome testimony on this ground).

92. *See, e.g.,* United States v. Lewellyn, 723 F.2d 615 (8th Cir. 1983) (rejected testimony based on a DSM-III diagnosis of pathological gambling after finding there was "little knowledge about pathological gambling within the community of mental health professionals" and that "not more than 20 or 25 doctors have had experience with pathological gambling").

93. For a general exposition of these points, *see* Paul Gianelli, *The Admissibility of Novel Scientific Evidence: Frye v. United States, A Half-Century Later,* 80 COLUM. L. REV. 1197 (1980).

94. 509 U.S. 579 (1993).

95. The adjectives describing the two approaches can be found in *Daubert. Id.* at 588–89.

96. *Black's Law Dictionary* defines *dicta* as follows: "The word is generally used as an abbreviated form of *obiter dictum,* 'a remark by the way'; that is, an observation or remark made by a judge in pronouncing an opinion upon a cause, concerning some rule, principle, or application of law, or the solution of a question suggested by the case at bar, but not necessarily involved in the case. . . ." BLACK'S LAW DICTIONARY 454 (6th ed. 1990). Dicta thus have some precedential value because they indicate the thinking of a court and the analysis that it might apply if a particular issue related to the case at hand were before the court. Nonetheless, because dicta are not part of the holding in regard to the question litigated, they are not controlling on subsequent or inferior courts.

97. 509 U.S. at 597.

98. *Id.* at 592–93.

99. *Id.* at 594–95.

100. Jones v. State, 862 S.W.2d 242, 245 (Ark. 1993) (dicta); State v. Cephas, 637 A.2d 20 (Del. Super. 1994); State v. Foret, 628 So. 2d 1116 (La. 1993); Comm. v. Lanigan, 641 N.E.2d 1342 (Mass. 1994); State v. Moore, 885 P.2d 457 (Mont. 1994); State v. Alberico, 861 P.2d 192 (N.M. 1993); State v. Futch, 860 P.2d 264 (Or. App. 1993); State v. Hofer, 512 N.W.2d 482 (S.D. 1994); State v. Brooks, 643 A.2d 226 (Vt. 1993); Wilt v. Buracker, 443 S.E.2d 196 (W. Va. 1993); Springfield v. State, 860 P.2d 435 (Wyo. 1993).

101. State v. Bible, 858 P.2d 1152 (Ariz. 1993); People v. Leahy, 882 P.2d 321 (Cal. 1994); Flanagan v. State, 625 So. 2d 827, 829 n.2 (Fla. 1993); State v. Dean, 523 N.W.2d 681 (Neb. 1994); People v. Wesley, 633 N.E.2d 451, 462 n.2 (N.Y. 1994).

102. Bible, 858 P.2d at 1183.

103. The Nebraska Supreme Court noted that the language of Nebraska Rule 702 is identical to Federal Rule 702, but it nonetheless declined to follow the lead of the United States Supreme Court, because the "increasing prevalence of expert evidence cautions against the admission of scientific evidence which is still the subject of dispute and controversy in the scientific community." State v. Dean, 246 Neb. at 692. In a lengthy discussion of the relative merits of *Frye* and *Daubert*, the California Supreme Court also noted its preference for a conservative approach to novel scientific evidence, in part because acceptance of such evidence reverberates as subsequent courts follow appellate courts upholding its use. People v. Leahy, 882 P.2d 321, 325 (Cal 1994). *Cf.* John Monahan & Laurens Walker, *Social Authority: Obtaining, Evaluating, and Establishing Social Science in Law,* 134 U. PA. L. REV. 477 (1986) and Gail S. Perry & Gary B. Melton, *Precedential Value of Judicial Notice of Social Facts:* Parham *as an Example,* 22 J. FAM. L. 633 (1984) (discussing precedential value of judges' conclusions about social reality).

104. *See Daubert,* 509 U.S. at 600 (Rehnquist, J., concurring in part and dissenting in part).

105. *Cf.* People v. Beckley, 456 N.W.2d 391, 404 (Mich. 1990). (rejecting application of *Frye* to clinical testimony because "'[p]sychologists, when called as experts, do not talk about things or objects; they talk about people. They do not dehumanize people with whom they deal by treating them as objects composed of interacting biological systems.'").

106. For more discussion of what scientific validity means, *see* § 1.02(c).

107. Bonnie & Slobogin, *supra* note 75, at 461. Many clinical theories are either not subject to falsification at all (e.g., Freudian theories, which can be used to explain any phenomenon) or are not sufficiently testable at this point in time (e.g., the repressed memory phenomenon). *See* James Richardson et al., *The Problems of Applying* Daubert *to Psychological Syndrome Evidence,* 79 JUDICATURE 10 (1995).

108. *See, e.g.,* Ronald Allen, *Expertise and the Daubert Decision,* 84 J. CRIM. L. & CRIMINOLOGY 1157 (1994); Kenneth J. Chesebro, *Galileo's Retort: Peter Huber's Junk Scholarship,* 42 AM. U. L. REV. 1637 (1993); Edward J. Imwinkelreid, *Attempts to Limit the Scope of the* Frye Stan-dard for the Admission of Scientific Evidence: Confronting the Real Cost of the General Acceptance Test, 10 BEHAV. SCI. & L. 441 (1992); Michael S. Jacobs, *Testing the Assumptions Underlying the Debate About Scientific Evidence: A Closer Look at Juror "Incompetence" and Scientific "Objectivity,"* 25 CONN. L. REV. 1083 (1993); Neil Vidmar, *Are Juries Competent to Decide Liability in Tort Cases Involving Scientific/Medical Issues? Some Data from Medical Malpractice,* 43 EMORY L.J. 885 (1994).

For a good debate on this issue, *see* David Faigman, *To Have and Have Not: Assessing the Value of Social Science to the Law as Science and Policy,* 38 EMORY L.J. 1005 (1989) and Taslitz, *supra* note 83.

109. 628 A.2d 696 (1993); *see also* State v. Luce, 628 A.2d 707 (N.H. 1993); State v. Chamberlain, 628 A.2d 704 (N.H. 1993). The New Hampshire cases, which illustrated especially problematic use of general clinical techniques to reach forensic conclusions, are discussed further in § 15.04(c)(4).

110. *See, e.g.,* United States v. Rincon, 28 F.3d 921 (9th Cir. 1994) (relying on *Daubert* to exclude expert testimony about eyewitnesses); Gier v. Educational Serv. United No. 16, 845 F. Supp. 1342 (D. Neb. 1994) (relying on *Daubert* to exclude expert testimony that seven mentally retarded children were abused at their school). As one commentator has stated, "Now, a proponent of scientific evidence must provide not only articles citing studies and research showing acceptance of the scientific principle, but also must provide detailed descriptions of the studies themselves so that the trial judge can determine whether the studies' conclusions were derived by the scientific method." Jennifer Sparks, *Admissibility of Expert Psychological Evidence in the Federal Courts,* 27 ARIZ. ST. L.J. 1315 1328 (1995). A similar view was presented by Stern, a prosecutor specialized in child abuse cases:

"Although the *Daubert* rule may be more sensible law than *Frye,* it imposes significant responsibilities on child abuse prosecutors. It is no longer enough to simply 'count noses' to see how many professionals agree or disagree with one particular view. Trial lawyers must be prepared to battle the merits of each new principle sought to be presented to a jury.

"To do so successfully will require the prosecution to be able to both intelligently support the scientific theory it advances and to challenge questionable science offered by the opposing side. Above all, it will mean that the prosecutor must more thoroughly understand the theories and methodologies involved.

"Prosecutors will need to learn and be able to debate the merits and weaknesses of each theory presented. Child abuse professionals, acting as expert witnesses, will also have enhanced responsibilities to help educate and inform prosecutors and judges. In addition, professionals will need to be prepared to counter contrary scientific experts." Paul Stern, *Science in the Courtroom: From the* Frye-Pan *to the Fire,* VIOLENCE UPDATE, Aug. 1994, at 5. Ironically, a push for more scientific evidence will increase the types of probabilistic evidence in front of the courts, which will create the tension described in § 1.03(c).

111. The suspect expert testimony was (1) being used by the state (2) to reinforce claims of child abuse which already had considerable credence, two considerations which we think cut against admissibility. See § 1.04(b).

112. *Cf.* Rosemary L. Flint, Note, *Child Sexual Abuse Accommodation Syndrome: Admissibility Requirements,* 23 AM. J. CRIM. L. 171, 190 (1995)(noting that Child Sexual Abuse Accommodation Syndrome may be the best evidence that will ever be available in child sexual abuse cases, as such abuse cannot be experimentally recreated, controlled, or evaluated).

113. Maureen O'Connor et al., *Mental Health Professional Expertise in the Courtroom,* in LAW, MENTAL HEALTH, AND MENTAL DISORDER 40, 51–54 (Bruce D. Sales & Daniel W. Shuman eds. 1996).

114. Consider this language from *Cressey,* which we think can just as easily be applied to testimony based on research: "We are not convinced that a thorough cross-examination can effectively expose any unreliable elements or assumptions in [the psychologist's] testimony. The methodology used in the psychological evaluations makes her presentation of evidence effectively beyond reproach. [The psychologist's] conclusions do not rest on one particular indicator or symptom, but rather on her interpretation of all the factors and information before her. So even though the defendant may be able to discredit several of the indicators, symptoms, or test results, the expert's overall opinion is likely to emerge unscathed. An expert using this methodology may candidly acknowledge any inconsistencies or potential shortcomings in the individual pieces of evidence she presents, but can easily dismiss the critique by saying that her evaluation relies on no one symptom or indicator and that her conclusions still hold true in light of all the other available factors and her expertise in the field. In such a case, the expert's conclusions are as impenetrable as they are unverifiable." 628 A.2d at 701.

115. For detailed overviews of the limits of authority for various types of mental health professionals, see the state-by-state series of monographs on law affecting psychological practice edited by Bruce D. Sales and published by the American Psychological Association. For empirical studies about judicial preferences for experts from different mental health disciplines, *see* Norman G. Poythress, *Psychological Issues in Criminal Proceedings: Judicial Preference Regarding Expert Testimony,* 10 CRIM. JUST. & BEHAV. 175 (1983); A. Daniel Yarmey & P. Karen Popiel, *Judged Value of Medical Versus Psychological Expert Witnesses,* 11 INT'L J. L. & PSYCHIATRY 195 (1988).

116. Fred Schindler et al., *A Study of the Causes of Conflict between Psychiatrists and Psychologists,* 32 HOSP. & COMMUNITY PSYCHIATRY 263 (1981). Continuing debates among the various mental health professional associations about the optimal limits of practice suggest that this conflict has not abated significantly in recent years.

117. MELTON ET AL., *supra* note 81, at 52–53. Licensure, another easily determinable criterion, is also a poor measure of competence. *See* Gerald P. Koocher, *Credentialing in Psychology: Close Encounters with Competence?,* 34 AM. PSYCHOLOGIST 696 (1979).

118. Russell Petrella & Norman G. Poythress, *The Quality of Forensic Examinations: An Interdisciplinary Study,* 51 J. CONSULTING & CLINICAL PSYCHOL. 6 (1983).

119. *See generally* George Dix & Norman G. Poythress, *Propriety of Medical Dominance of Forensic Mental Health Practice: The Empirical Evidence,* 23 ARIZ. L. REV. 961 (1981).

120. The other major group of mental health professionals, psychiatric nurses, has been omitted from this brief discussion because they have not been included in the relevant research. However, at least for those nurses with substantial (master's-level) training in mental health, there is no reason to believe that they would be less competent experts. Also, where the opinions being offered concern research reports rather than clinical impressions, other professionals (e.g., sociologists; experimental psychologists) may offer the most extensive and up-to-date testimony.

Chapter 2

1. 42 U.S.C. § 1395 (1975).

2. 42 U.S.C. § 2689 (1975) (repealed by Mental Health Systems Act (1980).

3. *See, e.g.,* 42 U.S.C. § 1396 (1983).

4. 42 U.S.C. § 12102 et seq. (1990).

5. 42 C.F.R. § 27802 (1975). Federal law applies in all cases involving a "drug abuse prevention function conducted, regulated, or directly or indirectly assisted by any department or agency of the United States." *Id.*

6. *See, e.g.,* Marbury v. Madison, 5 U.S. (1 Cranch) 137 (1803).

7. *See, e.g.,* McCulloch v. Maryland, 17 U.S. (4 Wheat.) 317 (1819).

8. In many states, the "appeal" of a misdemeanor conviction is a trial *de novo,* meaning that the "appellate" court retries the case from scratch. The de novo device developed because transcripts were not kept of misdemeanor proceedings.

9. 28 U.S.C. § 1251. *See also* U.S. CONST. art. III(d).

10. 28 U.S.C. §§ 1252, 1254.

11. 441 U.S. 418 (1979).

12. 494 U.S. 210 (1990).

13. *In re* Winship, 397 U.S. 358 (1970).

14. *See, e.g.,* United States v. Wade, 388 U.S. 218 (1967). However, the Court has held that a conviction does not violate the Sixth Amendment if the defendant received no prison time. Argersinger v. Hamlin, 407 U.S. 25 (1972).

15. U.S. CONST. amend. VI.

16. Gerstein v. Pugh, 420 U.S. 103 (1975); Riverside Cty. v. McLaughlin, 500 U.S. 44 (1991).

17. *See, e.g.,* 18 U.S.C. §§ 3141–3150 (1984).

18. Brady v. Maryland, 373 U.S. 83 (1963).

19. Charles Whitebread & Christopher Slobogin, Criminal Procedure: An Analysis of Cases and Concepts § 23.02(a) (1986).

20. McCarthy v. United States, 394 U.S. 459 (1969).

21. Project on Standards for Criminal Justice, Pleas of Guilty 1–2 (1968).

22. Apodaca v. Oregon, 406 U.S. 404 (1972); Johnson v. Louisiana, 406 U.S. 356 (1972).

23. 463 U.S. 880 (1983). See § 9.06.

24. 477 U.S. 399 (1986). See § 7.08(b).

25. Vitek v. Jones, 445 U.S. 488 (1980).

26. Michael McConville & Chester L. Mirsky, The Skeleton of Plea Bargaining, NEW L.J. 1373 (Oct. 9, 1992). Despite these perceptions of attorneys who represent the indigent, however, empirical findings suggest that court-appointed and public defender attorneys are fully as effective as privately retained counsel. See National Center for State Courts, Indigent Defenders: Get Tthe Job Done and Done Well (1992).

27. Neglect proceedings in which the state seeks custody over the child represent a unique category of case. See generally Chapter 15. They are not "civil" in the sense that term is used here, nor are they criminal or "quasi-criminal," as that term is used in this chapter. They are most closely analogous to administrative proceedings, described below, which involve an attempt by the state to deprive an individual of "property."

28. Fed. R. Civ. P. 35.

29. Fed. R. Civ. P. 26(a)(2).

30. Fed. R. Civ. P. 26(a)(1)(A).

31. Fed. R. Civ. P. 26(b)(4)(B).

32. See Fed. R. Civ. P. 26(b)(5).

33. Fed. R. Civ. P. 48.

34. See, e.g., Rennie v. Klein, 462 F. Supp. 1131 (D.N.J. 1978).

35. Addington v. Texas, 441 U.S. 418 (1979).

36. See, e.g., Lessard v. Schmidt, 349 F. Supp. 1078 (1972).

37. McKeiver v. Pennsylvania, 403 U.S. 528 (1971).

38. In re Winship, 397 U.S. 358 (1970); In re Gault, 387 U.S. 1 (1967).

Chapter 3

1. Many authors have noted that empathic understanding by the therapist and the credibility (as opposed to accuracy) of therapeutic interpretations are among the general (versus specific) sources of gain in therapy. See Thomas Borkovec & Sidney Nau, Credibility of Analogue Therapy Rationales, 3 J. Behav. Therapy & Exper. Psychiatry 257 (1972); Jerome Frank, Persuasion and Healing (3d ed. 1991); Nicholas Hobbs, Sources of Gain in Psychotherapy, 17 Am. Psychol. 741 (1962); Hans Strupp, Specific v. Nonspecific Factors in Psychotherapy and the Problem of Control, 23 Archives Gen. Psychiatry 393 (1970).

2. But see David L. Rosenhan, On Being Sane in Insane Places, 179 SCI. 250 (1973), in which Rosenhan and several colleagues intentionally presented bogus symptoms in order to become "patients" and to study the behaviors of mental health service providers.

3. Daniel Shuman, The Use of Empathy in Forensic Evaluations, 3 Ethics & Behav. 289 (1993).

4. "All tests share the need for a relatively quiet, distraction-free setting in administration. . . . When these conditions are not met in a single case, then the test norms may not apply in evaluating that individual's performance." Kirk Heilbrun, The Role of Psychological Testing in Forensic Assessment, 16 Law & Hum. Behav. 257–72, at 266 (1992).

5. The Eleventh Mental Measurements Yearbook (Jack J. Kramer & Jane C. Conoley eds. 1992).

6. The categories, with the number of tests in each shown in parentheses, were: Achievement (75); Developmental (155); Educational (90); Intellectual (150); Miscellaneous (113); Neuropsychological (23, counting batteries as one test each); Personality or "general scales" (578); Reading (144), Sensory–Motor (31); Speech/Hearing (90); and Vocations (510). Heilbrun, supra note 4, at 264 n.8.

7. American Psychiatric Association, Diagnostic and Statistical Manual of Mental Disorders (DSM-IV) (4th ed. 1994).

8. Supra note 5.

9. The brief for the American Psychological Association in the landmark case of Jenkins v. United States, 307 F.2d 637 (D.C. Cir. 1962), argued that "[i]n the diagnosis of mental disease and mental defect, including the causal relationships between mental disease or defect and overt behavior, a principle tool of the clinical psychologist is found in psychological tests. . . ." Erasmus L. Hoch & John Darley, A Case at Law, 17 Am. Psychol. 623, 632 (1962).

10. "Clinical psychologists generally utilize a standardized, self-report personality inventory in conjunction with one or two other tests usually of the projective type; however, any reliable psychological evaluation of a defendant should consist of an extensive battery of tests, both of the self-report personality inventory nature and projective techniques." Raymond M. Cameron, The Mental Health Expert: A Guide to Direct and Cross-Examination, 2 Crim. Just. J. 299, 309 (1979).

11. See Thomas Grisso, Evaluating Competencies: Forensic Assessments and Instruments (1986); Theodore Blau, Psychological Tests in the Courtroom, 15 Prof. Psychol.: Res. & Prac. 176–86 (1984); Heilbrun, supra note 4.

12. Heilbrun, supra note 4, at 265.

13. Inappropriate uses of testing to force inferences about legally relevant behavior may prove disastrous. Poythress reported the case of a psychologist who drew heavily on his interpretations of projective drawings on the Bender–Gestalt to support his testimony that a particular defendant in a criminal case was not inclined toward sexual acting out, as the charges against him sug-

gested. This testimony opened the door for rebuttal evidence, in the form of the defendant's otherwise inadmissible prior record, that the defendant had been implicated in three, and possibly four, prior sexual assaults. Norman G. Poythress, *Is There a Baby in the Bathwater? Psychological Tests and Expert Testimony* (paper presented at the meeting of the American Psychology–Law Society, Boston, Oct. 1981).

14. Legal competence to stand trial depends on whether the defendant has "sufficient present ability to consult with his lawyer with a reasonable degree of rational understanding . . . [and has a] rational as well as factual understanding of proceedings against him." Dusky v. United States, 362 U.S. 402 (1960). *See* § 6.02(b).

15. *Id.*

16. This unpublished opinion was communicated by a colleague who requested that the case citation remain undisclosed because of concerns about confidentiality of juvenile court records.

17. Robert D. Miller & Edward J. Germain, *The Retrospective Evaluation of Competency to Stand Trial*, 11 INT'L J. L. & PSYCHIATRY 113 (1988).

18. Steven Bank & Norman Poythress, *The Elements of Persuasion in Expert Testimony*, 10 J. PSYCHIATRY & L. 173 (1982).

19. Skepticism among jurists regarding the methods and research of psychiatry has been noted in the psycholegal literature and in case opinions. For instance, one justice characterized psychiatry as the "ultimate wizardry," David Bazelon, *Psychiatrists and the Adversary Process*, 230 SCI. AM. 18–23 (1974), while Supreme Court Justice Lewis Powell has referred to the use of research and statistical findings as "numerology," Ballew v. Georgia, 435 U.S. 223, 246 (1978) (Powell, J. concurring).

20. *Cf.* THE QUOTABLE LAWYER 111 (David Shrager & Elizabeth Prost eds. 1986)(attributing to Benjamin Disraeli the statement: "There are three kinds of lies; lies, damned lies, and statistics").

21. GRISSO, *supra* note 11.

22. *See, e.g.*, Robey's Checklist for the assessment of competence to stand trial. Ames Robey, *Criteria for Competency to Stand Trial: A Checklist for Psychiatrists*, 122 AM. J. PSYCHIATRY 616 (1965).

23. *See, e.g.*, Jeffrey S. Janofsky et al., *The Hopkins Competency Assessment Test: A Brief Method for Evaluating Patients' Capacity to Give Informed Consent*, 43 HOSP. & COMMUNITY PSYCHIATRY 132–36 (1992). The instrument is organized, inappropriately, around patients' comprehension of what doctors are supposed to do in the informed consent process, rather than around the information and abilities that patients actually need to give informed consent.

24. *See, e.g.*, BARRY BRICKLIN, BRICKLIN PERCEPTUAL SCALES: CHILD PERCEPTION OF PARENT SERIES (1990).

25. THOMAS GRISSO, JUVENILES' WAIVER OF RIGHTS: LEGAL AND PSYCHOLOGICAL COMPETENCE (1981).

26. GRISSO, *supra* note 11.

27. In particular, the MacArthur Research Foundation Network on Mental Health and the Law is in the process of refining, based on extensive and sophisticated research, instruments for evaluating criminal and civil

competencies, risk (i.e., danger to others), and coercion. This book refers to these instruments where relevant [*see, e.g.*, §§ 6.06(f), 9.09(c), 11.03(a)(2)], but the process of refinement is ongoing and thus our descriptions may be outdated.

28. *See* Kirk Heilbrun, *Response Style, Situation, Third Party Information and Competency to Stand Trial: Scientific Issues in Practice*, 14 LAW & HUM. BEHAV. 193–96 (1990); Kirk Heilbrun et al., *The Use of Third Party Information in Forensic Assessments: A Two-State Comparison*, 22 BULL. AM. ACAD. PSYCHIATRY & L. 399 (1994).

29. *See, e.g.*, Christopher Slobogin et al., *The Feasibility of a Brief Evaluation of Mental State at the Time of the Offense*, 8 LAW & HUM. BEHAV. 305 (1984) (recommending at least a two-stage process for insanity evaluations).

30. American Bar Association, Model Rules of Professional Conduct 4.2 ("In representing a client, a lawyer shall not communicate about the subject of the representation with a party the lawyer knows to be represented by another lawyer in the matter, unless the lawyer has the consent of the other lawyer or is authorized by law to do so").

31. *Cf.* American Bar Association, Model Rule of Professional Conduct 4.3: "In dealing on behalf of a client with a person who is not represented by counsel, a lawyer shall not state or imply that the lawyer is disinterested. When the lawyer knows or reasonably should know that the unrepresented person misunderstands the lawyer's role in the matter, the lawyer shall make reasonable efforts to correct the misunderstanding."

32. Although reports of amnesia may arise in a variety of cases, they may be particularly prevalent in pretrial evaluations of criminal defendants. Some studies indicate that as many as 60% of defendants involved in violent crime report amnesia symptoms. John Bradford & Selwyn Smith, *Amnesia and Homicide: The Padola Case and a Study of Thirty Cases*, 7 BULL. AM. ACAD. PSYCHIATRY & L. 219 (1979). *See also* Pamela J. Taylor & Michael L. Kopelman, *Amnesia for Criminal Offenses*, 14 PSYCHOL. MED. 581 (1984) (23% of those studied claimed amnesia).

33. For an excellent review of the literature on amnesia, *see* Daniel Schacter, *Amnesia and Crime: How Much Do We Really Know?* 41 AM. PSYCHOLOGIST 286 (1986). *See also* Dennis Koson & Ames Robey, *Amnesia and Competency to Stand Trial*, 130 AM. J. PSYCHIATRY 588 (1973).

34. ROBERT M. JULIEN, A PRIMER OF DRUG ACTION (1975).

35. *Id.* at 247.

36. For a concise discussion of different types of amnesia and clinical conditions associated with them, *see* Koson & Robey, *supra* note 33, at 588–92.

37. "Claims of practitioners notwithstanding, hypnotism has rarely, if ever, been shown under adequately controlled conditions, to improve the accuracy of subjects' recollections of details of complex natural events, such as crimes and accidents." David F. Hall & Elizabeth Loftus, *Recent Advances in Research on Eyewitness Testimony*, in PSYCHOLOGY, PSYCHIATRY, AND THE LAW: A CLINICAL AND FORENSIC HANDBOOK 417, at 426 (C. Patrick Ewing ed. 1985). For reviews of the literature on memory recovery

through hypnosis, *see* Martin Reiser, *Investigative Hypnosis,* in PSYCHOLOGICAL METHODS IN CRIMINAL INVESTIGATION AND EVIDENCE 151 (David C. Raskin ed. 1989); Marilyn C. Smith, *Hypnotic Memory Enhancement of Witnesses: Does It Work?,* 94 PSYCHOL. BULL. 387 (1983).

38. Gregory J. Murrey et al., *Hypnotically Created Pseudomemories: Further Investigation Into the "Memory Distortion or Response Bias" Question,* 101 J. ABNORMAL PSYCHOL. 75 (1992); Amanda J. Barnier & Kevin M. McConkey, *Reports of Real and False Memories: The Relevance of Hypnosis, Hypnotizability, and Context of Memory Test,* 101 J. ABNORMAL PSYCHOL. 521 (1992).

39. Martin Orne, *The Use and Misuse of Hypnosis in Court,* 27 INT'L J. CLINICAL & EXPERIMENTAL HYPNOSIS 311 (1979); David Speigel & Herbert Speigel, *Forensic Uses of Hypnosis,* in HANDBOOK OF FORENSIC PSYCHOLOGY 490 (Irving Weiner & Alan Hess eds. 1987).

40. Speigel & Speigel, *supra* note 39, at 500-01.

41. "It is clear that the validity of material produced under hypnosis is questionable, particularly when obvious motive exists to dissimulate. . . ." Robert D. Miller & Lawrence J. Stava, *Hypnosis and Dissimulation,* in CLINICAL ASSESSMENT OF MALINGERING AND DECEPTION 234, 249 (Richard Rogers ed. 1988) [hereinafter MALINGERING AND DECEPTION]. *See also* Richard Rogers & Robert M. Wettstein, *Drug-Assisted Interviews to Detect Malingering and Deception,* in MALINGERING AND DECEPTION, at 195–204.

42. Frederick C. Redlich et al., *Narcoanalysis and Truth,* 107 AM. J. PSYCHIATRY 586 (1951).

43. Martin J. Gerson & Victor M. Victoroff, *Experimental Investigation into the Validity of Confessions Obtained under Sodium Amytal Narcosis,* 9 J. CLINICAL PSYCHOPATHOLOGY 359–75 (1948).

44. Harley Stock, personal communication with Norman Poythress (Feb. 20, 1979).

45. Both malingering and defensiveness are captured by the broader term "dissimulation." Additional response styles not explicitly covered in this chapter include *reliable/honest* and *irrelevant.* The former deals with presentations in which the clinician judges that the client made a sincere attempt at accurate responding but inaccuracies occur anyway, attributable to poor understanding, misperception, or normal processes (e.g., normal forgetting) that result in mistakes. The latter refers to the situation in which the person fails to become engaged in the assessment process; responses may be random or irrelevant but are not systematically orchestrated to portray a particular clinical picture. For a broader discussion of response styles, *see* Richard Rogers, *Toward an Empirical Model of Malingering and Deception,* 2 BEHAV. SCI. & L. 93 (1984); MALINGERING AND DECEPTION, *supra* note 41.

46. For a comprehensive review of the early literature on the detection of malingering, *see* Jeffrey L. Geller et al., *Feigned Insanity in Nineteenth-Century America: Tactics, Trials, and Truth,* 8 BEHAV. SCI. & L. 3 (1990).

47. Richard Rogers, *Structured Interviews and Dissimulation* (1988), in MALINGERING AND DECEPTION, *supra* note 41, at 251. *See also* Rogers, *supra* note 45, at 95 (Table I).

48. Schacter, *supra* note 33, at 290–91.

49. *See* JAY ZISKIN & DAVID FAUST, COPING WITH PSYCHIATRIC AND PSYCHOLOGICAL TESTIMONY (4th ed. 1988) (especially Vol. II, Chap. 18, at 850–76).

50. James R. Ogloff, *The Admissibility of Expert Testimony Regarding Malingering and Deception,* 8 BEHAV. SCI. & L. 27 (1990).

51. Richard Rogers & James L. Cavanaugh, *Application of the SADS Diagnostic Interview to Forensic Psychiatry,* 9 J. PSYCHIATRY & L. 329 (1981); Richard Rogers et al., *Use of the SADS Diagnostic Interview in Evaluating Legal Insanity,* 40 J. CLINICAL PSYCHOL. 1538-41 (1984).

52. Jean Endicott & Robert L. Spitzer, *A Diagnostic Interview: The Schedule of Affective Disorders and Schizophrenia,* 35 ARCHIVES GEN. PSYCHIATRY 837 (1978).

53. RICHARD ROGERS ET AL., SIRS: STRUCTURED INTERVIEW OF REPORTED SYMPTOMS (1992) (available from Psychological Assessment Resources, Inc.)[hereinafter SIRS MANUAL].

54. One scale (*DS*) is designed to detect a defensive posture. The remaining 12 scales primarily target overendorsement or exaggeration of symptoms.

55. Although both the *simulation* design and the *known groups* design are useful and can potentially provide important information, each is subject to limitations and criticisms.

The simulation design is an analogue approach to the study of malingering because the investigator does not have access to a group of "real" malingering subjects. Rather, malingerers are experimentally created by differential sets of instructions. Some subjects are instructed to respond as if psychologically disturbed ("ill," "crazy," "insane," etc.) and represent feigners in the study; other subjects are instructed to respond honestly and constitute the control or comparison group. The performance of experimentally created malingerers is compared to that of honest responding controls, and analyses focus on test scores, profiles, or other indices that optimally discriminate and classify subjects into their correct groups. The simulation approach is subject to significant concerns regarding generalizability of findings to the clinical setting, particularly when researchers utilize relatively homogeneous and atypical (for the clinical setting) subjects, such as college students. Analogue subjects may be suspect in terms of their ability to conceptualize and fabricate indications of mental impairment in ways that true malingerers might; researchers can potentially overcome this problem to some degree by coaching subjects about the nature of mental illness or strategies for test taking, thus enhancing their ability to malinger more skillfully. Relatively few research studies have implemented this strategy, however. An even greater difficulty for researchers using simulation designs is to create a feasible analogue to the motivational state that exists in a real forensic assessment. Rewards to "fake bad" such as small amounts of money or course credit bear little resemblance to the motivational incentives of a plaintiff in a personal injury case who stands to win a judgment of several hundred thousand dollars, or that of a criminal defendant seeking to establish mental disorder as a mitigating factor to avoid capital punishment.

The known groups design contrasts the test performance of persons designated on independent and a priori grounds as "malingerers" with the performance of normal subjects or known clinical control groups. This design has more of a "real world" feel to it, although it too has limitations. Most obvious is concern about the criterion for identifying the members of the known malingering group; after all, if the criterion were all that good, the researchers probably would not be conducting the study. Further, if the research stimulus materials are presented independently of (usually after) the interaction that yielded the experimental classification of "malingerer," there is an assumption that the individual will continue to feign to some presumably significant degree on the research protocol. Whether this is a valid assumption is of course unknown. Although some theories would postulate malingering as a general response style, contemporary theories that define malingering as adaptive behavior give rise to concerns that, absent a need to feign in a particular situation, the individual might respond more "normally."

Because of the criterion problem and difficulty accessing groups of potential malingerers in clinical settings, more research on the use of psychometric tests to detect malingering has been conducted using simulation designs. Some studies of both types have been further weakened by experimenters' use of exclusively "normal" control groups for comparison; although distinguishing malingerers from normals is important, the more critical task for forensic examiners is distinguishing malingerers from persons who are truly symptomatic. Ideally, to establish the psychometric utility of a test of malingering, the instrument would have been developed and validated using both types of designs and clinical, as opposed to normal, controls.

56. Richard Rogers et al., *Standardized Assessment of Malingering: Validation of the Structured Interview of Reported Symptoms,* 3 PSYCHOL. ASSESSMENT: J. CONSULTING & CLINICAL PSYCHOL. 89 (1991).

57. Richard Rogers et al., *The SIRS as a Measure of Malingering: A Validation Study with a Correctional Sample,* 8 BEHAV. SCI. & L. 85 (1990).

58. Richard Rogers et al., *Detection of Malingering on the Structured Interview of Reported Symptoms (SIRS): A Study of Coached and Uncoached Simulators,* 3 PSYCHOL. ASSESSMENT: J. CONSULTING & CLINICAL PSYCHOL. 673 (1991).

59. Richard Rogers et al., *Faking Specific Disorders: A Study of the Structured Interview of Reported Symptoms (SIRS),* 48 J. CLINICAL PSYCHOL. 643 (1992).

60. Sensitivity reflects a test's capacity to select many or most of the individuals who possess the trait or exhibit the behavior that the test is designed to measure. *See* § 20.02.

61. Specificity is an index of the degree to which the test selects only those individuals possessing the trait or expressing the behavior that the test is designed to detect. *See* § 20.02.

62. Schretlen completed a comprehensive review of the published research on the detection of malingering using intelligence tests, the Rorschach, MMPI, and Bender–Gestalt, and concluded that psychological tests can accurately detect faking. A close and critical reading of his review, however, reveals that the actual clinical utility of a

number of the tests reviewed is yet to be demonstrated. David J. Schretlen, *The Use of Psychological Tests to Identify Malingered Symptoms of Mental Disorder,* 8 CLINICAL PSYCHOL. REV. 451 (1988).

63. Richard Rogers et al., *Feigning Neuropsychological Impairment: A Critical Review of Methodological and Clinical Considerations,* 13 CLINICAL PSYCHOL. REV. 255 (1993).

64. *Id.* at 260.

65. Schretlen, *supra* note 62, at 465.

66. *Id.* at 465.

67. Glenn G. Perry & Bill N. Kinder, *The Susceptibility of the Rorschach to Malingering: A Critical Review,* 54 J. PERSONALITY ASSESSMENT 47, at 53 (1990). "The results are extremely inconsistent and no reliable pattern of responses in a protocol that would indicate the presence of malingering has been identified. A few patterns have been suggested, but to date these have not been replicated. Perhaps a significant proportion of this heterogeneity, and failure to replicate, is due to unsound design and/or data analysis procedures. Stermac concluded that 'it is apparent that the issue of deception on projective tests has been inadequately investigated. Many of the studies described have serious methodological limitations [and] clinical applications are limited.'" Lana Stermac, *Projective Testing and Dissimulation,* in MALINGERING AND DECEPTION, *supra* note 41, at 168.

68. Schretlen, *supra* note 62, at 467.

69. *See, e.g.,* JOHN R. GRAHAM, THE MMPI: A PRACTICAL GUIDE 17–33 (1977); CHARLES L. GOLDEN, CLINICAL INTERPRETATION OF OBJECTIVE PSYCHOLOGICAL TESTS 65–75 (1979); JOHN R. GRAHAM, MMPI-2: ASSESSING PERSONALITY AND PSYCHOPATHOLOGY 22–51 (1990); ROGER L. GREENE, THE MMPI-2/MMPI: AN INTERPRETIVE MANUAL 49–133 (1991).

70. Roger L. Greene, *Assessment of Malingering and Defensiveness by Objective Personality Inventories,* in MALINGERING AND DECEPTION, *supra* note 41, at 123–58.

71. Schretlen, *supra* note 62, at 473; David T. Berry et al., *Detection of Malingering on the MMPI: A Meta-Analysis,* 11 CLINICAL PSYCHOL. REV. 585–98 (1991); Rudy Buigas et al., *Assessment of Malingering Using the MMPI-2: Which Index is Best?* (paper presented at the meeting of the American Psychology–Law Society, Santa Fe, March 1993).

72. Schretlen, *supra* note 62, at 473. *See also* David Schretlen, *A Limitation of Using the Wiener and Harmon Obvious and Subtle Scales to Detect Faking on the MMPI,* 46 J. CLINICAL PSYCHOL. 782, 785 (1990); Buigas et al., *supra* note 71.

73. Richard Rogers et al., *Feigning Schizophrenic Disorders on the MMPI-2: Detection of Coached Simulators,* 60 J. PERSONALITY ASSESSMENT 215, at 220 (1993).

74. *Id.* at 222 (citing authorities recommending that F scale scores ranging from 11 to 23 are optimal for detecting malingerers, whereas in their own study a score of $F \geq 28$ yielded the optimum classification). Similar concerns with the wide range of cutoff scores were voiced by Berry et al., *supra* note 71, at 593.

75. Schretlen, *supra* note 62, at 472. Traditionally, the recommended cutoff score for F-K is in the range of 10–12. For a recent study reporting problems applying

customary MMPI cutoff scores with forensic clients, *see* Deborah Roman et al., *Evaluating MMPI Validity in a Forensic Psychiatric Population: Distinguishing between Malingering and Genuine Psychopathology,* 17 CRIM. J. & BEHAV. 186 (1990).

76. Greene, *supra* note 70, at 148.

77. Rex J. Beaber et al., *A Brief Test for Measuring Malingering in Schizophrenic Individuals,* 142 AM. J. PSYCHIATRY 1478 (1985).

78. J. Roy Gillis et al., *Validity of the M Test: Simulation-Design and Natural Group Approaches,* 57 J. PERSONALITY ASSESSMENT 130 (1991); Glenn Paul Smith & Randy Borum, *Detection of Malingering in a Forensic Sample: A Study of the M Test,* 20 J. PSYCHIATRY & L. 505 (1993); Glenn Paul Smith, *Rule-out and Rule-In Scales for the M Test for Malingering: A Cross-Validation Study,* 21 BULL. AM. ACAD. PSYCHIATRY & L. 107 (1993).

79. Schretlen, *supra* note 62.

80. "Scatter" refers to the finding that fakers fail more of the easy items, but pass more of the harder ones, than do persons who are truly mentally deficient. "[W]idely used intelligence tests, such as the WAIS-R, are poorly adapted to 'scatter' analysis because they contain too few easy items and the items are arranged in an obvious hierarchical order." Schretlen, *supra* note 62, at 456.

81. Rogers et al., *supra* note 63, at 256.

82. *Id.* at 260–63.

83. David Schretlen & Hal Arkowitz, *A Psychological Test to Detect Prison Inmates Who Fake Insanity or Mental Retardation,* 8 BEHAV. SCI. & L. 75 (1992); David Schretlen et al., *Cross-Validation of a Psychological Test Battery to Detect Faked Insanity,* 4 PSYCHOL. ASSESSMENT 77 (1992).

84. In the case example described earlier, when confronted with the inconsistencies and the examiner's assertion that he had not been truthful, the defendant admitted to his dissimulation. He spoke at some length about his anxiety concerning his serious charges and his fears about possibly being sentenced to prison. Thereafter he appeared cooperative and candid in further efforts to complete the court-ordered evaluation.

85. *See, e.g.,* Department of Youth Servs. v. A Juvenile, 398 Mass. 516, 499 N.E.2d 812 (1986); Mayer v. Baiser, 147 Ill. App. 3d 150, 100 Ill. Dec. 649, 497 N.E.2d 827 (1986); MINN. R. EVID. R. 703. Even under Rule 703, the inadmissible evidence is not "substantive" evidence, but rather "merely" evidence supporting the expert's opinion, and the judge may so instruct.

86. *See, e.g.,* United States v. Lawson, 653 F.2d 299, 301–02 (7th Cir. 1981) (psychiatrist can describe staff reports, defendant's interviews with other physicians, information from the United States Marine Corps, reports from the FBI, and information from the United States Attorney's Office); United States v. Bilson, 648 F.2d 1238, 1239 (9th Cir. 1981) (psychiatrist could base sanity opinion on and describe psychological tests administered by unlicensed psychologist); United States v. Baca, 687 F.2d 1356, 1361 (10th Cir. 1982) (expert can give opinion as to defendant's competence based on another doctor's evaluations). *Cf.* Robert Sadoff, *Psychiatric Involvement in the Search for Truth,* 52 A.B.A. J. 251 (1966).

87. *See, e.g.,* Greenfield v. Commonwealth, 214 Va. 710, 204 S.E.2d 414 (1974).

88. FED. R. EVID. 801(d)(2).

89. FED. R. EVID. 803(b)(3).

90. FED. R. EVID. 803(b)(1).

91. *See, e.g.,* United States v. Gonzalez, 559 F.2d 1271 (5th Cir. 1977). *But see* United States v. Guinan, 836 F.2d 350 (7th Cir. 1988).

92. FED. R. EVID. 803(6) (Records of Regularly Conducted Activity). *See also* FED. R. EVID. 803(8)(Public Records and Reports). *Cf.* Williams v. Alexander, 309 N.Y. 283, 129 N.E.2d 417 (1955).

93. United States v. Oates, 560 F.2d 45 (2d Cir. 1977).

94. Note, *Hearsay Bases of Psychiatric Opinion Testimony: A Critique of Federal Rule of Evidence 703,* 51 S. CAL. L. REV. 129 (1977); Ronald L. Carlson, *Collision Course in Expert Testimony: Limitations on Affirmative Introduction of Underlying Data,* 36 FLA L. REV. 234 (1984).

95. For instance, many statements made to a social worker doing a family history may help form the basis for an opinion but may not be "significant." Or, a psychologist whose tests form part of the basis of an opinion may have left the state for another job. In both instances, requiring the out-of-court declarant to testify may not be useful.

96. For details, *see* ANDRE MOENSSENS ET AL., SCIENTIFIC EVIDENCE IN CRIMINAL CASES 607–14 (3d ed. 1986); David C. Raskin, *The Polygraph in 1986: Scientific, Professional and Legal Issues Surrounding Application and Acceptance of Polygraph Evidence,* 1986 UTAH L. REV. 29.

97. *See, e.g.,* MICHAEL J. SAKS & REID HASTIE, SOCIAL PSYCHOLOGY IN COURT 198 (1978); Benjamin Kleinmuntz & Julian J. Szucko, *On the Fallibility of Lie Detection,* 17 LAW & SOC'Y REV. 85, 86–87 (1981). Other problems with the research include possible bias in the selection of the sample of polygraph results and inadequate controls for variations in the analysts' skills. *Id.* at 93.

98. *Id.* at 96 (reporting false-positive rates from 18% to 55%); DAVID T. LYKKEN, A TREMOR IN THE BLOOD: USE AND ABUSES OF THE LIE DETECTOR 25 (1981) (reporting rates of 36–39%).

99. LYKKEN, *supra* note 98, ch. 13; SAKS & HASTIE, *supra* note 97, at 202 ("there is no scientific evidence to support the claim that [voice stress analyzers] are accurate beyond chance levels").

100. *See* Kleinmuntz & Szucko, *supra* note 97, at 99–100.

101. *See, e.g.,* United States v. Brevard, 739 F.2d 18 (4th Cir. 1984); People v. Baynes, 88 Ill. 2d 225, 58 Ill. Dec. 819, 430 N.E.2d 1070 (1981); Commonwealth v. Vitello, 376 Mass. 426, 381 N.E.2d 582, 596–99 (1978); People v. Anderson, 637, P.2d 354, 361–62 (Colo. 1981). Some courts will allow polygraph results for the sole purpose of determining whether a defendant's confession was voluntary. *See, e.g.,* United States v. Johnson, 816 F.2d 918, 923 (3d Cir. 1987).

102. Anderson v. United States, 788 F2.d 517, 519 (8th Cir. 1986); State v. Marti, 290 N.W.2d 570, 586–87 (Iowa 1980).

103. *See, e.g.,* United States v. Piccinonna, 885 F.2d

1529 (1989) (allowing polygraph results obtained following appropriate procedures (1) when stipulated; (2) to
impeach a witness; (3) to corroborate a witness whose
credibility has been attacked). This case summarizes the
case law in the area.

104. Orne, *supra* note 39, at 319.

105. *Id.* at 320.

106. 483 U.S. 44 (1987).

107. State *ex rel.* Collins v. Superior Ct., 132 Ariz.
180, 644 P.2d 1266 (1982); People v. Shirley, 31 Cal.3d
18, 641 P.2d 775, 784–86, 181 Cal. Rptr. 243, 252–54,
(1982); State v. Mack, 292 N.W.2d 764, 771 (Minn.
1980).

108. 86 N.J. 525, 543–46, 432 A.2d 86, 95–97
(1981).

109. A more extensive excerpt from *Hurd* is instructive:

"The first question a court must consider is the appropriateness of using hypnosis for the kind of memory loss
encountered. The reason for a subject's lack of memory is
an important factor in evaluating the reliability of hypnosis in restoring recall. [H]ypnosis often is reasonably reliable in reviving normal recall where there is a pathological reason, such as a traumatic neurosis, for the witness'
inability to remember. On the other hand, the likelihood
of obtaining reasonably accurate recall diminishes if hypnosis is used simply to refresh a witness' memory concerning details where there may be no recollection at all
or to 'verify' one of several conflicting accounts given by
a witness. A related factor to be considered is whether
the witness has any discernible motivation for not remembering or for 'recalling' a particular version of the
events. In either case, the possibility of creating self-serving fantasy is significant.

"Once it is determined that a case is of a kind likely to

yield normal recall if hypnosis is properly administered,
then it is necessary to determine whether the procedures
followed were reasonably reliable. Of particular importance are the manner of questioning and the presence of
cues or suggestions during the trance and the post-hypnot-
ic period. . . . An additional factor affecting the reliability
of the procedures is the amenability of the subject to hypnosis, since some experts believe that subjects capable of
entering deeper trances are usually more suggestible. . . .

"To provide an adequate record for evaluating the reliability of the hypnotic procedure, and to ensure a minimum level of reliability, we also adopt several procedural
requirements. . . . First, a psychiatrist or psychologist
experienced in the use of hypnosis must conduct the session. This professional should also be able to qualify as an
expert in order to aid the court in evaluating the procedures followed. . . . Second, the professional conducting
the hypnotic session should be independent of and not
regularly employed by the prosecutor, investigator or defense. . . . Third, any information given to the hypnotist
by law enforcement personnel or the defense prior to the
hypnotic session must be recorded, either in writing or
another suitable form. . . . Fourth, *before* inducing hypnosis the hypnotist should obtain a detailed description of
the facts as the subject remembers them. . . . Fifth, all
contacts between the hypnotist and the subject must be
recorded. . . . Sixth, only the hypnotist and the subject
should be present during any phase of the hypnotic session, including the pre-hypnotic testing and the post-hyp-
notic interview." *Id.* at 544–46. The court also held that
the party seeking to introduce the hypnotically induced
statements has the burden of proving they are reliable
enough to introduce into evidence.

110. McCormick on Evidence 633–34 (3d. ed.
1984).

Chapter 4

1. Schmerber v. California, 384 U.S. 757, 761
(1966). *See generally* Charles Whitebread & Christopher Slobogin, Criminal Procedure: An Analysis of
Constitutional Cases and Concepts ch. 15 (3d ed.
1993). For a full explication of the issues discussed in this
and the following section, see Christopher Slobogin, Estelle v. Smith: *The Constitutional Contours of the Forensic
Evaluation,* 31 Emory L.J. 71 (1982).

2. 218 U.S. 245 (1910).

3. Schmerber v. California, 384 U.S. 757, 765
(1966)(blood test); Gilbert v. California, 388 U.S. 263,
266–67 (1967)(handwriting sample); United States v.
Wade, 388 U.S. 218, 222–23 (1967) (lineup); Holt v.
United States, 218 U.S. 245 (1910) (clothing).

4. Thornton v. Corcoran, 407 F.2d 695, 700 (D.C.
Cir. 1969).

5. 451 U.S. 454 (1981).

6. *Id.* at 464 n.8.

7. Hoffman v. United States, 341 U.S. 479 (1951).

8. This ban applies in federal jurisdictions under 18
U.S.C. § 4244. Among the states that impose, by statute,

the ban or a limited version of it are Alabama, Alaska,
Arizona, Arkansas, Colorado, District of Columbia,
Florida, Hawaii, Illinois, Maine, Massachusetts, Michigan, Mississippi, Missouri, Montana, Nebraska, Nevada,
New Jersey, New Mexico, New York, North Dakota,
Ohio, Pennsylvania, South Carolina, South Dakota, Tennessee, Texas, Vermont, Virginia, Washington, Wisconsin and Wyoming. For a somewhat out-of-date compilation of statutes, *see generally* Samuel Brakel et al., The
Mentally Disabled and the Law, Table 12.6, col. 8
(1985).

9. 451 U.S. at 465.

10. Even if it can be assumed that the prosecutor acts
in good faith, the prosecutor "cannot be certain that
somewhere in the depths of his investigative apparatus,
often including hundreds of employees, there was not
some prohibited use of the compelled testimony." Kasti-
gar v. United States, 406 U.S. 441, 469 (1971) (Marshall,
J., dissenting). Discovering such abuse and proving it are
extremely difficult, "for all proof lies in the hands of the
government." James Rief, *The Grand Jury Witness and Com-*

pulsory Testimony Legislation, 10 Am. Crim. L. Rev. 829, 856–59 (1972).

11. Va. Code Ann. § 19.2-169.1(D).

12. 483 U.S. 402 (1987).

13. *See, e.g.*, Fla. R. Crim. P. 3.211(e) (providing that results of a competency report may be used only on that issue unless the defendant uses the report, or portions thereof "for any other purpose, in which case disclosure and use of the report, or any portion thereof, shall be governed by applicable rules of evidence and rules of criminal procedure"). Under this type of rule, if the defendant supports an insanity defense with an expert other than the one who conducted the competency examination, or with the same expert but based on a different evaluation, the competency results could not be used by the prosecution.

14. *See* cases collected in 17 A.L.R.4th 1274 (1982). In practice, however, indigent defendants are often evaluated by state-employed evaluators at the *state's* request well before formal notice is given. *See infra* text accompanying notes 22.

15. *Id. See in particular* United States v. Albright, 388 F.2d 719 (4th Cir. 1968); Alexander v. United States, 380 F.2d 33, 39 (8th Cir. 1967); State v. Swinburne, 324 S.W.2d 746 (Mo. 1959). *But see* Johnson v. People, 172 Colo. 72, 470 P.2d 37 (1970).

16. 451 U.S. at 465.

17. *See, e.g.*, State v. Huson, 73 Wash. 2d 660, 440 P.2d 192 (1968), *cert. denied*, 393 U.S. 1096 (1968); Ala. Stat. § 12.34.083 (1980). Some states bar the defense altogether. *See, e.g.*, State v. Richards, 495 N.W.2d 1987 (Minn. 1992). For criticism of these latter two approaches, *see* Slobogin, *supra note* 1, at 103–06.

18. Lee v. County Court, 267 N.E.2d 452, 461–62, 318 N.Y.S.2d 705, 719 (1971).

19. 18. Model Penal Code § 4.09 (1962). *See supra* note 8 for a list of states which have adopted this ban or one similar to it.

20. Fed. R. Crim. P. 12.2.

21. *See, e.g.*, Troiani v. Poole, 858 F. Supp. 1051 (1994); Woomer v. Aiken, 856 F.2d 677 (4th Cir. 1988); Devine v. Solem, 815 F.2d 1204 (8th Cir. 1987); United States v. Leonard, 609 F.2d 1163 (5th Cir. 1980). Presumably, the states governed by these circuit courts are constitutionally required to follow the dictates of these decisions. *See also* Lovette v. State, 636 So. 2d 1304 (Fla. 1994) (citing Fla. R. Crim. P. 3.216[a]); State v. Mulrine, 55 Del. 65, 183 A.2d 831 (1962); State v. Whitlow, 45 N.J. 3, 21, 210 A.2d 763, 772 (1965); 32 A.L.R.2d 434, 444 § 5 (1982 & Later Case Service, 1989).

22. *See, e.g.*, United States v. Alvarez, 519 F.2d 1036 (3d Cir. 1975); Houston v. State, 602 P.2d 784 (Ala. 1979); Pratt v. State, 39 Md. App. 442, 448, 387 A.2d 779, 783 (1978); People v. Hilliker, 29 Mich. App. 543, 547, 185 N.W.2d 831, 833 (1971).

23. Va. Code Ann. § 19.2-169.5(E) (1982).

24. Va. Code Ann. §§ 19.2-169.5(E) & 19.2-168.1.

25. *See, e.g.*, American Bar Association, Criminal Justice Mental Health Standards, standard 11-3.2 (1986) [hereinafter Standards].

26. *See* State v. Shaw, 471 P.2d 715 (Ariz. 1970); State *ex rel.* Boyd v. Green, 355 So. 2d 789 (Fla. 1978); Sanchez v. State, 562 P.2d 270 (Wyo. 1977).

27. *See generally* David W. Louisell & Geoffrey C. Hazard, *Insanity as a Defense: The Bifurcated Trial,* 49 Cal. L. Rev. 805 (1961).

28. Of the two dozen states that once required bifurcation, apparently only six states (California, Colorado, Maryland, New Mexico, New York, and Wisconsin) retain the procedure. Brakel et al., *supra* note 8, tbl. 12.6, col. 10.

29. Indiana, Maine, Massachusetts, Minnesota, New Jersey, North Dakota, Pennsylvania, and West Virginia permit the procedure on this basis. *Id.* col. 11. *See generally* 1 A.L.R. 4th 884 (1980); Note, *The Psychiatric Expert in the Criminal Trial: Are Bifurcation and the Rules Concerning Opinion Testimony on Ultimate Issue Constitutionally Compatible?* 70 Marq. L. Rev. 493 (1987).

30. *See, e.g.*, Gibson v. Zahradnick, 581 F.2d 75 (4th Cir. 1978).

31. Hollis v. Smith, 571 F.2d 685, 691 (2d Cir. 1978); Annot., 9 A.L.R.3d 990, 999–1001 (1966).

32. 451 U.S. at 462–63.

33. *Id.* at 469 n.13.

34. 387 U.S. 1 (1967).

35. *See, e.g.*, Lessard v. Schmidt, 349 F. Supp. 1078 (1972).

36. *See, e.g.*, Suzuki v. Yuen, 617 F.2d 173, 177–78 (9th Cir. 1980); Cramer v. Tyars, 488 P.2d 793 (Cal. 1979); State *ex rel.* Kiritsis v. Marion Probate Ct., 381 N.E. 2d 1245 (Ind. 1978); People *ex rel.* Keith v. Keith, 38 Ill. 2d 405, 231 N.E.2d 387 (1967). *See generally* 23 A.L.R.4th 563.

37. 478 U.S. 364 (1986).

38. *See also* French v. Blackburn, 428 F. Supp. 1351 (M.D.N.C. 1977), *aff'd,* 443 U.S. 901 (1979), which summarily affirmed a lower court holding that the Fifth Amendment does not apply to civil commitment.

39. 451 U.S. at 468.

40. 484 U.S. 436 (1966).

41. Miller and his colleagues found that few patients subject to commitment proceedings refuse to talk as a result of warnings. They speculate, based on other studies of the admission process, that this is because "most patients understand and recall little of what they are told on admission," that "many patients tend to perceive clinicians as helpers no matter what the situation," and that "warnings may actually seduce some patients into feeling secure enough to reveal more information than they otherwise would have done. . . ." Robert Miller et al., *The Right to Remain Silent during Psychiatric Examination in Civil and Criminal Cases—A National Survey and an Analysis,* 9 Int'l J. L. & Psychiatry 77, 91–92 (1986).

42. Coleman v. Alabama, 399 U.S. 1 (1970); Wade v. United States, 388 U.S. 218 (1967); Hamilton v. Alabama, 368 U.S. 52 (1961).

43. *See, e.g.*, People v. Rosenthal, 617 P.2d 551 (Colo. 1980); Houston v. State, 602 P.2d 784 (Alaska 1979).

44. *E.g.,* Hollis v. Smith, 571 F.2d 685 (2d Cir. 1978); United States v. Cohen, 530 F.2d 43 (5th Cir.),

cert. denied, 429 U.S. 855 (1976); McKenna v. State, 98 Nev. 38, 639 P.2d 557 (1982); Presnell v. State, 241 Ga. 49, 243 S.E.2d 496 (1978); People v. Larsen, 74 Ill. 2d 348, 385 N.E.2d 679 (1979); State v. Wilson, 26 Ohio App. 2d 23, 268 N.E.2d 814 (1971); Shepard v. Bowe, 250 Or. 288, 442 P.2d 238 (1968); Commonwealth v. Stukes, 435 Pa. 535, 257 A.2d 828 (1969). *See generally* Timothy E. Travers, Annot., *Right of Accused in Criminal Prosecution to Presence of Counsel at Court-Appointed or -Approved Psychiatric Examination,* 3 A.L.R.4th 910 (1995); Thomas M. Fleming, Annot., *Right of Party to Have Attorney or Physician Present during Physical or Mental Examination at Instance of Opposing Party,* 84 A.L.R. 5th 558 (1995).

45. 451 U.S. at 470 & n.14.

46. 388 U.S. 218 (1967).

47. For an example of a case in which the attorney's presence could have been useful, *see* United States v. Byers, No. 78-1451 (D.C. Cir. Dec. 24, 1980). A second decision in *Byers* was issued at 740 F.2d 1104 (D.C. Cir. 1984), after *Estelle v. Smith* was decided and reargument occurred.

48. Thornton v. Corcoran, 407 F.2d 695 (D.C. Cir. 1969); STANDARDS, *supra* note 25, standard 7-3.6(c)(ii), 7-3.6(d), and accompanying commentary.

49. *See* STANDARDS, *supra* note 25, standard 7-3(c)(i) and accompanying commentary.

50. *Compare* Zabkowicz v. West Bend Co. 585 F. Supp. 635, 636 (D. Wis. 1984) (attorney presence permitted because psychiatric examination "could easily be transformed into a *de facto* deposition") *to* Warrick v. Brode, 46 F.R.D. 427, 428 (D. Del. 1969) ("The very presence of a lawyer for the examined party injects a partisan character into what would otherwise be a wholly objective inquiry"). *See also* Stakley v. Allstate Ins. Co., 547 So. 2d 275 (Fla. 2d Dist. 1989) (attorney presence permitted if the client requests it, "absent any valid reason to prohibit the presence of a third party"); CHARLES WRIGHT & ARTHUR MILLER, FEDERAL PRACTICE & PROCEDURE § 2236 (1994).

51. Slobogin, *supra* note 1, at 132–34; Note, *The Indigent's Right to an Adequate Defense: Expert and Investigational Assistance in Criminal Proceedings,* 55 CORNELL L. REV. 632, 639–41 (1970).

52. *See, e.g.,* Travis H. Lewin, *Indigency Informal and Formal Procedures to Provide Partisan Psychiatric Assistance to the Poor,* 52 IOWA L. REV. 458, 487 (1966); Note, *supra* note 51, at 639–41.

53. GARY MELTON ET AL., COMMUNITY MENTAL HEALTH CENTERS AND THE COURTS: AN EVALUATION OF COMMUNITY-BASED FORENSIC SERVICES 23–42 (1985) (estimating approximately 40% savings using community-based resources).

54. 470 U.S. 68 (1985).

55. *See generally* 85 A.L.R. 4th 19 (1991). *See also* Granviel v. Lynaugh, 881 F.2d 185 (5th Cir. 1989) (holding that *Ake* requires no more than an "independent" court-appointed psychiatrist whose report is to be made available to both the prosecution and defense). *But see* Hammett v. State, 578 S.W.2d 699, 720–21 (Tex. Crim. App. 1979) (Odum, Roberts, & Phillips, JJ., concurring).

56. These states include Alabama, Alaska, Arkansas, Connecticut, Illinois, Kansas, Iowa, Michigan, South Dakota, North Dakota, Ohio, Oregon, Pennsylvania, Rhode Island, and Washington. *See* BRAKEL ET AL., *supra* note 8, tbl. 12.6, col. 7.

57. For a description of such a program in Virginia, *see* MELTON ET AL., *supra* note 53.

58. Note, *The Indigent's Right to Psychiatric Assistance: Ake v. Oklahoma,* 17 N.C. CENT. L.J. 208, 220–22 (1988).

59. *See, e.g.,* In re Gannon, 123 N.J. Super. 104, 301 A.2d 493, 494 (1973) (civil commitment).

60. 425 F. Supp. 1038 (E.D.N.Y. 1976), *aff'd,* 556 F.2d 556 (2d Cir. 1977).

61. Gray v. District Ct., 884 P.2d 286 (Colo. 1994). *See generally* Stephen Saltzburg, *Privileges and Professionals: Laywers and Psychiatrists,* 66 VA. L. REV. 597 (1980).

62. 519 F.2d 1036 (3d Cir. 1975). *See also* Houston v. State, 602 P.2d 784 (Ala. 1979); Pratt v. State, 39 Md. App. 442, 387 A.2d 779 (1978), *aff'd,* 284 Md. 516, 398 A.2d 421(1979).

63. The ABA recommends that the *Alvarez* rule be followed, except when "the prosecution establishes, to the court's satisfaction, that in bad faith the defendant secured evaluations by all available qualified [professionals] in the area thereby depriving the prosecution of the opportunity to obtain an adequate evaluation." STANDARDS, *supra* note 25, standard 7-3.3(b)(ii).

64. Carr v. Watkins, 227 Md. 578, 177 A.2d 841 (1962); Berry V. Moench, 8 Utah 2d 191, 331 P.2d 814 (1958). *Cf.* Roe v. Ingraham, 480 F.2d 102 (2d Cir. 1973); Hammond v. Setna Ins., Ohio, 243 F. Supp. 793 (1965).

65. Although the U.S. Supreme Court has barred pretrial discovery of case records under limited circumstances, Seattle Times v. Rhinehart, 467 U.S. 20 (1984), the First Amendment and state public-access laws push in the opposite direction in most cases. *See generally* Katherine Pownell, *The First Amendment and Pretrial Discovery Hearings: When Should the Press Have Access?* 36 UCLA L. REV. 609 (1989); Charles N. Davis, *Access to Discovery Records in Florida Criminal Trials: Public Justice and Public Records,* 6 FLA. J. L. & PUB. POL'Y 297 (1995). The typical exceptions to this public-access rule are juvenile records and presentence reports. *See* Jonathan Gough, *The Expungement of Adjudication Records of Juvenile and Adult Offenders: A Problem of Status,* 1966 WASH. L. Q. 147, 168–78; Albert Roche, *The Position for Confidentiality of the Presentence Investigation Report,* 29 ALBANY L. REV. 206 (1965).

66. Chandler v. Florida, 449 U.S. 560 (1981); Richmond Newspapers, Inc. v. Virginia, 448 U.S. 555 (1980).

67. Block v. Sacramento Clinical Labs, 131 Cal. App. 3d 306, 182 Cal. Rptr. 438 (1982); Commonwealth *ex rel.* Platt v. Platt, 266 Pa. Super. Ct. 276, 404 A.2d 410 (1979) (civil commitment hearing); McKay v. Commonwealth, 52 Pa. Comm. 24, 415 A.2d 910 (1980) (competency to operate a motor vehicle).

68. For a compilation of statutes, *see* Note, *Child Abuse: Helping Kids Who Are Hurting,* 74 MARQ. L. REV. 560 n.1 (1991).

69. For a listing of statutes, *see* Note, *A Psychotherapist's Duty to Protect,* 25 CREIGHTON L. REV. 1461, 1467–68 n.11 (1992).

70. The principal exception to the nondisclosure rule dictated by the attorney–client privilege is when the attorney's services are sought to enable the client to commit a future crime. *See* MCCORMICK ON EVIDENCE § 95 (1992). But the ethical rules also require or recommend that the attorney provide information necessary to prevent a crime that can cause death or seriously bodily harm, even if the attorney's services are not sought for that purpose. *See* American Bar Association, Model Rules of Professional Conduct, Rule 1.6.

71. Tarasoff v. Regents, Univ. of Cal., 551 P.2d 334 (Cal. 1976).

72. Cal. Stat. § 43.92. For an overview of relevant statutes, *see* Paul Appelbaum et al., *Statutory Approaches to Limiting Psychiatrists' Liability for Their Patients' Violent Acts,* 146 AM. J. PSYCHIATRY 821 (1989). An even more limited variation comes from Arizona, where liability attaches only if "the patient has communicated to the mental health provider an explicit threat of imminent serious physical harm or death to a clearly identified or identifiable victim or victims, and the patient has the apparent intent and ability to carry out such threat." Ariz. Stat. 36-517.02.

A few state courts have rejected *Tarasoff* altogether. *See, e.g.*, Boynton v. Burglass, 590 So. 2d 446 (Fla. App. 1991). A number of courts have refused to recognize a duty-to-warn claim under the particular circumstances of the case but have otherwise left the question open: Case v. United States, 523 F. Supp. 317 (S.D. Ohio 1981); *In re* Estate of Votteller, 327 N.W.2d 759 (Iowa 1982) (no duty to warn where victim knows of danger); Ross v. Central La. State Hosp., 392 So. 2d 698 (La. App. 1980) (no duty to warn of need for medications where evidence shows schizophrenia does not increase patient's dangerousness, and medication does not reduce it); Furr v. Spring Grove State Hosp., 53 Md. App. 474, 454 A.2d 414 (1983) (no duty to warn where victim not identifiable); Shaw v. Glickman, 45 Md. App. 718, 415 A.2d 625 (1980) (no duty to warn where patient does not divulge intent to injure third party); Cairl v. State, 323 N.W.2d 20 (Minn. 1982)(no duty to warn in the absence of specific threat to specific person); Sherrill v. Wilson, 653 S.W.2d 661 (Mo. 1983) (en banc) (no duty to control where danger directed at the general public); Leedy v. Harnett, 510 F. Supp. 1125 (M.D. Pa. 1981) (no duty to warn where danger posed to plaintiffs does not differ from that posed to anyone else patient may have contact with).

One study found that, as of 1989, approximately 50 professionals are sued each year for breach of the duty to protect, roughly two-thirds of whom settle before trial, and one-ninth of whom end up losing at trial. James C. Beck, *Current Status of the Duty to Protect,* in CONFIDENTIALITY VERSUS THE DUTY TO PROTECT: FORESEEABLE HARM IN THE PRACTICE OF PSYCHIATRY 9 (American Psychiatric Press, 1990). Interestingly, it also found that of all the published decisions regarding *Tarasoff,* only four imposed liability on the defendant. *Id.*

73. Apparently only one court has applied *Tarasoff* to the evaluation context. Hicks v. United States, 511 F.2d 407, 415–16 (D.C. Cir. 1975). Hawaii has granted court-ordered psychiatrists immunity from *Tarasoff*-type claims. Seibel v. Kemble, 631 P.2d 173 (Haw. 1981). Also unresolved is whether evaluators who reveal information as a result of *Tarasoff* can testify about that information at trial. *See* People v. Clark, 268 Cal. Rptr. 399 (1990) (allowing such testimony). *See also* Gregory B. Leong et al., *The Psychotherapist as Witness for the Prosecution: The Criminalization of Tarasoff,* 149 AM. J. PSYCHIATRY 1011 (1992); Robert Lloyd Goldstein & Joann Maria Calderone, *The Tarasoff Raid: A New Extension of the Duty to Protect,* 20 BULL. AM. ACAD. PSYCHIATRY & L. 335 (1992).

74. *See, e.g.,* Ryans v. Lowell, 197 N.J. Super. 266, 484 A.2d, 1253 (A.D. 1984); State v. Cole, 295 N.W.2d 29 (Iowa 1980); Chiasera v. Employers Mut. Liab. Ins., 101 Misc.2d 877, 422 N.Y.S. 2d 341 (Sup. Ct. 1979).

75. Thompson v. County of Alameda, 27 Cal. 3d 741, 614 P.2d 728, 167 Cal. Rptr. 70 (1980). But note that the same court expanded liability to some extent when it allowed recovery for injury to the threatened victim's son, as well as the victim, on the ground that the former injury was "foreseeable." Hedlund v. Superior Ct., 34 Cal. 3d 695, 669 P.2d 41, 194 Cal. Rptr. 805 (1983). *See also* Lipari v. Sears, Roebuck & Co., 497 F. Supp. 185 (D. Neb. 1980) (finding liability where no specific victim had been threatened, on theory that foreseeable violence may involve a "class of persons at risk"); Jablonski v. United States, 712 F.2d 391 (9th Cir. 1983) (psychological profile of assailant indicated he was likely to harm "women very close to him").

76. Using Arizona again as an example, the relevant statute states that the duty "is discharged by all of the following: 1. Communicating when possible the threat to all identifiable victims. 2. Notifying a law enforcement agency in the vicinity where the patient or any potential victim resides. 3. Taking reasonable steps to initiate proceedings for voluntary or involuntary hospitalization, if appropriate. 4. Taking any other precautions that a reasonable and prudent mental health provider would take under the circumstances." Ariz. Stat. § 36-517.02(B). The Maryland statute is similar but adds that the duty can be discharged by making "reasonable and timely efforts to . . . formulate a diagnostic impression and establish and undertake a documented treatment plan calculated to eliminate the possibility that the patient will carry out the threat." Md. Stat. § 5-315(c)(2)(ii).

77. *See* Note, *Where the Public Peril Begins: A Survey of Psycho-Therapists to Determine the Effects of Tarasoff,* 31 STAN. L. REV. 165 (1978). *See also* Daniel Givelber et al., *Tarasoff, Myth and Reality: An Empirical Study of Private Law in Actions,* 1984 WIS. L. REV. 443.

78. *Official Actions, Council on Psychiatry and Law,* 141 AM. J. PSYCHIATRY 487 (1984). For ethical rules, *see* American Medical Association, Principles of Medical Ethics of the American Medical Association, § 9; American Psychiatric Association, *Ethical Principles of Psychiatrists,* 141 AM. J. PSYCHIATRY 487 (1984); American Psychological Association, *Ethical Principles of Psychologists,* 47 AM. PSYCHOLOGIST 1597 (1992) (Principle 5.05).

79. Virtually every state recognizes a psychologist–patient privilege. Those that specifically recognize a social worker–patient privilege as well include Alabama, California, District of Columbia, Idaho, Illinois, Iowa, Kansas, Montana, Nevada, New York, Ohio, Pennsylvania, Rhode Island, South Carolina, Texas, Vermont, Virginia, and West Virginia. In Jaffee v. Redmond, 116 S. Ct. 1923 (1996), the U.S. Supreme Court adopted the psychotherapist–patient privilege for the federal courts and included social workers in the definition of psychotherapist. For a compilation of statutes, *see* Note, *Breaking the Silence: A Reconsideration of Michigan's Psychotherapist–Patient Privilege* 1361, 1364 n.11 (1993); *Jaffee,* 116 S. Ct. at 1930 n.17.

80. *See* Cynthia B. v. New Rochelle Hosp. Med. Ctr., 60 N.Y.2d 452, 470 N.Y.S.2d 122, 470 N.E.2d 363 (1983) (protective order may be obtained by treating hospital or doctor if disclosure "may be seriously detrimental to the interest of the patient, to uninvolved third parties, or to an important program of the custodian of the record").

81. For states that apply the balancing approach in the civil context, *see* CAL. EVID. CODE § 1010-28(f); CONN. GEN. STAT. ANN. § S2-146(c); ILL. ANN. STAT. ch. 91 h, § 810(a)(1); ME. REV. STAT. ANN. tit. 32, § 7005; MASS. ANN. LAWS ch. 233, § 20B(c); TENN. CODE ANN. § 24-1-207; VA. CODE ANN. § 8.01-400.2. Judge Hufstedler has argued that disclosures may not be compelled in a personal injury case over a claim of privilege beyond "the fact of treatment, the time and length of treatment, the cost of treatment, and the ultimate diagnosis unless the party seeking disclosure establishes in the trial court a compelling need for its production." Caesar v. Moutanos, 542 F.2d 1064, 1075 (9th Cir. 1976) (Hufstedler, J., concurring and dissenting). *But see Jaffee,* discussed *supra* in text accompanying note 82.

For nuances in the application of the privilege in the criminal context, see Note, *supra* note 79. For a general treatment of the privilege, *see* MCCORMICK ON EVIDENCE ch. 11 (1993).

82. 116 S. Ct. 1923 (1996).

83. For a general treatment of the informed consent doctrine, *see* Alan Meisel et al., *Toward a Model of the Legal Doctrine of Informed Consent,* 134 AM. J. PSYCHIATRY 285 (1977).

84. Although failure to inform the patient of relevant information is the gravamen of an informed consent claim, absence of injury will usually lead to a summary judgment in favor of the defendant; nominal damages are rarely granted in such cases (and are rarely sued for to begin with).

85. For a discussion of malpractice and negligent misdiagnosis actions, see RALPH SLOVENKO, PSYCHIATRY AND LAW 399–400 (1973). For a more recent treatment of these issues, see MICHAEL PERLIN, MENTAL DISABILITY LAW: CIVIL AND CRIMINAL §§ 12.01 *et seq.* (1989, with supplements), in particular, 12.04 (describing the erosion of the "locality" rule and the adoption of a national standard of prevailing norms), 12.13 (failure to diagnose illness accurately).

86. Note, *Medical Malpractice: The Liability of Psychiatrists,* 48 NOTRE DAME LAW. 693, 749 (1973).

87. These states include California, Massachusetts, Michigan, Missouri, Nevada, New York, Ohio, Oregon, and Pennsylvania. *See generally* R.F. Chase, *Annot., Liability for False Imprisonment Predicated upon Institution of, or Conduct in Connection with, Insanity Proceedings,* 30 A.L.R.3d 523, § 5 (1995).

88. American Academy of Psychiatry and the Law, *Ethical Guidelines for the Practice of Forensic Psychiatry AAPL Guidelines,* in AMERICAN ACADEMY OF PSYCHIATRY AND THE LAW MEMBERSHIP DIRECTORY xi–xiv (1993) [hereinafter AAPL Guidelines].

89. Committee on Ethical Guidelines for Forensic Psychologists, *Speciality Guidelines for Forensic Psychologists,* 15 LAW & HUM. BEHAV. 655 (1991) [hereinafter APLS Guidelines]. These guidelines were developed by Division 41 (a.k.a. the American Psychology–Law Society (APLS)) of the American Psychological Association in collaboration with the American Academy of Forensic Psychology, which has also endorsed the guidelines by a majority vote of its members. Some state organizations have also developed guidelines for forensic clinical practice. *See, e.g.,* MAINE SOCIETY OF FORENSIC PSYCHOLOGISTS, GUIDELINES FOR THE PRACTICE OF FORENSIC PSYCHOLOGY (1989).

90. AAPL Guidelines, *supra* note 88, § V, at xiv.

91. APLS Guidelines, *supra* note 89, §§ III.C. (p. 658), VI.A. (p. 661).

92. Abraham Fenster et al., *The Making of a Forensic Psychologist,* 6 PROF. PSYCHOL. 457 (1975); Norman G. Poythress, *A Proposal for Training in Forensic Psychology,* 34 AM. PSYCHOLOGIST 612 (1979).

93. Joseph D. Bloom et al., *Residence Curriculum in Forensic Psychiatry,* 137 AM. J. PSYCHIATRY 730 (1980); Seymour Pollack, *Forensic Psychiatry: A Specialty,* 2 BULL. AM. ACAD. PSYCHIATRY & L. 1 (1974); Robert Sadoff et al., *Survey of Teaching Programs in Law and Psychiatry,* 2 BULL. AM. ACAD. PSYCHIATRY & L. 67 (1974).

94. Richard J. Freeman & Ronald Roesch, *Psycholegal Education: Training for Forum and Function,* in HANDBOOK OF PSYCHOLOGY AND LAW 568 (Dorothy K. Kagehiro & William S. Laufer eds. 1992); Gary B. Melton, *Training in Psychology and Law,* in HANDBOOK OF FORENSIC PSYCHOLOGY 681 (Irving D. Weiner & Alan K. Hess eds. 1987); Kirk S. Heilbrun & Larry V. Annis, *Research and Training in Forensic Psychology: National Survey of Forensic Facilities,* 19 PROF. PSYCHOL.: RES. & PRAC. 211 (1988); Randy K. Otto et al., *Training and Credentialling in Forensic Psychology,* 8 BEHAVIORAL SCI. & L. 217 (1990); Alan J. Tomkins & James R.P. Ogloff, *Training and Career Options in Psychology and Law,* 8 BEHAVIORAL SCI. & L. 205 (1990).

95. Ronald Roesch et al., *Training Programs, Courses, and Workshops in Psychology and the Law,* in THE IMPACT OF SOCIAL PSYCHOLOGY ON PROCEDURAL JUSTICE 83 (Martin F. Kaplan ed. 1986).

96. 819 Park Avenue, Baltimore, Md. 21201.

97. 2100 E. Broadway, Suite 313, Columbia, Mo. 65201-6082. Although board certification requires a medical or doctoral degree and hundreds of hours of su-

pervision, it should be noted that such certification does not automatically translate into state certification or acceptance as an expert witness, as state law can vary significantly from that tested by these boards.

98. Two organizations provide forensic training for social workers: the National Organization of Forensic Social Work, P.O. Box 174, Milan, Mich. 48160, and the Forensic Practice Committee of the National Federation of Clinical Social Workers, Box 3740, Arlington, Va. 22203.

99. AAPL's address is 819 Park Avenue, Baltimore, Md. 21201.

100. Information about membership in APLS can be obtained from Cathy Oslzly, Law/Psychology Program, 209 Burnett Hall, University of Nebraska—Lincoln, Lincoln, Neb. 68588-0308.

101. Among the books in the field are the following, of varying length and quality: THEODORE BLAU, THE PSYCHOLOGIST AS EXPERT WITNESS (1981); STANLEY BRODSKY, TESTIFYING IN COURT: GUIDELINES AND MAXIMS FOR THE EXPERT WITNESS (1991); CHARLES EWING, PSYCHOLOGY, PSYCHIATRY, AND THE LAW: A CLINICAL AND FORENSIC HANDBOOK (1985); RICHARD GARDNER, FAMILY EVALUATION IN CHILD CUSTODY LITIGATION (1982); RICHARD GREEN & A. SCHAEFER, FORENSIC PSYCHOLOGY: A PRIMER FOR LEGAL AND MENTAL HEALTH PROFESSIONALS (1984); THOMAS GRISSO, EVALUATING COMPETENCIES: FORENSIC ASSESSMENTS AND INSTRUMENTS (1986); MICHAEL MALONEY, A CLINICIAN'S GUIDE TO FORENSIC PSYCHOLOGICAL ASSESSMENT (1985); DAVID SHAPIRO, PSYCHOLOGICAL EVALUATION AND EXPERT TESTIMONY, A PRACTICAL GUIDE TO FORENSIC WORK (1984); DANIEL SHUM., PSYCHIATRIC AND PSYCHOLOGICAL EVIDENCE (1986); HANDBOOK OF FORENSIC PSYCHOLOGY, supra note 94; JAY ZISKIN, COPING WITH PSYCHIATRIC AND LEGAL TESTIMONY—VOLS. 1–3 (5th ed. 1994); BARBARA A. WEINER & ROBERT M. WETTSTEIN, LEGAL ISSUES IN MENTAL HEALTH CARE (1993).

102. In some cases, of course, self-study, including reading relevant literature and statutes, and informal discussions with mental health and legal colleagues, may be sufficient to generalize into areas not drastically dissimilar from one's established areas of competence.

103. Thomas Grisso, *The Economic and Scientific Future of Forensic Psychological Assessment,* 42 AM. PSYCHOLOGIST 831, 836 (1987).

104. *See, e.g.,* § 8.04(b) & (e).

105. Linda Appenfeldt, *Court-Appointed Competency to Proceed to Trial Evaluations,* FLA. PSYCHOLOGIST (Nov. 1991) at 20.

106. APLS Guidelines, *supra* note 89, at 658.

107. Stanley L. Brodsky & Norman G. Poythress, *Expertise on the Witness Stand: A Practitioner's Guide,* in PSYCHOLOGY, PSYCHIATRY AND THE LAW: A CLINICAL AND FORENSIC HANDBOOK, *supra* note 101, at 389.

108. APLS Guidelines, *supra* note 89, § IV.A.3, at 658.

109. APLS Guidelines, *supra* note 89, § IV.A.4, at 658.

110. Some authorities recommend that the experts arrange to be paid for their evaluation time prior to testifying in court, thus avoiding the situation of testifying (presumably on behalf of) a party that owes them a large amount of money. *See* Stuart A. Greenberg & Francine B. Kulick, *The Role of the Mental Health Professional in Employment Litigation,* in MENTAL AND EMOTIONAL INJURIES IN EMPLOYMENT LITIGATION 141 (James J. MacDonald Jr. & Francine B. Kulick eds. 1994). This recommendation appears to flow more from considerations of trial tactics and appearances, however, than from ethical mandates.

111. AAPL Guidelines, supra note 88, § IV, at xiii.

112. APLS Guidelines, supra note 89, § IV.B,at 659.

113. *See, e.g.,* Dupree v. Malpractice Research Inc., 179 Mich. App. 254, 445 N.W.2d 498 (1989); Polo v. Gotchel, 225 N.J. Super. 429, 542 A.2d 947 (1987).

114. *See* the ethical codes of the American Psychiatric Association and the American Psychological Association, *supra* note 78. Analogously, lawyers are urged (but not required) to donate 50 hours of their time to pro bono service. American Bar Association, Model Rule of Professional Conduct, Rule 6.1.

One problem not answered by the clinical ethical codes is the appropriate response when clinicians who have agreed to be involved in a case on a *pro bono* basis are offered what amounts to full payment by parties who in fact prevailed. These situations, admittedly infrequent, are troublesome. On the one hand, the payment may be seen as a serendipitous and fair reward for someone who, in good faith, committed professional services to the public good with no expectation of personal benefit. Alternatively, accepting such payment leaves the clinician open to allegations of *de facto* contingency contracting under the guise of voluntary professional service.

115. APLS Guidelines, *supra* note 89, § IV.A.2, at 658.

116. Clinicians' objectivity might also be open to question if the results of their forensic evaluations turn out favorably for "their patients."

117. AAPL Guidelines, *supra* note 88, § II, at xi–xii.

118. *See generally* WHO IS THE CLIENT? (John Monahan ed. 1981).

119. Daniel Shuman, *The Use of Empathy in Forensic Evaluations,* 3 ETHICS & BEHAV. 289 (1993). Shuman would prohibit only "reflective" empathy (which he defines as a "quality of felt awareness of the experiences of another person"), while allowing "receptive" empathy (defined as "awareness of a person's perceptions and experiences"). Thus, he would prohibit the statement "I'll bet that made you angry" but would permit "I am not sure that I understood your response; were you angry?" We assume, for purposes of the following discussion, there is a significant difference between the two.

120. When an emergency situation forces the clinician to assume a therapeutic role and posture toward an individual, ethical guidelines related to problems with dual role relationships suggest that the examiner avoid providing further forensic services (e.g., forensic evaluation anticipating expert testimony) to that person unless that is reasonably unavoidable. APLS Guidelines, *supra* note 89, § VI.D.2, at 662.

121. A fuller excerpt of the relevant passage is as follows: "The use of empathetic techniques and tools of clarification and interpretation may lower a subject's usual defenses. It is difficult to provide guidelines to regulate such behavior, however, because in many cases these techniques represent the essence of the psychiatric examination. In addition, empathetic statements may be necessary to prevent the subject from suffering harm as the result of discussing psychologically distressing topics. A particularly troubling situation arises when the defendant responds to an empathetic interviewer by revealing damaging information as a penitential act or as an expression of guilt. One must ultimately rely on the judgment of the individual psychiatrist in this type of situation. What can be said is that the psychiatrist should consider terminating the examination whenever it appears that the subject is confused about the purpose of the encounter. A subject who appears to be slipping into a 'therapeutic' mindset should be reminded of the nontherapeutic intent of the assessment before the examination proceeds further." *Psychiatry in the Sentencing Process,* in AMERICAN PSYCHIATRIC ASSOCIATION, ISSUES IN FORENSIC PSYCHIATRY 203 (1984).

122. *See* AAPL Guidelines, *supra* note 88, § II, at xii, and APLS Guidelines, *supra* note 89, § IV.D.2, at 658.

123. Similar conflicts are found in other contexts. For example, psychiatrists who evaluate individuals for civil commitment may later be put in the role of attending psychiatrist following involuntary hospitalization.

124. A thoughtful discussion of these issues appears in the report of the National Institutes of Mental Health task force that reviewed procedures at St. Elizabeth's Hospital in Washington, D.C., prompted by concerns with the hospital's management of John Hinckley, a patient who attempted to assassinate President Ronald Reagan. *See Final Report of the National Institute of Mental Health (NIMH) Ad Hoc Forensic Advisory Panel,* 12 MENTAL & PHYSICAL DISABILITY L. REP. 77 (1988) [hereinafter NIMH Panel].

125. The NIMH panel concluded that in such contexts, therapists should be required to provide input into decisions regarding patient management and discharge planning:

"The panel also notes, however, that assessing the likelihood of future violent behavior of forensic patients requires the calibration of multiple factors including the patient's medical progress, underlying personality characteristics, and the environmental stresses that will likely be encountered upon release. The dynamics of a patient's committing offense may offer certain clues toward understanding and prediction. . . .

"The treatment staff needs to consider detailed information not only about the patient's medical progress but how multiple factors come together to make the next step safe. Some of the relevant information may be best understood and known by the patient's therapist. . . . This information should, therefore, be integrated into the forensic assessment and prediction process and documented.

"Many communications in therapy are not recorded on charts, shared directly with others on the treatment team nor do they become open later to court scrutiny and review. . . . The safeguards [for release decision making] should ensure that all clinically relevant information (even that learned in therapy) does go forward and is at least potentially available to the court in its role in release decisionmaking." *Id.* at 78–79.

Although the patient should be advised that the therapist may make limited disclosures to other hospital staff involved in a collateral forensic evaluation, efforts should be made to otherwise preserve the therapeutic role and relationship. Thus, the NIMH committee also advised: "The Panel recommends that patients' therapists not be subpoenaed to court to testify at release hearings." *Id.* at 79.

126. AAPL Guidelines, *supra* note 88, § II, at xii.

127. *Id.,* § II, at xi.

128. APLS Guidelines, *supra* note 89, § V.B, at 660.

129. W. Glenn Clingempeel et al., *A National Study of Ethical Dilemmas of Psychologists in the Criminal Justice System,* in WHO IS THE CLIENT, *supra* note 118, at 126.

130. This tension parallels that which arises in similar situations in the law, for example, when the "best" information for purposes of determining the "truth" may have to give way to "justice" concerns that an individual's privacy right not be sacrificed in the process of obtaining that evidence. *See* §7.02, discussing search and seizure law.

131. *See* American Psychological Association, Principle 5.01, *supra* note 78.

132. American Psychological Association, Principle 5.05, *supra* note 78, at 1604.

133. American Psychological Association, Principle D: Respect for People's Rights and Dignity, *supra* note 78, at 1599.

134. In this case, the clinical staff agreed to release a *post hoc* opinion regarding mental state at the time of the offense *only* if the defendant's attorney provided a written authorization for the amended report. The attorney refused to provide such a release, and no report was sent.

Chapter 5

1. *See* Symposium, *Justice and Mental Health Systems Interactions,* 16 LAW & HUM. BEHAV. 1 (1992).

2. Evaluations connected with private civil litigation (e.g., torts and, in most states, child custody disputes) are typically conducted by general mental health professionals and not subject to any "system" as such (although, as discussed in §16.01(b)(2), some states have established

special clinics for evaluation and mediation in child custody disputes). Although there is an overarching system for civil evaluations that are mandated by the *government* (e.g., worker's compensation, Social Security, and civil commitment determinations), these systems typically are relatively standardized because they commonly arise in administrative structures guided by detailed statutes or regulations. Also, even though such evaluations involve public law, their immediate consequences usually apply only to the subjects and their families (unlike criminal and juvenile cases, in which retribution and incapacitation are often immediate public concerns). Therefore, most of the controversy about the design of forensic service systems has focused on ways of providing criminal and juvenile evaluations, and our own discussion has a similar emphasis.

3. This section and §5.05 appeared earlier in somewhat different form in Gary B. Melton, *Expert Opinions: "Not for Cosmic Understanding,"* in PSYCHOLOGY IN LITIGATION AND LEGISLATION 55 (Bruce D. Sales & Gary Van den Bos eds. 1994).

4. *See* JEROME D. FRANK, PERSUASION AND HEALING (3d ed. 1991); PLACEBO: THEORY, RESEARCH, AND MECHANISMS (Leonard White et al. eds. 1985).

5. *See, e.g.*, American Psychological Association, *Ethical Principles of Psychologists and Code of Conduct,* 47 AM. PSYCHOLOGIST 1597 (1992) (Standard 7.03); Committee on Ethical Guidelines for Forensic Psychologists, *Specialty Guidelines for Forensic Psychologists,* 15 LAW & HUM. BEHAV. 655 (1991) (Guideline IV(D)).

6. Of course, this particular problem can be avoided—albeit often with some loss of efficiency and privacy—by conducting jail-based evaluations of defendants currently in custody. Nonetheless, the broader point is still applicable. General clinicians' forays into the legal system—often with great publicity—may affect other clients' and potential clients' trust. *Cf.* MURRAY LEVINE & HOWARD J. DOUECK, THE IMPACT OF MANDATED REPORTING ON THE THERAPEUTIC PROCESS: PICKING UP THE PIECES (1995).

7. GARY B. MELTON ET AL., COMMUNITY MENTAL HEALTH CENTERS AND THE COURTS: AN EVALUATION OF COMMUNITY-BASED FORENSIC SERVICES 113 (1985).

8. Payment for community-based evaluations came from court budgets while the much greater cost of state-financed hospital evaluations was not incurred by the referring agency. *Id.* at 90–92.

9. VA. CODE §§ 19.2-168.1 & -169.1 to 19.2-169.7.

10. *See, e.g.*, James R.P. Ogloff & Ronald Roesch, *Using Community Mental Health Centers to Provide Comprehensive Mental Health Services to Local Jails,* in LAW AND PSYCHOLOGY: THE BROADENING OF THE DISCIPLINE 241, 252–58 (James R.P. Ogloff ed. 1992).

11. Henry J. Steadman, *Boundary Spanners: A Key Component for the Effective Interactions of the Justice and Mental Health Systems,* 16 LAW & HUM. BEHAV. 75 (1992).

12. To be clear, as the discussion *infra* indicates, our desire to have most forensic assessments conducted by specialists in forensic mental health does not imply that the specialists should be located outside the regular community mental health system. Integration of forensic services into community mental health services is needed to avoid establishing a chronically underfunded and understaffed de facto corrections program and to assure responsiveness to people in conflict with their relatives and neighbors and in periods of great crisis. Such an approach may ultimately reduce unnecessary court referrals.

13. MELTON ET AL., *supra* note 7, at 43–55. It is important to note that samples of forensic clinicians in this study were probably atypical. One group consisted of community mental health professionals who had participated in an extensive training program at the Institute of Law, Psychiatry, and Public Policy at the University of Virginia. The other group was composed of diplomates certified by the American Board of Forensic Psychology. These groups showed that they possess a specialized body of knowledge commonly possessed by neither judges nor general mental health professionals.

14. This section is derived from Norman Poythress et al., *Pretrial Evaluations for Criminal Courts: Contemporary Models of Service Delivery,* 18 J. MENTAL HEALTH ADMIN. 198–207 (1991). Information about the number of states following the models is drawn from Thomas Grisso et al., *The Organization of Pretrial Evaluation Services: A National Profile,* 18 LAW & HUM. BEHAV. 377 (1994).

15. *See, e.g.*, RONALD ROESCH & STEPHEN GOLDING, COMPETENCY TO STAND TRIAL 188–91 (1980); A. Louis McGarry, *Competence for Trial and Due Process Via the State Hospital,* 122 AM. J. PSYCHIATRY 623 (1965); Ronald Roesch, *A Brief, Immediate Screening Interview to Determine Competency to Stand Trial: A Feasibility Study,* 5 CRIM. JUST. & BEHAV. 241 (1978).

16. *See generally* Ingo Keilitz et al., *Least Restrictive Treatment of Involuntary Patients: Translating Concepts into Practice,* 29 ST. LOUIS U. L.J. 691 (1985).

17. Of course, this approach could also be used in the inpatient context. By the same token, the more global approach could be used in the outpatient context, although it would be less feasible in many cases.

18. Thomas Grisso et al., personal communication, Sept. 11, 1995, at 50.

19. *Id.* at 50–51. *But see* Grisso et al., *supra* note 14, at 386, Table 6, for different figures: inpatient (27.2-day average); local outpatient (19-day average for private practitioner system, 27.1-day average for community-based system), and outpatient hospital (49-day average). The latter average is much higher than that reflected in the text, and may affect the cost assessment.

20. MELTON ET AL., *supra* note 7, at 27–42.

21. Norman Poythress, *Forensic Examiner Training in Alabama* (paper presented at the meeting of the American Psychology–Law Society, Williamsburg, VA, Mar. 1990).

22. *Supra* note 14.

23. *See generally* Gary B. Melton, *Community Psychology and Rural Legal Systems,* in RURAL PSYCHOLOGY (Alan W. Childs & Gary B. Melton eds. 1983) (discussing potential benefits of psychological consultation in the legal system in rural communities).

24. MELTON ET AL., *supra* note 7, at 43–67.

25. *Cf.* Thomas Grisso, *The Economic and Scientific Future of Forensic Psychological Assessment,* 42 AM. PSYCHOLOGIST 831 (1987) (discussing ways that market forces may diminish or increase the quality of forensic assessments).

26. *See, e.g.*, MELTON ET AL., *supra* note 7, at 79–83.

27. *Id. See generally* HENRY J. STEADMAN ET AL., THE

MENTALLY ILL IN JAIL: PLANNING FOR ESSENTIAL SERVICES (1989) (describing the state of mental health services in jails in the United States); Ogloff & Roesch, *supra* note 10, at 245–51 (discussing the rationale for jail-based mental health services, including forensic services). *See also* Karen A. Abram & Linda A. Teplin, *Co-Occurring Disorders among Mentally Ill Jail Detainees: Implications for Public Policy,* 46 AM. PSYCHOLOGIST 1036 (1991); Linda A. Teplin, *The Criminalization Hypothesis: Myth, Misnomer, or Management Strategy?,* in LAW AND MENTAL HEALTH: MAJOR DEVELOPMENTS AND RESEARCH NEEDS 149 (Saleem A. Shah & Bruce D. Sales eds. 1991) (discussing the risk of detention in jail for people with serious mental illnesses when therapeutic alternatives are believed to be unavailable).

28. A fundamental constitutional principle is that involuntary restrictions on liberty and intrusions on privacy should be no greater than necessary to meet the state's compelling interest. *See, e.g.,* Jackson v. Indiana, 406 U.S. 715, 717; Shelton v. Tucker, 364 U.S. 479, 488 (1960); Lake v. Cameron, 364 F.2d 657 (D.C. Cir. 1966). For application of this legal doctrine to the design of forensic mental health services, *see, e.g.,* CRIMINAL JUSTICE MENTAL HEALTH STANDARDS §§ 7-4.3, 7-4.9(a), 7-7.2(b), & 7-7.16 and accompanying commentary (Am. Bar Ass'n 1984).

29. For a discussion of the abuse of hospital-based evaluations of competency to stand trial, see § 6.03(c).

30. Most of this section is derived from MELTON ET AL., *supra* note 7, chs. 6, 7.

31. Douglas A. Hastings & Richard J. Bonnie, *A Survey of Pretrial Psychiatric Evaluations in Richmond, Virginia,* 1 DEVELOPMENTS MENTAL HEALTH L. 9–12 (1981); Ronald Roesch & Stephen Golding, *Legal and Judicial Interpretation of Competency to Stand Trial Statutes and Procedures,* 16 CRIMINOLOGY 420–29 (1978).

32. For an example of such a statute, see VA. CODE § 19.2-169.5 (dealing with the procedures for performing a competency evaluation and filing a report).

33. MELTON ET AL., *supra* note 7, at 98–99.

34. *See* Kirk S. Heilbrun & Lawrence V. Annis, *Research and Training in Forensic Psychology: National Survey of Forensic Facilities,* 19 PROF. PSYCHOL.: RES. & PRAC. 211 (1988); Howard V. Zonana et al., *Training and Credentialing in Forensic Psychology,* 8 BEHAVIORAL SCI. & L. 233 (1990); Randy Otto et al., *Training and Credentialing in Forensic Psychology,* 8 LAW & HUM. BEHAV. 217 (1990).

Each of the authors of this book is a present or former director of a forensic training program. We are convinced of the efficacy of specialized, interdisciplinary training for mental health professionals who seek to offer assistance to the legal system and for lawyers who might use such consultation. Therefore, we hope that specialized courses and internships in forensic mental health will become a standard feature of professional training programs. Unfortunately, there is far to go before such a goal will be reached.

35. *See* Grisso, *supra* note 25.

36. MELTON ET AL., *supra* note 7, at 53–54 & 94–100.

37. *See* CRIMINAL JUSTICE MENTAL HEALTH STANDARDS, *supra* note 28, Standard 7-1.3 and accompanying commentary.

38. *See, e.g.,* Gary B. Melton, *Effects of a State Law Permitting Minors to Consent to Psychotherapy,* 12 PROF. PSYCHOL. 647 (1981); Marsha B. Liss & Linda E. Weinberger, *Psychologists' Knowledge of Mental Health Laws, or I Didn't Know I Was Legally Responsible for That* (paper presented at the meeting of the American Psychology–Law Society, Chicago, Oct. 1983).

39. *Cf.* Lawrence H. Cohen et al., *Use of Psychotherapy Research by Professional Psychologists,* 41 AM. PSYCHOLOGIST 198 (1986) (describing clinical psychologists' reliance on oral communications from trusted colleagues and their limited reading of journals and research books); Thomas Grisso & Gary B. Melton, *Getting Child Development Research to Legal Practitioners: Which Way to the Trenches?,* in REFORMING THE LAW: IMPACT OF CHILD DEVELOPMENT RESEARCH 146 (Gary B. Melton ed. 1987).

40. *See, e.g.,* STEPHEN L. WASBY, SMALL TOWN POLICE AND THE SUPREME COURT: HEARING THE WORD (1976).

41. MELTON ET AL., *supra* note 7, at 100–01.

42. Robert Fein et al., *The Designated Forensic Professional Program: A State Government–University Partnership to Improve Forensic Mental Health Services,* 18 J. MENTAL HEALTH ADMIN. 223 (1991).

43. Stephen J. Morse, *Failed Explanations and Criminal Responsibility: Experts and the Unconscious,* 68 VA. L. REV. 971, 1053–54 (1982). Morse's conclusions are, as he admits, based on impressions rather than systematic evidence. However, there are several reasons to believe that forensic practice is near the bottom of the pecking order of mental health specialties. First, working conditions in forensic units have often been abysmal. Second, the double-agent status that forensic practice often creates [see Chapter 4] is uncomfortable for many mental health professionals. Third, forensic practice necessarily subjects one's work to public scrutiny in an adversary setting, a circumstance that some clinicians find stressful or even demeaning. Fourth, the clients of the forensic mental health system may themselves be perceived as undesirable. Fifth, forensic practice requires spending time away from "real" mental health work in preparation for legal proceedings.

Lending some empirical evidence for this hypothesis, Steadman and his colleagues found that there was 28% turnover within 15 to 20 months in the staff providing mental health services for inmates of jails that they studied. STEADMAN ET AL., *supra* note 27, at 107–09.

44. Otto et al., *supra* note 34, at 226–27.

45. *See* Fein et al., *supra* note 42.

46. An additional situation in which a noncertified clinician may be called as an expert might occur when the clinician has been treating a person for an extended period, during which the person allegedly becomes involved in a crime. The treating clinician's opinions may provide especially probative evidence concerning the defendant's mental state near or at the time of the offense. However, as we cautioned in § 4.05(c)(2), the ethically pure role in such a dual-role situation is to resist offering an expert

opinion and to act as a fact witness, recounting solely observations about behavior.

47. John Petrila, *Forensic Psychiatry and Community Mental Health,* 1 DEVELOPMENTS MENTAL HEALTH L. 1 (1981).

48. Henry J. Steadman et al., *Mentally Disordered Offenders: A National Survey of Patients and Facilities,* 6 LAW & HUM. BEHAV. 31 (1982).

49. *See, e.g.,* John Petrila & James L. Hedlund, *A Computer-Supported Information System for Forensic Services,* 34 HOSP. & COMMUNITY PSYCHIATRY 451 (1983).

50. Charles A. Kiesler, *Public and Professional Myths About Mental Hospitalization: An Empirical Reassessment of Policy-Related Beliefs,* 37 AM. PSYCHOLOGIST 1323 (1982).

51. *See* MELTON ET AL., *supra* note 7, at 92.

52. *Id.*

53. *See* Poythress et al., *supra* note 14, at 203.

54. It should also be noted that therapists—in contrast with evaluators—may not be entitled to fees for testimony, because they are considered fact witnesses, not experts. *See, e.g.,* Baird v. Larson, 59 Wash. App. 715 (1990).

55. An excellent example of such a form contract is provided by Stuart Greenberg in his materials on forensic evaluations. Dr. Greenberg can be reached at The Watermark Tower, 1109 First Avenue, Suite 310, Seattle, WA 98101-2945.

56. Greenberg, *id.,* also charges a nonrefundable fee any time that services are requested, even if the services are in fact never rendered. He states that this fee "inhibits attorneys from retaining me just so that the other side can't," pays for the "value to the attorney to be able to say to opposing counsel that they have retained this or that expert and that opposing counsel's client will be subject to thorough evaluation," and compensates for the loss of cases that have to be turned down because of anticipated (but, as it turns out, nonexistent) business. E-mail on Psylaw bulletin board (Jan. 3, 1995).

57. Forensic evaluations typically are not covered by insurance policies because such evaluations are occurring as part of a legal strategy; they are not "medically necessary." When coverage is thus limited, billing that implicitly or explicitly represents that the services were medically necessary would be fraudulent.

58. Lacking a more descriptive term without the surplus meaning of subject, we focus this section on the client. The disclosure process that is described is germane even if the individual to be evaluated has not sought the evaluation and thus, strictly speaking, is not a client.

59. Greenberg, *supra* note 55, has developed excellent materials on preevaluation disclosures by the clinician.

60. *See, e.g.,* Doe v. Roe, 93 Misc. 2d 201, 400 N.Y.S. 668 (1977); MacDonald v. Clinger, 84 App. Div. 2d 482, 446 N.Y.S. 801 (1982).

61. *See generally* HENRY A. DAVIDSON, FORENSIC PSYCHIATRY 338–41 (1965).

62. Note that this statement applies only to the forensic context. For reasons too complex to discuss here, keeping separate files may make some sense when

the entity to which the clinician is reporting is a managed care organization or an insurance company instead of a court.

63. *See, e.g.,* FED. R. CIV. P. 26(b).

64. American Psychological Association, *Ethical Principles of Psychologists and Code of Conduct,* 47 AM. PSYCHOLOGIST 1597 (1992) (Standard 2.02(b)).

65. *Id.* (Standard 2.09).

66. *Id.* (Standard 2.10). *See* Daniel Tranel, *The Release of Psychological Data to Nonexperts: Ethical and Legal Considerations,* 25 PROF. PSYCHOL.: RES. & PRAC. 33 (1994).

67. *See* Reid J. Meloy, *Psychological Test Data Protected . . . Again,* CALIF. PSYCHOLOGIST, Nov. 1991, at 21 (describing several cases, including *Detroit v. NLRB,* 440 U.S. 301 (1979)); Bruce Frumkin, *How to Handle Attorney Requests for Psychological Test Data,* in INNOVATIONS IN CLINICAL PRACTICE: A SOURCEBOOK 275 (Leon Vandecreek et al. eds. 1995). *See also* Standeford v. Winn-Dixie, F.3d (5th Cir. 1995) (unpublished).

68. Robert L. Sadoff, *Practical Issues in Forensic Psychiatric Practice,* in PRINCIPLES AND PRACTICE OF FORENSIC PSYCHIATRY 41, 45 (Richard Rosner ed. 1994).

69. *Id.* at 46.

70. Sadoff flatly states that "[i]t is not recommended to advertise one's wares or skills in legal journals or daily newspapers." *Id.* at 45.

71. 58 Fed. Reg. 557 (FTC Docket No. C-3406, Jan. 7, 1993).

72. 58 Fed. Reg. 17411 (FTC Docket No. C-3416, Apr. 2, 1993).

73. American Psychological Association, *supra* note 64, Principle 4.

74. Rules 5(c) & 5(d), quoted in William J. Curran, *Ethical Perspectives: Formal Codes and Standards,* in FORENSIC PSYCHIATRY AND PSYCHOLOGY 43, 56 (William J. Curran et al. eds. 1986).

75. FLA. STAT. § 490.009(2)(d)(e) (1995).

76. Blau provides an illustration of a general announcement that could be sent to colleagues, attorneys, and courts:

> JANE DOE, Ph.D.,
> takes pleasure in announcing the addition of
> FORENSIC CONSULTATION
> to her practice of clinical and child psychology.
>
> | | |
> |---|---|
> | Custodial evaluations | Marital dissolution mediation |
> | Competency evaluation | Assessment of psychological deficit |
> | 24 Oak Ridge Parkway Suite 145 [Phone number] | Hours by appointment |

THEODORE H. BLAU, THE PSYCHOLOGIST AS EXPERT WITNESS 27 (1984).

77. *Supra* note 25.

78. Grisso joined with Stephen Golding as primary authors of the American Psychology–Law Society's ethical guidelines. Committee on Ethical Guidelines for Forensic Psychologists, *Specialty Guidelines for Forensic Psy-*

chologists, 15 LAW & HUM. BEHAV. 655 (1991). These guidelines in turn formed the foundation for a special section on forensic practice in the American Psychological Association ethical code. American Psychological Association, *supra* note 64, § 7.

79. One way of disseminating research, not discussed in the text, is to change the *system,* to make it more receptive to such research. Grisso's colleague, Paul S. Appelbaum, has argued for such a specialized system for civil commitment decisions. Appelbaum, *Civil Commitment from a Systems Perspective,* 16 LAW & HUM. BEHAV. 61 (1992). Similarly, Melton has proposed development of a specialized bar in juvenile courts—to more effectively use and debunk psychological and psychiatric evidence on substantive issues in proceedings involving children and to apply developmental knowledge to improve the quality of representation of children. *See generally* Gary B. Melton, *Taking* Gault *Seriously: Toward a New Juvenile Court,* 68 NEB. L. REV. 146 (1989).

In describing prevailing approaches to criminal forensic evaluation, Grisso et al., *supra* note 14, found that *systematization*—establishment of a network of community programs providing evaluations—resulted in far more continuing education and quality control than occurred in states using either traditional inpatient models or ad hoc appointment of private practitioners. *Id.* at 389–90. The states using community agencies also had higher satisfaction with their forensic services. *Id.* at 390.

80. *See generally* REFORMING THE LAW: IMPACT OF CHILD DEVELOPMENT RESEARCH (Gary B. Melton ed. 1987); Gary B. Melton, *Bringing Psychology to the Legal System: Opportunities, Obstacles, and Efficacy,* 42 AM. PSYCHOLOGIST 488 (1987).

81. Grisso & Melton, *supra* note 39, at 146.

82. Thomas L. Hafemeister & Gary B. Melton, *The Impact of Social Science Research on the Judiciary,* in REFORMING THE LAW, *supra* note 80, at 27.

83. Gary B. Melton, *Guidelines for Effective Diffusion of Child Development Research into the Legal System,* in REFORMING THE LAW, *supra* note 80, at 280.

84. *See generally* CAROL H. WEISS & E. SINGER, REPORTING OF SOCIAL SCIENCE IN THE NATIONAL MEDIA (1988).

85. It is also interesting to note that the extent to which judges read literature, in *whatever* form, varies directly with the extent of their secretarial help. MELTON ET AL., *supra* note 7, at 76 ($r = .72$, in one sample of trial judges).

86. *See* WASBY, *supra* note 40.

87. Kathryn Olson & Aleisa C. McKinlay, *Peer Networking as a Method of Dissemination of Information to Judges about Child Sexual Abuse* (1993) (available from the Center on Children, Families, and the Law, University of Nebraska–Lincoln).

88. This process would be ideal for communication of information related to development or maintenance of a forensic service system. It also is an inexpensive way of providing external consultation by nationally recognized authorities about issues in using expert opinions in particular contexts.

89. *See supra* note 78 and accompanying text.

90. *See, e.g.,* Gary B. Melton, *Organized Psychology and Legal Policy-making: Involvement in the Post-*Hinckley *Debate,* 16 PROF. PSYCHOL.: RES. & PRAC. 810 (1985).

91. *See* Melton et al., *Psychologists as Law Professors,* 42 AM. PSYCHOLOGIST 502 (1987).

92. Section references refer to applicable parts of this book.

Chapter 6

1. Bruce Winick, *Incompetency to Stand Trial: Developments in the Law,* in MENTALLY DISORDERED OFFENDERS: PERSPECTIVES FROM LAW AND SOCIAL SCIENCE 3 (John Monahan & Henry Steadman eds. 1983).

2. *Id.* at 3–4. *See also* GROUP FOR THE ADVANCEMENT OF PSYCHIATRY, MISUSE OF PSYCHIATRY IN THE CRIMINAL COURTS: COMPETENCY TO STAND TRIAL (1974) (hereinafter GAP).

3. 2 WILLIAM BLACKSTONE, COMMENTARIES ON THE LAW OF ENGLAND 2181 (W. Jones ed. 1916). Blackstone also notes the requirement that the defendant be competent throughout all phases of the criminal process, going on to state that if the defendant "loses his senses" after conviction but prior to judgment, judgment shall not be pronounced, and if the defendant "becomes of nonsane memory" after judgment, execution shall be stayed. *Id.* at 2182.

4. Frith's Case, 22 How. St. Tr. 307 (1790).

5. JUSTIN MILLER, HANDBOOK ON CRIMINAL LAW 28–32 (1934). Although the substantive criminal law is

found in statute in this country, its original source was the English common law.

6. United States v. Lawrence, 26 F. Cas. 887 (D.C. Cir. 1835).

7. Youtsey v. United States, 97 F. 937, 940–41 (6th Cir. 1899).

8. Drope v. Missouri, 420 U.S. 162, 172 (1975). *See also* Dusky v. United States, 362 U.S. 402 (1960); Godinez v. Moran, 509 U.S. 389 (1993).

9. Note, *Incompetency to Stand Trial,* 81 HARV. L. REV. 454, 457–58 (1967).

10. *See also id.* at 458 ("In part there is the notion that the state is justified in imposing sanctions only where there is a possibility that the person convicted will realize the moral reprehensibility of his conduct").

11. Dusky v. United States, 362 U.S. 402 (1960).

12. *Id.*

13. As is true in other areas (e.g., civil commitment, discussed in Chapter 10), statutory definitions vary among the states. The statutory definitions are collected

in Robert J. Favole, *Mental Disability in the American Crimi-nal Process: A Four Issue Survey,* in MENTALLY DISORDERED OFFENDERS: PERSPECTIVES FROM LAW AND SOCIAL SCIENCE 247 (John Monahan & Henry Steadman eds. 1983).

14. One commentary has observed that despite the fact that concerns for fairness underlie the competency doctrine, "as a practical matter . . . these considerations cannot require that every defendant have 'a high degree of performance capacity.'. . . Many defendants lack the in-telligence or the legal sophistication to participate active-ly in the conduct of their defense. But enlarging the class of persons considered incompetent to stand trial to in-clude all such defendants would fundamentally alter the administration of the criminal law." Note, *supra* note 9, at 459. *See also* GAP, *supra* note 2, at 896 (cautioning that its competency criteria list is meant only to identify areas of inquiry and should not leave the impression that "enor-mous legal sophistication is required of both psychiatrist and defendant").

15. Favole, *supra* note 13, at 248–57 (Table 1).

16. People v. Lang, 113 Ill. 2d 407, 498 N.E.2d 1105 (1986); State v. Black, 815 S.W.2d 166 (Tenn. 1991); State v. Perry, 502 So. 2d 543 (La. 1986), *cert. denied,* 484 U.S. 872 (1987); Harper v. State, 579 N.E.2d 68 (Ind. 1991); Feguer v. United States, 302 F.2d 214 (8th Cir.), *cert. denied,* 371 U.S. 872 (1962). *See generally* Alan M. Goldstein & Marc Burd, *Role of Delusions in Trial Competen-cy Evaluations: Case Law and Implications for Forensic Practice,* 3 FORENSIC REP. 361 (1990).

17. Fl. R. Crim. Pro § 3.211(a)

18. CHARLES WHITEBREAD & CHRISTOPHER SLOBOGIN, CRIMINAL PROCEDURE § 26.01 (3d ed. 1993).

19. Richard J. Bonnie, *The Competence of Criminal De-fendants: A Theoretical Reformulation,* 10 BEHAVIORAL SCI. & L. 291 (1992); Richard J. Bonnie, *The Competence of Crim-inal Defendants: Beyond* Dusky & Drope, 47 U. MIAMI L. REV. 539 (1993).

20. *See, e.g.,* Lafferty v. Cook, 949 F.2d 1546 (10th Cir. 1991), *cert. denied,* 112 S. Ct. 1942 (1992); Martin v. Estelle, 546 F.2d 177, 180 (5th Cir.), *cert. denied,* 431 U.S. 971 (1977); Wieter v. Settle, 193 F. Supp. 318, 321–22 (W.D. Mo. 1961).

21. ABA CRIMINAL JUSTICE MENTAL HEALTH STAN-DARDS, standard 7-4.1 (1984)[hereinafter STANDARDS]. The commentary urges that the evaluation of competency consider whether the defendant has a perception of the process not distorted by mental illness or disability; (2) whether the defendant has the capacity to maintain the at-torney–client relationship, including the ability to discuss the facts with counsel without "paranoid distrust," and to discuss strategy; (3) whether the defendant can recall and relate factual information; (4) whether, if necessary, the defendant has the ability to testify in his or her own de-fense; and (5) whether these skills are proportional to the relative complexity and severity of the case. *Id.* at 7-152 to 7-154.

22. GAP, *supra* note 2, at 896–97.

23. 46 A.L.R.3d 544 (1972).

24. Commonwealth *ex rel.* Cummins v. Price, 421 Pa. 396, 218 A.2d 758, 763 (1966), *cert. denied,* 385 U.S.

869. The court also noted that "for over 100 years, lack of memory in murder cases has been a common and fre-quent defense." 218 A.2d at 760.

25. State v. McClendon, 103 Ariz. 103, 437 P.2d 421, 424, 425 (1968).

26. 391 F.2d 460 (1968).

27. 391 F.2d at 463–64.

28. 325 F. Supp. 485 (D. Tenn. 1971).

29. Bruce Winick, *Psychotropic Medication and Compe-tence to Stand Trial,* 1977 AM. B. FOUND. RES. J. 769, 773 (1977).

30. *Id.* at 775 (showing that, as of 1976, only 13 states imposed an automatic bar rule, a number that has surely decreased since that time).

31. 504 U.S. 127 (1992).

32. Winick, *supra* note 1, at 9.

33. Stuart E. Eizenstadt, *Mental Competency to Stand Trial,* 4 HARV. C.R.-C.L. L. REV. 379 (1969).

34. AMERICAN PSYCHIATRIC ASSOCIATION, THE PRINCI-PLES OF MEDICAL ETHICS, WITH ANNOTATIONS ESPECIALLY APPLICABLE TO PSYCHIATRY § 4, anno. 13, at 7 (1981). *See also* § 4.05(b)(1) for more detailed discussion of this is-sue.

35. STANDARDS, *supra* note 21, standard 7-3.2(d).

36. 383 U.S. 375 (1966).

37. Bruce Winick, *Incompetency to Stand Trial: An As-sessment of Costs and Benefits, and a Proposal for Reform,* 39 RUTGERS L. REV. 243, 265–66 (1987).

38. STANDARDS, *supra* note 21, standard 7-4.2(c).

39. Rodney J. Uphoff, *The Role of the Criminal Defense Lawyer in Representing the Mentally Impaired Defendant: Zeal-ous Advocate or Officer of the Court?* 1988 WIS. L. REV. 65.

40. *See* ABA Model Rule of Professional Conduct 1.2(c); Model Code of Professional Responsibility, DR 7-102(A)(7).

41. 383 U.S. 375 (1966). *See also* 18 USC § 4241(a).

42. 420 U.S. 162 (1975).

43. 420 U.S. at 180.

44. *See* Howard Owens et al., *The Judge's View of Com-petency Evaluations,* 15 BULL. AM. ACAD. PSYCHIATRY & L. 381 (1987).

45. Arthur H. Rosenberg & A. Louis McGarry, *Com-petency for Trial: The Making of an Expert,* 128 AM. J. PSYCHI-ATRY 82 (1972).

46. RONALD ROESCH & STEPHEN GOLDING, COMPE-TENCY TO STAND TRIAL 50–52 (1980).

47. *Id.* at 193–97; Ronald Roesch & Stephen Gold-ing, *Legal and Judicial Interpretation of Competency to Stand Trial,* 16 CRIMINOLOGY 420 (1978).

48. Jeffrey Geller & Eric D. Lister, *The Process of Crim-inal Commitment for Pretrial Psychiatric Examination: An Eval-uation,* 135 AM. J. PSYCHIATRY 53 (1978). *See also* ALAN STONE, MENTAL HEALTH AND THE LAW: A SYSTEM IN TRANSI-TION 63 (1976) (suggesting that, when police learn the strictures of "imminent dangerousness" in the context of civil commitment, they are more likely to rely on the criminal justice system to force entry of "crazy" people who are "disturbing the peace" into the mental health sys-tem).

49. Even for prisoners, there is a residual liberty in-

terest in avoiding forced psychiatric treatment. *See* Vitek v. Jones, 445 U.S. 480 (1980).

50. Typically, statutes providing for the hospitalization of defendants for evaluation of competency to stand trial fail to provide explicit authority for involuntary treatment of those defendants.

51. ROESCH & GOLDING, *supra* note 46, at 192.

52. Robert A. Burt & Norval Morris, *A Proposal for the Abolition of the Incompetency Plea,* 40 U. CHI. L. REV. 66, 88 (1972).

53. Joyce K. Laben et al., *Reform from the Inside: Mental Health Center Evaluations of Competency to Stand Trial,* 5 J. COMMUNITY PSYCHOL. 52 (1977). So that our biases are exposed, it is important to note that Petrila began the decentralization of the Missouri forensic system when he was Director of Forensic Services from 1979 to 1981, and Melton and Slobogin were involved in decentralizing the Virginia forensic system. *See* GARY MELTON ET AL., COMMUNITY MENTAL HEALTH CENTERS AND THE COURTS: AN EVALUATION OF COMMUNITY-BASED FORENSIC SERVICES (1985).

54. In 1979, at least 4 of the 12 federal circuits and 17 states allowed psychologists to testify on essentially the same footing as psychiatrists. These included California, Colorado, Georgia, Indiana, Kentucky, Maryland, Michigan, New Mexico, Oklahoma, Oregon, Pennsylvania, Rhode Island, South Dakota, Tennessee, Texas, Virginia, and Wisconsin. Comment, *The Psychologist as Expert Witness: Science in the Courtroom?,* 38 MD. L. REV. 539 nn. 21–22, 546, Appendix (1979).

55. Ronald Roesch & Stephen Golding, *Treatment and Disposition of Defendants to Stand Trial: A Review and Proposal,* 2 INT'L J. L. & PSYCHIATRY 349, 365 (1979). *See also* LABORATORY OF COMMUNITY PSYCHIATRY, COMPETENCY TO STAND TRIAL AND MENTAL ILLNESS (1974).

56. For an account of the increasing attention focused on the right to speedy trial, found in the Sixth Amendment, *see* WHITEBREAD & SLOBOGIN, *supra* note 18, ch. 25. For a treatment of the right to bail, derived from the Eighth Amendment, *see id.,* § 20.03.

57. Note, *supra* note 9, at 470.

58. Carter v. United States, 252 F.2d 608, 617–18 (D.C. Cir. 1957).

59. ROESCH & GOLDING, *supra* note 46, at 193.

60. *See* WHITEBREAD & SLOBOGIN, *supra* note 18, § 26.04.

61. James H. Reich & Linda Tookey, *Disagreement Between Court and Psychiatrist on Competency to Stand Trial,* 47 J. CLINICAL PSYCHIATRY 29 (1986) (reporting that the court disagreed with clinicians' recommendations regarding competency in only 1.7% (6/390) of cases). *See also* LABORATORY OF COMMUNITY PSYCHIATRY, *supra* note 55 (Massachusetts); HENRY STEADMAN, BEATING A RAP?: DEFENDANTS FOUND INCOMPETENT TO STAND TRIAL (1979) (New York); ROESCH & GOLDING, *supra* note 46 (North Carolina); John H. Hess & Hebert E. Thomas, *Incompetency to Stand Trial: Procedures, Results and Problems,* 119 AM. J. PSYCHIATRY 713 (1963) (Michigan); John Petrila, *The Insanity Defense and Other Mental Health Dispositions in Missouri,* 5 INT'L J. L. & PSYCHIATRY 81 (1982); Eric Pfeiffer

et al., *Mental Competency Evaluations for the Federal Courts,* 144 J. NERVOUS MENTAL DISEASE 320 (1967); Carl R. Vann, *Pretrial Determination and Judicial Decisionmaking: An Analysis of the Use of Psychiatric Information in the Administration of Criminal Justice,* 43 U. DET. L.J. 13 (1965); Wright Williams & Kent S. Miller, *The Processing and Disposition of Incompetent Mentally Ill Offenders,* 5 LAW & HUM. BEHAV. 245 (1981) (Florida); Stephen Hart & Richard Hare, *Predicting Fitness to Stand Trial: The Relative Power of Demographic, Criminal and Clinical Variables,* 5 FORENSIC REP. 53 (1992) (Canada).

62. 505 U.S. 437 (1992).

63. Bruce Winick, *Presumptions and Burdens of Proof in Determining Competency to Stand Trial: An Analysis of Medina v. California and the Supreme Court's New Due Process Methodology in Criminal Cases,* 47 MIAMI L. REV. 817 (1993).

At the same time, the Supreme Court has held unconstitutional a statute which placed the burden on the defendant to show incompetency by *clear and convincing evidence* (a standard of proof more difficult to meet than the preponderance level required by the California statute). Cooper v. Oklahoma, 116 S. Ct. 1373 (1996).

64. Roesch & Golding, *supra* note 55, at 349–50.

65. 406 U.S. 715 (1972).

66. *Id.* at 737–38.

67. STONE, *supra* note 48, at 212.

68. Roesch & Golding, *supra* note 55, at 355. These authors have summarized a dozen proposals that deal with limitations on treatment and/or disposition of criminal charges. They note that most of the proposals advocate a six-month limit on treatment, with an additional six months available if needed, an addendum that Stone, *supra* note 32, at 212, has also suggested. Other suggested time limits on commitment have ranged from 90 days, with a possible 90-day extension (the ABA), to six months with indefinite one-year extensions available (Law Reform Commission of Canada).

69. Grant Morris & J. Reid Meloy, *Out of Mind? Out of Sight: The Uncivil Commitment of Permanently Incompetent Criminal Defendants,* 27 U.C. DAVIS L. REV. 1, 11–17 (1993). *See also* Roesch & Golding, *supra* note 55, at 357 (Table 2).

70. *See, e.g.,* Fla. R. Crim. P. 3.213(a). In 1979, 27 states and the District of Columbia had *no* guidelines for dismissing charges. These states included Alabama, Alaska, Arkansas, California, Colorado, Delaware, the District of Columbia, Georgia, Hawaii, Indiana, Iowa, Kentucky, Louisiana, Mississippi, Missouri, Nebraska, Nevada, New Hampshire, New Jersey, New Mexico, Ohio, Oklahoma, South Dakota, Tennessee, Texas, Utah, Vermont and Virginia. Roesch & Golding, *supra* note 46, at 130.

71. New York's experience is illustrative. Anecdotal evidence suggests that hospital staff may be reluctant to move for complete dismissal of charges because facility control over the individual would be loosened. For instance, an individual committed as incompetent to stand trial receives no passes or furloughs unless an internal review by a forensic committee concurs that the person is

not dangerous, a procedure that is not required when a civilly committed patient is involved.

72. According to a 1979 study, 19 states and the District of Columbia provide for automatic hospitalization for incompetency. Roesch & Golding, *supra* note 55, at 357.

73. STEADMAN, *supra* note 61, at 103–04.

74. STANDARDS, *supra* note 21, standard 7-4.9.

75. *Id.*, standard 7-4.11.

76. Roesch & Golding, *supra* note 55, at 364.

77. James J. Gobert, *Competency to Stand Trial: A Pre- and Post-Jackson Analysis*, 40 TENN. L. REV. 659, 668 (1973).

78. Burt & Morris, *supra* note 52.

79. *Id.* at 76.

80. ABA CRIMINAL JUSTICE MENTAL HEALTH STANDARDS, standard 7-4.13 (1983) (first tentative draft).

81. *Id.* The ABA proposal actually specified that the hearing could take place either at 18 months or at 12 months, apparently reflecting ambivalence on the part of the drafters.

82. *Id.*, commentary at 7-239.

83. *Id.*, commentary at 7-240.

84. *See generally Id.*, standards 7-7.3 to 7-7.11.

85. STANDARDS, *supra* note 21, commentary at 7-245. Linda Fentiman, *Whose Right Is It Anyway?: Rethinking Competency to Stand Trial in Light of the Synthetically Sane Insanity Defendant*, 40 U. MIAMI L. REV. 1109 (1986); Note, *Antipsychotic Drugs and Fitness to Stand Trial: The Right of the Unfit Accused to Refuse Treatment*, 52 U. CHI. L. REV. 773 (1985).

86. ROESCH & GOLDING, *supra* note 46, at 41. *See also* United States v. Charters, 829 F.2d 479 (4th Cir. 1987), *rev'd* on review by the full panel of the Fourth Circuit, 863 F.2d 302 (4th Cir. 1988). *But see* Commonwealth v. Louraine, 453 N.E.2d 437 (Mass. 1983); People v. Hardesty, 362 N.W.2d 787 (Mich. 1984); State v. Hayes, 389 A.2d 1379 (N.H. 1978); State v. Law, 244 S.E.2d 302 (S.C. 1978). *See also* Winick, *supra* note 29.

87. 505 U.S. 437 (1992).

88. 494 U.S. 210 (1990).

89. STANDARDS, *supra* note 21, standard 7-4.14. *See also* GAP, *supra* note 2, at 904.

90. 389 A.2d 1379 (1978).

91. GAP, *supra* note 2, at 901; ROESCH & GOLDING, *supra* note 46, at 40.

92. *See, e.g.*, LABORATORY OF COMMUNITY PSYCHIATRY, *supra* note 55; GAP, *supra* note 2; ROESCH & GOLDING, *supra* note 46; THOMAS GRISSO, COMPETENCY TO STAND TRIAL EVALUATIONS: A MANUAL FOR PRACTICE (1988); Thomas Grisso, *Five-Year Research Update (1986–1990): Evaluations for Competence to Stand Trial*, 10 BEHAVIORAL SCI. & L. 353 (1992); Thomas Grisso, *Pretrial Clinical Evaluations in Criminal Cases: Past Trends and Future Directions*, 23 CRIM. JUST. & BEHAV. 90 (1996).

93. Steven K. Hoge et al., *Attorney–Client Decision Making in Criminal Cases: Client Competence and Participation as Perceived by Their Attorneys*, 10 BEHAVIORAL SCI. & L. 385 (1992). Attorneys doubted the competence of their clients in 14.8% of 122 *felony* cases. *Id.* at 389. Norman

G. Poythress et al., *Client Abilities to Assist Counsel and Make Decisions in Criminal Cases: Findings from Three Studies*, 18 LAW & HUM. BEHAV. 435 (1994). In three samples that included both felony and misdemeanor cases, attorneys doubted competence in 7.9%, 14.7%, and 11% of cases. *Id.* at 450.

94. In the study by Hoge et al., *supra* note 93, attorneys referred 52.6% of cases for evaluation of competence. *Id.* at 391. In the three studies by Poythress et al., *supra* note 93, only 20–45% of cases were referred for evaluation *Id.* at 450.

95. *See supra* note 93.

96. Lisa M. Berman & Yvonne H. Osborne, *Attorneys' Referrals for Competency to Stand Trial Evaluations: Comparisons of Referred and Nonreferred Clients*, 5 BEHAVIORAL SCI. & L. 373 (1980).

97. Henry J. Steadman et al., *Mentally Disordered Offenders: A National Survey of Patients and Facilities*, 6 LAW & HUM. BEHAV. 31, 33 (1982).

98. ROESCH & GOLDING, *supra* note 46, at 47–49.

99. Note, however, that as many states move to outpatient evaluation systems (see generally Chapter 5), the number of commitments (as opposed to evaluations) has decreased significantly. *See* Melton et al., *supra* note 53, at 23–42.

100. STEADMAN, *supra* note 61.

101. *Id.* at 30.

102. *Id.* at 30–33.

103. Steven K. Hoge et al., *The MacArthur Adjudicative Competence Study: Development and Validation of a Research Instrument*, 21 LAW & HUM. BEH. 141 (1997).

104. ROESCH & GOLDING, *supra* note 46, at 148–49.

105. A clinical judgment that the defendant may be incompetent moves these more traditional issues to the fore. In jurisdictions that require that treatment for competence restoration be provided in the least restrictive appropriate setting, examiners may also have to address the issue of whether the defendant meets criteria for involuntary hospitalization—typically a "dangerousness" standard. See § 6.07(c).

106. Norman G. Poythress & Harley Stock, *Competency to Stand Trial: A Historical Review and Some New Data*, 8 J. PSYCHIATRY & L. 131 (1980).

107. LABORATORY OF COMMUNITY PSYCHIATRY, *supra* note 55; Stephen L. Golding et al., *Assessment and Conceptualization of Competency to Stand Trial: Preliminary Data on the Interdisciplinary Fitness Interview*, 8 LAW & HUM. BEHAV. 321 (1984); Ronald Roesch, *Determining Competency to Stand Trial: An Examination of Evaluation Procedures in an Institutional Setting*, 47 J. CONSULTING & CLINICAL PSYCHOL. 542 (1979).

108. ROESCH & GOLDING, *supra* note 46, at 188–91. Ronald Roesch, *A Brief, Immediate Screening Interview to Determine Competency to Stand Trial: A Feasibility Study*, 5 CRIM. JUST. & BEHAV. 241 (1978).

109. Golding et al., *supra* note 107.

110. *See, e.g.*, ROESCH & GOLDING, *supra* note 46, at 188–91; Roesch, *supra* note 108.

111. *See* Golding et al., *supra* note 107.

112. *See* MELTON ET AL., *supra* note 53, at 11–12;

Russell C. Petrella & Norman G. Poythress, *The Quality of Forensic Examinations: An Interdisciplinary Study,* 51 J. Consulting & Clinical Psychol. 76 (1983).

113. A. Louis McGarry, *Competence for Trial and Due Process Via the State Hospital,* 122 Am. J. Psychiatry 623 (1965) (reporting a perfect correlation between diagnosis of psychosis and opinion of "incompetent" [31 cases] and nonpsychotic diagnosis and opinion of "competent" [75 cases]).

114. Robert A. Nicholson & William G. Johnson, *Prediction of Competency to Stand Trial: Contribution of Demographics, Type of Offenses, Clinical Characteristics and Psycholegal Ability,* 14 Int'l J. L. & Psychiatry 287 (1991). Forty-three percent of the variance in clinicians' judgments was explained, with diagnoses of psychoses (5%) and scores on the Georgia Court Competence Test (7%) accounting for independent components of variance. *See also* A.E. Daniel et al., *Factors Correlated with Psychiatric Recommendations of Incompetence,* 12 J. Psychiatry & L. 527 (1984) Clinicians' judgments correlated .40 with total scores on the Competency Screening Test. However, CST scores did not survive as an independent predictor in the discriminant function analysis, suggesting that clinicians may have given greater weight to diagnosis and symptoms than to impairment in functional legal abilities.

115. Robert A. Nicholson & Karen E. Kugler, *Competent and Incompetent Criminal Defendants: A Quantitative Review of Comparative Research,* 109 Psychol. Bull. 355 (1991).

116. *See, e.g.,* Laboratory of Community Psychiatry, *supra* note 55, at 100; Roesch & Golding, *supra* note 46, at 188–91; Golding et al., *supra* note 107. *See also* Poythress & Stock, *supra* note 106; Roesch, *supra* note 108.

117. *See generally* Melton et al., *supra* note 53, ch. 4.

118. *See* E. Fuller Torrey & Robert L. Taylor, *Cheap Labor from Poor Nations,* 130 Am. J. Psychiatry 428 (1973).

119. Ames Robey, *Criteria for Competency to Stand Trial: A Checklist for Psychiatrists,* 122 Am. J. Psychiatry 616 (1965).

120. Barry A. Bukatman et al., *What Is Competency to Stand Trial?,* 127 Am. J. Psychiatry 145 (1971).

121. Paul Lipsitt et al., *Competency for Trial: A Screening Instrument,* 128 Am. J. Psychiatry 105 (1971).

122. Laboratory for Community Psychiatry, *supra* note 55, at 98–116.

123. Golding et al., *supra* note 107.

124. Robert W. Wildman II et al., *The Georgia Court Competency Test: An Attempt to Develop a Rapid, Quantitative Measure of Fitness for Trial.* (unpublished manuscript, Forensic Services Division, Central State Hospital, Milledgeville, GA).

125. Caroline T. Everington & Ruth Luckasson, Competence Assessment for Standing Trial for Defendants with Mental Retardation (CAST-MR) (1992) (available from International Diagnostic Systems, Inc.).

126. George W. Barnard et al., *Competency to Stand Trial: Description and Initial Evaluation of a New Computer-Assisted Assessment Tool (CADCOMP),* 19 Bull. Am. Acad. Psychiatry & L. 367 (1991).

127. One or more of these instruments have been discussed by a number of reviewers. *See* Thomas Grisso, Evaluating Competencies: Forensic Assessments and Instruments 62–112 (1986) (reviewing the CST, CAI, IFI, and GCCT); Ronald Roesch & Stephen L. Golding, *Defining and Assessing Competency to Stand Trial,* in Handbook of Forensic Psychology 378 (Irving B. Weiner & Allen K. Hess eds. 1987) (reviewing the CST, CAI, and IFI); Ronald Roesch et al., *Competency to Stand Trial: Legal and Clinical Issues,* 2 Applied & Preventive Psychol. 43 (1993) (reviewing the CST, CAI, and IFI).

128. The scoring manual is provided in Laboratory of Community Psychiatry, *supra* note 55, at 75–88.

129. *Id.* at 91.

130. Lipsitt et al., *supra* note 121, at 107.

131. The usual false-negative rate found in the studies is below 7% and ranges as low as 0%. The exception is a study by Roesch & Golding, which obtained a false-negative rate of 23.8%. Roesch & Golding, *supra* note 1, at 181–83.

132. Samuel J. Brakel, *Presumption, Bias, and Incompetency in the Criminal Process,* 1974 Wis. L. Rev. 1105, 1118–19 (1974).

133. Robert A. Nicholson et al., *Instruments for Assessing Competency to Stand Trial: How Do They Work?,* 19 Prof. Psychol.: Res. & Prac. 383 (1988). *See also* Karen L. Ustad et al., *Restoration of Competency to Stand Trial: Assessment with the Georgia Court Competency Test and the Competency Screening Test,* 20 Law & Hum. Behav. 131 (1996).

134. Laboratory of Community Psychiatry, *supra* note 55, at 100.

135. Grisso, *supra* note 92, at 80.

136. "[T]he CAI currently may not have the status of an instrument; without the use of the quantified rating system, and with no standardized description of the interview process, the CAI's sole contribution would be a list of 13 legally relevant concepts and definitions." *Id.* at 84.

137. Jan Schreiber, *Assessing Competency to Stand Trial: A Case Study of Technology Diffusion in Four States,* 6 Bull. Am. Acad. Psychiatry & L. 439, 446 (1978).

138. Laboratory of Community Psychiatry, *supra* note 55, at 98–125.

139. Stephen L. Golding & Ronald Roesch, *Interdisciplinary Fitness Interview Training Manual* (1981) (unpublished manuscript). Professor Golding advises (personal communication) that a revised IFI is now available. However, as the published research on the IFI has examined the original instrument, we will limit our analysis and discussion to the original version.

140. Golding et al., *supra* note 107.

141. *Id.*

142. *Id.* at 333–34.

143. The description here is adapted from Grisso, *supra* note 92, at 101–02.

144. Wildman II et al., *supra* note 124.

145. Grisso, *supra* note 92, at 101.

146. Robert Nicholson et al., *A Comparison of Instruments for Assessing Competency to Stand Trial,* 12 Law & Hum. Behav. 313 (1988).

147. Nicholson et al., *supra* note 133, at 391–92; Ustad et al., *supra* note 133, at 143.

148. Robert A. Nicholson, *Defining and Assessing Competency to Stand Trial* (1992) (paper presented at the meeting of the American Psychological Association, Washington, D.C.).

149. Barnard et al., *supra* note 126. George W. Barnard et al., *Itemmetric and Scale Analysis of a New Computer-Assisted Competency Instrument (CADCOMP),* 10 BEHAVIORAL SCI. & L. 419 (1992).

150. Barnard et al., *supra* note 126, at 369.

151. *Id.* at 378. The developers claim that "using only the CADCOMP narrative report based on a computer assisted self-report of the defendant, a mental health clinician can arrive at a reliable competency judgment that is at least as valid as judgments based on other competency instruments."

152. *Id.* at 373. Other concerns regarding the validity of the CADCOMP stem from the limited sample to which it was applied in this initial study. The article indicates that "the median number of days between admission and time of testing was 77.5 days," *id.* at 374, and that "subjects had been in intensive residential treatment aimed at restoring their competence for an average of five months," *id.* at 375. In Florida forensic hospitals, 44% of persons admitted for competence restoration are found competent by hospital staff within three months of admission (Sally Cunningham, personal communication, Forensic Services Division of Florida Health and Rehabilitative Services, Sept. 1994). Thus, the subjects in this study are clearly not representative of the range of persons referred for evaluation and/or treatment on the issue of pretrial competence.

153. Ironically, the developers of the CADCOMP envision the CADCOMP as *more* efficient than existing instruments: "Considering the fact that other approaches, i.e., the CAI and IFI, require lengthy face-to-face interviews and produce no preliminary report, CADCOMP may offer a considerable efficiency advantage." *Id.* at 378.

154. Caroline T. Everington, *The Competence for Standing Trial for Defendants with Mental Retardation,* 17 CRIM. JUST. & BEHAV. 147, 148 (1990).

155. *Id.*

156. *Id.*

157. EVERINGTON & LUCKASSON, *supra* note 125, at 21.

158. *Id.* at 23.

159. *Id.* at 20–21.

160. *Id.* at 23 (Table 3), 31.

161. *Id.* at 24. Discriminant analysis yielded classification accuracy rates of 100%, 83% and 83% for sections I, II, and III respectively. *Id.*

162. For more recent data on the validity of the CAST-MR, *see* Caroline Everington and Charles Dunn, *A Second Validation Study of the Competence Assessment for Standing Trial for Defendants with Mental Retardation,* 22 CRIM. JUST. BEHAV. 44 (1995).

164. *Id.* at 21–22.

164. *Id.* at 18–19.

165. *See supra* note 18.

166. Bonnie (1993), *supra* note 19, at 572–76.

167. Nicholson, *supra* note 148, at 17.

168. The description here of the MacArthur research protocol is adapted from Hoge et al., *supra* note 103. For futher consideration of the conceptual backdrop for the intrument, *see* Ian Freckelton. *Rationality and Flexibility in Assessment of Fitness to Stand Trial,* 19 INT'L J. L. & PSYCHIATRY 39 (1996).

169. Hoge et al., *supra* note 103. Additional data from a pilot study of the research protocol is presented in Steven K. Hoge et al., *Mentally Ill and Non-Mentally Ill Defendants' Abilities to Understand Information Relevant to Adjudication: A Preliminary Study,* 24 BULL. AM. ACAD. PSYCHIATRY & L. 187 (1996).

170. "The actual utility of brief screening instruments for dealing with referrals for competency to stand trial evaluations has yet to be demonstrated." Grisso, *supra* note 92, at 359.

171. "CST evaluations typically involve little by way of assessment of a defendant's decisionmaking abilities. Yet decisionmaking about plea will be the final and decisive event for most defendants." *Id.* at 366.

172. *Cf.* William S. Davidson & John A. Saul, *Youth Advocacy in the Juvenile Court: A Clash of Paradigms,* in LEGAL REFORMS AFFECTING CHILD AND YOUTH SERVICES (Gary B. Melton ed., 1982) (juvenile courts are wedded to case-by-case analyses of juvenile delinquency).

173. ROESCH & GOLDING, *supra* note 46, at 89.

174. For a general description of the test from which the results described in the text were taken, *see* MELTON ET AL., supra note 53, ch. 3.

175. Some mental health professionals appear to disagree. *See* Stephen B. Lawrence, *Clinical Evaluation of Competence to Stand Trial,* in PSYCHOLOGY, PSYCHIATRY, AND THE LAW: A CLINICAL AND FORENSIC HANDBOOK 41 (Charles Patrick Ewing ed. 1985). "Long practical experience . . . indicated both judges and attorneys needed and preferred written reports which presented a *complete* picture of the defendant. Attorneys and judges want to know the defendant's life history and background, present mental status, level and degree of cognitive functioning, personality profile, diagnosis, and prognosis. Simply addressing the issue of legal competency to stand trial is too narrow a focus." *Id.* at 52. Although this statement accurately depicts what many attorneys "prefer," their "need" for all of this information is a different matter; perhaps, as discussed in § 6.03(c), Lawrence is referring to situations in which attorneys are using competency evaluations to achieve other aims.

176. Indeed, in some jurisdictions the law mandates that evaluation reports deal with this issue. *See, e.g.*, Fla. R. Crim. P. 3.210 (b) (1), which requires that mental health experts who opine that the defendant may be incompetent to proceed "shall report on . . . the treatment or treatments appropriate . . . the availability of acceptable treatment . . . the likelihood of the defendant attaining competence [and] . . . the probable duration of the treatment required to restore competence."

177. *See, e.g.*, Fla. R. Crim. P. 3.212(c)(3)(i). Although the requirement that an incompetent person meet

commitment criteria before inpatient care can take place is a well-intentioned attempt to prevent unnecessary deprivations of liberty, it can result in inappropriate placement. A certain proportion of those found incompetent do not meet commitment criteria yet may nonetheless require inpatient hospitalization to be restored. This group will be disserved by rules that, like Florida's, prevent such hospitalization.

178. For a review and discussion of these studies, *see* Robert A. Nicholson & John L. McNulty, *Outcome of Hospitalization for Defendants Found Incompetent to Stand Trial,* 10 BEHAVIORAL SCI. & L. 371 (1992).

179. Linda Pendleton, *Treatment of Persons Found Incompetent to Stand Trial,* 137 AM. J. PSYCHIATRY 1098 (1980); Dan L. Davis, *Treatment Planning for the Patient Who Is Incompetent to Stand Trial,* 36 HOSP. & COMMUNITY PSYCHIATRY 268 (1985); Robert J. Barth, *Training the Mentally Retarded to Be Competent to Stand Trial* (1989) (unpublished Ph.D. dissertation, University of South Florida,

Tampa); Alex M. Seigel & Amiram Elwork, *Treating Incompetence to Stand Trial,* 14 LAW & HUM. BEHAV. 57 (1990); D. Ridgley Brown, *A Didactic Group Program for Persons Found Unfit to Stand Trial,* 43 HOSP. & COMMUNITY PSYCHIATRY 732 (1992).

180. The lone exception is the study from Michigan (see Table 6.6), which is by far the earliest study and which relied on a much older (1972–73) database. As mental health professionals have become more aware over the past two decades of the functional nature of the construct of legal competence, fewer reports with high LOS have appeared in the literature. Even in this study, LOS varied considerably across hospitals in the Michigan system, with significantly lower LOS reported at Michigan's Center for Forensic Psychiatry, where staff would be expected to be more aware of the functional nature of legal competence.

181. *See also* text accompanying note 104 *supra.*

182. *See* Barth, *supra* note 179; Brown, *supra* note 179.

Chapter 7

1. *See generally* Hawaii v. Standard Oil, 405 U.S. 251 (1972).

2. *See generally* John Stuart Mill, *On Liberty,* in THE PHILOSOPHY OF JOHN STUART MILL (1961).

3. *See* Note, *Civil Commitment of the Mentally Ill: Developments in the Law,* 87 HARV. L. REV. 1190, 1217–18 (1974) (describing the "threshold requirement of incapacity" for exercise of the *parens patriae* authority).

4. 509 U.S. 389 (1993).

5. U.S. CONST. amend. IV ("The right of the people to be secure in their persons, houses, papers, and effects, against unreasonable searches and seizures, shall not be violated. . .").

6. Mapp v. Ohio, 367 U.S. 643 (1961).

7. For instance, the Supreme Court has held that one's authority to consent to search of a given area depends on whether one has "apparent authority" over the area. Illinois v. Rodriquez, 497 U.S. 177 (1990). Some research explores the extent to which laypeople and police agree on who has apparent authority over an area. Dorothy K. Kagehiro et al., *"Reasonable Expectation of Privacy" and Third-Party Consent Searches,* 15 LAW & HUM. BEHAV. 121 (1991). *See also* Dorothy Kagehiro & Ralph B. Taylor, *Third-Party Consent Searches: Legal vs. Social Perceptions of "Common Authority,"* 18 J. APPLIED SOC. PSYCHOL. 1274 (1988); Dorothy Kagehiro et al., *Consent to Search Another's Premises and Property: Comparing the Law of Criminal Procedure with Social Perceptions of Laypersons and Police Detectives* (forthcoming).

The Supreme Court has also held that the Fourth Amendment's rules only apply to police actions that intrude upon areas associated with "expectations of privacy society is prepared to recognize as reasonable." Katz v. United States, 389 U.S. 347 (1967). Some research investigates the extent to which society agrees with the Court's conclusions regarding the degree of privacy rea-

sonably expected in various situations. Christopher Slobogin & Joseph Schumacher, *Reasonable Expectations of Privacy and Autonomy in Fourth Amendment Cases: An Empirical Look at "Understandings Recognized and Permitted by Society,"* 42 DUKE L.J. 727, 760–62 (1993).

8. *See generally* CHARLES WHITEBREAD & CHRISTOPHER SLOBOGIN, CRIMINAL PROCEDURE: AN ANALYSIS OF CASES AND CONCEPTS §§ 12.02, 12.04 (3d ed. 1993).

9. Florida v. Rodriguez, 469 U.S. 1 (1984) (finding that a person's agreement to follow an officer to where the person's colleagues were being questioned by another officer "as clearly the sort of consensual encounter that implicates no Fourth Amendment interest").

10. Schneckloth v. Bustamonte, 412 U.S. 218 (1973).

11. Dorothy Kagehiro, *Perceived Voluntariness of Consent to Warrantless Police Searches,* 18 J. APPLIED SOC. PSYCHOL. 38 (1988). Kagehiro found that search requests phrased in an interrogatory fashion (e.g., "Would you mind if I came in and looked around?") result in higher perceived choice in permitting entry than did declarative requests (e.g., "I would appreciate it if I could come in and look around"). Interestingly, however, she found, in addition, that the former type of request resulted in a greater likelihood that entry would be granted and that questions would *not* be asked about the police objective. Thus, this research suggests that people subjected to a police request for consent may be more likely to assert their rights if the request is framed declaratively rather than interrogatively. The study also found that the more detail the police provide in their request about their objective, the less likely the person would feel free to ask the police to leave, once consent was given. Again, this type of research may assist the court in deciding the voluntariness of a given consent. *See also* James Wulach, *Psychological Evaluation of the Consent to Search,* 18 PSYCHIATRY & L. 319 (1990).

12. For a more comprehensive review of the law of confessions, *see generally* WHITEBREAD & SLOBOGIN, *supra* note 8, ch. 16. *See also* LAWRENCE S. WRIGHTSMAN & SAUL M. KASSIN, CONFESSIONS IN THE CLASSROOM (1993).

13. 297 U.S. 278 (1936).

14. For a listing of these cases through the late 1950s, *see* Spano v. New York, 360 U.S. 315 n.2 (1959).

15. *See* Fikes v. Alabama, 352 U.S. 191, 197. *But cf.* Yale Kamisar, *What Is an "Involuntary" Confession? Some Comments on Inbau and Reid's Criminal Interrogation and Confessions,* 17 RUTGERS L. REV. 728, at 755–59 (1963) (Supreme Court actually rarely directly analyzed the willfulness of the defendant's confession).

16. Ashcraft v. Tennessee, 322 U.S. 143 (1944).

17. Haynes v. Washington, 373 U.S. 1336 (1963).

18. Lynum v. Illinois, 372 U.S. 528 (1963).

19. Beecher v. Alabama, 408 U.S. 234 (1972).

20. *See* Escobedo v. Illinois, 378 U.S. 478 (1964); Massiah v. United States, 377 U.S. 201 (1964).

21. 384 U.S. 436 (1965).

22. The continuing viability of the due process voluntariness approach is discussed below in the text. The Supreme Court resurrected Sixth Amendment analysis in Brewer v. Williams, 430 U.S. 387 (1977). *See* Yale Kamisar, Brewer v. Williams, Massiah, *and* Miranda: *What Is Interrogation? When Does It Matter?,* 67 GEO. L. REV. 1 (1978). That analysis remains important in those cases in which the defendant has been formally charged (an event that usually takes place at least 24 to 48 hours after arrest) and the government deliberately elicits information from the accused. In such circumstances, defendants must knowingly and voluntarily waive their Sixth Amendment right, an inquiry in most respects identical to waiver analysis under Miranda. *See* WHITEBREAD & SLOBOGIN, *supra* note 8, § 16.04(c).

23. 384 U.S. at 444. As subsequent discussion in the text indicates, however, confessions obtained in violation of this rule may still be admissible under certain circumstances. *See* Michigan v. Tucker, 417 U.S. 433 (1974) (evidence derived from leads in statement taken in violation of *Miranda* held admissible); Milton v. Wainwright, 407 U.S. 371 (1972) (admission of confession taken in violation of defendant's right to counsel held to be harmless error); Harris v. New York, 401 U.S. 222 (1971) (statement obtained in violation of *Miranda* may be used to impeach defendant's testimony but not as part of prosecution's case-in-chief); New York v. Quarles, 467 U.S. 649 (1984) (statements obtained in the absence of warnings are admissible if necessary to ensure "public safety").

24. 384 U.S. at 444.

25. *Id.* at 444–45.

26. *See id.* at 455–57. *See also* Rhode Island v. Innis, 446 U.S. 291, 301 (1980).

27. *See* Spano v. New York, 360 U.S. 315, 326 (1959) (Douglas, J., concurring).

28. For an eloquent critique of this body of law, *see* Kamisar, *supra* note 22.

29. The one exception to this statement is when the defendant asks for an attorney. In such cases, the Court has adopted another per se rule providing that unless the defendant initiates contact, the police are forbidden to talk to the defendant until an attorney is present. Edwards v. Arizona, 451 U.S. 477 (1981); Minnick v. Mississippi, 498 U.S. 146 (1990).

30. In his concurring opinion in Rhode Island v. Innis, 446 U.S. 291 (1980), Chief Justice Burger, generally an opponent of defendant-oriented rules such as *Miranda*, stated: "The meaning of *Miranda* has become reasonably clear and law enforcement practices have adjusted to its strictures; I would neither overrule *Miranda*, disparage it, nor extend it at this late date." *Id.* at 304.

31. Oregon v. Hass, 420 U.S. 714 (1975); Harris v. New York, 401 U.S. 222 (1971).

32. Beckwith v. United States, 425 U.S. 341 (1976).

33. Berkemer v. McCarty, 468 U.S. 420 (1984).

34. Oregon v. Mathiason, 429 U.S. 492 (1977); California v. Beheler, 463 U.S. 1121 (1983).

35. 384 U.S. at 478–79.

36. Illinois v. Perkins, 496 U.S. 292 (1990).

37. North Carolina v. Butler, 441 U.S. 369 (1979); Connecticut v. Barrett, 479 U.S. 523 (1987).

38. Colorado v. Spring, 479 U.S. 564 (1987).

39. Moran v. Burbine, 475 U.S. 412 (1986).

40. The consensus may not be as universal as one would expect, however. A case decided shortly after *Miranda* is illustrative. In Davis v. North Carolina, 384 U.S. 737 (1966), Davis, accused of rape and murder, confessed after being held incommunicado for 16 days and being fed a diet of two sandwiches and peanuts daily (he lost 15 pounds during this period). At one point, he was required to walk 14 miles to disprove an alibi. Each of the lower courts through the Fourth Circuit held Davis's confession to be voluntary, as did two Supreme Court Justices (Clark and Harlan).

41. *See* Miranda v. Arizona, 384 U.S. at 515 (Harlan, J., dissenting).

42. 446 U.S. 291 (1980).

43. *See, e.g.,* Miller v. State, 496 N.E. 2d 1297 (Ind. 1986) (waiver valid though defendant "expected that he could exonerate himself by giving a statement"); Miller v. Fenton, 796 F.2d 598 (3d Cir. 1986) (waiver valid despite facts that detective exaggerated evidence against defendant, lied about whether victim was dead, and promised psychiatric help if defendant confessed); United States v. Velasquez 885 F.2d 1076 (3d Cir. 1989) (waiver valid despite false statement about co-defendant's confession); State v. Braun, 509 P.2d 742 (Iowa 1973) (same).

44. *See, e.g.,* Reck v. Pate, 367 U.S. 433 (1961) (mental retardation and physical illness); Blackburn v. Alabama, 361 U.S. 199 (1969) (history of mental illness); Fikes v. Alabama, 352 U.S. 191 (1957) (schizophrenia and high suggestibility); Townsend v. Sain, 372 U.S. 392 (1963) (administration of truth serum).

45. *See, e.g.,* Nebraska v. Smith, 494 N.W.2d 558 (Neb. 1993) (person with low intelligence and post-traumatic stress disorder symptoms made a valid waiver); Nebraska v. Melton, 478 N.W.2d 341 (Neb. 1992) (waiver was knowing, intelligent and voluntary despite fact that, the day after confession, the suspect was signed into a regional psychiatric treatment center); Louisiana v. Castille,

590 So. 2d 755 (La. Ct. App. 1991) (evidence of substance abuse at time of interrogation insufficient to render confession involuntary); State v. Osborne, 330 S.E.2d 447 (Ga. 1985) (lack of education and illiteracy not a bar to finding confession voluntary); State v. Jenkins, 268 S.E.2d 458 (Va. 1980) (subnormal intelligence not "necessarily dispositive").

46. As Perlin has summarized it, statements will be excluded only when "the mental subnormality is so great that an accused is incapable of understanding the meaning and effect of his confessions" (quoting Casias v. State, 452 S.W.2d 483, 488 [Tex. Crim. App. 1970]), or when the defendant's mental illness is combined with other circumstances so that it is not the "product of an essentially free and unconstrained choice by the maker" (quoting Jackson v. United States, 404 A.2d 911, 923 [D.C. App. 1979]). MICHAEL PERLIN, MENTAL DISABILITY LAW: CIVIL AND CRIMINAL (Vol. III) 270–71 (1989).

47. 479 U.S. 157 (1986).

48. Typically, the reliability of a confession is left up to the trier of fact. See Crane v. Kentucky, 476 U.S. 683 (1986).

49. Welsh White, Police Trickery in Inducing Confessions, 127 U. PA. L. REV. 581 (1979).

50. Although the ultimate determination of the fairness of these and other police tactics is a moral or legal one, behavioral scientists might provide legal policymakers with information both about the effectiveness of such tactics in evoking confessions and about defendants' subjective experience of these tactics. One means of gathering such data would be to present participants with hypothetical situations involving interrogation, as Grisso did with juveniles. See THOMAS GRISSO, JUVENILES' WAIVER OF RIGHTS: LEGAL AND PSYCHOLOGICAL COMPETENCE (1981). See infra note 64.

51. Joseph Grano, Voluntariness, Free Will, and the Law of Confessions, 65 VA. L. REV. 859 (1979).

52. Id. at 901, 904–05.

53. Id. at 906.

54. See, e.g., example of "confession" in § 8.06(b).

55. GRISSO, supra note 50. Adult norms are available for three of Grisso's measures. Id, ch. 5. The Comprehension of Miranda Rights (CMR) measure requires the defendant to paraphrase each of four Miranda statements: defendant's explanations are scored 2–1–0 for the presence of critical elements in each paraphrase. The Comprehension of Miranda—True/False (CM-TF) measure requires the defendant to match each of four Miranda statements to three alternative statements and to judge whether the alternative means the "same" as or something "different" from the Miranda statement with which it is paired, yielding a total score that ranges from 0 to 12. Finally, the Comprehension of Miranda Vocabulary (CMV) measure requires that the defendant define six critical words (e.g., "right" "consult") contained in the Miranda statements; these definitions are scored 2–1–0 for the inclusion of key definitional elements, yielding a score from 0 to 12.

Grisso's scales have also been tested with two populations of adults with mental retardation. It was found that both samples (one from a sheltered workshop and one composed of current probationers) scored significantly lower than either the adult or juvenile group studied by Grisso. Solomon M. Fulero & Caroline Everington, Assessing Competency to Waive Miranda Rights in Defendants with Mental Retardation, 19 LAW & HUM. BEHAV. 533 (1995).

56. Id. at 83.

57. Lawrence S. Leiken, Police Interrogation in Colorado: The Implementation of Miranda, 47 DENV. L.J. 1, 20 (1971); Richard H. Seeburger & R. Stanton Wettick, Miranda in Pittsburgh: A Statistical Study, U. PITT L. REV. 1, 26 (1967); Evelle J. Younger, Results of a Survey Conducted in the District Attorney's Office of Los Angeles County Regarding the Effect of the Miranda Decision upon the Prosecution of Felony Cases, 5 AM. CRIM. L.Q. 32 (1966); Project, Interrogations in New Haven: The Impact of Miranda, 76 YALE L.J. 1521 (1967).

58. See, e.g., ROBERT PERSKE, UNEQUAL JUSTICE (1991). The author recounts more than 25 cases involving people with developmental disabilities charged with crime. In one case, a man with an IQ of 49 who had confessed to a murder in Georgia stated on the witness stand in response to leading questions that he had also assassinated President Lincoln and President Kennedy. Id. at 17–18. Another involved a man with an IQ of 69 who, at police prodding, confessed to a number of crimes he could not have committed. Id. at 55. In a third case, part of the confession transcript read as follows:

Q: Did she tell you to tie her hands behind her back?
A: Ah, if she did, I did.
Q: Watcha use?
A: The ropes?
Q: No, not the ropes. Watcha use?
A: Only my belt.
Q: No, not your belt . . . remember . . . cutting the venetian blind cords?
A: Ah, it's the same rope.
Q: Yeah.
      . . .
Q: Okay, now tell us how it went, David—tell us how you did it.
A: She told me to grab the knife, and, and, stab her, that's all.
Q: (raising voice) David, no, David.
A: If it did happen, and I did it, and my fingerprints were on it—
      [The police had lied to the defendant about his fingerprints being at the scene.]
Q: (slamming hand on table and yelling) You hung her!
A: Okay, so I hung her.

Id. at 16.

59. See, e.g., Gisli H. Gudjonsson, Compliance in an Interrogative Situation: A New Scale, 10 PERSONALITY & INDIVIDUAL DIFFERENCES 535 (1989); Krishna K. Singh & Gisli H. Gudjonsson, The Internal Consistency of the "Shift" Factor on the Gudjonsson Suggestibility Scale, 8 PERSONALITY & INDIVIDUAL DIFFERENCE 265 (1987); Carol K. Sigelman et al., Evaluating Alternative Techniques of Questioning Mentally Retarded Persons, 86 AM. J. MENTAL DEFICIENCY 511 (1982).

60. Richard Angelo Leo, *The Impact of* Miranda *Revisited,* 86 J. CRIM. L. & CRIMINOLOGY 621, 689 n. 288 (1996) ("In both England and America, researchers have uncovered numerous documented cases of false confessions to police . . . in response to psychological [as opposed to physical] interrogation techniques").

61. Saul M. Kassin & Lawrence S. Wrightsman, *Confession Evidence, in* THE PSYCHOLOGY OF EVIDENCE AND TRIAL PROCEDURE 67–94 (Saul M. Kassin & Lawrence S. Wrightsman eds. 1985).

62. Gudjonsson has added to this category those who may be protecting the real offender. GISLI H. GUDJONSSON, THE PSYCHOLOGY OF INTERROGATIONS, CONFESSIONS AND TESTIMONY 227 (1992).

63. Richard Ofshe, *Coerced Confessions: The Logic of Seemingly Irrational Action,* 6 CULTIC STUDIES J. 6 (1989).

64. Most research in this regard has been on the effect of suggestive questioning on children, adults and those with mental retardation. For a review of the literature with respect to children and adults, *see, e.g.,* Stephen J. Ceci & Maggie Bruck, *The Suggestibility of the Child Witness: A Historical Review and Synthesis,* 113 PSYCHOL. BULL. 403 (1993). With respect to those with mental retardation, *see* PERSKE, *supra* note 58; Jim Ellis & Ruth Luckasson, *Mentally Retarded Criminal Defendants,* 53 GEO. WASH. L. REV. 414, 428–29, 445–52, 462–63 (1985) (reviewing research and law). *See generally* § 7.07(b)(2), this book.

On the effect of maximization techniques (e.g., exaggerating the evidence) and minimization techniques (e.g., suggesting leniency if a statement is made), regardless of the population involved, *see* Saul M. Kassin & Karlyn McNall, *Police Interrogations and Confessions: Communicating Promises and Threat by Pragmatic Implication,* 15 LAW & HUM. BEHAV. 233 (1991).

65. WHITEBREAD & SLOBOGIN, *supra* note 8, at 625.

66. Boykin v. Alabama, 395 U.S. 238 (1969).

67. In Henderson v. Morgan, 426 U.S. 637 (1976), the Court held that a plea is invalid unless the person understands the "critical" elements of the charge, including the *mens rea* requirement for the crime. The Court overturned Henderson's plea because he had not understood that intent was an element of second-degree murder, to which he had pled guilty.

68. This obviously includes the most likely sentence. The federal rules also require that the person be informed of minimum and maximum sentences, the effects of any special parole terms, and whether restitution of the victim might be required. Fed. R. Crim. P. 11(c). The ABA recommends that the defendant also be informed of any additional punishment that might be authorized by reason of a previous conviction. ABA Project on Standards for Criminal Justice, PLEAS OF GUILTY standard 14-1-4(a)(iii). However, "collateral" consequences of a plea (e.g., loss of the right to vote) need not be communicated. *See generally* WHITEBREAD & SLOBOGIN, *supra* note 8, 642–43.

69. *Cf.* Boykin v. Alabama, 395 U.S. 238 (1969).

70. *Cf.* Henderson v. Morgan, 426 U.S. 637 (1976) (judge need not make inquiry on record to determine understanding of charge pleaded to if there is "a representation [on the record] by defense counsel that the nature of the offense has been explained to the accused").

71. 478 F.2d 211 (9th Cir. 1973).

72. *Id.* at 214–25.

73. *Id.* at 215. *See also* United States v. Masthres, 539 F.2d 721, 726 (D.C. Cir. 1976).

74. 509 U.S. 389 (1993).

75. Note, *Competence to Plead Guilty: A New Standard,* 1974 DUKE L.J. 149, 170.

76. Bruce Winick, *Incompetency to Stand Trial: An Assessment of Costs and Benefits, and a Proposal for Reform,* 39 RUTGERS L. REV. 243, 271–72 (1987) (arguing that defendants who can articulate a preference for trial should be found competent, if their attorney acquiesces); Richard J. Bonnie, *The Competence of Criminal Defendants: A Theoretical Reformulation,* 10 BEHAVIORAL SCI. & L. 291 (1992) (disagreeing with Winick's "articulation" standard, and instead proposing a standard that requires the ability to give a plausible reason for the decision to go to trial before agreeing with a defendant's decision). For a more recent treatment of both approaches, *see* Bruce Winick, *Reforming Incompetency to Stand Trial and Plead Guilty: A Restated Proposal and a Response to Professor Bonnie,* 85 J. CRIM. L. & CRIMINOLOGY 571 (1995).

77. WHITEBREAD & SLOBOGIN, *supra* note 8, at 640.

78. 434 U.S. 357 (1978).

79. 397 U.S. 742 (1970).

80. Toward the end of its opinion the Court summed up its stance by stating: "[A] plea of guilty entered by one fully aware of the direct consequences, including the actual value of any commitments made to him by the court, prosecutor, or his own counsel, must stand unless induced by threats (or promises to discontinue improper harassment), misrepresentation (including unfulfilled or unfulfillable promises), or perhaps by promises that are by their nature improper as having no proper relationship to the prosecutor's business (e.g., bribes)." *Id.* at 755 (quoting Shelton v. United States, 246 F.2d 571 (5th Cir. 1957) (en banc)).

81. 422 U.S. 806 (1975).

82. *Id.* at 820.

83. Westbrook v. Arizona, 384 U.S. 150 (1966) (per curiam); Massey v. Moore, 348 U.S. 105 (1954).

84. 509 U.S. 389 (1993).

85. *Id.* at 400.

86. *Cf.* United States v. Mohawk, 20 F.3d 1480 (9th Cir. 1994) (government failed to prove waiver of counsel was knowing and intelligent).

87. 465 U.S. 168 (1984).

88. *See, e.g.,* Cordoba v. Harris, 473 F. Supp. 632 (S.D.N.Y. 1979).

89. A good example is the Colin Ferguson case, involving a defendant charged with the murder of six people on the Long Island Railroad. There a clearly mentally ill defendant was nonetheless allowed to proceed *pro se* after firing his lawyers, who had wanted to pursue a "black rage" defense. Because Ferguson was held to understand the consequences of his waiver, the court accepted it. Ferguson went on to defend himself on the ground that he did not commit the offense, despite overwhelming proof

to the contrary. *N.Y. Times,* Dec. 10, 1994, at 29, col. 5. *See also* People v. Miller, 167 Cal. Rptr. 816, 1818 (1980) (bizarre statements and actions alone do not make waiver invalid); State v. Evans, 610 P.2d 35 (Ariz. 1980) (diagnosis of paranoid schizophrenia does not make waiver invalid).

90. For a list of relevant cases, *see* Frendak v. United States, 408 A.2d 364, 373 nn. 13–14 (D.C. 1979).

91. 346 F.2d 812 (1965).

92. *Id.* at 818–19.

93. *See, e.g.,* United States v. Robertson, 507 F.2d 1148, 1161 (D.C. Cir. 1974) (separate opinion of Bazelon, C.J.). On the other hand, courts in some jurisdictions have appeared to rely exclusively on a test of whether the evidence points toward an insanity defense, lest a defendant innocent by reason of insanity be erroneously convicted. *See, e.g.,* State v. Smith, 564 P.2d 1154, 1156 (Wash. 1977) (en banc).

94. 408 A.2d 364 (1979).

95. 400 U.S. 25 (1970).

96. 422 U.S. 806 (1975).

97. 408 A.2d at 376.

98. *Id.* at 376–78.

99. *Id.* at 378.

100. 940 F.2d 1543 (D.C. Cir. 1991). The *Marble* court gave two reasons for its decision, both based on the post-*Whalem* changes in federal law: (1) because federal law has now made clear that insanity is an affirmative defense to be proven by the defendant [see § 8.02(b)], the defense should have the prerogative of deciding when to raise it, and (2) because federal law has now made clear that persons who are convicted are entitled to mental health treatment in a hospital if such treatment is necessary, imprisonment is no longer the only alternative to an insanity acquittal for the mentally ill offender. Of course, neither of these reasons confronts the *Whalem* court's conclusion that a blameless peson should not be convicted under any circumstances.

101. *See generally* Anne Singer, *The Imposition of the Insanity Defense on an Unwilling Defendant,* 41 OHIO ST. L.J. 637 (1980), *See also supra* note 93.

102. Some lower courts have so held. State v. Faragi, 498 A.2d 723, 728–30 (N.H. 1985).

103. 408 F.2d at 380 n.29. *See* Loren Roth et al., *The Dilemma of Denial in the Assessment of Competency to Refuse Treatment,* 139 AM. J. PSYCHIATRY 910 (1982).

104. Another example of such a situation involved a person charged with shooting a mail carrier who was convinced that during the Korean Way, J. Edgar Hoover had given him a "license to kill" at will. He refused to allow his attorney to assert an insanity defense, insisting instead that a photocopy of his "license to kill" be obtained and introduced into evidence so the judge and jury could see that he was innocent of any crime.

105. For reviews of the pre-1970s law, most of which came from cases rather than statutes, *see* George Collins & E. Clifton Bond, *Youth as a Bar to Testimonial Competence,* 8 ARK. L. REV. 100 (1954); Richard Thomas, *The Problem of the Child Witness,* 10 WYO. L.J. 214 (1956); Note, *The Competency of Children as Witnesses,* 39 VA. L. REV. 358

(1953). *See, e.g.,* United States v. Perez, 526 F.2d 859 (5th Cir. 1976); United States v. Schoefield, 465 F.2d 560 (D.C. Cir. 1975), *cert. denied,* 409 U.S. 881 (1972).

106. *See* Scott Rowley, *The Competency of Witnesses,* 24 IOWA L. REV. 482, 488 (1939).

107. The view endorsed by the Federal Rules goes back much further, however. Indeed, in the 1895 case of *Wheeler v. United States,* 159 U.S. 523 (1895), the United States Supreme Court held that the five-year-old son of a murder victim was properly qualified as a witness, using the following reasoning: "that the boy was not by reason of his youth, as a matter of law, absolutely disqualified as a witness is clear. While no one would think of calling as a witness an infant only two or three years old, there is no precise age which determines the question of competency. This depends on the capacity and intelligence of the child, his appreciation of the difference between truth and falsehood, as well as of his duty to tell the former. The decision on this question rests primarily with the trial judge, who sees the proposed witness, notices his manner, his apparent possession or lack of intelligence, and may resort to any examination which will tend to disclose his capacity and intelligence as well as his understanding of the obligation of an oath." *Id.* at 524. Even older is the English decision in Rex v. Brasier, 1 Leach 199, 168 Eng. Rep. 202 (1770), which stated that "there is no precise or fixed rule as to the time within which infants are excluded from giving evidence; but their admissibility depends upon the sense and reason they entertain of the danger and impropriety of falsehood, which is to be collected from their answers to questions propounded to them by the court, but if they are found incompetent to take an oath, their testimony cannot be received." *Id.* at 203.

108. The rule actually states that every person is competent to be a witness "except as otherwise provided in these rules." Rules that might limit the apparent broad scope of Rule 601 include Rule 401 (barring the admission of irrelevant information), Rule 403 (barring relevant information if there is a substantial danger it would mislead the jury or cause undue prejudice), Rule 602 (requiring that testimony be based on "personal knowledge"), and Rule 603 (requiring every witness to declare they will testify truthfully).

109. DAVID LOUISELL & CHRISTOPHER MUELLER, FEDERAL EVIDENCE § 252, at 18 (1979).

110. *See, e.g.,* 18 U.S.C. § 3509(c); ALA. CODE § 15-25-3(c) (1992); COLO. REV. STAT. § 13-90-106(1)(b)(II) (1990); MO. ANN. STAT. § 491.060(2)(1991). For other states, *see* John E.B. Myers, *The Competence of Young Children to Testify in Legal Proceedings,* 11 BEHAVIORAL SCI. & L. 121, 132 n.66 (1993).

111. *See, e.g.,* Moates v. State, 545 So. 2d 224 (Ala. Crim. App. 1989); People v. District Ct., 791 P.2d 682 (Colo. 1990).

112. JOHN HENRY WIGMORE, WIGMORE ON EVIDENCE § 509 (3d ed. 1940).

113. *See supra* note 108.

114. GLEN WEISSENBERGER, FEDERAL RULES OF EVIDENCE 221 (1996).

115. Myers, *supra* note 110, at 123.

116. *Id.* at 222–23. Although these criteria are most often found in cases addressing the competency of children, they are also used in evaluating the competency of other witnesses. *See, e.g.,* Commonwealth v. Anderson, 552 A.2d 1064 (1988) (holding that "competency considerations applicable to a child witness are also applicable to a retarded adult with the mental capacity of a child").

117. Marcia Johnson & Mary Foley, *Differentiating Fact from Fantasy: The Reliability of Children's Memory,* 40(2) J. Soc. Issues 33, 36 (1984).

118. Gail S. Goodman & Alison Clarke-Stewart, *Suggestibility in Children's Testimony: Implications for Sexual Abuse Investigations,* in The Suggestibility of Children's Recollections (John Doris ed. 1991), *cited in* Myers, *supra* note 110, at 123.

119. Ann Brown, *Judgments of Recency for Long Sequences of Pictures: The Absence of a Developmental Trend,* 15 J. Experimental Child Psychol. 473 (1943); Ann Brown & Joseph Campione, *Recognition Memory for Perceptually Similar Pictures in Preschool Children,* 15 J. Experimental Child Psychol. 356 (1972); Ann Brown & Marcia S. Scott, *Recognition Memory for Pictures in Preschool Children,* 11 J. Experimental Child Psychol. 401(1971); David Corsini et al., *Recognition Memory of Preschool Children for Pictures and Words,* 16 Psychonomic Sci. 192 (1969); Keith Nelson, *Memory Development in Children: Evidence from Nonverbal Tasks,* 25 Psychonomic Sci. 346 (1971); Marion Perlmutter & Nancy A. Myers, *Recognition Memory Development in 2-to-4-year-olds,* 10 Developmental Psychol. 447 (1974); Marion Perlmutter & Nancy A. Myers, *Young Children's Coding and Storage of Visual and Verbal Material,* 46 Child Dev. 215 (1975); Marion Perlmutter & Nancy A. Myers, *Recognition Memory in Preschool Children,* 12 Developmental Psychol. 271 (1976); Lionel Standing et al., *Perception and Memory for Pictures: Single-Trial Learning of 2500 Visual Stimuli,* 19 Psychonomic Sci. 73 (1970).

120. Gail S. Goodman & Rebecca S. Reed, *Age Differences in Eyewitness Testimony,* 10 Law & Hum. Beh. 317 (1986); Janat F. Parker et al., *Eyewitness Testimony of Children,* 16 J. Applied Psychol. 287 (1986).

121. Michael Leippe et al., *Eyewitness Memory for a Touching Experience: Accuracy Differences between Child and Adult Witnesses,* 76 J. Applied Psychol. 367 (1987).

122. *See generally* Beth M. Schwart-Kenney et al., *Improving Children's Person Identification,* 1 Child Maltreatment 121 (1996); Mary A. King & John C. Yuille, *Suggestibility and the Child Witness,* in Children's Eyewitness Memory 24 (Stephen J. Ceci et al., eds. 1987); Janat F. Parker & Lourdes E. Carranza, *Eyewitness Testimony of Children in Target-Present and Target-Absent Lineups,* 13 Law & Hum. Beh. 133 (1989).

123. Karen J. Saywitz et al., *Children's Memories of a Physician Examination Involving Genital Touch: Implications for Reports of Child Sexual Abuse,* 59 J. Consulting & Clinical Psychol. 682 (1991); Margaret S. Steward & David S. Steward, *The Development of a Model Interview for Young Child Victims of Sexual Abuse: Comparing the Effectiveness of Anatomical Dolls, Drawings, and Video Graphics* (Final Report to the National Center on Child Abuse and Neglect).

124. Barbara Vanoss Marin et al., *The Potential of Chil-* dren *as Eyewitnesses: A Comparison of Children and Adults on Eyewitness Tasks,* 3 Law & Hum. Behav. 295 (1979).

125. However, there is some research suggesting that a small proportion of young children (1–3%) report fantasy when asked about real-life events. Gail S. Goodman & Christine Aman, *Children's Use of Anatomically Detailed Dolls to Recount an Event,* 61 Child Dev. 1859 (1990); Leslie Rudy & Gail Goodman, *Effects of Participation on Children's Reports; Implications for Children's Testimony,* 27 Dev. Psychol. 527 (1991).

126. Rhona Flin et al., *The Effect of a Five-Month Delay on Children's and Adults' Eyewitness Memory,* 83 Brit. J. Psychol. 323 (1992).

127. Debra Ann Poole & Lawrence T. White, *Two Years Later: Effects of Question Repetition and Retention Interval on the Eyewitness Testimony of Children and Adults,* 29 Dev. Psychol. 844 (1993). *See also* Charles J. Brainerd et al., *Development of Forgetting and Reminiscence,* 55 Monographs Soc'y Res. Child Develop. 1 (1990).

128. David B. Pillemer & S. White, *Childhood Events Recalled by Children and Adults,* 21 Advances in Child Develop. & Beh. 297 (1989).

129. *See generally* Peggy J. Miller & Linda L. Sperry, *Early Talk about the Past: The Origins of Conversational Stories of Personal Experience,* 15 J. Child Lang. 293 (1988).

130. Gary Melton et al., *Empirical Research on Child Maltreatment and the Law,* 24 J. Clinical Child Psychol. 47, 58 (1995) (citing five studies). This article is an excellent review of the literature.

131. Debra Ann Poole & Lawrence T. White, *Tell Me Again and Again: Stability and Change in the Repeated Testimonies of Children and Adults,* in Memory and Testimony in the Child Witness 26–34 (Maria S. Zaragoza et al. eds. 1995) [hereinafter Memory and Testimony]. *See also* Amye R. Warren & Peggy Lane, *Effects of Timing and Type of Questioning on Eyewitness Accuracy and Suggestibility,* in Memory & Testimony, *supra,* at 56–57 (noting that "neutral questioning" may help maintain accuracy, if done early, but also noting that multiple neutral interviews are unlikely in the "real world").

132. Poole & White, *supra* note 131, at 42. This observation is also consistent with earlier laboratory studies suggesting marked age differences in free-recall ability that appear related to developmental differences in retrieval strategy. *See infra* note 137.

133. Karen J. Saywitz et al., *Can Children Provide Accurate Eyewitness Reports?,* 1 Violence Update 1 (Sept. 1990) ("One of the most stable findings of memory research is that young children spontaneously recall less information than older children and adults when asked open-ended questions."); Helen J. Emmerich & Brian P. Ackerman, *Developmental Differences in Recall: Encoding or Retrieval?,* 25 J. Experimental Child Psychol. 514 (1978); Akira Kobasigawa, *Utilization of Retrieval Cues by Children in Recall,* 45 Child Dev. 127 (1974); Marion Perlmutter & Margaret Ricks, *Recall in Preschool Children,* 27 J. Experimental Child Psychol. 423 (1979); Kenneth Ritter et al., *The Development of Retrieval Strategies in Young Children,* 5 Cognitive Psychol. 310 (1973).

134. Probably the leading case in this area is New

Jersey v. Michaels, 625 A.2d 489 (N.J. 1993), which held that, upon an appropriate showing, trial courts must hold "taint" hearings to determine whether suggestive interviewing has rendered a child's testimony inadmissible. *See also* People v. Delaney, 52 Cal. App. 765, 199 Pac. 896 (1921); Macale v. Lynch, 110 Wash. 444, 188 Pac. 517 (1920). To the courts, suggestibility is a particularly important issue when the defendant is a parent or other significant adult in the child's life. *See* Gelhaar v. State, 41 Wis. 2d 230, 163 N.W.2d 609 (1969); State v. Hung, 2 Ariz. App. 6, 406 P.2d 208 (1965); Richard Benedek & Elissa Benedek, *The Child's Preference in Michigan Custody Disputes,* AM. J. FAM. THERAPY 37, 40 (1979).

135. *See generally* ELIZABETH LOFTUS, EYEWITNESS TESTIMONY (1979).

136. For a general review, *see* Stephen J. Ceci & Maggie Bruck, *The Suggestibility of the Child Witness: A Historical Review and Synthesis,* 113 PSYCHOL. BULL. 403 (1993). *See also* Stephen J. Ceci et al., *Interviewing Preschoolers: Remembrance of Things Planted,* in THE CHILD WITNESS: COGNITIVE, SOCIAL AND LEGAL ISSUES (D. P. Peters ed. 1996); Stephen J. Ceci et al., *Age Differences in Suggestibility: Psycholegal Implications,* 117 J. EXPERIMENTAL PSYCHOL.: GEN. 38 (1987).

137. Karen J. Saywitz, *Improving Children's Testimony: The Question, the Answer, and the Environment,* in MEMORY AND TESTIMONY, *supra* note 131, 109 & 122 (summarizing Ceci et al., *supra* note 136). *See also* Goodman et al., *Children's Memory for a Stressful Event: Improving Children's Reports,* 1 J. NARRATIVE & LIFE HISTORY, 69 (1991) (finding that, when interviewed in an intimidating manner, three- and four-year-olds may answer abuse-related questions at an average commission error rate of 25%); Ann E. Tobey & Gail S. Goodman, *Children's Eyewitness Memory: Effects of Participation and Forensic Context,* 16 CHILD ABUSE & NEGLECT 779 (1992) (describing suggestivity of four-year-olds in response to police questioning).

However, there may not be a completely linear relationship between age and conformity. In research involving first-, fourth-, seventh-, and tenth-graders, Allen and Newtson observed adult influence on children's judgments to decrease sharply from first to fourth grade and then to *increase* slightly in tenth grade. This result was consistent across several forms of judgments: "visual" (judgment of length of line), "opinion" (e.g., "kittens make good pets"), and "delay of gratification" (e.g., "I would rather have 50 cents today than $1 tomorrow"). Vernon Allen & Darren Newtson, *Development of Conformity and Independency,* 22 J. PERSONALITY & SOC. PSYCHOL. 18 (1972).

For a general description of the suggesbility research, *see* articles published in 1 PSYCHOLOGY, PUBLIC POLICY & LAW (No. 2, 1995), which includes the amicus brief submitted by Maggie Bruck and Stephen Ceci in the case of New Jersey v. Michaels, 642 A.2d 1380 (N.J. 1994), described *supra* note 134.

138. Warren & Lane, *supra* note 131, at 58–59.

139. Jeffrey J. Haugaard et al., *Children's Definitions of the Truth and Their Competency as Witnesses in Legal Proceedings,* 15 LAW & HUM. BEHAV. 253 (1991).

140. *See generally* Gail S. Goodman & V. Helgeson,

Children as Witnesses: What Do They Remember? in HANDBOOK ON SEXUAL ABUSE OF CHILDREN (Lenore E. Auerbach Walker ed. 1988) (noting that children are more likely to be suggestible than adults when their memory is weaker or the questioner is "of relatively high status").

141. Eugene Fodor, *Resistance to Social Influence Among Adolescents as a Function of Moral Development,* 85 J. SOC. PSYCHOL. 121 (1971).

142. *See* Carol K. Sigelman et al., *The Responsiveness of Mentally Retarded Persons to Questions,* 17 EDUC. & TRAINING MENTALLY RETARDED 120, 123 (1982).

143. Marvin Rosen et al., *Investigating the Phenomenon of Acquiescence in the Mentally Handicapped: 2 Theoretical Models, Testimony Development and Normative Data,* 20 BRIT. J. MENTAL SUBNORMALITY 58, 58–68 (1974); Carol K. Sigelman et al., *When in Doubt, Say Yes: Acquiescence in Interviews with Mentally Retarded Persons,* 19 MENTAL RETARDATION 53 (1980).

144. John E.B. Myers, *The Testimonial Competence of Children,* 25 J. FAM. L. 287, 318 (1986).

145. John R. Christiansen, *Washington Survey: The Testimony of Child Witnesses: Fact, Fantasy, and the Influence of Pretrial Interviews,* 62 WASH. L. REV. 705, 717–18 (1987). At least one court has adopted this procedure. *See* New Jersey v. Michaels, described *supra* note 134.

146. For a general treatment of the law and psychology of repressed memories, *see* Julie M. Kosmond Murray, *Repression, Memory, and Suggestibility: A Call for Limitations on the Admissibility of Repressed Memory Testimony in Sexual Abuse Trials,* 66 COLO. L. REV. 477 (1995).

147. Riggs v. State, 235 Ind. 499, 135 N.E.2d 247 (1956). In that case, the trial court erred in not seeking such validation of testimony of a 12-year-old girl who was asked simply, "Did you have sexual intercourse with Hiram Riggs?" She answered affirmatively without any additional details. No evidence was presented of the girl's understanding of "sexual intercourse." *See also* Fitzgerald v. United States, 412 A.2d 1 (D.C. 1980) (jury instruction on corroboration of minors' allegation required in sex offense cases).

148. DAVID SHAFFER, DEVELOPMENTAL PSYCHOLOGY: THEORY, RESEARCH AND APPLICATIONS 285 (1985).

149. *See* JOHN H. FLAVELL, THE DEVELOPMENTAL PSYCHOLOGY OF JEAN PIAGET (1963), for a comprehensive review of Piagetian terminology, theory, and research.

150. The classical Piagetian assessment of this ability invokes a task of reproducing the view of a particular scene (i.e., a model of three mountains) from different vantage points. *See* JEAN PIAGET & BARBEL INHELDER, THE CHILD'S CONCEPTION OF SPACE (1956).

151. *See, e.g.,* ALTERNATIVES TO PIAGET: CRITICAL ESSAYS ON THE THEORY (Linda S. Siegel & Charles Brainerd eds. 1978) [hereinafter ALTERNATIVES].

152. Linda S. Siegel, *The Relationship of Language and Thought in the Preoperational Child: A Reconsideration of Nonverbal Alternative to Piagetian Tasks,* in ALTERNATIVES, *supra* note 151.

153. *See* Charles Brainerd, *Learning Research and Piagetian Theory,* in ALTERNATIVES, *supra* note 151.

154. Helene Borke, *Interpersonal Perception of Young*

Children: Egocentrism or Empathy? 5 DEVELOPMENTAL PSY-CHOL. 263 (1971); Helene Borke, *The Development of Empathy in Chinese and American Children between 3 and 6 Years of Age: A Cross-Cultural Study,* 9 DEVELOPMENTAL PSYCHOL. 102 (1973); Helene Borke, *Piaget's Mountains Revisited: Changes in the Egocentric Landscapes,* 11 DEVELOPMENTAL PSYCHOL. 240 (1975); Helene Borke, *Piaget's View of Social Interaction and the Theoretical Construct of Empathy,* in AL-TERNATIVES, *supra* note 151 [hereinafter *Piaget's View*].

155. *But see* Michael J. Chandler & Stephen Greenspan, *Ersatz Egocentrism: A Reply to H. Borke,* 7 DEVELOP-MENTAL PSYCHOL. 104 (1972) (Borke's tasks involved taking perspective of self rather than of others). For a reply *see* Helene Borke, *Chandler and Greenspan's "Ersatz Egocentrism": A Rejoinder,* 7 DEVELOPMENTAL PSYCHOL. 107 (1972).

156. *Piaget's View, supra* note 154, at 38.

157. *See supra* note 153 and accompanying text.

158. In a largely critical essay on the philosophical assumptions of Piagetian theory, Hall and Kaye made a similar point: "If psychologists are interested in describing the normal course of cognitive development, much of Piaget's theory may be of use. If, on the other hand, the theorist is interested in determining the child's ultimate capacity at any given time, he would use the approach exemplified by Trabasso." Vernon C. Hall & Daniel B. Kaye, *The Necessity of Logical Necessity in Piaget's Theory,* in ALTER-NATIVES, *supra* note 151, at 165–66.

159. Cathleen A. Carter et al., *Linguistic and Socioemotional Influences on the Accuracy of Children's Reports,* 29 LAW & HUM. BEH. 335 (1996) (finding that accuracy was significantly decreased when complex, developmentally inappropriate questions were used, and increased when children were interviewed by "a warm supportive interviewer").

160. For a review of the case law on these points, *see* Myers, *supra* note 144, at 318–24.

161. Rolf H. Monge et al., *An Evaluation of the Acquisition of Sexual Information through a Sex Education Class,* 13 J. SEX RES. 170 (1977).

162. *Id.* at 179 (only 38.4% of the students knew the meaning of the word *menstruation;* 13.1% knew the definition of *scrotum;* 14.1% knew what *coitus* means; 30.3% knew that *Fallopian tubes* were part of the female reproductive system, and 54.5% knew that *seminal vesicles* were part of the male reproductive system; the meaning of *menopause* was known by 27.5% of the students).

163. Hans Kreitler & Shulamith Kreitler, *Children's Concepts of Sexuality and Birth,* 37 CHILD DEV. 363 (1966).

164. State *ex rel.* R.R., 398 A.2d 76 (1979).

165. The *voir dire* in *Wheeler,* discussed *supra* note 107, was exemplary: "The boy . . . said among other things that he knew the difference between the truth and a lie; that if he told a lie the bad man would get him, and that he was going to tell the truth. When further asked what they would do to him in court if he told a lie, he replied they would put him in jail. He also said that his mother had told him that morning to 'tell no lie,' and in response to a question as to what the clerk said to him, when he held up his hand, he answered, 'Don't you tell no

story.'" 159 U.S. at 524.

"One commentator suggested a 'typical group of questions': What is your name? How old are you? Where do you live? Do you go to School? Do you go to Sunday School? Do you know what happens to anyone telling a lie? Do you know why you are here today? Would you tell a true story or a wrong story today? Suppose you told a wrong story, do you know what would happen? Do you know what an oath is? Did you ever hear of God?" Note, *supra* note 105, at 362. Besides raising a constitutional issue, these questions are probably of little probative value today in view of changing norms and, as indicated in the text below, are being used less frequently.

166. *See, e.g.,* People v. Norfleet, 371 N.W.2d 4338 (Mich. 1985) (child witness); State v. Pettis, 488 A.2d 704, 706 (R.I. 1985) (mentally retarded witness).

167. *See, e.g.,* Federal Rule of Evidence 603, which provides: "Before testifying, every witness shall be required to declare that the witness will testify truthfully, by oath or affirmation administered in a form calculated to awaken the witness' conscience and impress the witness' mind with the duty to tell the truth."

168. *See, e.g.,* N.Y. Crim. P. Law § 60.20 (1981); Fla. Stat. Ann. § 90.605(2) (1991).

169. Roger Burton, *Honesty and Dishonesty,* in MORAL DEVELOPMENT AND BEHAVIOR: THEORY, RESEARCH, AND SO-CIAL ISSUES (Thommas Lickona ed. 1976) [hereinafter MORAL DEVELOPMENT].

170. Nicholas Groth, *The Psychology of the Sexual Offender: Rape, Incest, and Child Molestation* (workshop presented by Psychological Associates of the Albermarle, Charlotte, NC, Mar. 1980).

171. Kay Bussey, *Lying and Truthfulness: Children's Definitions, Standards and Evaluative Reactions,* 63 CHILD DEV. 129, 135 (1992).

172. Haugaard et al., *supra* note 139.

173. *Id.* at 269. *See also* M. Devitt et al., *A Study of the Willingness of Children to Make False Accusations about a Serious Matter in a Realistic Setting* (paper presented at the meeting of the American Psychology–Law Society, Santa Fe, NM, Mar. 1994) (when parents direct children to lie, the rate of false allegations likely to increase).

174. *See* studies cited in Ellis & Luckasson, *supra* note 64, at 429 n. 78.

175. MORAL DEVELOPMENT, *supra* note 169.

176. JEAN PIAGET, THE MORAL DEVELOPMENT OF THE CHILD (1965).

177. Lawrence Kohlberg, *Stage and Sequence: The Cognitive-Developmental Approach to Socialization,* in HAND-BOOK OF SOCIALIZATION THEORY AND RESEARCH (David A. Goslin ed. 1969).

178. The correlation between moral judgments and moral behavior is in fact rather modest. *See* Walter Mischel & Harriet Mischel, *A Cognitive Social-Learning Approach to Morality and Self-Regulation,* in MORAL DEVELOP-MENT, *supra* note 169.

179. *Cf.* State v. Green, 383 S.E.2d 419 (N.C. 1989) (trial court did not abuse its discretion in finding that a seven-year-old was competent to testify when she testified that she knew what it meant to tell the truth and the

difference between right and wrong, notwithstanding that she also testified that her mother decided what the truth was and that she did not know what it meant to break a promise or what an oath was).

180. Lawrence Kohlberg, *From Is to Ought: How to Commit the Naturalistic Fallacy and Get Away with It,* in COGNITIVE DEVELOPMENT AND EPISTEMOLOGY (Walter Mischel ed. 1971). For critiques of Kohlberg's theory, *see* William Kurtines & Esther Greif, *The Development of Moral Thought: Review and Evaluation of Kohlberg's Approach,* 31 PSYCHOL. BULL. 453 (1974); Mischel & Mischel, *supra* note 178; Elizabeth Simpson, *Moral Development Research: A Case of Scientific Cultural Bias,* 17(2) HUM. DEV. 81 (1974).

181. Adherents to social learning theory, the major competing theory of moral development, would agree, *see* Mischel & Mischel, *supra* note 178. From their point of view, children's behavior would be influenced primarily by the rewards, punishments, and models available in a given situation (in interaction with a child's cognitive competencies).

182. Saywitz, *supra* note 137, at 136–37. *See also* Gail S. Goodman & Bette Bottoms, CHILD WITNESSES: UNDERSTANDING AND IMPROVING TESTIMONY 283 (1993) (reporting research of Rhona Flin); Gail Goodman et al., *Testifying in Criminal Court,* 57 MONOGRAPHS SOC'Y RES. CHILD DEV. 1 (1992); Julie A. Lipovsky, *The Impact of Court on Children: Research Findings and Practical Recommendations,* 9 J. INTERPERSONAL VIOLENCE 238 (1994). There are obvious ethical problems in inducing such stress. As an alternative, recall, conceptual skills, and the like might be evaluated in situations of naturally occurring stress, such as hospitalization. Experimentation might also be attempted in simulations of trials in courtrooms or simulated courtrooms.

183. Paul E. Hill & Samuel M. Hill, *Videotaping Children's Testimony: An Empirical View,* 85 MICH. L. REV. 809 (1987). *Cf.* Maryland v. Craig, 497 U.S. 836 (1990), in which the Supreme Court upheld such a procedure against a challenge that it violated the Sixth Amendment right of confrontation.

184. *See* Jodi A. Quas et al., *District Attorneys' Views of Legal Innovations for Child Witness,* AP-LS NEWS, Spring/Summer 1996, at 5 (of 153 prosecutor offices responding to survey, 0% used closed circuit TV, either one-way or two-way, and only .7% used videotaped depositions).

185. *Id.* at 5. *See also* Melton et al., *supra* note 130, at 64.

186. *Id.* at 64–65.

187. *Id.* at 64. *See also,* Lipovsky, *supra* note 182, at 636.

188. *See, e.g.,* Jonas v. State, 773 P.2d 960 (Alaska Ct. App. 1989); Barrera v. United States, 599 A.2d 1119 (D.C. 1991); State v. R.W., 514 A.2d 1287 (N.J. 1986).

189. Myers, *supra* note 144, at 348. Indeed, it appears that expert testimony on suggestibility, memory, or typical behavior of an abused child is very rare. Quas et al., *supra* note 184, at 6 (expert testimony occurred in from 0% to 3.9% of the cases, depending on the issue).

190. *See* Gail Goodman & Joseph Michelli, *Would You*

Believe a Child Witness?, 15(11) PSYCHOL. TODAY 80 (1981).

191. *See supra* text accompanying note 145.

192. John C. Yuille et al., *Interviewing Children in Sex Abuse Cases,* in CHILD VICTIMS, CHILD WITNESSES: UNDERSTANDING AND IMPROVING CHILDREN'S TESTIMONY: CLINICAL, DEVELOPMENTAL AND LEGAL IMPLICATIONS 95 (Gail Goodman & B. Bottoms eds. 1993). *See also* Ray Bull, *Innovative Techniques for the Questioning of Child Witnesses, Especially Those Who Are Young and Those with Learning Disability,* in MEMORY AND TESTIMONY, *supra* note 131, at 179, 182–88.

193. Judy S. DeLoache, *The Use of Dolls in Interviewing Young Children,* in MEMORY AND TESTIMONY, *supra* note 131, at 160, 178. Raskin and Esplin assert that "puppets, drawings, good touch/bad touch games, and toys are generally unnecessary and should be avoided whenever possible." *See also* David Raskin & Philip W. Esplin, *Statement Validity Assessment: Interview Procedures and Context Analysis of Children's Statements of Sexual Abuse,* 13 BEHAVIORAL ASSESSMENT 265, 270 (1991); Stephen J. Ceci & Maggie Bruck, *Children's Recollections: Translating Research into Policy* (50% of three-year-old children responded incorrectly when dolls used), cited in amicus brief, *supra* note 137, at 291.

194. *See, e.g.,* Melton, et al., *supra* note 130, at 68–69; Bull, *supra* note 192, at 187, citing several sources, including Margaret-Ellen Pipe & J. Clare Wilson, *Cues and Secrets: Influences on Children's Event Reports,* 30 DEVELOPMENTAL PSYCHOL. 515 (1994).

195. *See* Elizabeth Loftus & John Monahan, *Trial by Data: Psychological Research as Legal Evidence,* 35 AM. PSYCHOLOGIST 270 (1980).

196. Ronald P. Fisher & Michelle R. McCauley, *Improving Eyewitness Testimony with the Cognitive Interview,* in MEMORY AND TESTIMONY, *supra* note 131, at 141.

197. Saywitz, *supra* note 137, at 128–131. For other descriptions of techniques that enhance investigative and testimonial accuracy, *see* Carter, et al., *supra* note 159; Gail S. Goodman, et al., *Children's Testimony About a Stressful Event: Improving Children's Reports,* 1 J. NARRATIVE & LIFE HISTORY 69 (1991).

198. GRAHAM C. LILLY, AN INTRODUCTION TO THE LAW OF EVIDENCE § 10.2 (1987).

199. ABA Model Code of Judicial Conduct, Canon 3(9); ABA Standards for the Prosecution and Defense Functions §§ 3-5.8(b), 4-7.7(b).

200. EDWARD W. CLEARY ET AL., MCCORMICK ON EVIDENCE § 44 (3d ed. 1987).

201. LILLY, *supra* note 198, at 355–56.

202. For an account of the *Hiss* trial, *see* Judson Faulknor, 1950 Annual Survey of American Law of Evidence 804–08 (1950). *See also* United States v. Hiss, 88 F. Supp. 559 (S.D.N.Y. 1950).

203. *See generally* CLEARY, *supra* note 200, § 44. Many states still restrict credibility testimony to reputation evidence, however. *Id.*

204. 698 F.2d 1154 (11th Cir. 1983).

205. Chnapkova v. Koh, 985 F.2d 79 (2d Cir. 1993); United States v. Sessa, 806 F. Supp. 1063, 1069 (E.D.N.Y.

1992); United States v. Barnard, 490 F.2d 907 (9th Cir. 1973); United States v. DiBernardo, 552 F. Supp. 1315 (S.D. Fla. 1982).

206. 4 Cal. 4th 742, 842 P.2d 1192, 15 Cal. 2d 432, 454 (1992).

207. United States v. Zaure, 801 F.2d 336 (8th Cir. 1986) ("putting an impressively qualified expert's stamp on truthfulness goes too far . . . The jury may well . . . [accept] the opinion and [surrender] their own common sense in weighing testimony"); Munoz v. State, 763 S.W.2d 30, 32 (Tex. Ct. App. 1988) (holding in a murder trial that the testimony of psychiatric experts is generally not admissible to impeach because the benefit to be gained does not offset the delay, confusion, and expense of such testimony); People v. Miller, 481 N.W.2d 668 (Mich. App. 1987) ("It is well settled that an expert witness may not render an opinion as to a complainant's veracity").

208. United States v. Butt, 955 F.2d 77, 82 (1st Cir. 1992).

209. State v. Kim, 64 Haw. 598, 645 P.2d 1330 (1982); State v. Wilson, 8 Ohio App. 3d 216, 456 N.E.2d 1287 (1982); Hawkins v. Florida, 326 So. 2d 299 (Fla. Ct. App. 2d Dist. 1976).

210. Quoting Michael Juviler, *Psychiatric Opinion as to Credibility of Witnesses: A Suggested Approach,* 48 CAL. L. REV. 648, 674 (1960), *quoted in* State v. Vaughn, 171 Conn. 454, 370 A.2d 1002 (1976). *See also* WIGMORE ON EVIDENCE, §§ 934a, 924a.

211. *See, e.g.,* State v. Campbell, 127 N.H. 112, 116 498 A.2d 330, 333 (1985) (holding that psychiatric testimony on credibility of a rape complainant should be excluded because its prejudicial impact outweighs its probative value). *See generally* Leign B. Bienen, *A Question of Credibility: John Henry Wigmore's Use of Scientific Authority in Section 924a of the Treatise on Evidence,* 29 CAL. W. L. REV. 235 (1983).

212. *See generally* Patricia A. Tetreault, *Rape Myth Acceptance: A Case for Providing Educational Expert Testimony in Rape Jury Trials,* 7 BEHAVIORAL SCI. & L. 243 (1989).

213. State v. Oliver, 354 S.E.2d 527 (N.C. App. 1987); State v. Saldana, 324 N.W.2d 227, 231 (Minn. 1982); State v. Maule, 667 P.2d 96,98 (Wash. App. 1983). *But see* State v. D.R., 109 N.J. 348, 537 A.2d 667 (1988); State v. Myers, 382 N.W.2d 91 (Iowa 1986). *See generally* David McCord, *Expert Psychological Testimony About Child Complainants in Sexual Abuse Prosecutions—A Foray into the Admissibility of Novel Psychological Evidence,* 77 J. CRIM. L. & CRIMINOLOGY 1 (1986).

214. *See, e.g.,* ELIZABETH LOFTUS, *supra* note 135; GARY SOBEL, EYEWITNESS IDENTIFICATION: LEGAL AND PRACTICAL PROBLEMS (1972). For more recent research, *see* BRIAN L. CUTLER & STEPHEN D. PENROD, MISTAKEN IDENTIFICATION: THE EYEWITNESS, PSYCHOLOGY AND THE LAW (1995). *See also* C.A. Elizabeth Luss & Gary L. Wells, *Eyewitness Identification and the Selection of Distracters for Lineups,* 15 LAW & HUM. BEHAV. 43 (1991).

215. *See, e.g.,* United States v. Fosher, 590 F.2d 381 (1st Cir. 1979); State v. Reed, 226 Kan. 591, 601 P.2d 1125 (1979); United States v. Amaral, 488 F.2d 1148 (9th Cir. 1973).

216. People v. MacDonald, 37 Cal. 3d 351, 690 P.2d 709, 208 Cal. Rptr. 236 (1984); United States v. Downing, 753 F.2d 1224 (3d Cir. 1985).

217. *See, e.g.,* Hampton v. State, 92 Wis. 2d 450, 285 N.W.2d 868, 872 (1979); State v. Fontaine, 382 N.W.2d 374, 378 (N.D. 1987). Other courts have limited participation of the experts to assisting in the drafting of instructions which inform the jury of the relevant research regarding eyewitness testimony. State v. Warren, 230 Kan. 385, 635 P.2d 1236, 1244 (1981).

218. *See generally* Stephen Morse, *Crazy Behavior, Morals, and Science: An Analysis of Mental Health Law,* 51 S. CAL. L. REV. 527, 601–04 (1978).

219. Note that, to the extent the issue can be framed in terms of witness *competency* rather than witness *credibility,* the moving party may be better able to compel an evaluation. *But see supra* text accompanying notes 144–45. At the same time, unless there is significant evidence of mental disorder, the court is unlikely to grant such a motion. Furthermore, even if an evaluation is compelled, it is likely to be at the behest of the court rather than one of the parties, because witness competency is for the court to determine. Thus, for a competency evaluation, the court will probably select the evaluator and receive the report.

220. Fed. R. Civ. P. 35. In about half the states, parties to a civil suit do not even have the limited power granted by the federal rules; even *parties* cannot be compelled to undergo an evaluation. Even under the federal rules, the power to compel is limited; although the court is empowered, in the typical discovery abuse situations, to hold defaulting parties in contempt, it may *not* do so when the order requires a physical or mental examination.

221. Actually, Fed. Crim. R. P. 16(a)(1)(D) and 16(b)(1)(B) only provide for disclosure of the results of such mental examinations and tests; they do not authorize either side to compel them. However, most courts permit the prosecution to compel competency and sanity evaluations. *See* § 4.02(a), 402(b).

222. GENE R. SHREVE & PETER RAVEN-HANSEN, UNDERSTANDING CIVIL PROCEDURE § 75, at 297 (1993).

223. Schlagenhauf v. Holder, 379 U.S. 104, 110 (1964).

224. *See* Roberta J. O'Neale, *Court-Ordered Psychiatric Examination of a Rape Victim in a Criminal Rape Prosecution—Or How Many Times Must a Woman Be Raped?* 18 SANTA CLARA L. REV. 119 (1978). *See also* Marilyn T. MacCrimmon & Christine Boyle, *Equality, Fairness and Relevance: Disclosure of Therapists' Records in Sexual Assault Trials* (paper presented at Canadian Institute for the Administration of Justice [CIAJ] Conference, Vancouver, Canada, Oct. 17, 1993).

225. 4 WILLIAM BLACKSTONE, COMMENTARIES 24 (9th ed. 1978).

226. *See* Note, *The Eighth Amendment and the Execution of the Presently Incompetent,* 32 STAN. L. REV. 765 (1980); Note, *Mental Aberration and Post-Conviction Sanctions,* 15 SUFFOLK U. L. REV. 1219 (1981); Cameron v. Fisher, 320 F.2d 731 (D.C. Cir. 1976); State v. Hehman, 520 P.2d 507

(Ariz. 1974); Commonwealth v. Robinson, 431 A.2d 901 (Pa. 1981).

227. *See* Ford v. Wainwright, 477 U.S. 399, 405, 407–10, 412–13 (1986). *Ford* also lists two other reasons for the incompetency ban: Madness is punishment enough in itself, and an incompetent person cannot make peace with God.

228. 531 F.2d 83 (2d Cir. 1976).

229. The right comes in many forms. Some jurisdictions require that the court address the defendant personally, United States v. Byars, 290 F.2d 515 (6th Cir. 1961), whereas others hold that inquiry by the defense attorney is sufficient, Cummingham v. State, 575 P.2d 936 (Nev. 1978). Some limit the right to certain crimes, Brogan v. Banmiller, 136 A.2d 141 (Pa. App. 1957) (allocution applicable only to murder), and some do not permit its exercise when conviction is by plea. Goodloe v. State, 486 S.W.2d 430 (Mo. 1972).

230. 656 F.2d 512 (9th Cir. 1981).

231. For instance, many states require a showing of prejudice before a violation of the right is found and resentencing ordered. *See* Annot., 96 A.L.R.2d 1292, 1296.

232. Chavez v. United States, 531 F.2d 83 (2d Cir. 1976).

233. *See, e.g.,* Fla. R. Crim. P. 3.720(a).

234. *See* commentary to CRIMINAL JUSTICE MENTAL HEALTH STANDARDS, standard 7-5.2(1984) [hereinafter STANDARDS].

235. *Id.*, standard 7-5.2(a).

236. *Id.*, standard 7-5.2(b).

237. 477 U.S. 399 (1986).

238. FLA. STATS. § 922.07 (1986).

239. STANDARDS, *supra* note 234, standard 7-5.2(b).

240. STANDARDS, *supra* note 234, standard 7-5.8(d)(f).

241. 429 U.S. 1012 (1976).

242. *See generally* G. Richard Strafer, *Volunteering for Execution,* 74 J. CRIM. L. & CRIM. 860 (1983); Note, *Insanity of the Condemned,* 88 YALE L. J. 533 (1979).

243. 663 F.2d 1004 (10th Cir. 1981).

244. Stanley L. Brodsky, *Professional Ethics and Professional Morality in the Assessment of Competence for Execution: A Response to Bonnie,* 14 LAW & HUM. BEHAV. 91 (1990).

245. American Psychological Association, Board of Social and Ethical Responsibility in Psychology, *Agenda,* Meeting of May 5–7, 1989, at 117.

246. Richard Bonnie, *Dilemmas in Administering the Death Penalty: Conscientious Abstention, Professional Ethics, and the Needs of the Legal System,* 14 LAW & HUM. BEHAV. 67, 81–82 (1990).

247. National Medical Association, *Position Statement on the Role of the Psychiatrist in Evaluation and Treating "Death Row" Inmates* (undated), *cited in* Bonnie, *supra* note 246, at 84.

248. Bonnie, *supra* note 246, at 83–84.

249. *Id.* at 82–86. A third response would be to have nonprofessionals provide the treatment, something which may be feasible for some types of medical treatment but probably not for all psychiatric treatment. *See* Stacy A. Ragon, *A Doctor's Dilemma: Resolving the Conflict Between Physician Participation in Executions and the AMA's Code of Medical Ethics,* 20 DAYTON L. REV. 975 (1995).

250. David Wexler & Bruce Winick, *Therapeutic Jurisprudence as a New Approach to Mental Health Law Policy Analysis and Research,* 45 U. MIAMI L. REV. 979, 992–97 (1991).

251. For a full description of the litigation, *see* State v. Perry, 610 So. 2d 746 (La. 1992).

252. 494 U.S. 210 (1990).

253. 610 So. 2d at 751.

254. *Id.* at 747–48.

Chapter 8

1. For one treatment of the insanity defense that provides citations to virtually all the philosophical and empirical literature, *see* MICHAEL PERLIN, THE JURISPRUDENCE OF THE INSANITY DEFENSE (1994).

2. DAVID ABRAHAMSEN, THE PSYCHOLOGY OF CRIME 106 (1967); Stephen Morse, *Crazy Behavior, Morals, and Science: An Analysis of Mental Health Law,* 51 S. CAL. L. REV. 527 (1978); Joseph Weintraub, *Insanity as a Defense: A Panel Discussion,* 37 F.R.D. 365, 372 (1964); Abraham L. Halpern, *The Insanity Defense: A Juridical Anachronism,* 7 PSYCHIATRIC ANNALS 1 (1977); Abraham L. Halpern, *The Politics of the Insanity Defense,* 14 AM. J. FORENSIC PSYCHIATRY 1 (1993).

3. NORVAL MORRIS, MADNESS AND THE CRIMINAL LAW (1982).

4. 1 NAT'L COMM'N ON REFORM OF FED. CRIM. LAWS, WORKING PAPERS 248–52 (1970).

5. Mannfred Guttmacher, *Principal Difficulties with the Present Criteria of Responsibility and Possible Alternatives,* in

MODEL PENAL CODE § 171 Commentary (Tent. Draft No. 4 1995).

6. ABRAHAM GOLDSTEIN, THE INSANITY DEFENSE 223 (1967); Richard Bonnie, *The Moral Basis of the Insanity Defense,* 69 A.B.A. J. 194–97 (1983); Bernard Diamond, *With Malice Aforethought,* 2 ARCHIVES CRIM. PSYCHIATRY 1 (1957); Henry H. Hart, *The Aims of the Criminal Law,* 23 LAW & CONTEMP. PROBS. 401 (1958); Herbert Packer, Mens Rea *and the Supreme Court,* 1962 SUP. CT. REV. 107.

7. As Fletcher put it, "The issue of insanity requires us to probe our premises for blaming and punishing. In posing the question whether a particular person is responsible for a criminal act, we are forced to resolve our doubts about whether anyone is ever responsible for criminal conduct." GEORGE FLETCHER, RETHINKING CRIMINAL LAW 835 (1978).

8. After the *Hinckley* verdict in 1982, more than 40 bills proposing the abolition or modification of the de-

fense were introduced in the United States Congress, and similar bills were proposed in several state legislatures. *See* 6 MENTAL DISABILITY L. REP. 340 (1982). An ABC News poll indicated that 76% did not believe that justice had been done in the case. More recent polls indicate that 87% believe the insanity defense allows "too many guilty people to go free." RALPH SLOVENKO, PSYCHIATRY AND CRIMINAL CULPABILITY 1, 180 (1995).

9. Richard A. Pasewark et al., *Opinions about the Insanity Plea,* 8 J. FORENSIC PSYCHIATRY 8 (1981).

10. *Id.*

11. Michigan: Gerald Cooke & Cynthia Sikorski, *Factors Affecting Length of Hospitalization of Persons Adjudicated Not Guilty by Reason of Insanity,* 2 BULL. AM. ACAD. PSYCHIATRY & L. 251 (1974) (0.1% for offenses involving serious offenses such as homicide, assault, and burglary); New York: *Hearing before Subcomm. on Crim. Justice of House Comm. on the Judiciary,* 97th Cong. 2d. Sess. (July 22, 1982) (statement of Steadman) (0.16% of all felonies); St. Louis: John Petrila, *The Insanity Defense and Other Mental Health Dispositions in Missouri,* 5 INT'L J. L. & PSYCHIATRY 81 (1982) (0.2% of felonies); Richmond: Douglas Hastings & Richard Bonnie, *A Survey of Pretrial Psychiatric Evaluations in Richmond, Virginia,* 1 DEV. MENTAL HEALTH & L. 9 (1981) (0.5% of felonies); New Jersey: *Hearing Before Subcomm. on Crim. Justice of House Comm. on the Judiciary,* 97th Cong., 2d Sess. (Sept. 9, 1982) (statement of Rodriguez) (0.16%) [hereinafter Rodriguez Statement]; another treatment of the same information is found at Joseph H. Rodriguez et al., *The Insanity Defense Under Siege: Legislative Assaults and Legal Rejoinders,* 14 RUTGERS L.J. 397 (1983).

12. HENRY STEADMAN ET AL., BEFORE AND AFTER HINCKLEY: EVALUATING INSANITY DEFENSE REFORM (1993).

13. *Id.* at 52 (California), 68 & 107 (Georgia), 126 (Montana) (1993). The high rate in Montana was apparently due to the fact that postacquittal commitment there tended to be short and thus the defense was a relatively attractive alternative to conviction for those charged with minor felonies. *Id.* at 127 (60% of NGRIs in Montana were charged with minor felonies), 148 (acquittals less desirable in New York and California than in Montana, given longer commitment terms in first two states).

14. *See* David Brown, *Insanity Defense: Setting a Benchmark of Human Intellect and Will,* WASH. POST, Jan. 27, 1992, at A3.

15. Pasewark et al., *supra* note 9.

16. HENRY STEADMAN & JERALDINE BRAFF, *Defendants Not Guilty by Reason of Insanity,* in MENTALLY DISORDERED OFFENDERS: PERSPECTIVES FROM LAW AND SOCIAL SCIENCE, 109, 118 (John Monahan & Henry Steadman eds. 1983) (citing KENNETH FUKUNAGA, THE CRIMINALLY INSANE (1977)).

17. Henry Steadman et al., *Mentally Disordered Offenders: A National Survey of Patients and Facilities,* 6 LAW & HUM. BEHAV. 31, 36 (1982).

18. Rodriguez Statement, *supra* note 11.

19. STEADMAN ET AL., *supra* note 12, at 53 (California), 69 (Georgia), 77 (New York), 128 (Montana).

20. Henry Steadman et al., *Factors Associated with a Successful Insanity Plea,* 140 AM. J. PSYCHIATRY 401 (1983). *See also* Brown, *supra* note 14, at 51; Callahan et al., *The Volume and Characteristics of Insanity Defense Pleas: An Eight State Study,* 19 BULL. AM. ACAD. PSYCHIATRY & L. 331 (1991) (estimated 26% across eight states involved in Steadman study described in text).

21. The states, number of NGRI verdicts, ratio of verdicts to felony arrests, and sources for the data are as follows:

- Wyoming—1 between 1970 and 1972, 0.005% estimated. Richard A. Pasewark & Bruce Wayne Lanthorn, *Disposition of Persons Utilizing the Insanity Defense,* 5 J. HUM.ICS 87 (1977)
- Illinois—50 in 1979, 0.23%. REPORT OF THE (ILLINOIS) DEPARTMENT OF MENTAL HEALTH COMMITTEE ON CRIMINAL JUSTICE AND MENTAL HEALTH SYSTEM (1982) [hereinafter ILLINOIS REPORT].
- Florida—119 in 1981, 0.34%. CENTER FOR GOVERNMENTAL RESPONSIBILITY, THE INSANITY DEFENSE IN FLORIDA (1983).
- California—259 in 1980, 0.6%. William Turner & Beverly Ornstein, *Distinguishing the Wicked from the Mentally Ill,* 3 CAL. LAW. 42 (1983).
- New York—55 per year between 1976 and 1978, 0.65%. Henry Steadman, *Insanity Acquittals in New York State, 1965–1978,* 137 AM. J. PSYCHIATRY 321 (1980).

22. Steadman et al., *supra* note 17, at 33. In 1978, there were approximately 2,284,495 felony arrests. FBI UNIFORM CRIME REPORTS, CRIME IN THE UNITED STATES 185 (1979).

23. *See* Callahan et al., *supra* note 20.

24. In Oregon, between 1978 and 1980, 80% of NGRI verdicts were the result of agreements between prosecution and defense and did not go to trial, 17% were the result of bench trials, and only 3% had gone through a jury trial. Jeffrey Rogers et al., *Insanity Defenses: Contested or Conceded?,* 141 AM. J. PSYCHIATRY 885 (1984). A Michigan study found that 90% of those defendants found NGRI were adjudicated in nonjury trials, often through a quasi-plea-bargaining process. Gare A. Smith & James A. Hall, *Evaluating Michigan's Guilty but Mentally Ill Verdict,* 16 U. MICH. J.L. REF. 77, 94 (1982). *See also* Robert P. Bogenberger et al., *Follow-up of Insanity Acquittees in Hawaii,* 10 INT'L J. L. & PSYCHIATRY 382 (1987) (72.5% of NGRIs had a bench trial, 25% were found NGRI based on a plea agreement, and 2% were found NGRI by juries); Lisa A. Callahan et al., *The Volume and Characteristics of Insanity Defense Pleas: An Eight-State Study,* 19 BULL. AM. ACAD. PSYCHIATRY & L. 19 (1991) (of NGRI verdicts, 77.2% were by bench trial, 15.8% by plea, and 7.4% by jury); Andrew Blum, *Debunking Myths of the Insanity Plea,* NAT'L L.J., Apr. 20, 1992, at 9 (according to a study conducted by Policy Research Associates, only 7% of NGRIs are by a jury); Carmen Cirincione, *Revisiting the Insanity Defense: Contested or Consensus?,* 14 BEHAV. SCI. & L. 61 (1996) (multistate study showing only 14.4% NGRI adjudications were by jury trial).

25. Hastings & Bonnie, *supra* note 11 (100% in Rich-

mond, Virginia, in 1976); Richard A. Pasewark et al., *Characteristics and Disposition of Persons Found Not Guilty by Reason of Insanity in New York State, 1971–1976,* 136 AM. J. PSYCHIATRY 655, 658 (1979) (68.9% in New York in 1971–76); John Petrila et al., *The Pre-Trial Examination Process in Missouri: A Descriptive Study,* 9 BULL. AM. ACAD. PSYCHIATRY & L. 60 (1981) (65% in Missouri in 1978); Rodriguez Statement, *supra* note 11 (81% in New Jersey in 1982).

26. *See supra* note 8.

27. Note, *Commitment Following an Insanity Acquittal,* 94 HARV. L. REV. 605 (1981).

28. *See generally* James Ellis, *The Consequences of the Insanity Defense: Proposals to Reform Post-Acquittal Commitment Law,* 35 CATHOLIC U. L. REV. 1961 (1986).

29. Grant Morris, *Acquittal by Reason of Insanity,* in MENTALLY DISORDERED OFFENDERS: PERSPECTIVES FROM LAW AND SOCIAL SCIENCE 65, 70–72 (John Monahan & Henry Steadman eds. 1983); Note, *supra* note 27, at 605–06.

30. Morris, *supra* note 29, at 67–68; SAMUEL BRAKEL, JOHN PARRY, & BARBARA WEINER, THE MENTALLY DISABLED AND THE LAW 786–95 (1985) (chart).

31. Joseph Goldstein & Jay Katz, *Abolish the "Insanity Defense"—Why Not?,* 72 YALE L.J. 853 (1963).

32. Pasewark et al., *supra* note 25. Of those who had been released without supervision during this period, the average length of stay was about 15 months. Pasewark and his colleagues also found that those charged with more severe crimes spent more time in the hospital (e.g., a 1,102-day average for those charged with rape vs. a 398-day average for those charged with assault).

33. Rodriguez Statement, *supra* note 11, at 402 n. 32.

34. Michael Criss & Robert Racine, *Impact of Change in Legal Standard for Those Adjudicated Not Guilty by Reason of Insanity, 1975–1979 in Michigan,* 8 BULL. AM. ACAD. PSYCHIATRY & L. 261, 266–67 (1981). *See also* Lee J. Baldwin et al., *Factors Influencing Length of Hospitalization for NGRI Acquittees in a Maximum Security Facility,* 20 J. PSYCHIATRY & L. 257 (1992).

35. ILLINOIS REPORT, *supra* note 21.

36. Mark L. Pantle et al., *Comparing Institutionalization Periods and Subsequent Arrests of Insanity Acquittees and Convicted Felons,* 8 J. PSYCHIATRY & L. 305 (1980); Richard A. Pasewark et al., *Detention and Rearrest Rates of Persons Found Not Guilty by Reason of Insanity and Convicted Felons,* 139 AM. J. PSYCHIATRY 892 (1982); STEADMAN ET AL., *supra* note 12, at 98.

37. *Id.* at 59 (California); Rodriguez Statement, *supra* note 11 (New Jersey).

38. Harris et al., *Length of Detention in Matched Groups of Insanity Acquittees and Convicted Offenders,* 14 INT'L J.L. & PSYCHIATRY 223 (1991).

39. STEADMAN ET AL., *supra* note 12, at 117.

40. Betty L. Phillips & Richard A. Pasewark, *Insanity Pleas in Connecticut,* 8 BULL. AM. ACAD. PSYCHIATRY & L. 335 (1980).

41. Henry J. Steadman & Joseph J. Cocozza, *Selective Reporting and the Public's Misconceptions of the Criminally Insane,* 41 PUB. OPINION Q. 523 (1978).

42. Those studies which found that NGRIs had a lower recidivism rate include Stuart B. Silver et al., *Follow-up after Release of Insanity Acquittees, Mentally Disordered Offenders, and Convicted Felons,* 17 BULL. AM. ACAD. PSYCHIATRY & L. 387 (1989) (finding the NGRIs rearrest rate was significantly lower than the rearrest rate of convicted felons and of mentally disordered prisoners transferred for hospital treatment); Pantle et al., *supra* note 36; Pasewark et al., *supra* note 25. In the latter two studies, however, those found NGRI repeated more often than the felons. Phillips & Pasewark, *supra* note 40, found the recidivism rate to be about even.

The measures of recidivism are limited in all these studies. As indicated in § 9.09(b)(3), the official records (of arrests, etc.) used in these studies to determine recidivism are a relatively weak measure of criminality and tend to represent police efficiency as much as subject behavior.

43. *See, e.g.,* Stephen L. Bieber et al., *Predicting Criminal Recidivism of Insanity Acquittees,* 11 INT'L J. L. & PSYCHIATRY 105 (1980); Marnie E. Rice et al., *Recidivism among Male Insanity Acquittees,* 18 J. PSYCHIATRY & L. 379 (1990).

44. Joseph J. Cocozza et al., *Trends in Violent Crime among Ex-Mental Patients,* 16 CRIMINOLOGY 317 (1978).

45. Slovenko has asserted, without citation, that "[n]ationwide . . . the rate of recidivism among those discharged from prison (roughly, 60 percent) is more than double that of insanity acquittees (approximately 25 percent)." SLOVENKO, *supra* note 8, at 190.

46. 18 IDAHO CODE § 107 (1982); MONT. LAWS ch. 713 (1979); UTAH CODE § 76-2-304.5 (1983).

47. JOHN W. JONES, THE LAW AND LEGAL THEORY OF THE GREEKS 264 (1965); Anthony Platt & Bernard Diamond, *The Origins and Development of the "Wild Beast" Concept of Mental Illness and Its Relation to Theories of Criminal Responsibility,* 1 J. HIST. BEHAVIORAL SCI. 355 (1965).

48. Loftus E. Becker, *Durham Revisited: Psychiatry and the Problem of Crime,* in DIAGNOSIS AND DEBATE 43 (Richard Bonnie ed. 1977).

49. *Id.* at 44.

50. SIR MATTHEW HALE, PLEAS OF THE CROWN 14 (1847 ed.).

51. The "wild beast" language originated with Lord Bracton in 1265. J. BIGGS, THE GUILTY MIND 82 (1955).

52. Rex v. Arnold, 16 How. St. Tr. 695 (1724).

53. Anthony Platt & Bernard Diamond, *The Origins of the "Right and Wrong" Test of Criminal Responsibility,* 54 CAL. L. REV. 1227 (1966).

54. 10 Cl. & F. 200, 8 Eng. Rep. 718 (H.L. 1843).

55. ISSAC RAY, A TREATISE ON THE MEDICAL JURISPRUDENCE OF INSANITY (1833) (cited in Becker, *supra* note 48, at 50).

56. *See id.* at 34.

57. A. ZILBOORG, MIND, MEDICINE AND MAN 273 (1943).

58. Parsons v. State, 81 Ala. 577, 596, 2 So. 854 (1886).

59. *See* GOLDSTEIN, *supra* note 6, at 13; JAMES F. STEPHEN, A HISTORY OF THE CRIMINAL LAW OF ENGLAND 168 (1883).

60. *See, e.g.,* Commonwealth v. Woodhouse, 164

A.2d 98, 106 (Pa. 1960); Sollars v. State, 316 P.2d 917, 920 (Nev. 1957); Robert Waelder, *Psychiatry and the Problems of Criminal Responsibility,* 101 U. PA. L. REV. 378, 383 (1952); Barbara Wootton, *Book Review,* 77 YALE L.J. 1019, 1026–27 (1968) (reviewing ABRAHAM S. GOLDSTEIN, THE INSANITY DEFENSE [1967]).

61. SHELDON GLUECK, LAW AND PSYCHIATRY 54, 57–58 (1962); HENRY WEIHOFEN, MENTAL DISORDER AS A CRIMINAL DEFENSE 85 (1954).

62. Durham v. United States, 214 F.2d 862, 873–74 (D.C. Cir. 1954); Herbert Wechsler, *The Criteria of Criminal Responsibility,* 22 U. CHI. L. REV. 367, 375 (1954).

63. State v. Jones, 50 N.J. 369 (1871).

64. 214 F.2d 862 (D.C. Cir. 1954).

65. David L. Bazelon, *Equal Justice for the Unequal* (Isaac Ray Award Lecture, 1961), *reprinted in* D. L. BAZELON, QUESTIONING AUTHORITY: JUSTICE AND CRIMINAL LAW (1988).

66. *See, e.g.,* Blocker v. United States, 288 F.2d 853, 859 (D.C. Cir. 1961); O'Beirne v. Overholser, 193 F. Supp. 652, 660 (D.D.C. 1961).

67. *See* Becker, *supra* note 48, at 57, for a description of this event.

68. Richard Arens, *The* Durham *Rule in Action: Judicial Psychiatry and Psychiatric Justice,* 2 LAW & SOC'Y REV. 41 (1967) (acquittal rate went from 0.5% to 2.5%); Abe Krash, *The* Durham *Rule and Judicial Administration of the Insanity Defense in the District of Columbia,* 70 YALE L.J. 905, 948 (1961).

69. 312 F.2d 847 (D.C. Cir. 1962).

70. *Id.* at 850–51.

71. United States v. Brawner, 471 F.2d 969 (D.C. Cir. 1972).

72. Maine adopted the "product" test in 1964, ME. REV. STAT. ANN. tit. 15, § 102 (1964), but repealed its statute and adopted a modified version of the ALI test in 1975, ME. REV. STAT. ANN. tit. 17A, § 58 (1975).

73. MODEL PENAL CODE § 401(1) (Tent Draft No. 4 1955).

74. MODEL PENAL CODE § 4.01 comment.

75. MODEL PENAL CODE § 4.01(2).

76. United States v. Brawner, 471 F.2d 969, 1029 (D.C. Cir. 1972) (Bazelon, J., concurring) ("At no point in its opinion does the court explain why the boundary of a legal concept—criminal responsibility—should be marked by medical concepts, especially when the validity of the 'medical model' is seriously questioned by some eminent psychiatrists").

77. *See* David Bazelon, *The Morality of Criminal Law,* 49 U.S.C.L. REV. 385 (1976).

78. For instance, Moore has proposed that insanity be equated simply with "irrationality," with the latter term defined according to the intelligibility, consistency, and coherence of the beliefs leading to the crime. MICHAEL MOORE, LAW & PSYCHIATRY 244–45, 207 (1985). Morse has argued that a defendant should be found insane "if at the time of the offense the defendant was extremely crazy and the craziness affected the criminal behavior." Stephen Morse, *Excusing the Crazy: The Insanity Defense Reconsidered,* 58 S. CAL. L. REV. 780 (1985).

79. *But see* State v. Johnson, 399 A.2d 469, 476 (R.I. 1979) (adding mental disease or defect predicate to Bazelon's responsibility test).

80. CRIMINAL JUSTICE MENTAL HEALTH STANDARDS, standard 7-6.1 (1984) [hereinafter STANDARDS]; American Psychiatric Association, Statement on the Insanity Defense 12 (1982) [hereinafter APA STATEMENT].

81. STANDARDS, *supra* note 80, at 329–32; APA STATEMENT, *supra* note 80, at 11.

82. STANDARDS, *supra* note 80, at 341.

83. Bonnie, *supra* note 6, at 196–97.

84. 18 U.S.C. §402 (1984). The major difference between the two is that the ABA provision places the burden of disproving insanity on the prosecution, while the federal statute places the burden of proving insanity on the defendant by clear and convincing evidence [see § 8.02(c)(5)].

85. For a somewhat contradictory listing of the states with the ALI and *M'Naghten* tests, *see* 18 HOFSTRA L. REV. 1133, 1170 n.113 (1995) (see also note 94); 70 DENVER U. L. REV. 161 n.13 (1995).

86. RITA SIMON, THE JURY AND THE DEFENSE OF INSANITY 215 (1967).

87. Norman Finkel et al., *Insanity Defenses from the Jurors' Perspective,* 9 L. & PSYCHOL. REV. 77 (1985). *See also,* Norman Finkel & Christoper Slobogin, *Insanity Justification and Culpability: Toward a Unifying Schema,* 19 LAW & HUM. BEHAV. 447 (1995) (comparing federal and ALI tests).

88. Robert M. Wettstein et al., *A Prospective Comparison of Four Insanity Defense Standards,* 148 AM. J. PSYCHIATRY 21 (1991).

89. Richard Rogers & Charles R. Clark, *Diogenes Revisited: Another Search for the Ultimate NGRI Standard* (paper presented at the meeting of American Academy of Psychiatry and Law, Albuquerque, N.M., October 1985).

90. Ingo Keilitz, *Researching and Reforming the Insanity Defense,* in 39 RUTGERS L. REV. 47, 57–61 (1987).

91. STEADMAN ET AL., *supra* note 12, ch. 4.

92. STANDARDS, *supra* note 80, at 343.

93. *See, e.g.,* United States v. Brawner, 471 F.2d 969, 994 (D.C. Cir. 1972) (Bazelon, J., concurring); SEYMOUR HALLECK, PSYCHIATRY AND THE DILEMMAS OF CRIME 341–42 (1967). Morris makes much the same point but argues from this premise that rather than expanding the insanity defense, it should be eliminated: "It is hard to see why a special rule . . . should be made for the mentally ill." MORRIS, *supra* note 3, at 61.

94. MOORE, *supra* note 78, chs. 2, 6, argues that one's environment is usually irrelevant to responsibility determinations because it does not normally disturb our capacity for rational action, which, he argues, is the only criterion by which we can assess illness and criminal culpability.

95. Durham v. United States, 214 F.2d 862 (1954).

96. *See, e.g.,* McDonald v. United States, 312 F.2d 847, 851 (D.C. Cir. 1962); Snider v. Smith, 187 F. Suppl. 299 (1960); GOLDSTEIN, *supra* note 6, at 48.

97. Pollard v. United States, 282 F.2d 450 (6th Cir. 1960); Lee v. Thompson, 452 F. Supp. 165, 167–68

(1977); Government of the Virgin Islands v. Downey, 396 F. Supp. 349 (D.V.I. 1975).

98. Kane v. United States, 399 F.2d 730, 733–36 (9th Cir. 1969); State v. Hall, 214 N.W.2d 205 (Iowa 1974); People v. Kelly, 10 Cal. 3d 565, 517 P.2d 875, 111 Cal. Rptr. 171 (1973); Beasley v. State, 50 Ala. 149 (1874).

99. ME. REV. STAT. ANN. ch. 149, §39-A; Stacia E. Reynolds, *Battle of the Experts Revisited: 1983 Oregon Legislation on the Insanity Defense,* 20 WILLIAMETTE L. REV. 303 (1984).

100. CONN. PUB. ACTS 83–386 (1983).

101. *See, e.g.,* MICH. COMP. LAWS §§ 768.21a(a), 330.1400a.

102. The ABA version is found in STANDARDS, *supra* note 80, standard 7-6.1, which defines "mental disease or defect" as "(i) impairments of mind, whether enduring or transitory; or, (ii) mental retardation, which substantially affected the mental or emotional processes of the defendant at the time of the alleged offense." The American Psychiatric Association's version is found in the next sentence of the text.

103. APA STATEMENT, *supra* note 80, at 12.

104. GOLDSTEIN, *supra* note 6, at 33.

105. *See supra* note 25.

106. Indeed, Gerard has argued that the DSM should merely provide a starting point for the analysis. He requires, in addition to inclusion in the DSM, that the disorder (1) "characteristically" interfere with "a person's ability to make normal choices about legally relevant behavior," and (2) result from "physical malfunction" that, if not scientifically provable, is only inferrable when the person's "behavior is irrational in the sense of being contrary to the person's own self-interest in the short range, when viewed objectively . . . and . . . compulsive in the sense of being impervious to influence by the person's environment." Applying these criteria, he concluded that only four DSM disorders justify invoking the insanity defense: moderate or worse mental retardation, schizophrenia, the affective disorders (mania and depression), and brain syndromes that are not induced by the voluntary ingestion of some substance. Jules B. Gerard, *The Usefulness of the Medical Model to the Legal System,* in ALEXANDER BROOKS & BRUCE WINICK, CURRENT ISSUES IN MENTAL DISABILITY LAW 135, 154–68 (1987).

107. *See, e.g.,* United States v. Currens, 390 F.2d 751, 774 n.32 (3d Cir. 1961) (arguing that (1) psychopaths are not defined solely by a propensity to commit antisocial behavior and (2) denying the insanity defense to those with the psychopath label would impermissibly base the defense on categories rather than on individual traits).

108. People v. Doan, 141 Mich. App. 209, 366 N.W.2d 593 (1985).

109. *See also* Phillips & Pasework, *supra* note 40 (recounting that in Connecticut between 1970 and 1972, 40% of those found NGRI had personality disorders).

110. WAYNE R. LAFAVE & AUSTIN W. SCOTT, CRIMINAL LAW 312 (2d. ed. 1986).

111. American Psychiatric Association, DIAGNOSTIC AND STATISTICAL MANUAL OF MENTAL DISORDERS (4th ed. 1994), at xxiii [hereinafter DSM-IV].

112. Carter v. United States, 252 F.2d 608, 616 (D.C. Cir. 1957).

113. MOORE, *supra* note 78, chs. 1, 2, 6, 9, 10.

114. *See, e.g.,* Michael Corrado, *Automatism and a Theory of Action,* 39 EMORY L.J. 1991 (1990); Lloyd Weinreb, *Desert, Punishment and Criminal Responsibility,* 49 LAW & CONTEMP. PROBS. 47, 61 N. 27 (1986); John L. Hill, *Freedom, Determinism, and the Externalization of Responsibility in the Law: A Philosophical Analysis,* 76 GEO. L.J. 2045, 2059 (1988).

115. Scott W. Howe, *Reassessing the Individualization Mandate in Capital Sentencing: Darrow's Defense of Leopold and Loeb,* 79 IOWA L. REV. 994, 1033 (1994). *See also* Peter Arenella, *Convicting the Morally Blameless: Reassessing the Relationship Between Legal and Moral Accountability,* 39 UCLA L. REV. 1511, 1524–25 (1992): "[A] threshold conception of moral agency—one suitable for moral norms implicated by *mala in se* crimes—must include the following character-based attributes: the capacity to care for the interests of other human beings; the internalization of others' normative expectations, including self-identification as a participant in the community's blaming practices; the ability to engage in moral evaluation of one's character and acts; the capacity to respond to moral norms as a motivation for one's choices; and the power to control those firmly entrenched aspects of character that impair one's ability to act in accordance with one's moral judgments."

116. For further explication of Moore's thesis, *see* Christopher Slobogin, *A Rational Approach to Responsibility,* 83 MICH. L. REV. 820 (1985).

117. MODEL PENAL CODE § 4.01 comment (Tent. Draft No. 4 1955).

118. Francis Allen, *The Rule of the American Law Institute's Model Penal Code,* 45 MARQ. L. REV. 494, 501 (1972).

119. GOLDSTEIN, *supra* note 6, at 49–53.

120. *Id.* at 50.

121. Further evidence for this proposition comes from comparing the acquittal rates, expressed as a percentage of felony prosecutions, for the five states listed earlier. *Supra* note 21. Proceeding from the state with the lowest acquittal rate to the state with the highest would produce the following order: Wyoming, Illinois, Florida, California, New York. Yet Wyoming, Illinois, and California used the ALI test, Florida used *M'Naghten,* and New York used a liberalized version of *M'Naghten* during the period in which the relevant data were collected.

122. GOLDSTEIN, *supra* note 6, at 51–53.

123. MODEL PENAL CODE § 4.01 comment (Tent. Draft No. 4 1955).

124. *See, e.g.,* State v. Crenshaw, 98 Wash.2d 789, 659 P.2d 488 (1983).

125. 216 N.Y. 324, 110 N.E. 945 (1915).

126. Becker, *supra* note 48, at 46–48.

127. *Id.* at 48–49. *See* United States v. Freeman, 357 F.2d 606, 615–18 (2d Cir. 1966), for a slightly different view of the *M'Naghten* case.

128. *See, e.g.,* United States v. Kunak, 17 C.M.R. 346, 357–58 (1954).

129. GOLDSTEIN, *supra* note 6, at 70–75.

130. *See, e.g.,* State v. Levier, 601 P.2d 1116 (Kan.

1979); State v. Law, 244 S.E.2d 302 (S.C. 1978); Hill v. State, 339 So. 2d 1382 (Miss. 1976); State v. Jacobs, 205 N.W.2d 662 (Neb. 1973); Commonwealth v. Woodhouse, 164 A.2d 98, 106 (Pa. 1960); Sollars v. State, 316 P.2d 917; 920 (Nev. 1957); Hechtman, *Practice Commentaries following N.Y. Penal Law* § 30.05, at 69.

131. APA STATEMENT, *supra* note 80, at 11. These sentiments echo those of many scholars, among them Wooten, who noted that "[i]t is indeed apparent that some people, such as sadistic sexual perverts, suffer from temptations from which others are immune, [b]ut the fact that the impulse is unusual is no proof that it is irresistible." Wooton, *supra* note 60, at 1026–27 (1968). *See also* United States v. Lyons, 731 F.2d 243, 248–49 (5th Cir. 1984).

132. *See* Richard Rogers, *Empiricism v. Emotionalism,* 42 AM. PSYCHOLOGIST 840, 841–42 (1987).

133. Thompson v. Commonwealth, 193 Va. 704, 717, 70 S.E.2d 284, 291–92 (1952).

134. United States v. Chandler, 393 F.2d 920 (4th Cir. 1968).

135. United States v. Smeaton, 762 F.2d 796, 798–99 (9th Cir. 1985).

136. Thompson v. Commonwealth, 193 Va. 704, 717, 70 S.E.2d 284, 292 (1952); Rollins v. Commonwealth, 207 Va. 580, 151 S.E.2d 625 (1966).

137. Commonwealth v. Mosler, 4 Pa. 264 (1846).

138. United States v. Lewellyn, 723 F.2d 615 (8th Cir. 1983). *See also* Coffman v. United States, 290 F.2d 212 (5th Cir. 1961).

139. Blake v. United States, 407 F.2d 908 (5th Cir. 1969); *See also* United States v. Shapiro, 383 F.2d 680 (7th Cir. 1967) (stating that the volitional prong does not call for "complete destruction of the power to control one's acts," in reversing the conviction of a person with a "very impulsive personality with very weak control.").

140. *See* United States v. Smith, 404 F.2d 720, 725 (6th Cir. 1968); Wion v. United States, 325 F.2d 420, 426 n.7 (10th Cir. 1963) (both quoting from Warren Burger, *Comments on Psychiatry and the Law,* 32 F.R.D. 547, 560 (1962)).

141. *See, e.g.,* Jodie English, *The Light between Twilight and Dusk: Federal Criminal Law and the Volitional Insanity Defense,* 40 HASTINGS, L.J. 1, 13 (1988) (describing Aristotle's views); 4 BLACKSTONE'S COMMENTARIES 20 (1803).

142. Governor's Task Force to Review the Defense of Insanity, State of Maryland, *reported in* RITA SIMON & DAVID E. AARONSON, THE INSANITY DEFENSE 167 (1988).

143. *See* Slobogin, *supra* note 116, at 830 (noting that under Moore's definition of insanity, which asks simply whether the person was irrational, the degree to which one is "compelled" is irrelevant, unless the compulsion creates irrational thinking).

144. *See, e.g.,* MOORE, *supra* note 78, at 374 (speaking of unconscious compulsion as an "excuse in its own right").

145. The states that placed the burden on the defendant, as of 1993, are Colorado, Florida, Illinois, Iowa, Kansas, Maryland, Massachusetts, Michigan, Mississippi, Nebraska, New Mexico, New York, North Dakota, Oklahoma, South Dakota, and Tennessee.

146. 18 U.S.C. §402(b) (1984).

147. *See, e.g.,* Commonwealth v. Vogel, 440 Pa. 1, 2, 268 A. 2d 89, 90 (1970).

148. *See generally* Addington v. Texas, 441 U.S. 418 (1979); APA STATEMENT, *supra* note 80, at 12–13.

149. Again using the five-state acquittal rates described earlier, *supra* note 21, the three states with the lowest acqittal rates (Wyoming, Illinois, and Florida) place the burden on the prosecution, as does the state with the highest acquittal rate (New York), whereas the state with the second highest acquittal rate (California) places the burden on the defendant. Steadman et al., in more methodologically sound research, found that changing the burden and standard of proof in Georgia and New York did not reduce the success rate of insanity pleas, although it did reduce the use of the plea. STEADMAN ET AL., *supra* note 12, ch. 5.

150. STANDARDS, *supra* note 80, standard 7-6.9.

151. GOLDSTEIN, *supra* note 6, at 113.

152. *See, e.g.,* United States v. Dresser, 542 F.2d 737, 742 n.2 (8th Cir. 1976).

153. Fain v. Commonwealth, 78 Ky. 183 (1879); H.M. Advocate v. Fraser, 4 Couper 70 (1878).

154. *See generally* PETER LOW ET AL., CRIMINAL LAW: CASES AND MATERIALS 152–55 (2d ed. 1986). Most of the decisions finding automatism in such cases are British or Canadian. *But see* Featherstone v. Clark, 293 F. Supp. 508 (W.D. 1978); Sprague v. State, 52 Wis. 2d 89, 187 N.W.2d 784 (1971); California v. March, 338 P.2d 495 (Cal. Ct. App. 1959); Government of the Virgin Islands v. Smith, 278 F.2d 169 (3d Cir. 1960); Fulcher v. States, 633 P.2d 142 (Wyo. 1981).

155. Tift v. State, 17 Ga. App. 663, 88 S.E. 41 (1916). *Cf.* State v. Gooze, 14 N.J. Super. 277, 81 A.2d 811 (1951); People v. Decina, 2 N.Y. 2d 133 157 N.Y.S. 2d 558, 138 N.E.2d 799 (1956).

156. *See, e.g.,* LOW ET AL., *supra* note 154, at 152; Earl F. Rose, *Criminal Responsibility and Competency as Influenced by Organic Disease,* 35 MO. L. REV. 326 (1970).

157. Bratty v. Attorney-General for Northern Ireland, 3 All E.R. 535 (1961); Regina v. Kemp, 3 All E.R. 249 (1956). This concern over disposition has also given rise to the rather strange distinction, prevalent in Commonwealth countries but fortunately nonexistent here, between "sane automatism" (e.g., sleepwalking) and "insane automatism" (e.g., dissociation). *See generally* W.H. Holland, *Automatism and Criminal Responsibility,* 25 CRIM. L.Q. 95 (1982) (a Canadian publication).

158. Sanford Gifford et al., *An Unusual Adverse Reaction to Self-Medication with Prednisone: An Irrational Crime during a Fugue State,* 7 INT'L J. PSYCHIATRIC MED. 97 (1976). *See also* Thomas J. Luparello, *Features of Fugue: A Unified Hypothesis of Regression,* 18 J. AM. PSYCHOANALYTIC ASS'N 379, 380 (1970).

159. *See supra* cases cited note 97.

160. *See e.g.,* Washington v. Wheaton, 850 P.2d 507 (Wash. 1993).

161. *See, e.g.,* United States v. Denny-Shaffer, 2 F.3d 999 (10th Cir. 1993).

162. Elyn Saks, *Multiple Personality Disorder and Crimi-*

nal Responsibility, 25 U.C. DAVIS L. REV. 383, 452–54 (1992). On the other hand, Saks would not allow conviction even when the host sanely commits the crime unless "the appearance of other alters is so extremely limited that punishing the person-body does not seem problematic." *Id.* This rule is less likely to be accepted by a court, for obvious reasons.

163. MODEL PENAL CODE § 2.02 (Official Draft 1962).

164. The ABA has criticized use of this term because it suggests that clinical testimony on the issue of *mens rea* is a "doctrine" like the insanity defense, when in fact it is merely an evidentiary rule that permits relevant testimony on an issue pertinent to most criminal trials. STANDARDS, *supra* note 80, standard 7-6.2 and commentary. Though we agree with the ABA's position, many jurisdictions do not (*see* below). As a result, it is more accurate to refer to the general concept of clinical testimony on *mens rea* as a doctrine, and we continue to use the term "diminished capacity" as a shorthand designation for the various exceptions to the evidentiary principle noted below.

165. 64 Cal. 2d 310, 518 P.2d 341, 49 Cal. Rptr. 815 (1974).

166. 471 F.2d 923 (D.C. Cir. 1972).

167. *See, e.g.,* People v. Wolff, 61 Cal. 2d 795, 394 P.2d 959, 40 Cal. Rptr. 271 (1964); People v. Conley, 64 Cal. 2d 310, 411 P.2d 911, 49 Cal. Rptr. 815 (1966). The *Gorshen* case, described at the beginning of this chapter (see Case Study 8.1), could also be seen as an example of the California courts' confusing use of the term "diminished capacity." *See generally* Peter Arenella, *The Diminished Capacity and Diminished Responsibility Defenses: Two Children of a Doomed Marriage,* 77 COLUM. L. REV. 827 (1977).

168. Cal. Penal Code §§ 188, 189, 21.

169. More than two-thirds of the states that have the death penalty follow the Model Penal Code's formulation in requiring the sentencing authority to consider as possible "mitigating factors" (1) whether the capital offense "was committed while the defendant was under the influence of extreme mental or emotional disturbance" and whether (2) at the time of the offense, cognitive or volitional impairment was impaired by mental disease or defect or intoxication. LOW ET AL., *supra* note 154, at 811. *See also* Mary Bicknell, *Constitutional Law: The Eighth Amendment Does Not Prohibit the Execution of Mentally Retarded Convicts,* 43 OKLA. L. REV. 357 n. 129 (1990).

170. Because of the latter difficulty, Morse has proposed that a person who can show diminished responsibility arbitrarily receive half the punishment normally received for the crime. Stephen Morse, *Diminished Capacity: A Moral and Legal Conundrum,* 2 INT'L J. L. & PSYCHIATRY 271 (1979).

171. As of 1985, at least the following states had rejected the doctrine: Arizona, Delaware, District of Columbia, Florida, Georgia, Louisiana, Maryland, Minnesota, North Carolina, Ohio, Oklahoma, West Virginia, Wisconsin, and Wyoming. *See generally* Travis H.D. Lewin, *Psychiatric Evidence in Criminal Cases for Purposes Other Than the Defense of Insanity,* 26 SYRACUSE L. REV. 1051 (1975); LAFAVE & SCOTT, *supra* note 110, § 4.7 n.10.

172. The Insanity Defense Reform Act of 1984 states that, aside from the insanity defense described in the act, "[m]ental disease or defect does not otherwise constitute a defense." 18 U.S.C. §20(a).

173. A third, much less persuasive reason given by the courts that reject the diminished capacity doctrine is that people who lack *mens rea* due to mental disease or defect are not entitled to exculpation. As the court stated in State v. Johnson, 292 Md. 405, 439 A.2d 542 (1982): "[T]he introduction of expert psychiatric testimony concerning the defendant's mental aberrations when the basic sanity of the accused is not at issue conflicts with the governing principle of the criminal law that all legally sane individuals are equally capable of forming and possessing the same types and degrees of intent." Of course, this type of tautological reasoning proves nothing.

174. As of 1985, the following states had indicated, either by statute or judicial decision, that expert testimony on *mens rea* is admissible under certain circumstances: Alaska, Arkansas, California, Connecticut, Colorado, Hawaii, Idaho, Iowa, Kansas, Kentucky, Maine, Massachusetts, Michigan, Missouri, Montana, Nevada, New Jersey, New Mexico, New York, Oregon, Pennsylvania, Rhode Island, Tennessee (see Tennessee v. Phipps, 883 S.W.2d 138 [Tenn. Crim. App. 1994]), Texas, Utah, Vermont, and Washington. *See also* LAFAVE & SCOTT, *supra* note 110, §4.7 n.19; John Q. LaFond, *U.S. Mental Health Law and Policy: Future Trends Affecting Forensic Psychiatrists,* 11 AM. J. FORENSIC PSYCHIATRY 5 n. 47 (1990). The ABA has also recommended that such testimony be admitted. STANDARDS, *supra* note 80, standard 7-6.2. Finally, *see infra* notes 175–177 and accompanying text.

175. State v. Hines, 445 A.2d 314 (Conn. 1982); Commonwealth v. Walzack, 360 A.2d 914 (Pa. 1976); People v. Wetmore, 22 Cal. 3d 318, 583 P.2d 1308, 149 Cal. Rptr. 265 (1978).

176. *See* Sandstrom v. Montana, 442 U.S. 510 (1979).

177. *See* Hughes v. Mathews, 576 F.2d 1250 (7th Cir.), *cert. dismissed sub nom.,* Israel V. Hughes, 439 U.S. 801 (1978). *Cf.* Muench v. Israel, 715 F.2d 1124 (7th Cir. 1983). In Montana v. Egelhoff, 116 S. Ct. 2013 (1996), the Supreme Court rejected both of these arguments when made in support of a "voluntary intoxication" defense. However, it based this rejection largely on the grounds that the intoxication defense is of relatively "recent vintage." Defenses based on mental illness obviously are not [see § 8.02(b)], although the specific defense of diminished capacity defense is a very recent development. For more discussion of *Egelhoff,* see § 8.03(e), which examines the voluntary intoxication defense.

178. *See, e.g.,* Simpson v. State, 381 N.E.2d 122 (Ind. 1978); People v. Loving, 258 Cal. App. 2d 84, 65 Cal. Rptr. 425 (1968); Bradshaw v. State, 353 So. 2d 188 (Fla. App. 1st Dist. 1978); Waye v. Commonwealth, 219 Va. 683, 251 S.E.2d 202 (1979).

179. *See, e.g.,* United States v. Bright, 517 F.2d 584 (2d Cir. 1975).

180. Massachusetts and Texas clearly impose this limitation. The cases permitting expert testimony on

mens rea in Pennsylvania, Nevada, New Mexico, Rhode Island, and Washington were homicide cases, leaving it unclear whether they would restrict the use of such testimony to homicide charges only.

181. Only Colorado, New Jersey, and Oregon have specifically held that evidence of diminished capacity is admissible to negate general intent.

The situation in Model Penal Code jurisdictions is much more complicated than the text suggests. As defined in the Model Penal Code, both recklessness and negligence have subjective elements. *See* Model Penal Code § 2.02(2)(c), (d). Thus, technically, evidence of mental impairment might even be admissible to negate these mental states. *See generally* RALPH REISNER & CHRISTOPHER SLOBOGIN, LAW AND THE MENTAL HEALTH SYSTEM: CIVIL AND CRIMINAL ASPECTS 541–43 (1990).

182. *See, e.g.,* Ohio v. Wilcox, 436 N.E.2d 523 (Ohio 1982); State v. Schantz, 403 P.2d 521 (Ariz. 1965).

183. *See* Richard Bonnie & Christopher Slobogin, *The Role of Mental Health Professionals in the Criminal Process: The Case for Informed Speculation,* 66 VA. L. REV. 427, 473–77 (1980).

184. 517 F.2d 584 (2d Cir. 1975).

185. *See generally* Andrew Taslitz, *Myself Alone: Individualizing Justice Through Psychological Character Evidence,* 52 MD. L. REV. 1 (1993).

186. FEDERAL RULES OF EVIDENCE 404.

187. FEDERAL RULES OF EVIDENCE 404(a).

188. 553 F.2d 1073 (7th Cir. 1977).

189. 668 P.2d 874 (Ariz. 1981). *See also* State v. Christensen, 129 Ariz. 32, 628 P.2d 580 (1981) (holding it error to exclude testimony that the defendant had difficulty dealing with stress and that the stress associated with the offense caused his reaction to be more reflexive than reflective, and thus unpremeditated).

190. 247 F. Supp. 743 (S.D.N.Y. 1965). *See also* State v. Wood, 346 N.W.2d 481 (Iowa 1984), where the court allowed expert testimony that one of the participants was a passive–dependent personality who would follow others and therefore should not be convicted as an accomplice.

191. *See, e.g.,* People v. Jones, 156 Cal. App. 2d 279, 319 P.2d 458 (1957). *See also* Robert H. Woody & J.M. Shade, *Psychological Testimony on the Propensity for Sexual Child Abuse,* MICH. PSYCHOLOGIST 12 (March–April 1989).

192. *See, e.g.,* Freeman v. State, 486 P.2d 967 (Alaska 1971).

193. United States v. Webb, 625 F.2d 709 (5th Cir. 1980) (excluding testimony that defendant would not shoot a helicopter because this conclusion was "within the 'ken of lay jurors'"); United States v. MacDonald, 485 F. Supp. 1087 (E.D.N.C. 1979), aff'd 688 F.2d 224 (4th Cir. 1982) (rejecting testimony that defendant's personality was inconsistent with violent murders).

194. 88 N.J. 508, 443 A.2d 1020 (1982).

195. 310 N.W.2d 58 (Minn. 1981).

196. *See, e.g.,* Sanders v. State, 251 Ga. 70, 303 S.E.2d 13 (1983).

197. 337 N.W.2d 512 (Iowa 1983).

198. People v. James, 451 N.W.2d 611 (Mich. App. 1990); State v. McCoy, 400 N.W.2d 807 (Minn. App. 1987); In re Cheryl H., 153 Cal. App. 3d 1098, 200 Cal. Rptr. 789 (1984); State v. Myers, 359 N.W.2d 604 (Minn. 1984).

199. Henson v. State, 535 N.E.2d 1189 (Ind. 1989); State v. Marks, 231 Kan. 645, 647 P.2d 1292 (1982); State v. Huey, 145 Ariz. 59, 699 P.2d 1290 (1985); State v. Allewalt, 308 Md. 89, 517 A.2d 741 (1986). Note that in these states the defendant would also be able to show consent through proving the trauma symptoms are not present. *See generally* Toni Massaro, *Experts, Psychology, Credibility, and Rape: The Rape Trauma Syndrome Issue and Its Implications for Expert Psychological Testimony,* 69 MINN. L. REV. 395 (1985).

200. With respect to the rape-trauma syndrome, *see* State v. Saldana, 324 N.Wd.2d 227 (1982); Spencer v. General Elec. Co, 688 F. Supp. 1072 (E.D. Va. 1988); People v. Pullins, 145 Mich. App. 414, 378 N.W.2d 501 (1985); Commonwealth v. Zamarripa, 379 Pa. Super. 20, 549 A.2d 980 (1988). As to testimony that a child has been abused, *see* State v. Tracy, 482 N.W.2d 675 (Iowa 1992) (holding that expert was impermissibly testifying as to the child victim's truthfulness); People v. Beckley, 434 Mich. 691, 456 N.W.2d 391 (1990); People v. Reinhardt, 188 Mich. App. 80, 469 N.W.2d 22 (1991) (limiting such testimony to whether the child's symptoms are "typical" of that normally found in sexually abused children; specific testimony that the child victim was abused is impermissible).

201. 36 Cal. 3d 236, 681 P.2d 291, 203 Cal. Rptr. 450 (1984).

202. For further explication of this concept, *See* Slobogin, *supra* note 116, at 846–47.

203. 397 U.S. 358 (1970).

204. *See, e.g.,* Mullaney v. Wilbur, 421 U.S. 684 (1975) (holding that the state must disprove provocation beyond a reasonable doubt).

205. LAFAVE & SCOTT, *supra* note 110, § 5.7, at 454–61.

206. *Id.,* §7.10, at 653–660.

207. *Id.* at 432–33.

208. *Id.* at 659.

209. MODEL PENAL CODE § 3.04.

210. MODEL PENAL CODE § 210.3.

211. MODEL PENAL CODE § 2.09.

212. The initial research identifying this syndrome was conducted by Walker. *See* LENORE WALKER, THE BATTERED WOMAN (1979). Scores of researchers have since refined the concept, and scores of commentators and courts have since considered its application under a number of legal doctrines, including insanity, provocation, and, as described here, self-defense. *See generally* Regina A. Schuller & Neil Vidmar, *Battered Woman Syndrome Evidence in the Courtroom: A Review of the Literature,* 16 LAW & HUM. BEHAV. 273 (1992); Meredith B. Cross, *The Expert as Educator: A Proposed Approach to the Use of Battered Women Syndrome Expert Testimony,* 35 VAND. L. REV. 753 (1982).

213. State v. Norman, 378 S.E.2d 8 (N.C. 1989). *Cf.* Jahnke v. State, 682 P.2d 991 (Wyo. 1984) (rejecting evi-

dence of battered-child syndrome to support self-defense claim).

214. State v. Kelly, 97 N.J. 178, 478 A.2d 364 (1984); Ibn-Tamas v. United States, 455 A.2d 893 (D.C. App. 1983); Smith v. State, 277 S.E.2d 678 (Ga. 1981); Hawthorne v. State, 408 So. 2d 801 (Fla. App. 1982). Note that the syndrome has also been used by the *state* to rebut a defendant's insanity defense. State v. Baker, 424 A.2d 177 (N.H. 1980).

215. 2 All E.R. 801 (1954).

216. 563 F.2d 1331 (9th Cir. 1977). *See also* Kanaras v. State, 54 Md. App. 568, 460 A.2d 61 (1983) (defendant was "passive" and "easily led" and therefore coerced into theft, housebreaking and felony murder).

217. *See generally* CHARLES WHITEBREAD & CHRISTOPHER SLOBOGIN, CRIMINAL PROCEDURE ch. 20 (3d. ed. 1993).

218. United States v. Bestanipour, 41 F.3d 1178 (7th Cir. 1994); United States v. Hill, 655 F.2d 512 (3d Cir. 1981). *Cf.* United States v. Newman, 849 F.2d 156 (5th Cir. 1988).

219. *See, e.g.,* People v. Kelly, 10 Cal. 3d 565, 516 P.2d 875, 11 Cal. Rptr. 171 (1973); Chittum v. Commonwealth, 211 Va. 12, 174 S.E.2d 779 (1970); Cirack v. State, 201 So. 2d 706 (Fla. 1967); Beasley v. State, 50 Ala. 149 (1874). *See generally* LAFAVE & SCOTT, *supra* note 110, § 4.10(g), at 395 n.62.

220. 214 N.W. 2d 205 (Iowa 1974).

221. *See* LAFAVE & SCOTT, *supra* note 110, § 4.10, at 387–93.

222. Paul Robinson, *Causing the Condition of One's Own Defense: A Study in the Limits of Theory in Criminal Law Doctrine,* 71 VA. L. REV. 1 (1985).

223. 116 S. Ct. 2013 (1996).

224. LAFAVE & SCOTT, *supra* note 110, § 4.10, at 393–94. *See also* Minneapolis v. Altimus, 306 Minn. 462, 238 N.W.2d 851 (1976); MODEL PENAL CODE §§ 2.08(4), 5(c) (1962).

225. LAFAVE & SCOTT, *supra* note 110, at 393–94.

226. *See, e.g.,* Driver v. Hinnant, 346 F.2d 761 (4th Cir. 1966). *Cf.* Robinson v. California, 370 U.S. 660 (1962).

227. United States v. Moore, 486 F.2d 1139 (D.C. Cir. 1973); United States v. Sullivan, 406 F.2d 180 (2d Cir. 1969); People v. Vorrero, 227 N.E.2d 18 (N.Y. 1967); Roberts v. State, 41 Wis. 2d 537, 164 N.W.2d 525 (1969).

228. Alaska, Delaware, Georgia, Illinois, Indiana, Kentucky, Maryland, Michigan, New Mexico, South Carolina, South Dakota, and Utah. *See* LaFond, *supra* note 174, at n.38.

229. *See* MICH. COMP. LAWS ANN. §§ 768.29a(2), 768.36 (1982).

230. *See, e.g.,* BARBARA WOOTEN, CRIME AND THE CRIMINAL LAW (1963). This proposal, in turn, is to be distinguished from the move in some states (e.g., Oregon) changing the insanity verdict from not guilty by reason of insanity to guilty except for insanity. This type of legislation does not eliminate the insanity defense, but merely changes the verdict label, apparently in an effort to send a message to the public that the person has been found to have committed a criminal act, and perhaps also to suggest that the person will not be released immediately from custody.

231. *See* statutes cited *supra* note 46.

232. State v. Byers, 861 P.2d 860 (Mont. 1993), *cert. denied,* 114 S. Ct. 1380 (1994); State v. Search, 798 P.2d 914 (1990).

233. According to Smith & Hall, *supra* note 24, at 101, the percentage of acquittals since passage of Michigan's GBMI law has increased slightly. *See also* Christopher Slobogin, *The GBMI Verdict: An Idea Whose Time Should Not Have Come,* 53 GEO. WASH. L. REV. 494, 506–10 (1985) (canvassing National Center for State Court data, which suggest that in only one of four states studied—Georgia—did insanity acquittals drop after introduction of the verdict). Another study of Georgia found that the decrease in the acquittal rate in that state may have been due largely to a federal court's decision a year before the adoption of the GBMI verdict eliminating Georgia's practice of automatically committing insanity acquittees. STEADMAN ET AL., *supra* note 12, at 108–11. At the same time, it found that the rate of insanity pleas increased significantly after adoption of the verdict. *Id.* at 106–08.

234. Steadman and his colleagues found that, in Georgia, those found GBMI for violent offenses were confined longer than those found NGRI *and* those found guilty. STEADMAN ET AL., *supra* note 12, at 117–19. What is not clear from this research, however, is whether those who received longer sentences would have been found NGRI in the absence of the GBMI verdict. In fact, it is very possible that this group is composed of the most dangerous offenders, who under the pre-GBMI system would have been convicted and confined for relatively longer periods analogous to those now experienced by those found GBMI. In other words, Steadman et al.'s findings may merely indicate that the GBMI verdict has changed nothing but the label assigned the most dangerous, noninsane defendants. *See* Smith & Hall, *supra* note 24, at 95–100 (finding that most people in GBMI group come from the guilty group, not the NGRI group).

235. *See, e.g.,* People v. Murphy, 416 Mich. 453, 331 N.W.2d 152 (1982) (striking down a jury's GBMI verdict as against the weight of the evidence and directing an insanity acquittal); Michigan v. Fultz, 111 Mich. App. 587, 314 N.W.2d 702 (1981) (same, except GBMI verdict came from a bench trial).

236. *See, e.g.,* People v. Crews, 122 Ill. 2d 266, 119 Ill. Dec. 308, 522 N.E.2d 1167 (1988).

237. DEL. CODE ANN. tit. 11, § 408.

238. *See, e.g.,* the Michigan jury instruction, which after stating that "[i]n most respects a verdict of guilty but mentally ill is the same as a verdict of guilty," continues "[t]he distinction is that the verdict of guilty but mentally ill imposes upon the Department of Corrections an obligation to provide appropriate psychiatric treatment during the period of imprisonment or while the defendant is on probation." Michigan Criminal Jury Instructions CJI 7:8:10 (1977).

239. Indeed, one mental health administrator assert-

ed that roughly 75% of those found GBMI in Michigan are sent to prison and receive "no treatment." Testimony of William Meyer, in MYTHS & REALITIES: A REPORT OF THE NATIONAL COMMISSION ON THE INSANITY DEFENSE 333 (1983). This testimony also indicated that most GBMI offenders are sex offenders who are relatively untreatable; yet a study of GBMI offenders in Michigan found that 72% needed treatment. *See generally* Slobogin, *supra* note 233, at 518 n.115; *see also* Smith & Hall, *supra* note 24, at 104–06 (finding that GBMI offenders were no more likely to receive treatment than other prisoners); STEADMAN ET AL., *supra* note 12, at 116 (finding that only 2% of those found GBMI in Georgia were hospitalized); Keilitz, *supra* note 90, at 77. 240. Most state statutes make clear that treatment is not a "right" but is to be provided GBMI offenders in the discretion of state. *See, e.g.,* ILL. REV. STAT. ch. 38, § 1005-2-6; N.M. STAT. ANN. § 31.9.4; S.D. CODIFIED LAWS ANN. § 23A-27-38; UTAH CODE ANN. § 77-35-21.5(4); 42 PA. CONS. STAT. § 9727(b); GA. CODE ANN. § 17-7-131(g). Several state courts have explicitly held that there is no right to treatment under GBMI statutes. *See, e.g.,* People v. Marshall, 114 Ill. App.3d 217, 448 N.E.2d 969 (1983). Even in Michigan, where the courts have held that GBMI offenders have a right to treatment, the right is seldom enforced. *See* Slobogin, *supra* note 233, at 513–14 n.90.

241. *See* Robert J. Favole, *Mental Disability in the American Criminal process: A Four Issue Survey,* in MENTALLY DISORDERED OFFENDERS: PERSPECTIVES FROM LAW AND SOCIAL SCIENCE 281–95 (John Monahan & Henry J. Steadman eds. 1983) (chart showing that all fifty states have some provision for transferring prisoners to mental health facilities).

242. *See* SIMON, *supra* note 86, at 178 (concluding that jurors would prefer such a compromise verdict). *See also* Gary Melton et al., *The Effects of the Addition of a GBMI Verdict,* NIMH Grant No. RO1MH39243, *reported in* REISNER & SLOBOGIN, LAW & THE MENTAL HEALTH SYSTEM 81 (1995 suppl.) (finding that field and laboratory studies "offer substantial evidence that GBMI . . . does not make juries' decisions easier [and] does not decrease their attention to extraneous issues [although it] does offer a compromise verdict that permits avoidance of hard questions of criminal responsibility.").

243. *See, e.g.,* STANDARDS, *supra* note 80, standard 7-6.8.

244. Richard C. Boldt, *The Construction of Responsibility in the Criminal Law,* 140 U. PA. L. REV. 2245 n.169 (1992) ("the [GBMI] movement seems to have stalled and there has been little new legislative or judicial initiative in those states that did not develop "GBMI" verdicts by 1986").

245. Much of the material in this section is drawn from Norman G. Poythress & Christopher Slobogin, *Psychological Constructs Relevant to Defenses of Insanity and Diminished Capacity,* in SCIENTIFIC REFERENCE MANUAL (David L. Faigman et al. eds. 1997).

246. Data for the first three samples, in the order in which they appear in the table, are from the following studies: Cooke & Sikorski, *supra* note 11; Criss & Racine,

supra note 34; Pasewark et al., *supra* note 25. The data for the last three samples are from STEADMAN ET AL., *supra* note 12, at 74–83 (New York data); 50–62 (California data); 105–119 (Georgia data). Some condensing of the original data was necessary to make the studies more nearly comparable. The data are not directly comparable in all categories; for example, "prior criminal record" was recorded by Cooke and Sikorski as prior conviction, while the other studies used prior arrest as the measure. Further, the percentages in Table 8.1 are rounded to the nearest whole percent; in some instances the figures are extracted directly from the studies cited; in other instances they are based on our calculations of data presented. When calculations were made by us, only the n for which data were available was used in determining percentages.

247. *See also* Petrila, *supra* note 11, Table 11 (reporting that a study of pretrial evaluations in Missouri in 1978 revealed that only 1 of 127 defendants recommended as NGRI was diagnosed as having a personality disorder).

248. James Gleick, *Getting Away with Murder,* NEW TIMES 21 (Aug. 1978).

249. Rodney C. Howard & Charles R. Clark, *When Courts and Experts Disagree: Discordance Between Insanity Recommendations and Adjudications,* 9 LAW & HUM. BEHAV. 385 (1985).

250. *Supra* note 34.

251. Smith & Hall, *supra* note 24, at 95–100.

252. W. ALLEN HAUSER & DALE C. HESDORFFER, EPILEPSY: FREQUENCY, CAUSES, AND CONSEQUENCES 2 (1990).

253. For a description of various types of seizures, *see* Ernst Neidermeyer, *Neurologic Aspects of the Epilepsies,* in PSYCHIATRIC ASPECTS OF EPILEPSY 99 (Dietrich Blumer ed. 1984).

254. Many persons who suffer from seizures report a conscious subjective experience, called an *aura,* that occurs at the beginning of the seizure. This experience may involve perceptual aberrations (hallucinations) or affective disturbances including the sudden onset of fear. Some persons describe the aura as a mixture between reality and dreaming; others report a sense of déjà vu. Memory for this brief portion of the seizure is retained. *Id.* at 104.

255. Gregory D. Cascino, *Complex Partial Seizures: Clinical Features and Differential Diagnosis,* 15 PSYCHIATRIC CLINICS N. AM. 373, 376 (1992).

256. Some writers have erroneously used the terms "complex partial seizures," "psychomotor epilepsy," and "temporal lobe epilepsy" interchangeably. These terms are not equivalents. About 20% of patients with temporal lobe EEG focus will never have a seizure, and about 20% of patients who experience a psychomotor seizure will fail to reveal a temporal lobe focus on repeated EEG. Janice R. Stevens, *Psychiatric Implications of Psychomotor Epilepsy,* 14 ARCHIVES GEN. PSYCHIATRY 461, 461 (1966).

257. Cascino, *supra* note 255, at 374.

258. "[S]trikingly complex activities can be performed. A patient may disrobe, may go out for a long walk, may drive a car, may perform household chores, such as washing dishes or cleaning the floor, and so on."

Frank D. Benson, *Interictal Behavior Disorder in Epilepsy*, 9 PSYCHIATRIC CLINICS N. AM. 283, 285 (1986). Such automatisms, however, "always occur out of context with environmental activities, and they have short duration (measured in minutes) during which the victim is recovering orientation." *Id.*

259. *See* JOSE M. R. DELGADO, PHYSICAL CONTROL OF THE MIND (1969); Burr Eichelman, *The Limbic System and Aggression in Humans*, 7 NEUROSCIENCE & BIOBEHAVIORAL REV. 391 (1983); Burr Eichelman, *Bridges from the Animal Laboratory to the Study of Violent or Criminal Individuals*, in MENTAL DISORDER AND CRIME 194 (Sheilah Hodgins ed. 1993).

260. Orrin Devinsky & David Bear, *Varieties of Aggressive Behavior in Temporal Lobe Epilepsy*, 141 AM. J. PSYCHIATRY 651, 653 (1984).

261. STEVEN WHITMAN & BRUCE P. HERMANN, PSYCHOPATHOLOGY IN EPILEPSY 296 (1986).

262. *Id.* at 288–89.

263. David M. Treiman, *Epilepsy and Violence: Medical and Legal Issues*, 27 EPILEPSIA (suppl. 2) s77, s78 (1986) (describing a study of 229 EEGs taken on 212 such individuals; only 14 of 212 (6.6%) had minimally or slightly abnormal EEGs, and none of the EEG abnormalities were interpreted as epileptiform). Neidermeyer, *supra* note 253, at 106, similarly concluded that "[m]ost cases of rage attacks show no EEG evidence of temporal lobe epilepsy."

264. Antonio V. Delgato-Escueta et al., *The Nature of Aggression during Epileptic Seizures*, 305 NEW ENG. J. MED. 711 (1981). In this study, the expert panel viewed videotaped recordings of 33 epileptic attacks involving 19 patients. The attacks "appeared suddenly, without evidence of planning, and lasted an average of 29 seconds. . . . Aggressive acts were stereotyped, simple, unsustained, and never supported by consecutive series of purposeful movements." *Id.* at 715.

265. Ernst A. Rodin, *Psychomotor Epilepsy and Aggressive Behavior*, 28 ARCHIVES GEN. PSYCHIATRY 210 (1973). In this study the author chemically induced seizures in 150 patients at an epilepsy clinic and photographed their behavior during the seizure and postictal period. Zero incidents of aggressive behavior occurred.

266. Dietrich Blumer, *Temporal Lobe Epilepsy and Its Psychiatric Significance*, in PSYCHIATRIC ASPECTS, *supra* note 253, 15 171–98.

267. Delgato-Escueta et al., *supra* note 264, at 715.

268. Devinsky & Bear, *supra* note 260, at 654.

269. David Bear et al., *Behavioral Alterations in Patients with Temporal Lobe Epilepsy*, in PSYCHIATRIC ASPECTS OF EPILEPSY, *supra* note 253, at 201–02.

270. *See* Sidney Levin, *Epileptic Clouded States*, 116 J. NERVOUS & MENTAL DISEASE 215 (1952) (describing 52 cases in which abnormal mental states developed from 24 hours to 7 days postseizure); S.J. Logsdail & B.K. Toone, *Post-ictal Psychoses*, 152 BRIT. J. PSYCHIATRY 246 (1988) (describing 14 cases of psychosis or confusion immediately postseizure or within one week of apparent return to normal functioning).

271. MICHAEL R. TRIMBLE, THE PSYCHOSES OF EPILEPSY 137 (1991).

272. Affective warmth and interpersonal cohesion are often retained in persons who are diagnosed with both epilepsy and psychosis. *Id.* at 134.

273. Paul Fedio, *Behavioral Characteristics of Patients with Temporal Lobe Epilepsy*, 9 PSYCHIATRIC CLINICS N. AM. 267, 273 (1986) ("Interictal psychosis may, at times, have no direct relation to seizure activity . . ."); Logsdail & Toone, *supra* note 270, at 249 ("There was no particular association between EEG abnormalities [and psychotic symptom onset]"). For some individuals there is also the phenomenon of "forced normalization" or "alternative psychosis" in which symptoms of psychosis appear only when the seizure disorder is relatively under control. *See, e.g.*, Ann Pakalnis et al., *Forced Normalisation*, 44 ARCHIVES NEUROLOGY 289 (1987).

274. "There are discordant views that TLE produces a distinct personality syndrome. . . ." Fedio, *supra* note 273, at 270.

275. For a comprehensive discussion of behaviors thought to constitute the "interictal syndrome" of TLE patients, *see* David Bear et al., *Interictal Behavior in Hospitalized Temporal Lobe Epileptics: Relationship to Idiopathic Psychiatric Syndromes*, 45 J. NEUROLOGY, NEUROSURGERY & PSYCHIATRY 481 (1982).

276. Behaviors that appear to best discriminate the interictal behavior of persons with TLE from controls include viscosity (interpersonal adhesiveness or clinging behavior), circumstantiality (excessive use of detail in verbal reports), hypergraphia (excessive writing behavior), hyposexuality (reduced sexual interest and activity), and increased interest in religious and/or philosophical matters (sometimes evidenced by frequent religious conversions). *Id.*; Fedio, *supra* note 273, at 273–74.

277. Bear et al., *supra* note 275, at 482 (persons with TLE were no more prone to aggression, or less likely to engage in angry outbursts, compared to controls).

278. "It is further remarkable how even during extreme outbursts a measure of control seems to be present: the rage is frightening, furniture is destroyed, a family member is struck, but rarely is someone injured." Dietrich Blumer, *Epilepsy and Violence*, in RAGE/HATE/ASSAULT AND OTHER FORMS OF VIOLENCE 207, 210 (Denis F. Madden & John R. Lion eds. 1976).

279. "[P]atients with temporal lobe epilepsy may display disparate forms of aggressive behavior and . . . the more frequent, clinically important, and mechanistically significant aggressive behaviors do not occur during the ictal period. . . . Most of the aggressive acts follow a provocation, although it may seem a trivial one to others. The aggressive act may be planned out in clear consciousness over a significant period of time. . . . The patient characteristically recalls and acknowledges his behavior and may experience sincere remorse concerning the consequences." Devinsky & Bear, *supra* note 260, at 654.

280. Dietric Blumer & Frank Benson, *Personality Changes with Frontal and Temporal Lobe Lesions*, in PSYCHIATRIC ASPECTS, *supra* note 253.

281. *See supra* notes 273–79 and accompanying text.

282. A. Earl Walker, *Murder or Epilepsy?*, 133 J. NERVOUS & MENTAL DISEASE 430 (1961).

283. Harold E. Himwich et al., *Changes in Cerebral Bloodflow and Arteriovenous Oxygen Difference during Insulin Hypoglycemia*, 93 J. NERVOUS & MENTAL DISEASE 362, 364 (1941).

284. Harold E. Himwich, *A Review of Hypoglycemia, Its Physiology and Pathology, Symptomatology and Treatment*, 11 AM. J. DIGESTIVE DISEASES 1, 4–5 (1944).

285. William H. Lyle, *Temporary Insanity: Some Practical Considerations in a Legal Defense*, 8 J. ORTHOMOLECULAR PSYCHIATRY (1979).

286. Richard C. W. Hall et al., *Endocrine Disease and Behavior*, 4 INTEGRATIVE PSYCHIATRY 122, 125–26 (1986). Physiological signs that may be present include dilated pupils, hypertension, and tachycardia. *Id.*

287. The transitory nature of the episode is also of diagnostic importance and has been dramatically demonstrated in the treatment of individual cases. Wilder wrote: "As a rule (hypoglycemic states) are promptly reversible by an intravenous injection of glucose. . . . The effect is so miraculous that the needle is still in the patient's vein and a severe coma or psychosis has already been transformed into complete normalcy." Joseph Wilder, *Sugar Metabolism and Its Relation to Criminology*, in HANDBOOK OF CORRECTIONAL PSYCHOLOGY 101 (Robert Mitchell Lindner & Robert Victor Seliger eds. 1947).

288. V. Markku Linnoila & Matti Virkkunen, *Aggression, Suicidality, and Serotonin*, 53 (10 suppl.) J. CLINICAL PSYCHIATRY 46 (1992).

289. *Id.* at 49–50. Type II alcoholism occurs in individuals whose biological fathers severely abused alcohol and have significant histories of involvement with the criminal justice system and alcoholism treatment programs but whose mothers' history is relatively normal. The relative risk for heritability of alcoholism in offspring from this parentage is 9x. C. Robert Cloninger et al., *Inheritance of Alcohol Abuse: Cross-fostering Analysis of Adopted Men*, 38 ARCHIVES GEN. PSYCHIATRY 861, 866–67 (1981).

290. A low 5-hydroxyindoleacetic acid (5-HIAA) level in cerebrospinal fluid has been one of the most consistent markers for impulsive (but not planned) aggressive behavior. Linnoila & Virkkunen, *supra* note 288, at 46–47.

291. Hall et al., *supra* note 286, at 122.

292. *See, e.g.*, Thomas Lingenfelser et al., *Cognitive and Psychomotor Function During Severe Insulin-induced Hypoglycaemia in Insulin-dependent Diabetic Patients*, 25 NEUROPSYCHOBIOLOGY 161 (1992). A. Wirsen et al., *Neuropsychological Performance Differs Between Type 1 Diabetic and Normal Men During Insulin-induced Hypoglycaemia*, 9 DIABETIC MED. 156 (1992). Daniel J. Cox et al., *Disruptive Effects of Acute Hypoglycemia on Speed of Cognitive and Motor Performance*, 16 DIABETES CARE 1391 (1993).

293. Robert D. Gittler, *Spontaneous Hypoglycemia*, 62 N.Y. ST. J. MED. 236, 239 (1962).

294. Lyle, *supra* note 285.

295. DSM-IV, *supra* note 111, at 477 (1994).

296. Descriptive studies note that persons with MPD frequently endorse some symptoms associated with schizophrenia, particularly auditory hallucinations. Colin A. Ross et al., *Schneiderian Symptoms in Multiple Personality Disorder and Schizophrenia*, 31 COMPREHENSIVE PSYCHIATRY 111 (1990). However, some experts distinguish between the "voices" heard by persons with schizophrenia, which are typically described as originating "outside" the person's head, from those described by persons with MPD, which often take the form of commentaries or conversations inside the head; the latter are construed as commentaries by or conversations among alters.

297. *Compare* Michael F. Clearly, *Dissociative States—Disproportionate Use as a Defense in Criminal Proceedings*, 1 AM. J. FORENSIC PSYCHOL. 157, 159 (1983) (a review of discharge diagnoses from several mental health agencies concluding that dissociative disorder as a primary diagnosis in psychiatric populations is "much less than one-tenth of one percent [0.1%]") *with* Colin A. Ross, *Epidemiology of Multiple Personality Disorder and Dissociation*, 14 PSYCHIATRICS CLINICS N. AM. 503, 505 (1991) (about 10% of the persons surveyed met DSM-III-R criteria for dissociative disorder of some kind) and Colin A. Ross et al., *The Frequency of Multiple Personality Disorder among Psychiatric Patients*, 148 AM. J. PSYCHIATRY 1717 (1990) (5.4% of 299 inpatients met diagnostic criteria for MPD; several studies reviewed by these authors yielded estimates from 1–5%, with a single study reporting an outlier estimate of 16%).

298. Other authors agree with Clearly. *See* Paul Chodoff, *Comment*, 144 AM. J. PSYCHIATRY 124 (1987) (reporting having observed only one "very doubtful case" in forty years of practicing psychiatry, and informal polling of colleagues in private practice who report no, or at most one to two cases); Corbett H. Thigpen & Harvey M. Cleckley, *On the Incidence of Multiple Personality Disorder: A Brief Communication*, 32 INT'L J. CLINICAL & EXPERIMENTAL HYPNOSIS 63 (1984) (reporting having seen only 1 case of MPD in "tens of thousands" of patients in over three decades of practicing psychiatry).

299. Eve M. Bernstein & Frank W. Putnam, *Development, Reliability, and Validity of a Dissociation Scale*, 174 J. NERVOUS & MENTAL DISEASE 727 (1986).

300. Richard J. Lowenstein, *An Office Mental Status Examination for Complex Chronic Dissociative Symptoms and Multiple Personality Disorder*, 14 PSYCHIATRIC CLINICS N. AM. 567 (1991). Colin A. Ross et al., *The Dissociative Disorders Interview Schedule: A Structured Interview*, 2 DISSOCIATION: PROGRESS DISSOCIATIVE DISORDERS 169 (1989). Marlene Steinberg et al., *The Structured Clinical Interview for DSM-III—Dissociative Disorders: Preliminary Report on a New Diagnostic Instrument*, 147 AM. J. PSYCHIATRY 76 (1990).

301. "The premorbid personality of a person who experiences dissociative states usually reveals emotional immaturity, self-centeredness and episodic emotional disturbances in childhood and adolescence." Robert Showalter et al., *The Spousal-Homicide Syndrome*, 3 INT'L J. L. & PSYCHIATRY 117, 133 (1980). Consistent with this clinical impression, one study reported that 64% of persons diagnosed with MPD also met criteria for borderline personality disorder. Colin A. Ross et al., *Structured Interview Data on 102 Cases of Multiple Personality Disorder from Four Centers*, 147 AM. J. PSYCHIATRY 596, 598–99 (1990).

302. The ratio of women to men diagnosed with MPD is about 9:1. Ross et al., *supra* note 301, at 598 (reporting 90.2% women in the sample); Philip M. Coons et al., *Multiple Personality Disorder: A Clinical Investigation of 50 Cases,* 176 J. NERVOUS & MENTAL DISEASE 519, 520 (1988) (reporting 92% women in the sample). Colin Ross et al., *Multiple Personality Disorder: An Analysis of 236 Cases,* 34 CAN. J. PSYCHIATRY 413, 414 (1989) (reporting 87.7% women in the sample).

303. *Id.* at 416 (79.2% of MPD subjects reported extensive sexual abuse and 74.9% reported extensive physical abuse). Frank Putnam et al., *The Clinical Phenomenology of Multiple Personality Disorder: Review of 100 Cases,* 47 J. CLINICAL PSYCHIATRY 285, 290 (1986) (97 of 100 persons diagnosed with MPD reported overwhelming and abusive experiences). Coons et al., *supra* note 302, at 521 (96% of the sample reported physical or sexual abuse in childhood).

304. In one study of 236 cases, the mean number of alters at the time of reporting was 15.7. Ross et al., *supra* note 302 at 415. The distribution of reported number of alters is positively skewed. Another study reported the mean number of alters was 13.3, but the median was only 9 and the mode (most commonly occurring frequency) was 3. Putnam et al., *supra* note 303, at 288.

305. Putnam et al., *supra* note 303, at 289 (89% of adult MPDs reported that their alter appeared before age 12).

306. Martin T. Orne et al., *On the Differential Diagnosis of Multiple Personality in the Forensic Context,* 32 INT'L J. CLINICAL & EXPERIMENTAL HYPNOSIS 118 (1984).

307. Paul S. Appelbaum & Alexander Greer, *Who's On Trial? Multiple Personalities and the Insanity Defense,* 45 HOSP. & COMMUNITY PSYCHIATRY 965 (1994).

308. The study of stress-related disorders has developed primarily in the context of war, including the study of war neurosis (combat-related stress) and victims of the holocaust. It has expanded into research on the impact of natural disasters (e.g., hurricanes) and industrial accidents and thence to specific individual experiences (e.g., rape or assault). For a review, *see* Philip A. Saigh, *History, Current Nosology, and Epidemiology,* in POSTTRAUMATIC STRESS DISORDER: A BEHAVIORAL APPROACH TO ASSESSMENT AND TREATMENT 1 (Philip A. Saigh ed. 1992).

309. AMERICAN PSYCHIATRIC ASSOCIATION, DIAGNOSTIC AND STATISTICAL MANUAL OF MENTAL DISORDERS (3rd ed. 1980) [hereinafter DSM-III].

310. According to DSM-IV, the stressor must involve "direct personal experience of an event that involves actual or threatened death or serious injury, or other threat to one's physical integrity; or witnessing an event that involves death, injury, or a threat to the physical integrity of another person; or learning about unexpected or violent death, serious harm, or threat of death or injury experienced by a family member or other close associate," which event must trigger "intense fear, helplessness or horror (or in children with response must involve disorganized or agitated behavior)." DSM-IV, *supra* note 111, at 424.

311. Examples of reexperiencing include distressing recollections, perceptions, or dreams about the event;

acting or feeling as if the event were recurring, including hallucinations or dissociative flashbacks; and, as noted in the text, intense psychological distress or physiological reactivity when exposed to events that symbolize or are similar to the event. *Id.* at 428.

312. Examples of avoidance and numbing include efforts to avoid thinking about the trauma or places associated with it, inability to recall important aspects of the trauma, diminished interest or participation in significant activities, feeling detached or estranged from others, restricted affect, and a sense of a foreshortened future. *Id.*

313. Examples of increased arousal include difficulty falling or staying asleep, irritability, or outbursts of anger; difficulty concentrating; hypervigilance; and exaggerated startle response. *Id.*

314. Landy F. Sparr & Roland M. Atkinson, *Posttraumatic Stress Disorder as an Insanity Defense: Medicolegal Quicksand,* 143 AM. J. PSYCHIATRY 608 (1986); Anthony S. Higgins, *Post-traumatic Stress Disorder and Its Role in the Defense of Vietnam Veterans,* 15 LAW & PSYCHOL. REV. 259 (1991); Alan A. Stone, *Post-traumatic Stress Disorder and the Law: Critical Review of the New Frontier,* 21 BULL. AM. ACAD. PSYCHIATRY & L. 23 (1993).

315. Brett T. Litz et al., *Assessment of Posttraumatic Stress Disorder,* in POSTTRAUMATIC STRESS DISORDER: A BEHAVIORAL APPROACH TO ASSESSMENT AND TREATMENT 50, 57 (Philip A. Saigh ed. 1992).

316. Thomas W. Miller et al., *Assessment of Life Stress Events: The Etiology and Measurement of Traumatic Stress Disorder,* 38 INT'L J. SOC. PSYCHIATRY 215 (1992) (describing 10 measures).

317. Anthony Feinstein & Ray Dolan, *Predictors of Post-Traumatic Stress Disorder Following Physical Trauma: An Examination of the Stressor Criterion,* 21 PSYCHOL. MED. 85 (1991); Naomi Breslau & Glenn C. Davis, *Posttraumatic Stress Disorder: The Stressor Criterion,* 150 J. NERVOUS & MENTAL DISEASE 255 (1987).

318. Susan D. Solomon & Glorisa J. Canino, *Appropriateness of DSM-III-R Criteria for Posttraumatic Stress Disorder,* 31 COMPREHENSIVE PSYCHIATRY 227 (1990).

319. Flashback experiences among Vietnam veterans have been described as "sudden, discrete experience(s), leading to actions, where the manifest psychic content is only indirectly related to the war; in addition the veteran does not have conscious awareness of reliving events in Vietnam." Herbert J. Cross, *Social Factors Associated with Post-traumatic Stress Disorder in Vietnam Veterans,* in POSTTRAUMATIC STRESS DISORDER: ASSESSMENT, DIFFERENTIAL DIAGNOSIS AND FORENSIC EVALUATION 73, 85 (Carroll L. Meek ed. 1990).

320. Teodoro Ayllon et al., *Interpretations of Symptoms: Fact or Fiction,* 3 BEHAV. RES. & THERAPY 1 (1965). *See generally* Stephen Morse, *Failed Explanations and Criminal Responsibility: Experts and the Unconscious,* 68 VA. L. REV. 971 (1982).

321. David Behar, *Flashbacks and Posttraumatic Stress Symptoms in Combat Veterans,* 28 COMPREHENSIVE PSYCHIATRY 459, 463 (1987).

322. Landy F. Sparr et al., *Military Combat, Posttraumatic Stress Disorder, and Criminal Behavior in Vietnam Veter-*

ans, 15 Bull. Am. Acad. Psychiatry & L. 141, 152 (1987).

323. A.A. Sandberg et al., *An XYY Human Male,* 2 Lancet 488 (1961).

324. Michael Craft, *The Current Status of XYY and XXY Syndromes: A Review of Treatment Implications,* 1 Int'l J. L. & Psychiatry 319, 319–20 (1978).

325. 42 A.L.R.2d (1972); Note, *The XYY Chromosomal Abnormality: Use and Misuse in the Legal Process,* 9 Harv. J. Legis. 469, 484 (1972).

326. Lissy F. Jarvik et al., *Human Aggression and the Extra Y Chromosome: Fact or Fantasy,* 28 Am. Psychologist 674 (1973).

327. Stanley Walzer et al., *The XYY Genotype,* 29 Ann. Rev. Med. 563 (1978).

328. Craft, *supra* note 324.

329. Walzer et al., *supra* note 327.

330. Jarvik et al., *supra* note 326, at 679–80.

331. Craft, *supra* note 324, at 321.

332. "Since it is probable that there is considerable variability in the phenotypic development of XYY males, it is inappropriate to allude to an XYY syndrome. The term syndrome implies a degree of symptom consistency that is not supported by the data available at this time." Walzer et al., *supra* note 327, at 568.

333. DSM-IV, *supra* note 111, at 609. Additional diagnoses in this category not covered in this review include intermittent explosive disorder and trichotillomania (compulsive hair pulling).

334. *Id.*

335. *Id.* at 615.

336. *Id.* at 613.

337. *Id.*

338. *Id.*

339. For kleptomania the person experiences an "increasing sense of tension immediately before committing the theft" and "[p]leasure, gratification, or relief at the time of committing the theft." *Id.* at 613. For pyromania the person experiences "tension or affective arousal before the act" and "[p]leasure, gratification, or relief when setting fires, or when witnessing or participating in their aftermath." *Id.* at 615.

340. *Id.* at 618.

341. *Id.*

342. *Id.*

343. Two of the better reviews of the disorders discussed in this section are: Michael J. Popkin, *Impulse Control Disorders Not Elsewhere Classified,* in Comprehensive Textbook of Psychiatry—V, Vol. 2, 1145–54 (Benjamin J. Sadock ed. 1989); Susan L. McElroy et al., *The DSM-III Impulse Control Disorders Not Elsewhere Classified: Clinical Characteristics and Relationship to Other Psychiatric Disorders,* 149 Am. J. Psychiatry 318 (1992). Popkin noted that these disorders "have been the subject of much theorizing and speculation but distressingly little systematic study." *Id.* at 1145. McElroy et al. echoed this appraisal, noting that "as a group [these disorders] remain poorly studied." *Id.* at 319.

344. Marcus J. Goldman, *Kleptomania: Making Sense of the Nonsensical,* 148 Am. J. Psychiatry 986 (1991).

345. Susan L. McElroy et al., *Kleptomania: Clinical Characteristics and Associated Psychopathology,* 21 Psychol. Med. 93 (1991).

346. *See, e.g.,* Jeffrey L. Geller, *Firesetting in the Adult Psychiatric Population,* 38 Hosp. & Community Psychiatry 501 (1987); Jeffrey L. Geller et al., *Adult Lifetime Prevalence of Firesetting Behaviors in a State Hospital Population,* 63 Psychiatric Q. 129 (1992).

347. Henry R. Lesieur & Sheila B. Blume, *The South Oaks Gambling Screen (SOGS): A New Instrument for the Identification of Pathological Gamblers,* 144 Am. J. Psychiatry 1184 (1987). Rachel A. Volberg & Steven M. Banks, *A Review of Two Measures of Pathological Gambling in the United States,* 6 J. Gambling Stud. 153 (1990).

348. Robert Ladouceur, *Prevalence Estimates of Pathological Gambling in Quebec,* 36 Can. J. Psychiatry 732 (1991); Roger C. Bland et al., *Epidemiology of Pathological Gambling in Edmonton,* 38 Can. J. Psychiatry 108 (1993).

349. McElroy et al., *supra* note 343, at 653.

350. One review reported that women constituted 81% of reported cases. Marcus J. Goldman, *Kleptomania: An Overview,* 22 Psychiatric Annals 68 (1992). Women constituted 75% of the 20 cases described by McElroy et al., *supra* note 345.

351. "Although shoplifting is rampant, kleptomania is unlikely to explain more than a tiny fraction of such 'offenses.' Fewer than 5% of arrested shoplifters give a history that is consistent with kleptomania." Popkin, *supra* note 343, at 1148.

352. Jeffrey L. Geller & Gregory Bertsch, *Fire-setting Behavior in the Histories of a State Hospital Population,* 142 Am. J. Psychiatry 464 (1985).

353. Geller et al., *supra* note 346, at 129.

354. Geller & Bertsch, *supra* note 352 (half the group of fire setters had a history limited to a single episode).

355. In one study of 191 nongeriatric inpatients, none of those who had set illegal fires had a diagnosis of pyromania. *Id.* at 466.

356. *Id.* at 464.

357. Louis H. Gold, *Psychiatric Profile of the Firesetter,* 7 J. Forensic Sci. 404 (1962). Lee B. Macht & John E. Mack, *The Firesetter Syndrome,* 31 Psychiatry 277 (1968).

358. "Though much has been written on firesetting behavior, the literature provides little practical information . . . beyond a multiplicity of diverse and arbitrary classification systems, a variety of motivational factors, and a number of narrowly defined profiles or composites of arsonists." Anthony Olen Rider, *The Firesetter: A Psychological Profile,* FBI Law Enforcement Bulletin (Jun.–Aug. 1980). "There is no adequate description of the typical arsonist, for there is not now, nor has there ever been, such a character." Jeffrey L. Geller, *Arson in Review: From Profit to Pathology,* 15 Psychiatric Clinics N. Am. 623 (1992).

359. Donald I. Templer et al., *Correlates of Pathological Gambling Propensity in Prison Inmates,* 34 Comprehensive Psychiatry 347 (1993).

360. The lower estimate was reported by Roger C. Bland et al., *Epidemiology of Pathological Gambling in Edmonton,* 38 Can. J. Psychiatry 108 (1993); the higher es-

timate was reported by Robert Ladouceur, *Prevalence Estimates of Pathological Gambling in Quebec,* 36 CAN. J. PSYCHIATRY 732, 733 (1991). The variance in prevalence estimates may be attributable to site differences or to methodological differences (e.g., the studies used different diagnostic instruments and different administration procedures, i.e., telephone vs. face-to-face interviews).

361. Darrell W. Bolen et al., *Personality Traits of Pathological Gamblers* (paper presented at the Second Annual Conference on Gambling, Lake Tahoe, Nevada, 1975) (reporting a mean IQ of 112.7 for ten persons in therapy for pathological gambling), *cited in* Julie D. Moravec & Patrick H. Munley, *Psychological Test Findings on Pathological Gamblers in Treatment,* 18 INT'L J. ADDICTIONS 1003, 1004 (1983). In their own study Moravec and Munley obtained a mean IQ estimate of 116.78 in 23 veterans in a Veterans Administration pathological gambling treatment program. *Id.* at 1006.

362. In a study reviewed by McElroy et al., *supra* note 343, at 320, 72% of a treatment group of 25 persons diagnosed with pathological gambling experienced an episode of major depression after attempting to quit gambling. Bland et al., *supra* note 360, at 109, reported that 40% of their sample of persons meeting criteria for pathological gambling also met criteria for antisocial personality disorder, 63.3% met criteria for alcohol abuse or dependence, and 33% met criteria for affective disorder.

363. "The tendency to incendiarism is linked with urethral eroticism through the desire to urinate while watching the flames (a regression to psychosexual infantilism, a masturbation equivalent)." Gold, *supra* note 357, at 406.

364. Alex P. Blaszczynski & Neil McConaghy, *The Medical Model of Pathological Gambling: Current Shortcomings,* 5 J. GAMBLING BEHAVIOR 42 (1989).

365. For a discussion, see *id.* at 45–46.

366. McElroy et al., *supra* note 343, at 323–25. The authors are quick to note, however, that "this hypothesis does *not* argue that impulse disorders are caused by affective spectrum disorder, but rather, that they may share the same underlying physiologic abnormality as other forms." *Id.* at 324.

367. "[T]heir diagnostic validity, individually and as a category, remains in question." *Id.* at 323.

368. *See, e.g.,* Ronald K. Siegel, *Cocaine Hallucinations,* 135 AM. J. PSYCHIATRY 309 (1978); Theo C. Maschreck et al., *Characteristics of Freebase Cocaine Psychosis,* YALE J. BIOLOGICAL MED. 115 (1988); Solomon H. Snyder, *Amphetamine Psychosis: A "Model" Schizophrenia Mediated by Catecholaimines,* 130 AM. J. PSYCHIATRY 61 (1973); Robert Erard et al., *The PCP Psychosis: Prolonged Intoxication or Drug-Precipitated Functional Illness?* 12 J. PSYCHEDELIC DRUGS 142 (1980). *See also* DSM-IV, *supra* note 111, at 192 (listing the following disorders—substance-induced delirium, substance-induced persisting dementia, and substance-induced psychotic disorder, among others).

369. HERBERT FINGARETTE & ANN FINGARETTE HASSE, MENTAL DISABILITIES AND CRIMINAL RESPONSIBILITY ch. 11 (1979). Some studies they cite include HERRICK WALLGREN & HERBERT BARRY, ACTIONS OF ALCOHOL 806

(1970); Julius Merry, *The Loss of Control Myth,* 1 LANCET 1257 (1966).

370. FINGARETTE & HASSE, *supra* note 369, at 184–85.

371. *Id.* at 178.

372. *Id.* at 182.

373. *See, e.g.,* ALFRED RAY LINDESMITH, ADDICTION AND OPIATES (1968); John A. O'Donnell, *A Follow-Up of Narcotic Addicts,* 34 AM. J. OF ORTHOPSYCHIATRY 948 (1964); LEE N. ROBINS, A FOLLOW-UP OF VIETNAM DRUG USERS, SPECIAL ACTIONS OFFICE FOR DRUG ABUSE PREVENTION, EXECUTIVE OFFICE OF THE PRESIDENT (1973).

374. FINGARETTE & HASSE, *supra* note 369, at 165.

375. ROBINS, *supra* note 373.

376. FINGARETTE & HASSE, *supra* note 369, at 165.

377. George F. Koob, *The Reward System and Cocaine Abuse,* in BIOLOGICAL BASIS OF SUBSTANCE ABUSE 351 (Stanley Korenman & Jack D. Barchas eds. 1993).

378. Frank H. Gawin, *Cocaine Addiction: Psychology, Neurophysiology, and Treatment,* in *id.* at 424, 429. This author also states, "[I]n cocaine dependence . . . conditioned craving may be more intense than in other addictive disorders." *Id.* at 431.

379. Edgar H. Adams & Nicholas J. Kozel, *Trends in the Prevalence and Consequences of Cocaine Abuse,* 61 NIDA RES. MONOGRAPH 35 (1985).

380. Frank H. Gawin & Herbert D. Kleber, *Cocaine Use in America: Epidemiologic and Clinical Perspectives,* 61 NIDA RES. MONOGRAPH 182 (1985).

381. Florida v. Zamora, 361 So. 2d 776 (Fla. App. 1978). In a more recent case, Ronald Ray Howard, a crack cocaine dealer who murdered a Texas highway patrol officer, asserted that the violent lyrics of "rap" music had "caused" him to shoot the trooper. The jury was not convinced and he was convicted of first degree murder. U.S.A. TODAY, July 15, 1994, at 3a.

382. United States v. Hearst, 412 F. Supp. 889 (N.D. Cal. 1976).

383. *See generally,* Richard Bonnie, *Excusing and Punishing in Criminal Adjudication: A Reality Check,* 5 CORNELL J. L. & PUB. POL'Y 10 (1995); Stephen Morse, *The "New Syndrome Excuse Syndrome,"* 14 CRIM. JUST. ETHICS 3 (1995).

384. Julie Horney, *Menstrual Cycles and Criminal Responsibility,* 2 LAW & HUM. BEHAV. 25 (1978); Judith Abplanalp, *Premenstrual Syndrome,* 3 BEHAVIORAL SCI. & L. 103 (1985). For a particularly critical view of the scientific basis for a defense based on premenstrual syndrome, see Harry B. Balcer, *Menstruation and Crime: A Critical Review of the Literature from the Perspective of Clinical Criminology,* 5 BEHAVIORAL SCI. & L. 307 (1987).

385. Richard Rada, *Plasma Androgens and the Sex Offender,* 8 BULL. AM. ACAD. PSYCHIATRY & L. 456 (1980).

386. Alexander Capron, *Fetal Alcohol and Felony,* HASTINGS CENTER REPORT (May–June 1992).

387. This defense was floated by William Kunstler and other attorneys of Colin Ferguson after he was charged with killing six people on the Long Island Railroad. Ferguson later fired his attorneys and represented himself, rejecting the insanity defense and instead arguing that he did not commit the crime. For a description of

this defense in context, *see* Jeffrey Rosen, *The Trials of William Kunstler,* N.Y. TIMES [Review of Books]. Sept. 18, 1994, at 16, col. 3.

388. Jacob H. Conn, *The Myth of Coercion through Hypnosis: A Brief Communication,* 19 INT'L J. CLINICAL & EXPERIMENTAL HYPNOSIS 95 (1981).

389. Pasewark, Pantle, and Steadman, for instance, identified three groups of NGRI acquittees who probably should not benefit from the defense but nonetheless periodically do; they are drawn from women who commit infanticide, law enforcement officials who kill in the course of duty, and people whose plight as a "victim" of their victim makes them sympathetic. Pasewark et al., *supra* note 25.

390. Another proponent of this approach, who has elaborated upon it further in forensic contexts, is Stephen Morse. *See* Stephen Morse, *Brain and Blame,* 84 GEO. L.J. 527 (1996); Stephen Morse, *Culpability and Control,* 142 U. PA. L. REV. 1587 (1994); Stephen Morse, *Causation, Compulsion, and Involuntariness,* 22 BULL. ACAD. PSYCHIATRY & L. 159 (1994).

391. *See* PERLIN, *supra* note 1, at 14 (discussing the "vividness" effect, in which statistically undue prominence is given to abnormal insanity cases).

392. PETER DIXON, THE OFFICIAL RULES (1978).

393. Harley Stock & Norman Poythress, *Psychologists' Opinions on Competency and Sanity: How Reliable?* (paper presented at the American Psychological Association Annual Convention, New York, Aug. 1979).

394. Kenneth K. Fukunaga et al., *Insanity Plea: Inter-Examiner Agreement and Concordance of Psychiatric Opinion and Court Verdict,* 5 LAW & HUM. BEHAV. 325 (1981).

395. Lawrence Raifman, *Interjudge Reliability of Psychiatrists' Evaluations of Criminal Defendants' Competency to Stand Trial and Legal Sanity* (paper presented at the American Psychology–Law Society Convention, Baltimore, Oct. 1979).

396. The three studies, in the order listed in the table, are Richard Rogers et al., *An Empirical Approach to Insanity Evaluations,* 37 J. CLINICAL PSYCHOL. 683 (1981); Richard Rogers et al., *Evaluating Insanity: A Study of Construct Validity,* 8 LAW & HUM. BEHAV. 293 (1984); Richard Rogers et al., *The RCRAS and Legal Insanity: A Cross-Validation Study,* 39 J. CLINICAL PSYCHOL. 544 (1983).

397. Available from Psychological Assessment Resources Inc., Odessa, Fla. *See also* Richard Rogers & James Cavanaugh, *The Rogers Criminal Responsibility Assessment Scales,* 160 ILL. MED. J. 164 (1981).

398. Michael R. Phillips et al., *Psychiatry and the Criminal Justice System: Testing the Myths,* 145 AM. J. PSYCHIATRY 605 (1988).

399. "[C]linicians' determinations were not always independent—a second evaluator may have read the previous evaluator's report." *Id.* at 608.

400. *See* GARY MELTON ET AL., COMMUNITY MENTAL HEALTH CENTERS AND THE COURTS: AN EVALUATION OF COMMUNITY-BASED FORENSIC SERVICES ch. 4 (1985).

401. *See* Petrila et al., *supra* note 25, at 60 (reporting that a study of pretrial evaluations in state institutions in Missouri in 1978 revealed that only 1 of 127 defendants

recommended as NGRI was diagnosed as having a personality disorder). *See also* Richard W. Jeffrey et al., *Insanity Plea: Predicting Not Guilty by Reason of Insanity Adjudications,* 16 BULL. AM. ACAD. PSYCHIATRY & L. 35 (1988) (using discriminant function analyses to predict forensic clinicians opinions and court decisions in 133 defendants evaluated at Colorado State Hospital, a diagnosis of personality disorder was a significant factor predicting a clinical opinion that the defendant was *sane* and a legal outcome of *guilty*). Janet I. Warren et al., *Criminal Offense, Psychiatric Diagnosis, and Psycholegal Opinion: An Analysis of 894 Pretrial Referrals,* 19 BULL. AM. ACAD. PSYCHIATRY & L. 63 (1991) (diagnoses most strongly associated with clinical recommendations of *sane* were personality disorders and substance abuse disorders).

402. Robert J. Stoller & Robert H. Geertsma, *The Consistency of Psychiatrists' Clinical Judgments,* 137 J. NERVOUS & MENTAL DISEASE 58 (1963). Nested in the 565 items were 8 "nonsense" items that were deemed by the investigators to be fanciful, extremely esoteric, and completely beyond the data demonstrated in the interview. Several of these items involved psychodynamic symbolism—for example, "At this point, the patient's depreciation of the introjected father's penis is revealed," or "The loss of a boy friend is painful for the patient because it reawakens her secondary envy of mother's breast." Though the psychiatrists had been instructed to give inapplicable items a rating of 0, three of the nonsense items were scored across all six categories of applicability; four others were scored in five of the possible six categories.

403. *Id.*

404. Morse, *supra* note 320, at 1022.

405. Anasseril E. Daniel & Phillip W. Harris, *Female Offenders Referred for Pre-Trial Psychiatric Evaluation,* 9 BULL. AM. ACAD. PSYCHIATRY & L. 40 (1981).

406. Fukanaga et al., *supra* note 394.

407. Poythress, unpublished data (1982).

408. Richard Rogers et al., *Legal Outcome and Clinical Findings: A Study of Insanity Evaluations,* 14 BULL. AM. ACAD. PSYCHIATRY & L. 219 (1986).

409. As Bonnie and Slobogin have argued, there is a natural skepticism in judges and jurors who serve in criminal cases which serves as a check against undue weight being assigned to mental health expert opinions. Bonnie & Slobogin, *supra* note 183, at 493. Some empirical findings support the existence of this natural skepticism. *See* Diane L. Bridgeman & David Marlowe, *Jury Decision-Making: An Empirical Study Based on Actual Felony Trials,* 64 J. APPLIED PSYCHOL. 91 (1979); Randolf B.A. Read et al., *Psychiatrists and the Jurors' Dilemma,* 6 BULL. AM. ACAD. PSYCHIATRY & L. 1 (1978); Rita Simon, *The Dynamics of Jury Behavior,* in THE ROLE OF THE FORENSIC PSYCHOLOGIST (Gerald Cooke ed. 1980).

410. *Supra* note 397.

411. *Id.* at 1.

412. *Id.* at 10–11.

413. *Id.* at 33.

414. *See generally* Stephen Morse, *Crazy Behavior, Morals, and Science: An Analysis of Mental Health Law,* 51 S.

CAL. L. REV. 527 (1978); Comment, *The Psychologist as Expert Witness: Science in the Courtroom,* 38 MD. L. REV. 539 (1979).

415. *See* Rogers et al., *supra* notes 396, 408.

416. For another critique of the RCRAS, *see* Stephen L. Golding and Ronald Roesch, *The Assessment of Criminal Responsibility: Approach to a Current Controversy,* in HANDBOOK OF FORENSIC PSYCHOLOGY 395–432 (Irving B. Weiner & Allen K. Hess eds. 1987). Professor Rogers's response to criticisms of the RCRAS have been noted in Richard Rogers & Charles P. Ewing, *The Measurement of Insanity: Debating the Merits of the R-CRAS and its Alternatives,* 15 INT'L J. L. & PSYCHIATRY 113 (1992).

417. For a discussion of investigative reporting as a possible clinical procedure, *see* Murray Levine, *Investigative Reporting as a Research Method: An Analysis of Bernstein and Woodward's* ALL THE PRESIDENT'S MEN, 35 AM. PSYCHOLOGIST 626 (1980).

418. Christopher Slobogin et al., *The Feasibility of a Brief Evaluation of Mental State at the Time of the Offense,* 8 LAW & HUM. BEHAV. 305 (1984).

419. Morse, *supra* note 320, at 1049.

420. Carol K. Sigelman et al., *When in Doubt, Say Yes: Acquiescence in Interviews with Mentally Retarded Persons,* 19 MENTAL RETARDATION 53 (1981).

421. Raymond M. Cameron, *The Mental Health Expert: A Guide to Direct and Cross-Examination,* 2 CRIM. JUST. J. 299, 309 (1979).

422. Norman Poythress, *Is There a Baby in the Bath Water?: Psychological Tests and Expert Testimony* (paper presented at the American Psychology–Law Society Convention, Boston, 1981).

423. *See also* Lawrence S. Kubie, *The Ruby Case: Who or What Was on Trial?,* 1 J. PSYCHIATRY & L. 472 (1973).

424. In a study of 107 pretrial examinations at a Massachusetts hospital, diagnosis perfectly predicted insanity opinion. Each of 31 cases diagnosed as psychotic was recommended as not criminally responsible; none of the nonpsychotic defendants received such a recommendation. A. Louis McGarry, *Competency for Trial and Due Process via the State Hospital,* 122 AM. J. PSYCHIATRY 623 (1965).

425. Morse, *supra* note 414, at 604–15.

426. The term "chemically induced" is somewhat of an overstatement. The behavioral symptoms of some disorders can be induced by the administration of certain drugs, though the long-term impact is not to induce the long-range (prognostic) features. *See* ROBERT M. JULIEN, A PRIMER OF DRUG ACTION (1985); Michael H. Stone, *Drug-Related Schizophrenic Syndromes,* 11 INT'L J. PSYCHIATRY 391 (1973).

427. To some extent, the battle over diagnosis in the Hinckley case, maligned by many commentators, may nonetheless have helped the jury understand the degree of Hinckley's dysfunction. *See generally* REISNER & SLOBOGIN, *supra* note 181, at 379–92.

428. *See, e.g.,* Heinz Hafner & Wolfgang Boker, *Mentally Disordered Violent Offenders,* 8 SOCIAL PSYCHIATRY 220 (1973).

429. For an excellent analysis of the limits of clinical inquiry into such legally defined mental elements as "intent," *see* Charles R. Clark, *Clinical Limits of Expert Testimony on Diminished Capacity,* 5 INT'L J. L. & PSYCHIATRY 155 (1982).

430. Morse, *supra* note 414, at 612–13, 618–19.

431. Though there is one psychodynamic model, there are several schools of thought invoking psychodynamic concepts—Freudian, Jungian, Adlerian, and so forth. For our purposes, their similarities—especially the focus on unconscious determinants of behavior—are more important than their differences.

432. *See, e.g.,* Pollard v. United States, 282 F.2d 450 (6th Cir. 1960). In California, which for a period required that the defendant "meaningfully" and "maturely" consider his or her actions, *see, e.g.,* People V. Wolff, 61 Cal. 2d 795, 394 P.2d 959, 40 Cal. Rptr. 271 (1964), such formulations were also offered in support of a diminished capacity defense. *See, e.g.,* People v. Gorshen, 51 Cal. 2d 716, 336 P.2d 492 (1959). Since 1981, when California's legislature reinstated the traditional, consciousness-oriented notion of intent, CAL. PENAL CODE § 1026.5 (1985), this kind of testimony should no longer be relevant on the *mens rea* issue.

433. Eugene Revitch, *Sexually Motivated Burglaries,* 6 BULL. AM. ACAD. PSYCHIATRY & L. 277 (1978).

434. For a comprehensive critique of psychodynamic explanations of criminal behavior, *see* Morse, *supra* note 320, at 1022.

435. *Supra* note 320.

436. *Id.* at 3.

437. *See also* Stoller & Geertsma, *supra* note 402.

438. The theory used to explain behavior may significantly influence third-party judgments about the responsibility of the actor. *See* Amerigo Farina et al., *Some Consequences of Changing People's Views Regarding the Nature of Mental Illness,* 87 J. ABNORMAL PSYCHOL. 272 (1978).

Chapter 9

1. ARTHUR CAMPBELL, THE LAW OF SENTENCING 24–41 (1978).

2. Daniel D. Nagin, *General Deterrence: A Review of the Empirical Evidence,* in DETERRENCE AND INCAPACITATION: ESTIMATING THE EFFECTS OF CRIMINAL SANCTIONS ON CRIME RATES 95, 135–36 (Alfred Blumstein et al. eds. 1978).

3. Bentham made the classical statement in support of deterrence in JEREMY BENTHAM, THE RATIONALE OF PUNISHMENT (1830). *See also* Johannes Andenaes, *The General Preventive Effects of Punishment,* 144 U. PA. L. REV. 949 (1966); RICHARD POSNER, ECONOMIC ANALYSIS OF LAW (2d ed. 1977).

4. These three goals of punishment are often called

"individual prevention" goals, to emphasize their offender-specific orientation. PETER LOW et al., CRIMINAL LAW: CASES AND MATERIALS 21–28 (2d ed. 1986).

5. As such it tends to conflict with the free will premise of the criminal justice system [*see* §§ 1.03(a); 9.04(b)]. For an elaboration of this thesis, *see* HERBERT PACKER, THE LIMITS OF THE CRIMINAL SANCTION 73–75 (1968).

6. For a scathing report on the lack of treatment for many individuals with mental illness confined in jails, *see* E. Fuller Torrey et al., *Criminalizing the Serious Mentally Ill: The Abuse of Jails as Mental Hospitals* (1992) (joint report of the National Alliance for the Mentally Ill and Public Citizen's Health Research Group). There have been attempts to create uniform minimum standards for the delivery of health services in prisons, but federal courts have found many state prison systems to be constitutionally deficient in delivering mental health care, a situation unlikely to improve as states struggle with dramatic increases in prison population. For a good summary of these issues, *see* Fred Cohen & Joel Dvoskin, *Inmates with Mental Disorders: A Guide to Law and Practice*, 16 MENTAL & PHYSICAL DISABILITY L. REP. 339 (1992).

7. NICHOLAS KITTRIE & ELYCE ZENOFF, SANCTIONS, SENTENCING AND CORRECTIONS: LAW, POLICY AND PRACTICE 368 (1981). In 1978, there were 307,384 individuals imprisoned in the United States, distributed between federal (29,803 inmates) and state (277,581 inmates) prisons, and the vast majority of these inmates were serving terms longer than one year. There were also more than 158,000 individuals in local jails, some of them awaiting trial and most others serving time for misdemeanor convictions. *Id.* at 362. These figures rose sharply through the 1980s, so that by 1992 there were 847,271 people in prison (65,706 in federal prisons and 781,565 in state prisons), and the jail population had risen to 444,584. *Statistical Abstract of the United States*, United States Department of Commerce, Bureau of the Census, Table 339 & Table 338 (1994).

8. Rutherford Campbell, *Sentencing: The Use of Psychiatric Information and Presentence Reports*, 60 KY. L.J. 285, 288 (1972).

9. Alan Dershowitz, *The Role of Psychiatry in the Sentencing Process*, 1 INT'L J. L. & PSYCHIATRY 63, 63–64 (1978).

10. Gray Cavender & Michael Mushenko, *The Adoption and Implementation of Determinate-based Sanctioning Policies: A Critical Perspective*, 17 GEO. L. REV. 425, 434 (1983).

11. *Id.*

12. TRANSACTIONS OF THE NATIONAL CONGRESS ON PRISONS AND REFORMATORY DISCIPLINE (Albany 1871) (Weeds & Parsons eds. 1970), *quoted by* Dershowitz, *supra* note 9, at 65.

13. Cavender & Meshenko, *supra* note 10, at 430.

14. Dershowitz, *supra* note 9, at 6.

15. Williams v. New York, 337 U.S. 241, 247 (1948).

16. Dershowitz, *supra* note 9, at 6.

17. *See, e.g.*, Gary Mason, *Indeterminate Sentencing:*

Cruel and Unusual Punishment, or Just Plain Cruel? 16 NEW ENG. J. CRIM. & CIV. CONFINEMENT 89 (1990).

18. Andrew Von Hirsch, *Recent Trends in American Criminal Sentencing Theory*, 42 MD. L. REV. 6, 29 (1983). For further discussion of this issue, see § 9.07(b).

19. One of the most influential articles in this regard was Robert Martinson, *What Works?: Questions and Answers about Prison Reform*, 1974 PUB. INTEREST 22, which concluded that "with few and isolated exceptions, the rehabilitative efforts that have been reported so far had no appreciable effect on recidivism." This article is discussed further in § 9.07(b).

20. John Monahan & Mary Ruggiero, *Psychological and Psychiatric Aspects of Determinate Criminal Sentencing*, 3 INT'L J. L. & PSYCHIATRY 143 (1980).

21. David Greenberg & Drew Humphries, *The Cooptation of Fixed Sentencing Reform*, 26 CRIME & DELINQ. 206, 208 (1980).

22. Albert Alschuler, *Sentencing Reform and Prosecutorial Power: A Critique of Recent Proposals for "Fixed" and "Presumptive" Sentencing*, 126 U. PA. L. REV. 550, 552–53 (1978).

23. John Hogarth, *Can Psychiatry Aid Sentencing?*, 2 INT'L J. L. PSYCHIATRY 499, 501 (1979). Hogarth concludes that psychiatry has a role, but only if as an initial step coerced treatment in the name of rehabilitation is ended, thereby rendering the therapist offender relationship benign.

24. A major influence in this shift of opinion was a book by MARVIN FRANKEL, CRIMINAL SENTENCES: LAW WITHOUT ORDER (1973). Frankel, a former judge, started with the premise that "the almost wholly unchecked and sweeping favors we give to judges in the fashioning of sentences are terrifying and intolerable for a society that professes devotion to the role of law." *Id.* at 5. In Chapter 9 of the book, he proposed a "Commission on Sentencing," a proposal eventually adopted by Congress and a number of states.

25. Lisa Stansky, *Breaking Up Prison Gridlock*, A.B.A. J. 70, 71 (May 1996) (stating that only 29 states still retain "completely or partially" indeterminate sentencing schemes); Michael Tonry, *Real Offense Sentencing: The Model Sentencing and Correction Act*, 72 J. CRIM. L. & CRIMINOLOGY 1550, 1551 (1981). A state-by-state review as of 1984 is provided in Sandra Shane-Dubow et al., *Sentencing Reform in the United States: History, Content, and Effect* (U.S. Department of Justice, National Institute of Justice, 1985). The authors characterize the following states as determinate sentencing states: Arizona, California, Colorado, Connecticut, Illinois, Indiana, Maine, Minnesota, New Jersey, New Mexico, North Carolina, Ohio, Pennsylvania, Tennessee, and Washington. *Id.*, Table 28. Since 1985, several other states, including Florida, have adopted determinate sentencing.

26. The Sentencing Reform Act of 1984 is found at 18 U.S.C. §§ 3551–3625, 3673, 3742, and 28 U.S.C. §§ 991–998. The United States Supreme Court upheld the constitutionality of the statute in Mistretta v. United States, 480 U.S. 361 (1989).

27. Todd Clear et al., *Discretion and the Determinate*

Sentence: Its Distribution, Control, and Effect on Time Served, 24 CRIME & DELINQ. 428 (1978); Stephen Lagoy et al., *A Comparative Assessment of Determinate Sentencing in the Four Pioneer States*, 24 CRIME & DELINQ. 385 (1978); Blake Nelson, *The Minnesota Sentencing Guidelines: The Effects of Determinate Sentencing on Disparities in Sentencing Decisions*, 10 LAW & INEQUALITY 217 (1992).

The relationship of race to sentencing has received particular attention. *See, e.g.*, Alfred Blumstein, *Racial Disproportionality of U.S. Prison Populations Revisited*, 64 U. COLO. L. REV. 743 (1993); Debra Dailey, *Prison and Race in Minnesota*, 64 U. COLO. L. REV. 761 (1993); Samuel Myers, *Racial Disparities in Sentencing: Can Sentencing Reforms Reduce Discrimination in Punishment?*, 64 U. COLO. L. REV. 781 (1993). The first two articles emphasize the important role that plea charging and bargaining have on the process because each suggests that these and other collateral factors may "push" African Americans into offense categories with harsher penalties. The third article suggests that African Americans were denied parole in the federal system much more frequently than whites, and that the statistical difference could not be explained simply by factors related to parole (e.g., characteristics that might put the person at a higher risk for recidivism).

28. *See, e.g., Symposium on Federal Sentencing*, 66 S. CAL. L. REV. 99 (1992); *Symposium: Punishment*, 101 YALE L.J. 1681 (1992); *Symposium: Making Sense of the Federal Sentencing Guidelines*, 25 U.C. DAVIS L. REV. 563 (1992).

29. Michael Tonry, *The Success of Judge Frankel's Sentencing Conversion*, 64 U. COLO. L. REV. 713 (1993). *See, e.g.*, Daniel Freed, *Federal Sentencing in the Wake of Guidelines: Unacceptable Limits on the Discretion of Sentences*, 101 YALE L. J. 1681 (1992); Gerald Heaney, *The Reality of Guidelines Sentencing: No End to Disparity*, 28 AM. CRIM. L. REV. 161 (1991). Heaney, who studied sentencing under the guidelines in three federal districts in 1989, also concluded that prosecutors and probation officers, because of their influence over the charge, had even more influence under the federal guidelines than before. *Id.* at 170–75. He also found evidence of continuing racial disparity in sentencing. *Id.* at 203–08.

30. Stephen Fennell & William Hall, *Due Process at Sentencing: An Empirical and Legal Analysis of the Disclosure of Presentence Reports in Federal Courts*, 93 HARV. L. REV. 1613, 1621–22 (1980).

31. Andrew Von Hirsch & Kathleen Hanrahan, *Determinate Penalty Systems in America: An Overview*, 27 CRIME & DELINQ. 289, 291 (1981).

32. Von Hirsch, *supra* note 18. Von Hirsch points out that incapacitation and deterrence could play roles in a determinate sentence scheme. However, the notion of "commensurate" punishment or "just deserts" (i.e., the idea that the offender is punished in proportion to the severity of the offense) seems to have had the most impact as a conceptual underpinning for statutory revision. In large part, this development is probably due to the influence that Von Hirsch himself has had on this movement. His book, DOING JUSTICE (1976), has become a basic text of advocates of determinate sentencing.

33. Von Hirsch & Hanrahan, *supra* note 31, at 294.

34. Cavender & Mushenko, *supra* note 10, at 447 n. 81 (reporting that, as of 1983, Alaska, Arizona, California, New Jersey, New Mexico, and North Carolina had adopted presumptive sentencing).

35. As of 1983, Colorado, Illinois, Indiana, Missouri, and Tennessee used a definite sentencing scheme. *Id.* at 447 n. 82. Maine used a variation on this type of sentencing. *Id.*, at 462, Table 2.

36. The states using sentencing commissions included Alaska, Arkansas, Colorado, Delaware, Ohio, Minnesota, North Carolina, Pennsylvania, Tennessee, Texas, Utah, and Washington. Leonard Orland & Kevin Reitz, *Epilogue: A Gathering of State Sentencing Commissions*, 64 U. COLO. L. REV. 837 (1993).

37. Cavender & Mushenko, *supra* note 10, at 448.

38. Lagoy et al., *supra* note 27, at 385.

39. In 1986, 86% of federal criminal cases ended in a plea. In 1988, 91% of felony convictions in the 75 most populous counties in the United States resulted through a guilty plea. U.S. DEPARTMENT OF JUSTICE, SOURCEBOOK OF CRIMINAL JUSTICE STATISTICS 502 (Table 5.25), 526 (Table 5.51), *cited in* Robert Scott & William Stuntz, *Plea Bargaining as Contract*, 101 YALE L.J. 1909 (1992).

40. *See, e.g.*, Albert Alschuler, *The Failure of Sentencing Guidelines: A Plea for Less Aggregation*, 58 U. CHI. L. REV. 901 (1991); Eric Berlin, *Comment: The Federal Sentencing Guidelines' Failure to Eliminate Sentencing Disparity: Governmental Manipulations before Arrest*, 1993 WIS. L. REV. 187 (1993). Both articles argue that prosecutors and investigative officers wield significant control over sentencing, primarily through decisions categorizing the offense to be charged and pleaded (which ultimately forms the basis for the sentence). Studies of plea-bargaining practices in three cities under the federal sentencing guidelines found manipulation of plea bargaining by prosecutors, particularly to avoid imposition of mandatory minimum sentences in some cases. Ilene Nagel & Stephen Schulhofer, *A Tale of Three Cities: An Empirical Study of Charging and Bargaining Practices under the Federal Guidelines*, 66 S. CAL. L. REV. 501 (1992); Stephen Schulhofer & Ilene Nagel, *Negotiated Pleas under the Federal Sentencing Guidelines: The First Fifteen Months*, 27 AM. CRIM. L. REV. 231 (1989). They conclude that "prosecutorial discretion, in charging and in the plea negotiation process, poses obstacles" to ending sentencing disparity in federal law. Nagel & Schulhofer, *supra* at 501.

41. Studies of efforts at banning or sharply curtailing plea bargaining in Alaska, Wayne County (Michigan), and "Hampton" County (a pseudonym for another Michigan county) are summarized in RESEARCH ON SENTENCING: THE SEARCH FOR REFORM ch. 4 (Alfred Blumstein et al. Eds. 1983). The reviewers conclude that plea-bargaining bans and mandatory and determinate sentencing laws have produced "modest changes" in sentencing outcome, primarily in the direction of some increases of prison use for marginal offenders who might not previously have received a prison sentence. *Id.* at 185–86. They also found that partial bans on plea bargaining were readily circumvented (e.g., a ban on sentence bargaining produced an increase in charge bargaining). *Id.* at 185, 196–98.

42. Alschuler, *supra* note 22, at 551.

43. Approximately a dozen states have provisions for jury sentencing. CAMBPELL, *supra* note 1, at 227 n. 24 and accompanying text.

44. The United States Supreme Court has noted that "we begin with the general proposition that once it is determined that a sentence is within the limitations set forth in the statute under which it is imposed, appellate review is at an end." Dorszynski v. United States, 418 U.S. 424, 431 (1974).

45. Morrissey v. Brewer, 408 U.S. 471, 477 (1972).

46. *E.g.*, Maine and Minnesota.

47. *See generally* Lagoy et al., *supra* note 27, at 390, 396 (discussing the diminished role of the parole boards in California and Illinois).

48. *See* Victoria Palacios, *Go and Sin No More: Rationality and Release Decisions by Parole Boards*, 45 S. CAL. L. REV. 567, (1993–1994).

49. Mempa v. Rhay, 389 U.S. 128 (1967); Townsend v. Burke, 334 U.S. 736 (1948).

50. George Dix, *Expert Prediction Testimony in Capital Sentencing: Evidentiary and Constitutional Considerations*, 19 AM. CRIM. L. REV. 1, 15 (1981).

51. *See, e.g.*, Harmelin v. Michigan, 501 U.S. 957 (1991) (finding that individualized sentencing hearings are not required except in capital cases). This case is discussed in G. David Hackney, *Recent Developments: A Trunk Full of Trouble*: Harmelin v. Michigan, 27 HARV. C.R.-C.L. L. REV. 262 (1992).

52. United States v. Tucker, 404 U.S. 443 (1972).

53. In articulating this exception, the Supreme Court barred the use by a sentencing judge of two prior convictions that were later found to be constitutionally invalid (because obtained when the defendant did not have counsel). *Id.* But it has also allowed a sentencing judge to take into account a defendant's prior refusal to cooperate with a government investigation of other individuals, Roberts v. United States, 445 U.S. 552 (1980), as well as a belief that the defendant testified falsely at trial, United States v. Grayson, 438 U.S. 41 (1978).

54. James Weismann, *Sentencing Due Process: Evolving Constitutional Principles*, 18 WAKE FOREST L. REV 523, 524–28 (1982).

55. CAMPBELL *supra* note 1, at 416. For a discussion of the bases for parole board action, *see* Robert Dawson, *The Decision to Grant or Deny Parole: A Study of Parole Criteria in Law and Practice*, 1966 WASH. U. L.Q. 23 (1966).

56. The parolee is entitled to the following procedural rights before parole may be revoked: (1) a "probably cause" finding, with notice to the parolee that parole has been violated, and (2) a revocation hearing, where the parolee is entitled to written notice, the disclosure of adverse evidence, an opportunity to be heard in person and to present witnesses, an opportunity to confront and cross-examine adverse witnesses (unless the hearing officer finds "good cause" not to allow this), a neutral and detached hearing officer (who need not be a judge or a lawyer), and a written statement giving the decision and the reasons for it. Morrissey v. Brewer, 408 U.S. 471, 484–488 (1972). Legal counsel is not guaranteed in all cases; rather, it need only be provided when the facts are "complex" and/or the petitioner appears to be incapable of "speaking effectively for himself." Gagnon v. Scarpelli, 445 U.S. 480 (1981).

57. Williams v. New York, 337 U.S. 241, 247 (1948).

58. *Id. See also* Roberts v. United States, 445 U.S. 552 (1980).

59. United States v. Jones, 899 F.2d 1097, 1102–03 (11th Cir. 1990). An excellent summary of federal appeals court decisions on the federal sentencing guidelines is found in *Guidelines Sentencing: An Outline of Appellate Case Law on Selected Issues* (published periodically by the Federal Judicial Center).

60. Weismann, *supra* note 54, at 524.

61. James Weismann, *Determinate Sentencing and Psychiatric Evidence: A Due Process Examination*, 27 ST. LOUIS U. L.J. 343 (1983).

62. Fed. R. Crim. P. 32(c)(1) (1994).

63. This description of the preparation of the presentence report and its contents is taken primarily from Fennell & Hall, *supra* note 30, at 1623–28. *See also* John Schmolesky & Timothy Thorson, *The Importance of the Presentence Investigation Report after Sentencing*, 18 CRIM. L. BULL. 406, 408 (1982).

64. Heaney, *supra* note 29.

65. Fennell & Hall, *supra* note 30, at 1626.

66. Hogarth, *supra* note 23, at 500.

67. Dershowitz, *supra* note 9, has concluded that the continued role of psychiatry in the sentencing process is uncertain, because the objectives of most sentencing reform efforts are the reduction of discretion in sentencing and renewed emphasis on the *crime* that has been committed rather than the *criminal* who has committed it.

68. Monahan & Ruggiero, *supra* note 20, at 143. It is also difficult to overestimate the desire of defense counsel to bring to the attention of the court any factor in mitigation of the defendant's actions. For example, in 1981, when nearly everyone was predicting the demise of the rehabilitative model, an article by a defense attorney appeared predicting the increased use of social and behavioral scientists on behalf of the defense. G. Thomas Gitchoff, *Expert Testimony at Sentencing*, NAT'L J. CRIM. DEF. 101, 107 (1981).

69. These factors are listed in *Research Project: Minnesota Sentencing Guidelines*, 5 HAMLINE L. REV. 273, 412–15 (1982).

70. In 1980, 45 states had habitual offender statutes. *See* Comment, *The Constitutional Infirmities of Indiana's Habitual Offender Statute*, 13 IND. L. REV. 597, 597 n. 1 (1980). By 1994, ten states and the federal government had amended these statutes to increase both the types of convictions which determine eligibility and the duration of sentence once the statute is found to apply. Donna Hunzeker, *Significant State Anti-Crime Legislation* 1 (May 1994) (publication of the Sentencing Project, Washington, D.C.).

71. IND. CODE § 35-50-2-8(d)(e) (Supp. 1983).

72. Hallye Jordan, *Three Strikes Hit Mostly the Non-Violent*, 108 LOS ANGELES DAILY J. 1 (Jan. 9, 1995).

73. Comment, *Selective Incapacitation: Reducing Crime Through Predictions of Recidivism*, 96 HARV. L. REV. 511, 512 (1983).

74. *Id.* at 513.

75. Jordan, *supra* note 72, at 1.

76. In the period studied, of more than 7,400 second- and third-strike cases, 70% were charged with nonviolent, nonserious offenses, generally drug possession or petty theft. The vast majority of individuals sentenced as "two-" and "three-" strikers were convicted of nonviolent or nonserious offenses. If limited to more serious crimes, on the other hand, the law may not have much impact. In Illinois, which enacted the equivalent of a three-strikes law in 1978, only 92 of the nearly 25,000 people imprisoned between the effective date of the statute and early 1994 received mandatory life sentences under the law, suggesting very little protection of the public. Harvey Berkman, *Few Felons Out in Three Strikes*, 16 NAT'L L.J. 3 (1994).

77. 445 U.S. 263 (1980).

78. 463 U.S. 277 (1983).

79. Note, *Rummel v. Estelle: Sentencing Without a Rational Basis*, 32 SYRACUSE L. REV. 803 (1981); Comment, *Salvaging Proportionate Prison Sentencing: A Reply to Rummel v. Estelle*, 15 U. MICH. J. L. REFORM 285 (1982).

80. SAMUEL BRAKEL & RONALD S. ROCK, THE MENTALLY DISABLED AND THE LAW 25 (1971).

81. GROUP FOR THE ADVANCED OF PSYCHIATRY, PSYCHIATRY AND SEX PSYCHOPATH LEGISLATION: THE 30S TO THE 80S, 950 n.15 (1977) [hereinafter GAP].

82. George Dix, *Special Dispositional Alternatives for Abnormal Offenders*, in MENTALLY DISORDERED OFFENDERS: PERSPECTIVES FROM LAW AND SOCIAL SCIENCE 133, 134–35 (John Monahan & Henry Steadman eds. 1983).

83. Note, *Washington's New Violent Sexual Predator Commitment System: An Unconstitutional Law and an Unwise Policy Choice*, 14 U. PUGET SOUND L. REV. 105, 110 n. 27 (1990).

84. Annotation, *Standard of Proof Required under Statute Providing for Commitment of Sexual Offenders or Sexual Psychopaths*, 96 A.L.R.3d 840, 842 (1979).

85. GAP, *supra* note 81, at 842.

86. Comment, *Commitment of Sexual Psychopaths and the Requirements of Procedural Due Process*, 44 FORDHAM L. REV. 923, 933, nn. 68–69 (1976).

87. GAP, *supra* note 81, at 861–67.

88. 386 U.S. 605 (1967).

89. Minnesota *ex rel.* Pearson v. Probate Ct., 309 U.S. 270 (1940).

90. *See* Allen v. Illinois, 478 U.S. 364 (1986) [discussed in § 4.02(d)].

91. GAP, *supra* note 81, at 935.

92. AMERICAN BAR ASSOCIATION, CRIMINAL JUSTICE MENTAL HEALTH STANDARDS, standard 7-8.1.

93. *Id.* at 457–58.

94. GAP, *supra* note 81, at 935.

95. *Id.* at 936.

96. *Id.* at 937.

97. *Id.*

98. Rorie Sherman, *Psychiatric Gulag or Wise Safekeep-*

ing?, NAT'L L.J., Sept. 5, 1994, at A1, A24 (noting that since 1990, five states—Washington, Minnesota, Kansas, and New Jersey—had passed new sex offender laws).

99. Note, *A Framework for Post-Sentence Sex Offender Legislation: Perspectives on Prevention, Registration, and the Public's "Right" to Know*, 48 VANDERBILT L. REV. 219, 221–22 n. 10 (1995).

100. *Id.*, at 239. *See also Recent Legislation: Criminal Law—Sex Offender Notification Statute—Washington State Community Protection Act Serves as Model for Other Initiatives by Lawmakers and Communities*, 108 HARV. L. REV. 787 (1995).

101. State v. Ward, 123 Wash. 2d 488, 869 P.2d 1062 (1994).

102. Procedurally, the statute works as follows. Near or at the expiration of the criminal sentence, the state files a petition alleging the person to be a sexually violent predator. If the court finds probable cause for the petition, the individual is transferred for evaluation and within 45 days a court hearing is held to determine whether the state can prove beyond a reasonable doubt that the person is a sexually violent predator. If so, the individual is committed to a facility for "control, care, and treatment" until "safe to be at large." WASH. REV. CODE § 71.09.060(1).

103. WASH. REV. CODE § 71.09.020(1).

104. *In re* Young, 122 Wash. 2d 1, 857 P.2d 989, 992 (1993) (quoting the Act's legislative history).

105. For an excellent review of these and other practical and ethical problems associated with these statutes, *see* Robert Wettstein, *A Psychiatric Perspective on Washington's Sexually Violent Predators Statute*, 15 U. PUGET SOUND L. REV. 597 (1992).

106. *See generally* Alan Dershowitz, *The Origins of Preventive Confinement in Anglo-American Law*, 43 U. CIN. L. REV. 781 (1974).

107. Note, *Civil Commitment of the Mentally Ill: Developments in the Law*, 87 HARV. L. REV. 1190, 1230 (1974).

108. *Cf.* United States v. Salerno, 481 U.S. 739 (1987) (upholding preventive detention prior to trial and providing examples of analogous situations).

109. John Monahan, *The Case for Prediction in the Modified Desert Model of Criminal Sentencing*, 5 INT'L J.L. & PSYCHIATRY 103–13 (1982).

110. 504 U.S. 71 (1990).

111. Foucha had been found insane based on testimony that he had a drug-induced psychosis. Upon recovery, he was diagnosed as an antisocial personality, which the Court assumed, based on a concession by the state, was not a "mental disease." At another point in its opinion the Court expressed concern that Louisiana's law "would permit the State to hold indefinitely any other insanity acquittee not mentally ill who could be shown to have a *personality disorder* that may lead to criminal conduct" [Emphasis added]. Ultimately, however, there is no clear message from the Court as to what might constitute a mental illness for purposes of this exception to the ban on preventive confinement, probably because the Court did not focus on the issue and has very little expertise on it.

112. *But see* Stephen J. Morse, *Culpability and Control*,

142 U. Pa. L. Rev. 1587, 1636 (1994) (suggesting that "the psychopath lacks attributes that give people perhaps the best reasons not to harm others . . . [and thus] seems 'morally insane,' unable successfully to reason practically about moral issues, to include moral concerns among his reasons for action").

113. 122 Wash. 2d 1, 857 P.2d 989 (1993).

114. It can be argued in any event that treatability cannot be a valid criterion for punishment, in that it is a status just as is dangerousness. Christopher Slobogin, *The Jurisprudence of Dangerousness as a Criterion in the Criminal Process,* in Law, Mental Health, and Mental Disorder ch. 10 (Bruce Sales & Daniel Shuman eds. 1996).

115. ___ U.S. ___ (June 23, 1997).

116. *In re* Blodgett, 510 N.W.2d 910 (Minn. 1994).

117. State *ex rel.* Pearson v. Probate C., 205 Minn. 545, 287 N.W. 297 (1939). *See In re* Linehan, 518 N.W.2d 609 (Minn. 1994).

118. 518 N.W.2d 609 (Minn. 1994).

119. One expert had testified that Linehan was "extremely impulsive" when under the influence of alcohol but that he normally was a "stable, intact and fairly controlled personality" whose behavior was "planful" and "controlled." 518 N.W.2d at 613.

120. *Id.* at 614.

121. *See* Barefoot v. Estelle, 463 U.S. 880 (1983).

122. 18 U.S.C. §§ 5005–5026.

123. Pub. L. No. 98-473, 98 Stat. 2014 (1984).

124. Note, *Sentencing of Youthful Misdemeanants under the Youth Corrections Act: Eliminating Disparities Created by the Federal Magistrate Act of 1979,* 51 Fordham L. Rev. 1254 (1983).

125. Wilfred Reitz, *Federal Youths Corrections Act: The Continuing Charade,* 13 U. Rich. L. Rev. 743 (1979).

126. 18 U.S.C. §5006(d).

127. 18 U.S.C. § 4216.

128. 18 U.S.C. § 5010(b).

129. 18 U.S.C. § 5017.

130. 18 U.S.C. § 5021.

131. 18 U.S.C. §§ 4251–4255.

132. Pub. L. No. 98-473, 98 Stat. 2077 (1984).

133. Patricia Brown, *Considering Post-Arrest Rehabilitation of Addicted Offenders under the Federal Sentencing Guidelines,* 10 Yale L. & Pol'y Rev. 520 (1992). Brown argues, contrary to the federal statute, that the courts should be permitted to consider the successful rehabilitation of an offender between arrest and sentencing as a mitigating factor. Although the number of incarcerated individuals with substance abuse problems has grown exponentially in recent years because of revised sentencing policies, treatment capacity remains often woefully inadequate. For one discussion of a model program for treating addicted offenders calling for an expansion of such programs, *see* Karen Klocke, *Drug-Related Crime and Addicted Offenders: A Proposed Response,* 5 Notre Dame J. L. Ethics & Pub. Pol'y 639 (1991).

134. 28 U.S.C.A § 2902 (West 1994).

135. Pamela Casey, *The Evolving Role of Courts,* 15 APLS News 3 (No. 2, 1995). *See also* Jack Lehman, *The Movement Towards Therapeutic Jurisprudence: An Inside Look at the Origin and Operation of America's First Drug Courts,* Nat'l Jud. C. Alumni Mag. 13 (Winter 1995).

136. Furman v. Georgia, 408 U.S. 238 (1972).

137. *Id.* 293 (Brennan, J.).

138. *Id.* at 251 (Douglas, J.).

139. Woodson v. North Carolina, 428 U.S. 280, 305 (1976).

140. *Id.* (striking down the mandatory imposition of the death sentence upon conviction of first-degree murder).

141. 438 U.S. 586, 597 (1978).

142. *See generally* George Dix, *Appellate Review of the Decision to Impose Death,* 68 Geo. L. Rev. 97 (1979), for a description of typical statutes.

143. The one exception is Connecticut, which prohibits imposing the death penalty if any statutory mitigating factor is found. Conn. Stat. § 53a-46a(d).

144. About 24 states have such provisions. *See* Richard Bonnie, *Psychiatry and the Death Penalty: Emerging Problems in Virginia,* 66 Va. L. Rev. 167, 184 (1980).

145. *See* Note, *Constitutional Law: The Eighth Amendment Does Not Prohibit the Execution of Mentally Retarded Convicts,* 43 Okla. L. Rev. 357, 371 n. 130 (1990), for a listing of state statutory provisions making mental retardation and other conditions and situations mitigating factors. In Penry v. Lynaugh, 492 U.S. 361 (1989), the Supreme Court held that prohibiting consideration of mental retardation as a mitigating factor in capital cases was unconstitutional, although it did not ban execution of those with mental retardation. Eleven states have nonetheless done so. Jonathan L. Bing, *Protecting the Mentally Retarded from Capital Punishment: State Efforts since Penry and Recommendations for the Future,* 22 N.Y.U. Rev. L. & Soc. Change 59, 114 (1996).

146. These factors are all taken from Florida cases. Florida Public Defenders Association, Defending Capital Cases ch. 3 (1992).

147. *See, e.g.,* Fla. Stat. § 921.141(5). In some states, however, nonstatutory aggravating factors may be considered.

148. Colorado, Idaho, Maryland, New Mexico, Oklahoma, Oregon, Texas, Virginia, and Washington. *See* Claudia M. Worrell, *Psychiatric Prediction of Dangerousness in Capital Sentencing: The Quest for Innocent Authority,* 5 Behavioral Sci. & L. 433, 434 (1987). *See generally* George Dix, *Expert Prediction Testimony in Capital Sentencing: Evidentiary and Constitutional Considerations,* 19 Am. Crim. L. Rev. 1, 4 n. 20 (1981).

149. Va. Code Ann. § 19.2-264.4(c).

150. Jurek v. Texas, 428 U.S. 262 (1976).

151. 463 U.S. 880 (1983).

152. 476 U.S. 1 (1986).

153. Miller v. State, 373 So. 2d 882 (Fla. 1979). *See also* Huckaby v. State, 343 So. 2d 29, 34 (Fla. 1977).

154. Zant v. Stephens, 462 U.S. 862, 885 (1976). *See generally* Randy Hertz & Robert Weisberg, *In Mitigation of the Penalty of Death: Lockett v. Ohio and the Capital Defendant's Right to Consideration of Mitigating Circumstances,* 69 Cal. L. Rev. 317 (1981); Note, *A Continuing Source of Aggravation: The Improper Consideration of Mitigating Factors*

in Death Penalty Sentencing, 41 HASTINGS L. REV. 409 (1990).

155. *Barefoot*, 463 U.S. at 896 (Blackmun, J., dissenting).

156. *See generally* Dix, *supra* note 142; Bonnie, *supra* note 144.

157. Gardner v. Florida, 430 U.S. 349 (1977).

158. In 1981, three states (Idaho, Louisiana, and Virginia) specified that the rules of evidence did apply and six states (Alabama, Florida, Montana, Nevada, Tennessee, and Washington) specified that rules of evidence did not apply. Dix, *supra* note 148, at 9 nn. 39, 40.

159. 470 U.S. 68 (1985).

160. Kevin Clancy et al., *Sentence Decisionmaking: The Logic of Sentence Decisions and the Extent and Sources of Sentence Disparity*, 72 CRIM. L. & CRIMINOL. 524, 535 (1981). Factors that influenced sentence disparity included (1) the judges' overall value orientations about the functions of the criminal sanction, (2) judgments about the appropriate goal of case-specific sentences, (3) perceptions about the severity of the sentences themselves, (4) a predisposition to impose relatively harsh or lenient sanctions, and (5) the manner in which each judge perceived the seriousness of the particular attributes of a given case. *Id.* at 553–54. *See also* Brian Forst & Charles Wellford, *Punishment and Sentencing: Developing Sentencing Guidelines Empirically from Principles of Punishment*, 33 RUTGERS L. REV. 799 (1981).

161. Shari S. Diamond, *Order in the Court: Consistency in Criminal Court Decisions*, in 2 PSYCHOL. & L. 123 (American Psychological Association Master Lecture Series, James Scheirer & Barbara Hammonds eds. 1983).

162. *See generally* William Austin & Mary Kristine Utne, *Sentencing: Discretion and Justice in Judicial Decision-Making*, in PSYCHOLOGY IN THE LEGAL PROCESS (Bruce Sales ed. 1977).

163. Thomas M. Uhlman & N. Darlene Walker, *"He Takes Some of My Time; I Take Some of His": An Analysis of Judicial Sentencing Patterns in Jury Cases*, 14 LAW & SOC'Y REV. 323 (1980).

164. George W. Baab & William R. Furgeson, *Comment: Texas Sentencing Patterns: A Statistical Study*, 45 TEX. L. REV. 471 (1967).

165. *Id.* at 485–86.

166. *See, e.g.*, Carol Bohmer, *Bad or Mad?— The Psychiatrist in the Sentencing Process*, 4 J. PSYCHIATRY & L. 23 (1976).

167. *See generally* Keith A. Findley & Meredith J. Ross, Comment, *Access, Accuracy and Fairness: The Federal Presentence Investigation Report Under Julian and the Sentencing Guidelines*, 1989 WIS. L. REV. 837. *See also* Elizabeth Lear, *Is Conviction Irrelevant?*, 40 UCLA L. REV. 1179, 1203 (1993) ("hearsay statements contained in the presentence report often provide the sole justification for a substantially greater term of imprisonment under the [federal sentencing] Guidelines").

168. Schmolesky & Thorson, *supra* note 63, at 407–11.

169. *Id.* at 423. *See also* the articles and cases cited by these authors at nn. 91–95 and accompanying text; John

C. Coffee, *The Future of Sentencing Reform: Emerging Legal Issues in the Individualization of Justice*, 73 MICH. L. REV 1361 (1975).

170. Fed. R. Crim. P. 32(3)(A).

171. *Id.*

172. *Id.*

173. Fennell & Hall, *supra* note 30.

174. *Id.* at 1652.

175. Nathan Sidley, *The Evaluation of Prison Treatment and Preventive Detention Programs: Some Problems Faced by the Patuxent Institution*, 2 BULL. AM. ACAD. PSYCHIATRY & L. 73 (1974).

176. Vladimir J. Konecni et al., *Prison or Mental Hospital: Factors Affecting the Processing of Persons Suspected of Being "Mentally Disordered Sex Offenders*," in NEW DIRECTIONS IN PSYCHOLEGAL RESEARCH 87–124 (Paul Lipsitt & Bruce D. Sales eds. 1980) (if the 9 cases in which the court ordered a continuance for further psychiatric studies are discounted, the concordance rate for the remaining 104 cases is 99%).

177. *Id.*

178. The prominence of social control over humanistic motivations in the incarceration of these special-track offenders may also be reflected in the relative lack of treatment provided. One study of treatment at the Center for the Diagnosis and Treatment of Dangerous Persons, in Massachusetts, revealed that patients received an average of 2.41 hours of treatment per month. R. Kirkland Schwitzgebel, *Professional Accountability in the Treatment and Release of Dangerous Persons*, in PERSPECTIVES IN LAW AND PSYCHOLOGY 139 (Bruce D. Sales ed. 1977).

179. Ian G. Campbell, *The Influence of Psychiatric Presentence Reports*, 4 INT'L J. L. & PSYCHIATRY 89 (1981).

180. *Id.* at 104.

181. Charles E. Smith, *A Review of the Presentence Diagnostic Procedure Study in North Carolina*, 8 N.C. CEN. L.J. 17, 31 n. 27 (1976).

182. In Bohmer's study, courts' agreement with psychiatric recommendations was 42% when incarceration was advised, and 37% when probation was advised. Bohmer, *supra* note 166, at 34–35.

183. Dershowitz, *supra* note 9, at 68.

184. Bohmer, *supra* note 166, at 36.

185. *Cf.* RALPH REISNER & CHRISTOPHER SLOBOGIN, LAW & THE MENTAL HEALTH SYSTEM: CIVIL AND CRIMINAL ASPECTS 770 (2d ed. 1990) (noting that roughly 14% of all convicted felons may be psychotic).

186. NATIONAL INSTITUTE OF CORRECTIONS, OFFENDER NEEDS ASSESSMENT: MODELS AND APPROACHES (1984).

187. *Id.*

188. *Supra* note 19.

189. *See, e.g.*, Von Hirsch, *supra* note 18, at 9.

190. *See* Ted Palmer, *Martinson Revisited*, 1975 J. RES. CRIME & DELINQ. 133 (1975); Herbert C. Quay, *The Three Faces of Evaluation: What Can Be Expected to Work?*, 4 CRIM. JUSTICE & BEHAV. 341 (1977).

191. Don A. Andrews et al., *Does Correctional Treatment Work? A Clinically Relevant and Psychologically Informed Meta-Analysis*, 28 CRIMINOLOGY 369 (1990).

192. Mark W. Lipsey, *Juvenile Delinquency Treatment: A*

Meta-Analytic Inquiry into the Variability of Effects, in META-ANALYSIS FOR EXPLANATION 83 (Thomas D. Cook et al. Eds. 1992).

193. For a thorough discussion of the debate on the efficacy of corrections treatment in reducing recidivism, *see* DON A. ANDREWS & JAMES BONTA, THE PSYCHOLOGY OF CRIMINAL CONDUCT 181 (1994).

194. For additional discussion of treatment for criminal offenders, *see* ALEXANDER B. SMITH & LOUIS BERLIN, TREATING THE CRIMINAL OFFENDER (3d ed. 1988).

195. ANDREWS & BONTA, *supra* note 193, at 189.

196. For a meta-analysis of the studies, *see* William L. Marshall et al., *Treatment Outcome with Sex Offenders*, 11 CLINICAL PSYCHOL. REV. 465 (1991). Marshall and his colleagues conclude that some treatments do work, but several scholars have criticized this conclusion. *See, e.g.*, Vernon L. Quinsey et al., *Assessing Treatment Efficacy in Outcome Studies of Sex Offenders*, 8 J. INTERPERSONAL VIOLENCE 512 (1993). Marshall responded in William L. Marshall, *The Treatment of Sex Offenders: What Does the Outcome Data Tell Us? A Reply to Quinsey, Harris, Rice and Lalumiere*, 8 J. INTERPERSONAL VIOLENCE 524 (1993), and provided an updated review in William L. Marshall & William D. Pithers, *A Reconsideration of Treatment Outcome with Sex Offenders*, 21 CRIM. JUSTICE & BEHAVIOR 10 (1994). *See also* Lita Furby et al., *Sex Offender Recidivism: A Review*, 105 PSYCHOL. BULL. 3 (1989); Gordon C.N. Hall, *Sexual Offender Recidivism Revisited: A Meta-Analysis of Recent Treatment Studies*, 63 J. CONSULTING & CLINICAL PSYCHOL. 802 (1995); Mark Small, *The Legal Context of Mentally Disordered Sex Offender (MDSO) Treatment Programs*, 19 CRIMINAL JUSTICE & BEHAV. 127, 133 (1992).

197. CAMPBELL, *supra* note 1, at 95.

198. Linda Caravello et al., *An Investigation of Treatment Recommendations Made by a Court Clinic*, 9 BULL. AM. ACAD. PSYCHIATRY & L. 224 (1981). Selective referrals alone do not account for the high frequency of treatment-oriented recommendations. Psychiatrists' commitment to the medical model may bias them toward dispositional attributions of the offenders' social problems.

199. Eileen F. Morrison, *Victimization in Prison: Implications for the Mentally Ill Inmate and for Health Professionals*, 5 ARCHIVES PSYCHIATRIC NURSING 17 (1991).

200. This bias may be particularly hard to resist for the clinician who is familiar with the appalling conditions in many prison settings.

201. Carol Bohmer, *The Court Psychiatrist: Between Two Worlds*, 16 DUQ. L. REV. 601 (1977–78).

202. Allen Bartholomew, *Some Problems of the Psychiatrist in Relation to Sentencing*, 15 CRIM. L.Q. 325, 333 (1973). Bartholomew notes the danger of psychiatrists recommending themselves as treaters but does not address the ethical issue.

203. *See, e.g.*, Kirk Heilbrun et al., *The Treatment of Mentally Disordered Offenders: A National Survey of Psychiatrists*, 20 BULL. AM. ACAD. PSYCHIATRY & L. 475 (1992) (reporting available treatment in public mental hospitals for sex offenders and convicted inmates who are mentally ill); Ron Jemelke et al., *The Mentally Ill in Prisons: A Review*, 40 HOSP. & COMMUNITY PSYCHIATRY 481 (1989).

204. DAVID WEXLER, CRIMINAL COMMITMENTS AND DANGEROUS MENTAL PATIENTS: LEGAL ISSUES OF CONFINEMENT, TREATMENT, AND RELEASE 22 (1976) ("In practice, students of the indeterminate sentence have repeatedly observed that patients and inmates are drawn to game-playing—known colloquially as 'shamming,' 'conning,' or, in the parole release context, 'programming'—in order to convince their keepers that rehabilitative efforts have been successful and that release is in order").

205. James Podgers, *The Psychiatrist's Role in Death Sentence Debated*, 66 A.B.A. J. 1509 (1980) (quoting David Goldberger).

206. Monica A. Walker, *Measuring the Seriousness of Crimes*, 18 BRIT. J. CRIM. 348 (1978); Monahan & Ruggiero, *supra* note 20, at 146.

207. Bonnie, *supra* note 144, at 185.

208. For instance, one study found that sentence outcomes were affected by whether defense attorneys had available to them a report from a mental health professional supporting an insanity defense (with approximately two-thirds of the defendants with a report allowed to plead to lesser charges, as compared to only one-fourth of similarly charged defendants without such a report). Norman G. Poythress, *Whether to Plead Insane: A Study in Attorney–Client Decision Making* (paper presented at the Biennial Conference of the American Psychology—Law Society, Mar. 1994).

209. Bonnie has noted that this is particularly relevant in capital cases: "The substantive inquiry in a capital sentencing proceeding . . . is not restricted to behavioral impairments arising out of mental disease or defect. The door in this sense is open to the full spectrum of explanations that may be offered. . . . " Bonnie, *supra* note 144, at 184–85. This leaves the clinician free to explore unconventional (i.e., non-DSM) syndromes or levels of emotional or psychological impairment that fall short of diagnostic significance. *See, e.g.*, C. Robert Showalter et al., *The Spousal-Homicide Syndrome*, 3 INT'L J. L. & PSYCHIATRY 117 (1980); J. Richard Ciccone & Gary B. Kaskey, *Life Events and Antisocial Behavior*, 7 BULL. AM. ACAD. PSYCHIATRY & L. 63 (1979). *See also* Richard J. Bonnie & Christopher Slobogin, *The Role of Mental Health Professionals in the Criminal Process: The Case for Informed Speculation*, 66 VA. L. REV. 427, 473–92 (1980).

210. HARRY KALVEN & HANS ZEISEL, THE AMERICAN JURY 301–05 (1971).

211. Gerald Cooke & Eric Pogany, *The Influence on Judges' Sentencing Practices of a Mental Evaluation*, 3 BULL. AM. ACAD. PSYCHIATRY & L. 245 (1975).

212. William Austin, *The Concept of Desert and Its Influence on Simulated Decision Makers' Sentencing Decisions*, 3 LAW & HUM. BEHAV. 163 (1979).

213. George Dix, *Participation by Mental Health Professionals in Capital Murder Sentencing*, 1 INT'L J. L. & PSYCHIATRY 283, 292 (1978).

214. Joel Henderson & G. Thomas Gitchoff, *Using Experts and Victims in the Sentencing Process*, 17 CRIM. L. BULL. 226 (1981).

215. A clear example of the importance of methodology in questionnaire research is found in the critique by

Dohrenwend, Egri, and Mendelsohn of an earlier study by Srole and colleagues, LEO SROLE ET AL., MENTAL HEALTH IN THE METROPOLIS (1962), showing that many of the significant results of the earlier study were methodological artifacts. Bruce Dohrenwend et al., *Psychiatric Disorder in the General Population: A Study of the Problem of Clinical Judgment*, 127 AM. J. PSYCHIATRY 1304 (1971).

216. This precise language is taken from ALA. CODE § 13a-5-51(5) (1975).

217. For a list of jurisdictions, *see supra* note 148.

218. Dangerousness evaluations can arise in a diversity of situations, including civil commitment [Chapter 10], confinement of persons adjudicated not guilty by reason of insanity [§ 10.10(a)], bail determinations [§ 2.04(a)(1)], parental fitness determinations in child custody [Chapter 16], and evaluations regarding allegations of parental abuse and neglect [Chapter 15]. These considerations are more or less implicit in other evaluation contexts as well. In competence-to-stand-trial assessments (Chapter 6), some states invoke the principle of least restrictive treatment alternative in deciding where to place a defendant for treatment to restore competence. In these states, the evaluator may also be required to opine whether the person meets civil commitment criteria under a "dangerous to others" standard to guide the court's decision about placement [*see* § 6.07(c)].

219. John Monahan & Saleem Shah, *Dangerousness and Commitment of the Mentally Disordered in the United States*, 15 SCHIZOPHRENIA BULL. 541 (1989). *See also* Saleem Shah, *Dangerousness: Some Definitional, Conceptual, and Public Policy Issues*, in PERSPECTIVES IN LAW & PSYCHOLOGY—I: THE CRIMINAL JUSTICE SYSTEM 91 (Bruce D. Sales ed. 1977).

220. 463 U.S. 354 (1983).

221. Davis v. Lhim, 335 N.W.2d 481 (Mich. App. 1983).

222. Florida v. Baker, #CF 89-4023A1 (Cir. C. Polk County 1990) (unreported).

223. Well over half the states do not require proof of an overt act for civil commitment purposes. REISNER & SLOBOGIN, *supra* note 185, at 644 ("approximately ten states have such provisions").

224. Edward P. Mulvey & Charles W. Lidz, *Clinical Considerations in the Prediction of Dangerousness in Mental Patients*, 4 CLINICAL PSYCHOL. REV. 379, 380 (1984) [citations omitted] ("[I]t is not always clear to the clinician exactly what is being predicted. . . . What faces the clinician as a result is an interpretive task for which the judgment about the risk posed by a patient is as much of an ethical dilemma as an empirical question").

225. *Id.* at 379.

226. "As far as assessments of likely response to certain institutional treatments and later criminal recidivism are concerned, the usual psychiatric and psychological evaluations have limited, often unknown or undemonstrated, usefulness." Saleem A. Shah, *Recent Research on Crime and Mental Disorder: Some Implications for Programs and Policies*, in MENTAL DISORDER AND CRIME 303, 310 (Sheilah Hodgins ed. 1993). *Cf.* Terrill R. Holland, *Diagnostic Labelling: Individual Difference in the Behavior of Clini-*

cians Conducting Presentence Evaluations, 6 CRIM. JUSTICE BEHAV. 187 (1979); Michael Garvey, *The Criminal: A Psychiatric Viewpoint*, 8 J. PSYCHIATRY & L. 457–64 (1980).

227. Megargee concluded that no psychological test has been developed "which will adequately postdict, let alone predict, violent behavior." Edwin I. Megargee, *The Prediction of Violence with Psychological Tests*, in CURRENT TOPICS IN CLINICAL AND COMMUNITY PSYCHOLOGY 98, 145 (Charles Spielberger ed. 1970). Monahan noted Megargee's earlier conclusion and found that the subsequent decade of research on psychological tests "would do little to modify his conclusion." JOHN MONAHAN, PREDICTING VIOLENT BEHAVIOR: AN ASSESSMENT OF CLINICAL TECHNIQUES 80 (1981).

228. DANIEL KAHNEMAN ET AL., JUDGMENT UNDER UNCERTAINTY (1982). For a consideration of cognitive biases in forensic contexts, *see* Randy Borum et al., *Improving Clinical Judgment and Decision Making in Forensic Evaluation*, 21 J. PSYCHIATRY & L. 35 (1993).

229. Joseph Cocozza & Henry J. Steadman, *Prediction in Psychiatry: An Example of Misplaced Confidence in Experts*, 25 SOC. PROBS. 266 (1978); Henry J. Steadman, *Some Evidence on the Inadequacy of the Concept and Determination of Dangerousness in Law and Psychiatry*, 1 J. PSYCHIATRY & L. 409 (1979); Henry J. Steadman & Joseph Cocozza, *Psychiatry, Dangerousness, and the Repetitively Violent Offender*, 69 J. CRIM. L. & CRIMINOLOGY 226 (1978).

230. Steadman, *supra* note 229, at 419, described more than 18 criteria of dangerousness cited in court psychiatric reports.

231. *Id.* at 421.

232. Loren J. Chapman & Jean P. Chapman, *Genesis of Popular but Erroneous Psychodiagnostic Observations*, 72 J. ABNORMAL PSYCHOL. 193 (1967); Loren J. Chapman & Jean P. Chapman, *Illusory Correlation as an Obstacle to the Use of Valid Psychodiagnostic Signs*, 74 J. ABNORMAL PSYCHOL. 271 (1969).

233. Stephen H. Dinwiddie & Sean Yutzy, *Dangerous Delusions? Misidentification Syndromes and Professional Negligence*, 21 BULL. AM. ACAD. PSYCHIATRY & L. 513 (1993).

234. John Monahan & Henry Steadman, *Crime and Mental Disorder: An Epidemiological Approach,* in CRIME AND JUSTICE: AN ANNUAL REVIEW OF RESEARCH (Norval Morris & Michael Tonry eds. 1983).

235. Richard Levinson & George Ann Ramsay, *Dangerousness, Stress, and Mental Health Evaluations*, 20 J. HEALTH & SOC. BEHAV. 178 (1979).

236. Scott M. Reichlin & Joseph D. Bloom, *Effects of Publicity on a Forensic Hospital*, 21 BULL. AM. ACAD. PSYCHIATRY & L. 475 (1993).

237. Clinicians' liability for the dangerous actions of their clients is a more realistic concern in decisions about hospital discharges than in the area of presentence evaluations. However, the political influences attendant to publicity about such cases is similar.

238. This has been observed in studies from a variety of legal contexts. *See* Cocozza & Steadman, *supra* note 229 (reporting 86.7% concordance rate between psychiatrists' predictions of dangerousness and judges' decisions to commit individuals determined incompetent for trial);

Norman G. Poythress, *Mental Health Expert Testimony: Current Problems*, 5 J. PSYCHIATRY & L. 201 (1977) (see in particular Table 2, showing several studies of high concordance rates between psychiatrists' predictions of dangerousness and judges' decisions to civilly commit).

239. For a broader discussion of these and other statistics in violence prediction research, *see* Stephen Hart et al., *A Note on Portraying the Accuracy of Violence Predictions*, 17 LAW & HUM. BEHAV. 695 (1993).

240. For an excellent historical analysis of mental health policy in the United States, *see* JOHN Q. LAFOND & MARY DURHAM, BACK TO THE ASYLUM: THE FUTURE OF MENTAL HEALTH LAW AND POLICY IN THE UNITED STATES (1992).

241. Bernard Rubin, *Prediction of Dangerousness in Mentally Ill Criminals*, 27 ARCHIVES GEN. PSYCHIATRY 397, 397–98 (1972) ("Even in the most careful, painstaking, laborious and lengthy clinical approach to the prediction of dangerousness, false positives may be at a minimum of 60% to 70%"). MONAHAN, *supra* note 227, at 77 ("The 'best' clinical research currently in existence indicates that *psychiatrists and psychologists are accurate in no more than one out of three predictions of violent behavior over a several-year period among institutionalized populations that had both committed violence in the past (and thus had high base rates for it) and who were diagnosed as mentally ill*").

242. Stephen J. Pfohl, *From Whom Will We Be Protected?: Comparative Approaches to the Assessment of Dangerousness*, 2 INT'L J. L. PSYCHIATRY 55 (1979).

243. *Id.* at 60.

244. 451 U.S. 454 (1981).

245. George Dix, *The Death Penalty, "Dangerousness," Psychiatric Testimony, and Professional Ethics*, 5 AM. J. CRIM. L. 151, 158 (1977).

246. *Id.*

247. *Id.* at 172.

248. The Texas Court of Criminal Appeals affirmed the jury's imposition of the death penalty, though not without a scathing dissent from Judge Odom, who commented: "I am unable to find that much of the testimony offered was from this side of the twilight zone." Quoted *id.* at 165.

249. Bruce Ennis & Thomas Litwack, *Flipping Coins in the Courtroom: Psychiatry and the Presumption of Expertise*, 62 CAL. L. REV. 693 (1974). *See also* JAY ZISKIN & DAVID FAUST, COPING WITH PSYCHIATRIC AND PSYCHOLOGICAL TESTIMONY (1988). A brief by the American Psychiatric Association in Barefoot v. Estelle, 463 U.S. 880 (1983), argued that psychiatric predictions of dangerousness are so unreliable that they should be proscribed at capital sentencing.

250. *See, e.g.*, Dix, *supra* note 245.

251. ALAN STONE, LAW, PSYCHIATRY, AND MORALITY 109 (1984).

252. *See* the review by Randy Otto, *Prediction of Dangerous Behavior: A Review and Analysis of "Second Generation" Research*, 5 FORENSIC REP. 103 (1992), for a depiction of this literature.

253. 463 U.S. at 901 n.7.

254. Thomas R. Litwack et al., *The Assessment of Dangerousness and Prediction of Violence: Recent Research and Future Prospects*, 64 PSYCHIATRY Q. 245 (1993); Norman Poythress, *Expert Testimony on Violence and Dangerousness: Roles for Mental Health Professionals*, 5 FORENSIC REP. 135, 142–45 (1992); Thomas R. Litwack & Louis B. Schlesinger, *Assessing and Predicting Violence: Research, Law, and Applications*, in HANDBOOK OF FORENSIC PSYCHOLOGY 205 (Irving Weiner & Alan Hess eds. 1987); David T. Lykken, *Predicting Violence in the Violent Society*, 2 APPLIED & PREVENTIVE PSYCHOL. 13 (1993); Robert Menzies et al., *The Dimensions of Dangerousness: Evaluating the Accuracy of Psychometric Predictions of Violence Among Forensic Patients*, 9 LAW & HUM. BEHAV. 49 (1985); John Monahan, *Risk Assessment of Violence Among the Mentally Disordered: Generating Useful Knowledge*, 11 INT'L J. L. & PSYCHIATRY 249 (1988); Christopher Slobogin, *Dangerousness and Expertise*, 139 U. PA. L. REV. 97, 110–17 (1984).

255. For a sophisticated discussion of this issue, *see* Edward P. Mulvey & Charles W. Lidz, *Measuring Patient Violence in Dangerousness Research*, 17 LAW & HUM. BEHAV. 277 (1993).

256. Henry J. Steadman et al., *Designing a New Generation of Risk Assessment Research*, in VIOLENCE AND MENTAL DISORDER: DEVELOPMENTS IN RISK ASSESSMENT 307 (1994).

257. Edward P. Mulvey, *The Advantages and Challenges of Relying on Collateral Reports of Subject Violence* (paper presented at the biennial meeting of the American Psychology–Law Society, 1992).

258. *Supra* note 256, at 310.

259. John Monahan, *The Prediction of Violent Behavior: Toward a Second Generation of Theory and Policy*, 141 AM. J. PSYCHIATRY 10, 11 (1984).

260. For an excellent review of this literature, *see* Otto, *supra* note 252, although note that Otto calculated *false-positive error rate* rather than *percent-false-positive rate* in evaluating these studies. *See supra* note 239 and accompanying text.

261. Charles W. Lidz et al., *The Accuracy of Predictions of Violence to Others*, 269 J. AM. MED. ASS'N 1007–11 (1993).

262. John Monahan & Henry Steadman, *Toward a Rejuvenation of Risk Assessment Research*, in VIOLENCE & DISORDER, *supra* note 256, at 5.

263. Ironically, the apparent consistency and conclusiveness of the research may have led to a reduction in research efforts to study and improve predictions of violence. While a significant number of studies have examined psychiatric predictions in inpatient settings, *see* Otto, *supra* note 252, Monahan and Steadman found only a single study of the validity of clinical predictions of violence in the community between 1979 and 1993. Monahan & Steadman, *supra* note 262, at 5.

264. Results from this study have begun to appear in the literature. *See supra* note 261; *infra* Table 9.4 n. o.

265. For a description of this study, *see supra* Steadman et al., note 256.

266. Marc Miller & Norval Morris, *Predictions of Dangerousness: An Argument for Limited Use*, 3 VIOLENCE & VICTIMS 263, 269 (1988).

267. To develop actuarial predictors, it is necessary to identify two samples of subjects from the population whose violence potential is to be predicted. Researchers can then measure the first sample (derivation sample) on a large number of variables (clinical, behavioral, demographic, etc.) thought a priori to have some relevance to the prediction of dangerousness. The derivation sample can then be followed for some designated period to see which subjects actually behave violently. When the derivation sample has been partitioned into "dangerous" and "nondangerous" subgroups, a statistical procedure such as discriminant function can be applied to determine which of the previously measured variables are most useful in distinguishing the two subgroups. The original number of predictors can be substantially reduced by eliminating those that have little or no discriminating power. Finally, an equation can be developed to indicate how the remaining variables should be weighed and combined to yield a prediction. The equation can then be applied to the second sample (cross-validation) to estimate the true discriminating power of the equation.

For a good example of research attempting to develop an actuarial approach to violence recidivism, *see* Grant T. Harris et al., *Violent Recidivism of Mentally Disordered Offenders: The Development of a Statistical Prediction Instrument*, 20 CRIM. JUSTICE & BEHAV. 315 (1993).

268. Slobogin, *supra* note 254, at 141–48.

269. *See, e.g.*, John S. Carroll, *Judgments of Recidivism Risk: The Use of Base-Rate Information in Parole Decisions*, in NEW DIRECTIONS IN PSYCHOLEGAL RESEARCH 68 (Paul Lipsitt & Bruce D. Sales eds. 1980).

270. Alan Tawshunski, *Note: Admissibility of Mathematical Evidence in Criminal Trials*, 21 AM. CRIM. L. REV. 55 (1983).

271. Some reasonably successful statistical approaches for predicting parole failure have been developed. *See* ANDREWS & BONTA, *supra* note 193, ch. 9. For a discussion of the limits on the utility of actuarial predictions in violence prediction, *see* Poythress, *supra* note 254, at 142–45.

272. In the limited literature that exists, the index of concern has been the percentage of false-positive errors—individuals labeled by the predictive procedure as likely to be violent who were not, on follow-up, found to have been violent. One study found 66% false positives using statistical techniques versus 85% using clinical techniques. Joseph Cocozza & Henry Steadman, *Some Refinements in the Measurement and Prediction of Dangerous Behavior*, 131 AM. J. PSYCHIATRY 1012 (1974). Another reported 78% statistical versus 84% clinical. Henry Steadman & Joseph Cocozza, *The Dangerousness Standard and Psychiatry: A Cross-National Issue in the Social Control of the Mentally Ill*, 63 SOC. RES. 649 (1979). A third study reported 80% statistical versus 85.5% clinical. TERRENCE THORNBERRY & JOSEPH JACOBY, THE CRIMINALLY INSANE: A FOLLOW-UP OF MENTALLY ILL OFFENDERS (1979). In some of these studies, the actual error rates associated with statistical prediction may have been underestimated due to investigators' failure to use cross-validated predictor equations; thus, the true differences between these approaches may

be smaller than the reported differences. At the same time, for reasons noted earlier [see § 9.09(b)(3)], the false positive rates in these studies for *both* statistical and clinical techniques are likely, overall, to be overestimates.

273. Paul E. Meehl, *When Shall We Use Our Heads Instead of the Formula?* 4 J. COUNSELING PSYCHOL. 268 (1957).

274. However, it may not be a simple matter of counting up features from a master list in a simple additive fashion. *See* § 9.09(c).

275. *Supra* note 256, at 303.

276. MONAHAN, *supra* 227, at 126.

277. *See generally supra* note 254.

278. Jeffrey W. Swanson, *Mental Disorder, Substance Abuse, and Community Violence: An Epidemiological Approach*, in VIOLENCE AND MENTAL DISORDER, *supra* note 256, at 101, 120.

279. *Supra* note 256 at 303–04.

280. Timothy J. Harpur et al., *Two-Factor Conceptualization of Psychopathy: Construct Validity and Assessment Implications*, 1 PSYCHOL. ASSESSMENT: J. CONSULTING & CLINICAL PSYCHOL. 6 (1989); Robert D. Hare et al., *The Revised Psychopathy Checklist: Reliability and Factor Structure*, 2 PSYCHOL. ASSESSMENT: J. CONSULTING & CLINICAL PSYCHOL. 338 (1990).

281. *See supra* note 227.

282. James R. P. Ogloff et al., *Treating Criminal Psychopaths in a Therapeutic Community Program*, 8 BEHAVIORAL SCI. & L. 181 (1990).

283. Some persons who meet criteria for APD will also score in the clinical range on the PCL-R, as items that load on factor 2 of the PCL-R substantially overlap with DSM behavioral criteria for APD. Factor 1, however, retains a number of "personality" features that fit with Cleckley's classic definition of psychopathy rather than the DSM diagnosis. HERVEY CLECKLEY, THE MASK OF SANITY (4th ed. 1964). Thus, an Axis II diagnosis of APD is an incomplete proxy for PCL-R assessment, and APD, although associated with violence, does not predict as well as does PCL-R.

284. David Farrington et al., *Long-Term Criminal Outcomes of Hyperactivity–Impulsivity–Attention Deficit and Conduct Problems in Childhood*, in STRAIGHT AND DEVIOUS PATHWAYS FROM CHILDHOOD TO ADULTHOOD 62 (Lee Robins & Michael Rutter eds. 1990); Lykken, *supra* note 254; Patterson & Yoerger, *supra* Table 9.4 n. m.

285. Barbara Maughan, *Childhood Precursors of Aggressive Offending in Personality-Disordered Adults*, in MENTAL DISORDER AND CRIME, *supra* note 226, at 119.

286. *Id.*

287. For a thorough and lucid analysis of the underlying, and often unexamined assumptions in social support research, *see* Karen S. Rook & David Dooley, *Applying Social Support Research: Theoretical Problems and Future Directions*, 41 J. SOC. ISSUES 5 (1985).

288. Joan Fiore et al., *Social Network Interactions: A Buffer or a Stress*, 11 AM. J. COMMUNITY PSYCHOL. 423 (1983). Proferred support may be perceived as a stressor because it is unwanted, too controlling, or fails to meet the person's expectations.

289. Gondolf et al., *supra* Table 9.4 n. o, at 192–93.

290. John Monahan, *Mental Disorder and Violent Behavior: Perceptions and Evidence*, 47 AM. PSYCHOLOGIST 511 (1992); JEFFREY W. SWANSON et al., *Psychotic Symptoms and Disorders and the Risk of Violent Behavior in the Community*, 6 CRIM. BEHAV. & MEN. HEALTH 309 (1996).

291. The multipliers reported in Table 9.4 are derived from epidemiological studies that used self-report of violence as the dependent measure. A relationship between mental disorder and violence is also reported in a large study from Finland, where solved murders were used as the dependent measure. Compared to undiagnosed persons, risk multipliers for murder were: major affective disorder, 2×; schizophrenia, 7×; personality disorder, 10×; APD with alcoholism, 20×. Jari Tuhonen et al., *Criminality Associated with Mental Disorders and Intellectual Deficiency*, 50 ARCHIVES GEN. PSYCHIATRY 917 (1993).

292. Swanson, *supra* note 278.

293. For discussions of the literature on delusions and violence, *see* Alec Buchanan, *Acting on Delusion: A Review*, 23 PSYCHOL. MED. 123 (1993); Karel W. DePauw & T. Krystyna Szulecka, *Dangerous Delusions: Violence and the Misidentification Syndromes*, 152 BRIT. J. PSYCHIATRY 91 (1988); Pamela J. Taylor, *Motives for Offending among Violent and Psychotic Men*, 147 BR. J. PSYCHIATRY 491 (1985); Pamela J. Taylor et al., *Delusions and Violence*, in VIOLENCE AND MENTAL DISORDER, *supra* note 256, at 161–82. The presence of delusional ideas appears to be a factor (along with recognition of the hallucinated voice) that influences whether a person will act on hallucinatory commands. *See* John Junginger, *Predicting Compliance with Command Hallucinations*, 147 AM. J. PSYCHIATRY 245 (1990).

294. Estroff & Zimmer, *supra* Table 9.4, n. q, at 276.

295. Charles Lidz, personal communication, regarding unpublished findings from the NIMH supported dangerousness study (*supra* note 261 and accompanying text).

296. Link & Steve, *supra* Table 9.4 n. u, at 156.

297. "If one were to compare the available objective evidence, recidivistic offenders (those with 3+ convictions for serious or felonious crimes) . . . would clearly surpass persons with 'major mental disorders' . . . in terms of the danger and threat posed to the community." Shah, *supra* note 226, at 312.

298. For example, sexual sadistic murderers, about whom relatively little is known, only infrequently display the characteristics featured in Table 9.4. *See* Park Elliott Dietz et al., *The Sexually Sadistic Criminal and His Offenses*, 18 BULL. AM. ACAD. PSYCHIATRY & L. 163 (1990).

299. Shah, *supra* note 226, at 307.

300. Edward P. Mulvey and Charles W. Lidz, *Conditional Prediction: A Model for Research on Dangerousness to Others in a New Era*, 18 INT'L J. L. & PSYCHIATRY 129 (1995).

Chapter 10

1. *See* Jacobson v. Massachusetts, 197 U.S. 11, 26 (1905): "The possession and enjoyment of all rights are subject to such reasonable conditions as may be deemed by the governing authority of the country essential to the safety, health, peace, good order and morals of the community. Even liberty itself, the greatest of all rights, is not unrestricted license to act according to one's will."

2. Hawaii v. Standard Oil Co., 405 U.S. 251, 257 (1972) (quoting WILLIAM BLACKSTONE, COMMENTARIES 47).

3. The notion that criminal offenses must be explicitly defined is a principle of constitutional dimension. *See generally* Lanzetta v. New Jersey, 306 U.S. 451, 453 (1939); HERBERT PACKER, THE LIMITS OF THE CRIMINAL SANCTIONS 88–91. (1968).

4. Addington v. Texas, 441 U.S. 418, 428 (1978).

5. *Id.*

6. Even most indeterminate sentencing schemes have an outer limit on imprisonment. *See* § 9.03(a).

7. RICHARD J. BONNIE, PSYCHIATRISTS AND THE LEGAL PROCESS: DIAGNOSIS AND DEBATE 24–26 (1977).

8. ALAN STONE, MENTAL HEALTH AND THE LAW: A SYSTEM IN TRANSITION 45 (1975).

9. THOMAS SZASZ, LAW, LIBERTY, AND PSYCHIATRY 240 (1963).

10. Stephen Morse, *A Preference for Liberty: The Case Against Involuntary Commitment of the Mentally Disordered*, 70 CAL. L. REV. 54 (1982).

11. The first of the lawsuits, and the most important in terms of influence, was Lessard v. Schmidt, 349 F. Supp. 1078 (E.D. Wis. 1972). It is discussed in more detail throughout this chapter.

12. The seminal right-to-treatment case is Wyatt v. Stickney, 325 F. Supp. 781 (M.D. Ala. 1971), *aff'd sub nom.*, Wyatt v. Aderholdt, 503 F.2d 1305 (5th Cir. 1974). These cases had enormous influence on subsequent litigation in this area. *See* Letter, *The Wyatt Standards: An Influential Force in State and Federal Rules,* 28 HOSP. & COMMUNITY PSYCHIATRY 374 (1977).

13. *See, e.g.,* Washington v. Harper, 494 U.S. 210 (1990); Project Release v. Cuomo, 722 F.2d 960 (2d Cir. 1983); Rogers v. Comm'r Dep't of Mental Health, 390 Mass. 489, 458 N.E.2d 308 (1983).

14. SAMUEL J. BRAKEL & RONALD S. ROCK, THE MENTALLY DISABLED AND THE LAW 1 (1971).

15. *Id.* at 1–2.

16. *Id.* at 2.

17. *Id.*

18. *Id.*

19. *Id.* For further discussion of the development of English law, *see* Alan Dershowitz, *The Origins of Preventive Confinement in Anglo-American Law, Part I: The American Experience*, 43 U. CIN. L. REV. 1 (1974).

20. BRAKEL & ROCK, *supra* note 14, at 6.

21. *Id.* at 4.

22. *Id.* For further discussion of the development of American law, *see* Alan Dershowitz, *The Origin of Preventive*

Confinement in Anglo-American Law, Part II: The American Experience, 43 U. CIN. L. REV. 781 (1974).

23. BRAKEL & ROCK, *supra* note 14, at 6.

24. *Id.* at 36.

25. Dershowitz, *supra* note 22, at 789.

26. For example, a Mrs. E.P. Packard, committed for three years solely on the word of her husband and because she expressed opinions he did not like, campaigned for increased safeguards at the time of commitment. *Id.* at 7–8.

27. The person primarily responsible for public concern with the problems of persons with mental disorder and the dramatic increase in the creation of institutions for the disabled was Dorothea Dix, whose efforts resulted in federal grant of land to the states for the establishment of hospitals and the building of at least 32 hospitals in this country and abroad. *Id.* at 8 n. 39 and text.

28. *Id.* at 60.

29. *Id.*

30. NANCY M. COLEMAN & LAURENCE GILBERT, STALKING THE LEAST RESTRICTIVE ALTERNATIVE: LITIGATIVE AND NON-LITIGATIVE STRATEGIES FOR THE INDIGENT MENTALLY DISABLED 12 (1979) (and citations therein).

31. U.S. Dep't of Commerce, *Statistical Abstract of the United States* Table 203 (115th ed.) (in 1990, there were 90,300 patients in state and county mental health hospitals, another 80,300 in private hospitals, and approximately 80,000 more in general hospitals, Veterans Administration hospitals, outpatient clinics, and other facilities). Note that in 1993, there were also roughly 74,000 people diagnosed as having mental retardation who were institutionalized in government-run facilities. *Id.*, Table 202.

32. For a discussion of psychotropic medications and their impact, *see* 2 THE PRESIDENT'S COMMISSION ON MENTAL HEALTH, TASK FORCE REPORT: NATURE AND SCOPE OF THE PROBLEM 55–56 (1978) (and citations therein).

33. Mental Retardation Facilities and Community Mental Health Centers Construction Act, 42 U.S.C. § 217 *et seq.* (1963).

34. *Developments in the Law: Civil Commitment of the Mentally Ill*, 87 HARV. L. REV. 1190, 1207–08 (1974). This article is an exhaustive discussion of civil commitment law, including a description of case law, statutory law, and commentary up to the time of its publication. It is recommended to those interested in delving more deeply into the jurisprudential bases for civil commitment. *See also* John Q. LaFond, *Law and the Delivery of Involuntary Mental Health Services*, 64 AM. J. ORTHOPSYCHIATRY 209 (1994).

35. Proschaska v. Brinegar, 251 Iowa 834, 102 N.W.2d 870, 872 (1960).

36. DAVID WEXLER, MENTAL HEALTH LAW: MAJOR ISSUES 23 (1981).

37. *See, e.g.,* SZASZ, *supra* note 9; THOMAS SZASZ, PSYCHIATRIC JUSTICE 269 (1965).

38. One of the best known is David Rosenhan, *On Being Sane in Insane Place*, 179 SCI. 150 (1973). In this study, eight individuals, feigning mental illness, were admitted to a number of mental health facilities. Staff members reportedly never detected the deception.

39. The most influential article arguing this position is probably Bruce Ennis & Thomas Litwak, *Psychiatry and the Presumption of Expertise: Flipping Coins in the Courtroom*, 62 CAL. L. REV. 693 (1974).

40. Humphrey v. Cady, 405 U.S. 504, 509 (1972).

41. 406 U.S. 715 (1972) [discussed in § 6.04].

42. *Id.* at 737. Wexler observes that this invitation was "rather rudely retracted in some later cases," noting the Court's increased tendency to decide cases on narrow grounds—a tendency Wexler attributes tentatively to the difficulty of the issues the cases raised. WEXLER, *supra* note 36, at 52 n. 13.

43. Lessard v. Schmidt, 349 F. Supp. 1078, 1094 (E.D. Wis. 1972) (quoting Joseph Livermore et al., *On the Justification for Civil Commitment*, 117 U. PA. L. REV. 75, 80 [1968].

44. Commonwealth *ex rel.* Finken v. Roop, 339 A.2d 764, 778 (Pa. Ct. App. 1978).

45. *Id.*

46. 1 MENTAL HEALTH LAW PROJECT, LEGAL RIGHTS OF THE MENTALLY DISABLED 37 (1975).

47. STONE, *supra* note 8, at 1.

48. Wyatt v. Stickney, 325 F. Supp. 781 (M.D. Ala. 1971), *aff'd sub nom.,* Wyatt v. Aderholt, 503 F.2d 1305 (5th Cir. 1974).

49. For the impact of the *Wyatt* litigation, *see* Letter, *supra* note 12; *Special Project, the Remedial Process in Institution Reform Litigation*, 78 COLUM. L. REV. 784 (1978).

50. R. Dennis Scott, *The Treatment Barrier*, 46 BRIT. J. MED. PSYCHIATRY 45, 46 (1973).

51. *See, e.g.,* Amerigo Farina et al., *People's Reactions to a Former Mental Health Patient Moving to Their Neighborhood*, 2 J. COMMUNITY PSYCHOL. 108 (1974).

52. Mary Durham & John Q. LaFond, *The Empirical Consequences and Policy Implications of Broadening the Statutory Criteria for Civil Commitment*, 3 YALE L. POL'Y REV. 395, 428–31 (1985).

53. State *ex rel.* Hawks v. Lazaro, 202 S.E.2d 109, 120 (W. Va. 1974).

54. Lessard v. Schmidt, 349 F. Supp. 1078 (E.D. Wis 1973), *vacated on other grounds,* 414 U.S. 473 (1973), *on remand,* 379 F. Supp. 1376 (E.D. Wis. 1974), *vacated on other grounds,* 421 U.S. 957 (1975) *on remand,* 413 F. Supp. 1318 (E.D. Wis. 1976).

55. *Id.* at 1089.

56. *Id.*

57. *In re* Ballay, 182 F.2d 648, 659 (D.C. Cir. 1973).

58. State *ex rel.* Hawks v. Lazaro, 202 S.E.2d at 121.

59. Other patient advocates sought to limit the use of commitment by making provision of institutional care prohibitively expensive. This strategy formed the underpinning of at least some of the lawsuits filed challenging institutional conditions. MENTAL HEALTH LAW PROJECT, *supra* note 46, at 40.

60. 387 U.S. 1 (1967).

61. *Id.* at 11.

62. Alan Dershowitz, *Psychiatry in the Legal Process, A Knife Cuts Both Ways*, in THE PATH OF THE LAW FROM 1967, 71–83 (Alfred D. Sutherland ed. 1968).

63. For a general discussion, *see* Note, *Overt Dangerous*

Behavior as a Constitutional Requirement for Civil Commitment of the Mentally Ill, 44 U. CHI. L. REV. 562 (1977). The courts have split on whether an overt act is constitutionally required as part of the proof of dangerousness. *Compare* Project Release v. Prevost, 722 F.2d 960 (2d Cir. 1983), *and In re* Salen, 228 S.E.2d 649 (N.C. Ct. App. 1976) (overt act not required), *with* Goldy v. Beal, 429 F. Supp. 640 (M.D. Pa. 1976), and Lynch v. Baxley, 386 F. Supp. 378 (M.D. Ala. 1974) (overt act required).

64. *See, e.g.,* Dixon v. Attorney Gen., 325 F. Supp. 966 (N.D. Pa. 1971); Wessel v. Pryor, 461 F. Supp. 1144 (E.D. Ark. 1978); State *ex rel.* Hawks v. Lazaro, 202 S.E.2d 109 (W. Va. 1974).

65. 422 U.S. 563 (1975).

66. *Id.* at 573.

67. *Id.* at 576.

68. For instance, the "without more" language could be construed to mean that a state may confine a nondangerous person if it provides treatment. From this, one could argue that there is a constitutional right to treatment for nondangerous people who are committed. However, later statements by the Court belie that interpretation. *See, e.g.,* Pennhurst St. Sch. & Hosp. v. Halderman, 451 U.S. 1 (1981) (in which the Court stated that it had "never found that the involuntarily committed have a constitutional 'right to treatment,' much less the voluntarily committed") and text accompanying notes 69–71 *infra.* Some commentators criticized *Donaldson* for its caution. *See, e.g.,* Joseph Mancilla, *The Right to Treatment Case—That Wasn't,* 30 U. MIAMI L. REV. 486 (1976). Others acknowledged the limited nature of the holding but argued that the Court's focus on the liberty interest of patients was a necessary step toward a broader affirmation of treatment rights. *See, e.g.,* Note, O'Connor v. Donaldson: *The Supreme Court Sidesteps the Right to Treatment,* 13 CAL. W. L. REV. 168 (1976). For an elaboration of the latter point, *see* Ron Spece, *Preserving the Right to Treatment: A Critical Assessment and Constructive Development of Constitutional Right to Treatment Theories,* 20 ARIZ. L. REV. 1 (1978).

69. 422 U.S. at 580 (Burger, C.J., concurring).

70. Donaldson v. O'Connor, 493 F.2d 507, 520 (5th Cir. 1974).

71. 422 U.S. at 582.

72. *Id.* at 582–83.

73. 441 U.S. 418 (1978).

74. *In re* Winship, 397 U.S. 358 (1970).

75. 441 U.S. at 426.

76. *Id.* at 428.

77. *Id.* at 429.

78. *Id.*

79. 442 U.S. 584 (1979).

80. *Id.* at 591.

81. J.R. v. Parham, 413 F. Supp. 112, 139 (1976).

82. 442 U.S. at 600.

83. *Id.* at 600–01.

84. *Id.* at 605.

85. *Id.* at 602. To some extent, this statement by the Court was belied by its own decisions. For instance, just three years before *Parham* the Court had held that a state

could not grant parents an absolute veto over a minor child's decision to have an abortion, Planned Parenthood v. Danforth, 428 U.S. 52 (1976), a right which, while important, is no more important than the child's liberty interest.

86. 442 U.S. at 603.

87. *Id.* at 606–07.

88. *Id.* at 607.

89. *Id.* at 609.

90. *Id.*

92. *See, e.g.,* Youngberg v. Romeo, 457 U.S. 307 (1982), where the Supreme Court directed the federal judiciary to defer to the judgment exercised by professionals charged with administration and treatment decision; Washington v. Harper, 494 U.S. 219 (1994) (a competent prisoner has no right to refuse psychotropic medication if he is considered dangerous to self or others, or gravely disabled).

92. *See, e.g.,* Project Release v. Prevost, 722 F.2d 960 (2d Cir. 1983) (relying on medical judgment and administrative processes for determining a patient's capacity to consent to treatment); United States v. Charters, 863 F.2d 302 (4th Cir. 1988) (relying on a medical decision-making process to determine the right to refuse).

93. *See, e.g.,* the dissent of Justice Brennan in the *Parham* case, 442 U.S. at 625, in which he criticized the majority opinion; in large measure his remarks were based on the criticisms of clinical expertise noted earlier in this chapter.

94. *See, e.g.,* Gary B. Melton, *Family and Mental Hospital as Myths: Civil Commitment of Minors,* in CHILDREN, MENTAL HEALTH, AND THE LAW (N. Dickon Reppucci et al. eds. 1984). Michael Perlin, *An Invitation to the Dance: An Empirical Response to Chief Justice Warren Burger's "Time-Consuming Procedural Minuets" Theory* in Parham v. J.R., 9 BULL. AM. ACAD. PSYCHIATRY & L. 149 (1981).

95. John Parry, *Involuntary Civil Commitment in the 90s: A Constitutional Perspective,* 18 MENTAL & PHYSICAL DISABILITY L. REP. 320, 322 (1994) (noting that "not much has changed" in terms of commitment criteria and procedures "in the past ten years," despite the Supreme Court's retrenchment).

96. TEX. REV. CIVIL STAT. art. 5547-4(k) (Supp. 1982–83).

97. VT. STAT. ANN. tit. 18, § 7101 (17) (S8pp. 1984).

98. *See, e.g.,* FLA. STAT. ANN. § 394.455(3).

99. *See, e.g.,* ARIZ. REV. STAT. ANN. § 36-501(22).

100. For further explication of this issue, *see* § 8.02(c)(1).

101. Ten states do so either in their definition of mental illness or in other sections of the commitment statute. Paul Stiles & John Petrila, *Report to Florida Legislature on State Mental Health Statutes* 1–2 (Oct. 4, 1995).

102. Loren Roth, *A Commitment Law for Patients, Doctors, and Lawyers,* 136 AM. J. PSYCHIATRY 1121 (1979).

103. STONE, *supra* note 8, at 66–70.

104. On the other hand, the individual's ability to control his or her antisocial behavior, which may be closely related to the capacity to make treatment decisions, *is* relevant to police power commitment. If the person's

mental disorder makes that person unresponsive to the dictates of the criminal law (in other words, "insane" for purposes of criminal culpability), the state should have authority to commit, based on a danger to others rationale. *See* Christopher Slobogin, *Dangerousness as a Criterion in the Criminal Process,* in Law, Mental Health, and Mental Disorder 360, 368–70 (Bruce Sales & Daniel Shuman eds. 1996).

105. *See* Del. Code. Ann. 16 § 5001(1) (mental illness is that which "renders such person unable to make responsible decisions with respect to his hospitalization"); Kan. Stat. Ann. § 59-2902(h) (a mentally ill person "lacks capacity to make an informed decision concerning treatment").

106. Roth, *supra* note 102, at 1121.

107. *See* Rebecca Dresser, *Ulysses and the Psychiatrists: A Legal and Policy Analysis of the Voluntary Commitment Contract,* 16 Harv. C.R.-C.L. L. Rev. 777 (1982).

108. 494 U.S. 113, at 135, 136 (1990).

109. As *Zinermon* merely held that the plaintiff–patient had a cause of action against the state of Florida, it did not definitively resolve this issue, however.

110. Unfortunately, these provisions are often honored in the breach. *See* § 10.04(c). Commentators have expressed doubt that admitting facilities make much effort to determine whether an individual has the capacity to make the admission decision; they suggest that many "voluntary" patients are in fact patients who either are subtly coerced into accepting the label or in fact are unable to understand its implications. *See* Dresser, *supra* note 107, at 838; Janet Gilboy & John Schmidt, *"Voluntary"Hospitalization of the Mentally Ill,* 66 N.W. U. L. Rev. 429, 443 (1972). The latter is true particularly with populations for whom the "voluntary" label seems clearly fictitious— for example, minors admitted by parents or guardians, and the mentally retarded, who are most often admitted by another party. Whether *Zinermon* will change these practices remains to be seen.

111. Alaska Stat. § 47.30.070(i) (1984).

112. Fla. Stat. § 394.467(1)(A)2.b (1995).

113. Suzuki v. Yuen, 7617 F.2d 173, 176 (9th Cir. 1980).

114. *See, e.g.,* Haw. Rev. Stat. § 334-1; Ky. Rev. Stat. Ann. § 202A.030; N.M. Stat. Ann. § 43-1-3(E).

115. Pa. Stat. Ann. tit. 50, § 7301(a).

116. It also could be seen as an attempt to avoid deprivation of liberty based simply on the "status" of being mentally ill and dangerous. *Cf.* Robinson v. California, 370 U.S. 660 (1962) (finding that punishment of a person simply for being addicted is a violation of the Eighth Amendment's prohibition against cruel and unusual punishment). However, most courts would not consider commitment to be "punishment" for purposes of the Eighth Amendment. *Cf.* Youngberg v. Romeo, 457 U.S. 307 (1982).

117. People v. Sansone, 309 N.E.2d 733, 735 (1974); *In re* Salem, 228 S.E.2d 649 (N.C. Ct. App. 1976).

118. Alexander Brooks, *Defining the Dangerousness of the Mentally Ill: Involuntary Civil Commitment,* in Mentally Abnormal Offenders (M. & A. Craft eds. 1984).

119. Alaska Stat. § 47.30.070(i).

120. Pa. Stat. Ann. tit. 50, § 7301(a).

121. 422 U.S. at 575.

122. *See* Anthony B. Clapper, *Finding a Right in State Constitutions for Community Treatment of the Mentally Ill,* 142 U. Pa. L. Rev. 739–83 n. 183 (1993) (citing 39 states). *See also* Edward B. Beis, *State Involuntary Commitment Statutes,* 7 Mental Health and the Law (1983).

123. Nev. Rev. Stat. § 433A.310(1).

124. *See* Beis, *supra* note 122.

125. *See* Clifford Stromberg & Alan Stone, *A Model State Law on Civil Commitment of the Mentally Ill,* 20 Harv. J. on Legis. 275, 301–03 (1983).

126. Robert Miller, *Need for Treatment Criteria for Involuntary Civil Commitment: Impact in Practice,* 139 Am. J. Psychiatry 1380 (1992).

127. *See, e.g.,* 34 Hosp. & Community Psychiatry (Sept. 1983), much of which is devoted to this subject.

128. When the Coalition for the Homeless brought suit to compel New York State to provide housing for the homeless mentally ill, Mayor Koch of New York was quoted as saying, "I hope [plaintiffs have] success in [the] suit in getting the state to reinstitutionalize those who need it . . ." N.Y. Times, May 21, 1982, sect. A, at 1, col. 1.

129. *See* Parry, *supra* note 95, Table, at 330–36 (citing 32 states).

130. Del. Code Ann. 16 § 50001(1).

131. A number of courts also struck down need for treatment statutes on vagueness grounds. *See, e.g.,* Commonwealth *ex rel.* Finken v. Roop, 339 A.2d 764 (Pa. 1975); State *ex rel.* Hawks v. Lazaro, 202 S.E.2d 109 (W. Va. 1975). *But see* Paul Appelbaum, *Is the Need for Treatment Constitutionally Acceptable as a Basis for Civil Commitment?,* 12 Law, Medicine & Health Care 144 (1984) (arguing that more precisely defined criteria, perhaps akin to the predicted deterioration standard, should pass constitutional muster).

132. *See, e.g.,* Lynch v. Baxley, 386 F. Supp. 378, 391–92 (M.D. Ala. 1974) ("[t]he state may well have an obligation under the police power to restrain the liberty of the threatening individual, even though his condition is not amenable to any currently available treatment").

133. *Cf. Donaldson,* 422 U.S. at 584–85 (Burger, C.J., concurring) (states are not "powerless" to provide "care in a sheltered environment" for those mentally ill who are "untreatable" but otherwise "will suffer real harm to themselves").

134. Kirkland Schwitzgebel, *Survey of State Civil Commitment Statutes,* in Civil Commitment and Social Policy: An Evaluation of the Massachusetts Mental Health Reform Act of 1970, 54 (1981).

135. *See, e.g.,* Appelbaum, *supra* note 131; Stromberg & Stone, *supra* note 125; Browning Hoffman & Robert C. Dunn, *Beyond* Rouse *and* Wyatt: *An Administrative Law Model for Expanding and Implementing the Mental Patient's Right to Treatment,* 61 Va. L. Rev. 297 (1975).

136. Stone, *supra* note 8, at 66–67.

137. Roth, *supra* note 102, at 1122.

138. *Id.*; Stone, *supra* note 8, at 67.

139. Roth, *supra* note 102, at 1123.

140. *Id.*

141. *Id.* at 1124–25.

142. STONE, *supra* note 8, at 70.

143. *Id.*

144. Morse, *supra* note 10, at 87–93.

145. Browning Hoffman & Laurence Foust, *Least Restrictive Treatment of the Mentally Ill: A Doctrine in Search of Its Senses,* 14 SAN DIEGO REV. 1100, 1112–15 (1977). At the time of their article, the authors counted 20 states that referred explicitly to the doctrine in their commitment laws. *Id.* at 48, n. 49. For updated surveys, *see* Clapper, *supra* note 122, at 785 n. 191 (describing 29 states requiring treatment in the least restrictive environment "if available"); Parry, *supra* note 95, table, at 330–36 (reporting that 23 states require least-restrictive-alternative treatment and an additional 8 states' statutes require investigations of "other" treatment alternatives).

146. Lake v. Cameron, 364 F.2d 657 (D.C. Cir. 1966).

147. *See, e.g.,* Welsch v. Likens, 373 F. Supp. 487 (D. Minn. 1974). The Supreme Court, on the other hand, has seemed less receptive to the idea that the doctrine has constitutional status. *See, e.g.,* Youngberg v. Romeo, 457 U.S. 307 (1982) ("The Constitution only requires that the courts make certain that professional judgment in fact was exercised. It is not appropriate for the courts to specify which of several professionally acceptable choices should have been made").

148. In Shelton v. Tucker, 364 U.S. 479 (1960), the Court struck down an Arkansas law requiring teachers to list affiliations with organizations. The Court announced that even a legitimate governmental purpose "cannot be pursued by means that broadly stifle fundamental personal liberties when the end can be more narrowly achieved. The breadth of legislative abridgment must be viewed in the light of less drastic means for achieving the same basic purpose." *Id.* at 488.

149. Hoffman & Foust, *supra* note 145.

150. David Chambers, *Alternatives to Civil Commitment of the Mentally Ill,* 70 MICH. L. REV. 1107, 1168 (1972).

151. *See, e.g.,* Dixon v. Weinberger, 405 F. Supp. 974 (D.D.C. 1975), ordering creation of suitable residential facilities that would allow the implementation of patients' rights to be treated in the least restrictive environment.

152. *See, e.g.,* Leslz v. Kavanagh, 807 F.2d 1243 (5th Cir. 1987); Phillips v. Thompson, 715 F.2d 365, 368 (7th Cir. 1983).

153. In Pennhurst St. Sch. & Hosp. v. Haldemann, 451 U.S. 1, 29 (1981), the Court stated that it had never imposed on the states "such open-ended and *potentially* burdensome obligations as providing 'appropriate' treatment in the 'least restrictive environment,'" nor did the legislation before it (the Developmentally Disabled Assistance and Bill of Rights Act) do so.

154. *See, e.g.,* Garrity v. Gallen, 522 F. Supp. 171 (D.N.H. 1981), in which the court held that there was no constitutional or federal statutory right held by patients entitling them to the development of community-based treatment programs and facilities. *See generally* Jan Costello & James Preis, *Beyond Least Restrictive Alternative Doctrine: A Constitutional Right to Treatment for Mentally Disabled Persons in the Community,* 20 LOY. L.A. L. REV. 1527 (1987).

155. For a more detailed treatment of the issues addressed in this subsection, *see* Christopher Slobogin, *Involuntary Treatment in the Community of People Who Are Violent and Mentally Ill,* 45 HOSP. & COMMUNITY PSYCHIATRY 685 (1994).

156. E. Fuller Torrey & Robert J. Kaplan, *A National Survey of the Use of Outpatient Commitment,* 46 PSYCHIATRIC SERVICES 778 (1995); Ingo Keilitz et al., *Least Restrictive Treatment of Involuntary Patients: Translating Concepts Into Practice,* 29 ST. LOUIS U. L.J. 691, 708 (1985).

157. HAW. REV. STAT. § 334-121 (1985). North Carolina defines the criteria for outpatient commitment to require a treatment history indicating a need for treatment to prevent further disability or deterioration which "would predictably result in dangerousness." N.C. GEN. STAT. § 122C-271(a) (1) (1989). Both statutes also require a finding that the person is unable to make an informed decision to seek or comply with recommended treatment voluntarily and a finding that the person is incapable of surviving safely in the community. *Id.*

158. Susan Stefan, *Preventive Commitment: The Concept and Its Pitfalls,* 11 MENTAL DISABILITY L. REP. 288 (1987).

159. SAMUEL BRAKEL ET AL., THE MENTALLY DISABLED AND THE LAW 203 (1985).

160. Perhaps for this reason, outpatient commitment is seldom used. Robert Miller, *Commitment to Outpatient Treatment: A National Survey,* 36 HOSP. & COMMUNITY PSYCHIATRY 265 (1985) (outpatient commitment represents only 5% of all dispositions in those jurisdictions which authorize it).

161. *See* Jeffrey L. Geller, *Rights, Wrongs, and the Dilemma of Coerced Community Treatment,* 143 AM. J. PSYCHIATRY 1259, 1261 (1986).

162. For instance, in the leading case of Lessard v. Schmidt, 349 Supp. 1078 (E.D. Wis. 1972), a three-judge federal district court held that involuntary commitment is constitutionally justified only if there is an "extreme likelihood that if the person is not confined he will do immediate harm to himself or others." *See also* Suzuki v. Alba, 438 F. Supp. 1006 (D. Haw. 1977); Mignone v. Vincent, 411 F. Supp. 1386, 1389 (S.D.N.Y. 1976).

163. Hachter v. Wachtel, 269 S.E.2d 849, 852 (W. Va. 1980); Commonwealth v. Nassar, 380 Mass. 908, 406 N.E.2d 1286 (1980).

164. *See, e.g.,* Wolonsky v. Balson 58 Ohio App. 2d 25, 387 N.E.2d 625 (1976); People v. De Anda, 114 Cal. App. 3d 488, 170 Cal. Rptr. 830, 833–37 (1983); State v. Collins, 381 So. 2d 449 (La. 1980).

165. *See* Mary L. Durham & John Q. LaFond, *The Empirical Consequences and Policy Implications of Broadening the Statutory Criteria for Civil Commitment,* 3 YALE L. & POL'Y REV. 395, 401 (1985) (under a predicted deterioration standard adopted in Washington, "new patients stayed in hospitals longer than other patients and become chronic users of the state mental hospitals").

166. *Cf.* Stromberg & Stone, *supra* note 125, at 380 (arguing for release of all but a small group of involuntarily committed people within 100 days).

167. In California, the decision is made by attending staff, a mental health professional designated by the county, or a police officer, who has the authority to have an individual admitted on an emergency basis. CAL. WELF. INST. CODE § 5150.

168. Emergency admissions in Washington are effected either by a mental health professional designated by the county or by a police officer. WASH. REV. CODE. ANN. tit. 71.05.140.

169. N.Y. MENTAL HYGIENE LAW §§ 9.37, 9.39.

170. VA. CODE ANN. § 37.1-67.1.

171. For example, in New York, the statute requires only an "opinion" by the director of county mental health services that the individual is mentally ill, needs immediate care and treatment, and presents a likelihood of serious harm to self or others. N.Y. MENTAL HYGIENE LAW § 9.37. In Washington, the mental health professional is required to conduct an investigation of allegations that the person meets the criteria, but no standard governs the determination that emergency care is needed. WASH. REV. CODE ANN. tit. 71.05.150. In Virginia, the judge or magistrate need only rely upon a sworn petition of the applicant, although he or she can also act upon his or her own motion, in which case "probable cause" is required. VA. CODE ANN. § 37.1-67.1.

172. CAL. WELF. INST. CODE § 5150.

173. VA. CODE ANN. § 37.1-67.3.

174. WASH. REV. CODE ANN. tit. 71.05.200.

175. N.Y. MENTAL HYGIENE LAW § 9.39.

176. CAL. WELF. INST. CODE § 5157.

177. *Id.*

178. VA. CODE ANN § 37.1-67.1.

179. CAL. WELF. INST. CODE § 5150.

180. WASH. REV. CODE ANN. tit. 71.05.140.

181. N.Y. MENTAL HYGIENE LAW § 9.39.

182. *Id.*

183. National Center for State Courts, *Guidelines for Involuntary Civil Commitment,* 10 MENTAL DISABILITY L. REP. 409, 427 (1986). *See also* Uri Avirtur, *Screening Services in Civil Commitment of the Mentally Ill: An Attempt to Balance Individual Liberties with Needs for Treatment,* 21 BULL. AM. ACAD. PSYCHIATRY & L. 195 (1993).

184. NATIONAL CENTER FOR STATE COURTS, A MODEL FOR THE APPLICATION OF THE LEAST RESTRICTIVE ALTERNATIVE DOCTRINE IN INVOLUNTARY CIVIL COMMITMENT 291–323 (1984).

185. *Id.* at 428.

186. New York law provides only for the giving of "notice" to the patient. N.Y. MENTAL HYGIENE LAW § 9.39. This provision was challenged on constitutional grounds but was upheld because nothing in the record proved that patients were failing to receive "notice" that was "due." Project Release v. Prevost, 722 F.2d 960 (2d Cir. 1983). The court's reasoning on this issue is more a model of circularity than of clarity.

187. WASH. REV. CODE ANN. tit. 71.05.460; VA. CODE ANN. § 37.1-67.3; CAL. WELF. INST. CODE § 5157.

As noted, all patients in New York are entitled to the services of the Mental Hygiene Legal Service.

188. In New York, the patient (or any relative or friend on his or her behalf) may file within 30 days for review of a judicial decision authorizing detention, in which case a jury is summoned to hear the case. N.Y. MENTAL HYGIENE LAW § 9.35. In Virginia, the person has the right to appeal within 30 days for *de novo* hearing in front of a jury. VA. CODE ANN. § 37.1-67.6.

189. See *supra* note 73 and accompanying text.

190. Virginia, for example, does not exclude hearsay evidence at the commitment proceeding. The court may accept written certification of the examining physician's findings. VA. CODE ANN. § 37.1-67.3.

191. In Washington, the individual has the right to remain silent, though in certain circumstances the physician–patient privilege may be deemed waived by the court. WASH. REV. CODE ANN. tits. 71.05.200, 71.05.250. In the other jurisdictions under discussion, the right does not apply. *See, e.g.,* Conservatorship of Mitchell, 114 Ca. 3d 606, 170 Cal. Rptr. 759 (1981).

192. An independent clinician is available to the patient in Washington. WASH. REV. CODE ANN. tit. 71.05.470. California provides an interpreter if necessary.

193. In Stamus v. Leonhardt, 414 F. Supp. 439 (S.D. Iowa 1976), the court struck down a provision permitting exclusion of the respondent from the hearing when it would be "injurious" to the subject or "attended with no advantage."

194. In many states the hearing is closed unless the respondent requests that it be open, while in others the question is left up to the court and in still others it is closed. RALPH REISNER & CHRISTOPHER SLOBOGIN, LAW AND THE MENTAL HEALTH SYSTEM: CIVIL AND CRIMINAL ASPECTS 719 (1988).

195. VA. CODE ANN. § 37.1-67.3.

196. *Id.*

197. WASH. REV. CODE ANN. tit. 71.05.240.

198. WASH. REV. CODE ANN. tit. 71.05.280-320.

199. WASH. REV. CODE ANN. §§ 5251, 5252.

200. WASH. REV. CODE ANN. § 5256.4.

201. WASH. REV. CODE ANN. § 5257.

202. WASH. REV. CODE ANN. §§5350–71.

203. N.Y. MENTAL HYGIENE LAW §§ 9.27, 9.31.

204. N.Y. MENTAL HYGIENE LAW § 9.27.

205. N.Y. MENTAL HYGIENE LAW § 9.31.

206. It also closely tracks the model for the commitment of children proposed by Justice Brennan in his concurring and dissenting opinion in the *Parham* case. Although vigorously criticizing Chief Justice Burger's analysis, Brennan agreed that nonjudicial forms of admission for children might be constitutionally permissible if followed within a reasonable time by judicial hearing with procedural protection for the patient. 422 U.S. at 632–33 (Brennan, J., concurring and dissenting).

207. *See* Jillane T. Hinds, *Involuntary Outpatient Commitment for the Chronically Mentally Ill,* 69 NEB. L. REV. 346, 356 (1990).

208. *Id.* at 358–59. Unfortunately, clinics are not al-

ways notified, which can create significant problems. *See* Robert Miller & Paul Fiddleman, *Outpatient Commitment: Treatment in the Least Restrictive Environment?,* 35 HOSP. & COMMUNITY PSYCHIATRY 147 (1984).

209. *See* David Wexler, *Health Care Compliance Principles and the Insanity Acquittee Conditional Release Process,* 27 CRIM. L. BULL. 18, 20–22 (1991). Even when the issue involved is conditional release of insanity acquittees, many states do not require a hearing unless the court so moves, or unless the prosecuting attorney objects to the proposed conditional release. *Id.*

210. *Id.*

211. *See* Donald Meichenbaum & Dennis Turk, FACILITATING TREATMENT ADHERENCE: A PRACTITIONER'S GUIDEBOOK (1987).

212. *See* OR. REV. STAT. §§ 161.327 to 161.336.

213. Wexler criticizes the Board's procedures in this area, noting that after its hearing, the Board deliberates in closed session and issues its findings and order based on a majority vote. "Such a model does not comport ideally with the model developed earlier . . . : a single judge holding a hearing to review a previously negotiated agreement, questioning the patient about the agreement, putting the final touches on it; extracting from the patient a public commitment to comply, setting a follow-up hearing at which the same judge will preside, and, in the presence of the patient, entering an order approving the patient's temporary release according to the terms and conditions set out in the agreement." Wexler, *supra* note 209, at 216–17.

214. *See* Jeffrey L. Rogers et al., *Oregon's Psychiatric Security Review Board: A Comprehensive System for Managing Insanity Acquittees,* 484 ANNALS AM. ACAD. POL. & SOC. SCI. 86 (1986); Joseph Bloom et al., *Lifetime Police Contacts of Discharged PSRB Clients,* 8 INT'L J. L. & PSYCHIATRY 189 (1986).

215. *Cf.* Griffin v. Wisconsin, 483 U.S. 868 (1987) (Fourth Amendment governs search of a probationer's home). *See generally* Patricia Griffin et al., *Designing Conditional Release Systems for Insanity Acquittees,* 18 J. MENTAL HEALTH ADMIN. 231 (1991).

216. 408 U.S. 471 (1972).

217. *See, e.g.,* Dietrich v. Brooks, 27 Or. App. 821, 558 P.2d 357 (1976); *In re* Richardson, 481 A.2d 473 (D.C. 1984) (requiring only an affidavit by the hospital superintendent within 24 hours of rehospitalization citing recent behavior by the patient).

218. G.T. v. Vermont (Vt. 1992) (No. 92-941); Application of True v. Dept. of Health & Welfare, 103 Idaho 151, 645 P.2d 891 (1982); *In re* Peterson, 360 N.W.2d 33 (Minn. 1984).

219. *See, e.g.,* Birls v. Wallis, 619 F. Supp. 481 (M.D. Ala. 1985); Hinds, *supra* note 207, at 376–80.

220. *Id.*

221. For further discussion of the advantages and disadvantages of voluntary hospitalization, *see* GROUP FOR THE ADVANCEMENT OF PSYCHIATRY, FORCED INTO TREATMENT: THE ROLE OF COERCION IN CLINICAL PRACTICE (1994); Susan C. Reed & Dan A. Lewis, *The Negotiation of Voluntary Admission in Chicago's State Mental Hospitals,* 18 J.

PSYCHIATRY & L. 137 (1990); Francine Cournos et al., *Report of the Task Force on Consent to Voluntary Hospitalization,* 21 BULL. AM. ACAD. PSYCHIATRY & L. 293 (1993): Steven K. Hoge, *On Being "Too Crazy" to Sign into a Mental Hospital: The Issue of Consent to Psychiatric Hospitalization,* 22 BULL. AM. ACAD. PSYCHIATRY & L. 431 (1994).

222. BRAKEL ET AL., *supra* note 159, at 178–79.

223. *See* Alicia Lucksted & Robert D. Coursey, *Consumer Perceptions of Pressure and Force in Psychiatric Treatments,* 46 PSYCHIATRIC SERVICES 146 (1995); Reed & Lewis, *supra* note 221; *supra* note 110.

224. 494 U.S. 113 (1990).

225. Winick has argued that, at least when the person "assents," competency to make treatment decisions should not be a requirement for voluntary admission, given the benefits of "voluntary" as opposed to "involuntary" treatment. Bruce Winick, *Competency to Consent to Voluntary Hospitalization: A Therapeutic Jurisprudence Analysis of* Zinerman v. Burch, 14 INT'L J. L. & PSYCHIATRY 169 (1991).

226. *See* Normal G. Poythress et al., *Capacity to Consent to Voluntary Hospitalization: Searching for a Satisfactory* Zinerman *Screen* 24 BULL. AM. ACAD. PSYCHIATRY & L. 439 (1996) (using an instrument developed by the MacArthur Foundation Research Network, the authors found that 55% of 120 persons brought to crisis stabilization units for involuntary psychiatry evaluation demonstrated impairment in the capacity to understand at least one of four items of information relevant to voluntary admission); Grace G. Olin & Harry S. Olin, *Informed Consent in Voluntary Mental Admissions,* 132 AM. J. PSYCHIATRY 938, 940 (1975) (reporting a "massive lack of comprehension by patients of their voluntary status"); Paul S. Applebaum et al., *Empirical Assessment of Competency to Consent to Psychiatric Hospitalization,* 138 AM. J. PSYCHIATRY 1170, 1175 (1981) (reporting that "according to any meaningful standard a large number, perhaps a majority, of psychiatric patients may not be competent to sign themselves into the hospital."); Steward Levine et al., *Competency of Geropsychiatric Patients to Consent to Voluntary Hospitalization,* 2 AM. J. GERIATRIC PSYCHIATRY 300 (1994).

227. Cournos, *supra* note 221, at 300.

228. *See also* Charles A. Kiesler, *Public and Professional Myths about Mental Hospitalization: An Empirical Reassessment of Policy Related Beliefs,* 37 AM. PSYCHOLOGIST 1323 (1982); Charles A. Kiesler & Amy E. Sibulkin, *Episodic Rate of Mental Hospitalization,* 141 AM. J. PSYCHIATRY 44 (1984).

229. John Q. LaFond & Mary L. Durham, BACK TO THE ASYLUM: THE FUTURE OF MENTAL HEALTH LAW AND POLICY IN THE UNITED STATES 144–45 (1992) ("Studies clearly demonstrate that when legislative reforms have been enacted to limit the use of involuntary commitment, there has been an immediate decrease in the number of commitments for at least two years. But the decline in admission rates is short-lived."); Michael R. Bagby & Leslie Atkinson, *The Effects of Legislative Reform on Civil Commitment Admission Rates: A Critical Analysis,* 6 BEHAVIORAL SCI. & L. 45 (1988) (finding that "15 of the 17 independent data sets showed that increases in civil com-

mitment rates followed initial post-reform decreases" and that "[a]ll three studies which included extended post-reform observations revealed that admissions rates eventually approach pre-reform levels").

230. In general, law effects have been assessed through time-series designs. *See, e.g.,* Felix v. Milliken, 463 F. Supp. 1360 (E.D. Mich. 1978). For discussion of the strengths and weaknesses of such "quasi-experimental" research designs, *see generally* DONALD T. CAMPBELL & JULIAN STANLEY, EXPERIMENTAL AND QUASI-EXPERIMENTAL DESIGNS FOR RESEARCH (1966); EXPERIMENTATION IN THE LAW: REPORT OF THE FEDERAL JUDICIAL CENTER ADVISORY COMMITTEE ON EXPERIMENTATION IN THE LAW 107–12 (1981). *See also* 33 NEB. SYMP. ON MOTIVATION (Gary Melton ed. 1985) (examining the circumstances under which law affects behavior).

231. James Luckey & John Berman, *Effects of a New Commitment Law on Involuntary Admissions and Service Utilization Patterns,* 3 LAW & HUM. BEHAV. 149 (1979).

232. Nebraska uses an interdisciplinary quasi-judicial board for civil commitment. NEB. REV. STAT. §§ 83-1017, 83-1018, and 83-1035 through 83-1081. This administrative mechanism has been held to provide sufficient protection of the respondent's right to due process. Doremus v. Farrell, 407 F. Supp. 509 (D. Neb. 1975). Nebraska's procedures are also unusual in that the county attorney, who is also the criminal prosecutor, functions as both gatekeeper (e.g., in determining whether there is cause to hospitalize someone involuntarily) and prosecutor in commitment proceedings. NEB. REV. STAT. §§ 83-1024 and 83-1053. Although there is considerable potential for abuse in such a situation (e.g., the county attorney can move to civilly commit an individual when evidence is too weak for him or her to pursue criminal prosecution), the procedure is a particularly close analogue to prosecutorial gatekeeping in the criminal process. See § 2.04(a).

233. The methodological problems of pre–post designs can be greatly attenuated if there are *repeated* prechange and postchange observations. The research then compares the slope of curves prior to and following the "interruption" by a change in the law. *See* Donald T. Campbell, *Reforms as Experiments,* 24 AM. PSYCHOLOGIST 409 (1969).

234. Between 1956 and 1980, the number of patients in public mental hospitals dropped from 551,390 to 132,000, but the annual admission rate almost doubled, from 185,597 to 390,000. BRAKEL ET AL., *supra* note 159, at 47.

235. *See* Morse, *supra* note 10, at 67–79.

236. The often flagrant failure to apply the legal standards for civil commitment has been documented in numerous jurisdictions. *See, e.g.,* Virginia A. Hiday, *Reformed Commitment Procedures: An Empirical Study in the Courtroom,* 11 LAW SOC'Y REV. 651 (1977); Virginia A. Hiday, *The Role of Counsel in Civil Commitment: Changes, Effects, Determinants,* 5 U. PSYCHIATRY & L. 551 (1977); Virginia A. Hiday, *Court Discretion: Application of the Dangerousness Standard in Civil Commitment,* 5 LAW & HUM. BEHAV. 275 (1981); Virginia A. Hiday & Stephen Markell, *Components*

of Dangerousness: Legal Standards in Civil Commitment, 3 INT'L J. L. PSYCHIATRY 405 (1980); Paul D. Lipsitt & David Lelos, *Decision Markers in Law and Psychiatry and the Involuntary Commitment Process,* 17 COMMUNITY MENTAL HEALTH J. 114 (1981); Serena Stier & Kurt Stoebe, *Involuntary Hospitalization of the Mentally Ill in Iowa: The Failure of the 1975 Legislation,* 64 IOWA L. REV. 1284 (1979); Carol Warren, *Involuntary Commitment for Mental Disorder: The Application of California's Lanterman–Petris–Short Act,* 11 LAW & SOC'Y REV. 629 (1977); David Wexler & Stanley Scoville, *The Administration of Psychiatric Justice: Theory and Practice in Arizona,* 13 ARIZ. L. REV. 1 (1971); James Wickham, *Hospitalization of the Mentally Ill in Idaho and the Need for Reform,* 16 IDAHO L. REV. 211 (1980); Jerome Yesavage, *A Study of Mandatory Review of Civil Commitment,* 41 ARCHIVES GEN. PSYCHIATRY 229 (1984); Thomas Zander, *Civil Commitment in Wisconsin: The Impact of* Lessard v. Schmidt, 1976 WIS. L. REV. 503. Harold Bursztajn et al., *Process Analysis for Judge's Commitment Decisions: A Preliminary Empirical Study,* 143 AM. J. PSYCHIATRY 170 (1986).

237. Robert Miller, *Need for Treatment Criteria for Involuntary Civil Commitment: Impact in Practice,* 149 AM. J. PSYCHIATRY 1380 (1992) (a survey of eight states which changed to broader commitment standards finding that the change *decreased* admissions in at least five states and concluding that measurement of legal effects is very difficult in this area); John Monahan et al., *The Stone–Roth Model of Civil Commitment and the California Dangerousness Standard: An Operational Comparison,* 39 ARCHIVES GEN. PSYCHIATRY 1267 (1982); Jonathan Marx & Richard Levinson, *Statutory Change and "Street-Level" Implementation of Psychiatric Commitment,* 27 SOC. SCI. MED. 1247 (1988), *But see* Bagby & Atkinson, *supra* note 229, at 58 (legislative provisions that have sought to expand medical prerogatives result in a sustained increase in civil commitments, in part because mental health professionals perceive legalistic laws as an unnecessary constraint in the treatment of the mentally ill).

Compare also Ken Hoge et al., *An Empirical Comparison of the Stone and Dangerousness Criteria for Civil Commitment,* 146 AM. J. PSYCHIATRY 170 (1989) (resident psychiatrists applying Stone's proposal [see § 10.03(f)] would drastically *reduce* the number committed when compared to a dangerousness standard (from 296 to 32)), *with* Steven Segal et al., *Civil Commitment in the Psychiatric Emergency Room,* 45 ARCHIVES GEN. PSYCHIATRY 753 (1988) (clinicians' rating of danger and grave disability under legalistic statutes closely related to most severely ill on diagnostic and symptomatic assessments of mental disorder).

238. Hoffman & Foust, *supra* note 145, at 1126. To some extent, however, the neglect of the least restrictive alternative notion may be due to a belief that community resources are lacking and that hospitalization therefore represents the best alternative. Eric Turkheimer & Charles D. H. Parry, *Why the Gap? Practice and Policy in Civil Commitment Hearings,* 47 AM. PSYCHOLOGIST 646 (1992).

239. This thesis was suggested by Alan Stone, *Psychiatric Abuse and Legal Reform: Two Ways to Make a Bad Situation Worse,* 5 INT'L J. L. & PSYCHIATRY 9, 10–16 (1982).

Several studies seem to debunk the criminalization these. *See* Kenneth L. Appelbaum et al., *Are Pretrial Commitments for Forensic Evaluation Used to Control Nuisance Behavior?*, 42 HOSP. & COMMUNITY PSYCHIATRY 603 (1992); Virginia Hiday, *Civil Commitment and Arrests: An Investigation of the Criminalization Thesis*, 180 J. NERVOUS MENTAL DISORDER 184 (1992); Thomas M. Arvanites, *A Comparison of Civil Patients and Incompetent Defendants: Pre and Post Deinstitutionalization*, 18 BULL. AM. ACAD. PSYCHIATRY & L. 393 (1990). Linda A. Teplin, *The Criminalization Hypothesis: Myth, Misnomer, or Management Strategy*, LAW & MENTAL HEALTH: MAJOR DEVELOPMENTS AND RESEARCH NEEDS 149 (Saleem Shah & Bruce D. Sales eds. 1991).

240. *See generally* John Thibaut & Laurens Walker, *A Theory of Procedure*, 66 CAL. L. REV. 541 (1978).

241. *See generally* the studies cited *supra* notes 231 & 236.

The Supreme Court acknowledged the research on the sloppiness of commitment procedures in Parham v. J.R., 442 U.S. 584, 609 (1979), but curiously used the literature to support *loosening* of procedural rigor. The Court suggested that the "illusory" nature of civil commitment made the hearing nothing more than "time-consuming procedural minuets" unworthy of judges' and clinicians' time. *Id.* at 605. Morse has also concluded that legalization of civil commitment has not, and will not, result in formal, adversary procedures and adequate rigor of legal decisionmaking. However, he reaches a policy conclusion opposite to that of the Supreme Court. Rather than accept an inherent, intolerably high number of erroneous commitments, he argues that civil commitment should simply be abolished. Morse, *supra* note 10, at 67–79.

242. Stier & Stoebe, *supra* note 236.

243. *See, e.g.*, Naomi Leavitt & Patricia L. Maykuth, *Conformance to Attorney Performance Standards: Advocacy Behavior in a Maximum Security Prison Hospital*, 13 LAW & HUM. BEHAV. 217 (1989) (competency of representation in civil commitment cases substantially lower than in criminal commitment cases, even after implementation of attorney performance standards defining minimally adequate representation); Charles D. Parry & Eric Turkheimer, *Length of Hospitalization and Outcome of Commitment and Recommitment Hearings*, 43 HOSP. & COMMUNITY PSYCHIATRY 65 (1992) (focusing on recommitment hearings); the articles by Hiday, *supra* note 236; Wexler & Scoville, *supra* note 236; Elliott Andalman & David Chambers, *Effective Counsel for Persons Facing Civil Commitment: A Survey, a Polemic, and a Proposal*, 45 MISS. L.J. 43 (1974); Fred Cohen, *The Function of the Attorney and the Commitment of the Mentally Ill*, 44 TEX. L. REV. 424 (1966); State *ex rel.* Memmel v. Mundy, 75 Wis. 2d 276, 249 N.W.2d 573 (1977).

244. Israel Zwerling et al., *"No-Commitment Week": A Feasibility Study*, 135 AM. J. PSYCHIATRY 1198 (1978).

245. As Perlin has stated, "[I]n some instances where mental health reform legislation does not meet the paternalistic needs of mental health professionals, the statutes are simply subverted." Michael Perlin, *Morality and Pretextuality, Psychiatry and Law: Of "Ordinary Common Sense,"*

Heuristic Reasoning, and Cognitive Dissonance, 19 BULL AM. ACAD. PSYCHIATRY & L. 131, 139 (1991). Perlin cites Bagby & Atkinson, *supra* note 229, at 28, and Bagby et al., *Effects of Mental Health Legislative Reform in Ontario*, 28 CAN. PSYCHOL. 21 (1987). Of course, this subversion could not take place without the acquiescence of the legal profession. *See also* Charles Lidz et al., *Civil Commitment: The Consistency of Clinicians and the Use of Legal Standards*, 146 AM. J. PSYCHIATRY 176 (1989) (finding that danger to self or others and grave disability accounted for only about 70% of commitments).

246. Norman Poythress, *Psychiatric Expertise in Civil Commitment: Training Attorneys to Cope with Expert Testimony*, 2 LAW & HUM. BEHAV. 1 (1978). *See also* Leavitt & Maykuth, *supra* note 243.

247. *See, e.g.*, Stone, *supra* note 239, at 19. In extemporaneous remarks at the Sixth International Symposium on Law and Psychiatry, University of Virginia, June 13, 1981, Seymour Halleck, a well-known scholar in forensic psychiatry at the University of North Carolina, argued that psychiatric residents should not be permitted to commit patients. Halleck's reasoning was that the experience is corrupting, in that it teaches psychiatry as social control rather than as healing, and may predispose some psychatrists to the expression of power for its own sake.

248. Scott M. Reichlin & Joseph D. Bloom, *Effects of Publicity on a Forensic Hospital*, 21 BULL. AM. ACAD. PSYCHIATRY & L. 475 (1993); Norman Poythress & Stanley L. Brodsky, *In the Wake of a Negligent Release Law Suit: An Investigation of Professional Consequence and Institutional Impact on a State Psychiatric Hospital*, 16 LAW & HUM. BEHAV. 155 (1992).

249. Charles Kiesler, *Mental Hospitals and Alternative Care: Noninstitutionalization as Potential Public Policy for Mental Patients*, 37 AM. PSYCHOLOGIST 349, at 359 (1982).

250. *Id.*

251. *Id.* at 357–58.

252. *Id.* at 357.

253. *Id.* at 358–59.

254. It does not appear that this class of people was directly studied by the research reported in Kiesler, given the likelihood that few courts would have allowed such persons to be randomly assigned to an outpatient program. *See* Mark Mills & Bonnie Cummins, *Deinstitutionalization Reconsidered*, 5 INT'L J. L. & PSYCHIATRY 271, 276 (1982) (a review of studies concluding that the studies showing clearly favorable outcomes for community treatment had excluded the most severely disturbed patients, while those that included this group show community treatment was not as successful).

255. Mary Test, *Effective Treatment of the Chronically Mentally Ill: What Is Necessary*, 37 J. SOC. ISSUES 71, 82 (1981) (comprehensive community services can eliminate the need for hospitalization "for all but 15 to 25%" of chronically ill individuals).

256. *See* Morse, *supra* note 10, at 79–84. For a discussion of the types of inpatient programs most likely to benefit persons with serious mental illness, see Gordon L. Paul & Anthony A. Menditto, *Effectiveness of Inpatient*

Treatment Programs for Mentally Ill Adults in Public Psychiatric Facilities, 1 APPLIED & PREVENTIVE PSYCHOL. 41 (1992).

257. *Id. See also* Frank Johnson, *The Constitution and the Federal District Judge,* 54 TEX. L. REV. 903, 909 (1976) (discussing the recalcitrance of Alabama authorities in implementing a court order to provide humane care and treatment).

258. State hospitals are generally perceived as undesirable places in which to work, and financial inducements alone have often failed to facilitate recruitment and retention of professional staff for state hospitals. Stonewall Stickney, Wyatt v. Stickney; *Background and Postscript,* in THE RIGHT TO TREATMENT FOR MENTAL PATIENTS 29, 39–41 (Stuart E. Golann & William Fremouw eds. 1976); Stone, *supra* note 239, at 20–21.

259. E. Fuller Torrey & Robert L. Taylor, *Cheap Labor from Poor Nations,* 130 AM. J. PSYCHIATRY 428 (1973).

260. *See generally* ERVING GOFFMAN, ESSAYS ON THE SOCIAL SITUATION OF MENTAL PATIENTS AND OTHER INMATES (1961); Michael S. Goldstein, *The Sociology of Mental Health and Illness,* 5 ANN. REV. SOC. 381 (1979).

261. *Cf.* American Psychological Association, *Ethical Principles of Psychologists,* 36 AM. PSYCHOLOGIST 633 (1981), Principles 1f, 3c, and 8c, discussed generally in § 4.05(a).

262. *See generally* ALTERNATIVES TO MENTAL HOSPITAL TREATMENT (Leonard I. Stein & Mary Ann Test eds. 1978); Kiesler, *supra* note 249; Morse, *supra* note 10, at 84–87 and accompanying citations.

263. *See* Kiesler, *supra* note 228, at 1331.

264. *See* Lynn Kahle & Bruce Sales, *Due Process of Law and the Attitudes of Professionals Toward Civil Commitment,* in NEW DIRECTIONS IN PSYCHOLOGICAL RESEARCH 265 (Paul Lipsitt & Bruce Sales eds. 1979).

265. Charles Kiesler, *Mental Health Policy as a Field of Inquiry for Psychology,* 35 AM. PSYCHOLOGIST 1066, 1073–74 (1980).

266. *See, e.g.,* Zander, *supra* note 236, at 523, 524–26, 530–31, 539–42, 549–51, 552–54 (describing civil commitment hearings in Dane County, Wisconsin).

267. *See* David Wexler, *The Structure of Civil Commitment: Patterns, Pressures, and Interactions in Mental Health Legislation,* 7 LAW & HUM. BEHAV. 1 (1983).

268. *See* studies cited *supra* note 236.

269. AMERICAN BAR ASSOCIATION, MODEL CODE OF PROFESSIONAL RESPONSIBILITY Canon 7.

270. In their role as "counselors," attorneys often themselves define the course that clients should follow. *See generally* DOUGLAS ROSENTHAL, LAWYER AND CLIENT: WHO'S IN CHARGE? (1974).

271. AMERICAN BAR ASSOCIATION, MODEL CODE OF PROFESSIONAL RESPONSIBILITY, Ethical Consideration (EC) 7–11.

272. *Id.,* EC 7–12.

273. *See, e.g.,* Samuel Brakel, *Legal Schizophrenia and the Mental Health Lawyer: Recent Trends in Civil Commitment Litigation,* 6 BEHAVIORAL SCI. & L. 3 (1988); Samuel Brakel, *Legal Aid in Mental Hospitals,* 1981 A.B.F. RES. J. 21 (1981); Robert H. Woody, *Public Policy and Legal Aid in Mental Hospitals: The Dimensions of the Problem and Their Im-*

plications for Legal Education and Practice, 1982 A.B.F. RES. J. 237 (1982).

274. *See* John J. Ensminger & Thomas D. Liguori, *The Therapeutic Significance of the Civil Commitment Hearing: An Unexplored Potential,* 6 J. PSYCHIATRY & L. 5 (1978). *See also* Tom R. Tyler, *The Psychological Consequences of Judicial Procedures: Implications for Civil Commitment Hearings,* 46 SMU L. REV. 433 (1992). *But see* Sumner J. Sydeman et al., *Procedural Justice in the Context of Civil Commitment: A Critique of Tyler's Analysis,* 3 PSYCHOL. PUB. POL'Y & L. (in press).

275. *See* MICHAEL SAKS & REID HASTIE, SOCIAL PSYCHOLOGY IN COURT 119–33 (1978).

276. WEXLER, *supra* note 36, at 99.

277. *See, e.g.,* *Preparation and Trial of a Civil Commitment Case,* 5 MENTAL DISABILITY L. REP. 201, 281 (1981); Christopher Slobogin, *The Attorney's Role in Civil Commitment,* 1 MENTAL HEALTH LEGAL STUD. CTR. NEWSL. 1, 2 (1979).

278. ARIZ. REV. STAT. ANN. § 36-537.

279. The Division of Mental Health Advocacy in the Department of the Public Advocate in New Jersey exemplifies the utility of integrating mental health professionals with legal aid for the mentally disabled. *See* Perlin, *supra* note 94, at 156.

280. *See* Robert Farrell, *The Right of an Indigent Civil Commitment Defendant to Psychiatric Assistance of His Choice at State Expense,* 11 IDAHO L. REV. 141 (1975). *But see In re Gannon,* 123 N.J. Super. 104, 301 A.2d 493 (Somerset Co. 1973).

281. WILLIAM J. FREMOUW ET AL., SUICIDE RISK: ASSESSMENT AND RESPONSE GUIDELINES (1990) [hereinafter SUICIDE RISK]; ASSESSMENT AND PREDICTION OF SUICIDE (Ronald W. Maris et al. eds. 1992) [hereinafter ASSESSMENT AND PREDICTION]; SUICIDE: GUIDELINES FOR ASSESSMENT, MANAGEMENT AND TREATMENT (Bruce Bongar ed. 1992) [hereinafter GUIDELINES].

282. *See* SUICIDE RISK, *supra* note 281, chs. 3–5, 7.

283. David C. Clark & Jan Fawcett, *Review of Empirical Risk Factors for Evaluation of the Suicidal Patient,* in GUIDELINES, *supra* note 281, at 16–48.

284. For literature on suicide in children and adolescents, *see* Mae. E. Sokol & Cynthia R. Pfeffer, *Suicidal Behavior of Children,* in GUIDELINES, *supra* note 281, at 69–83; Alan L. Berman & David A. Jobes, *Suicidal Behavior of Adolescents,* in GUIDELINES, *supra* note 281, at 84–105; Madelyn S. Gould et al., *The Clinical Prediction of Adolescent Suicide,* in ASSESSMENT AND PREDICTION, *supra* note 281, at 130–44.

285. SUICIDE RISK, *supra* note 281, at 35, Table 4.1.

286. Based on data from the National Center for Health Statistics presented by Clark & Fawcett, *supra* note 283, at 17, Table 2.1, the 1989 data regarding suicide in the United States showed an annual rate of 19.9 per 100,000 for men, compared to only 4.8 per 100,000 for women.

287. Clark & Fawcett, *supra* note 283, at 17.

288. It has been suggested that age-related risk differences as calculated from 1980s epidemiological data are "slight" compared to earlier years' data, leading to the

conclusion that "[t]oday the age of the person being evaluated contributes little useful information to the estimation of suicide risk." *Id.*

289. *Id.* The authors cite data from Normal Kreitman, *Suicide, Age, and Marital Status,* 18 PSYCHOL. MED. 121 (1988) showing that, among marital categories, the highest suicide rate is among young persons who are recently widowed, but that this association attenuates with age. They also argue that *"marital status* functions as a proxy for the variable *responsibility for children under age 18 years,"* and that these responsibilities (not marital status) are associated with lower risk. *Id.*

290. *Id.* at 18–19. The authors note further that perhaps as many as two-thirds of people who meet diagnostic criteria for psychiatric illness never contact a mental health professional or seek services, and that 43–48% of persons who die by suicide have never seen a mental health professional in their lives. *Id.* at 20–21.

291. SUICIDE RISK, *supra* note 281, at 24, Table 3.1.

292. *Id.*

293. Clark & Fawcett, *supra* note 283, at 34, Table 2.5.

294. *Id.* at 38, Table 2.6.

295. *Id.*

296. *Id.* at 40, Table 2.7.

297. *Id.* at 40.

298. *Id.*

299. *Id.* at 31.

300. SUICIDE RISK, *supra* note 281, at 39.

301. William A. Scheftner et al., *Family History and Five-Year Suicide Risk,* 153 BRIT. J. PSYCHIATRY 805 (1988).

302. Clark & Fawcett, *supra* note 283, at 38.

303. "The interviewer who has a matter-of-fact approach about morbid and suicidal thinking makes it easier for the patient to volunteer information and probably elicits more complete data." *Id.* at 22.

304. SUICIDE RISK, *supra* note 281, at 43–44.

305. These measures and interpretation of scores regarding risk level are discussed in SUICIDE RISK, *supra* note 281, ch. 5. *See also* Joseph M. Rothberg & Carol Geer-Williams, *A Comparison and Review of Suicide Prediction Scales,* in ASSESSMENT AND PREDICTION, *supra* note 281, at 202.

306. Clark & Fawcett, *supra* note 283, at 26–27 [Emphasis in original].

307. Betsy S. Comstock, *Decision to Hospitalize and Alternatives to Hospitalization,* in GUIDELINES, *supra* note 281, at 207.

308. *Id.* at 210–11.

309. Alex D. Pokorny, *Prediction of Suicide in Psychiatric Patients: A Prospective Study,* 40 ARCH. GEN. PSYCHIATRY 249, 257 (1983).

310. *Id.* at 255.

311. *Id.*

312. *See, e.g.,* NEB. REV. STAT. § 83-1009.

313. *See, e.g.,* CAL. WELF. INST. CODE §§ 5350, ¶ 5371.

314. Issues in the use of guardianship are discussed in Phillip Massad & Bruce Sales, *Guardianship: An Alternative to Institutionalization?,* 24 AM. BEHAV. SCIENTIST 755 (1981).

315. For a review of this literature, *see* Randy K. Otto, *Prediction of Dangerous Behavior: A Review and Analysis of "Second-Generation" Research,* 5 FORENSIC REPORTS 103 (1992).

316. Charles W. Lidz et al., *The Accuracy of Predictions of Violence to Others,* 269 J. AM. MED. ASS'N 1007 (1993) (47% false positives). One earlier study found young male paranoid schizophrenics admitted on an emergency basis to be especially prone to violence in the hospital, regardless of whether they had committed an overt violent act prior to admission. Ethan Rofman et al., *The Prediction of Dangerous Behavior in Emergency Civil Commitment,* 137 AM. J. PSYCHIATRY 1061 (1980). However, that conclusion must be tempered by acknowledgment of serious methodological problems with the study. *See* Loren Roth, *Dangerousness: In the Eye of the Beholder?,* 138 AM. J. PSYCHIATRY 995 (1981). In a better-designed study of short-term predictions of violent behavior, Werner, Rose, Yesavage, and Seeman found that psychiatrists' predictions were not significantly correlated with the actual assaultiveness of patients in the hospital. Paul Werner et al., *Psychiatrists' Judgments of Dangerousness in Patients on an Acute Care Unit,* 141 AM. J. PSYCHIATRY 263 (1984).

317. *See, e.g.,* People v. Keith, 38 Ill. 2d 405, 410–11, 231 N.E.2d 387, 390 (1967).

318. The Supreme Court rejected a definitive link between the Fifth Amendment and criminal proceedings in *In re* Gault, 387 U.S. 1, 49 (1967): "[T]he availability of the privilege does not turn upon the type of proceeding in which its protection is invoked, but upon the nature of the statement or admission and the exposure which it invites. The privilege may, for example, be claimed in a civil or administrative proceeding, if the statement is or may be inculpatory." However, this language was rejected in Allen v. Illinois, 478 U.S. 364 (1986) [discussed in § 4.02(d)].

319. Andersen v. Maryland, 427 U.S. 463, 475 (1976); Bellis v. United States, 417 U.S. 85, 88 (1974); United States v. White, 322 U.S. 694, 698 (1944).

320. The imposition of sanctions for refusing to talk in civil commitment hearings is problematic. For example, should a mute catatonic person be held in contempt of court? *Cf.* Christopher Slobogin, Estelle v. Smith: *The Constitutional Contours of the Forensic Evaluation,* 32 EMORY L.J. 71, 103–06 (1982).

321. *See Preparation and Trial of a Civil Commitment Case,* 5 MENTAL DISABILITY L. REP. 201, 205–06 (1981), and cases cited therein.

322. As indicated in § 10.04(a)(1), even under relatively legalistic statutes there may be no right to counsel at the temporary detention hearing. *See, e.g.,* VA. CODE ANN. § 37.1-67.3. Under "medical" statutes, there may be a right to consult counsel after admission but no automatic appointment of counsel. *See, e.g.,* N.Y. MENTAL HYGIENE LAW § 9.07.

323. State statutes may require the presentation of information about the process and rights within it. Regardless, though, such "warnings" are ethically required. *See* American Psychological Association, *supra* note 261, Principles 6 and 8A [§ 4.05(d)]. In presenting the rele-

vant information, clinicians should try to ensure that, insofar as possible, respondents actually understand the rights and their applicability in their own cases. Too frequently, clinicians obey the letter but not the spirit of the law through rote recitation of rights and subtle coercion to cooperate. *See generally* CHARLES LIDZ ET AL., INFORMED CONSENT: A STUDY OF DECISIONMAKING IN PSYCHIATRY (1984).

324. *See In re* Scott L., 469 A.2d 1336 (N.H. 1983).

325. Ensminger & Liguori, *supra* note 274, at 21.

326. *Cf.* Stone, *supra* note 8, at 19–20. Because the "prescreener" is based in a community mental health center, he or she can be especially important in making the proper links among prehospital community-based care, the hospital, and community-based aftercare.

327. *See* Wexler, *supra* note 267.

328. 442 U.S. 584 (1979).

329. *See* JANE KNITZER, UNCLAIMED CHILDREN: THE FAILURE OF PUBLIC RESPONSIBILITY TO CHILDREN AND ADOLESCENTS IN NEED OF MENTAL HEALTH SERVICES 54–57, 113–29 (1982); Perlin, *supra* note 94, at 150.

330. Melton, *supra* note 94; Perlin *supra* note 94. *See also* Gail S. Perry & Gary B. Melton, *Precedential Value of Judicial Notice of Social Facts:* Parham *as an Example*, 22 J. FAM. L. (1984); James Ellis, *Volunteering Children: Parental Commitment of Minors to Mental Institutions*, 62 CAL. L. REV. 840 (1974).

331. *See, e.g.*, J.L. v. Parham, 412 F. Supp. 112, 124 (M.D. Ga. 1976); KNITZER, *supra* note 329, at 11–12 nn. 23, 46; Robin S. Barack, *Hospitalization of Emotionally Disturbed Children: Who Gets Hospitalized and Why*, 56 AM. J. ORTHOPSYCHIATRY 317 (1986) (no differences in diagnosis, academic achievement, intellectual functioning and gender between inpatients and special-class students; the key difference was that, for the former group, a critical event had occurred within a month prior to admission).

332. *See, e.g.*, KNITZER, *supra* note 329, at 11 n. 21.

333. *See, e.g.*, 412 F. Supp. at 112, 124; L. OLSON, A POINT IN TIME STUDY OF CHILDREN AND ADOLESCENTS IN STATE HOSPITALS 5 (1981).

334. *See generally* KNITZER, *supra* note 329, at 67–78. *See also infra* note 334.

335. Herbert Quay, *Residential Treatment*, in PSYCHOPATHOLOGICAL DISORDERS OF CHILDHOOD 387, 390 (Herbert Quay & John S. Werry eds. 2d ed. 1979); Bertrand Winsberg et al., *Home vs. Hospital Care of Children with Behavior Disorders: A Controlled Investigation*, 37 ARCHIVES GEN. PSYCHIATRY 413 (1980).

336. *See* Robert Miller & Emmet Kenney, *Adolescent Delinquency and the Myth of Hospital Treatment*, 12 CRIME DELINQ. 38 (1966).

337. Highly intrusive treatments are common in some residential schools and group homes. *See, e.g.*, Milonas v. Williams, 691 F.2d 941 (10th Cir. 1982).

338. There is evidence that, as juvenile justice standards tighten, juvenile mental health admissions increase. *See* Carol Warren, *New Forms of Social Control: The Myth of Deinstitutionalization*, 24 AM. BEHAV. SCIENTIST 724 (1981).

339. Many hospitalized youth are wards of the state.

The lack of accountability of their guardians is well documented. *See, e.g.*, Malcolm Bush & Andrew Gordon, *Client Choice and Bureaucratic Accountability: Possibilities for Responsiveness in a Social Welfare Bureaucracy*, 34(4) J. SOC. ISSUES 22 (1978).

340. *See* Perlin, *supra* note 94, at 156–60.

341. 445 U.S. 480 (1980).

342. *Id.* at 568–70.

343. *Id.* at 567–70.

344. *See, e.g.*, Michael Churgin, *The Transfer of Inmates to Mental Health Facilities: Developments in the Law*, in MENTALLY DISORDERED OFFENDERS: PERSPECTIVES FROM LAW AND SOCIAL SCIENCE 207, 219–23 (John Monahan & Henry Steadman eds. 1983).

345. AMERICAN BAR ASSOCIATION, CRIMINAL JUSTICE MENTAL HEALTH STANDARDS, standard 7-10.5 (1984) [hereinafter STANDARDS].

346. *Id.*

347. *See* Churgin, *supra* note 344, at 226–27.

348. GARY MELTON ET AL., COMMUNITY MENTAL HEALTH CENTERS AND THE COURTS: AN EVALUATION OF COMMUNITY-BASED FORENSIC SERVICES (1985); Robert J. Favole, *Mental Disability in the American Criminal Process: A Four Issue Survey*, in MENTALLY DISORDERED OFFENDERS: PERSPECTIVES FROM LAW AND SOCIAL SCIENCE 247, 283 (John Monahan & Henry Steadman eds. 1983) ("Only West Virginia and Indiana have statutes that seem sure to withstand a *Vitek*-type challenge"); Eliot Hartstone et al., Vitek *and Beyond: The Empirical Context of Prison-to-Hospital Transfers*, 45 LAW CONTEMP. PROBS. 125 (1982) (*Vitek* will have an impact only if Department of Corrections hospitals are included).

349. John Monahan et al., *Prisoners Transferred to Mental Hospitals*, in MENTALLY DISORDERED OFFENDERS: PERSPECTIVES FROM LAW AND SOCIAL SCIENCE 233 (John Monahan & Henry Steadman eds. 1983).

350. STANDARDS, *supra* note 345, standard 7-10.4.

351. *See* Estelle v. Gamble, 429 U.S. 97 (1976).

352. STANDARDS, *supra* note 345, standards 7-10.1 through 7-10.5.

353. In 1988, only 5% of American prisons provided treatment programs that included a therapeutic community. *See* Margaret Severson, *Redefining the Boundaries of Mental Health Services: A Holistic Approach to Inmate Mental Health*, 56 FEDERAL PROBATION 57 (1992).

354. *See* Loren Roth, *Correctional Psychiatry*, in MODERN LEGAL PSYCHIATRY AND FORENSIC SCIENCE 677, 684–87 (William J. Curran et al. eds. 1980).

355. *See* § 9.07(c)(3).

356. There are no formal studies on the treatment available in transfer facilities. However, Monahan and colleagues reported that their "impression from visiting several transfer facilities is that they are 'hospitals' in name only." Monahan et al., *supra* note 349, at 243. *See also supra* note 353.

357. *See, e.g.*, Appelbaum et al., *supra* note 239. William H. Snow & Katharine Briar, *The Convergence of the Mentally Disordered and the Jail Population*, 15 J. OFFENDER COUNSELING SERV. & REHAB. 147 (1990).

358. *See generally* National Institute of Health, DEVELOPING JAIL MENTAL HEALTH SERVICES: PRACTICES AND PRINCIPLES (1986).

359. Bette Runck, *NIMH Report: Study of 43 Jails Shows Mental Health Services and Inmate Safety Are Compatible,* 34 HOSP. & COMMUNITY PSYCHIATRY 1007 (1983).

360. For reviews, see Donald H.J. Hermann, *Assault on the Insanity Defense: Limitations on the Effectiveness and Effect of the Defense of Insanity,* 14 RUTGERS L.J. 241, 312–59 (1983); Grant Morris, *Acquittal by Reason of Insanity: Developments in the Law,* in MENTALLY DISORDERED OFFENDERS: PERSPECTIVES FROM LAW AND SOCIAL SCIENCE 65, 70–72 (John Monahan & Henry Steadman eds. 1983).

361. Hermann, *supra* note 360, at 329–59; Note, *Commitment Following an Insanity Acquittal,* 84 HARV. L. REV. 605 (1981).

362. Addington v. Texas, 441 U.S. 418 (1979).

363. *See* Hermann, *supra* note 360, at 337–38. This can be a significant difference when amorphous issues such as mental illness and dangerousness are involved. The ABA would place the burden on the state by clear and convincing evidence, as in civil commitment. STANDARDS, *supra* note 345, standard 7-7.4(b).

364. Note, *supra* note 361, at 605–07.

365. *Id.* at 339–42.

366. *In re* Franklin, 496 P.2d 465, 471 & n. 6 (Cal. 1972); Chase v. Kearns, 278 A.2d 132, 134 (Me. 1971); *In re* Lewis, 403 A.2d 1115, 1117 (Del. 1979).

367. In some jurisdictions, insanity acquittals occur most frequently in cases involving property crimes. *See, e.g.,* John Petrila, *The Insanity Defense and Other Mental Health Dispositions in Missouri,* 5 INT'L J.L. & PSYCHIATRY 81, 95 (1982); Rogers & Bloom, *supra* note 214, at 192.

368. Note, *Commitment and Release of Persons Found Not Guilty by Reason of Insanity: A Georgia Perspective,* 15 GA. L. REV. 1065, 1079 (1981) (the more serious antisocial behavior usually associated with criminal proceedings does not necessarily correlate with a greater likelihood of recidivism).

369. In such jurisdictions, a reasonable doubt as to sanity cannot be said to imply clear and convincing evidence of mental illness, even at the time of the offense.

370. 463 U.S. 354 (1983). For a critique of *Jones,* see Donald Hermann, *Automatic Commitment and Release of Insanity Acquittees: Constitutional Dimensions,* 14 RUTGERS L.J. 667 (1983); James Ellis, *The Consequences of the Insanity Defense: Proposals to Reform Post-Acquittal Commitment Law,* 35 CATH. U. L. REV. 961 (1986).

371. 463 U.S. at 364.

372. *Id.* at 366.

373. *Id.* at 368. The ABA would limit the length of criminal commitment to the maximum term the individual would have received had he or she been convicted. STANDARDS, *supra* note 345, standard 7-7.7. The acquittee may petition for release periodically; at these hearings, the *state* would bear the burden of proof. *Id.,* Standard 7-7.8.

374. 504 U.S. 71 (1992).

375. ___ U.S. ___ (decided June 23, 1997). *Hendricks* addressed the constitutionality of a sexual predator statute. *See* § 9.04(b). But its rationale seems applicable to insanity acquittees as well. Even if *Hendricks* does not apply and *Foucha* is construed to require both "serious" mental illness and dangerousness for commitment, if a diagnosis can be characterized as a mental disorder separate from a dangerousness finding (which is true even of the antisocial personality diagnosis at issue in *Foucha*), then proof of that diagnosis plus dangerousness could well satisfy *Foucha.*

376. Henry Steadman & Jeraldine Braff, *Defendants Not Guilty by Reason of Insanity,* in MENTALLY DISORDERED OFFENDERS: PERSPECTIVES FROM LAW AND SOCIAL SCIENCE 109, 118–19 (John Monahan & Henry Steadman eds. 1983) (citing several studies and noting a lack of "basic information"); Note, *supra* note 368, at 1079.

377. *See* BRAKEL ET AL., *supra* note 159, Table 205.

378. 113 S. Ct. 2637 (1993).

379. The Court also justified this holding by asserting that the extent of disability and dangerousness is easier to diagnose for mentally retarded people than for mentally ill people. Even if this were true, this reasoning directly contradicts the Court's reasoning in *Addington v. Texas* [see § 10.02(d)], where the Court justified a lower standard of proof for commitment because of the *difficulty* of making psychiatric judgments.

380. *See generally* Gunnar Dwybad & Stanley Herr, *Unnecessary Coercion: An End to Involuntary Civil Commitment of Retarded Persons,* 31 STAN. L. REV. 753 (1979).

381. FLA. STAT. § 393.063(23) (1986).

382. FLA. STAT. § 393.11(1)(c).

383. FLA. STAT. § 393.11(1)(b).

384. FLA. STAT. § 393.11(2)(c).

385. FLA. STAT. § 394.467(1)(a)(2).

386. FLA. STAT. § 393.115(1).

387. *See, e.g.,* United States v. Shorter, 343 A.2d 569, 571–72 (D.C. 1975).

388. James Ellis & Ruth Luckasson, *Mentally Retarded Criminal Defendants,* 53 GEO. WASH. L. REV. 414, 466–70 (1985).

389. STANDARDS, *supra* note 345, standards 7-7.4(b), 7-7.8.

390. Thomas L. Hafemeister & Ali J. Amirshahi, *Civil Commitment for Drug Dependency: The Judicial Response,* 26 LOY. L.A. L. REV. 39 n. 20 (1992).

391. In addition to Hafemeister & Amirshahi, *supra* note 390, a good source of information on these types of statutes, relied on below, is BRAKEL ET AL., *supra* note 159, at 41–43.

392. *See, e.g.,* the Federal Narcotic Addict Rehabilitation Act (NARA) of 1966, 42 U.S.C. §§ 3401–3442 (1988).

393. Ortega v. Rasor, 291 F. Supp. 748 (S.D. Fla. 1968). *See also* Lolley v. Charter Woods Hosp., 572 So. 2d 1223 (Ala. 1990); *In re* Redcloud, 359 N.W.2d 710 (Minn. Ct. App. 1984).

394. *See, e.g., In re* Stokes, 546 A.2d 356 (D.C. 1988);

Dudley v. State *ex rel.* Dudley, 730 S.W.2d 51 (Tex. 1987).

395. WEXLER, *supra* note 36, at 37–39.

396. *Id.* at 42–44.

397. *Id.* at 39.

398. For a summary of research on the effectiveness of treatment of drug addicts, *see* Larry Gostin, *An Alternative Public Health Vision for a National Drug Strategy: "Treatment Works,"* 28 HOUS. L. REV. 285, 299–302 (1991).

Chapter 11

1. *President's Commission for the Study of Ethical Problems in Medicine and Biomedical and Behavioral Research,* 1 MAKING HEALTH CARE DECISIONS 44–45 (1982).

2. Even John Stuart Mill, who generally believed that the power of the government should be strictly curtailed, agreed that these two exceptions, narrowly defined, were necessary. *John Stuart Mill, On Liberty,* in THE PHILOSOPHY OF JOHN STUART MILL 196–97 (1961); Mary Ellen Waithe, *Why Mill Was For Paternalism,* 6 INT'L J. L. & PSYCHIATRY 101 (1983).

3. *See, e.g.,* Loren Roth et al., *Tests of Competency to Consent to Treatment,* 134 AM. J. PSYCHIATRY 279 (1997).

4. James F. Drane, *The Many Faces of Competency,* THE HASTINGS CENTER REP. 17 (April, 1985).

5. Elyn Saks, *Competency to Refuse Treatment,* 69 N.C. L. REV. 945, 995 (1991).

6. *Id.* at 997.

7. The history of guardianship law is reviewed in John Regan, *Protective Services for the Elderly: Commitment, Guardianship, and Alternatives,* 13 WM. & MARY L. REV. 569, 570–73 (1972).

8. *See In re* Gault, 387 U.S. 1, 16–17 (1967).

9. All but seven states and the District of Columbia distinguish between guardianship (conservatorship) of the estate and guardianship of the person. BRUCE D. SALES ET AL., DISABLED PERSONS AND THE LAW: STATE LEGISLATIVE ISSUES 461 (1982).

10. CAL. WELF. INST. CODE §§ 5350–71.

11. According to Tor and Sales, "the legal distinction between plenary and limited guardianship [is] well entrenched today." Phillip B. Tor & Bruce D. Sales, *A Social Science Perspective on the Law of Guardianship: Directions for Improving the Process and Practice,* 18 PSYCHOL. & L. REV. 1, 26 (1994). *See also* John Parry & Sally Balch Hurme, *Guardianship Monitoring and Enforcement Nationwide,* 15 MENTAL & PHYSICAL DISABILITY L. REP. 304 (1991).

12. Lawrence Friedman & Mark Savage, *Taking Care: The Law of Conservatorship in California,* 61 S. CAL. L. REV. 273, 283 (1988); Roger Peters et al., *Guardianship of the Elderly in Tallahassee, Florida,* 25 GERONTOLOGIST 532, 536 (1985); Lawrence Frolik, *Plenary Guardianship: An Analysis, A Critique and a Proposal for Reform,* 23 ARIZ. L. REV. 599, 653 (1981); MELVIN T. AXILBUND, EXERCISING JUDGEMENT FOR THE DISABLED; REPORT OF AN INQUIRY INTO LIMITED GUARDIANSHIP, PUBLIC GUARDIANSHIP AND PROTECTIVE SERVICES IN SIX STATES (ABA Commission on the Mentally Disabled ed. 1979);

13. Tor & Sales, *supra* note 11, at 27–28.

14. *See generally* CHILDREN'S COMPETENCE TO CONSENT (Gary B. Melton et al. eds. 1983) [hereinafter CHIL-

DREN'S COMPETENCE]; Gary B. Melton, *Toward "Personhood" for Adolescents: Autonomy and Privacy as Values in Public Policy,* 38 AM. PSYCHOLOGIST 99 (1983).

15. For example, minors generally are unable to enter contracts, except for "necessaries." *See, e.g.,* Halbam v. Lemke, 99 Wis. 2d 241, 298 N.W. 2d 562 (1980).

16. Some states have enacted provisions providing provisions for minors' independent consent to treatment. *See generally* Walter J. Wadlington, *Consent for Medical Care for Minors: The Legal Framework,* in CHILDREN'S COMPETENCE, *supra* note 14, at 57.

17. A special showing that the minor is "mature" will often be required before he or she is permitted to exercise self-determination. *See* Walter Wadlington, *Minors and Health Care: The Age of Consent,* 73 OSGOODE HALL L.J. 115 (1973). The mature-minor rule has had its most controversial application in abortion law. *See* Gary Melton, *Minors and Privacy: Are Legal and Psychological Concepts Compatible?,* 62 NEB. L. REV. 455, 463–72 (1983).

18. SALES ET AL., *supra* note 9, at 464.

19. *See, e.g.,* Parham v. J.R., 442 U.S. 182 (1979). *But see* WALTER WADLINGTON ET AL., CHILDREN IN THE LEGAL SYSTEM 182 (1983) (noting that assumptions about the "natural bonds of affection" in Blackstone and Kent refer to the treatment of bastards).

20. *See* SALES ET AL., *supra* note 9, at 13–14; B. ENNIS & L. SIEGEL, THE RIGHTS OF MENTAL PATIENTS; THE BASIC ACLU GUIDE TO MENTAL PATIENT'S RIGHTS 74–77 (1973).

21. SAMUEL BRAKEL ET AL., THE MENTALLY DISABLED AND THE LAW 258–59 (1985).

22. See SALES ET AL., *supra* note 9, at 462.

23. *See supra* note 10.

24. SALES ET AL., *supra* note 9, at 463.

25. As Alexander and Lewin state: "Dependents institute proceedings to secure their needs. Co-owners of property find incompetency proceedings convenient ways to secure the sale of realty. Heirs institute actions to preserve their dwindling inheritances. Beneficiaries of trusts or estates seek incompetency as an expedient method of removing as trustee one who is managing the trust or estate in a manner adverse to their interests. All of these motives may be honest and without any intent to cheat . . . , but none of the proceedings are commenced to assist the debilitated." GEORGE J. ALEXANDER & TRAVIS H.D. LEWIN, THE AGED AND THE NEED FOR SURROGATE MANAGEMENT 135 (1972).

26. Regan, *supra* note 7, at 605.

27. *See, e.g.,* Guardianship of Roe, 383 Mass. 45, 421 N.E.2d 40 (1981), in which the court justified a rejection of the clear and convincing standard of proof used in civil

commitment in favor of the lower preponderance standard with the following language: "We do not feel that more harm will befall an individual who is erroneously subjected to guardianship than to an individual who is in need of a guardian but is erroneously denied one. If an individual is erroneously subjected to a guardianship, then [state law] allows such a ward to file a petition for the removal of his guardian." *Id.* at 47. The latter statement is disingenuous at best, in light of the evidence. *See infra* notes 35–38 and accompanying text.

See also Rud v. Dahl, 4578 F.2d 674, 679 (7th Cir. 1978), where the court stated that counsel is not required because "the nature of the intrusion on liberty interests from an adjudication of incompetency is far less than the intrusion resulting from other types of proceedings in which the presence of counsel has been mandated." Of course, in those states in which a guardian can commit the ward, this statement is patently false. The court also concluded, in somewhat circular reasoning, that counsel was not needed because the rules of evidence did not apply at guardianship proceedings and because mandatory appointment of counsel would dissipate the ward's assets.

28. In a study conducted by the Associated Press of 2,200 guardianship files from numerous jurisdictions, allegations were found to be absent in one out of three files. Associated Press Special Report, *Guardians of the Elderly: An Ailing System,* L.A. TIMES, Sept. 27, 1987, at 2, 20, 28 (describing study) (hereinafter AP Study).

29. Regan, *supra* note 7, at 605–06; AP Study, *supra* note 28 (only 14 states require that notification of a proceeding include information about the proposed wards' rights to oppose the petition and the rights they may lose); Peters et al., *supra* note 12, at 535.

30. *See, e.g.*, Rud v. Dahl, 578 F.2d 674, 679 (7th Cir. 1978); AP Study, *supra* note 28 (legal representation is absent in a majority of cases, is not mandated in a number of states and is discretionary with the judge in others); Richard R. Pleak & Paul Appelbaum, *The Clinician's Role in Protecting Patients' Rights in Guardianship Proceedings*, 36 HOSP. & COMMUNITY PSYCHIATRY 77, 78 (1985) (in none of 27 guardianship proceedings observed was counsel present); Friedman & Savage, *supra* note 12, at 283 (only 16 to 44% are represented during guardianship process).

31. SALES ET AL., *supra* note 9, at 463 (22 states provide the respondent with a right to a jury).

32. The right to be present is guaranteed in only 38 states, *id.*, and that right is often waivable with only a doctor's certificate that the respondent is unable to attend. *See also* AP Study, *supra* note 28 (only a small percentage of guardianship records indicated that elderly wards attended their hearings).

33. At least one study has found that attorneys in guardianship proceedings saw their roles as investigators, not as advocates. Kris Bulcroft et al., *Elderly Wards and Their Legal Guardians: Analysis of County Probate Records in Ohio and Washington,* 31 GERONTOLOGIST 156, 157 (1991). This result is not surprising given analogous results in studies observing attorneys at commitment proceedings. See § 10.05(c).

34. A number of states provide for court-appointed

guardians *ad litem* in place of, or in addition to, the respondent's attorney. Judith McCue, *The States Are Acting to Reform Their Guardianship Statutes,* TRUSTS & ESTATES 32 (July, 1992), *cited* in Tor & Sales, *supra* note 11, at 23. One study in Illinois confirmed that court-appointed guardians *ad litem* will often make recommendations to which the proposed ward is opposed. Madelyn A. Iris, *Guardianship and the Elderly: A Multi-Perspective View of the Decisionmaking Process,* 28 GERONTOLOGIST 39 (1988).

35. SALES ET AL., *supra* note 9, at 464.

36. In the AP study, only 16% of the files contained annual reports mandated by statute. AP study, *supra* note 28. Another survey found that more than one-third of the jurisdictions surveyed failed to take action against guardians who failed to file periodic reports. Parry & Hurme, *supra* note 11, at 305. A third study found that many judges, court personnel and guardians are not even aware of the monitoring requirements. Sally B. Hurme, STEPS TO ENHANCE GUARDIANSHIP MONITORING 17, *cited* in Tor & Sales, *supra* note 11, at 31.

37. "In a study of 200 wards with public guardians, competency was restored to only four, possibly because the files for these cases were the few with up-to-date status reports." Tor & Sales, *supra* note 11, at 25.

38. *Id.* at 24.

39. A review of standards as of 1993 is found in Phillip Tor, *Finding Incompetency in Guardianship: Standardizing the Process*, 35 ARIZ. L. REV. 739 (1993). *See also* Dorothy Siemon et al., *Public Guardianship: What It Is and What Does It Mean,* 27 CLEARINGHOUSE REV. 588, 590–93 (1993) (tables).

40. George Alexander, *Premature Probate: A Different Perspective on Guardianship for the Elderly,* 31 STAN. L. REV. 1003, 1015–16 (1979).

41. NATIONAL CONFERENCE OF COMMISSIONERS ON UNIFORM STATE LAW, UNIFORM PROBATE CODE § 5 (4th ed. 1975).

42. *In re* Boyer, 646 P.2d 1085 (Utah 1981).

43. Bobbe S. Nolan, *Functional Evaluation of the Elderly in Guardianship Proceedings,* 12 L. MED. & HEALTH CARE 210 (1984).

44. Cal. Code § 5350.

45. N.H. REV. STATE. ANN. § 464–1:2 (VII) (1992).

46. In re Oltmer, 336 N.W.2d 560 (Neb. 1983).

47. *Id.* at 562 (Krivosha, C.J., Caporale, J., dissenting).

48. Plumer v. Early, 190 Cal. Rptr. 578 (3d Dist. 1983).

49. Tor, *supra* note 39, at 752. In those states that do, examination is often supposed to be by a physician, although in some states a psychologist or a multidisciplinary team may conduct it. SALES ET AL., *supra* note 9, at 463.

50. AP Study, *supra* note 28 (of 2,200 randomly sampled files, only 2 of 3 had such evidence).

51. H. Russel Searight et al., *The Community Competence Scale: Preliminary Reliability and Validity,* 11 AM. J. COMMUNITY PSYCHOLOGY 609 (1983). *See also* T. Anderton, *The Elderly, Incompetency, and Guardianship* (unpublished M.S. thesis, St. Louis University, 1979) and Patricia A. Loeb, *Validity of the Community Competence Scale with the*

Elderly (unpublished Ph.D. dissertation, St. Louis University, 1983), cited in THOMAS GRISSO, EVALUATING COMPETENCIES: FORENSIC ASSESSMENTS AND INSTRUMENTS 297 (1986).

52. *E.g.*, "[t]he CCS is in need of research showing that the scores on various competency subscales correspond to external indicators of the same specific functional abilities that the subscales claim to measure." GRISSO, *supra* note 51, at 301.

53. The instrument was derived from surveys of professionals and elderly nonprofessionals as to the components of competency for an elderly person. Anderton, *supra* note 51. This approach "provides the CCS with a firm base in terms of content validity." GRISSO, *supra* note 51, at 298.

54. The Multidimensional Functional Assessment Questionnaire and the Philadelphia Geriatric Center Multilevel Assessment Inventory, both developed for use with the elderly, are evaluated in GRISSO, *supra* note 51, at 284–95. *See also* Stephen J. Anderer, *A Model for Determining Competency* in *Guardianship Proceedings*, 14 MENTAL & PHYSICAL DISABILITY L. REP. 107 (1990); Arpiar G. Saunders & Mitchell M. Simon, *Individual Functional Assessment: An Instruction Manual*, 11 MENTAL & PHYSICAL DISABILITY L. REP. 60 (1987).

55. In the preliminary research for the CCS, the concept of competency to live in the community was found to be unitary, without differentiation of management of property and persons. Anderton, *supra* note 51.

56. For a discussion of the alternatives, *see* Robert Hodgson, *Guardianship of Mentally Retarded Persons: Three Approaches to a Long Neglected Problem*, 37 ALB. L. REV. 407 (1973). According to the Associated Press study of guardianship involving elderly wards, 70% of the guardians are family members. AP Study, *supra* note 28.

57. Frolik, *supra* note 12, at 646–49.

58. Consider, for example, the circumstance in which a wealthy elderly man takes a young woman as his paramour and wills most of his estate to her.

59. *See* Robert Wettstein & Loren Roth, *The Psychiatrist as Legal Guardian*, 145 AM. J. PSYCHIATRY 600 (1988).

60. *See, e.g.*, Rogers v. Comm'r, Dep't of Mental Health, 390 Mass. 489 (1983); *In re* Roe, 421 N.E.2d 40 (Mass. 1981); Saikewicz v. Superintendent of Belchertown State Hosp., 370 N.E.2d 417 (Mass. 1977); *In re* Grady, 426 (N.J. 1981); *In re* Quinlan, 335 A.2d 647 (N.J. 1976), *cert. denied*, 429 U.S. 922 (1976).

61. What could be called a third model involves having a court, rather than the guardian, apply one of these two tests. For instance, court permission is usually required for "extraordinary" interventions, such as sterilization. *See, e.g.*, *In re* Hayes, 93 Wash. 228, 608 P.2d 635 (1980). Courts are divided, however, as to whether hospitalization is an "extraordinary" intervention. *Compare*, *e.g.*, Von Luce v. Rankin, 588 S.W.2d 445 (Ark. 1979) (prohibiting a guardian from "volunteering in" a ward, at least if the ward protests), *with* Parham v. J.R., 442 U.S. 584 (1979) (permitting parents or state agency to "volunteer in" a child, at least if a mental health professional finds the child to be in need of treatment).

62. 497 U.S. 261 (1990).

63. *See, e.g.*, *In re* Jeffers, 606 N.E.2d 727 (Ill. Ct. App. 1992) (rejecting the substituted judgment test in the context of a guardian's consent to medicating the ward because "the incompetency of an incompetent person in a vegetative state does not lead him to pose a danger to himself or others while the incompetency of the mental health incompetent does[,] . . . the choices involved in the present case hold far less drastic consequences than the choices of a guardian on behalf of a person in a vegetative state[,] and . . . a person who suffers from mental incompetency might never have had the competency to make a reasoned decision regarding medication, as opposed to a person who lives in a vegetative coma)." *See also In re* Guardianship of L.W., 482 N.W.2d 60 (Wis. 1992).

64. *See* Gary Melton & Elizabeth Scott, *Evaluation of Mentally Retarded Persons for Sterilization: Contributions and Limits of Psychological Consultation*, 15 PROF. PSYCHOL.: RES. PRAC. 34, 35–36 (1984). *Cf. In re* Hayes, 93 Wash. 228, 608 P.2d 635 (1980), and *In re* Grady, 85 N.J. 235, 426 A.2d 467 (1981). Parry has argued that the best-interests test is, as a practical matter, the only test that can be applied unless the person has expressed his or her wishes or his or her wishes are shown by clear and convincing evidence. John Parry, *A Unified Theory of Substitute Consent*, 11 MENTAL & PHYSICAL DISABILITY L. REP. 378 (1987).

65. For example, an individual may have a personal preference to avoid particular kinds of side effects (e.g., loss of hair), even if it means enduring other consequences that most people would find more noxious.

66. For an example of the difficulties in applying a subjective substituted judgment standard, *see* Saikewicz v. Superintendent of Belchertown State Hosp., 370 N.E.2d 417 (Mass. 1977), in which the court attempted to discern the subjective wishes of a profoundly retarded man.

67. *See generally* Judith Areen, *The Legal Status of Consent Obtained from Families of Adult Patients to Withhold or Withdraw Treatment*, 258 J. AM. MED. ASS'N 229 (1987).

68. A durable power of attorney is to be distinguished from a traditional power of attorney, which does not survive the incapacity of the principal.

69. 42 U.S.C. § 1395 (1991).

70. FLA. STAT. §§ 765.101 et. seq.

71. MINN. STAT. § 253b.03(6d).

72. 497 U.S. 261 (1990).

73. For a decision upholding such advanced directives, see *In re* Guardianship of Browning, 568 So. 2d 4 (Fla. 1990).

74. *See, e.g.*, *In re* Rosa M. 597 N.Y.S.2d 544 (Sup. Ct. 1991) (involving refusal of electroconvulsive therapy by the patient's surrogate decisionmaker).

75. Although the doctrine of informed consent has deep roots in Anglo-American reverence for individual liberty, the doctrine really did not develop until the 1960s. JAY KATZ, THE SILENT WORLD OF DOCTOR AND PATIENT 59–80 (1984); CHARLES LIDZ ET AL., INFORMED CONSENT: A STUDY OF DECISIONMAKING IN PSYCHIATRY 11–12 (1984) [hereinafter INFORMED CONSENT]. The first

informed consent case is usually considered to be Salgo v. Leland Stanford Jr. Univ. Bd. of Trustees, 317 P.2d 170 (Cal. Dist. Ct. App. 1957).

76. *See* KATZ, *supra* note 75, at 49; Wadlington, *supra* note 16, at 59.

77. *See* KATZ, *supra* note 75, at 69–71; Wadlington, *supra* note 16, at 64–65.

78. INFORMED CONSENT, *supra* note 75, at 4.

79. *See* KATZ, *supra* note 75.

80. *Id.* at 86–87.

81. Alan Stone, *Psychiatric Abuse and Legal Reform: Two Ways to Make a Bad Situation Worse*, 5 INT'L J. L. & PSYCHIATRY 9, 20–22 (1982).

82. *See generally* INFORMED CONSENT, *supra* note 75, at 5, 22–23.

83. The challenge came in Canterbury v. Spence, 464 F.2d 772 (D.C. Cir. 1972), *cert. denied*, 409 U.S. 1064 (1972).

84. *See, e.g.*, Natanson v. Kline, 350 P.2d 1093, *reh'g denied*, 354 P.2d 670 (Kan. 1960).

85. The leading case in this regard is Canterbury v. Spence, *supra* note 83.

86. *See, e.g.*, id.

87. The subjective test has rarely been adopted. INFORMED CONSENT, *supra* note 75, at 343 nn. 35–36 and accompanying text.

88. *Id.* at 12.

89. RALPH REISNER & CHRISTOPHER SLOBOGIN, LAW AND THE MENTAL HEALTH SYSTEM: CIVIL AND CRIMINAL ASPECTS 186 (1990). Roughly 14 states adopt the more patient-oriented standard.

90. BARRY R. FURROW ET AL., HEALTH LAW (1897). The authors provide two less persuasive reasons as well: the physician does not have enough time to give all the information patients may request and the physician should not be subjected to the hindsight of the patient and the second guessing of the jury.

91. Largey v. Rothman, 110 N.J. 204, 540 A.2d 504 (1988).

92. KATZ, *supra* note 75, at 83.

93. *See, e.g.*, Mitchell v. Robinson, 334 S.W.2d 11 (Mo. 1960) (speaking of whether treatment was "immediately necessary to save [the person's] life or sanity").

94. *See, e.g.*, Cobbs v. Grant, 502 P.2d 1 (Cal. 1972) (dictum stating that "a medical doctor need not make disclosure of risks when the patients requests that he not be informed").

95. Canterbury v. Spence, 464 F.2d 772 (D.C. Cir. 1972).

96. Cobbs v. Grant, 502 P.2d 1 (Cal. 1972).

97. Weithorn has described well some models for such shared responsibility. Lois Weithorn, *Involving Children in Decisions Affecting Their Own Welfare: Guidelines for Professionals*, in CHILDREN'S COMPETENCE, *supra* note 14.

98. *See* KATZ, *supra* note 75, especially ch. 6.

99. STANDARDS REGARDING CONSENT FOR TREATMENT AND RESEARCH INVOLVING CHILDREN (Division of Child, Youth & Family Services, American Psychological Association 1982).

100. *See generally* Bruce Winick, *Competency to Consent to Treatment: The Distinction between Assent and Objection*, 28 HOUS. L. REV. 15 (1991).

101. A physician might seek such consultation, for example, before performing an abortion on a minor. *See* Melton, *supra* note 17, at 468 n. 68 and accompanying text.

102. *See, e.g.*, VA. CODE ANN. § 54–325.12(B), which provides a sterilization procedure.

103. *See* Melton, *supra* note 17, at 492.

104. Loren Roth et al., *Tests of Competency to Consent to Treatment*, 134 AM. J. PSYCHIATRY 279 (1977).

105. *See* Paul Appelbaum & Thomas Grisso, *The MacArthur Treatment Competence Study (I)*, 19 LAW & HUM. BEHAV. 105 (1995) (arguing, based on a comprehensive review of the legal and clinical literature, that the first four constructs discussed later in the text represent the relevant legal landscape).

106. *See* Richard Bonnie, *The Competence of Criminal Defendants: Beyond* Dusky *and* Drope, 47 U. MIAMI L. REV. 539, 573–74 (1993).

107. *See* Saks, *supra* note 5; Grant Morris, *Judging Judgment: Assessing the Competence of Mental Patients to Refuse Treatment*, 32 SAN DIEGO L. REV. 343 (1995). *See generally*, Loren Roth et al., *The Dilemma of Denial in the Assessment of Competency to Refuse Treatment*, 139 AM. J. PSYCHIATRY 910 (1982).

108. William Thompson, *Psychological Issues in Informed Consent*, in 3 MAKING HEALTH CARE DECISIONS 83, 86–103 (The President's Commission for the Study of Ethical Problems in Medicine and Biomedical and Behavioral Research ed. 1983).

109. ALAN STONE, MENTAL HEALTH AND LAW: A SYSTEM IN TRANSITION 65–70 (1975).

110. *Id.* at 68–69.

111. For an advocate of the latter view, *see* Saks, *supra* note 5.

112. *See, e.g.*, Kaimowitz v. Department of Mental Health, No. 73–19434–AW (Cir. Ct. Wayne County, Mich., July 10, 1973) (institutionalized patients unable to give voluntary consent to psychosurgery), *abstracted in* 13 CRIM. L. REP. 2452 (1973), *reprinted in* ALEXANDER BROOKS, LAW, PSYCHIATRY, AND THE MENTAL HEALTH SYSTEM 902 (1974). *See also* DAVID WEXLER, MENTAL HEALTH LAW: MAJOR ISSUES 193–212 (1981).

113. The management of patients' consent to various forms of treatment and to hospitalization itself is vividly described in KATZ, *supra* note 75; INFORMED CONSENT, *supra* note 75.

114. Thomas Grisso & Linda Vierling, *Minors' Consent to Treatment*, 9 PROF. PSYCHOL. 412, 421–23 (1978); Gary Melton, *Decision Making by Children, Psychological Risks and Benefits*, in CHILDREN'S COMPETENCE, *supra* note 14, at 21, 24–26.

115. Gary Melton, *Sexually Abused Children and the Legal System: Some Policy Recommendations*, 13 AM. J. FAM. THERAPY 61 (1985).

116. 720 F.2d 266 (3d Cir. 1983).

117. 738 F.2d 1 (1st Cir. 1984). *See also* Rogers v. Com'r Dep't Mental Health 458 N.E.2d 308 (Mass. Sup. Jud. Ct. 1983).

118. For a brief review of cases during the height of the controversy, *see* John Parry, *Right to Refuse Psychotropic Medication,* 8 MENTAL & PHYSICAL DISABILITY L. REP. 83 (1984).

119. For a review of the various constitutional bases for the right to refuse, *see* 2 MENTAL DISABILITY L. REP. 43–50 (1977).

120. *See, e.g.,* Rogers v. Okin, 634 F.2d 650, 650 n. 1 (1st Cir. 1980) (explicitly excluding consideration of other powerful psychotropic medication, such as lithium and the antidepressants).

121. Brief of *amici curiae* American Psychological Association, American Orthopsychiatric Association, and National Mental Health Association in Mills v. Rogers, at 4–5 (citations omitted). Other side effects include extrapyramidal symptoms such as "muscle spasm, irregular flexing, writhing or grimacing movements, and protrusion of the tongue (dystonic reactions); motor restlessness, and inability to stay still (akathesia); and mask-like face, drooping, stiffness and rigidity, shuffling gait, and tremors (pseudo-Parkinsonian syndrome) and[, routine] nonmuscular physical side effects [such as] drowsiness, dizziness, blurred vision, dry mouth, torn-up stomach, low blood pressure, palpitations, skin rashes, and constipation." *Id.* On tardive dyskinesia, *see* Mark R. Munetz et al., *Tardive Dyskinesia and Informed Consent: Myths and Realities,* 10 BULL. AM. ACAD. PSYCHIATRY & L. 77 (1982). Phenothiazines also have adverse psychological side effects. They sometimes impair concentration or create agitation or depression, and the physical side effects may induce stigma or shame. Brief of *amicis curiae, supra,* at 6–8. *See also* Alexander Brooks, *The Right to Refuse Antipsychotic Medications: Law and Policy,* 39 RUTGERS L. REV. 339, 347–50 (1987); Note, Washington v. Harper: *Forced Medication and Substantive Due Process,* 25 CONN. L. REV. 265, 266–71 (1992).

122. Brooks, *supra* note 121, at 350–52 (citing research indicating that "medications are extensively administered for the convenience of staff rather than for treatment purposes and are commonly used in a counter-therapeutic manner").

123. THEODORE H. SARBIN & JAMES C. MANCUSO, SCHIZOPHRENIA: MEDICAL DIAGNOSIS OR MORAL VERDICT? 144–50 (1980).

124. Brooks, *supra* note 121, at 351 (describing findings in Rennie v. Klein, 476 F. Supp. 1294, 1302 (D.N.J. 1979), that "[p]olypharmacy, the universally condemned use of more than one antipsychotic drug at a time, was widespread"). *See also* William A. Hargreaves et al., *Effects of the Jamison–Farabee Consent Decree: Due Process Protection for Involuntary Psychiatric Patients Treated with Psychoactive Medication,* 144 AM. J. PSYCHIATRY 188, 192 (1985).

125. *See, e.g.,* Rogers v. Okin, 634 F.2d 650, 651 (1st Cir. 1980) (noting lack of contest over existence of some right to refuse).

126. For a description of the psychological and fiscal costs of the right to refuse, *see* Brooks, *supra* note 121, at 37–74.

127. 494 U.S. 210 (1990).

128. Parham v. J.R., 442 U.S. 584 (1979) [discussed in § 10.10(a)]; Vitek v. Jones, 445 U.S. 480 (1980) [discussed in § 10.10(c)].

129. Bruce Winick, *New Directions in the Right to Refuse Mental Health Treatment: The Implications of Riggins v. Nevada,* 2 WM. & MARY BILL RTS. J. 205 (1993).

130. *See, e.g.,* Rogers v. Okin, 478 F. Supp. 1342, 1367 (1979); *Cf.* Aden v. Younger, 57 Cal. App. 3d 662, 129 Cal. Rptr. 535, 546 (4th Dist. 1976) (finding that psychosurgery and electroshock therapy infringed upon freedom of thought and thus could only be used if the state can show a compelling state interest).

131. *See, e.g.,* Nelson v. Heyne, 335 F. Supp. 451, 455 (N.D. Ind. 1972); *Cf.* Knecht v. Gillman, 488 F.2d 1136 (8th Cir. 1973) (finding that aversive conditioning violates the Eighth Amendment when not used for treatment purposes).

132. *See* discussion on informed consent doctrine, § 11.03(a).

133. *See, e.g.,* Rogers v. Okin, 634 F.2d 650 (1st Cir. 1980); Scott v. Plante, 532 F.2d 939, 946 n. 9 (3d Cir. 1976).

134. No court has contemplated holding that an incompetent person should have such a right. This posture makes sense if the medication is needed to restore competency. On the other hand, even an incompetent person should be able to avoid medication that is not administered for treatment purposes.

135. 504 U.S. 127 (1992).

136. Riggins had argued that the medication affected his demeanor and mental state during trial, thus denying him the right to show the jury his true mental state, which he thought was relevant to his insanity defense. The Court avoided addressing this argument [*see* § 6.04(d) for further discussion of the issue], and instead focused its opinion on the issues discussed in the text.

137. 457 U.S. 307 (1982) (holding that whether the right to treatment has been violated depends on whether "professional judgment was exercised" in arriving at the treatment plan).

138. *But see* Susan Stefan, *Leaving Civil Rights to the "Experts": From Defense to Abdication under the Professional Judgment Standard,* 102 YALE L.J. 639 (1992). Stefan distinguishes between "positive rights" (where the claimant is asking the state for something, as with the right to treatment) and "negative rights" attempting to avoid state intervention (as with the right to refuse). She argues that whereas *Youngberg*'s professional judgment standard is appropriate where positive rights are involved, applying that standard in negative-rights situations inappropriately allows the scope of a right protecting the individual from the state to be determined by doctors instead of courts.

139. *See, e.g.,* United States v. Charters, 863 F.2d 302 (4th Cir. 1988); Dautremont v. Broadlawns Hosp., 827 F.2d 291 (8th Cir. 1987).

140. *See, e.g.,* Parham v. J.R., 442 U.S. 584 (1979) (permitting commitment of minor on sayso of mental health professional; no judge or attorney required).

141. *See, e.g.,* Rogers v. Commissioner, 458 N.W.2d 308 (1983).

142. *See, e.g.,* Rennie v. Klein, 462 F. Supp. 1131,

1147 (D.N.J. 1978); Dautremont v. Broadlawns Hosp., 827 F.2d 291 (8th Cir. 1987).

143. Even an administrative procedure is costly. A study of the administrative review process at Napa State Hospital put the cost of outside reviewers, advocates, lost staff time, and so on at $300,000 per year for that hospital and estimated that the cost of instituting such a program at all five California state hospitals would be between one million and one and a half million dollars. Hargreaves et al., *supra* note 124.

144. In New Jersey, switching from an external review system to an internal one dropped the proportion of cases in which there was discontinuation or a reduction of dosages from 59% to 2.5%. Brief for New Jersey Dep't of Public Advocate in *Harper v. Washington,* at 38–54, *cited in* 494 U.S. 210, 252 n. 22 (Stevens, J., dissenting). *But see* Franklin Hickman et al., *Right to Refuse Psychotropic Medication: An Interdisciplinary Proposal,* 6 MENTAL DISABILITY L. Rep. 122, 130 (1982) (external psychiatrist affirmed treatment recommendation in 100% of cases, whereas internal reviewer affirmed in only 75% of the cases). The difference may lie in the composition of the review board. *Cf.* Brooks, *supra* note 121, at 373 (speculating that relatively low 67% affirmance rate of Minnesota Treatment Review Panel was due to fact that review board had only one physician).

145. This procedure was required in *Rennie,* supra note 142.

146. Refusals range from 2.4% to 15% of the total civil patient population. Brooks, *supra* note 121, at 373. However, they can range much higher with forensic populations. Robert Miller et al., *The Right to Refuse Treatment in a Forensic Patient Population: Six-Month Review,* 17 BULL. AM. ACAD. PSYCHIATRY & L. 107 (1989) (finding a refusal rate of 75%).

147. *See, e.g.,* Rogers v. Commissioner, 390 Mass. 489, 458 N.E.2d 308, 322 (1983) (requiring a finding of "imminent" dangerousness before forcible medication may occur). A few states have also adopted statutes that may be *less* protective, *see, e.g.,* UTAH CODE ANN. § 64–7–36(10) (a civilly committed patient is deemed to be incompetent for making treatment decisions), although they are still to be tested under *Harper* and *Riggins. Cf.* State *ex rel.* Jones v. Gerhardstein, 416 NW.2d 883 (Wis. 1987) (holding that, under a statute similar to Utah's, forcible medication is not permissible until a court has found the patient incompetent).

148. *See, e.g.,* Aden v. Younger, 57 Cal. App. 3d 662, 129 Cal. Rptr. 535 (1976) (recognizing that "[p]atients have a right to refuse psychosurgery" and that "[n]o shock treatments may be given if the patient is able to give informed consent and refuses," as well as sanctioning heightened review procedures for patient consent to such procedures); Knecht v. Gillman, 488 F.2d 1136 (1973) (permitting consent to anectine conditioning only if a physician certifies the inmate is "mentally competent to understand fully" the risks and benefits, and holding that consent may be revoked at any time).

149. *See generally* KATZ, *supra* note 75; Paul R. Benson, *Informed Consent: Drug Information Disclosed to Patients*

Prescribed Antipsychotic Medication, 172 J. NERVOUS & MENTAL DISEASE 642 (1983).

150. Lynn Epstein & Louis Lasagna, *Obtaining Informed Consent: Form or Substance?* 123 ARCHIVES INTERNAL MED. 682 (1969).

151. T. M. Grunder, *On the Readability of Surgical Consent Forms,* 302 NEW ENG. J. MED. 900 (1980); Gary Morrow, *How Readable Are Subject Consent Forms?,* 244 J. Am. Med. Ass'n 56 (1980); Allan Berg & Karleen B. Hammitt, *Assessing the Psychiatric Patient's Ability to Meet the Literacy Demands of Hospitalization,* 31 HOSP. & COMMUNITY PSYCHIATRY 266 (1980); Gerald S. Coles et al., *Literacy Skills of Long-Term Hospitalized Mental Patients,* 29 HOSP. & COMMUNITY PSYCHIATRY 512 (1978).

152. INFORMED CONSENT, *supra* note 75, at 93–94.

153. *See, e.g., id.* at 86–88.

154. *See, e.g., id.* at 187–88.

155. A sensitive discussion of these issues is presented in KATZ, *supra* note 75, at 165 et seq.

156. INFORMED CONSENT, *supra* note 75, at 25.

157. Paul Slovic et al., *Informing People About Risk,* in PRODUCT LABELING AND HEALTH RISKS: BANBURY REPORT 165 (Lovis A. Morris et al. eds. 1980).

158. Millet G. Morgan et al., *Powerline Frequency Electric and Magnetic Fields: A Pilot Study of Risk Perception,* 5 RISK ANALYSIS 139 (1985).

159. Charles Keown et al., *Attitudes of Physicians, Pharmacists, and Lay Persons toward Seriousness and Need for Disclosure of Prescription Drug Side Effects,* 3 HEALTH PSYCHOL. 1 (1984).

160. Steven J. Sherman et al., *Imagining Can Heighten or Lower the Perceived Likelihood of Contracting a Disease: The Mediating Effect of Ease of Imagery,* 11 PERSON & SOC. PSYCHOL. BULL. 118 (1985).

161. William C. Thompson, *Research on Human Judgment and Decision Making: Implications for Informed Consent and Institutional Review,* in RESEARCH ETHICS: A PSYCHOLOGICAL APPROACH ch. 2 (Barbara H. Stanley et al. eds. 1996) (hereinafter RESEARCH ETHICS). The foregoing citations on risk perception were taken from this piece.

162. Thomas Grisso & Paul Appelbaum, *The MacArthur Treatment Competency Study (III): Abilities of Patients to Consent to Psychiatric and Medical Treatment,* 19 LAW & HUM. BEHAV. 149, 173 (1995).

163. *Id.*

164. As the researchers put it, "a fixed inability to understand should not automatically be presumed on the basis of a patient's initial failure to comprehend the disclosure." *Id.* at 173.

165. INFORMED CONSENT, *supra* note 75, at 26–28.

166. *Id.,* at 24.

167. David Soskis, *Schizophrenic and Medical Inpatients as Informed Drug Consumers,* 35 ARCHIVES GEN. PSYCHIATRY 645 (1978).

168. Richard Jaffe, *Problems of Long-Term Informed Consent,* 14 BULL. AM. ACAD. PSYCHIATRY & L. 163 (1986).

169. Barbara Stanley et al., *The Functional Competency of Elderly at Risk,* 28 GERONTOLOGIST 53 (1988).

170. Loren Roth et al., *Competency to Decide about Treatment or Research: An Overview of Some Empirical Data,* 5

INT'L J.L. & PSYCHIATRY 29 (1982); Michael Irwin et al., *Psychotic Patients' Understanding of Informed Consent*, 142 AM. J. PSYCHIATRY 1351 (1985); Jeffrey S. Janofsky et al., *The Hopkins Competency Assessment Test: A Brief Method for Evaluating Patients' Capacity to Give Informed Consent*, 43 HOSP. & COMMUNITY PSYCHIATRY 132 (1992); Paul R. Benson et al., *Information, Disclosure, Subject Understanding, and Informed Consent in Psychiatric Research*, 12 LAW & HUM. BEHAV. 455 (1988).

171. Munetz et al., *supra* note 121, at 85. *See also* James C. Beck, *Patients' Competency to Give Informed Consent to Medication*, 37 HOSP. & COMMUNITY PSYCHIATRY 400 (1986).

172. Grisso & Appelbaum, *supra* note 162.

173. For a description of these instruments, *see* Thomas Grisso et al., *The MacArthur Treatment Competence Study (II): Measures of Abilities Related to Competence to Consent to Treatment*, 19 LAW & HUM. BEHAV. 127 (1995). *See also infra* text accompanying notes 197–200.

174. James M. Gold & Philip D. Harvey, *Cognitive Deficits in Schizophrenia*, 16 PSYCHIATRIC CLINICS N. AM. 295 (1993).

175. *See, e.g.*, Linda Clare et al., *Memory in Schizophrenia: What Is Impaired and What Is Preserved*, 31 NEUROPSY-CHOLGIA 1225 (1993).

176. Grisso & Appelbaum, *supra* note 162, at 169.

177. *Id.* at 171.

178. *Id.* at 172.

179. *See* Gary Melton, *Developmental Psychology and the Law: The State of the Art*, 22 J. FAM. L. 445, 463–65 (1984), and the studies cited there. *See generally* CHILDREN'S COMPETENCE, *supra* note 14.

180. *See, e.g.*, Lois Weithorn & Susan Campbell, *The Competency of Children and Adolescents to Make Informed Treatment Decisions*, 53 CHILD DEV. 1589 (1982).

181. Howard S. Adelman et al., *Competence of Minors to Understand, Evaluate, and Communicate about Their Psychoeducational Problems*, 16 PROF. PSYCHOL.: RES. & PRAC. 426 (1985); Howard S. Adelman & Linda Taylor, *Children's Reluctance Regarding Treatment: Incompetence, Resistance, or an Appropriate Response?*, 15 SCH. PSYCHOL. REV. 91 (1986); Rochelle T. Bastien & Howard S. Adelman, *Noncompulsory versus Legally Mandated Placement, Perceived Choice, and Response to Treatment among Adolescents*, 52 J. CONSULTING & CLINICAL PSYCHOL. 171 (1984); David S. Holmes & Robert G. Urie, *Effects of Preparing Children for Psychotherapy*, 43 J. CONSULTING & CLINICAL PSYCHOL. 311 (1975); Barbara L. Bonner & Francis L. Everett, *Influence of Client Preparation and Problem Severity on Attitudes and Expectations in Child Psychotherapy*, 17 PROF. PSYCHOL.: RES. & PRAC. 223 (1986). *See also* Charles Lewis, *Decision Making Related to Health: When Could/Should Children Behave Responsibly?*, in CHILDREN'S COMPETENCE, *supra* note 14.

182. Herbert Kelman, *The Rights of the Subject in Social Research: An Analysis in Terms of Relative Power and Legitimacy*, 27 AM. PSYCHOLOGIST 989 (1972).

183. Thomas Grisso, *Voluntary Consent to Research Participation in the Institutional Context*, in RESEARCH ETHICS, *supra* note 161, ch. 3.

184. *See* ERVING GOFFMAN, ASYLUMS (1971).

185. Catherine E. Rosen, *Why Clients Relinquish Their Rights to Privacy under Sign-Away Pressures*, 8 PROF. PSYCHOLOGY 17 (1977) (100% of patients agreed to allow hospital to include personal data on a computer record until a sentence was added to the consent form that treatment would not depend on whether they so agreed, at which point the compliance rate dropped to 41% in one clinic and 20% in another).

186. *See generally* KATZ, *supra* note 75; INFORMED CONSENT, *supra* note 75, at 315 (doctors tended to offer information not as though patients were expected to decide whether or not to accept the treatment but as though the doctors were being kind enough to tell patients what needed to be done, behavior that interacted with patient's self-doubts to produce a lack of assertiveness).

187. Loren Roth & Paul Appelbaum, *Involuntary Treatment in Medicine and Psychiatry*, 141 AM. J. PSYCHIATRY 202 (1984).

188. *See generally, Interpersonal Relations in Health Care*, 35(1) J. SOC. ISSUES (1979).

189. *Cf.* JACK W. BREHM, A THEORY OF PSYCHOLOGICAL REACTANCE (1966).

190. Michael Saks, *Social Psychological Contributions to a Legislative Subcommittee on Organ and Tissue Transplants*, 33 AM. PSYCHOLOGIST 680 (1978).

191. *Cf.* Shalom Schwartz, *Elicitation of Moral Obligation and Self-Sacrificing Behavior: An Experimental Study of Volunteering to Be a Bone Marrow Donor*, 15 J. PERSONALITY & SOC. PSYCHOL. 283 (1970).

192. William Thompson, *Psychological Issues in Informed Consent*, in 3 MAKING HEALTH CARE DECISIONS (President's Commission for the Study of Ethical Problems in Medicine and Biomedical and Behavioral Research eds. 1983).

193. *See, e.g.*, Weithorn & Campbell, *supra* note 180.

194. Although the phenothiazines doubtless help many patients, there are also equally effective psychological therapies in many cases. BERTRAM P. KARON & GARY R. VANDENBOS, PSYCHOTHERAPY OF SCHIZOPHRENIA: THE TREATMENT OF CHOICE (1981).

195. 634 F.2d at 654.

196. In addition to the MacCAT-T described in the text, *see* Michael Lavin, *The Hopkins Competency Assessment Test: A Brief Method for Evaluating Patients' Capacity to Give Informed Consent*, 43 HOSP. & COMMUNITY PSYCHIATRY 646 (1992); Thomas Gutheil & Harold Bursztajn, *Clinicians' Guidelines for Assessing and Presenting Subtle Forms of Patient Incompetence in Legal Settings*, 143 AM. J. PSYCHIATRY 1020 (1986); Santo W. Bentivegna & Kathleen Garvey, *Applications of Hartman's Competency to Consent and Right to Refuse Treatment Concepts*, 8 AM. J. FORENSIC PSYCHOL. 25 (1990).

197. Grisso et al. *supra* note 173, at 130–36.

198. *Id.*

199. *See generally* 2 PSYCHOL., PUB. POL'Y & L. 1–216 (1996), which is devoted to an assessment of the MacArthur Treatment Competency Project.

200. Christopher Slobogin, *"Appreciation" as a Measure of Competency: Some Thoughts about the MacArthur Group's*

Approach, 2 PSYCHOL. PUB. POL'Y & L. 18 (1996).

201. Patricia Keith-Spiegel, *Children and Consent to Participate in Research*, in CHILDREN'S COMPETENCE, *supra* note 14, at 179, 180–81.

202. A notable and relatively common example would be drug research, in which the effect on humans and particular groups (e.g., children) is not completely predictable from animal studies.

203. 132 *J. Am. Med. Ass'n* 1090 (1946).

204. 45 C.F.R. pt. 46 (1983).

205. *See, e.g.*, 10 C.F.R. pt. 745 (1984) (Dep't of Energy); 16 C.F.R. pt. 1028 (1984) (Consumer Product Safety Comm'n); 21 C.F.R. pts, 50, 56 (1983) (Food & Drug Administration).

206. Confidentiality may be substantially more limited than most researchers and participants imagine. *See* DOROTHY NELKIN, SCIENCE AS INTELLECTUAL PROPERTY: WHO CONTROLS SCIENTIFIC RESEARCH? chs. 3 and 4 (1983); Roberta Morris et al., *Research and the Freedom of Information Act*, 36 AM. PSYCHOLOGIST 819 (1981).

207. 45 C.F.R. §§ 45.116(a), (b) (1983).

208. A common issue in social–psychological research is the use of deception so as to minimize the effects of participants' knowledge of the purpose of the experiment. *See* Jeffrey Geller, *Alternatives to Deception: Why, What, and How?*, in THE ETHICS OF SOCIAL RESEARCH: SURVEYS AND EXPERIMENTS (Joan E. Sieber ed. 1982).

209. 45 C.F.R. § 46.116(c) (1983).

210. 45 C.F.R. § 46.102(g).

211. NATIONAL COMMISSION FOR THE PROTECTION OF HUM. SUBJECTS OF BIOMEDICAL AND BEHAVIORAL RESEARCH, THE BELMONT REPORT: ETHICAL PRINCIPLES AND GUIDELINES FOR THE PROTECTION OF HUM. SUBJECTS OF RESEARCH (1979).

212. In addition, there are special regulations for research on fetuses, pregnant women, and *in vitro* fertilization. 45 C.F.R. pt. 46(B) (1983).

213. 45 C.F.R. § 46.306.

214. 45 C.F.R. § 46.305(a) (2).

215. 45 C.F.R. §§ 46.402(b), 46,402(c), and 46.408.

216. 45 C.F.R. §§ 46.405, 46.406, and 46.407.

217. 45 C.F.R. § 46.409.

218. 45 C.F.R. § 46.408(c).

219. Proposed regulations were published at 43 Fed. Reg. 53,590 (1978).

220. *See, e.g.*, Barbara Stanley & Michael Stanley, *Psychiatric Patients in Research: Protecting Their Autonomy*, 22 COMPREHENSIVE PSYCHIATRY 420 (1981).

221. For such an integration, *see* Barbara Stanley, *Informed Consent and Competence: A Review of Empirical Research* (paper presented at workshop of the National Institute of Mental Health on "Empirical Research on Informed Consent with Subjects of Uncertain Competence," Jan. 12, 1981).

222. Lois Weithorn, *Children's Capacities to Decide about Participation in Research*, 5(2) IRB: A REVIEW OF HUM. SUBJECTS RESEARCH 1 (1983), and studies cited therein.

223. Rona Abramovitch et al., *Children's Capacity to Agree to Psychological Research: Knowledge of Risks and Benefits and Voluntariness*, 5 ETHICS & BEHAV. 25 (1995).

224. *Id.* at 36–45.

225. Barbara Stanley et al., *Preliminary Findings on Psychiatry Patients as Research Participants: A Population at Risk?*, 138 AM. J. PSYCHIATRY 669 (1981).

226. Loren Roth et al., *Competency to Decide about Treatment or Research*, 5 INT'L J. L. & PSYCHIATRY 29 (1982); Lisa Grossman & Frank Summers, *A Study of the Capacity of Schizophrenic Patients to Give Informed Consent*, 31 HOSP. & COMMUNITY PSYCHIATRY 205 (1980).

227. *See, e.g.*, Audrey T. McCollum & A. Herbert Schwartz, *Pediatric Research Hospitalization: Its Meaning to Parents*, 3 PEDIATRIC RESEARCH 199 (1969).

228. Thompson, *supra* note 161, at 89–91.

229. *See, e.g.*, Patricia Keith-Spiegel & Thomas Maas, *Consent to Research: Are There Developmental Differences?* (paper presented at the meeting of the APA, Los Angeles, Aug. 1981).

230. Most state statutes simply use this phrase or some variation on it and provide no further definition. 11 AM. JUR. *Testamentary Capacity* §§ 159, 161 (1985).

231. This test was first established in the case of Banks v. Goodfellow, 1870 5 Q.B. 549. For a discussion of this case, the evolution of the doctrine of testamentary capacity, and some reflections on the role of the expert witness in assisting the courts in determining whether capacity exists, *see* Willis Spaulding, *Testamentary Competency: Reconciling Doctrine with the Role of the Expert Witness*, 9 LAW & HUM. BEHAV. 113 (1985).

232. *Wills*, 79 AM. JUR. 2d § 71 at 329 (1975) [hereinafter *Wills*].

233. *See generally id.* §§ 77–101.

234. For a discussion, *see* 18 AM. JUR. 2d, *Mentally Disordered Testator's Execution of Will during Lucid Interval* § 1 (1979).

235. *Wills, supra* note 232, § 87, at 341.

236. THOMAS SZASZ, LAW, LIBERTY AND PSYCHIATRY 75–76 (1963). A similar view is expressed in Note, *Testamentary Capacity in a Nutshell: A Psychiatric Reevaluation*, 18 STAN. L. REV. 1119 (1996). *But see* M. C. Slough, *Testamentary Capacity: Evidentiary Aspects*, in 2 LANDMARK PAPERS ON ESTATE PLANNING: WILLS, ESTATES, AND TRUSTS 594, 610–11 (Arthur Winard ed. 1968).

237. John Langbein, *Living Probate: The Conservatorship Model*, 77 MICH. L. REV. 63, 67 (1978).

238. Daniel Friedlander, *Comtemporary Ante-Mortem Statutory Formulations: Observations and Alternatives*, 32 CASE W. RES. L. REV. 823 (1982).

239. *See generally* Irwin N. Perr, *Wills, Testamentary Capacity and Undue Influence*, 9 BULL. AM. ACAD. PSYCHIATRY & L. 15 (1981); John Hogan, *When Does Influence Become Undue?*, 7 LOY. U. CHI. L. J. 629 (1976).

240. Spaulding, *supra* note 231, at 138.

241. *Id.* at 133–38.

242. Note, *supra* note 236, at 1139.

243. WALTER BROMBERG, THE USES OF PSYCHIATRY IN THE LAW: A CLINICAL VIEW OF FORENSIC PSYCHIATRY 254 (1979).

Chapter 12

1. JEFFREY O'CONNELL & R. HENDERSON, TORT LAW: NO-FAULT AND BEYOND 1–2 (1975). The authors provide an excellent summary of the development of the principle of "fault" as a determinant in adjudicating the compensability of injuries.

2. *Id.* at 3–6.

3. RESTATEMENT (SECOND) OF THE LAW OF TORTS § 6 cmt. (1965).

4. JAMES A. DOOLEY, MODERN TORT LAW: LIABILITY AND LITIGATION 8 (rev. ed. by Barry A. Lindahl 1983).

5. *See generally The American Law Institute's Reporters' Study on Enterprise Responsibility for Personal Injury,* 30 SAN DIEGO L. REV. 371 (1993); Jeffrey O'Connell & James Guinivan, *An Irrational Combination: The Relative Expansion of Liability Insurance and Contraction of Loss Insurance,* 49 OHIO ST. L.J. 757 (1988).

6. *Workmen's Compensation,* 82 AM. JUR. 2d §§ 1–731 at 27 (1992) [hereinafter *Workmen's Compensation*].

7. *See generally* LARSON'S WORKMEN'S COMPENSATION LAW §§ 4.20–5.30 (rev. ed. by Matthew Bender 1993) [hereinafter LARSON'S]. This multivolume work, updated periodically, is the most comprehensive description of the workers' compensation system available. It is an excellent and exhaustive compendium of information on every facet and phase of this system. Most law libraries will have a copy, and workers' compensation boards should as well.

8. We use the term "mental injury" rather than "psychiatric injury" because the latter term implies that these proceedings are limited to psychiatrists when, in fact, nearly any clinical profession may find itself involved in evaluating mental injury in the workers' compensation or tort context; indeed, Bromberg has noted that "every type of medical specialist is currently utilized in studying industrial, automobile, and household injuries. The list extends from surgeons to neurologists, neurosurgeons, orthopedic specialists, psychiatrists, electromyographers, electroencephalographers, nuclear medicine specialists (brain scan and tomography), plastic surgeons, otolargologists, ophthalmologists, radiologists, dermatologists, internists, psychiatric and clinical psychologists." WALTER BROMBERG, THE USES OF PSYCHIATRY IN THE LAW: A CLINICAL VIEW OF FORENSIC PSYCHIATRY 311 (1979). *But see infra* notes 124–25 and accompanying text.

9. Note, *Determining the Compensability of Mental Disabilities,* 55 U.S.C. L. REV. 193, 195 (1981).

10. *Workmen's Compensation, supra* note 6, at 27.

11. LARSON'S, *supra* note 7, § 4.50.

12. *Id.* The development of workers' compensation law was also influenced by the experience of railroad workers, who often were injured on the job and experienced difficulty in obtaining compensation through traditional tort remedies. Edward M. Brown, *Regulating Damage Claims for Emotional Injuries Before the First World War,* 8 BEHAVIORAL SCI. & L. 421 (1990).

13. Ellen Smith Pryor, *Mental Disabilities and the Disability Fabric,* in MENTAL DISORDER, WORK DISABILITY AND THE LAW 153, at 157 (Richard J. Bonnie & John Monahan eds. 1996).

14. LARSON'S, *supra* note 7, at 2–6 to 2–7.

15. Pryor, *supra* note 13, at 157–58.

16. *Workmen's Compensation, supra* note 6, at 30–31, O'CONNELL & HENDERSON, *supra* note 1, at 74.

17. Charles R. O'Keefe, Jr., *The Guides to the Evaluation of Permanent Impairment and Workers' Compensation in Indiana,* 27 IND. L. REV. 647, 649 (1994).

18. O'CONNELL & HENDERSON, *supra* note 1, at 74.

19. *Workmen's Compensation, supra* note 6, at 515.

20. *Id.* at 492.

21. *Id.* at 499.

22. *Id.* at 502.

23. *Id.* at 541.

24. *Id.* at 536.

25. Lawrence Joseph, *The Causation Issue in Workers' Compensation Mental Disability Cases: An Analysis, Solutions and a Perspective,* 36 VAND. L. REV. 263, 286 (1983).

26. *Workmen's Compensation, supra* note 6, at 560–61.

27. Pryor, *supra* note 186–87, at 12.

28. "The purpose of the workers' compensation acts is not limited to the payment of compensation to injured employees during the period of their incapacity, but extends as well to persons who are dependent upon such an employee for support, and who are deprived of such support by reason of his death. . . . [I]t may be said that dependency means that the claimant looked to and relied on the contributions of the worker for support and maintenance, in whole or in part." *Workmen's Compensation, supra* note 6, at 180, 182.

29. LARSON'S, *supra* note 7, § 2.40.

30. *Id.*

31. Compensable diseases and injuries include the following: anthrax, apoplexy, cerebral hemorrhage, stroke, paralysis, heart attack, and other ailments; injuries by animals or insects; arm and wrist injuries; assaults, attacks, and shootings; damage to or loss of artificial limbs or members; injuries while indulging in recreation, amusements, athletic contests, entertainments, and employer-sponsored social affairs, such as outings, picnics, parties, etc.; back injuries; from fires, caustics, electricity, acids, or boiling water, and blisters; cancer; compressed air illness; drowning; Dupuytreau's contracture; electric shock, emphysema, fright, shock, or excitement; explosions; injuries from heat, cold, storm, lightning, and diseases resulting from exposure; eye injury, face injuries, and occasionally, disfigurement; injuries from falling, thrown, or flying objects; injuries from falling, slipping, or tripping; foot injuries and infections or diseases; head injuries; hearing loss or interference; hernia; infection; inhalation of gases, fumes, dust, and so forth; leg or hip injuries; injuries from machinery, equipment, and vehicles; mental, emotional, or nervous disorders; muscle injuries; nerve injuries; occupational diseases; overwork or exhaustion; pneumonia; poisoning; radiation injuries or diseases; sexual organ injuries; silicosis and other dust diseases; skin diseases; tuberculosis; typhoid fever contracted from drinking contaminated water furnished by an employer;

and ulcers. *See generally Workmen's Compensation, supra* note 6.

32. *Id.* at 261.

33. LARSON'S, *supra* note 7, § 6.00.

34. *Id.*

35. *Id.*

36. *Id.*, § 6.50.

37. *Workmen's Compensation, supra* note 6, at 262; LARSON'S, *supra* note 7, §§ 14.00 et seq.

38. Note, *supra* note 9, at 210–11.

39. *Workmen's Compensation, supra* note 6, at 340–42.

40. *Id.* at 340, 381–83.

41. *Id.* at 343 n. 70.

42. LARSON'S, *supra* note 7, §§ 38.00 *et seq.*

43. *Id.,* §§ 38.80, 38.81.

44. *Id.*

45. Annot., 97 A.L.R. 3d 161, 168 (1980) [hereinafter Annot.].

46. *Id.*

47. For a recent review of state law in this regard, see Marc A. Antonetti, *Labor Law: Workers' Compensation Statutes and the Recovery of Emotional Distress Damages in the Absence of Physical Injury,* 1990 ANN. SURV. AM. L. 671 (1990).

48. LARSON'S, *supra* note 7, § 42.22.

49. *Id.,* § 42.20.

50. Annot., *supra* note 45, at 169.

51. Joseph, *supra* note 25, at 288.

52. *Id.* at n. 104. The case citations from which these examples derive are omitted here but are supplied in the source.

53. LARSON'S, *supra* note 7, § 42.21.

54. *Id.*

55. Joseph, *supra* note 25, at 291.

56. LARSON'S, *supra* note 7, § 42.23. A 1990 review found that the following ten states deny workers' compensation for any kind of mental injury: Alabama, Florida, Georgia, Kansas, Minnesota, Montana, Nebraska, New Mexico, Ohio, and Oklahoma. Fourteen other states only permitted compensation for mental injury in situations of unusual stress. These included Arizona, Arkansas, Colorado, Illinois, Indiana, Maine, Tennessee, Massachusetts, Washington, New York, Rhode Island, Wisconsin, Pennsylvania, and Wyoming. A number of other states permitted recovery but had not yet decided whether unusual stress was required; these included Delaware, Louisiana, Maryland, Mississippi, Missouri, Texas, and Virginia. A handful of states permitted recovery for mental–mental injuries regardless of the quality of the stress, including Alaska, California, West Virginia, Kentucky, Michigan, New Jersey, Oregon, and Hawaii. Finally, some states had not yet decided whether to compensate mental–mental injuries, including Connecticut, Idaho, Iowa, Nevada, New Hampshire, North Carolina, North Dakota, South Carolina, South Dakota, Utah, and Vermont. Jimmy P. Mann & John Neece, *Workers' Compensation for Law Enforcement Related Post Traumatic Stress Disorder,* 8 BEHAVIORAL SCI. & L. 447, 456 (1990).

57. *See* Katherine Lippel, *Compensation for Mental–Mental Claims under Canadian Law,* 8 BEHAVIORAL

SCI. & L. 375 (1990). Lippel, who is generally critical of the Canadian approach, writes that "the choice of policymakers is to risk overcompensation in some cases, or to guarantee undercompensation in all cases. Today, in most Canadian jurisdictions, it is impossible to deny that many legitimate claims are being refused, . . . sometimes in clear violation of the letter or the spirit of the statute." *Id.* at 397.

58. *See supra* note 56. For a discussion of the increasingly common phenomenon of a state legislature adopting a more restrictive rule for compensating mental injuries after the state courts permit broader compensation, *see* Note, *Mental/Mental Claims under the Louisiana Worker's Compensation Act after* Sparks v. Tulane Medical Center Hospital and Clinic: *A Legislative Death Knell?,* 50 LA. L. REV. 609 (1990).

59. Annot., *supra* note 45, at 173.

60. Sparks v. Tulane Med. Ctr. Hosp. & Clinic, 546 So. 2d 138 (La. 1989). Sparks' job at Tulane Medical Center was to distribute medical supplies. She complained during her tenure on several occasions that coworkers were using drugs. She became the target of vandalism on the job and was told by a supervisor that a number of her coworkers wanted "to kick" her "butt." *Id.* at 141. She then left work, complaining of headaches and difficulty in sleeping. She also entered psychiatric care. Interestingly, she recovered damages despite statutory language that required the injury to be the result of "violence to the physical structure of the body."

61. LA. REV. STAT. ANN. § 23:1021(7)(a)–(c) (1991). *See* Note, *supra* note 60, for a fuller description of the case.

62. Annot., *supra* note 45, at 173.

63. Jose v. Equifax, Inc., 556 S.W.2d 82, 84 (Tenn. 1977).

64. CAL. STAT. § 3208.3(a)(b) (1995). Other states have also required claimants to show employment contributed to mental impairment by a certain percentage, ranging from 10% to 75%. Pryor, *supra* note 13, at 44.

65. Michael Staten & John Umbeck, *Compensating Stress-Induced Disability: Incentive Problems,* in SAFETY AND THE WORK FORCE 103, 107 (John D. Worrall ed. 1983).

66. *Sticking It to Business: Companies Struggle with an Out-of-Control Workers' Compensation System,* U.S. NEWS & WORLD REP., Mar. 8, 1993, at 59; O'Keefe, *supra* note 17, at 647. Another study, conducted in 1992, found that although the average number of workers' compensation claims dropped between 1989 and 1991 the average cost per claim (mental and physical) jumped by over $1,350. *Workers' Compensation Costs,* NEWSDAY, Apr. 27, 1993, at 33.

67. *See* William H. Miller, *The Costs of Workers' Compensation,* INDUS. WK., Aug. 17, 1992, at 22. Inflation in medical costs affected the workers' compensation system in at least three ways. First, by the end of the 1980s the percentage of expenditures for medical care had risen from approximately one-third to 40%. *Id.* Second, the workers' compensation system traditionally has not incorporated the same type of cost-containment measures imposed in the insurance-financed general health care

sector (e.g., states traditionally have prohibited the use of employee copayments and deductibles). Third, workers' compensation often has covered expenditures that insurance would not cover. *Id.* For example, workers' compensation will pay for long-term physical therapy, whereas most insurance plans would not provide such coverage or would impose strict limitations on use. Roger Thompson, *Health Reform Aims at Workers' Comp.*, NATION'S BUSINESS, May 1993, at 34.

68. In California, one in eight workers' compensation claims results in litigation. John G. Kilgour, *Workers' Compensation Problems and Solutions: The California Experience,* 1992 LAB. L.J. 84, 89 (Feb. 1992). One estimate suggested that, in California in 1990, one and a half billion dollars was spent obtaining seven billion dollars in compensation. Mark D. Fefer, *What to Do about Workers' Compensation,* FORTUNE, June 29, 1992, at 80.

69. Miller, *supra* note 67.

70. Donald T. DeCarlo & Martin Minkowitz, *Workers' Compensation and Employers' Liability Law: National Developments and Trends,* 25 TORT & INS. L.J. 521, 526 (1990). This article also discusses a variety of court rulings applying and interpreting workers' compensation statutes.

71. *See* N.M. Helvcian, *Workers Compensation Paranoia: Mental Stress Claims,* cited in Pryor, *supra* note 13, at 44–45 (finding, based on data from the National Council of Compensation Insurance from 1979 through 1990, that the incidence of mental stress claims in ten states increased through the mid-1980s, peaked in 1987, and has since abated); S. Marley, *Tort Reform Tops Concerns,* BUSINESS INSURANCE, April 18, 1994 (nationwide poll of risk managers showing that stress-related workers' compensation claims are no longer on the list of major concerns).

72. Bruce Sales & George Perrin, *Artificial Legal Standards in Mental–Emotional Injury Litigation,* 11 BEHAVIORAL SCI. & L. 193 (1993).

73. Reforms have included legislation permitting the use of employee-paid deductibles in workers' compensation policies, the establishment of antifraud units, and efforts to achieve cost savings by permitting workers' compensation systems to contract with a health service plan to be the exclusive provider of medical care for work and nonwork injuries and illnesses. *See generally* Ruth A. Brown, *Workers' Compensation: State Enactments in 1992,* MONTHLY LAB. REV., Jan. 1993, at 50. This article provides a state by state review of significant statutory developments in workers' compensation in 1992.

74. Pryor, *supra* note 13, at 46. *See also* Antonetti, *supra* note 47, at 698: "[M]ental–mental claims have gained recognition in an expanding number of jurisdictions through judicial interpretation. In recent years, however, a new trend has developed. Legislatures, concerned about overburdening employers with liability for mental–mental claims, have narrowed the range of compensable claims. This trend will likely continue for a number of years as legislatures seek to chart a middle ground between their constituencies of workers and employers").

75. Note, *supra* note 9, at 211.

76. DOOLEY, *supra* note 4, at 8.

77. *Id.*

78. *Id.*

79. *See generally* WILLIAM PROSSER, LAW OF TORTS (4th ed. 1971).

80. *Id.* at 324.

81. *Id.* at 327.

82. 17 Cal. 3d 425, 557 P.2d 334, 131 Cal. Rptr. 14 (1976).

83. RALPH SLOVENKO, PSYCHIATRY AND LAW 278 (1973).

84. RESTATEMENT (SECOND) OF THE LAW OF TORTS § 282 (1965).

85. HOWARD L. OLECK, OLECK'S TORT LAW PRACTICE MANUAL 127 (1982).

86. *Id.*

87. SLOVENKO, *supra* note 83, at 278.

88. *Id.* at 296 (quoting Lord Chancellor Francis Bacon).

89. *Id.* at 297.

90. *Id.* at 298.

91. Arthur C. Roberts & Allen P. Wilkinson, *Developing a Positive Picture at Trial,* 19(1) TRIAL 56 (1983).

92. William H. Theis, *The Intentional Infliction of Emotional Distress: A Need for Limits on Liability,* 27 DEPAUL L. REV. 275, 275 (1977).

93. Ronald E. Goins, *Intentional Infliction of Emotional Distress—Escaping the Impact Rule in Arkansas,* 35 ARK. L. REV. 533, 536–37 (1981).

94. *Id.* at 533–36.

95. Thomas F. Lambert, Jr., *Tort Liability for Psychic Injuries: Overview and Update,* 37 A.T.L.A. L.J. 1 (1978).

96. MARILYN MINZER ET AL., 1 DAMAGES IN TORT ACTIONS 6–3 (1991). All but Kentucky, Indiana, Maine, Rhode Island, Vermont, West Virginia, and Wyoming are said to recognize the tort. *Compare* David B. Millard, *Intentionally and Negligently Inflicted Emotional Distress: Toward a Coherent Reconciliation,* 15 IND. L. REV. 617, 631 n. 94 (1982) (finding only 38 states that recognize the tort).

97. MINZER ET AL., *supra* note 96, at 6-3–6-13.

98. *Id.* at 6–32.

99. *Id.* at 6–40.

100. *Id.* at 6–43 (citing RESTATEMENT [SECOND] OF THE LAW OF TORTS).

101. *Id.* at 6-44–6-45.

102. OLECK, *supra* note 85, at 77.

103. Such conduct has included the following: assaults, interference with the enjoyment of property, threats, discrimination, defamation, false imprisonment, malicious prosecution, interference with business relationships, wrongful eviction, unlawful suspension from a labor union, detention by an undertaker of the dead body of the plaintiff's son for the purpose of collecting an account, fraudulent inducement to enter a bigamous marriage, breach of promise to marry, sending a package containing a dead rat instead of an expected loaf of bread, and failure to provide prompt ambulance service. MINZER ET AL., *supra* note 96, at 6-60–6-68.

104. *Id.* at 6–139.

105. Annot., 20 A.L.R. 4th 773, 777 (1983).

106. Annot., 40 A.L.R. 3d 1290, 1293–94 (1971).

107. MINZER ET AL., *supra* note 96, at 6–144–6–145.

108. RESTATEMENT (SECOND) OF THE LAW OF TORTS § 46 cmt. j (1965).

109. MINZER ET AL., *supra* note 96, at 6–88.

110. According to a recent survey, 15 states recognized the tort of negligent infliction of emotional distress without requiring the presence of a physical injury: Alabama, California, Connecticut, Hawaii, Illinois, Iowa, Louisiana, Missouri, Montana, Nebraska, New York, North Carolina, Ohio, Texas and West Virginia. Mary Donovan, *Is the Injury Requirement Obsolete in a Claim for Fear of Future Consequences?*, 41 UCLA L. REV. 1337, 1396 n. 72 (1994).

111. Note, *Administering the Tort of Negligent Infliction of Mental Distress: A Synthesis*, 4 CARDOZO L. REV. 487, 488–89 & n. 9 (1993).

112. *See, e.g.,* Dillon v. Legg, 441 P.2d 912 (Cal. 1968). Although the California courts expanded *Dillon* considerably in the following 20 years, in Thing v. LaChusa, 771 P.2d 814 (Cal. 1989), the California Supreme Court reaffirmed that "in the absence of physical injury or impact to the plaintiff himself, damages for emotional distress should be recoverable only if the plaintiff: (1) is closely related to the injury victim; (2) is present at the scene of the injury-producing event at the time it occurs and is then aware that it is causing injury to the victim and; (3) as a result suffers emotional distress beyond that which would be anticipated in a disinterested witness."

113. *See, e.g.,* Bowen v. Lumbermens Mut. Casualty, Co., 517 N.W.2d 432 (Wis. 1994).

114. Dunphy v. Gregor, 642 A.2d 372 (N.J. 1994) (fiance).

115. These different policy limitations on recovery are discussed in Lambert, Jr., *supra* note 95. *See also* Note, *Negligent Infliction of Emotional Distress—Bystander Recovery*, 21 DUQ. L. REV. 797 (1983); David J. Leibson, *Recovery of Damages for Emotional Distress Caused by Physical Injury to Another*, 15 J. FAM. L. 163 (1976–77); MINZER ET AL., *supra* note 96, at 5-22–5-25.

116. Culbert v. Sampson's Supermarkets, Inc., 444 A.2d 433 (Me. 1982), *discussed in* Note, *supra* note 115.

117. Shepard v. Superior Ct., 76 Cal. App. 3d 16, 142 Cal. Rptr. 612 (1977).

118. This case is discussed in detail in Helen L. Collins, *Torts—Strict Product Liability—Recovery for Emotional Distress*, 17 DUQ. L. REV. 535 (1978–79).

119. MINZER ET AL., *supra* note 96, at 6–81.

120. Martin Blinder, *The Abuse of Psychiatric Disability Determinations*, 1979 MED. TRIAL TECH. Q. 84, 86 (1979).

121. William F. Sheeley, CLINICAL PSYCHIATRY NEWS, June 1980, quoted in Eric H. Marcus, *Compensation Payments—Blessing or Curse*, 1983 MED. TRIAL TECH. Q. 319, 321 (1983).

122. Eric H. Marcus, *Causation in Psychiatry: Realities and Speculations*, 1983 MED. TRIAL TECH. Q. 424, 430 (1983). Marcus also calls judicial efforts to apply clinical concepts in workers' compensation cases "both logically and psychiatrically fallacious."

123. *Id.* at 431–32.

124. Karen Merrikin et al., *Recognition of Psychologists in Workers' Compensation Law*, 18 PROF. PSYCHOL.: RES. & PRAC. 260 (1987).

125. Jacob P. Panzarella, *The Nature of Work, Job Loss, and the Diagnostic Complexities of Psychologically Injured Workers*, 21 PSYCHIATRIC ANNALS 10 (1991).

126. HENRY DAVIDSON, FORENSIC PSYCHIATRY 92 (2d ed. 1965).

127. *Id.* at 65.

128. BROMBERG, *supra* note 8, at 322.

129. Note, *supra* note 9, at 213.

130. The AMA *Guides, infra* note 132, at 293, suggest that the Wechsler Adult Intelligence Scale (WAIS), the Minnesota Multiphasic Personality Inventory (MMPI), the Rorschach, and the Thematic Apperception Test (TAT) may be useful in establishing the existence of a mental disorder in this context.

131. Roberts & Wilkinson, *supra* note 91, at 58–59.

132. American Medical Association, *Guides to the Evaluation of Permanent Impairment* (4th ed. rev. 1993) [hereinafter AMA *Guides*].

133. Willis J. Spaulding, *A Look at the AMA Guides to the Evaluation of Permanent Impairment: Problems in Workers' Compensation Claims Involving Mental Disability*, 8 BEHAVIORAL SCI. & L. 361, 369 (Table 3) (1990). The states that had adopted the guidelines are Alabama, Alaska, Arizona, Arkansas, Colorado, Connecticut, Delaware, the District of Columbia, Florida, Georgia, Hawaii, Idaho, Indiana, Iowa, Louisiana, Maryland, Massachusetts, Mississippi, Montana, Nebraska, Nevada, New Hampshire, New Mexico, North Dakota, Ohio, Oklahoma, Oregon, Rhode Island, South Carolina, South Dakota, Tennessee, Texas, Utah, Vermont, Washington, and Wyoming.

134. Allen Enslow, *Psychiatric Disorders and Work Function*, 21 PSYCHIATRIC ANNALS 27 (1991).

135. *See* cases summarized in Herbert Lasky, *Psychiatry and California Workers' Compensation Laws: A Threat and a Challenge*, 17 CAL. W. L. REV. 1 (1980).

136. Andrew D. Whyman & Robert J. Underwood, *The Psychiatric Examination in Workers' Compensation*, 21 PSYCHIATRIC ANNALS 36, 52 (1991).

137. AMA *Guides, supra* note 132, at 291.

138. Mental and behavioral disorders are covered in Chapter 14 of the AMA *Guides*, at 291–302.

139. SLOVENKO, *supra* note 83, at 294.

140. LESTER KEISER, THE TRAUMATIC NEUROSES 41 (1968).

141. *Id.* at 300.

142. Because the traumatic stressor and presumed causal relationship to emotional disorder are inherent in the diagnosis, PTSD has become particularly popular in civil litigation. *See* Alan A. Stone, *Post-traumatic Stress Disorder and the Law: Critical Review of the New Frontier*, BULL. AM. ACAD. PSYCHIATRY & L. 23 (1993). *See generally* Landy F. Sparr & James K. Boehnlein, *Posttraumatic Stress Disorder in Tort Actions: Forensic Minefield*, 18 BULL. AM. ACAD. PSYCHIATRY & L. 283 (1990).

143. AMERICAN PSYCHIATRIC ASSOCIATION, DIAGNOSTIC AND STATISTICAL MANUAL OF MENTAL DISORDERS 424 (4th ed. 1994).

144. AMERICAN PSYCHIATRIC ASSOCIATION, DIAGNOSTIC AND STATISTICAL MANUAL OF MENTAL DISORDERS 236 (3d ed. 1980).

145. J. David Kinzie et al., *Posttraumatic Stress Disorder among Survivors of Cambodian Concentration Camps,* 141 AM. J. PSYCHIATRY 645 (1984).

146. William W. Eaton et al., *Impairment in Holocaust Survivors after 33 Years: Data from an Unbiased Community Sample,* 139 AM. J. PSYCHIATRY 773 (1982).

147. Lenore C. Terr, *Psychic Trauma in Children: Observations following the Chowchilla School Bus Kidnapping,* 138 AM. J. PSYCHIATRY 14 (1981).

148. James L. Tichener & Frederic T. Kapp, *Family and Character Change at Buffalo Creek,* 133 AM. J. PSYCHIATRY 295 (1976); Kai T. Erikson, *Loss of Communality at Buffalo Creek,* 133 AM. J. PSYCHIATRY 302 (1976); Charles B. Wilkinson, *Aftermath of a Disaster: The Collapse of the Hyatt Regency Hotel Skywalks,* 140 AM. J. PSYCHIATRY 1134 (1983). For a comprehensive meta-analysis of disaster studies, *see* Anthony V. Rubonis & Leonard Bickman, *Psychological Impairment in the Wake of Disaster: The Disaster–Psychopathology Relationship,* 109 PSYCHOLOG. BULL. 384 (1991).

149. Richard J. Alexander, *"Burning Out" versus "Punching Out,"* 6 J. HUM. STRESS 37 (1980) (describing the gradual "burning out" of air traffic controllers).

150. *See generally* KEISER, *supra* note 140; M. TRIMBLE, POST-TRAUMATIC NEUROSIS: FROM RAILWAY SPINE TO THE WHIPLASH (1981).

151. Rubonis & Bickman, *supra* note 148, at 395–96.

152. Steven M. Southwick et al., *Abnormal Noradrenergic Function in Posttraumatic Stress Disorder,* 50 ARCHIVES GEN. PSYCHIATRY 266, 267 (1993) (80% of PTSD subjects met criteria for lifetime diagnosis of depression; 85% met criteria for alcohol dependence); Brett T. Litz et al., *Assessment of Posttraumatic Stress Disorder,* in POSTTRAUMATIC STRESS DISORDER: A BEHAVIORAL APPROACH TO ASSESSMENT AND TREATMENT 58 (Philip A. Saigh ed. 1992) (studies reviewed suggest 60–100% of PTSD victims have secondary diagnoses, commonly substance abuse or dependence) [hereinafter POSTTRAUMATIC STRESS DISORDER]; David Behar, *Flashbacks and Posttraumatic Stress Symptoms in Combat Veterans,* 28 COMPREHENSIVE PSYCHIATRY 459, 461 (1987) (reporting that of 37 veterans referred to an outpatient clinic for PTSD, 95.4% met criteria for one or more additional psychiatric disorders).

153. David W. Foy et al., *Etiology of Posttraumatic Stress Disorder,* in POSTTRAUMATIC STRESS DISORDER, *supra* note 152, at 28.

154. Behar, *supra* note 152, at 459.

155. Brett T. Litz et al., *Assessment of Posttraumatic Stress Disorder,* in POSTTRAUMATIC STRESS DISORDER, *supra* note 152, at 57. Thomas W. Miller et al., *Assessment of Life Stress Events: The Etiology and Measurement of Traumatic Stress Disorder,* 38 INT'L J. SOC. PSYCHIATRY 215 (1992) (describing ten measures including special scales from conventional tests, such as the MMPI, and special instruments focused on combat-related or civilian accident/disaster events).

156. Wilkinson, *supra* note 148, at 1136.

157. SLOVENKO, *supra* note 83, at 300.

158. Roberts & Wilkinson, *supra* note 91, at 58.

159. *Id.*

160. *Id.*

161. Joseph T. Smith, *The Expert Witness: Maximizing Damages for Psychic Injuries,* 18 (4) TRIAL 51 (1982). Smith summarizes some of the literature concerning psychological impact upon individuals who have undergone stressful events, as well as the grieving process and the characteristics of pathological grief.

162. *Id.* at 51.

163. BROMBERG, *supra* note 8, at 318–22.

164. *Id.* at 332–33.

165. Id. at 334–35.

166. *Id.*

167. Robert H. Woody, *The Pain/Intelligence Nexus in Personal Injury Litigation,* 1979 MED. TRIAL TECH. Q. 249 (1979).

168. BROMBERG, *supra* note 8, at 331. For a detailed discussion of malingering, *see* DAVIDSON, *supra* note 126, ch. 12.

169. BROMBERG, *supra* note 8, at 331.

170. *Id.*

171. For studies showing an increase in the number of stressful life events prior to many "accidents," *see* review by Hanna Levinson et al., *Recent Life Events and Accidents: The Role of Sex Differences,* 9 J. HUM. STRESS 4 (1983). Another article described the following scenario: "A person who has developed a psychiatric disability after a compensable accident was under great psychological stress before the accident. He sent out signals of being accident prone and that 'an accident was waiting to happen.'" The authors concluded that "[t]he accident did not cause the disability, for it was 'subconsciously' caused by the patient himself. Therefore, the nature of the accident is unimportant in understanding the disability." Alexander Hirschfeld & Robert C. Behan, *The Accident Process: I. Etiological Considerations of Industrial Injuries,* 186 J. AM. MED. ASS'N 193 (1963). *But see* Herbert C. Modlin, *The Post Accident Anxiety Syndrome: Psychosocial Aspects,* 123 AM. J. PSYCHIATRY 1008 (1967) (finding no increase in stressful life events prior to accidents). *See generally* Elliott M. Heiman & Stephen B. Shanfield, *Psychiatric Disability Assessment: Clarification of Problems,* 19 COMPREHENSIVE PSYCHIATRY 449 (1978).

172. *See, e.g.,* Mardi Horowitz et al., *Life Event Questionnaires for Measuring Presumptive Stress,* 39 PSYCHOSOMATIC MED. 413 (1977); Diane T. Fairbank & Richard Hough, *Life Event Classifications and the Event–Illness Relationship,* 5 J. HUM. STRESS 41 (1979); J. Gavin Andrews, *Life Event Stress and Psychiatric Illness,* 8 PSYCHOL. MED. 545 (1978); Alex Zautra & Ernst Beier, *The Effects of Life Crisis on Psychological Adjustment,* 6 AM. J. COMMUNITY PSYCHOL. 125 (1978). *But see* Peggy A. Thoits, *Undesirable Life Events and Psychophysiological Distress: A Problem of Operational Confounding,* 46 AM. SOC. REV. 97 (1981); Richard H. Rahe, *Life Change Events and Mental Illness: An Overview,* 5 J. HUM. STRESS 2 (1979) (a review concluding that most studies have found a low, positive correlation (0.16–0.36) between recent life change events and psychological distress, and that the literature to date fails to compellingly

demonstrate the superiority of any aspect of life event assessment over a simple counting of the number of life change events).

173. Barbara S. Dohrenwend et al., *Exemplification of a Method for Scaling Life Events: The PERI Life Events Scale,* 19 J. HEALTH SOC. BEHAV. 205 (1978).

174. Other available scales include the Social Readjustment Rating Scale, *see* Thomas H. Holmes & Richard H. Rahe, *The Social Readjustment Rating Scale,* 11 J. PSYCHOSOMATIC RES. 213 (1967), and the Life Experiences Survey, *see* Irwin G. Sarason et al., *Assessing the Impact of Life Changes: Development of the Life Experiences Survey,* 46 J. CONSULTING & CLINICAL PSYCHOL. 932 (1978). Both of these are considerably briefer (43 and 47 items, respectively) than the PERI Life Events Scale. Different scales have been designed to assess different aspects of the life change experience. Fairbank and Hough, *supra* note 172, focus on the individual's perceived sense of control over the events, whereas Sarason et al., *supra,* focus on the subject's perception of the impact of the change event (positive or negative impact). Both of these are variations on the original Holmes and Rahe assessment, which focuses on the number of life change events in a given time frame.

175. Franklin G. Erbaugh & John D. Benjamin, *Trauma and Mental Disorder,* in TRAUMA AND DISEASE 56 (L. Bradhy & S. Kahn eds. 1937).

176. Herbert Lasky, *Psychiatric Disability Evaluation of the Injured Worker: Legal Overview,* in 21 PSYCHIATRIC ANNALS 16 (1991).

177. AMA *Guides, supra* note 132, at 291–92.

178. Allen J. Enslow, *Psychiatric Disorders and Work Function,* in 21 PSYCHIATRIC ANNALS 27, 29–31 (1991).

179. *Id.*

180. AMA *Guides, supra* note 132, at 4. *See also id.* at 4–5 ("it is a straightforward matter to verify whether or not a numerical rating of impairment is substantiated in accordance with the criteria contained in the *Guides*").

181. AMA *Guides, supra* note 132.

182. *Id.* at 1–3.

183. Blinder, *supra* note 120, at 88.

184. Harley C. Shands, *Comments on "Causal Relation" in Workmen's Compensation Proceedings,* J. PSYCHIATRY & L. 245, 253 (1974).

185. Carroll M. Brodsky, *A Psychiatrist's Reflections on the Workers' Compensation System,* 8 BEHAVIORAL SCI. & L. 331, 345 (1990). *See also* Jayne Patrick, *Personality Characteristics of Work-Ready Workers' Compensation Clients,* 44 J. CLINICAL PSYCHOL. 1009 (1988) (concluding that workers' compensation claimants are not a homogeneous group, and that those judged work-ready scored in the average range on the MMPI, the WAIS-R, and the Wide Range Interest and Opinion Test).

186. John Gardner, *Early Referral and Other Factors Affecting Vocational Rehabilitation Outcome for the Workers' Compensation Client,* 34 REHABILITATION COUNSELING 197 (1991) (studying 1,173 workers' compensation cases in Florida from March–May 1985 and concluding that early referrals [i.e., within six months of the injury] resulted in better rates of job return and lower expenditures in benefits); Rochelle V. Habeck et al., *Employer Factors Related to Workers' Compensation Claims and Disability Management,* 34 REHABILITATION COUNSELING 210 (1991) (finding among 24 hospitals in the Northeast, which had similar incidence and severity of injuries, a "dramatic variability" in the costs and consequences of those injuries, with the single most important cause of variation being the organization's internal system of risk management and its postinjury response).

187. A good summary of the workers' compensation evaluation and report is found in Andrew Whyman & Robert Underwood, *The Psychiatric Examination in Workers' Compensation,* 21 PSYCHIATRIC ANNALS 36 (1991).

188. Blinder, *supra* note 120, at 84–85.

189. *See* Roberts & Wilkinson, *supra* note 91.

Chapter 13

1. 42 U.S.C. §§ 12101–12213 (1994).

2. 135 CONG. REC. § 10770 n. 1.

3. In reaching this conclusion, Congress relied in part on a survey conducted by Louis Harris and Associates in 1986. LOUIS HARRIS & ASSOCIATES, THE ICD SURVEY OF DISABLED AMERICANS: BRINGING DISABLED AMERICANS INTO THE MAINSTREAM. Harris found that nearly two-thirds of Americans with disabilities were unemployed, *id.* at 47. He also discovered many other examples of disenfranchisement among the disabled. For instance, nearly two-thirds of those with a disability had not attended a movie in the year prior to the survey. *Id.* at 37, 39. Other sources recounted other types of discrimination encountered by people with disability; for example, children with Down's syndrome were denied admission to a zoo because the zookeeper thought the children would upset the chimpanzees. S. REP. NO. 116, 101st Cong., 1st Sess. 7 (1989); H.R. REP.NO. 485, 101st Cong., 2d Sess., pt. 2, at 30 (1990).

4. *See supra* note 3. *See also* Report of Senate Committee on Labor and Human Resources, Report No. 101–116, at 9 (Aug. 30, 1989). The percentage of people with a mental disability who *are* employed is difficult to estimate, in part because people who are employed may be reluctant to reveal the existence of a mental disability for fear of reprisal. Jones and his colleagues, *infra* note 8, at 32, recount a 1986 report from the United States Bureau of the Census suggesting that in 1984 there were 154,565,000 people in the work force between the ages of 16 and 64, of whom 22,514,000 were disabled in some way. Of that group it was estimated that 1,473,000 people were impaired because of a psychiatric problem, including people suffering from serious depression (434,000), mental retardation (605,000), nervous or emotional problems (640,000), and senility or Alzheimer's disease (64,000). *See generally* Laura J. Milazzo-Sayre et al., *Serious and Severe Mental Illness and Work: What Do We Know?,* in MENTAL DISORDER, WORK DISABILITY &

THE LAW 13–24 (Richard J. Bonnie & John Monahan eds. 1996).

5. 42 U.S.C. § 12101(a)(1) (1994).

6. 42 U.S.C. § at 12101(a)(9).

7. *See, e.g.*, NICK KATES ET AL., THE PSYCHOLOGICAL IMPACT OF JOB LOSS (1990); MARIE JAHODA, EMPLOYMENT AND UNEMPLOYMENT: A SOCIAL–PSYCHOLOGICAL ANALYSIS (1982); Ralph Catalano et al., *Using ECA Survey Data to Examine the Effect of Job Layoffs on Violent Behavior*, 44 HOSP. & COMMUNITY PSYCHIATRY 874 (1993). Other commentators have argued that despite the clear relationship between job status and mental health, policymakers in the field of mental health have failed to devote the resources necessary to understand and respond to mental health issues of the unemployed. Samuel H. Osipow & Louise F. Fitzgerald, *Unemployment and Mental Health: A Neglected Relationship*, 2 APPLIED & PREVENTIVE PSYCHOL. 59 (1993).

8. Brian J. Jones et al., *A Survey of Fortune 500 Corporate Policies Concerning the Psychiatrically Handicapped*, J. REHABILITATION 31 (Oct.–Dec. 1991). The authors found that of 127 respondents to their survey, only 13 had a "formal policy (i.e., written regulation) specifically concerning the hiring of the psychiatrically handicapped." *Id.* at 33.

9. 29 U.S.C. § 719, 793, 794. For a detailed discussion of the Rehabilitation Act, *see* BONNIE TUCKER & BRUCE A. GOLDSTEIN, LEGAL RIGHTS OF PERSONS WITH DISABILITIES: AN ANALYSIS OF FEDERAL LAW chs. 3–9 (1992).

10. 42 U.S.C. § 12112(a) (1994).

11. In an excellent summary and discussion of the ADA, Burgdorf observes that a distinguishing feature of the ADA is "the extensive statutory language devoted to defining discrimination and establishing standards to prohibit it." He attributes this specificity to a reluctance on the part of Congress to leave the development of legal standards under the Act "to the vagaries of the regulatory and judicial processes," and the "idiosyncracies of disability discrimination, which demand more statutory guidance than general mandates not to discriminate." Robert L. Burgdorf, *The Americans with Disabilities Act: Analysis and Implications of a Second-Generation Civil Rights Statute*, 26 HARV. C.R.-C.L. L. REV. 413, 509–10 (1991). Burgdorf notes that this specificity may become a problem because statutory flaws must be amended by Congress rather than dealt with by courts or regulatory bodies.

12. 42 U.S.C. § 12112(b)(1)–(7) (1994).

13. 42 U.S.C. § 12111(8) (1994).

14. 42 U.S.C. § 12102(2) (1994).

15. John Parry, *Mental Disability Coverage and Important Terms of the Americans with Disabilities Act*, in MENTAL DISABILITIES AND THE AMERICANS WITH DISABILITIES ACT: A PRACTITIONER'S GUIDE TO EMPLOYMENT, INSURANCE, TREATMENT, PUBLIC ACCESS AND HOUSING 2 (1994). *See also* School Board v. Arline, 480 U.S. 273, 284 (1987), which held that the analogous provisions of the Rehabilitation Act "acknowledged that society's accumulated myths and fears about disability and diseases are as handicapping as are the physical limitations that flow from actual impairment."

16. For instance, Senator Jesse Helms linked pedophiles, people with schizophrenia, those with manic–depressive illness, transvestites, and people who are HIV positive, and declared that none should be covered by the ADA. 135 Cong. Rec. S.10765–01 (1989).

17. 29 C.F.R. § 1630.2(h)(2). An excellent discussion of the ADA and learning disabilities can be found at Paul D. Grossman, *Employment Discrimination Law for the Learning Disabled Community*, 15 LEARNING DISABILITY Q. 287 (1992). For two cases addressing the subject of learning disabilities and the ADA, *see* Wynne v. Tufts Univ. Sch. of Medicine, 976 F.2d 791 (1st Cir. 1992) (Tufts Medical School acted reasonably in attempting to accommodate plaintiff's learning disability by arranging for tutors, examinations at Tufts' expense, and other assistance and was not required to change the way it administered examinations); Pandazides v. Virginia Bd. of Educ., 1994 U.S. App. Lexis 672 (4th Cir. 1994) (reinstating a claim from a learning-disabled plaintiff that the defendant should modify the administration of its tests for certification as a teacher.

18. *See* Paul F. Mickey, Jr. & Maryelena Pardo, *Dealing with Mental Disabilities under the ADA*, 9 LAB. L. REP. 531 (1993).

19. *Id.* at 534.

20. 42 U.S.C. § 12114(a) & (b) (1994). *See also* U.S Equal Employment Opportunity Commission, *A Technical Assistance Manual on the Employment Provisions (Title I) of the Americans with Disabilities Act* at II-7 (1992)[hereinafter EEOC Manual]. On April 30, 1997, guidelines dealing specifically with people who have a mental disorder were issued by the EEOC. *See* N.Y. TIMES, April 30, 1997, at A1, A15.

21. 42 U.S.C. § 12211(a) & (b) (1994).

22. 42 U.S.C. § 12211(b)(1)-(3) (1994). Other excluded conditions include transvestism, pedophilia, transsexualism, exhibitionism, voyeurism, gender identity disorders not resulting from physical impairments, other sexual behavior disorders, and compulsive gambling.

23. EEOC Manual, *supra* note 20, at II-2.

24. *Id.* at II-3.

25. Hindman v. GTE Data Services, Inc., 63 U.S.L.W. 2096 (M.D. Fla. 1994).

26. 29 C.F.R. § 1630(j)(2)(i)-(iii) (1993).

27. Laura Lee Hall, *Making the ADA Work for People with Psychiatric Disabilities*, in MENTAL DISORDER, WORK DISABILITY AND THE LAW, *supra* note 4, 241, at 244.

28. EEOC Manual, *supra* note 20, at II-3.

29. Christopher Bell, *The Americans with Disabilities Act, Mental Disability, and Work*, in MENTAL DISORDER, WORK DISABILITY AND THE LAW, *supra* note 4, 203 at 208.

30. John Parry, *Mental Disabilities Under the ADA: A Difficult Path to Follow*, 17 MENTAL & PHYSICAL DISABILITY L. REP. 100, 102 (1993).

31. Mickey & Pardo, *supra* note 18, at 534.

32. EEOC Manual, *supra* note 20, at II-9.

33. EEOC Manual, *supra* note 20, at II-10.

34. EEOC Manual, *supra* note 20, at II-11.

35. *Id.*

36. 42 U.S.C. § 12111(8) (1994).

37. EEOC Manual, *supra* note 20, at II-11–II-12.

38. *Id.* at II-12.

39. 29 C.F.R. § 1630.2(n)(1) (1993).

40. 29 C.F.R. § 1630.2(n)(2)(i) (1993); *EEOC Title I Regulations and Interpretive Appendix* B-19 [hereinafter EEOC Appendix].

41. 29 C.F.R. § 1630.2(n)(2)(ii) (1993).

42. 29 C.F.R. § 1630.2(n)(2)(iii) (1993).

43. 29 C.F.R. § 1630.2(n)(3)(ii)–(vii) (1993). For additional commentary on the essential functions idea, *see* Margaret H. Edwards, *The ADA and the Employment of Individuals with Mental Disabilities,* 18 EMPLOYEE REL. L.J. 347, 359–62 (1992–93); Michael T. Brannick et al., *Job Analysis, Personnel Selection, and the ADA,* 2 HUM. RESOURCE MGMT REV. 171, 176 (1992). *See also* EEOC Manual, *supra* note 20, at II-19, II-20 (discussing the need for and content of a job analysis).

44. 29 C.F.R. § 1630.2(n)(3)(i) (1993).

45. 967 F.2d 794 (2d Cir 1992).

46. 1993 WESTLAW 106166 (S.D.N.Y. 1993).

47. No. 03940027 (EEOC May 12, 1994), *reported at* 18 MENTAL AND PHYSICAL DISABILITY L. REP. 426 (1994).

48. 42 U.S.C. § 12112(5)(A) (1994).

49. 42 U.S.C. § 12112(5)(B) (1994).

50. For instance, the reasonable accommodation principle has been called a "major element of disability nondiscrimination regulations and caselaw under the Rehabilitation Act." Burgdorf, *supra* note 11, at 460. *See also* U.S. COMMISSION ON CIVIL RIGHTS, ACCOMMODATING THE SPECTRUM OF INDIVIDUAL ABILITIES 102 (1983) ("discrimination against handicapped people cannot be eliminated if programs, activities, and tasks are always structured in the ways that people with 'normal' physical and mental abilities customarily undertake them. Adjustments or modifications of opportunities to permit handicapped people to participate fully have been broadly termed 'reasonable accommodation'").

51. EEOC Manual, *supra* note 20, at III-2.

52. 42 U.S.C. § 12111(9)(A)–(B) (1994).

53. 42 U.S.C. § 12111.

54. EEOC Manual, *supra* note 20, at III-15.

55. LAURA L. MANCUSO, CASE STUDIES ON REASONABLE ACCOMMODATION FOR WORKERS WITH PSYCHIATRIC DISABILITIES (1993). Mancuso, who explores in some depth the experiences of ten workers with a mental disability, concludes from her interviews that the decision to disclose or not disclose the existence of a mental disability is a major decision and source of conflict for employees and applicants. She identifies several benefits from disclosing the existence of a disability, including the fact that disclosure permits the worker to ask for and be involved in creating a reasonable accommodation. In addition, it permits a worker to have a job coach come to the work site and communicate with the employer, makes it easier to come to work at a time of heightened symptoms, is likely to be consistent with the process of recovery, and permits coworkers to offer support. She also notes several potential hazards from disclosure, including being teased or harassed by coworkers, risking the possibility that despite the ADA the employer may find a reason not to hire based on the disability, limiting the opportunities

for career advancement, and creating conflict with one's self perception or beliefs. Related to the latter point, "[t]here appears to be no consensus as to how, when, to whom or what information should be disclosed in the accommodation process. Poor self-awareness or self-denial may also make disclosure difficult." Bell, *supra* note 29, at 212.

56. DEBORAH ZUCKERMAN, KATHLEEN DEBENHAM, & KENNETH MOORE, THE ADA AND PEOPLE WITH MENTAL ILLNESS: A RESOURCE MANUAL FOR EMPLOYERS 36 (1993). The authors identify several related barriers to reasonable accommodation, including a lack of resources to cover a person's job if he or she takes leave because of illness and concern on the part of the employer and other employees that accommodations will lower standards. This publication, published jointly by the American Bar Association and the National Mental Health Association, is a good guide to issues associated with implementing the ADA in the area of employment for people with mental illness.

57. ZUCKERMAN, *supra* note 56, at 25.

58. One study found, for instance, that employees with a mental disability most frequently cited a flexible or part-time schedule as a helpful accommodation. MANCUSO, *supra* note 55, at 47.

59. Edwards, *supra* note 43, at 381–82.

60. No. 01931927 (EEOC May 5, 1994), *reported in* 18 MENTAL & PHYSICAL DISABILITY L. REP. 527 (1994).

61. *See also* Mackie v. Runyon, 804 F.Supp.1508 (M.D. Fla. 1992) (a postal employee who was unable because of an alleged disability to work the night shift was unable to perform the "essential functions" of a job that historically was scheduled almost exclusively for the night shift); Hilton-Boy v. Shalala, No. 03930059 (EEOC Sept. 10, 1993), *reported in* 18 MENTAL & PHYSICAL DISABILITY L. REP. 168 (1994) (a woman disabled by stress syndrome and major clinical depression not "qualified" to carry out a claims technician job and unable to suggest any ways in which she could be reasonably accommodated).

62. EEOC Manual, *supra* note 20, at VII-7.

63. Edwards, *supra* note 43, at 379 ("accommodating the employee with a mental disability by reassigning the employee to another position has been particularly problematic for courts under the Rehabilitation Act. A number of decisions have said that no such reassignment is required when the individual is not otherwise qualified or is no longer qualified for his or her present position").

64. *See, e.g.,* Shea v. Tisch, 870 F.2d 786 (1st Cir. 1989).

65. "Reasonable accommodation may include . . . reassignment to a vacant position." 42 U.S.C. § 12111(9)(B) (1994).

66. *See* 42 U.S.C. § 12112(b)(2) (1994).

67. Judith A. Cook et al., *Field-Testing a Post-Secondary Faculty In-Service Training for Working with Students Who Have Psychiatric Disabilities,* 17 PSYCHOSOCIAL REHABILITATION J. 157 (1993).

68. EEOC Manual, *supra* note 20, at III-33.

69. 29 C.F.R. § 1630.2(o).

70. *See, e.g.,* Jessica Wolf & Stephen DiPietro, *From Patient to Student: Supported Education Programs in Southwest*

Connecticut, 15 Psychosocial Rehabilitation J. 61 (1992); M.D. Tashjian et al., Best Practice Study of Vocational Rehabilitation Services to Severely Mentally Ill Persons (Washington, D.C.: Policy Study Associates, 1989), *cited in* Hall, *supra* note 27, at 267, 271.

71. Bell, *supra* note 29, at 215–216.

72. Jean Campbell & Caroline Kaufmann, *Equality and Difference in the ADA: Unintended Consequences for Employment of People with Mental Health Disabilities,* in Mental Disorder, Work Disability and the Law, *supra* note 4, 221, at 233–34.

73. 42 U.S.C. § 12113(b) (1994).

74. 42 U.S.C. § 12111(3).

75. 29 C.F.R. § 1630.2(r) (1993).

76. EEOC Appendix, *supra* note 40, at B-28–B-29.

77. Edwards, *supra* note 43, at 375–76. *See also* Ramachandar v. Sobol, 838 F. Supp. 100 (1993) (physician who refused to take lithium for a manic–depressive illness and who as a result practiced while impaired is not entitled to accommodation: The law "does not require professional licensing authorities, against their best judgment, to play Russian roulette with public health. Reasonable accommodation, in the context of permitting a physician to practice medicine, necessarily is accommodation that eliminates significant risk to patients.").

78. No. 03920107 (EEOC Nov. 23, 1993), *reported in* 18 Mental & Physical Disability L. Rep. 270 (1994).

79. *See also* Davis v. West, No. 03930085 (EEOC Dec. 16, 1993), *reported in* 18 Mental & Physical Disability L. Rep. 270 (1994) (postal worker who crashed while under the influence of alcohol and drugs can be fired despite availability of treatment, given the public safety risk); Daniels-Merritt v. Johnson, 1993 U.S. Dist. LEXIS 18331 (W.D. Mo. 1993) (demotion and then discharge of an employee permissible despite allegation that she could work under a different supervisor, in part because of "paranoia directed toward the high level management officials" and in part because she was virtually impossible to work with or supervise, despite several counseling sessions). *But see* Hindman v. GTE Data Services, Inc., 63 U.S.L.W. 2096 (M.D. Fla. 1994) (court refused to grant summary judgment to GTE despite the plaintiff's violation of company policy in bringing a gun to work; the court found that the company should have investigated the possibility of leaves of absence to accommodate the employee's problems with poor judgment).

80. 687 F. Supp. 1214, 1219 (S.D. Ohio 1988).

81. 42 U.S.C. § 12112(b)(6) (1994).

82. EEOC Manual, *supra* note 20, at IV-1.

83. Zuckerman, *supra* note 56, at 30–31; *Interviewing under the ADA: Know What Not to Ask,* Personnel J. (Supp.) 5 (June 1992).

84. EEOC Manual, *supra* note 20, at V-1.

85. *Id.* at V-18.

86. For a general discussion of the status of psychological testing under the ADA, *see* David W. Arnold & Alan J. Thiemann, *To Test or Not to Test: The Status of Psychological Testing under the Americans with Disabilities Act (ADA),* 6 J. Bus. & Psychol. 503 (1992); Scott L. Martin & Karen B. Slora, *Employee Selection by Testing,* HR Mag. June

1991, at 68. Both of these articles conclude that psychological testing is generally unaffected by the ADA. Arnold and Thiemann note that tests designed to detect a mental impairment "represent a small minority of the tests which are used in employment settings. The vast majority of tests used in employment settings are used to assess applicants with respect to qualities which are not even remotely similar to those contained in the definition of impairment." *Id.* at 505. Although these articles seem generally persuasive, the authors of both articles are employed by firms who design and/or administer such tests as part of the employment process and so may be perceived as having a stake in the outcome of this issue. As noted in the text, for instance, the above quotation may be overly sanguine about the status of testing: Even though it may not test for a disability, a test that has the practical effect of screening out people with a disability violates the ADA.

87. EEOC Manual, *supra* note 20, at V-18.

88. EEOC Manual, *supra* note 20, at V-19. An example of the latter situation comes from DiPompo v. West Point Military Academy, 770 F. Supp. 887 (S.D.N.Y. 1991). There a firefighter with a successful record at two other firefighting companies applied for a job at West Point. The job at West Point, unlike his previous employment, required employees to read and interpret written material regarding toxic substances. The applicant had minimal reading skills because of his dyslexia. The court rejected his argument that the job should be restructured, finding that it was not reasonable under the Rehabilitation Act to require West Point to hire a reader so that the applicant could become a firefighter.

89. EEOC Manual, *supra* note 20, at V-19.

90. *Id.* at V-20–V-21.

91. 42 U.S.C. § 12117(a) (1994).

92. The description of this process is taken from the EEOC Manual, *supra* note 20, sect. X.

93. For a general discussion of the enforcement provisions for each of the titles of the ADA, *see* Kristi Bleger, *The Americans with Disabilities Act: Enforcement Mechanisms,* 16 Mental & Physical Disability L. Rep. 347 (1992).

94. Liz Spayd, *The Disabilities Act, One Year Later,* Wash. Post, July 29, 1993, at 23.

95. *Id.*

96. Wilma Randle, *Disabilities Act Strains Enforcement Apparatus,* Chi. Trib., Oct. 31, 1992, at 1.

97. This example, which is used throughout the next three subsections as well, is taken from Doe v. Region 13 Mental Health–Mental Retardation Comm'n, 704 F.2d 1402 (5th Cir. 1983), in which the court found that the plaintiff's depression was an impairment under the Rehabilitation Act but that she was not qualified to perform her job as a therapist. The court did not reach the reasonable accommodation or direct threat issues.

98. *See, e.g.,* studies cited *supra* notes 56, 70. *See also* Ellen S. Fabian et al., *Reasonable Accommodations for Workers with Serious Mental Illness: Type, Frequency, and Associated Outcomes,* 17 Psychosocial Rehabilitation J. 163 (1993); Loretta K. Haggard, *Reasonable Accommodation of Individuals with Mental Disabilities and Psychoactive Substance Use Disorders Under Title I of the Americans with Disabilities Act,*

43 J. URB. & CONTEMP. L. 343 (1993); Laura L. Mancuso, *Reasonable Accommodation for Workers with Psychiatric Disabilities,* 14 PSYCHOSOCIAL REHABILITATION J. 3 (1990).

99. 42 U.S.C. §§ 3601 *et seq.* (1994).

100. 134 Cong. Rec. H. 4603 (statement of Rep. Peter Rodino). Senator Edward Kennedy, chief sponsor of the FHAA in the Senate, referred to the enforcement provisions of the original Fair Housing Act as a "toothless tiger." 100th Cong, 2d Sess., 134 Cong. Record S. 10454 (Aug. 1, 1988).

101. *Recent Developments: Fair Housing Amendments Act of 1988,* 24 HARV. C.R.-C.L. L. REV. 248 (1989).

102. The focus here is on discrimination based on handicap. The statutory amendments also made illegal discrimination in the sale or rental of housing based on "familial status." 42 U.S.C. § 3602(k) (1994 Supp.). For a general discussion of the latter issue, *see* Michael Seng, *Discrimination Against Families with Children and Handicapped Persons Under the 1988 Amendments to the Fair Housing Act,* 22 J. MARSHALL L. REV. 541 (1989).

103. James Kushner, *The Fair Housing Amendments Act of 1988: The Second Generation of Fair Housing,* 42 VAND. L. REV. 1049 (1989); Harold Ellis, *Neighborhood Opposition and the Permissible Purposes of Zoning,* 7 J. LAND USE & ENVTL L. 275 (1992).

104. *See generally* James Alisky & Kenneth Iczkowski, *Barriers to Housing for Deinstitutionalized Psychiatric Patients,* 41 HOSP. & COMMUNITY PSYCHIATRY 93, 94 (1990); Barry Trute et al., *Social Rejection of the Mentally Ill: A Replication Study of Public Attitude,* 24 SOC. PSYCHIATRY & PSYCHIATRIC EPIDEMIOLOGY 69 (1989); Note: *The Impact of Federal Antidiscrimination Laws on Housing for People with Mental Disabilities,* 59 GEO. WASH. L. REV. 413 (1991).

105. For discussion of the central role housing plays in enabling people to live in a community, *see* THE HOMELESS MENTALLY ILL: A TASK FORCE REPORT OF THE AMERICAN PSYCHIATRIC ASSOCIATION (Richard Lamb ed. 1984); Priscilla Ridgeway & Anthony Zipple, *The Paradigm Shift in Residential Services: From the Linear Continuum to Supported Housing Approaches,* 13 PSYCHOSOCIAL REHABILITATION J. 11 (1990); Beth Tanzman, *An Overview of Surveys of Mental Health Consumers' Preferences for Housing and Support Services,* 44 HOSP. & COMMUNITY PSYCHIATRY 450 (1993).

106. Robert Drake et al., *Housing Instability and Homelessness Among After-Care Patients of an Urban State Hospital,* 40 HOSP. & COMMUNITY PSYCHIATRY 46, 47 (1989). In addition, an absence of adequate housing can prolong hospitalization for many individuals. Sharon Salit & Luis Marcos, *Have General Hospitals Become Chronic Care Institutions for the Mentally Ill?,* 148 AM. J. PSYCHIATRY 892 (1991).

107. 473 U.S. 432 (1985).

108. 42 U.S.C. § 3604(f) (1994 Supp.).

109. 42 U.S.C. § 12112(b)(4) prohibits discrimination against a "qualified individual because of the known disability of an individual with whom the qualified individual is known to have a relationship or association."

110. Note, however, that the FHAA excludes certain transactions from its coverage. Most notably, a private home sale by an individual who owns no more than three private homes and makes a sale without a broker is exempt from the FHAA. This exclusion was part of the original Fair Housing Act, and applies as well under the FHAA. Michigan Protection & Advocacy Services, Inc. v. Babin, 799 F. Supp. 695 (E.D. Mich. 1992).

111. H. Rep. No. 485, Pt. 3 101st Cong., 1st Sess.

112. 42 U.S.C. § 3602(h) (1994 Supp.).

113. *Id.*

114. 54 Fed. Reg. 3232.

115. 24 C.F.R. § 100.202(c) (1993).

116. 42 U.S.C. § 3604(3)(A) (1994 Supp.).

117. *Id.*

118. For example, the FHAA requires that for most multifamily dwellings constructed 30 months after the enactment of the FHAA, doors for entering and leaving the dwelling have to be sufficiently wide to permit passage by an individual in a wheelchair. 42 U.S.C. § 3604(3)(c) (1994 Supp.).

119. 42 U.S.C. § 3604(f)(9) (1994 Supp.).

120. 100 C.F.R. § 200(d).

121. 1988 U.S. Code & Cong. Admin. News 2190.

122. John Petrila, *Enforcement of the Fair Housing Amendments Act to Benefit People with Mental Disability,* 45 HOSP. & COMMUNITY PSYCHIATRY 156 (1994). Petrila summarizes cases decided in the area of mental disability under the FHAA and concludes that the FHAA "appears to be emerging as an important tool with which mentally disabled people can obtain housing." *See also* Robert L. Schonfeld & Seth P. Stein, *Fighting Municipal "Tag-Team": The Federal Fair Housing Amendments Act and Its Use in Obtaining Access to Housing for Persons with Disabilities,* 21 FORDHAM URB. L.J. 299 (1994).

123. 42 U.S.C. § 3607(b).

124. H.R. Rep. No. 711, 100th Cong., 1st Sess. 24 (1988).

125. 115 S. Ct. 417 (1995).

126. 974 F.2d 43 (6th Cir. 1992).

127. In another case, Cason v. Rochester Hous. Auth., 748 F. Supp. 1002 (W.D.N.Y. 1990), a court ruled that it was illegal for the city housing authority to force people with diagnoses of major mental illness (in this case, schizophrenia) to prove that they had the ability to live independently before being granted public housing. The court ruling was based on the rationale that no other group of people had to make such a showing, and that the requirement therefore was discriminatory, based on "unsubstantiated prejudices and fears regarding those with mental and physical disabilities." *Id.* at 1008.

128. 823 F. Supp. 1285 (D. Md. 1993).

129. *See also* Ardmore v. City of Akron, 1990 WESTLAW 385236 (N.D. Ohio 1990) (striking down similar notice and hearing requirements).

130. 578 N.Y.S.2d 1004 (1991).

131. 787 F. Supp. 872 (W.D. Wis. 1991).

132. *See also* Horizon House Developmental Services, Inc. v. Township of Upper Southampton, 804 F. Supp. 683 (E.D. Pa. 1992) (finding a requirement that group homes be separated by at least one thousand feet discriminatory on its face and therefore violative of the FHAA).

133. 720 F. Supp. 720 (S.D. Ill. 1989).

134. *Id.* at 726. Another court reached a similar conclusion in a case in which a community argued that recovering alcoholics and substance abusers were dangerous, because the only "proof" that they posed a direct threat to the community was the "speculative conclusions of the neighbors." Oxford House-Evergreen v. City of Plainfield, 760 F. Supp. 1329 (D.N.J. 1991).

135. 820 F. Supp. 636 (D.N.H. 1993).

136. For example, in Talley v. Lane, 13 F.3d 1031 (7th Cir. 1994), a federal court of appeals affirmed a summary judgment for defendant in a case in which a plaintiff had been convicted for offenses involving narcotics possession. *See also* Housing Auth. v. Pappion, 540 So. 2d 567 (La. Ct. App. 1989), involving a tenant with a diagnosis of schizophrenia who allegedly had threatened other residents and engaged in other disruptive behavior. The reviewing court upheld his eviction, despite evidence that the tenant was now taking medication that had eliminated the complained of behaviors. This case is criticized by one commentator on the ground that the court should have given the tenant a "second chance" as a reasonable accommodation. Note, *supra* note 104, at 445.

137. *See generally* 42 U.S.C. §§ 3610 *et seq.* for the statutory provisions concerning enforcement of the FHAA.

138. 42 U.S.C. §§ 401 *et seq.*

139. 42 U.S.C. §§ 1381 *et seq.*

140. Prior to 1972, the Social Security program was a mixture of federal and state responsibility, with states using disparate substantive and procedural criteria in administering the program. In 1972, Congress enacted a comprehensive overhaul of the Social Security Administration and directed the Administration to create a program with standardized criteria and rules. Since that time, these disability programs largely have been the product of federal law. *See generally* Rachelle Lombardi, *The Evaluation of Children's Impairments in Determining Disability under the Supplemental Security Income Program,* 57 FORDHAM L. REV. 1107 (1989).

141. *Id.*

142. Mark D. DeBofsky, *Social Security Disability Law: A Game Plan,* TRIAL 18 (June 1988).

143. For instance, individuals qualifying for SSDI become entitled to Medicare, whereas those qualifying for SSI generally become eligible for Medicaid. *Id.* at 18. *See also* Michael C. Parks, *The Relationship between Medicaid and Social Security Administration Disability Determinations: An Introduction for Advocates,* CLEARINGHOUSE REV. 1566 (April 1992). Parks's article provides a very good introduction for those wishing to acquire more information on the complex relationship between SSA determinations and state determinations of Medicaid eligibility.

144. Statement of Peter J. McGough, Associate Director, Human Resources Division, General Accounting Office, before the Senate Special Comm. on Aging, 98th Cong., 1st Sess. 6 (1983) [hereinafter GAO Testimony].

145. City of New York v. Heckler, 578 F. Supp. 1109 (E.D.N.Y.), *aff'd,* 742 F.2d 729 (2d Cir. 1984), *aff'd sub nom.,* Bowen v. City of New York, 476 U.S. 467 (1986).

Prior to *Heckler*, the policies pursued by the SSA resulted in a precipitous decline in the numbers of people receiving favorable SSI determinations and approximately 500,000 having benefits terminated; furthermore, people with mental disability were singled out for such terminations. Richard E. Levy, *Social Security Claimants with Developmental Disabilities: Problems of Policy and Practice,* 39 KAN. L. REV. 529, 530–40 (1991). After the Supreme Court's ruling, the SSA changed its policy to one of encouraging people to apply for benefits, and funded outreach programs designed to locate people who were eligible for benefits but had not yet applied. *See, e.g.,* SSI Outreach Demonstration Program for FY 1992, 56 Fed. Reg. 4784 (Sept. 20, 1991) (announcing the availability of funds and requesting applications for "cooperative agreements which increase outreach efforts to needy aged, blind, and disabled individuals who are potentially eligible for the SSI program").

146. In 1984, Congress enacted the Social Security Disability Benefits Reform Act of 1984, 42 U.S.C. § 1305, directing SSA to revise the criteria for determining whether an individual had a mental impairment and whether the impairment had a significant impact on the person's ability to work.

147. This definition is found in the SSDI statutory scheme at 42 U.S.C. § 423(d)(1)(A) (1991), and in the SSI scheme at 42 U.S.C. § 1382c(a)(3)(A) (1991).

148. This requirement is contained at 42 U.S.C. § 423 (d)(2)(A) (1991) for SSDI and at 42 U.S.C. § 1382c(a)(3)(B) (1991) for SSI.

149. *See generally* 20 C.F.R. §§ 404.1505 through 404.1599 (1993).

150. 20 C.F.R. § 404.1510 (1993).

151. Levy, *supra* note 145, at 545–50.

152. 20 C.F.R. § 404.1520(1993).

153. 20 C.F.R. § 404.1521(b) (1993).

154. *See, e.g.,* Moore v. Sullivan, U.S. App. LEXIS 3312 (5th Cir. 1990) (holding that schizophrenia can meet the duration requirement even if it had been in remission for some period during last 12 months); Singletary v. Bowen, 798 F.2d 818 (5th Cir. 1986).

155. Bowen v. Yuckert, 482 U.S. 137, 141 (1987). *See also* Bowen v. City of New York, 476 U.S. 467, 471 (1986), in which the Court observed that "if a claimant's condition meets or equals the listed impairments, he is conclusively presumed to be disabled and entitled to benefits."

156. 20 C.F.R. Pt. 404, subpt. P., app. I, ch. 12.00. At various times, the SSA has indicated in regulation that it might let the mental impairment listings lapse or significantly revise them. However, that has not happened to date, and the listings apply at least through 1997.

157. 20 C.F.R. Pt. 404, subpt. P., app. I, ch. 12.00 (1993).

158. 20 C.F.R. § 404.1520(e)(1993).

159. 20 C.F.R. § 404.1520(f)(1993).

160. 20 C.F.R. § 404.1545 (1993).

161. Christensen v. Bowen, 633 F. Supp. 1214, 1216 (N.D. Cal. 1986); Ceballos v. Bowen, 649 F. Supp. 693, 704 (S.D.N.Y. 1986).

162. 42 U.S.C. § 423(d)(3) (1991).

163. Lebus v. Harris, 526 F. Supp. 56, 60 (N.D. Cal. 1981).

164. Bell, *supra* note 29, at 218.

165. Publ. L. No. 104–193 (the Personal Responsibility and Work Opportunity Reconciliation Act of 1996).

166. 42 U.S.C. § 1382c(a)(3) (1993).

167. 493 U.S. 521 (1990).

168. *Id.* at 535 n. 15 (citing House Committee on Ways and Means, *Background Material and Data on Programs Within the Jurisdiction of the Committee on Ways and Means,* 101st Cong., 1st Sess. 46 [1989]).

169. Other data from the House Ways and Means Committee report, *supra* note 168, indicated that SSA had significantly reduced the proportion of cases in which it found that individuals had an impairment meeting or comparable to those on the listings. In 1975, for instance, a match between the individual and list was found in 43.9% of the cases; in 1983, that figure had fallen to 8.3%, rising slightly in the next few years to 11.0% in 1988. *See* Richard P. Weishaupt & Robert E. Rains, Sullivan v. Zebley: *New Disability Standards for Indigent Children to Obtain Government Benefits,* 35 Soc. Sec. Rep. Ser. 3 n. 115 (1992). These figures suggested the importance of the additional steps for adults, because if SSA was engaged in an effort to reduce benefit eligibility by applying the impairment criteria restrictively, the additional steps provided another opportunity for an individual to gain benefits.

170. 493 U.S. at 539.

171. 20 C.F.R. § 416.924 (1993).

172. 20 C.F.R. § 416.924(f) (1993).

173. *Id.*

174. *See generally* 20 C.F.R. § 416.924e(b)(1)–(3) (1993). The remaining developmental categories are age 3 to attainment of age 6, age 6 to attainment of age 16, and age 16 to attainment of age 18.

175. 20 C.F.R. § 416.924c (1993). The SSA defined these domains in the following manner. *Cognition*—the ability to learn through perception, reasoning, or intuition and to retain, use, and manifest the acquired knowledge in action or communication. *Communication*—the ability to receive, comprehend, and express messages in order to meet one's needs or to obtain or convey information; with respect to speech, it refers to audibility, intelligibility, and efficiency of speech production. *Motor skills*—the ability to use one's body and extremities in gross and fine motions to relate to the physical environment and serve one's own or others' physical needs or purposes. *Social skills*—the ability to form, develop, and sustain relationships with other people on a personal and social basis, to respond appropriately within one's own social role or to the social roles of others, and to conduct oneself according to the manners and mores of the social group. *Personal/behavioral patterns* referred to activities and behaviors entailed in self-help (feeding, dressing), self-regulation (maintaining proper nutrition, sleep, regulating mood), self-improvement (increasing self-help behavior through learning new skills), self-protection

(taking necessary safety precautions), and self-control (adapting to changes in environment or activity, controlling impulsive or aggressive behaviors that could otherwise result in harm to oneself, others, or property). Office of Disability, SSA, HHS, *Determining Disability for a Child Under 18: Title XVI,* Instructor's Guide sec. IV, at 9.

176. *Id.* The SSA defined *responsiveness to stimuli* as physical and emotional behaviors in reaction to visual, auditory, or tactile stimulation, manifesting an infant's sensitivity to stimuli within a range of normal, hypersensitive (excessive response, such as overexcitability or fearfulness), or hyposensitive (minimal or absent response, as in withdrawal or apathy). *Concentration, persistence, and pace* referred to the ability to sustain a focus on, and pay attention to, an activity or task, and to perform the activity or complete the task at a reasonable or age-appropriate rate. *Id.*

177. Julie Clark, *Determining Disability for Children: Implementation of Sullivan v. Zebley, Part I: The New Sequential Evaluation Process—An Overview,* Clearinghouse Rev., 246, 247 (July 1991).

178. 42 U.S.C. § 1382c(a)(3) (1996).

179. *Id.*

180. The Bazelon Center for Mental Health Law, *The Impact of Children's SSI Program Changes in Welfare Reform* 1,2 (Aug. 7, 1996).

181. *Id.*

182. 20 C.F.R. § 416.924(c) (1993). Although the SSA is likely to promulgate new regulations to implement the 1996 amendments, the portion of the regulations discussed in this and the next paragraph are unlikely to change significantly.

183. 20 C.F.R. § 416.924(d) (1993).

184. 20 C.F.R. § 416.924(e) (1993).

185. *Id.*

186. *See generally* Ronald Gilbert & J. Douglas Peters, *The Social Security Disability Claim,* 24(6) Prac. Law. 47, 53 (1979).

187. 42 U.S.C. § 421 (1991); 20 C.F.R. § 404.1503 (1993).

188. Sam O. Opaku, *The Psychiatrist and the Social Security Disability Insurance and Supplemental Security Income Programs,* 39 Hosp. & Community Psychiatry 879 (1988).

189. Francis J. O'Byrne, *How to Prepare the Social Security Disability Case,* 35(3) Prac. Law. 61, 62 (1989). The Secretary of Health and Human Services may overrule the state agency's conclusion, however. 20 C.F.R. § 404.1503(d) (1993).

190. *See generally* 20 C.F.R. §§ 404.929 *et seq.* (1993).

191. Alan K. Goldhammer, *Evidentiary Considerations in Disability Adjudication—A Judge's Perspective,* 44 Admin. L. Rev. 445–52 (1992).

192. For a discussion of the role of a vocational expert in these hearings, *see* R. Michael Booker, *A Guide to the Effective Use of Vocational Experts in Social Security Disability Hearings,* 9 Am. J. Trial Advoc. 237 (1985).

193. Thompson v. Schweiker, 549 F. Supp. 51, 52 (D. Ore. 1982); Christensen v. Bowen, 633 F. Supp. 1214, 1222 (N.D. Cal. 1986).

194. 20 C.F.R. § 404.1517 (1993).

195. Ceballos v. Bowen, 649 F. Supp. 693, 697 (S.D.N.Y. 1986); Murray v. Heckler, 722 F.2d 499, 501–02 (9th Cir. 1983).

196. O'Byrne, *supra* note 189, at 63.

197. 20 C.F.R. § 404.953 (1993).

198. The district court in *Heckler, supra* note 145, found that "the mentally ill are particularly vulnerable to bureaucratic errors. Some do not even understand the communications they receive from SSA. Others are afraid of the system. Even with help from social workers and others, many do not appeal denials or terminations. An erroneous termination or denial of benefits to a mentally ill person means more than that he or she will no longer receive benefits. To many it may mean a severe medical setback. [A psychiatrist] testified that one of her patients who had not been hospitalized for fifteen years was hospitalized as a result of the trauma of having benefits cut off. This was not a unique case. Some slip into acute paranoia while others become suicidal." 578 F. Supp. at 1115.

199. Special Report: *Guidelines for Psychiatric Evaluation of Social Security Disability Claimants,* 34 HOSP. & COMMUNITY PSYCHIATRY 1044, 1048 (1983) [hereinafter Special Report].

200. 20 C.F.R. § 404, subpt. P, app. 1, C1–4.

201. For an excellent summary of these issues, *see* Opaku, *supra* note 188.

202. The PRTF and related forms can be obtained by writing to Social Security Administration, Office of Disability, Division of Medical and Vocational Policy, 3–A-10

Operations Building, 6401 Security Bldg., Baltimore, MD 21235.

203. 20 C.F.R. § 404.1520a(3)(c)(1) (1993).

204. This example is from Booker, *supra* note 192, app. 2.

205. Commentary, *Disability Determination: Psychiatrists Needed,* 36 HOSP. & COMMUNITY PSYCHIATRY 337 (1985).

206. GAO testimony, *supra* note 144, at 16.

207. Special Report, *supra* note 199, at 1048. As another example, the APA notes that statements such as "this patient has a severe ongoing depression that completely immobilizes him" are inadequate because the regulations require support for this conclusion by "symptoms, signs, and laboratory findings." *Id.* at 1047 n. 196.

208. SSA Program Circular, Office of the New York Regional Comissioners, No. 6-79 (Aug. 22, 1979).

209. *Id.* at 3.

210. 20 C.F.R. § 404, subpt P., app. 1, § 12.00(C) (4) (1993).

211. 20 C.F.R. § 404.1530(a) (1993).

212. Special report, *supra* note 199, at 1048–51.

213. *Id.* at 1048–51.

214. 55 Fed. Reg. 51,210 (No. 239, 1990).

215. 20 C.F.R. pt. 404, subpt. P., app. 1, ch. 112.00 (1993).

216. 20 C.F.R. pt. 404, subpt. P., app. 1, § 112.00E (1993).

217. 20 C.F.R. pt. 404, subpt. P., app. 1, § 112.00F (1993).

Chapter 14

1. GARY B. MELTON ET AL., PSYCHOLOGICAL EVALUATIONS FOR THE COURTS: A HANDBOOK FOR MENTAL HEALTH PROFESSIONALS AND LAWYERS 291 (1st ed. 1987) (notes omitted).

2. *See, e.g.,* BARRY C. FELD, JUSTICE FOR CHILDREN: THE RIGHT TO COUNSEL AND THE JUVENILE COURTS (1993).

3. *See* MICHAEL A. JONES & BARRY KRISBERG, IMAGES AND REALITY: JUVENILE CRIME, YOUTH VIOLENCE AND PUBLIC POLICY (1994); James C. Howell et al., *Trends in Juvenile Crime and Youth Violence,* in SERIOUS, VIOLENT, AND CHRONIC JUVENILE OFFENDERS: A SOURCEBOOK 1 (James C. Howell et al. eds. 1995) [hereinafter SOURCEBOOK].

4. Ira M. Schwartz, *Juvenile Crime-Fighting Policies: What the Public Really Wants,* in JUVENILE JUSTICE AND PUBLIC POLICY: TOWARD A NATIONAL AGENDA 214 (Ira M. Schwartz ed. 1992) [hereinafter PUBLIC POLICY].

5. GENERAL ACCOUNTING OFFICE, JUVENILE JUSTICE: JUVENILES PROCESSED IN CRIMINAL COURT AND CASE DISPOSITIONS (Aug. 1995) (Report No. GAO/GGD-95–170). The number of transfers increased 68% between 1988 and 1992, nearly three times faster than the number of juvenile cases overall. JEFFREY A. BUTTS, DELINQUENCY CASES IN JUVENILE COURT, 1992, 1–2 (July

1994). It is likely that transfers have increased still more rapidly in the mid-1990s as many state legislatures have made transfer easier by broadening the range of cases potentially subject to it and loosening the procedural requirements that prosecutors must address in transfer cases. Howell et al., *supra* note 3, at 21–22; Lemov, *The Assault on Juvenile Justice,* GOVERNING, Dec. 1994, at 26, 26–27.

6. MELTON ET AL., *supra* note 1, at 291.

7. Although the term "infant" has come to have a colloquial meaning referring to very young children, in law the use is broader—for example, it is synonymous in some contexts with "minor"—and suggests both the continual raising of the threshold age for special status and the law's lack of recognition of the differences among children of various ages. The virtual absence of the term "adolescence" from legal commentary is illustrative. *See* FRANKLIN E. ZIMRING, THE CHANGING LEGAL WORLD OF ADOLESCENCE xi–xii (1982).

8. WAYNE R. LAFAVE & AUSTIN W. SCOTT, CRIMINAL LAW 351–52 (1972).

9. *See generally* JOSEPH KETT, RITES OF PASSAGES (1977); David Bakan, *Adolescence in America: From Idea to Social Fact,* in TWELVE TO SIXTEEN: EARLY ADOLESCENCE

73–89 (Jerome Kagan & Robert Coles eds. 1971); Joseph Kett, *The History of Age Grouping in America,* in YOUTH: TRANSITION TO ADULTHOOD 9–29 (James S. Coleman ed. 1974).

10. *See* ANTHONY PLATT, THE CHILD SAVERS: THE INVENTIONS OF DELINQUENCY (2d ed. 1977); Bakan, *supra* note 9.

11. G. STANLEY HALL, ADOLESCENCE: ITS PSYCHOLOGY AND ITS RELATIONS TO PHYSIOLOGY, ANTHROPOLOGY, SOCIOLOGY, SEX, CRIME, RELIGION, AND EDUCATION (1904).

12. *See generally* KETT, *supra* note 9.

13. The first juvenile code (in Illinois) was not enacted until 1899. The development of the juvenile court was coincident with the adoption of compulsory education and child labor laws. *See* Bakan, *supra* note 9. These developments were paralleled by events in Scandinavia, where like-minded reformers established an administrative, therapeutic system for juvenile justice and child welfare. TOVE STANG DAHL, CHILD WELFARE AND SOCIAL DEFENCE (1985).

14. The *parens patriae* power is based on the state's duty to protect dependent persons and their property. The application of this power to quasi-criminal jurisprudence is dubious; it is certainly outside the centuries-old common-law meaning of the term. *In re* Gault, 387 U.S. 1, 16–17 (1967).

15. This practice of using civil terms (e.g., "respondent" instead of "defendant") persists in most jurisdictions, despite the repudiation of the concept that the juvenile court is *really* civil.

16. *In re* Gault, 387 U.S. 1, 14 n.14.

17. The *legal realism* school of jurisprudence, which was especially influential in the first half of this century, is based on a belief that the law is not a static, "natural" whole, but that it should respond to social realities and needs. *See generally* PAUL ROSEN, THE SUPREME COURT AND SOCIAL SCIENCE (1972); Calvin Woodard, *The Limits of Legal Realism: An Historical Perspective,* 54 VA. L. REV. 689 (1968).

18. The use of the term "science" is arguably a misnomer in that the reformers were actually interested in the application of *social welfare* principles to the law. The "science" involved was to be experts' judgments of the best interests of the child, as derived from new penological principles. *See generally* PLATT, *supra* note 10.

19. *See* WALTER F. MURPHY & C. HERMAN PRITCHETT, COURTS, JUDGES, AND POLITICS: AN INTRODUCTION TO THE JUDICIAL PROCESS 5 (3d ed. 1979).

20. Address to the National Council of Juvenile Court Judges (1950), *cited in* Lamar T. Empey, *Introduction: The Social Construction of Childhood and Juvenile Justice,* in THE FUTURE OF CHILDHOOD AND JUVENILE JUSTICE 1, 25 (Lamar T. Empey ed. 1979).

21. *Social facts* are the "recurrent patterns of behavior on which policy must be based." DONALD L. HOROWITZ, THE COURTS AND SOCIAL POLICY 45 (1977).

22. Kent v. United States, 383 U.S. 541, 556 (1966).

23. 387 U.S. 1 (1967).

24. *Id.* at 28.

25. *Id.* at 19.

26. *Id.* at 18.

27. *Id.* at 26.

28. *Id.* at 13.

29. For the range of questions about children's rights that the U.S. Supreme Court has considered, *see* Gary B. Melton, *Rights of Adolescents,* in 2 ENCYCLOPEDIA OF ADOLESCENCE 930 (Richard M. Lerner et al. eds. 1991).

30. 387 U.S. at 31–57.

31. *Id.* at 17.

32. 387 U.S. at 19.

33. McKeiver v. Pennsylvania, 403 U.S. 528, 547, 551 (1971).

34. *See, e.g.,* W. VAUGHAN STAPLETON & LEE E. TEITELBAUM, IN DEFENSE OF YOUTH: A STUDY OF THE ROLE OF COUNSEL IN AMERICAN JUVENILE COURTS (1972); Anthony Platt & Ruth Friedman, *The Limits of Advocacy: Occupational Hazards in Juvenile Court,* 116 U. PA. L. REV. 1156 (1968). A national study conducted by Patricia J. Falk and Gail S. Perry at the University of Nebraska–Lincoln in the early 1980s, although limited by a low response rate, suggested that juvenile court judges are still reluctant to permit full adversariness. They were more likely than juvenile attorneys themselves to favor attorneys' adoption of a guardian's role. *See* Perry, *infra* note 35.

Recent research shows that the right to counsel is still given only lip service in many juvenile courts. Juvenile respondents, especially in nonmetropolitan areas, often have no legal counsel; in some jurisdictions, the majority of respondents are unrepresented. FELD, *supra* note 2; GENERAL ACCOUNTING OFFICE, JUVENILE JUSTICE: REPRESENTATION RATES VARIED AS DID COUNSEL'S IMPACT ON COURT OUTCOMES (June 1995) (Report No. GAO/GGD-95–139); Stevens H. Clarke & Gary G. Koch, *Juvenile Court: Do Lawyers Make a Difference?,* 14 LAW & SOC'Y REV. 263 (1980).

35. *See, e.g.,* JUVENILE JUSTICE STANDARDS RELATING TO COUNSEL FOR PRIVATE PARTIES (1980); STAPLETON & TEITELBAUM, *supra* note 34; Vance L. Cowden & Geoffrey R. McKee, *Competency to Stand Trial in Juvenile Delinquency Proceedings: Cognitive Maturity and the Attorney–Client Relationship,* 33 J. FAM. L. 629, 636–37 (1995), and citations therein; Elyce E. Ferster et al., *The Juvenile Justice System: In Search of the Role of Counsel,* 39 FORDHAM L. REV. 375 (1971); Richard Kay & Daniel Segal, *The Role of the Attorney in Juvenile Court Proceedings: A Non-Polar Approach,* 61 GEO. L.J. 1401 (1973); Patrick D. McAnany, *Gault Attorneys in the Second Decade: Some Normative Reflections,* 29 JUV. & FAM. CT. J. 37 (1978); Theodore McMillan & Dorothy L. McMurtry, *The Role of the Defense Lawyer in Juvenile Court: Advocate or Social Worker?,* 14 ST. LOUIS U. L.J. 561 (1970); Gail S. Perry, Attorney Representational Styles in Juvenile Court: Eenie, Meenie, Miney, Moe (1983) (unpublished M.A. thesis, University of Nebraska–Lincoln).

36. For a particularly thoughtful exposition of the realities of juvenile justice amid the conflicts between treatment and punishment, *see* State *ex rel.* D.D.H. v. Dostert, 269 S.E.2d 401 (W. Va. 1980).

37. Schwartz, *supra* note 4. *See also* IRA M. SCHWARTZ ET AL., COMBATTING JUVENILE CRIME: WHAT THE PUBLIC REALLY WANTS (Apr. 1992) (monograph available from

the Center for the Study of Youth Policy, University of Pennsylvania School of Social Work).

38. JONES & KRISBERG, *supra* note 3, at 1–2.

39. Schwartz, *supra* note 4, at 215.

40. Lemov, *supra* note 5, at 27.

41. Ten states redefined their codes during that period to deemphasize the rehabilitative goal of the juvenile court, and numerous states moved toward a modified "just deserts" approach providing generally for dispositions proportionate to the offense and specifically for mandatory minimum terms or determinate terms for serious offenses. Barry C. Feld, *Juvenile Court Meets Principle of Offense: Punishment, Treatment, and the Difference It Makes,* 68 B.U. L. REV. 821 (1988); Barry C. Feld, *The Punitive Juvenile Court and the Quality of Procedural Justice: Disjunctions between Rhetoric and Reality,* 36 CRIME & DELINQ. 443, 447–51 (1990).

42. One commentator has argued that such apparently divergent goals are reconciled in the context of youthful offender statutes that typically provide for a period of incarceration followed by intensive supervision in the community. Julianne P. Sheffer, Note, *Serious and Habitual Offender Statutes: Reconciling Punishment and Rehabilitation Within the Juvenile Justice System,* 48 VAND. L. REV. 479 (1995).

43. The various views are discussed in § 14.03(b)(3).

44. Howell et al., *supra* note 3, at 21–22.

45. Mark Soler, *Juvenile Justice in the Next Century: Programs or Politics?,* ABA CRIM. JUST. MAG., Winter 1996, at 27. The spate of new transfer statutes invites a comparable wave of appeals asserting that such laws violate due process and equal protection. However, courts have been uniform in upholding the federal constitutionality of provisions for direct filing in criminal courts by prosecutors and for mandatory transfer in serious cases. State *ex rel.* A. L., 638 A.2d 814, 818 (N.J. Super. A.D. 1994). *See also* State v. Martin, 191 Wis. 647, 530 N.W.2d 420 (Ct. App. 1995). *But see* State v. Mohi, 267 Utah Adv. Rep. 7, 1995 Utah LEXIS 37 (holding that a provision for direct filing without guidance to prosecutors about the standard to be used was so arbitrary that it violated the Utah Constitution's requirement for "uniform operation" of the law).

46. VA. CODE ANN. §§ 16.1-226–1-348 (Cum. Supp. 1995). For an overview of the Virginia juvenile code and an analysis of recent developments concerning it, *see* Robert E. Shepherd, Jr., *Legal Issues Involving Children,* 28 U. RICH. L. REV. 1075 (1994).

47. VA. CODE ANN. § 16.1-227.

48. VA. CODE ANN. § 16.1-227(4). *See also* VA. CODE ANN. §§ 16.1-227(1), 16.1-227(3) (requiring consideration of public safety in applying the principle that the intake officer and the judge should pursue the least restrictive alternative for the juvenile).

49. VA. CODE ANN. § 16.1-285.1.

50. Virginia is scheduled to move to a *family court* model, but the implementation of the legislation, which connotes broad court involvement in family issues, has been delayed because of a political disagreement about funding for it. Shepherd, *supra* note 46, at 1076.

51. VA. CODE ANN. § 16.1-269.1.

52. VA. CODE ANN. § 16.1-246(C). Another euphemism for arrest that is often used is "taking the child into custody." *See* FL. STAT. § 39.037.

53. The intake process is omitted in cases involving violations of traffic laws, game and fish laws, surfing ordinances, curfew ordinances, and animal control violations. In such cases, law enforcement officers may issue summons, as in the adult criminal court. VA. CODE ANN. § 16.1-260(F).

54. *See, e.g.,* CENTER FOR THE STUDY OF YOUTH POLICY, ARKANSAS AND ARIZONA REFORMING TROUBLED YOUTH CORRECTIONS SYSTEMS (1992); CENTER FOR THE STUDY OF YOUTH POLICY, MISSOURI AND HAWAII: LEADERS IN YOUTH CORRECTION POLICY (1992); CENTER FOR THE STUDY OF YOUTH POLICY, YOUTH CORRECTIONS AND THE QUIET REVOLUTION (1985) (reporting on reform efforts in Oregon and Utah); BARRY KRISBERG & JAMES F. AUSTIN, REINVENTING JUVENILE JUSTICE 142–70 (1993).

55. The authorities cited *supra* note 54 describe the catalytic influence in some states of judicial examination of inhumane conditions in juvenile training schools.

56. IDAHO CODE § 16–1801 (Cum. Supp. 1995).

57. Federal juvenile justice policy in the Clinton Administration emphasizes a reliance on graduated sanctions as well as a multifaceted approach to prevention and treatment. *See generally* JOHN J. WILSON & JAMES C. HOWELL, COMPREHENSIVE STRATEGY FOR SERIOUS, VIOLENT, AND CHRONIC JUVENILE OFFENDERS (1994); Barry Krisberg et al., *Graduated Sanctions for Serious, Violent, and Chronic Juvenile Offenders,* in SOURCEBOOK, *supra* note 3, at 142.

58. Exceptions are the volumes on Abuse and Neglect, Noncriminal Misbehavior, and Schools and Education.

59. *See* JUVENILE JUSTICE STANDARDS: SUMMARY AND ANALYSIS (1982).

60. For a summary of these provisions, with special emphasis on forensic mental health, *see* Stephen J. Morse & Charles H. Whitebread II, *Mental Health Implications of the Juvenile Justice Standards,* in LEGAL REFORMS AFFECTING CHILD AND YOUTH SERVICES 5 (Gary B. Melton ed. 1982).

61. The decriminalization of status offenses has yet to be endorsed by the ABA. *See supra* note 58 and accompanying text.

62. The text that came closest to addressing this question was a footnote excerpting a conclusory statement from a position paper prepared for the Project: "Juveniles may be viewed as incomplete adults, lacking in full moral and experiential development, extended unique jural status in other contexts, and deserving of the social moratorium extended by this and all other societies of which I am aware." ABA JOINT COMMISSION ON JUVENILE JUSTICE STANDARDS, JUVENILE JUSTICE STANDARDS RELATING TO DISPOSITIONS 19 n. 5 (1980).

63. Barry C. Feld, *Criminalizing Juvenile Justice: Rules of Procedure for the Juvenile Court,* 69 MINN. L. REV. 141, 276 (1984).

64. Barry C. Feld, *Criminalizing the Juvenile Court: A Research Agenda for the 1990s,* in PUBLIC POLICY, *supra* note 4, at 59, 60. *See also* Janet E. Ainsworth, *Re-imagining Childhood and Reconstructing the Legal Order: The Case for*

Abolishing the Juvenile Court, 69 N.C. L. REV. 1083 (1991); Katherine H. Federle, *The Abolition of the Juvenile Court: A Proposal for the Preservation of Children's Legal Rights,* 16 J. CONTEMP. L. 23 (1990).

65. For example, Melton has debunked assumptions (1) that juveniles typically are so cognitively and socially incompetent that they cannot fairly be held accountable for their behavior, (2) that juveniles, relative to adults, are so malleable that they can be assumed to be especially amenable to treatment, and (3) that formal adversary procedures are not conducive to rehabilitation. Gary B. Melton, *Taking* Gault *Seriously: Toward a New Juvenile Court,* 68 NEB. L. REV. 146, 150–64 (1989).

66. *See, e.g., id.* at 167–77. *See also* IRA M. SCHWARTZ, (IN)JUSTICE FOR JUVENILES: RETHINKING THE BEST INTERESTS OF THE CHILD (1989). Schwartz argues for the following seven reforms: (1) a clear acknowledgment that "the court's primary purpose is to administer justice" (quoting Gary B. Melton, *Should the Juvenile Court Be Abolished?,* DIV. CHILD, YOUTH, & FAM. SERVICES NEWSL., Fall 1986, at 4, 11); (2) application to juvenile respondents of all rights of adult defendants except the right to waive counsel; (3) access by the public and the media to juvenile proceedings; (4) mandatory rotation of juvenile judges; (5) removal of human services and correctional programs from judicial administration; (6) abolition of status-offense jurisdiction and diversion of minor delinquency; and (7) restructuring of the juvenile court as a division of a court of general jurisdiction. SCHWARTZ, *supra* at 160–64. SCHWARTZ concludes that if such reforms fail to be implemented so that there is due respect for juveniles' autonomy and dignity, "then it would be advisable to eliminate the juvenile court's jurisdiction over delinquency cases and have them handled in the adult criminal courts." *Id.* at 164.

67. *See, e.g.,* Martin R. Gardner, *Punitive Juvenile Justice: Some Observations on a Recent Trend,* 10 INT'L J. L. & PSYCHIATRY 129 (1987); Martin R. Gardner, *The Right of Juvenile Offenders to Be Punished: Some Implications of Treating Kids as Persons,* 68 NEB. L. REV. 182 (1989).

68. *See, e.g.,* Irene Merker Rosenberg, *Leaving Bad Enough Alone: A Response to the Juvenile Court Abolitionists,* 1993 WIS. L. REV. 163. "Experience with juvenile transfer suggests that criminal court jurisdiction—in effect, the model favored by the abolitionists—is not likely to be fully satisfactory. Criminal courts are less likely than juvenile courts to take some action to hold juveniles accountable, and adult correctional systems are less likely than juvenile programs to prevent recidivism." Howell et al., *supra* note 3, at 22–23.

69. *See, e.g.,* Melton, *supra* note 65.

70. For an articulate expression by a leading judge of the view that the various public purposes can be accommodated through judicial leadership within the existing juvenile court, *see* Leonard P. Edwards, *The Juvenile Court and the Role of the Juvenile Court Judge,* 43 (2) JUV. & FAM. CT. J. 1 (1992).

71. Barry C. Feld, *Violent Youth and Public Policy: A Case Study of Juvenile Justice Law Reform,* 79 MINN. L. REV. 965, 1099 (1995).

72. Convention on the Rights of the Child, U.N. Doc. A/Res/44/25 art. 40(1) (1989).

73. For example, responding to research showing that many juvenile respondents are not represented by counsel, *see supra* note 34, Minnesota now provides for appointed counsel, or standby counsel if the child waives the right to counsel, and for consultation with an attorney prior to acceptance of a waiver in all cases involving felony or gross misdemeanor charges or possible out-of-home placement. *See* Feld, *supra* note 71, at 1116–17 and citations therein.

74. Juvenile courts in the United States handle approximately 1.5 million cases per year—a number that is increasing steadily not only for serious juvenile delinquency but also for status offense cases. HOWARD N. SNYDER & MELISSA SICKMUND, JUVENILE OFFENDERS AND VICTIMS: A NATIONAL REPORT 126, 138–39 (Aug. 1995).

75. The following discussion focuses on the clinician's role in juvenile delinquency cases and, to a lesser extent, status-offense cases. Section 10.10(a) and Chapters 15, 16, and 17 deal with other clinical issues that may arise in juvenile court.

76. *See, e.g.,* S.C. CODE ANN . § 44–23–410 (Law Co-Op. 1986).

77. *See, e.g.,* State *ex rel.* Causey, 363 So. 2d 472 (La. 1978); *In re* S.W.T., 277 N.W.2d 507 (Minn. 1979). *See generally* Cowden & McKee, *supra* note 35; Thomas Grisso et al., *Competence to Stand Trial in Juvenile Court,* 10 INT'L J. L. & PSYCHIATRY 1 (1987).

78. *See* Grisso et al., *supra* note 77.

79. *See, e.g., In re* C.W.M., 407 A.2d 617 (D.C. App. 1979).

80. 421 U.S. 519, 529 (1975).

81. This situation may be changing as legislatures more often predicate transfer to criminal court on the nature of the pending charge and as questions arise about the applicability of offenses committed while a juvenile under "three-strikes" laws that provide for onerous penalties for repeated offenses.

82. *See, e.g.,* JUVENILE JUSTICE STANDARDS RELATING TO TRANSFER BETWEEN COURTS § 2.2(C)(3) (1980).

83. *See, e.g.,* James F. Austin & Barry Krisberg, *Wider, Stronger, and Different Nets: The Dialectics of Criminal Justice Reform,* 18 J. RESEARCH CRIME & DELINQ. 165 (1981); Thomas G. Blomberg, *Diversion's Disparate Results and Unresolved Questions: An Integrative Evaluation Perspective,* 20 J. RESEARCH CRIME & DELINQ. 24 (1983); Mark Ezell, *Juvenile Diversion: The Ongoing Search for Alternatives,* in JUVENILE JUSTICE AND PUBLIC POLICY: TOWARD A NATIONAL AGENDA 45, 51–52 (Ira M. Schwartz ed. 1992); Edward P. Mulvey & Ann Hicks, *The Paradoxical Effect of a Juvenile Code Change in Virginia,* 10 AM. J. COMMUNITY PSYCHOL. 705 (1982); Paul Nejelski, *Diversion: Unleashing the Hounds of Heaven?,* in PURSUING JUSTICE FOR THE CHILD 94 (Margaret Rosenheim ed. 1976).

84. WALTER WADLINGTON ET AL., CHILDREN IN THE LEGAL SYSTEM 550 (1983).

85. It has been our experience that clinical reports are often used for evidence of mitigation, preparatory to striking a bargain (1) to reduce the charges in exchange

for a guilty plea, (2) to drop the charges, or (3) to recommend probation in exchange for a guarantee of participation in a treatment program. In some jurisdictions, even most insanity defenses are the result of prosecution stipulation. *See e.g.*, John Petrila, *The Insanity Defense and Other Mental Health Dispositions in Missouri,* 5 INT'L J. L. & PSYCHIATRY 81 (1982): § 8.02 (a)(3).

86. Typically, there is a subset of waiver cases in which transfer of jurisdiction is mandatory or based largely or completely on the seriousness of the offense and the goal of protecting public safety. However, most transfer cases involve discretionary decisions in which amenability to treatment is a central consideration. Only one-third of the transfers in 1992 involved violent offenses. FELD, *supra*, at 2. Moreover, the decision is a matter of broad judicial discretion to weigh a multiplicity of factors in most jurisdictions and, therefore, a question that invites expert opinion. *Cf.* United States v. Juvenile Male #1, 47 F.3d 68, 71 (2d Cir. 1995) (noting that "no court of appeals has ever found that a district court abused its discretion by failing to balance properly the six statutory factors").

87. WADLINGTON ET AL., *supra* note 84, at 516. *See generally* Edward P. Mulvey, *Judging Amenability to Treatment in Juvenile Offenders,* in CHILDREN, MENTAL HEALTH, AND THE LAW 195 (N. Dickon Reppucci et al. eds. 1984).

88. Whether a respondent is found to be not innocent should, of course, turn on whether the state can prove its charges beyond reasonable doubt—not whether the defense attorney or the judge thinks that the respondent is in need of, or amenable to, treatment.

89. *See supra* notes 34–35.

90. The ABA's MODEL CODE OF PROFESSIONAL RESPONSIBILITY EC 7–11, 7–12 gives ambiguous guidance as to the proper style of representation of a questionably competent client. See discussion af this issue in the civil commitment context [§ 10.06] and in custody and abuse proceedings [§ 16.03(f)(2)]

91. Thomas Grisso, *Juveniles' Consent in Delinquency Proceedings,* in CHILDREN'S COMPETENCE TO CONSENT 131, 144–45 (Gary B. Melton et al. eds. 1983). *See generally* Thomas Grisso & Thomas Lovinguth, *Lawyers and Child Clients: A Call for Research,* in THE RIGHTS OF CHILDREN: LEGAL AND PSYCHOLOGICAL PERSPECTIVES 215 (James S. Henning ed. 1982).

92. THOMAS GRISSO, JUVENILES' WAIVER OF RIGHTS: LEGAL AND PSYCHOLOGICAL COMPETENCE (1981).

93. *Id.*; Gary B. Melton, *Children's Concepts of Their Rights,* 9 J. CLINICAL CHILD PSYCHOL. 186 (1980); Gary B. Melton & Susan P. Limber, *What Rights Mean to Children: Children's Own Views,* in IDEOLOGIES OF CHILDREN'S RIGHTS 167 (Michael Freeman & Philip Veerman eds. 1992).

94. GRISSO, *supra* note 92, at 118–20.

95. *Id.*

96. *Id.* at 59–93.

97. *Id.* at 83–84.

98. *See id.* at 64 nn. 6–7, and cases cited therein.

99. *See* Resolution of the ABA on Learning Disabilities and the Juvenile Justice System (adopted by the House of Delegates, Aug. 1983).

100. NANCY DUNIVANT, A CAUSAL ANALYSIS OF THE RELATIONSHIP BETWEEN LEARNING DISABILITIES AND JUVENILE DELINQUENCY (1984); NANCY DUNIVANT, IMPROVING ACADEMIC SKILLS AND PREVENTING DELINQUENCY OF LEARNING-DISABLED JUVENILE DELINQUENTS: EVALUATION OF THE ACLD REMEDIAL PROGRAM (1984).

101. We do not mean to imply that adult defendants do not sometimes have similar views. Nonetheless, it has been our experience that adults much more frequently perceive forensic evaluations as a possible opportunity to "beat the rap." On the other hand, juveniles more often are anxious or resistant about the evaluation, presumably because of the developmentally appropriate concern with fashioning an identity. *See* ERIK ERIKSON, IDENTITY: YOUTH AND CRISIS (1968). In that connection, it is threatening to perceive an identity fragile because of immaturity as even more tenuous because of mental disorder. Also, for some youths, delinquent values and identification—and, therefore, unwillingness to perceive themselves as needing help—may solidify connection with a delinquent peer culture. *See* § 14.06(b).

102. Depressed adolescents often engage in aggressive behavior. *See e.g.*, John A. Chiles et al., *Depression in an Adolescent Delinquent Population,* 37 ARCH. GEN. PSYCHIATRY 1179 (1980). Indeed, the co-occurrence of antisocial and oppositional behavior with low self-esteem, suicidal ideation and behavior, and general depression is common. AMERICAN PSYCHIATRIC ASSOCIATION, DIAGNOSTIC AND STATISTICAL MANUAL OF MENTAL DISORDERS 87–89, 92–93 (4th ed. 1994).

103. For instance, there is a question whether juveniles may be constitutionally transferred to criminal courts if they are treatable, but the state has failed to develop the necessary programs. Haziel v. United States, 404 F.2d 1275, 1280 (D.C. Cir. 1968).

104. Mulvey, *supra* note 87, at 201.

105. VA. CODE ANN. § 16.1-278.8 (Cum. Supp. 1995). *See also* VA. CODE ANN. § 16.1-249 (allowing placement of juveniles in jail, although apart from adult inmates).

106. There is an argument to be made, however, that conditions of probation must be "fair and rationally related to a sensible plan for rehabilitation." CHARLES H. WHITEBREAD & MONRAD PAULSEN, JUVENILE LAW AND PROCEDURE 176 (1974).

107. VA. CODE ANN. § 16.1-278 (1982).

108. *See supra* note 103.

109. The right to treatment in juvenile justice has been based on a theory that if liberty is deprived for the purpose of treatment (as the juvenile justice system has purported to do), due process then requires that treatment be provided. *See e.g.*, Nelson v. Heyne, 491 F.2d 352 (7th Cir. 1974); Morgan v. Sproat, 432 F. Supp. 1130 (S.D. Miss. 1977); Pena v. N.Y. State Div. for Youth, 419 F. Supp. 203 (S.D.N.Y. 1976); Morales v. Turman, 364 F. Supp. 166 (E.D. Tex. 1973); Inmates of Boys Training School v. Affleck, 346 F. Supp. 1354 (D.R.I. 1973). This theory is likely to become increasingly less persuasive, however, as states revise the purpose statements in their juvenile codes to deemphasize or eliminate rehabilitation

as a primary goal. *See* SNYDER & SICKMUND, *supra* note 74, at 71 (listing the express purposes of state juvenile codes).

110. THE REHABILITATION OF CRIMINAL OFFENDERS: PROBLEMS AND PROSPECTS (Lee Sechrest et al. eds. 1979). The National Academy panel saw no basis for the belief that juveniles would be especially amenable to treatment: "It may be implicitly assumed by many that age is an important element in classification because it is, or should be, easier to rehabilitate youthful offenders. That seems a dubious prospect at best. By any measure currently available, rates of involvement in criminal activity subsequent to adjudication are at least as high for juveniles as for adults with similar offense histories. It could be argued that given the same circumstances it might be more difficult to rehabilitate juveniles than adults because their very youth is indicative that they have no prolonged periods of satisfactory behavior patterns to which they might be restored by proper treatment. In fact, however, very little is known about differential treatment or potential for rehabilitation of juveniles and adults. Certainly when the treatment methods that have been employed are examined, there do not appear to have been any startling differences between what has been tried with juveniles and adults. The one exception is temporary foster home placement of juveniles, but that tactic has never been subjected to a controlled test of its efficacy." *Id.* at 50–51.

111. Melton, *supra* note 65, at 161–62.

112. Mark W. Lipsey, *Juvenile Delinquency Treatment: A Meta-Analytic Inquiry into the Variability of Effects*, in META-ANALYSIS FOR EXPLANATION: A CASEBOOK 83 (1992).

113. *Cited in* SNYDER & SICKMUND, *supra* note 74, at 160.

114. *See, e.g.*, George J. DuPaul & Tanya L. Eckert, *The Effects of Social Skills Curricula: Now You See Them, Now You Don't*, 9 SCHOOL PSYCHOL. Q. 113 (1994). *Cf.* Stephen M. Cox et al., *A Meta-Analytic Assessment of Delinquency-Related Outcomes of Alternative Education Programs*, 19 CRIME & DELINQ. 219 (1995) (showing no effect of such programs on recidivism). Otherwise well-designed and well-funded behavioral programs often have failed to reduce recidivism (even though in-program gains were impressive) when they did not include significant efforts to change the family and community. Helene E. Cavior & Annesley Schmidt, *Test of the Effectiveness of a Differential Treatment Strategy at the Robert F. Kennedy Center*, 5 CRIM. JUST. & BEHAV. 131 (1978); V. Scott Johnson, *Behavior Modification in the Correctional Setting*, 4 CRIM. JUSTICE & BEHAV. 397 (1971).

115. In that connection, the current fascination with boot camps is especially troublesome. We are aware of no research that suggests that boot camps and other shock incarceration approaches are any more effective than traditional training schools in reducing recidivism. *See* Scott W. Henggeler & Sonja K. Schoenwald, *Boot Camps for Juvenile Offenders: Just Say No*, 3 J. CHILD & FAM. STUDIES 243–48 (1994); Dale K. Sechrest, *Prison "Boot Camps" Do Not Measure Up*, FEDERAL PROBATION, Sept. 1989, at 15. Criminal justice authorities worry that such approaches may increase hypermasculine, "tough-guy" responses that

are common in delinquent peer groups and that they also may stimulate increased aggression by staff. *See e.g.*, Merry Morash & Lila Rucker, *A Critical Look at the Idea of Boot Camp as a Correctional Reform*, 36 CRIME & DELINQ. 204 (1990).

116. For reviews pointing out the positive directions of recent intervention research, *see, e.g.*, PETER W. GREENWOOD & FRANKLIN E. ZIMRING, ONE MORE CHANCE: THE PURSUIT OF PROMISING INTERVENTION STRATEGIES FOR CHRONIC JUVENILE OFFENDERS (1985) (report by the Rand Corporation); Barry Krisberg et al., *Graduated Sanctions for Serious, Violent, and Chronic Juvenile Offenders*, in SOURCEBOOK, *supra* note 3, at 142; David C. Tate et al., *Violent Juvenile Delinquents: Treatment Efficacy and Implications for Future Action*, 50 AM. PSYCHOL. 777 (1995); Barry Krisberg & David Onek, *Proven Prevention and Intervention Programs for Serious, Violent and Chronic Juvenile Offenders* (1994) (unpublished report by the National Council on Crime and Delinquency).

117. *E.g.*, Charles M. Borduin et al., *Multisystemic Treatment of Serious Juvenile Offenders: Long-Term Prevention of Criminality and Violence*, 63 J. CONSULTING & CLIN. PSYCHOL. 569 (1995); Scott W. Henggeler & Charles M. Borduin, *Multisystemic Treatment of Serious Juvenile Offenders and their Families*, in HOME-BASED SERVICES FOR TROUBLED CHILDREN 113 (Ira M. Schwartz & Philip AuClaire eds. 1995); Scott W. Henggeler et al., *Family Preservation Using Multisystemic Therapy: An Effective Alternative to Incarcerating Serious Juvenile Offenders*, 60 J. CONSULTING & CLIN. PSYCHOL. 953 (1992) [hereinafter *Alternative*]; Scott W. Henggeler et al., *Family Preservation Using Multisystemic Treatment: Long-term Follow-up to a Clinical Trial with Serious Juvenile Offenders*, 2 J. CHILD & FAM. STUDIES 283 (1993) [hereinafter *Follow-up*]; Scott W. Henggeler et al., *Multisystemic Treatment of Juvenile Offenders: Effects on Adolescent Behavior and Family Interaction*, 22 DEVELOPMENTAL PSYCHOL. 132 (1986); David G. Scherer et al., *Multisystemic Family Preservation Therapy with Rural and Minority Families of Serious Adolescent Offenders: Preliminary Findings from a Controlled Clinical Trial*, 2 J. EMOTIONAL & BEHAV. DISORDERS 198 (1994).

118. These principles are elaborated in SCOTT W. HENGGELER & CHARLES M. BORDUIN, FAMILY THERAPY AND BEYOND: A MULTISYSTEMIC APPROACH TO TREATING THE BEHAVIOR PROBLEMS OF CHILDREN AND ADOLESCENTS (1990); SCOTT W. HENGGELER ET AL., TREATMENT MANUAL FOR FAMILY PRESERVATION USING MULTISYSTEMIC THERAPY (1994) (available from the Family Services Research Center, Department of Psychiatry and Behavioral Sciences, Medical University of South Carolina, 171 Ashley Avenue, Charleston, SC 29425–0742).

119. *Alternative, supra* note 117; *Follow-up, supra* note 117.

120. Borduin et al., *supra* note 117.

121. *See, e.g.*, Joseph L. Massimo & Milton F. Shore, *The Effectiveness of a Vocationally Oriented Psychotherapy*, 33 AM. J. ORTHOPSYCHIATRY 634 (1963); Milton F. Shore & Joseph L. Massimo, *Comprehensive Vocationally Oriented Psychotherapy for Adolescent Delinquent Boys: A Follow-Up Study*, 36 AM. J. ORTHOPSYCHIATRY 609 (1966); Milton F. Shore

& Joseph L. Massimo, *Five Years Later: A Follow-Up Study of Comprehensive Vocationally Oriented Psychotherapy*, 39 AM. J. ORTHOPSYCHIATRY 769 (1969); Milton F. Shore & Joseph L. Massimo, *After Ten Years: A Follow-Up Study of Comprehensive Vocationally Oriented Psychotherapy*, 43 AM. J. ORTHOPSYCHIATRY 128 (1973); Milton F. Shore & Joseph L. Massimo, *Fifteen Years After Treatment: A Follow-Up Study of Comprehensive Vocationally Oriented Psychotherapy*, 49 AM. J. ORTHOPSYCHIATRY 240 (1979).

In the program described in these articles, therapists were on call 24 hours a day. The breadth of their work was illustrated by the following description: "In essence, the therapist entered all areas of the adolescent's life. Job finding, court appearances, pleasure trips, driving lessons when appropriate, locating and obtaining a car, arranging for a dentist appointment, going for glasses, shopping for clothes with a first pay check, opening a bank account and other activities require this maximum commitment." Massimo & Shore, *supra*, at 636.

122. *See generally* Williams S. Davidson II & Robin Redner, *The Prevention of Juvenile Delinquency: Diversion from the Juvenile Justice System*, in 14 OUNCES OF PREVENTION: A CASEBOOK FOR PRACTITIONERS 123 (Richard H. Price et al. eds. 1988).

123. The prevention model and the research associated with it are described in DAN OLWEUS, BULLYING AT SCHOOL: WHAT WE KNOW AND WHAT WE CAN DO (1993). Melton is currently principal investigator in a large-scale quasi-experiment to test the efficacy of Olweus's approach in the United States.

124. The problem of juveniles' violence against other family members is most often a reflection of violence as a pattern of interaction in the family. *See, e.g.*, GERALD PATTERSON, COERCIVE FAMILY PROCESS (1982); Shelley Post, *Adolescent Parricide in Abusive Families*, 61 CHILD WELF. 445 (1982).

125. Especially in status offense cases, parents are often complainants because of their children's "uncontrollability," promiscuity, or running away. *See* JOHN MURRAY, STATUS OFFENDERS: A SOURCEBOOK 6 (1983).

126. In some jurisdictions, this authority extends to holding the parents' accountable for their children's behavior. *See* Gilbert Geis & Arnold Binder, *Sins of their Children: Parental Responsibility for Juvenile Delinquency*, 5 NOTRE DAME J. L. ETHICS & PUB. POL'Y 303 (1991).

127. *See, e.g.*, SCOTT W. HENGGELER, DELINQUENCY IN ADOLESCENCE 39–42 (1989), and citations therein; Valerie Johnson & Robert J. Pandina, *Effects of the Family Environment on Adolescent Substance Use, Delinquency, and Coping Styles*, 17 AM. J. DRUG & ALCOHOL ABUSE 71 (1991).

128. TERENCE P. THORNBERRY, VIOLENT FAMILIES AND YOUTH VIOLENCE (Dec. 1994) (Fact Sheet #21, published by the Office of Juvenile Justice and Delinquency Prevention [OJJDP], U.S. Department of Justice). The project as a whole is summarized in several publications: DAVID HUIZINGA ET AL., URBAN DELINQUENCY AND SUBSTANCE ABUSE: INITIAL FINDINGS (Mar. 1994) (monograph published by OJJDP); Terence P. Thornberry et al., *The Prevention of Serious Delinquency and Violence: Implications from the Program of Research on the Causes and Correlates of Delinquency*, in SOURCEBOOK, *supra* note 3, at 213; *Tribute to Marvin E. Wolfgang: Symposium on the Causes and Correlates of Juvenile Delinquency*, 82 J. CRIM. L. & CRIMINOLOGY 1 (1991).

129. In such a circumstance, the parents themselves often have a history of criminality, especially aggressiveness, and thus may model violent and antisocial behavior but may be unable or unwilling to establish clear positive norms. HENGGELER, *supra* note 127, at 45–46, and citations therein.

130. *See supra* note 124.

131. *See, e.g.*, LEONARD ERON ET AL., LEARNING OF AGGRESSION IN CHILDREN 75–78 (1971); E. Mavis Hetherington & Barclay Martin, *Family Interaction*, in PSYCHOPATHOLOGICAL DISORDERS OF CHILDHOOD 30 (Herbert C. Quay & John Werry eds. 2d ed. 1979), and citations therein.

132. Hetherington & Martin, *supra* note 131, at 266.

133. *See, e.g.*, Stephanie M. Green et al., *Child Psychopathology and Deviant Family Hierarchies*, 1 J. CHILD & FAM. STUDIES 341 (1992); Barton J. Mann et al., *An Investigation of Systemic Conceptualizations of Parent-Child Coalitions and Symptom Change*, 58 J. CONSULTING & CLIN. PSYCHOL. 336 (1990).

134. *See, e.g.*, Emily W. Herbert & Donald Baer, *Training Parents as Behavior Modifiers: Self-Recording of Contingent Attention*, 5 J. APPLIED BEHAV. ANALYSIS 139 (1972); Gretchen K. Lobitz & Stephen M. Johnson, *Normal versus Deviant Children: A Multimethod Comparison*, 3 J. ABNORMAL CHILD PSYCHOL. 353 (1975); Robert Wahler, *Oppositional Children: A Quest for Parental Reinforcement Control*, 3 J. APPLIED BEHAV. ANALYSIS 159 (1968).

135. HENGGELER, *supra* note 127, at 47–48.

136. HUIZINGA ET AL., *supra* note 128, at 14.

137. Mark Warr, *Parents, Peers, and Delinquency*, 72 SOC. FORCES 247 (1993).

138. *Id.*

139. *Id.* at 20.

140. HUIZINGA ET AL., *supra* note 128, at 14.

141. HENGGELER, *supra* note 127, at 50; HUIZINGA ET AL., *supra* note 128, at 16.

142. The Causes and Correlates study, HUIZINGA ET AL., *supra* note 128, showed that juvenile-justice involvement is very common in some neighborhoods. For example, about one-third of 15-year-old males in high-crime neighborhoods in Denver and Rochester report having been arrested at least once. *Id.* at 9–10. In the Denver sample (analogous Rochester data are unavailable), the proportion rises to 41% by age 17. Moreover, adolescent-onset delinquency often "is part of the conforming process that normally occurs within adolescent friendship groups"—so much so that delinquents often are even more attached to their friends than are other adolescents. HENGGELER, *supra* note 128, at 51.

143. Albert J. Reiss, Jr., & David P. Farrington, *Advancing Knowledge about Co-offending: Results from a Prospective Longitudinal Survey of London Males*, 82 J. CRIM. L. & CRIMINOLOGY 360, 362 (1991).

144. AMERICAN PSYCHIATRIC ASSOCIATION, *supra* note 102, at 87.

145. Except where otherwise indicated, the description herein of characteristics of gangs is based on James C. Howell, *Recent Gang Research: Program and Policy Implications,* 40 CRIME & DELINQ. 495 (1994).

146. In the Rochester sample in the Causes and Correlates study, HUIZINGA ET AL., *supra* note 128, at 18, 7% of ninth- and tenth-graders owned illegal guns, and 3% owned legal guns. Illegal gun ownership was highly related to delinquency, and illegal gun owners often were gang members whose friends also owned illegal guns. On the other hand, youths who owned guns legally typically had fathers who use guns for sport and hunting. *See generally* Clifford R. O'Donnell, *Firearm Deaths Among Children and Youth,* 50 AM. PSYCHOL. 771 (1995).

147. John M. Hagedorn, *Neighborhoods, Markets, and Gang Drug Organization,* 31 J. RESEARCH IN CRIME & DELINQ. 264, 290 (1994).

148. HUIZINGA ET AL., *supra* note 128, at 16.

149. Of course, the norm in juvenile justice, especially in institutional settings, has been to organize groups of delinquents—a structure that increases the likelihood of further delinquent identification and group delinquent behavior.

150. *See, e.g.,* JAMES GARBARINO, CHILDREN AND FAMILIES IN THE SOCIAL ENVIRONMENT 167–68 (1982); Eleanor Maccoby et al., *Community Integration and the Social Control of Juvenile Delinquency,* 14 J. SOC. ISSUES 38 (1958); Ora Simcha-Fagan & Joseph E. Schwartz, *Neighborhood and Delinquency: An Assessment of Contextual Effects,* 24 CRIMINOLOGY 667 (1986). Increased risk for delinquency among youth is present in impoverished neighborhoods even when family variables and race are controlled. HUIZINGA ET AL., *supra* note 128, at 15–16.

151. *See generally* U.S. ADVISORY BOARD ON CHILD ABUSE AND NEGLECT: A NEW NATIONAL STRATEGY FOR THE PROTECTION OF CHILDREN (1993).

152. PANEL ON HIGH-RISK YOUTH, LOSING GENERATIONS: ADOLESCENTS IN HIGH-RISK SETTINGS 14 (1993).

153. *See* William S. Davidson II & John A. Saul, *Youth Advocacy in the Juvenile Court: A Clash of Paradigms,* in LEGAL REFORMS AFFECTING CHILD AND YOUTH SERVICES 29 (Gary B. Melton ed. 1982).

154. *See supra* note 122.

155. GARY B. MELTON, CHILD ADVOCACY: PSYCHOLOGICAL ISSUES AND INTERVENTIONS 54–64 (1983); William S. Davidson II & Charles A. Rapp, *A Multiple Strategy Model of Child Advocacy,* 21 SOC. WORK 225 (1976).

156. *See* Gary B. Melton, *Children, Families, and the Courts in the Twenty-First Century,* 66 S. CAL. L. REV. 1993, 2040–47 (1993).

157. Daniel W. Edwards et al., *National Health Insurance, Psychotherapy, and the Poor,* 34 AM. PSYCHOL. 411 (1979); Raymond Lorion, *Socioeconomic Status and Traditional Treatment Approaches Reconsidered,* 79 PSYCHOL. BULL. 263 (1973); Raymond Lorion, *Patient and Therapist Variables in the Treatment of Low-Income Patients,* 81 PSYCHOL. BULL. 344 (1974).

158. A significant issue of equal protection exists when one of two juveniles equally amenable to treatment (given unlimited resources) is transferred to criminal court and the other is not because the latter youth's family has more resources available or simply is more willing to cooperate.

159. Laura Weinstein, *Project Re-Ed Schools for Emotionally Disturbed Children: Effectiveness as Viewed by Referring Agencies, Parents, and Teachers,* 35 EXCEPTIONAL CHILDREN 703 (1969).

160. HUIZINGA ET AL., *supra* note 128, at 15.

161. *Id.*

162. MELTON, *supra* note 155, at 68–69.

163. *See* Charles H. King, *The Ego and the Integration of Violence in Homicidal Youth,* 45 AM. J. ORTHOPSYCHIATRY 134 (1975).

164. For discussions of the relationship between cognitive and affective development, see MELTON, *supra* note 155, at 73–81; Robert Brooks, *Psychoeducational Assessment: A Broader Perspective,* 10 PROF. PSYCHOL. 708 (1979). Among the studies showing the significance of social perceptions and skills as factors in delinquency are the following: T. J. Dishion et al., *Skill Deficits and Male Adolescent Delinquency,* 12 J. ABNORMAL CHILD PSYCHOL. 37 (1984); Kenneth A. Dodge, *Social Cognition and Children's Aggressive Behavior,* 51 CHILD DEV. 162 (1980); Kenneth A. Dodge et al., *The Assessment of Intention-Cue Detection Skills in Children: Implications for Developmental Psychopathology,* 55 CHILD DEV. 163 (1982); Kenneth A. Dodge et al., *Hostile Attributional Biases in Severely Aggressive Adolescents,* 99 J. ABNORMAL PSYCHOL. 385 (1990); Ronald G. Slaby & Nancy G. Guerra, *Cognitive Mediators of Aggression in Adolescent Offenders: I. Assessment,* 24 DEV. PSYCHOL. 580 (1988).

165. *See* GERALD SPIVACK ET AL., THE PROBLEM-SOLVING APPROACH TO ADJUSTMENT (1976).

166. *See* Brooks, *supra* note 164.

167. When a behavior problem is related to a special educational need, the procedural protections of IDEA and its guarantee of a free appropriate public education apply. *See, e.g.,* S-1 v. Turlington, 635 F.2d 342 (5th Cir. 1981); Doe v. Koger, 480 F. Supp. 225 (N.D. Ind. 1979); Howard S. v. Friendswood Indep. School Dist., 454 F. Supp. 634 (S.D. Tex. 1978); Stuart v. Nappi, 443 F. Supp. 1234 (D. Conn. 1978).

168. Daniel Offer et al., *The Mental Health Professional's Concept of the Normal Adolescent,* 38 ARCH. GEN. PSYCHIATRY 149 (1981).

169. Patrick H. Tolan, *Delinquent Behaviors and Male Adolescent Development: A Preliminary Study,* 17 J. YOUTH & ADOLESCENCE 413 (1988). Most adolescents engage in some delinquent behavior, but most who come into contact with the juvenile justice system do so only once. SNYDER & SICKMUND, *supra* note 74, at 49, 158–60.

170. John Monahan, *Childhood Predictors of Adult Criminal Behavior,* in EARLY CHILDHOOD INTERVENTION AND JUVENILE DELINQUENCY (F.N. Dutile et al. eds. 1982).

171. SNYDER & SICKMUND, *supra* note 74, at 158.

172. *See* HENGGELER, *supra* note 127, at 29–30, and citations therein. *See also* references cited *supra* note 164.

173. David C. Tate et al., *Violent Juvenile Delinquents: Treatment Effectiveness and Implications for Future Action,* 50 AM. PSYCHOL. 777, 778–79 (1995).

174. HENGGELER, *supra* note 127, at 35.

175. AMERICAN PSYCHIATRIC ASSOCIATION, *supra* note 102, at 86–87.

176. SNYDER & SICKMUND, *supra* note 74, at 159.

177. *Id.* at 160.

178. Terence P. Thornberry et al., *Testing Interactional Theory: An Examination of Reciprocal Causal Relationships Among Family, School, and Delinquency,* 82 J. CRIM. L. & CRIMINOLOGY 3, 33 (1991).

179. HENGGELER, *supra* note 127, at 72–76, and citations therein.

180. *See, e.g.*, Judith V. Becker & Meg S. Kaplan, *Cognitive Behavioral Treatment of the Juvenile Sex Offender,* in THE JUVENILE SEX OFFENDER 264 (Howard E. Barbaree et al. eds. 1993).

181. Charles Borduin et al., *Multisystemic Treatment of Adolescent Sexual Offenders,* 35 INT'L J. OFFENDER THERAPY & COMP. CRIMINOLOGY 105 (1990).

182. HENGGELER, *supra* note 127, at 100–03.

183. Gary B. Melton, *Testimony Before the U.S. Senate Subcomm. on Juvenile Justice on the Subject of Status Offenses and Child Protection* at 10 (May 21, 1991) (written statement).

184. *Id.* at 4–8 (footnotes omitted).

185. JANE KNITZER, UNCLAIMED CHILDREN: THE FAILURE OF PUBLIC RESPONSIBILITY TO CHILD AND ADOLESCENTS IN NEED OF MENTAL HEALTH SERVICES 11–12 n. 24 (1982). Consistent with the referral route from juvenile courts, the most common diagnosis in children's inpatient facilities is a conduct disorder, and many have involvement in the juvenile justice system. *See, e.g.*, Alan E. Kazdin, *Overt and Covert Antisocial Behavior: Child and Family Characteristics Among Psychiatric Inpatient Children,* 1 CHILD & FAM. STUDIES 3 (1992); Dean X. Parmelee et al., *Children and Adolescents Discharged from Public Psychiatric Hospitals: Evaluation of Outcome in a Continuum of Care,* 4 J. CHILD & FAM. STUDIES 43 (1995)

186. *See* Barry Krisberg & Ira M. Schwartz, *Rethinking Juvenile Justice,* 29 CRIME & DELINQ. 333, 360 (1983); Ira M. Schwartz et al., *The "Hidden" System of Juvenile Control,* 30 CRIME & DELINQ. 371 (1984); Carol Warren, *New Forms of Social Control: The Myth of Deinstitutionalization,* 24 AM. BEHAV. SCIENTIST 724 (1981).

187. *See, e.g.*, Herbert C. Quay, *Mental Health Administrators' Attitudes Toward "Children's Rights": A National Survey* (paper presented at the meeting of the American Psychological Association, Anaheim, CA, Aug. 1983).

188. Jean Ann Linney, *Deinstitutionalization in the Juvenile Justice System,* in CHILDREN, MENTAL HEALTH, AND THE LAW 211, 224 (N. Dickon Reppucci et al. eds. 1984).

189. Edward P. Mulvey, *Family Courts: The Issue of Reasonable Goals,* 6 LAW & HUM. BEHAV. 49 (1982).

190. In general, voluntary consent is likely to enhance the efficacy of services. *See* Gary B. Melton, *Decision Making by Children: Psychological Risks and Benefits,* in CHILDREN'S COMPETENCE TO CONSENT 21, 30–31 (Gary B. Melton et al. eds. 1983).

191. *See* Charles F. Carroll & N. Dickon Reppucci, *Meanings That Professionals Attach to Labels for Children,* 46 J. CONSULTING & CLINICAL PSYCHOL. 372 (1978).

192. Morse & Whitebread, *supra* note 60, at 23–24.

Chapter 15

---

1. *See* GARY B. MELTON, CHILD ADVOCACY: PSYCHOLOGICAL ISSUES AND INTERVENTIONS 3–9 (1983). *Cf.* GARY B. MELTON ET AL., NO PLACE TO GO: CIVIL COMMITMENT OF MINORS (forthcoming) (describing the complex relation of child and parent interests in decisions about psychiatric hospitalization).

2. A panel of the National Research Council concluded: "Despite vigorous debate over the last two decades, little progress has been made in constructing clear, reliable, valid, and useful definitions of child abuse and neglect. The difficulties in constructing definitions include such factors as lack of social consensus over what forms of parenting are dangerous or unacceptable; uncertainty about whether to define maltreatment based on adult characteristics, adult behavior, child outcome, environmental context, or some combination; conflict over whether standards of endangerment or harm should be used in constructing definitions; and confusion as to whether similar definitions should be used for scientific, legal, and clinical purposes." NATIONAL RESEARCH COUNCIL, UNDERSTANDING CHILD ABUSE AND NEGLECT 5 (1993).

3. *See generally* NATIONAL COMMISSION ON FAMILY FOSTER CARE, A BLUEPRINT FOR FOSTERING INFANTS, CHILDREN, AND YOUTHS IN THE 1990S (1991); U.S. ADVISORY BOARD ON CHILD ABUSE AND NEGLECT (ABCAN), NEIGHBORS HELPING NEIGHBORS: A NEW NATIONAL STRATEGY FOR THE PROTECTION OF CHILDREN 27–30 (1993) [hereinafter ABCAN] (discussing possible responses to the foster-care crisis).

4. *See* Gary B. Melton, *Child Protection: Making a Bad Situation Worse?,* 35 CONTEMP. PSYCHOL. 213 (1990).

5. DOUGLAS J. BESHAROV, RECOGNIZING CHILD ABUSE: A GUIDE FOR THE CONCERNED 23 (1990) (also noting that, "[u]nfortunately, these laws are often vague and can be understood only within the context of court decisions and agency practices"); WALTER J. WADLINGTON ET AL., CHILDREN IN THE LEGAL SYSTEM 789 (1983). For histories and critiques of the reporting laws, *see* ABCAN, *supra* note 3, at 9–11; SETH C. KALICHMAN, MANDATED REPORTING OF SUSPECTED CHILD ABUSE: ETHICS, LAW, AND POLICY (1993); MURRAY LEVINE & HOWARD J. DOUECK ET AL., THE IMPACT OF MANDATED REPORTING ON THE THERAPEUTIC PROCESS: PICKING UP THE PIECES (1995).

6. *See generally* LEVINE & DOUECK, *supra* note 5 (discussing effects of therapists' reports of suspected child maltreatment to Child Protective Services).

7. Reports of suspected child maltreatment in the United States now exceed three million per year. Daro,

infra note 8. This number is nearly three times larger than the figure for 1980. ABCAN, *supra* note 3, at 8. When the battered-child syndrome was first identified in the early 1960s (the impetus to adoption of reporting laws), it was estimated to affect about *300* cases. C. Henry Kempe et al., *The Battered Child Syndrome*, 181 J. AM. MED. ASS'N 17 (1962).

8. In 1995, 3.1 million reports of suspected child maltreatment were recorded in the United States. Deborah Daro, *Current Trends in Child Abuse Reporting and Fatalities: NCPCA's 1995 Annual Fifty-State Survey*, APSAC [AMERICAN PROFESSIONAL SOCIETY ON THE ABUSE OF CHILDREN] ADVISOR, Summer 1996, at 21. Among the officially substantiated cases (only about one-third of those reported), *id.*, at least one-fourth received no services at all other than an investigation, *id.* at 22. The sheer scale of the problem and the equally striking enormity of the failure to respond adequately to it led the U.S. Advisory Board on Child Abuse and Neglect to describe the situation in 1990 as a "national emergency," U.S. ADVISORY BOARD ON CHILD ABUSE AND NEGLECT (ABCAN), CHILD ABUSE AND NEGLECT: CRITICAL FIRST STEPS IN RESPONSE TO A NATIONAL EMERGENCY (1990), an emergency which has persisted and worsened. *See, e.g.*, ABCAN, THE CONTINUING CHILD PROTECTION EMERGENCY: A CHALLENGE TO THE NATION (1993).

9. A task panel of the American Psychological Association concluded: "The stunning frequency of reports masks substantial underreporting. Studies of mental health professionals' compliance with mandatory reporting show, on average, that more than 30% of clinicians sometimes suspect that one of their cases involves child maltreatment but fail to report it. Such negligence often is related to an ethical dilemma that is perceived to be present in the decision whether to report suspected maltreatment, and that creates considerable stress for most professionals facing such a decision. Clinicians often believe that reporting maltreatment is not in their clients' best interest and that it conflicts with professional standards of protection of clients' privacy. . . .

"Complicating the dilemma is the fact that reporting hinges on identification of situations that constitute maltreatment and warrant reporting. The laws themselves, however, are of limited assistance in such judgments. The vagueness of legal standards for child abuse and neglect may result in both underreporting and overreporting. Most often, because professionals regard reporting as a serious matter, they desire some level of confidence in their opinions before reporting, even though the law requires reporting of mere suspicions. Clinicians have a "reporting threshold" when they believe there is sufficient evidence of serious actual or potential harm to a child to warrant state action. Vagueness of statutes decreases confidence in those judgments, so that the complexity of the case and the degree of specificity in the legal standard interact to affect decisions whether to report suspected maltreatment." Gary B. Melton et al., *Empirical Research on Child Maltreatment and the Law*, 24 J. CLIN. CHILD PSYCHOL. 47, 51 (Supp. 1995) (citations omitted).

10. There is often an additional discretionary judg-ment, generally made by the prosecuting attorney but often with consultation by social services and mental health professionals, about whether criminal child abuse charges will be brought. In some cases, there may also be an administrative process, a tort action, or both. For example, an allegation that a child care professional has abused a child may result in action to suspend or revoke the license of the professional and the facility in which he or she worked and to seek monetary damages from each. For overviews of the legal process in child protection cases and the issues that may arise, *see, e.g.,* JOHN E. B. MYERS, LEGAL ISSUES IN CHILD ABUSE AND NEGLECT (1992); Josephine A. Bulkley et al., *Child Abuse and Neglect Laws and Legal Proceedings*, in THE APSAC HANDBOOK ON CHILD MALTREATMENT 271 (John Briere et al. eds. 1996) [hereinafter APSAC HANDBOOK].

11. *See generally* BARBARA NELSON, MAKING AN ISSUE OF CHILD ABUSE: POLITICAL AGENDA SETTING FOR SOCIAL PROBLEMS (1984) (discussing the history of child protection legislation).

12. *See* ANTHONY PLATT, THE CHILD SAVERS: THE INVENTION OF DELINQUENCY (2d ed. 1977); Robert H. Mnookin, *Children's Rights: Beyond Kiddie Libbers and Child Savers*, 7 J. CLIN. CHILD PSYCHOL. 163 (1978).

13. *See, e.g.*, James Garbarino et al., *Who Owns the Children? An Ecological Perspective on Public Policy*, in LEGAL REFORMS AFFECTING CHILD AND YOUTH SERVICES 43 (Gary B. Melton ed. 1982).

14. *See, e.g.*, Michael S. Wald, *State Intervention on Behalf of "Neglected" Children: A Search for Realistic Standards*, 27 STAN. L. REV. 985 (1975). Long a professor at Stanford Law School, Wald is now director of social services in San Francisco.

15. Wald was the reporter for the volume on JUVENILE JUSTICE STANDARDS RELATING TO ABUSE AND NEGLECT (tentative draft 1977) [hereinafter STANDARDS].

16. JOSEPH GOLDSTEIN ET AL., BEFORE THE BEST INTEREST OF THE CHILD (1979); JOSEPH GOLDSTEIN ET AL., BEYOND THE BEST INTEREST OF THE CHILD (1973).

17. GOLDSTEIN ET AL., BEFORE THE BEST INTERESTS OF THE CHILD, *supra* note 16, at Child Placement Code of Hampstead-Haven,¶10.5.

18. *Id.*, ¶30.9.

19. *Cf.* BESHAROV, *supra* note 5, at 12–19 (lamenting the number of unfounded reports of child maltreatment), 123–33 (advocating reporting of parents with mental illness, mental retardation, substance abuse, or "inability to care for a newborn," even when no harm to their children has occurred).

20. *See* Melton et al., *supra* note 9, at 48.

21. For policies and practices recommended by advocates in domestic violence programs to shield battered mothers and their children, *see, e.g.,* Barbara J. Hart, Parental Abduction and Domestic Violence (Nov. 1992) (paper presented at the meeting of the American Prosecutors Research Institute); Barbara J. Hart, Safety Planning for Children: Strategizing for Unsupervised Visits with Batterers (1990) (unpublished manuscript, Pennsylvania Coalition Against Domestic Violence).

Especially when the violent spouse is the husband

(rather than the wife) and there are frequent acts of violence against the spouse, there is a high probability of physical child abuse. Susan M. Ross, *Risk of Physical Abuse to Children of Spouse Abusing Parents*, 20 CHILD ABUSE & NEGLECT 589 (1996).

22. Although sexual abuse and severe physical abuse cases (especially parent-inflicted fatalities) dominate news reports about child maltreatment, about half of recorded suspected cases and a similar proportion of substantiated cases involve allegations of neglect. NATIONAL CENTER ON CHILD ABUSE AND NEGLECT, CHILD MALTREATMENT 1994: REPORTS FROM THE STATES TO THE NATIONAL CENTER ON CHILD ABUSE AND NEGLECT 3–6 (1996); Daro, *supra* note 8, at 21.

In beginning one of its reports with several typical case examples, ABCAN, *supra* note 3, described the families as follows: "Their stories are not dramatic. They are not the sort that appear on the front pages of newspapers or the covers of news magazines. The adults involved are not evil people.

"But the families in the stories are people in real trouble who have many problems, few resources, and little access to help. The children are at significant risk, the community has failed to provide the help necessary to ensure their safe and healthy development, and the child protection system as currently designed may even interfere with the help that is needed." *Id.* at 1.

23. ABCAN, *supra* note 3 (in 1990, declaring a national emergency); U.S. ADVISORY BOARD ON CHILD ABUSE AND NEGLECT, CREATING CARING COMMUNITIES: BLUEPRINT FOR AN EFFECTIVE FEDERAL POLICY ON CHILD ABUSE AND NEGLECT (1991) [hereinafter ABCAN, CREATING CARING COMMUNITIES]; U.S. ADVISORY BOARD ON CHILD ABUSE AND NEGLECT, THE CONTINUING CHILD PROTECTION EMERGENCY: A CHALLENGE TO THE NATION (1993); ABCAN, *supra* note 3 (in 1993, presenting a new national strategy for child protection); U.S. ADVISORY BOARD ON CHILD ABUSE AND NEGLECT, A NATION'S SHAME: FATAL CHILD ABUSE AND NEGLECT IN THE UNITED STATES (1995).

24. ABCAN, *supra* note 3, at 2–3.

25. *Id.* at 3.

26. *Id.* at 80.

27. *Id.* at 11.

28. *Id.* at 10.

29. ABCAN, CREATING CARING COMMUNITIES, *supra* note 23, at 35–49. Both on their own and because of the influence of ABCAN, several other boards and commissions in the 1990s adopted a similar perspective. *See* Patricia Schene, *Child Abuse and Neglect Policy: History, Models, and Future Directions*, in APSAC HANDBOOK, *supra* note 10, at 385. Several foundations also launched initiatives designed to implement the proposals of ABCAN and similar groups. *See, e.g.*, Leslie Mitchel & Anne Cohn Donnelly, *Healthy Families America: Building a National System*, APSAC ADVISOR, Winter 1993, at 9 (describing a national initiative led by the National Committee to Prevent Child Abuse and funded by Ronald McDonald Children's Charities); Center for the Study of Social Policy, *A Community-Based Approach to Child Protection* (Jan. 1995) (background paper for an initiative by the Edna McConnell Clark Foundation);

Edna McConnell Clark Foundation, *Community Partnerships for the Protection of Children* (June 1995) (guidelines for grant applications). *See also* Gary B. Melton, *Infant Home Visitation: One Step Toward Creation of Caring Communities*, APSAC ADVISOR, Winter 1993, at 5 (describing ABCAN's logic in making recommendations that resulted in the Healthy Families America initiative noted *supra*).

30. *Id.* at 46.

31. ABCAN, *supra* note 3. Background papers that ABCAN used in its deliberations were published in PROTECTING CHILDREN FROM ABUSE AND NEGLECT: FOUNDATIONS FOR A NEW NATIONAL STRATEGY (Gary B. Melton & Frank D. Barry eds. 1994) [hereinafter PROTECTING CHILDREN].

32. Summarizing survey data, Straus concluded that "more than 90 percent of American parents hit toddlers and most continue to hit their children for years. For at least one out of five, and probably closer to half of all children, hitting begins when they are infants and does not end until they leave home." MURRAY A. STRAUS, BEATING THE DEVIL OUT OF THEM: CORPORAL PUNISHMENT IN AMERICAN FAMILIES 3 (1994). Although the severity and frequency of corporal punishment have been declining, *ed.* at 25–29, it is still very common: "[A]t least two-thirds of mothers of toddlers hit them three or more times a week." *Id.* at 25.

33. Demographic differences in use of corporal punishment are less pronounced than many may believe, and the direction of the differences that may exist are probably contrary to the beliefs of many people. Middle-class parents may be somewhat more likely sometimes to use corporal punishment on adolescents, *id.* at 45, although the frequency of their use is somewhat less than that of lower-class parents, *id.* at 46–47. In other words, lower-class parents are relatively unlikely to hit their teenage children at all, but if they do, they do so relatively often. When data are summed across all ages, social class is unrelated to use of corporal punishment, *id.* at 56, and whites are slightly more likely to use corporal punishment than are African Americans or Hispanic Americans, *id.* at 56–57.

34. STANDARDS, *supra* note 15, § 2.1(A).

35. *Id.*, commentary at 63.

36. *Id.*, commentary at 63–64.

37. FLA. STAT. ANN. § 415.503(13) (West 1996).

38. FLA. STAT. ANN. § 415.503(9)(a). Florida recently expanded its definition to include any instance in which a caregiver "[i]nflicts, or allows to be inflicted, physical, mental, or emotional harm." 1996 Fla. Laws ch. 96–402 § 21.

39. WYO. STAT. ANN. § 14-3-202(a)(ii)(B) (1996) (emphasis added).

40. *E.g.*, ILL. ANN. STAT. ch. 325, para. 5/3(e) (Smith-Hurd 1996). Florida recently changed its definition focusing on an "[i]njury sustained as a result of excessive corporal punishment," FLA. STAT. ANN. § 415.503(9)(a)(1) (West 1996), to specify that: "Corporal discipline may be considered excessive or abusive when it results in any of the following or other similar injuries:

a. Sprains, dislocations, or cartilage damage.

b. Bone or skull fractures.

c. Brain or spinal cord damage.

d. Intracranial hemorrhage or injury to other internal organs.

e. Asphysiation, suffocation, or drowning.

f. Injury resulting from the use of a deadly weapon.

g. Burns or scalding.

h. Cuts, lacerations, punctures, or bites.

i. Permanent or temporary disfigurement.

j. Permanent or temporary loss or impairment of a body part or function."

1996 Fla. Laws ch. 96-402 § 21.
For an interesting case defining "reasonable" corporal punishment, *see* Hawaii V. Crouser, 911 P.2d. 725 (Haw. 1996).

41. N.Y. FAM. CT. ACT § 1012f(I)(B) (McKinney 1996).

42. *E.g.*, MD. ANN. CODE art. 27, § 35C(2)(I) (1995).

43. A number of courts have upheld the constitutionality of broad standards (e.g., "cruelty") for child abuse. *E.g.*, People v. Jennings, 641 P.2d 276 (Colo. 1982); Bowers v. State, 283 Md. 115, 389 A.2d 341 (1978); State v. Sinica, 372 N.W.2d 445 (Neb. 1985). *But see* State v. Meinert, 225 Kan. 816, 594 P.2d 232 (1979).

44. STANDARDS, *supra* note 15, § 2.1(B).

45. *Id.*, commentary at 65–66.

46. *E.g.*, N.J. STAT. ANN. § 9:6-8.9D(2) (West 1995); N.Y. SOC. SERV. LAW § 371(4a)(I)(B) (Consol. 1996); R.I. GEN. LAWS § 40-11-2(1)(e) (1995).

47. *E.g.*, TENN. CODE ANN. § 37-1-102(12)(B) (1996).

48. Kelly Weisberg, *The "Discovery" of Sexual Abuse: Experts' Role in Legal Formulation*, 18 U.C. DAVIS L. REV. 1 (1984).

49. In the past decade, the proportion of child protective cases involving child sexual abuse has declined significantly (from 16% to 10% of all reports). Daro, *supra* note 8, at 21.

50. Reflecting the increased prosecutorial activity, appellate cases involving sexual abuse rose dramatically during the late 1980s and early 1990s. Melton et al., *supra* note 9, at 47–48. For a review of research on the frequency of criminal trials in sexual abuse cases, *see id.* at 55.

51. STANDARDS, *supra* note 15, § 2.1(D) and commentary.

52. *Id.*, commentary at 70–71.

53. *Id.*, commentary at 72.

54. *See, e.g.*, ALA. CODE § 13-A-6-66 (1996); ALASKA STAT. § 11.41.436 (1995); ARK. CODE ANN. § 5-14-108 (MICHIE 1995); CAL. PENAL CODE § 288.5 (DEERING 1996); ILL. ANN. STAT. ch. 720, para. 5/12-15 (Smith-Hurd 1996); KY. REV. STAT. ANN. § 510.110 (Michie/Bobbs-Merrill 1995).

55. Georgia and Kansas are among the states that do not specifically define "sexual abuse" in their criminal statutes. *See infra* note 56.

56. *See, e.g.*, ALASKA STAT. § 47.17.290 (1995); GA. CODE ANN. § 9-3-33.1 (1996) (defining sexual abuse by reference to the penal code sections dealing with rape, in-cest, carnal knowledge, and sexual battery); KAN. STAT. ANN. § 38-1052(12)(c) (1995) (defining sexual abuse by reference to criminal statutes). *Compare, e.g.*, ALA. CODE § 26-14-1 (1996); ARK. CODE ANN. § 9-27-303 (Michie 1995); KY. REV. STAT. ANN. § 117(49) (Michie/Bobbs-Merrill 1995).

57. *See, e.g.*, JAMES GARBARINO ET AL., THE PSYCHOLOGICALLY BATTERED CHILD (1986); PSYCHOLOGICAL MALTREATMENT OF CHILDREN AND YOUTH (Marla R. Brassard et al. eds. 1987).

58. There is substantial evidence for adverse psychological effects on children as a result of their parents' divorce. *See generally* Paul R. Amato, *Life-Span Adjustment of Children to Their Parents' Divorce*, FUTURE OF CHILDREN, Spring 1994, at 143. Many of these effects persist even into adulthood. Paul R. Amato & Bruce Keith, *Parental Divorce and Adult Well-Being: A Meta-Analysis*, 53 J. MARRIAGE & FAM. 43 (1991). *See, e.g.*, Howard S. Friedman et al., *Psychosocial and Behavioral Predictors of Longevity: The Aging and Death of "Termites,"* 50 AM. PSYCHOL. 69 (1995). Given these impacts and the fact that divorce is clearly willful behavior on the part of at least one parent, could it be termed "abusive"?

59. STANDARDS, *supra* note 15, § 2.1(C).

60. WYO. STAT. ANN. § 14-3-202(ii)(A) (1996).

61. *See, e.g.*, State v. Ballard, 341 So. 2d 957 (Ala. App. 1976); State v. Meinert, 594 P.2d 232 (Kan. 1979). *But see* People v. Smith, 678 P.2d 886 (Cal. 1984); People v. Jennings, 641 P.2d 276 (Colo. 1982); Mahun v. State, 377 So. 2d 1158 (Fla. 1979); State v. Freeman, 409 So. 2d 581 (La. 1982); State v. Sinica, 372 N.W.2d 445 (Neb. 1985); Bludsworth v. State, 646 P.2d 558 (Nev. 1982); State v. Daniels, 400 N.E.2d 399 (Ohio 1980).

62. JEANNE GIOVANNONI & ROSINA M. BECERRA, DEFINING CHILD ABUSE (1979).

63. *Id.*

64. Kempe et al., *supra* note 7.

65. *See supra* note 5.

66. *See supra* notes 7–8.

67. In international work on child protection policy, Melton has been struck by what appears to be a natural evolution of child protection efforts. Other Western countries have tended to be on the same path as the United States, but several years delayed. Thus the substantial increase in sexual abuse cases has come later to Europe, and the range of responses considered–notwithstanding great debate about their efficacy–has been very similar in most countries to that in the United States.

Perhaps even more to the point, in newly democratic societies there seems to be a similar evolution. When people are freed to consider domestic violations of human decency and individual rights, their first impulse is to try to ferret out cases of severe child abuse–to enact a reporting law and to establish an investigation system. Soon this system becomes overwhelmed, and calls occur for its reform.

See also David Finkelhor, *Introduction*, in APSAC HANDBOOK, *supra* note 10, at ix (describing the evolution of the child protection movement).

68. *See supra* note 22.

69. *See, e.g.*, THE BACKLASH: CHILD PROTECTION UNDER FIRE (John E. B. Myers ed. 1994); David Finkelhor, *"The Backlash" in Sociological Perspective*, APSAC ADVISOR, Fall 1995, at 1.

We suspect that there are few contexts in which social science researchers and human service professionals are as polarized as they are in matters pertaining to child maltreatment, particularly in regard to the response of the criminal justice system. For a flavor of this debate, *see* Symposium, *Suggestibility of Child Witnesses: The Social Science Amicus Brief in* State of New Jersey v. Margaret Kelly Michaels, 1 PSYCHOL., PUB. POL, & L. 243 (1995).

70. *See, e.g.*, STRAUS, *supra* note 32, at 19–48; Robert F. Drinan, *Saving Our Children: Focusing the World's Attention on the Abuse of Children*, 26 LOY. U. CHI. L. REV. 137 (1995); Gary B. Melton, *Socialization in the Global Community: Respect for the Dignity of Children*, 46 AM. PSYCHOL. 66 (1991).

71. Ross D. Parke & C. W. Collmer, *Child Abuse: An Interdisciplinary Analysis*, in 5 REVIEW OF CHILD DEVELOPMENT RESEARCH 509, 513 (E. Mavis Hetherington ed. 1975).

72. JAMES GARBARINO & ANNE GARBARINO, EMOTIONAL MALTREATMENT OF CHILDREN 8 (1980).

73. *Id.* at 18–20.

74. DAVID GIL, VIOLENCE AGAINST CHILDREN: PHYSICAL ABUSE IN THE UNITED STATES 6 (1970).

75. Katherine K. Christoffel et al., *Standard Definitions for Childhood Injury Research: Excerpts of a Conference Report*, 89 PEDIATRICS 1027 (1992).

76. NATIONAL RESEARCH COUNCIL, *supra* note 2, at 57–77.

77. *Id.* at 345.

78. In an expansive review covering even evidence for evolutionary and genetic factors in child maltreatment, Belsky has clearly stated the need for an ecological approach that examines the interaction among multiple determinants of abuse and neglect: "When the etiology of child maltreatment is considered, there is no shortage of causal agents that are invoked to explain the occurrence of physical child abuse and neglect. Some of the factors are historical (e.g., societal attitudes toward family privacy) and some are contemporaneous (e.g., poverty); some are cultural (e.g., tolerance of violence) and some are situational (e.g., crying episode); and some are attributes of parents (e.g., hostile personality) and some of children (e.g., difficult temperament). Although past reviewers of the literature have identified psychiatric or psychological models of maltreatment, which focus attention on the characteristics of the perpetrator, sociological models, which focus attention on the contextual conditions that give rise to abuse and neglect, and social–interactional or effect-of-child-on-caregiver models, which underscore the dyadic nature of problematic parenting, it is clear today that no one such model is adequate. . . .

"[C]hild maltreatment is now widely recognized to be multiply determined by a variety of factors operating through transactional processes at various levels of analysis (i.e., life-course history to immediate situational to historical–evolutionary) in the broad ecology of parent–child relations. Moreover, it is well appreciated that what determines whether child maltreatment will take place is the balance of stressors and supports or of potentiating (i.e., risk) and compensatory (i.e., protective factors). When stressors (of a variety of kinds: parent, child, social conditions) outweigh supports (also of a variety of kinds), or when potentiating factors [overbalance] compensatory ones, the probability of child maltreatment increases. In other words . . . there not only appears to be no single cause of child maltreatment, but no necessary or sufficient causes. All too sadly, there are many pathways to child abuse and neglect." Jay Belsky, *Etiology of Child Maltreatment: A Developmental–Ecological Analysis*, 114 PSYCHOL. BULL. 413, 413 (1993).

79. *See, e.g.*, URIE BRONFENBRENNER, THE ECOLOGY OF HUM. DEVELOPMENT: EXPERIMENTS BY NATURE AND DESIGN (1979); JAMES GARBARINO, CHILDREN AND FAMILIES IN THE SOCIAL ENVIRONMENT (1982).

80. "Behavioral repertoire" refers to the range of behaviors available to an individual in a particular situation.

81. For a brief review of the literature on the significance of child characteristics in the etiology of child maltreatment, *see* NATIONAL RESEARCH COUNCIL, *supra* note 2, at 123–25. *See also* Robert T. Ammerman, *The Role of the Child in Physical Abuse: A Reappraisal*, 6 VIOLENCE & VICTIMS 87 (1991) (arguing that aggressive and disobedient behavior by children may maintain, but probably does not create, physical abuse).

82. *See generally* EXTENDING FAMILIES: THE SOCIAL NETWORKS OF PARENTS AND THEIR CHILDREN (Moncrief Cochran et al. Eds. 1990).

83. Martha Farrell Erickson & Byron Egeland, *Child Neglect*, in APSAC HANDBOOK, *supra* note 10, at 4, 13.

84. *See generally* Gary B. Melton, *The Improbability of Prevention of Sexual Abuse*, in CHILD ABUSE PREVENTION 168 (Diane J. Willis et al. eds. 1992) (arguing that a broad strategy of family strengthening is most likely to have the effect of preventing sexual abuse, but that such a strategy will have stronger effects on other potential childhood problems).

85. Lucy Berliner & Diana M. Elliott, *Sexual Abuse of Children*, in APSAC HANDBOOK, *supra* note 10, at 51, 53 (citations omitted).

86. *See, e.g., id.*; NATIONAL RESEARCH COUNCIL, *supra* note 2, at 133.

87. *Gallup Poll Finds Far More of America's Children Are Victims of Physical and Sexual Abuse Than Officially Reported*, 14 ABA JUV. & CHILD WELFARE L. REP. 171, 172 (1996); Leroy Pelton, *The Role of Material Factors in Child Abuse and Neglect*, in PROTECTING CHILDREN, *supra* note 31, at 131, 135.

88. David A. Wolfe, *The Role of Intervention and Treatment Services in the Prevention of Child Abuse and Neglect*, in PROTECTING CHILDREN, *supra* note 31, at 224, 225.

89. Richard J. Gelles, *Child Abuse as Psychopathology: A Sociological Critique and Reformulation*, 43 AM. J. ORTHOPSYCHIATRY 611 (1973).

90. John J. Spinetta & David Rigler, *The Child Abusing Parent: A Psychological Review*, 77 PSYCHOL. BULL. 296, 299 (1972).

91. *See, e.g.*, NATIONAL RESEARCH COUNCIL, *supra* note 2, at 111–15; Erickson & Egeland, *supra* note 83, at 13–14; David J. Kolko, *Child Physical Abuse*, in APSAC HANDBOOK, *supra* note 10, at 21, 24–25; Wolfe, *supra* note 88, at 224–25.

92. NATIONAL RESEARCH COUNCIL, *supra* note 2, at 111 (citations omitted).

There may be stronger evidence for distinctiveness in family dynamics than abuser characteristics. *See, e.g.*, James M. Gaudin, Jr. et al., *Family Functioning in Neglectful Families*, 20 CHILD ABUSE & NEGLECT 363 (1995) (relative to a comparison group of low-income families enrolled in public-support programs, neglectful families were substantially less organized, less democratic, more chaotic, less verbally expressive, and less positive in their affect). It is noteworthy that there nonetheless was wide variation among the neglectful families in Gaudin et al.'s study.

93. *See, e.g.*, NATIONAL RESEARCH COUNCIL, *supra* note 2, at 115–16; Erickson & Egeland, *supra* note 83, at 13; Kolko, *supra* note 91, at 25–26. *See also* Joel S. Milner et al., *Empathic Responsiveness and Affective Reactivity to Infant Stimuli in High- and Low-Risk for Physical Abuse Mothers*, 19 CHILD ABUSE & NEGLECT 767 (1995) (study showing that high-risk mothers' empathy did not differ in response to changes in infants' affect).

94. Mindy S. Rosenberg & N. Dickon Reppucci, *Abusive Mothers: Perceptions of Their Own and Their Children's Behavior*, 51 J. CONSULTING & CLINICAL PSYCHOL. 674 (1983).

95. It is noteworthy that the focus of Parents Anonymous groups generally is the enhancement of the parents' sense of competence. *See* Virginia Murphy-Berman & Gary B. Melton, *The Self-Help Movement and Neighborhood Support for Troubled Families* (1996) (manuscript in review).

96. Pelton, *supra* note 87, at 153 (citations omitted).

97. James Garbarino & Ann Crouter, *Defining the Community Context of Parent–Child Relations: The Correlates of Child Maltreatment*, 49 CHILD DEV. 604 (1978); James Garbarino & Kathleen Kostelny, *Neighborhood-Based Programs*, in PROTECTING CHILDREN, *supra* note 31, at 304, 315–22; James Garbarino et al., *Child Maltreatment as a Community Problem*, 16 CHILD ABUSE & NEGLECT 455 (1992); James Garbarino et al., *Children in Dangerous Environments: Child Maltreatment in the Context of Community Violence*, in CHILD ABUSE, CHILD DEVELOPMENT, AND SOCIAL POLICY 167 (Dante Cicchetti & Sheree Toth eds. 1993) [hereinafter CHILD ABUSE AND POLICY]; James Garbarino & Deborah Sherman, *High-Risk Neighborhoods and High-Risk Families: The Human Ecology of Child Maltreatment*, 51 CHILD DEV. 188 (1980).

Other researchers have replicated Garbarino's findings. *See, e.g.*, Claudia J. Coulton et al., *Community Level Factors and Child Maltreatment Rates*, 66 CHILD DEV. 1262 (1995); Gay Young & Tamra Gately, *Neighborhood Impoverishment and Child Maltreatment: An Analysis from the Ecological Perspective*, 9 J. FAM. ISSUES 240 (1988). *See also* Gary B. Melton, *It's Time for Neighborhood Research and Action*, 16 CHILD ABUSE & NEGLECT 909 (1992) (commenting on the implications of Garbarino et al.'s work).

The overall significance of neighborhood factors in child development is well established. *See, e.g.*, NATIONAL RESEARCH COUNCIL, LOSING GENERATIONS: ADOLESCENTS IN HIGH-RISK SETTINGS (1993); Jeanne Brooks-Gunn et al., *Do Neighborhoods Influence Child and Adolescent Development?*, 99 AM. J. SOC. 353 (1993); Claudia J. Coulton & Shanta Pandey, *Geographic Concentration of Poverty and Risk to Children in Urban Neighborhoods*, 35 AM. BEHAV. SCIENTIST 238 (1992).

98. Garbarino & Crouter, *supra* note 97.

99. Garbarino & Sherman, *supra* note 97.

100. Richard J. Gelles & Murray A. Straus, *Violence in the American Family*, 35(2) J. SOC. ISSUES 15, 33 (1979).

101. Neglectful mothers often report that their own mothers are seldom positive toward them (e.g., they do not really listen or provide companionship to them) and that their male partners are relatively unlikely to provide them with instrumental support (e.g., babysitting). Carol Coohey, *Neglectful Mothers, Their Mothers, and Partners: The Significance of Mutual Aid*, 19 CHILD ABUSE & NEGLECT 743 (1993).

102. Carol Coohey, *Child Maltreatment: Testing the Social Isolation Hypothesis*, 20 CHILD ABUSE & NEGLECT 241, 249–50, 251 (1996) (citations omitted).

103. ROSS A. THOMPSON, PREVENTING CHILD MALTREATMENT THROUGH SOCIAL SUPPORT: A CRITICAL ANALYSIS (1995) [hereinafter THOMPSON, PREVENTING CHILD MALTREATMENT]; Ross A. Thompson, *Social Support and the Prevention of Child Maltreatment*, in PROTECTING CHILDREN, *supra* note 31, at 40.

104. THOMPSON, PREVENTING CHILD MALTREATMENT, *supra* note 103, at 17.

105. *Id.* at 29, 100–01, 112.

106. *Id.* at 163.

107. *See supra* notes 101–02.

108. THOMPSON, PREVENTING CHILD MALTREATMENT, *supra* note 103, at 179.

109. Pelton, *supra* note 87, at 131.

110. *Id.* at 137.

111. Isabel Wolock & Bernard Horowitz, *Child Maltreatment and Material Deprivation among AFDC Families*, 53 SOC. SERV. REV. 175 (1979).

112. Pelton, *supra* note 87, at 149–50.

113. *Id.* at 145–47.

114. ABCAN, *supra* note 3, at 21–22 [Emphasis and footnotes omitted].

115. Pelton, *supra* note 87, at 132–42.

116. *Id.* at 154, and citations therein.

117. *Id.*

118. *Id.* at 155.

119. For an overview of the gaps in knowledge about child maltreatment and a discussion of the related problems of research policy, *see* Gary B. Melton & Mary Fran Flood, *Research Policy and Child Maltreatment: Developing the Scientific Foundation for Effective Protection of Children*, 18 CHILD ABUSE & NEGLECT 1 (Supp. 1994). *See also* Catherine Marneffe, *Child Abuse Treatment: A Fallow Land*, 20 CHILD ABUSE & NEGLECT 379, 379 (1996) (lamenting the lack of articles on treatment in CHILD ABUSE AND NEGLECT).

120. David A. Wolfe, *The Role of Intervention and Treatment Services in the Prevention of Child Abuse and Neglect*, in PROTECTING CHILDREN, *supra* note 31, at 224, 258.

121. *Id.* at 259.

122. *See generally* NATIONAL RESEARCH COUNCIL, *supra* note 2, at 261–65 (there is minimal evidence for efficacy of parent and family interventions in cases of child maltreatment, and the favorable results that have been obtained have been rendered equivocal by methodological limitations).

123. Melton et al., *supra* note 9, at 55–56, and citations therein.

124. Anne H. Cohn & Deborah Daro, *Is Treatment Too Late? What Ten Years of Evaluative Research Tell Us*, 11 CHILD ABUSE & NEGLECT 433, 440 (1987).

125. Judith V. Becker et al., *Empirical Research on Child Abuse Treatment: Report by the Child Abuse and Neglect Treatment Working Group, American Psychological Association*, 24 J. CLIN. CHILD PSYCHOL. 23, 37 (Supp. 1994).

126. Pelton, *supra* note 87, at 159–66. This principle applies to secondary prevention as well as treatment programs. *See, e.g.*, DEBORAH DARO ET AL., PREVENTING CHILD ABUSE: AN EVALUATION OF SERVICES TO HIGH-RISK FAMILIES (1993). *See also* Becker et al., *supra* note 125, at 36 (comparing the efficacy of multisystemic treatment and other home-based service models).

127. *See, e.g.*, Becker et al., *supra* note 125, at 24 (effects of physical abuse), 25–26 (effects of sexual abuse), 30 (effects of neglect); Erickson & Egeland, *supra* note 83, at 8–13 (effects of neglect). Even when social class is controlled, neglected children (relative to nonmaltreated children) have lower grades, more suspensions, more disciplinary referrals, and more grade repetitions. Kathleen A. Kendall-Tackett & John Eckenrode, *The Effects of Neglect on Academic Achievement and Disciplinary Problems: A Developmental Perspective*, 20 CHILD ABUSE & NEGLECT 161 (1996).

128. GENERAL ACCOUNTING OFFICE, FOSTER CARE: HEALTH NEEDS OF MANY YOUNG CHILDREN ARE UNKNOWN AND UNMET 1 (1995).

129. NATIONAL RESEARCH COUNCIL, *supra* note 2, at 256.

130. This official neglect has occurred even while foster care expenditures have increased dramatically. Federal expenditures under Title IV-E rose from $546 million in 1985 to $2.9 billion just a decade later. *Id.* at 4.

131. *Id.* at 2.

132. *Id.* at 5.

133. NATIONAL RESEARCH COUNCIL, *supra* note 2, at 256–57; Becker et al., *supra* note 125, at 25, 30; Wolfe, *supra* note 120, at 244–46.

134. Sheree L. Toth & Dante Cicchetti, *Child Maltreatment: Where Do We Go from Here in Our Treatment of Victims?*, in CHILD ABUSE AND POLICY, *supra* note 97, at 399. For a consensus statement about characteristics of high-quality treatment of abused and neglected children and their families, *see* Vicki Flerx & Susan P. Limber, *Treatment of Abused and Neglected Children and Their Families: Summary of the Wild Dunes International Conference* (paper presented at the meeting of the International Society for

Prevention of Child Abuse and Neglect, Dublin, Aug. 1996).

135. ABCAN, *supra* note 3, at 2, 9–11, and citations therein.

136. *Id.* at 9–10 (footnote omitted).

137. This differentiation is commonly known as *dual tracking. See* FLA. STAT. ch. 415.5017 (1995); MO. REV. STAT. § 210.109 (1996).

138. *See, e.g.*, NEB. REV. STAT. § 28.713 (1996).

139. *See, e.g.*, Virginia Murphy-Berman, *A Conceptual Framework for Thinking about Risk Assessment and Case Management in Child Protective Service*, 18 CHILD ABUSE & NEGLECT 193 (1994); Michael S. Wald & Maria Woolverton, *Risk Assessment: The Emperor's New Clothes?*, 69 CHILD WELFARE 483 (1990).

140. This problem may be alleviated by establishment of limitations on admission in criminal proceedings of information gathered for the purpose of child protection and related services. *See* Murray Levine & Eric Doherty, *The Fifth Amendment and Therapeutic Requirements to Admit Abuse*, 18 CRIM. JUST. & BEHAV. 98 (1991).

141. *See, e.g.*, FLA. STAT. ch. 415.5055 (1995); NEB. REV. STAT. § 28-728 (Supp. 1996). *See also* Task Force on Multidisciplinary Assessment, Final Report (Jan. 1996) (report to the Massachusetts commissioner of social services).

142. For a debate on the use of child interview specialists, *see* Paul Stern & Bill Walsh, *Professional Exchange: The Role of Child Interview Specialists*, APSAC ADVISOR, Summer 1995, at 10.

143. ALASKA STAT. § 47.10.142 (1994).

144. ARK. CODE ANN. § 12-12-516(a)(1) (1995).

145. *See also* CAL. WELF. & INST. CODE § 319(a)–(d) (1996), which provides that a child taken into protective custody shall be released to the parents unless: "(a) there is a substantial danger to the physical health of the minor or the minor is suffering severe emotional damage, and there are no reasonable means by which the minor's physical or emotional health may be protected without removing the minor from the parents' or guardians' physical custody; (b) there is substantial evidence that the [parent or guardian] is likely to flee the jurisdiction of the court; (c) the minor has left a placement in which he or she was placed by the juvenile court; (d) the minor indicates an unwillingness to return home, if the minor has been physically or sexually abused by a person residing in the home."

146. For an overview of these laws and their implementation, *see* DEBRA WHITCOMB, WHEN THE VICTIM IS A CHILD (2d ed. 1992).

147. Melton et al., *supra* note 9, at 64, and citations therein; Jodi A. Quas, *District Attorneys' Views of Legal Innovations for Child Witnesses*, AP-LS NEWS, Spring/Summer 1996, at 5.

148. *Id.* at 99.

149. Maryland V. Craig, 497 U.S. 836 (1987); Coy v. Iowa, 487 U.S. 1012 (1988); Kentucky v. Stincer, 482 U.S. 730 (1987); Globe Newspaper Co. v. Superior Ct., 457 U.S. 596 (1982). *See also* Idaho v. Wright, 497 U.S. 805 (1990) (considering the admissibility of an allegedly abused child's hearsay statements).

150. *See* San Antonio Indep. School Dist. v. Rodriquez, 411 U.S. 1 (1973) (articulating the doctrine of strict scrutiny of intrusions on rights expressly or implicitly guaranteed by the Constitution).

151. *See* Mark A. Small & Gary B. Melton, *Evaluation of Child Witnesses for Confrontation by Criminal Defendants*, 25 PROF. PSYCHOL.: RESEARCH & PRAC. 228, 229 (1994), and citations therein. The Association's brief in Maryland v. Craig, 497 U.S. 836 (1990), was written largely by a team of psychologists (principally Gail S. Goodman, Murray Levine, and Gary B. Melton, with assistance by counsel David W. Ogden) and was subsequently published at 15 LAW & HUM. BEHAV. 13 (1990).

152. 497 U.S. 836 (1987).

153. *Id.* at 855.

154. *Id.*

155. *Id.* at 856.

156. *Id.*

157. *Id.* at 860 (citation omitted).

158. *Id.* at 856.

159. *Id.*

160. *Id.*

161. *See, e.g.*, NEB. REV. STAT. § 29-1926 (1996).

162. *See* Small & Melton, *supra* note 151, at 230. The application of *Craig* is also unclear in states that have confrontation clauses that appear to be more restrictive than the Sixth Amendment to the U.S. Constitution. *See* Mark A. Small, *Constitutional Challenges to Child Witness Protection Legislation: An Update*, 9 VIOLENCE & VICTIMS 369 (1994) (discussing the application of *Craig* to state constitutional provisions requiring *face-to-face* confrontation).

163. *Id.* at 232 (citation omitted).

164. *See supra* note 161.

165. Small & Melton, *supra* note 151, at 232.

166. Melton et al., *supra* note 9, at 68 (citations omitted).

167. Gary B. Melton, *Children as Partners for Justice: Next Steps for Developmentalists*, 57 MONOGRAPHS OF SOC'Y FOR RESEARCH IN CHILD DEV., Serial No. 229, at 153, 157 (1992), *discussing* Gail S. Goodman et al., *Testifying in Criminal Court*, 57 MONOGRAPHS SOC'Y FOR RES. IN CHILD DEV. (Serial No. 229), at 1 (1992).

168. *Id.*

169. Judy Cashmore, *The Use of Closed-Circuit Television for Child Witnesses in the ACT* (report to the Australian Law Reform Commission, Oct. 1992).

170. Helen L. Westcott & Graham M. Davies, *Sexually Abused Children's and Young People's Perspectives on Investigative Interviews* (unpublished manuscript, Public Policy Department, National Society for Prevention of Cruelty to Children, London, England, 1994).

171. *See* Small & Melton, *supra* note 151, at 231.

172. *See* Melton et al., *supra* note 9, at 62–66, and citations therein. *See generally* Gary B. Melton, *Children as Legal Actors*, in HANDBOOK OF PSYCHOLOGY AND LAW 275 (Dorothy K. Kagehiro & William S. Laufer eds. 1991) (discussing children's competence and experience in various legal roles, including witness).

173. *See* Josephine Bulkley, *Recent Supreme Court Decisions Ease Child Abuse Prosecutions: Use of Closed-Circuit Tele-*vision and Children's Statements of Abuse under the Confrontation Clause, 16 NOVA L. REV. 687, 689–90 (1992).

174. For such a primer, see MYERS, *supra* note 10, at 33–52.

175. 497 U.S. 805 (1990).

176. Justice O'Connor wrote the opinion for the Court in both cases. *Wright* was decided by a 5–4 vote that deviated markedly from the Court's usual ideological division. O'Connor was joined by the two most liberal members of the Court at the time (Brennan and Marshall), a centrist (Stevens), and perhaps the most conservative Justice (Scalia). Justice Kennedy wrote a dissenting opinion that also attracted Justices across the ideological spectrum (from left to right: Blackmun, White, and Rehnquist).

177. 448 U.S. 56 (1980).

178. 497 U.S. at 815.

179. "The residual hearsay exception . . . accommodates ad hoc instances in which statements not otherwise falling within a recognized hearsay exception . . . might nevertheless be sufficiently reliable to be admissible at trial." *Id.* at 817 (discussing Fed. R. Evid. 803(24) and the congruent Idaho state evidentiary rule).

180. *Id.*

181. *Id.* at 819.

182. *Id.*

183. *Id.* at 822–23.

184. *Id.* at 820.

185. *Id.* at 822.

186. *Id.* at 821–22.

187. *Id.* at 820 (citations omitted).

188. John E. B. Meyers, *Steps Toward Forensically Relevant Research*, 57 MONOGRAPHS OF SOC'Y FOR RES. IN CHILD DEV. (Serial No. 229), at 143, 150 (1992).

189. *Id.*

190. Josephine A. Bulkley et al., *Child Abuse and Neglect Laws and Legal Proceedings*, in APSAC HANDBOOK, *supra* note 10, at 271, 288–89.

191. *See also* Melton et al., *supra* note 9, at 57–60; Karen J. Saywitz & Gail S. Goodman, *Interviewing Children In and Out of Court*, in APSAC HANDBOOK, *supra* note 10, at 297.

192. 497 U.S. at 824–25.

193. MYERS, *supra* note 10, at 53.

194. *Id.* at 52–54.

195. In many states, the exception is not limited either to physicians or even to health professionals focusing exclusively on physical care. Bulkley et al., *supra* note 10, at 285, and citations therein. *See, e.g., In re* M.P., 882 P.2d 1180 (Wash. App. 1994).

196. 502 U.S. 346 (1992).

197. United States v. Tome, 61 F.3d 1446 (10th Cir. 1995).

198. The law generally presumes spontaneous statements to be more reliable than those elicited by questioning. Indeed, a traditional hearsay exception applies to "excited utterances" (statements about an event that are made spontaneously without time for reflection). Because of the diverse circumstances in which children disclose abuse, some courts have admitted spontaneous statements made

long after the event discussed. *See* Bulkley et al., *supra* note 10, at 285, and citations therein. Perhaps of relevance here is the base rate for false reports of abuse made by children, with estimates ranging from 2% to 33%. *See generally*, E. Mikkelsen, et al., *False Sexual Abuse Allegations by Children and Adolescents: Context Factors and Clinical Subtypes*, 45 AM. J. PSYCHOTHERAPY 556 (1992).

199. Webb v. Lewis, 33 F.3d 1079 (9th Cir. 1994).

200. John E. B. Myers, the leading proponent of liberal use of mental health professionals' opinions on the case in chief in child maltreatment cases, *see infra* note 203, has flatly rejected testimony that directly focuses on the child's credibility: "All U.S. courts agree that expert witnesses are not to comment directly on the credibility of individual children or on the credibility of sexually abused children as a group. Thus, expert witnesses should not say that a child told the truth or was believable when describing abuse." Myers, *Expert Testimony*, in APSAC HANDBOOK, *supra* note 10, at 319, 335–36.

201. State v. Milbradt, 756 P.2d 620, 624 (Or. 1988).

202. Yount v. State, 872 S.W.2d 706 (Tex. Crim. App. 1993).

203. *See, e.g.*, John E. B. Myers et al., *Expert Testimony in Child Sexual Abuse Litigation*, 68 NEB. L. REV. 1 (1989); AMERICAN PROFESSIONAL SOCIETY ON THE ABUSE OF CHILDREN, GUIDELINES FOR PSYCHOSOCIAL EVALUATION OF SUSPECTED SEXUAL ABUSE IN YOUNG CHILDREN (1990). Although the APSAC GUIDELINES, *id.* at 6, indicate that mental health professionals "may directly state that abuse did or did not occur," they also state flatly that "[t]he evaluator should take care to communicate that mental health professionals have no special ability to detect whether an individual is telling the truth."

204. *See* Gary B. Melton, *Doing Justice and Doing Good: Conflicts for Mental Health Professionals*, FUTURE OF CHILDREN, Summer/Fall 1994, at 102, 117 nn. 60–61.

205. Lois B. Oberlander, *Psycholegal Issues in Child Sexual Abuse Evaluations: A Survey of Forensic Mental Health Professionals*, 19 CHILD ABUSE & NEGLECT 475 (1995).

206. Across the United States, there are nearly 40 professional classifications named in child abuse reporting laws, and numerous states now encompass "any person" within the scope of their statutes. SETH C. KALICHMAN, MANDATED REPORTING OF SUSPECTED CHILD ABUSE: ETHICS, LAW, AND POLICY 24 (1993).

207. For elaboration of our view on this and other uses of expert testimony in child abuse cases, *see* Gary B. Melton & Susan Limber, *Psychologists' Involvement in Cases of Child Maltreatment*, 44 AM. PSYCHOL. 1225 (1989) (policy statement of the American Psychological Association Division of Child, Youth, and Family Services).

208. *See* Myers, *supra* note 200, at 332–33, and citations therein.

209. Michael E. Lamb, *The Investigation of Child Sexual Abuse: An Interdisciplinary Statement*, 3(4) J. CHILD SEXUAL ABUSE, 93, 97 (1994).

210. *See, e.g.*, Jon R. Conte & Lucy Berliner, *The Impact of Sexual Abuse on Children: Empirical Findings*, in HANDBOOK ON SEXUAL ABUSE OF CHILDREN 72 (Lenore Walker ed. 1988); Howard Dubowitz et al., *A Follow-Up Study of Behavior Problems Associated with Sexual Abuse*, 17 CHILD ABUSE & NEGLECT 743 (1993).

211. Myers, *supra* note 200, at 327–30, presents a useful visual depiction of the base-rate problem. However, he partially misses its import by subsequently focusing on sexualized behavior, the symptoms that are most disproportionately common among sexually abused children. *Id.* at 330–32. Because a large proportion of a small population still may be smaller than a small proportion of a large population and because sexualized behavior is exhibited by only a minority of the sexually abused population, the base-rate problem still applies. *See* Angela Browne & David Finkelhor, *Initial and Long-Term Effects: A Review of the Research*, in A SOURCEBOOK ON CHILD SEXUAL ABUSE 143, 151 (David Finkelhor ed. 1986). Indeed, the example given is a wonderful illustration of why syndrome evidence is inherently misleading and prejudicial.

212. *See, e.g.*, Steward v. State, 652 N.E.2d 490 (Ind. 1995).

213. *See, e.g.*, Estelle v. McGuire, 502 U.S. 62 (1991); State v. Moyer, 727 P.2d 31 (Ariz. App. 1986); State v. Dumlao, 491 A.2d 404 (Conn. App. 1987); Price v. Comm'r, 445 S.E.2d 642 (Va. App. 1994).

214. *See generally* Carole Jenny, *Medical Issues in Sexual Abuse*, in APSAC HANDBOOK, *supra* note 10, at 195; Charles F. Johnson, *Physical Abuse: Accidental Versus Intentional Trauma in Children*, in APSAC HANDBOOK, *supra* note 10, at 206.

215. 310 N.W.2d 58 (Minn. 1981).

216. *See* Fed. R. Evid. 404.

217. 310 N.W.2d at 64.

218. *See, e.g.*, Haakanson v State, 760 P.2d 1030 (Ala. App. 1988); People v. Walkey, 177 Cal. App. 3d 268 (1986); People v. Lucero, 724 P.2d 1374 (Colo. App. 1986); Sanders v. State, 251 Ga. 70, 303 S.E.2d 13 (1983); State v. Pulizzano, 155 Wis. 2d 633, 456 N.W.2d 325 (1990). These cases are criminal cases in which the state attempted to introduce evidence of battering-parent syndrome, efforts rejected by the courts. Such evidence is admissible if the *defendant* introduces his or her character in an effort to show it *unlikely* that the defendant engaged in the charged conduct. Otherwise, the courts invariably view the proffered evidence as highly prejudicial. For a general discussion, see Thomas N. Bulleit, Jr., Note, *The Battering Parent Syndrome: Inexpert Testimony as Character Evidence*, 17 U. MICH. J. L. REF. 653 (1984).

219. *See* Fed. R. Evid. 403.

220. The burden is in effect shifted to the defendant, who must convince the jury that he or she is one of the X% of persons with his or her characteristics who is not a battering parent.

Although the potential use of character evidence to inculpate defendants has received the greatest attention, defense attorneys do occasionally try to admit behavioral-science testimony as character evidence designed to suggest that a defendant with certain characteristics would be unlikely or perhaps even psychologically unable to offend against children. The lack of strong psychological traits that correlate with child maltreatment [see §

15.03(d)(1)] means that evidence on this point, if presented accurately, is unlikely to assist either the defendant or the factfinder. Notably, the search for a profile of child sexual abusers has been largely futile. William D. Murphy & Timothy A. Smith, *Sex Offenders Against Children: Empirical and Clinical Issues*, in APSAC HANDBOOK, *supra* note 10, at 175, 177. Accordingly, courts have been reluctant to admit testimony by defense experts on offender profiles. Myers, *supra* note 200, at 336.

221. 42 U.S.C. § 675(5)(B) (West Supp. 1996).

222. The Adoption Assistance and Child Welfare Act of 1980 requires states to make "reasonable efforts" to return each foster child to his or her biological or adoptive family. 42 U.S.C.S. § 671(a)(15) (West Supp. 1996).

223. *See* DONALD T. KRAMER, LEGAL RIGHTS OF CHILDREN 96 (2d ed. 1994) (noting the difficulty of "clearly isolating it [disposition] as a separate and distinct part of a case").

224. *See, e.g.,* S.C. CODE ANN. § 20-7-762 (Law. Co-op. Cum. Supp. 1995) (providing that the family court must review and approve a CPS-prepared dispositional plan indicating "any changes in parental behavior that must be made and any services which will be provided to the family to ensure, to the greatest extent possible, that the child will not be endangered").

225. *See supra* notes 221–22. *But see* Suter v. Artist M., 503 U.S. 347 (1992) (holding that Congress did not create an enforceable private right of action to reasonable efforts by the state; instead, states are required only to develop a plan for each effort that is approved by the Secretary of Health and Human Services).

226. *E.g.,* IND. CODE ANN. § 31-6-4-19(b) (West 1996); MASS. GEN. LAWS ANN. ch. 119 § 29B (West 1993).

227. 42 U.S.C.S. § 671(a)(15) (West Supp. 1996).

228. *See supra* note 139. *See also* ABCAN, CREATING CARING COMMUNITIES, *supra* note 23, at 109 (describing child maltreatment as "the most underresearched major social problem"); Melton & Flood, *supra* note 119, at 4 (listing major gaps in knowledge about child abuse and neglect, including the facts that knowledge is lacking about "the validity of predictions by workers in the various sectors of the child protection system," that "little research is available to guide workers in assessing risk of imminent danger to children," and that "[t]here is insufficient research about treatment to match families to treatment approaches").

229. NATIONAL RESEARCH COUNCIL, *supra* note 2, at 275.

230. *See, e.g.,* STANDARDS, *supra* note 15, § 8.2; MODEL STATUTE FOR TERMINATION OF PARENTAL RIGHTS § 12(1) (National Council of Juvenile and Family Court Judges) [hereinafter MODEL STATUTE], *reprinted in* WALTER J. WADLINGTON ET AL., CHILDREN IN THE LEGAL SYSTEM 789 (1983).

231. CAL. FAM. CODE § 7828 (West 1994).

232. N.Y. FAM. CT. ACT §§ 622 & 623 (McKinney 1983).

233. The difficulty of the issue is reflected in the Supreme Court's seemingly conflicting decisions in San-

tosky v. Kramer, 455 U.S. 745 (1982) (termination of parental rights requires clear and convincing evidence) and Lassiter v. Department of Social Services, 452 U.S. 18 (1981) (no right to counsel in such proceedings). *See* Douglas Besharov, *Terminating Parental Rights: The Indigent Parent's Right to Counsel after* Lassiter v. North Carolina, 15 FAM. L.Q. 205 (1981); Patricia J. Falk, Note, *Why Not Beyond a Reasonable Doubt?*, 62 NEB. L. REV. 602 (1983).

234. State v. Robert H., 118 N.H. 713, 716, 393 A.2d 1387, 1389 (1978).

235. Santosky v. Kramer, 455 U.S. 745, 764 (1982).

236. NEB. REV. STAT. § 43-292(4) (1994).

237. NEB. REV. STAT. § 43-292(5).

238. MODEL STATUTE, *supra* note 230, § 12(1).

239. *Id.*, §§ 12(1), 12(2).

240. *Id.*, § 12(3).

241. VA. CODE ANN. § 16.1-283(B) *et. seq.* (Michie 1996).

242. N.Y. SOC. SERV. LAW § 384-b(7)(a) (McKinney 1992).

243. Howard A. Davidson, *Improving the Judicial Handling of Civil Child Maltreatment Cases*, in FAMILIES IN COURT 63, 79 (Meredith Hofford ed. 1989).

244. *Id.* at 78–80.

245. In the current initiative undertaken by the Edna McConnell Clark Foundation for child protection reform, demonstration programs often have drawn from domestic violence programs and have routinely developed safety plans for families. The innovation, consistent with the notion that isolation is a critical factor in the causation and recurrence of child maltreatment [see § 15.03(d)(2)], is that community members ("natural helpers") often join in community safety agreements in which they agree to offer support and/or monitoring and parents agree to cooperate in the plan, which is ratified by CPS. Patricia Schene, Remarks to a Study Group Supported by the Edna McConnell Clark Foundation and Conducted by the Institute for Families in Society, University of South Carolina (Oct. 4, 1996).

246. Like a few other U.S. jurisdictions, Arizona has explicit statutory authority for mediation in child protection cases. ARIZ. REV. STAT. ANN. § 8-546.10 (Cum. Supp. 1994). The Arizona program is clouded, however, by the fact that the agency with authority to conduct mediation (i.e., the state attorney general's office) also is the entity that represents the state in civil child protection matters.

For examples of other programs for mediation of child protection cases, *see, e.g.,* Jane Maresca, *Mediating Child Protection Cases*, 74 CHILD WELFARE 731 (1995); Margaret Shaw & W. Patrick Phear, *Innovation in Dispute Resolution: Case Status Conferences for Child Protection and Placement Proceedings in the State of Connecticut*, 29 FAM. & CONCILIATION CTS. REV. 270 (1991); Nancy Thoenes, *Mediation and the Dependency Court: The Controversy and Three Courts' Experience*, 29 FAM. & CONCILIATION CTS. REV. 246 (1991). For a useful overview of the debates about these programs and of the process of their implementation, *see* Center for Policy Research, Alternatives to Adjudication in Child Abuse and Neglect Cases (1992) (final report to the State Justice Institute in re Grant No. SJI-89-03C-022).

247. Bernard Mayer, *Mediation in Child Protection Cases: The Impact of Third-Party Intervention on Parental Compliance Attitudes*, MEDIATION Q., Summer 1989, at 89.

248. Shaw & Phear, *supra* note 246.

249. *See supra* note 245.

250. *See* MARK HARDIN, FAMILY GROUP CONFERENCES IN CHILD ABUSE AND NEGLECT CASES: LEARNING FROM THE EXPERIENCE OF NEW ZEALAND (1996); Gary B. Melton, Foreign Innovations in Dispute Resolution in Matters Related to Juvenile Justice and Child Protection (Oct. 1992) (report to the Committee on Family Relations, 2020 Vision Project, Judicial Council of California; discussion primarily of the New Zealand family group conferences and the Scottish hearings system).

251. As of Fall 1995, five North American jurisdictions reported demonstration projects using family group conferences (California, Illinois, Newfoundland, Oregon, Vermont). Karen Farestad et al., *International Survey of Innovative Programs with CPS Linkages* 4 (report by the American Humane Association to the Edna McConnell Clark Foundation, Feb. 1996). This number continues to expand. Melton is currently involved in designing a trial of family group conferences in South Carolina.

252. *See* Alsager v. District Ct., 406 F. Supp. 10 (S.D. Iowa 1975), *aff'd*, 545 F.2d 1137 (8th Cir. 1976) (statute permitting termination on ground of "unfitness" is unconstitutionally vague). There is a plausible argument that statutes that provide for termination on the ground of unfitness resulting from "mental illness" are void for vagueness unless there is further definition. *Cf. Developments in the Law: Civil Commitment of the Mentally Ill*, 87 HARV. L. REV. 1190, 1253–58 (1974) (analyzing use of "mental illness" as the statutory threshold for civil commitment).

253. The courts do not require that the child suffer actual harm before terminating parental rights. *See, e.g., In re* Appeal in Maricopa County Juvenile Action No. JS-501568, 869 P.2d 1224 (Ariz. App. 1994) (mother's minimal efforts to engage in drug treatment during the first year of her child's out-of-home placement did not preclude a finding that she had been negligent in remediating the conditions leading to the placement); *In re* J.P., 633 N.E.2d 27 (Ill. App. 1994); *In re* T.J.O., 527 N.W.2d 417 (Iowa App. 1994) (the parents had not addressed their substance abuse and relationship problems, and the child had already bonded with foster parents); *In re* K.M.B., 883 S.W.2d 123 (Mo. App. 1994) (court did not require medical evidence to show that the mother was an unfit parent and a substance abuser, given record of 13 failed attempts at treatment and facts that one child had observed her taking drugs and another had been exposed to drugs *in utero*).

In cases involving parents with mental illness, the courts have focused on the parents' difficulties in caring for their children. For example, the Alabama Supreme Court upheld the termination of parental rights of parents with mental illness because they had not provided an adequate, safe residence for their child. *Ex parte State Dep't Hum. Resources*, 624 So. 2d 589 (Ala. 1993). *See also* E.C. v. District of Columbia, 589 A.2d 1245 (D.C. App. 1991) (mental illness by itself does not justify termina-

tion of parental rights, but its effects on the children can do so). Courts have reached similar conclusions regarding parents with mental retardation. *See, e.g.*, Egly v. Blackford County Dep't Pub. Welfare, 592 N.E.2d 1232 (Ind. 1992).

254. *See, e.g.*, HENRY GRUNEBAUM ET AL., MENTALLY ILL MOTHERS AND THEIR CHILDREN (1975); Bertram Cohler et al., *Disturbance of Attention Among Schizophrenic, Depressed, and Well Mothers and their Children*, 18 J. CHILD PSYCHOL. & PSYCHIATRY 115 (1977); Carol Kauffman et al., *Superkids: Competent Children of Psychotic Mothers*, 136 AM. J. PSYCHIATRY 11 (1979); Arnold Sameroff et al., *The Early Development of Children Born to Mentally Ill Women*, in CHILDREN AT RISK FOR SCHIZOPHRENIA 482 (Norman W. Watt et al. eds. 1983).

It might be expected that the greatest risk would be incurred by children of parents with schizophrenia. If parents are behaving in ways that are out of touch with reality and are unable to form relationships, it would be unsurprising to find that their children would suffer from the experience of unpredictability, deviant social norms in the home (in contrast to school and neighborhoods), and emotional distance in the family. In fact, there is now a rather substantial research literature (including the authorities noted above) indicating lower social competence, on the average, among children of parents with schizophrenia than among children of parents without known mental illnesses. But their competence is no lower than that of children of parents with other mental disorders (e.g., depression), although one might expect these latter parents to provide a less deviant environment. Of still greater policy significance, the differences between children of parents with schizophrenia and children of parents without mental illnesses tend to disappear when appropriate controls are added for social class.

255. As Markikangas and Angst noted, "Familial aggregation [heightened risk] of depression may result from shared genes, common environmental factors, or a combination thereof." Kathleen Ries Merikangas & Jules Angst, *The Challenge of Depressive Disorders in Adolescence*, in PSYCHOSOCIAL DISTURBANCES IN YOUNG PEOPLE: CHALLENGES FOR PREVENTION 131, 144 (Michael Rutter ed. 1995).

256. *See, e.g.*, Bruce E. Compas, *Promoting Successful Coping During Adolescence*, in PSYCHOSOCIAL DISTURBANCES IN YOUNG PEOPLE, *supra* note 255, at 247, 252, 255–56, 260.

257. Carol T. Mowbray et al., *Motherhood for Women with Serious Mental Illness: Pregnancy, Childbirth, and the Postpartum Period*, 65 AM. J. ORTHOPSYCHIATRY 21, 25 (1995).

258. *Id.* at 26.

259. *See id.* at 32–35.

260. *Id.* at 31.

261. *Id.* at 32.

262. Most of the research on children of parents with serious mental illness has focused on early childhood, *see supra* note 254, presumably under the hypothesis that a parent's schizophrenic disorder and the accompanying affective shallowness and mental preoccupations would inhibit the development of an attachment between the par-

ent and the child. However, it may be that the most significant effects occur later in development, when an abnormal style of information processing in the family might adversely affect a child's ability to deal with school tasks. *See* David Reiss, *Families and the Etiology of Schizophrenia*, 14 SCHIZOPHRENIA BULL. 9 (1975).

263. Given the relatively high stress and social and economic challenges that accompany living with a serious mental illness, it is unsurprising that pregnancy is typically perceived as a crisis by women with serious mental illness, and that they are at relatively high risk of postpartum psychotic or depressive episodes. Mowbray et al., *supra* note 257, at 25–29. The hypothesis is plausible but, as far as we are aware, unstudied that there are some risks to adult patients' mental health and, by extension, to the well-being of the family when stressors that arise naturally in the development of children (e.g., transition to junior high) occur.

264. Patricia M. Crittenden, *Social Networks, Quality of Child Rearing, and Child Development*, 56 CHILD DEV. 1299 (1985).

265. Mild mental retardation tends to be identified primarily by the schools. After completion of schooling, most people with mild mental retardation are no longer labeled retarded. *See generally* JAME MERCER, LABELING THE MENTALLY RETARDED: CLINICAL AND SOCIAL SYSTEM PERSPECTIVES ON MENTAL RETARDATION (1973).

266. *Id.*

267. M.L.E. Lubs & J.A. Maes, *Recurrence Risk in Mental Retardation*, in 3 RESEARCH TO PRACTICE IN MENTAL RETARDATION (Peter Mittler ed. 1977).

268. ELIZABETH REED & SHELDON C. REED, MENTAL RETARDATION: A FAMILY STUDY (1965).

269. Stephen Magura & Alexandre B. Laudet, *Parental Substance Abuse and Child Maltreatment: Review and Implications for Intervention*, 18 CHILDREN & YOUTH SERVICES REV. 193, 194–95 (1996).

270. DAVID FINKELHOR, CHILD SEXUAL ABUSE: NEW THEORY AND RESEARCH 44 (1984); Glenace E. Edwall & Norman G. Hoffman, *Correlates of Incest Reported by Adolescent Girls in Treatment for Substance Abuse*, in HANDBOOK ON SEXUAL ABUSE OF CHILDREN 94, 98 (Lenore E. A. Walker ed. 1988). Although it is probably incorrect to say that alcohol abuse itself *causes* sexual abuse, disinhibition resulting from intoxication is often a contributing factor. Moreover, there is little doubt that parental alcohol abuse is one of the many factors increasing the stress of children in incestuous families. Indeed, alcohol abuse by nonoffending mothers is common in such families. Lorna P. Cammaert, *Nonoffending Mothers*, in HANDBOOK ON CHILD SEXUAL ABUSE OF CHILDREN, *supra*, at 309, 312.

271. Theodore Jacob et al., *The Alcoholic's Spouse, Children and Family Interactions: Substantive Findings and Methodological Issues*, 39 J. STUD. ALCOHOL 1231 (1978).

272. GEORGE VAILLANT, THE NATURAL HISTORY OF ALCOHOLISM 65 (1983).

273. Robert J. Rotunda et al., *Family Systems and Alcohol Misuse: Research on the Effects of Alcoholism on Family Functioning and Effective Family Interventions*, 26 PROF. PSYCHOL.: RESEARCH & PRAC. 95 (1995).

274. *Id.* at 95.

275. *Id.* at 95–96.

276. *Id.* at 99. For a recent example of a failure to find significant differences in psychosocial functioning between adult children of alcoholics and other adults, *see* Chris Segrin & Michelle Mize Menees, *The Impact of Coping Styles and Family Communication on the Social Skills of Children of Alcoholics*, 57 J. STUD. ALCOHOL 29 (1996).

277. Rotunda et al., *supra* note 273, at 99.

278. *See* Polly E. Bijurr et al., *Parental Alcohol Use, Problem Drinking, and Children's Injuries*, 267 J. AM. MED. ASS'N 3166 (1992) (finding that child injuries are more likely to occur when mothers are problem drinkers, especially if they are married to men who also are moderate or heavy drinkers).

279. For a compilation of relevant cases (most of them ending in drug-abusing parents' loss of custody or parental rights altogether), *see* Mary E. Taylor, Annotation, *Parent's Use of Drugs as Factor in Award of Custody of Children, Visitation Rights, or Termination of Parental Rights*, 20 A.L.R.5th 534 (1994).

280. *See, e.g.*, John W. Kydd, *Abandoning Our Children: Mothers, Alcohol and Drugs*, 69 DENV. U. L. REV. 359 (1992); Jennifer M. Mone, Note, *Has Connecticut Thrown Out the Baby with the Bath Water? Termination of Parental Rights and In re Valerie D.*, 19 FORDHAM URB. L.J. 535 (1992); Victoria J. Swenson & Cheryl Crabbe, *Pregnant Substance Abusers: A Problem That Won't Go Away*, 25 ST. MARY'S L.J. 589 (1994).

281. *See* U.S. GENERAL ACCOUNTING OFFICE, FOSTER CARE: PARENTAL DRUG ABUSE HAS ALARMING IMPACT ON YOUNG CHILDREN (Apr. 1994) (Report No. GAO/HEHS-94-89) (describing the impact of increased referrals to foster care of children of drug abusing parents).

282. Theresa Lawton Hawley et al., *Children of Addicted Mothers: Effects of the "Crack Epidemic" on the Caregiving Environment and the Development of Preschoolers*, 65 AM. J. ORTHOPSYCHIATRY 364, 365–67 (1995).

283. *Id.* at 368–73.

284. *Id.* at 370. The magnitude of this disparity may have been an artifact of the referral pattern of the particular treatment program studied, in that CPS was a principal source of referrals. *Id.* at 370–71.

285. *Id.* at 371–73.

286. *E.g.*, Richard Barth & Barbara Needell, *Outcomes for Drug-Exposed Children Four Years Post-Adoption*, 18 CHILDREN & YOUTH SERVICES REV. 37 (1996) (no difference between drug-exposed and non-drug-exposed children—at least as categorized by their adoptive parents—in adoptive parent satisfaction and most indicators of child development); Magura & Laudet, *supra* note 269, at 198–200 (describing the environmental problems that often accompany parental drug abuse); Asher Ornoy et al., *The Developmental Outcome of Children Born to Heroin-Dependent Mothers, Raised at Home or Adopted*, 20 CHILD ABUSE & NEGLECT 385 (1996) (environmental influence on child development is stronger than the effects of prenatal exposure to heroin).

287. In a study comparing urban African American families in which children entered foster care because of

parental drug abuse with those in which children entered foster care for other reasons, poverty and housing problems were much more common factors in the former group. CLARICE WALKER ET AL., PARENTAL DRUG ABUSE AND AFRICAN AMERICAN CHILDREN IN FOSTER CARE: ISSUES AND STUDY FINDINGS 2 (1991).

288. Magura & Laudet, *supra* note 269, at 204. *See also* NATIONAL COUNCIL OF JUVENILE AND FAMILY COURT JUDGES, PROTOCOL FOR MAKING REASONABLE EFFORTS TO PRESERVE FAMILIES IN DRUG-RELATED DEPENDENCY CASES (Jan. 1992) (describing factors and options for juvenile and family court judges to consider in making dispositional decisions in child protection cases involving parental drug abuse).

289. Mary Fran Flood, *Innovative (and Successful!) Programs: A Presentation for Rural Nebraska Communities on Program Options for Helping Substance Using Pregnant Women and Parents* 13–14 (unpublished manuscript, Center on Children, Families, and the Law, University of Nebraska—Lincoln, 1992).

290. U.S. GENERAL ACCOUNTING OFFICE, COCAINE TREATMENT: EARLY RESULTS FROM VARIOUS APPROACHES 2 (June 1996) (Report No. GAO/HEHS-96-80).

291. *See, e.g.*, WALKER ET AL., *infra* note 331, at 27–30.

292. James P. Gleeson & Lynn C. Craig, *Kinship Care in Child Welfare: An Analysis of States' Policies*, 16 CHILDREN & YOUTH SERVICES REV. 7, 24 (1994).

293. CHILD WELFARE LEAGUE OF AMERICA, KINSHIP CARE: A NATURAL BRIDGE 16 (1994) [hereinafter CWLA].

294. *Id.* at 27. For a state-by-state review of policies on kinship care, see Gleeson & Craig, *supra* note 292.

295. *See* Mark Hardin, *Sizing Up Welfare Reform's Impact on Child Protection*, 15 CHILD L. PRAC. 104, 104–05 (1996), *discussing* Personal Responsibility and Work Opportunity Reconciliation Act of 1996, Pub. L. 104-193, § 5 (to be codified at 42 U.S.C. § 671(a)(18)).

296. CWLA, *supra* note 293, at 13.

297. As noted *infra*, relative caregivers typically are offered fewer resources than are nonrelative foster parents. In Miller v. Youakim, 440 U.S. 125 (1979), the U.S. Supreme Court held that states cannot discriminate against kinship care providers under the federal foster care program (Title IV-E of the Social Security Act). However, denial of state-financed foster-care payments to kinship-care providers was upheld in subsequent cases. Lipscomb v. Simmons, 962 F.2d 1374 (9th Cir. 1992); King v. McMahon, 230 Cal. Rptr. 911 (1986).

298. Gleeson & Craig, *supra* note 292, at 28.

299. CWLA, *supra* note 293, at 17–18.

300. Howard Dubowitz et al., *A Profile of Kinship Care*, 72 CHILD WELFARE 153 (1993).

301. *Id.* at 159. Similarly, a survey of kinship care providers in California showed that most expected the children for whom they were caring to live with them until they reached adulthood. Jill Duerr Berrick et al., *A Comparison of Kinship Foster Homes and Foster Family Homes: Implications for Kinship Foster Care as Family Preservation*, 16 CHILDREN & YOUTH SERVICES REV. 56-57 (1994).

302. Dubowitz et al., *supra* note 300, at 160–61.

303. *Id.* at 161.

304. Although adolescents in kinship care do not expect their relatives to support them, they (unlike youth in traditional foster homes) do expect to be able to live with relatives. Alfreda P. Iglehart, *Kinship Foster Care: Placement, Service, and Outcome Issues*, 16 CHILDREN & YOUTH SERVICES REV. 107 (1994).

305. Dubowitz et al., *supra* note 300, at 160.

306. CWLA, *supra* note 293, at 35. With similar ambivalence, other commentators have noted that "[w]hen children are placed in kinship foster care, the ultimate 'permanency plan' very often becomes long-term foster care and emancipation." Jill Duerr Berrick & Richard P. Barth, *Research on Kinship Foster Care: What Do We Know? Where Do We Go from Here?*, 16 CHILDREN & YOUTH SERVICES REV. 1 (1994).

307. Howard Dubowitz et al., *Children in Foster Care: How Do They Fare?*, CHILDREN & YOUTH SERVICES REV. 85 (1994).

308. CWLA, *supra* note 293, at 20–21.

309. Dubowitz et al., *supra* note 300, at 158; Berrick et al., *supra* note 301, at 42; Gleeson & Craig, *supra* note 292, at 10.

310. CWLA, *supra* note 293, at 57.

311. *Id.*

312. *Id.* at 49–50.

313. *Id.* at 44.

314. *Id.* at 63.

315. Nicole S. LeProhn, *The Role of the Kinship Foster Parent: A Comparison of the Role Conceptions of Relative and Non-Relative Foster Parents*, 16 CHILDREN & YOUTH SERVICES REV. 65 (1994). This sense of responsibility carries over in most cases to assurance that siblings can remain together. Dubowitz et al., *supra* note 300, at 161.

316. CWLA, *supra* note 293, at 64; Berrick et al., *supra* note 301, at 53.

317. *See, e.g.*, CAROL STACK, ALL OUR KIN: STRATEGIES FOR SURVIVAL IN A BLACK COMMUNITY (1974).

318. CWLA, *supra* note 293, at 18–19.

319. Berrick et al., *supra* note 301, at 49.

320. *See* Gary B. Melton, *The Child's Right to a Family Environment: Why Children's Rights and Family Values Are Compatible*, 51 AM. PSYCHOLOGIST 1234 (1996) (discussing the right to a family environment, pursuant to the Convention on the Rights of the Child).

321. Berrick & Barth, *supra* note 306, at 4.

322. *See supra* notes 127, 210 and accompanying text.

323. A study of more than 200 validated cases of sexual abuse in El Paso showed denial in only 6% and recantation in only 4% of cases of disclosure. Ninety-six percent of the affected children made a partial or full disclosure during at least one interview with CPS or the police. Child sexual abuse accommodation syndrome—a clinical description of recantation and other responses to sexual abuse—was rare. April R. Bradley & James M. Wood, *How Do Children Tell? The Disclosure Process in Child Sexual Abuse*, 20 CHILD ABUSE & NEGLECT 881 (1996). For commentary on this study, *see* David P. H. Jones, *Gradual Disclosure by Sexual Assault Victims: A Sacred Cow?*, 20 CHILD ABUSE & NEGLECT 879 (1996).

324. *See* Melton et al., *supra* note 9, at 57–60, and citations therein.

325. *Id.* at 59–60.

326. Gary B. Melton, *Children as Partners for Justice: Next Steps for Developmentalists*, MONOGRAPHS SOC'Y FOR RESEARCH IN CHILD DEV. (Serial No. 229), at 153, 154.

327. *Id.* at 301.

328. Karen J. Saywitz & Gail S. Goodman, *Interviewing Children In and Out of Court: Current Research and Practice Implications*, in APSAC HANDBOOK, *supra* note 10, at 297, 310–11. For other practical guidance, *see* L. Dennison Reed, *Findings from Research on Children's Suggestibility and Implications for Conducting Child Interviews*, 1 CHILD MALTREATMENT 105 (1996).

329. Melton et al., *supra* note 9, at 66, and citations therein. Similar issues apply in regard to the suggestiveness of ordinary interviews. Amye R. Warren et al., *It Sounds Good in Theory, But . . . : Do Investigative Interviewers Follow Guidelines Based on Memory Research?*, 1 CHILD MALTREATMENT 231 (1996).

330. Nancy W. Perry et al., *When Lawyers Question Children: Is Justice Served?*, 19 LAW & HUM. BEHAV. 609 (1995).

331. ANNE GRAFFAM WALKER, HANDBOOK ON QUESTIONING CHILDREN: A LINGUISTIC PERSPECTIVE (1994) (available from the ABA Center on Children and the Law, 740 Fifteenth St., NW, Washington, DC 20005). *See also* Anne Graffam Walker & Amye R. Warren, *The Language of the Child Abuse Interview: Asking the Questions, Understanding the Answers*, in TRUE AND FALSE ALLEGATIONS OF CHILD SEXUAL ABUSE: ASSESSMENT AND CLOSE MANAGEMENT 153 (Tara Ney ed. 1995) (problems that arise when adults make erroneous assumptions about children's comprehension).

332. *Cognitive Interviewing*, July/Aug. 1995, at 2.

333. *See* R. Edward Geiselman et al., *Effects of Cognitive Questioning Techniques on Children's Recall Performance*, in CHILD VICTIMS, CHILD WITNESSES: UNDERSTANDING AND IMPROVING TESTIMONY 71 (Gail S. Goodman & Bette L. Bottoms eds. 1993); Karen J. Saywitz et al., *Effects of Cognitive Interviewing and Practice on Children's Recall Performance*, 77 J. APPLIED PSYCHOL. 744 (1992); NATIONAL INSTITUTE OF JUSTICE, NEW APPROACH TO INTERVIEWING CHILDREN: A TEST OF ITS EFFECTIVENESS (1992).

334. Karen J. Saywitz & Lynn Snyder, *Improving Children's Testimony with Preparation*, in CHILD VICTIMS, CHILD WITNESSES, *supra* note 333, at 117, 134–38.

335. *Id.* at 126–29; Karen J. Saywitz et al., *Helping Children Tell What Happened: A Follow-up Study of the Narrative Elaboration Procedure*, 1 CHILD MALTREATMENT 200 (1996).

336. Saywitz & Snyder, *supra* note 334, at 131–33.

337. THOMAS GRISSO, EVALUATING COMPETENCIES: FORENSIC ASSESSMENTS AND INSTRUMENTS 188-267 (1986).

338. Karen S. Budd & Michelle J. Holdsworth, *Issues in Clinical Assessment of Minimal Parenting Competence*, 25 J. CLIN. CHILD PSYCHOL. 2 (1996).

339. For a detailed review of the CAP's psychometric properties by its developer, *see* Joel S. Milner, *Assessing Physical Child Abuse Risk: The Child Abuse Potential Inventory*, 14 CLIN. PSYCHOL. REV. 547 (1994).

340. Gary B. Melton, *Review of the Child Abuse Potential Inventory, Form VI*, in THE TENTH MENTAL MEASUREMENTS YEARBOOK 153, 153 (Jane C. Conoley & Jack Kramer eds. 1989).

341. *Id.* at 154–55.

342. Lucy Berliner & Jon Conte, *Sexual Abuse Evaluations: Conceptual and Empirical Observations*, 17 CHILD ABUSE & NEGLECT 111, 115 (1993). For data on the procedures used in presentation of the dolls, *see* Barbara W. Boat & Mark D. Everson, *Concerning Practices of Interviewers When Using Anatomical Dolls in Child Protective Services Investigations*, 1 CHILD MALTREATMENT 96 (1996).

343. *See, e.g.*, Gerald P. Koocher et al., *Psychological Science and the Use of Anatomically Detailed Dolls in Child Sexual-Abuse Assessments*, 118 PSYCHOL. BULL. 1999 (1995) (report of the American Psychological Association Working Group on Anatomical Dolls); Lamb, *supra* note 209, at 100; Melton et al., *supra* note 9, at 67–69; Glenn Wolfner et al., *The Use of Anatomically Detailed Dolls in Sexual Abuse Evaluations: The State of the Science*, 2 APPLIED & PREVENTIVE PSYCHOL. 1 (1993); AMERICAN PROFESSIONAL SOCIETY ON THE ABUSE OF CHILDREN, USE OF ANATOMICAL DOLLS IN CHILD SEXUAL ABUSE ASSESSMENTS § V(A) (1995).

344. Melton et al., *supra* note 9, at 68 (citing and concurring with Wolfner et al., *supra* note 343, page citations omitted).

345. Koocher et al., *supra* note 343, at 218.

346. *Id.* at 211.

347. STANLEY L. BRODSKY, TESTIFYING IN COURT: GUIDELINES AND MAXIMS FOR THE EXPERT WITNESS 182 (1991).

348. *Id.* at 184.

349. Such actions sometimes raise constitutional issues and always pose ethical problems. Melton, *supra* note 204, at 107; Melton & Limber, *supra* note 207, at 1229.

350. Melton, *supra* note 204.

351. This phenomenon is most directly observed in "child advocacy centers," which often operate under the auspice of the prosecutor's office. *See id.* at 104–06.

352. The remainder of this section is adapted from *id.* at 108–09.

353. *See, e.g.*, Dan Slater & Valerie Hans, *Public Opinion of Forensic Psychiatry Following the* Hinckley *Verdict*, 141 AM. J. PSYCHIATRY 675 (1984).

354. A forward-looking view—a focus on what can be done, not primarily on whether there has been compliance—is likely to mitigate the role conflicts even in dispositional assessment itself.

355. CAL. WELF. & INST. CODE §§ 15610 *et seq.* (West Cum. Supp. 1996).

356. CAL. WELF. & INST. CODE § 15610.23 defines dependent adult to include "any person . . . between the age of 18 and 64 years, who has physical or mental limitations that restrict his or her ability to carry out normal activities or to protect his or her rights including, but not limited to, persons who have physical or developmental disabilities or whose physical or mental abilities have diminished because of age," or who is an inpatient in a health facility.

357. CAL. WELF. & INST. CODE § 15610.27.

358. *See, e.g.*, CAL. WELF. & INST. CODE § 15610.30

(defining "fiduciary abuse" to include instances in which the caregiver for a dependent adult "takes, secretes, or appropriates . . . [the dependent adult's] money or property, to any use or purposes not in the due and lawful execution of his or her trust").

359. CAL. PENAL CODE § 368(a)–(b) (West 1996).

360. Terry Fulmer, *Elder Abuse*, in ABUSE AND VICTIMIZATION ACROSS THE LIFE SPAN 188, 188–90 (Martha B. Straus ed. 1988).

361. RICHARD J. GELLES & CLAIRE PEDRICK CORNELL, INTIMATE VIOLENCE IN FAMILIES 101 (2d ed. 1990).

362. *Id.* at 101.

363. Fulmer, *supra* note 360, at 189.

364. *Id.* at 190.

365. GELLES & CORNELL, *supra* note 361, at 100.

366. *Id.* at 103.

367. *Compare, e.g.*, John Briere & Jon Conte, *Self-Reported Amnesia for Abuse in Adults Molested as Children*, 6 J. TRAUMATIC STRESS 21 (1993), *and* Linda Meyers Williams, *Recall of Childhood Trauma: A Prospective Study of Women's Memories of Child Sexual Abuse*, 62 J. CONSULTING & CLIN. PSYCHOL. 1167 (1994), *and* Linda Meyers Williams, *What Does It Mean to Forget Child Sexual Abuse?: A Reply to Loftus, Garry, and Feldman (1994)*, 62 J. CONSULTING & CLIN. PSYCHOL. 1182 (1994) [hereinafter Williams, *What Does It Mean to Forget Child Sexual Abuse?*], *with* Elizabeth F. Loftus, *The Reality of Repressed Memories*, 48 AM. PSYCHOL. 518 (1993), *and* Elizabeth F. Loftus et al., *Forgetting Sexual Trauma: What Does It Mean When 38% Forget?*, 62 J. CONSULTING & CLIN. PSYCHOL. 1177 (1994).

368. For a critique of this approach, *see* Kenneth S. Pope, *Memory, Abuse, and Science: Questioning Claims about the False Memory Syndrome Epidemic*, 51 AM. PSYCHOL. 957 (1996).

369. At least 19 states have adopted a delayed discovery rule for tort cases involving child abuse, and a few have applied the rule in criminal proceedings. Loftus, *supra* note 367, at 520.

370. Briere & Conte, *supra* note 367.

371. Williams, *Recall of Childhood Trauma, supra* note 367.

372. Williams, *What Does It Mean to Forget Child Sexual Abuse?, supra* note 367, at 1184–85.

373. Loftus, *supra* note 367, at 521.

374. *E.g., id.* at 530–33.

375. *E.g., id.* at 530–33.

376. Bette L. Bottoms et al., *An Analysis of Ritualistic and Religion-Related Child Abuse Allegations*, 20 LAW & HUM. BEHAV. 1 (1996) [hereinafter Bottoms et al., *Ritualistic Abuse*]; Bette L. Bottoms et al., *In the Name of God: A Profile of Religion-Related Child Abuse*, 51 J. SOC. ISSUES, No. 2, at 85 (1995).

377. Bottoms et al., *Ritualistic Abuse, supra* note 376, at 26.

378. *Id.* at 25–26.

379. *Id.* at 21–22.

380. *Id.* at 24–25.

381. *Id.* at 21–24.

382. *Id.* at 9–11.

383. *See, e.g.*, Kenneth V. Lanning, *Ritual Abuse: A Law Enforcement View or Perspective*, 15 CHILD ABUSE & NEGLECT 171 (1991).

384. Bottoms et al., *Ritualistic Abuse, supra* note 376, at 27.

385. Loftus, *supra* note 367, at 534.

386. Several journals are devoted exclusively to research and practice related to child abuse and neglect. CHILD ABUSE & NEGLECT; CHILD ABUSE REVIEW; CHILD MALTREATMENT; JOURNAL OF CHILD SEXUAL ABUSE. Several others consistently include articles on the topic. *E.g.*, CHILDREN & YOUTH SERVICES REVIEW; JOURNAL OF INTERPERSONAL VIOLENCE. In recent years, special issues on child maltreatment have also appeared in CRIMINAL JUSTICE & BEHAVIOR; JOURNAL OF CLINICAL CHILD PSYCHOLOGY; PSYCHOLOGY, PUBLIC POLICY & LAW.

Chapter 16

1. *See generally* Patricia H. Shiono & Linda Sandham Quinn, *Epidemiology of Divorce*, FUTURE OF CHILDREN, Spring 1994, at 15. In 1990, 11.3% (7.2 million) of American children lived in married stepfamilies, 9.5% (6 million) lived with a divorced single parent, and 7.6% (4.9 million) lived with a separated or widowed parent. *Id.* at 21. Each year, more than one million children experience a divorce. *Id.* at 23. When *de facto* divorces are added to those that are formalized, two-thirds of all first marriages end in dissolution. Teresa Castro-Martin & Larry L. Bumpass, *Recent Trends and Differentials in Marital Disruption*, 26 DEMOGRAPHY 37 (1989).

2. *See, e.g.*, SALVADOR MINUCHIN, FAMILIES AND FAMILY THERAPY (1974).

3. Divorce cases might be best conceptualized as a system of private bargaining. *See* Robert H. Mnookin &

Lewis Kornhauser, *Bargaining in the Shadow of the Law: The Case of Divorce*, 88 YALE L.J. 950 (1979).

4. GARY B. MELTON ET AL., COMMUNITY MENTAL HEALTH CENTERS AND THE LAW: AN EVALUATION OF COMMUNITY-BASED FORENSIC SERVICES 71–72 (1985). The sample was drawn from judges attending a course at the University of Virginia and thus was unrepresentative, although courts in 24 states and territories were included. *Id.* at 69–72.

5. *Id.* at 70–73.

6. Robert D. Felner et al., *Child Custody Resolution: A Study of Social Science Involvement and Impact*, 18 PROF. PSYCHOL.: RESEARCH & PRAC. 468, 470 (1987).

7. Although the Juvenile Justice Standards would establish a family court with jurisdiction over both delinquency and divorce, JUVENILE JUSTICE STANDARDS RELAT-

ING TO COURT ORGANIZATION AND ADMINISTRATION (1980), relatively few states have adopted such a model.

8. Judges tend to weigh "responsibility" issues more heavily than do clinicians. Carol R. Lowery, *Child Custody Decisions in Divorce Proceedings: A Survey of Judges,* 12 PROF. PSYCHOL. 492 (1981). Conceivably, however, the moral development literature might give some clues as to the parent more likely to socialize moral values. Thomas Grisso, *Forensic Assessment in Juvenile and Family Cases: The State of the Art* 16 (keynote address to the Summer Institute on Mental Health Law, University of Nebraska–Lincoln, June 1, 1984).

9. Our usual injunction against ultimate-issue testimony is, of course, relevant, even if the scientific basis were more extensive.

10. Grisso, *supra* note 8, at 8–9.

11. *See Guidelines for Child Custody Evaluations in Divorce Proceedings,* 49 AM. PSYCHOL. 677, 677 (1994) [hereinafter *Guidelines*], and citations therein.

12. *Id. The Guidelines* are discussed *infra* § 16.01(c).

13. MELTON ET AL., *supra* note 4, at 74.

14. Felner et al., *supra* note 6, at 471.

15. *Id.* at 472.

16. *See generally* Stephen J. Morse, *Crazy Behavior, Morals, and Science: An Analysis of Mental Health Law,* 51 S. CAL. L. REV. 527 (1978).

17. Stephen J. Morse, *Law and Mental Health Professionals: The Limits of Expertise,* 9 PROF. PSYCHOL. 389, 395 (1978).

18. *See* Andre P. Derdeyn, *Child Custody Consultation,* 45 AM. J. ORTHOPSYCHIATRY 791, 795 (1975). The child's lack of standing may frustrate his or her sense of fairness. Gary B. Melton & E. Allan Lind, *Procedural Justice in Family Court: Does the Adversary Model Make Sense?,* in LEGAL REFORMS AFFECTING CHILD AND YOUTH SERVICES 65, 70–71 (Gary B. Melton ed. 1982). The inadequacy of advocacy for children's wishes by guardians *ad litem* is explored in Kim J. Landsman & Martha L. Minow, *Note, Lawyering for the Child: Principles of Representation in Custody and Visitation Disputes Arising from Divorce,* 87 YALE L.J. 1126 (1978).

19. 466 U.S. 429 (1984).

20. *Id.* at 431.

21. *Id.* at 434.

22. Jeffrey Z. Rubin, *Experimental Research on Third-Party Intervention in Conflict: Toward Some Generalizations,* 87 PSYCHOL. BULL. 379 (1980).

23. Lynn Mather et al., *"The Passenger Decides on the Destination and I Decide on the Route": Are Divorce Lawyers "Expensive Cab Drivers"?,* 9 INT'L J. L. & FAM. 286 (1995).

24. Such an approach would be especially appropriate in a jurisdiction requiring parents to develop a specific plan for post-divorce parental responsibilities. *See* Jane W. Ellis, *Plans, Protections and Professional Interventions in Divorce Custody Reform and the Role of Legal Professionals,* 24 U. MICH. J. L. REFORM 67 (1990).

25. *See* Richard E. Crouch, *Divorce Mediation and Legal Ethics,* 16 FAM. L.Q. 219 (1982). *See also* Association of Family and Conciliation Courts, MODEL STANDARDS OF PRACTICE FOR CHILD CUSTODY EVALUATION, Standard VI(C) [hereinafter MODEL STANDARDS]. The Standard states "the evaluator should . . . be cautious about switching roles to that of either mediator or therapist. Such a change of roles would render future testimony and/or reevaluations invalid by virtue of the change in objectivity and neutrality."

26. More than 30 states now have compulsory mediation for parents involved in disputes about child custody and visitation. Sanford N. Katz, *Historical Perspective and Current Trends in the Legal Process of Divorce,* FUTURE OF CHILDREN, Spring 1994, at 44, 54.

27. Peter A. Dillon & Robert E. Emery, *Divorce Mediation and Resolution of Child Custody Disputes: Long-Term Effects,* 66 AM. J. ORTHOPSYCHIATRY 131, 131 (1996).

28. *Id.* at 131–32. One of the authors of the article cited, Robert Emery, is the leading researcher on mediation and generally a strong proponent of such programs.

29. *Id.* at 132–33.

30. *Id.* at 133. A nine-year follow-up of participants in one experiment did show some evidence—by mothers' but not by fathers' reports—of greater visitation by the noncustodial parent and greater interparental communication. *Id.* at 138. Such sustained positive effects on parental behavior might reasonably be expected to translate into a better quality of life for the children.

31. Katherine Kitzman & Robert E. Emery, *Child and Family Coping One Year After Mediated and Litigated Child Custody Disputes,* 8 J. FAM. PSYCHOL. 150 (1994).

32. *See, e.g.,* ROBERT E. EMERY, RENEGOTIATING FAMILY RELATIONSHIPS: DIVORCE, CHILD CUSTODY, AND MEDIATION 178–80 (1994); Isolina Ricci et al., *Profile: Child Custody Mediation Services in California Superior Courts,* 30 FAM. & CONCILIATION CTS. REV. 229, 232 (1992). EMERY, *supra* at 183–84, has warned: "Ironically, perhaps the major concern about custody mediation from the perspective of administration of justice is that it may be too successful. In their enthusiasm about diverting cases from court, judges and other court personnel sometimes overemphasize agreement rates as a measure of the success or failure of mediation. This can lead to subtle pressures on mediators to become increasingly coercive in order to obtain a goal that may be a dubious indicator of success. Mediators occasionally need to remind themselves and others about the intervention's more ambitious goals of empowerment, education, and protecting ongoing relationships against unnecessary conflict."

33. Gary B. Melton, *Children, Families, and the Courts in the Twenty-first Century,* 66 S. CAL. L. REV. 1993, 2024–25 (1993).

34. *See, e.g.,* Robert H. Mnookin et al., *Private Ordering Revisited: What Custodial Arrangements Are Parents Negotiating?,* in DIVORCE REFORM AT THE CROSSROADS 37, 60–61 (Stephen D. Sugarman & Herma Hill Kay eds. 1990) (roughly one-fifth of petitioners and half of respondents in divorce actions in California proceeded *pro se*).

35. One-fourth of the fathers and the majority of the mothers using public mediation services in California are unemployed or earning wages below the poverty level, and the majority present other difficult problems, such as

domestic violence. Charlene F. Depner, Trends in the Characteristics of Users of Juvenile and Family Courts: Child Custody, Visitation, Family Court Services (June 1992) (paper prepared for a meeting of the Consortium on Children, Families, and the Law).

36. Guidelines, supra note 11.

37. Id. at 677.

38. Id. at 678.

39. Id. at 679.

40. Id. at 679.

41. Id. at 678.

42. Id. at 678.

43. Id. at 678. Cf. STANLEY L. BRODSKY, TESTIFYING IN COURT: GUIDELINES AND MAXIMS FOR THE EXPERT WITNESS 160–63 (1991) (describing the conflicts that therapists experience when they are called to testify in a custody dispute involving one of their clients). See also MODEL STANDARDS, supra note 25, Standard VI(B)("a person who has been a . . . therapist for any or all members of the family should not perform a custody evaluation because the previous knowledge and relationship may render him or her incapable of being completely neutral and incapable of having unbiased objectivity").

44. The mandate to interview all relevant parties applies unless there is a focus on the needs or competence of only a single individual in the family, or the question does not require a clinical evaluation (e.g., it focuses instead on research or a critique of a clinician's method). Guidelines, supra note 11, at 678–79.

45. Id.

46. Id. at 679. See also MODEL STANDARDS, supra note 25, Standards III, IV (recommending multiparty and multisource evaluations), VI(E) ("evaluators shall not make statements of fact or inference about parties whom they have not seen").

47. Elizabeth Scott & Andre P. Derdeyn, Rethinking Joint Custody, 45 OHIO ST. L.J. 455, 464–65 nn. 41–42 (1984).

48. Id. See Chapsky v. Wood, 26 Kan. 650 (1881).

49. See, e.g., Hines v. Hines, 185 N.W. 9 (Iowa 1921).

50. See Robert H. Mnookin, Child-Custody Adjudication: Judicial Functions in the Face of Indeterminancy, 39 LAW & CONTEMP. PROBS. 226 (1975).

51. See generally Andre P. Derdeyn, Child Custody in Historical Perspective, 133 AM. J. ORTHOPSYCHIATRY 1369 (1976).

52. See, e.g., State ex rel. Watts v. Watts, 350 N.Y.S.2d 285 (Fam. Ct. 1973). Cf. In re Doe, 418 S.E.2d 3 (Ga. 1992) (when both parents are legal custodians, they have equal responsibility for decisions about the child).

53. See, e.g., CAL. FAM. CODE § 3080 (Deering 1995).

54. E.g., Wheeler v. Gill, 413 S.E.2d 860 (S.C. App. 1992); Malone v. Malone, 842 S.W.2d 621 (Tenn. App. 1992); McCreery v. McCreery, 237 S.E.2d 167 (Va. 1977).

55. See, e.g., In re Clingingsmith, 838 P.2d 417 (Mont. 1992).

56. Race of a parent's new spouse is one such factor. See supra notes 19–21 and accompanying text.

57. See, e.g., In re Converse, 826 P.2d 937 (Mont. 1992); Sukin v. Sukin, 842 P.2d 922 (Utah App. 1992).

58. Linda Whobrey Rohman et al., Social Science and the Best Interests Standard: Another Case for Informed Speculation, in PSYCHOLOGY AND CHILD CUSTODY DETERMINATIONS: ROLES, KNOWLEDGE, AND EXPERTISE 59, 62 n. 2 (Lois A. Weithorn ed. 1987), and accompanying text.

59. Uniform Marriage and Divorce Act § 402, 9A U.L.A. 561 (1987).

60. 140 N.W.2d 152 (Iowa 1966).

61. Id. at 155.

62. Id. at 156.

63. Id. at 154.

64. Id. at 156.

65. Mnookin, supra note 50, at 262.

66. JOSEPH GOLDSTEIN ET AL., BEYOND THE BEST INTERESTS OF THE CHILD (1973).

67. See Richard E. Crouch, An Essay on the Critical and Judicial Reception of "Beyond the Best Interests of the Child," 13 FAM. L.Q. 49 (1979).

68. Daniel Katkin et al., Above and Beyond the Best Interests of the Child: An Inquiry into the Relationship Between Law and Social Action, 8 LAW & SOC'Y REV. 669 (1974); Gary B. Melton, The Psychologist's Role in Juvenile and Family Law, 7 J. CLIN. CHILD PSYCHOL. 189, 190 (1978).

69. GOLDSTEIN ET AL., supra note 66, at 9–20. But see Michael S. Wald, Thinking about Public Policy toward Abuse and Neglect of Children: A Review of Beyond the Best Interests of the Child, 78 MICH. L. REV. 645, 655–70 (1980).

70. GOLDSTEIN ET AL., supra note 66, Child Placement Code of Hampstead-Haven ¶ 30.5.

71. Id. at 101.

72. There is substantial evidence that infants form multiple attachments, although they tend to prefer the primary caretaker in times of stress. These studies are reviewed with attention to their implications for policy in W. Glenn Clingempeel & N. Dickon Reppucci, Joint Custody After Divorce: Major Issues and Goals for Research, 91 PSYCHOL. BULL. 102, 112–13 (1982); Ross A. Thompson, The Father's Case in Child Custody Disputes: The Contributions of Psychological Research, in FATHERHOOD AND FAMILY POLICY 53, 90–94 (Michael E. Lamb & Abraham Sagi eds. 1983).

73. GOLDSTEIN ET AL., supra note 66, at 153.

74. Id. at 54, 62–63.

75. Mnookin & Kornhauser, supra note 3, at 981–83.

76. N. Dickon Reppucci, The Wisdom of Solomon: Issues in Child Custody Determination, in CHILDREN, MENTAL HEALTH, AND THE LAW 59, 65 (N. Dickon Reppucci et al. eds. 1984).

77. GOLDSTEIN ET AL., supra note 66, Child Placement Code of Hampstead-Haven ¶ 10.5.

78. Cf. Michael W. Agopian, Parental Child Stealing: Participants and the Victimization Process, 5 VICTIMOLOGY 263 (1980).

79. It should be noted that the concept of a primary attachment figure is controversial within psychology. Some researchers have noted that children commonly have multiple attachment figures and that attachments change across time. See, e.g., MICHAEL E. LAMB ET AL., INFANT–MOTHER ATTACHMENT (1985).

80. Richard Neely, *The Primary Caretaker Rule: Child Custody and the Dynamics of Greed*, 3 YALE L. & POL'Y REV. 168 (1984).

81. *See, e.g.*, Lenz v. Lenz, 430 N.W.2d 168 (Minn. 1988); Foreng v. Foreng, 509 N.W.2d 38 (N.D. 1993); Note, *A Step Backward: The Minnesota Supreme Court Adopts a "Primary Caretaker" Presumption in Child Custody Cases*, 70 MINN. L. REV. 1344 (1986).

82. Arguably, there is a maternal bias in the rule because it focuses on the sorts of parental behavior that are more common among mothers and ignores those that are more common among fathers. *Cf.* Eleanor E. Maccoby, *Divorce and Custody: The Rights, Needs, and Obligations of Mothers, Fathers, and Children*, in THE INDIVIDUAL, THE FAMILY AND SOCIAL GOOD: PERSONAL FULFILLMENT IN TIMES OF CHANGE 135, 153–58 (Gary B. Melton ed. 1995) (describing differences in parental behavior between men and women and indicating their balance within "coparenting"). As a practical matter, the primary-caretaker rule may simply offer a facially neutral way to ensure that mothers are typically awarded custody of young children—a tender-years presumption for an era of *de jure* gender equality. *See* Shearer v. Shearer, 448 S.E.2d 165, 170–71 (W. Va. 1994) (Neely, J., dissenting) (attacking "rampant gender bias" in the West Virginia judiciary's application of the primary-caretaker rule).

83. *See* David L. Chambers, *Rethinking the Substantive Rules for Custody Disputes in Divorce*, 83 MICH. L. REV. 477 (1984).

84. Shearer v. Shearer, 448 S.E.2d 165, 167 (W. Va. 1994) (quoting Garska v. McCoy, 278 S.E.2d 357 (W. Va. 1981).

85. Noting the emotional and financial costs involved in attempting to discern psychological parenthood, Scott has argued for an *approximation standard*, in which postdivorce arrangements would parallel predivorce parental child care as much as possible. Elizabeth S. Scott, *Pluralism, Parental Preference, and Child Custody*, 80 CAL. L. REV. 615 (1992).

86. *Shearer*, 448 S.E.2d at 168 (quoting David M. v. Margaret M., 385 S.E.2d 912, 923 [W. Va. 1989]).

87. Although almost all mothers regard themselves as having been the principal caregiver, the majority of divorcing fathers view themselves as having had a preseparation level of involvement in their children's lives equal to or greater than that of their wives. ELEANOR E. MACCOBY & ROBERT H. MNOOKIN, DIVIDING THE CHILD: SOCIAL AND LEGAL DILEMMAS OF CUSTODY 67 (1992). This disparity reflects differences in perceptions of responsibilities for economic support and childrearing per se. *Id.* at 68–70. When the disparity is large, there is a high probability of substantial or intense legal conflict. *Id.* at 145.

88. Scott & Derdeyn, *supra* note 47, at 469–70. The movement was spurred in part by fathers' groups. *Id.* at 462 nn. 30–31, and accompanying text.

89. CAL. FAM. CODE § 3080 (Deering 1995). *See* Scott & Derdeyn, *supra* note 47, at 456 n. 3.

90. *See Survey of American Law*, 11 FAM. L. REP. 3015, 3019 (1985).

91. *Id.* at 472.

92. *See, e.g.*, MACCOBY & MNOOKIN, *supra* note 87, at 106.

93. *See, e.g.*, CAL. FAM. CODE § 3080.

94. *E.g.*, FLA. STAT. ANN. § 61.13(2)(b) (West Supp. 1994); LA. CIV. CODE ANN. art. 146(C) (West Supp. 1994).

95. *See* Scott & Derdeyn, *supra* note 47, at 475–77, and citations therein.

96. *Id.* at 472–73 and citations therein.

97. *Id.* at 475–77.

98. *Id.* at 476–77.

99. Although family law—like other domains of law particularly relevant to the lives of children—is commonly believed to be especially open to the insights of the social and behavioral sciences, it has been remarkably impervious to social realities. *See generally* Gary B. Melton, *The Clashing of Symbols: Prelude to Child and Family Policy*, 42 AM. PSYCHOL. 345 (1987); Gary B. Melton, *The Significance of Law in the Everyday Lives of Children and Families*, 22 GA. L. REV. 851 (1988).

To the extent that the law has changed, controversies remain about whether the law has reflected or caused the sea change in family life that has occurred in the past generation. Accordingly, for example, some states are considering whether to reform their laws to make divorce harder to obtain. *See* Martha Heller, *Note: Should Breaking-up Be Harder to Do?: The Ramifications a Return to a Fault-Based System Would Have upon Domestic Violence*, 4 VA. J. SOC. POL'Y & L. 263, 263–64 (1996).

100. Some of the changes that have occurred in family law—and in the types of cases affecting domestic relations courts—are natural by-products of the increase in divorce itself. For example, the number and diversity of blended families have increased dramatically, and courts have been faced with questions about stepparents' rights when a parent and a stepparent separate or divorce. Similarly, when parents go their separate ways (often hundreds or thousands of miles apart), grandparents may become effectively isolated from their grandchildren, and law on grandparents' rights has developed accordingly.

Other changes in family form and, correspondingly, family law have been the by-products of biotechnological developments. The increasing diversity of biological relationships poses problems for a legal system that has used biological parenthood as the principal marker for parental rights. *See, e.g.*, Vickie L. Henry, *A Tale of Three Women: A Survey of the Rights and Responsibilities of Unmarried Women Who Conceive by Alternative Insemination and a Model for Legislative Reform*, 19 AM. J. L. & MED. 285 (1993). Pauline M. Pagliocca et al., *Parenting and the Law*, in 3 HANDBOOK OF PARENTING 437, 438–40 (Marc H. Bornstein, ed., 1995).

101. Patricia J. Falk, *The Prevalence of Social Science in Gay Rights Cases: The Synergistic Influences of Historical Context, Justificatory Citation, and Dissemination Efforts*, 41 WAYNE L. REV. 1, 13–20 (1994).

102. *E.g.*, *In re* Wiarda, 505 N.W.2d 506 (Iowa Ct. App. 1993); Hall v. Hall, 291 N.W.2d 143 (Mich. Ct. App. 1980); G. A. v. D. A., 745 S.W.2d 726 (Mo. Ct.

App. 1987); Tucker v. Tucker, 910 P.2d 1209 (Utah 1996); Bottoms v. Bottoms, 457 S.E.2d 102 (Va. 1995). The court in *G.A.* was especially distressed that the lesbian mother was *openly* living with her lover. In *Tucker,* the court was concerned by the moral example of living with a lesbian partner while still married.

103. *E.g.,* Irish v. Irish, 300 N.W.2d 739 (Mich. Ct. App. 1980); H. v. P., 643 S.W.2d 865 (Mo. Ct. App. 1982); L. v. D., 630 S.W.2d 240 (Mo. Ct. App. 1982).

104. *E.g.,* Teegarden v. Teegarden, 642 N.E.2d 1007 (Ind. Ct. App. 1994); Woodruff v. Woodruff, 260 S.E.2d 775 (N.C. Ct. App. 1979); In re Marriage of Ashling, 599 P.2d 475 (Or. Ct. App. 1979); Conkel v. Conkel, 509 N.E.2d 983 (Ohio Ct. App. 1987); In re Marriage of Calquinto, 718 P.2d 7 (Wash. Ct. App. 1983); Blew v. Verta, 617 A.2d 31 (Pa. Super. 1992); Van Driel v. Van Driel, 525 N.W.2d 37 (S.D. 1994).

105. *See, e.g.,* Greathouse v. Shreve, 891 S.W.2d 387 (Ky. 1995); Uhing v. Uhing, 488 N.W.2d 366 (Neb. 1992).

106. *See, e.g.,* In re Miller, 825 P.2d 189 (Mont. 1992); Adams v. Adams, No. A-91–437, Westlaw 120294 (Neb. Ct. App. Apr. 20, 1993).

107. *See, e.g.,* Zvorak v. Beireis, 519 N.W.2d 87, 88–89 (Iowa 1994), and citations therein (the principle of best interests of the child must accommodate "the strong societal interest in preserving the natural parent–child relationship," to the extent that the court may even "remove children from conscientious, well-intentioned custodians with a history of providing good care to the children and place them with a natural parent," *id.* at 89); La. Civ. Code Ann. art. 133 (West 1996) (a third party may obtain custody of a child only if an award of custody to the parent would result in substantial harm to the child).

A case in which a stepparent actually did obtain custody is an illustration of the strong presumption in favor of a biological parent competing with a third party. In Henderson v. Mabry, 838 S.W.2d 537 (Tenn. Ct. App. 1992), a custodial mother died and left children who had lived with her and their stepfather for five years. The court found that it would be in the children's best interest to remain in the custody of the stepfather, but the court also ordered liberal visitation for the biological father so that he might recover custody ultimately.

108. *See, e.g.,* Taylor v. Kennedy, 649 So. 2d 270 (Fla. Ct. App. 1995); In re Sedelmeier, 491 N.W.2d 86 (S.D. 1992). *Cf.* In re Simmons, 486 N.W.2d 788 (Minn. App. 1992) (permitting visitation by a stepparent but denying access to a child's confidential records and other rights accorded to a child's parents). *But see* In re Durento, 854 P.2d 1352 (Colo. Ct. App. 1992) (permitting visitation by a stepparent when it would be in the child's best interest).

109. *See, e.g.,* Carter v. Taylor, 611 So. 2d 874 (Miss. 1992); Bubac v. Boston, 600 So. 2d 951 (Miss. 1992). *See also* Malpass v. Hodson, 424 S.E.2d 470 (S.C. 1992) (a mother's attempt to recover custody from the grandparents is dependent on her parental fitness, the amount of contact she has had with the child, the circumstances under which temporary relinquishment occurred, and the

degree of attachment between the child and the grandparents). *Cf.* Ray v. Burns, 832 S.W.2d 431 (Tex. Ct. App. 1992) (grandmother awarded joint custody in a case in which the mother had an "unstable, disorganized, and chaotic lifestyle").

110. Ross A. Thompson et al., *Grandparents' Visitation Rights: Legalizing the Ties That Bind,* 44 Am. Psychol. 1217 (1989).

111. Shiono & Quinn, *supra* note 1, at 26. This decrease has been especially marked among African American families, although grandparents in African American families still are substantially more likely to be in a central child-caring role than are grandparents in white families. *Id. See also,* § 15.05(e).

112. Thompson et al., *supra* note 110, at 1219.

113. *Id.* at 1220.

114. *Id.* at 1220–21.

115. *Id.* at 1221.

116. Mnookin & Kornhauser, *supra* note 3, at 981–83.

117. A *longitudinal* study is one in which the participants are observed at various points across time.

118. *E.g.,* E. Mavis Hetherington, *Divorce: A Child's Perspective,* 34 Am. Psychol. 851 (1979) [hereinafter Hetherington, *Divorce*]; E. Mavis Hetherington, *Family Relations Six Years After Divorce,* in Remarriage and Stepparenting Today 125 (Kay Pasley & Marilyn Ihinger-Tallman eds. 1987); E. Mavis Hetherington, *Parents, Children, and Siblings Six Years After Divorce,* in Relationships within Families 311 (Robert A. Hinde & Joan Stevenson eds., 1988); E. Mavis Hetherington, *Coping with Family Transitions: Winners, Losers, and Survivors,* 60 Child Dev. 1 (1989); E. Mavis Hetherington, *An Overview of the Virginia Longitudinal Study of Divorce and Remarriage with a Focus on Early Adolescence,* 7 J. Fam. Psychol. 39 (1993); E. Mavis Hetherington et al., *Divorced Fathers,* 25 Fam. Coordinator 417 (1976); E. Mavis Hetherington et al., *The Aftermath of Divorce,* in Mother/Child Father/Child Relationships 110 (Joseph Stevens & Marilyn Mathews eds. 1978); E. Mavis Hetherington et al., *The Development of Children in Mother-Headed Families,* in The American Family: Dying or Developing? 117 (David Reiss & Howard Hoffman eds. 1979); E. Mavis Hetherington et al., *The Effects of Divorce on Parents and Children,* in Nontraditional Families 233 (Michael E. Lamb ed. 1982); E. Mavis Hetherington et al., *Family Interaction and the Social, Emotional, and Cognitive Development of Children Following Divorce,* in The Family: Setting Priorities 114 (Victor C. Vaughn & T. Berry Brazelton eds. 1979); E. Mavis Hetherington et al., *Play and Social Interaction in Children Following Divorce,* 35 J. Soc. Issues 26 (1979).

119. Judith S. Wallerstein & Sandra Blakeslee, Second Chances: Men, Women, and Children a Decade after Divorce (1989); Judith S. Wallerstein & Joan B. Kelly, Surviving the Breakup: How Children and Parents Cope with Divorce (1980); Joan B. Kelly & Judith S. Wallerstein, *Part-Time Parent, Part-Time Child: Visiting after Divorce,* 6 J. Clin. Child Psychol. 51 (1977); Joan B. Kelly & Judith S. Wallerstein, *The Effects of Parental Divorce: Experiences of the Child in Early Latency,* 46 Am. J. Orthopsy-

CHIATRY 20 (1976); Judith S. Wallerstein, *The Long-Term Effects of Divorce on Children: A Review*, 30 J. AM. ACAD. CHILD & ADOLESCENT PSYCHIATRY 349 (1991); Judith S. Wallerstein, *Children of Divorce: Preliminary Report of a Ten-Year Follow-Up of Young Children*, 54 AM. J. ORTHOPSYCHIATRY 444 (1984) [hereinafter Wallerstein, *Ten-Year Follow-up*]; Judith S. Wallerstein & Shauna B. Corbin, *Daughters of Divorce: Report from a Ten-Year Follow-Up*, 59 AM. J. ORTHOPSYCHIATRY 593 (1989); Judith S. Wallerstein & Joan B. Kelly, *The Effects of Parental Divorce: Experiences of the Child in Later Latency*, 46 AM. J. ORTHOPSYCHIATRY 256 (1976); Judith S. Wallerstein & Joan B. Kelly, *The Effects of Parental Divorce: The Experiences of the Preschool Child*, 14 J. AM. ACAD. CHILD PSYCHIATRY 600 (1975); Judith S. Wallerstein & Joan B. Kelly, *The Effects of Parental Divorce: The Adolescent Experience*, in CHILDREN AT PSYCHIATRIC RISK 479 (E. J. Anthony & Cyrille Koupernik eds. 1974).

120. Although the Virginia and California projects were seminal, the literature has expanded significantly beyond these longitudinal projects. *See generally* Paul R. Amato, *Life-Span Adjustment of Children to Their Parents' Divorce*, FUTURE OF CHILDREN, Spring 1994, at 143. A particularly important large-scale investigation was undertaken by two well-known senior scholars, psychologist Eleanor E. Maccoby and lawyer Robert H. Mnookin. MACCOBY & MNOOKIN, *supra* note 87. Although limited to a single jurisdiction (California) that has typically been a pacesetter in family law, Maccoby and Mnookin's study is unique in the scope of its data on the process of divorcing and in its insights about the various procedures and dispositions in practice. *See also* Maccoby, *supra* note 82, at 135 (discussing gender roles and divorce policy in the light of data on parents' postdivorce behavior).

Interestingly, the magnitude of differences between children from divorced and intact families has decreased across time. Amato, *supra*, at 149. This recent shift in research findings is probably attributable to increasing acceptance of divorce (and, therefore, less stigmatization of children experiencing it) coupled with a decrease in legal and social barriers (and, therefore, less conflict prior to and during divorce). The trend in data about child adjustment is paralleled by evidence that noncustodial fathers are increasingly involved with their children. Ross A. Thompson, *The Role of the Father after Divorce*, FUTURE OF CHILDREN, Spring 1994, at 210, 223.

121. *A quasi-experimental* study is one in which there is an attempt to minimize uncontrolled variables but no random assignment of participants to experimental conditions, as in a true experiment. In particular, the Virginia study, discussed in the publications cited in note 118 *supra*, permitted comparisons with children in intact families at various points across time.

122. The Virginia group subsequently undertook an analogous longitudinal study of early adolescents' response to divorce and remarriage. E. Mavis Hetherington & W. Glenn Clingempeel, *Coping with Marital Transitions*, 37(2–3) MONOGRAPHS SOC'Y FOR RES. IN CHILD DEV. (Serial No. 227), at 1 (1992).

123. Thompson, *supra* note 72, at 83. *See generally* Paul R. Amato, *Life-Span Adjustment of Children to Their*

Parents' Divorce, FUTURE OF CHILDREN, Spring 1994, at 143.

124. *See generally* E. MARK CUMMINGS & PATRICK DAVIES, CHILDREN AND MARITAL CONFLICT: THE IMPACT OF FAMILY DISPUTE AND RESOLUTION (1994); Robert E. Emery, *Interparental Conflict and the Children of Discord and Divorce*, 92 PSYCHOL. BULL. 310 (1982).

The pernicious influence of parental conflict is illustrated by the fact that problems in parent–child relations are detectable 8 to 12 years *before* divorce. Paul R. Amato & Alan Booth, *A Prospective Study of Divorce and Parent–Child Relationships*, 58 J. MARRIAGE & FAM. 356 (1996). This finding is consistent with other studies showing children to have heightened behavior problems years before their parents' divorce. *See id.* at 357, and citations therein.

Moreover, the effects of parental conflict can be long-lasting. Perhaps because parental divorce raises the risk of personal divorce, the former is associated, over the lifespan, with increased risk of premature mortality. Howard S. Friedman et al., *Psychosocial and Behavioral Predictors of Longevity: The Aging and Death of "Termites,"* 50 AM. PSYCHOL. 69 (1995). Pooling data from 37 studies involving 80,000 adults, Amato and Keith found that parental divorce in childhood increased the risk in adulthood of mental health problems, low education, low job status, low standard of living, unsatisfying marriage, divorce, single parenthood, and physical health problems. Paul R. Amato & Bruce Keith, *Parental Divorce and Adult Well-Being: A Meta-Analysis*, 53 J. MARRIAGE & FAM. 43 (1991). It should be noted, however, that the effect sizes (the proportions of variance in adult well-being accounted for by the experience of parental divorce) often were small. Amato, *supra* note 123, at 146.

125. The Hetherington and Clingempeel study, *supra* note 122, showed an effect of divorce apart from parental competence. *See* Eleanor E. Maccoby, *Family Structure and Children's Adjustment: Is Quality of Parenting the Major Mediator?*, 57(2–3) MONOGRAPHS SOC'Y FOR RES. IN CHILD DEV. (Serial No. 227), at 230 (1992). Children who have experienced parental divorce face increased risk of low academic achievement, conduct problems, low self-esteem, low social competence, and poor parent–child relations. Amato, *supra* note 123, at 145. Differences between children who have experienced parental divorce and those who have not persist across the lifespan. *See supra* note 124.

126. Hetherington, *Divorce, supra* note 118, at 855.

127. *See infra* note 134.

128. E. Mavis Hetherington, *An Overview of the Virginia Longitudinal Study of Divorce and Remarriage with a Focus on Early Adolescence*, 7 J. FAM. PSYCHOL. 39, 48 (1993).

129. Hetherington, *Divorce, supra* note 118, at 856. *Cf.* James R. Turner, *Divorced Fathers Who Win Contested Custody of Their Children: An Exploratory Study*, 54 AM. J. ORTHOPSYCHIATRY 498 (1984) (some fathers who sought and won custody had not been very involved with their children prior to the divorce; others had been intensely involved).

130. Wallerstein, *Ten-Year Follow-Up, supra* note 119. Hetherington and Clingempeel's work, *supra* note 122,

shows that adjustment problems persist for adolescents in stepfamilies, even though the earlier research with younger children showed that problems abated over time.

131. *See supra* note 130 and citations therein.

132. Besides neglecting the fact that divorced families commonly become blended families, social scientists have given remarkably little attention to the role of extended family members in facilitating (or exacerbating) children's adjustment to divorce. Among children living with divorced or separated mothers, 23% of white and 30% of black children live with a second adult; for children living with divorced or separated fathers, the comparable figures are 22% and 20%. Donald J. Hernandez, *Demographic Trends and the Living Arrangements of Children,* in IMPACT OF DIVORCE, SINGLE PARENTING, AND STEPPARENTING ON CHILDREN 3, 14 (E. Mavis Hetherington & Josephine D. Arasteh eds. 1988).

133. The complexity of known relevant factors—especially those that are extrafamilial—and the limitations of such research for clinical use were succinctly illustrated in an overview by Behrman and Quinn: "Variables that are believed to account for children's adjustment to divorce include the amount and nature of involvement of the non-custodial parent, the custodial parent's adjustment to divorce and his or her parenting skills, interparental conflict before and after divorce, economic hardship, and other life stresses (for example, moving, changing schools, parental remarriage). Little is known about how these factors interact to affect a child's response to divorce among children of different ethnic and racial backgrounds, what the long-term effects are on individual children, and how various legal and therapeutic interventions influence the outcomes for children." Richard E. Behrman & Linda Sandham Quinn, *Children and Divorce: Overview and Analysis,* FUTURE OF CHILDREN, Spring 1994, at 4, 6.

134. Clingempeel & Reppucci, *supra* note 72, at 117, and studies cited therein. Such factors may be especially important "[w]here there is concern about the capacity of both parents to protect the child from the interparental conflict and their own disturbed attitudes and behavior." Janet R. Johnston, *High-Conflict Divorce,* FUTURE OF CHILDREN, Spring 1994, at 165, 179.

135. *Id.* at 115, and studies cited therein.

136. *See id.* at 117; Susan B. Steinman, *The Experience of Children in a Joint-Custody Arrangement: A Report of a Study,* 51 AM. J. ORTHOPSYCHIATRY 403, 411–12 (1981).

137. Concluding that "[r]esponsive adults such as teachers, coaches, or parents of friends can help children maintain feelings of self-worth, competence, and self-control," Hetherington and Stanley-Hagen also noted that siblings and peers are potent sources of support for many older children and adolescents—a double-edged sword, given evidence that children in divorced and remarried families are especially vulnerable to peer pressure. E. Mavis Hetherington & Margaret M. Stanley-Hagen, *Parenting in Divorced and Remarried Families,* in 3 HANDBOOK OF PARENTING 233, 249 (Marc H. Bornstein ed. 1995).

138. *See* Hetherington, *Divorce, supra* note 118, at 852 & 854.

139. This statement should not be read to imply that parent–child and mother–father relationships are unimportant to adolescents: "The factors most powerfully associated with good adolescent adjustment [when the youth's parents had divorced] were (a) having a close relationship with a residential parent who monitored well and remained involved in decisions concerning the young persons' life and (b) not feeling caught in the middle of parent conflict." Eleanor E. Maccoby et al., *Postdivorce Roles of Mothers and Fathers in the Lives of Their Children,* 7 J. FAM. PSYCHOL. 24, 36 (1993).

Adolescents maintained close relationships with both parents even when their only direct contact with the non-resident parent was over summer vacation. *Id.* Adolescents further almost always made clear that they visited their nonresident parent because they enjoyed being with him or her. *Id.* at 37.

140. Hetherington & Clingempeel, *supra* note 122, at 206.

141. Behrman & Quinn, *supra* note 133, at 9.

142. Maccoby, *supra* note 82, at 159.

143. Thompson, *supra* note 72, at 83–84 (citations omitted).

144. *See supra* note 51 and accompanying text.

145. Kelin Elliott Gersick, *Fathers by Choice: Characteristics of Men Who Do and Do Not Seek Custody of their Children Following Divorce* (unpublished doctoral dissertation, Harvard University, 1975 *cited in* Thompson, *supra* note 72, at 66, 92–93.

146. For a particularly thoughtful and well-informed discussion of the dilemmas—especially the related gender issues—in reconstituting families and rearing children in various family constellations, *see* Eleanor E. Maccoby, *Divorce and Custody: The Rights, Needs, and Obligations of Mothers, Fathers, and Children,* in THE INDIVIDUAL, THE FAMILY, AND SOCIAL GOOD: PERSONAL FULFILLMENT IN TIMES OF CHANGE 135 (Gary B. Melton ed. 1995).

147. Ross D. Parke, *Fathers and Families,* in 3 HANDBOOK OF PARENTING 27, 31–33 (Marc H. Bornstein ed. 1995); Thompson, *supra* note 72, at 74–77.

148. Hetherington & Stanley-Hagen, *supra* note 137, at 238, and citations therein.

149. Thompson, *supra* note 120, at 219 (footnotes omitted).

150. John W. Santrock & Richard A. Warshak, *Father Custody and Social Development in Boys and Girls,* 35 (4) J. SOC. ISSUES 112 (1979).

151. *Id.*

152. Hetherington & Stanley-Hagen, *supra* note 137, and citations therein.

153. *Id.*

154. *Id.* at 238.

155. Although remarriage presents some obvious advantages in economic support for children and emotional support for custodial parents, many newly remarried parents find new problems of monitoring, control, and attachment, in part because of unclarity about the role that stepparents should play in childrearing. The effects of parental remarriage include complex interactions of the child's age and gender and his or her previous relationship with the custodial parent. *See generally id.* at 241–46.

Moreover, the quality of a new marriage is highly related to the stepparent–stepchild relationship. Mark A. Fine & Lawrence A. Kurdek, *Relation between Marital Quality and (Step)Parent–Child Relationship Quality for Parents and Stepparents in Stepfamilies,* 9 J. FAM. PSYCHOL. 216 (1995). This fact provides additional evidence for the need to consider relationships beyond those between parents and children in describing the options for custody and visitation. It also gives another reason to be humble in making predictions about the effects of potential dispositions, because a parent may have no specific plans to remarry at the time an evaluation is conducted.

156. Mothers' availability is related to sons' academic achievement. Lois W. Hoffman, *Maternal Employment: 1979,* 34 AM. PSYCHOL. 859, 863 (1979). Father absence, especially as a result of divorce, adversely affects adolescent girls' ability to relate easily to boys. E. Mavis Hetherington, *Effects of Father Absence on Personality Development in Adolescent Daughters,* 7 DEV. PSYCHOL. 313 (1972).

157. "Keeping the children together" appears to be one of the strongest determinants of *de facto* custody arrangements. In families that have more than one child, the children almost always live in the same household. MACCOBY & MNOOKIN, *supra* note 87, at 77. Courts generally support this approach. *See, e.g.*, Wiskoski v. Wiskoski, 629 A.2d 996 (Pa. Super. 1993); Mitzel v. Black Cloud-Warberg, 511 N.W.2d 816 (S.D. 1994).

158. Douglas B. Downey & Brian Powell, *Do Children in Single-Parent Households Fare Better Living with Same-Sex Parents?,* 55 J. MARRIAGE & FAM. 55 (1993).

159. MACCOBY & MNOOKIN, *supra* note 87, at 99.

160. *Id.* at 73.

161. *Id.* at 169.

162. *Id.* at 103.

163. *Id.* at 93.

164. *Id.*

165. Hetherington & Stanley-Hagen, *supra* note 137, at 240 (citations omitted).

166. *See* Robert D. Felner & Lisa Terre, *Joint Custody: A Simplistic Solution,* FAM. ADVOC., Summer 1986, at 7.

167. Carol R. Lowery, *Maternal and Joint Custody: Differences in the Decision Process,* 10 LAW & HUM. BEHAV. 303, 313 (1986).

168. Johnston, *supra* note 134, at 176.

169. MACCOBY & MNOOKIN, *supra* note 87, at 104.

170. *Id.* at 150–51.

171. *Id.* at 159.

172. *Id.* at 159.

173. *Id.* at 243.

174. Hetherington & Stanley-Hagen, *supra* note 137, at 241. Children typically adjust well when their divorced parents are disengaged from each other "provided their parents do not interfere with each other's parenting, conflict is low, and the children are not asked to act as go-betweens." *Id.*

Although conflict rarely turns into cooperation, disengagement often does so: "We conclude that the existence of initial overt conflict and angry communication weakens or wipes out the chances that parents will be able to do business together effectively at a later time when anger has cooled. Our findings suggest that if parents cannot initially cooperate, they can keep the door open for later improvements in co-parenting by initially reducing communication." Maccoby & Mnookin, *supra* note 87, at 248.

175. MACCOBY & MNOOKIN, *supra* note 87, at 193.

176. Hetherington & Stanley-Hagen, *supra* note 137, at 240.

177. *Id.* at 107.

178. *Id.* at 108.

179. *See* Amato, *supra* note 120, at 148.

180. James H. Bray & E. Mavis Hetherington, *Families in Transition: Introduction and Overview,* 7 J. FAM. PSYCHOL. 3, 3 (1993); Frank F. Furstenberg, Jr., *History and Current Status of Divorce in the United States,* FUTURE OF CHILDREN, Spring 1994, at 29, 32; Donald J. Hernandez, *Demographic Trends and the Living Arrangements of Children,* in IMPACT OF DIVORCE, SINGLE PARENTING, AND STEPPARENTING ON CHILDREN 3 (E. Mavis Hetherington & Josephine D. Arasteh eds. 1988); Luis M. Laosa, *Ethnicity and Single Parenting in the United States,* in IMPACT OF DIVORCE, SINGLE PARENTING, AND STEPPARENTING ON CHILDREN 23 (E. Mavis Hetherington & Josephine Arasteh eds. 1988); Patricia H. Shiono & Linda Sandham Quinn, *Epidemiology of Divorce,* FUTURE OF CHILDREN, Spring 1994, at 15, 19.

181. Joy D. Teachman & Kathleen M. Paasch, *Financial Impact of Divorce on Children and their Families,* FUTURE OF CHILDREN, Spring 1994, at 63, 67.

182. Gary B. Melton, *Developmental Psychology and the Law: The State of the Art,* 22 J. FAM. L. 445, 472 n. 119 (1984), and accompanying text.

Incarceration by itself generally does not justify termination of visitation rights. *See, e.g.*, Lewis v. Lewis, 637 A.2d 70 (D.C. 1994); Smith v. Smith, 869 S.W.2d 55 (Ky. Ct. App. 1994); Sullivan v. Shaw, 650 A.2d 882 (Pa. Super. 1994). *Cf.* Debra Ratterman, *Statutes on Children of Arrested or Incarcerated Parents,* 13 ABA JUV. & CHILD WELFARE L. REP. 139 (1994) (review of law on child protection proceedings involving incarcerated parents).

183. Patricia J. Falk, *Lesbian Mothers: Psychosocial Assumptions in Family Law,* 44 AM. PSYCHOL. 941, 942–43 (1989). For more recent reviews that were not as directly focused on judges' concerns but that reached the same conclusions and were based largely on the same studies, see AMERICAN PSYCHOLOGICAL ASSOCIATION, LESBIAN AND GAY PARENTING: A RESOURCE FOR PSYCHOLOGISTS (1995) (includes annotated bibliography); Charlotte J. Patterson, *Children of Lesbian and Gay Parents,* 63 CHILD DEV. 1025 (1992); Charlotte J. Patterson, *Lesbian and Gay Parenthood,* in 3 HANDBOOK OF PARENTING 255 (Marc H. Bornstein ed. 1995); Fiona Tasker & Susan Golombok, *Adults Raised as Children in Lesbian Families,* 65 AM. J. ORTHOPSYCHIATRY 203, 203–06 (1995).

184. Falk, *supra* note 183, at 946.

185. *See supra* note 183.

186. Falk, *supra* note 183, at 943–46.

Although many would question the underlying assumption of some courts that homosexuality itself is a negative outcome, a study recently conducted in England did show that adults reared in lesbian households were significantly more likely to have been involved in a same-gender sexual relationship than were a comparison sample of adults reared in heterosexual single-parent households. Tasker & Golombok, *supra* note 183, at 210. They also were more likely to have considered the possibility of a homosexual relationship. *Id.* at 211. Among the 25 adult children of lesbian mothers, two identified as lesbians and were involved in a current lesbian relationship. Id. at 211. Although the difference was not statistically significant in the small sample, 36% of the participants reared in lesbian households (compared with 20% of the participants reared in single-parent heterosexual households) reported having been sexually attracted to a person of the same gender. *Id.* at 210. All 25 of the adult children of lesbian mothers had had opposite-gender sexual relationships as well. *Id.* at 210–11. Therefore, the Tasker and Golombok study suggests that having a lesbian mother "widen[s] the adolescent's view of . . . acceptable sexual behavior to include same-gender sexual relationships," but that the experience infrequently leads to a lesbian or gay identity. *Id.* at 212.

187. Patterson, *Lesbian and Gay Parenthood, supra* note 183, at 261.

188. Patterson, *Children of Lesbian and Gay Parents, supra* note 183, at 1029, and citations therein.

189. Patterson summarized the literature as follows: "Although both lesbians and gay men may become parents in any of a variety of ways, the preponderance of research to date has focused on children who were born in the context of heterosexual marriages, whose parents divorced, and whose mothers have identified themselves as lesbians. . . . Of the many other ways in which children might come to be brought up by lesbian or gay parents (e.g., through foster parenting, adoptive parenting, co-parenting, or multiple parenting arrangements), no systematic research has yet appeared." *Id.* at 1029.

190. *Id.* at 1035–36, and citations therein.

191. *See, e.g.*, Woodruff v. Woodruff, 44 N.C. App. 350, 260 S.E.2d 775 (1979) (gay father could have unsupervised overnight visitation with his son, but the trial court had properly ordered the father not to allow his lover to be present during such visits). *But see, e.g.*, Doe v. Doe, 16 Mass. App. 499, 452 N.E.2d 293 (1983) (rejecting the argument that an open lesbian relationship did not bar a mother's participation in joint custody when the son was "very comfortable" in her home and he had not been teased by peers in the mother's neighborhood about her relationship).

192. Whether through statutory or common law, all states now provide for consideration of the child's wishes in custody and visitation cases. Catherine A. Crosby-Currie, *Children's Involvement in Contested Custody Cases: Practices and Experiences of Legal and Mental Health Professionals,* 20 LAW & HUM. BEHAV. 289, 289–92 (1996). For illustrative cases, *see, e.g.*, Knook v. Knook, 621 A.2d 267 (Conn. 1993); In re Andersen, 603 N.E.2d 70 (Ill. Ct. App. 1992); In re Erickson, 491 N.W.2d 799 (Iowa Ct. App. 1992); In re Black, 837 P.2d 407 (Mont. 1992); Van

Gorder v. Van Gorder, 591 N.Y.S.2d 915 (App. Div. 1992); Zucker v. Zucker, 589 N.Y.S.2d 908 (App. Div. 1992); Gould v. Miller, 488 N.W.2d 42 (N.D. 1992); McMillen v. McMillen, 602 A.2d 845 (Pa. 1992); Harris v. Harris, 832 S.W.2d 352 (Tenn. Ct. App. 1992).

193. NEB. REV. STAT. § 42–364(2)(B) (1995).

194. Ellen Greenberg Garrison, *Children's Competence to Participate in Divorce Custody Decisionmaking,* 20 J. CLINICAL CHILD PSYCHOL. 78 (1991).

195. *See generally* CHOICE AND PERCEIVED CONTROL (Lawrence Perlmuter & Richard A. Monty eds. 1979); Gary B. Melton, *Decision Making by Children: Psychological Risks and Benefits,* in CHILDREN'S COMPETENCE TO CONSENT 21 (Gary B. Melton et al. eds. 1983).

196. Elizabeth S. Scott et al., *Children's Preference in Adjudicated Custody Decisions,* 22 GA. L. REV. 1035, 1046–47 (1988).

197. *Id.* at 1047

198. *Id.* at 1048–49.

199. *Id.* at 1047. Similar findings about judges' habits in regard to child involvement in custody cases were obtained in a subsequent two-state study. Crosby-Currie, *supra* note 192.

200. *Better Lawyering: New ABA Standards for the Child's Attorney,* 15 CHILD L. PRAC. 6, 6 (Standard A-1) (1996). The ABA Standards and related commentary were originally published in *American Bar Association Standards of Practice for Lawyers Who Represent Children in Abuse and Neglect Proceedings,* 29 FAM. L.Q. 375 (1995). For extensive commentary on these standards, *see* Symposium, *Ethical Issues in the Legal Representation of Children,* 64 FORDHAM L. REV. 1279 (1996). *See also* Marvin R. Ventrell, *Clarifying the Role of the Child's Attorney: New Scholarship Provides Guidance,* GUARDIAN, Spring 1996, at 3 (discussion by the executive director of the National Association of Counsel for Children of the themes of the ABA Standards and the Fordham issue).

201. *Better Lawyering, supra* note 200, at 6 (Standards B-2(1), B-4).

202. *Id.* (Standard B-4(3)). *See also id.* (Standard B-2(1)).

203. *Id.* (Standard A-2).

204. *Id.* at 7 (Standard C-1).

205. *Id.* (Standard D-2).

206. *Id.* at 8 (Standard D-5).

207. *Id.* (Standard D-7).

208. *Id.* at 9–10 (Standard I-2).

209. *Id.* at 7 (Standard C-2).

210. *Id.* (Standards C-2(4), C-2(6)).

211. This position is also recommended by Derdeyn, *supra* note 18, at 795, and the MODEL STANDARDS, *supra* note 25, Standard I(A) ("If there is a court-connected office of evaluation and conciliation, the evaluation shall be referred to that office for assignment to a qualified evaluator. If there is no such related office or if the evaluation is to be handled privately, the court shall appoint an evaluator or one must be agreed to by both parties and approved by the court."). One consequence of this position is that contact with any counsel, other than with respect

to scheduling or administative matters, should probably be reduced to writing and copied to other counsel.

212. One instance in which access to one parent (and the child) might be sufficient is when that parent's competence is in question and he or she seeks only to rebut that argument. Even in that example, though, it would be very helpful to have the other parent's perpective to focus the evaluation appropriately. *See supra* text accompanying notes 39–40.

213. A stark example of treating clinicians' tendency to take sides in custody disputes was presented by Derdeyn, *supra* note 18, at 788–99.

214. *Psychotherapist privilege* is the privilege to keep information gathered in therapy from being admitted into evidence in a legal proceeding. In federal courts, and in many states, it applies to communications with social workers and psychologists as well as with psychiatrists. See § 4.04(c).

215. Psychotherapist privilege is not available at all in about one-third of the states, and it is often not available to clients of social workers and sometimes psychologists. Gary B. Melton & Nancy S. Ehrenreich, *Ethical and Legal Issues in Mental Health Services for Children*, in Handbook of Clinical Child Psychology 1035, 1046–47 (C. Eugene Walker & Michael C. Roberts eds. 2d ed. 1992).

216. It is at least arguable that when a client divulges information in the presence of another client (especially a spouse with whom he or she may become involved in litigation), he or she has waived any expectation of privacy. On the other hand, such a rule would frustrate the purposes of psychotherapist privilege, and it might deter spouses from seeking counseling in an attempt to save their marriage or resolve issues outside court. *Cf.* Minnesota v. Andring, 342 N.W.2d 128 (Minn. 1984) (privilege applicable in group therapy).

217. The question of whether the child or a parent owns the privilege in child therapy is unclear. Melton & Ehrenreich, *supra* note 215, at 1047. The issue is still more muddled in exercise of the privilege in custody disputes. Because of the potential conflict of interest, at least one court has required appointment of a guardian *ad litem* to decide whether to exercise privilege on behalf of a child when the child was too young to exercise it competently. Nagle v. Hooks, 460 A.2d 49 (Md. Ct. Spec. App. 1983).

218. It has been argued that marriage counselor privilege cannot be invoked in a custody dispute because the exclusion of reliable evidence relevant to the parents' fitness interferes with the child's constitutional right to due process. M. v. K., 452 A.2d 477 (N.J. Super. Law Div. 1982).

219. *See, e.g.,* Marc J. Ackerman, Clinician's Guide to Child Custody Evaluations (1995); Barry Bricklin, The Custody Evaluation Handbook: Research-Based Solutions and Applications (1995); Stanley Kissel & Nelson W. Freeling, Evaluating Children for Courts Using Psychological Tests (1990); Mary E. Lindley, A Manual on Investigating Child Custody Reports (1988); Benjamin M. Schutz, Ellen B. Dixon, Joanne

C. Lindenberger, & Neil J. Ruther, Solomon's Sword: A Practical Guide to Conducting Child Custody Evaluations (1989); Diane Skafte, Child Custody Evaluations: A Practical Guide (1985); Philip M. Stahl, Conducting Child Custody Evaluations: A Comprehensive Guide (1994); Psychology and Child Custody Determinations: Knowledge, Roles and Expertise (Lois A. Weithorn ed. 1987). The quality of the guidance provided varies greatly across these various volumes.

220. Thomas Grisso, Evaluating Competencies: Forensic Assessments and Instruments 200 (1986) (citation omitted).

221. "[Testing] can provide information . . . to determine fitness in being able to parent adequately. . . . Psychological testing can also reveal the emotional make-up of the child and parents and can provide information about such dimensions as maturity, anti-social tendencies, propensity to anxiety and depression, and dangerousness to self and others. . . . Psychological testing may provide important information regarding which parent may be more capable to raise a child and also in resolving visitation issues." Kissel & Freeling, *supra* note 219, at 5.

222. "Many tests were evaluated and examined in the preparation of this chapter. We found no tests that directly measure the domain of functional parent abilities. Although some instruments sample parental attitudes and beliefs, there is insufficient evidence to correlate these attitudes with actual behavior." Schutz, Dixon, Lindenberger, & Ruther, *supra* note 219, at 69.

223. "Projective measures have not been shown to have the requisite psychometric properies to render them reliable or valid for predicting custodial functioning." Lois A. Weithorn & Thomas Grisso, *Psychological Evaluations in Divorce Custody: Problems, Principles, and Procedures,* in Psychology and Child Custody Determinatons: Knowledge, Roles and Expertise 165 (Lois A. Weithorn Ed. 1987).

224. William G. Keilin $ Larry J. Bloom, *Child Custody Evaluation Practices: A Survey of Experienced Professionals*, 17 Prof. Psychol. Res. & Prac. 338, 339 (1986).

225. *Id.*

226. Among those respondents who use psychological tests, the tests most frequently cited for use with adults were the Minnesota Multiphasic Personality Inventory (used in 87.7% of cases), Rorschach Inkblots (67.3%), Thematic Apperception Test (67.3%), Wechsler Adult Intelligence Scale (66.8%), Bender–Gestalt drawings (82.5%), and projective drawings (80%). Among the tests most frequently cited for use with children were intelligence tests (85.1%), Thematic Apperception Test or Children's Apperception Test (74.7%), and various projective drawing tests (79.4–94.3%). *Id.* at 340–41, Tables, 3 4.

227. "Each parent is generally administered the Minnesota Multiphasic Personality Inventory (MMPI). *When appropriate,* projective personality tests . . . and intellectual assessments . . . are used." *Id.* at 344 (emphasis added).

228. David Brodzinsky, *On the Use and Misuse of Psychological Testing in Child Custody Evaluations*, 24 PROF. PSYCHOL.: RES. & PRAC. 213, 214 (1993). Brodzinsky goes on to note: "Psychological tests were developed primarily to address clinical questions, especially those related to clinical diagnosis and treatment planning . . . but these data are only indirectly tied to the substantive issue involved in custody and visitation disputes. . . . [W]e do not know how valid they are in addressing those issues that are of primary concern to the court." *Id*. at 214–15.

229. "It requires many inferential leaps to connect [traditional tests] with parental competencies we are attempting to measure." SCHUTZ ET AL, *supra* note 219, at 67. *See also* Karen S. Budd & Michelle J. Holdsworth, *Issues in Clinical Assessment of Minimal Parenting Competence*, 25 J. CLINICAL CHILD PSYCHOL. 2, 4 (1996), and citations therein.

230. Brodzinsky, *supra* note 228, at 213. "There is a clear need for standardized assessment procedures that are geared specifically to the issues confronting the child custody evaluator. Such procedures, though, whether they are clinician-administered tests or self-report questionnaires, must have proven reliability and validity for forensic purposes. Unfortunately, the current array of tests and questionnaires typically used by custody evaluators does not meet these criteria." *Id*. at 218.

231. MARC J. ACKERMAN & KATHLEEEN SCHOENDORF, ACKERMAN–SHOENDORF SCALES FOR PARENT EVALUATION OF CUSTODY (1992).

232. BARRY BRICKLIN, BRICKLIN PERCEPTUAL SCALES (1990).

233. Brodzinsky, *supra* note 228, at 218. The author's ambivalence in endorsing these measures, however, is reflected in the following language: "[C]onsiderable caution must be exercised in interpreting the data derived from these and other measures in terms of custody and visitation recommendations. . . . [These measures] represent a valuable addition to the field of child custody evaluation . . . [and] are likely to provide information that is particularly relevant to the issues before the court. Future research, however, will need to resolve the dilemma regarding validation of these measures." *Id*.

234. SCHUTZ ET AL., *supra* note 219, at 64, 70–71, endorse the use of the Bricklin Perceptual Scale (BPS).

235. Gary B. Melton, *Review of the Ackerman–Schoendorf Scales for Parent Evaluation of Custody*, in MENTAL MEASUREMENTS YEARBOOK 222 (Jane C. Conoley & James C. Impara eds. 12th ed. 1995) [hereinafter TWELFTH MENTAL MEASUREMENTS].

236. *Id*. at 23.

237. Joyce A. Arditti, *Review of the Ackerman–Schoendorf Scales for Parent Evaluation of Custody*, in TWELFTH MENTAL MEASUREMENTS, *supra* note 235, at 20–22. Arditti notes poor scale reliability, absence of predictive validity data and concurrent validity data, and the particular demographic characterics of the small standardization sample (*n* = 100 couples, 96.9% white) that may limit the ASPECT's use with ethnically diverse families. *Id*. at 21.

238. Robert A. Nicholson. "To date, there are no studies examining the relationship between scores on these measures and independent criteria of parenting capacity in custody cases." *Id*.

239. A Psychlit review, using key word searches based on the test author's name, ASPECT, and "child custody" failed to reveal any published journal articles from 1987–96 on this measure. We note, however, that some description of the research on the ASPECT appears in ACKERMAN, *supra* note 219.

240. For a further description of these measures, *see* BRICKLIN, *supra* note 219, Chapters 4–7.

241. The nonverbal response is viewed by the author as "more closely aligned with, and reflective of, unconscious mental sources than with conscious sources. . . . [T]he unconscious is seen as our inner computer, that part of us that collects the thousands of interactions we have with others, 'weights' them according to our own special and unique value systems, and yields what we all experience as gut-level dispositions." BRICKLIN, *supra* note 219, at 77–78.

242. "The Scales rest on too many assumptions, the most egregious of which is that children who stick a stylus into a long black line have unconsciously chosen the spot on the line which reveals their unconscious attitudes. . . . Even this reviewer, who is a believer in Freud and clinical intuition, has difficulty with that idea, especially in view of the meager theories and statistics presented in its defense." Marcia B. Shaffer, *Review of the Bricklin Perceptual Scales*, in ELEVENTH MENTAL MEASUREMENTS YEARBOOK 118–19 (Jack J. Kramer & Jane C. Conoley eds. 1992) [hereinafter ELEVENTH MENTAL MEASUREMENTS].

243. Regarding the BPS, one reviewer noted that "data that are presented are limited by very small samples (ranging from 12 to 36). The usual descriptive statistics are not presented; samples are only described as adversarial and nonadversarial." Rosa A. Hagin, *Review of the Bricklin Perceptual Scales*, in ELEVENTH MENTAL MEASUREMENTS, *supra* note 242, at 117–18.

Regarding the PORT: "The development of the PORT is incompletely described in the test manual. Because several references are made to standardization and to statistical data, the potential user is led to believe that norms exist or that comparison data from something resembling a standardization sample are contained in the test manual. They are not. . . . Very little information is provided about [30 children in the development sample] except to imply that most were being seen in someone's private practice and that none were presently in the throes of divorce or custody proceedings. No demographic information is provided." Janet F. Carlson, *Review of the Perception-of-Relationships-Test*, in TWELFTH MENTAL MEASUREMENTS, *supra* note 235, at 746.

Regarding the PPCP, after commenting that no norms for clinical interpretation are provided in the manual, one author noted that "the PPCP directions allude to 'parents in our sample' [p. 5] and 'Scale data collected so far (*N* = 60)' [p. 6] but no other information is provided. Therefore we have no data about how parents from different socioeconomic, educational, and cultural backgrounds might be expected to respond to the PPCP." Robert W. Hiltonsmith, *Review of the Parent Perception of Child Profile*, in TWELFTH MENTAL MEASUREMENTS, *supra* note 235, at 738.

244. Regarding the PORT, "it is apparent that reliability of the PORT has not been addressed adequately. . . . [T]he PORT has serious flaws regarding its psychometric properties. . . . The test author broaches the subjects of standardization, statistical data, validation, and reliability, however, and the PORT does not measure up favorably." Carlson, *supra* note 243, at 747. "The validity support is meagre . . . and there are no reliability data. . . . At best it is an exploratory tool to gather impressions." Judith Conger, *Review of Perception-of-Relationships-Test*, in TWELFTH MENTAL MEASUREMENTS, *supra* note 235, at 747–48.

Regarding the PASS: "Lack of information concerning validity and reliability is a serious limitation of the PASS. No information is included in the manual. Evidence supporting the validity of inferences concerning parent awareness skills constructed from PASS scores, and evidence supporting the reliability of scores is necessary before this instrument can be considered for clinical use." Lisa G. Bischoff, *Review of the Parent Awareness Skills Survey*, in TWELFTH MENTAL MEASUREMENTS, *supra* note 235, at 735–36.

Regarding the PPCP, "No reliability data are presented. . . . No validity data are presented. The PPCP includes little or no information on scoring, norms, reliability, or validity." Hiltonsmith, *supra* note 243, at 738.

245. See *supra* note 239 for a description of the Psychlit search strategy used in an effort to uncover the published research for these measures. One largely descriptive article was published by the author in 1992. Barry Bricklin, *Data-based Tests in Custody Evaluations*, 20 AM. J.

FAM. THERAPY 254 (1992). The author's reseach is also described in his 1995 book, BRICKLIN, *supra* note 219.

246. Budd & Holdsworth, *supra* note 229. *See also*, Michaela C. Heinze & Thomas Grisso, *Review of Instruments Assessing Parenting Competencies Used in Child Custody Evaluations*, 14 BEH. SCI & L. 293 (1996).

247. Concerning the PPCP, one reviewer concluded that "[t]he lack of validity and reliability suggests that any scores obtained from the instrument probably should not be used in report writing." Mary L. Kelley, *Review of the Parent Perception of Child Profile*, in TWELFTH MENTAL MEASUREMENTS, *supra* note 235, at 738–39. Obviously, we extend this recommendation to all of the specialty measures discussed in this section.

248. Rebecca A. Clay, *Courts Reshape Image of "the Good Mother*," APA MONITOR, Dec. 1995, at 31, 31.

249. *Id.*

250. *See, e.g.*, R.H. v. B.F., 653 N.E.2d 195 (Mass. 1995); FLA. STAT. ANN. § 61.13(2)(b)(2) (West 1995); LA. REV. STAT. ANN. § 9:364 (West 1996); MICH. COMP. LAWS ANN. § 722.23 (West 1996); N.D. CENT. CODE § 14-09-06.2(1)(j) (1995); VT. STAT. ANN. tit. 15, § 655 (1995); VA. CODE ANN. § 20-124.3 (1996).

251. LA. REV. STAT. ANN. § 9:364(C) (West 1996). The Louisiana statute is similar to Arizona and Wyoming laws. Michelli v. Michelli, 655 So. 2d 1342, 1346 n. 3 (La. Ct. App. 1995), and citations therein.

252. *See, e.g.*, Thompson v. Thompson, 651 N.E.2d 222 (Ill, Ct. App. 1995) (denying a 17-year-old boy standing to seek an order placing his custody with his aunt and uncle, who had cared for him after the death of his divorced mother).

253. *See, e.g.*, William A. Galston, *Needed: A Not-So-Fast Divorce Law*, N.Y. TIMES, Dec. 27, 1995, at A15.

254. *Guidelines, supra* note 11, at 678.

Chapter 17

1. 20 U.S.C. §§ 1400–1485.
2. 20 U.S.C. §§ 1400(c), 1412(5)(B).
3. 20 U.S.C. §§ 1400(b)(1), (3), (4).
4. 20 U.S.C. § 1400(b)(9).
5. *Abuse and Neglect of Children in Institutions, 1979: Hearings Before the Subcomm. on Child and Human Development of the Senate Comm. on Labor and Human Resources,* 96th Cong., 1st Sess. (1979).
6. *Id.* at 5 (statement of Dr. Phyllis Kaplan).
7. L. LIPPMAN & I. GOLDBERG, THE RIGHT TO EDUCATION 29 (1973).
8. David Neal & David L. Kirp, *The Allure of Legalization Reconsidered: The Case of Special Education*, 48 LAW & CONTEMP. PROB. 63, 69 (1985).
9. LIPPMAN & GOLDBERG, *supra* note 7, at 8–9. *See also* Larry P. v. Riles, 343 F. Supp. 1306 (N.D. Cal. 1972), *aff'd*, 502 F.2d 963 (9th Cir. 1974) (finding that although blacks formed 28.5% of the school district's population, black children comprised 66% of

classes for the educable mentally retarded, and enjoining the use of then current IQ tests as racially discriminatory).

10. Neal & Kirp, *supra* note 8, at 68.
11. Christopher Slobogin, *Treatment of the Mentally Disabled: Rethinking the Community-First Idea*, 69 NEB. L. REV. 413, 418–19 (1990).
12. 484 U.S. 305 (1988).
13. 20 U.S.C. § 1401(a)(1).
14. 20 U.S.C. § 1401(a)(15).
15. 34 C.F.R. § 300.5(b)(8).
16. 20 U.S.C. § 1412(18)(A-D).
17. 458 U.S. 176 (1982).
18. *Id.* at 200.
19. *Id.* at 203.
20. *See generally,* Slobogin, *supra* note 11, at 425–429..
21. 853 F.2d 171 (3d Cir. 1988).
22. Burke County Bd. Educ. v. Denton, 895 F.2d

973, 980 (4th Cir. 1990); Evans v. District No. 17, 841 F.2d 824, 831 (8th Cir. 1988); Brown v. Wilson County School Bd., 747 F. Supp. 436, 442 (M.D. Tenn. 1990).

23. *See In re* Conklin, 946 F.2d 306, 320–21 (4th Cir. 1991) (summary of statutes).

24. 20 U.S.C.A. § 1401(17).

25. 468 U.S. 883 (1984).

26. 20 U.S.C.A. § 1412(5)(B).

27. 20 U.S.C.A. §§ 1401(a)(1)(A), 1412(5)(B).

28. Alan Gartner & Dorothy Lipsky, *Beyond Special Education: Toward a Quality System for All Students,* 57 HARV. EDUC. REV. 367 (1987) (74% of all children educated in "pull-out" classes); Douglas Biklen, *The Least Restrictive Environment: Its Application to Education,* in LEGAL REFORMS AFFECTING CHILD AND YOUTH SERVICES (G. Melton ed. 1982); St. Louis Parents Ass'n, 591 F. Supp. 1416, 1451 n. 73 (W.D. Mo. 1984) (85% of handicapped are educated in specially designed buildings); Florida Advocacy Center for Persons with Disabilities, Position Paper (1987) (87.2% of mentally handicapped in Florida are placed in special class or separate schools), *cited in* Slobogin, *supra* note 11, at 426 n. 56.

29. Janet Sansone & Naomi Zigmond, *Evaluating Mainstreaming through an Analysis of Students' Schedules,* 52(5) EXCEPTIONAL CHILDREN 452 (1986).

30. *See, e.g.,* Martha Minow, *Learning to Live with the Dilemma of Difference: Bilingual and Special Education,* 48 LAW & CONTEMP. PROBS. 157 (1985) (noting that mainstreaming can exacerbate stereotyping of the disabled unless differences are treated as aspects of the community's identity rather than as evidence of inequality or lower status); Jonathan Taylor, *Caught in the Continuum: A Critical Analysis of the Principles of the Least Restrictive Environment,* 13 J. A. SEVERELY HANDICAPPED 41 (1988) (arguing that the least-restrictive-environment idea is outmoded and should be replaced by a policy of integration, meaning the elimination of social, cultural, economic, and administrative barriers to community integration and encouragement of relationships between people with developmental disabilities and nondisabled people).

31. 700 F.2d 1058 (6th Cir.), *cert. denied,* 464 U.S. 864 (1983).

32. The child was currently attending a regular school in a "segregated" classroom with other disabled children. As a result, he was provided a limited opportunity for mainstreaming because he attended lunch, gym, and recess with nondisabled students.

33. 700 F.2d at 1063.

34. 874 F.2d 1036 (5th Cir. 1989).

35. Greer v. Rome City, 950 F.2d 688 (11th Cir. 1991). See also Bd. v. Holland, 14F. 3rd 1398 (9th Cir. 1994).

36. 20 U.S.C. § 1412(2)(C).

37. 20 U.S.C. § 1415(b)(1)(C).

38. 20 U.S.C. § 1413(a)(3); 34 C.F.R. § 300.382. Congress believed that the in-service training would gradually increase knowledge of special education needs and thus increase the accuracy of referrals and reduce the need for screening on the assessment staff. *Id.*

39. 20 U.S.C. § 1412(5)(C); 34 C.F.R. § 300.532(a)–(e).

40. William H. Clune & Mark H. Van Pelt, *A Political Method of Evaluating the Education for All Handicapped Children Act of 1975 and the Several Gaps of Gap Analysis,* 48 LAW & CONTEMP. PROBS. 7, at 57 n. 239 (recounting studies showing that placement decisions often reached without input of parents).

41. 20 U.S.C. § 1401(19)(A)–(E).

42. *See generally* 20 U.S.C. § 1400.

43. 34 C.F.R. § 300.532(f).

44. 20 U.S.C. § 1412(5)(c).

45. *Id.*

46. Clune & Van Pelt, *supra* note 40, at 11.

47. 20 U.S.C. § 1415(b)(2).

48. Clune & Van Pelt, *supra* note 40, at 13.

49. 20 U.S.C. § 1415(e).

50. 34 C.F.R. § 300.534(b).

51. For a general treatment of this issue, *see* Joseph Ellis & Daniel Geller, *Disciplining Handicapped Students: An Administrator's Dilemma,* 77 INT'L ASS'N SEC. SCHOOL PRINCIPALS 22, 24 (1993).

52. 421 U.S. 921 (1975).

53. 419 U.S. 565 (1975).

54. 484 U.S. 305 (1988).

55. *Id.* at 328

56. 20 U.S.C. § 1414(e)(3).

57. Ellis & Geller, *supra* note 51, at 37.

58. 34 C.F.R. §§ 300.530–300.532.

59. 34 C.F.R. § 300.540–43.

60. A particularly useful guide in this regard, and one on which we relied in this section of the chapter, is Betsy B. Waterman, *Assessing Children for the Presence of A Disability,* NICHCY NEWS DIG. 1 (1994) (disseminated by the National Information Center for Children and Youth with Disabilities, P.O. Box 1492, Washington, D.C. 20013-1492 (single copy free).

61. *Id.* at 9–10.

62. For various versions of such checklists, *see* H.LEE SWANSON & BILLY L. WATSON, EDUCATION AND PSYCHOLOGICAL ASSESSMENT OF EXCEPTIONAL CHILDREN (2d ed. 1989); GERALD WALLACE ET AL. EDUCATIONAL ASSESSMENT OF LEARNING PROBLEMS, TESTING FOR TEACHING (1992).

63. *Id.* at 19.

64. CHERI HOY & NOEL GREGG, ASSESSMENT: THE SPECIAL EDUCATOR'S ROLE 46 (1994).

65. Waterman, *supra* note 60, at 10.

66. C. HOY & N. GREGG, *supra* note 64; WALLACE, LARSEN, & ELKSININ, *supra* note 62; T.E. Sewell, *Dynamic Assessment as a Nondiscriminatory Procedure,* in DYNAMIC ASSESSMENT: AN INTERACTIONAL APPROACH TO EVALUATION LEARNING POTENTIAL 426 (Carol S. Lidz ed. 1987); WILLIAM H. BERDINE & STACIE A. MEYER, ASSESSMENT IN SPECIAL EDUCATION (2d ed. 1987).

67. *See, e.g.,* Mary E. Franklin, *Culturally Sensitive Instructional Practices for African-American Learners with Disabilities,* 59(2) EXCEPTIONAL CHILDREN 115 (1992).

68. Waterman, *supra* note 60, at 9.

_____*Chapter 18*_____

1. Bruce Ennis & Thomas Litwack, *Psychiatry and the Presumption of Expertise: Flipping Coins in the Courtroom,* 62 CAL. L. REV. 693, 695 (1974).

2. David Faust & Jay Ziskin, *The Expert Witness in Psychology and Psychiatry,* 241 SCI. 31, 31 (1988).

3. *See id.*; Comment, *The Psychologist as Expert Witness: Science in the Courtroom,* 38 MD. L. REV. 539 (1979); Stephen Morse, *Crazy Behavior, Morals and Science: An Analysis of Mental Health Law,* 51 S. CAL. L. REV. 527 (1978). This feeling is probably most prevalent in criminal cases, where mental health professionals are often viewed as "fuzzy apologists for criminals." S.A. Strauss, *Psychiatric Testimony, with Special Reference to Cases of Post-Traumatic Neurosis,* 1 FORENSIC SCI. 77 (1972).

4. *See, e.g.,* Debra J. Saunders, *Battered-Woman "Expert" Behaves True to Form,* St. Petersburg Times, Feb. 7, 1995 ("[Lenore] Walker . . . has been a paid witness—a so-called expert—who has built a cottage industry justifying murders. . . . [Walker] has made a career out of blaming murder victims"); Roberta W. Shell, *Psychiatric Testimony: Science or Fortune Telling?,* 7 BARRISTER 6 (1980) ("One New Jersey psychiatrist reportedly received $10,000 for a single psychiatric consultation. Such large fees lead some observers to question how well the neutrality of the witness holds up under the pressure of pleasing a client who is paying high prices for a particular verdict"). *See generally* Ralph Slovenko, *The Lawyer and the Forensic Expert: Boundaries of Ethical Practice,* 5 BEHAVIORAL SCI. & L. 119 (1987).

5. David Bazelon, a federal judge well-known for his interest in mental health issues and once a spirited advocate for psychiatric testimony, eventually came to this belief. David Bazelon, *Psychiatry and the Adversary Process,* 230 SCI. AM. 18 (1974). As he put it: "One might hope that psychiatrists would open up their reservoirs of knowledge in the courtroom. Unfortunately in my experience they try to limit their testimony to conclusory statements couched in psychiatric terminology. Thereafter they take shelter in a defensive resistance to questions about the facts that are or ought to be in their possession. They thus refuse to submit their opinions to the scrutiny that the adversary process demands." *Id.* at 18. *See also* GARY MELTON ET AL., COMMUNITY MENTAL HEALTH CENTERS AND THE COURTS: AN EVALUATION OF COMMUNITY-BASED SERVICES 56–66 (1985) (judges, defense attorneys, and prosecutors rated hospital reports inferior in terms of separating fact from opinion, presenting the factual basis of opinions, focusing on relevant and appropriate legal issues, and clarity of writing).

6. Richard Bonnie, *Morality, Equality, and Expertise: Renegotiating the Relationship Between Psychiatry and the Criminal Law,* 12 BULL. AM. ACAD. PSYCHIATRY & L. 5, 5–6 (1984).

7. For a comprehensive discussion of many issues raised in this chapter, *see* HAROLD A. FEDER, SUCCEEDING AS AN EXPERT WITNESS: INCREASING YOUR IMPACT AND INCOME (1991).

8. Stanley L. Brodsky & Norman G. Poythress, *Expertise on the Witness Stand: A Practitioner's Guide,* in PSYCHOLOGY, PSYCHIATRY AND THE LAW: A CLINICAL AND FORENSIC HANDBOOK 389, 391 (C.P. Ewing ed. 1985).

9. Arguably, such feedback is *required* in a competency-to-stand-trial evaluation [see § 6.07(a)] but is otherwise discretionary with the clinician.

10. For additional guidelines on forensic report writing, *see* Robert Bluglass, *The Psychiatric Court Report,* 19 MED. SCI. & L. 121 (1979); GERALD H. VANDENBERG, COURT TESTIMONY IN MENTAL HEALTH: A GUIDE FOR MENTAL HEALTH PROFESSIONALS AND ATTORNEYS (1993).

11. A. Louis McGarry, *Competency for Trial and Due Process via the State Hospital,* 122 AM. J. PSYCHIATRY 623 (1965).

12. In the *Hinckley* case, one psychiatrist submitted his findings in a 900-page report. The sheer volume, we suspect, might have ensured that the jurors would be unlikely to read or understand everything included.

13. *See, e.g.,* ETHICAL PRINCIPLES OF PSYCHOLOGISTS AND CODE OF CONDUCT § 7.04 ("in forensic testimony and reports, psychologists testify truthfully, honestly, and candidly and, consistent with applicable legal procedures, describe fairly the bases for their testimony and conclusions. Whenever necessary to avoid misleading, psychologists acknowledge the limits of their data or conclusions").

14. Russell C. Petrella & Norman Poythress, *Forensic Evaluations for Criminal Courts—An Interdisciplinary Study* (1979) (unpublished manuscript on file with the Department of Training and Research, Center for Forensic Psychiatry, P.O. Box 2060, Ann Arbor, MI 48106).

15. ERWIN P. BETTINGHAUS, PERSUASIVE COMMUNICATION (1973).

16. "The witness with the cultivated courtroom manner, rather than with the superior knowledge and greater integrity, may make the best appearance and carry the jury. The premium thus placed on personality and patter is so great that lawyers become more interested in retaining a good testifier than in retaining a good witness." Andre Moenssens, *The "Impartial" Medical Expert: A New Look at an Old Issue,* 25 MED. TRIAL TECH. Q. 63, 67 (1978).

17. As outlined in § 2.04(b), however, objections on privilege and relevancy grounds may require a delay while a judge deliberates on them.

18. For a discussion of primacy and recency effects, *see* RONALD L. APPELBAUM & KARL W.E. ANATOL, STRATEGIES FOR PERSUASIVE COMMUNICATION (1974).

19. W. McGuire, *Inducing Resistance to Persuasion,* in ADVANCES IN EXPERIMENTAL SOCIAL PSYCHOLOGY (Leonard Berkowitz ed. vol. 1 1964). *See also,* Kipling D. Williams et al., *The Effects of Stealing Thunder in Criminal and Civil Trials,* 17 LAW & HUM. BEHAV. 597 (1993).

20. Brodsky & Poythress, *supra* note 8, at 392–94.

21. Thomas Grisso, *The Differences between Forensic Psy-*

chiatry and Forensic Psychology, 21 BULL. AM. ACAD. PSYCHIA-
TRY & L. 133 (1993).

22. Empirical studies using survey methods have
documented judges' preferences for psychiatrists over
clinical psychologists, and both of these groups of experts over nonpsychiatric physicians, academic psychologists, social workers, and psychiatric nurses. Norman G.
Poythress, *Psychological Issues in Criminal Proceedings: Judicial Preference Regarding Expert Testimony,* 10 CRIM. JUSTICE
& BEHAV. 175 (1983); A. Daniel Yarmey & P. Karen
Popiel, *Judged Value of Medical versus Psychological Expert
Witnesses,* 11 INT'L J. L. & PSYCHIATRY 195 (1988).
Whether the expert judgments of psychiatrists are qual-
itatively different in ways that would support these judi-
cial biases has been questioned. *See* George E. Dix and
Norman G. Poythress, *Propriety of Medical Dominance of
Forensic Mental Health Practice: The Empirical Evidence,* 23
ARIZ. L. REV. 961 (1981).

23. This line of questioning may also serve an inoculating function, as described in text accompanying note
19 *supra.*

24. Frye v. United States, 293 F. 1013 (D.C. Cir.
1923).

25. FED. R. EVID. 703.

26. This ploy will be more common when one side
has a privately retained expert and the other does not.
The privately retained expert will be cast as the "hired
gun" whereas the other side's court appointed expert will
be cast as more neutral. When both parties have retained
their own experts, they are equally vulnerable to this line
of questioning and thus it may be omitted as not advantageous.

27. For a sampling of empirical studies on the
relative importance of "expertise" (credentials) versus
"trustworthiness," *see* Michael H. Birnbaum & Steven
E. Stegner, *Source Credibility in Social Judgment: Bias, Expertise and the Judge's Point of View,* 37 J. PERS. & SOC. PSY-
CHOL. 48 (1979); Elliott McGinnies & Charles D. Ward,
*Better Liked than Right: Trustworthiness and Expertise as Fac-
tors in Credibility,* 6 PERS. SOC. PSYCHOL. BULL. 467
(1980).

28. *See supra* note 13.

29. Thomas Dixon & Robert Blondis, *Cross-Examina-
tion of Psychiatric Witnesses in Civil Commitment Proceedings,* 1
MENTAL DISABILITY L. REP. 164 (1976); Stan Twardy & V.
Siomopoulos, *Medical Testimony—Mental Health Proceed-
ing—Direct and Cross-Examination of a Defendant's Clinical
Psychologist—Part I,* 23 MED. TRIAL TECH. Q. 66 (1977);
Stan Twardy & V. Siomopoulos, *Medical Testimony—Mental
Health Proceeding—Direct and Cross-Examination of a Defen-
dant's Clinical Psychiatrist— Part II,* 23 MED. TRIAL TECH. Q.
187 (1977); Raymond M. Cameron, *The Mental Health Ex-
pert: A Guide to Direct and Cross-Examination,* 2 CRIM. JUST.
J. 299 (1979); JAY ZISKIN & DAVID FAUST, COPING WITH
PSYCHIATRIC AND PSYCHOLOGICAL TESTIMONY (4th ed.
1988).

30. Stanley L. Brodsky, *The Mental Health Professional
on the Witness Stand: A Survival Guide,* in PSYCHOLOGY IN
THE LEGAL PROCESS 269 (Bruce D. Sales ed. 1977); STAN-

LEY L. BRODSKY, TESTIFYING IN COURT: GUIDELINES AND
MAXIMS FOR THE EXPERT WITNESS (1991); Brodsky &
Poythress, *supra* note 8. *See also* GROUP FOR THE AD-
VANCEMENT OF PSYCHIATRY, THE MENTAL HEALTH PROFES-
SIONAL AND THE LEGAL SYSTEM (GAP Report No. 131
1991).

31. *See, e.g.,* Irwin Perr, *Cross-Examination of the Psychiatrist, Using Publications,* 5 BULL. AM. ACAD. PSYCHIATRY
& L. 327 (1977); Seymour Pollack, *Cross-Examination of
the Psychiatrist Using Publications: Point—Counter Point,* 5
BULL. AM. ACAD. PSYCHIATRY & L. 332 (1977).

32. Fred N. Diem, *Evidence—The Use of Learned Trea-
tises on Cross-Examination of a Medical Expert—Treatises
Which an Expert Has Used in His Studies are Acceptable for the
Sole Purpose of Impeaching His Testimony,* 6 TEX. TECH. L.
REV. 237 (1974).

33. *See, e.g.,* FLA. STAT. § 90.706.

34. Norman Poythress, *Coping on the Witness Stand:
Learned Responses to "Learned Treatises,"* 11 PROF. PSYCHOL.
139 (1980).

35. However, they have fallen in disfavor in recent
years. In 1975, the Federal Rules of Evidence incorporated Rule 705, which states: "The expert may testify in
terms of opinion or inference and give reasons therefore
without first testifying to the underlying facts or data, unless the court requires otherwise. The expert may in any
event be required to disclose the underlying facts or data
on cross-examination."

The first sentence of this rule was designed to abolish any "hypothetical question" requirement, which had
existed in many jurisdictions as a way of allowing the
court to decide whether any part of the opinion was
based on inadmissible evidence and of ensuring that the
factfinder was aware of all the facts underlying a given
opinion. The first concern has diminished in light of
rules relaxing the requirements for expert data [see
§ 3.08] and the latter concern is dealt with by the second sentence of the rule. As the commentary to Rule
705 states: "The hypothetical question has been the
target of a great deal of criticism as encouraging partisan
bias, affording an opportunity for summing up in the
middle of the case, and as complex and time consuming.
While [Rule 705] allows counsel to make disclosure
of the underlying facts or data as a preliminary to the
giving of an expert opinion, if he chooses, the instances
in which he is required to do so are reduced. This is
true whether the expert bases his opinion on data furnished him at secondhand or observed by him at first-
hand."

36. Hesitations ("uh," "er"), qualifiers ("probably,"
"maybe"), and intensifiers ("most certainly") are among
the features of witness's speech identified as *powerless*
speech (i.e., less persuasive). *See* Bonnie Erickson et al.,
*Speech Style and Impression Formation in a Court Setting: The
Effects of "Powerful" and "Powerless" Speech,* 14 J. EXPERIMENTAL
SOC. PSYCHOL. 266 (1978); WILLIAM O'BARR, LINGUISTIC
EVIDENCE: LANGUAGE, POWER, AND STRATEGY IN THE
COURTROOM (1982).

37. Stanley Brodsky, *Competence on the Witness Stand:*

The Art of Testimony (paper presented at the Fifth Annual Symposium on Mental Health Law, Miami, Fla., April 7, 1995).

38. Scott Sundby, *The Jury as Critic: An Empirical Look at How Capital Juries Perceive Expert and Lay Testimony,* VA. L. REV. (1997).

39. Anthony Champagne et al., *An Empirical Examination of the Use of Expert Witnesses in American Courts,* 31 JURIMETRICS J. 375, 377 (1991). *See also,* Daniel W. Shuman et al., *An Empirical Examination of the Use of Expert Witnesses in the Courts—Part II: A Three City Study,* 34 JURIMETRICS J. 193 (1994).

40. *See also* Paul Rosenthal, *Nature of Jury Response to the Expert Witness,* 28 J. FORENSIC SCI. 528 (1983); R. L. Tanton, *Jury Preconceptions and Their Effect on Expert Scientific Testimony,* 24 J. FORENSIC SCI. 681, 691 (1979).

41. Daniel W. Shuman et al., *Assessing the Believability of Expert Witnesses: Science in the Jurybox,* 37 JURIMETRICS 23 (1996). *See also, supra* note 27.

42. *See, e.g.,* MELTON ET AL., *supra* note 5, at 99 (members of advisory committee for Virginia's forensic evaluation "expressed a desire that such language be required in every report . . ."); Norman Poythress, *Concerning Reform in Expert Testimony: An Open Letter from a Practicing Psychologist,* 6 LAW & HUM. BEHAV. 39 (1982).

43. Norman Poythress, *Conflicting Postures for Mental Health Expert Witnesses: Prevailing Attitudes of Trial Court Judges* (1981) (unpublished manuscript on file with the Department of Training and Research, Center for Forensic Psychiatry, POB 2060, Ann Arbor, MI 48106).

44. Specifically, the third aspect corresponds with the first and second inference levels (application of meaning to a behavioral image and perception of a general mental state), the fourth aspect corresponds with the third and fourth inference levels (formulation of a perceived mental state to fit into theoretical constructs or research literature and diagnosis), the fifth and sixth correspond with the fifth inference level (relationship of formulation or diagnosis to the legally relevant behavior), and the last two aspects correspond with the last two inference levels (penultimate and ultimate legal issue). The first two aspects, dealing with statistical information) have no corresponding inference level.

45. Note, however, the rejection of statistical and actuarial data may be understandable in light of the well-documented difficulty that decisionmakers have in bringing statistical information describing group behavior to bear on decisions about individuals. *See* § 1.03(c). *See also* John Carroll, *Judgments of Recidivism Risk: The Use of Base-Rate Information in Parole Decisions,* in NEW DIRECTIONS IN PSYCHOLEGAL RESEARCH 68 (Paul Lipsitt & Bruce D. Sales eds. 1980).

46. Brodsky & Poythress, *supra* note 8, at 407–08. The "allegiance" effect may be a very subtle one. Laboratory studies of the psychology of witness behavior suggest that the mere fact of being called by one party may influence witnesses to testify in terms that are discernible to third party observers (e.g., mock judges) as more favorable to the side that has "called" them. Neil Vidmar & Nancy MacDonald Laird, *Adversary Social Roles: Their Effects on Witnesses' Communication of Evidence and the Assessment of Adjudicators,* 44 J. PERSONALITY & SOC. PSYCHOL. 888 (1983). This subtle effect may be enhanced by pretrial interactions with attorneys in the course of preparing for testimony. Blair H. Sheppard & Neil Vidmar, *Adversary Pretrial Procedures and Testimonial Evidence: Effects of Lawyer's Role and Machiavellianism,* 39 J. PERSONALITY & SOC. PSYCHOL. 320 (1983).

47. Until 1984, the best known example of an evidentiary rule permitting ultimate-issue testimony was Federal Rule of Evidence 704; although it was amended in that year to prohibit ultimate issue testimony concerning mental disease or defect, many states have not gone along with this change. *See, e.g.,* FLA. STAT. § 90.703. Of course, as noted in Chapter 1, even the original version of Rule 704 was modified by Rule 702's injunction that experts may only testify based on specialized knowledge; however, this limitation typically did not prevent experts from testifying as to a person's sanity or competency (which explains why the 1984 amendment was needed).

For an example of a statute requiring ultimate issue testimony, *see* MICH. STAT. ANN. 28.1043, § 20a(6)(c) (examiners' reports "shall contain . . . the opinion [of the examiner] on the issue of the defendant's insanity at the time the alleged offense was committed").

48. Stephen Morse, *Reforming Expert Testimony: A Response from the Tower (and the Trenches),* 6 LAW & HUM. BEHAV. 45 (1982). Morse notes that attorneys often take their business elsewhere when he informs them that he will not testify to ultimate issues. Anecdotally, a colleague recalled his experience setting up private practice in New York. One attorney told him candidly, "This is how forensic psychology works—I send you money, and you send me an opinion I can use in court." Paul Revland, personal communication.

49. James Bradley, *Overconfidence in Ignorant Experts,* 17 BULL. PSYCHONOMIC SOC'Y 82 (1981).

50. Joost Meerloo, *Emotionalism in the Jury and the Court of Justice: The Hazards of Psychiatric Testimony,* 139 J. NERVOUS & MENTAL DISEASE 294 (1964).

51. *See, e.g.,* Richard Rogers & Charles P. Ewing, *Ultimate Opinion Proscriptions: A Cosmetic Fix and a Plea for Empiricism,* 13 LAW & HUM. BEHAV. 357 (1989).

52. Christopher Slobogin, *The Ultimate Issue Issue,* 7 BEHAVIORAL SCI. & L. 259 (1989).

53. However, there is some evidence to suggest that mental health professionals would welcome evidentiary restraints that would prohibit ultimate-issue testimony. *See* Gary B. Melton, *Organized Psychology and Legal Policymaking: Involvement in the Post-Hinckley Debate,* 16 PROF. PSYCHOL. RES. & PRAC. 810 (1985).

54. *Report of the Task Force on the Role of Psychology in the Criminal Justice System, Recommendation 5,* in WHO IS THE CLIENT? (John Monahan ed. 1980).

55. The clinical staff at one state forensic hospital

routinely includes the following statement in reports to the court: "The staff at [_____] hospital recognize and respect that judgments regarding a criminal defendant's competency to stand trial and criminal responsibility are to be made by a judge or jury, not by mental health professionals. As such, our opinions should be regarded as only advisory."

56. *See* Poythress, *supra* note 43, at 40–41.

Index

Index